## THE COOKBOOK USED IN MORE AMERICAN KITCHENS THAN ANY OTHER IS NOW BETTER THAN EVER.

Homemakers of America have clearly shown their overwhelming preference for the BETTER HOMES AND GARDENS® NEW COOK BOOK, making it the bestselling cookbook of all time. Why? Because it has over 1200 delicious recipes (professional home economists duplicate the working conditions and time limitations you face every day), plus meal planning guides and menus, hundreds of kitchen-tested cooking tips, recipes for appliances, easy meals, and great new entertainment ideas.

Now, with an eye to important changes in American tastes and attitudes about food, the folks at Better Homes and Gardens® have streamlined your whole meal-making experience, cut out unnecessary steps and introduced completely new time- and money-saving techniques. The incomparable result is a wide variety of delightful old favorites, exciting international classics and tempting new flavors which preserve the Better Homes and Gardens® tradition of foods that are as speedy and easy to prepare as they are delicious to eat.

# BETTER HOMES AND GARDENS®

# NEW COOK BOOK

**BANTAM BOOKS**

TORONTO · NEW YORK · LONDON · SYDNEY · AUCKLAND

*This low-priced Bantam Book
has been completely reset in a type face
designed for easy reading, and was printed
from new plates. It contains the complete
text of the original hard-cover edition.*
NOT ONE WORD HAS BEEN OMITTED.

BETTER HOMES AND GARDENS® NEW COOK BOOK

*A Bantam Book / published by arrangement with
Meredith Corporation*

### PRINTING HISTORY

*Meredith edition originally published November 1930*

*Better Homes and Gardens® Family Book Service
edition October 1963*
*Latest revised edition published August 1981*

*Bantam edition / October 1979*
*4 printings through January 1981*
*Bantam Revised edition / October 1982*
*11 printings through October 1987*

*The red plaid cover design is Registered in
U. S. Patent and Trademark Office.*

ISBN 0-553-22528-6

*Published simultaneously in the United States and Canada*

*Bantam Books are published by Bantam Books, Inc.
Its trademark, consisting of the words "Bantam
Books" and the portrayal of a rooster, is Registered
in U. S. Patent and Trademark Office and in other
countries. Marca Registrada. Bantam Books, Inc.,
666 Fifth Avenue, New York, New York 10103.*

PRINTED IN THE UNITED STATES OF AMERICA

O    20  19  18  17  16  15  14

# Contents

| | |
|---|---|
| Nutrition Analysis | ix |
| Appetizers & Snacks | 1 |
| Barbecue | 25 |
| Beverages | 73 |
| Breads | 95 |
| Cakes | 163 |
| Candy | 201 |
| Canning & Freezing | 223 |
| Cookies | 289 |
| Desserts | 329 |
| Eggs & Cheese | 367 |
| Fish & Seafood | 407 |
| Meat | 443 |
| Pies | 537 |
| Poultry | 577 |
| Rice, Pasta & Cereal | 631 |

| | |
|---|---|
| Salads & Dressings | 653 |
| Sauces & Relishes | 707 |
| Soups & Stews | 731 |
| Vegetables | 767 |
| Special Helps | 819 |
| Index | 887 |
| Measurements | 935 |

# All About This Book

From cover to cover, this Better Homes and Gardens® *New Cook Book* will be your best friend in the kitchen. To give you superb results from your cooking—and to help you enjoy your success—is why we created this book. So whether you're an experienced cook or a first-timer, our recipes will make you a big hit with your family and friends.

Selecting recipes for this revised edition has been a great challenge because we wanted our book to be a collection of the very best. As we made our selections, we tried to reflect the growing number of new food products, trends in cooking, and important changes in your tastes, preferences, and attitudes about food. So we carefully evaluated our old edition, weighing each recipe that we added and each one that we omitted. The result is this book. And it's filled with delightful old favorites, tempting international classics, and exciting new flavors.

Proper nutrition, a balanced diet, and good health are concerns all of us share. And because of this interest, we've added a new feature to our book—nutrition analysis charts. These charts tell you at a glance every recipe's content of calories, vitamins, and minerals so you know exactly how much nutrition you're getting from the prepared foods. This can be a great help as you plan your daily diet. (For more information on nutrition analysis, see the next page.)

Since busy schedules have become our way of life, we placed an emphasis on ease of cooking. Our recipes are written with streamlined preparation methods and simplified techniques. The "old favorites" were updated to make them even more reliable, with clearer, easier-to-understand cooking procedures. And time-saving microwave and crockery cooker directions are given with some of the recipes to make your cooking even easier.

Because food costs are on the rise, most of our recipes are prepared "from scratch" to help you stretch your food dollar. Expensive ultra-convenience and specialty foods aren't used.

Since another way to get a grip on rising food costs is to budget food expenditures and plan meals in advance, we've included a Special Helps chapter to make you a better-informed consumer and a smarter shopper. It's packed with lots of useful ideas and tips. Serving your family money-saving main dishes is still another way to cut food costs, and we offer you a wide selection of such recipes in the chapters on Eggs and Cheese, Meat, Poultry, Fish and Seafood, Soups and Stews, and Rice, Pasta, and Cereal. And because gardening and preserving your own fresh vegetables and fruits are once again popular, we help you successfully and safely can or freeze at home with an extensive chapter on the basics of food preservation.

Whether you're entertaining friends or preparing family meals, we hope all of our recipes bring you joy and good eating.

# Nutrition Analysis

Nutrition labeling on packaged foods has enabled you to know what vitamins and minerals you're eating and what nutritional values you're getting from each serving. Now you can get this same type of information from the recipes in your *New Cook Book*. Every recipe in this book is accompanied by a nutrition analysis, which gives values for the number of calories and the amount of protein, carbohydrate, fat, sodium, and potassium in an individual serving. Protein, carbohydrate, and fat are given in gram weights, and sodium and potassium in milligrams. The analysis also gives the percentages of the United States Recommended Daily Allowances (U.S. RDA) for protein, vitamin A, vitamin C, thiamine, riboflavin, niacin, and iron per serving.

Use the nutrition analyses to compare the nutritional values of individual recipes. Plan your daily menus by finding recipes that meet your calorie and nutritional needs. For ease of comparison, we've put the nutrition analyses in chart form at the beginning of each chapter. To see how this works, compare the nutrition analysis of Barbecued Bacon Burgers and Basic Grilled Burgers. Going across the chart, you'll see that a serving of Barbecued Bacon Burgers is higher in calories, protein, carbohydrate, fat, sodium, and potassium than one of Basic Grilled Burgers. If calories and carbohydrate values are of concern to you, you'll notice that the Basic Grilled Burgers recipe contains half the calories and no carbohydrate. But when you compare the two recipes for their percentages of U.S. RDAs per serving, you'll see that Barbecued Bacon Burgers is higher in protein, vitamin A, vitamin C, thiamine, riboflavin, niacin, calcium, and iron. So now the decision depends on your personal nutritional needs.

To obtain each nutrition analysis, we used these guidelines.
• If a recipe lists ingredients for a frosting, topping, filling, or dressing within the recipe, the analysis for these ingredients is included in the nutrition analysis for the recipe. (For example, see the Yellow Citrus Cake recipe. The analysis includes the recipe for Lemon Filling in the total nutrition analysis.)
• If a recipe lists a suggested sub-recipe with a page reference, the suggested recipe is not included in the nutrition analysis.

Instead, it is listed separately, with its own nutrition analysis. To obtain the total nutrition analysis for a serving of the complete recipe, look up the analysis for both recipes and add them together. (For example, see the Banana Cake recipe with the suggested frosting, Creamy Butter Frosting. The total nutrition analysis requires adding the two analyses together.)

• Suggested garnishes and ingredients listed as "optional" or "if desired" were omitted in the analyses.

• If a food is marinated and then brushed with the marinade during cooking, or if a basting sauce is used, the nutrition analysis includes the entire amount of marinade or sauce.

• When two ingredient options appear in a recipe (such as butter or margarine), the nutrition analysis was calculated using the first choice of ingredients.

• When a recipe ingredient has a variable weight (such as a 3- to 3½-pound beef chuck pot roast), the nutrition analysis was calculated using the lesser weight of the ingredient.

• If a recipe gives two serving sizes (such as "Makes 4 to 6 servings"), the nutrition analysis was calculated using the first choice.

• The nutrition analyses for recipes calling for fresh ingredients were calculated using measurements for raw fruits, vegetables, and meats.

# In Our Test Kitchen

Every recipe Better Homes and Gardens® publishes is tested in our Test Kitchen until is meets our high standards of quality. Along with the Test Kitchen Director and a panel of editors, our Test Kitchen home economists perfect each recipe's preparation, texture, color and flavor.

You can be confident about every Better Homes and Gardens® recipe you prepare. Each one is tested until it earns the Test Kitchen Seal of Approval—assuring that it looks appealing, tastes good, and is practical to prepare and serve.

## WHY 21 MILLION PEOPLE TRUST THIS ALL-TIME FAVORITE BEST SELLER

- 1,251 Test Kitchen-tested recipes
- Over 80 illustrated cooking tips
- Nutrition Analysis for every recipe
- 21 tabbed chapter dividers
- Exciting new dishes, plus many old favorites
- Time-saving ideas for today's busy cooks
- Many made-from-scratch recipes
- Shopping tips and storage information
- Canning and freezing instructions
- 246 illustrations, many in mouthwatering color
- Meal planning and nutrition basics

For more than half a century, people have counted on the Better Homes and Gardens® *New Cook Book* to help them prepare delicious, nutritious dishes that turn out right every time. So many, in fact, that they have made this the best-selling hard-cover cookbook of all time! We believe it will become a reliable friend in your kitchen, too.

# BETTER HOMES AND GARDENS®

# NEW COOK BOOK

# Appetizers & Snacks

# Appetizers & Snacks

# Appetizers & Snacks

# Appetizers & Snacks

# Appetizers

# Appetizers & Snacks

| Recipes | | | | | | | | Percent of U.S. RDA Per Serving | | | | | | | |
|---|---|---|---|---|---|---|---|---|---|---|---|---|---|---|---|
| | Servings (fraction of recipe) | Calories | Protein (grams) | Carbohydrate (grams) | Fat (grams) | Sodium (milligrams) | Potassium (milligrams) | Protein | Vitamin A | Vitamin C | Thiamine | Riboflavin | Niacin | Calcium | Iron |
| Appetizer Clam Shells | 1/6 | 110 | 4 | 11 | 6 | 428 | 120 | 7 | 5 | 17 | 4 | 6 | 4 | 5 | 11 |
| Appetizer Fruit Combo | 1/6 | 104 | 1 | 26 | 0 | 13 | 325 | 2 | 55 | 79 | 7 | 4 | 4 | 3 | 5 |
| Baked Ham-Stuffed Mushrooms | 1/24 | 21 | 1 | 2 | 1 | 45 | 63 | 2 | 1 | 1 | 2 | 4 | 3 | 1 | 1 |
| Beer-Cheese Fondue | 1/4 | 444 | 29 | 5 | 33 | 1064 | 114 | 44 | 27 | 0 | 0 | 28 | 2 | 92 | 6 |
| Blue Cheese-Onion Dip | 1/32 | 58 | 1 | 1 | 5 | 62 | 24 | 2 | 2 | 1 | 1 | 2 | 0 | 2 | 0 |
| Broiled Grapefruit Halves | 1/6 | 92 | 1 | 20 | 1 | 26 | 157 | 2 | 1 | 62 | 3 | 2 | 1 | 2 | 4 |
| Cheese Ball | 1/28 | 64 | 2 | 1 | 6 | 43 | 34 | 2 | 7 | 4 | 1 | 3 | 0 | 2 | 1 |
| Cheese-Ham Ball | 1/40 | 43 | 2 | 0 | 4 | 86 | 16 | 2 | 3 | 1 | 0 | 2 | 0 | 2 | 1 |
| Cheese-Wine Log | 1/48 | 30 | 2 | 0 | 2 | 101 | 10 | 3 | 2 | 0 | 0 | 2 | 0 | 4 | 1 |
| Chicken and Crab Wontons | 1/40 | 33 | 2 | 2 | 2 | 117 | 21 | 3 | 1 | 1 | 1 | 1 | 2 | 1 | 1 |
| Chicken Liver Pate | 1/27 | 55 | 5 | 1 | 4 | 40 | 30 | 7 | 43 | 6 | 2 | 27 | 10 | 0 | 8 |
| Chili con Queso | 1/28 | 39 | 2 | 1 | 3 | 76 | 57 | 3 | 4 | 9 | 1 | 2 | 1 | 6 | 1 |
| Cocktail Meatballs w/Tangy Cranberry Sauce | 1/40 | 41 | 1 | 3 | 3 | 24 | 27 | 2 | 1 | 2 | 1 | 1 | 1 | 0 | 1 |
| Crab Cocktail | 1/4 | 52 | 8 | 2 | 2 | 488 | 161 | 13 | 11 | 11 | 3 | 3 | 5 | 3 | 3 |
| Creamy Dill Dip | 1/32 | 66 | 1 | 1 | 7 | 64 | 18 | 1 | 2 | 1 | 1 | 1 | 0 | 0 | 0 |
| Creamy Onion Dip | 1/24 | 55 | 1 | 1 | 6 | 63 | 20 | 1 | 1 | 1 | 0 | 1 | 0 | 1 | 1 |
| Crunch Party Mix | 1/16 | 418 | 11 | 32 | 32 | 719 | 235 | 17 | 11 | 6 | 16 | 13 | 32 | 6 | 13 |
| Dilled Salmon Dip | 1/40 | 46 | 2 | 0 | 4 | 51 | 32 | 3 | 4 | 2 | 0 | 2 | 2 | 2 | 0 |
| Egg Rolls | 1/10 | 101 | 6 | 9 | 4 | 457 | 84 | 10 | 3 | 5 | 6 | 6 | 9 | 3 | 6 |

# Nutrition Analysis Chart

| | | | | | | | | | | | | | | |
|---|---|---|---|---|---|---|---|---|---|---|---|---|---|---|
| Egg Salad Triangles | 1/20 | 51 | 2 | 3 | 4 | 171 | 23 | 3 | 3 | 0 | 2 | 2 | 1 | 1 | 3 |
| Fluffy Fruit Dip | 1/24 | 39 | 1 | 3 | 3 | 6 | 24 | 1 | 2 | 0 | 1 | 1 | 0 | 1 | 0 |
| Fruit-Crab Cocktail | 1/8 | 278 | 7 | 19 | 21 | 184 | 628 | 11 | 21 | 107 | 14 | 11 | 11 | 6 | 6 |
| Guacamole | 1/16 | 48 | 1 | 2 | 5 | 68 | 175 | 1 | 2 | 8 | 2 | 3 | 2 | 0 | 1 |
| Hot Broccoli Dip | 1/32 | 18 | 0 | 1 | 2 | 22 | 27 | 1 | 5 | 8 | 0 | 0 | 1 | 0 | 0 |
| Italian Appetizer Artichokes | 1/2 | 286 | 7 | 16 | 25 | 101 | 525 | 11 | 25 | 42 | 8 | 15 | 4 | 21 | 7 |
| Oyster Cocktail | 1/4 | 77 | 10 | 4 | 2 | 83 | 147 | 15 | 7 | 63 | 11 | 12 | 14 | 11 | 35 |
| Oysters Rockefeller | 1/4 | 200 | 13 | 12 | 11 | 547 | 429 | 20 | 130 | 100 | 17 | 21 | 18 | 21 | 47 |
| Party Ham Sandwiches | 1/16 | 92 | 3 | 6 | 6 | 222 | 51 | 4 | 2 | 1 | 4 | 3 | 3 | 2 | 3 |
| Pineapple-Orange Ice | 1/6 | 82 | 2 | 20 | 0 | 1 | 156 | 1 | 2 | 34 | 4 | 1 | 1 | 1 | 1 |
| Salmon Mousse | 1/96 | 50 | 2 | 1 | 4 | 112 | 34 | 3 | 1 | 1 | 0 | 1 | 3 | 1 | 1 |
| Shrimp Cocktail | 1/4 | 106 | 22 | 2 | 1 | 160 | 261 | 33 | 0 | 6 | 2 | 2 | 18 | 7 | 10 |
| Shrimp-Cucumber Appetizer Spread | 1/20 | 35 | 2 | 0 | 3 | 39 | 18 | 3 | 2 | 1 | 0 | 1 | 1 | 1 | 1 |
| Smoky Cheese Ball | 1/56 | 75 | 2 | 1 | 7 | 71 | 21 | 3 | 5 | 0 | 1 | 2 | 0 | 4 | 1 |
| Swedish Meatballs | 1/60 | 55 | 3 | 2 | 4 | 77 | 64 | 4 | 2 | 3 | 1 | 2 | 3 | 1 | 3 |
| Swiss Cheese-Ham Spread | 1/48 | 47 | 1 | 0 | 4 | 65 | 16 | 2 | 4 | 1 | 0 | 2 | 0 | 3 | 1 |
| Tomato-Chili Guacamole | 1/21 | 38 | 1 | 2 | 4 | 52 | 152 | 1 | 2 | 9 | 2 | 3 | 2 | 0 | 1 |

# Appetizers & Snacks

Prepare some of your snacks or appetizers ahead of time to avoid a last-minute rush. After preparation, wrap or cover foods so they are airtight (use moisture-vaporproof material for the freezer). Chill or freeze the food quickly. Use refrigerated foods within 24 hours or within the time given in the recipe to avoid loss of flavor and quality.

## Oysters Rockefeller

|   |   |
|---|---|
| 1 | **10-ounce package frozen chopped spinach** |
| 24 | **oysters in shells** |
| 2 | **tablespoons chopped onion** |
| 2 | **tablespoons snipped parsley** |
| 2 | **tablespoons butter or margarine, melted** |
| ½ | **teaspoon salt** |
|   | **Several drops bottled hot pepper sauce** |
| ¼ | **cup fine dry bread crumbs** |
| 1 | **tablespoon butter or margarine, melted** |
|   | **Rock salt** |

Oven 450°

Cook spinach according to package directions. Drain well; press out excess water. Set aside. Thoroughly wash oysters in shells. Open each with an oyster knife or other blunt-tipped knife. With a knife remove oysters and dry. Discard flat top shells; thoroughly wash deep bottom shells. Place each oyster in a shell half.

Stir together cooked spinach, chopped onion, snipped parsley, 2 tablespoons melted butter or margarine, salt, hot pepper sauce, and dash *pepper*. Top *each* oyster shell with 1 *table-spoon* of the spinach mixture.

In a small bowl toss together bread crumbs and the 1 tablespoon melted butter or margarine. Sprinkle about ½ *tea-spoon* of the buttered crumbs over *each* spinach-topped oyster.

Line a shallow baking pan with rock salt to about ½-inch depth. (Or, use crumpled aluminum foil to keep shells from

## Appetizer juices

For a light and nonfilling appetizer, serve a small glass of juice. Try an icy-cold fruit juice garnished with fresh fruit or a mint sprig. Or, heat fruit juice (or a mixture of fruit juices) with cloves and stick cinnamon for a warming appetizer.

Vegetable juices such as tomato, carrot, or vegetable juice cocktail served cold or hot also are excellent meal starters. If desired, add herbs, seasoned salt, Worcestershire sauce, or bottled hot pepper sauce for extra spiciness.

tipping.) Arrange oysters atop salt or crumpled foil. Bake in a 450° oven about 10 minutes or till heated through. Makes 4 servings.

## Appetizer Clam Shells

½ **cup finely chopped onion**
¼ **cup finely chopped green pepper**
1 **tablespoon butter or margarine**
2 **tablespoons all-purpose flour**
1 **tablespoon grated Parmesan cheese**
¼ **teaspoon salt**
 **Dash Worcestershire sauce**
 **Dash bottled hot pepper sauce**
½ **cup finely crushed rich round crackers (12 crackers)**
1 **7½-ounce can minced clams**
½ **cup chopped water chestnuts**
1 **tablespoon butter or margarine, melted**

Oven 350°

In a saucepan cook onion and green pepper in the 1 tablespoon butter or margarine till tender but not brown. Stir in *flour*; add cheese, salt, Worcestershire sauce, and hot pepper sauce. Add ¼ *cup* of the crushed crackers; mix well. Stir in the *undrained* clams and the water chestnuts; cook and stir till thickened and bubbly. Divide among 6 coquille shells, baking shells, or individual baking dishes. Combine the remaining crackers and the 1 tablespoon melted butter or margarine; sprinkle atop mixture in each shell. Bake in a 350° oven about 15 minutes or till heated through. Garnish with cherry tomatoes and parsley, if desired. Makes 6 servings.

## Swedish Meatballs

| | |
|---|---|
| ½ | **cup chopped onion** |
| 3 | **tablespoons butter or margarine** |
| 1 | **beaten egg** |
| 1 | **cup light cream** |
| 1½ | **cups soft bread crumbs** |
| ¼ | **cup finely snipped parsley** |
| 1¼ | **teaspoons salt** |
| | **Dash ground nutmeg** |
| | **Dash ground ginger** |
| | **Dash pepper** |
| 1½ | **pounds ground beef*** |
| 2 | **tablespoons all-purpose flour** |
| 1 | **teaspoon instant beef bouillon granules** |
| ½ | **teaspoon instant coffee crystals** |

Cook onion in *1 tablespoon* of the butter or margarine till tender. In a mixing bowl combine egg and cream; stir in cooked onion, bread crumbs, parsley, salt, nutmeg, ginger, and pepper. Add ground beef or meats; mix well. Chill mixture. Shape chilled meat mixture in ¾- to 1-inch balls.

Brown meatballs, half at a time, in the remaining 2 tablespoons butter or margarine; remove from skillet. Stir flour, bouillon granules, and coffee crystals into pan drippings; add 1¼ cups *water*. Cook and stir till thickened and bubbly. Add meatballs. Cover; simmer about 30 minutes, basting meatballs occasionally. Makes about 60 meatballs.

*\*Or,* use a mixture of ¾ pound *ground beef,* ½ pound *ground veal,* and ¼ pound *ground pork* for the meatballs.

## Appetizer Fruit Combo

    1   15¼-ounce can pineapple chunks (juice
        pack)
    3   cups cantaloupe *or* honeydew melon balls
    1   cup strawberries, halved lengthwise
    ¼   cup orange marmalade
    2   tablespoons orange liqueur

Drain pineapple chunks, reserving juice. In a mixing bowl combine pineapple chunks, melon balls, and strawberries. Combine the reserved pineapple juice, marmalade, and orange liqueur; pour over fruits. Stir gently. Chill 1 to 2 hours; stir occasionally. Serves 6.

## Cocktail Meatballs

    1   beaten egg
    2   tablespoons fine dry bread crumbs
    2   tablespoons thinly sliced green onion
    2   tablespoons finely chopped green pepper
    ¼   teaspoon dried thyme, crushed
    ½   pound lean ground beef
        Cooking oil
        Tangy Cranberry Sauce

Combine egg, bread crumbs, green onion, green pepper, thyme, ½ teaspoon *salt,* and dash *pepper.* Add ground beef; mix well. Shape beef mixture into ¾-inch meatballs. (Allow meatballs to stand at room temperature 30 minutes before cooking.)

Pour cooking oil into a metal fondue cooker to no more than ½ capacity or to a depth of 2 inches. Heat over range to 350°. Add 1 teaspoon *salt* to the hot oil. Transfer cooker to a fondue burner. Spear individual meatballs with a fondue fork; cook in hot oil about 1 minute or till browned. Transfer meatballs to a dinner fork; dip into warm Tangy Cranberry Sauce. Makes about 40 meatballs.

**Tangy Cranberry Sauce:** Combine one 8-ounce can *jellied cranberry sauce,* 3 tablespoons *bottled steak sauce,*

2 teaspoons *brown sugar,* 2 teaspoons *cooking oil,* and 1 teaspoon *prepared mustard.* Beat till smooth with a rotary beater. Heat through. Makes 2 cups.

## Pineapple-Orange Ice

> ¾ **cup water**
> ¼ **cup sugar**
> 1½ **cups unsweetened pineapple juice**
> ¾ **cup orange juice**
> **Finely shredded orange peel or mint sprigs (optional)**

In a small saucepan combine water and sugar. Bring to boiling; reduce heat and simmer, uncovered, for 5 minutes. Cool slightly. Stir in pineapple juice and orange juice; pour into an 8x8x2-inch pan. Cover pan with foil and freeze about 5 hours or till mixture is firm. To serve, break up mixture with a spoon till mushy. Spoon into individual sherbet glasses. Trim with shredded orange peel or mint sprigs, if desired. Makes 6 servings.

## Cheese Ball

> 1 **8-ounce package cream cheese, softened**
> ½ **cup dairy sour cream**
> ¼ **cup butter or margarine, softened**
> 2 **tablespoons finely chopped pimiento**
> 1 **tablespoon snipped parsley**
> 1 **teaspoon grated onion**
> ⅓ **cup finely chopped nuts**
> ⅓ **cup snipped parsley**

Combine cream cheese, sour cream, and butter or margarine; beat with electric mixer till fluffy. Stir in pimiento, 1 tablespoon parsley, and onion. Chill. Shape into a ball. Coat with nuts and ⅓ cup parsley. Makes about 1¾ cups.

**Dilled Salmon Dip:** Prepare as above, *except* omit nuts and ⅓ cup parsley. Stir in one 7¾-ounce can *salmon,* drained, flaked, and skin and bones removed, and ¼ teaspoon dried *dillweed.* Cover; chill. Add milk, if necessary, to make of dipping consistency. Makes 2½ cups.

**Swiss Cheese-Ham Spread:** Prepare as above, *except* omit nuts and ⅓ cup parsley. Have 1 cup shredded *Swiss cheese* at room temperature. Combine Swiss cheese, cheese ball mixture, one 3-ounce can *deviled ham,* and 1 teaspoon *prepared mustard.* Beat till almost smooth. Cover; chill. Makes 3 cups.

## Cheese-Wine Log

> 2 cups shredded sharp cheddar cheese, softened
> 1 3-ounce package cream cheese, softened
> ⅓ cup dry white wine
> 1 tablespoon finely chopped green onion
> 1 teaspoon prepared horseradish
> 1 2½-ounce package (about 1 cup) smoked beef, finely snipped
> Assorted crackers

In a small mixer bowl beat softened cheeses till nearly smooth; gradually beat in wine. Add onion and prepared horseradish. Chill mixture about 1 hour or till slightly firm. Shape mixture into 2 logs, each about 6 inches long. Roll each in *half* of the beef. Wrap and chill till ready to serve. Serve with crackers. Makes 2.

# Baked Ham-Stuffed Mushrooms

- **24** fresh mushrooms, 1½ to 2 inches in diameter
- **¼** cup chopped green onion
- **1** tablespoon butter *or* margarine
- **2** teaspoons all-purpose flour
- **¼** teaspoon dried savory, crushed
- **2** tablespoons dry white wine
- **½** cup finely chopped, fully cooked ham
- **2** tablespoons grated Parmesan cheese
- **¼** cup fine dry bread crumbs                    Oven 350°

Wash mushrooms; drain. Remove stems from mushrooms; reserve caps. Chop stems to make 1 cup. Cook chopped stems and green onion in butter or margarine just till tender. Stir in flour, savory, and ⅛ teaspoon *pepper;* add wine and 2 tablespoons *water.* Cook and stir till thickened and bubbly; stir in ham and Parmesan. Fill mushroom caps with ham mixture. Place mushrooms in a 15x10x1-inch baking pan. Top with bread crumbs. Bake in a 350° oven for 15 to 20 minutes or till tender. Makes 24.

# Fruit-Crab Cocktail

- **½** cup mayonnaise *or* salad dressing
- **2** tablspoons catsup
- **1** tablespoon lemon juice
  Dash bottled hot pepper sauce
  Few drops Worcestershire sauce
- **1** pound crab legs, cooked, chilled, and shelled, *or* one 6-ounce can crab meat, drained, cartilage removed, and cut into pieces
- **4** oranges, peeled and sectioned
- **2** avocados, peeled, seeded, and thinly sliced
- **1** grapefruit, peeled and sectioned
  Bibb lettuce leaves

For dressing, combine mayonnaise, catsup, lemon juice, pepper sauce, and Worcestershire. Arrange crab meat, orange sections, avocado slices, and grapefruit sections in 8 lettuce-lined cocktail cups or glasses. Pour dressing over crab mixture. Serves 8.

---

## Salmon Mousse

---

    1   15½-ounce can salmon
    2   envelopes unflavored gelatin
    2   cups mayonnaise or salad dressing
    ½   cup chili sauce
    2   tablesppoons lemon juice
    1   tablespoon Worcestershire sauce
    ½   teaspoon dried dillweed
    ¼   teaspoon pepper
    1   6½-ounce can tuna, drained and finely
          flaked
    4   hard-cooked eggs, finely chopped
    ½   cup pimiento-stuffed olives, finely chopped
    ¼   cup finely chopped onion
        Party rye bread or assorted crackers

Drain salmon, reserving liquid; add water, if necessary, to equal ½ cup liquid. Bone and finely flake salmon; set aside. Sprinkle gelatin over reserved salmon liquid. Place over hot water and stir to dissolve. In a mixing bowl gradually blend dissolved gelatin into mayonnaise. Stir in chili sauce, lemon juice, Worcestershire sauce, dillweed, and pepper. Fold in flaked salmon, tuna, hard-cooked eggs, olives, and onion. Turn into a 6-cup mold. Chill till firm. Unmold. Garnish with additional pimiento-stuffed olives, if desired. Serve with party rye bread or crackers. Makes 6 cups.

## Smoky Cheese Ball

*Finely chopped walnuts, peanuts, or toasted almonds make a crunchy coating—*

    2  8-ounce packages cream cheese, softened
    2  cups shredded smoky cheddar cheese (8
       ounces)
    ½  cup butter or margarine, softened
    2  tablespoons milk
    2  teaspoons steak sauce
    1  cup finely chopped nuts
       Assorted crackers

In a mixer bowl combine cream cheese, shredded cheddar cheese, softened butter, milk, and steak sauce. Beat mixture with electric mixer till fluffy. Chill slightly; shape into a ball. Place chopped nuts on waxed paper; gently roll cheese ball over nuts to coat. Serve with crackers. Makes about 3½ cups.

## Cheese-Ham Ball

    1  8-ounce package cream cheese
    1  cup shredded American cheese (4 ounces)
    1  4½-ounce can deviled ham
    2  tablespoons finely chopped pimiento
    1  teaspoon grated onion
    1  tablespoon milk
       Snipped parsley (optional)
       Assorted crackers

Have cheeses at room temperature. In a small mixer bowl combine *half* of the cream cheese and all of the American cheese; beat with electric mixer till blended. Beat in deviled ham; stir in pimiento and onion. Chill mixture for 2 to 3 hours. Shape into a ball on a serving plate. Combine remaining cream cheese and the milk; beat smooth. Spread over ham mixture; chill well. Sprinkle with snipped parsley, if desired. Serve with crackers. Makes 1½ cups.

## Shrimp-Cucumber Appetizer Spread

> 1 **3-ounce package cream cheese, softened**
> 2 **tablespoons mayonnaise *or* salad dressing**
> 1 **tablespoon catsup**
> 1 **teaspoon prepared mustard**
>   **Dash garlic powder**
> 1 **4½-ounce can shrimp, drained and**
>   **chopped**
> ¼ **cup finely chopped cucumber**
> 1 **teaspoon finely chopped onion**
>   **Melba toast**

In a mixing bowl stir together the cream cheese and mayonnaise or salad dressing; stir in catsup, mustard, and garlic powder. Stir in chopped shrimp, cucumber, and onion. Spread mixture over melba toast. Garnish with additional shrimp and cucumber, if desired. Makes 1¼ cups spread.

## Shrimp Cocktail

> 1 **pound fresh *or* frozen shelled shrimp,**
>   **cooked, drained, and chilled**
>   **Lettuce**
>   **Cocktail Sauce (see recipe, page 724)**
>   **Lemon wedges**

Arrange cooked and chilled shrimp in lettuce-lined cocktail cups or glasses. Serve with about *1 tablespoon* of the Cocktail Sauce spooned atop each serving. Garnish each serving with a lemon wedge. Makes 4 servings.

**Oyster Cocktail:** Prepare as above, *except* use 1 pint shucked *oysters*, drained and chilled. Omit shrimp.

**Crab Cocktail:** Prepare as above, *except* use one 7-ounce can *crab meat*, drained, flaked, and cartilage removed; *or* one 6-ounce package frozen *crab meat*, thawed and flaked. Add 1 cup finely chopped *celery* to the crab meat; mix well. Omit shrimp.

## Egg Salad Triangles

    4   hard-cooked eggs, chopped
    2   tablespoons chopped pimiento-stuffed
        olives
    1   tablespoon finely chopped green onion
    3   tablespoons mayonnaise *or* salad dressing
    2   teaspoons prepared mustard
    5   slices white sandwich bread
        Sliced pimiento-stuffed olives (optional)

Combine chopped eggs, chopped olives, and green onion; stir in mayonnaise or salad dressing and mustard. Remove crusts from bread, if desired. Spread each slice of bread with about ¼ cup of the egg mixture. Cut each slice of bread diagonally into quarters. If desired, garnish each sandwich with sliced pimiento-stuffed olives. Makes 20 sandwiches.

## Chicken Liver Pâté

    1   pound chicken livers
   ¼   cup chopped onion
    2   tablespoons butter *or* margarine
    3   tablespoons mayonnaise *or* salad dressing
    2   tablespoons lemon juice
    2   tablespoons butter *or* margarine, softened
    8   drops bottled hot pepper sauce
   ½   teaspoon dry mustard
        Assorted crackers

In a skillet cover and cook livers and onion in 2 tablespoons butter or margarine about 5 minutes or till livers are no longer pink, stirring occasionally. Drain; reserve 3 tablespoons drippings. Process liver-onion mixture and reserved drippings in a food processor or blender. (*Or*, put liver-onion mixture through the fine blade of a meat grinder; stir reserved drippings into ground mixture.) Add mayonnaise or salad dressing, lemon juice, 2 tablespoons butter, pepper sauce, mustard, ½ teaspoon *salt*, and dash *pepper*; mix well. Place in a well-oiled 2-cup mold or bowl. Cover; chill for 6 hours or overnight. Unmold. If desired, garnish with chopped hard-cooked egg, snipped chives, or parsley. Serve with crackers. Makes about 1⅔ cups.

## Party Ham Sandwiches

- **1   4½-ounce can deviled ham**
- **¼  cup finely chopped celery**
- **¼  cup finely chopped dill pickle**
- **1   tablespoon mayonnaise or salad dressing**
- **4   slices firm-textured white bread**
- **4   slices firm-textured rye bread**
- **1   4-ounce container whipped cream cheese**
  - **Snipped parsley**
  - **Pimiento strips**

Combine deviled ham, celery, dill pickle, and mayonnaise or salad dressing. Cover; chill. Remove crusts from bread, if desired. Spread white bread slices with ham mixture, top with rye bread slices. Frost tops with cream cheese. Cut each sandwich diagonally into quarters. Decorate sandwiches with parsley or pimiento. Makes 16 sandwiches.

## Chicken and Crab Wontons

    1   **whole small chicken breast**
    1   **clove garlic, minced**
    1   **tablespoon cooking oil**
    1   **cup chopped Chinese cabbage**
  ½   **cup finely chopped pea pods**
  ¼   **cup chopped water chestnuts**
    2   **tablespoons chopped onion**
  ½   **cup canned** *or* **cooked crab meat**
    1   **beaten egg**
    2   **tablespoons soy sauce**
    1   **teaspoon dry sherry**
  ¼   **teaspoon salt**
  ⅛   **teaspoon pepper**
  40   **wonton skins**
        **Cooking oil or shortening for deep-fat
          frying**
        **Sweet-Sour Sauce and Hot Chinese
          Mustard (see recipes, pages 723 and
          718)**

To make filling, skin, bone, and finely chop chicken. In a skillet cook chicken and garlic in the 1 tablespoon cooking oil about 2 minutes. Add vegetables; cook 2 to 3 minutes more. Flake crab meat. In a bowl combine crab, chicken-vegetable mixture, egg, soy sauce, sherry, salt, and pepper. Cool slightly.

To wrap wontons, place a wonton skin with one point toward you. Spoon about *2 teaspoons* of the filling just off center of skin. Fold bottom point of wonton skin over filling. Roll wonton once to cover filling, leaving about 1 inch unrolled at the top of the skin. Grasp the left- and right-hand corners and bring together below filling. Overlap corners. Repeat with remaining wonton skins and filling.

Fry wontons, a few at a time, in deep hot oil or shortening (365°) for 2 to 3 minutes or till golden brown. Use a slotted spoon or wire strainer to remove wontons. Drain on paper toweling. Serve warm with Sweet-Sour Sauce and Hot Chinese Mustard. Makes 40 wontons.

***Egg Rolls:*** Prepare filling as above, *except* use 10 *egg roll* *skins.* To wrap egg rolls, place an egg roll skin with one point toward you. Spoon about ¼ *cup* of the filling diagonally across and just below center of skin. Fold bottom point of skin over filling; tuck point under filling. Fold side corners over, forming an envelope shape. Roll up toward remaining corner; moisten point and press firmly to seal. Repeat with remaining egg roll skins and filling. Deep-fat fry and serve as above. Makes 10.

## Italian Appetizer Artichokes

> **2    small artichokes**
> **Lemon juice**
> **1    8-ounce container (1 cup) sour cream with**
> **French onion**
> **2    tablespoons finely chopped green pepper**
> **1    tablespoons snipped parsley**
> **1    teaspoon lemon juice**
> **½    teaspoon dried oregano, crushed**
> **2    to 3 tablespoons milk**

Wash artichokes; trim stems and remove loose outer leaves. Cut off 1 inch of tops; snip off sharp leaf tips. Brush edges with some lemon juice. In a large kettle cover and cook artichokes in boiling salted water about 25 minutes or till a leaf pulls out easily. Drain upside down. Chill thoroughly.

To make the dip, combine sour cream with French onion, green pepper, parsley, 1 teaspoon lemon juice, and the oregano. Add milk to make of dipping consistency. Chill.

To eat, pull off a leaf and dip the base of the leaf in the dip. Draw through teeth, eating only the tender flesh. Continue till a cone of young leaves appears. Pull away the cone, eating the little bit of soft flesh. Scoop out and discard the fuzzy "choke." Eat the remaining heart with a fork, dipping each piece in the dip. Makes 2 servings.

## Broiled Grapefuit Halves

    **3 grapefruit**
    **3 teaspoons butter or margarine**
    **3 tablespoons brown sugar**
    **¾ teaspoon ground cinnamon**
    **Maraschino cherries**

Have grapefruit at room temperature. Cut each in half; then cut a thin slice from the bottom of each half to balance grapefruit. Cut around each section to loosen fruit from shell. Remove core from each half; dot each half with ½ *teaspoon* butter or margarine. Combine brown sugar and cinnamon; sprinkle over grapefruit. Place on broiler rack or in a shallow baking pan; broil 4 inches from heat about 8 minutes or till heated through and topping is bubbly. Garnish with maraschino cherries. Serves 6.

## Crunch Party Mix

    **1 cup cooking oil**
    **2 tablespoons Worcestershire sauce**
    **1 teaspoon garlic salt**
    **1 teaspoon seasoned salt**
    **Several drops bottled hot pepper sauce**
    **7 cups round toasted oat cereal (6 ounces)**
    **5 cups small pretzels (8 ounces)**
    **3 cups salted mixed nuts (1 pound)**
    **3 cups bite-sized shredded wheat squares (6 ounces)**
    **¼ cup grated Parmesan cheese**    Oven 250°

In a saucepan heat together the oil, Worcestershire, garlic salt, seasoned salt, and hot pepper sauce. In a large roasting pan combine the oat cereal, pretzels, nuts, and shredded wheat squares. Stir oil mixture well; drizzle over cereal mixture, tossing to coat evenly. Bake in a 250° oven for 2 hours, stirring every 30 minutes. Remove from oven; sprinkle with Parmesan; toss lightly. Makes about 16 cups.

## Hot Broccoli Dip

1   **10-ounce package frozen chopped broccoli**
1   **teaspoon instant beef bouillon granules**
1   **cup dairy sour cream**
1   **teaspoon Worcestershire sauce**
   **Dash garlic powder**
   **Raw vegetable dippers, assorted crackers,**
     **or breadsticks**

Cook broccoli according to package directions. Drain; reserve ⅓ cup liquid, adding water, if necessary. Stir bouillon granules into reserved liquid.

In a blender container combine broccoli, reserved broccoli liquid, and sour cream. Cover; blend till smooth, stopping to scrape down sides of container as necessary. Pour broccoli mixture into a saucepan. Stir in Worcestershire sauce and garlic powder; heat through. Transfer to a fondue pot; place over a fondue burner. Serve with raw vegetables, crackers, or breadsticks. Makes 2 cups.

## Beer-Cheese Fondue

2   **cups shredded Swiss cheese (8 ounces)**
2   **cups shredded American cheese (8 ounces)**
1   **tablespoon cornstarch**
½   **teaspoon dry mustard**
1   **teaspoon Worcestershire sauce**
   **Few drops bottled hot pepper sauce**
⅔   **cup beer**
   **French bread, cut into bite-size pieces,**
     **each with 1 crust**

Have the cheeses at room temperature. In a mixing bowl combine cheeses with cornstarch and dry mustard; toss to coat. Add Worcestershire sauce and hot pepper sauce; mix well.

In a saucepan heat beer just till warm. Gradually add cheese mixture, stirring constantly over medium-low heat till the cheese is melted.

Quickly transfer cheese mixture to a fondue pot; place over a fondue burner. Spear a bread cube with a fondue fork, piercing the crust last. Dip bread into cheese mixture, swirling to coat bread. (The swirling is important to keep the mixture in motion so it doesn't set up.) If mixture thickens while standing, stir in some additional warmed beer. Makes 4 to 6 servings.

---

## Fondue dippers

Many foods, even leftovers, make suitable and interesting fondue dippers. Cut dippers into bite-size pieces. A general guideline is to allow 10 to 12 pieces per serving for appetizer fondues. Try these dippers:

French or Italian bread, hard rolls, English muffins, breadsticks, bagels, or pretzels. (Cut bread and rolls into cubes so that each piece has one crust.)

Beef, chicken, turkey, ham, or seafood. (Serve meats precooked.)

Cherry tomatoes, carrot slices, cooked or raw broccoli or cauliflower, green pepper pieces, cooked artichokes, or cooked mushrooms.

---

## Creamy Dill Dip

   1   **cup dairy sour cream**
   1   **cup mayonnaise or salad dressing**
   1   **tablespoon minced dried onion**
   1   **tablespoon dried dillweed**
   ½   **teaspoon seasoned salt**
       **Assorted fresh vegetable dippers or crisp**
       **crackers**

Thoroughly combine sour cream, mayonnaise or salad dressing, minced dried onion, dillweed, and seasoned salt. Cover and chill thoroughly to blend flavors. Serve with fresh vegetable dippers or crackers. Makes 2 cups dip.

## Creamy Onion Dip

> **1 cup dairy sour cream**
> **½ cup mayonnaise *or* salad dressing**
> **2 tablespoons *regular* onion soup mix**
> **2 tablespoons snipped parsley**
> **Potato chips, corn chips, *or* crisp crackers**

Thoroughly combine sour cream, mayonnaise or salad dressing, onion soup mix, and parsley. Cover; chill till serving time. Serve with your choice of chips or crackers. Makes 1½ cups.

**Blue Cheese-Onion Dip:** Prepare Creamy Onion Dip as above, *except* stir in ½ cup crumbled *blue cheese*, ⅓ cup chopped *walnuts*, and 2 tablespoons *milk*. Makes 2 cups.

## Fluffy Fruit Dip

> **1 cup dairy sour cream**
> **⅓ cup apricot *or* peach preserves, *or* orange marmalade**
> **¼ cup finely chopped walnuts**
> **2 to 3 tablespoons milk**
> **Assorted fresh or canned fruit dippers, chilled**

In a small bowl combine sour cream, preserves or marmalade (cut up any large pieces of fruit), and walnuts; mix well. Stir in enough milk to make mixture of dipping consistency; chill. To serve, insert wooden picks into chilled fruit pieces. Dunk fruit into chilled dip. Makes 1½ cups dip.

# Guacamole

2 **medium avocados, seeded and peeled**
1 **thin slice of small onion**
1 **tablespoon lemon juice**
1 **clove garlic, minced**
½ **teaspoon salt**
**Assorted fresh vegetable dippers**

In a blender container combine avocados, onion, lemon juice, garlic, and salt. Blend till smooth, scraping down sides of container as necessary. Place in a serving bowl. Cover and chill before serving. Serve as a dip with fresh vegetables. Makes about 1 cup.

   ***Tomato-Chili Guacamole:*** Prepare Guacamole as above, *except* stir in 1 small *tomato,* peeled and finely chopped, and 2 tablespoons finely chopped canned *green chili peppers.* Cover; chill before serving. Makes 1⅓ cups.

# Chili con Queso

½ **cup finely chopped onion**
1 **tablespoon butter *or* margarine**
2 **medium tomatoes, peeled, seeded, and chopped**
1 **4-ounce can green chili peppers, rinsed, seeded, and chopped**
¼ **teaspoon salt**
1 **cup shredded cheddar cheese (4 ounces)**
1 **cup shredded Monterey Jack cheese food (4 ounces)**
**Milk**
**Tortilla chips *or* corn chips**

In a medium saucepan cook onion in butter or margarine till tender but not brown. Stir in tomatoes, chili peppers, and salt. Simmer, uncovered, for 10 minutes. Add cheeses, a little at a time, stirring just till melted. Stir in a little milk if mixture becomes too thick. Heat through over low heat. Transfer to a small serving bowl; serve warm with tortilla chips or corn chips. Makes about 1¾ cups.

**Barbecue**

**Barbecue**

**Barbecue**

**Barbecue**

**Barbecue**

**Barbecue**

**Barbecue**

**Barbecue**

# Barbecue

| Recipes | Servings (fraction of recipe) | Calories | Protein (grams) | Carbohydrate (grams) | Fat (grams) | Sodium (milligrams) | Potassium (milligrams) | Percent of U.S. RDA Per Serving | | | | | | | |
|---|---|---|---|---|---|---|---|---|---|---|---|---|---|---|---|
| | | | | | | | | Protein | Vitamin A | Vitamin C | Thiamine | Riboflavin | Niacin | Calcium | Iron |
| Apple-Peanut-Buttered Pork Steaks | 1/4 | 728 | 35 | 19 | 57 | 165 | 684 | 54 | 0 | 8 | 109 | 24 | 49 | 3 | 30 |
| Bacon-Wrapped Franks | 1/4 | 889 | 26 | 46 | 66 | 2059 | 382 | 39 | 6 | 6 | 3 | 42 | 29 | 30 | 18 |
| Barbecued Bacon Burgers | 1/6 | 605 | 27 | 25 | 43 | 774 | 446 | 42 | 5 | 5 | 11 | 24 | 20 | 6 | 25 |
| Basic Grilled Burgers | 1/4 | 304 | 20 | 0 | 24 | 337 | 325 | 31 | 1 | 1 | 0 | 6 | 24 | 1 | 17 |
| Basted Poultry-on-a-Spit w/Herb-Butter Basting Sauce | 1/8 | 245 | 22 | 0 | 22 | 140 | 4 | 33 | 26 | 0 | 2 | 5 | 26 | 2 | 12 |
| Basted Poultry-on-a-Spit w/Sweet-Sour Basting Sauce | 1/8 | 242 | 22 | 26 | 22 | 171 | 6 | 33 | 17 | 2 | 2 | 5 | 27 | 2 | 16 |
| Basted Poultry-on-a-Spit w/Wine Basting Sauce | 1/8 | 187 | 22 | 2 | 22 | 36 | 9 | 33 | 19 | 3 | 1 | 5 | 26 | 2 | 13 |
| Beef Teriyaki | 1/6 | 429 | 27 | 7 | 33 | 1840 | 477 | 32 | 1 | 6 | 2 | 7 | 14 | 5 | 24 |
| Blue Cheese Burgers | 1/4 | 530 | 27 | 33 | 31 | 794 | 412 | 41 | 6 | 2 | 6 | 10 | 20 | 6 | 24 |
| Calico Rice Bake | 1/6 | 218 | 8 | 24 | 10 | 605 | 104 | 12 | 53 | 2 | 6 | 8 | 7 | 16 | 8 |
| Caraway-Cheese Spread w/bread | 1/20 | 98 | 3 | 14 | 3 | 158 | 35 | 5 | 2 | 0 | 0 | 8 | 5 | 17 | 3 |
| Cheesy Butter Spread w/bread | 1/28 | 103 | 3 | 14 | 14 | 186 | 36 | 5 | 2 | 1 | 1 | 8 | 5 | 8 | 4 |
| Cheesy Potato-Carrot Foil Bake | 1/6 | 307 | 8 | 16 | 24 | 317 | 444 | 12 | 91 | 30 | 10 | 8 | 8 | 17 | 6 |
| Company Pork Loin Roast | 1/10 | 608 | 32 | 10 | 48 | 543 | 633 | 49 | 8 | 10 | 102 | 23 | 43 | 3 | 28 |
| Corn-Stuffed Pork Chops | 1/6 | 802 | 45 | 8 | 65 | 400 | 754 | 69 | 7 | 23 | 140 | 33 | 57 | 4 | 39 |
| Country-Style Barbecued Ribs | 1/6 | 805 | 28 | 17 | 70 | 733 | 681 | 43 | 12 | 33 | 88 | 20 | 37 | 4 | 29 |

# Nutrition Analysis Chart

| | | | | | | | | | | | | | |
|---|---|---|---|---|---|---|---|---|---|---|---|---|---|
| Crab-Bacon Bites | 1/24 | 96 | 3 | 2 | 8 | 199 | 36 | 4 | 1 | 4 | 2 | 2 | 1 | 2 |
| Fiesta Beef Kebabs | 1/6 | 358 | 24 | 14 | 23 | 678 | 524 | 36 | 59 | 9 | 14 | 29 | 3 | 21 |
| Fish in a Basket | 1/4 | 363 | 28 | 8 | 23 | 482 | 445 | 44 | 0 | 18 | 13 | 24 | 4 | 5 |
| Foil-Barbecued Shrimp | 1/6 | 243 | 29 | 3 | 13 | 533 | 377 | 45 | 14 | 3 | 3 | 25 | 11 | 15 |
| Foil-Wrapped Clambake | 1/8 | 655 | 35 | 20 | 50 | 707 | 772 | 54 | 26 | 16 | 17 | 30 | 13 | 23 |
| Frank-Vegetable Kebabs | 1/6 | 291 | 10 | 9 | 24 | 853 | 469 | 16 | 95 | 12 | 12 | 12 | 3 | 11 |
| Garlic Spread w/bread | 1/9 | 145 | 3 | 14 | 24 | 237 | 32 | 4 | 0 | 0 | 4 | 5 | 3 | 4 |
| Glazed Ham Slice | 1/6 | 395 | 18 | 25 | 25 | 1157 | 388 | 27 | 7 | 49 | 13 | 22 | 2 | 17 |
| Grilled Acorn Squash | 1/6 | 170 | 3 | 35 | 4 | 51 | 894 | 5 | 53 | 8 | 15 | 7 | 8 | 13 |
| Grilled Rock Lobster Tails | 1/4 | 232 | 27 | 2 | 13 | 340 | 321 | 41 | 2 | 2 | 3 | 23 | 9 | 13 |
| Grilled Salmon Steaks | 1/6 | 350 | 23 | 1 | 28 | 152 | 395 | 35 | 16 | 12 | 9 | 18 | 4 | 4 |
| Grilled Turkey Pieces | 1/10 | 301 | 35 | 1 | 16 | 701 | 44 | 54 | 2 | 8 | 43 | 52 | 3 | 22 |
| Grilled Whole Potatoes | 1 | 185 | 4 | 33 | 6 | 6 | 782 | 6 | 51 | 0 | 4 | 14 | 1 | 6 |
| Herbed Spread w/bread | 1/9 | 145 | 3 | 14 | 9 | 237 | 32 | 4 | 0 | 8 | 4 | 5 | 3 | 4 |
| Herb-Seasoned Vegetables | 1/4 | 249 | 6 | 34 | 12 | 336 | 913 | 9 | 160 | 13 | 15 | 11 | 13 | 13 |
| Italian-Seasoned Vegetable Kebabs | 1/4 | 119 | 4 | 12 | 7 | 401 | 704 | 6 | 63 | 11 | 28 | 24 | 4 | 8 |
| Lamb Shish Kebabs | 1/6 | 424 | 20 | 9 | 34 | 432 | 767 | 31 | 93 | 19 | 31 | 40 | 3 | 12 |
| Lemon-Marinated Chuck Roast | 1/8 | 428 | 29 | 3 | 35 | 536 | 489 | 45 | 9 | 9 | 16 | 35 | 2 | 25 |
| Marinated Fish Kebabs | 1/6 | 167 | 16 | 9 | 7 | 715 | 574 | 25 | 84 | 8 | 12 | 18 | 4 | 10 |
| Marinated Leg of Lamb | 1/10 | 439 | 27 | 1 | 36 | 309 | 457 | 42 | 9 | 16 | 20 | 39 | 2 | 12 |
| Marinated Shrimp Appetizers | 1/30 | 62 | 6 | 1 | 4 | 149 | 73 | 9 | 2 | 0 | 1 | 5 | 2 | 3 |
| Meat and Potato Bake | 1/4 | 488 | 22 | 34 | 29 | 1303 | 990 | 34 | 51 | 28 | 20 | 26 | 18 | 18 |
| Mustard-Parsley Spread w/bread | 1/13 | 125 | 14 | 6 | 218 | 36 | 4 | 5 | 5 | 8 | 4 | 40 | 3 | 4 |
| Onion-Stuffed Steak | 1/6 | 875 | 31 | 2 | 81 | 591 | 48 | 11 | 5 | 10 | 21 | 40 | 4 | 28 |
| Parmesan Spread w/bread | 1/16 | 121 | 3 | 14 | 6 | 208 | 34 | 5 | 0 | 8 | 5 | 5 | 4 | 4 |
| Pineapple-Glazed Chicken | 1/12 | 199 | 24 | 9 | 7 | 169 | 71 | 37 | 22 | 5 | 29 | 37 | 2 | 15 |
| Pizza Burgers | 1/10 | 503 | 29 | 27 | 30 | 741 | 433 | 44 | 14 | 17 | 22 | 27 | 24 | 23 |
| Pizza-Frank Sandwiches | 1/6 | 657 | 25 | 31 | 47 | 1634 | 358 | 39 | 4 | 31 | 25 | 26 | 17 | 23 |
| Polish Sausage-Krauters | 1/4 | 486 | 25 | 7 | 39 | 2392 | 456 | 38 | 11 | 36 | 18 | 25 | 3 | 22 |

# Nutrition Analysis Chart

## Percent of U.S. RDA Per Serving

| Recipes | Servings (fraction of recipe) | Calories | Protein (grams) | Carbohydrate (grams) | Fat (grams) | Sodium (milligrams) | Potassium (milligrams) | Protein | Vitamin A | Vitamin C | Thiamine | Riboflavin | Niacin | Calcium | Iron |
|---|---|---|---|---|---|---|---|---|---|---|---|---|---|---|---|
| Quick Garlic Cubed Steaks | 1/6 | 399 | 26 | 21 | 23 | 563 | 411 | 40 | 7 | 5 | 16 | 17 | 33 | 3 | 23 |
| Roasted Corn on the Cob w/Herbed Butter | 1/8 | 183 | 3 | 19 | 12 | 273 | 239 | 5 | 16 | 17 | 8 | 6 | 7 | 1 | 3 |
| Roasted Pork Chops | 1/6 | 854 | 44 | 19 | 66 | 959 | 864 | 67 | 10 | 21 | 139 | 31 | 58 | 5 | 38 |
| Saucy Lamb Riblets | 1/4 | 743 | 29 | 24 | 59 | 1183 | 690 | 44 | 15 | 16 | 15 | 23 | 44 | 4 | 15 |
| Skillet-Fried Fish | 1/6 | 280 | 20 | 17 | 14 | 789 | 388 | 31 | 42 | 0 | 0 | 14 | 16 | 10 | 5 |
| Smoked Mustard-Glazed Ribs | 1/6 | 759 | 27 | 26 | 61 | 586 | 557 | 42 | 0 | 5 | 86 | 19 | 35 | 5 | 28 |
| Smoked Short Ribs | 1/6 | 811 | 33 | 9 | 69 | 647 | 652 | 51 | 19 | 10 | 11 | 18 | 41 | 3 | 30 |
| Spiced Orange-Apricot Ribs | 1/6 | 738 | 27 | 21 | 60 | 1110 | 502 | 42 | 24 | 11 | 86 | 20 | 35 | 3 | 26 |
| Spicy Barbecued Chicken | 1/12 | 203 | 24 | 6 | 9 | 284 | 78 | 37 | 22 | 5 | 5 | 29 | 37 | 2 | 15 |
| Steak and Shrimp Kebabs | 1/6 | 394 | 22 | 23 | 24 | 386 | 730 | 35 | 6 | 79 | 79 | 15 | 29 | 2 | 20 |
| Sweet-Sour Ham | 1/14 | 377 | 30 | 15 | 21 | 1709 | 629 | 47 | 0 | 43 | 61 | 20 | 33 | 7 | 27 |
| Teriyaki Appetizer Ribs | 1/26 | 172 | 6 | 3 | 15 | 430 | 123 | 10 | 0 | 1 | 20 | 5 | 8 | 1 | 7 |
| Wine-Sauced Shoulder Chops | 1/8 | 524 | 26 | 2 | 44 | 118 | 450 | 40 | 5 | 13 | 16 | 19 | 38 | 2 | 11 |

# Barbecue

Becoming familiar with basic barbecuing techniques makes cooking *outdoors* over the charcoal grill even more pleasant.

Follow the manufacturer's directions for your grill. If the firebox needs a foundation for the charcoal, you can line the firebox of a brazier-type grill with heavy-duty foil and top it with a one-inch base of pea gravel, coarse grit, or expanded mica insulation pellets. Change the liner when it gets full of greasy drippings. You can wash gravel or grit bedding to dry and use again. Discard the insulation pellets. Determine the approximate amount of briquettes you'll need. Small, short-cooking foods need fewer briquettes than thicker meat cuts. Mound briquettes and start them with liquid lighter or jelly fire starter, following label directions. Or, omit the fuel fire starters and use an electric starter. *Don't use gasoline or kerosene!* Once started, let the coals burn until they die down to a glow. Arrange the coals (see tip box, page 71) with long-handled tongs.

To check the temperature of the coals, hold your hand, palm side down, above the coals at the distance the food will be cooking. Start counting "one thousand one, one thousand two," etc. If you need to remove your hand after 2 seconds, the coals are *Hot;* 3 seconds, *Medium-hot;* 4 seconds, *Medium;* and 5 or 6 seconds; *Slow.*

As food cooks, control flare-ups by spacing coals farther apart or using a pump-spray bottle filled with water. Don't douse the coals!

Use a meat thermometer to check the doneness of roasts. Insert it so the tip reaches the thickest part of the meat, without touching fat, bone, or the metal spit rod. Check the final temperature by pushing the thermometer a little farther into the meat. If the temperature drops, cook longer.

When turning steaks, use tongs to avoid piercing the meat. If you don't have tongs, insert the fork into a strip of fat and flip the steak with the aid of a turner.

The cooking times for chicken, ribs, and chops can be shortened with the use of a microwave oven. Just partially micro-cook these foods before placing them on the grill.

# Grilling Chart

| Type of Food | Cut or portion (placed 4 inches above coals) | Weight or thickness | Temperature of coals* |
|---|---|---|---|
| **Beef** | Burgers | ½ inch | Medium-hot |
| | | | Medium |
| | | ¾ inch | Medium-hot |
| | | | Medium |
| | Porterhouse, T-bone, or sirloin steak | 1 inch | Medium-hot |
| | | 1½ inches | Medium-hot |
| | | | Medium |
| | Chuck blade steak | 1 inch | Medium |
| | | 2½ inches | Medium |
| **Lamb** | Rib chops | 1 inch | Medium |
| | | 1½ inches | Medium |
| | Shoulder chops | 1 inch | Medium |
| | | 1½ inches | Medium |
| **Pork** | Loin chops | 1 inch | Medium |
| | | 1½ inches | Medium |
| | Blade steak | ¾ inch | Medium |
| | Loin back ribs or spareribs | 5-6 pounds | Medium |
| **Ham** | Fully cooked slice | ½ inch | Medium-hot |
| | | 1 inch | Medium |
| | Canned | 5 pounds | Medium |
| **Chicken** | Broiler-fryer halves | 2½-3 pounds | Medium-hot |
| | Roasting chicken, unstuffed | 3-4 pounds | Medium |
| **Turkey** | Unstuffed | 6-8 pounds | Medium |
| | | 12-16 pounds | Medium |
| **Fish** | Salmon or halibut steaks | ¾ inch | Medium |
| | | 1-1½ inches | Medium-hot |
| | Trout, snapper, or whitefish fillets | 6-8 ounces each | Medium-hot |
| | | | Medium |
| **Seafood** | Shrimp (large) | 2 pounds | Hot |

*Estimate by holding hand, palm down, about 4 inches above hot coals. Count seconds you can hold position. Holding 2 seconds = *Hot* coals; 3 seconds = *Medium-hot;* 4 seconds = *Medium;* and 5 or 6 seconds = *Slow.*

# A basic guide for cooking foods on the grill

| Approximate total cooking times | | | | Comments |
| Open Grill | | Covered grill | | |
| Rare | Medium | Rare | Medium | |
| --- | --- | --- | --- | --- |
| 8-10 min. | 10-12 min. | 7-9 min. | 8-10 min. | Allow four burgers per |
| 10-12 min. | 12-15 min. | 8-10 min. | 10-12 min. | pound. |
| 10-12 min. | 12-15 min. | 8-10 min. | 10-12 min. | Allow three burgers |
| 12-15 min. | 14-18 min. | 10-12 min. | 12-15 min. | per pound. |
| 12-18 min. | 15-20 min. | 8-10 min. | 10-15 min. | Check doneness by |
| 18-20 min. | 20-25 min. | 10-15 min. | 15-18 min. | cutting a slit in meat |
| 20-25 min. | 25-30 min. | 15-18 min. | 18-22 min. | near bone. |
| 12-18 min. | 15-20 min. | 8-10 min. | 12-18 min. | |
| 50-60 min. | 55-65 min. | 45-55 min. | 50-60 min. | Use foil tent on open grill. |
| | 20-25 min. | | 20-25 min. | Check doneness by cutting a slit in meat |
| 25-30 min. | 28-32 min. | 20-25 min. | 23-28 min. | near bone. |
| | 22-28 min. | | 18-22 min. | |
| 28-32 min. | 30-35 min. | 20-25 min. | 25-30 min. | |
| | **Well-done** | | **Well-done** | |
| | 22-25 min. | | 18-22 min. | A wire grill basket aids in turning. |
| | 30-35 min. | | 25-30 min. | |
| | 15-20 min. | | 15-20 min. | |
| | | | 1¼-1½ hrs. | |
| | 10-15 min. | | 10-15 min. | Slash fat edge of ham slice. |
| | 25-35 min. | | 20-30 min. | |
| | 1½-1¾ hrs. | | 1¼-1¾ hrs. | Use foil tent on open grill. |
| | 45-50 min. | | 40-45 min. | |
| | | | 2-2½ hrs. | |
| | | | 3-3¾ hrs. | Meat thermometer inserted in thigh |
| | | | 3½-4½ hrs. | should register 185° |
| | 17-22 min. | | 15-20 min. | Use a wire grill basket. |
| | 10-17 min. | | 10-15 min. | |
| | 10-17 min. | | 10-15 min. | Use a wire grill basket. |
| | 17-20 min. | | 15-17 min. | |
| | 15-18 min. | | 15-18 min. | |

# Spit-Roasting Chart

| Type of food | Cut | Weight | Temperature of coals* |
|---|---|---|---|
| **Beef** | Rolled rib roast | 5-6 pounds | Medium |
| | Tenderloin roast | 2½ pounds | Medium-hot |
| | Eye of round | 3-4 pounds | Medium-hot |
| | Boneless rump roast | 3-4 pounds | Slow |
| **Lamb** | Leg | 5-7 pounds | Medium |
| **Pork** | Boneless loin roast | 5-6 pounds | Medium |
| | Loin back ribs or spareribs | 3-4 pounds | Slow |
| **Ham** | Boneless piece | 9-10 pounds | Medium |
| | Canned | 5 pounds | Medium |
| **Chicken** | Whole | 2½-3 pounds | Medium-hot |
| | | | Medium |
| **Cornish Hens** | 4 birds | 1-1½ pounds each | Medium-hot |
| **Duckling** | Whole domestic | 4-6 pounds | Medium-hot |
| **Turkey** | Unstuffed | 6-8 pounds | Medium |
| | 2 rolled turkey roasts | 28 ounces each | Medium-hot |
| | Boneless turkey roast | 5-6 pounds | Medium-hot |

*Estimate temperature of coals by holding hand, palm down, about 4 inches above hot coals. Count the seconds you can hold position. Holding 2 seconds indicates *Hot* coals; 3 seconds, *Medium*-hot coals; 4 seconds, *Medium* coals; and 5 or 6 seconds, *Slow* coals.

# A Guide for cooking meat and poultry on a spit

| Approximate roasting time | | | Comments |
|---|---|---|---|
| **Covered grill**\*\* | | | |
| **Rare** | **Medium** | **Well-done** | |
| 2-2½ hrs. | 2½-3 hrs. | | |
| 40-45 min. | 45-50 min. | | |
| 1¼-1½ hrs. | 1½-2 hrs. | | |
| | 1¼-1¾ hrs. | 1½-2 hours | Have meat rolled and tied. |
| 1 hr. | 1 ½-2 hrs. | 1¾-2¼ hours | Have shank cut off short. Balance diagonally on spit. |
| | | 4-4½ hours | Have meat rolled and tied. |
| | | 1-1¼ hours | Thread on spit accordion style. |
| | | 2-2¼ hours | |
| | | 1¼-1½ hours | Tie securely after mounting on spit. |
| | | 1½-1¾ hours | |
| | | 1½-2 hours | |
| | | 1½-1¾ hours | |
| | | 1½-1¾ hours | A deep foil drip pan is essential. |
| | | 3¼-4½ hours | Push holding forks deep into bird. |
| | | 1¾-2¼ hours | Purchase frozen; thaw completely. |
| | | 2½-3½ hours | |

\*\*Use a covered grill when cooking on the rotisserie. Or, if you have a brazier with a half-hood, cover the open side with heavy-duty foil, making it into a covered grill.

# Beef

## Beef Teriyaki

1½    pounds boneless beef tenderloin or sirloin
      steak
½     cup soy sauce
2     tablespoons cooking oil
2     tablespoons molasses
2     teaspoons dry mustard
1     teaspoon ground ginger
4     cloves garlic, halved

Partially freeze beef; thinly slice across grain into approximately 3-inch strips. For marinade, combine soy sauce, oil, molasses, mustard, ginger, garlic, and ¼ cup *water*; mix well. Add meat to marinade; let stand 15 minutes at room temperature. Drain meat, reserving marinade. Thread meat strips accordion style on 12 skewers. If desired, halve preserved kumquats crosswise and add a kumquat half to the end of each skewer. Grill skewers over *hot* coals 5 to 7 minutes or to desired doneness. Turn and baste occasionally with marinade. Serves 6.

## Smoked Short Ribs

      Hickory chips
4     pounds beef plate short ribs, cut into
      serving-size pieces
1     10¾-ounce can condensed tomato soup
¾     cup dry red wine
¼     cup finely chopped onion
2     tablespoons cooking oil
1     tablespoon prepared mustard
2     teaspoons chili powder
1     teaspoon paprika
1     teaspoon celery seed

About an hour before cooking time, soak hickory chips in enough water to cover. Drain chips. In a covered grill place *slow* coals on both sides of drip pan. Sprinkle coals with hickory chips. Place ribs, bone side down, on grill. Lower grill hood. Grill ribs about 1½ hours or till done, adding hickory chips every 20 minutes. Meanwhile, in a saucepan mix tomato soup, next 7 ingredients, and ¼ teaspoon *salt*. Heat sauce on grill. Brush ribs with sauce. Grill, uncovered, about 20 minutes more; brush often with sauce. Serves 6.

---

## Steak and Shrimp Kebabs

*A takeoff on the "surf and turf" entrée, this version is a grilled kebab—*

- ½ **pound fresh or frozen shrimp, shelled**
- ½ **cup catsup**
- ¼ **cup water**
- ¼ **cup finely chopped onion**
- 1 **tablespoon brown sugar**
- 3 **tablespoons lemon juice**
- 2 **tablespoons cooking oil**
- 2 **teaspoons prepared mustard**
- 2 **teaspoons Worcestershire sauce**
- ½ **teaspoon chili powder**
- 1 **pound beef sirloin steak, cut into 1-inch pieces**
- 2 **zucchini, cut diagonally into 1-inch pieces**
- 2 **fresh ears of corn, cut into 1-inch pieces**
- 2 **small onions, cut into wedges**
- 1 **green pepper or red sweet pepper, cut into squares**
- 6 **cherry tomatoes**

Thaw shrimp, if frozen. For sauce, in a small saucepan combine the catsup, water, chopped onion, and brown sugar. Stir in the lemon juice, cooking oil, prepared mustard, Worcestershire sauce, and chili powder. Simmer the sauce, uncovered, 10 minutes, stirring once or twice.

Meanwhile, on 6 skewers thread sirloin steak pieces alternately with shelled shrimp, zucchini pieces, corn pieces, onion wedges, and green or red pepper squares.

Grill kebabs over *medium-hot* coals to desired doneness; allow 15 to 17 minutes for medium-rare meat. Turn the kebabs often and brush with the sauce. Garnish the end of each skewer with a cherry tomato before serving. Makes 6 servings.

## Onion-Stuffed Steak

> **2 beef porterhouse steaks, cut 1½ inches thick (about 1½ pounds each), *or* 1 beef sirloin steak, cut 1½ inches thick (about 2 to 2½ pounds)**
> **½ cup sliced green onion**
> **1 large clove garlic, minced**
> **3 tablespoons butter *or* margarine**
> **Dash celery salt**
> **¼ cup dry red wine**
> **2 tablespoons soy sauce**
> **1 cup sliced fresh mushrooms**

Slash fat edges of steak at 1-inch intervals (don't cut into meat). Slice pockets in each side of meat, cutting almost to bone. In a skillet cook onion and garlic in *1 tablespoon* of the butter. Add celery salt and dash *pepper*. Stuff pockets with onion mixture; skewer closed. Mix wine and soy sauce; brush on meat. Grill over *medium-hot* coals for 8 to 10 minutes; brush often with soy mixture. Turn; grill 8 to 10 minutes more for rare. Brush often with soy mixture. In a small skillet cook mushrooms in the remaining 2 tablespoons butter till tender. Slice steak across grain. Pass mushrooms to spoon atop steak. Serves 6.

# Fiesta Beef Kebabs

    ½    cup catsup
    ½    envelope *regular* onion soup mix
    ¼    cup vinegar
    ¼    cup cooking oil
    2    tablespoons sugar
    1    tablespoon prepared mustard
         Dash bottled hot pepper sauce
  1½    pounds beef top round steak, cut into
             1-inch pieces
    2    green *or* red sweet peppers

For marinade, combine first 7 ingredients, ½ cup *water*, and
¼ teaspoon *salt*. Bring to boiling. Cover; simmer 20 minutes.
Cool to room temperature. Add meat. Cover; simmer 20
minutes. Cool to room temperature. Add meat. Cover; refrigerate overnight. Turn meat occasionally. Drain beef; reserve
marinade. Cut peppers into 1-inch squares. On 6 skewers
alternate beef and peppers. Grill over *medium-hot* coals to
desired doneness; allow about 15 minutes for rare. Baste
kebabs with marinade. Serves 6.

# Lemon-Marinated
# Chuck Roast

    1    3- to 3½-pound beef chuck pot roast, cut
             1½ inches thick
    1    teaspoon prepared mustard
    1    teaspoon finely shredded lemon peel
    ⅓    cup lemon juice
    ⅓    cup cooking oil
    2    tablespoons sliced green onion
    1    tablespoon sugar
    1    tablespoon Worcestershire sauce
  1½    teaspoons salt
    ⅛    teaspoon pepper

Slash fat edges of roast. Place meat in a shallow baking dish. For marinade, place mustard and lemon peel in a small bowl; gradually stir in lemon juice. Add oil, onion, sugar, Worcestershire sauce, salt, and pepper. Pour over roast. Cover; let stand 6 hours or overnight in refrigerator, turning meat several times. Remove roast from marinade; reserve marinade. Pat excess moisture from roast with paper toweling.

Grill roast over *medium-hot* coals for 17 to 20 minutes. Turn; cook 17 to 20 minutes more for rare to medium-rare or to desired doneness. Heat reserved marinade on grill. Remove roast to a serving platter. Carve meat across the grain into thin slices. Spoon marinade over roast. Makes 8 servings.

## Quick Garlic Cubed Steaks

- ¼ **cup butter or margarine**
- 2 **tablespoons Worcestershire sauce**
- 2 **tablespoons lemon juice**
- 1 **teaspoon finely snipped parsley**
- ½ **teaspoon celery salt**
- 1 **clove garlic, minced**
- 6 **beef cubed steaks**
- 6 **slices French bread, toasted**

In a saucepan melt butter; stir in Worcestershire, lemon juice, parsley, celery salt, and garlic. Brush butter mixture on both sides of steaks. Place steaks in a wire grill basket. Grill over *hot* coals for 1 to 2 minutes. Turn basket over and grill for 1 to 2 minutes more. Season steaks with salt and pepper. Place each steak atop a toasted bread slice. Spoon remaining butter mixture over steaks. Serves 6.

## Basic Grilled Burgers

- 1 **pound ground beef**
- ½ **teaspoon salt**
  **Dash pepper**

Mix beef, salt, and pepper. Form into four 4-inch patties. Grill over *medium-hot* coals for 5 to 6 minutes; turn and grill 4 to 5 minutes more. Serve on buns, if desired. Serves 4.

**Variations:** Add any of the following to the basic meat mixture: 2 tablespoons chopped *green onion;* 2 tablespoons drained *sweet pickle relish;* 2 tablespoons chopped *pimiento-stuffed olives;* 1 tablespoon prepared *horseradish;* or ¼ teaspoon minced *dried garlic.*

---

## Pizza Burgers

---

    1   **beaten egg**
    1   **8-ounce can pizza sauce**
    ¼   **cup fine dry bread crumbs**
    ¼   **cup grated Parmesan cheese**
    2   **tablespoons snipped parsley**
    ¼   **teaspoon dried oregano, crushed**
    ¼   **teaspoon fennel seed, crushed**
    ¼   **teaspoon garlic salt**
    2   **pounds ground beef**
    2   **tablespoons chopped onion**
    2   **tablespoons chopped pimiento-stuffed
          olives or chopped pitted ripe olives**
   10   **slices French bread, toasted and buttered**
   10   **slice mozzarella cheese**
   10   **tomato slices**

Combine egg and ½ cup of the pizza sauce; stir in crumbs, Parmesan, parsley, oregano, fennel, garlic salt, and dash *pepper.* Add beef; mix well. Divide into 10 equal portions. Shape meat into oval patties ½ inch thick.

In a saucepan combine remaining pizza sauce, onion, olives, and 1 tablespoon *water.* Bring to boiling; reduce heat. Simmer, uncovered, 5 minutes; stir occasionally. Grill burgers over *medium* coals about 7 minutes. Turn and cook about 7 minutes more for medium doneness. Brush with some pizza sauce mixture during the last 5 minutes. Top *each* bread slice with cheese, a burger, lettuce, and tomato. Pass remaining sauce. Serves 10.

## Barbecued Bacon Burgers

    **6**   **slices bacon**
    **1**   **beaten egg**
    **3**   **tablespoons rolled oats**
    **3**   **tablespoons finely chopped green pepper**
    **2**   **tablespoons catsup**
 **1½**   **teaspoons prepared horseradish**
 **1½**   **teaspoons prepared mustard**
  **¾**   **teaspoon salt**
  **⅛**   **teaspoon pepper**
 **1½**   **pounds ground beef**
    **6**   **hamburger buns, split and toasted**

In a skillet cook bacon till almost done, but not crisp. Cut bacon strips in half crosswise. In a mixing bowl combine egg, oats, green pepper, catsup, horseradish, mustard, salt, and pepper. Add ground beef; mix well. Shape into six 4-inch patties. Arrange patties in a greased wire grill basket. Place 2 half-slices of bacon criss-crossed atop each burger to form an "X." Close basket. Grill burgers over *medium* coals, turning often, for 18 to 20 minutes, or to desired doneness. Serve on buns. Makes 6 servings.

## Blue Cheese Burgers

  **½**   **cup chopped water chestnuts**
   **3**   **tablespoons crumbled blue cheese**
   **2**   **tablespoons chopped pimiento-stuffed**
        **olives (optional)**
   **1**   **tablespoon Worcestershire sauce**
  **½**   **teaspoon salt**
   **1**   **pound ground beef *or* ground lamb**
        **Prepared mustard (optional)**
   **4**   **Kaiser rolls *or* hamburger buns, split,**
        **toasted, and buttered**

In a mixing bowl thoroughly combine chopped water chest-nuts, blue cheese, olives, Worcestershire sauce, and salt. Add ground meat; mix well. Shape into four 4-inch patties. Grill burgers over *medium-hot* coals for 5 to 6 minutes. Turn and grill 4 to 5 minutes more for medium doneness. If desired, spread some mustard on cut surfaces of Kaiser rolls or hamburger buns. Serve burgers on rolls or buns. Serves 4.

# Poultry

## Spicy Barbecued Chicken

*Be sure to brush all of the sauce on the chicken pieces during the last 10 minutes of grilling—*

| | |
|---|---|
| ¼ | cup finely chopped onion |
| 1 | clove garlic, minced |
| 2 | tablespoons cooking oil |
| ¾ | cup catsup |
| ⅓ | cup vinegar |
| 1 | tablespoon Worcestershire sauce |
| 2 | teaspoons brown sugar |
| 1 | teaspoon celery seed |
| 1 | teaspoon dry mustard |
| ½ | teaspoon salt |
| ¼ | teaspoon pepper |
| ¼ | teaspoon bottled hot pepper sauce |
| 2 | 2½- to 3-pound broiler-fryer chickens |

For sauce, in a saucepan cook chopped onion and minced garlic in cooking oil till onion is tender but not brown. Stir in the catsup, vinegar, Worcestershire sauce, brown sugar, celery seed, dry mustard, salt, pepper, and bottled hot pepper sauce. Bring mixture to boiling. Reduce heat and simmer sauce, uncovered, for 10 minutes, stirring once or twice during cooking.

Meanwhile, cut the chickens into quarters. Break the wing, hip, and drumstick joints of chickens so that the pieces will remain flat during grilling. Twist wing tips under back. Season chicken pieces with additional salt.

Place chicken pieces, bone side down, over *medium-hot*

coals. Grill chicken for 25 minutes or till bone side is well browned. Turn chicken. Grill 20 to 25 minutes more or till chicken is tender. Brush chicken often with sauce during the last 10 minutes of grilling, using all of the sauce. Makes 12 servings.

## Pineapple-Glazed Chicken

>     1   8¼-ounce can crushed pineapple
>     ½   cup chili sauce or hot-style catsup
>     2   tablespoons brown sugar
>     1   tablespoon prepared mustard
>     2   2½- to 3-pound broiler-fryer chickens,
>             halved lengthwise
>         Cooking oil
>         Salt

For sauce, drain pineapple, reserving ¼ cup syrup. Combine pineapple, reserved syrup, chili sauce or catsup, sugar, and mustard.

Break wing, hip, and drumstick joints of chickens; twist wing tips under back. Brush chickens lightly with oil; season with salt. Grill chickens over *medium-hot* coals, bone side down, for 25 to 30 minutes or till bone side is well browned. Turn chickens. Grill 20 minutes more. Turn chickens again. Spoon sauce atop. Grill 5 to 10 minutes more or till chickens are done. Makes 12 servings.

## Grilled Turkey Pieces

>     1   6- to 7-pound turkey
>     ⅓   cup cooking oil
>     ⅓   cup soy sauce
>     ⅓   cup thinly sliced green onion or finely
>             chopped onion
>    1½   teaspoons ground turmeric
>    1½   teaspoons ground ginger
>     ¾   teaspoon dry mustard
>     1   clove garlic, minced

Have the meatman cut turkey in half lengthwise. At home, thaw turkey, if frozen. Cut into pieces: 2 wings, 2 drumsticks, 2 thighs, 4 breast pieces, and 2 back pieces.

For marinade, combine oil, soy sauce, onion, turmeric, ginger, mustard, and garlic. Place turkey in a large plastic bag. Add marinade and close the bag. Marinate turkey in refrigerator 6 hours or overnight. Drain, reserving marinade. In a covered grill place thighs and breast pieces over *slow* coals. Lower hood and grill about 30 minutes, turning pieces occasionally. Add drumsticks, wings, and back pieces. Lower hood; grill about 1 hour more or till turkey is tender, turning pieces occasionally. During the last 15 minutes, brush pieces with reserved marinade. Serves 10.

## Basted Poultry-on-a-Spit

**4   1- to 1½-pound Cornish game hens *or* two 2½- to 3-pound whole broiler-fryer chickens**
**Sweet-Sour Basting Sauce *or* Wine Basting Sauce *or* Herb-Butter Basting Sauce**

For Cornish game hens, season the cavity of each hen with a little salt and pepper. Run the spit rod through each hen crosswise, below the breastbone; pinch the tines of the holding forks together and push into each hen. (Space birds about 1 inch apart on rod.) With four 18-inch cords, use one cord to tie each hen. (Tie the tail to crossed legs. Bring cord around to back, cross and bring around and across breast, securing wings to body. Tie a knot; cut off loose ends.) Test for balance.

For chickens, season cavity of each with a little salt and pepper. Skewer neck skin to back of chickens. Mount one chicken on spit rod; secure with 2 holding forks and tie with cord (see tip on page 44). Add a third fork and second chicken. Secure with a fourth fork; tie with cord. Test for balance.

Place *medium-hot* coals around the drip pan. Attach spit; position pan directly under meat. Turn on motor; lower grill hood. Grill hens or chickens for 1½ to 1¾ hours or till leg joints move easily. Baste occasionally during the last 30 minutes with a basting sauce. Pass extra sauce, if desired. Serves 8.

***Sweet-Sour Basting Sauce:*** In a saucepan combine one 10-ounce jar *currant jelly*, 3 tablespoons *vinegar*, 1 tablespoon *soy sauce*, ½ teaspoon *garlic powder*, and ½ teaspoon ground *ginger*; heat and stir just to boiling. Makes 1¼ cups sauce.

***Wine Basting Sauce:*** In a saucepan combine ½ cup *dry white wine*; 2 tablespoons *butter or margarine*; 2 tablespoons *lemon or lime juice*; 2 teaspoons *cornstarch*; 1 teaspoon *sugar*, ½ teaspoon dried *savory or* dried *marjoram*, crushed; and dash *pepper*. Cook and stir till thickened and bubbly; cook and stir 2 minutes more. Makes about 1 cup sauce.

## Mounting birds on a spit

Place a holding fork on the spit rod with tines toward the point. Insert the rod through the bird lengthwise. Pinch the fork tines together and push them into the breast of the bird.

Next, tie the wings to the body using a 24-inch cord. Start the cord at the back and loop it around each wing. Wrap it around the wings again. Tie in the center of the breast (illustration).

Loop an 18-inch cord around the tail, then across the crossed legs; tie tightly to hold bird securely. Pull together the cords attached to the wings and legs (right illustration), and tie tightly. Secure the bird with a second holding fork, and test for balance.

**Herb-Butter Basting Sauce:** In a saucepan combine ½ cup *butter or margarine;* 1 teaspoon *onion juice or grated onion;* ½ teaspoon dried *oregano,* crushed; ½ teaspoon dried *basil,* crushed; ¼ teaspoon *pepper;* and several dashes bottled *hot pepper sauce.* Heat and stir till hot. Makes about ½ cup sauce.

# Sausages & Franks

## Polish Sausage-Krauters

> **8 Polish sausages or large frankfurters**
> **1 8-ounce can sauerkraut, drained and snipped**
> **¼ cup chili sauce**
> **2 tablespoons finely chopped onion**
> **1 teaspoon caraway seed**

Slit sausages or frankfurters lengthwise, cutting almost to ends and only ¾ of the way through. Combine sauerkraut, chili sauce, onion, and caraway seed. Stuff about *2 tablespoons* of the mixture into the slit of each sausage or frankfurter; secure with wooden picks. Grill over *hot* coals for 10 to 12 minutes, turning frequently. Remove picks. Serve in frankfurter buns, if desired. Serves 4.

# Bacon-Wrapped Franks

    8  slices bacon
    8  frankfurters or fully-cooked bratwursts
    2  tablespoons Dijon-style mustard or
         prepared mustard
    2  tablespoons thinly sliced green onion or
         finely chopped onion
    2  slices American, Swiss, brick, or Muenster
         cheese
         Bottled barbecue sauce
    8  frankfurter buns, split and toasted

Partially cook bacon. Drain; set aside. Slit frankfurters or bratwursts lengthwise, cutting almost to ends and only ¾ of the
way through. Spread inside of each frank or bratwurst with
some mustard; add some of the onion. Cut each slice of
cheese into 4 strips. Lay 1 strip of cheese inside each frank or
bratwurst. Wrap each frank with a strip of bacon; secure with
wooden picks.

Grill over *hot* coals for 10 to 12 minutes, brushing with
barbecue sauce and turning frequently so bacon cooks crisp
on all sides. Remove picks. Serve frankfurters or bratwursts in
toasted buns. Makes 4 servings.

## Pizza-Frank Sandwiches

  1   **beaten egg**
 ¼   **cup milk**
 ¾   **cup soft bread crumbs**
 ¼   **cup grated Parmesan cheese**
  2   **tablespoons snipped parsley**
 ½   **teaspoon garlic salt**
 ½   **pound bulk Italian sausage**
 ½   **pound ground beef**
  6   **frankfurters**
  1   **8-ounce can pizza sauce**
  2   **tablespoons chopped onion**
  2   **tablespoons sliced pimiento-stuffed olives**
  6   **frankfurter buns, split**
 ⅓   **cup shredded mozzarella cheese**

Combine egg and milk; stir in crumbs, Parmesan, parsley, garlic salt, and dash *pepper*. Add sausage and beef; mix thoroughly. Divide into 6 equal portions. Shape meat around frankfurters, leaving ends open; roll each between waxed paper to make of uniform thickness. Chill. In a saucepan combine pizza sauce, onion, and olives. Simmer uncovered, 5 minutes; stir occasionally. Grill frankfurters over *medium* coals about 5 minutes or till meat is set. Turn and grill about 10 minutes more or till meat is done. Brush with pizza sauce mixture during last 5 minutes. Toast buns. Serve franks on buns. Spoon remaining sauce atop sandwiches; sprinkle with cheese. Serves 6.

## Frank-Vegetable Kebabs

  1   **10-ounce package frozen brussels sprouts**
  1   **small onion, cut into wedges**
  3   **tomatoes, cut into wedges**
  8   **frankfurters or fully-cooked bratwursts, cut into thirds**
 ¼   **cup butter or margarine**
 ½   **teaspoon dried basil, crushed**

Cook sprouts and onion in boiling salted water about 5 minutes or till barely tender; drain. On 6 skewers thread brussels sprouts, onion, tomatoes, and franks or bratwurst. In a saucepan combine butter, basil, ¼ teaspoon *salt*, and dash *pepper*; heat till butter melts. Grill kebabs over *medium* coals for 10 to 12 minutes, turning often and brushing frequently with butter mixture. Makes 6 servings.

# Pork & Ham

## Sweet-Sour Ham

- 1 **5-pound canned ham**
- 1 **20-ounce can pineapple slices**
- ¼ **cup dry sherry or dry white wine**
- 3 **tablespoons vinegar**
- 2 **tablespoons soy sauce**
- 2 **tablespoons honey**
- 1 **tablespoon cooking oil**
- 1 **clove garlic, minced**
  **Dash salt**
- 2 **small green peppers, cut into 1½-inch squares**
- 14 **cherry tomatoes**
- 2 **limes, cut into wedges**

Insert the spit rod through center of ham.* Secure with holding forks; test for balance. Insert a meat thermometer near center of ham, not touching the rod. In a covered grill place *medium* coals around drip pan. Attach spit; position drip pan under meat. Turn on motor; lower grill hood or cover with a foil tent. Grill ham over *medium* coals about 1¼ hours or till done and meat thermometer registers 140°.

Meanwhile, prepare the sauce. Drain pineapple, reserving ⅔ cup syrup. In a saucepan combine reserved syrup, sherry, vinegar, soy, honey, cooking oil, garlic, and salt. Boil mixture down to equal ⅔ cup (about 10 minutes); stir occasionally.

During the last 30 minutes of cooking, brush ham often with sauce; pass remaining sauce.

Before serving, quarter each pineapple slice. Thread 14 small bamboo skewers with green pepper squares, pieces of pineapple, a cherry tomato, and a lime wedge. Serve with ham. Makes 14 servings.

**\*Note:** If your grill does not have a spit, place ham directly on grill over drip pan. Lower hood or tent the grill with heavy-duty foil. Grill ham over *medium* coals for 1 hour. Lift foil tent; turn ham. Insert meat thermometer and brush with sauce. Cover grill again with foil tent. Bake ham about 30 minutes more or till thermometer registers 140°.

---

## Glazed Ham Slice

½ **cup hot-style catsup**
½ **cup apricot preserves, pineapple preserves,**
    **or orange marmalade**
2 **tablespoons finely chopped onion**
1 **tablespoon cooking oil**
1 **tablespoon prepared mustard**
1 **teaspoon Worcestershire sauce**
1 **1½- to 2-pound fully cooked ham slice, cut**
    **1 inch thick**

For glaze, in a saucepan combine catsup, preserves or marmalade, onion, oil, mustard, and Worcestershire sauce. Simmer, uncovered, for 5 minutes, stirring once or twice.

Slash fat edge of ham slice to prevent curling. Grill ham slice over *medium* coals for 10 to 15 minutes; brush lightly with glaze. Turn ham and grill 10 to 15 minutes more or till done, brushing with glaze the last 10 minutes. Reheat glaze in a small saucepan on edge of grill. To serve, cut ham into slices; pass heated glaze. Makes 6 to 8 servings.

## Meat and Potato Bake

    4  large baking potatoes
       Cooking oil
    1  12-ounce can luncheon meat
    4  slices American cheese, cut in half
          diagonally (3 ounces)
       Grated Parmesan cheese
       Butter or margarine

Rub potatoes with cooking oil. Wrap each potato in an 18x12-inch rectangle of heavy-duty foil; seal edges well. Grill over *medium* coals for 1½ hours or till done; turn occasionally. (Or, cook over *medium-slow* coals for 1½ to 2 hours or till done.)

Remove from grill; unwrap. Slice each potato crosswise into four pieces. Cut meat in half crosswise; cut each half into six slices crosswise. Insert slices of meat between potato pieces. Reassemble potato; rewrap in foil, closing top. (Or, skewer potato together and omit foil.)

Grill 10 to 15 minutes more or till heated through; turn twice. Remove foil; place 2 cheese triangles atop each potato. Sprinkle with Parmesan; serve with butter. Serves 4.

## Corn-Stuffed Pork Chops

    6  pork loin chops, cut 1½ inches thick
   ¼  cup chopped green pepper
   ¼  cup chopped onion
    1  tablespoon butter or margarine
    1  beaten egg
 1½  cups toasted bread cubes
   ½  cup cooked whole kernel corn
    2  tablespoons chopped pimiento
   ½  teaspoon salt
   ¼  teaspoon ground cumin
       Dash pepper

Cut a pocket in each chop by cutting from fat side almost to bone edge. Season cavity of each with a little salt and pepper.

For stuffing, in a small saucepan cook green pepper and onion in butter till tender but not brown. Combine egg, bread cubes, corn, pimiento, salt, cumin, and pepper. Pour cooked pepper and onion over bread cube mixture; toss lightly. Spoon about ¼ cup of the stuffing into each pork chop. Securely fasten pocket opening with wooden picks. Grill over *medium* coals about 20 minutes. Turn meat; grill 15 to 20 minutes more or till done. Before serving, remove picks. Serves 6.

---

## Roasted Pork Chops

- **1  cup chopped onion**
- **1  clove garlic, minced**
- **2  tablespoons cooking oil**
- **¾  cup catsup**
- **¼  cup lemon juice**
- **3  tablespoons sugar**
- **2  tablespoons Worcestershire sauce**
- **1  tablespoon prepared mustard**
- **1  teaspoon salt**
- **¼  teaspoon bottled hot pepper sauce**
- **6  pork loin chops or rib chops, cut 1¼ to 1½ inches thick**

For sauce, in a saucepan cook onion and garlic in hot cooking oil till tender but not brown. Stir in catsup and next 6 ingredients. Simmer, uncovered, 5 minutes, stirring once or twice. Sprinkle chops with salt. Place chops in a wire grill basket. Grill chops over *medium* coals about 25 minutes. Turn meat and grill about 20 minutes more or till done, brushing with sauce occasionally. Makes 6 servings.

## Company Pork Loin Roast

     1  **cup catsup**
    ½  **cup water**
    ¼  **cup wine vinegar**
     2  **tablespoons cooking oil**
     2  **tablespoons minced dried onion**
     2  **tablespoons Worcestershire sauce**
     1  **tablespoon brown sugar**
     1  **teaspoon mustard seed**
     1  **teaspoon dried oregano, crushed**
     1  **bay leaf**
    ½  **teaspoon salt**
    ¼  **teaspoon pepper**
    ¼  **teaspoon chili powder**
     1  **4- to 5-pound boneless pork loin roast**

For sauce, in a saucepan combine catsup, water, wine vinegar, oil, onion, Worcestershire sauce, brown sugar, mustard seed, oregano, bay leaf, salt, pepper, and chili powder. Bring to boiling; reduce heat. Simmer the sauce, uncovered, 20 minutes; remove bay leaf.

In a covered grill place *medium* coals on both sides of drip pan. Place roast on grill; insert a meat thermometer near center of roast. Lower hood or cover with a foil tent. Grill for 2 to 2½ hours or till meat thermometer registers 170° for well-done. Brush with sauce frequently during last 30 minutes of grilling. Makes 10 servings.

## Apple-Peanut-Buttered Pork Steaks

    ½  **cup apple butter**
     2  **tablespoons peanut butter**
    ¼  **teaspoon finely shredded orange peel**
     2  **tablespoons orange juice**
     4  **pork shoulder blade steaks, cut ¾ inch
         thick (2 pounds)**

Blend apple butter into peanut butter; add orange peel and juice. Season steaks with a little salt and pepper. Grill over *medium* coals about 15 minutes. Turn steaks; brush with apple butter mixture. Grill 15 to 20 minutes more. Brush on remaining mixture. Serves 4.

**Note:** If desired, use 1¼-inch-thick steaks. Grill 25 minutes. Turn and grill about 25 minutes more or till done. Makes 8 servings.

---

## Spiced Orange-Apricot Ribs

    1  **teaspoon ground ginger**
    1  **teaspoon ground coriander**
   ½  **teaspoon paprika**
    4  **pounds pork loin back ribs *or* spareribs**
       **Hickory chips**
       **Apricot Glaze**

Combine ginger, coriander, paprika, 1 teaspoon *salt,* and ¼ teaspoon *pepper;* rub onto meaty side of ribs. Cover and refrigerate for 2 hours. About an hour before cooking time, soak hickory chips in enough water to cover.

Lace ribs accordion style on a spit rod. Secure ribs with holding forks. Place *hot* coals around a shallow foil drip pan. Drain hickory chips; sprinkle some over coals. Attach spit; position drip pan under meat. Turn on motor; lower grill hood or cover with a foil tent. Grill ribs over *hot* coals about 1 hour or till done. Sprinkle the coals with dampened hickory chips every 20 minutes. Brush ribs frequently with Apricot Glaze during the last 15 minutes of cooking. Heat and pass remaining glaze. Garnish ribs with orange slices, if desired. Serves 6.

***Apricot Glaze:*** Combine ½ cup *apricot preserves,* ¼ cup *orange juice,* 3 tablespoons *soy sauce,* and 1 tablespoon *lemon juice.*

## Country-Style Barbecued Ribs

    **4**   **pounds pork country-style ribs**
    **1**   **cup chopped onion**
    **1**   **clove garlic, minced**
  **¼**   **cup cooking oil**
    **1**   **8-ounce can tomato sauce**
  **¼**   **cup packed brown sugar**
  **¼**   **cup lemon juice**
    **2**   **tablespoons Worcestershire sauce**
    **2**   **tablespoons prepared mustard**
    **1**   **teaspoon celery seed**

Cook ribs, covered, in enough boiling salted water to cover, 45 to 60 minutes or till tender. Drain. Cook onion and garlic in hot oil till tender. Stir in tomato sauce, next 5 ingredients, ½ cup *water*, 1 teaspoon *salt*, and ¼ teaspoon *pepper*. Simmer, uncovered, 15 minutes; stir once or twice. Grill ribs over *slow* coals about 45 minutes or till done; turn every 15 minutes. Brush with sauce till coated. Serves 6.

## Smoked Mustard-Glazed Ribs

*Choose country-style ribs, loin back ribs, or spareribs for this barbecue recipe—*

    **4**   **pounds pork country-style ribs *or* 6 pounds pork loin back ribs *or* spareribs**
    **2**   **tablespoons sugar**
    **1**   **teaspoon salt**
    **1**   **teaspoon paprika**
    **1**   **teaspoon ground turmeric**
       **Hickory chips**
  **½**   **cup packed brown sugar**
  **⅓**   **cup vinegar**
  **¼**   **cup prepared mustard**
  **¼**   **cup chopped onion**
    **2**   **cloves garlic, minced**
  **½**   **teaspoon celery seed**
    **1**   **small onion, thinly sliced**

Thoroughly rub the ribs with a mixture of sugar, salt, paprika, and turmeric. Cover; refrigerate ribs for 4 hours. About an hour before cooking time, soak hickory chips in enough water to cover; drain well.

In a covered grill place *slow* coals on both sides of drip pan. Sprinkle coals with dampened hickory chips. Place ribs, bone side down, on grill; lower grill hood. Grill ribs over *slow* coals about 30 minutes. Turn meat and grill about 25 to 30 minutes more. Sprinkle coals with dampened hickory chips every 20 minutes.

Meanwhile, in a small saucepan combine brown sugar, vinegar, prepared mustard, chopped onion, garlic, and celery seed. Bring mixture to boiling, stirring till sugar dissolves. Brush mixture on both sides of ribs; grill, uncovered, 10 to 15 minutes more or till ribs are done. Heat any remaining sauce. Transfer ribs to a warm platter. Top ribs with sliced onion and additional sauce. Makes 6 servings.

# Fish & Seafood

## Foil-Wrapped Clambake

|   |   |
|---|---|
| 48 | clams in shells |
| 4 | quarts cold water |
| ⅓ | cup salt |
| 8 | chicken drumsticks |
|   | Salt |
|   | Pepper |
| 8 | fresh ears of corn |
|   | Rockweed *or* large bunch parsley |
| 4 | frozen lobster tails, thawed and halved lengthwise |
| 1 | 16-ounce package frozen fish fillets, thawed and cut into 8 pieces |
| 1 | pound butter, melted |

Thoroughly wash clams in shells. In a large kettle combine cold water and ⅓ cup salt. Place clams in salt water mixture; let stand 15 minutes. Rinse well. Repeat salt water soaking and rinsing twice more.

In a covered grill place chicken drumsticks over *hot* coals. Grill about 10 minutes. Season with salt and pepper. Turn back husks of corn. Use a stiff brush to remove silk. Lay husks back in place.

Tear off sixteen 36x18-inch pieces of heavy-duty foil. Place 1 sheet crosswise over a second sheet. Repeat, making a total of 8 sets. Lay a handful of rockweed or parsley in the center of each foil set. Cut eight 18-inch squares of cheesecloth; place 1 square atop rockweed or parsley. For each package arrange the following on cheesecloth: 6 clams in shells, 1 precooked chicken drumstick, 1 ear of corn, ½ of a lobster tail, and 1 piece of fish. Securely tie opposite ends of cheesecloth together. Seal opposite ends of foil together; seal well.

Place foil packages, seam side up, on grill. Lower grill hood. Grill over *hot* coals about 45 minutes. Serve with individual cups of hot, melted butter. Makes 8 servings.

## Skillet-Fried Fish

- **6 fresh or frozen pan-dressed trout or other fish (about 6 ounces each)**
- **⅔ cup yellow cornmeal**
- **¼ cup all-purpose flour**
- **2 teaspoons salt**
- **½ teaspoon paprika**
  **Dash cayenne (optional)**
- **1 5⅓-ounce can (⅔ cup) evaporated milk**
  **Cooking oil**

Thaw fish, if frozen. Thoroughly stir together cornmeal, flour, salt, paprika, and cayenne. Dip fish in evaporated milk, then coat with seasoned cornmeal mixture.

Heat a small amount of cooking oil in a heavy, large skillet over *hot* coals till oil is hot. Cook fish, a few at a time, in hot oil 4 to 5 minutes or till lightly browned. Turn and cook 4 to 5 minutes more or till fish flakes easily when tested with a fork. Add more oil as needed. Drain the fish on paper toweling before serving. Makes 6 servings.

## Fish in a Basket

4 **fresh or frozen whole pan-dressed lake or
brook trout or perch (about 10 to 12
ounces each)**
⅓ **cup all-purpose flour**
½ **teaspoon salt**
⅛ **teaspoon pepper**
¼ **cup butter or margarine, melted**

Thaw fish, if frozen. In a bowl combine flour, salt, and pepper.
Dip fish in seasoned flour, coating thoroughly. Place coated fish
in a well-greased wire grill basket. Grill fish over *hot* coals
about 10 minutes. Turn fish and baste with melted butter. Grill
about 10 minutes more or till fish flakes easily when tested
with a fork; baste often with butter. Makes 4 servings.

**Note:** Wire grill baskets are indispensable for foods that are
difficult to turn, such as fish or shrimp. A hinged basket is more
versatile, since it adjusts to the thickness of foods.

## Grilled Salmon Steaks

3 **fresh or frozen salmon steaks or other fish
steaks (1 to 1½ inches thick)**
½ **cup cooking oil**
¼ **cup snipped parsley**
¼ **cup lemon juice**
2 **tablespoons grated onion**
1 **teaspoon dry mustard**
¼ **teaspoon salt**

Thaw fish, if frozen. Place fish in a shallow dish. For marinade,
combine oil, parsley, lemon juice, onion, mustard, salt, and
dash *pepper*. Pour over fish. Marinate, covered, in the refrigerator 6 hours. Drain, reserving marinade. Place fish in a
well-greased wire grill basket. Grill over *medium-hot* coals 8 to
10 minutes or till fish is lightly browned. Baste with marinade
and turn. Brush again with marinade; grill 8 to 10 minutes
more or till fish flakes easily when tested with a fork. Makes 6
servings.

## Marinated Fish Kebabs

1 **pound fresh or frozen haddock fillets**
3 **tablespoons cooking oil**
3 **tablespoons dry sherry**
3 **tablespoons soy sauce**
2 **green onions, finely chopped**
2 **cloves garlic, minced**
1 **tablespoon brown sugar**
1 **teaspoon dry mustard**
⅛ **teaspoon pepper**
1 **large green pepper**
6 **mushroom caps**
12 **cherry tomatoes**

Thaw fish, if frozen. Cut fish into 1-inch pieces. For marinade, in a bowl combine oil, dry sherry, soy sauce, garlic, brown sugar, dry mustard, and pepper. Place fish pieces in marinade. Cover; marinate at room temperature for 1 hour. Drain fish, reserving marinade. Cut green pepper into 1-inch squares. Pour some boiling water over green pepper and mushrooms in a bowl. Let stand 1 minute; drain. On 6 skewers alternate fish, green pepper, cherry tomatoes, and mushrooms. Grill kebabs over *medium* coals for 8 to 10 minutes or till fish is done, turning and basting frequently with marinade. Serves 6.

## Foil-Barbecued Shrimp

2 **pounds fresh or frozen large shrimp, shelled and deveined**
6 **tablespoons butter or margarine**
½ **cup snipped parsley**
¾ **teaspoon curry powder**
1 **clove garlic, minced**
½ **teaspoon salt**
**Dash pepper**

Thaw shrimp, if frozen. In a saucepan melt butter; stir in parsley, curry powder, garlic, salt, and pepper. Add shrimp; stir to coat. Divide shrimp mixture equally among six 12x18-inch pieces of heavy-duty foil. Fold foil around shrimp, sealing the edges well.

Grill foil-wrapped shrimp packages over *hot* coals about 8 minutes. Turn and grill 7 to 8 minutes more or till done. Serve in foil packages, if desired. Makes 6 servings.

## Grilled Rock Lobster Tails

> **4** **frozen rock lobster tails (about 5 ounces each)**
> **¼** **cup butter *or* margarine, melted**
> **2** **teaspoons lemon juice**
> **Dash ground ginger**
> **Dash chili powder**

Thaw rock lobster tails. Cut off the thin undershell membrane with kitchen scissors. Bend tail back to crack shell or insert long skewers lengthwise between shell and meat to prevent curling. (To butterfly rock lobster tails, partially thaw tails; snip through center of hard top shell with kitchen scissors. With a sharp knife cut through the meat, but *not through undershell.* Spread open.)

For sauce, combine melted butter, lemon juice, ginger, and chili powder; brush over lobster meat. With meat side up, grill lobster tails over *hot* coals about 7 minutes. Brush with sauce; turn shell side up. Grill 7 to 8 minutes more or till meat has lost its transparency and is opaque. Makes 4 servings.

# Lamb & Breads

## Marinated Leg of Lamb

*You don't have to have a rotisserie to grill a leg of lamb. Just start with a boned piece of meat—*

- **1 5- to 6-pound leg of lamb**
- **½ cup cooking oil**
- **⅓ cup lemon juice**
- **¼ cup finely chopped onion**
- **2 tablespoons finely snipped parsley**
- **1 teaspoon salt**
- **¾ teaspoon dried basil, crushed**
- **½ teaspoon dried thyme, crushed**
- **¼ teaspoon dried tarragon, crushed**

Have your meatman bone the leg of lamb and slit the meat lengthwise so you can spread it flat on the grill like a thick steak. For marinade, in a bowl combine the oil, lemon juice, chopped onion, parsley, salt, basil, thyme, and tarragon. Place lamb in a large plastic bag set in a deep bowl. Pour lemon juice marinade over the lamb and close bag. Refrigerate meat 4 to 6 hours, turning bag occasionally to coat lamb evenly with marinade.

Drain lamb, reserving marinade. Insert two long skewers through meat at right angles making a +, *or* place meat in a wire grill basket. (The skewers or grill basket make it easier to turn the meat and keep it from curling during cooking.)

Grill meat over *medium* coals, turning every 15 minutes, to desired doneness. Allow about 1½ hours for medium or 2 hours for well-done lamb. Baste the meat frequently with reserved marinade.

To serve, place lamb on a carving board, removing the skewers or removing the basket. Cut lamb across the grain into thin slices. Makes 10 servings.

**Note:** This marinade is equally good on a bone-in leg of lamb such as the one pictured in the tip box at right. See the chart on pages 30 and 32 for cooking times.

## Wine-Sauced Shoulder Chops

- ¼ **cup thinly sliced green onion**
- 1 **2-ounce can (¼ cup) sliced pimiento, drained and chopped**
- ½ **teaspoon dried oregano, crushed**
- ¼ **teaspoon dried tarragon, crushed**
- ¼ **teaspoon lemon pepper *or* pepper**
- 2 **tablespoons olive *or* cooking oil**
- 1 **tablespoon cornstarch**
- 1 **tablespoon Worcestershire sauce**
- ½ **cup dry white wine**
- 8 **lamb shoulder chops, cut ¾ to 1 inch thick**

For sauce, cook onion, pimiento, herbs, and pepper in hot oil till onion is tender. Combine cornstarch, Worcestershire, and ⅓ cup *cold water;* stir into onion mixture. Cook and stir till bubbly. Add wine. Keep sauce warm.

Grill chops over *medium* coals for 10 to 12 minutes. Turn chops; grill 10 to 12 minutes more or till done, brushing frequently with sauce. Pass remaining sauce. Serves 8.

---

### Roast on a spit

*Boneless roasts:* Insert spit rod through center of roast; secure with holding forks. Test for balance, holding one end of the rod in each hand; turn gently. If meat turns unevenly, readjust forks or rod. *Bone-in roasts:* To allow for the bone's weight, insert the rod diagonally as shown at left. Adjust holding forks and test for balance as above.

## Lamb Shish Kebabs

| | |
|---|---|
| ¾ | cup chopped onion |
| ⅓ | cup lemon juice |
| 3 | tablespoons olive oil |
| 1 | teaspoon salt |
| ¾ | teaspoon dried thyme, crushed |
| ¼ | teaspoon pepper |
| 1½ | pounds boneless lamb, cut into 1-inch pieces |
| 12 | large fresh mushrooms |
| 2 | medium green peppers, cut into 1½-inch pieces |
| 3 | medium tomatoes, quartered |

For marinade, in a bowl combine onion, lemon juice, olive oil, salt, thyme, and pepper. Add meat. Cover and refrigerate several hours or overnight. Drain meat, reserving marinade. Pour some boiling water over mushrooms and green pepper in a bowl. Let stand 1 to 2 minutes; drain.

Thread meat on skewers alternately with tomatoes, green pepper, and mushrooms. Grill over *medium* coals about 25 minutes, brushing with marinade and turning skewers often. (For firm-cooked tomatoes, grill on separate skewers 8 to 10 minutes.) Makes 6 servings.

## Saucy Lamb Riblets

| | |
|---|---|
| 3 | to 4 pounds lamb breast riblets, cut into 2- to 3-rib pieces |
| ½ | cup finely chopped onion |
| 1 | tablespoon cooking oil |
| ¾ | cup catsup |
| 3 | tablespoons Worcestershire sauce |
| 2 | tablespoons brown sugar |
| 2 | tablespoons vinegar |
| ¾ | teaspoon salt |
| | Dash bottled hot pepper sauce |

Trim excess fat from riblets. Cook riblets, covered, in boiling salted water for 30 to 40 minutes. Drain. Meanwhile, cook onion in hot oil till tender. Add remaining ingredients and ¼ cup *water;* heat through. Grill riblets over *medium-hot* coals for 8 to 10 minutes. Brush riblets with some of the catsup mixture; turn and continue grilling for 10 minutes more or till riblets are hot and glazed. Brush riblets again with sauce before serving. Pass extra sauce with meat. Makes 4 main-dish servings or 10 to 12 appetizer servings.

## Grilled Bread Fix-Ups

*Match a bread or roll with a spread—*
**French or Italian Bread:** Cut a *1-pound loaf* into 1-inch diagonal slices, cutting to, but not through, bottom crust. Spread your choice of spread between every other slice of bread. Wrap loosely in heavy-duty foil. Place on edge of grill. Grill over *slow* coals about 15 minutes or till heated through, turning frequently.* Makes about 15 servings.

**Dinner or Hard Rolls:** Split 10 to 12 *dinner rolls* in half. (For hard rolls, split each roll horizontally, cutting to, but not through, opposite side of roll.) Spread your choice of spread on cut surfaces of each roll; reassemble rolls. Wrap loosely in heavy-duty foil. Grill over *slow* coals about 10 minutes or till heated through, turning twice.* Makes 10 to 12 servings.

**Rye or Wheat Bread:** Spread your choice of spread on one side of 12 *bread slices.* Place slices together, forming 6 sandwiches; stack sandwiches. Wrap loosely in heavy-duty foil. Grill over *slow* coals for 12 minutes or till heated through.* Pull slices apart to serve. Makes 12 servings.

**Mustard-Parsley Spread:** Combine 6 tablespoons *butter,* softened; 2 tablespoons finely snipped *parsley;* 2 teaspoons *prepared mustard;* and ½ teaspoon dried *oregano,* crushed.

**Garlic Spread:** Stir together 6 tablespoons *butter,* softened, and ½ teaspoon *garlic powder.*

**Parmesan Spread:** Combine 6 tablespoons *butter,* softened; ¼ cup grated *Parmesan cheese;* and 1 tablespoon snipped *chives.*

***Caraway-Cheese Spread:*** Stir together one 4-ounce container *whipped cream cheese with pimientos,* 1 tablespoon thinly sliced *green onion,* and 1 teaspoon *caraway seed.*

***Cheesy Butter Spread:*** Cream together ¾ cup shredded *Swiss, cheddar, Monterey Jack,* or *American cheese;* ¼ cup *butter or margarine,* softened; 2 tablespoons finely snipped *parsley;* and 2 teaspoons *prepared horseradish.*

***Herbed Spread:*** Cream together 6 tablespoons *butter,* softened; ½ teaspoon dried *marjoram,* crushed; ½ teaspoon dried *thyme,* crushed; and ¼ teaspoon *garlic powder.*

**\*Note:** Or, wrap loosely in foil and place on a baking sheet. Bake in a 350° oven for 15 to 20 minutes or till heated through.

# Vegetables

## Roasted Corn on the Cob

**Fresh ears of corn**
**Butter or Herbed Butter**
**Salt**
**Pepper**

Remove husks from the fresh corn. Remove silks with a stiff brush or by hand. Spread each ear of corn with about *1 tablespoon* of the butter or the Herbed Butter. Sprinkle corn with a little salt and pepper. Wrap securely in heavy-duty foil. Roast ears over *medium-hot* coals about 30 minutes or till corn is tender, turning several times.

***Herbed Butter:*** In a bowl cream together ½ cup *butter or margarine,* softened; ½ teaspoon *salt;* ½ teaspoon dried *rosemary,* crushed; and ½ teaspoon dried *marjoram,* crushed. Keep mixture at room temperature for 1 hour to blend flavors. Makes about ½ cup—enough for 8 ears of corn.

## Grilled Whole Potatoes

> Potatoes
> Cooking oil
> Shredded Swiss or cheddar cheese
>    (optional)
> Sliced green onion (optional)
> Butter (optional)
> Dairy sour cream (optional)

Tear off 6x9-inch pieces of heavy-duty foil—one for *each* potato. Brush potatoes with some cooking oil. Wrap one potato in each piece of foil. Grill over *medium-slow* coals till tender, 1½ to 1¾ hours, or till potatoes are tender, turning occasionally. Remove foil. Open potatoes with tines of fork and push ends to fluff. Top with shredded Swiss or cheddar cheese, sliced green onion, butter, or sour cream, if desired.

## Cheesy Potato-Carrot Foil Bake

> 4 slices bacon
> 3 large potatoes
> 3 medium carrots, shredded
> ¼ cup sliced green onion
>    Salt
>    Pepper
> ¼ cup butter or margarine
> ½ teaspoon caraway seed
> 1 cup shredded Monterey Jack cheese (4 ounces)

Cook bacon till crisp; drain and crumble. Set aside. Tear off a 36x18-inch piece of heavy-duty foil. Fold in half to make an 18-inch square. Fold up sides, using your fist to form a pouch. Thinly slice potatoes into pouch; add carrots and green onion. Sprinkle with a little salt and pepper; dot with butter and sprinkle with caraway. Fold edges of foil to seal pouch securely, leaving space for expansion of steam.

Grill over *slow* coals 55 to 60 minutes or till done; turn

several times. Open package; stir in crumbled bacon and cheese. Close pouch; return to grill for about 1 minute or till cheese melts. Makes 6 servings.

## Grilled Acorn Squash

- 3 medium acorn squash
- 2 tablespoons butter or margarine
- 2 tablespoons brown sugar
- 2 tablespoons water
    Brown sugar
- 1 apple, cut into wedges

Rinse squash. Cut in half lengthwise; remove seeds. Prick insides with the tines of a fork; season cavities with salt and pepper. Add *1 teaspoon* each of butter, brown sugar, and water to each squash. Wrap each half, cut side up, in a 12x18-inch piece of heavy-duty foil; seal securely. Place cut side up on grill. Grill over *medium* coals 50 to 60 minutes or till tender. Open foil. Stir to fluff squash; sprinkle with additional brown sugar. Top with wedges of apple. Makes 6 servings.

## Italian-Seasoned Vegetable Kebabs

- 12 fresh large mushrooms
- 2 small zucchini, cut into 1-inch bias-sliced pieces
- 3 tablespoons Italian salad dressing
- 2 tablespoons lemon juice
- 1 teaspoon Worcestershire sauce
- ¼ teaspoon salt
- 12 cherry tomatoes

Pour some boiling water over mushrooms in a bowl. Let stand 1 minute; drain. On four skewers alternately thread mushrooms and zucchini. Combine Italian salad dressing, lemon juice, Worcestershire sauce, and salt. Grill kebabs over *medi-*

um coals about 12 minutes, turning and brushing often with salad dressing mixture. Thread cherry tomatoes on ends of skewers; grill 5 to 8 minutes more or till heated through, turning and brushing often with salad dressing mixture. Makes 4 servings.

---

## Grilling frozen vegetables

Tear off a 36x18-inch piece of heavy-duty foil. Fold in half to make an 18-inch square. Fold up sides, using your fist to form a pouch.

Place one 10-ounce package *frozen vegetables* in center of pouch. Season with *salt* and *pepper*; top with a pat of *butter or margarine*. Fold edges of foil to seal pouch securely, leaving space for expansion of steam. Grill over *medium-hot* coals till vegetables are cooked. Allow about 20 minutes for peas and other small vegetables; allow more time for larger vegetables. Turn the package of vegetables frequently.

---

## Herb-Seasoned Vegetables

8   **small onions**
4   **large carrots, cut into 1½-inch pieces**
4   **small pattypan squash**
2   **green peppers**
¼   **cup butter or margarine, melted**
¼   **teaspoon dried rosemary, crushed**
¼   **teaspoon dried marjoram, crushed**
¼   **teaspoon salt**
    **Dash pepper**

In a saucepan cook onions and carrots in a small amount of boiling salted water about 20 minutes or till nearly tender;

drain. Cut squash into 1-inch wedges; cut peppers into 1-inch squares. Combine butter, rosemary, marjoram, salt, and pepper. On four skewers alternately thread vegetables. Grill over *medium* coals about 20 minutes or till done. Turn and brush frequently with butter mixture. Serves 4.

## Calico Rice Bake

| 1 | 16-ounce can mixed vegetables, drained |
| 1⅓ | cups quick-cooking rice |
| 1⅓ | cups water |
| 1 | cup shredded cheddar cheese (4 ounces) |
| ¾ | teaspoon salt |
| ½ | teaspoon onion salt |
| ¼ | teaspoon dried rosemary, crushed |
| ⅛ | teaspoon pepper |
| 2 | tablespoons butter *or* margarine |

Tear off a 36x18-inch piece of heavy-duty foil. Fold in half to make an 18-inch square. Fold up sides, using your fist to form a pouch. In a bowl thoroughly combine vegetables, rice, water, cheese, salt, onion salt, rosemary, and pepper. Place mixture in pouch; dot with butter. Fold edges of foil to seal pouch securely. Grill over *medium-hot* coals about 30 minutes or till done. Before serving, open pouch and fluff rice with a fork. Makes 6 servings.

# Appetizers

## Marinated Shrimp Appetizers

2 **pounds fresh or frozen large shrimp, shelled and deveined**
½ **cup cooking oil**
½ **cup lime juice**
3 **tablespoons dry white wine**
1 **tablespoon snipped chives**
1 **clove garlic, minced**
1½ **teaspoons salt**
½ **teaspoon dried dillweed**
**Several dashes bottled hot pepper sauce**

Thaw shrimp, if frozen. Place in a shallow baking dish. For marinade, combine oil, lime juice, wine, chives, garlic, salt, dillweed, and hot pepper sauce. Pour marinade mixture over shrimp. Cover and refrigerate 4 to 6 hours or overnight. Occasionally spoon marinade over shrimp.

Remove the shrimp, reserving marinade. Thread shrimp on skewers or place in a wire grill basket. Grill over *hot* coals for 8 to 10 minutes or till done, turning and brushing often with reserved marinade. Serve on wooden picks. Makes about 30 appetizers.

## Teriyaki Appetizer Ribs

4 **pounds meaty pork spareribs, sawed in half across bones**
½ **cup soy sauce**
2 **tablespoons cooking oil**
2 **tablespoons lemon juice**
1 **tablespoon brown sugar**
2 **cloves garlic, minced**
1 **teaspoon ground ginger**
2 **tablespoons honey**

Cut meat into 2-rib portions. For marinade, mix soy, oil, lemon juice, brown sugar, garlic, ginger, and ¼ teaspoon *pepper*. Place ribs in a shallow baking dish; pour marinade over. Cover; refrigerate 4 to 6 hours. Occasionally spoon marinade over. Remove ribs; reserve marinade. Grill ribs over *slow* coals, bone side down, about 25 minutes. (Add less-meaty ribs after 10 minutes of grilling.) Turn ribs, meaty side down; grill 15 to 20 minutes more. Stir honey into reserved marinade; brush ribs frequently during last 5 minutes. Makes about 26.

## Crab-Bacon Bites

      1   **7-ounce can crab meat**
      1   **beaten egg**
     ¼   **cup tomato juice**
     ½   **cup fine dry bread crumbs**
      1   **tablespoon grated Parmesan cheese**
      1   **tablespoon finely chopped green onion**
      1   **tablespoon lemon juice**
     ¼   **teaspoon Worcestershire sauce**
           **Dash bottled hot pepper sauce**
     12   **slices bacon, cut in half**
           **Nonstick vegetable spray coating**

Drain, flake, and remove cartilage from crab; set aside. Combine egg, next 7 ingredients, and ¼ teaspoon *salt*. Add crab meat; mix well. In a skillet partially cook bacon; drain on paper toweling. Shape crab mixture into 24 logs, about 1½ inches long. Wrap each log with a half-slice of bacon; fasten securely with wooden picks. Spray cold grill with vegetable spray coating. Grill logs over *hot* coals about 10 minutes or till evenly browned, turning several times. Makes 24 appetizers.

# Arranging coals for barbecuing

For spit-roasting, place a foil drip pan under meat and spread coals in a circle around the firebox. (The drip pan catches drippings and helps to avoid flare-ups. You can make one out of heavy-duty foil.)

When cooking large pieces of meat in a covered grill, center the drip pan in the firebox and pile coals on both long sides of the pan. Place meat on grate over drip pan.

For foods cooked flat, such as steaks, chops, and burgers, spread coals over the entire firebox. Place coals about ½ inch apart.

For kebabs, line up coals in parallel rows, placing some around edges of grill. Place kebabs on grate over spaces between briquette rows.

# Beverages

# Beverages

# Beverages

# Beverages

# Beverages

# Beverages

# Beverages

# Beverages

# Beverages

Percent of U.S. RDA Per Serving

| Recipes | Servings (fraction of recipe) | Calories | Protein (grams) | Carbohydrate (grams) | Fat (grams) | Sodium (milligrams) | Potassium (milligrams) | Protein | Vitamin A | Vitamin C | Thiamine | Riboflavin | Niacin | Calcium | Iron |
|---|---|---|---|---|---|---|---|---|---|---|---|---|---|---|---|
| Apricot Swizzle | 1/7 | 155 | 0 | 41 | 0 | 1 | 103 | 0 | 10 | 18 | 1 | 1 | 1 | 1 | 1 |
| Bloody Marys | 1/16 | 67 | 1 | 4 | 0 | 254 | 202 | 1 | 14 | 25 | 3 | 2 | 4 | 1 | 4 |
| Café Almond | 1/1 | 133 | 1 | 4 | 9 | 13 | 94 | 1 | 8 | 1 | 3 | 3 | 2 | 2 | 0 |
| Café Benedictine | 1/1 | 197 | 2 | 5 | 16 | 26 | 130 | 3 | 13 | 1 | 5 | 3 | 2 | 2 | 0 |
| Café Columbian | 1/1 | 179 | 2 | 16 | 10 | 23 | 147 | 2 | 8 | 1 | 3 | 1 | 3 | 3 | 2 |
| Café Israel | 1/1 | 225 | 2 | 27 | 10 | 32 | 200 | 3 | 8 | 1 | 4 | 1 | 4 | 3 | 4 |
| Champagne Fruit Punch | 1/90 | 88 | 0 | 16 | 0 | 2 | 127 | 0 | 1 | 25 | 3 | 1 | 1 | 1 | 1 |
| Chocolate Milk Shake | 1/2 | 428 | 11 | 57 | 19 | 164 | 522 | 17 | 15 | 4 | 6 | 30 | 2 | 34 | 4 |
| Chocolate Soda | 1/1 | 349 | 7 | 51 | 15 | 103 | 347 | 11 | 12 | 2 | 4 | 18 | 1 | 20 | 4 |
| Choco-Nutty Milk Shake | 1/2 | 522 | 15 | 60 | 27 | 261 | 622 | 23 | 15 | 4 | 8 | 31 | 14 | 35 | 6 |
| Citrus Rum Punch | 1/30 | 117 | 0 | 16 | 0 | 1 | 72 | 0 | 0 | 27 | 2 | 1 | 2 | 0 | 0 |
| Cocoa | 1/5 | 177 | 7 | 24 | 7 | 86 | 333 | 11 | 5 | 3 | 3 | 19 | 2 | 21 | 3 |
| Coffee | 1/1 | 3 | 0 | 1 | 0 | 2 | 81 | 0 | 0 | 0 | 0 | 0 | 4 | 0 | 1 |
| Coffee-and-Cream Milk Shake | 1/2 | 338 | 10 | 34 | 18 | 145 | 444 | 16 | 15 | 4 | 4 | 29 | 3 | 34 | 1 |
| Coffee Chocolate | 1/6 | 197 | 7 | 22 | 11 | 82 | 340 | 10 | 5 | 3 | 3 | 18 | 3 | 20 | 4 |
| Creamy Reception Punch | 1/36 | 92 | 2 | 15 | 3 | 19 | 113 | 2 | 26 | 4 | 4 | 4 | 1 | 5 | 1 |
| Double Chocolate Soda | 1/1 | 349 | 7 | 51 | 15 | 103 | 347 | 11 | 12 | 2 | 2 | 18 | 1 | 20 | 4 |
| Easy Sherbet Punch | 1/36 | 90 | 0 | 22 | 1 | 4 | 9 | 1 | 1 | 1 | 1 | 1 | 0 | 1 | 1 |
| Eggnog | 1/15 | 160 | 4 | 9 | 8 | 81 | 89 | 6 | 10 | 2 | 1 | 8 | 0 | 6 | 2 |
| Frisky Sours | 1/9 | 174 | 1 | 22 | 0 | 1 | 184 | 1 | 4 | 79 | 5 | 1 | 1 | 2 | 1 |

# Nutrition Analysis Chart

| | | | | | | | | | | | | | | |
|---|---|---|---|---|---|---|---|---|---|---|---|---|---|---|
| Frosty Cranberry Cocktail | 1/1 | 123 | 1 | 11 | 11 | 0 | 1 | 254 | 1 | 32 | 3 | 1 | 2 | 3 | 1 |
| Fruit Cooler | 1/6 | 213 | 1 | 53 | 0 | 3 | 434 | 2 | 4 | 68 | 10 | 3 | 3 | 4 | 5 |
| Fruit-Flavored Float | 1/8 | 268 | 5 | 43 | 9 | 73 | 224 | 8 | 7 | 3 | 14 | 1 | 17 | 2 |
| Grenadine Punch | 1/22 | 79 | 0 | 17 | 0 | 6 | 92 | 0 | 2 | 36 | 2 | 0 | 1 | 1 |
| Hot Buttered Rum Mix | 1/12 | 360 | 1 | 27 | 18 | 207 | 108 | 2 | 14 | 0 | 1 | 3 | 5 | 4 |
| Hot Chocolate | 1/6 | 196 | 7 | 22 | 11 | 82 | 313 | 10 | 5 | 3 | 18 | 2 | 20 | 4 |
| Hot Mulled Cider | 1/8 | 176 | 0 | 45 | 0 | 7 | 331 | 1 | 1 | 18 | 4 | 3 | 3 | 11 |
| Iced Tea | 1/5 | 0 | 0 | 0 | 0 | 0 | 0 | 0 | 0 | 0 | 0 | 0 | 0 | 0 |
| Individual Cocktails | 1/10 | 181 | 0 | 21 | 0 | 1 | 142 | 0 | 7 | 8 | 1 | 1 | 1 | 3 |
| Irish Coffee | 1/1 | 154 | 1 | 9 | 0 | 12 | 72 | 1 | 8 | 1 | 2 | 2 | 3 | 0 |
| Lemonade or Limeade | 1/6 | 139 | 0 | 36 | 0 | 1 | 58 | 0 | 0 | 31 | 0 | 0 | 0 | 1 |
| Nonalcoholic Punch | 1/22 | 74 | 0 | 19 | 0 | 0 | 64 | 0 | 3 | 4 | 1 | 0 | 0 | 1 |
| Orange-Grape Cooler | 1/12 | 88 | 1 | 22 | 0 | 1 | 172 | 1 | 1 | 54 | 5 | 1 | 1 | 1 |
| Orange Spiced Tea | 1/37 | 32 | 0 | 7 | 0 | 1 | 146 | 1 | 3 | 50 | 4 | 1 | 1 | 1 |
| Party Punch Base | 1/5 | 167 | 0 | 43 | 0 | 2 | 282 | 1 | 14 | 16 | 2 | 2 | 2 | 6 |
| Pastel Punch | 1/36 | 105 | 1 | 22 | 0 | 12 | 91 | 2 | 3 | 27 | 2 | 3 | 3 | 0 |
| Quantity Fruit Punch | 1/90 | 71 | 0 | 18 | 0 | 1 | 97 | 0 | 1 | 25 | 3 | 1 | 1 | 1 |
| Sangria | 1/20 | 98 | 0 | 11 | 0 | 4 | 136 | 1 | 1 | 36 | 3 | 1 | 3 | 2 |
| Slushy Punch | 1/25 | 87 | 0 | 22 | 0 | 1 | 148 | 1 | 1 | 35 | 3 | 1 | 2 | 0 |
| Spicy Chocolate | 1/6 | 196 | 7 | 22 | 11 | 82 | 313 | 10 | 5 | 3 | 4 | 18 | 2 | 20 | 4 |
| Spiked Party Punch | 1/14 | 134 | 0 | 15 | 0 | 1 | 101 | 0 | 5 | 6 | 1 | 1 | 1 | 2 |
| Spiked Slushy Punch | 1/28 | 106 | 0 | 20 | 0 | 1 | 132 | 1 | 2 | 32 | 3 | 1 | 1 | 1 |
| Strawberry Milk Shake | 1/2 | 492 | 11 | 73 | 19 | 146 | 575 | 17 | 16 | 130 | 8 | 34 | 5 | 36 | 6 |
| Strawberry Spritzer | 1/24 | 81 | 0 | 20 | 0 | 2 | 113 | 0 | 0 | 31 | 2 | 2 | 1 | 3 |
| Tea or Sun Tea | 1/5 | 0 | 0 | 0 | 0 | 0 | 0 | 0 | 0 | 0 | 0 | 0 | 0 | 0 |
| Vanilla Milk Shake | 1/2 | 337 | 10 | 34 | 18 | 144 | 416 | 16 | 15 | 4 | 6 | 29 | 34 | 1 |
| Vanilla Soda | 1/1 | 257 | 6 | 28 | 14 | 83 | 241 | 9 | 12 | 2 | 16 | 1 | 19 | 1 |
| White Wine Punch | 1/23 | 91 | 0 | 12 | 0 | 4 | 120 | 0 | 3 | 3 | 0 | 1 | 1 | 3 |
| Yogurt Sip | 1/5 | 137 | 2 | 19 | 1 | 25 | 138 | 3 | 8 | 39 | 2 | 6 | 6 | 2 |

# Beverages

There are as many ways to use and serve beverages as there are recipes for them. With some imagination, a beverage can be an intriguing accompaniment to a meal, an appetizer, a dessert, or simply a refreshment to enjoy by itself. Explore the many varieties offered to you in this chapter.

Remember this rule of thumb when you're determining serving sizes for beverages. Generally an 8-ounce serving is used for a meal accompaniment, and a 4-ounce serving for a cocktail-type beverage served alone.

Several recipes that call for carbonated beverages as ingredients recommend that you slowly pour the carbonated beverage down the side of the punch bowl or glass. This will prevent any loss of carbonation when adding the beverage to the other ingredients.

## Beverage dress-ups

Use one of the following extra touches to give beverages a festive look:

Stud orange, lemon, or lime slices with whole cloves and float atop punches.

For sweet drinks, wet glass rims with orange or lemon slices, then dip the rims in granulated sugar.

To avoid diluting iced drinks, freeze soda water, tonic, or carbonated beverages in cube shapes to use instead of ice.

Float an ice ring (see directions on page 78) or fruit-filled ice cubes in punches. First, fill the refrigerator tray half-full of water and freeze. Then add cranberries, small lemon wedges, or berries and finish filling the tray with water; freeze solid.

During the warmer summer months, try to allow enough freezer space to keep tall glasses or mugs chilled for cold drinks.

## Quantity Fruit Punch

- **8** cups water
- **1** 16-ounce can frozen orange juice concentrate
- **1** 12-ounce can frozen lemonade concentrate
- **2** 46-ounce cans unsweetened pineapple juice
- **2½** cups sugar
- **¼** cup lime juice
  Ice cubes
- **4** 28-ounce bottles ginger ale, chilled
- **2** 28-ounce bottles carbonated water, chilled
  Fresh strawberries, halved lengthwise (optional)
  Oranges, thinly sliced (optional)

Combine water and the frozen concentrates; stir to dissolve. Stir in pineapple juice, sugar, and lime juice; stir to dissolve sugar. Chill. To serve, pour *half* of the mixture of juices over ice in a large punch bowl. Slowly pour in *2 bottles* of the ginger ale and *1 bottle* of the carbonated water; stir gently to mix. Garnish with strawberries and orange slices, if desired. Repeat with remaining ingredients when needed. Makes 90 (4-ounce) servings.

**Champagne Fruit Punch:** Prepare Quantity Fruit Punch as above, *except* substitute four 750-milliliter bottles of *champagne or dry white wine* for the ginger ale.

## Citrus Rum Punch

Prepare Ice Ring in advance. Combine 5 cups *water,* one 12-ounce can frozen *limeade concentrate,* one 6-ounce can frozen *lemonade concentrate,* and one 6-ounce can frozen *orange juice concentrate;* stir to dissolve. Pour into a large punch bowl; stir in one 750-milliliter bottle of *rum.* Slowly pour in one 28-ounce bottle of chilled *carbonated water;* stir gently to mix. Place Ice Ring in punch bowl. Makes 30 (4-ounce) servings.

***Ice Ring:*** Drain one 8-ounce can *pineapple slices;* halve slices. In a 6½-cup ring mold arrange the halved pineapple slices and 8 *maraschino cherries.* Slowly fill ring mold with water. Freeze till solid.

## Slushy Punch

>     3    **cups water**
>     1    **cup sugar**
>     2    **ripe medium bananas, cut up**
>     3    **cups unsweetened pineapple juice**
>     1    **6-ounce can frozen orange juice**
>          **concentrate, thawed**
>     1    **6-ounce can frozen lemonade concentrate,**
>          **thawed**
>     2    **tablespoons lemon juice**
>     1    **28-ounce bottle carbonated water, chilled**
>          **Orange slices *or* fresh mint leaves**
>          **(optional)**

In a 3-quart saucepan combine water and sugar. Bring to boiling, stirring till sugar is dissolved. Boil syrup gently, uncovered, for 3 minutes; remove from heat and cool.

Meanwhile, in a blender container combine cup-up ripe bananas and *half* of the unsweetened pineapple juice. Cover and blend till smooth. Stir banana mixture into cooled syrup. Stir in remaining pineapple juice, the thawed orange juice and lemonade concentrates, and lemon juice.

Turn fruit mixture into a 13x9x2-inch baking pan. Freeze for several hours. (*Or,* cover with moisture-vaporproof wrap. Seal, label, and freeze for as long as 2 months. If desired, break up partially frozen mixture and store in smaller containers to use as needed.)

To serve, remove fruit mixture from freezer, let stand at room temperature for 30 minutes (*or,* for 5 to 10 minutes if mixture has liquor in it; see recipe below). To form a slush, scrape a large spoon across the surface of the frozen mixture. Spoon into a punch bowl. Slowly pour in carbonated water, stir gently to mix. Garnish with orange slices or fresh mint leaves, if desired. Makes 25 (4-ounce) servings.

**Spiked Slushy Punch:** Prepare Slushy Punch as above, *except* add 1½ cups *light rum or vodka* along with the fruit juices. Continue as directed. Makes 28 (4-ounce) servings.

**Note:** For individual servings, spoon or scoop slush into each glass. Slowly pour in carbonated water, using equal amounts of slush and carbonated water. Stir gently to mix. Garnish as above.

## Party Punch Base

- ⅓ **cup sugar**
- 12 **inches stick cinnamon, broken**
- ½ **teaspoon whole cloves**
- 3 **cups apple juice, chilled**
- 1 **12-ounce can apricot nectar, chilled**
- ¼ **cup lemon juice**

In a small saucepan combine sugar, cinnamon, cloves, and ½ cup *water;* bring to boiling. Reduce heat; cover and simmer 10 minutes. Strain out spices and discard. Chill. Combine with apple juice, apricot nectar, and lemon juice. Makes 5 cups Party Punch Base. Use in the following party punches:

**White Wine Punch:** Prepare Party Punch Base as above. In a punch bowl combine Party Punch Base and two 750-milliliter bottles of chilled *dry white wine.* Stir to mix. Makes 23 (4-ounce) servings.

**Spiked Party Punch:** Prepare Party Punch Base as above. In a punch bowl combine Party Punch Base with 2 cups *vodka, bourbon, brandy, or rum.* Stir to mix. Makes 14 (4-ounce) servings.

**Individual Cocktails:** Prepare Party Punch Base as above. For each cocktail, pour 1 jigger *vodka, bourbon, brandy,* or *rum* over *ice* in a glass. Add about ½ cup Party Punch Base; stir. Makes 10 (4-ounce) cocktails.

**Nonalcoholic Punch:** Prepare Party Punch Base as above. Combine Party Punch Base with two 28-ounce bottles of chilled *lemon-lime or grapefruit carbonated beverage.* Makes 22 (4-ounce) servings.

## Bloody Marys

| | |
|---|---|
| 1 | 46-ounce can tomato juice |
| 1½ | to 2 cups vodka |
| 2 | tablespoons lemon juice |
| 1 | tablespoon Worcestershire sauce |
| 1 | teaspoon prepared horseradish |
| ½ | teaspoon salt |
| | Few drops bottled hot pepper sauce |

In a large pitcher combine all ingredients. Cover; refrigerate several hours or overnight. Pour into salt-rimmed glasses. Serve each with a celery-stick stirrer, if desired. Makes 16 (4-ounce) servings.

## Creamy Reception Punch

| | |
|---|---|
| 2 | quarts vanilla ice cream |
| 4 | cups orange juice |
| ½ | cup lemon juice |
| 2 | 28-ounce bottles lemon-lime carbonated beverage, chilled |

Spoon vanilla ice cream by tablespoons into a large punch bowl. Add orange juice and lemon juice, stirring to muddle ice cream. Slowly pour in chilled lemon-lime carbonated beverage; stir gently to mix. Makes 36 (4-ounce) servings.

**Pastel Punch:** Prepare Creamy Reception Punch as above, *except* substitute 1 quart *orange sherbet* for 1 of the quarts of vanilla ice cream. Add one 10-ounce jar *undrained maraschino cherries*.

**Easy Sherbet Punch:** Prepare Creamy Reception Punch as above, *except* substitute 2 quarts of fruit-flavored *sherbet* for ice cream and add an additional 28-ounce bottle of carbonated beverage. Omit fruit juices.

# Grenadine Punch

1½   **cups water**
1   **6-ounce can frozen orange juice concentrate**
1   **cup lemon juice**
1   **cup grenadine syrup, chilled**
½   **cup light corn syrup**
    **Ice cubes**
2   **28-ounce bottles ginger ale, chilled**

In a large bowl or pitcher combine water and orange juice concentrate; stir to dissolve. Stir in lemon juice, chilled grenadine syrup, and light corn syrup. Carefully pour over ice cubes in a punch bowl. Slowly pour in the chilled ginger ale; stir gently to mix. Makes about 22 (4-ounce) servings.

# Fruit Cooler

1   **envelope unsweetened raspberry-flavored soft drink mix**
½   **cup sugar**
1   **46-ounce can unsweetened pineapple juice**
½   **cup orange juice**
¼   **cup lemon juice**
    **Ice cubes**

Add raspberry-flavored soft drink mix and sugar to pineapple juice. Stir to dissolve. Add remaining fruit juices. Chill. Serve over ice. Makes about 6 (8-ounce) servings.

## Apricot Swizzle

>     2  cups water
>     1  12-ounce can apricot nectar
>     1  6-ounce can frozen lemonade concentrate,
>        thawed
>    ¼  cup sugar
>     2  tablespoons instant tea powder
>        Ice cubes
>     1  28-ounce bottle ginger ale, chilled

Combine water, nectar, lemonade concentrate, sugar, and tea powder; stir till sugar and tea dissolve. Pour over ice in a punch bowl. Slowly pour in ginger ale; stir gently to mix. Makes about 7 (8-ounce) servings.

## Fruit-Flavored Float

>     1  cup sugar
>     1  envelope unsweetened lemon-lime- or
>        cherry-flavored soft drink mix
>     2  cups milk
>     1  quart vanilla ice cream
>     1  28-ounce bottle carbonated water, chilled

Combine sugar and fruit-flavored soft drink mix. Add milk; stir to dissolve sugar. Pour mixture into 8 tall glasses. Spoon about ½ cup of the ice cream into each glass. Slowly pour in the chilled carbonated water to fill each glass. Stir gently to mix. (Or, mix and serve in a large punch bowl, if desired.) Makes about 8 (8-ounce) servings.

## Eggnog

  6   **egg yolks**
  ¼   **cup sugar**
  2   **cups milk**
  ½   **cup light rum\***
  ½   **cup bourbon\***
  1   **teaspoon vanilla**
  ¼   **teaspoon salt**
  1   **cup whipping cream**
  6   **egg whites**
  ¼   **cup sugar**
      **Ground nutmeg**

In a small mixer bowl beat egg yolks till blended. Gradually add ¼ cup sugar, beating at high speed till thick and lemon colored. Stir in milk; stir in rum, bourbon, vanilla, and salt. Chill thoroughly.

Whip cream. Wash beaters well. In a large mixer bowl beat egg whites till soft peaks form. Gradually add remaining ¼ cup sugar, beating to stiff peaks. Fold yolk mixture and whipped cream into egg whites. Serve immediately. Sprinkle nutmeg over each serving. Makes about 15 (4-ounce) servings.

**\*Note:** For a nonalcoholic eggnog, prepare Eggnog as above, *except* omit the rum and bourbon and increase the milk to *3 cups.*

## Cocoa

  ⅓   **cup sugar**
  ⅓   **cup unsweetened cocoa powder**
      **Dash salt**
  ½   **cup water**
  3½  **cups milk**
  ½   **teaspoon vanilla**
      **Marshmallows or whipped cream (optional)**

In a saucepan combine sugar, cocoa, and salt. Stir in water. Bring mixture to boiling, stirring constantly. Cook and stir 1 minute more. Stir in milk. Heat just to boiling; *do not boil.* Remove from heat; stir in vanilla. Beat with a rotary beater till frothy. Serve in cups or mugs. Top each serving with a few marshmallows or a dollop of whipped cream, if desired. Makes 5 (6-ounce) servings.

## Sangria

   **4**   **oranges**
   **2**   **lemons**
   **2**   **750-milliliter bottles dry red wine**
   **⅓**   **cup sugar**
   **¼**   **cup brandy**
   **2**   **cups carbonated water, chilled**

Using a potato peeler, cut the outer peel from *one* orange into a spiral strip, being careful not to remove any white membrane. Place peel in a 2-quart container. Squeeze peeled orange, *2* more of the oranges, and *1* of the lemons; add juice to peel. Cut the remaining orange into wedges and the remaining lemon into thin slices; add to fruit juices along with wine, sugar, and brandy. Stir to dissolve sugar; chill. Pour into a punch bowl or two pitchers; remove orange peel. Slowly pour in carbonated water; stir gently. Makes 20 (4-ounce) servings.

## Hot Chocolate

   **1**   **cup water**
   **2**   **squares (2 ounces) unsweetened chocolate**
   **⅓**   **cup sugar**
        **Dash salt**
   **4**   **cups milk**
        **Whipped cream *or* marshmallows**
          **(optional)**

In a saucepan combine water, chocolate, sugar, and salt. Cook and stir over medium-low heat till chocolate melts. Gradually stir in milk; heat just to boiling. *Do not boil.* Remove from heat; beat with a rotary beater till frothy. Serve in cups or mugs. Top each serving with a dollop of whipped cream or a few marshmallows, if desired. Makes 6 (6-ounce) servings.

**Coffee Chocolate:** Prepare Hot Chocolate as above, *except* stir 2 tablespoons *instant coffee crystals* into chocolate-water mixture before heating.

**Spicy Chocolate:** Prepare Hot Chocolate as above, *except* stir 1 teaspoon ground *cinnamon* and ¼ teaspoon ground *nutmeg* into chocolate-water mixture before heating.

## Orange-Grape Cooler

>       2   **cups water**
>       1   **6-ounce can frozen orange juice**
>           **concentrate**
>    1½   **cups white grape juice, chilled**
>      ¼   **cup lemon juice**
>      ¼   **cup honey**
>       1   **12-ounce bottle lemon-lime carbonated**
>           **beverage, chilled**
>           **Ice Ring (see recipe, page 78) or ice cubes**

In a punch bowl combine water and orange juice concentrate; stir to dissolve. Stir in white grape juice, lemon juice, and honey. Slowly pour in carbonated beverage; stir gently to mix. Float Ice Ring in punch bowl or serve over ice. Makes 12 (4-ounce) servings.

## Vanilla Milk Shake

>       2   **cups vanilla ice cream (1 pint)**
>       1   **cup milk**

Place vanilla ice cream in a blender container; add milk. Cover; blend till mixture is smooth. Pour into glasses. Serve immediately. Makes about 2 (8-ounce) servings.

**Chocolate Milk Shake:** Prepare Vanilla Milk Shake as above, *except* add ¼ cup *chocolate-flavored syrup* with the milk.

**Choco-Nutty Milk Shake:** Prepare Vanilla Milk Shake as above, *except* add ¼ cup *chocolate-flavored syrup* and 2 tablespoons *peanut butter* with the milk.

**Coffee-and-Cream Milk Shake:** Prepare Vanilla Milk Shake as above, *except* blend 2 teaspoons *instant coffee crystals* with the milk.

**Strawberry Milk Shake:** Prepare Vanilla Milk Shake as above, *except* blend one *undrained* 10-ounce package frozen *strawberries or raspberries,* thawed, with the milk.

**Note:** If desired, add 2 tablespoons *instant malted milk powder* to blender container with the milk for any of the above milk shakes.

---

# Hot Buttered Rum Mix

    1   cup butter or margarine, softened
    1   cup packed brown sugar
    ½   cup sifted powdered sugar
    1   teaspoon ground nutmeg
    1   teaspoon ground cinnamon
    2   cups vanilla ice cream, softened (1 pint)
        Rum
        Boiling water

In a small mixer beat together softened butter or margarine, brown sugar, powdered sugar, nutmeg, and cinnamon till well combined. Beat in the softened ice cream. Turn mixture into a 4-cup freezer container. Seal and freeze. (Mixture will not freeze solid.) Makes about 4 cups mix.

To serve, spoon about ⅓ cup of the ice cream mixture into a mug; add *1 jigger* of rum and *½ cup* boiling water. Stir well.

---

# Vanilla Soda

    1   to 2 cups vanilla ice cream
    1   cup carbonated water, ginger ale, or
          lemon-lime carbonated beverage,
          chilled

Add a large spoonful of vanilla ice cream to a chilled 14- to 16-ounce glass. Add enough carbonated water, ginger ale, or lemon-lime carbonated beverage to half-fill the glass; stir gently to mix. Add one or two scoops more vanilla ice cream to ice cream mixture in glass. Fill with remaining carbonated water, ginger ale, or lemon-lime carbonated beverage. Makes 1 (14- to 16-ounce) serving.

**Chocolate Soda:** Prepare Vanilla Soda as above, *except* stir in 2 tablespoons *chcolate-flavored syrup* with the first spoonful of vanilla ice cream; mix well.

**Double Chocolate Soda:** Prepare Vanilla Soda as above, *except* substitute *chocolate ice cream* for the vanilla ice cream and stir in 2 tablespoons *chocolate-flavored syrup* with the first spoonful of chocolate ice cream; mix well.

---

## Lemonade or Limeade

---

  **1  cup sugar**
  **1  cup lemon juice *or* lime juice**
     **Ice cubes**

Combine sugar, lemon or lime juice, and 5 cups *water;* stir to dissolve sugar. Serve over ice. Garnish with lemon or lime slices, if desired. Makes 6 (8-ounce) servings.

---

## Hot Mulled Cider

---

  **8  cups apple cider *or* apple juice**
**½  cup packed brown sugar**
     **Dash ground nutmeg**
  **6  inches stick cinnamon**
  **1  teaspoon whole allspice**
  **1  teaspoon whole cloves**
  **8  thin orange wedges *or* slices**
  **8  whole cloves**

In a large saucepan combine apple cider or juice, brown sugar, and nutmeg. *For spice bag,* place cinnamon, allspice, and the

1 teaspoon cloves in cheesecloth and tie; add to cider mixture. Bring to boiling. Reduce heat; cover and simmer 10 minutes. Remove spice bag and discard. Serve cider in mugs with a clove-studded orange wedge in each. Makes 8 (8-ounce) servings.

## Frosty Cranberry Cocktail

> 1  **6-ounce can frozen cranberry juice cocktail concentrate**
> ¾  **cup light rum**
> 1  **medium banana, cut up**
> 2  **tablespoons lemon juice**
> 4  **cups ice cubes**

In a blender container combine cranberry juice, rum, banana, and lemon juice. Cover; blend till smooth. Add *half* of the ice cubes; cover. Blend till smooth. Add remaining ice cubes. Cover; blend till slushy. Pour into glasses. Garnish each with banana slices, if desired. Makes 7 (4-ounce) servings.

## Frisky Sours

> 1  **6-ounce can frozen orange-grapefruit juice concentrate**
> 1  **6-ounce can frozen lemonade concentrate**
> 1½  **cups whiskey**
> 1½  **cups cold water**
>  **Ice cubes (optional)**

In a blender container combine first 4 ingredients. Cover; blend just till mixed. Serve over ice, if desired. Makes 9 (4-ounce) servings.

# Strawberry Spritzer

> **3** 10-ounce packages frozen sliced
>      strawberries
> **6** cups white grape juice
> **1** 28-ounce bottle carbonated water, chilled

Let strawberries stand at room temperature 20 minutes. Place 2 of the *undrained* packages of strawberries in a blender container. Cover and blend till smooth. In a large punch bowl or pitcher combine blended strawberries, grape juice, and remaining *undrained* package of strawberries.

To serve, slowly pour in carbonated water; stir gently to mix. Add red food coloring, if desired. Makes 24 (4-ounce) servings.

# Yogurt Sip

> **1** 10-ounce package frozen peach slices
> **1** cup plain yogurt (8 ounces)
> ¼ cup peach brandy *or* other brandy
> ¼ cup light rum
> **1** tablespoon honey
>      Ground nutmeg

Let peaches stand at room temperature 10 minutes. In a blender container combine yogurt, brandy, rum, and honey. Add *undrained* peaches. Cover; blend till smooth. Pour into glasses; top with nutmeg. Makes 5 (4-ounce) servings.

# Coffee

> ¾ cup water (for each 6-ounce cup)
> **1** to 2 tablespoons ground coffee (for each
>      6-ounce cup)

**Percolator Coffee:** Pour water into a percolator; stand the stem and basket firmly in the pot. Measure coffee into basket. Replace basket lid and cover pot. Bring water to boiling;

reduce heat and perk gently 5 to 8 minutes. Let stand for a minute or two; remove basket. Keep coffee warm over low heat.

***Drip Coffee:*** Measure coffee into basket of pot. Measure water. *For electric drip coffee makers,* pour cold water into upper compartment. Place pot on heating element; allow water to drip through coffee basket. *For nonelectric drip coffee makers,* pour boiling water over coffee in basket. Simply allow water to drip into bottom section.

When coffee has finished dripping, remove basket; discard grounds. Stir the brewed coffee and serve. Keep warm over low heat.

## Dessert Coffee

½ **cup hot strong coffee**
**Desired coffee flavoring**
**(see choices below)**
**Whipped cream**
**Ground cinnamon *or* nutmeg**

In a coffee cup or mug stir together hot coffee and desired flavoring. Top with a dollop of whipped cream; sprinkle with cinnamon or nutmeg. Makes 1 (6-ounce) serving.

***Café Israel:*** Stir 2 tablespoons *chocolate-flavored syrup* and 2 tablespoons *orange liqueur* into coffee.

***Café Columbian:*** Stir 2 tablespoons *coffee liqueur* and 1 tablespoon *chocolate-flavored syrup* into coffee.

***Irish Coffee:*** Stir 1 tablespoon *Irish whiskey* and 2 teaspoon *sugar* into coffee.

***Café Benedictine:*** Stir 2 tablespoons *Benedictine* and 2 tablespoons *light cream* into coffee.

***Café Almond:*** Stir 2 tablespoons *Amaretto* into coffee.

## Tea

**Boiling water**
3 **to 6 teaspoons loose tea *or* 3 to 6 tea bags**
4 **cups boiling water**

Warm a teapot by rinsing it with boiling water. Measure loose tea into a tea ball. Empty teapot; add tea ball or tea bags to pot. Immediately add the 4 cups boiling water to teapot. Cover pot and let steep 3 to 5 minutes. Remove tea ball or bags; stir tea and serve at once. Makes 5 (6-ounce) servings.

**Iced Tea:** Prepare Tea as above, *except* use 4 to 8 teaspoons loose tea or 4 to 8 tea bags. Cool. Pour over *ice cubes* in glasses; pass sugar and lemon, if desired.

Keep tea at room temperature to avoid clouding. If tea does become cloudy, restore the clear amber color by adding a little boiling water to the tea.

## Sun Tea

 4  tea bags
    Ice cubes

In a 2-quart clear glass container place tea bags. Add 1½ quarts *cold water;* cover. Let stand in full sun 2 to 3 hours or till of desired strength. Remove tea bags. Serve over ice. Store in refrigerator. Makes 1½ quarts.

**Note:** You don't need the sun to brew Sun Tea. Simply prepare as directed above, *except* let stand at room temperature several hours or till of desired strength.

## Orange Spiced Tea

 1  cup orange-flavored instant breakfast drink
    powder
 1  cup instant tea powder
 1  3-ounce envelope (about ⅓ cup)
    sugar-sweetened lemonade mix
 ½  teaspoon ground cinnamon
 ½  teaspoon ground cloves

Combine all ingredients. Store in a tightly covered container. Stir before using. To use, stir *1 tablespoon* of the mix into 1 cup *boiling or cold water.* Makes about 2⅓ cups tea mix.

# Wine Guide

Are you confused about choosing the right wine to serve with certain foods? You'll be glad to learn that most of the strict "wine rules" are out the window these days. Here are more-relaxed guidelines to help you enjoy wine to its fullest.

Wines can be divided into four general classes: appetizer, dinner, dessert, and sparkling wines. The name of the class generally indicates the use of each wine.

*Appetizer wines,* also called aperitifs, are those served before a meal or as a cocktail.

*Dinner wines,* also called table wines, include red, white, and rosé wines. They usually are served with the main course. Red dinner wines are predominantly dry and rich, and sometimes have a tart or astringent character, so they are best with hearty or highly seasoned foods. White dinner wines are lighter in flavor and can be very dry and tart or slightly sweet and fragrant. Serve white wines with delicately flavored foods so that the flavor of the wine does not overpower the entrée.

| Wines | Serving Temperature | Best With |
|---|---|---|
| **Appetizer Wines**<br>Sherry (dry), Vermouth, Flavored Wines | Cool room temperature (around 65°F.) *or* chilled (around 50°F.) | All appetizer foods—canapés, hors d'oeuvres, soups, dips |
| **Red Dinner Wines**<br>Burgundy, Cabernet Sauvignon, Gamay, Chianti, Pinot Noir, Petite Sirah, Ruby Cabernet, Barbera, Zinfandel | Cool room temperature (around 65°F.) | Hearty foods—all red meats, including beef, pork, game; cheese, egg, and pasta dishes; highly seasoned foods |
| **Rosé Wines** | Chilled (around 50°F.) | Ham, fried chicken, picnic foods, shellfish, cold beef |
| **White Dinner Wines**<br>Chablis, Rhine, Sauterne (dry), Chardonnay, Chenin Blanc, White Riesling, French Colombard, Sauvignon Blanc | Chilled (around 50°F.) | Light foods—poultry, fish and shellfish, ham, veal |
| **Dessert Wines**<br>Port, Tokay, Muscatel, Catawba, Sauterne (sweet), Aurora, Sherry | Cool room temperature (around 65°F.) | All desserts—fruits, nuts, cakes, dessert cheeses |
| **Sparkling Wines**<br>Champagne, Sparkling Burgundy, Sparkling Rosé, Cold Duck | Chilled (around 45°F.) | All foods and occasions |

Rosé wine is an all-purpose dinner wine, compatible with any food. Rosé wines, which are simply pale red wines, may be sweet or dry, or even lightly carbonated.

In cooking, the flavor of wine should subtly enhance the natural food flavors. Dry red wines are generally used in main dishes such as stews and sauces for red meats. Dry white wines work well with white sauces or poultry dishes.

*Dessert wines* are heavier-bodied and sweeter, and are served as the dessert or as a dessert accompaniment. You also can add them to your favorite dessert sauce.

*Sparkling wines,* served either by themselves or as an accompaniment, make any occasion special. They taste equally good before, during, or at the end of the meal. The driest ones are labeled "brut."

Store unopened wines at a cool, constant temperature (about 60 F.). Store corked bottles on their sides so the wine will stay in contact with the cork and keep it moist.

# Breads

# Breads

# Breads

# Breads

# Breads

# Breads

# Breads

# Breads

# Breads

| Recipes | Servings (fraction of recipe) | Calories | Protein (grams) | Carbohydrate (grams) | Fat (grams) | Sodium (milligrams) | Potassium (milligrams) | Percent of U.S. RDA Per Serving | | | | | | | |
|---|---|---|---|---|---|---|---|---|---|---|---|---|---|---|---|
| | | | | | | | | Protein | Vitamin A | Vitamin C | Thiamine | Riboflavin | Niacin | Calcium | Iron |
| Anadama Bread | 1/36 | 118 | 3 | 21 | 2 | 189 | 83 | 5 | | | 11 | 7 | 7 | 7 | 2 |
| Any-Fruit Coffee Cake | 1/16 | 432 | 5 | 64 | 19 | 386 | 116 | 8 | 14 | 4 | 14 | 10 | 8 | 8 | 7 |
| Apple Fritter Rings | 1/16 | 101 | 4 | 19 | 3 | 30 | 85 | 3 | | 4 | 4 | 2 | 2 | 2 | 2 |
| Apple-Raisin Muffins | 1/10 | 201 | 4 | 27 | 9 | 259 | 96 | 6 | 2 | 1 | 11 | 8 | 8 | 6 | 5 |
| Applesauce Coffee Cake | 1/8 | 307 | 5 | 37 | 16 | 420 | 87 | 8 | 13 | | 14 | 9 | 9 | 7 | 8 |
| Apricot-Orange Bread | 1/18 | 175 | 3 | 33 | 4 | 182 | 155 | 4 | 17 | 20 | 9 | 5 | 5 | 6 | 6 |
| Bagels | 1/12 | 180 | 5 | 38 | 1 | 551 | 66 | 8 | | | 21 | 9 | 14 | 14 | 8 |
| Banana Nut Bread | 1/16 | 154 | 3 | 22 | 6 | 169 | 85 | 4 | 2 | 2 | 7 | 5 | 8 | 4 | 4 |
| Banana-Nut Muffins | 1/10 | 237 | 5 | 28 | 12 | 181 | 155 | 7 | 2 | 4 | 12 | 8 | 8 | 7 | 6 |
| Barbecue Breadsticks | 1/24 | 56 | 2 | 9 | 1 | 106 | 30 | 2 | | 0 | 5 | 4 | 4 | 3 | 2 |
| Basic Muffins | 1/10 | 184 | 4 | 23 | 7 | 258 | 55 | 6 | 2 | | 10 | 8 | 8 | 6 | 4 |
| Batter Rolls | 1/18 | 160 | 4 | 21 | 7 | 132 | 60 | 5 | 1 | 0 | 11 | 9 | 6 | 7 | 4 |
| Beer-Cheese Triangles | 1/10 | 129 | 3 | 17 | 5 | 352 | 27 | 5 | | 0 | 8 | 6 | 6 | 5 | 4 |
| Biscuits Supreme | 1/10 | 195 | 4 | 21 | 11 | 247 | 49 | 5 | | 0 | 11 | 7 | 7 | 7 | 4 |
| Bismarks w/Butterscotch Filling | 1/24 | 165 | 4 | 25 | 5 | 164 | 80 | 6 | 3 | 0 | 10 | 9 | 9 | 6 | 5 |
| Bismarks w/Chocolate Filling | 1/24 | 166 | 4 | 25 | 6 | 156 | 74 | 6 | 2 | 0 | 10 | 9 | 9 | 6 | 5 |
| Blueberry Buckle | 1/8 | 468 | 6 | 67 | 20 | 256 | 101 | 9 | 7 | 9 | 18 | 13 | 13 | 11 | 9 |
| Blueberry Muffins | 1/10 | 200 | 4 | 27 | 9 | 258 | 64 | 6 | 2 | 3 | 10 | 8 | 8 | 6 | 5 |
| Boston Brown Bread | 1/20 | 53 | 2 | 10 | 1 | 65 | 85 | 2 | | | 3 | 3 | 4 | 3 | 5 |
| Breadsticks | 1/24 | 56 | 2 | 9 | 1 | 644 | 29 | 2 | | 0 | 5 | 4 | 4 | 3 | 2 |

# Nutrition Analysis Chart

| Item | Serving | | | | | | | | | | | | |
|---|---|---|---|---|---|---|---|---|---|---|---|---|---|
| Buckwheat Pancakes | 1/8 | 127 | 19 | 4 | 244 | 146 | 7 | 3 | 1 | 8 | 4 | 2 | 3 |
| Buttermilk Biscuits | 1/10 | 191 | 21 | 10 | 290 | 51 | 5 | 3 | 0 | 11 | 7 | 7 | 5 |
| Buttermilk Doughnuts | 1/18 | 139 | 23 | 3 | 125 | 48 | 6 | 2 | 0 | 10 | 8 | 6 | 4 |
| Buttermilk Pancakes | 1/10 | 98 | 16 | 2 | 243 | 67 | 5 | 1 | 1 | 8 | 4 | 5 | 3 |
| Cake Doughnuts w/Chocolate Glaze | 1/16 | 240 | 38 | 8 | 174 | 71 | 6 | 5 | 0 | 12 | 8 | 7 | 6 |
| Cake Doughnuts w/Orange Glaze | 1/16 | 227 | 41 | 5 | 156 | 53 | 6 | 4 | 2 | 12 | 8 | 7 | 5 |
| Caramel-Pecan Rolls | 1/24 | 223 | 33 | 9 | 174 | 86 | 6 | 4 | 0 | 12 | 8 | 7 | 6 |
| Cardamom Braid | 1/24 | 89 | 14 | 3 | 75 | 34 | 3 | 2 | 0 | 7 | 5 | 4 | 3 |
| Cheese Bread | 1/36 | 70 | 11 | 2 | 144 | 21 | 4 | 1 | 0 | 6 | 5 | 4 | 3 |
| Cheese Muffins | 1/10 | 206 | 23 | 10 | 297 | 60 | 8 | 3 | 0 | 10 | 9 | 6 | 5 |
| Cheese-Nut Bread | 1/18 | 223 | 29 | 10 | 251 | 85 | 9 | 3 | 1 | 11 | 10 | 6 | 5 |
| Cheese Spoon Bread | 1/6 | 359 | 22 | 25 | 748 | 82 | 19 | 26 | 2 | 11 | 10 | 3 | 5 |
| Cherry-Pecan Bread | 1/18 | 213 | 27 | 11 | 207 | 81 | 5 | 6 | 0 | 10 | 6 | 3 | 4 |
| Chocolate Cake Doughnuts w/Chocolate Glaze | 1/16 | 265 | 43 | 9 | 174 | 86 | 7 | 5 | 0 | 12 | 9 | 7 | 7 |
| Chocolate Swirl Coffee Cake | 1/12 | 447 | 61 | 20 | 250 | 163 | 12 | 14 | 0 | 23 | 19 | 14 | 12 |
| Chocolate Yeast Doughnuts | 1/16 | 225 | 34 | 8 | 157 | 84 | 7 | 2 | 0 | 13 | 11 | 9 | 7 |
| Cinnamon Crisps | 1/24 | 228 | 35 | 9 | 146 | 78 | 5 | 4 | 0 | 11 | 8 | 6 | 5 |
| Cinnamon Rolls | 1/24 | 176 | 29 | 5 | 149 | 89 | 6 | 5 | 0 | 11 | 8 | 7 | 6 |
| Cinnamon Swirl Bread | 1/36 | 129 | 23 | 2 | 147 | 55 | 6 | 2 | 0 | 11 | 9 | 7 | 5 |
| Cocoa Ripple Ring | 1/12 | 252 | 33 | 12 | 225 | 97 | 6 | 2 | 0 | 8 | 7 | 5 | 6 |
| Corn Bread | 1/8 | 238 | 31 | 10 | 813 | 121 | 6 | 5 | 1 | 12 | 10 | 8 | 6 |
| Corn Sticks | 1/20 | 95 | 13 | 4 | 325 | 48 | 4 | 2 | 0 | 5 | 4 | 2 | 2 |
| Cornmeal Biscuits | 1/10 | 194 | 21 | 11 | 247 | 61 | 5 | 5 | 0 | 10 | 6 | 6 | 4 |
| Cranberry Muffins | 1/10 | 207 | 29 | 9 | 258 | 63 | 6 | 2 | 2 | 10 | 8 | 6 | 5 |
| Cranberry-Orange Bread | 1/18 | 159 | 29 | 4 | 181 | 89 | 4 | 2 | 20 | 9 | 5 | 4 | 4 |
| Croissants | 1/48 | 100 | 9 | 6 | 118 | 25 | 2 | 5 | 0 | 5 | 4 | 3 | 2 |

# Nutrition Analysis Chart

| Recipes | Servings (fraction of recipe) | Calories | Protein (grams) | Carbohydrate (grams) | Fat (grams) | Sodium (milligrams) | Potassium (milligrams) | Protein | Vitamin A | Vitamin C | Thiamine | Riboflavin | Niacin | Calcium | Iron |
|---|---|---|---|---|---|---|---|---|---|---|---|---|---|---|---|
| | | | | | | | | \<-- Percent of U.S. RDA Per Serving --\> | | | | | | | |
| Date-Apple Coffee Bread | 1/18 | 174 | 3 | 33 | 4 | 149 | 175 | 4 | 2 | 2 | 1 | 9 | 6 | 6 | 8 |
| Date-Nut Muffins | 1/10 | 242 | 4 | 32 | 11 | 258 | 150 | 7 | 2 | 2 | 0 | 12 | 9 | 7 | 7 |
| Dinner Rolls | 1/30 | 98 | 3 | 15 | 1 | 104 | 37 | 4 | 3 | 0 | 0 | 8 | 6 | 5 | 3 |
| Easy-Mix White Bread | 1/36 | 89 | 3 | 17 | 1 | 127 | 45 | 4 | 0 | 0 | 0 | 9 | 7 | 6 | 3 |
| Egg Bread | 1/36 | 119 | 4 | 20 | 2 | 147 | 55 | 6 | 2 | 0 | 0 | 11 | 9 | 7 | 5 |
| French Bread | 1/20 | 90 | 3 | 19 | 0 | 442 | 34 | 4 | 0 | 0 | 0 | 11 | 7 | 7 | 4 |
| French Toast | 1/5 | 694 | 10 | 136 | 13 | 549 | 430 | 16 | 14 | 1 | 1 | 32 | 23 | 10 | 22 |
| Garden Biscuits | 1/10 | 196 | 3 | 21 | 11 | 248 | 57 | 5 | 4 | 2 | 2 | 11 | 8 | 7 | 4 |
| German Stollen | 1/48 | 94 | 3 | 16 | 2 | 74 | 70 | 3 | 2 | 3 | 3 | 4 | 4 | 3 | 3 |
| Hamburger/Frankfurter Buns | 1/12 | 246 | 6 | 39 | 7 | 261 | 93 | 10 | 0 | 7 | 0 | 20 | 15 | 12 | 8 |
| Herb Bagels | 1/12 | 180 | 5 | 38 | 0 | 551 | 66 | 8 | 0 | 0 | 0 | 21 | 14 | 14 | 8 |
| Homemade Biscuit Mix | 1 cup | 2140 | 34 | 260 | 106 | 3542 | 324 | 52 | 0 | 0 | 0 | 137 | 75 | 85 | 51 |
| Homemade Biscuit Mix Biscuits | 1/10 | 146 | 3 | 18 | 7 | 237 | 39 | 4 | 0 | 0 | 2 | 6 | 6 | 6 | 3 |
| Homemade Biscuit Mix Muffins | 1/12 | 205 | 6 | 25 | 10 | 303 | 61 | 6 | 2 | 10 | 0 | 12 | 9 | 7 | 3 |
| Homemade Biscuit Mix Pancakes | 1/10 | 171 | 4 | 18 | 9 | 255 | 69 | 7 | 3 | 0 | 0 | 10 | 9 | 6 | 5 |
| Honey-Wheat Muffins | 1/12 | 152 | 3 | 24 | 6 | 155 | 57 | 4 | 1 | 1 | 1 | 7 | 5 | 4 | 4 |
| Hot Cross Buns | 1/18 | 236 | 5 | 37 | 8 | 109 | 110 | 7 | 2 | 2 | 1 | 14 | 12 | 2 | 7 |
| Hush Puppies | 1/24 | 62 | 2 | 10 | 2 | 155 | 51 | 3 | 1 | 1 | 1 | 4 | 3 | 27 | 2 |
| Individual French Loaves | 1/8 | 336 | 10 | 69 | 0 | 1656 | 128 | 16 | 0 | 0 | 0 | 41 | 27 | 0 | 16 |
| Jelly Muffins | 1/10 | 196 | 4 | 25 | 6 | 259 | 58 | 6 | 2 | 1 | | 10 | 8 | 6 | 5 |

# Nutrition Analysis Chart

| | | | | | | | | | | | | | | | | |
|---|---|---|---|---|---|---|---|---|---|---|---|---|---|---|---|---|
| Julekage | 1/32 | 161 | 3 | 29 | 4 | 111 | 145 | 4 | 4 | 10 | 11 | 12 | 8 | 6 | 3 | 5 |
| Kuchen | 1/16 | 225 | 4 | 37 | 7 | 139 | 80 | 7 | 7 | 1 | 12 | 17 | 10 | 7 | 3 | 6 |
| Light Rye Bagels | 1/12 | 165 | 5 | 35 | 1 | 550 | 72 | 7 | 0 | 0 | 17 | 17 | 12 | 12 | 1 | 7 |
| Molasses-Oatmeal Bread | 1/36 | 117 | 3 | 20 | 3 | 189 | 83 | 5 | 1 | 0 | 11 | 11 | 7 | 6 | 2 | 6 |
| Nut Bread | 1/18 | 198 | 4 | 29 | 8 | 207 | 80 | 6 | 1 | 1 | 11 | 11 | 8 | 6 | 5 | 5 |
| Onion Bagels | 1/12 | 208 | 5 | 39 | 3 | 586 | 78 | 8 | 2 | 1 | 21 | 21 | 14 | 14 | 1 | 8 |
| Orange-Cinnamon Sourdough Rolls | 1/12 | 206 | 4 | 37 | 4 | 290 | 64 | 7 | 3 | 1 | 17 | 17 | 11 | 11 | 8 | 6 |
| Orange-Date Coffee Cake | 1/12 | 312 | 4 | 41 | 15 | 208 | 165 | 6 | 3 | 10 | 12 | 12 | 8 | 7 | 5 | 8 |
| Orange Sticky Rolls | 1/9 | 302 | 5 | 45 | 12 | 286 | 67 | 6 | 4 | 5 | 13 | 13 | 9 | 8 | 5 | 5 |
| Pancakes | 1/8 | 129 | 3 | 20 | 4 | 239 | 72 | 6 | 2 | 1 | 9 | 9 | 9 | 5 | 3 | 4 |
| Parmesan Breadsticks | 1/24 | 61 | 2 | 9 | 2 | 105 | 31 | 3 | 1 | 0 | 5 | 5 | 5 | 3 | 0 | 2 |
| Party Pita Bread | 1/24 | 81 | 2 | 13 | 2 | 134 | 22 | 3 | 0 | 0 | 5 | 8 | 5 | 3 | 2 | 3 |
| Peasant Bread | 1/36 | 70 | 2 | 14 | 1 | 127 | 59 | 3 | 1 | 0 | 8 | 8 | 6 | 5 | 0 | 4 |
| Pecan Biscuit Spirals | 1/15 | 160 | 3 | 17 | 9 | 230 | 53 | 4 | 7 | 1 | 9 | 9 | 5 | 5 | 1 | 4 |
| Pita Bread | 1/12 | 162 | 4 | 26 | 5 | 267 | 44 | 6 | 0 | 0 | 15 | 15 | 10 | 10 | 3 | 6 |
| Popovers | 1/6 | 159 | 6 | 18 | 7 | 219 | 100 | 9 | 5 | 1 | 11 | 11 | 12 | 6 | 1 | 6 |
| Poppy Seed or Sesame Seed Bagels | 1/12 | 187 | 6 | 38 | 1 | 556 | 71 | 9 | 1 | 0 | 21 | 21 | 15 | 14 | 1 | 9 |
| Potato Bread | 1/36 | 92 | 2 | 18 | 2 | 184 | 83 | 4 | 0 | 2 | 10 | 10 | 6 | 7 | 1 | 4 |
| Powdered Sugar Icing | 1/12 | 33 | 0 | 8 | 0 | 1 | 3 | 0 | 0 | 0 | 0 | 0 | 0 | 0 | 0 | 0 |
| Prune Kuchen | 1/16 | 269 | 5 | 49 | 7 | 140 | 204 | 7 | 13 | 1 | 13 | 13 | 12 | 9 | 4 | 10 |
| Pumpernickel | 1/32 | 87 | 2 | 17 | 1 | 207 | 83 | 3 | 0 | 0 | 8 | 8 | 6 | 3 | 1 | 5 |
| Pumpkin Muffins | 1/10 | 215 | 4 | 31 | 9 | 260 | 140 | 6 | 17 | 1 | 11 | 11 | 9 | 6 | 5 | 6 |
| Pumpkin Nut Bread | 1/18 | 178 | 3 | 27 | 7 | 125 | 146 | 5 | 19 | 1 | 8 | 8 | 6 | 6 | 4 | 7 |
| Raisin Bread | 1/36 | 142 | 4 | 26 | 4 | 149 | 117 | 6 | 2 | 0 | 12 | 12 | 9 | 7 | 3 | 6 |
| Russian Black Bread | 1/32 | 126 | 3 | 25 | 2 | 256 | 122 | 5 | 5 | 4 | 15 | 15 | 12 | 11 | 2 | 8 |
| Rye Bread | 1/24 | 122 | 3 | 25 | 1 | 91 | 63 | 5 | 5 | 0 | 7 | 7 | 7 | 7 | 1 | 6 |
| Sesame Swirls | 1/18 | 159 | 3 | 15 | 10 | 249 | 66 | 5 | 7 | 0 | 8 | 8 | 6 | 5 | 4 | 4 |

# Nutrition Analysis Chart

The last eight columns ("Protein" through "Iron") are expressed as **Percent of U.S. RDA Per Serving**.

| Recipes | Servings (fraction of recipe) | Calories | Protein (grams) | Carbohydrate (grams) | Fat (grams) | Sodium (milligrams) | Potassium (milligrams) | Protein | Vitamin A | Vitamin C | Thiamine | Riboflavin | Niacin | Calcium | Iron |
|---|---|---|---|---|---|---|---|---|---|---|---|---|---|---|---|
| Soft Pretzels | 1/16 | 158 | 4 | 28 | 4 | 2274 | 75 | 7 | 1 | 0 | 0 | 14 | 11 | 9 | 5 |
| Sour Cream Biscuits | 1/10 | 235 | 3 | 21 | 3 | 252 | 63 | 5 | 4 | 0 | 0 | 11 | 8 | 7 | 6 |
| Sourdough Bread | 1/32 | 94 | 3 | 20 | 3 | 151 | 30 | 4 | 0 | 0 | 0 | 11 | 7 | 7 | 1 |
| Sourdough Starter | 1 cup | 1647 | 49 | 346 | 5 | 15 | 638 | 75 | 0 | 0 | 0 | 198 | 136 | 133 | 78 |
| Spicy Buttermilk Coffee Cake | 1/16 | 280 | 9 | 43 | 11 | 178 | 154 | 6 | 2 | 2 | 0 | 10 | 8 | 6 | 7 |
| Spoon Bread | 1/6 | 326 | 9 | 21 | 3 | 687 | 270 | 14 | 24 | 3 | 2 | 9 | 18 | 18 | 6 |
| Sticky Nut Rolls | 1/12 | 261 | 3 | 38 | 5 | 225 | 80 | 5 | 3 | 0 | 0 | 10 | 7 | 5 | 8 |
| Streusel Coffee Cake | 1/8 | 356 | 5 | 53 | 8 | 254 | 182 | 8 | 3 | 1 | 1 | 14 | 9 | 6 | 9 |
| Sunflower Seed Muffins | 1/12 | 186 | 4 | 25 | 4 | 157 | 112 | 6 | 1 | 1 | 1 | 15 | 6 | 4 | 6 |
| Sunshine Muffins | 1/8 | 161 | 3 | 28 | 4 | 308 | 78 | 5 | 2 | 5 | 5 | 10 | 7 | 3 | 5 |
| Swedish Limpa | 1/24 | 123 | 3 | 25 | 3 | 91 | 64 | 5 | 0 | 1 | 1 | 11 | 7 | 7 | 6 |
| Sweet Rolls | 1/24 | 133 | 3 | 21 | 3 | 130 | 49 | 5 | 3 | 0 | 0 | 11 | 8 | 7 | 5 |
| Three-C Bread | 1/24 | 157 | 3 | 21 | 3 | 120 | 71 | 4 | 22 | 2 | 2 | 7 | 5 | 4 | 4 |
| Waffles | 1/3 | 734 | 17 | 64 | 17 | 795 | 321 | 26 | 12 | 2 | 2 | 36 | 38 | 26 | 15 |
| White Bread (Conventional Method) | 1/36 | 90 | 3 | 17 | 1 | 128 | 42 | 4 | 1 | 0 | 0 | 9 | 7 | 2 | 3 |
| Whole Wheat Bread | 1/32 | 87 | 2 | 17 | 1 | 134 | 51 | 4 | 0 | 0 | 0 | 8 | 4 | 1 | 4 |
| Whole Wheat Pita Bread | 1/12 | 153 | 4 | 24 | 5 | 268 | 98 | 7 | 0 | 0 | 0 | 14 | 6 | 9 | 6 |
| Yeast Doughnuts | 1/16 | 167 | 4 | 25 | 6 | 148 | 67 | 7 | 2 | 2 | 0 | 13 | 11 | 8 | 6 |
| Zucchini Nut Loaf | 1/16 | 152 | 2 | 22 | 6 | 110 | 49 | 4 | 1 | 1 | 3 | 6 | 4 | 1 | 3 |

# Yeast Breads

When making yeast breads, you'll want your loaves to look and taste extra special. Below are some helpful hints we recommend for achieving a perfect product every time.

Although you can still make bread the conventional "soften-the-yeast" way, consider the newer easy-mix method. It eliminates the yeast-softening step since you combine the dry yeast directly with the flour.

Here's how to identify the stage of dough specified for your bread: *Soft dough* is too sticky to knead and is often used for batter breads. *Moderately soft dough* is slightly sticky, may be kneaded on a floured surface, and is used for most sweet breads. *Moderately stiff dough* is somewhat firm to the touch, kneads easily on a floured surface, and is used for most unsweet breads. *Stiff dough* is firm to the touch and is easily rolled on a floured surface. French bread dough is an example.

When the recipe gives a range on the amount of flour, start by adding the smaller amount. And remember, flour used in kneading is also part of this measured amount.

Don't place dough in a hot area to rise because excessive heat will kill the yeast. A good spot is in an unheated oven with a large pan of hot water set on the lower rack under the bowl of dough. The optimum rising temperature is 80°.

Do not add flour after rising starts. This produces dark streaks and a coarse texture.

Don't let loaves rise too long or to the top of the pan. If the dough rises much over twice its original size, the cell walls become thin; since the dough rises further in the oven, the cells may collapse and the bread may fall.

Before baking, gently brush the top of the loaf with shortening, butter, margarine, or oil for a browner crust. Brush with milk, water, or beaten egg for a crispy and shiny crust. For a softer crust, brush the top with butter or margarine after baking.

## Easy-Mix White Bread

5¾ to 6¼ cups all-purpose flour
1 package active dry yeast
2¼ cups milk
2 tablespoons sugar
1 tablespoon shortening
2 teaspoons salt                    Oven 375°

In a large mixer bowl combine *2½ cups* of the flour and the yeast. In a saucepan heat milk, sugar, shortening, and salt just till warm (115° to 120°) and shortening is almost melted; stir constantly. Add to flour mixture. Beat at low speed of electric mixer ½ minute, scraping sides of bowl. Beat 3 minutes at high speed. Stir in as much remaining flour as you can mix in with a spoon. Turn out onto a lightly floured surface. Knead in enough remaining flour to make a moderately stiff dough that is smooth and elastic (6 to 8 minutes total). Shape into a ball. Place in a greased bowl; turn once. Cover; let rise in a warm place till double (about 1¼ hours).

Punch down; turn out onto a lightly floured surface. Divide dough in half. Cover; let rest 10 minutes. Lightly grease two 8x4x2-inch loaf pans. Shape each half of dough into a loaf by patting or rolling. To pat dough, gently pull the dough into a loaf shape, tucking the edges beneath. Place in pans. Brush loaves with melted butter. Cover; let rise in a warm place till nearly double (45 to 60 minutes). Bake in a 375° oven about

### Easy-mix method

Do not use the easy-mix method in Canada. Differences in the yeast make it impossible to get good results. Instead, here's how to convert recipes to the conventional method.

Change ¼ *cup* of the liquid to warm *water;* add yeast to dissolve. Heat remaining liquid and continue as directed in the conventional method (see recipe at right).

45 minutes or till done. Remove from pans; cool. Makes 2 loaves.

---

## White Bread (Conventional Method)

1 **package active dry yeast**
¼ **cup warm water (110° or 115°)**
2 **cups milk**
2 **tablespoons sugar**
1 **tablespoon shortening**
2 **teaspoons salt**
5¾ **to 6¼ cups all-purpose flour**
   **Melted butter**                          Oven 375°

Soften yeast in warm water. In a saucepan heat milk, sugar, shortening, and salt just till warm (115° to 120°) and shortening is almost melted; stir constantly. Turn into a large mixing bowl. Stir in *2 cups* of the flour; beat well. Add the softened yeast; stir till smooth. Stir in as much of the remaining flour as you can mix in with a spoon. Turn out onto a lightly floured surface. Knead in enough of the remaining flour to make a moderately stiff dough that is smooth and elastic (6 to 8 minutes total). Shape into a ball. Place in a lightly greased bowl; turn once to grease surface. Cover; let rise in a warm place till double (about 1¼ hours).

Punch down; turn out onto a lightly floured surface. Divide dough in half. Shape into two balls. Cover; let rest 10 minutes. Grease two 8x4x2-inch loaf pans. Shape each ball of dough into a loaf. Place in pans. Brush loaves with some melted butter or margarine. Cover; let rise in a warm place till nearly double (45 to 60 minutes). Bake in a 375° oven about 45 minutes or till bread tests done. Test by tapping the top with your finger. A hollow sound means the loaf is properly baked. Remove from pans; cool on a wire rack. Makes 2 loaves.

**Note:** To make bread in advance, prepare dough for White Bread, using either the conventional or easy-mix method. After dough has risen, shape each ball of dough into a loaf and place in pans. Cover loaves loosely with clear plastic wrap.

Refrigerate up to 24 hours. When ready to bake, remove bread from refrigerator and uncover. Brush with some melted butter or margarine. Let stand in a warm place till loaves nearly double; puncture any surface bubbles with a wooden pick. Bake as above.

## French Bread

| 5½ | to 6 cups all-purpose flour |
| 2 | packages active dry yeast |
| 2 | teaspoons salt |
| 2 | cups warm water (115° to 120°) |
| | Cornmeal |
| 1 | slightly beaten egg white (optional) |
| 1 | tablespoon water (optional)    Oven 375° |

In a large mixer bowl combine *2 cups* of the flour, the yeast, and salt. Add warm water. Beat at low speed of electric mixer for ½ minute, scraping sides of bowl constantly. Beat 3 minutes at high speed. Stir in as much of the remaining flour as you can mix in with a spoon. Turn out onto a lightly floured surface. Knead in enough of the remaining flour to make a stiff dough that is smooth and elastic (8 to 10 minutes total). Shape into a ball. Place in a lightly greased bowl; turn once to grease surface. Cover; let rise in a warm place till double (1 to 1¼ hours).

Punch down; turn out onto a lightly floured surface. Divide in half. Cover; let rest 10 minutes. Roll each half into a 15x12-inch rectangle. Roll up tightly from long side; seal well. Taper ends. (*Or,* shape into individual loaves or hard rolls as below.) Place, seam side down, on a greased baking sheet sprinkled with cornmeal. If desired, brush with a mixture of egg white and water. Cover; let rise till nearly double (about 45 minutes). With a sharp knife, make 3 or 4 diagonal cuts about ¼ inch deep across tops of loaves. Bake in a 375° oven 40 to 45 minutes. If desired, brush again with egg white mixture after 20 minutes of baking. Cool. Makes 2 loaves.

***Individual French Loaves:*** Cut each half of dough into quarters, making 8 pieces total. Shape into balls. Cover; let rest 10 minutes. Shape each ball into a 6-inch loaf; taper ends.

Place 2½ inches apart on a greased baking sheet sprinked with cornmeal. Press down ends of loaves. Brush with egg white mixture, if desired. Cover; let rise till nearly double (about 45 minutes). Make 3 shallow cuts diagonally across the top of each loaf. Bake in a 375° oven for 25 to 30 minutes. If desired, brush again with egg white mixture after 15 minutes of baking. Makes 8 loaves.

**Note:** Italian Bread is similar to French Bread, but loaves are often shorter and thicker.

---

## Molasses-Oatmeal Bread

---

  5¾ **to 6¼ cups all-purpose flour**
  2 **packages active dry yeast**
  1¾ **cups water**
  1 **cup quick-cooking rolled oats**
  ½ **cup light molasses**
  ⅓ **cup shortening**
  1 **tablespoon salt**
  2 **eggs**
   **Quick-cooking rolled oats**
  1 **beaten egg white (optional)**
  1 **tablespoon water**
   **(optional)**                    Oven 375°

In a large mixer bowl combine *2 cups* of the flour and yeast. In a saucepan heat the 1¾ cups water, the 1 cup rolled oats, light molasses, shortening, and salt just till warm (115° to 120°) and shortening is almost melted; stir constantly. Add to flour mixture. Add the 2 eggs. Beat at low speed of electric mixer for ½ minute, scraping sides of bowl constantly. Beat 3 minutes at high speed. Stir in as much of the remaining flour as you can mix in with a spoon. Turn out onto a lightly floured surface. Knead in enough of the remaining flour to make a moderately soft dough that is smooth and elastic (3 to 5 minutes total). Shape into a ball. Place in a lightly greased bowl; turn once to grease surface. Cover; let rise in a warm place till double (about 1½ hours).

Punch down; turn out onto a lightly floured surface. Divide dough in half. Cover; let rest 10 minutes. Grease two 9x5x3-inch loaf pans. If desired, coat each pan with about 3 *tablespoons* rolled oats.

Shape dough into loaves. Place loaves in pans. Cover; let rise till nearly double (45 to 60 minutes). If desired, brush loaves with a mixture of egg white and 1 tablespoon water; sprinkle tops lightly with additional rolled oats. Bake in a 375° oven for 40 to 45 minutes or till done. Cover loosely with foil the last 15 minutes of baking to prevent overbrowning. Remove from pans; cool on a wire rack. Makes 2 loaves.

## Rye Bread

Oven 350°

In a large mixer bowl combine 2½ cups *all-purpose flour*, 2 packages *active dry yeast*, and 1 tablespoon *caraway seed*. Stir together 2 cups warm *water* (115° to 120°), ½ cup packed *brown sugar*, 1 tablespoon *cooking oil*, and 1 teaspoon *salt*; add to flour mixture. Beat at low speed of electric mixer ½ minute, scraping bowl. Beat 3 minutes at high speed. Stir in 2½ cups *rye flour* and as much of ¾ to 1¼ cups *all-purpose flour* as you can mix in with a spoon. Turn out onto a floured surface. Knead in enough remaining all-purpose flour to make a moderately stiff dough that is smooth and elastic (6 to 8 minutes total). Place in a greased bowl; turn. Cover; let rise in a warm place till double (about 1½ hours).

Punch down; divide in half. Cover; let rest 10 minutes. Shape into two 4½-inch round loaves on greased baking sheets. Cover; let rise till nearly double (40 minutes). Bake in a 350° oven 40 to 45 minutes. Cool. Makes 2.

## Whole Wheat Bread

Oven 375°

In a larger mixer bowl combine 2 cups *all-purpose flour* and 1 package *active dry yeast*. Heat 1¾ cups *water*, ⅓ cup packed *brown sugar*, 3 tablespoons *shortening*, and 2 teaspoons *salt* just till warm (115° to 120°), stirring constantly. Add to flour mixture. Beat at low speed of electric mixer ½ minute, scraping bowl. Beat 3 minutes at high speed. Stir in 2 cups *whole wheat flour* and as much of 1 to 1½ cups *all-purpose flour* as you can mix in with a spoon. On a lightly floured surface knead in enough remaining all-purpose flour to make a moderately stiff dough (6 to 8 minutes total). Shape into a ball in a lightly greased bowl; turn once. Cover; let rise in a warm place till double (1 to 1½ hours).

Punch dough down; turn out onto a lightly floured surface. Divide in half. Cover; let rest 10 minutes. Shape into loaves; place in 2 greased 8x4x2-inch loaf pans. Cover; let rise till nearly double (about 1 hour). Bake in a 375° oven about 45 minutes. Cover the loaves with foil the last 20 minutes to prevent overbrowning. Makes 2 loaves.

## German Stollen

|   |   |
|---|---|
| 4 | to 4½ cups all-purpose flour |
| 1 | package active dry yeast |
| ¼ | teaspoon ground cardamom |
| 1¼ | cups milk |
| ½ | cup butter or margarine |
| ¼ | cup granulated sugar |
| 1 | teaspoon salt |
| 1 | slightly beaten egg |
| 1 | cup raisins |
| ¼ | cup chopped mixed candied fruits and peels |
| ¼ | cup dried currants |
| ¼ | cup chopped blanched almonds |
| 2 | tablespoons finely shredded orange peel |
| 1 | tablespoon finely shredded lemon peel |
| 1 | cup sifted powdered sugar |
| 2 | tablespoons hot water |
| ½ | teaspoon butter or margarine     Oven 375° |

In a large mixer bowl combine *2 cups* of the flour, the yeast, and cardamom. In a saucepan heat milk, the ½ cup butter, granulated sugar, and salt just till warm (115° to 120°) and butter is almost melted; stir constantly. Add to flour mixture.

Add egg. Beat at low speed of electric mixer for ½ minute; scrape sides of bowl constantly. Beat 3 minutes at high speed. Stir in as much of the remaining flour as you can mix in with a spoon. Stir in raisins, candied fruits and peels, currants, almonds, and orange and lemon peels.

Turn out onto a lightly floured surface. Knead in enough of the remaining flour to make a moderately soft dough that is smooth and elastic (3 to 5 minutes total). Shape into a ball. Place in a greased bowl; turn once. Cover; let rise in a warm place till double (about 1¾ hours). Punch down; turn out onto a lightly floured surface. Divide into thirds. Cover; let rest 10 minutes.

Roll one third of the dough into a 10x6-inch rectangle. Without stretching, fold the long side over to within 1 inch of the opposite side; seal. Place on a greased baking sheet; repeat with remaining dough.

Cover; let rise till nearly double (about 1 hour). Bake in a 375° oven for 18 to 20 minutes or till golden. Combine the powdered sugar, hot water, and ½ teaspoon butter or margarine; brush over warm bread. Makes 3.

## Cheese Bread

Oven 350°

In a large mixer bowl combine 1½ cups *all-purpose flour* and 1 package *active dry yeast*. Heat 1½ cups shredded *American or Swiss cheese*, 1¼ cups *water*, ¼ cup *sugar*, and 1½ teaspoons *salt* just till warm (115° to 120°), stirring constantly. Add to flour mixture; add 1 *egg*. Beat at low speed of electric mixer for ½ minute, scraping bowl. Beat 3 minutes at high speed. Stir in as much of 2 to 2½ cups *all-purpose flour* as you can mix in with a spoon. On a floured surface knead in enough of the remaining all-purpose flour to make a moderately stiff dough that is smooth and elastic (6 to 8 minutes total). Shape into a ball in a greased bowl; turn once. Cover; let rise in a warm place till double (1 to 1¼ hours).

Punch down; divide in half. Cover; let rest 10 minutes. Shape into 2 loaves; place in greased 8x4x2-inch loaf pans. Cover; let rise till nearly double (about 45 minutes). Bake in a

350° oven 40 to 45 minutes. Cover with foil the last 20 minutes to prevent overbrowning. Cool on a wire rack. Makes 2 loaves.

## Swedish Limpa

Oven 350°

In a large mixer bowl combine 2½ cups *all-purpose flour*, 2 packages *active dry yeast*, and 1 tablespoon *caraway seed*. Stir together 2 cups warm *water* (115° to 120°), ½ cup packed *brown sugar*, 2 tablespoons finely shredded *orange peel*, 1 tablespoon *cooking oil*, and 1 teaspoon *salt*. Add to flour mixture. Beat at low speed of electric mixer for ½ minute, scraping bowl. Beat 3 minutes at high speed. Stir in 2½ cups *rye flour* and as much of ¾ to 1¼ cups *all-purpose flour* as you can mix in with a spoon. On a floured surface knead in enough remaining all-purpose flour to make a moderately stiff dough that is smooth and elastic (6 to 8 minutes total). Shape into a ball in a greased bowl; turn once. Cover; let rise in a warm place till double (1¼ to 1½ hours).

Punch down; divide in half. Cover; let rest 10 minutes. Shape into two 4½-inch round loaves on greased baking sheets. Cover; let rise till nearly double (about 40 minutes). Bake in a 350° oven 40 to 45 minutes. Makes 2.

## Pumpernickel

Oven 350°

Combine 2 cups *all-purpose flour*, 3 packages *active dry yeast*, and 1 tablespoon *caraway seed*. Mix 1½ cups warm *water* (115° to 120°), ½ cup light *molasses*, 2 tablespoons *cooking oil*, and 1 tablespoon *salt*. Add to flour mixture. Beat at low speed of electric mixer ½ minute, scraping bowl. Beat 3 minutes at high speed. Stir in 2 cups *rye flour* and as much of ¾ to 1¼ cups *all-purpose flour* as you can mix in with a spoon. On a floured surface knead in enough of the remaining all-purpose flour to make a moderately stiff dough that is smooth and elastic (6 to 8 minutes total). Shape into a ball in a greased bowl; turn once. Cover; let rise till double (about 1½ hours).

Punch down; divide in half. Cover; let rest 10 minutes. Shape into 2 round loaves. Place on a greased baking sheet sprinkled with *cornmeal*. Flatten slightly with hand to a 6- to 7-inch diameter. Cover; let rise till nearly double (30 to 45 minutes). Bake in a 350° oven 35 to 40 minutes or till well browned. Makes 2.

## Anadama Bread

| | |
|---|---|
| **6¼** | **to 6¾ cups all-purpose flour** |
| **½** | **cup cornmeal** |
| **2** | **packages active dry yeast** |
| **½** | **cup dark molasses** |
| **⅓** | **cup shortening** |
| **2** | **eggs** Oven 375° |

Combine *3 cups* flour, cornmeal, and the yeast. Heat molasses, shortening, 2 cups *water,* and 1 tablespoon *salt* just till warm (115° to 120°); stir constantly. Add to flour mixture; add eggs. Beat at low speed of electric mixer ½ minute. Beat 3 minutes at high speed. Stir in as much remaining flour as you can mix in with a spoon. On a floured surface knead in enough remaining flour to make a moderately soft dough (3 to 5 minutes total). Shape into a ball in a greased bowl; turn once. Cover; let rise in a warm place till double (1 to 1¼ hours). Punch down; divide in half. Cover; let rest 10 minutes. Grease two 9x5x3-inch loaf pans. Shape dough into 2 loaves; place in pans. Cover; let rise till nearly double (45 to 60 minutes). Bake in a 375° oven 35 to 40 minutes. Makes 2.

# Russian Black Bread

3½  to 4 cups all-purpose flour
4   cups rye flour
2   cups whole bran cereal
2   packages active dry yeast
2   tablespoons instant coffee crystals
2   tablespoons caraway seed
1   tablespoon sugar
1   teaspoon fennel seed, crushed
2½  cups water
⅓   cup molasses
¼   cup butter or margarine
1   square (1 ounce) unsweetened chocolate
2   tablespoons vinegar
½   cup cold water
1   tablespoon cornstarch                    Oven 375°

In a large mixer bowl combine *3 cups* of the all-purpose flour, *1 cup* of the rye flour, the whole bran cereal, the yeast, coffee crystals, caraway seed, sugar, fennel seed, and 1 tablespoon *salt*. In a saucepan heat together the 2½ cups water, molasses, butter or margarine, chocolate, and vinegar just till warm (115° to 120°) and chocolate and butter are almost melted; stir constantly. Add molasses mixture to flour mixture in mixer bowl. Beat at low speed of electric mixer ½ minute, scraping bowl. Beat 3 minutes at high speed. Stir in remaining 3 cups rye flour and as much of the remaining all-purpose flour as you can mix in with a spoon.

Turn out onto a lightly floured surface. Knead in enough remaining all-purpose flour to make a moderately stiff dough that is smooth and elastic (6 to 8 minutes total). (Dough may be slightly sticky because of the rye flour.) Shape into a ball. Place in a greased bowl; turn once. Cover; let rise in a warm place till nearly double (1¼ to 1½ hours).

Punch down; divide in half. Shape each half into a ball. Place on greased baking sheets. Flatten slightly with palm of hand to a 6- to 7-inch diameter. Cover; let rise till nearly double (30 to 45 minutes). Bake in a 375° oven for 50 to 60 minutes or till well browned and bread sounds hollow when tapped. Remove from baking sheets; cool.

Meanwhile, in a small saucepan combine the ½ cup cold water and cornstarch. Cook and stir till thickened and bubbly; cook 1 minute more. Brush over *hot* bread. Makes 2 loaves.

## Potato Bread

   **1    medium potato, peeled and cubed**
**1½    cups water**
   **2    packages active dry yeast**
   **6    to 6½ cups all-purpose flour**
   **3    tablespoons sugar**
   **2    tablespoons shortening**
   **1    tablespoon salt**
        **All-purpose flour or cornmeal**
          **(optional)**                           Oven 375°

In a medium saucepan cook potato in the water about 12 minutes or till tender; *do not drain.* Cool cubed potato mixture to 110° to 115°. Set aside ½ *cup* of the cooking liquid. Mash potato in the remaining liquid; add enough warm water to make 2 cups mashed potato mixture.

In a large mixer bowl soften yeast in the reserved ½ cup potato liquid. Add mashed potato mixture, *2 cups* of the flour, the sugar, shortening, and salt. Beat at low speed of electric mixer for ½ minute, scraping sides of bowl constantly. Beat 3 minutes at high speed.

Stir in as much of the remaining flour as you can mix in with a spoon. Turn out onto a lightly floured surface. Knead in enough of the remaining flour to make a moderately stiff dough that is smooth and elastic (6 to 8 minutes total). Shape into a ball. Place in a lightly greased bowl; turn once to grease surface. Cover; let rise in a warm place till double (about 1 hour).

Punch down; turn out onto a lightly floured surface. Divide dough in half. Cover; let rest 10 minutes. Shape each half into a loaf. Place in two greased 8x4x2-inch loaf pans. Cover; let rise till nearly double (about 35 minutes).

If desired, brush tops with a little water and dust lightly with additional flour or cornmeal. Bake in a 375° oven for 40 to 45 minutes or till bread tests done, covering with foil the last 15 minutes of baking to prevent overbrowning. Remove from pans; cool on a wire rack. Makes 2 loaves.

## Egg Bread

| | |
|---|---|
| 6¾ | to 7¼ cups all-purpose flour |
| 2 | packages active dry yeast |
| 2 | cups milk |
| ¼ | cup sugar |
| ¼ | cup butter or margarine |
| 2 | teaspoons salt |
| 3 | eggs |

Oven 375°

In a large mixer bowl combine *3 cups* of the flour and the yeast. In a saucepan heat milk, sugar, butter, and salt just till warm (115° to 120°) and butter is almost melted; stir constantly. Add to flour mixture; add eggs. Beat at low speed of electric mixer ½ minute, scraping bowl. Beat 3 minutes at high speed. Stir in as much remaining flour as you can mix in with a spoon. Turn out onto a lightly floured surface. Knead in enough remaining flour to make a moderately stiff dough that is smooth and elastic (6 to 8 minutes total). Shape into a ball. Place in a lightly greased bowl; turn once to grease surface. Cover; let rise in a warm place till double (about 1¼ hours).

Punch down; divide dough in half. Cover; let rest 10 minutes. Shape into 2 loaves. Place in two greased 9x5x3-inch loaf pans. Cover; let rise till nearly double (35 to 45 minutes). Bake in a 375° oven 35 to 40 minutes or till done, covering with foil the last 15 minutes to prevent overbrowning. Remove from pans; cool on a wire rack. Makes 2 loaves.

***Cinnamon Swirl Bread:*** Prepare Egg Bread dough as above, *except* instead of shaping into loaves, roll each half of dough into a 15x7-inch rectangle. Brush entire surface lightly with *water.* Combine ½ cup *sugar* and 2 teaspoons ground *cinnamon;* sprinkle half of the sugar mixture over each rectangle. Beginning with narrow end, roll up jelly roll style; seal edge and ends. Place, sealed edges down, in greased loaf pans. Continue as directed above. Drizzle warm loaf with Powdered Sugar Icing (see recipe, page 121).

***Raisin Bread:*** Prepare Egg Bread dough as above, *except* stir in 2 cups plumped *raisins* when stirring in flour with a spoon. To plump raisins, cover raisins in a saucepan with water. Bring to boiling. Remove from heat and let stand 5 minutes; drain. Drizzle warm loaf with Powdered Sugar Icing (see recipe, page 121).

## Julekage

Oven 350°

In a large mixer bowl combine 2½ cups *all-purpose flour*, 2 packages *active dry yeast*, and ¾ teaspoon ground *carda-mom*. In a saucepan heat 1¼ cups *milk*, ½ cup *sugar*, ½ cup *butter or margarine*, and 1 teaspoon *salt* just till warm (115° to 120°) and the butter is almost melted; stir constantly. Add heated milk mixture to flour mixture; add 1 *egg*. Beat at low speed of electric mixer for ½ minute. Beat 3 minutes at high speed, scraping sides of bowl constantly. Stir in 1 cup chopped *mixed candied fruits and peels*, 1 cup *light raisins*, and as much of 2 to 2½ cups *all-purpose flour* as you can mix in with a spoon.

Turn out onto a lightly floured surface. Knead in enough of the remaining all-purpose flour to make a moderately stiff dough that is smooth and elastic (6 to 8 minutes total). Shape dough into a ball. Place in a lightly greased bowl; turn once to grease surface. Cover; let rise in a warm place till double (about 1½ hours).

Punch dough down; divide dough in half. Cover; let rest 10 minutes. Shape into 2 round loaves; place on greased baking sheets. Flatten each slightly to a 6-inch diameter. Cover; let rise till nearly double (45 to 60 minutes). Stir together 1 slightly beaten *egg yolk* and 2 tablespoons *water;* brush over loaves. Bake in a 350° oven 35 minutes or till done. Cool on a wire rack.

In a mixing bowl combine 1 cup sifted *powdered sugar*, ¼ teaspoon *vanilla*, and enough *milk* to make of drizzling consistency. Drizzle over cooled loaves. Decorate with almonds and candied cherries, if desired. Slice to serve. Makes 2 round loaves.

---

## Cardamom Braid

Oven 375°

---

In a large mixer bowl combine ¾ cup *all-purpose flour,* 1 package *active dry yeast,* and 1 teaspoon ground *cardamom.* Heat ¾ cup *milk,* ⅓ cup *sugar,* ¼ cup *butter or margarine,* and ½ teaspoon *salt* just till warm (115° to 120°); stir constantly. Add to flour mixture; add 1 egg. Beat at low speed of electric mixer for ½ minute. Beat 3 minutes at high speed. Stir in as much of 1¾ to 2¼ cups *all-purpose flour* as you can mix in with a spoon. On a lightly floured surface knead in enough remaining flour to make a moderately soft dough that is smooth and elastic (3 to 5 minutes total). Shape into a ball. Place in a greased bowl; turn once. Cover; let rise till double (about 1¼ hours).

Punch down; divide into thirds. Cover; let rest 10 minutes. Roll each ball into a 16-inch-long rope. Braid, referring to tip on page 117. Cover; let rise till nearly double (about 40 minutes). Lightly brush with milk; sprinkle with 1 tablespoon *sugar.* Bake in a 375° oven about 20 minutes. Cool on a wire rack. Makes 1.

---

## Peasant Bread

Oven 375°

---

In a large mixer bowl combine 2 cups *all-purpose flour* and 2 packages *active dry yeast.* Heat 1¾ cups *water,* ¼ cup *dark molasses,* 2 tablespoons *cooking oil,* and 2 teaspoons *salt* just till warm (115° to 120°); stir constantly. Add to flour mixture. Beat at low speed of electric mixer ½ minute, scraping bowl. Beat 3 minutes at high speed. Stir in 1½ cups *rye flour,* ½ cup *whole bran cereal,* ⅓ cup *yellow cornmeal,* 1 tablespoon *cara-way seed,* and as much of 1 to 1½ cups *all-purpose flour* as you can mix in with a spoon. On a lightly floured surface knead in enough remaining all-purpose flour to make a moderately stiff dough that is smooth and elastic (6 to 8 minutes total). Shape into a ball in a greased bowl; turn once. Cover; let rise in a warm place till double (1 to 1¼ hours).

Punch down; turn out onto a floured surface. Divide in half. Cover; let rest 10 minutes. Shape into 2 loaves; place in two greased 8x4x2-inch loaf pans. Cover; let rise till nearly double (30 to 45 minutes). Bake in a 375° oven 35 to 40 minutes. Makes 2 loaves.

## Kuchen

   **3    cups all-purpose flour**
   **1    package active dry yeast**
   **¾    cup milk**
   **6    tablespoons butter or margarine**
   **⅓    cup sugar**
   **½    teaspoon salt**
   **2    eggs**
   **1    beaten egg**
   **3    tablespoons light cream or milk**
   **1    cup sugar**
**1½    teaspoons ground cinnamon**
   **2    cups thinly sliced peeled apple, sliced
            rhubarb, sliced Italian plums, or cottage
            cheese**                                   Oven 400°

In a mixer bowl combine 1½ cups of the flour and the yeast. In a saucepan heat ¾ cup milk, butter, ⅓ cup sugar, and salt just till warm (115° to 120°) and butter is almost melted, stirring constantly. Add to flour mixture; add 2 eggs. Beat at low speed of electric mixer ½ minute, scraping bowl. Beat 3 minutes at high speed. Stir in remaining flour. Divide in half. With lightly floured fingers, pat into two greased 9x1½-inch round baking pans, pressing up sides to form a rim. Cover; let rise in a warm place till double (45 to 50 minutes).

Combine the beaten egg and 3 tablespoons cream or milk. Stir in 1 cup sugar and the cinnamon. (If cottage cheese is used, stir into the sugar-cream mixture.) Arrange fruit atop

# How to braid breads

You can give your favorite kneaded yeast bread or coffee cake an intriguing twist by shaping it into a braid. For picture-perfect results, just follow these simple directions.

Plan to make one braid from a recipe based on 3½ to 4 cups flour, and two braids from a recipe based on 5 to 6 cups of flour.

*Preparing the dough:* Mix up the bread dough following recipe instructions. Knead the dough and let it rise in a warm place till double. Punch down. For each braid, divide the dough into thirds and shape each portion into a ball. Cover and let rest 10 minutes so dough will be easier to handle. On a lightly floured surface roll each ball into an evenly thick rope about 16 inches long. Line up the three ropes, 1 inch apart, on a greased baking sheet.

*Braiding the bread:* Begin in the middle of the ropes and work toward the ends. (Working from the middle is easier and helps avoid stretching the dough, which results in an uneven loaf.) Braid the ropes loosely so the dough has room to expand without cracking or losing its shape. Gently straighten the ropes on the baking sheet. Pinch the ends of the ropes together and tuck the sealed portion under the braid so the ropes won't come apart during baking. Cover the braid and let rise in a warm place till almost double. For a crisp, shiny crust, brush the braid with a mixture of 1 *egg yolk* and 1 tablespoon *milk*. If desired, sprinkle with a little *sugar, sesame seed,* or *poppy seed* atop each braid. Bake as directed in the recipe.

risen dough. Carefully spoon sugar-cream mixture over fruit. Bake in a 400° oven for 20 to 25 minutes. Cool slightly. Cut into wedges; serve warm. Makes 2 coffee cakes.

**Note:** If using apples or rhubarb, simmer sliced fruit in water 2 minutes or just till tender. Drain; place atop dough.

**Prune Kuchen:** Prepare Kuchen dough as above. While dough is rising, make prune filling. In a saucepan combine 2 cups *coarsely snipped prunes* and enough water to come 1 inch above prunes. Simmer 10 minutes; drain. Spoon cooked prunes atop risen dough. Finish Kuchen as directed.

---

# Chocolate Swirl Coffee Cake

|   |   |
|---|---|
| **4** | **to 4½ cups all-purpose flour** |
| **2** | **packages active dry yeast** |
| **¾** | **cup sugar** |
| **⅔** | **cup water** |
| **½** | **cup butter or margarine** |
| **⅓** | **cup evaporated milk** |
| **½** | **teaspoon salt** |
| **4** | **egg yolks** |
| **¾** | **cup semisweet chocolate pieces** |
| **⅓** | **cup evaporated milk** |
| **2** | **tablespoons sugar** |
| **½** | **teaspoon ground cinnamon** |
| **¼** | **cup all-purpose flour** |
| **¼** | **cup sugar** |
| **1** | **teaspoon ground cinnamon** |
| **¼** | **cup butter or margarine** |
| **¼** | **cup chopped nuts** |

Oven 350°

In a large mixer bowl combine *1½ cups* of the flour and the yeast. In a saucepan heat ¾ cup sugar, water, ½ cup butter or margarine, ⅓ cup evaporated milk, and salt just till warm (115° to 120°) and butter is almost melted, stirring constantly. Add to flour mixture; add egg yolks. Beat at low speed of electric mixer for ½ minute, scraping bowl often. Beat 3 minutes at high speed. Stir in as much of the remaining flour as you can mix in with a spoon. Turn out onto a lightly floured surface. Knead in enough of the remaining flour to make a moderately soft dough that is smooth and elastic (3 to 5 minutes total). Shape into a ball. Place in a lightly greased bowl; turn once to grease surface. Cover; let rise in a warm place till double (about 2 hours).

Punch down. Cover; let rest 10 minutes. Meanwhile, combine chocolate pieces, ⅓ cup evaporated milk, 2 tablespoons sugar, and ½ teaspoon cinnamon. Stir over low heat till chocolate is melted; cool. Roll dough into an 18x10-inch rectangle. Spread with chocolate mixture; roll up from long side. Join and seal ends. Place in a greased 10-inch tube pan. Combine ¼ cup flour, ¼ cup sugar, and 1 teaspoon cinnamon. Cut in ¼ cup butter or margarine; stir in nuts. Sprinkle over dough. Cover; let rise till nearly double (about 1¼ hours). Bake on lower rack in a 350° oven for 45 to 50 minutes. Cool 15 minutes; remove from pan. Makes 1 large coffee cake.

## Cinnamon Crisps

| | |
|---|---|
| 3½ to 4 cups | all-purpose flour |
| 1 | package active dry yeast |
| 1¼ | cups milk |
| ¼ | cup granulated sugar |
| ¼ | cup shortening |
| 1 | teaspoon salt |
| 1 | egg |
| ½ | cup granulated sugar |
| ½ | cup packed brown sugar |
| ¼ | cup butter or margarine, melted |
| ½ | teaspoon ground cinnamon |
| ¼ | cup butter or margarine, melted |
| 1 | cup granulated sugar |
| ½ | cup chopped pecans |
| 1 | teaspoon ground cinnamon        Oven 400° |

In a large mixer bowl combine *2 cups* flour and the yeast. Heat milk, ¼ cup granulated sugar, shortening, and salt just till warm (115° to 120°); stir constantly. Add to flour mixture; add egg. Beat at low speed of electric mixer ½ minute, scraping sides of bowl constantly. Beat 3 minutes at high speed. Stir in as much of the remaining flour as you can mix in with a spoon. On a lightly floured surface knead in enough of the remaining flour to make a moderately soft dough that is smooth and elastic (3 to 5 minutes total). Shape into a ball. Place in a lightly greased bowl; turn once to grease surface. Cover; let rise in a warm place till double (1 to 1½ hours).

Punch down; divide in half. Cover; let rest 10 minutes. Roll *half* of the dough into a 12-inch square. Combine ½ cup granulated sugar, brown sugar, ¼ cup melted butter or margarine, and ½ teaspoon ground cinnamon; spread *half* over dough. Roll up jelly roll style; seal seams. Cut into 12 rolls. Place on greased baking sheets 3 to 4 inches apart. Flatten each roll to about 3 inches in diameter. Repeat with remaining dough and cinnamon-sugar mixture. Cover; let rise till nearly double (about 30 minutes). Cover with waxed paper. Use a rolling pin to flatten to ⅛-inch thickness; remove paper. Brush rolls with ¼ cup melted butter. Combine 1 cup granulated sugar, pecans, and 1 teaspoon ground cinnamon. Sprinkle over rolls. Cover with waxed paper; roll flat. Remove paper. Bake in a 400° oven 10 to 12 minutes. Remove from baking sheets immediately. Makes 24.

## Sweet Rolls

Oven 375°

In a mixer bowl combine 2 cups *all-purpose flour* and 1 package *active dry yeast*. Heat 1 cup *milk,* ⅓ cup *sugar,* ⅓ cup *butter,* and 1 teaspoon *salt* just till warm (115° to 120°); stir constantly. Add to flour mixture; add 2 *eggs.* Beat at low speed of electric mixer for ½ minute. Beat 3 minutes at high speed. Stir in as much of 2 to 2½ cups *all-purpose flour* as you can mix in with a spoon. On a floured surface knead in enough remaining all-purpose flour to make a moderately stiff dough that is smooth and elastic (6 to 8 minutes total). Shape into a ball in a greased bowl; turn once. Cover; let rise in a warm place till double (about 1 hour). Punch down; divide in half. Cover; let rest 10 minutes. Shape and bake as below. Makes 24.

***Caramel-Pecan Rolls:*** Prepare Sweet Roll dough as directed. Divide dough in half. Roll one half into a 12x8-inch rectangle. Melt 3 tablespoons *butter or margarine;* brush *half* over dough. Combine ½ cup *granulated sugar* and 1 teaspoon ground *cinnamon;* sprinkle *half* over dough. Roll up jelly roll style, beginning from longest side. Seal seams. Cut into 12 pieces. Repeat with remaining dough. Combine ⅔ cup packed *brown sugar,* ¼ cup *butter,* and 2 tablespoons *light corn syrup;* cook and stir till blended. Divide between two 9x1½-inch round baking pans. Sprinkle *each* pan with ¼ cup chopped *pecans.* Place rolls in prepared pans. Cover; let rise till nearly double (about 30 minutes). Bake in a 375° oven 20 to 25 minutes. Invert onto a serving plate.

***Cinnamon Rolls:*** Prepare Sweet Roll dough as directed; divide in half. Roll one half of dough into a 12x8-inch rectangle. Melt 3 tablespoons *butter;* spread half over dough. Combine ½ cup *granulated sugar* and 2 teaspoons ground *cinnamon;* sprinkle half over dough. Measure ¾ cup *raisins;* sprinkle *half* over dough. Roll up jelly roll style, beginning from longest side. Seal. Slice into 12 pieces. Place in a greased 9x1½-inch round baking pan. Repeat with remaining. Cover; let rise till nearly double (about 30 minutes). Bake in a 375° oven 20 to 25 minutes. Cool slightly; remove from pans. Drizzle with Powdered Sugar Icing.

***Powdered Sugar Icing:*** Combine 1 cup sifted *powdered sugar,* ¼ teaspoon *vanilla,* and enough *milk* for drizzling.

---

## Yeast Doughnuts

**3**   **to 3½ cups all-purpose flour**
**2**   **packages active dry yeast**
**¾**   **cup milk**
**⅓**   **cup granulated sugar**
**¼**   **cup shortening**
**1**   **teaspoon salt**
**2**   **eggs**
    **Shortening *or* cooking oil for deep-fat frying**
    **Powdered Sugar Icing (see recipe, page 121) or granulated sugar**

In a large mixer bowl combine 1½ *cups* of the flour and the yeast. In a saucepan heat milk, sugar, ¼ cup shortening, and salt just till warm (115° to 120°) and shortening is almost melted; stir constantly. Add to flour; add eggs. Beat at low speed of electric mixer ½ minute, scraping bowl often. Beat 3 minutes at high speed. Stir in as much of the remaining flour as you can mix in with a spoon. Turn out onto a lightly floured surface. Knead in enough of the remaining flour to make a moderately soft dough that is smooth and elastic (3 to 5 minutes total). Shape into a ball. Place in a lightly greased bowl; turn once to grease surface. Cover; let rise in a warm place till double (1 to 1¼ hours).

Punch down; turn out onto a lightly floured surface. Divide in half. Cover; let rest 10 minutes. Roll each half of dough to ½-inch thickness. Cut with a floured doughnut cutter. Cover; let rise till *very light* (45 to 60 minutes). Heat oil or shortening to 375°. Carefully add 2 to 3 doughnuts; fry about 1 minute, Turn and fry about 1 minute more; drain. Glaze with Powdered Sugar Icing or shake in a bag of granulated sugar. Makes 16 to 18.

**Chocolate Yeast Doughnuts:** Prepare Yeast Doughnut dough as above, *except* add 2 squares (2 ounces) *semisweet chocolate,* cut up, to milk mixture. Heat till chocolate melts; stir constantly. If necessary, cool till just warm (115° to 120°). Continue as directed. For chocolate glaze, combine 1 cup sifted *powdered sugar;* 2 teaspoons hot *water;* 1 square (1 ounce) *semisweet chocolate,* melted; 1 tablespoon *butter or margarine,* melted; and ½ teaspoon *vanilla.* Add some additional water, if necessary, to make of drizzling consistency.

## Hot Cross Buns

3½  to 4 cups all-purpose flour
2  packages active dry yeast
1  teaspoon ground cinnamon
¾  cup milk
½  cup cooking oil
⅓  cup granulated sugar
¾  teaspoon salt
3  eggs
⅔  cup dried currants
1  egg white
1½  cups sifted powdered sugar
¼  teaspoon vanilla
Dash salt                        Oven 375°

In a large mixer bowl combine 1½ cups of the flour, the yeast, and cinnamon. In a saucepan heat milk, oil, granulated sugar, and ¾ teaspoon salt just till warm (115° to 120°); stir constantly. Add to flour mixture; add eggs. Beat at low speed of electric mixer for ½ minute, scraping sides of bowl constantly. Beat 3 minutes at high speed. Stir in currants and as much of the remaining flour as you can mix in with a spoon. Turn dough out onto a lightly floured surface. Knead in enough of the remaining flour to make a moderately soft dough that is smooth and elastic (3 to 5 minutes total). Shape into a ball. Place in a lightly greased bowl; turn once to grease surface. Cover; let rise in a warm place till double (about 1½ hours).

Punch down; turn out onto a lightly floured surface. Cover; let rest 10 minutes. Divide dough into 18 pieces; form each piece into a smooth ball. Place on a greased baking sheet 1½ inches apart. Cover; let rise till nearly double (30 to 45 minutes). With a sharp knife cut a shallow cross in each; brush tops with some of the slightly beaten egg white (reserve remaining egg white). Bake in a 375° oven for 12 to 15 minutes or till golden. Cool slightly.

Meanwhile, combine powdered sugar, vanilla, dash salt, and the reserved portion of beaten egg white. Add additional milk, if necessary, to make of piping consistency. Pipe crosses on tops of buns. Makes 18.

## Bismarcks

In a large mixer bowl combine 1½ cups *all-purpose flour* and 2 packages *active dry yeast*. In a saucepan heat together ¾ cup *milk*, ⅓ cup *granulated sugar*, ¼ cup *shortening*, and 1 teaspoon *salt* just till warm (115° to 120°) and shortening is almost melted; stir constantly. Add to flour mixture; add 2 *eggs*. Beat at low speed of electric mixer ½ minute, scraping bowl. Beat 3 minutes at high speed. Stir in as much of 1½ to 2 cups *all-purpose flour* as you can mix in with a spoon. Turn out onto a lightly floured surface. Knead in enough of the remaining flour to make a moderately soft dough that is smooth and elastic (3 to 5 minutes total). Shape into a ball. Place in a lightly greased bowl; turn once to grease surface. Cover; let rise in a warm place till double (45 to 60 minutes).

Punch down; divide dough in half. Cover; let rest 10 minutes. Roll out each half to about ½-inch thickness. Cut with a floured 2½-inch biscuit cutter, pressing straight down. Reroll and cut trimmings.

Cover; let rounds of dough rise in a warm place till *very light* (about 30 minutes). Heat *cooking oil* or *shortening* to 375°. Fry, 2 or 3 at a time, about 1 minute per side or till golden brown; drain. Using a sharp knife, cut a wide slit in the side of each bismarck. Using a spoon, insert *2 teaspoons* Chocolate or Butterscotch Filling into *each* bismarck. Or, fit a decorating bag with a medium writing tube; fill bag with desired filling. Insert tube into slit in each bismarck and squeeze in about *2 teaspoons* filling. Roll in sifted *powdered sugar*. Makes 24.

***Chocolate Filling:*** In a small saucepan combine ½ cup *granulated sugar*, 2 tablespoons *all-purpose flour*, and ¼ teaspoon *salt*. Add 1 cup *milk* and 1 square (1 ounce) *unsweetened chocolate*, cut up. Cook and stir over medium heat till thickened and bubbly. Cook and stir 2 minutes more. Gradually stir *half* of the hot mixture into 1 beaten *egg*; return to remaining hot mixture in pan. Cook and stir till just bubbly. Remove from heat. Stir in 1 tablespoon *butter or margarine* and 1 teaspoon *vanilla*. Cover surface with clear plastic wrap. Cool without stirring. Makes 1¼ cups.

***Butterscotch Filling:*** Prepare Chocolate Filling as above, *except* omit chocolate. Substitute an equal amount of packed *brown sugar* for the granulated sugar, and increase the butter or margarine from *1 to 2 tablespoons.*

## Dinner Rolls

**4   to 4½ cups all-purpose flour**
**1   package active dry yeast**
**1   cup milk**
**⅓   cup sugar**
**⅓   cup butter, margarine, *or* shortening**
**1   teaspoon salt**
**2   eggs**                                    Oven 375°

In a large mixer bowl combine *2 cups* of the flour and the yeast. In a saucepan heat milk, sugar, butter, and salt just till warm (115° to 120°) and butter is almost melted; stir constantly. Add to flour mixture; add eggs. Beat at low speed of electric mixer for ½ minute, scraping sides of bowl constantly. Beat 3 minutes at high speed. Stir in as much remaining flour as you can mix in with a spoon. Turn out onto a floured surface. Knead in enough remaining flour to make a moderately stiff dough that is smooth and elastic (6 to 8 minutes total). Shape into a ball. Place in a greased bowl; turn once. Cover; let rise in a warm place till double (about 1 hour).

Punch down; divide dough in half. Cover; let rest 10 minutes. Shape into desired rolls (see tip on page 126). Cover; let rise till nearly double (about 30 minutes). Bake in a 375° oven for 12 to 15 minutes or till golden. Makes 2 to 2½ dozen rolls.

**Brown-and-Serve Rolls:** Prepare Dinner Rolls as above. Shape into desired rolls (see tip on page 126). Cover; let rise till nearly double (about 30 minutes). Bake in 325° oven about 10 minutes; *do not brown.* Remove from pans; cool. Wrap, label, and freeze.

To serve, open packages containing desired number of rolls. Thaw rolls in package at room temperature for 10 to 15 minutes. Unwrap completely. Bake on ungreased baking sheets in a 400° oven about 10 minutes or till golden.

**Hamburger and Frankfurter Buns:** Prepare Dinner Rolls as above; let rise till double. Punch dough down; divide into 12 portions. Cover; let rest 10 minutes. *For hamburger*

## Shaping dinner rolls

**To make Cloverleaves,** lightly grease 24 muffin cups. Divide each *half* of dough into 36 pieces. Shape each piece of dough into a ball, pulling edges under to make a smooth top. Place 3 balls in each greased muffin cup, smooth side up, as shown. Let rise and bake as directed. Makes 24 rolls.

**To make Parker House Rolls,** lightly grease baking sheets. On a lightly floured surface roll out each *half* of dough to ¼-inch thickness. Cut with a floured 2½-inch round cutter. Brush with melted *butter or margarine.* Make an off-center crease in each round. Fold so large half overlaps slightly, as shown. Place 2 to 3 inches apart on baking sheets. Let rise and bake as directed. Makes 30 rolls.

**To make Butterhorns,** lightly grease baking sheets. On a lightly floured surface roll each *half* of dough into a 12-inch circle. Brush with melted *butter.* Cut each circle into 12 wedges. To shape, begin at wide end of wedge and roll toward point, as shown. Place, point down, 2 to 3 inches apart on baking sheets. Let rise and bake as directed. Makes 24 rolls.

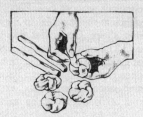

**To make Rosettes,** lightly grease baking sheets. Divide each *half* of dough into 16 pieces.

On a lightly floured surface roll each piece into a 12-inch rope. Tie in a loose knot, leaving two long ends. Tuck top end under roll. Bring bottom end up; tuck into center of roll, as shown. Place 2 to 3 inches apart on baking sheets. Let rise and bake as directed. Makes 32 rolls.

*buns,* shape each portion into an even circle, folding edges under. Press flat between hands. *For frankfurter buns,* shape into rolls about 5½ inches long, tapering ends. Place on a greased baking sheet. Cover; let rise till nearly double (about 30 minutes). Bake in a 375° oven for 12 to 15 minutes or till golden. Remove buns from sheet; cool. Makes 12 buns.

## Bagels

> 4¼ to 4¾ cups all-purpose flour
> 2 packages active dry yeast
> 1½ cups warm water (110° to 115°)
> 3 tablespoons sugar
> 1 tablespoon salt
> 1 tablespoon sugar
>
> Oven 375°

In a mixer bowl combine *1½ cups* of the flour and the yeast. Combine warm water, the 3 tablespoons sugar, and salt. Pour over flour mixture. Beat at low speed of electric mixer ½ minute, scraping bowl. Beat 3 minutes at high speed. Stir in as much remaining flour as you can mix in with a spoon.

Turn out onto a lightly floured surface. Knead in enough remaining flour to make a moderately stiff dough that is smooth and elastic (6 to 8 minutes total). Cover; let rest 10 minutes.

Cut into 12 portions; shape each into a smooth ball. Punch a hole in the center of each. Pull gently to make a 1½- to 2-inch hole. Place on a greased baking sheet. Cover; let rise 20 minutes. Broil 5 inches from heat 3 to 4 minutes, turning once (tops should not brown). Heat 1 gallon *water* and the 1 tablespoon sugar to boiling; reduce heat. Cook 4 or 5 bagels at a time for 7 minutes, turning once; drain. Place on a greased baking sheet. Bake in a 375° oven for 25 to 30 minutes. Makes 12.

**Light Rye Bagels:** Prepare Bagels as above, *except* substitute 1¼ cups *rye flour* for the first 1¼ cups of the all-purpose flour.

**Herb Bagels:** Prepare Bagels as above, *except* add 2 teaspoons dried *marjoram,* crushed; *or* 1 teaspoon dried *dillweed;* or 1 teaspoon dried *tarragon,* crushed; *or* ½ teaspoon *garlic powder* to the flour-yeast mixture.

**Onion Bagels:** Prepare Bagels as above, *except* cook ½ cup finely chopped *onion* in 3 tablespoons *butter* till tender but not brown. Brush onion mixture over tops of bagels after first 15 minutes of baking.

**Poppy Seed or Sesame Seed Bagels:** Prepare Bagels as above, *except* before baking, brush tops with beaten *egg;* sprinkle with *poppy seed* or toasted *sesame seed.*

## Breadsticks

      **2   to 2½ cups all-purpose flour**
      **1   package active dry yeast**
     **¾   cup milk**
      **2   tablespoons shortening**
      **1   tablespoon sugar**
      **1   teaspoon salt**                      Oven 375°

In a small mixer bowl combine ¾ cup of the flour and the yeast. In a saucepan heat milk, shortening, sugar, and salt just till warm (115° to 120°) and shortening is almost melted, stirring constantly. Add to flour mixture. Beat at low speed of electric mixer for ½ minute, scraping sides of bowl constantly. Beat 3 minutes at high speed. Stir in as much of the remaining flour as you can mix in with a spoon. Turn out onto a lightly floured surface. Knead in enough of the remaining flour to make a stiff dough that is smooth and elastic (8 to 10 minutes total). Shape into a ball. Place in a lightly greased bowl; turn once to grease surface. Cover; let rise in a warm place till double (45 to 60 minutes).

Punch down; turn out onto a lightly floured surface. Divide dough into 4 portions. Cover; let rest 10 minutes. Divide each portion into 6 pieces. Roll each piece into a rope 8 inches long. Place on greased baking sheets. Cover; let rise in a warm place till nearly double (about 30 minutes). If desired, brush with a mixture of egg white and water, and sprinkle with coarse salt or sesame seed.

Bake in a 375° oven for 10 to 15 minutes or till golden brown. (For drier breadsticks, after baking 10 minutes, decrease oven temperature to 300° and bake 25 to 30 minutes longer.) Makes 24 breadsticks.

***Parmesan Breadsticks:*** Prepare Breadsticks as above, *except* stir ⅓ cup grated *Parmesan cheese* into the ¾ cup flour and yeast. Omit sprinkling with coarse salt or seed.

***Barbecue Breadsticks:*** Prepare Breadstick dough as above, *except* decrease the milk to ⅔ *cup* and stir 2 tablespoons bottled *barbecue sauce* and 1 teaspoon *minced dried onion* into the milk-shortening mixture in saucepan. Omit sprinkling breadsticks with coarse salt or seed. For drier barbecue breadsticks, bake in a 375° oven for 10 minutes; decrease temperature to 300° and bake only 15 to 20 minutes longer.

---

## Croissants

|  |  |  |
|---|---|---|
| 1½ | cups butter or margarine | |
| ⅓ | cup all-purpose flour | |
| 2 | packages active dry yeast | |
| ½ | cup warm water (110° to 115°) | |
| ¾ | cup milk | |
| ¼ | cup sugar | |
| 1 | teaspoon salt | |
| 1 | egg | |
| 3¾ | to 4¼ cups all-purpose flour | |
| 1 | egg yolk | |
| 1 | tablespoon milk | Oven 375° |

Cream butter or margarine with ⅓ cup flour. Roll butter mixture between two sheets of waxed paper into a 12x6-inch rectangle. Chill at least 1 hour.

Soften yeast in warm water. Heat ¾ cup milk, sugar, and salt till sugar dissolves. Cool to lukewarm; turn milk mixture into a large mixing bowl. Add softened yeast and 1 egg; beat well.

Stir in *2 cups* of the flour; beat well. Stir in as much of the remaining flour as you can mix in with a spoon. Turn out onto a lightly floured surface. Knead in enough of the remaining flour to make a moderately soft dough that is smooth and elastic (3 to 5 minutes total). Let rest 10 minutes.

Roll into a 14-inch square. Place *chilled* butter mixture on one half of dough; fold over other half and seal edges. Roll into a 21x12-inch rectangle; seal edges. Fold into thirds. Roll into a 21x12-inch rectangle. Fold and roll twice more; seal edges. Chill after each rolling. Fold into thirds to 12x7 inches. Cover; chill several hours or overnight.

Cut dough crosswise into fourths. Roll each fourth into a 12-inch circle. Cut each circle into 12 wedges. Roll up each wedge loosely, starting from the side opposite the point.

Place on ungreased baking sheets, point down; curve ends. Cover; let rise till double (30 to 45 minutes). Beat egg yolk with 1 tablespoon milk; brush on rolls. Bake in a 375° oven for 12 to 15 minutes. Remove from baking sheets. Makes 48.

---

## Brioche

---

|   |   |   |
|---|---|---|
| **1** | **package active dry yeast** | |
| **¼** | **cup warm water (110° to 115°)** | |
| **½** | **cup butter or margarine** | |
| **⅓** | **cup sugar** | |
| **½** | **teaspoon salt** | |
| **4** | **cups all-purpose flour** | |
| **½** | **cup milk** | |
| **4** | **eggs** | |
| **1** | **tablespoon water** | Oven 375° |

Soften yeast in ¼ cup warm water. Cream butter or margarine, sugar, and salt. Add *1 cup* of the flour and the milk to creamed mixture. Separate *one* of the eggs; set egg white aside. Blend yolk with remaining 3 eggs; add to creamed mixture. Add softened yeast; beat well. Stir in the remaining flour till smooth. Turn into a greased bowl. Cover; let rise in a warm place till double (about 2 hours).

Refrigerate overnight; punch down. Turn out onto a lightly floured surface. Divide dough into quarters; set one aside. Divide each of the remaining quarters into 8 pieces, making a total of 24. With floured hands, form each piece into a ball, tucking under edges. Place each in a greased muffin cup. Divide reserved dough into 24 pieces; shape into balls.

With a floured finger, make an indentation in each large ball. Press a small ball into each indentation. Blend reserved egg white and 1 tablespoon water; brush over rolls. Cover; let rise till nearly double (40 to 45 minutes). Bake in a 375° oven about 15 minutes, brushing again after 7 minutes. Makes 24.

***To use individual brioche pans,*** prepare dough and divide into quarters as above; set one aside. Divide each remaining quarter into 6 pieces, making a total of 18. Form into balls; place in 18 greased individual brioche pans. Divide reserved dough into 18 pieces; shape into balls and place one atop each larger ball. Let rise; bake as directed above. Makes 18.

---

## Soft Pretzels

|        |                                  |           |
|--------|----------------------------------|-----------|
| 4      | to 4½ cups all-purpose flour     |           |
| 1      | package active dry yeast         |           |
| 1½     | cups milk                        |           |
| ¼      | cup sugar                        |           |
| 2      | tablespoons cooking oil          |           |
| 1½     | teaspoons salt                   |           |
| 3      | tablespoons salt                 |           |
| 2      | quarts boiling water             |           |
| 1      | slightly beaten egg white        |           |
|        | Coarse salt *or* sesame seed     | Oven 350° |

In a mixer bowl combine *2 cups* of the flour and the yeast. In a saucepan heat milk, sugar, oil, and 1½ teaspoons salt just till warm (115° to 120°); stir constantly. Add to flour mixture. Beat at low speed of electric mixer for ½ minute, scraping bowl.

Beat 3 minutes at high speed. Stir in as much of the remaining flour as you can mix in with a spoon. Turn out onto a lightly floured surface. Knead in enough of the remaining flour to make a moderately stiff dough that is smooth and elastic (6 to 8 minutes total). Shape into a ball. Place in a lightly greased bowl; turn once to grease surface. Cover; let rise in a warm place till double (about 1½ hours).

Punch down; turn out onto a lightly floured surface. Cover; let rest 10 minutes. Roll into a 12x8-inch rectangle. Cut into 16 strips, each 12 inches long and ½ inch wide. Roll each into a rope 16 inches long.

To shape into pretzels, start by shaping one rope of dough into a circle, overlapping about 4 inches from each end and leaving ends free. Take one end of dough in each hand and twist at the point where dough overlaps. Carefully lift ends across to the opposite edge of the circle. Tuck ends under edge to make a pretzel shape; moisten and press ends to seal. Let rise, uncovered, 20 minutes.

Dissolve 3 tablespoons salt in the boiling water. Lower 3 or 4 pretzels at a time into boiling water; boil for 2 minutes, turning once. Remove with a slotted spoon to paper toweling, let stand a few seconds, then place ½ inch apart on a well-greased baking sheet. Brush with a mixture of egg white and 1 tablespoon *water*. Sprinkle lightly with coarse salt or sesame seed. Bake in a 350° oven 25 to 30 minutes or till golden brown. Makes 16 pretzels.

## Pita Bread

| | |
|---|---|
| 1 | **package active dry yeast** |
| 1¼ | **cups warm water (110° to 115°)** |
| 3¼ | **to 3¾ cups all-purpose flour** |
| ¼ | **cup shortening** |
| 1½ | **teaspoons salt** |

Oven 450°

In a large mixer bowl soften yeast in warm water. Add *2 cups* of the flour, the shortening, and salt. Beat at low speed of electric mixer for ½ minute, scraping sides of bowl. Beat 3 minutes at high speed. Stir in as much of the remaining flour as you can mix in with a spoon. Turn out onto a lightly floured surface. Knead in enough of the remaining flour to make a moderately soft dough that is smooth and elastic (3 to 5 minutes total). Cover; let rest in a warm place about 15 minutes. Divide into 12 equal portions. Roll each between floured hands into a *very* smooth ball. Cover with plastic wrap or a damp cloth; let rest 10 minutes. Using fingers, gently flatten balls without creasing dough. Cover; let rest 10 minutes. (Keep dough pieces covered till ready to use.)

On a well-floured surface lightly roll one piece of dough at a time into a 7-inch round, *turning dough over once.* Do not stretch, puncture, or crease dough. (Work with enough flour so dough does not stick.) Place on a baking sheet.

Bake 2 at a time in a 450° oven about 3 minutes or till dough is puffed and softly set. Turn over with a spatula; bake about 2 minutes more or till dough begins to lightly brown. Repeat with remaining dough, baking one batch before rolling and baking the next batch.

To serve, slice bread crosswise to form a pocket; generously fill each pocket with desired filling. (Allow any extra bread to just cool before wrapping for storage.) Makes 12 pita rounds.

**Whole Wheat Pita Bread:** Prepare Pita Bread as above, *except* substitute 2 cups *whole wheat flour* and 1¼ to 1¾ cups *all-purpose flour* for the 3¼ to 3¾ cups all-purpose flour.

**Party Pita Bread:** Prepare Pita Bread as above, *except* divide the dough into 24 equal portions. Roll into 4-inch rounds and bake about 2 minutes on each side. To serve, slice bread crosswise to form a pocket; fill with desired filling. Makes 24.

## Batter Rolls

Oven 375°

In a large mixer bowl combine 2 cups *all-purpose flour* and 1 package *active dry yeast.* In a saucepan heat 1¼ cups *milk,* ½ cup *shortening,* ¼ cup *sugar,* and 1 teaspoon *salt* just till warm (115° to 120°) and shortening is almost melted; stir constantly. Add to flour mixture; add 1 *egg.* Beat at low speed of electric mixer for ½ minute, scraping sides of bowl constantly. Beat 3 minutes at high speed. Add 1¼ cups *all-purpose flour;* beat at low speed about 2 minutes or till batter is smooth.

Cover; let rise in a warm place till double (about 1 hour). Beat down with a wooden spoon. Let rest 5 minutes. Spoon into greased muffin cups, filling each half full. Cover; let rise till nearly double (about 30 minutes). Brush tops lightly with *milk;* sprinkle with 1 tablespoon *poppy seed or sesame seed,* if desired. Bake in a 375° oven 15 to 18 minutes. Makes 18.

## Sourdough Starter

> **1    package active dry yeast**
> **2½   cups warm water (110° to 115°)**
> **2    cups all-purpose flour**
> **1    tablespoon sugar or honey**

Dissolve yeast in ½ *cup* of the water. Stir in remaining 2 cups water, the flour, and sugar or honey. Beat till smooth. Cover with cheesecloth. Let stand at room temperature for 5 to 10 days or till bubbly; stir 2 or 3 times each day. (Fermentation time depends upon room temperature. A warmer room hastens the fermentation process.)

To store, transfer Sourdough Starter to a jar and cover with cheesecloth; refrigerate. *Do not cover jar tightly with a metal lid.* To use Starter, bring desired amount to room temperature. To replenish Starter after using, stir ¾ cup *all-purpose flour,* ¾ cup *water,* and 1 teaspoon *sugar or honey* into remaining amount. Cover; let stand at room temperature at least 1 day or till bubbly. Refrigerate for later use.

If Starter isn't used within 10 days, stir in 1 teaspoon *sugar or honey.* Repeat every 10 days until used.

## Sourdough Bread

Oven 400°

Bring 1 cup *Sourdough Starter* to room temperature. Dissolve 1 package *active dry yeast* in 1½ cups warm *water* (110° to

115°). Stir in 2½ cups *all-purpose flour*, 2 teaspoons *salt*, 2 teaspoons *sugar*, and the Sourdough Starter. Combine 2½ cups *all-purpose flour* and ½ teaspoon *baking soda*; stir into sourdough mixture. Stir in as much of ½ to 1 cup *all-purpose flour* as you can mix in with a spoon. On a lightly floured surface knead in enough of the remaining flour to make a moderately stiff dough that is smooth and elastic (6 to 8 minutes total). Shape into a ball in a greased bowl; turn once. Cover; let rise in a warm place till double (1 to 1½ hours).

Punch down; divide in half. Cover; let rest 10 minutes. Shape each half into a 6-inch round or 9x4-inch oblong loaf on a greased baking sheet. With a sharp knife, make criss-cross slashes across tops. Cover; let rise till nearly double (about 1 hour). Bake in a 400° oven 35 to 40 minutes. Cool. Makes 2.

# Orange-Cinnamon
# Sourdough Rolls

> ¾ **cup Sourdough Starter**
> 2 **cups self-rising flour**
> ½ **cup buttermilk *or* sour milk**
> 4 **tablespoons butter, melted**
> ½ **cup sugar**
> 1 **tablespoon grated orange peel**
> 2 **teaspoons ground cinnamon**
> **Powdered Sugar Icing (see recipe,
> page 121)**                                    Oven 450°

Bring Sourdough Starter to room temperature. Combine self-rising flour, buttermilk, and Starter. Turn dough out onto a lightly floured surface; knead 15 times. Roll into a 12-inch square. Brush with *3 tablespoons* of the melted butter. Combine sugar, orange peel, and cinnamon; sprinkle over dough. Roll up, jelly roll style; seal seam. Slice into 12 pieces; place, cut side down, in a greased 9x9x2-inch baking pan. Brush with the remaining melted butter. Bake in a 450° oven 20 to 25 minutes or till golden. Immediately turn out onto a wire rack; drizzle with Powdered Sugar Icing. Makes 12.

# Quick Breads

It's easy to understand why quick breads are so popular. First of all, there's such a wide variety of taste-tempting breads from which to choose. And, they're relatively speedy to prepare and bake, especially when you take into account the rising time necessary for yeast bread preparation.

Although biscuits, muffins, and nut breads play a particularly tasty role in rounding out the meal, the quick bread family isn't limited to the bread plate. In fact, feathery pancakes and crisp waffles can serve as part of the main dish. And doughnuts often star as the meal-ending dessert.

The following are quick bread tips and explanations.

Baking powder, baking soda, steam, or air—rather than yeast—leaven quick breads.

Most quick breads are best served hot from the oven—with plenty of butter!

Most nut breads should be stored for at least a day. The flavors will mellow and the loaf will slice more easily.

After baking, turn nut breads out of the pan and cool on a wire rack. Place cooled bread in an airtight container, or wrap it in foil or clear plastic wrap.

A crack down the center of a nut loaf is no mistake—it's typical.

Serve nut breads cut in very thin slices with simple spreads: soft butter, cream cheese, jam, or jelly.

Dip tops of warm muffins in melted butter or margarine and then in sugar for a sweet and sparkling crusty topping.

## Boston Brown Bread

In a mixing bowl stir together ½ cup *whole wheat flour*, ¼ cup *all-purpose flour*, ¼ cup *yellow cornmeal*, ½ teaspoon *baking powder*, ¼ teaspoon *baking soda*, and ¼ teaspoon *salt*. In another mixing bowl combine 1 *egg*, ¼ cup *light molasses*, 2 tablespoons *sugar*, and 2 teaspoons *cooking oil*. Add flour mixture and ¾ cup *buttermilk or sour milk* alternately to the molasses mixture; beat well. Stir in ¼ cup *raisins*.

Turn batter into two well-greased 16-ounce vegetable cans.

Cover cans tightly with foil. Place cans on a rack set in a large Dutch oven. Pour hot water into Dutch oven to a depth of 1 inch. Bring to boiling; reduce heat. Cover; simmer 2½ to 3 hours or till done. Add boiling water as needed. Remove cans from pan; let stand 10 minutes. Remove bread from cans. Serve warm. Makes 2.

---

### Making sour milk

When you don't have any buttermilk on hand, substitute an equal amount of "soured" milk for the buttermilk.

To make sour milk, combine 1 tablespoon *lemon juice or vinegar* and enough whole *milk* to make *1 cup* total liquid. Let the mixture stand 5 minutes before using in the recipe.

---

# Date-Apple Coffee Bread

| | |
|---|---|
| 1 | tablespoon instant coffee crystals |
| 1 | cup boiling water |
| 1⅓ | cups snipped pitted dates (8 ounces) |
| 2¼ | cups all-purpose flour |
| ¾ | cup packed brown sugar |
| 2 | teaspoons baking powder |
| ½ | teaspoon salt |
| ½ | teaspoon baking soda |
| 1 | beaten egg |
| 2 | medium apples, peeled, cored, and shredded (1 cup) |
| ½ | cup chopped walnuts |
| 2 | tablespoons butter or margarine, melted |

Oven 350°

Dissolve coffee crystals in boiling water; pour over dates. Set aside. In a large mixing bowl stir together flour, brown sugar, baking powder, salt, and soda. Combine egg, shredded apple, walnuts, melted butter or margarine, and coffee-date mixture. Add to flour mixture, stirring just till moistened. Turn into a greased 9x5x3-inch loaf pan. Bake in a 350° oven for 60 to 65 minutes or till a wooden pick inserted near center comes out clean. Cool in pan 10 minutes. Remove from pan; cool on a wire rack. Makes 1.

## Cranberry-Orange Bread

| | |
|---|---|
| 3 | **medium oranges** |
| 1 | **beaten egg** |
| 2 | **tablespoons cooking oil** |
| 2 | **cups all-purpose flour** |
| ¾ | **cup granulated sugar** |
| 1½ | **teaspoons baking powder** |
| 1 | **teaspoon salt** |
| ½ | **teaspoon baking soda** |
| 1 | **cup coarsely chopped fresh or frozen cranberries** |
| ½ | **cup chopped walnuts** |
| 1 | **cup sifted powdered sugar** |

Oven 350°

Finely shred peel from 1 orange; reserve peel. Squeeze juice from all oranges. Measure ¾ cup of the juice; reserve remaining orange juice.

In a mixing bowl combine the ¾ cup orange juice, *1 teaspoon* of the shredded orange peel, egg, and cooking oil. In another mixing bowl, stir together flour, granulated sugar, baking powder, salt, and baking soda. Add orange juice mixture to dry ingredients; stir just till moistened. Fold in chopped cranberries and walnuts.

Turn batter into one lightly greased 8x4x2-inch loaf pan *or* three 6x3x2-inch loaf pans. Bake in a 350° oven for 50 to 60 minutes for a large pan (30 to 40 minutes for smaller pans) or till a wooden pick inserted near center comes out clean. Cool bread 10 minutes in pan; remove from pan. Cool thoroughly on a wire rack.

For glaze, stir *1 tablespoon* of the reserved orange juice into powdered sugar. Add more orange juice to make of drizzling consistency. Drizzle glaze atop cooled loaves; garnish with reserved shredded orange peel. Makes 1 large or 3 small loaves.

**Apricot-Orange Bread:** Prepare Cranberry-Orange Bread as above, *except* substitute 1 cup snipped *dried apricots* for the cranberries. Pour boiling water over apricots; let stand about 5 minutes. Drain well before folding into batter.

---

## Zucchini Nut Loaf

|   |   |
|---|---|
| 1½ | **cups all-purpose flour** |
| 1 | **teaspoon ground cinnamon** |
| ½ | **teaspoon baking soda** |
| ½ | **teaspoon salt** |
| ½ | **teaspoon ground nutmeg** |
| ¼ | **teaspoon baking powder** |
| 1 | **cup sugar** |
| 1 | **cup finely shredded unpeeled zucchini** |
| 1 | **egg** |
| ¼ | **cup cooking oil** |
| ¼ | **teaspoon finely shredded lemon peel** |
| ½ | **cup chopped walnuts** |

Oven 350°

In a mixing bowl stir together flour, cinnamon, baking soda, salt, nutmeg, and baking powder; set aside. In a mixing bowl beat together sugar, shredded zucchini, and egg. Add oil and lemon peel; mix well. Stir flour mixture into zucchini mixture. Gently fold in chopped nuts. Turn batter into a greased 8x4x2-inch loaf pan. Bake in 350° oven for 55 to 60 minutes or till a wooden pick inserted near center comes out clean. Cool in pan 10 minutes. Remove from pan; cool thoroughly on a rack. Wrap and store loaf overnight before slicing. Makes 1.

## Cherry-Pecan Bread

Oven 350°

In a mixing bowl thoroughly stir together 2 cups *all-purpose flour*, 1 teaspoon *baking soda*, and ½ teaspoon *salt*; set aside. In a large mixer bowl beat together ¾ cup *sugar*, ½ cup *butter or margarine*, 2 *eggs*, and 1 teaspoon *vanilla* till light and fluffy. Add flour mixture and 1 cup *buttermilk or sour milk* alternately to beaten mixture. Beat just till blended after each addition. Fold in 1 cup chopped *pecans* and 1 cup chopped *maraschino cherries*. Turn batter into a lightly greased 9x5x3-inch loaf pan. Bake in a 350° oven for 55 to 60 minutes. Cool in pan 10 minutes. Remove from pan; cool. If desired, glaze with Powdered Sugar Icing (see recipe, page 121). Makes 1 loaf.

## Banana Nut Bread

| | |
|---|---|
| 1¾ | **cups all-purpose flour** |
| 1¼ | **teaspoons baking powder** |
| ½ | **teaspoon baking soda** |
| ⅔ | **cup sugar** |
| ⅓ | **cup shortening** |
| 2 | **eggs** |
| 2 | **tablespoons milk** |
| 1 | **cup mashed ripe banana** |
| ¼ | **cup chopped nuts** |

Oven 350°

Stir together flour, baking powder, soda, and ¾ teaspoon *salt*. Set aside.

In a mixer bowl beat sugar and shortening with electric mixer till light, scraping sides of bowl often. Add eggs, one at a time, and the milk, beating till smooth after each addition. Add flour mixture and banana alternately to creamed mixture, beating till smooth after each addition. Fold in nuts.

Turn batter into a lightly greased 8x4x2-inch loaf pan. Bake in a 350° oven for 60 to 65 minutes or till a wooden pick inserted near center comes out clean. Cool in pan 10 minutes. Remove from pan; cool. For easier slicing, wrap and store overnight. Makes 1.

## Three-C Bread

2½　cups all-purpose flour
1　cup sugar
1　teaspoon baking powder
1　teaspoon baking soda
½　teaspoon ground mace
3　beaten eggs
½　cup cooking oil
½　cup milk
2　cups shredded carrots
1⅓　cups flaked coconut
½　cup chopped maraschino cherries　Oven 350°

Stir together flour, sugar, baking powder, soda, mace, and ½ teaspoon *salt*. Combine eggs, oil, and milk. Add to dry ingredients; mix well. Stir in carrots, coconut, and cherries. Pour into 3 greased 21-ounce pie filling cans. Bake in a 350° oven for 1 to 1½ hours. (Or, pour batter into one greased 9x5x 3-inch loaf pan. Bake in a 350° oven 45 to 50 minutes.) Cool in cans 10 minutes. Remove from cans; cool completely. Wrap and store overnight before slicing. Makes 3.

## Pumpkin Nut Bread

2　cups all-purpose flour
2　teaspoons baking powder
½　teaspoon salt
½　teaspoon ground ginger
¼　teaspoon baking soda
¼　teaspoon ground cloves
1　cup packed brown sugar
⅓　cup shortening
2　eggs
1　cup canned pumpkin
¼　cup milk
½　cup coarsely chopped walnuts
½　cup raisins　　　　　　　　　　Oven 350°

In a mixing bowl stir together flour, baking powder, salt, ginger, baking soda, and cloves; set aside. In a large mixer bowl beat together brown sugar and shortening till well combined; beat in eggs. Add pumpkin and milk; mix well. Add flour mixture to sugar-pumpkin mixture, mixing well. Stir in chopped nuts and the raisins.

Turn batter into a greased 9x5x3-inch loaf pan. Bake in a 350° oven for 55 to 60 minutes or till a wooden pick inserted near center comes out clean. Cool in pan 10 minutes. Remove from pan; cool thoroughly on a wire rack. Wrap and store overnight before slicing. Makes 1 loaf.

## Nut Bread

      3  **cups all-purpose flour**
      1  **cup sugar**
      4  **teaspoon baking powder**
      1  **teaspoon salt**
      1  **beaten egg**
    1⅔  **cups milk**
     ¼  **cup cooking oil**
     ¾  **cup chopped nuts**                Oven 350°

Stir together the flour, sugar, baking powder, and salt. Combine egg, milk, and oil; add to dry ingredients, stirring just till combined. Stir in nuts. Turn into a greased 9x5x3-inch loaf pan. Bake in a 350° oven about 1 to 1¼ hours. Cool in pan 10 minutes. Remove from pan; cool on a rack. Wrap and store overnight before slicing. Makes 1.

  **Cheese-Nut Bread:** Prepare Nut Bread as above, *except* add 1 cup shredded *cheese* (4 ounces) to batter with nuts.

## Any-Fruit Coffee Cake

| | |
|---|---|
| 4 | cups chopped apples, apricots, peaches, pineapple, *or* whole blueberries |
| 1 | cup water |
| 2 | tablespoons lemon juice |
| 1¼ | cups sugar |
| ⅓ | cup cornstarch |
| 3 | cups all-purpose flour |
| 1 | cup sugar |
| 1 | tablespoon baking powder |
| 1 | teaspoon salt |
| 1 | teaspoon ground cinnamon |
| ¼ | teaspoon ground mace |
| 1 | cup butter or margarine |
| 2 | slightly beaten eggs |
| 1 | cup milk |
| 1 | teaspoon vanilla |
| ½ | cup sugar |
| ½ | cup all-purpose flour |
| ¼ | cup butter or margarine |
| ½ | cup chopped walnuts |

Oven 350°

In a saucepan combine choice of fruit and the water. Simmer, covered, about 5 minutes or till fruit is tender. Stir in lemon juice. Mix the 1¼ cups sugar and cornstarch; stir into fruit mixture. Cook and stir till thickened and bubbly. Cool.

In a mixing bowl stir together the 3 cups flour, 1 cup sugar, baking powder, salt, cinnamon, and mace. Cut in the 1 cup butter or margarine till mixture resembles fine crumbs. Combine eggs, milk, and vanilla. Add to flour mixture, mixing till blended. Spread *half* of the batter in a greased 13x9x2-inch baking pan or two greased 8x8x2-inch baking pans.

Spread the cooled fruit mixture over the batter. Spoon the remaining batter in small mounds over the fruit mixture, spreading out as much as possible. Combine the ½ cup sugar and ½ cup flour; cut in the ¼ cup butter or margarine till mixture resembles coarse crumbs. Stir in nuts. Sprinkle nut mixture over batter in pan. Bake in a 350° oven 45 to 50 minutes for a 13x9x2-inch pan (40 to 45 minutes for two 8x8x2-inch baking pans) or till cake tests done. Cool. Makes 1 large coffee cake or 2 small coffee cakes.

---

## Spicy Buttermilk Coffee Cake

|       |                                        |            |
|-------|----------------------------------------|------------|
| 2½    | cups all-purpose flour                 |            |
| 2     | cups packed brown sugar                |            |
| ⅔     | cup shortening                         |            |
| 2     | teaspoons baking powder                |            |
| ½     | teaspoon baking soda                   |            |
| ½     | teaspoon ground cinnamon               |            |
| ½     | teaspoon ground nutmeg                 |            |
| 1     | cup buttermilk *or* sour milk          |            |
| 2     | beaten eggs                            |            |
| ⅓     | cup chopped nuts                       | Oven 375°  |

Combine flour, brown sugar, and ½ teaspoon *salt*. Cut in shortening till mixture is crumbly; set aside ½ *cup* crumb mixture. To remaining crumb mixture add baking powder, soda, and spices; mix well. Add buttermilk or sour milk and eggs; mix well. Pour into two greased 8x1½-inch or 9x1½-inch round baking pans. Combine reserved crumbs with nuts; sprinkle atop cakes. Bake in a 375° oven for 20 to 25 minutes. Serve warm. Makes 2 coffee cakes.

---

## Orange-Date Coffee Cake

|       |                                          |           |
|-------|------------------------------------------|-----------|
| 2     | cups all-purpose flour                   |           |
| ½     | cup granulated sugar                     |           |
| 1     | tablespoon baking powder                 |           |
| 1     | beaten egg                               |           |
| ½     | cup milk                                 |           |
| ½     | cup cooking oil                          |           |
| ½     | cup snipped pitted dates                 |           |
| 2     | teaspoons finely shredded orange peel    |           |
| ½     | cup orange juice                         |           |
| ½     | cup chopped walnuts                      |           |
| ½     | cup packed brown sugar                   |           |
| 2     | tablespoons butter *or* margarine, softened |        |
| 1     | teaspoon ground cinnamon                 | Oven 375° |

Stir together flour, granulated sugar, baking powder, and ½ teaspoon *salt*. Make a well in the center. Combine egg, milk, and oil; add all at once to dry ingredients. Stir just till well mixed. Combine dates, orange peel, and orange juice; stir into batter just till blended. Spread evenly in a greased 11x7x1½-inch baking pan. Combine walnuts, brown sugar, butter, and cinnamon; sprinkle over batter. Bake in a 375° oven about 30 minutes. Makes 1.

## Blueberry Buckle

| | |
|---|---|
| ¾ | **cup sugar** |
| ½ | **cup shortening** |
| 1 | **egg** |
| 2½ | **cups all-purpose flour** |
| 2½ | **teaspoons baking powder** |
| ½ | **cup milk** |
| 2 | **cups blueberries** |
| ½ | **cup sugar** |
| ½ | **teaspoon ground cinnamon** |
| ¼ | **cup butter *or* margarine** |

Oven 350°

Beat ¾ cup sugar and shortening till light and fluffy. Add egg; beat well. Stir together *2 cups* of the flour, the baking powder, and ¼ teaspoon *salt*. Add flour mixture and milk alternately to beaten mixture. Beat till smooth after each addition. Spread in a greased 8x8x2-inch or 9x9x2-inch baking pan. Top with blueberries. Combine the remaining ½ cup flour, ½ cup sugar, and cinnamon; cut in butter or margarine till crumbly. Sprinkle over blueberries. Bake in a 350° oven for 45 to 50 minutes. Cut into squares. Serve warm. Makes 1 coffee cake.

## Streusel Coffee Cake

| | |
|---|---|
| 1½ | cups all-purpose flour |
| ¾ | cup granulated sugar |
| 2 | teaspoons baking powder |
| ½ | teaspoon salt |
| 1 | beaten egg |
| ½ | cup milk |
| ¼ | cup cooking oil |
| ½ | cup raisins |
| ½ | cup chopped nuts |
| ¼ | cup packed brown sugar |
| 1 | tablespoon all-purpose flour |
| 1 | tablespoon butter or margarine, softened |
| 1 | teaspoon ground cinnamon        Oven 375° |

Stir together the 1½ cups flour, granulated sugar, baking powder, and salt. Combine egg, milk, and oil. Add to flour mixture; mix well. Stir in raisins. Turn into a greased 9x9x2-inch baking pan. Combine nuts, brown sugar, 1 tablespoon flour, butter or margarine, and cinnamon; sprinkle over batter. Bake in a 375° oven about 25 minutes. Makes 1 coffee cake.

## Cocoa Ripple Ring

| | |
|---|---|
| ¾ | cup granulated sugar |
| ½ | cup shortening |
| 2 | eggs |
| 1½ | cups all-purpose flour |
| 2 | teaspoons baking powder |
| ⅔ | cup milk |
| ⅓ | cup presweetened cocoa powder |
| ⅓ | cup chopped walnuts        Oven 350° |

Beat granulated sugar and shortening till fluffy. Add eggs; beat well. Stir together flour, baking powder, and ¾ teaspoon *salt*. Add flour mixture and milk alternately to beaten mixture, beating till smooth after each addition.

Spoon ⅓ of the batter (1 cup) into a greased 9-inch fluted tube pan, 6½-cup ring mold, or 9x9x2-inch baking pan. Combine cocoa and nuts; sprinkle *half* over batter. Repeat layers, ending with batter. Bake in a 350° oven 30 to 35 minutes. Cool in pan 5 minutes; turn out onto a serving platter. Dust with sifted powdered sugar, if desired. Makes 1.

---

## Applesauce Coffee Cake

    1¾    **cups all-purpose flour**
     ½    **cup sugar**
     ½    **cup butter or margarine**
     2    **beaten eggs**
     1    **teaspoon vanilla**
    1½    **teaspoons baking powder**
     ½    **teaspoon baking soda**
     1    **cup chunk-style applesauce**
     ¼    **cup chopped nuts**
     ½    **teaspoon ground cinnamon**          Oven 375°

Stir together ¾ *cup* of the flour and the sugar; cut in butter or margarine till crumbly. Set aside ½ *cup* of the crumb mixture for topping. To remaining crumb mixture, add eggs and vanilla; beat by hand till smooth.

Stir together remaining 1 cup flour, the baking powder, soda, and ½ teaspoon *salt*. Add dry ingredients and applesauce alternately to beaten mixture, stirring after each addition. Turn into a greased 8x8x2-inch baking pan. Stir nuts and cinnamon into reserved crumb mixture; sprinkle atop. Bake in a 375° oven 30 minutes or till done. Serve warm. Makes 1.

## Sticky Nut Rolls

| | |
|---|---|
| ½ | cup light corn syrup or maple-flavored syrup |
| ⅓ | cup packed brown sugar |
| 3 | tablespoons butter or margarine, melted |
| 1 | tablespoon water |
| ⅓ | cup coarsely chopped pecans or walnuts |
| 2 | cups all-purpose flour |
| 1 | tablespoon baking powder |
| ½ | teaspoon salt |
| ⅓ | cup shortening |
| ¾ | cup milk |
| ¼ | cup granulated sugar |
| ½ | teaspoon ground cinnamon |

Oven 425°

In a saucepan combine syrup, brown sugar, butter or margarine, and water. Cook and stir over low heat till brown sugar is dissolved; *do not boil*. Spread in bottom of a 9x9x2-inch baking pan. Sprinkle nuts over.

In a mixing bowl stir together flour, baking powder, and salt. Cut in shortening till mixture resembles coarse crumbs. Make a well in center. Add milk all at once, stirring just till dough clings together. Turn dough out onto a lightly floured surface. Knead dough gently 15 to 20 strokes. Roll into a 12x10-inch rectangle. Combine granulated sugar and cinnamon; sprinkle over dough. Roll up jelly roll style, beginning with long side. Slice into 1-inch pieces. Place, cut side down, in prepared pan. Bake in a 425° oven 30 minutes or till golden. Loosen sides and invert onto a serving plate. Serve warm. Makes 12 rolls.

**Orange Sticky Rolls:** Prepare Sticky Nut Rolls as above, *except* in the saucepan substitute ¾ cup *granulated sugar* for the syrup and brown sugar. Stir in the butter or margarine, 1 tablespoon finely shredded *orange peel*, and 2 tablespoons *orange juice*. Omit the water. Bring mixture to boiling over medium heat; cook and stir 1 minute. Set aside *2 tablespoons* orange mixture; pour remainder into an 8x8x2-inch baking pan. Omit nuts.

Continue as directed above for dough. Roll dough out into a 12x9-inch rectangle. Spread dough with reserved orange mixture. Mix the ¼ cup granulated sugar and cinnamon; sprinkle over dough. Roll up; slice into 9 pieces. Arrange in pan. Bake about 20 minutes or till golden. Makes 9.

## Cake Doughnuts

*For a fast topping, shake doughnuts in a mixture of sugar and cinnamon—*

> 3¼ **cups all-purpose flour**
> 2 **teaspoons baking powder**
> ½ **teaspoon salt**
> ½ **teaspoon ground cinnamon**
> ¼ **teaspoon ground nutmeg**
> 2 **beaten eggs**
> ⅔ **cup granulated sugar**
> 1 **teaspoon vanilla**
> ⅔ **cup milk**
> ¼ **cup butter or margarine, melted**
> **Shortening or cooking oil for deep-fat frying**
> **Chocolate Glaze or Orange Glaze**

Stir together flour, baking powder, salt, ½ teaspoon cinnamon, and nutmeg. In a large mixer bowl combine eggs, ⅔ cup granulated sugar, and vanilla; beat till thick. Combine milk and melted butter or margarine. Add flour mixture and milk mixture alternately to egg mixture; beat just till blended after each addition. Cover; chill about 2 hours.

On a lightly floured surface roll dough to ½-inch thickness. Cut with a floured 2½-inch doughnut cutter. Fry in deep, hot fat (375°) about 1 minute per side or till golden, turning once with a slotted spoon. Drain on paper toweling. Cool. Drizzle with Chocolate Glaze or Orange Glaze. Makes 16.

**Chocolate Glaze:** Melt 1½ squares (1½ ounces) *unsweetened chocolate* and 2 tablespoons *butter;* cool. Stir in 1½ cups sifted *powdered sugar* and 1 teaspoon *vanilla.* Add enough boiling water to make of drizzling consistency.

**Orange Glaze:** In a mixing bowl combine 2 cups sifted *powdered sugar,* 1 teaspoon finely shredded *orange peel,* and 2 to 3 tablespoons *orange juice.*

**Chocolate Cake Doughnuts:** Prepare Cake Doughnut

dough as above, *except* omit spices, increase granulated sugar to *1 cup,* and add 1 square (1 ounce) melted and cooled *unsweetened chocolate* with the milk and butter. Roll dough and fry as directed. Drizzle with *Chocolate Glaze.*

## Buttermilk Doughnuts

3¼ **cups all-purpose flour**
1 **teaspoon baking soda**
½ **teaspoon baking powder**
½ **teaspoon ground nutmeg**
⅛ **teaspoon salt**
2 **slightly beaten eggs**
½ **cup sugar**
2 **tablespoons butter or margarine, melted**
1 **cup buttermilk or sour milk**
**Shortening or cooking oil for deep-fat frying**

In a mixing bowl stir together flour, baking soda, baking powder, nutmeg, and salt; set aside. In a large mixer bowl beat eggs and sugar till thick and lemon colored. Stir in melted butter or margarine. Add flour mixture and buttermilk or sour milk alternately to egg mixture; beat just till blended after each addition. Cover; chill dough about 2 hours.

Turn dough out onto a lightly floured surface. Roll to ½-inch thickness; cut with a 2½-inch doughnut cutter. Fry in deep, hot fat (375°) about 1 minute per side or till golden, turning once. Drain on paper toweling. While warm, sprinkle with additional sugar, if desired. Makes 18.

## Apple Fritter Rings

Core and peel 4 large tart cooking *apples;* cut into ½-inch-thick rings and set aside. In a mixing bowl thoroughly stir together 1 cup *all-purpose flour,* 2 tablespoons *sugar,* 1 teaspoon *baking powder,* and dash *salt.* Combine 1 beaten *egg,* ⅔ cup *milk,* and 1 teaspoon *cooking oil;* add all at once to flour mixture, stirring just till combined.

In a skillet that is at least 2 inches deep, heat 1 inch *shortening or cooking oil* to 375°. Dip apple slices in batter one at a time. Fry fritters in hot fat about 1½ minutes per side or till golden brown, turning once. Drain on paper toweling. Sprinkle hot fritters with a mixture of ¼ cup *sugar* and ½ teaspoon ground *cinnamon.* Serve hot. Makes 16 fritters.

---

## Homemade Biscuit Mix

---

**10** **cups all-purpose flour**
**⅓** **cup baking powder**
**¼** **cup sugar**
**4** **teaspoons salt**
**2** **cups shortening that does not require refrigeration**

In a large mixing bowl stir together flour, baking powder, sugar, and salt. With a pastry blender cut in shortening till mixture resembles coarse crumbs. Store in a covered airtight container up to six weeks at room temperature.

To use, spoon mix lightly into a measuring cup; level off with a straight-edged spatula. (For longer storage, place in a sealed freezer container and store in the freezer for up to six months. To use, allow mix to come to room temperature.) Makes 12½ cups.

**Biscuits:** Place 2 cups *Homemade Biscuit Mix* in a bowl: make a well in center. Add ½ cup *milk.* Stir with a fork just till dough follows fork around bowl. Turn dough out onto lightly floured surface. Knead gently for 10 to 12 strokes. Roll or pat to ½-inch thickness. Cut dough with a floured 2½-inch biscuit cutter, dipping cutter in flour between cuts. Bake on an ungreased baking sheet in a 450° oven for 10 to 12 minutes or till golden brown. Makes 10 biscuits.

**Muffins:** In a mixing bowl combine 3 cups *Homemade Biscuit Mix* and 3 tablespoons *sugar.* In another bowl mix 1 beaten *egg* and 1 cup *milk;* add all at once to dry ingredients. Stir till moistened (batter should be lumpy). Fill greased muffin cups ⅔ full. Bake in a 400° oven for 20 to 25 minutes or till golden. Makes 12 muffins.

**Pancakes:** Place 2 cups *Homemade Biscuit Mix* in a

bowl. Add 2 beaten *eggs* and 1 cup *milk* all at once to biscuit mix, stirring till blended but still slightly lumpy.

Pour about ¼ *cup* of the batter onto a hot, lightly greased griddle or heavy skillet. Cook till golden brown, turning to cook other side when pancakes have a bubbly surface and slightly dry edges. Makes 10 pancakes.

## Beer-Cheese Triangles

> **2** **cups packaged biscuit mix or Homemade Biscuit Mix (see recipe, page 151)**
> **½** **cup shredded cheddar cheese (2 ounces)**
> **½** **cup beer**           Oven 450°

In a mixing bowl stir together packaged biscuit mix or Homemade Biscuit Mix and shredded cheese. Make a well in the center; add beer all at once. Stir just till mixture clings together. Knead gently on a lightly floured surface for 5 strokes. Roll or pat dough into a 6-inch circle. Cut into 10 wedges. Place on a greased baking sheet. Bake in a 450° oven for 8 to 10 minutes. Makes 10.

## Pecan Biscuit Spirals

> **2** **cups all-purpose flour**
> **2** **tablespoons granulated sugar**
> **1** **tablespoon baking powder**
> **½** **teaspoon salt**
> **½** **cup butter or margarine**
> **1** **beaten egg**
> **½** **cup milk**
> **1** **tablespoon butter or margarine, melted**
> **¼** **cup finely chopped pecans**
> **3** **tablespoons brown sugar or granulated sugar**     Oven 450°

In a mixing bowl stir together flour, 2 tablespoons granulated sugar, baking powder, and salt. Cut in ½ cup butter or margarine till mixture resembles coarse crumbs. Make a well in the center. Combine egg and milk; add all at once to dry mixture. Stir just till dough clings together. Knead gently on a lightly floured surface for 12 to 15 strokes.

Roll dough into a 15x8-inch rectangle. Brush with 1 tablespoon melted butter or margarine. Combine pecans and 3 tablespoons brown sugar or granulated sugar; sprinkle over dough. Fold dough in half lengthwise to make a 15x4-inch rectangle. Cut into fifteen 1-inch wide strips. Holding a strip at both ends, carefully twist in opposite directions twice, forming a spiral. Place on a lightly greased baking sheet, pressing both ends down. Bake in a 450° oven about 10 minutes or till golden brown. Serve warm. Makes 15 spirals.

## Biscuits Supreme

> 2 **cups all-purpose flour**
> 4 **teaspoons baking powder**
> 2 **teaspoons sugar**
> ½ **teaspoon cream of tartar**
> ½ **teaspoon salt**
> ½ **cup shortening**
> ⅔ **cup milk**                    Oven 450°

Stir together flour, baking powder, sugar, cream of tartar, and salt. Cut in shortening till mixture resembles coarse crumbs. Make a well in the center; add milk all at once. Stir just till dough clings together. Knead gently on a lightly floured surface for 10 to 12 strokes. Roll or pat to ½-inch thickness. Cut with a 2½-inch biscuit cutter*, dipping cutter in flour between cuts. Transfer to an ungreased baking sheet. Bake in a 450° oven for 10 to 12 minutes or till golden. Serve warm. Makes 10 to 12 biscuits.

**Buttermilk Biscuits:** Prepare Biscuits Supreme as above, *except* stir ¼ teaspoon *baking soda* into flour mixture and substitute ¾ cup *buttermilk* for the milk.

**Cornmeal Biscuits:** Prepare Biscuits Supreme as above,

**\*Note:** If you do not have a biscuit cutter, pat the dough into a ½-inch-thick rectangle. Cut the dough into squares, triangles, or strips using a sharp knife.

*except* use only *1½ cups* all-purpose flour and add ½ cup yellow *commeal*. If desired, stir ¼ teaspoon *ground sage* into flour mixture.

**Garden Biscuits:** Prepare Biscuits Supreme as above, *except* add 2 tablespoons finely chopped *carrot,* 1 tablespoon finely snipped *parsley,* and 1 teaspoon finely chopped *green onion* to flour mixture with the milk; mix well.

**Sour Cream Biscuits:** Prepare Biscuits Supreme as above, *except* use 1 cup dairy *sour cream* and only *2 table-spoons* milk.

## Sesame Swirls

| | |
|---|---|
| 2½ | cups all-purpose flour |
| 1 | tablespoon baking powder |
| 1 | teaspoon salt |
| ½ | cup butter or margarine |
| 1 | cup dairy sour cream |
| ¼ | cup milk |
| 1 | slightly beaten egg |
| ⅓ | cup sesame seed, toasted |

Oven 425°

Stir together flour, baking powder, and salt. Cut in butter or margarine till mixture resembles coarse crumbs. Stir sour cream and milk together. Add all at once to dry mixture. Stir just till dough clings together. Knead gently on a well-floured surface (10 to 12 strokes). Roll dough into a 15x12-inch rectangle. Brush with some of the egg. Sprinkle with sesame seed. Roll up jelly roll style, starting with long side. Cut into 18 slices using a piece of ordinary thread; place on a greased baking sheet. Brush tops with remaining egg. Bake in a 425° oven 15 to 18 minutes. Makes 18 biscuits.

## Hush Puppies

  1   beaten egg
  1   cup buttermilk *or* sour milk
  ½   cup finely chopped onion
  ¼   cup water
1¾   cups cornmeal
  ½   cup all-purpose flour
  1   tablespoon sugar
  2   teaspoons baking powder
  1   teaspoon salt
  ½   teaspoon baking soda
      Shortening *or* cooking oil for deep-fat
         frying

In a mixing bowl stir together egg, buttermilk or sour milk, onion, and water; set aside. In a large mixing bowl combine cornmeal, flour, sugar, baking powder, salt, and baking soda. Add egg mixture to cornmeal mixture; stir just till moistened. Drop batter by tablespoons into deep hot fat (375°). Fry about 2 minutes or till golden brown, turning once. Drain on paper toweling. Serve hot with butter or margarine, if desired. Makes about 24.

## Corn Bread

  1   cup all-purpose flour
  1   cup yellow cornmeal
  ¼   cup sugar
  4   teaspoons baking powder
  ¾   teaspoon salt
  2   eggs
  1   cup milk
  ¼   cup cooking oil *or* shortening,
         melted                                Oven 425°

Stir together flour, cornmeal, sugar, baking powder, and salt. Add eggs, milk, and oil or melted shortening. Beat just till smooth (do not overbeat). Turn into a greased 9x9x2-inch baking pan. Bake in a 425° oven for 20 to 25 minutes. Makes 8 or 9 servings.

**Corn Sticks:** Prepare Corn Bread batter as above. Spoon batter into greased corn stick pans, filling pans ⅔ full. Bake in a 425° oven for 12 to 15 minutes. Makes 20 sticks.

---

## Spoon Bread

2 cups milk
1 cup yellow cornmeal
1 cup milk
2 tablespoons butter *or* margarine
1 teaspoon salt
1 teaspoon baking powder
3 beaten egg yolks
3 stiff-beaten egg whites
  Butter *or* margarine                         Oven 325°

In a saucepan stir 2 cups milk into cornmeal. Cook, stirring constantly, till very thick and pulling away from sides of pan. Remove from heat. Stir in 1 cup milk, 2 tablespoons butter or margarine, salt, and baking powder. Stir about *1 cup* of the hot mixture into egg yolks; return all to saucepan. Gently fold in egg whites. Turn into a greased 2-quart casserole. Bake in a 325° oven about 50 minutes or till a knife inserted near center comes out clean. Serve immediately with butter or margarine. Makes 6 servings.

**Cheese Spoon Bread:** Prepare Spoon Bread batter as above, *except* stir ½ cup grated *Parmesan cheese* (2 ounces) into cooked cornmeal mixture with the 2 tablespoons butter or margarine.

## Basic Muffins

1¾ **cups all-purpose flour**
¼ **cup sugar**
2½ **teaspoons baking powder**
¾ **teaspoon salt**
1 **beaten egg**
¾ **cup milk**
⅓ **cup cooking oil**                          Oven 400°

In a large mixing bowl stir together the flour, sugar, baking powder, and salt. Make a well in the center. Combine egg, milk, and oil. Add egg mixture all at once to flour mixture. Stir just till moistened; batter should be lumpy. Grease muffin cups or line with paper bake cups; fill ⅔ full. Bake in a 400° oven for 20 to 25 minutes or till golden. Remove from pans; serve warm. Makes 10 to 12 muffins.

**Blueberry Muffins:** Prepare Basic Muffins as above, *except* combine ¾ cup fresh or frozen *blueberries,* thawed, and *2 tablespoons* additional sugar. Add 1 teaspoon finely shredded *lemon peel,* if desired. Carefully fold into batter.

**Cranberry Muffins:** Prepare Basic Muffins as above, *except* coarsely chop 1 cup fresh or frozen *cranberries* and combine with ¼ *cup* additional sugar. Fold into batter.

**Apple-Raisin Muffins:** Prepare Basic Muffins as above, *except* stir ½ teaspoon ground *cinnamon* into the flour mixture. Fold 1 cup chopped peeled *apple* and ¼ cup *raisins* into batter.

**Jelly Muffins:** Prepare Basic Muffins as above, *except* spoon 1 teaspoon *jelly* atop batter in *each* muffin cup before baking.

**Date-Nut Muffins:** Prepare Basic Muffins as above, *except* fold ⅔ cup coarsely chopped pitted *dates* and ⅓ cup chopped *walnuts or pecans* into the batter.

**Cheese Muffins:** Prepare Basic Muffins as above, *except* stir ½ cup shredded *cheddar or Swiss cheese* into flour mixture.

**Banana-Nut Muffins:** Prepare Basic Muffins as above, *except* decrease milk to ½ *cup.* Stir in 1 cup mashed *banana* and ½ cup chopped *nuts* into batter.

**Pumpkin Muffins:** Prepare Basic Muffins as above, *except* increase sugar to ⅓ cup. Add ½ cup canned *pumpkin* to egg mixture. Stir ½ teaspoon ground *cinnamon* and ½ teaspoon ground *nutmeg* into flour mixture. Stir ½ cup *raisins* into batter.

## Honey-Wheat Muffins

| | |
|---|---|
| 1 | **cup all-purpose flour** |
| ½ | **cup whole wheat flour** |
| 2 | **teaspoons baking powder** |
| ½ | **teaspoon salt** |
| 1 | **beaten egg** |
| ½ | **cup milk** |
| ½ | **cup honey** |
| ¼ | **cup cooking oil** |
| ½ | **teaspoon finely shredded lemon peel** |

Oven 375°

Stir together all-purpose flour, whole wheat flour, baking powder, and salt; make a well in the center. Combine egg, milk, honey, oil, and lemon peel; add all at once to dry ingredients, stirring just till moistened (batter should be lumpy). Grease muffin cups or line with paper bake cups; fill ⅔ full. Bake in a 375° oven about 20 minutes. Makes 12.

**Sunflower Seed Muffins:** Prepare Honey-Wheat Muffins as above, *except* stir ½ cup shelled *sunflower seeds* into the flour mixture. Makes 12 muffins.

## Sunshine Muffins

| | |
|---|---|
| 1 | **8¼-ounce can crushed pineapple** |
| | **Milk** |
| 1½ | **cups packaged biscuit mix or Homemade Biscuit Mix (see recipe, page 151)** |
| 3 | **tablespoons sugar** |
| 1 | **beaten egg** |
| 1 | **tablespoon sugar** |
| 1 | **tablespoon finely shredded orange peel** |

Oven 400°

Drain pineapple, reserving syrup. Add enough milk to syrup to measure ¾ cup liquid. Combine packaged biscuit mix or Homemade Biscuit Mix and the 3 tablespoons sugar. Combine egg, the reserved pineapple liquid, and ¼ cup of the drained pineapple; add all at once to dry ingredients, stirring just till moistened, Grease muffin cups or line with paper bake cups; fill ⅔ full. Stir together remaining drained pineapple, 1 tablespoon sugar, and orange peel. Spoon about *1 tablespoon* pineapple mixture atop batter in *each* muffin cup. Bake in a 400° oven for 20 to 25 minutes or till golden. Makes 8 to 10 muffins.

## Pancakes

**1¼** **cups all-purpose flour**
 **2** **tablespoons granulated sugar**
 **2** **teaspoons baking powder**
 **1** **beaten egg**
 **1** **cup milk**
 **1** **tablespoon cooking oil**

Stir together flour, granulated sugar, baking powder, and ½ teaspoon *salt*. Combine egg, milk, and oil; add all at once to flour mixture, stirring till blended but still slightly lumpy. Pour about ¼ *cup* batter onto a hot, lightly greased griddle or heavy skillet for each standard-size pancake *or* about *1 tablespoon* batter for each dollar-size pancake. Cook till golden brown, turning to cook other side when pancakes have a bubbly surface and slightly dry edges. Makes about eight 4-inch pancakes or about 30 dollar-size pancakes.

**Buttermilk Pancakes:** Prepare Pancake batter as above, *except* reduce baking powder to *1 teaspoon* and add ½ teaspoon *baking soda* to the flour mixture; substitute 1⅓ cups *buttermilk or sour milk* for the 1 cup milk. Add additional buttermilk to thin the batter, if necessary. Makes about 10 pancakes.

**Buckwheat Pancakes:** Prepare Pancake batter as above, *except* substitute ¾ cup *whole wheat flour* and ½ cup *buckwheat flour* for the 1¼ cups all-purpose flour, and substitute 2 tablespoons *brown sugar* for the granulated sugar. Increase milk to 1¼ *cups*. Makes 8.

## French Toast

**3** beaten eggs
**¾** cup milk
**1** tablespoon sugar
**⅛** teaspoon ground cinnamon (optional)
**10** slices dry white bread
Butter, margarine, *or* cooking oil
Maple-flavored syrup

In a shallow bowl beat together eggs, milk, sugar, cinnamon, and ¼ teaspoon *salt*. Dip bread in egg mixture, coating both sides. In a skillet cook bread on both sides in a small amount of hot butter, margarine, or oil over medium-high heat till golden brown; add more butter as needed. Serve with maple-flavored syrup. Makes 5 servings.

## Waffles

**1¾** cups all-purpose flour
**1** tablespoon baking powder
**2** egg yolks
**1¾** cups milk
**½** cup cooking oil *or* shortening, melted
**2** egg whites

In a large mixing bowl stir together flour, baking powder, and ½ teaspoon *salt*. In a small mixing bowl beat egg yolks with a fork. Beat in milk and cooking oil or melted shortening. Add to flour mixture all at once. Stir mixture till blended but still slightly lumpy.

In a small mixer bowl beat egg whites till stiff peaks form. Gently fold beaten egg whites into flour-milk mixture, leaving a few fluffs of egg white. *Do not overmix.*

Pour batter onto grids of a preheated, lightly greased waffle baker. Close lid quickly; do not open during baking. Use a fork to help lift the baked waffle off grid.

To keep baked waffles hot for serving, place in a single layer on a wire rack placed atop a baking sheet in a warm oven. Makes three 9-inch waffles.

## Popovers

| | |
|---|---|
| 1½ | **teaspoons shortening** |
| 2 | **beaten eggs** |
| 1 | **cup milk** |
| 1 | **tablespoon cooking oil** |
| 1 | **cup all-purpose flour** |

Oven 450°

Grease six 6-ounce custard cups with ¼ *teaspoon* of the shortening for *each* cup. Place custard cups on a 15x10x1-inch baking pan or baking sheet and place in oven; preheat oven to 450°. Meanwhile, in a 4-cup liquid measure or mixing bowl combine beaten eggs, milk, and oil. Add flour and ½ teaspoon *salt*. Beat with electric mixer or rotary heater till mixture is smooth. Remove pan from oven. Fill the hot custard cups *half* full. Return to oven. Bake in a 450° oven for 20 minutes. Reduce oven to 350°; bake 15 to 20 minutes more or till *very firm*. (If popovers brown too quickly, turn off oven and finish baking in the cooling oven till very firm.) A few minutes before removing from oven, prick each popover with a fork to let steam escape. Serve hot. Makes 6.

# Cakes

# Cakes

# Cakes

# Cakes

# Cakes

# Cakes

# Cakes

# Cakes

# Cakes

Percent of U.S. RDA Per Serving

| Recipes | Servings (fraction of recipe) | Calories | Protein (grams) | Carbohydrate (grams) | Fat (grams) | Sodium (milligrams) | Potassium (milligrams) | Protein | Vitamin A | Vitamin C | Thiamine | Riboflavin | Niacin | Calcium | Iron |
|---|---|---|---|---|---|---|---|---|---|---|---|---|---|---|---|
| Angel Cake | 1/12 | 157 | 4 | 36 | 0 | 89 | 51 | 6 | 0 | 0 | 0 | 0 | 5 | 0 | 0 |
| Applesauce Spice Cake | 1/12 | 382 | 5 | 66 | 12 | 430 | 169 | 8 | 9 | 1 | 14 | 9 | 7 | 3 | 9 |
| Banana Cake | 1/12 | 300 | 5 | 50 | 10 | 339 | 125 | 7 | 3 | 3 | 13 | 10 | 8 | 3 | 6 |
| Black Forest Cake | 1/12 | 661 | 6 | 92 | 31 | 402 | 199 | 10 | 20 | 2 | 11 | 12 | 6 | 7 | 9 |
| Broiled Coconut Topping | 1/9 | 132 | 1 | 13 | 9 | 55 | 85 | 3 | 3 | 1 | 1 | 1 | 1 | 1 | 4 |
| Busy-Day Cake | 1/9 | 228 | 4 | 34 | 9 | 227 | 58 | 6 | 2 | 0 | 10 | 10 | 8 | 6 | 5 |
| Butter Frosting | 1/12 | 199 | 0 | 38 | 6 | 73 | 10 | 0 | 5 | 0 | 0 | 0 | 1 | 0 | 1 |
| Butterscotch Marble Cake | 1/12 | 462 | 6 | 65 | 21 | 317 | 133 | 10 | 6 | 0 | 2 | 2 | 8 | 1 | 9 |
| Carrot Cake | 1/12 | 404 | 5 | 52 | 20 | 327 | 137 | 7 | 64 | 4 | 11 | 11 | 9 | 6 | 4 |
| Chocolate Butter Frosting | 1/12 | 226 | 1 | 39 | 9 | 76 | 57 | 1 | 5 | 0 | 0 | 0 | 2 | 2 | 2 |
| Chocolate Cake Roll | 1/10 | 274 | 4 | 36 | 14 | 146 | 114 | 7 | 13 | 0 | 8 | 4 | 8 | 4 | 5 |
| Chocolate Chip Cake | 1/12 | 436 | 5 | 53 | 24 | 291 | 131 | 8 | 1 | 0 | 9 | 9 | 10 | 6 | 6 |
| Chocolate Icing | 1/12 | 124 | 0 | 18 | 6 | 38 | 27 | 1 | 2 | 0 | 0 | 0 | 1 | 1 | 1 |
| Chocolate Marble Cake | 1/12 | 233 | 4 | 32 | 11 | 247 | 71 | 6 | 9 | 0 | 9 | 9 | 7 | 5 | 5 |
| Chocolate Sour Cream Frosting | 1/12 | 206 | 1 | 29 | 11 | 52 | 62 | 1 | 5 | 0 | 0 | 0 | 2 | 2 | 2 |
| Coconut-Pecan Frosting | 1/12 | 186 | 3 | 14 | 14 | 72 | 115 | 4 | 5 | 1 | 4 | 4 | 4 | 1 | 3 |
| Cream Cheese Frosting | 1/12 | 125 | 1 | 17 | 7 | 65 | 7 | 1 | 5 | 0 | 0 | 0 | 1 | 0 | 1 |
| Creamy Butter Frosting | 1/12 | 203 | 1 | 37 | 6 | 76 | 10 | 1 | 6 | 0 | 0 | 0 | 1 | 1 | 1 |
| Creamy White Frosting | 1/16 | 221 | 0 | 28 | 13 | 2 | 6 | 0 | 0 | 0 | 0 | 0 | 0 | 0 | 0 |
| Dark Fruitcake | 1/40 | 266 | 3 | 48 | 8 | 125 | 386 | 5 | 5 | 26 | 13 | 7 | 6 | 5 | 10 |

# Nutrition Analysis Chart

| | | | | | | | | | | | | | | |
|---|---|---|---|---|---|---|---|---|---|---|---|---|---|---|
| Date Cake | 1/12 | 309 | 4 | 44 | 14 | 147 | 182 | 7 | 2 | 0 | 10 | 7 | 7 | 3 | 8 |
| Devil's Food Cake | 1/12 | 313 | 5 | 49 | 12 | 330 | 113 | 8 | 3 | 0 | 11 | 9 | 7 | 2 | 8 |
| Feathery Fudge Cake | 1/12 | 327 | 4 | 47 | 15 | 337 | 93 | 6 | 10 | 0 | 10 | 7 | 6 | 2 | 7 |
| Fluffy White Frosting | 1/12 | 67 | 1 | 17 | 0 | 8 | 8 | 1 | 0 | 0 | 1 | 1 | 0 | 0 | 0 |
| Fudge Frosting | 1/12 | 278 | 1 | 56 | 7 | 105 | 71 | 2 | 4 | 0 | 1 | 3 | 0 | 0 | 3 |
| German Chocolate Cake | 1/12 | 269 | 4 | 36 | 12 | 220 | 79 | 7 | 9 | 0 | 9 | 9 | 5 | 4 | 5 |
| Gingerbread | 1/8 | 284 | 4 | 38 | 13 | 236 | 242 | 5 | 1 | 0 | 11 | 7 | 6 | 5 | 4 |
| Golden Chiffon Cake | 1/12 | 287 | 5 | 40 | 12 | 294 | 56 | 8 | 7 | 1 | 2 | 6 | 1 | 3 | 4 |
| Hot Milk Sponge Cake | 1/9 | 186 | 3 | 34 | 4 | 148 | 49 | 5 | 5 | 0 | 7 | 7 | 4 | 3 | 5 |
| Italian Cream Cake | 1/16 | 257 | 6 | 45 | 7 | 121 | 113 | 9 | 5 | 1 | 7 | 9 | 4 | 9 | 4 |
| Jelly Roll | 1/10 | 161 | 3 | 33 | 2 | 112 | 43 | 5 | 5 | 1 | 4 | 6 | 2 | 5 | 2 |
| Lady Baltimore Cake | 1/12 | 420 | 5 | 64 | 17 | 293 | 260 | 8 | 1 | 2 | 14 | 11 | 8 | 6 | 8 |
| Lemon Butter Frosting | 1/12 | 197 | 0 | 38 | 6 | 71 | 10 | 0 | 5 | 4 | 0 | 1 | 0 | 0 | 0 |
| Lemon Filling | 1/12 | 72 | 0 | 14 | 2 | 13 | 9 | 1 | 3 | 3 | 1 | 1 | 0 | 0 | 1 |
| Light Fruitcake | 1/36 | 234 | 3 | 39 | 8 | 82 | 228 | 4 | 6 | 24 | 11 | 5 | 5 | 3 | 6 |
| Mocha Butter Frosting | 1/12 | 204 | 1 | 39 | 6 | 73 | 40 | 1 | 5 | 0 | 0 | 1 | 0 | 1 | 1 |
| Nutmeg Cake with Toasted Meringue Topping | 1/12 | 337 | 5 | 56 | 11 | 265 | 130 | 8 | 6 | 1 | 11 | 10 | 6 | 5 | 8 |
| Orange Butter Frosting | 3/12 | 198 | 0 | 38 | 6 | 71 | 13 | 0 | 5 | 5 | 0 | 0 | 0 | 0 | 0 |
| Orange Sponge Cake | 1/12 | 186 | 5 | 36 | 3 | 74 | 66 | 7 | 6 | 10 | 8 | 8 | 4 | 2 | 5 |
| Peanut Butter Frosting | 1/12 | 195 | 2 | 39 | 4 | 51 | 59 | 3 | 0 | 0 | 1 | 1 | 6 | 1 | 1 |
| Penuche Frosting | 1/12 | 236 | 0 | 43 | 8 | 102 | 73 | 0 | 6 | 0 | 0 | 1 | 1 | 2 | 4 |
| Peppermint Frosting | 1/12 | 295 | 0 | 38 | 17 | 3 | 3 | 8 | 0 | 0 | 0 | 1 | 0 | 1 | 0 |
| Peppermint-Stick Frosting | 1/12 | 113 | 1 | 28 | 0 | 15 | 9 | 1 | 0 | 1 | 0 | 1 | 1 | 0 | 1 |
| Petits Fours Icing | 1/36 | 91 | 0 | 23 | 0 | 0 | 1 | 0 | 0 | 0 | 0 | 0 | 0 | 0 | 0 |
| Petits Fours | 1/26 | 192 | 1 | 38 | 4 | 97 | 24 | 2 | 0 | 0 | 3 | 3 | 2 | 0 | 1 |
| Pineapple Upside-Down Cake | 1/8 | 345 | 3 | 57 | 12 | 217 | 109 | 5 | 4 | 3 | 12 | 7 | 7 | 4 | 8 |
| Poppy Seed Cake | 1/12 | 421 | 7 | 66 | 16 | 498 | 250 | 11 | 14 | 3 | 15 | 11 | 10 | 5 | 11 |
| Pound Cake | 1/12 | 303 | 4 | 33 | 17 | 279 | 47 | 7 | 16 | 0 | 10 | 8 | 6 | 2 | 6 |

# Nutrition Analysis Chart

| Recipes | Servings (fraction of recipe) | Calories | Protein (grams) | Carbohydrate (grams) | Fat (grams) | Sodium (milligrams) | Potassium (milligrams) | Protein | Vitamin A | Vitamin C | Thiamine | Riboflavin | Niacin | Calcium | Iron |
|---|---|---|---|---|---|---|---|---|---|---|---|---|---|---|---|
| | | | | | | | | Percent of U.S. RDA Per Serving | | | | | | | |
| Powdered Sugar Icing | 1/12 | 33 | 0 | 8 | 0 | 1 | 3 | 0 | 0 | 0 | 0 | 0 | 0 | 0 | 0 |
| Pumpkin Molasses Cake | 1/12 | 307 | 5 | 53 | 9 | 314 | 242 | 7 | 21 | 2 | 13 | 13 | 10 | 8 | 12 |
| Rocky-Road Frosting | 1/12 | 184 | 1 | 26 | 10 | 51 | 64 | 2 | 3 | 0 | 1 | 1 | 1 | 1 | 4 |
| Seafoam Frosting | 1/12 | 92 | 1 | 23 | 0 | 16 | 87 | 1 | 1 | 0 | 0 | 0 | 1 | 0 | 5 |
| Seven-Minute Frosting | 1/12 | 102 | 1 | 26 | 0 | 9 | 8 | 1 | 1 | 0 | 0 | 0 | 1 | 0 | 0 |
| Sour Cream Chocolate Cake | 1/12 | 306 | 4 | 41 | 15 | 196 | 101 | 6 | 4 | 0 | 9 | 9 | 8 | 5 | 7 |
| Spice Nut Cake | 1/12 | 349 | 5 | 48 | 16 | 320 | 135 | 8 | 3 | 1 | 12 | 12 | 10 | 6 | 9 |
| White Cake Supreme | 1/12 | 304 | 4 | 42 | 13 | 291 | 70 | 7 | 1 | 0 | 9 | 9 | 9 | 6 | 3 |
| White Cake Supreme Cupcakes | 1/30 | 122 | 2 | 17 | 5 | 116 | 28 | 3 | 0 | 0 | 4 | 4 | 4 | 2 | 1 |
| Yellow Cake | 1/12 | 315 | 5 | 52 | 10 | 363 | 79 | 8 | 9 | 0 | 13 | 13 | 11 | 8 | 6 |
| Yellow Cake Cupcakes | 1/30 | 126 | 2 | 21 | 4 | 145 | 31 | 3 | 4 | 0 | 5 | 5 | 4 | 3 | 2 |
| Yellow Citrus Cake | 1/12 | 301 | 4 | 42 | 13 | 224 | 62 | 7 | 3 | 4 | 10 | 10 | 8 | 6 | 5 |

# Cakes

Cakes are grouped into three classes; those made with shortening (conventional and quick-mix), those made without shortening (angel and sponge), and combination angel and shortening types (chiffon).

For a shortening-type cake, grease and lightly flour bottoms of pans, or line bottoms with waxed paper. Pans for angel, sponge, and chiffon cakes should not be greased, unless specified.

A shortening-type cake is done when a cake tester or wooden pick inserted in the center comes out clean. The cake also will shrink slightly from the sides of the pan. Angel, sponge, and chiffon cakes are done when the cake springs back when touched lightly with your finger.

Cool shortening layer cakes in their pans on wire racks 10 minutes (loaf cakes, 15 minutes), then loosen edges. Place an inverted rack on the cake and turn all over; carefully lift off the pan. Put a second rack over the cake and invert again so the top side is up. Invert angel, sponge, and chiffon cakes in their pans as they are removed from the oven to prevent them from shrinking or falling.

## Tips for using the nutrition analysis chart

The nutrition analysis for each cake and frosting recipe in this chapter is listed separately in the chart on preceding pages To obtain the total nutrition analysis for a serving of cake frosted with the suggested frosting (or any other frosting listed in the chapter), look up the analysis for both the cake and the frosting and add them. If a cake recipe lists ingredients for a frosting, topping, or filling within the recipe, the analysis for these ingredients is included in the nutrition analysis for the cake.

## White Cake Supreme

    2   cups all-purpose flour
    1   tablespoon baking powder
    1   teaspoon salt
   ¾   cup shortening
  1½   cups sugar
  1½   teaspoons vanilla
    1   cup milk
    5   egg whites                          Oven 375°

Grease and lightly flour two 9x1½-inch round baking pans.
Combine flour, baking powder, and salt. In a mixer bowl beat
shortening on medium speed of electric mixer about 30 seconds. Add sugar and vanilla and beat till fluffy. Add dry
ingredients and milk alternately to beaten mixture, beating on
low speed after each addition. Wash beaters. In a small mixer
bowl beat egg whites till stiff peaks form. Gently fold into flour
mixture. Turn into prepared pans. Bake in 375° oven about 20
minutes or till cake tests done. Cool 10 minutes on wire racks.
Remove from pans. Cool. Serves 12.

   ***Chocolate Chip Cake:*** Prepare White Cake Supreme as
above, *except* pour *half* of the batter into 2 prepared pans.
Sprinkle ⅓ cup *semisweet chocolate pieces* over batter in *each*
pan. Add remaining batter, spreading evenly; sprinkle *each*
with ⅓ cup more *chocolate pieces*. Bake as above. Serves 12.

   ***Lady Baltimore Cake:*** Prepare White Cake Supreme as
above, *except* spread 1 layer with Date-Nut Filling and frost
cake with Seven-Minute Frosting (see recipe, page 194). For
Date-Nut Filling, combine ¼ of the *Seven-Minute Frosting;* 1
cup chopped, pitted *dates or figs;* ½ cup *raisins;* ½ cup
chopped *candied cherries;* and ½ cup chopped *pecans.* Frost
cake with remaining frosting. Serves 12.

   ***Cupcakes:*** Grease and lightly flour muffin pans or line
with paper bake cups; set aside. Prepare White Cake Supreme
as above. Fill each cup half full. Bake in a 375° oven 18 to 20
minutes or till done. Cool on a wire rack. Frost with desired
frosting. Makes 30.

   ***Petits Fours:*** Grease and lightly flour a 13x9x2-inch baking pan. Prepare White Cake Supreme as above; turn into

prepared pan. Bake in a 375° oven for 25 minutes. Cool 10 minutes on a wire rack; remove from pan. Cool thoroughly. Cut into 1½-inch squares, diamonds, or circles. Ice with Petits Fours Icing (see recipe, page 196). Makes 36 to 40.

## Yellow Citrus Cake

|       |                                              |
| ----- | -------------------------------------------- |
| 2     | cups all-purpose flour                       |
| 2½    | teaspoons baking powder                      |
| ¾     | teaspoon salt                                |
| ⅔     | cup shortening                               |
| 1½    | cups sugar                                   |
| 1     | tablespoon grated orange peel                |
| 1½    | teaspoons grated lemon peel                  |
| 3     | eggs                                         |
| ⅔     | cup milk                                     |
| 2     | tablespoons lemon juice                      |
|       | Lemon Filling                                |
|       | Fluffy White Frosting (see recipe, page 196) |

Oven 350°

Grease and lightly flour two 8x1½-inch *or* 9x1½-inch round baking pans. Combine the first 3 ingredients. Beat shortening about 30 seconds. Add sugar and peels; beat till well combined. Add eggs, one at a time, beating 1 minute after each. Add dry ingredients, milk, and lemon juice alternately to beaten mixture, beating after each addition. Turn into pans. Bake in a 350° oven for 30 minutes or till done. Cool 10 minutes on wire racks. Remove from pans; cool. Halve layers horizontally, making 4 cake layers. Spread Lemon Filling between layers. Frost top and sides with Fluffy White Frosting. Serves 12.

***Lemon Filling:*** Combine ¾ cup *sugar*, 2 tablespoons *cornstarch*, and dash *salt*; stir in ¾ cup cold *water*. Add 2 beaten *egg yolks*, 1 teaspoon grated *lemon peel*, and 3 tablespoons *lemon juice*. Cook and stir till bubbly; cook 1 minute more. Stir in 1 tablespoon *butter*. Cover surface with waxed paper; cool.

## Busy-Day Cake

| | |
|---|---|
| 1½ | **cups all-purpose flour** |
| ¾ | **cup sugar** |
| 2½ | **teaspoons baking powder** |
| ¾ | **cup milk** |
| ⅓ | **cup shortening** |
| 1 | **egg** |
| 1½ | **teaspoons vanilla** |

Oven 375°

Grease and lightly flour a 9x9x2-inch baking pan. In a small mixer bowl combine all ingredients and ½ teaspoon *salt*. Beat with electric mixer till combined. Beat 2 minutes on medium speed. Turn into pan. Bake in a 375° oven 25 to 30 minutes or till done. Cool. Serves 9.

## Yellow Cake

| | |
|---|---|
| 2¾ | **cups all-purpose flour** |
| 2½ | **teaspoons baking powder** |
| ½ | **cup butter *or* margarine** |
| 1¾ | **cups sugar** |
| 1½ | **teaspoons vanilla** |
| 2 | **eggs** |
| 1¼ | **cups milk** |

Oven 375°

Grease and lightly flour two 8x1½-inch *or* 9x1½-inch round baking pans. Combine flour, baking powder, and 1 teaspoon *salt*. Beat butter about 30 seconds. Add sugar and vanilla; beat till well combined. Add eggs, one at a time, beating 1 minute after each. Add dry ingredients and milk alternately to beaten mixture, beating after each addition. Turn into pans. Bake in a 375° oven for 30 to 35 minutes or till done. Cool 10 minutes on wire racks. Remove from pans. Cool. Serves 12.

***Cupcakes:*** Grease and lightly flour muffin pans or line with paper bake cups. Prepare Yellow Cake as above. Fill each cup half full. Bake in a 375° oven 18 to 20 minutes or till done. Cool on a wire rack. Makes 30.

## Pineapple Upside-Down Cake

| | |
|---|---|
| 1 | 8-ounce can pineapple slices |
| 2 | tablespoons butter or margarine |
| ½ | cup packed brown sugar |
| 4 | maraschino cherries, halved |
| 1½ | cups all-purpose flour |
| 2½ | teaspoons baking powder |
| ⅓ | cup shortening |
| ¾ | cup granulated sugar |
| 1 | egg |
| 1½ | teaspoons vanilla |

Oven 350°

Drain pineapple; reserve liquid. Halve slices. Melt butter in a 9x1½-inch round baking pan. Stir in brown sugar and *1 tablespoon* reserved pineapple liquid. Add water to remaining liquid to make ⅔ cup. Arrange pineapple and cherries in pan. Combine flour, baking powder, and ¼ teaspoon *salt*. Beat shortening about 30 seconds. Add granulated sugar; beat till well combined. Add egg and vanilla; beat 1 minute. Add dry ingredients and the ⅔ cup liquid alternately to beaten mixture, beating after each addition. Spread in pan. Bake in a 350° oven 40 minutes. Cool 5 minutes; invert onto a plate. Serve warm. Serves 8.

## Banana Cake

| | |
|---|---|
| 2½ | cups all-purpose flour |
| 1½ | cups sugar |
| 1½ | teaspoons baking powder |
| 1 | teaspoon baking soda |
| 1 | teaspoon salt |
| ½ | cup shortening |
| 1 | cup mashed ripe banana |
| ⅔ | cup buttermilk *or* sour milk |
| 2 | eggs |
| 1 | teaspoon vanilla |
| | Creamy Butter Frosting (see recipe, page 195) |

Oven 350°

Grease and lightly flour two 9x1½-inch round baking pans. In a mixer bowl combine the first 5 ingredients. Add shortening and banana; beat on low speed of electric mixer till combined. Add buttermilk or sour milk, eggs, and vanilla; beat 2 minutes on medium speed. Turn batter into prepared pans. Bake in a 350° oven for 30 minutes or till done. Cool 10 minutes on wire racks. Remove from pans; cool thoroughly. Frost with Creamy Butter Frosting. Makes 12 servings.

## Pound Cake

|       |                          |            |
|-------|--------------------------|------------|
| 1     | cup butter *or* margarine |           |
| 4     | eggs                     |            |
| 2     | cups all-purpose flour   |            |
| 1     | teaspoon baking powder   |            |
| ¼     | teaspoon salt            |            |
| ¼     | teaspoon ground nutmeg   |            |
| 1     | cup sugar                |            |
| 1½    | teaspoons vanilla        | Oven 325°  |

Bring butter or margarine and eggs to room temperature. Grease and flour a 9x5x3-inch loaf pan. Stir together flour, baking powder, salt, and nutmeg. In a large mixer bowl beat the butter or margarine on medium speed of electric mixer about 30 seconds. Gradually add sugar, beating 6 minutes or till fluffy. Add vanilla. Add the eggs, one at a time, beating 1 minute after each; scrape bowl frequently. Gradually add dry ingredients to egg mixture, beating on low speed just till thoroughly combined. Turn batter into pan. Bake in a 325° oven for 55 to 65 minutes or till done. Cool 15 minutes on a wire rack. Remove from pan. Cool. Makes 12 servings.

# Pumpkin Molasses Cake

2½ cups all-purpose flour
2 teaspoons grated orange peel
1 teaspoon baking soda
½ teaspoon salt
½ teaspoon ground cinnamon
½ teaspoon ground ginger
½ cup butter *or* margarine
1½ cups packed brown sugar
2 eggs
¾ cup buttermilk *or* sour milk
½ cup canned pumpkin
¼ cup light molasses
Powdered sugar                      Oven 350°

Grease and lightly flour a 13x9x2-inch baking pan. Combine the first 6 ingredients. Beat butter about 30 seconds. Add brown sugar and beat till well combined. Add eggs, one at a time, beating 1 minute after each. Combine buttermilk, pumpkin, and molasses. Add dry ingredients and buttermilk mixture alternately to beaten mixture, beating after each addition. Turn into pan. Bake in a 350° oven for 30 to 35 minutes or till done. Cool on a wire rack. Sprinkle with powdered sugar. Serves 12.

# Carrot Cake

2 cups all-purpose flour
2 cups sugar
1 teaspoon baking powder
1 teaspoon baking soda
1 teaspoon salt
1 teaspoon ground cinnamon
3 cups finely shredded carrot
1 cup cooking oil
4 eggs
Cream Cheese Frosting
(see recipe, page 197)          Oven 325°

Grease and lightly flour a 13x9x2-inch baking pan (or two 9x1½-inch round baking pans). In a mixer bowl combine the first 6 ingredients. Add next 3 ingredients, beating with electric mixer till combined. Beat on medium speed for 2 minutes. Turn into pan(s). Bake in a 325° oven for 50 to 60 minutes in the 13x9x2-inch pan or till done. (For two 9-inch layers, bake in a 325° oven for 40 minutes or till done.) Cool on a wire rack. (Remove layers from pans after cooling 10 minutes. Cool well.) Frost with Cream Cheese Frosting. Serves 12 to 15.

---

## Nutmeg Cake with Toasted Meringue Topping

|  |  |
|---|---|
| 2 | cups all-purpose flour |
| 2 | teaspoons ground nutmeg |
| 1 | teaspoon baking soda |
| 1 | teaspoon baking powder |
| ¼ | teaspoon salt |
| ¼ | cup butter *or* margarine |
| ¼ | cup shortening |
| 1½ | cups sugar |
| ½ | teaspoon vanilla |
| 3 | eggs |
| 1 | cup buttermilk *or* sour milk |
|  | Toasted Meringue Topping |
| ½ | cup flaked coconut |

Oven 350°

Grease and lightly flour a 13x9x2-inch baking pan. Combine the first 5 ingredients. In a mixer bowl beat together butter and shortening on medium speed of electric mixer about 30 seconds. Add sugar and vanilla and beat till well combined. Add eggs, one at a time, beating 1 minute after each. Add dry ingredients and buttermilk or sour milk alternately to beaten mixture, beating on low speed after each addition. Turn into pan. Bake in a 350° oven about 30 minutes or till done. Meanwhile, just before cake is removed from oven, prepare Toasted Meringue Topping; quickly spread topping over hot cake. Sprinkle with coconut. Bake in a 350° oven 5 minutes or till meringue is golden. Cool on a wire rack. Store in refrigerator. Makes 12 to 15 servings.

*Toasted Meringue Topping:* In a small mixer bowl beat 2 *egg whites* and ½ teaspoon *vanilla* on medium speed of electric mixer for 2 minutes or till soft peaks form. Gradually add ¾ cup packed *brown sugar*, 1 tablespoon at a time, beating on high speed for 4 minutes more or till mixture forms stiff, glossy peaks.

## To make sour milk

Place 1 tablespoon vinegar in a 2-cup glass measure. Add enough fresh milk to make 1 cup liquid. Stir well and allow to stand at room temperature 5 minutes before using.

---

# Gingerbread

---

| | |
|---|---|
| 1½ | **cups all-purpose flour** |
| ¾ | **teaspoon ground ginger** |
| ¾ | **teaspoon ground cinnamon** |
| ½ | **teaspoon baking powder** |
| ½ | **teaspoon baking soda** |
| ½ | **teaspoon salt** |
| ½ | **cup shortening** |
| ¼ | **cup packed brown sugar** |
| 1 | **egg** |
| ½ | **cup light molasses** |
| ½ | **cup boiling water**               Oven 350° |

Grease and lightly flour a 9x1½-inch round baking pan. Combine the first 6 ingredients. In a mixer bowl beat shortening on medium speed of electric mixer about 30 seconds. Add brown sugar; beat till fluffy. Add egg and molasses; beat 1 minute. Add dry ingredients and water alternately to beaten mixture, beating after each addition. Turn into prepared pan. Bake in a 350° oven 30 to 35 minutes or till done. Cool 10 minutes on a wire rack. Remove from pan; serve warm. Makes 8 servings.

## Spice Nut Cake

|     |                                                           |
| --- | --------------------------------------------------------- |
| 2   | cups all-purpose flour                                    |
| 1   | cup granulated sugar                                      |
| 1   | teaspoon salt                                             |
| 1   | teaspoon baking powder                                    |
| ¾   | teaspoon baking soda                                      |
| ¾   | teaspoon ground cloves                                    |
| ¾   | teaspoon ground cinnamon                                  |
| ⅔   | cup shortening                                            |
| ¾   | cup packed brown sugar                                    |
| 1   | cup buttermilk *or* sour milk                             |
| 3   | eggs                                                      |
| ½   | cup chopped walnuts                                       |
|     | Orange Butter Frosting (see recipe, page 195)             |

Oven 350°

Grease and lightly flour two 9x1½-inch round baking pans. In a mixer bowl combine the first 7 ingredients. Add shortening, brown sugar, and buttermilk or sour milk, mixing till all the flour is moistened. Beat 2 minutes. Add eggs; beat 2 minutes more. Stir in nuts. Turn into pans. Bake in a 350° oven for 30 to 35 minutes. Cool 10 minutes on wire racks. Remove from pans; cool. Frost with Orange Butter Frosting. Makes 12 servings.

---

## Applesauce Spice Cake

|      |                            |
| ---- | -------------------------- |
| 2½   | cups all-purpose flour     |
| 1½   | teaspoons baking soda      |
| 1    | teaspoon salt              |
| 1    | teaspoon ground cinnamon   |
| ¾    | teaspoon ground nutmeg     |
| ½    | teaspoon ground cloves     |
| ¼    | teaspoon baking powder     |
| ½    | cup butter *or* margarine  |
| 2    | cups sugar                 |
| 2    | eggs                       |
| 1    | 16-ounce can applesauce    |
| ¾    | cup raisins                |
| ½    | cup chopped nuts           |

Oven 350°

Grease and lightly flour a 13x9x2-inch baking pan. Combine the first 7 ingredients. In a mixer bowl beat butter with electric mixer for 30 seconds. Add sugar and beat till well combined. Add eggs, one at a time, beating 1 minute after each. Add dry ingredients and applesauce alternately to beaten mixture, beating on low speed after each addition. Stir in raisins and nuts. Turn into pan. Bake in a 350° oven for 45 minutes or till done. Cool on a wire rack. Serves 12 to 15.

# Date Cake

1⅓  **cups snipped pitted dates (8 ounces)**
1   **cup boiling water**
1½  **cups all-purpose flour**
1   **teaspoon baking soda**
½   **cup shortening**
1   **cup sugar**
1   **teaspoon vanilla**
2   **eggs**
¾   **cup chopped walnuts**                   Oven 350°

Grease and lightly flour a 13x9x2-inch baking pan. Combine dates and boiling water; cool to room temperature. Stir together the flour, baking soda, and ¼ teaspoon *salt*. In a large mixer bowl beat shortening about 30 seconds. Add sugar and vanilla and beat till fluffy. Add eggs, one at a time, beating 1 minute after each. Add dry ingredients and cooled *undrained* date mixture alternately to beaten mixture, beating after each addition. Stir in nuts. Spread in pan. Bake in a 350° oven for 30 to 35 minutes. If desired, serve each piece with a dollop of whipped cream. Serves 12.

## High altitude chart

Use this chart to adjust all cake ingredients listed. Experiment to discover the best formula; where two amounts appear, try the smaller first, and adjust next time, if necessary.

| Ingredients | 3,000 feet | 5,000 feet | 7,000 feet |
| --- | --- | --- | --- |
| Liquid: Add for each cup | 1 to 2 tablespoons | 2 to 4 tablespoons | 3 to 4 tablespoons |
| Baking powder: Decrease for each teaspoon | ⅛ teaspoon | ⅛ to ¼ teaspoon | ¼ teaspoon |
| Sugar: Decrease for each cup | 0 to 1 tablespoon | 0 to 2 tablespoons | 1 to 3 tablespoons |

# German Chocolate Cake

|  |  |
| --- | --- |
| 1 | 4-ounce package German sweet chocolate |
| 1⅔ | cups all-purpose flour |
| 1 | teaspoon baking soda |
| ½ | cup butter or margarine |
| 1 | cup sugar |
| 1 | teaspoon vanilla |
| 3 | egg yolks |
| ⅔ | cup buttermilk or sour milk |
| 3 | stiff-beaten egg whites |
|  | Coconut-Pecan Frosting (see recipe, page 197) |

Oven 350°

Grease and lightly flour two 8x1½-inch round baking pans. Heat chocolate and ⅓ cup *water* till chocolate melts; cool. Combine flour, soda, and ½ teaspoon *salt*. Beat butter about 30 seconds. Add sugar and vanilla; beat till fluffy. Add egg yolks, one at a time, beating 1 minute after each. Beat in chocolate mixture. Add dry ingredients and buttermilk alternately to beaten mixture, beating after each addition. Fold in egg whites. Turn into pans. Bake in a 350° oven for 30 to 35 minutes. Cool 10 minutes. Remove from pans; cool. Fill and frost top with Coconut-Pecan Frosting. Serves 12.

---

## Devil's Food Cake

---

        2¼    **cups all-purpose flour**
         ½    **cup unsweetened cocoa powder**
        1½    **teaspoons baking soda**
         1    **teaspoon salt**
         ½    **cup shortening**
         1    **cup sugar**
         1    **teaspoon vanilla**
         3    **egg yolks**
        1⅓    **cups cold water**
         3    **egg whites**
         ¾    **cup sugar**
              **Seafoam Frosting (see recipe, page 194)**
         1    **square (1 ounce) unsweetened chocolate**
         ½    **teaspoon shortening**                    Oven 350°

Grease and lightly flour two 9x1½-inch round baking pans. Stir together flour, cocoa powder, baking soda, and salt. In a large mixer bowl beat the ½ cup shortening on medium speed of electric mixer about 30 seconds. Add the 1 cup sugar and vanilla and beat till fluffy. Add egg yolks, one at a time, beating on medium speed for 1 minute after each. Add dry ingredients and water alternately to beaten mixture, beating on low speed after each addition till just combined.

Thoroughly wash the beaters. In a small mixer bowl beat egg whites till soft peaks form; gradually add the ¾ cup sugar, beating till stiff peaks form. Fold egg white mixture into batter; combine well. Turn batter into prepared pans. Spread batter evenly. Bake in a 350° oven for 30 to 35 minutes or till cake tests done. Cool 10 minutes on wire racks. Remove from pans; cool thoroughly on racks. Fill and frost with Seafoam Frosting. Melt chocolate with the ½ teaspoon shortening to drizzle around edge of frosted cake. Makes 12 servings.

---

## Black Forest Cake

|       | Cherry filling |            |
|-------|----------------|------------|
| 1     | slightly beaten egg |       |
| 1⅔    | cups granulated sugar |     |
| 1½    | cups milk |                 |
| 3     | squares (3 ounces) unsweetened chocolate, cut up | |
| 1¾    | cups all-purpose flour |    |
| 1     | teaspoon baking soda |      |
| ½     | cup shortening |            |
| 1     | teaspoon vanilla |          |
| 2     | eggs |                      |
|       | Golden Butter Frosting | Oven 350° |

Prepare Cherry Filling. Grease and lightly flour two 9x1½-inch round baking pans. Combine beaten egg, ⅔ *cup* granulated sugar, ½ *cup* milk, and chocolate. Cook and stir till mixture just boils; cool. Combine flour, soda, and ½ teaspoon *salt*. Beat shortening 30 seconds. Add remaining 1 cup granulated sugar and vanilla; beat till fluffy. Add the 2 eggs, one at a time, beating 1 minute after each. Add dry ingredients and remaining 1 cup milk alternately to beaten mixture, beating after each addition. Stir in chocolate mixture. Turn into pans. Bake in a 350° oven for 25 to 30 minutes. Cool 10 minutes on racks. Remove from pans; cool.

To assemble, place 1 cake layer on a serving plate. Using *1 cup* Golden Butter Frosting, make a ½-inch border (1 inch high) around top of layer. Use ½ *cup* of the frosting to make a solid circle in center of cake, about 2½ inches in diameter and 1 inch high. Spread chilled Cherry Filling between border and circle. Place second cake layer on top. Frost top and sides with remaining frosting. If desired, garnish with maraschino cherries and chocolate curls. Chill. Let stand at room temperature 20 minutes before serving. Serves 12.

**Cherry Filling:** Drain one 16-ounce can pitted *dark sweet cherries,* reserving ½ cup syrup. Halve cherries and pour ⅓ cup *Kirsch or cherry liqueur* over, let stand 2 hours. Combine 4 teaspoons *cornstarch* and reserved cherry syrup; add cherry-Kirsch mixture. Cook and stir till bubbly. Cook and stir 2 minutes more. Cool; cover and chill.

**Golden Butter Frosting:** Beat 1 cup *butter* till fluffy. Beat in 2¼ cups sifted *powdered sugar* till smooth. Add 3 *egg yolks,* beating till mixture is fluffy. Add 2¼ cups sifted *powdered sugar,* beating till smooth.

---

# Feathery Fudge Cake

|   |   |
|---|---|
| **2** | **cups all-purpose flour** |
| **1¼** | **teaspoons baking soda** |
| **½** | **teaspoon salt** |
| **⅔** | **cup butter or margarine** |
| **1¾** | **cups sugar** |
| **1** | **teaspoon vanilla** |
| **2** | **eggs** |
| **3** | **squares (3 ounces) unsweetened chocolate, melted and cooled** |
| **1¼** | **cups cold water** |

Oven 350°

Grease and lightly flour two 9x1½-inch round baking pans. Combine the first 3 ingredients. In a mixer bowl beat butter on medium speed of electric mixer about 30 seconds. Add sugar and vanilla and beat till well combined. Add eggs, one at a time, beating 1 minute after each. Beat in cooled chocolate. Add dry ingredients and cold water alternately to beaten mixture, beating after each addition. Turn into pans. Bake in a 350° oven for 30 to 35 minutes or till done. Cool 10 minutes on wire racks. Remove from pans. Cool. Makes 12 servings.

## Sour Cream Chocolate Cake

1¾   cups all-purpose flour
1    teaspoon baking soda
½    teaspoon salt
½    cup shortening
1½   cups sugar
½    teaspoon vanilla
2    eggs
3    squares (3 ounces) unsweetened
        chocolate, melted and cooled
½    cup dairy sour cream
1    cup cold water                    Oven 350°

Grease and lightly flour two 8x1½-inch *or* 9x1½-inch round baking pans. Stir together flour, baking soda, and salt. In a mixer bowl beat shortening on medium speed of electric mixer about 30 seconds. Add sugar and vanilla and beat till well combined. Add eggs, one at a time, beating 1 minute after each. Stir in cooled chocolate and sour cream. Add dry ingredients and cold water alternately to beaten mixture, beating on low speed after each addition till just combined. Turn into pans. Bake in 350° oven for 30 to 35 minutes or till done. Cool 10 minutes on wire racks. Remove from pans. Cool. Make 12 servings.

# Light Fruitcake

|    |                                                      |
|----|------------------------------------------------------|
| 3  | cups all-purpose flour                               |
| 1  | teaspoon baking powder                               |
| 1  | cup butter *or* margarine                            |
| 1  | cup sugar                                            |
| 4  | eggs                                                 |
| ½  | cup orange juice*                                    |
| ¼  | cup light corn syrup                                 |
| 1  | teaspoon lemon extract                               |
| 12 | ounces whole red or green candied cherries (2 cups)  |
| 8  | ounces diced mixed candied fruits and peels (1¼ cups) |
| 1  | cup light raisins                                    |
| 1  | cup chopped candied pineapple                        |
| 1  | cup chopped walnuts                    Oven 300°     |

Thoroughly grease a 5½-cup ring mold and six 4½x2½x1½-inch individual loaf pans (*or*, use one 5½-cup ring mold and a 10x3½x2½-inch loaf pan). Stir together flour and baking powder. In a large mixer bowl beat butter or margarine with electric mixer about 30 seconds. Add sugar and beat till fluffy. Add eggs, one at a time, beating 1 minute after each. Combine orange juice, corn syrup, and lemon extract. Add dry ingredients and orange juice mixture alternately to beaten mixture, beating on low speed after each addition till just combined. Combine cherries, fruits and peels, raisins, pineapple, and nuts; fold into batter. Turn batter into prepared pans. (For small loaf pans use ¾ cup batter each.)

Bake in a 300° oven for 50 to 60 minutes (70 minutes for larger loaf pan) or till cakes test done. Place cakes in pans on wire racks; cool thoroughly. Remove from pans.

Wrap in wine- brandy-, or fruit juice-moistened cheesecloth. Overwrap with foil, clear plastic wrap, or place in an airtight container. Store at least 1 week in refrigerator. (Store 3 to 4 weeks for a blended and mellow flavor.) Remoisten cheesecloth as needed if cakes are stored longer than 1 week. Makes 36 servings.

**\*Note:** If desired, use ¼ cup orange juice and ¼ cup dry white wine instead of the ½ cup orange juice.

## Dark Fruitcake

|       |                                                       |
|-------|-------------------------------------------------------|
| 3     | cups all-purpose flour                                |
| 2     | teaspoons baking powder                               |
| 2     | teaspoons ground cinnamon                             |
| 1     | teaspoon salt                                         |
| ½     | teaspoon ground nutmeg                                |
| ½     | teaspoon ground allspice                              |
| ½     | teaspoon ground cloves                                |
| 16    | ounces diced mixed candied fruits and peels (2½ cups) |
| 1     | 15-ounce package (3 cups) raisins                     |
| 1     | 8-ounce package (1⅓ cups) pitted whole dates, snipped |
| 8     | ounces whole red or green candied cherries (1⅓ cups)  |
| 1     | cup slivered almonds                                  |
| 1     | cup pecan halves                                      |
| ½     | cup chopped candied pineapple                         |
| 4     | eggs                                                  |
| 1¾    | cups packed brown sugar                               |
| 1     | cup orange juice                                      |
| ¾     | cup butter or margarine, melted and cooled            |
| ¼     | cup light molasses                     Oven 300°      |

Grease three 8x4x2-inch loaf pans or two 10x3½x2½-inch loaf pans. Line bottom and sides of pans with brown paper (brown paper prevents overbrowning); grease paper. Stir together flour, baking powder, cinnamon, salt, nutmeg, allspice, and cloves. Add fruits and peels, raisins, dates, cherries, almonds, pecans, and pineapple; mix till well coated. Beat eggs till foamy. Add brown sugar, orange juice, butter or margarine, and molasses; beat till combined. Stir into fruit mixture. Turn batter into pans, filling each about ¾ full.

Bake in a 300° oven for 2 hours or till cakes test done. (Cover all pans loosely with foil after 1 hour of baking to prevent overbrowning.) Place cakes in pans on wire racks; cool thoroughly. Remove from pans.

Wrap in wine-, brandy-, or fruit juice-moistened cheese-cloth. Overwrap with foil. Store in refrigerator. (Store 3 to 4 weeks for a blended and mellow flavor.) Remoisten cheese-cloth as needed after 1 week. Makes 40 servings.

## Angel Cake

1½   cups sifted powdered sugar
1    cup sifted cake flour *or* sifted all-purpose flour
1½   cups egg whites (11 or 12 large)
1½   teaspoons cream of tartar
1    teaspoon vanilla
1    cup granulated sugar                    Oven 350°

Sift together powdered sugar and cake or all-purpose flour; repeat sifting twice. In a large mixer bowl beat egg whites, cream of tartar, vanilla, and ¼ teaspoon *salt* at medium speed of electric mixer till soft peaks form. Gradually add granulated sugar, about 2 tablespoons at a time. Continue beating till stiff peaks form. Sift about ¼ of the flour mixture over whites; fold in lightly by hand. If bowl is too full, transfer to a larger bowl. Repeat, folding in remaining flour mixture by fourths. Turn into an *ungreased* 10-inch tube pan. Bake on lowest rack in a 350° oven about 40 minutes or till done. Invert cake in pan; cool completely. Loosen cake from pan; remove. Serves 12.

## Golden Chiffon Cake

7    eggs
2¼   cups sifted cake flour *or* 2 cups all-purpose flour
1½   cups sugar
1    tablespoon baking powder
½    cup cooking oil
2    teaspoons grated lemon peel
1    teaspoon vanilla
½    teaspoon cream of tartar                Oven 325°

Separate egg yolks from whites. In a large mixer bowl sift together cake or all-purpose flour, sugar, baking powder, and

1 teaspoon *salt;* makes a well in the center. Add oil, egg yolks, peel, vanilla, and ¾ cup cold *water.* Beat at low speed of electric mixer till combined, then on high speed about 5 minutes or till satin smooth. Thoroughly wash beaters. In a large mixing bowl combine egg whites and cream of tartar; beat till stiff peaks form. Pour batter in a thin stream over surface of egg whites; fold in gently by hand. Pour into an *ungreased* 10-inch tube pan. Bake in a 325° oven 65 to 70 minutes. Invert; cool completely. Loosen cake from pan; remove. Serves 12.

## Orange Sponge Cake

| | |
|---|---|
| 1¼ | **cups all-purpose flour** |
| ⅓ | **cup sugar** |
| 6 | **egg yolks** |
| 1 | **tablespoon grated orange peel** |
| ½ | **cup orange juice** |
| ⅔ | **cup sugar** |
| 6 | **egg whites** |
| 1 | **teaspoon cream of tartar** |
| ½ | **cup sugar** |

Oven 325°

Combine flour and ⅓ cup sugar. In a small mixer bowl beat yolks at high speed of electric mixer 6 minutes or till thick. Combine orange peel and juice; add to yolks, beating at low speed till combined. Gradually add ⅔ cup sugar and ¼ teaspoon *salt,* beating at medium speed till sugar dissolves. Gradually add ¼ of the flour mixture to yolk mixture, beating at low speed till combined. Repeat with remaining flour, ¼ at a time, beating a total of 2 minutes. Thoroughly wash beaters. Combine egg whites and cream of tartar; beat at medium speed till soft peaks form. Gradually add the ½ cup sugar, beating till stiff peaks form. Stir *1 cup* of the whites into yolk mixture. By hand, fold yolk mixture into remaining whites. Turn into an *ungreased* 10-inch tube pan. Bake in a 325° oven about 60 minutes. Invert; cool. Remove from pan. Serves 12.

# Hot Milk Sponge Cake

1   **cup all-purpose flour**
1   **teaspoon baking powder**
2   **eggs**
1   **cup sugar**
½   **cup milk**
2   **tablespoons butter or margarine**
    **Broiled Coconut Topping (see recipe,**
      **page 197)**            Oven 350°

Grease a 9x9x2-inch baking pan. Combine flour, baking powder, and ¼ teaspoon *salt*. In a small mixer bowl beat eggs at
high speed 4 minutes or till thick. Gradually add sugar; beat at
medium speed 4 to 5 minutes or till sugar dissolves. Add dry
ingredients to egg mixture; stir just till combined. Heat milk
with butter till butter melts; stir into batter and mix well. Turn
into pan. Bake in a 350° oven for 20 to 25 minutes. Frost
while warm with Broiled Coconut Topping. Serve warm. Serves
9.

# Jelly Roll

½   **cup all-purpose flour**
1   **teaspoon baking powder**
¼   **teaspoon salt**
4   **egg yolks**
½   **teaspoon vanilla**
⅓   **cup granulated sugar**
4   **egg whites**
½   **cup granulated sugar**
    **Sifted powdered sugar**
½   **cup jelly or jam**            Oven 375°

Grease and lightly flour a 15x10x1-inch jelly roll pan. Stir
together flour, baking powder, and salt. In a small mixer bowl
beat egg yolks and vanilla at high speed of electric mixer 5
minutes or till thick and lemon colored. Gradually add the ⅓ cup
sugar, beating till sugar dissolves. Thoroughly wash beaters.

In a large mixer bowl beat egg whites at medium speed till soft peaks form. Gradually add the ½ cup sugar; continue beating till stiff peaks form. Fold yolk mixture into whites. Sprinkle flour mixture over egg mixture; fold in gently, just till combined. Spread batter evenly into prepared pan. Bake in a 375° oven for 12 to 15 minutes or till done. Immediately loosen edges of cake from pan and turn out onto a towel sprinkled with sifted powdered sugar. Starting with narrow end, roll warm cake and towel together; cool on a wire rack. (See tip box below.) Unroll; spread cake with jelly or jam to within 1 inch of edges. Roll up cake. Makes 10 servings.

**Note:** Jelly rolls can be made with a variety of fillings. Try pudding, pie filling, whipped cream (plain or with fruit folded in), or softened ice cream. Freeze ice-cream-filled jelly rolls; refrigerate others.

**Chocolate Cake Roll:** Prepare Jelly Roll as above, *except* sift ¼ cup unsweetened *cocoa powder* together with dry ingredients. Continue as directed. Whip 1 cup *whipping cream;* fill baked and cooled cake with cream. Roll. For chocolate glaze, combine ½ cup *granulated sugar,* 4 teaspoons *cornstarch,* and dash *salt.* Stir in ½ cup *water;* add 1 square (1 ounce) *unsweetened chocolate,* cut up. Cook and stir till thickened and bubbly and chocolate melts. Cook 2 minutes more. Remove from heat; stir in 2 tablespoons *butter or margarine* and ½ teaspoon *vanilla.* Frost rolled cake with hot glaze. Chill till serving time.

## **Jelly roll pointers**

Roll the cake while it's still warm to prevent tearing. Starting with the narrow end, roll the warm cake and the towel together, as shown. The towel prevents the cake from sticking together as it cools.

## Chocolate Marble Cake

| 1¾ | cups all-purpose flour |
| 2½ | teaspoons baking powder |
| ¼ | teaspoon salt |
| ½ | cup butter or margarine |
| 1 | cup sugar |
| 1 | teaspoon vanilla |
| 2 | eggs |
| ⅔ | cup milk |
| 1 | square (1 ounce) unsweetened chocolate, melted and cooled |
| ¼ | teaspoon baking soda |

Oven 350°

Grease and lightly flour a 9x5x3-inch loaf pan. Combine flour, baking powder, and salt. Beat butter about 30 seconds. Add sugar and vanilla and beat till fluffy. Add eggs, one at a time, beating 1 minute after each. Add dry ingredients and milk alternately to beaten mixture, beating after each addition. Combine cooled chocolate, baking soda, and 2 tablespoons *hot water*; stir into ⅓ of the batter. Spoon light and dark batters alternately into loaf pan. Zigzag a spatula through batter. Bake in a 350° oven for 45 to 50 minutes or till done. Cool 15 minutes on a wire rack. Remove from pan. Cool thoroughly. Serves 12.

## Poppy Seed Cake

| 1½ | cups all-purpose flour |
| 1½ | cups whole wheat flour |
| ⅓ | cup poppy seeds |
| 2½ | teaspoons baking soda |
| ¾ | cup butter or margarine |
| 1½ | cups honey |
| 1 | teaspoon vanilla |
| 4 | eggs |
| ½ | cup buttermilk or sour milk |
| 1 | small banana, mashed (⅓ cup) |
| ½ | cup raisins |

Oven 350°

Grease and lightly flour a 10-inch fluted tube pan. Combine the first 4 ingredients and ½ teaspoon *salt*. Beat butter about 30 seconds. Add honey and vanilla; beat till fluffy. Add eggs, one at a time, beating 1 minute after each. Combine buttermilk or sour milk and banana. Add dry ingredients and buttermilk mixture alternately to beaten mixture, beating after each addition. Stir in raisins. Turn into pan; spread batter evenly. Bake in a 350° oven for 50 to 55 minutes or till done. Cool 15 minutes on a wire rack. Invert onto a wire rack; remove pan. Cool thoroughly. Serves 12.

## Butterscotch Marble Cake

|       |                                                       |
| ----- | ----------------------------------------------------- |
| 1     | **package 2-layer-size white cake mix**               |
| 1     | **4-serving-size package *instant* butterscotch pudding mix** |
| ¼     | **cup cooking oil**                                   |
| 4     | **eggs**                                              |
| ½     | **cup chocolate-flavored syrup**                      |
| ½     | **recipe Chocolate Icing (see recipe, page 199)**     |

Oven 350°

Grease and lightly flour a 10-inch fluted tube pan. In a large mixer bowl combine cake mix, pudding mix, oil, eggs, and 1 cup *water*. Beat at low speed of electric mixer till combined, then at medium speed for 2 minutes. Reserve 1½ cups batter. Turn remaining batter into pan. Stir together reserved batter and the chocolate syrup. Pour chocolate mixture atop butterscotch batter. Swirl with a metal spatula or spoon to marble. Bake in a 350° oven about 60 minutes or till done. Cool 15 minutes on a wire rack. Invert onto rack; remove pan. Cool. Glaze with Chocolate Icing. Serves 12.

## Italian Cream Cake

| | |
|---|---|
| 1½ | cups all-purpose flour |
| 1½ | teaspoons baking powder |
| ¼ | teaspoon salt |
| 3 | eggs |
| 1½ | cups granulated sugar |
| ¾ | cup milk |
| 1 | tablespoon butter *or* margarine |
| ¾ | cup granulated sugar |
| 3 | tablespoons cornstarch |
| ¾ | cup milk |
| 1 | 15-ounce container (2 cups) ricotta cheese |
| 1½ | teaspoons vanilla |
| ½ | cup semisweet chocolate pieces, coarsely chopped |
| 2 | tablespoons candied citron or candied fruits and peels, finely chopped |
| 2 | tablespoons pistachio nuts, ground |
| | Green food coloring (optional) |
| | Creamy White Frosting (see recipe, page 193) |

Oven 350°

Line two 9x1½-inch round baking pans with foil. Combine flour, baking powder, and salt. In a large mixer bowl beat eggs on high speed of electric mixer 4 minutes or till thick and lemon colored. Gradually add the 1½ cups sugar and beat 4 minutes. Add dry ingredients to egg mixture, beating on low speed just till combined. Heat the ¾ cup milk and butter just till butter melts. Add milk mixture, beating on low speed till combined. Pour into pans. Bake in a 350° oven for 25 to 30 minutes. Cool completely; remove from pans. Cut layers in half horizontally for a total of 4 layers.

For filling, combine the ¾ cup sugar and cornstarch in a saucepan; slowly stir in ¾ cup milk. Cook and stir till thickened and bubbly. Cover surface with waxed paper; cool without stirring. Beat ricotta cheese on medium speed of electric mixer till creamy; beat in cornstarch mixture and vanilla. Stir in chocolate pieces and candied fruit. Spread filling on 3 of the cake layers; stack. Top with remaining cake layer.

If desired, tint pistachio nuts with a few drops green food

coloring; set aside. Frost sides and top of cake with Creamy White Frosting. Sprinkle tinted pistachio nuts around edge of cake. Chill several hours or overnight before serving. Makes 16 servings.

# Frostings

### How to frost and cut cakes the professional way

Cool cake before frosting. Use a pastry brush or your hand to brush loose crumbs from sides of each layer. To keep serving plate clean, arrange strips of waxed paper around edge of plate, as shown. Place cake layer, top side down, on plate. Spread about ¼ of the frosting over the first layer. Place second layer, top side up, over frosted layer.

Spread sides of cake with a thin coat of frosting to seal in crumbs. Use about ⅔ of the remaining frosting to spread a thicker layer over the sides, making decorative swirls, as shown. Spread remaining frosting atop cake, joining frosted sides at edge. Swirl frosting with a spatula. Carefully remove waxed paper strips from under cake.

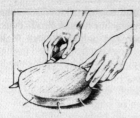

To split a cake layer, insert wooden picks halfway up the sides of each cake layer for a cutting guide, as shown. Slice layer in half horizontally with a sharp, long-bladed knife. Spread a filling or frosting between layers. When frosting three or more layers, position the first two layers as directed at left. Always place top layer with top side up.

Use a sharp, thin-bladed knife to cut a frosted cake into wedges. Insert the point of the knife into center of cake. Hold the knife at an angle with the point down. Slice with an up-and-down motion, pulling the knife toward you.

When cutting cakes with fluffy frosting, dip the knife into hot water before cutting the cake to prevent the frosting from sticking. Clean frosting and crumbs from the knife by occasionally wiping with a damp cloth.

When cutting a foam-type cake, use a cake breaker, a knife with a serrated blade, or an electric knife. To use a cake breaker, press the prongs gently through the cake and turn the handle away from the slice until the cake separates. When using a knife for cutting the cake, cut with a gentle back-and-forth motion.

For tube cakes, place the cake top side down on a serving plate to make frosting and cutting easier.

## Creamy White Frosting

- **1** **cup shortening**
- **1½** **teaspoons vanilla**
- **½** **teaspoon lemon extract**
- **4½** **to 4¾ cups sifted powdered sugar**
- **3** **to 4 tablespoons milk**

Beat shortening, vanilla, and lemon extract on medium speed of electric mixer for 30 seconds. Gradually add about *half* of the powdered sugar, beating well. Add *2 tablespoons* of the milk. Gradually beat in remaining powdered sugar and enough milk to make of spreading consistency (1 to 2 tablespoons). Frosts tops and sides of two 8- or 9-inch layers.

**Note:** Add additional powdered sugar to make of stiffer consistency for decorative flowers or borders.

*Peppermint Frosting:* Prepare Creamy White Frosting as above, *except* use ¼ teaspoon *peppermint extract* instead of the ½ teaspoon lemon extract.

## Seven-Minute Frosting

> 1½  **cups granulated sugar**
> ⅓  **cup cold water**
> 2  **egg whites**
> 2  **teaspoons light corn syrup or ¼ teaspoon cream of tartar**
> 1  **teaspoon vanilla**

In the top of a double boiler combine sugar, cold water, egg whites, corn syrup or cream of tartar, and dash *salt*. Beat 30 seconds on low speed of electric mixer. Place over boiling water (upper pan should not touch water). Cook about 7 minutes while beating constantly on high speed of electric mixer or till frosting forms stiff peaks. Remove from heat; add vanilla. Beat 2 to 3 minutes or till of spreading consistency. Frosts tops and sides of two 8- or 9-inch layers or one 10-inch tube cake.

*Peppermint-Stick Frosting:* Prepare Seven-Minute Frosting as above, *except* use ¼ teaspoon *peppermint extract* instead of vanilla. Garnish cake with crushed *peppermint-stick candy.*

*Seafoam Frosting:* Prepare Seven-Minute Frosting as above, *except* use 1¼ cups packed *brown sugar* instead of the granulated sugar, and ¼ cup *cold water* instead of the ⅓ cup cold water.

## Butter Frosting

     **6   tablespoons butter**
 **4½   to 4¾ cups sifted powdered sugar**
   **¼   cup milk**
 **1½   teaspoons vanilla**

In a small mixer bowl beat butter till light and fluffy. Gradually add about *half* of the powdered sugar, beating well. Beat in the milk and the vanilla. Gradually beat in remaining powdered sugar, then additional milk, if necessary, to make frosting of spreading consistency. Frosts tops and sides of two 8- or 9-inch layers.

**Creamy Butter Frosting:** Prepare Butter Frosting as above, *except* beat in 1 egg instead of the ¼ cup milk. After adding remaining powdered sugar, beat in enough milk, if necessary, to make frosting of spreading consistency. Cover; store in refrigerator.

**Chocolate Butter Frosting:** Prepare Butter Frosting as above, *except* add 2 squares (2 ounces) *unsweetened chocolate,* melted and cooled, with the vanilla.

**Mocha Butter Frosting:** Prepare Butter Frosting as above, *except* add ¼ cup unsweetened *cocoa powder* and 1 teaspoon instant *coffee crystals* to the butter; continue as directed, adding additional milk, if necessary, to make frosting of spreading consistency.

**Orange or Lemon Butter Frosting:** Prepare Butter Frosting as above, *except* add 1 teaspoon finely shredded *orange peel* or ½ teaspoon finely shredded *lemon peel* with vanilla. Use *orange juice or lemon juice* instead of milk.

**Peanut Butter Frosting:** Prepare Butter Frosting as above, *except* use smooth or crunchy *peanut butter* instead of the butter, and add additional milk, if necessary, to make frosting of spreading consistency.

## Powdered Sugar Icing

     **1   cup sifted powdered sugar**
   **¼   teaspoon vanilla**
        **Milk**

In a mixing bowl stir together powdered sugar, vanilla, and enough milk to make of drizzling consistency (about 1½ tablespoons). Drizzle over top of a 10-inch tube cake.

## Fluffy White Frosting

> 1 **cup sugar**
> ¼ **teaspoon cream of tartar**
> 2 **egg whites**
> 1 **teaspoon vanilla**

In a saucepan combine sugar, cream of tartar, ⅓ cup *water,* and dash *salt.* Cook and stir till bubbly and sugar dissolves. In a mixer bowl combine egg whites and vanilla. Add sugar syrup very slowly to unbeaten egg whites while beating constantly at high speed of electric mixer about 7 minutes or till stiff peaks form. Frosts tops and sides of two 8- or 9-inch layers or one 10-inch tube cake.

## Petits Fours Icing

> 3 **cups granulated sugar**
> 1½ **cups hot water**
> ¼ **teaspoon cream of tartar**
> 1 **teaspoon vanilla**
> **Sifted powdered sugar**

In a 2-quart saucepan combine granulated sugar, hot water, and cream of tartar. Cover and cook till boiling. Uncover; clip candy thermometer to saucepan. Cook till temperature of mixture is 226° on candy thermometer. Remove from heat. Cool at room temperature to 110°. Stir in vanilla. Stir in enough sifted powder sugar (about 2½ cups) to make of pouring consistency. Tint with food coloring, if desired. Spoon over cake pieces. Frosts about 36 petits fours.

## Cream Cheese Frosting

> 1 **3-ounce package cream cheese**
> ¼ **cup butter or margarine**
> 1 **teaspoon vanilla**
> 2 **cups sifted powdered sugar**

In a mixer bowl beat together cream cheese, butter or margarine, and vanilla till light and fluffy. Gradually add powdered sugar, beating till smooth. Spread over cooled cake; sprinkle with chopped nuts, if desired. Frosts tops of two 8- or 9-inch layers. Cover; store in the refrigerator.

## Coconut-Pecan Frosting

> 1 **egg**
> 1 **5⅓-ounce can (⅔ cup) evaporated milk**
> ⅔ **cup sugar**
> ¼ **cup butter or margarine**
> **Dash salt**
> 1⅓ **cups flaked coconut**
> ½ **cup chopped pecans**

In a saucepan beat egg slightly. Stir in milk, sugar, butter or margarine, and salt. Cook and stir over medium heat about 12 minutes or till thickened and bubbly. Stir in coconut and pecans. Cool thoroughly. Spread on cake. Frosts top of one 13x9-inch cake or tops of two 8- or 9-inch layers.

## Broiled Coconut Topping

> ½ **cup packed brown sugar**
> 3 **tablespoons butter or margarine, softened**
> 2 **tablespoons milk**
> 1 **cup flaked coconut**

In a mixer bowl beat brown sugar and butter or margarine till fluffy. Stir in milk. Stir in coconut; spread over warm cake in pan. Broil 4 inches from heat 3 to 4 minutes or till golden. Serve warm. Frosts top of a 9x9-inch cake. (Double recipe for top of one 13x9-inch cake.)

## Penuche Frosting

  ½  **cup butter or margarine**
  1  **cup packed brown sugar**
  ¼  **cup milk**
  3  **cups sifted powdered sugar**

In a medium saucepan melt butter or margarine; stir in brown sugar. Cook and stir till bubbly. Remove from heat. Add milk; beat vigorously till smooth. By hand, beat in enough of the powdered sugar to make of spreading consistency. Quickly frost the top of one 13x9-inch cake or tops of two 8- or 9-inch layers.

## Rocky-Road Frosting

  1  **cup tiny marshmallows**
  2  **squares (2 ounces) unsweetened**
      **chocolate, cut up**
  ¼  **cup butter or margarine**
  2  **to 2¼ cups sifted powdered sugar**
  1  **teaspoon vanilla**
  1  **cup tiny marshmallows**
  ½  **cup coarsely chopped walnuts**

In a saucepan combine 1 cup marshmallows, chocolate, butter, and ¼ cup *water*. Cook and stir over low heat till marshmallows and chocolate are melted. Cool slightly. Add 2 cups powdered sugar and vanilla; beat by hand about 2 minutes or till smooth and of spreading consistency. If necessary add additional powdered sugar. Stir in 1 cup marshmallows and walnuts. Frosts top of a 13x9-inch cake.

## Chocolate Sour Cream Frosting

*Frosting becomes stiffer when refrigerated—*
 1   **6-ounce package (1 cup) semisweet chocolate pieces**
 ¼   **cup butter *or* margarine**
 ½   **cup dairy sour cream**
 1   **teaspoon vanilla**
 2½   **cups sifted powdered sugar**

In a saucepan melt chocolate and butter over low heat, stirring frequently. Cool about 10 minutes. Stir in sour cream, vanilla, and ¼ teaspoon *salt*. Gradually add powdered sugar, beating by hand till smooth and of spreading consistency. Frosts two 8- or 9-inch layers. Store in refrigerator.

## Chocolate Icing

 1   **4-ounce package German sweet chocolate, broken up**
 3   **tablespoons butter *or* margarine**
 1½   **cups sifted powdered sugar**

In a small saucepan melt together the chocolate and butter over low heat. Remove from heat; stir in powdered sugar and 3 tablespoons *hot water*. Add more hot water, if needed, to make of pouring consistency. Spoon over cake. Glazes top of a 10-inch tube cake.

## Fudge Frosting

 3   **cups sugar**
 3   **tablespoons light corn syrup**
 2   **squares (2 ounces) unsweetened chocolate, cut up**
 ¼   **teaspoon salt**
 1   **cup milk**
 ¼   **cup butter *or* margarine**
 1   **teaspoon vanilla**

Butter sides of a heavy 3-quart saucepan. In it combine sugar, corn syrup, chocolate, and salt; stir in milk. Cook and stir over medium heat till all the sugar dissolves and the chocolate melts. (Avoid splashing the sides of pan with chocolate mixture.) Clip a candy thermometer to side of pan. Continue cooking over medium heat till thermometer registers 234° (soft-ball stage), stirring only as necessary to prevent sticking. (The chocolate mixture should boil gently over entire surface.) Watch closely; the temperature rises quickly above 220°. If you do not have a candy thermometer, use the cold water test, referring to the Candy chapter, page 207.

Remove saucepan from heat; add butter or margarine. Don't stir in the butter; simply place it on top of the mixture and let the heat melt it. Let mixture cool, without stirring, till candy thermometer registers 110°. (At this temperature, the bottom of the pan should feel comfortably warm.)

Add vanilla. Using a spoon, beat the mixture vigorously with an up-and-over motion for 5 to 6 minutes or till mixture is of spreading consistency. This is the critical step in making fudge frosting. Be sure to check the consistency frequently so that the frosting doesn't become too stiff. Pour and spread *immediately* atop a 13x9-inch cake. The frosting will be smooth and satiny, but will soon become too stiff to spread. Work quickly, using a small, metal spatula to spread frosting. To smooth small areas that set up too fast, dip the spatula in warm water and then smooth over these areas. Frosts top of a 13x9-inch cake.

**Note:** If frosting is overbeaten, it can be used as fudge candy.

**Candy**

**Candy**

**Candy**

**Candy**

**Candy**

**Candy**

**Candy**

**Candy**

# Candy

**Percent of U.S. RDA Per Serving** (columns: Protein, Vitamin A, Vitamin C, Thiamine, Riboflavin, Niacin, Calcium, Iron)

| Recipes | Servings (fraction of recipe) | Calories | Carbohydrate (grams) | Protein (grams) | Fat (grams) | Sodium (milligrams) | Potassium (milligrams) | Protein | Vitamin A | Vitamin C | Thiamine | Riboflavin | Niacin | Calcium | Iron |
|---|---|---|---|---|---|---|---|---|---|---|---|---|---|---|---|
| Almond Opera Fudge | 1/32 | 74 | 14 | 1 | 2 | 12 | 23 | 1 | 1 | 0 | 0 | 2 | 0 | 1 | 1 |
| Brown Sugar Nut Brittle | 1/72 | 64 | 10 | 1 | 3 | 50 | 39 | 2 | 1 | 0 | 1 | 0 | 3 | 1 | 2 |
| Caramel Apples | 1/14 | 427 | 84 | 3 | 10 | 149 | 347 | 5 | 10 | 8 | 8 | 10 | 1 | 15 | 13 |
| Caramel Corn | 1/8 | 199 | 30 | 1 | 9 | 218 | 89 | 1 | 7 | 0 | 0 | 2 | 1 | 2 | 7 |
| Caramels | 1/80 | 77 | 13 | 1 | 3 | 40 | 43 | 1 | 2 | 0 | 0 | 1 | 1 | 3 | 1 |
| Carob Candy Squares | 1/24 | 103 | 16 | 3 | 4 | 35 | 135 | 4 | 1 | 0 | 2 | 1 | 4 | 2 | 3 |
| Cherry Divinity | 1/36 | 78 | 20 | 0 | 0 | 21 | 9 | 0 | 0 | 1 | 0 | 0 | 0 | 0 | 1 |
| Cherry Opera Fudge | 1/32 | 70 | 15 | 0 | 1 | 9 | 14 | 0 | 1 | 0 | 0 | 1 | 1 | 1 | 0 |
| Chocolate Caramels | 1/80 | 80 | 13 | 1 | 3 | 40 | 49 | 1 | 2 | 0 | 0 | 2 | 0 | 3 | 2 |
| Chocolate-Covered Cherries | 1/60 | 89 | 13 | 1 | 4 | 27 | 44 | 1 | 1 | 0 | 0 | 1 | 2 | 3 | 2 |
| Chocolate Nut Balls | 1/30 | 72 | 7 | 1 | 5 | 22 | 42 | 2 | 1 | 0 | 1 | 1 | 4 | 0 | 2 |
| Choco-Scotch Crunchies | 1/36 | 83 | 9 | 2 | 5 | 49 | 54 | 3 | 0 | 0 | 1 | 1 | 4 | 1 | 2 |
| Cream Cheese Mints (molded) | 1/72 | 20 | 4 | 0 | 0 | 3 | 1 | 0 | 0 | 0 | 0 | 0 | 0 | 0 | 0 |
| Cream Cheese Mints (patties) | 1/48 | 31 | 6 | 0 | 1 | 4 | 2 | 0 | 1 | 0 | 0 | 0 | 0 | 0 | 0 |
| Divinity | 1/36 | 68 | 17 | 0 | 0 | 21 | 3 | 0 | 0 | 0 | 0 | 0 | 0 | 0 | 1 |
| Easy Fudge | 1/48 | 70 | 11 | 0 | 3 | 29 | 39 | 1 | 2 | 0 | 0 | 1 | 0 | 2 | 1 |
| Easy Walnut Penuche | 1/48 | 67 | 10 | 0 | 3 | 20 | 29 | 1 | 1 | 0 | 0 | 0 | 3 | 1 | 1 |
| Fondant | 1/24 | 69 | 18 | 0 | 0 | 1 | 1 | 0 | 0 | 0 | 0 | 0 | 0 | 0 | 0 |
| Fondant Mint Patties | 1/36 | 49 | 12 | 0 | 0 | 5 | 0 | 0 | 0 | 0 | 0 | 0 | 3 | 0 | 0 |
| Glazed Nuts | 1/12 | 155 | 12 | 3 | 12 | 113 | 138 | 5 | 2 | 0 | 3 | 10 | 3 | 4 | 5 |

# Nutrition Analysis Chart

| | | | | | | | | | | | | | | | |
|---|---|---|---|---|---|---|---|---|---|---|---|---|---|---|---|
| Nut Brittle | 1/72 | 64 | 1 | 10 | 3 | 49 | 29 | 2 | 1 | 0 | 1 | 0 | 3 | 1 | 2 |
| Old-Fashioned Molasses Taffy | 1/48 | 70 | 0 | 14 | 2 | 27 | 74 | 0 | 2 | 0 | 0 | 0 | 0 | 2 | 3 |
| Old-Time Fudge | 1/40 | 64 | 1 | 11 | 2 | 10 | 26 | 1 | 1 | 0 | 1 | 1 | 0 | 1 | 1 |
| Old-Time Popcorn Balls | 1/13 | 190 | 1 | 47 | 0 | 91 | 25 | 2 | 0 | 0 | 2 | 1 | 1 | 1 | 5 |
| Opera Fudge | 1/32 | 64 | 0 | 13 | 1 | 8 | 11 | 0 | 0 | 0 | 1 | 0 | 1 | 1 | 0 |
| Peanut Caramel Apples | 1/14 | 487 | 6 | 86 | 15 | 150 | 419 | 9 | 10 | 8 | 7 | 11 | 10 | 15 | 14 |
| Penuche | 1/48 | 58 | 0 | 11 | 2 | 9 | 28 | 0 | 1 | 0 | 1 | 0 | 0 | 1 | 1 |
| Peppermint Bonbons | 1/42 | 54 | 0 | 9 | 2 | 24 | 17 | 1 | 1 | 0 | 0 | 1 | 0 | 1 | 0 |
| Remarkable Fudge | 1/112 | 70 | 1 | 10 | 4 | 24 | 24 | 1 | 2 | 0 | 1 | 1 | 0 | 2 | 1 |
| Rocky Road | 1/48 | 70 | 1 | 8 | 4 | 10 | 45 | 2 | 1 | 0 | 2 | 0 | 0 | 2 | 2 |
| Saltwater Taffy | 1/48 | 56 | 0 | 13 | 0 | 77 | 1 | 0 | 0 | 0 | 0 | 0 | 0 | 0 | 2 |
| Sea Foam Candy | 1/54 | 43 | 0 | 9 | 1 | 5 | 35 | 0 | 0 | 0 | 0 | 0 | 0 | 1 | 2 |
| Southern Pralines | 1/30 | 156 | 1 | 22 | 8 | 21 | 92 | 1 | 2 | 0 | 4 | 1 | 0 | 2 | 3 |
| Sugared Popcorn | 1/6 | 143 | 1 | 19 | 7 | 0 | 32 | 2 | 0 | 3 | 1 | 1 | 0 | 0 | 2 |
| Toffee Butter Crunch | 1/48 | 81 | 0 | 6 | 7 | 47 | 25 | 1 | 3 | 0 | 1 | 0 | 0 | 1 | 1 |
| Walnut Divinity | 1/36 | 78 | 0 | 18 | 1 | 21 | 11 | 1 | 0 | 0 | 0 | 0 | 0 | 0 | 1 |

# Candy

The secret of making good candy is to follow recipe directions exactly. And the secret of keeping candy at its best is to store it properly.

Fudge and fondant will stay fresh and creamy for several weeks if tightly wrapped in waxed paper, foil, or clear plastic wrap. Store the wrapped candy in an airtight container in a cool, dry place.

Taffy and caramels should be individually wrapped to keep out moisture and prevent them from sticking together. Store wrapped candy in an airtight container in a cool, dry place. Brittles also should be protected from dampness by storing them in an airtight container.

Keep chocolate-dipped candies in bonbon cups and store them in a cool, dry place.

Divinity is not a good keeper, since it dries out quickly. So, eat it while it's fresh.

Popcorn balls will freeze well. Wrap each popcorn ball separately in clear plastic wrap, then freeze in moisture-vaporproof material till ready to use.

## Old-Time Fudge

    2  cups sugar
   ¾  cup milk
    2  squares (2 ounces) unsweetened
          chocolate, cut up
    1  teaspoon light corn syrup
    2  tablespoons butter *or* margarine
    1  teaspoon vanilla
   ½  cup coarsely chopped nuts

Butter the sides of a heavy 2-quart saucepan. In it combine sugar, milk, chocolate, corn syrup, and dash *salt*. Cook and stir over medium heat till sugar dissolves and mixture comes to boiling. Continue cooking to 234° (soft-ball stage), stirring only as necessary to prevent sticking (mixture should boil gently over entire surface). Immediately remove from heat; add butter or margarine but *do not stir*. Cool, without stirring, to lukewarm (110°), for 35 to 40 minutes. Add vanilla and nuts. Beat vigorously for 7 to 10 minutes or till fudge becomes very thick and just loses its gloss. Immediately spread in a buttered 9x5x3-inch loaf pan. Score into squares while warm; cut when firm. Makes about 1¼ pounds.

## Remarkable Fudge

- **4 cups sugar**
- **2 5⅓-ounce cans evaporated milk**
- **1 cup butter or margarine**
- **1 12-ounce package (2 cups) semisweet chocolate pieces**
- **1 7-ounce jar marshmallow creme**
- **1 cup chopped walnuts**
- **1 teaspoon vanilla**

Butter the sides of a heavy 3-quart saucepan. In it combine sugar, evaporated milk, and butter or margarine. Cook and stir over medium heat till mixture comes to boiling. Cook to 236° (soft-ball stage), about 12 minutes, stirring frequently (mixture should boil gently over entire surface). Remove from heat. Add remaining ingredients; stir till combined and chocolate is melted. Turn into a buttered 9x9x2-inch or 13x9x2-inch pan. Score into squares while warm; cut when firm. If fudge is soft, chill. Makes about 3½ pounds.

## Opera Fudge

- **2 cups sugar**
- **½ cup milk**
- **½ cup light cream**
- **1 tablespoon light corn syrup**
- **1 tablespoon butter *or* margarine**
- **1 teaspoon vanilla**

Butter the sides of a heavy 2-quart saucepan. In it combine sugar, milk, cream, corn syrup, and ½ teaspoon *salt*. Cook and stir over medium heat till mixture boils. Cook to 238° (soft-ball stage), stirring only to prevent sticking (mixture should boil gently over entire surface). Remove from heat. Add butter or margarine and vanilla but *do not stir.* Cool, without stirring, to lukewarm (110°). Beat vigorously about 10 minutes or till mixture becomes very thick, starts to lose its gloss, and becomes creamier. Spread in a buttered 8x4x2-inch loaf pan. Score while warm; cut when firm. Makes about 1 pound.

*Cherry Opera Fudge:* Prepare Opera Fudge as above, *except* stir in ¼ cup chopped candied *cherries* before spreading into pan.

*Almond Opera Fudge:* Prepare Opera Fudge as above, except add ¼ teaspoon *almond extract* with vanilla; stir in ⅓ cup chopped toasted *almonds* before spreading into pan.

## Penuche

| | |
|---|---|
| 1½ | **cups granulated sugar** |
| 1 | **cup packed brown sugar** |
| ⅓ | **cup light cream** |
| ⅓ | **cup milk** |
| 2 | **tablespoons butter *or* margarine** |
| 1 | **teaspoon vanilla** |
| ½ | **cup chopped pecans *or* walnuts** |

Butter the sides of a heavy 2-quart saucepan. In it combine granulated sugar, brown sugar, cream, milk, and butter or margarine. Cook over medium heat, stirring constantly, till sugars dissolve and mixture comes to boiling. Continue cooking to 236° (soft-ball stage), stirring only as necessary to prevent sticking (mixture should boil gently over entire surface). Immediately remove from heat; cool, without stirring, to lukewarm (110°). Add vanilla. Beat vigorously about 10 minutes or till mixture becomes very thick and starts to lose its gloss. Quickly stir in nuts. Immediately turn into a buttered 8x4x2-inch or 9x5x3-inch loaf pan. Score into squares while warm; cut when firm. Makes about 1½ pounds.

# Candy testing

Using a candy thermometer is the best way to ensure success in candy making. Use this test to check the accuracy of the thermometer each time you use it. Place the thermometer in boiling water. If it registers either below or above 212°F., add or subtract the same number of degrees from the recipe temperature and cook to that temperature. For an accurate reading, make sure the thermometer bulb is completely covered with liquid, not just foam, and see that it doesn't touch the pan bottom.

Use the *cold water test* if a thermometer is not available. Remove the pan of candy from heat. Immediately drop a few drops of the syrup into a cup of very cold (but not icy) water. Use fresh water and a clean spoon for each test. Form the drops into a ball with your fingers. The firmness of the ball indicates the syrup's temperature. Retest every 2 to 3 minutes till the desired stage is reached.

| Stage | Cold Water Test |
| --- | --- |
| Thread (230°-234°) | Candy syrup that is dropped from a spoon spins a 2-inch thread. |
| Soft-ball (234°-240°) | Candy syrup can be shaped into a ball that flattens when it is removed from water. |
| Firm-ball (244°-248°) | Candy syrup can be shaped into a firm ball that does not flatten when removed from water. |
| Hard-ball (250°-266°) | Candy syrup forms a hard. but pliiable ball. |
| Soft-crack (270°-290°) | Candy syrup separates into threads that are not hard or brittle. |
| Hard-crack (300°-310°) | Candy syrup separates into brittle threads. |

## Southern Pralines

1½   **cups granulated sugar**
1½   **cups packed brown sugar**
1    **cup light cream**
3    **tablespoons butter or margarine**
2    **cups pecan halves**

In a heavy 3-quart saucepan stir together granulated sugar, brown sugar, and cream. Bring to boiling over medium heat, stirring constantly. Cook to 234° (soft-ball stage), for 20 to 25 minutes, stirring only as necessary to prevent sticking. Remove from heat; add butter or margarine but *do not stir*. Let mixture stand with thermometer in pan. Cool, without stirring, to 150°, about 30 minutes. Quickly stir in pecans. Beat candy for 2 to 3 minutes or till slightly thickened and glossy. Drop candy from a tablespoon onto a baking sheet lined with waxed paper. If candy becomes too stiff to drop easily from a spoon, add a few drops hot water and stir. Makes about 30 pralines.

## Fondant

*Storing the fondant overnight makes the candy smooth and creamy—*

2    **cups sugar**
1½   **cups water**
2    **tablespoons light corn syrup or ⅛ teaspoon
       cream of tartar**

Butter the sides of a heavy 1½-quart saucepan. In it combine sugar, the water, and corn syrup or cream of tartar. Cook and stir over medium heat till sugar dissolves and mixture comes to boiling. Cover and cook for 30 to 45 seconds. Uncover, cook to 240° (soft-ball stage), for 20 to 25 minutes, without stirring (mixture should boil gently over entire surface).

Immediately pour mixture onto a platter. *Do not scrape pan.* Cool for 45 to 50 minutes or till candy feels only slightly warm to the touch; do not stir candy.

Using a spatula or a wooden spoon, scrape candy from

edge of platter toward the center, the beat vigorously for 5 to 6 minutes or till fondant is creamy and stiff. Knead fondant with fingers about 2 minutes or till smooth and free of lumps. Form into a ball. Wrap fondant in clear plastic wrap; let ripen for 24 hours at room temperature. (Ripening is necessary for smooth and creamy fondant.)

Make Fondant Mint Patties or stuff pitted dates, prunes, or figs with fondant. Roll stuffed fruit in sifted powdered sugar, if desired. *Or,* dip molded fondant into melted chocolate (see tip box, page 211). Makes about ¾ pound fondant.

***Fondant Mint Patties:*** Heat and stir ripened fondant in the top of a double boiler over hot, not boiling, water just till melted and smooth. Remove double boiler from heat but leave fondant over the hot water. Stir in 1 tablespoon softened *butter or margarine,* a few drops *oil of peppermint or oil of cinnamon,* and a few drops *food coloring,* if desired. Drop mixture from a spoon onto waxed paper, swirling tops. (If necessary, mint patties can be reheated and dropped again.) Makes about 3 dozen.

## Divinity

    2½  **cups sugar**
     ½  **cup light corn syrup**
     2  **egg whites**
     1  **teaspoon vanilla**

In a heavy 2-quart saucepan combine sugar, corn syrup, ½ cup *water,* and ¼ teaspoon *salt.* Cook and stir till sugar dissolves and mixture boils. Cook over medium heat to 260° (hard-ball stage), without stirring (mixture should boil gently over entire surface). As temperature nears 250°, beat egg whites to stiff peaks. Gradually pour hot syrup in a thin stream over egg whites, beating constantly at high speed of electric mixer. Add vanilla; beat 4 to 5 minutes more or till mixture holds its shape. Drop from a teaspoon onto waxed paper. (*Or,* spread in a butter 10x6x2-inch dish. Cool; cut into squares.) Makes about 3 dozen pieces.

***Cherry Divinity:*** Prepare Divinity as above, *except* stir in

½ cup chopped *candied cherries* after the 4 to 5 minutes of beating.

**Walnut Divinity:** Prepare Divinity as above, *except* stir in ½ cup coarsely chopped *walnuts* after the 4 to 5 minutes of beating.

## Sea Foam Candy

|     |                                    |           |
| --- | ---------------------------------- | --------- |
| 2   | cups packed dark brown sugar       |           |
| ¼   | cup dark corn syrup                |           |
| 2   | egg whites                         |           |
| 1   | teaspoon vanilla                   |           |
| ½   | cup chopped walnuts                | Oven 300° |

In a buttered heavy 2-quart saucepan combine sugar, corn syrup, and ¼ cup *water*. Cook and stir till sugar dissolves and mixture comes to boiling. Cook over medium heat to 260° (hard-ball stage), without stirring. Remove from heat. In a large mixer bowl beat egg whites with electric mixer to stiff peaks. Gradually pour the hot syrup in a thin stream over beaten egg whites, beating constantly at high speed for 6 minutes. Add vanilla; beat 10 minutes more or till mixture forms soft peaks and begins to lose its gloss. Stir in nuts. Let stand 2 minutes. Drop by level teaspoonfuls onto a buttered baking sheet. Bake in a 300° oven for 20 minutes. Makes 4½ dozen.

## Chocolate-Covered Cherries

|      |                                              |
| ---- | -------------------------------------------- |
| 60   | maraschino cherries with stems               |
| 3    | tablespoons butter or margarine, softened    |
| 3    | tablespoons light corn syrup                 |
| ¼    | teaspoon salt                                |
| 2    | cups sifted powdered sugar                   |
| 1½   | pounds candy-making milk chocolate, cut up   |

# Dipping chocolates

Dip caramels, nuts, candied fruits, or fondant into melted chocolate for a luscious treat. (Mold fondant centers a day or two in advance so they won't leak through chocolate.)

Use at least 1 pound of candy-making milk chocolate *or* confectioners' coating for dipping, finely chopped. Place water in the bottom of a double boiler so that it comes to within ½ inch of the bottom of the smaller pan; bring to boiling. Remove from heat. Put about *half* the chocolate or confectioners' coating in the top of the double boiler; set over the hot water till chocolate or coating begins to melt. Add remaining chocolate or coating, about ½ cup at a time, *stirring constantly* till melted and smooth. Stir constantly till candy reaches 130°. Refill bottom of double boiler with *cool* water to within ½ inch of the bottom of the smaller pan. Stir constantly till chocolate cools down to 83° (96° for confectioners' coating). This helps prevent dullness or streaking.

Drop desired centers, one at a time, into chocolate or coating; turn with a long-tined fork to coat. Lift candy out with the fork but do not pierce. Draw the bottom of the fork across the rim of the pan to remove excess coating. Invert candy onto waxed paper, twisting the fork slightly as candy falls to swirl the top. Repeat with remaining centers.

Work quickly and stir the chocolate or coating frequently to keep it evenly heated. The melted candy will stay at dipping temperature (chocolate 80° to 85°; confectioners' coating 92° to 96°) about 30 minutes. If it cools, replace water with *lukewarm* water (110°). Let dipped candy stand till set. Cover; store candy in a cool, dry place.

Drain cherries thoroughly on paper toweling. Combine butter or margarine, corn syrup, and salt. Stir in powdered sugar; knead mixture till smooth (chill mixture if too soft).

Shape 1 *teaspoon* of the sugar mixture around each cherry. Place coated cherries on a baking sheet lined with waxed paper; chill.

In a heavy 1-quart saucepan melt chocolate over low heat, stirring constantly. Holding by cherry stems, dip coated cherries, one at a time, into chocolate. Spoon chocolate over cherries to coat. Place cherries on a baking sheet lined with waxed paper. Chill. Store in refrigerator in a covered container. Let candies ripen in refrigerator for one or two weeks before serving. Makes 60.

## Caramels

- 1  **cup butter or margarine**
- 1  **16-ounce package (2¼ cups packed) brown sugar**
- 1  **cup light corn syrup**
- 1  **14-ounce can (1¼ cups) *sweetened condensed* milk**
- 1  **teaspoon vanilla**

Generously butter a 9x9x2-inch pan; set aside. In a heavy 3-quart saucepan melt the 1 cup butter or margarine. Add sugar and dash *salt;* stir thoroughly. Stir in corn syrup. Gradually add condensed milk; stir constantly. Cook over medium heat, stirring occasionally, to 245° (firm-ball stage), for 15 to 20 minutes (mixture should boil gently over entire surface). Remove from heat; stir in vanilla. Pour into buttered pan. When cool, cut into squares with a wet, sharp knife. Wrap each piece in clear plastic wrap. Makes about 2½ pounds.

***Chocolate Caramels:*** Prepare Caramels as above, *except* add 2 squares (2 ounces) *unsweetened chocolate,* cup up, with the milk.

## Caramel Apples

  **14**    **small tart apples**
  **½**    **cup butter** *or* **margarine**
   **2**    **cups packed brown sugar**
   **1**    **cup light corn syrup**
   **1**    **14-ounce can (1¼ cups)** *sweetened*
            *condensed* **milk**
   **1**    **teaspoon vanilla**

Wash and dry apples; remove stems. Insert a *wooden skewer* into the stem end of each apple. In a heavy 3-quart saucepan melt butter. Stir in sugar, corn syrup, and dash *salt;* mix well. Bring to boiling over medium heat, stirring constantly. Stir in condensed milk. Cook, stirring constantly, to 245° (firm-ball stage), for 12 to 15 minutes (mixture should boil gently over entire surface). Remove from heat; add vanilla. Dip each apple into caramel mixture; turn to coat. Set on a buttered baking sheet; chill. Makes 14 coated apples.

   **Peanut Caramel Apples:** Prepare Caramel Apples as above, *except* dip bottom half of apples into 1 cup chopped *peanuts* immediately after dipping apples into caramel.

## Saltwater Taffy

   **2**    **cups sugar**
   **1**    **cup light corn syrup**
   **2**    **tablespoons butter** *or* **margarine**
  **¼**    **teaspoon oil of peppermint (optional)**
   **7**    **drops green food coloring (optional)**

Butter the sides of a 2-quart saucepan. In it combine sugar, corn syrup, 1 cup *water,* and 1½ teaspoons *salt.* Cook over medium heat, stirring constantly, till sugar is dissolved. Continue cooking to 265° (hard-ball stage), without stirring (mixture should boil gently over entire surface).

   Remove from heat; stir in butter or margarine. Add flavoring and food coloring, if desired. Pour into a buttered 15x10x1-inch pan. Cool about 20 minutes or till easily handled. Butter hands and pull candy till difficult to pull. Cut into fourths; pull each piece into a long strand about ½ inch thick. With buttered scissors snip taffy into bite-sizes pieces. Wrap each in clear plastic wrap. Store overnight. Makes 1½ pounds.

## Glazed Nuts

    1½   **cups blanched whole almonds, cashews,**
         **raw peanuts, *or* pecan halves**
    ½    **cup sugar**
    2    **tablespoons butter *or* margarine**

In a heavy 8-inch skillet combine nuts, sugar, and butter or margarine. Cook over medium heat, stirring constantly, for 6 to 8 minutes or till sugar is melted and golden in color and nuts are toasted. Spread nuts on a buttered baking sheet or aluminum foil; separate into clusters. Sprinkle lightly with *salt*. Cool. Makes about ½ pound.

## Nut Brittle

    2    **cups sugar**
    1    **cup light corn syrup**
    ½    **cup water**
    ¼    **cup butter *or* margarine**
    ½    **teaspoon salt**
    2    **to 3 cups raw *or* roasted shelled peanuts**
         ***or* other coarsely chopped nuts (16**
         **ounces)**
    1½   **teaspoons baking soda**

Butter the sides of a heavy 3-quart saucepan. In it combine sugar, corn syrup, water, butter or margarine, and salt. Cook and stir till sugar dissolves and mixture comes to boiling. Cook, stirring occasionally, to 275° (soft-crack stage) and till syrup turns a golden color (mixture should boil gently over entire surface). Add nuts and continue cooking, stirring often, to 295° and till syrup is a clear golden color. Remove from heat. Quickly stir in soda. Immediately pour hot mixture into two buttered 15x10x1-inch pans or baking sheets. If desired, use two forks to lift and pull candy as it cools to stretch it thin. Cool; break into pieces. Makes about 2¼ pounds.

**Brown Sugar Nut Brittle:** Prepare Nut Brittle as above, *except* use only *1 cup* granulated sugar and add 1 cup packed *brown* sugar. Cook over medium heat, stirring constantly, to 275° and till syrup turns a deep golden color (mixture should boil gently over entire surface). Add nuts; cook, stirring often, to 295° and till syrup is a dark golden color. Continue as directed.

---

## Toffee Butter Crunch

- 1 **cup butter *or* margarine**
- 1 **cup sugar**
- 3 **tablespoons water**
- 1 **tablespoon light corn syrup**
- ½ **cup coarsely chopped pecans *or* toasted almonds**
- ¾ **cup semisweet or milk chocolate pieces**
- ½ **cup finely chopped pecans *or* toasted almonds**

Butter the sides of a heavy 2-quart saucepan. In it melt the 1 cup butter or margarine. Add sugar, water, and corn syrup. Cook over medium heat to 290° (soft-crack stage), stirring frequently (mixture should boil gently over entire surface). Watch carefully after 280°. Remove from heat. Quickly stir in the ½ cup *coarsely* chopped nuts. Immediately turn into a buttered 13x9x2-inch pan. Wait for 2 to 3 minutes for toffee surface to firm, then sprinkle with chocolate pieces. Let stand for 1 to 2 minutes. When chocolate is softened, spread evenly over toffee; sprinkle with the ½ cup *finely* chopped nuts. Chill till chocolate is firm; break into pieces. Makes about 1½ pounds.

## Old-Time Popcorn Balls

| | |
|---|---|
| **20** | **cups popped popcorn (about 1 cup unpopped)** |
| **2** | **cups sugar** |
| **1** | **cup water** |
| **½** | **cup light corn syrup** |
| **1** | **teaspoon vinegar** |
| **½** | **teaspoon salt** |
| **1** | **teaspoon vanilla** |

Oven 300°

Remove all unpopped kernels from popped corn. Put popcorn in a large roasting pan; keep warm in a 300° oven. Butter the sides of a 2-quart saucepan. In it combine sugar, water, corn syrup, vinegar, and salt. Cook to 270° (soft-crack stage), stirring frequently (mixture should boil gently over entire surface). Remove from heat; stir in vanilla. Slowly pour mixture over hot popcorn. Stir just till mixed. Butter hands; using a buttered cup, scoop up popcorn mixture. Shape with buttered hands into 2½- to 3-inch balls. Make 13 to 15.

## Old-Fashioned Molasses Taffy

| | |
|---|---|
| **2** | **cups sugar** |
| **1½** | **cups water** |
| **1** | **cup molasses** |
| **½** | **cup butter or margarine** |
| **¼** | **cup light corn syrup** |

Butter the sides of a heavy 3-quart saucepan. In it combine sugar, water, molasses, butter or margarine, and corn syrup. Cook over low heat, stirring constantly, till sugar is dissolved. Continue cooking to 265° (hard-ball stage), without stirring (mixture should boil gently over entire surface). Pour onto a buttered platter or shallow baking pan.

Cool 10 to 15 minutes or till easy to handle. Butter hands lightly and pull candy till light in color and difficult to pull. On a counter top rub and twist candy into ropes, ½ inch in diameter. With buttered scissors cut candy into 1-inch pieces. Wrap each piece individually in clear plastic wrap. Makes about 1½ pounds candy.

## Easy Fudge

- ½ **cup butter or margarine**
- ⅓ **cup water**
- 1 **16-ounce package powdered sugar**
- ½ **cup nonfat dry milk powder**
- ½ **cup unsweetened cocoa powder**
  **Dash salt**
- ½ **cup chopped nuts**

In a small saucepan heat together butter or margarine and water just to boiling, stirring to melt butter or margarine. Sift together powdered sugar, dry milk powder, cocoa powder, and salt into a large mixer bowl. (If powdered sugar mixture seems lumpy, sift again.) Add melted butter mixture. Stir till well blended; stir in chopped nuts. Turn into a buttered 8x8x2-inch pan. Chill several hours. Cut into squares. Makes about 1½ pounds.

## Chocolate Nut Balls

- 1 **6-ounce package (1 cup) semisweet chocolate pieces**
- 2 **tablespoons butter or margarine**
- 1 **egg**
- 1 **cup sifted powdered sugar**
- ½ **teaspoon vanilla**
  **Dash salt**
- ½ **cup flaked coconut**
- ½ **cup chopped peanuts**
  **Flaked coconut**

In a medium saucepan melt semisweet chocolate pieces and butter or margarine over low heat, stirring frequently. Remove pan from heat; cool to lukewarm.

Beat in egg till smooth and glossy. Add sifted powdered

sugar, vanilla, and salt; mix well. Stir in the ½ cup flaked coconut and the chopped peanuts. Chill about 1 hour. Form into 1-inch balls; roll in additional flaked coconut. Arrange on a baking sheet. Chill at least 3 hours or till firm. Makes about 2½ dozen balls.

## Peppermint Bonbons

    1   **pound confectioners' coating for dipping**
    ½   **cup whipping cream**
    1¼  **teaspoon peppermint extract**
        **Crushed peppermint candies**

In a heavy 2-quart saucepan melt confectioners' coating over low heat, stirring frequently. Remove from heat. Stir in whipping cream and peppermint extract. Beat at high speed of electric mixer till smooth. Chill in *freezer* for 20 to 30 minutes or till candy is stiff enough to be shaped.

Form candy into balls, using 2 teaspoons candy for each ball. Roll balls in crushed peppermint candies. Arrange on a baking sheet. Store in refrigerator. Makes 3½ dozen.

## Caramel Corn

    8   **cups popped popcorn**
    ¾   **cup packed brown sugar**
    6   **tablespoons butter or margarine**
    3   **tablespoons light corn syrup**
    ¼   **teaspoon baking soda**
    ¼   **teaspoon vanilla**                    Oven 300°

Remove all unpopped kernels from popped corn. Put popcorn into a 17x12x2-inch baking pan. In a 1½-quart saucepan combine sugar, butter or margarine, corn syrup, and ¼ teaspoon *salt*. Cook and stir over medium heat till butter melts and mixture comes to boiling. Cook, without stirring, for 5 minutes more. Remove from heat. Stir in baking soda and vanilla. Pour over popcorn; gently stir to coat popcorn. Bake

in a 300° oven for 15 minutes; stir. Bake 5 to 10 minutes
more. Remove corn to a large bowl; cool. Makes 8 cups.

---

## Sugared Popcorn

---

   ⅓  **cup unpopped popcorn**
   **3  tablespoons cooking oil**
   ⅓  **cup sugar**

Combine popcorn and ¼ cup *water;* set aside. In a 3-quart
saucepan heat oil. Stir sugar into hot oil. Add popcorn and
water mixture; cover. Pop the corn quickly over high heat,
shaking pan constantly. At the end of the peak of popping,
remove pan from heat to prevent sugar from burning. Makes
about 6 cups.

---

## Easy Walnut Penuche

---

   **6  tablespoons butter *or* margarine**
   **1  cup packed brown sugar**
   ¼  **cup milk**
   2½ **cups sifted powdered sugar**
   **1  cup chopped walnuts**

In a 1½-quart saucepan melt butter or margarine; add brown
sugar. Cook over low heat for 2 minutes; stir constantly.
Increase heat to medium; add milk. Cook and stir till mixture
boils. Remove from heat; cool 30 minutes. Gradually stir in
powdered sugar till mixture is of fudge consistency. Stir in
nuts. Spread in a buttered 9x5x3-inch or 8x4x2-inch loaf pan.
Chill. Cut into squares. Makes 1½ pounds.

## Carob Candy Squares

- ½ cup honey
- ½ cup creamy peanut butter
- ½ cup unsweetened carob powder or 1 square (1 ounce) unsweetened chocolate, melted
- 1 cup roasted soybeans or dry-roasted peanuts
- 1 cup raisins, cut-up pitted dates, or cut-up pitted figs
- 1 cup flaked coconut

In a saucepan stir together honey and peanut butter over low heat till melted. Remove from heat; stir in carob powder or chocolate till well combined. Stir in soybeans or peanuts, raisins, dates, or figs, and ¾ *cup* of the coconut till well coated. Press mixture into a 9x5x3-inch loaf pan lined with waxed paper. Sprinkle top of candy with remaining coconut. Cover; chill till firm. Cut into squares. Store, covered, in refrigerator. Makes 24 pieces.

## Choco-Scotch Crunchies

- 1 6-ounce package (1 cup) butterscotch pieces
- 1 6-ounce package (1 cup) semisweet chocolate pieces
- 1 3-ounce can (2½ cups) chow mein noodles
- 1 cup salted peanuts or cashews
- 1 cup tiny marshmallows

In a medium saucepan melt butterscotch and chocolate pieces over low heat, stirring occasionally. Remove from heat. Stir in chow mein noodles, nuts, and marshmallows. Drop from a teaspoon onto waxed paper. Refrigerate till firm. Makes 3 to 4 dozen.

**Microwave directions:** In a large nonmetal bowl combine butterscotch and chocolate pieces. Cook, uncovered, in a counter-top microwave oven on high power for about 2½ minutes or till melted. Stir after each minute. Stir in chow mein noodles, nuts, and marshmallows. Drop from a teaspoon onto waxed paper. Chill till firm.

## Rocky Road

>    **2   8-ounce bars milk chocolate, cut up**
>    **3   cups tiny marshmallows**
>    **¾   cup coarsely chopped nuts**

In a medium saucepan slowly melt milk chocolate over low heat, stirring constantly. Remove from heat. Stir in marshmallows and chopped nuts. Spread in a buttered 8x8x2-inch pan. Chill till chocolate is firm. Cut into squares. Makes 1½ pounds candy.

**Microwave directions:** Place cut-up chocolate in a medium nonmetal bowl. In a counter-top microwave oven cook on high power for 2 minutes or till chocolate is melted, stirring once, Stir in marshmallows and nuts. Spread in a buttered 8x8x2-inch pan. Chill till firm. Cut into squares. Makes 1½ pounds.

## Cream Cheese Mints

*These mints can be frozen for up to 1 month—*
>    **1   3-ounce package cream cheese, softened**
>    **½   teaspoon peppermint extract**
>    **3   cups sifted powdered sugar**
>    **Few drops food coloring**
>    **Granulated sugar**

In a small mixer bowl combine softened cream cheese and peppermint extract. Gradually beat in powdered sugar with electric mixer till mixture is smooth. (Knead in the last of the powdered sugar with your hands.) Knead in food coloring till evenly distributed.

Sprinkle small candy molds lightly with granulated sugar.

Press about ½ to ¾ *teaspoon* cream cheese mixture into each mold. Remove from mold. (*Or*, form mixture into ¾-inch balls. Dip each ball in granulated sugar, place on waxed paper. Flatten each with the bottom of a juice glass or with the tines of a fork.) Let dry overnight. Makes 6 to 8 dozen molded mints or about 4 dozen patties.

# Canning
## & Freezing

**Canning**
**& Freezing**

**Canning**
**& Freezing**

**Canning**
**& Freezing**

**Canning**

# Canning & Freezing

**Percent of U.S. RDA Per Serving**

| Recipes | Servings (fraction of recipe) | Calories | Protein (grams) | Carbohydrate (grams) | Fat (grams) | Sodium (milligrams) | Potassium (milligrams) | Protein | Vitamin A | Vitamin C | Thiamine | Riboflavin | Niacin | Calcium | Iron |
|---|---|---|---|---|---|---|---|---|---|---|---|---|---|---|---|
| Apple Butter | 1/128 | 41 | 0 | 11 | 0 | 0 | 35 | 0 | 0 | 2 | 0 | 0 | 0 | 0 | 1 |
| Apple Jelly | 1/64 | 48 | 0 | 12 | 0 | 0 | 24 | 0 | 1 | 1 | 0 | 0 | 0 | 0 | 0 |
| Apple Juice | 1/12 | 219 | 1 | 55 | 1 | 4 | 416 | 1 | 7 | 25 | 8 | 4 | 2 | 2 | 6 |
| Applesauce | 1/24 | 120 | 0 | 30 | 0 | 2 | 167 | 0 | 3 | 10 | 3 | 2 | 2 | 2 | 3 |
| Apples, sweetened | 1/8 | 82 | 0 | 21 | 0 | 1 | 69 | 0 | 1 | 2 | 1 | 1 | 0 | 0 | 1 |
| Apples, unsweetened | 1/8 | 34 | 0 | 9 | 0 | 1 | 69 | 0 | 0 | 2 | 1 | 1 | 0 | 0 | 0 |
| Apricot Nectar | 1/16 | 75 | 1 | 19 | 1 | 1 | 150 | 1 | 29 | 9 | 1 | 2 | 2 | 2 | 2 |
| Apricots, sweetened | 1/8 | 88 | 1 | 22 | 1 | 1 | 218 | 1 | 42 | 13 | 2 | 2 | 2 | 2 | 2 |
| Asparagus, w/salt | 1/8 | 18 | 2 | 3 | 0 | 135 | 188 | 3 | 12 | 37 | 8 | 8 | 5 | 5 | 4 |
| Beans, Green, w/salt | 1/8 | 18 | 2 | 4 | 0 | 137 | 134 | 2 | 7 | 17 | 3 | 4 | 1 | 1 | 3 |
| Beans, Lima, w/salt | 1/8 | 96 | 7 | 17 | 0 | 135 | 504 | 10 | 5 | 37 | 12 | 5 | 5 | 5 | 12 |
| Beans, Wax, w/salt | 1/8 | 15 | 1 | 3 | 0 | 137 | 134 | 1 | 3 | 18 | 3 | 3 | 1 | 1 | 3 |
| Beef (Chuck), canned | 1/8 | 150 | 21 | 0 | 7 | 37 | 168 | 32 | 0 | 0 | 0 | 3 | 9 | 16 | 15 |
| Beets, w/salt | 1/8 | 27 | 1 | 6 | 0 | 170 | 177 | 1 | 1 | 9 | 2 | 2 | 2 | 1 | 3 |
| Blackberries, sweetened | 1/8 | 90 | 1 | 22 | 1 | 1 | 123 | 1 | 3 | 25 | 2 | 1 | 2 | 1 | 4 |
| Blackberries, unsweetened | 1/8 | 42 | 1 | 9 | 1 | 1 | 122 | 1 | 3 | 25 | 1 | 1 | 2 | 1 | 4 |
| (Blackberry) Freezer Jam | 1/80 | 43 | 0 | 11 | 0 | 0 | 13 | 0 | 0 | 3 | 0 | 0 | 0 | 0 | 4 |
| Blueberries, canned w/sugar | 1/8 | 69 | 1 | 17 | 0 | 1 | 59 | 1 | 1 | 17 | 3 | 1 | 3 | 2 | 2 |
| Blueberries, frozen sweetened | 1/8 | 93 | 1 | 24 | 1 | 1 | 59 | 1 | 1 | 17 | 3 | 1 | 3 | 2 | 2 |
| Blueberries, unsweetened | 1/8 | 45 | 1 | 11 | 1 | 1 | 59 | 1 | 1 | 17 | 3 | 1 | 3 | 2 | 4 |

# Nutrition Analysis Chart

|  | | | | | | | | | | | | | | |
|---|---|---|---|---|---|---|---|---|---|---|---|---|---|---|
| Boysenberries, sweetened | 1/8 | 90 | 22 | 1 | 1 | 123 | 1 | 3 | 25 | 1 | 2 | 1 | 2 | 4 |
| Boysenberries, unsweetened | 1/8 | 42 | 9 | 1 | 1 | 122 | 1 | 3 | 25 | 1 | 2 | 1 | 2 | 4 |
| Bread and Butter Pickles | 1/48 | 95 | 24 | 0 | 4 | 101 | 1 | 3 | 10 | 1 | 2 | 1 | 1 | 3 |
| Broccoli | 1/4 | 24 | 4 | 3 | 14 | 196 | 4 | 48 | 88 | 4 | 7 | 2 | 5 | 4 |
| Cantaloupe, sweetened | 1/8 | 77 | 20 | 1 | 10 | 201 | 1 | 54 | 44 | 2 | 1 | 2 | 1 | 2 |
| Cantaloupe, unsweetened | 1/8 | 24 | 6 | 1 | 10 | 201 | 1 | 54 | 44 | 2 | 1 | 2 | 1 | 2 |
| Carrots, w/salt | 1/8 | 31 | 7 | 1 | 168 | 251 | 1 | 152 | 10 | 3 | 2 | 2 | 3 | 3 |
| Cauliflower | 1/4 | 14 | 3 | 1 | 7 | 148 | 2 | 1 | 65 | 4 | 3 | 2 | 1 | 3 |
| Cherries, Dark Sweet, canned w/sugar | 1/8 | 115 | 29 | 0 | 2 | 139 | 1 | 2 | 12 | 2 | 3 | 1 | 2 | 2 |
| Cherries, Dark Sweet, canned w/syrup or frozen sweetened | 1/8 | 99 | 25 | 0 | 2 | 139 | 1 | 2 | 12 | 2 | 3 | 1 | 2 | 2 |
| Cherries, Dark Sweet, unsweetened | 1/8 | 51 | 13 | 0 | 1 | 139 | 1 | 2 | 12 | 2 | 3 | 1 | 2 | 2 |
| Cherries, Tart Red, canned w/sugar | 1/8 | 109 | 28 | 0 | 2 | 149 | 1 | 16 | 13 | 3 | 3 | 2 | 2 | 2 |
| Cherries, Tart Red, canned w/syrup or frozen sweetened | 1/8 | 93 | 24 | 0 | 2 | 143 | 1 | 16 | 13 | 3 | 3 | 2 | 2 | 2 |
| Cherries, Tart Red, unsweetened | 1/8 | 45 | 11 | 1 | 2 | 148 | 1 | 16 | 13 | 3 | 3 | 2 | 2 | 2 |
| Chicken with bone, canned | 1/6 | 223 | 0 | 33 | 0 | 0 | 52 | 26 | 0 | 8 | 40 | 50 | 0 | 19 |
| Cinnamon-Apple Jelly | 1/64 | 48 | 12 | 0 | 0 | 24 | 0 | 0 | 1 | 0 | 0 | 0 | 0 | 0 |
| Clams, frozen | 1/4 | 93 | 1 | 16 | 41 | 267 | 24 | 2 | 19 | 8 | 12 | 7 | 8 | 21 |
| Corn, Cream-Style, w/salt | 1/4 | 69 | 16 | 1 | 133 | 136 | 4 | 7 | 10 | 6 | 5 | 5 | 0 | 3 |
| Corn, on the Cob | 1 | 79 | 18 | 1 | 0 | 231 | 4 | 16 | 16 | 8 | 6 | 7 | 0 | 3 |
| Corn Relish | 1/192 | 15 | 4 | 0 | 71 | 35 | 1 | 2 | 8 | 1 | 1 | 1 | 0 | 1 |
| Corn, Whole Kernel, w/salt | 1/4 | 69 | 16 | 1 | 133 | 136 | 4 | 7 | 10 | 6 | 5 | 5 | 0 | 3 |
| Crab, frozen | 1/4 | 156 | 3 | 32 | 240 | 377 | 50 | 0 | 0 | 2 | 3 | 27 | 11 | 15 |
| Dill Pickles | 1/16 | 4 | 1 | 0 | 413 | 34 | 0 | 1 | 3 | 1 | 0 | 0 | 1 | 1 |
| Fish, w/salt | 1/4 | 176 | 0 | 21 | 192 | 339 | 33 | 51 | 0 | 11 | 8 | 17 | 3 | 3 |
| Fruit Juice Jelly (Apple) | 1/96 | 41 | 11 | 0 | 9 | 12 | 0 | 0 | 1 | 0 | 0 | 0 | 0 | 0 |
| Gooseberries, canned w/sugar | 1/8 | 54 | 14 | 0 | 1 | 116 | 1 | 4 | 41 | 6 | 2 | 1 | 2 | 2 |
| Gooseberries, frozen sweetened | 1/8 | 78 | 20 | 0 | 1 | 117 | 1 | 4 | 41 | 6 | 2 | 1 | 1 | 2 |

# Nutrition Analysis Chart

Percent of U.S. RDA Per Serving

| Recipes | Servings (fraction of recipe) | Calories | Protein (grams) | Carbohydrate (grams) | Fat (grams) | Sodium (milligrams) | Potassium (milligrams) | Protein | Vitamin A | Vitamin C | Thiamine | Riboflavin | Niacin | Calcium | Iron |
|---|---|---|---|---|---|---|---|---|---|---|---|---|---|---|---|
| Gooseberries, unsweetened | 1/8 | 30 | 1 | 7 | 0 | 1 | 116 | 1 | 4 | 41 | 2 | 6 | 2 | 11 | 2 |
| Grape Jam | 1/96 | 44 | 0 | 11 | 0 | 0 | 18 | 0 | 0 | 1 | 1 | 2 | 1 | 0 | 0 |
| Grape Juice Concentrate | 1/30 | 71 | 1 | 17 | 0 | 2 | 75 | 1 | 0 | 3 | 3 | 2 | 1 | 0 | 0 |
| Honeydew Melon, sweetened | 1/8 | 81 | 1 | 20 | 0 | 10 | 214 | 1 | 1 | 33 | 2 | 2 | 2 | 3 | 2 |
| Honeydew Melon, unsweetened | 1/8 | 28 | 1 | 7 | 0 | 10 | 213 | 1 | 1 | 33 | 2 | 2 | 2 | 3 | 2 |
| Kosher Dill Pickles | 1/16 | 4 | 0 | 1 | 0 | 413 | 35 | 0 | 1 | 3 | 0 | 0 | 0 | 0 | 0 |
| Lamb (Shoulder), canned | 1/8 | 144 | 19 | 0 | 19 | 46 | 210 | 29 | 0 | 0 | 0 | 7 | 12 | 2 | 11 |
| Lobster, frozen | 1/4 | 156 | 32 | 1 | 3 | 240 | 377 | 50 | 1 | 0 | 0 | 2 | 3 | 27 | 15 |
| Loganberries, sweetened | 1/8 | 93 | 1 | 23 | 0 | 1 | 123 | 1 | 3 | 29 | 1 | 3 | 1 | 2 | 5 |
| Loganberries, unsweetened | 1/8 | 45 | 1 | 11 | 0 | 1 | 122 | 1 | 3 | 29 | 1 | 2 | 2 | 1 | 5 |
| Mint-Apple Jelly | 1/64 | 48 | 0 | 12 | 0 | 0 | 24 | 0 | 0 | 1 | 0 | 0 | 0 | 0 | 0 |
| Mixed Pickles | 1/48 | 78 | 1 | 20 | 1 | 145 | 125 | 1 | 22 | 29 | 2 | 2 | 1 | 0 | 3 |
| Orange Marmalade | 1/80 | 52 | 0 | 14 | 0 | 2 | 18 | 0 | 0 | 11 | 0 | 1 | 0 | 0 | 0 |
| Oysters, frozen | 1/4 | 79 | 10 | 4 | 2 | 88 | 145 | 16 | 7 | 0 | 3 | 11 | 13 | 15 | 37 |
| Peach-Banana Jam | 1/112 | 43 | 0 | 11 | 0 | 0 | 25 | 0 | 3 | 2 | 1 | 0 | 0 | 1 | 0 |
| Peaches, sweetened | 1/8 | 81 | 1 | 21 | 0 | 1 | 172 | 1 | 23 | 10 | 3 | 1 | 3 | 4 | 3 |
| Peaches, unsweetened | 1/8 | 33 | 1 | 8 | 0 | 1 | 172 | 1 | 23 | 10 | 3 | 1 | 3 | 4 | 3 |
| Peach Jam | 1/96 | 49 | 0 | 13 | 0 | 0 | 25 | 0 | 3 | 2 | 1 | 0 | 0 | 1 | 0 |
| Peach-Plum Jam | 1/96 | 49 | 0 | 13 | 0 | 0 | 18 | 0 | 2 | 1 | 0 | 1 | 0 | 0 | 0 |
| Pears, sweetened | 1/8 | 103 | 1 | 26 | 0 | 2 | 108 | 1 | 0 | 6 | 1 | 1 | 2 | 1 | 1 |

# Nutrition Analysis Chart

| Food | Serving | | | | | | | | | | | | | |
|---|---|---|---|---|---|---|---|---|---|---|---|---|---|---|
| Peas, Green, w/salt | 1/8 | 61 | 5 | 10 | 0 | 135 | 229 | 9 | 33 | 17 | 6 | 11 | 2 | 8 |
| Peppers, Sweet, w/salt | 1/4 | 12 | 0 | 3 | 0 | 273 | 107 | 4 | 107 | 3 | 2 | 1 | 0 | 2 |
| Plum Jam | 1/64 | 46 | 0 | 12 | 0 | 0 | 35 | 0 | 2 | 0 | 0 | 1 | 0 | 1 |
| Plums, sweetened | 1/8 | 93 | 0 | 24 | 0 | 1 | 158 | 1 | 9 | 2 | 2 | 2 | 1 | 3 |
| Plums, unsweetened | 1/8 | 45 | 0 | 11 | 0 | 1 | 157 | 1 | 9 | 2 | 2 | 2 | 1 | 3 |
| Pork (Shoulder), canned | 1/8 | 171 | 19 | 0 | 10 | 46 | 212 | 0 | 0 | 28 | 11 | 18 | 1 | 13 |
| Quick Mustard Pickles | 1/40 | 34 | 1 | 9 | 0 | 137 | 73 | 1 | 19 | 1 | 1 | 1 | 1 | 2 |
| Raspberries (Red), sweetened | 1/8 | 83 | 1 | 21 | 0 | 1 | 104 | 1 | 26 | 1 | 3 | 3 | 1 | 3 |
| Raspberries (Red), unsweetened | 1/8 | 35 | 1 | 8 | 0 | 1 | 103 | 1 | 26 | 1 | 3 | 3 | 1 | 3 |
| (Red Raspberry) Freezer Jam | 1/80 | 42 | 0 | 11 | 0 | 0 | 11 | 0 | 3 | 0 | 0 | 0 | 0 | 0 |
| Rhubarb, sweetened | 1/8 | 58 | 0 | 15 | 0 | 1 | 153 | 1 | 9 | 1 | 3 | 1 | 6 | 3 |
| Rhubarb, unsweetened | 1/8 | 10 | 0 | 2 | 0 | 1 | 153 | 1 | 9 | 1 | 3 | 1 | 6 | 3 |
| Rutabagas | 1/8 | 32 | 1 | 8 | 0 | 4 | 167 | 1 | 50 | 3 | 3 | 4 | 5 | 2 |
| Scallops, frozen | 1/4 | 127 | 26 | 4 | 2 | 301 | 540 | 40 | 0 | 8 | 4 | 7 | 13 | 19 |
| Shrimp, frozen | 1/4 | 156 | 32 | 3 | 1 | 240 | 377 | 50 | 0 | 2 | 3 | 27 | 11 | 15 |
| Spiced Peaches | 1/20 | 232 | 1 | 60 | 0 | 2 | 213 | 1 | 12 | 1 | 3 | 5 | 1 | 3 |
| Strawberries, sweetened | 1/8 | 76 | 1 | 19 | 0 | 1 | 123 | 1 | 73 | 2 | 3 | 2 | 2 | 4 |
| Strawberries, unsweetened | 1/8 | 28 | 1 | 6 | 0 | 1 | 122 | 1 | 73 | 2 | 3 | 2 | 2 | 4 |
| (Strawberry) Freezer Jam | 1/80 | 41 | 0 | 11 | 0 | 0 | 13 | 0 | 8 | 0 | 0 | 0 | 0 | 0 |
| Strawberry Jam | 1/112 | 52 | 0 | 13 | 0 | 0 | 18 | 0 | 11 | 0 | 0 | 0 | 0 | 1 |
| Sweet Pickle Slices | 1/56 | 91 | 0 | 24 | 0 | 4 | 76 | 2 | 6 | 1 | 1 | 0 | 1 | 3 |
| Sweet Potatoes, canned w/salt | 1/8 | 116 | 2 | 27 | 0 | 143 | 248 | 3 | 180 | 7 | 4 | 3 | 3 | 4 |
| Sweet Potatoes, sugar pack | 1/8 | 134 | 1 | 29 | 0 | 28 | 197 | 2 | 109 | 4 | 2 | 2 | 3 | 5 |
| Syrup, Heavy | 1/104 | 35 | 0 | 9 | 0 | 0 | 0 | 0 | 0 | 0 | 0 | 0 | 0 | 0 |
| Syrup, Medium | 1/88 | 26 | 0 | 7 | 0 | 0 | 0 | 0 | 0 | 0 | 0 | 0 | 0 | 0 |
| Syrup, Thin | 1/80 | 19 | 0 | 5 | 0 | 0 | 0 | 0 | 0 | 0 | 0 | 0 | 0 | 0 |
| Syrup, Very Heavy | 1/124 | 43 | 0 | 11 | 0 | 0 | 0 | 0 | 0 | 1 | 0 | 0 | 0 | 0 |
| Syrup, Very Thin | 1/76 | 10 | 0 | 3 | 0 | 0 | 0 | 0 | 0 | 0 | 0 | 0 | 0 | 0 |
| Tomato Catsup | 1/64 | 24 | 1 | 6 | 0 | 135 | 129 | 1 | 20 | 2 | 1 | 2 | 1 | 2 |

# Nutrition Analysis Chart

| Recipes | Servings (fraction of recipe) | Calories | Protein (grams) | Carbohydrate (grams) | Fat (grams) | Sodium (milligrams) | Potassium (milligrams) | Percent of U.S. RDA Per Serving | | | | | | | |
|---|---|---|---|---|---|---|---|---|---|---|---|---|---|---|---|
| | | | | | | | | Protein | Vitamin A | Vitamin C | Thiamine | Riboflavin | Niacin | Calcium | Iron |
| Tomatoes, w/salt | 1/8 | 32 | 2 | 7 | 0 | 271 | 346 | 2 | 24 | 48 | 6 | 4 | 5 | 2 | 4 |
| Tomato Juice | 1/20 | 36 | 2 | 8 | 0 | 165 | 403 | 3 | 30 | 63 | 7 | 4 | 6 | 2 | 5 |
| Tomato Juice Cocktail | 1/20 | 43 | 2 | 9 | 0 | 233 | 435 | 3 | 30 | 67 | 7 | 4 | 6 | 3 | 5 |
| Turnips | 1/8 | 20 | 1 | 4 | 0 | 32 | 174 | 1 | 0 | 39 | 2 | 3 | 2 | 3 | 2 |
| Veal (Chuck), canned | 1/8 | 165 | 20 | 0 | 9 | 34 | 156 | 30 | 0 | 0 | 4 | 12 | 22 | 1 | 14 |
| Vegetable Relish | 1/160 | 15 | 0 | 4 | 0 | 1 | 47 | 0 | 3 | 14 | 1 | 1 | 1 | 0 | 1 |
| Watermelon, sweetened | 1/8 | 74 | 0 | 19 | 0 | 1 | 80 | 1 | 9 | 9 | 2 | 1 | 1 | 1 | 2 |
| Watermelon, unsweetened | 1/8 | 21 | 0 | 5 | 0 | 1 | 80 | 1 | 9 | 9 | 2 | 1 | 1 | 1 | 2 |
| Whole Cranberry Sauce | 1/224 | 23 | 0 | 6 | 0 | 0 | 5 | 0 | 0 | 1 | 0 | 0 | 0 | 0 | 0 |
| Winter Squash, w/salt | 1/8 | 34 | 1 | 9 | 0 | 134 | 294 | 2 | 18 | 18 | 3 | 5 | 2 | 2 | 4 |

# Preservation Basics

Canning and freezing are the two main ways to store foods for year-round enjoyment. In canning, heat destroys troublesome organisms in food, and the sealed containers prevent recontamination of the food. During freezing, the very cold temperature slows down the growth and activity of organisms and enzymes.

Safe canning depends on the proper combination of time and temperature. The 212° F. temperature used in a boiling water bath for a specified time is sufficient heat for canning high-acid foods such as fruits, tomatoes, pickles, relishes, jams, and preserves. However, you must process low-acid foods such as vegetables, poultry, meats, and fish at 240° F. or 250° F. for a specified time. This is done under pressure. Processing procedures are important; therefore, it's essential that you carefully follow the directions given for each type of food.

In freezing, quick freezing at low temperatures (0° F. or below) is important. If the storage temperature increases above 0° F., the length of storage time decreases.

For canning and freezing, the quality of the food and sanitation are both important. Select quality fruits and vegetables and wash them carefully. Also, it's important to keep your work area clean and dry.

Labeling is essential for both canned and frozen products. You may think you'll remember what's in a container and when it was packed, but after a time you may forget details about seasonings and the date packed.

For canned foods, label jars with contents and date, and if you're canning several batches on the same day, include the batch number. After jars are properly sealed, remove the metal screw bands from the flat metal lids if this type of closure is used. Store canned products in a dry, cool, dark place.

For frozen foods, include the amount of food as well as the contents and date of packaging on the label. For handy reference of frozen foods, keep an inventory beside the freezer indicating when the foods were added so that you can use the products within their specified storage time limits. Cross off foods as they're removed from the freezer.

# Canning

Check over your equipment before starting to can foods. Then read the information on filling jars for the various packs and on how to process by either of the canning processes.

## Equipment

**Canners:** You'll need a water-bath canner for processing fruits, tomatoes, pickles, relishes, jams, and preserves. It's a large, deep kettle with a lid and rack or basket for holding the jars. Any large kettle will work if it's deep enough to allow one to two inches of water to boil freely over the tops of the jars during processing and if it has an open rack and a tight-fitting lid.

Use a pressure canner for low-acid foods such as meats, fish, poultry, and vegetables. This type of canner has a jar rack, a locking lid with a gasket, a pressure gauge or weight, a safety release, and a steam vent.

**Jars:** Use only standard mason jars. These canning jars are tempered and designed just for canning, and have a specially threaded mouth for proper sealing with metal or zinc lids. Jars from commercially prepared foods may not seal properly and may break during processing.

Discard canning jars with chips or cracks. The edges of jar rims must be smooth to ensure a good seal.

**Lids:** Two-piece closures, consisting of screw bands and flat metal lids with sealing compound, are the most widely used for home canning. Follow the manufacturer's directions carefully when preparing them. To use flat metal lids, place the prepared lid on the jar rim with the sealing compound next to the glass. Screw the band firmly by hand to hold the lid in place. The flat lids are designed for one-time use, but screw bands can be reused if they're not bent or rusty.

Zinc caps are available, although they're not as popular as the two-piece lids. The porcelain-lined metal cap always must be used with a new rubber ring. (Discard any zinc caps with damaged porcelain.) To use zinc caps, wet and slip the flexible rubber ring over the mouth of the jar and fit it snugly against the jar's shoulder. Wipe the rubber ring and rim after filling. Then screw the zinc cap down firmly against the rubber ring and unscrew it about ¼ inch. Immediately after processing, grasp the jar and cap firmly with potholders and screw the zinc cap down tightly to complete the seal.

**Other Equipment:** Besides canners, lids, and jars, other useful items include a large kettle or Dutch oven, a wide-mouth funnel, a jar lifter, a slotted spoon or ladle, liquid measuring cups, knives, a wooden board, a vegetable brush, a food mill, a colander or sieve, a timer, and a nonmetal utensil for releasing air bubbles from filled jars.

## The General Canning Process

There are two methods for packing food into containers. They are the cold-pack (raw-pack) and hot-pack methods. In cold-packing, uncooked food is firmly packed into the jar and covered with boiling liquid— syrup, water, or juice. (Loosely pack lima beans, corn, and peas when cold-packing.) In hot-packing, food is partially cooked and then loosely packed into jars that are then filled with boiling liquid.

Regardless of whether the hot- or cold-packing method is used, follow these guidelines:

1. Wash the jars in hot sudsy water and rinse thoroughly. Pour boiling water over jars and let them stand in hot water

### Safety reminder

Always boil home-canned vegetables (except tomatoes), meat, poultry, and fish for 10 to 20 minutes (20 minutes for corn or spinach) before tasting or using. Add water, if necessary, to avoid sticking. *Do not* taste these products cold from the jar.

until ready to fill. Prepare lids for the jars following the manufacturer's directions.

2. Prepare enough food at one time for one full canner. Work as quickly as possible.

3. Pack food into hot jars, leaving the headspace indicated in the recipe (see the tip box on page 235). A cloth placed under the jar prevents it from slipping and catches any spills while filling the jars.

4. Ladle or pour boiling liquid over the food, maintaining the specified headspace.

5. Release any air bubbles in the jar by gently working a wooden spoon or other nonmetal utensil down the side of the filled jar. Add additional liquid if needed.

6. Wipe off the rim of the jar with a clean, damp cloth or paper toweling. Any bits of food on the rim could prevent a perfect seal.

7. Add the prepared lids following the manufacturer's directions.

8. Process filled jars in either a water-bath canner or a pressure canner, depending on the type of food. Follow the procedure and recipe timings exactly. Times given in recipes are for processing at sea level. Adjust for altitudes of 1,000 feet or more above sea level for water-bath canning, and for 2,000 feet or more above sea level for pressure canning (read the tip boxes below and on page 237).

9. Remove processed jars to a rack to cool. Complete the seal for zinc cap closures. Allow air to circulate around jars, but keep the area free of drafts.

---

### Water-bath canning altitude adjustment

If the processing time specified in a recipe is 20 minutes or less, add 1 minute for each 1,000 feet above sea level. If the time is more than 20 minutes, add 2 minutes for each 1,000 feet above sea level.

10. After jars are completely cooled, check for a seal. To test jars with flat lids, press the center of the lid on a cooled jar. If the dip in the lid holds, the jar is sealed. If the lid bounces up and down when pressed, the jar isn't sealed. Other types of caps won't leak when a sealed jar is tipped.

If a jar isn't sealed, check it for flaws. Repack and reprocess the contents using a clean jar and a new lid for the full length of processing time. Or, refrigerate the food and use it within a day or two.

11. Label and store the jars in a dry, cool, dark place.

## Water-Bath Processing

Set the canner with rack on the range. Add 4 to 5 inches of water. Cover and start heating over high heat. Heat additional water.

Next, prepare the syrup, if needed, and keep it warm but not boiling. Prepare the food while water heats in the canner. When the water is hot, fill each jar following recipe directions, and place on the rack in the canner so it can heat as other jars are filled. Jars should not touch. Replace the canner cover each time you add a jar to minimize the escape of steam. When the last jar has been added, fill the canner with boiling water so that the water is 1 to 2 inches over the jar tops. Replace the cover; heat water to a brisk, rolling boil. Now begin the processing timing. Recipe timings are for canning at sea level; be sure to make altitude adjustment if needed (see the tip box on page 232).

Keep the water boiling gently during processing, adding boiling water if the level drops. If water stops boiling when you add water, stop counting the processing time, turn up the heat, and wait for a full boil before resuming counting. At the end of the processing time, turn off the heat and remove the jars. Cool completely and check the seals.

## Tips for Canning Fruit

• Select fresh, ripe, yet firm fruit. Sort fruit according to size and ripeness to ensure even cooking during processing.

• Wash fruit gently and thoroughly under cold running water. Or, wash in several changes of water, lifting fruit out of the water each time so dirt doesn't settle on it.
• Treat certain fruits (those that darken easily, such as apricots, peaches, and pears) with ascorbic acid color keeper during preparation. Follow package directions for the proportions of color keeper to water. Or, use a solution of 2 tablespoons salt and 2 tablespoons lemon juice per gallon of water. Drain fruit thoroughly.

---

### Syrups for canning and freezing fruit

To prepare the syrup, in a saucepan heat the specified amount of sugar and water listed below until the sugar dissolves. (Syrups suggested for canning include very thin, thin, medium, and heavy syrups. Those for freezing include thin, medium, heavy, and very heavy syrups.)

After heating, skim off the top, if necessary. Plan on using about 1 to 1½ cups syrup for each quart of canned fruit, or about ½ to ⅔ cup syrup per pint of frozen fruit. Cool the syrup before using for freezing; heat it before using for canning.

| Type of Syrup | Sugar (cups) | Water (cups) | Yield (cups) |
|---|---|---|---|
| Very Thin | 1 | 4 | 4¾ |
| Thin | 2 | 4 | 5 |
| Medium | 3 | 4 | 5½ |
| Heavy | 4¾ | 4 | 6½ |
| Very Heavy | 7 | 4 | 7¾ |

## Headspace in canning

In canning recipes, a specific headspace is indicated. Headspace is the space between the top of the food and liquid and the rim of the jar. Too little or too much space may prevent a complete seal.

## Pressure Canning

Low-acid foods, such as vegetables (except tomatoes), meats, poultry, and fish *must* be processed in a pressure canner to destroy the heat-resistant bacteria that could cause food poisoning. A higher temperature (240° F. to 250° F.) can only be reached in a pressure canner.

First, read the instructions packed with the pressure canner to become familiar with the canner's operation. Make sure all parts are clean and in working order. If your canner has a spring-dial gauge, have it checked for accuracy. Contact your County Extension Service for the nearest testing location.

When ready to start canning, set the canner with rack on the range and add 2 or 3 inches of boiling water or the amount specified by the canner manufacturer. Turn the heat to low.

Next, prepare enough vegetables or meat for one canner load. Fill each jar and place it in the canner. Jars should not touch. When the last jar is added, cover and lock the canner. Turn the heat up. When steam starts to come out of the open vent or petcock, reduce the heat so steam flows freely at a moderate rate. Let steam flow steadily for 10 minutes or more to exhaust air from inside the canner.

Close the vent and increase pressure. Refer to your canner instructions for specific details. Turn up and maintain the heat till you reach 10 to 15 pounds pressure, as the recipe directs.

Adjust the heat to maintain constant pressure. Constant pressure is important because any fluctuations will draw liquid out of the jars.

Pounds of pressure in the recipes are for canning at less than 2,000 feet above sea level; make adjustments for altitude, if necessary (see the tip box at right). Processing times are for canners of 12-quart size or larger.

Remove the canner from heat and set out of drafts on a wire rack or wooden board. Allow the pressure to return to normal on its own. Do not run water over the canner or rush cooling. Follow the canner's instructions for opening the pressure canner. Be sure to lift the cover away from you to avoid a blast of hot steam. If food is still boiling vigorously in jars, wait a few minutes before removing from the canner. Cool jars 2 to 3 inches apart on towels or a wooden board in a draft-free area. Check for proper sealing on the jars after they are completely cooled.

**Remember to boil the foods processed in the pressure canner for 10 to 20 minutes (20 minutes for corn or spinach) before tasting or using. Add water, if necessary. Do not taste these products cold from the jar. This includes all home-canned vegetables (except tomatoes), meats, poultry, and fish.**

## Tips for Canning Vegetables

• Select fresh, young, and tender produce, and minimize the time between picking and canning. Process small batches, enough for one canner load, to maintain the quality of the food.

• Wash vegetables thoroughly but don't let them stand in water. Lift them up and down in the water to help remove soil. Each time the water is changed, lift out the vegetables so dirt doesn't settle on them.

• Be sure to allow for the headspace specified in the recipe (see the tip box on page 235). Vegetables with a high starch content, such as corn, peas, and lima beans, expand while being processed in the canner. Be sure to note the headspace specified in the recipes when packing these starchy vegetables.

## Pressure canning altitude adjustment

The pounds of pressure specified in the recipes in this chapter apply to processing at elevations under 2,000 feet above sea level. Make the following adjustment for the type of gauge on your canner:

*For spring-dial gauges:* Instead of 10 pounds pressure at 2,000 feet, process at 11 pounds pressure; at 4,000 feet, process at 12 pounds pressure. For each additional 2,000 feet, add 1 pound of pressure.

*For weight gauges:* Above 2,000 feet, follow the manufacturer's directions for altitude adjustments.

## Using a Pressure Saucepan

A pressure saucepan (4- to 8-quart) may be used for canning pint jars if it has a rack and an accurate gauge that maintains 10 or 15 pounds of pressure. Before using the pressure saucepan, read the instructions carefully, then proceed with processing as directed.

**To adjust timing for a pressure saucepan,** add 20 minutes to the processing time given in recipes for pint jars in a pressure canner at 10 pounds pressure, and add 10 minutes to the time at 15 pounds pressure. This extra time makes up for the faster heating and cooling periods in the smaller saucepan. After processing, let the pressure return to zero before opening the pan. Do not put the pressure saucepan under cold water. Remove jars and set aside to cool.

## Open-Kettle Canning

This method of canning is used **only** for making jelly when the hot jelly is poured into sterilized glasses and sealed with paraffin (see page 283). Because of the large amount of sugar in jellies, they can safely be canned by this process. Preserves and jams should be processed in a water-bath canner.

## Detecting Spoilage

Inspect each home-canned jar carefully before serving. Detecting the presence of microorganisms is a matter of using your eyes, nose, and good sense. If the jar has leaked, shows patches of mold, or has a foamy or murky appearance, discard the food.

The odor from the opened jar should be pleasant and characteristic of the product canned. If the food doesn't look or smell right, don't use it. Some harmful toxins do not change the appearance or smell of home-canned vegetables and meats, although an off-odor may show up when the product is boiled. If you have any doubts, destroy the food.

Fortunately, these toxins are destroyed by boiling the food for 10 to 20 minutes (20 minutes for corn and spinach). If the product looks and smells good after the suggested boiling time, it's safe to eat. *Never* taste low-acid foods cold from the jar.

# Freezing

Freezing is a relatively easy way to preserve foods. Here is general information on equipment, the freezing process, and specifics on how to freeze fruits and vegetables.

## Equipment

**Containers:** Probably the most important item for freezing foods is the container or wrapping. You'll want a tightly sealed product so foods won't develop off-flavors, or lose their color, moisture, or nutritive value.

Commonly used containers include freezer bags of various sizes, rigid plastic containers, and wide-top freezing/canning jars. Select rigid containers for liquid or semiliquid foods, and freezing bags for dry-packs.

Be sure that any wrappings used for freezing are moistureproof and vaporproof, and that they can be tightly sealed. When sealing with tape, use freezer tape. All packaging materials should be able to withstand temperatures of 0° F. for extended times.

**Other Equipment:** An essential piece of equipment for freezing vegetables is a large kettle and a basket for blanching. Another important item is a timer for accurate timing of blanching. You probably have any other needed items already in your kitchen.

## The General Freezing Process

1. Select top-quality, fresh, ripe but firm fruit, and garden-fresh, tender vegetables. Choose varieties that are best for freezing (check your local County Extension Service).

2. Wash fruits and vegetables in cold water, and prepare them according to the individual recipes. Keep your work area clean.

3. Pack food tightly into containers, leaving the recommended headspace (see the tip box on page 235). Some loosely packing vegetables require no headspace. The headspace allows food and/or liquid to expand during freezing, and helps prevent cracked containers and freezer-burned products.

4. Follow the manufacturer's directions for sealing the container. For a good seal, wipe the sealing edges of the containers.

5. Label containers with their contents, amount, and the date of freezing.

6. Freeze in small batches at 0° F. or below. It's best to place items against freezer coils or plates and to leave space between packages so that air can circulate freely until the packages are solidly frozen. Don't add too much to the freezer at one time.

7. Store the frozen foods at 0° F. or below. A freezer thermometer is a good investment. Check individual recipes for storage times.

## Freezing Fruits

1. Select the fruit and decide on the type of pack. Use syrup-pack for desserts (chilled fruit in syrup) and sugar-pack for cooking, since there is little liquid. Unsweetened packed fruit may be lower in quality but is handy for special-diet cookery.

2. If needed, prepare the syrup according to the tip box on page 234. Chill the syrup, then wash and prepare the fruit. Don't use galvanized cookware, iron utensils, or chipped enamelware in preparing the fruit.

3. Wash and prepare fruit. If necessary, treat fruit during preparation with ascorbic acid color keeper to control darkening. Follow the label directions for proportions.

4. Pack the fruit into freezer containers, leaving the proper **headspace** (see the tip box on page 235).

*For sugar-, syrup-, and water-packs:* leave a 1/2-inch headspace for pint containers with straight or slightly flared sides and wide-top openings; leave a 1-inch headspace for quart containers with wide-top openings.

For containers with narrow-top openings or glass canning jars (don't use the glass canning jars for fruits packed in water), leave a ¾-inch headspace for pints and a 1½-inch headspace for quarts.

For *unsweetened, dry packs (no sugar or liquid):* leave a ½-inch headspace for pint and quart containers.

5. Place a piece of crumpled parchment paper or plastic wrap atop the fruit to hold it under the juice or syrup.

6. Seal, label, and freeze the fruit.

7. Thaw fruit in sealed containers for best color and flavor. Thaw in the refrigerator or in a bowl of cool water. For cooking, fruits need to be thawed only enough to separate. Serve uncooked fruits when there are a few ice crystals still remaining in the fruit.

## Freezing Vegetables

1. Select, wash, and prepare vegetables; pre-cook, following directions in recipes. The pre-cooking, also called blanching,

impedes the enzyme action, thus helping to retain the color, texture, and flavor of the food. Most vegetables are blanched in water.

2. To blanch in water, heat water to boiling in a large kettle with a lid. *Use a minimum of 1 gallon water for each pound of vegetables.* Place the vegetables in a blanching basket (or wire basket) and lower into the boiling water. Cover and start counting the time immediately. (Heat 1 minute longer at 5,000 or more feet above sea level.) Maintain high heat during blanching.

To steam-blanch vegetables, such as broccoli, use a kettle with a tight lid and a rack 3 inches above the kettle bottom. Add an inch or two of water to the kettle and boil. Place vegetables in a single layer in the basket, and lower onto the rack. Cover the kettle and steam for the specified time. (Steam 1 minute longer at 5,000 or more feet above sea level.) Maintain high heat during steaming.

3. Remove the vegetables immediately from the water or steam and plunge the basket of vegetables into a large quantity of ice water. Allow as much time for cooling as for blanching. Drain vegetables thoroughly.

4. Pack blanched vegetables tightly into freezer containers, leaving the appropriate headspace given in the recipe (some vegetables require no headspace).

5. Seal, label, and freeze vegetables.

## Freezing Other Foods

Besides fruits and vegetables, there are many other foods that can be frozen. They include meats, fish, shellfish, and poultry. Certain relishes and specially developed jam recipes also can be preserved in the freezer. Check the recipes in this chapter for freezing instructions.

# Fruits

## Apples

**Selecting:** Choose ripe, full-flavored apples that are crisp and firm in texture.

**Preparing:** Allow 2½ to 3 pounds *apples* for each quart. Rinse; remove stems and blossom ends. Peel; core. Halve, quarter, or slice.

Dip apples into *water* containing *ascorbic acid color keeper*, or *salt* and *lemon juice*. (Follow package directions for proportions of color keeper to water, or use 2 tablespoons salt and 2 tablespoons lemon juice for each gallon of water.) Drain well.

For freezing, if desired, steam apples for a firmer texture. Place on a rack above water in a covered kettle. Bring to boiling. Steam for 1½ to 2 minutes. Cool.

**Water-Bath Canning:** *Hot-Pack:* In a kettle prepare desired *syrup*. Allow 1 to 1½ cups syrup for each quart. Bring syrup to boiling; reduce heat. Prepare apples as above; add to syrup and return to boiling. Remove from heat. Spoon apples into hot, clean jars, leaving a ½-inch headspace. Return syrup to boiling. Add enough boiling syrup to cover, leaving a ½-inch headspace. Wipe rims; adjust lids. Process in a boiling water bath for 20 minutes for quarts or pints (start timing when water boils).

**Freezing:** *Unsweetened-Pack:* Prepare apples as above. Stir ½ teaspoon *ascorbid acid color keeper* into each 4 cups *cold water*. Allow 1 to 1½ cups water for each quart. Pack apples into moisture-vaporproof freezer containers, leaving headspace (see page 240). Add enough of the water to cover apples, leaving the proper headspace. Seal, label, and freeze.

*Syrup-Pack:* Prepare desired *syrup*; chill. Allow 1 to 1½ cups syrup for each quart. Prepare apples as above. Stir ½ teaspoon *ascorbic acid color keeper* into each 4 cups cold syrup. Pack apples into moisture-vaporproof freezer containers, leaving headspace (see page 240). Add enough syrup to cover apples, leaving the proper headspace. Seal, label, and freeze.

*Sugar-Pack:* Prepare apples as above. Dissolve ¼ teaspoon *ascorbic acid color keeper* in ¼ cup *cold water*. In a large bowl sprinkle ascorbic acid color keeper mixture and ½ cup *sugar* over each 4 cups apples. Stir to mix. Pack apples tightly into moisture-vaporproof freezer containers, leaving the proper headspace (see page 240). Seal, label, and freeze.

## Apple Butter

| 6 | **pounds tart cooking apples, cored and quartered (18 cups)** |
| 5 | **cups apple cider *or* apple juice** |
| 1 | **cup cider vinegar** |
| 4 | **cups sugar** |
| 2 | **teaspoons ground cinnamon** |
| ½ | **teaspoon ground cloves** |
| ½ | **teaspoon ground allspice** |

**Preparing:** In a kettle or Dutch oven combine apples, cider or juice, and vinegar. Bring to a boil. Cover; simmer for 30 minutes, stirring occasionally. Press through a food mill or sieve. Measure 16 cups pulp. Return pulp to kettle. Stir in remaining ingredients. Bring to a boil. Simmer, uncovered, for 1½ to 2 hours or till very thick, stirring often.

**Water-Bath Canning:** Prepare butter as above. Spoon hot butter into hot, clean jars, leaving a ½-inch headspace. Wipe rims; adjust lids. Process in boiling water bath for 10 minutes for half-pints or pints (start timing when water boils). Makes 8 to 9 half-pints.

**Freezing:** Prepare butter as above. Cool. Spoon butter into moisture-vaporproof freezer containers, leaving the proper headspace. Seal, label, and freeze. Makes 8 to 9 half-pints.

## Applesauce

| 8 | **pounds cooking apples, cored and quartered (24 cups)** |
| 1 | **to 1½ cups sugar** |

**Preparing:** In a kettle combine apples and 2 cups *water*. If desired, add 10 inches stick cinnamon. Bring to a boil. Cover and simmer for 8 to 10 minutes; stir often. Remove cinnamon.

Press apples through a food mill or sieve. Return pulp to kettle. Stir in sugar. If necessary, add ½ to 1 cup *water* for desired consistency. Bring to a boil.

**Water-Bath Canning:** Prepare applesauce as above. Spoon boiling applesauce into hot, clean jars, leaving a ½-inch headspace. Wipe rims; adjust lids. Process in boiling water bath for 20 minutes for pints or quarts (start timing when water boils). Makes 6 pints.

**Freezing:** Prepare applesauce as above. Cool. Spoon applesauce into moisture-vaporproof freezer containers, leaving headspace. Seal, label, and freeze. Makes 6 pints.

## Apple Juice

**10    pounds cooking apples, cored and coarsely chopped (36 cups)**

**Preparing:** In a kettle combine apples and 3 cups *water*. Bring to a boil; reduce heat. Cover and simmer for 40 minutes; stir occasionally. Strain apple mixture through a jelly bag or several layers of cheesecloth. When cool, squeeze to extract remaining juice. Strain juice again; return to kettle. If desired, stir in 1 tablespoon sugar for each 2 cups juice. Bring to a boil.

**Water-Bath Canning:** Prepare juice as above. Pour boiling juice into hot, clean jars, leaving a ½-inch headspace. Wipe jar rims; adjust lids. Process in boiling water bath for 15 minutes for pints or quarts (start timing when water boils). Makes 3 to 4 pints.

**Freezing:** Prepare juice. Cool. Pour into moisture-vaporproof freezer containers; leave a ½-inch headspace (for wide-top containers). Seal, label, and freeze. Makes 3 to 4 pints.

## Apricots

**Selecting:** Choose firm, fully ripe apricots that are plump and golden yellow in color.

**Preparing:** Allow 1½ to 2½ pounds *apricots* for each quart. Thoroughly rinse apricots.

For freezing, peel apricots to prevent skins from toughening.

Immerse whole apricots in *boiling water* for 20 to 30 minutes. At once plunge into *cold water* to stop cooking. (Do not let apricots soak in water.) Remove skins.

Halve and pit peeled or unpeeled apricots.

Prevent darkening during preparation by dipping the cut-up apricots into *water* containing *ascorbic acid color keeper,* or *salt* and *lemon juice.* (Follow package directions for proportions of color keeper to water, or use 2 tablespoons salt and 2 tablespoons lemon juice for each gallon water.) Drain well.

**Water-Bath Canning:** *Cold-Pack:* Prepare desired *syrup;* allow 1 to 1½ cups for each quart. Bring syrup to boiling; reduce heat. Prepare apricots as above. Spoon into hot, clean jars, leaving a ½-inch headspace. Return syrup to boiling. Add boiling syrup to cover, leaving a ½-inch headspace. Return syrup to boiling. Add boiling syrup to cover, leaving a ½-inch headspace. Wipe rims; adjust lids. Process in boiling water bath for 30 minutes for quarts or 25 minutes for pints (start timing when water boils).

*Hot-Pack:* In a kettle or Dutch oven prepare desired *syrup.* Allow 1 to 1½ cups syrup for each quart. Bring syrup to boiling; reduce heat. Prepare apricots as at left; add to syrup and return to boiling. Remove from heat. Spoon apricots into hot, clean jars, leaving a ½-inch headspace. Return syrup to boiling. Add boiling syrup to cover apricots, leaving a ½-inch headspace. Wipe jar rims; adjust lids. Process in boiling water bath for 25 minutes for quarts or 20 minutes for pints (start timing when water begins to boil).

**Freezing:** *Syrup-Pack:* Prepare desired *syrup;* chill. Allow 1 to 1½ cups for each quart. Prepare peeled apricots. Stir ¾ teaspoon *ascorbic acid color keeper* into each 4 cups cold syrup. Pack apricots tightly into moisture-vaporproof freezer containers; leave the proper headspace (see page 240). Add syrup to cover; leave the proper headspace. Seal; label; freeze.

*Sugar-Pack:* Prepare peeled apricots. Dissolve ¼ teaspoon *ascorbic acid color keeper* in ¼ cup *cold water.* In a large bowl sprinkle ascorbic acid color keeper mixture and ½ cup *sugar* over each 4 cups apricots; stir. Pack tightly into moisture-vaporproof freezer containers, leaving the proper headspace (see page 240). Seal, label, and freeze.

## Apricot Nectar

2 **pounds apricots, halved and pitted**
1 **cup sugar**

**Preparing:** Measure 6 cups apricots. In an 8- to 10-quart kettle combine apricots and 5 cups *water.* Bring to a boil; reduce heat and simmer 5 to 10 minutes or till soft, stirring occasionally. Remove from heat. Press mixture through a food mill or sieve. Measure 7 cups. Return pulp to kettle; add sugar. Bring juice to boiling, stirring to dissolve sugar.

**Water-Bath Canning:** Prepare nectar as above. Pour boiling nectar into hot, clean jars, leaving a ½-inch headspace. Wipe jar rims; adjust lids. Process in boiling water bath for 15 minutes for pints or quarts (start timing when water boils). Makes about 4 pints.

**Freezing:** Prepare the nectar. Cool thoroughly. Pour into moisture-vaporproof freezer containers; leave a ½-inch headspace (with wide-top containers.) Seal, label, and freeze. Makes about 4 pints.

## Berries

**Selecting:** Choose berries that are plump, firm, and full colored.

**Preparing:** Allow 1½ to 3 pounds *blackberries, blueberries, boysenberries, gooseberries, loganberries, raspberries,* or *strawberries* for each quart. Strawberries are not recommended for canning because they fade, lose flavor, and do not retain their shape during canning. Sort and rinse berries, removing stems and leaves. Drain well.

**Water-Bath Canning:** *Cold-Pack:* Use for soft berries, such as blackberries, boysenberries, loganberries, and raspberries.

Prepare desired *syrup;* allow 1 to 1½ cups for each quart. Bring to boiling; reduce heat. Prepare berries as above. Spoon into hot, clean jars, leaving a ½-inch headspace. Lightly shake jar to pack closely (do not crush). Return syrup to boiling. Add boiling syrup to cover; leave a ½-inch headspace. Wipe jar rims; adjust lids. Process in boiling water bath for 20 minutes for quarts or 15 minutes for pints (start timing when water boils).

*Hot-Pack:* Use for firm berries, such as blueberries and gooseberries.

Prepare berries as above. In a kettle sprinkle ¼ to ½ cup *sugar* over each 4 cups berries. Gently stir to mix. Let stand for 30 minutes. Add ¼ cup *water* to each 4 cups berries. Slowly bring to boiling, stirring gently to dissolve sugar. Spoon into hot, clean jars, leaving a ½-inch headspace. If there is not enough liquid to cover berries, add *boiling water* to cover, leaving a ½-inch headspace. Wipe rims; adjust lids. Process in boiling water bath for 15 minutes for quarts or 10 minutes for pints (start timing when water boils).

**Freezing:** *Unsweetened-Pack:* Prepare berries as above. If desired, slice strawberries. Pack into moisture-vaporproof freezer containers or bags, leaving the proper headspace (see page 240). Lightly shake to pack berries closely (do not crush). Seal, label, and freeze.

*Syrup-Pack:* Prepare desired *syrup;* chill. Allow 1 to 1½ cups syrup for each quart. Prepare berries as above. If desired, slice strawberries. Pack into moisture-vaporproof freezer containers, leaving the proper headspace (see page 240). Lightly shake container to pack closely (do not crush). Add enough cold syrup to cover berries, leaving the proper headspace. Seal, label, and freeze.

*Sugar-Pack:* Prepare berries as directed at left. If desired, slice strawberries. In a large bowl sprinkle ½ cup *sugar* over each 4 cups berries. Gently stir to mix. If desired, let berries stand 30 minutes to dissolve sugar. Pack berries into moisture-vaporproof freezer containers, leaving the proper headspace (see page 240). Lightly shake container to pack berries closely (do not crush). Seal, label, and freeze.

## Cherries

**Selecting:** Choose cherries that are fresh, firm, bright, and a good dark color for either tart red or dark sweet cherries.

**Preparing:** Allow 2 to 2½ pounds unpitted *dark sweet* or *tart red cherries* for each quart. Sort and rinse cherries, removing the stems and leaves. Drain well. If desired, pit the cherries.

**Water-Bath Canning:** *Cold-Pack:* Prepare desired *syrup;* allow 1 to 1½ cups syrup for each quart. Bring to boiling; reduce heat. Prepare cherries as above. Spoon cherries into hot, clean jars; leave a ½-inch headspace. Lightly shake jars to pack closely. Return syrup to boiling. Add boiling syrup to cover cherries; leave a ½-inch headspace. Wipe rims; adjust lids. Process in boiling water bath for 25 minutes for quarts or 20 minutes for pints (start timing when water boils).

*Hot-Pack:* Prepare cherries as above. In a kettle or Dutch oven sprinkle ⅔ to ¾ cup *sugar* over each 4 cups cherries. Gently stir to mix. Let stand for 2 hours. If additional juice is necessary, add about ½ cup *water* to each 4 cups cherries. Slowly bring to boiling, stirring gently to dissolve sugar. Spoon cherry mixture into hot, clean jars, leaving a ½-inch headspace. If there is not enough liquid to cover cherries, add *boiling water* to cover, leaving a ½-inch headspace. Wipe jar rims; adjust lids. Process in boiling water bath for 15 minutes for quarts or 10 minutes for pints (start timing when water boils).

**Freezing:** *Unsweetened-Pack:* Prepare cherries as above. Dip cherries into *water* containing *ascorbic acid color keeper* (follow package directions for proportions of color keeper to water). Drain well. Pack cherries into moisture-vaporproof freezer containers or bags, leaving the proper headspace (see page 240). Lightly shake containers or bags to pack cherries closely. Seal, label, and freeze.

*Syrup-Pack:* Prepare desired *syrup;* chill. Allow 1 to 1½ cups syrup for each quart. Prepare cherries as directed at left. Stir ½ teaspoon *ascorbic acid color keeper* into each 4 cups cold syrup. Pack cherries into moisture-vaporproof freezer containers, leaving the proper headspace (see page 240). Lightly shake containers to pack cherries closely. Add enough cold syrup to cover cherries, leaving the proper headspace. Seal, label, and freeze.

*Sugar-Pack:* Prepare cherries as directed at left. Dissolve ¼ teaspoon *ascorbic acid color keeper* in ¼ cup *cold water*. In a large bowl sprinkle color keeper mixture and ½ cup *sugar* over each 4 cups cherries. Gently stir to mix. Pack cherries into moisture-vaporproof freezer containers, leaving the proper headspace. Lightly shake containers to pack cherries closely. Seal, label, and freeze.

## Whole Cranberry Sauce

**3** pounds fresh cranberries (12 cups)
**6** cups sugar
**6** cups water

**Preparing:** Thoroughly rinse the cranberries. In an 8- to 10-quart kettle or Dutch oven combine sugar and water. Bring to boiling; cook and stir for 5 minutes. Add fresh cranberries; cook about 5 minutes or till cranberry skins pop. Remove from heat.

**Water-Bath Canning:** *Hot-Pack:* Prepare cranberry sauce as above. Spoon hot cranberry sauce into hot, clean jars, leaving a ½-inch headspace. Wipe jar rims; adjust lids. Process in boiling water bath for 10 minutes for pints or quarts (start timing when water boils). Makes 7 to 8 pints.

**Freezing:** Prepare Whole Cranberry Sauce as above. Cool. Spoon into moisture-vaporproof freezer containers, leaving a ½-inch headspace. Seal, label, and freeze. Makes 7 to 8 pints.

**Serving:** Stir canned sauce before serving.

## Grape Juice Concentrate

**14** cups Concord grapes (about 6 pounds)
**2** cups water
**1½** cups sugar

**Preparing:** In a 6-quart kettle or Dutch oven combine grapes and water; cover. Bring to boiling. Reduce heat; cook over low heat about 30 minutes or till grapes are very tender, stirring occasionally. Remove from heat. Strain through a jelly bag or several layers of cheesecloth set in a colander. Discard grape seeds and skins. Chill strained juice for 24 hours. Carefully strain the chilled juice again, leaving sediment in bottom. In a kettle or Dutch oven combine strained grape juice and sugar; bring to boiling.

**Water-Bath Canning:** Prepare grape juice as above. Pour boiling juice into hot, clean jars, leaving a ½-inch headspace. Wipe jar rims; adjust lids. Process juice in boiling water bath for 10 minutes for pints (start timing when water boils). Makes 5 pints.

**Freezing:** Prepare grape juice. Cool. Pour into moisture-vaporproof freezer containers; leave a ½-inch headspace (for wide-top containers). Seal, label, and freeze. Makes 5 pints.

**Serving:** Dilute each pint of canned or frozen Grape Juice Concentrate with 1 cup *water*. If necessary, add additional water for desired strength. Mix well. Cover and chill thoroughly.

## Melons

**Selecting:** Choose firm-fleshed, well-colored, ripe melons.

**Preparing:** Allow about 4 pounds *cantaloupes, watermelons,* or *honeydew melons* for each quart. Cut melons in half. Remove seeds and rind. Cut melons into slices, cubes, or balls.

**Freezing:** *Unsweetened-Pack:* Prepare melons as above. Pack melon pieces tightly into moisture-vaporproof freezer containers or freezer bags, leaving the proper headspace (see page 240). Seal, label, and freeze.

*Syrup-Pack:* Prepare desired *syrup;* chill. Allow 1 to 1½ cups syrup for each quart. Prepare melons as above. Pack melon pieces tightly into moisture-vaporproof freezer containers (see page 240), leaving the proper headspace. Add enough cold syrup to cover melons, leaving the proper headspace. Seal, label, and freeze.

## Peaches

**Selecting:** Choose plump peaches with a soft, creamy-to-yellow background color.

**Preparing:** Allow 2 to 3 pounds peaches for each quart. Rinse. To peel, immerse in *boiling water* for 20 to 30 seconds. Plunge into *cold water*. Remove skins. Halve; pit.

Prevent darkening during preparation by dipping peaches into *water* containing *ascorbic acid color keeper,* or *salt* and *lemon juice.* (Follow package directions for proportions of color keeper to water, or use 2 tablespoons salt and 2 tablespoons lemon juice for each gallon of water.) Drain well.

**Water-Bath Canning:** *Cold-Pack:* Prepare desired *syrup;* allow 1 to 1½ cups syrup for each quart. Bring to a boil;

reduce heat. Prepare peaches as above. Spoon peach halves, cavity side down and layers overlapping, into hot, clean jars; leave a ½-inch headspace. Return syrup to boiling. Add boiling syrup to cover; leave a ½-inch headspace. Wipe jar rims; adjust lids. Process in boiling water bath for 30 minutes for quarts or 25 minutes for pints (start timing when water boils).

*Hot-Pack:* In a kettle prepare desired *syrup;* allow 1 to 1½ cups syrup for each quart. Bring to boiling; reduce heat. Prepare peaches as above; add to syrup and return to boiling. Remove from heat. Spoon peach halves, cavity side down and layers overlapping, into hot, clean jars, leaving a ½-inch headspace. Return syrup to boiling. Add enough boiling syrup to cover, leaving a ½-inch headspace. Wipe rims; adjust lids. Process in boiling water bath for 25 minutes for quarts or 20 minutes for pints (start timing when water boils).

**Freezing:** *Unsweetened-Pack:* Prepare peaches as above; slice, if desired. Stir 1 teaspoon *ascorbic acid color keeper* into each 4 cups *cold water;* allow 1 to 1½ cups for each quart. Pack peaches tightly into moisture-vaporproof freezer containers; leave the proper headspace (see page 240). Add the water to cover; leave the proper headspace. Seal, label, and freeze.

*Syrup-Pack:* Prepare desired *syrup;* chill. Allow 1 to 1½ cups per quart. Prepare peaches as above; slice, if desired. Stir ½ teaspoon *ascorbic acid color keeper* into each 4 cups cold syrup. Pack peaches tightly into moisture-vaporproof freezer containers, leaving the proper headspace. Add cold syrup to cover; leave the proper headspace. Seal; label; freeze.

*Sugar-Pack:* Prepare peaches as directed at left; slice, if desired. Dissolve ¼ teaspoon *ascorbic acid color keeper* in ¼ cup *cold water;* sprinkle with ½ cup *sugar* over each 4 cups peaches. Stir. Pack peaches tightly into moisture-vaporproof freezer containers, leaving the proper headspace. Seal, label, and freeze.

## Spiced Peaches

|   |   |
|---|---|
| 5 | **cups sugar** |
| 1 | **cup vinegar** |
| 12 | **inches stick cinnamon, broken** |
| 2 | **teaspoons whole cloves** |
| 5 | **pounds small peaches** |

**Preparing:** For syrup, in a kettle combine sugar, vinegar, spices, and 2 cups *water*. Bring to boiling; reduce heat. Peel peaches. If desired, halve and pit. To prevent darkening, add peaches to syrup as they are peeled; simmer about 5 minutes. Remove from heat.

**Water-Bath Canning:** Spoon the peaches into hot, clean jars; leave a ½-inch headspace. Return syrup to boiling. Add the boiling syrup to cover; leave a ½-inch headspace. Wipe rims; adjust lids. Process in boiling water bath 20 minutes (start timing when water boils). Makes 5 or 6 pints.

## Pears

**Selecting:** Choose pears by appearance and feel. Color depends on variety. Select pears that are free of bruises and cuts and those that are uniformly firm-soft.

**Preparing:** Allow 2 to 3 pounds *pears* for each quart. Rinse pears; peel, halve, and core, removing stems and blossom ends.

Prevent darkening during preparation by dipping pears into *water* containing *ascorbic acid color keeper,* or *salt* and *lemon juice.* (Follow package directions for proportions of color keeper to water, or use 2 tablespoons salt and 2 tablespoons lemon juice for each gallon of water.) Drain. *Don't freeze pears.*

**Water-Bath Canning:** *Cold-Pack:* Prepare desired *syrup;* allow 1 to 1½ cups syrup for each quart. Bring to boiling; reduce heat. Prepare pears as above. Spoon pear halves, cavity side down and layers overlapping, into hot, clean jars; leave a ½-inch headspace. Return syrup to boiling. Add boiling syrup to cover pears; leave a ½-inch headspace. Wipe rims; adjust lids. Process in boiling water bath for 30 minutes for quarts or 25 minutes for pints (start timing when water boils).

*Hot-pack:* In a kettle prepare desired *syrup.* Allow 1 to 1½ cups syrup for each quart. Bring to boiling; reduce heat. Prepare pears as at left; add to syrup and return to boiling. Remove from heat. Spoon pear halves, cavity side down and layers overlapping, into hot, clean jars, leaving a ½-inch headspace. Return syrup to boiling. Add boiling syrup to cover pears, leaving a ½-inch headspace. Wipe rims; adjust lids.

Process in boiling water bath for 25 minutes for quarts or 20 minutes for pints (start timing when water boils).

## Plums

**Selecting:** Choose firm-fleshed, meaty varieties. Plums should be fairly firm to slightly soft.

**Preparing:** Allow 1¼ to 2½ pounds of *plums* for each quart. Thoroughly rinse plums and remove stems. Drain well. Prick plum skins. For freezing, halve and pit plums.

**Water-Bath Canning:** *Cold Pack:* Prepare desired *syrup;* allow 1 to 1½ cups syrup for each quart. Bring to a boil; reduce heat. Prepare plums as above. Spoon plums into hot, clean jars; leave a ½-inch headspace. Return syrup to boiling. Add enough boiling syrup to cover plums; leave a ½-inch headspace. Wipe jar rims; adjust lids. Process in boiling water bath for 25 minutes for quarts or 20 minutes for pints (start timing when water boils).

*Hot-Pack:* Prepare desired *syrup.* Allow 1 to 1½ cups syrup for each quart. Bring syrup to boiling; reduce heat. Prepare plums as above; add to syrup and return to boiling. Simmer for 2 minutes. Remove from heat. Cover and let stand 20 to 30 minutes. Spoon plums into hot, clean jars, leaving a ½-inch headspace. Return syrup to boiling. Add boiling syrup to cover, leaving a ½-inch headspace. Wipe jar rims; adjust lids. Process in boiling water bath for 25 minutes for quarts or 20 minutes for pints (start timing when water boils).

**Freezing:** *Unsweetened-Pack:* Prepare plums as above. Dip halved plums into *water* containing *ascorbic acid color keeper.* (Follow package directions for proportions of color keeper to water.) Drain well. Pack plums tightly into moisture-vaporproof freezer containers or bags, leaving the proper headspace (see page 240). Seal, label, and freeze.

*Syrup-Pack:* Prepare desired *syrup;* chill. Allow 1 to 1½ cups syrup per quart. Prepare plums. Stir ½ teaspoon *ascorbic acid color keeper* into each 4 cups syrup. Pack plums into moisture-vaporproof freezer containers; leave headspace (see page 240). Add syrup to cover; leave headspace. Seal; label; freeze.

*Sugar-Pack:* Prepare plums as directed at left. Dissolve ¼

teaspoon *ascorbic acid color keeper* in ¼ cup *cold water;* sprinkle with ½ cup *sugar* over each 4 cups plums. Stir to mix. Pack plums tightly into moisture-vaporproof freezer containers, leaving the proper headspace (see page 240). Seal, label, and freeze.

## Rhubarb

**Selecting:** Choose stalks of rhubarb that are fresh looking, firm, bright, and glossy.

**Preparing:** Allow 1 to 2 pounds *rhubarb* for each quart. Discard woody ends and leaves. Rinse; drain. Slice stalks into ½-inch pieces.

For freezing, blanch rhubarb by immersing pieces into boiling water for 1 minute. At once, plunge into cold water for 1 minute; drain.

**Water-Bath Canning:** *Hot-Pack:* Prepare rhubarb as above. In a kettle sprinkle ½ to 1 cup *sugar* over each 4 cups rhubarb pieces; mix well. Let stand 1 hour. Slowly bring to a boil; simmer 1 minute. Remove from heat; spoon into hot, clean jars, leaving a ½-inch headspace. Wipe rims; adjust lids. Process in boiling water bath for 10 minutes for pints or half-pints (start timing when water boils).

**Freezing:** *Unsweetened-Pack:* Prepare rhubarb as above. Pack blanched rhubarb into moisture-vaporproof freezer containers or bags, leaving headspace (see page 240). Lightly shake to pack closely. Seal, label, and freeze.

*Syrup-Pack:* Prepare desired *syrup*. Chill. Allow 1 to 1½ cups syrup for each quart. Prepare rhubarb as above. Pack blanched rhubarb into moisture-vaporproof freezer containers, leaving the proper headspace. Lightly shake to pack closely. Add cold syrup to cover, leaving headspace. Seal, label, and freeze.

*Sugar-Pack:* Prepare rhubarb as above. Sprinkle ½ cup *sugar* over each 3 cups blanched rhubarb pieces (4 cups raw). Stir to mix and dissolve sugar. Pack tightly into moisture-vaporproof freezer containers, leaving headspace. Lightly shake. Seal; label; freeze.

# Vegetables

## Asparagus

**Selecting:** Choose young, tender stalks of asparagus with compact, closed tips.

**Preparing:** Allow 2½ to 4½ pounds *asparagus* for each quart. Wash; drain. Trim off scales. Break off woody bases at the point where spears snap easily. Sort according to stalk thickness. Leave stalks whole, trimming to fit jars, or cut into 1½- to 2-inch pieces.

**Pressure Canning:** *Cold-Pack:* Prepare asparagus as above. Pack as tightly as possible, without crushing, into hot, clean jars, leaving a ½-inch headspace. Add ½ teaspoon *salt* for quarts or ¼ teaspoon for pints. Pour in *boiling water;* leave a ½-inch headspace. Wipe rims; adjust lids. Process in pressure canner at 10 pounds pressure for 30 minutes for quarts or 25 minutes for pints. At 15 pounds pressure, process quarts or pints 15 minutes.

*Hot-Pack:* Prepare asparagus as above. In a large kettle or Dutch oven bring *water* (enough to cover asparagus) to boiling. Add asparagus and boil 3 minutes. Pack hot asparagus loosely into hot, clean jars, leaving a ½-inch headspace. Add ½ teaspoon *salt* for quarts or ¼ teaspoon for pints. Pour in boiling cooking liquid; leave a ½-inch headspace. Wipe rims; adjust lids. Process in pressure canner at 10 pounds pressure for 30 minutes for quarts or 25 minutes for pints. At 15 pounds pressure, process quarts or pints 15 minutes.

*Boil at least 10 minutes before tasting home-canned asparagus; add water if needed.*

**Freezing:** Prepare asparagus as above. Place asparagus, according to size, in a blanching basket. Submerge 1 pound asparagus in 1 gallon *boiling water* in a large kettle. Cover and boil 2 minutes for small spears, 3 minutes for medium spears, and 4 minutes for large spears.

Remove basket from boiling water; immediately plunge into *ice water.* Cool for same amount of time as blanched. Drain well. Package into moisture-vaporproof freezer containers, alternating tips and stem ends for whole spears. Shake containers lightly to pack asparagus closely (do not crush), leaving a ½-inch headspace. Seal, label, and freeze.

Store in freezer up to 8 to 10 months. Cook, without thawing, in a small amount of boiling salted water 5 to 10 minutes.

## Beans—Green or Wax

*Do not use home-canned green beans for cold salads unless they have been boiled after canning—*

**Selecting:** Choose young, long, straight pods that snap crisply when bent.

**Preparing:** Allow 1½ to 2½ pounds *green or wax beans* for each quart. Wash beans; drain well. Remove ends and strings. Leave whole or cut into 1- or 2-inch pieces. For French-style, slice diagonally end-to-end.

**Pressure Canning:** *Cold-Pack:* Prepare beans as above. Pack as tightly as possible, without crushing, into hot, clean jars, leaving a ½-inch headspace. Add ½ teaspoon *salt* for quarts or ¼ teaspoon for pints. Pour in *boiling water,* leaving a ½-inch headspace. Wipe jar rims; adjust lids. Process in pressure canner at 10 pounds pressure for 25 minutes for quarts or 20 minutes for pints. At 15 pounds pressure, process quarts or pints 15 minutes.

*Hot-Pack:* Prepare beans as above. In a large kettle bring *water* (enough to cover beans) to boiling. Add beans and cook 5 minutes on high heat. Remove from heat. Pack hot beans loosely into hot, clean jars, leaving a ½-inch headspace. Add ½ teaspoon *salt* for quarts or ¼ teaspoon for pints. Pour in boiling cooking liquid, leaving a ½-inch headspace. Wipe rims; adjust lids. Process in pressure canner at 10 pounds pressure for 25 minutes for quarts or 20 minutes for pints. At 15 pounds pressure, process quarts or pints 15 minutes.

*Boil at least 10 minutes before tasting home-canned beans; add water if needed.*

**Freezing:** Prepare beans as above, *except* cut into 2- to 4-inch pieces. Place in a blanching basket. Submerge 1 pound beans in 1 gallon *boiling water* in a large kettle. Cover; boil 3 minutes. Begin timing at once.

Remove basket from boiling water; immediately plunge into *ice water.* Cool for same amount of time as blanched. Drain well. Package into moisture-vaporproof freezer containers. Shake containers lightly to pack beans closely (do not crush), leaving a ½-inch headspace. Seal, label, and freeze.

Store in freezer up to 8 to 10 months. Cook without thawing, in a small amount of boiling salted water 5 to 10 minutes.

## Beans—Lima or Butter

**Selecting:** Choose bright, dark green, crisp, full, young, and tender-skinned pods. The shelled beans should be plump with a tender, green or greenish-white skin.

**Preparing:** Allow 3 to 5 pounds *lima or butter beans* in pods for each quart. Thoroughly rinse the beans in pods; drain well. Shell beans; rinse again. Drain. Sort by size.

**Pressure Canning:** *Cold-Pack:* Prepare beans as above. Pack beans loosely (do not crush) into hot, clean jars. For small beans, leave a 1-inch headspace for pints and 1½ inches for quarts; for large beans, leave a ¾-inch headspace for pints and 1 inch for quarts. Add ½ teaspoon *salt* for quarts or ¼ teaspoon for pints. Pour in *boiling water*, leaving a ½-inch headspace. Wipe jar rims; adjust lids. Process in pressure canner at 10 pounds pressure for 50 minutes for quarts or 40 minutes for pints. At 15 pounds pressure, process quarts or pints 30 minutes.

*Hot Pack:* Prepare beans as above. In a large kettle bring *water* (enough to cover beans) to boiling. Add beans and boil 3 minutes. Pack hot beans loosely (do not crush) into hot, clean jars, leaving a 1-inch headspace. Add ½ teaspoon *salt* for quarts or ¼ teaspoon for pints. Pour in boiling cooking liquid, leaving a ½-inch headspace. Wipe jar rims; adjust lids. Process in pressure canner at 10 pounds pressure for 50 minutes for quarts, or 40 minutes for pints. At 15 pounds pressure, process quarts or pints 30 minutes.

*Boil at least 10 minutes before tasting home-canned beans; add water if needed.*

**Freezing:** Prepare beans as above. Place beans, according to size, in a blanching basket. Submerge 1 pound beans in 1 gallon *boiling water* in a large kettle. Cover and boil 2 minutes for small beans and 4 minutes for large beans; begin timing at once.

Remove basket from boiling water; immediately plunge basket into *ice water*. Cool for same amount of time as blanched. Drain well. Package into moisture-vaporproof freezer containers. Pack beans loosely (do not crush), leaving a ½-inch headspace. Seal, label, and freeze.

Store in freezer up to 8 to 10 months. Cook, without thawing, in a small amount of boiling salted water 5 to 10 minutes.

## Beets

**Selecting:** Choose round, small to medium beets with a smooth, firm, deep red flesh and a slender tap root. Large beets may be woody. Spring beets are often sold in bunches with tender, young tops still intact (to allow for weight of tops, buy about ½ pound more for each pound of beets needed).

**Preparing:** Allow 2 to 3½ pounds *beets* for each quart. Thoroughly scrub beets but do not peel. Cut off all but 1 inch of stems and roots; wash. In a large kettle bring water (enough to cover beets) to boiling. Add beets and cook 15 minutes. Cool slightly and slip off skins; trim. Cube, slice, or leave small beets whole. *Beets are not recommended for cold-pack canning.*

**Pressure Canning:** *Hot-Pack:* Prepare beets as above. Pack the hot beets into hot, clean jars, leaving a ½-inch headspace. Add ½ teaspoon *salt* for quarts or ¼ teaspoon for pints. Pour in *boiling water,* leaving a ½-inch headspace. Wipe jar rims; adjust lids. Process in pressure canner at 10 pounds pressure for 35 minutes for quarts or 30 minutes for pints. At 15 pounds pressure process quarts or pints 15 minutes.

*Boil at least 10 minutes before tasting home-canned beets; add water if needed.*

**Freezing:** Select beets as above. Thoroughly scrub beets but do not peel. Sort according to size. Trim off tops, leaving ½-inch stems. Cook till tender in boiling water to cover (small beets, 25 to 30 minutes; medium beets, 35 to 50 minutes). Drain; cool. Slip off skins. Cube or slice. Package into moisture-vaporproof feezer containers. Shake containers lightly to pack loosely; leave a ½-inch headspace. Seal, label, and freeze.

Store in freezer up to 8 to 10 months. Cook 1 pint, covered, without thawing, in 1 cup *boiling salted water* 5 to 6 minutes, breaking up frozen block of beets during cooking.

# Broccoli

**Selecting:** Choose firm, tender stalks bearing small, crisp leaves. The dark green or purplish-green buds should be tightly closed.

**Preparing:** Allow about 1 pound *broccoli* for each pint. Wash broccoli. Combine 4 cups *cold water* and 2 tablespoons *salt*. Immerse broccoli in salt-water mixture for 30 minutes to remove insects. Rinse thoroughly; drain. Remove outer leaves and tough part of stalks. Cut broccoli stalks lengthwise into uniform spears 5 to 6 inches long or to fit *freezer container* (cut so buds are about 1 inch in diameter).

**Freezing:** Prepare broccoli as at left. Place in a blanching basket. Submerge 1 pound broccoli in 1 gallon *boiling water* in a large kettle. Cover and boil 3 minutes; begin timing at once. Or, steam in a blanching basket 5 minutes (see directions on page 241). Remove from boiling water or steam; immediately plunge broccoli into *ice water*. Cool same amount of time as blanched. Drain well. Package into moisture-vaporproof freezer containers; leave no headspace. Seal; label; freeze.

Store in freezer up to 8 to 10 months. Cook, covered and without thawing, in a small amount of boiling salted water 5 to 7 minutes.

# Carrots

**Selecting:** Choose firm, well-shaped, bright golden carrots. Avoid carrots that are shriveled, soft, or cracked. Cut off any tops.

**Preparing:** Allow 2 to 3 pounds *carrots* for each quart. Wash and trim. Peel; rinse. Leave tiny carrots whole. For larger carrots, dice, slice, or cut into 2-inch strips.

**Pressure Canning:** *Cold-Pack:* Prepare carrots as above. Pack carrots as tightly as possible into hot, clean jars, leaving a 1-inch headspace. Add ½ teaspoon *salt* for quarts or ¼ teaspoon for pints. Pour in *boiling water,* leaving a ½-inch headspace. Wipe rims; adjust lids. Process in pressure canner at 10 pounds pressure for 30 minutes for quarts or 25 minutes for pints. At 15 pounds pressure, process quarts or pints 15 minutes.

*Hot-Pack:* Prepare carrots as above. In a large kettle or Dutch oven bring *water* (enough to cover carrots) to boiling. Add carrots and boil 3 minutes. Pack hot carrots into hot, clean jars, leaving a ½-inch headspace. Add ½ teaspoon *salt* for quarts or ¼ teaspoon for pints. Pour in boiling cooking liquid, leaving a ½-inch headspace. Wipe jar rims; adjust lids. Process in pressure canner at 10 pounds pressure for 30 minutes for quarts or 25 minutes for pints. At 15 pounds pressure, process quarts or pints 15 minutes.

*Boil at least 10 minutes before tasting home-canned carrots; add water if needed.*

**Freezing:** Prepare carrots as at left. Place carrots in a blanching basket. Submerge 1 pound carrots in 1 gallon *boiling water* in a large kettle. Cover and boil 5 minutes for tiny whole carrots and 2 minutes for sliced carrots or carrots cut into strips.

Remove from boiling water; immediately plunge into *ice water.* Cool for same amount of time as blanched. Drain. Package into moisture-vaporproof freezer containers. Pack carrots closely (do not crush), leaving a ½-inch headspace. Seal, label, and freeze.

Store in freezer up to 8 to 10 months. Cook, without thawing, in a small amount of boiling salted water 5 to 10 minutes.

---

# Cauliflower

---

**Selecting:** Choose a heavy, compact, white or creamy white head with bright green leaves.

**Preparing:** Allow about 1⅓ pounds *cauliflower* for each pint. Wash cauliflower. Combine 4 cups *cold water* and 2 tablespoons *salt.* Immerse cauliflower in salt-water mixture for 30 minutes to remove insects. Rinse thoroughly; drain. Remove the leaves and woody stem. Break the head into uniform flowerets about 1 inch in diameter.

**Freezing:** Prepare cauliflower as above. Place cauliflower in a blanching basket. Submerge 1 pound cauliflower in 1 gallon *boiling water* in a large kettle. Cover and boil 3 minutes; begin timing at once. Remove from boiling water; immediately plunge cauliflower into *ice water*. Cool for same amount of time as blanched. Drain well. Package into moisture-vaporproof freezer containers; leave no headspace. Seal, label, and freeze.

Store in freezer up to 8 to 10 months. Cook, covered and without thawing, in a small amount of boiling salted water 5 to 6 minutes.

---

### Safety reminder

Always boil home-canned vegetables (except tomatoes) for 10 to 20 minutes (20 minutes for corn or spinach) before tasting or using. Add water, if necessary, to avoid sticking.

---

## Corn—Cream Style

**Selecting:** Choose young but mature ears of corn with even rows of shiny, plump, milky kernels. Look for fresh, green husks; avoid wormy ears. For best flavor, use corn right after picking or purchasing. If it can't be used at once, store it unhusked, in the coolest part of the refrigerator.

**Preparing:** Allow 1½ to 3 pounds fresh ears of *corn* for each pint. Remove husks. Scrub with a stiff brush to remove silks. Rinse thoroughly in cool water. Use a sharp knife to cut off just the kernel tips, then scrape the corn with the dull edge of a knife.

**Pressure Canning:** *Cold-Pack:* Prepare cream-style corn as above. Pack corn loosely into hot, clean *pint* jars, leaving a 1½-inch headspace. (Do not shake or press down.) Add ¼ teaspoon *salt* for each pint. Pour in *boiling water,* leaving a ½-inch headspace. Wipe jar rims; adjust lids. Process in pressure canner at 10 pounds pressure for 95 minutes for pints (quarts are not recommended). At 15 pounds pressure, process pints 80 minutes.

*Hot-Pack:* Prepare cream-style corn as above. In a large kettle bring to boiling 1¼ to 2 cups *water* for each 4 cups corn. Add corn and boil 3 minutes. Pack hot corn into hot, clean *pint* jars, leaving a 1-inch headspace. Add ¼ teaspoon *salt* for each pint. Wipe jar rims; adjust lids. Process in pressure canner at 10 pounds pressure for 85 minutes for pints. At 15 pounds pressure, process pints 80 minutes.

*Boil at least 20 minutes before tasting home-canned corn. Add water and stir occasionally to prevent sticking.*

**Freezing:** Prepare corn as above, *except* do not cut corn off cob. To blanch ears of corn, place about 6 at a time in a large amount of *boiling water* in a large kettle. Cover and boil 4 minutes; begin timing at once.

Using tongs, remove corn from boiling water and immediately plunge into *ice water*. Cool for same amount of time as blanched. Drain. For cream-style corn, use a sharp knife to cut off just the kernel tips, then scrape the corn with the dull edge of a knife. Pack into moisture-vaporproof freezer containers. Shake containers lightly to pack corn closely, leaving a ½-inch headspace. Seal, label, and freeze.

Store in freezer up to 8 to 10 months. Cook, without thawing, in a small amount of boiling salted water for 5 to 10 minutes.

## Corn—On-the-Cob

**Selecting:** Choose corn as in recipe for Corn—Cream-Style.

**Preparing:** Remove husks from fresh ears of *corn*. Scrub with a stiff brush to remove silks. Rinse thoroughly in cool water.

**Freezing:** Prepare corn as above. To blanch ears of corn, place about 6 at a time in a large amount of *boiling water* in a large kettle. Cover and boil 7 minutes for small ears, 9 minutes for medium ears, and 11 minutes for large ears; begin timing at once.

Using tongs, remove corn from boiling water and immediately plunge ears of corn into *ice water*. Cool for same amount of time as blanched. Drain well.

Wrap each drained ear of corn individually in flexible wrapping material such as freezer paper or heavy-duty foil. Mold to the shape of the ear of corn, removing as much air as possible.

Bundle 4 to 6 ears of corn of uniform size together in a large plastic freezer bag. Seal, label, and freeze.

Store corn-on-the-cob in freezer up to 4 to 6 months. Cook, without thawing, in an uncovered pan in enough boiling salted water to cover ears 5 to 10 minutes.

## Corn—Whole Kernel

**Selecting:** Choose as in Corn—Cream-Style.

**Preparing:** Allow 1½ to 3 pounds fresh ears of *corn* for each pint. Remove husks. Scrub with a stiff brush to remove silks. Rinse well in cool water. Cut corn from cob at two-thirds depth; *do not scrape the cob.*

**Pressure Canning:** *Cold-Pack:* Prepare corn as above. Pack corn loosely into hot, clean, *pint* jars, leaving a 1-inch headspace. (Do not shake or press down.) Add ¼ teaspoon *salt* for each pint. Pour in *boiling water,* leaving a ½-inch headspace. Wipe jar rims; adjust lids. Process in pressure canner at 10 pounds pressure for 55 minutes for pints (quarts are not recommended). At 15 pounds pressure, process pints 50 minutes.

*Hot-Pack:* Prepare corn as above. In a large kettle bring to boiling 2 cups *water* for each 4 cups corn. Add corn and boil 3 minutes. Pack hot corn loosely into hot, clean *pint* jars, leaving a 1-inch headspace. Add ¼ teaspoon *salt* for each pint. Pour in boiling cooking liquid, leaving a 1-inch headspace. Wipe jar rims; adjust lids. Process in pressure canner at 10 pounds pressure for 55 minutes for pints. At 15 pounds pressure, process pints 50 minutes.

*Boil at least 20 minutes before tasting home-canned corn; add water if needed.*

**Freezing:** Remove husks and silks from corn. Rinse well in cool water. To blanch ears of corn, place about 6 at a time in a large amount of *boiling water* in a large kettle. Cover and boil 4 minutes; begin timing at once.

Using tongs, remove corn from boiling water and immediately plunge ears of corn into *ice water.* Cool for same amount of time as blanched. Drain well. Cut corn from cob at two-thirds depth; *do not scrape cob.* Package into moisture-vaporproof freezer containers. Shake containers lightly to pack corn closely, leaving a ½-inch headspace. Seal, label, and freeze up to 8 to 10 months. Cook, without thawing, in a small amount of boiling salted water 5 to 10 minutes.

# Peas (Green)

**Selecting:** Choose bright green, moist, crisp, well-filled pods.

**Preparing:** Allow 3 to 6 pounds *peas* in shells for each quart. Thoroughly rinse the unshelled peas in water; drain. Shell fresh peas; thoroughly rinse again and drain well.

**Pressure Canning:** *Cold-Pack:* Prepare peas as above. Pack peas loosely, without crushing, into hot, clean jars, leaving a 1-inch headspace. Add ½ teaspoon *salt* for quarts or ¼ teaspoon for pints. Pour in *boiling water*, leaving a 1-inch headspace. Wipe jar rims; adjust lids. Process in pressure canner at 10 pounds pressure for 40 minutes for quarts or pints. At 15 pounds pressure, process quarts or pints 30 minutes.

*Hot-Pack:* Prepare peas as above. In a large kettle or Dutch oven bring *water* (enough to cover peas) to boiling. Add peas and boil 3 minutes. Pack hot peas loosely, without crushing, into hot, clean jars, leaving a 1-inch headspace. Add ½ teaspoon *salt* for quarts or ¼ teaspoon for pints. Pour in boiling cooking liquid, leaving a 1-inch headspace. Wipe jar rims; adjust lids. Process in pressure canner at 10 pounds pressure for 40 minutes for quarts or pints. At 15 pounds pressure, process quarts or pints 30 minutes.

*Boil at least 10 minutes before tasting home-canned peas; add water if needed.*

**Freezing:** Prepare peas as above. Place peas in a blanching basket. Submerge 1 pound shelled peas in 1 gallon *boiling water* in a large kettle. Cover and boil 2 minutes; begin timing at once.

Remove basket from water; immediately plunge basket into *ice water*. Cool for same amount of time as blanched. Drain well. Package into moisture-vaporproof freezer containers. Shake containers lightly to pack peas loosely (do not crush), leaving a ½-inch headspace. Seal, label, and freeze.

Store in freezer up to 8 to 10 months. Cook, without thawing, in ½ cup *boiling salted water* 5 to 10 minutes.

## Peppers (Sweet)

**Selecting:** Although usually sold while still green, bell peppers will turn bright red if allowed to mature fully. Select well-shaped, firm, crisp, unblemished vegetables that have a bright green or red color.

**Preparing:** Allow ½ to ¾ pound *sweet peppers* for each pint. Wash. Remove the stems, seeds, and inner membranes of peppers before using. Cut into large pieces or leave whole (use wide-mouth jars for large pieces).

**Pressure Canning:** *Hot-Pack:* Prepare peppers as above. In a large kettle or Dutch oven bring *water* (enough to cover peppers) to boiling. Add peppers and boil 3 minutes. Pack blanched peppers into hot, clean *pint* jars, leaving a 1-inch headspace. Add 1 tablespoon *vinegar* and ½ teaspoon *salt* for each pint. Pour in boiling cooking liquid, leaving a 1-inch headspace. Wipe jar rims; adjust lids. Process in pressure canner at 10 pounds pressure for 35 minutes for pints. At 15 pounds pressure, process pints 30 minutes.

*Boil at least 10 minutes before tasting home-canned peppers; add water if needed.*

**Freezing:** Prepare peppers as above. Cut into halves or strips, or chop peppers. (For chopped peppers, spread pieces in a single layer in a shallow pan and place in freezer just till frozen.) Package peppers into moisture-vaporproof freezer containers. Shake containers lightly to pack closely; leave no headspace. Seal, label, and freeze.

Store in freezer up to 8 to 10 months. Use in soups, stews, meat loafs, and casseroles.

## Sweet Potatoes

**Selecting:** Choose firm sweet potatoes with uniform shape and skin color. Don't choose decayed, soft, or shriveled vegetables.

**Preparing:** Allow 2 to 3 pounds *sweet potatoes* for each quart. Thoroughly scrub potatoes; remove ends and woody portion.

In a covered saucepan cook whole sweet potatoes (do not

puncture with a fork) in enough *boiling water* to cover for 20 to 30 minutes or just until skins slip off easily. Remove skins; cut sweet potatoes into chunks.

**Pressure Canning:** *Hot-(Wet-) Pack:* Prepare sweet potatoes as above. Pack hot potatoes as tightly as possible, without crushing, into hot, clean jars, leaving a 1-inch headspace. Add ½ teaspoon *salt* for quarts or ¼ teaspoon for pints. Pour in *boiling* water, leaving a 1-inch headspace. Wipe jar rims; adjust lids. Process in pressure canner at 10 pounds pressure for 90 minutes for quarts or 55 minutes for pints. At 15 pounds pressure, process quarts or pints 50 minutes.

*Boil at least 10 minutes before tasting home-canned potatoes; add water if needed.*

**Freezing:** *Sugar-Pack:* Prepare sweet potatoes as above, *except* do not cook or cut up. Bake whole sweet potatoes in a 375° oven for 40 to 45 minutes or till just tender. Cool; peel and cut into halves crosswise or into thick slices. While preparing sweet potatoes, treat with a color keeper to prevent vegetables from darkening. (Either drop peeled potatoes in water containing ascorbic acid color keeper for 4 to 5 minutes—follow directions on package for proportions of color keeper to water—or use a solution of ¼ cup lemon juice per gallon of water.) Drain well.

Combine 1 cup packed *brown sugar* and ½ teaspoon ground *ginger*. Roll each piece of sweet potato into the sugar mixture till well coated. (This is enough sugar mixture for about 3 pounds potatoes or for 2 quarts.)

Package halves or slices into moisture-vaporproof freezer containers. Shake containers lightly to pack sweet potatoes, leaving a ½-inch headspace. Seal, label, and freeze.

Store in freezer up to 8 to 10 months. Thaw 1 quart sweet potato pieces till easy to separate. Then, layer in a 10x6x2-inch baking dish. Dot with 1 to 2 tablespoons *butter or margarine*. Bake, covered, in a 350° oven for 30 minutes. Uncover and bake sweet potato mixture about 10 minutes longer.

## Tomatoes

**Selecting:** Red tomatoes come in a variety of sizes and shapes, but in all cases select slightly underripe to ripe, firm tomatoes that are unblemished and well-shaped. Don't use any tomatoes with *spots, cracks,* or those that are *overripe, soft,* or *decayed.*

**Preparing:** Allow 2½ to 3 pounds *tomatoes* for each quart. Thoroughly wash and remove stems; drain. Put tomatoes into a wire-mesh basket. Dip into *boiling water* in a large kettle or Dutch oven for 30 seconds (water must be kept at or near boiling). Remove from boiling water and immediately dip tomatoes into *cold water.* When cool, slip off the skins and remove cores and stem ends. Pack small or medium tomatoes whole, but cut large tomatoes into quarters or eighths. Use a small spoon to scrape out excess seeds, if desired.

**Water-Bath Canning:** *Cold-Pack:* Prepare tomatoes as above. Pack tomatoes as tightly as possible into hot, clean jars, leaving a ½-inch headspace. Use a wooden spoon to press tomatoes gently till the juice runs out. Add more tomatoes and press gently to fill spaces. Add 1 teaspoon *salt* for quarts or ½ teaspoon for pints. *Add no water.* Wipe jar rims; adjust lids. Process in boiling water bath for 45 minutes for quarts or 35 minutes for pints (start timing when water boils).

*Hot-Pack:* Prepare tomatoes as above, *except* leave tomatoes whole or cut into halves. In a large kettle or Dutch oven bring tomatoes slowly to boiling, stirring constantly but gently. Boil, uncovered, 5 minutes. Pack hot tomatoes and some juice into hot, clean jars, leaving a ½-inch headspace. Add 1 teaspoon *salt* for quarts or ½ teaspoon for pints. *Add no water.* Wipe jar rims; adjust lids. Process in boiling water bath 45 minutes for quarts or 35 minutes for pints (start timing when water boils).

**Freezing:** Prepare tomatoes as above. In a large kettle bring tomatoes slowly to boiling, stirring constantly. Cover; simmer 10 minutes or till tender. Set kettle into ice water; cool. Package into moisture-vaporproof freezer containers. Closely pack tomatoes; leave proper headspace. Add 1 teaspoon *salt* for quarts or ½ teaspoon for pints. Seal, label, and freeze.

Store in freezer up to 8 to 10 months. Use tomatoes in cooked dishes, such as casseroles.

# Tomato Juice

### 8 pounds ripe but firm tomatoes

**Preparing:** Thoroughly wash tomatoes. Remove stems; drain. Cut out stem ends and cores, if present. Cut tomatoes into pieces. Measure about 19 cups tomato pieces.

In an 8- to 10-quart kettle or Dutch oven bring tomatoes slowly to boiling, stirring frequently. Cover and simmer about 15 minutes or till soft; stir often to prevent sticking. Press tomatoes through a food mill or sieve to extract juice; measure 12 cups juice. Return tomato juice to kettle and bring to boiling; boil 5 minutes, stirring often.

**Water-Bath Canning:** Prepare juice as above. Pour juice into hot, clean jars, leaving a ½-inch headspace. To tomato juice add ½ teaspoon *salt* for quarts or ¼ teaspoon for pints. Wipe jar rims; adjust lids. Process in boiling water bath for 35 minutes for quarts or 35 minutes for pints (start timing when water boils). Makes 5 to 6 pints.

**Freezing:** Prepare juice as above. Cool. Pour into moisture-vaporproof freezer containers; leave a ½-inch headspace (with wide-top containers). To juice add ½ teaspoon *salt* for quarts or ¼ teaspoon for pints. Seal, label, and freeze. Makes 5 to 6 pints.

***Tomato Juice Cocktail:*** Prepare tomato juice as above, *except* add 1 cup chopped *celery* and ½ cup chopped *onion* with uncooked tomatoes in the kettle or Dutch oven. Bring mixture slowly to boiling, stirring constantly but gently. Cover and simmer about 15 minutes or till soft; stir often to prevent sticking.

Press mixture through a food mill or sieve to extract juice; measure 12 cups juice. Return juice to kettle and bring to boiling; boil gently, uncovered, about 15 minutes, stirring often to prevent sticking. Measure 9½ to 10 cups juice. Stir in ¼ cup *lemon juice*, 1 tablespoon *sugar*, 2 teaspoons *salt*, 2 teaspoons *Worcestershire sauce*, 1 to 2 teaspoons *prepared horseradish*, and ¼ teaspoon *bottled hot pepper sauce*. Simmer 10 minutes.

**Water-Bath Canning:** Prepare cocktail as above. Pour into hot, clean jars, leaving a ½-inch headspace. Wipe jar rims; adjust lids. Process in boiling water bath for 15 minutes for quarts or 10 minutes for pints (start timing when water boils). Makes 5 to 6 pints.

**Freezing:** Freeze as above for Tomato Juice, *except* omit the salt.

## Tomato Catsup

| | |
|---|---|
| 1 | **cup white vinegar** |
| 1½ | **inches stick cinnamon, broken** |
| 1½ | **teaspoons whole cloves** |
| 1 | **teaspoon celery seed** |
| 8 | **pounds tomatoes (24 medium)** |
| 1 | **medium onion, chopped (½ cup)** |
| ¼ | **teaspoon cayenne** |
| 1 | **cup sugar** |

**Preparing:** In a saucepan mix the first 4 ingredients. Cover; bring to boiling. Remove from heat; let stand. Wash, core, and quarter tomatoes. Drain in a colander; discard liquid. Place tomatoes in a large kettle. Add onion and cayenne. Bring to boiling; cook 15 minutes. Stir often. Put mixture through a food mill; discard seeds and skins. Add sugar to tomato juice. Bring to boiling; simmer about 1½ to 2 hours or till reduced by half. (Measure depth with a ruler at start and finish.) Strain vinegar mixture into tomatoes; discard spices. Add 4 teaspoons *salt*. Simmer about 30 minutes or till of desired consistency, stirring often.

**Water-Bath Canning:** Prepare catsup as above. Pour hot catsup into hot, clean pint jars, leaving a ½-inch headspace. Wipe jar rims; adjust lids. Process in boiling water bath for 10 minutes for pints (start timing when water boils). Makes 2 pints.

**Freezing:** Prepare catsup as above. Set kettle into a sink of ice water; cool. Package into moisture-vaporproof freezer containers, leaving a ½-inch headspace. Seal, label, and freeze up to 8 to 10 months. Makes 2 pints.

## Turnips and Rutabagas

**Selecting:** Choose smooth, firm, tender turnips and rutabagas of small or medium size.

**Preparing:** Remove tops. Wash *turnips* and *rutabagas;*
peel off skin. Slice or cube.

**Freezing:** Prepare vegetables as above; place in blanching
basket. Submerge 1 pound vegetables in 1 gallon *boiling
water.* Cover; boil 2 minutes. Remove vegetables from water;
immediately plunge into *ice water.* Cool same amount of time
as blanched. Drain well. Package into moisture-vaporproof
freezer containers; leave no headspace. Seal, label, and freeze
up to 8 to 10 months. Cook, covered and without thawing, in
a small amount of boiling salted water 5 to 10 minutes.

## Winter Squash or Pumpkin

**Selecting:** Winter squash is the common name for a number
of varieties. Select squash that are heavy for their size, with
hard rinds and good coloring and shaping for their variety.

**Preparing:** Allow 1½ to 3 pounds *winter squash or pumpkin* for each quart. Wash; halve and remove seeds. Peel; cut
into 1-inch cubes. *Do not can mashed squash or pumpkin.*

**Pressure Canning:** *Cold-Pack:* Prepare squash or pumpkin as above. Pack squash or pumpkin cubes loosely into hot,
clean jars, leaving a ½-inch headspace. Add ½ teaspoon *salt*
for quarts and ¼ teaspoon for pints. Pour in *boiling water,*
leaving a ½-inch headspace. Wipe jar rims; adjust lids. Process
in pressure canner at 10 pounds pressure for 90 minutes for
quarts or 55 minutes for pints. At 15 pounds pressure, process
quarts or pints 20 minutes.

*Hot-Pack:* Prepare vegetable as above. In a large kettle
bring *water* (enough to barely cover squash or pumpkin cubes)
to boiling. Add cubes and boil 3 minutes. Pack hot vegetables
into hot, clean jars, leaving a ½-inch headspace. Add ½
teaspoon *salt* for quarts or ¼ teaspoon for pints. Pour in
boiling cooking liquid, leaving a ½-inch headspace. Wipe jar
rims; adjust lids. Process in pressure canner at 10 pounds

pressure for 90 minutes for quarts or 55 minutes for pints. At 15 pounds pressure, process quarts or pints 20 minutes.

*Boil at least 10 minutes before tasting home-canned vegetables; add water if needed.*

**Freezing:** Wash squash or pumpkin; halve and remove seeds. Cook before freezing. To bake squash, place halves or serving-size pieces, cut side down, in a baking pan. Cover with foil; bake in a 350° oven for 30 minutes. Turn cut side up; bake, covered, till tender (20 to 30 minutes more for acorn, buttercup, or butternut squash; 45 to 50 minutes more for Hubbard, banana, or spaghetti squash).

*Or,* in a covered pan cook squash in a small amount of boiling salted water till tender (allow 15 minutes for cubes). Cool quickly by placing pan in a sink of ice water.

Remove pulp from rind and mash or press through a sieve or food mill. Package into moisture-vaporproof freezer containers. Shake containers lightly to pack squash, leaving a ½-inch headspace. Seal, label, and freeze up to 8 to 10 months. Cook, covered and without thawing, 10 minutes. Season. Cook, uncovered, 10 minutes longer, stirring occasionally.

# Meat, Fish, & Poultry

## Meat

**Selecting:** Choose beef, veal, lamb, pork, or venison for canning or freezing.

**Preparing:** Chill *meat* immediately after slaughter. Refrigerate purchased meat and can as soon after purchase as possible. Cut chilled meat into cubes or strips that will pack easily into canning jars. Remove gristle, bones, and as much fat as possible. Keep your work area and utensils very clean.

**Pressure Canning:** *Hot-Pack:* Simmer meat in a small amount of water or meat stock in a covered pan till medium-done; stir occasionally. Season meat lightly with salt. Drain. Pack the hot meat loosely into hot, clean jars, leaving a 1-inch headspace. Pour in *boiling water or stock,* leaving a 1-inch headspace. Wipe jar rims; adjust lids. Process in pressure canner at 10 pounds pressure for 90 minutes for quarts or 75 minutes for pints.

*Boil canned meat in a small amount of water for 15 to 20 minutes before tasting or using.*

**Freezing:** Have fresh meat cut into desired cuts. Avoid packing more bone than necessary. Keep packages small—make them in family-size portions. Separate individual portions of chops or steaks with two layers of waxed paper for easy separation. Wrap in moisture-vaporproof material. Package ground meat in freezer containers or plastic freezer bags, or form into patties. Seal, label, and freeze.

Storage time at 0° F. is: beef steaks and roasts, 6 to 12 months; lamb and veal chops and roasts, 6 to 9 months; pork chops and roasts, 3 to 6 months; ground meat, 3 to 4 months; ham, 2 months; and bacon, 1 month.

To thaw, place in refrigerator in original wrap. Do not refreeze meat once it has thawed.

# Fish

**Selecting:** Use only very fresh, thoroughly cleaned fish. Bass, mackerel, salmon, or trout are varieties that can or freeze well.

**Preparing:** Allow 2 to 3 pounds whole *fish* for each pint. Remove head, fins, and tail. Split the fish but do not remove backbone. Remove skin, if desired. Cut the fish into jar-size lengths. Soak fish in a brine solution made in the proportion of 1 cup *salt* to 1 gallon *water* for 30 to 60 minutes, depending upon the thickness of the fish. Drain and rinse fish; discard brine.

**Pressure Canning:** *Cold-Pack:* Pack fish so that skin side of pieces is next to glass. Pack fish into hot, clean *pint* jars with wide mouths, leaving a 1-inch headspace. Add ¼ teaspoon *salt* to each jar. *Do not add liquid.* Wipe rims; adjust lids. Process in pressure canner at 10 pounds pressure for 100 minutes for pints (quarts are not recommended).

*Boil in a small amount of water for 10 minutes before tasting or using fish.*

**Freezing:** Any firm-fleshed, fresh, chilled fish is suitable for freezing. Dress and wash fish as for cooking. Cut into steaks or fillets, if desired, and dip these portions into a solution of ⅔ cup *salt* to 1 gallon *water* for 30 seconds. Wrap fish in moisture-vaporproof material. Seal, label, and freeze.

Store in freezer up to 6 to 9 months. To thaw, place in refrigerator in original wrap or cook frozen, allowing extra time.

## Shellfish

**Preparing for Freezing:** Shuck *oysters, clams,* or *scallops;* freeze immediately in freezer containers, leaving a 1½-inch headspace.

Cook *crabs* or *lobsters* as for eating; chill in refrigerator. Remove meat from shells; wrap meat in moisture-vaporproof material.

Freeze *shrimp,* uncooked, either in shells or shelled. Remove heads. Wrap for freezing.

Seal, label, and freeze. Storage time at 0° F. is: oysters, clams, scallops, and shrimp, 3 months; crab or lobster, 1 month. Cook shrimp while frozen. Thaw other shellfish in refrigerator in original wrap. Cook oysters, clams, and scallops as for fresh varieties.

## Poultry

**Selecting:** Choose chicken, duck, turkey, or game birds for canning or freezing.

**Preparing:** Allow 3½ to 4¼ pounds *chicken* for each quart canned with bone, and 5½ to 6¼ pounds per quart without bone. Rinse chilled, dressed chicken in cold water. Pat dry with a clean cloth. Cut up; remove visible fat. Boil, steam, or bake chicken till medium-done—pink color should be almost gone. Remove bone, if desired, but do not remove skin.

**Pressure Canning:** *Hot-Pack:* Prepare poultry as at left. Pack chicken pieces loosely into hot, clean jars. Place thigh and drumsticks with skin next to glass and fit breast pieces into center, leaving a 1-inch headspace. If desired, add 1 teaspoon *salt* for quarts or ½ teaspoon for pints. Pour in *boiling water or broth*, leaving a 1-inch headspace. Wipe rims; adjust lids. Process in pressure canner at 10 pounds pressure—for poultry with bones, process 75 minutes for quarts or 65 minutes for pints; for deboned poultry, process 90 minutes for quarts or 75 minutes for pints.

*Boil in a small amount of water for 15 to 20 minutes before tasting or using poultry.*

**Freezing:** Chill clean, dressed birds. Disjoint and cut up bird or leave whole. Wrap in moisture-vaporproof material. Wrap and freeze giblets separately. Seal, label, and freeze.

Storage time at 0° F. is: chicken, 12 months; turkey, 6 months; and giblets, 3 months.

To thaw, place in refrigerator in original wrap. Do not refreeze poultry once thawed.

## Wrap for freezing

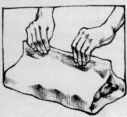

Use suitable wrapping 1½ times the circumference of the food. With food in center, join sides of wrap at top. Fold edges down in series of locked folds, pressing wrap against food. Crease. Seal ends, pressing to remove air. Bring ends of wrap against package; secure with freezer tape.

# Pickles & Relishes

Using the proper ingredients and equipment is important for making pickle products. Select a cucumber variety developed for pickling, and try to use the cucumbers as soon as possible after harvesting. Choose unwaxed cucumbers when pickling whole cucumbers; be sure to remove the blossoms.

Use granulated pickling or canning salt. Iodized table salt may cause the pickles to darken, and uniodized table salt may make the brine cloudy.

Choose a high-grade vinegar of 4 to 6 percent acid (40- to 60-grain). Either cider vinegar or white distilled vinegar can be used; however, use cider vinegar for most pickles. Use white vinegar when a light-colored product is desired. Never dilute the vinegar more than indicated in the recipe. Instead, for a less-sour product, add sugar.

Do not use copper, brass, galvanized, or iron utensils for making pickles. Instead, choose equipment made of stoneware, aluminum, glass, or stainless steel.

You'll need a water-bath canner with a rack for processing all pickles and relishes. Or, you can substitute any large kettle (with a rack) that's deep enough to hold jars and still have room for at least an inch or two of water to boil over the jar tops.

Standard canning jars and lids also are important for canning. Do not use jars or lids from commercially prepared foods.

## Causes of Poor Pickles

*Shriveled pickles:* salt, sugar, or vinegar solution is too strong.

*Hollow pickles:* cucumbers not as fresh as they should be, or are poorly developed.

*Soft or slippery pickles:* too little salt or acid, an imperfect seal, or insufficient heat.

## Vegetable Relish

| | |
|---|---|
| 8 | medium tomatoes, peeled, cored, and cut up (about 2¾ pounds) |
| 6 | medium zucchini, quartered lengthwise (about 3⅔ pounds) |
| 3 | large sweet red peppers, stems and seeds removed, and cut up (about 1 pound) |
| 3 | large green peppers, stems and seeds removed, and cut up (about 1 pound) |
| 2 | medium onions |
| 4 | cloves garlic |
| ¼ | cup pickling salt |
| 2 | cups vinegar |
| 2 | cups sugar |
| 1 | cup water |
| 2 | teaspoons dried thyme, crushed |
| 2 | bay leaves |
| ½ | teaspoon pepper |

**Preparing:** Using the coarse blade of a food grinder, grind tomatoes, zucchini, red and green peppers, onions, and garlic. Place in a colander to drain excess liquid. In a large nonmetal container sprinkle ground vegetables with pickling salt; let stand overnight. Rinse and drain well.

In a large kettle or Dutch oven combine vinegar, sugar, water, dried thyme, bay leaves, and pepper. Bring vinegar mixture to boiling, stirring to dissolve sugar. Stir in ground vegetable mixture. Bring mixture to boiling. Remove from heat.

**Water-Bath Canning:** Ladle hot relish mixture into hot, clean pint jars, leaving a ½-inch headspace. Wipe jar rims; adjust lids. Process in boiling water bath for 10 minutes for pints (start timing when water boils). Makes 5 to 6 pints.

**Freezing:** Prepare relish as above. Remove kettle or Dutch oven from heat. Cool mixture quickly by setting pan in a sink of ice water. Pack relish in pint freezer containers, leaving a ½-inch headspace. Seal, label, and freeze. Makes 5 to 6 pints.

# Corn Relish

| | |
|---|---|
| **16** | to 20 fresh ears of corn |
| **2** | cups water |
| **3** | cups chopped celery (6 stalks) |
| **1½** | cups chopped sweet red pepper (3 medium) |
| **1½** | cups chopped green pepper (3 medium) |
| **1** | cup chopped onion (2 medium) |
| **2** | cups vinegar |
| **1½** | cups sugar |
| **2** | tablespoons salt |
| **2** | teaspoons celery seed |
| **⅓** | cup all-purpose flour |
| **2** | tablespoons dry mustard |
| **1** | teaspoon ground turmeric |

**Preparing:** Husk and silk corn. Cut corn from cobs; do not scrape cobs. Measure 8 cups cut corn. In an 8- to 10-quart kettle or Dutch oven combine corn and the 2 cups water. Bring to boiling; boil gently, covered, about 12 minutes or till corn is nearly tender. Add celery, red and green peppers, onion, vinegar, sugar, salt, and celery seed. Boil, uncovered, 5 minutes longer, stirring occasionally.

Stir flour, dry mustard, and turmeric with ½ cup *cold water*. Add to corn mixture. Cook and stir till thickened and bubbly; cook 1 to 2 minutes longer.

**Water-Bath Canning:** Pack relish into hot, clean pint jars, leaving a ½-inch headspace. Wipe jar rims; adjust lids. Process in boiling water bath for 15 minutes for pints (start timing when water boils). Makes 6 pints.

## Processing pickles and relishes

It's essential to process home-canned pickles and relishes in a water-bath canner. The processing destroys organisms that cause spoilage, and en- sures the keeping quali- ty. Follow the general canning process on page 231 and the information on water-bath processing on page 233.

## Sweet Pickle Slices

| | |
|---|---|
| 1¼ | cups pickling salt |
| 4 | to 5 pounds 3- to 4-inch pickling cucumbers, washed |
| 6 | cups sugar |
| 4 | cups vinegar |
| ½ | cup prepared horseradish |
| 8 | inches stick cinnamon |
| ¾ | teaspoon celery seed |

**Preparing:** Stir pickling salt into 10 cups *boiling water;* pour over cucumbers in a large nonmetal container. Cool. Cover with a weighted plate to keep cucumbers in brine. Let stand 7 days. Drain. Cover cucumbers with hot water; let stand 24 hours. Drain. Cover again with hot water; let stand 24 hours. Drain; slice cucumbers and return to container. Mix remaining ingredients; bring to boiling. Slowly pour over cucumbers. Cool; cover. Let stand overnight. Each morning for 4 days, drain cucumbers, reserving liquid. Reheat the liquid; pour over cucumbers. Cool; cover each time. On the fifth day, remove cinnamon; bring liquid to boiling.

**Water-Bath Canning:** Pack cucumbers and liquid into hot, clean pint jars; leave a ½-inch headspace. Wipe rims; adjust lids. Process in boiling water bath 10 minutes for pints (start timing when water boils). Makes 7 or 8 pints.

## Bread and Butter Pickles

**4** quarts sliced medium cucumbers
**8** medium white onions, sliced
**3** cloves garlic
**⅓** cup pickling salt
**5** cups sugar
**3** cups cider vinegar
**2** tablespoons mustard seed
**1½** teaspoons turmeric
**1½** teaspoons celery seed

**Preparing:** In a large bowl combine first 4 ingredients. Stir in a large amount of *cracked ice*. Let stand 3 hours; drain well. Remove garlic. In a large kettle combine remaining ingredients; add drained mixture. Bring to a boil.

**Water-Bath Canning:** Pack pickles and liquid into hot, clean jars, leaving a ½-inch headspace. Wipe rims; adjust lids. Process 5 minutes for pints or half-pints (start timing when water boils). Makes 6 pints.

## Dill Pickles

*For each quart:*
**½** pound 4-inch pickling cucumbers (5 or 6 cucumbers)
**4** heads fresh dill *or* 2 tablespoons dillseed
**1** teaspoons mustard seed
**1¾** cups water
**¾** cup cider vinegar
**1** tablespoon pickling salt

**Preparing:** Thoroughly rinse cucumbers; remove stems and blossom ends. Pack cucumbers loosely into hot, clean quart jar(s), leaving a ½-inch headspace. Add dill and mustard seed to each quart. Make a brine by combining water, vinegar, and salt. Bring to boiling.

**Water-Bath Canning:** Slowly pour hot brine over cucumbers, leaving a ½-inch headspace. Wipe jar rim; adjust lid.

Process in boiling water bath for 15 minutes for quarts (start timing when water boils). Let pickles stand at least 1 week before opening. Makes 1 quart.

## Kosher Dill Pickles

*For each quart:*
- **½ pound 4-inch pickling cucumbers (5 or 6 cucumbers)**
- **4 heads fresh dill or 2 tablespoons dillseed**
- **1 clove garlic**
- **1 small piece dried hot red pepper (optional)**
- **2¼ cups water**
- **¾ cup vinegar**
- **1 tablespoon pickling salt**

**Preparing:** Thoroughly rinse cucumbers; remove stems and blossom ends. Pack cucumbers loosely into hot, clean quart jar(s), leaving a ½-inch headspace. Add dill, garlic, and red pepper. Make a brine by combining water, vinegar, and salt. Bring to boiling.

**Water-Bath Canning:** Slowly pour hot brine over cucumbers, leaving a ½-inch headspace. Wipe jar rim; adjust lid.

Process in boiling water bath for 15 minutes for quarts (start timing when water boils). Let pickles stand at least 1 week before opening. Makes 1 quart.

## Mixed Pickles

**10** pickling cucumbers, cut into 1-inch chunks (about 2 pounds)
**6** green peppers, cut into strips
**6** green tomatoes, cut into wedges
**¾** cup pickling salt
**6** large carrots, peeled and cut into strips (4 cups)
**4** cups sugar
**2½** cups cider vinegar
**3** tablespoons celery seed
**3** tablespoons mustard seed
**1** tablespoon pickling salt
**2** teaspoons turmeric

**Preparing:** In a large nonmetal container cover the first 3 ingredients with a mixture of the ¾ cup salt and 6 cups *water*. Cover; let stand in a cool place overnight. Drain; rinse. Place in a large kettle. Cook carrots in boiling salted water 5 minutes; drain. Add carrots to cucumber mixture. Combine remaining ingredients. Pour over vegetables. Bring to a boil.

**Water-Bath Canning:** Fill hot, clean pint jars; leave a ½-inch headspace. Wipe rims; adjust lids. Process 10 minutes for pints (start timing when water boils). Makes 6 pints.

## Quick Mustard Pickles

**2** pounds medium pickling cucumbers or zucchini, washed
**1** pound head cauliflower, broken into flowerets
**2** cups white vinegar
**1⅓** cups sugar
**2½** teaspoons dry mustard
**2½** teaspoons prepared horseradish
**2** teaspoons celery seed

**Preparing:** Cut cucumbers into ½-inch chunks or ¼-inch slices; measure 6 cups. Pack cucumbers and cauliflower into hot, clean pint jars, leaving a ½-inch headspace. In a saucepan mix remaining ingredients, 1⅓ cups *water,* and 2½ teaspoons *salt.* Bring to a boil.

**Water-Bath Canning:** Pour hot pickling liquid over vegetables in jars; leave a ½-inch headspace. (Liquid will be cloudy due to mustard.) Wipe rims; adjust lids. Process in boiling water bath 10 minutes for pints (start timing when water boils). Makes 5 pints.

# Jellies & Jams

As with pickles and relishes, the proper equipment and techniques are essential for successfully making jellies and jams.

## Equipment

A large 8- to 10-quart kettle or Dutch oven is an important piece of equipment for both cooked jams and jellies. For jelly-making, an accurate thermometer and a jelly bag or cheesecloth and colander also are needed. Use hot, sterilized jars (boiled 10 minutes) and paraffin or flat metal lids and screw bands for sealing. For jams and other spreads, use standard half-pint canning jars with flat metal lids and screw bands. Jam-type spreads must be processed in a boiling water bath; consequently, a covered water-bath canner and rack also are essential pieces of equipment.

## Preparation

**Jelly:** Wash jars in sudsy water; rinse. Sterilize in boiling water 10 minutes. Let stand in water till ready to fill; drain. Prepare lids following manufacturer's directions. (*Or,* if using paraffin, melt it over hot water.)

## Jelly test

To test jelly without a thermometer, dip a metal spoon into the jelly. Hold it over the kettle and watch for two drops that run together and sheet off the spoon.

For jelly without added pectin, prepare juice, then cook with sugar till the jellying point is reached. A thermometer is useful for measuring the jellying point, which is 8° above the boiling point of water. (*Or*, see the tip box above for how to test for the jellying stage without a thermometer.) Follow recipe directions for cooking jelly with added pectin.

Remove from heat and skim off foam with a metal spoon. Ladle jelly into hot, sterilized jars, leaving a ¼-inch headspace. Wipe rims.

To seal with flat metal lids and screw bands, place a lid with sealing compound next to the glass and screw the band down firmly. Invert jar a few seconds to sterilize lid. Turn right side up; cool. When cool, check the seal by feeling for an indentation in the center of the lid.

To seal with paraffin, spoon a thin layer of melted paraffin over surface of hot jelly. Rotate jar so paraffin clings to sides. Prick air bubbles. After paraffin hardens, spoon another thin layer over first layer for a total thickness of ⅛ inch. Cool; cover paraffin.

**Jams, Preserves, and Marmalades:** For cooked spreads, wash jars and lids in sudsy water; rinse. Let stand in water till ready to fill; drain. Heat 4 to 5 inches of water in a water-bath canner with rack. Prepare a jam-type spread following recipe directions. Ladle into hot, clean jars, leaving a ¼-inch headspace. Wipe rims. Place lid with sealing compound next to glass; screw band down firmly.

Place jars on a rack in a water-bath canner; add boiling

water till level is 1 to 2 inches above tops of jars. Cover; continue heating till water boils. Once water is boiling, start counting the processing time. While processed jars are cooling, invert jars for 30 minutes to prevent fruit from floating. When completely cooled, check seal by feeling for an indentation in the center of the lid.

For uncooked or freezer-type jams, follow the individual recipe directions.

## Storing

After jars are sealed, you can remove the metal screw bands from two-piece lids. Label jars with contents and date. Store jellies and jams in a cool, dry place.

## Apple Jelly

> **3 pounds tart apples, cut into chunks**
> **3 cups sugar**

**Preparing:** In an 8- to 10-quart kettle combine apples and 5 cups *water*. Bring to boiling; reduce heat. Cover; simmer about 30 minutes or till very soft, stirring occasionally.

Strain through a jelly bag or several layers of cheesecloth set in a colander; do not squeeze. Measure juice. Add enough water to measure 4 cups liquid. In a kettle heat and stir apple juice and sugar till dissolved. Bring to a full rolling boil (a boil that cannot be stirred down). Boil hard, uncovered, for 11 to 13 minutes or till thermometer registers 220° (syrup sheets off a metal spoon). Remove from heat; skim off foam with a metal spoon. Ladle into hot, sterilized jars, leaving a ¼-inch headspace. Seal, using metal lids or paraffin. Makes 4 half-pints.

*Cinnamon-Apple Jelly:* Prepare as directed above, *except* add 4 to 6 inches *stick cinnamon*, broken, with sugar. Remove before skimming.

*Mint-Apple Jelly:* Prepare as directed above, *except* tie 1 cup lightly packed *fresh mint leaves* in a cheesecloth bag; press mint with a rolling pin. Add mint and 6 drops *green food coloring* to kettle with juice and sugar. Remove mint before skimming off foam.

---

# Fruit Juice Jelly

**4** **cups unsweetened apple, grape, orange, or pineapple juice or cranberry juice cocktail (not low-calorie)**
**1** **1¾-ounce package powdered fruit pectin**
**¼** **cup lemon juice**
**4½** **cups sugar**

**Preparing:** In an 8- to 10-quart kettle combine juice, pectin, and lemon juice. Bring to a full rolling boil (a boil that cannot be stirred down). Stir in sugar. Return to a full rolling boil. Boil hard 1 minute; stir constantly. Remove from heat; quickly skim off foam with a metal spoon. Ladle into hot, sterilized jars; leave a ¼-inch headspace. Seal, using metal lids or paraffin. Makes 6 half-pints.

---

# Freezer Jam

**4** **cups blackberries, raspberries, or strawberries, caps removed**
**4** **cups sugar**
**¼** **teaspoon ground nutmeg**
**½** **of a 6-ounce package (1 foil pouch) liquid fruit pectin**
**2** **tablespoons lemon juice**

**Preparing:** Crush berries; measure 2 cups. In a large bowl combine the 2 cups crushed berries, the sugar, and nutmeg. Let stand 10 minutes. Combine pectin and lemon juice. Add to berry mixture; stir for 3 minutes.

**Freezing:** Ladle at once into clean jars or moisture-vaporproof freezer containers, leaving a ½-inch headspace. Seal; label. Let stand several hours at room temperature or till jam is set. Store up to 3 weeks in refrigerator or 1 year in freezer. Makes 5 half-pints.

## Peach Jam

2½ to 3 pounds peaches (10 to 12)
 1 1¾-ounce package powdered fruit pectin
 2 tablespoons lemon juice
5½ cups sugar

**Preparing:** Peel, pit, and coarsely grind peaches; measure 4 cups. In an 8- to 10-quart kettle combine ground peaches, pectin, and lemon juice. Bring to a full rolling boil (a boil that cannot be stirred down), stirring constantly. Stir in sugar. Return to a full rolling boil. Boil hard, uncovered, for 1 minute; stir constantly. Remove from heat; quickly skim off foam with a metal spoon.
  **Water-Bath Canning:** Ladle jam at once into hot clean half-pint jars, leaving a ¼-inch headspace. Wipe jar rims; adjust lids. Process in boiling water bath for 15 minutes (start timing when water boils). Makes 6 to 7 half-pints.
  *Peach-Banana Jam:* Prepare jam as above, *except* chop 1 slightly green medium *banana* and add to kettle with peaches. Makes 7 half-pints.
  *Peach-Plum Jam:* Prepare jam as above, *except* coarsely grind 1¼ pounds *peaches;* measure *2 cups.* Pit and finely chop ¾ pound fully ripe *Italian prune plums;* measure *2 cups.* Add to kettle with peaches. Makes 6 half-pints.

## Strawberry Jam

8 cups strawberries, caps removed
1 1¾-ounce package powdered fruit pectin
2 tablespoons lemon juice
7 cups sugar

**Preparing:** In a large bowl crush strawberries; measure 4½ cups. In an 8- to 10-quart kettle combine crushed berries, pectin, and lemon juice. Bring to a full rolling boil (a boil that cannot be stirred down). Stir in sugar. Return to a full rolling boil. Boil hard, uncovered, for 1 minute, stirring constantly. Remove from heat; quickly skim off foam with a metal spoon.

**Water-Bath Canning:** Ladle jam at once into hot, clean half-pint jars, leaving a ¼-inch headspace. Wipe jar rims; adjust lids. Process in boiling water bath for 15 minutes (start timing when water boils). Makes 7 to 8 half-pints.

## Grape Jam

    3½  **pounds Concord grapes**
     2  **cups water**
    4½  **cups sugar**

**Preparing:** Wash and stem grapes—make sure to include some grapes that are green. (Should have about 10 cups stemmed grapes.) Remove and reserve skins from *half* of the grapes. Leave skins on remaining grapes. In an 8- to 10-quart kettle combine the skinned and unskinned grapes. Cover and cook about 10 minutes or till grapes are very soft. Sieve cooked grape mixture to remove seeds and skins; discard seeds and cooked skins. Measure 3 cups of strained pulp and return to kettle.

Stir in water and reserved uncooked grape skins. Cook mixture, covered, for 10 minutes. Uncover and stir in sugar. Bring mixture to a full rolling boil (a boil that cannot be stirred down), stirring frequently. Boil, uncovered, about 12 minutes or till syrup sheets off a metal spoon. Remove from heat; quickly skim off foam with a metal spoon.

**Water-Bath Canning:** Ladle jam at once into hot, clean half-pint jars, leaving a ¼-inch headspace. Wipe jar rims; adjust lids. Process in boiling water bath for 15 minutes (start timing when water boils). Makes 6 half-pints.

## Plum Jam

    3  **pounds red plums (about 22 medium)**
    3  **cups sugar**
    2  **tablespoons lemon juice**

**Preparing:** Halve, pit, and coarsely grind plums; measure 4 cups ground plums. In an 8- to 10-quart kettle or Dutch oven combine plums, sugar, and lemon juice. Let mixture stand for 1 hour. Bring mixture to a full rolling boil (a boil that cannot be stirred down). Boil hard, uncovered, for 16 minutes or till syrup sheets off a metal spoon. Remove from heat; quickly skim off foam with a metal spoon.

**Water-Bath Canning:** Ladle jam at once into hot, clean half-pint jars, leaving a ¼-inch headspace. Wipe jar rims; adjust lids. Process in boiling water bath for 15 minutes (start timing when water boils). Makes 4 to 5 half-pints.

# Orange Marmalade

|       |                                                              |
| ----- | ------------------------------------------------------------ |
| **4** | **medium oranges**                                           |
| **1** | **medium lemon**                                             |
| **1½**| **cups water**                                               |
| **⅛** | **teaspoon baking soda**                                     |
| **5** | **cups sugar**                                               |
| **½** | **of a 6-ounce package (1 foil pouch) liquid fruit pectin** |

**Preparing:** Score orange and lemon peels into 4 lengthwise sections. Remove peels; scrape off white portion. Cut peels into very thin strips. Combine peels, water, and baking soda. Bring to boiling. Cover; simmer for 10 minutes. *Do not drain.* Remove membrane from fruits. Section fruits, reserving juices; discard seeds. Add sectioned fruits and juices to peel. Return to boiling. Cover and simmer for 20 minutes. Measure 3 cups. In an 8- to 10-quart kettle combine the 3 cups fruit mixture and sugar. Bring to a full rolling boil; boil, uncovered, 1 minute. Remove from heat; stir in pectin. Skim off foam.

**Water-Bath Canning:** Ladle marmalade into hot, clean half-pint jars, leaving a ¼-inch headspace. Wipe jar rims; adjust lids. Process in boiling water bath for 15 minutes (start timing when water boils). Makes 5 to 6 half-pints.

**Cookies**

**Cookies**

**Cookies**

**Cookies**

**Cookies**

**Cookies**

**Cookies**

**Cookies**

# Cookies

## Percent of U.S. RDA Per Serving

| Recipes | Servings (fraction of recipe) | Calories | Protein (grams) | Carbohydrate (grams) | Fat (grams) | Sodium (milligrams) | Potassium (milligrams) | Protein | Vitamin A | Vitamin C | Thiamine | Riboflavin | Niacin | Calcium | Iron |
|---|---|---|---|---|---|---|---|---|---|---|---|---|---|---|---|
| Almond Cookies | 1/48 | 86 | 1 | 10 | 5 | 35 | 13 | 2 | 2 | 0 | 0 | 3 | 2 | 0 | 1 |
| Apple-Filled Oatmeal Cookies | 1/30 | 98 | 1 | 14 | 4 | 62 | 57 | 2 | 2 | 3 | 0 | 4 | 2 | 1 | 3 |
| Apricot-Filled Oatmeal Bars | 1/30 | 108 | 1 | 15 | 5 | 77 | 47 | 2 | 2 | 4 | 0 | 4 | 2 | 1 | 3 |
| Banana Drop Cookies w/ Banana Butter Frosting | 1/60 | 71 | 1 | 11 | 3 | 47 | 29 | 1 | 1 | 2 | 1 | 2 | 2 | 0 | 1 |
| Basic Drop Cookie | 1/30 | 70 | 1 | 9 | 3 | 75 | 14 | 1 | 1 | 2 | 0 | 2 | 2 | 0 | 1 |
| Berliner Kranser | 1/36 | 86 | 1 | 8 | 5 | 64 | 11 | 2 | 2 | 5 | 0 | 3 | 2 | 0 | 0 |
| Blonde Brownies | 1/48 | 90 | 1 | 13 | 4 | 54 | 51 | 2 | 2 | 2 | 0 | 3 | 2 | 2 | 2 |
| Chocolate Cake Brownies w/ Chocolate Frosting | 1/36 | 161 | 2 | 21 | 8 | 69 | 70 | 3 | 3 | 4 | 0 | 3 | 3 | 2 | 3 |
| Chocolate Chip Cookies | 1/72 | 93 | 1 | 11 | 6 | 48 | 40 | 2 | 2 | 1 | 0 | 2 | 2 | 1 | 2 |
| Chocolate-Cream Cheese Brownies | 1/16 | 189 | 3 | 22 | 11 | 86 | 72 | 5 | 5 | 5 | 0 | 3 | 4 | 2 | 4 |
| Chocolate-Peanut Cookies | 1/40 | 66 | 1 | 7 | 4 | 57 | 33 | 2 | 2 | 1 | 0 | 2 | 1 | 2 | 2 |
| Chocolate Revel Bars | 1/72 | 127 | 2 | 18 | 6 | 107 | 78 | 3 | 3 | 3 | 0 | 4 | 4 | 2 | 4 |
| Chocolate Syrup Brownies w/ Quick Chocolate Glaze | 1/32 | 176 | 2 | 25 | 8 | 64 | 82 | 4 | 4 | 5 | 0 | 4 | 3 | 1 | 4 |
| Coconut Macaroons | 1/20 | 46 | 1 | 7 | 2 | 6 | 18 | 1 | 1 | 0 | 1 | 0 | 1 | 0 | 1 |
| Crisp Pecan Dainties | 1/78 | 51 | 1 | 6 | 3 | 40 | 14 | 1 | 1 | 2 | 0 | 3 | 1 | 0 | 1 |
| Crispy Chocolate-Peanut | | | | | | | | | | | | | | | |

# Nutrition Analysis Chart

| | | | | | | | | | | | | | | | | |
|---|---|---|---|---|---|---|---|---|---|---|---|---|---|---|---|---|
| Butter Bars | 1/36 | 92 | 2 | 10 | 5 | 62 | 68 | 4 | 2 | 1 | 2 | 2 | 1 | 6 | 1 | 4 |
| Date-Orange Bars | 1/24 | 86 | 1 | 12 | 4 | 47 | 68 | 2 | 2 | 2 | 3 | 2 | 2 | 2 | 2 | 3 |
| Double Chocolate Drops w/ Mocha Frosting | 1/42 | 130 | 1 | 18 | 7 | 51 | 66 | 2 | 1 | 0 | 3 | 2 | 2 | 2 | 2 | 3 |
| English Toffee Bars | 1/48 | 105 | 1 | 11 | 7 | 48 | 45 | 2 | 3 | 0 | 3 | 2 | 2 | 2 | 1 | 3 |
| Filled Sugar Cookies | 1/36 | 136 | 1 | 20 | 6 | 80 | 69 | 2 | 2 | 1 | 5 | 3 | 5 | 4 | 0 | 4 |
| Finnish Chestnut Fingers | 1/30 | 64 | 1 | 8 | 4 | 46 | 27 | 1 | 2 | 0 | 3 | 2 | 2 | 1 | 1 | 4 |
| Fudge Brownies | 1/16 | 173 | 2 | 19 | 11 | 78 | 62 | 4 | 6 | 0 | 4 | 3 | 2 | 2 | 0 | 4 |
| Ginger Crinkles | 1/49 | 80 | 1 | 12 | 3 | 60 | 38 | 1 | 0 | 0 | 3 | 2 | 2 | 1 | 1 | 2 |
| Hermits | 1/36 | 84 | 1 | 12 | 4 | 66 | 63 | 2 | 2 | 0 | 3 | 2 | 2 | 1 | 1 | 3 |
| Holiday Pineapple-Filled Spritz | 1/60 | 97 | 1 | 13 | 5 | 63 | 19 | 1 | 4 | 1 | 4 | 2 | 2 | 2 | 0 | 1 |
| Jam Thumbprints | 1/36 | 84 | 1 | 8 | 5 | 60 | 23 | 2 | 3 | 0 | 3 | 2 | 2 | 2 | 1 | 2 |
| Lebkuchen w/ Lemon Glaze | 1/28 | 152 | 2 | 33 | 1 | 28 | 157 | 3 | 1 | 6 | 8 | 6 | 5 | 5 | 3 | 7 |
| Lemon Squares | 1/16 | 130 | 2 | 20 | 5 | 99 | 22 | 3 | 5 | 2 | 4 | 3 | 3 | 2 | 1 | 2 |
| Lemon Tea Cookies w/ Lemon Glaze | 1/48 | 61 | 1 | 10 | 2 | 50 | 12 | 1 | 2 | 1 | 2 | 2 | 2 | 1 | 1 | 1 |
| Lemon-Yogurt Cookies | 1/36 | 95 | 1 | 14 | 4 | 66 | 35 | 2 | 1 | 0 | 2 | 3 | 1 | 2 | 1 | 2 |
| Meringue-Topped Bars | 1/24 | 158 | 2 | 23 | 7 | 90 | 63 | 3 | 5 | 0 | 4 | 3 | 2 | 2 | 1 | 4 |
| Oatmeal Cookies | 1/36 | 71 | 1 | 9 | 4 | 53 | 25 | 2 | 1 | 0 | 3 | 1 | 1 | 1 | 1 | 2 |
| Oatmeal Refrigerator Cookies | 1/60 | 70 | 1 | 7 | 4 | 76 | 30 | 2 | 2 | 0 | 2 | 1 | 1 | 1 | 1 | 2 |
| Old-Fashioned Raisin Bars | 1/72 | 54 | 1 | 8 | 2 | 24 | 26 | 2 | 0 | 0 | 2 | 1 | 0 | 1 | 0 | 1 |
| Orange-Chip Cookies | 1/60 | 68 | 1 | 9 | 4 | 34 | 17 | 1 | 1 | 1 | 3 | 2 | 2 | 2 | 0 | 2 |
| Peanut Butter Cookies | 1/48 | 63 | 1 | 7 | 3 | 70 | 30 | 2 | 2 | 0 | 2 | 1 | 1 | 3 | 1 | 1 |
| Peanut Butter-Oatmeal Bars | 1/36 | 116 | 2 | 14 | 6 | 85 | 64 | 3 | 3 | 0 | 3 | 2 | 3 | 4 | 1 | 3 |
| Peanut Butter Slices | 1/60 | 73 | 1 | 7 | 4 | 60 | 26 | 2 | 1 | 0 | 2 | 1 | 1 | 3 | 0 | 1 |
| Pecan Tassies | 1/24 | 116 | 1 | 11 | 8 | 66 | 50 | 2 | 5 | 0 | 4 | 2 | 2 | 2 | 1 | 3 |
| Pfeffernuesse | 1/60 | 67 | 1 | 12 | 2 | 44 | 48 | 2 | 2 | 0 | 4 | 2 | 2 | 2 | 1 | 3 |
| Pineapple-Coconut Drops | 1/36 | 79 | 1 | 9 | 5 | 63 | 28 | 2 | 1 | 1 | 3 | 1 | 1 | 1 | 1 | 2 |

# Nutrition Analysis Chart

| Recipes | Servings (fraction of recipe) | Calories | Protein (grams) | Carbohydrate (grams) | Fat (grams) | Sodium (milligrams) | Potassium (milligrams) | Protein | Vitamin A | Vitamin C | Thiamine | Riboflavin | Niacin | Calcium | Iron |
|---|---|---|---|---|---|---|---|---|---|---|---|---|---|---|---|
| | | | | | | | | Percent of U.S. RDA Per Serving | | | | | | | |
| Pinwheel Cookies | 1/72 | 68 | 1 | 10 | 3 | 40 | 34 | 1 | 1 | 1 | 0 | 3 | 2 | 2 | 2 |
| Prune-Filled Oatmeal Bars | 1/30 | 156 | 2 | 24 | 6 | 78 | 108 | 2 | 3 | 5 | 2 | 5 | 3 | 3 | 6 |
| Pumpkin Bars | 1/36 | 128 | 2 | 16 | 7 | 115 | 45 | 2 | 2 | 17 | 1 | 4 | 3 | 2 | 2 |
| Pumpkin Drop Cookies | 1/48 | 73 | 1 | 11 | 3 | 45 | 64 | 1 | 2 | 8 | 1 | 3 | 2 | 2 | 3 |
| Raisin-Filled Oatmeal Bars | 1/30 | 142 | 2 | 24 | 5 | 79 | 120 | 2 | 2 | 4 | 0 | 5 | 2 | 2 | 5 |
| Ranger Cookies | 1/48 | 68 | 2 | 10 | 3 | 58 | 44 | 1 | 1 | 3 | 1 | 3 | 2 | 2 | 2 |
| Refrigerator Cookies | 1/60 | 67 | 1 | 7 | 4 | 48 | 18 | 1 | 1 | 2 | 0 | 2 | 1 | 1 | 1 |
| Rolled Cream Cheese Cookies | 1/60 | 53 | 1 | 7 | 3 | 26 | 10 | 1 | 1 | 0 | 0 | 2 | 1 | 0 | 3 |
| Rolled Ginger Cookies | 1/60 | 95 | 1 | 15 | 4 | 47 | 62 | 1 | 2 | 2 | 0 | 5 | 3 | 1 | 1 |
| Rolled Sugar Cookies | 1/36 | 77 | 1 | 10 | 4 | 54 | 10 | 1 | 2 | 0 | 0 | 2 | 2 | 0 | 2 |
| Sandies | 1/36 | 103 | 1 | 8 | 8 | 62 | 28 | 1 | 2 | 2 | 0 | 5 | 2 | 2 | 1 |
| Santa's Whiskers | 1/80 | 59 | 1 | 7 | 3 | 29 | 16 | 1 | 1 | 1 | 0 | 2 | 1 | 1 | 2 |
| Seven-Layer Bars | 1/36 | 137 | 2 | 15 | 8 | 76 | 90 | 2 | 3 | 3 | 0 | 1 | 4 | 4 | 4 |
| Snickerdoodles | 1/66 | 79 | 1 | 12 | 3 | 61 | 11 | 1 | 2 | 3 | 0 | 3 | 2 | 0 | 2 |
| Sour Cream Nut Drops w/ Browned Butter Frosting | 1/48 | 99 | 1 | 14 | 5 | 66 | 41 | 1 | 2 | 3 | 0 | 3 | 2 | 1 | 2 |
| Spicy Oatmeal-Raisin Cookies | 1/40 | 73 | 1 | 9 | 4 | 57 | 38 | 1 | 2 | 2 | 0 | 3 | 2 | 1 | 2 |
| Spritz | 1/60 | 81 | 1 | 9 | 5 | 63 | 9 | 1 | 1 | 4 | 0 | 3 | 2 | 0 | 1 |
| Toffee Bars | 1/48 | 105 | 1 | 11 | 7 | 48 | 45 | 1 | 2 | 3 | 1 | 3 | 2 | 1 | 3 |
| Whole Wheat Cookies | 1/60 | 69 | 1 | 8 | 4 | 48 | 27 | 1 | 2 | 1 | 0 | 3 | 1 | 1 | 2 |

# Cookies

**Bar Cookies:** Test cakelike bars for doneness with a wooden pick. Fudgelike bars are done when a slight imprint remains after touching lightly. Cool bar cookies before frosting unless otherwise specified. The yield of bar cookies depends on the size of the pan as well as the size of the serving. Generally, thicker and richer bars should be cut into smaller pieces. Bar cookies can be cut into diamond shapes by making diagonal cuts in one direction and cuts straight across in the other direction.

**Drop Cookies:** When dropping dough on a cookie sheet, allow ample room for cookies to spread during baking. Prevent excessive spreading of cookies by chilling dough, dropping onto a cooled cookie sheet, baking at the correct temperature, and mounding dough when dropping it. Cool baked cookies on wire racks. When storing, do not mix soft and crisp varieties in the same container, or the crisp types will become soft.

**Shaped Cookies:** Cookie dough can be flattened with the bottom of a glass that has been dipped in sugar, with the tines of a fork, or with your thumb, or certain dough can be shaped by putting it through a cookie press. For best results with a cookie press, keep the dough pliable to obtain well-defined patterns.

**Rolled and Refrigerated Cookies:** For rolled cookies, roll a small amount of dough at a time, keeping the rest chilled. Use a pastry cloth and a stockinette cover for the rolling pin. Roll from center to edge as for piecrust. Using a lightly floured cutter, start cutting at the edge of dough and work toward the center. Be sure the dough is chilled; unchilled dough takes up too much flour, which causes cookies to be tough. Excessive rerolling of pieces of dough also causes toughness.

Chill dough for refrigerator cookies thoroughly before slicing. Use a sawing motion with a sharp knife when slicing cookies to retain shape. For extra crisp cookies, slice thin and bake till lightly browned.

# Bar Cookies

## Chocolate-Cream Cheese Brownies

| | |
|---|---|
| 1 | **6-ounce package (1 cup) semisweet chocolate pieces** |
| 2 | **tablespoons butter or margarine** |
| ½ | **cup all-purpose flour** |
| ½ | **teaspoon baking powder** |
| 2 | **eggs** |
| 1½ | **teaspoons vanilla** |
| 1 | **cup sugar** |
| ½ | **cup chopped walnuts** |
| 1 | **3-ounce package cream cheese, softened** |
| 1 | **beaten egg** |

Oven 350°

Grease and lightly flour an 8x8x2-inch baking pan. Melt chocolate and butter; cool. Stir together flour, baking powder, and ¼ teaspoon *salt*. In a mixer bowl beat 2 eggs and *1 teaspoon* of the vanilla; gradually add ¾ *cup* of the sugar. Continue beating eggs till thick and lemon colored. Add dry ingredients to egg mixture; beat till well combined. Stir in chocolate mixture; stir in nuts. Beat cheese and remaining ¼ cup sugar till fluffy. Stir in remaining egg and ½ teaspoon vanilla. Spread *half* of the chocolate mixture in pan. Pour cheese mixture over; top with remaining chocolate mixture. Swirl layers to marble, if desired. Bake in a 350° oven about 45 minutes. Cool on a wire rack. Cut into bars. Makes 16.

## Fudge Brownies

| | |
|---|---|
| ½ | **cup butter or margarine** |
| 2 | **squares (2 ounces) unsweetened chocolate** |
| 1 | **cup sugar** |
| 2 | **eggs** |
| 1 | **teaspoon vanilla** |
| ¾ | **cup all-purpose flour** |
| ½ | **cup chopped walnuts** Oven 350° |

Grease an 8x8x2-inch baking pan. Melt butter and chocolate. Remove from heat; stir in sugar. Add eggs and vanilla; beat *lightly* just till combined (don't overbeat or brownies will rise too high, then fall). Stir in flour and nuts. Spread batter in pan. Bake in a 350° oven for 30 minutes. Cool. Cut into bars. Makes 16.

## Chocolate Syrup Brownies

| | |
|---|---|
| ½ | **cup butter or margarine** |
| 1 | **cup sugar** |
| 4 | **eggs** |
| 1 | **16-ounce can (1½ cups) chocolate-flavored syrup** |
| 1¼ | **cups all-purpose flour** |
| 1 | **cup chopped walnuts** |
| | **Quick Chocolate Glaze** Oven 350° |

Grease a 13x9x2-inch baking pan. Beat butter for 30 seconds; add sugar and beat till fluffy. Add eggs and beat just till combined. Stir in syrup, then flour. Stir in walnuts. Turn into pan. Bake in a 350° oven for 30 to 35 minutes. Cool slightly; pour Quick Chocolate Glaze atop. Cool. Cut into bars. Makes 32.

**Quick Chocolate Glaze:** Combine ⅔ cup *sugar*, 3 tablespoons *milk*, and 3 tablespoons *butter*. Heat till boiling; boil 30 seconds. Stir in ½-cup *semisweet chocolate pieces* till melted.

## Chocolate Cake Brownies

  1½  **cups all-purpose flour**
   2  **teaspoons baking powder**
  ½  **cup butter or margarine**
  1¼  **cups sugar**
   2  **eggs**
   3  **squares (3 ounces) unsweetened**
       **chocolate, melted and cooled**
   1  **teaspoon vanilla**
   1  **cup milk**
   1  **cup chopped walnuts**
     **Chocolate Frosting**        Oven 350°

Grease a 15x10x1-inch baking pan. Combine flour, baking powder, and ½ teaspoon *salt*. Beat butter for 30 seconds; add sugar and beat till fluffy. Add eggs, melted chocolate, and vanilla; beat well. Add dry ingredients and milk alternately to beaten mixture, beating after each addition. Stir in walnuts. Turn batter into pan. Bake in a 350° oven 18 to 20 minutes. Cool on a wire rack. Frost with Chocolate Frosting. Cut into bars. Makes 36.

   ***Chocolate Frosting:*** Combine 3 tablespoons *butter*, 2 squares (2 ounces) *unsweetened chocolate*, and ¼ cup *milk*; heat till chocolate melts. Stir in 3 cups sifted *powdered sugar*. Thin with *milk*, if needed, to spread.

## Blonde Brownies

   2  **cups all-purpose flour**
   2  **teaspoons baking powder**
  ½  **cup butter or margarine**
   2  **cups packed brown sugar**
   2  **eggs**
   1  **teaspoon vanilla**
   1  **cup chopped walnuts**      Oven 350°

Grease a 13x9x2-inch baking pan. Combine flour, baking powder, and ¼ teaspoon *salt*. Melt butter; remove from heat.

Stir in sugar. Add eggs and vanilla; stir till combined. Stir dry ingredients and walnuts into sugar mixture. Spread in pan. Bake in a 350° oven 20 to 25 minutes. Cut into bars while warm. Makes 48.

---

## Apricot-Filled Oatmeal Bars

1½  **cups all-purpose flour**
1½  **cups quick-cooking rolled oats**
 1  **cup packed brown sugar**
½  **teaspoon baking soda**
¾  **cup butter or margarine**
 1  **cup apricot preserves**                Oven 375°

Stir together flour, oats, brown sugar, and soda. Cut in butter till mixture is crumbly. Pat ⅔ of the crumbs in the bottom of an ungreased 13x9x2-inch baking pan; spread with preserves. Sprinkle with remaining crumbs. Bake in a 375° oven for 25 to 30 minutes. Cool on a wire rack. Cut into bars. Makes 30.

**Raisin-Filled Oatmeal Bars:** Prepare Apricot-Filled Oatmeal Bars as above, *except* omit apricot preserves and use raisin filling. For raisin filling, in a saucepan combine ¼ cup *granulated sugar* and 1 tablespoon *cornstarch*. Stir in 2 cups *raisins* and 1 cup *water*. Cook and stir till bubbly. Spread atop crumb mixture. Continue as directed.

**Prune-Filled Oatmeal Bars:** Prepare Apricot-Filled Oatmeal Bars as above, *except* omit apricot preserves and use prune filling. For prune filling, in a saucepan combine 1 cup snipped, pitted *prunes,* ⅔ cup *water,* and ½ of a 6-ounce can (⅓ cup) *lemonade concentrate.* Cover; simmer 5 minutes. Mix ½ cup packed *brown sugar,* ½ cup chopped *walnuts,* and 2 tablespoons all-purpose *flour;* stir into prune mixture. Cook and stir till very thick. Spread atop crumb mixture. Continue as directed.

## Date-Orange Bars

- 1 cup all-purpose flour
- 1/2 teaspoon baking powder
- 1/4 teaspoon baking soda
- 1/4 cup butter *or* margarine
- 1/2 cup packed brown sugar
- 1 egg
- 1 teaspoon finely shredded orange peel
- 1/4 cup milk
- 1/4 cup orange juice
- 1/2 cup chopped walnuts
- 1/2 cup snipped pitted dates
  Powdered sugar
  Oven 350°

Grease an 11x7x1½-inch baking pan. Stir together flour, baking powder, and soda. Beat butter or margarine for 30 seconds; add brown sugar and beat till fluffy. Add egg and orange peel; beat well. Combine milk and orange juice. Add dry ingredients and milk mixture alternately to beaten mixture, beating after each addition. Stir in walnuts and dates. Spread in pan. Bake in a 350° oven about 25 minutes. Cool on a wire rack. Sift powdered sugar over top. Cut into bars. Makes 24.

## Toffee Bars

- 1 cup butter *or* margarine
- 1 cup packed brown sugar
- 1 egg yolk
- 1 teaspoon vanilla
- 2 cups all-purpose flour
- 1 6-ounce package (1 cup) semisweet
     chocolate pieces
- 1 cup chopped walnuts *or* pecans
  Oven 350°

Beat butter for 30 seconds; add brown sugar and beat till fluffy. Add egg yolk and vanilla; beat well. Gradually add flour to beaten mixture, beating constantly. Stir in chocolate pieces and nuts. Press evenly in an ungreased 15x10x1-inch baking pan. Bake in a 350° oven for 15 to 18 minutes. Cut into bars while warm. Makes 48.

**English Toffee Bars:** Prepare Toffee Bars as above, *except* omit chocolate pieces and nuts in the dough; bake as directed. Immediately sprinkle chocolate pieces over top and let stand till softened; then spread evenly. Sprinkle with finely chopped nuts.

---

# Chocolate Revel Bars

|       |                                                   |
|-------|---------------------------------------------------|
| 3     | cups quick-cooking rolled oats                    |
| 2½    | cups all-purpose flour                            |
| 1     | teaspoon baking soda                              |
| 1     | cup butter or margarine                           |
| 2     | cups packed brown sugar                           |
| 2     | eggs                                              |
| 4     | teaspoons vanilla                                 |
| 1     | 14-ounce can (1⅓ cups) *sweetened condensed milk* |
| 1½    | cups semisweet chocolate pieces                   |
| 2     | tablespoons butter or margarine                   |
| ½     | cup chopped walnuts          Oven 350°            |

Combine oats, flour, soda, and 1 teaspoon *salt*. Beat the 1 cup butter for 30 seconds; add brown sugar and beat till fluffy. Add eggs and 2 *teaspoons* of the vanilla; beat well. Stir dry ingredients gradually into beaten mixture, stirring till well combined. Heat together sweetened condensed milk, chocolate pieces, 2 tablespoons butter, and ½ teaspoon *salt* over low heat, stirring till smooth. Remove from heat. Stir in walnuts and the remaining 2 teaspoons vanilla. Pat ⅔ of the oat mixture in the bottom of an ungreased 15x10x1-inch baking pan. Spread chocolate mixture over dough. Dot with remaining oat mixture. Bake in a 350° oven for 25 to 30 minutes. Cool on a wire rack. Cut into bars. Makes 72.

## Seven-Layer Bars

- ½ cup butter *or* margarine
- 1½ cups finely crushed graham crackers
- 1 6-ounce package (1 cup) semisweet chocolate pieces
- 1 6-ounce package (1 cup) butterscotch pieces
- 1 3½-ounce can (1⅓ cups) flaked coconut
- ½ cup chopped walnuts
- 1 14-ounce can (1⅓ cups) *sweetened condensed milk*                  Oven 350°

Melt butter; stir in crushed graham crackers. Pat crumb mixture evenly in bottom of an ungreased 13x9x2-inch baking pan. Layer, in order, chocolate pieces, butterscotch pieces, coconut, and walnuts. Pour sweetened condensed milk evenly over all. Bake in a 350° oven 30 minutes; cool. Cut into bars. Makes 36.

## Old-Fashioned Raisin Bars

- 2 cups all-purpose flour
- 1 teaspoon baking soda
- 1 teaspoon ground cinnamon
- 1 teaspoon ground nutmeg
- ¼ teaspoon ground cloves
- 1 cup raisins
- ½ cup shortening *or* cooking oil
- ½ cup granulated sugar
- ½ cup honey
- 1 slightly beaten egg
- ¾ cup chopped walnuts
  Powdered sugar                                      Oven 350°

Grease a 15x10x1-inch baking pan. Stir together flour, soda, cinnamon, nutmeg, cloves, and ¼ teaspoon *salt*. In a 2-quart saucepan combine raisins, shortening or oil, and 1 cup *water;* bring to boiling. Remove from heat; cool 10 minutes. Stir in granulated sugar, honey, and egg. Add dry ingredients to raisin mixture; stir till smooth. Stir in walnuts. Turn into pan. Bake in a 350° oven for 18 to 20 minutes. Cool on a wire rack. Sift powdered sugar over top. Cut into bars. Makes about 72.

## Lemon Squares

> **6**   **tablespoons butter *or* margarine**
> **¼**   **cup granulated sugar**
> **1**   **cup all-purpose flour**
> **2**   **eggs**
> **¾**   **cup granulated sugar**
> **2**   **tablespoons all-purpose flour**
> **¼**   **teaspoon finely shredded lemon peel**
> **3**   **tablespoons lemon juice**
> **¼**   **teaspoon baking powder**        Oven 350°

Grease an 8x8x2-inch baking pan. Beat butter for 30 seconds; add the ¼ cup sugar and ¼ teaspoon *salt,* beating till fluffy. Stir in the 1 cup flour. Pat dough onto bottom of pan. Bake in a 350° oven for 15 minutes. Meanwhile, beat eggs; add remaining ¾ cup sugar, 2 tablespoons flour, lemon peel, lemon juice, and baking powder. Beat 3 minutes or till slightly thickened. Pour over baked layer. Bake in a 350° oven 25 to 30 minutes longer or till light golden brown around edges and center is set. Cool. Sift powdered sugar over top, if desired. Cut into squares. Makes 16.

## Peanut Butter-Oatmeal Bars

   **1   cup all-purpose flour**
   **1   cup quick-cooking rolled oats**
  **½   teaspoon baking soda**
  **½   cup butter or margarine**
  **½   cup granulated sugar**
  **½   cup packed brown sugar**
   **1   egg**
  **⅓   cup peanut butter**
  **¼   cup milk**
  **½   teaspoon vanilla**
   **1   6-ounce package (1 cup) semisweet
       chocolate pieces**
  **¼   cup sifted powdered sugar**
   **2   tablespoons peanut butter**
   **2   to 3 tablespoons milk**        Oven 350°

Grease a 13x9x2-inch baking pan. Combine flour, oats, soda, and ¼ teaspoon *salt*. Beat butter for 30 seconds; add sugars and beat till fluffy. Add egg, the ⅓ cup peanut butter, the ¼ cup milk, and vanilla; beat well. Add dry ingredients to beaten mixture, beating till smooth. Spread mixture in pan. Bake in a 350° oven for 18 to 20 minutes. Immediately sprinkle chocolate pieces over top; let stand till softened, then spread evenly. Cool. Combine powdered sugar and the 2 tablespoons peanut butter. Gradually add enough milk to make of drizzling consistency. Drizzle over top. Let stand several hours before cutting into bars. Makes 36.

# Crispy Chocolate-Peanut Butter Bars

- ½ cup light corn syrup
- ¼ cup packed brown sugar
- 1 cup peanut butter
- 2 cups crisp rice cereal
- 1 cup cornflakes, slightly crushed
- 1 6-ounce package (1 cup) semisweet chocolate pieces
- 1 teaspoon vanilla

In a 2-quart saucepan combine corn syrup, brown sugar, and dash *salt*. Cook and stir till mixture comes to a full boil. Stir in peanut butter. Remove from heat. Stir in cereals, chocolate pieces, and vanilla. Press into an ungreased 9x9x2-inch pan. Chill 1 hour. Cut into bars. Makes 36.

# Pumpkin Bars

- 2 cups all-purpose flour
- 2 teaspoons baking powder
- 2 teaspoons ground cinnamon
- 1 teaspoon baking soda
- 4 beaten eggs
- 1 16-ounce can pumpkin
- 1½ cups sugar
- 1 cup cooking oil
  Cream Cheese Frosting (see recipe, page 197)

Oven 350°

Stir together flour, baking powder, cinnamon, soda, and 1 teaspoon *salt*. Combine eggs, pumpkin, sugar, and oil; beat till combined. Add dry ingredients; beat till well combined. Spread batter in an ungreased 15x10x1-inch baking pan. Bake in a 350° oven for 25 to 30 minutes. Cool. Frost with Cream Cheese Frosting. Cut into bars. Makes 36.

## Meringue-Topped Bars

| | |
|---|---|
| 1½ | cups all-purpose flour |
| ¼ | teaspoon baking soda |
| ½ | cup butter *or* margarine |
| ¾ | cup packed brown sugar |
| 3 | eggs |
| 1 | teaspoon vanilla |
| ¼ | teaspoon cream of tartar |
| ¾ | cup granulated sugar |
| 1 | 6-ounce package semisweet chocolate pieces *or* two 1⅛-ounce bars chocolate-coated English toffee, chopped |

Oven 350°

Stir together flour, soda, and ¼ teaspoon *salt*. For crust, beat butter for 30 seconds; add brown sugar and beat till fluffy. Separate egg whites from egg yolks; set whites aside. Add egg yolks and vanilla to beaten mixture; beat well. Gradually add dry ingredients to beaten mixture, beating constantly. Spread in an ungreased 13x9x2-inch baking pan. Bake in a 350° oven for 10 minutes. Wash beaters. For meringue, combine egg whites and cream of tartar; beat till soft peaks form. Gradually add granulated sugar; beat till stiff peaks form. Sprinkle chocolate pieces or chopped toffee bars over hot crust. Spread meringue atop. Bake 30 minutes more or till golden brown. Cut into bars while warm. Makes 24.

# Drop Cookies

## Basic Drop Cookies

  1¼   **cups all-purpose flour**
  ½   **teaspoon baking soda**
  ¼   **cup butter or margarine**
  ¼   **cup shortening**
  ½   **cup granulated sugar**
  ¼   **cup packed brown sugar**
  1   **egg**
  1   **teaspoon vanilla**          Oven 375°

Grease a cookie sheet. Combine flour, soda, and ½ teaspoon *salt*. Beat butter and shortening with electric mixer for 30 seconds. Add sugars and beat till fluffy. Add egg and vanilla; beat well. Add dry ingredients to beaten mixture; beat well. Drop from a teaspoon 2 inches apart onto a greased cookie sheet. Bake in a 375° oven for 8 to 10 minutes. Remove; cool on a wire rack. Makes 30 to 36.

    ***Lemon-Yogurt Cookies:*** Prepare Basic Drop Cookie dough as above, *except* stir in ½ cup *lemon yogurt* and ½ cup chopped toasted *almonds*. Bake as directed. Cool about 1 minute before removing to a wire rack. When cool, frost with a mixture of 2 cups sifted *powdered sugar* and ¼ cup *lemon yogurt*. Makes 36.

    ***Chocolate-Peanut Cookies:*** Prepare Basic Drop Cookie dough as above, *except* use *1* cup all-purpose flour and add 3 tablespoons *milk* to beaten mixture. Stir in 1½ squares (1½ ounces) *unsweetened chocolate,* melted and cooled, and ½ cup chopped *peanuts*. Bake as directed. Makes 40.

    ***Pineapple-Coconut Drops:*** Prepare Basic Drop Cookie dough as above, *except* stir ¼ teaspoon ground *ginger* into dry ingredients. Stir in 1 cup *coconut*, ½ cup well-drained crushed *pineapple*, and ½ cup chopped *nuts*. Bake as directed. Makes 36 to 40.

    ***Spicy Oatmeal-Raisin Cookies:*** Prepare Basic Drop Cookie dough as above, *except* use *1 cup* all-purpose flour, ½ teaspoon each ground *cinnamon* and *nutmeg,* and add 2 tablespoons *milk* to beaten mixture. Stir in 1 cup quick-cooking *rolled oats*, ½ cup *raisins*, and ½ cup chopped *nuts*. Bake as directed. Makes 40.

## Chocolate Chip Cookies

|       |                                                    |           |
|-------|----------------------------------------------------|-----------|
| 2½    | **cups all-purpose flour**                         |           |
| 1     | **teaspoon baking soda**                           |           |
| ½     | **teaspoon salt**                                  |           |
| ½     | **cup butter or margarine**                        |           |
| ½     | **cup shotening**                                  |           |
| 1     | **cup packed brown sugar**                         |           |
| ½     | **cup granulated sugar**                           |           |
| 2     | **eggs**                                           |           |
| 1½    | **teaspoons vanilla**                              |           |
| 1     | **12-ounce package (2 cups) semisweet chocolate pieces** | |
| 1     | **cup chopped walnuts or pecans**                  | Oven 375° |

Stir together flour, soda, and salt. In a mixer bowl beat butter and shortening on medium speed of electric mixer for 30 seconds. Add sugars and beat till fluffy. Add eggs and vanilla; beat well. Add dry ingredients to beaten mixture, beating till well combined. Stir in chocolate pieces and nuts. Drop from a teaspoon 2 inches apart onto an ungreased cookie sheet. Bake in a 375° oven for 8 to 10 minutes or till done. Remove; cool. Makes about 72.

# Ranger Cookies

| 1¼ | cups all-purpose flour |
| ½ | teaspoon baking powder |
| ½ | teaspoon baking soda |
| ¼ | teaspoon salt |
| ½ | cup butter *or* margarine |
| ½ | cup granulated sugar |
| ½ | cup packed brown sugar |
| 1 | egg |
| 1 | teaspoon vanilla |
| 2 | cups crisp rice cereal |
| 1 | 3½-ounce can flaked coconut |
| 1 | cup pitted dates, snipped, *or* raisins |

Oven 375°

Stir together flour, baking powder, soda, and salt. In a mixer bowl beat butter for 30 seconds. Add sugars and beat till fluffy. Add egg and vanilla; beat well. Add dry ingredients to beaten mixture, beating till well combined. Stir in cereal, coconut, and dates or raisins. Drop from a teaspoon 2 inches apart onto an ungreased cookie sheet. Bake in a 375° oven for 8 to 10 minutes. Cool about 1 minute before removing to a wire rack. Makes 48.

# Pumpkin Drop Cookies

| 2 | cups all-purpose flour |
| 1 | teaspoon baking powder |
| 1 | teaspoon ground cinnamon |
| ½ | teaspoon baking soda |
| ½ | teaspoon ground nutmeg |
| ½ | cup butter *or* margarine |
| 1 | cup packed brown sugar |
| 1 | egg |
| 1 | cup canned pumpkin |
| 1 | teaspoon vanilla |
| 1 | cup raisins |
| ½ | cup chopped walnuts |

Oven 375°

Grease a cookie sheet. Stir together flour, baking powder, cinnamon, soda, and nutmeg. In a mixer bowl beat butter for 30 seconds; add brown sugar and beat till fluffy. Add egg, pumpkin, and vanilla; beat well. Add dry ingredients to beaten mixture, beating till well combined. Stir in raisins and walnuts. (Dough will be soft.) Drop from a teaspoon 2 inches apart onto a greased cookie sheet. Bake in a 375° oven for 8 to 10 minutes. Cool on a wire rack. Makes about 48.

## Banana Drop Cookies

Oven 375°

Grease a cookie sheet. Stir together 2 cups all-purpose *flour*, 1½ teaspoons *baking powder*, ½ teaspoon ground *cinnamon*, ¼ teaspoon *baking soda*, ¼ teaspoon *salt*, and ¼ teaspoon ground *cloves*. In a mixer bowl beat ½ cup *butter or margarine* for 30 seconds. Add 1 cup *granulated sugar* and beat till fluffy. Add 2 *eggs* and ½ teaspoon *vanilla*; beat well. Add dry ingredients and 1 cup mashed *banana* (2 medium) alternately to beaten mixture, beating after each addition. Stir in ½ cup chopped *walnuts*. Drop from a teaspoon 2 inches apart onto a well-greased cookie sheet. Bake in a 375° oven for 10 to 12 minutes. Remove from cookie sheet immediately; cool on a wire rack. Frost cooled cookies with Banana Butter Frosting. Makes 60.

***Banana Butter Frosting:*** Stir together 2 cups sifted *powdered sugar*, ¼ cup mashed *banana* (1 small), 2 tablespoons softened *butter*, and ½ teaspoon *vanilla*; mix well. If necessary, add additional powdered sugar to make of spreading consistency.

## Hermits

|       |                             |           |
|-------|-----------------------------|-----------|
| 1½    | cups all-purpose flour      |           |
| ½     | teaspoon baking soda        |           |
| ½     | teaspoon ground cinnamon    |           |
| ¼     | teaspoon ground nutmeg      |           |
| ¼     | teaspoon ground cloves      |           |
| ½     | cup butter or margarine     |           |
| ¾     | cup packed brown sugar      |           |
| 1     | egg                         |           |
| 2     | tablespoons milk            |           |
| 1     | teaspoon vanilla            |           |
| 1     | cup raisins                 |           |
| ½     | cup choppped walnuts        | Oven 375° |

Grease a cookie sheet. Combine flour, soda, spices, and ¼ teaspoon *salt*. Beat butter for 30 seconds; add brown sugar and beat till fluffy. Add egg, milk, and vanilla; beat well. Add dry ingredients to beaten mixture, beating till well combined. Stir in raisins and walnuts. Drop from a teaspoon 2 inches apart onto a greased cookie sheet. Bake in a 375° oven for 10 to 12 minutes. Cool. Makes 36.

## Apple-Filled Oatmeal Cookies

|       |                                |           |
|-------|--------------------------------|-----------|
|       | **Filling**                    |           |
| 1     | cup all-purpose flour          |           |
| 1     | teaspoon baking powder         |           |
| ½     | teaspoon ground cinnamon       |           |
| ⅛     | teaspoon ground cloves         |           |
| ½     | cup butter or margarine        |           |
| ½     | cup packed brown sugar         |           |
| 1     | egg                            |           |
| ¼     | cup milk                       |           |
| ¾     | cup quick-cooking rolled oats  | Oven 375° |

Grease a cookie sheet. Prepare Filling. Combine flour, baking powder, spices, and ⅛ teaspoon *salt*. Beat butter for 30 seconds; add brown sugar and beat till fluffy. Add egg; beat well.

Add dry ingredients and milk alternately, beating after each addition. Stir in oats. Drop from a teaspoon 2 inches apart onto a greased cookie sheet. Make a depression in the center of each; fill with a teaspoon of Filling. Bake in a 375° oven 10 to 12 minutes. Makes 30.

**Filling:** Combine 1½ cups finely diced peeled *apple*, ½ cup *granulated sugar*, ⅓ cup *raisins*, ⅓ cup chopped *pecans*, and 2 tablespoons *water*. Cook and stir till thick and apple is tender.

## Double Chocolate Drops

  1½   **cups all-purpose flour**
  ½    **teaspoon baking powder**
  ½    **teaspoon baking soda**
  ½    **cup shortening**
  2    **squares (2 ounces) unsweetened chocolate**
  1    **cup packed brown sugar**
  1    **egg**
  ½    **cup buttermilk or sour milk**
  1    **teaspoon vanilla**
  1    **6-ounce package (1 cup) semisweet**
       **chocolate pieces**
  ½    **cup chopped walnuts**
       **Mocha Frosting**                          Oven 350°

Grease a cookie sheet. Stir together flour, baking powder, soda, and ¼ teaspoon *salt*. Melt shortening and unsweetened chocolate over low heat. Cool 10 minutes. Stir in brown sugar, egg, buttermilk or sour milk, and vanilla; mix till smooth. Stir dry ingredients into saucepan mixture; mix well. Stir in chocolate pieces and nuts. Drop from a teaspoon 2 inches apart onto a greased cookie sheet. Bake in a 350° oven about 10 minutes. Cool about 1 minute before removing to a wire rack. Frost with Mocha Frosting. Makes about 42.

**Mocha Frosting:** Beat together ¼ cup *butter or margarine*, 2 tablespoons unsweetened *cocoa powder*, and 2 teaspoons instant *coffee crystals*. Stir in 2½ cups sifted *powdered sugar*, 1½ teaspoons *vanilla*, and enough *milk* to make of spreading consistency (about 2 to 3 tablespoons).

## Coconut Macaroons

**2**  **egg whites**
**½**  **teaspoon vanilla**
   **Dash salt**
**⅔**  **cup sugar**
**1**  **3½-ounce can (1⅓ cups) flaked**
   **coconut**                                    Oven 325°

Grease a cookie sheet. Beat egg whites, vanilla, and salt till soft peaks form. Gradually add sugar, beating till stiff peaks form. Fold in coconut. Drop from a teaspoon 1½ inches apart onto a greased cookie sheet. Bake in a 325° oven about 20 minutes. Cool on a wire rack. Makes 20 to 24.

## Sour Cream Nut Drops

Oven 375°

Grease a cookie sheet. Stir together 2 cups all-purpose *flour*, 1 teaspoon *baking powder*, ½ teaspoon *baking soda*, ½ teaspoon ground *cinnamon*, ¼ teaspoon *salt*, and ¼ teaspoon ground *nutmeg*. Beat ½ cup *butter or margarine* for 30 seconds; add 1 cup packed *brown sugar* and beat till fluffy. Add 1 *egg* and ½ teaspoon *vanilla*; beat well. Add dry ingredients and ½ cup *dairy sour cream* alternately to beaten mixture, beating after each addition. Stir in 1 cup chopped *cashews or pecans*. Drop from a teaspoon 2 inches apart onto a greased cookie sheet. Bake in a 375° oven 8 to 10 minutes or till lightly browned. Remove from cookie sheet immediately; cool on a wire rack. Frost tops of cooled cookies with Browned Butter Frosting. Makes 48.

**Browned Butter Frosting:** In a small saucepan heat and stir 3 tablespoons *butter or margarine* until browned. Remove from heat. Slowly beat in 2 cups sifted *powdered sugar*, 2 tablespoons *milk*, and 1 teaspoon *vanilla*.

## Lemon Tea Cookies

```
  2    teaspoons lemon juice
  ½    cup milk
 1¾    cups all-purpose flour
  1    teaspoon baking powder
  ¼    teaspoon baking soda
  ½    cup butter or margarine
  ¾    cup sugar
  1    egg
  1    teaspoon finely shredded lemon peel
       Lemon Glaze                          Oven 350°
```

Stir 2 teaspoons lemon juice into milk; set aside. Stir together flour, baking powder, soda, and ¼ teaspoon *salt*. Beat butter for 30 seconds; add sugar and beat till fluffy. Add egg and lemon peel; beat well. Add dry ingredients and milk mixture alternately to beaten mixture, beating well after each addition. Drop from a teaspoon 2 inches apart onto an ungreased cookie sheet. Bake in a 350° oven 12 to 14 minutes. Remove at once to a wire rack; brush Lemon Glaze over. Makes 48.

**Lemon Glaze:** Stir together ¾ cup *sugar* and ¼ cup *lemon juice*.

# Shaped Cookies

## Jam Thumbprints

- 1½ **cups all-purpose flour**
- ¼ **teaspoon salt**
- ⅔ **cup butter or margarine**
- ⅓ **cup sugar**
- 2 **egg yolks**
- 1 **teaspoon vanilla**
- 2 **slightly beaten egg whites**
- ¾ **cup finely chopped walnuts**
- ⅓ **cup cherry or strawberry preserves**

Oven 350°

Stir together flour and salt. Beat butter for 30 seconds; add sugar and beat till fluffy. Add egg yolks and vanilla; beat well. Add dry ingredients to beaten mixture, beating till well combined. Cover and chill 1 hour. Shape into 1-inch balls; roll in egg whites, then roll in finely chopped walnuts. Place 1 inch apart on an ungreased cookie sheet. Press down centers with thumb. Bake in a 350° oven for 15 to 17 minutes. Cool on a wire rack. Just before serving, fill centers with preserves. Makes 36.

## Peanut Butter Cookies

- 1¼ **cups all-purpose flour**
- ¾ **teaspoon baking soda**
- ¼ **teaspoon salt**
- ½ **cup butter or margarine**
- ½ **cup peanut butter**
- ½ **cup granulated sugar**
- ½ **cup packed brown sugar**
- 1 **egg**
- ½ **teaspoon vanilla**

Oven 375°

Stir together flour, soda, and salt. In a mixer bowl beat butter for 30 seconds. Add peanut butter and sugars; beat till fluffy. Add egg and vanilla; beat well. Add dry ingredients to beaten mixture; beat till well combined. Shape dough into 1-inch balls; roll in granulated sugar, if desired. Place 2 inches apart on an ungreased cookie sheet; crisscross with the tines of a fork. Bake in a 375° oven about 10 minutes. Cool about 1 minute before removing to a wire rack. Makes 48.

---

## Oatmeal Cookies

|   |   |
|---|---|
| 1 | **cup all-purpose flour** |
| ½ | **teaspoon baking powder** |
| ½ | **teaspoon baking soda** |
| ¼ | **cup shortening** |
| ¼ | **cup butter or margarine** |
| ½ | **cup granulated sugar** |
| ⅓ | **cup packed brown sugar** |
| 1 | **egg** |
| 2 | **tablespoons milk** |
| ½ | **teaspoon vanilla** |
| 1 | **cup quick-cooking rolled oats** |
| ¼ | **cup chopped walnuts** |

Oven 375°

Stir together flour, baking powder, baking soda, and ¼ teaspoon *salt*. In mixer bowl beat shortening and butter for 30 seconds; add sugars and beat till fluffy. Add egg, milk, and vanilla; beat well. Add dry ingredients to beaten mixture, beating till well combined. Stir in oats and walnuts. Chill dough 2 hours; form 1-inch balls. Dip tops of balls in additional granulated sugar, if desired. Place on an ungreased cookie sheet. Bake in a 375° oven for 10 to 12 minutes. Makes 36.

## Snickerdoodles

| | |
|---|---|
| 3¾ | cups all-purpose flour |
| ½ | teaspoon baking soda |
| ½ | teaspoon cream of tartar |
| 1 | cup butter *or* margarine |
| 2 | cups sugar |
| 2 | eggs |
| ¼ | cup milk |
| 1 | teaspoon vanilla |
| 3 | tablespoons sugar |
| 1 | teaspoon ground cinnamon |

Oven 375°

Grease a cookie sheet. Stir together flour, soda, cream of tartar, and ½ teaspoon *salt*. Beat butter for 30 seconds; add the 2 cups sugar and beat till fluffy. Add eggs, milk, and vanilla; beat well. Add dry ingredients to beaten mixture, beating till well combined. Form dough into 1-inch balls; roll in a mixture of the 3 tablespoons sugar and the cinnamon. Place balls 2 inches apart on a cookie sheet; flatten slightly with the bottom of a drinking glass. Bake in a 375° oven about 8 minutes or till light golden. Makes about 66.

## Sandies

| | |
|---|---|
| 1 | cup butter *or* margarine |
| ⅓ | cup granulated sugar |
| 2 | teaspoons vanilla |
| 2 | cups all-purpose flour |
| 1 | cup chopped pecans |
| ¼ | cup powdered sugar |

Oven 325°

Beat butter for 30 seconds; add granulated sugar and beat till fluffy. Add vanilla and 2 teaspoons *water*; beat well. Stir in flour and pecans. Shape into 1-inch balls or 1½x½-inch fingers. Place on an ungreased cookie sheet. Bake in a 325° oven about 20 minutes. Cool completely. Gently shake a few cookies at a time in a bag with powdered sugar. Makes 36.

## Ginger Crinkles

|       |                                |
| ----- | ------------------------------ |
| 2¼    | cups all-purpose flour         |
| 2     | teaspoons baking soda          |
| 1     | teaspoon ground ginger         |
| 1     | teaspoon ground cinnamon       |
| ½     | teaspoon ground cloves         |
| 1     | cup packed brown sugar         |
| ¾     | cup shortening *or* cooking oil |
| ¼     | cup molasses                   |
| 1     | egg          Oven 375°         |

Stir together the first 5 ingredients and ¼ teaspoon *salt*. Combine the remaining ingredients and beat well. Add dry ingredients to beaten mixture, beating well. Form 1-inch balls. Roll in granulated sugar, if desired; place 2 inches apart on an ungreased cookie sheet. Bake in 375° oven about 10 minutes. Makes 48.

## Almond Cookies

Oven 325°

Stir together 2¾ cups all-purpose *flour,* I cup *sugar,* ½ teaspoon *baking soda,* and ½ teaspoon *salt.* Cut in 1 cup *lard* till mixture resembles cornmeal. Combine 1 slightly beaten *egg,* 2 tablespoons *milk,* and 1 teaspoon *almond extract;* add to flour mixture. Mix well. Shape dough into 1-inch balls. Place 2 inches apart on an ungreased cookie sheet. Place a blanched *almond half* atop *each* cookie; press to flatten slightly. Bake in a 325° oven for 16 to 18 minutes. Cool on a wire rack. Makes 48.

# Pfeffernuesse

|         |                                  |
|---------|----------------------------------|
| 4       | cups all-purpose flour           |
| ½       | cup granulated sugar             |
| 1¼      | teaspoons baking soda            |
| 1½      | teaspoons ground cinnamon        |
| ½       | teaspoon ground cloves           |
| ½       | teaspoon ground nutmeg           |
| ¾       | cup light molasses               |
| ½       | cup butter *or* margarine        |
| 2       | beaten eggs                      |
|         | Sifted powdered sugar    Oven 350° |

Combine flour, sugar, soda, spices, and dash *pepper*. In a saucepan combine molasses and butter; heat and stir till butter melts. Cool to room temperature. Stir in eggs. Add dry ingredients to molasses mixture; mix well. Cover and chill several hours or overnight. Grease a cookie sheet. Shape dough into 1-inch balls. Place on a greased cookie sheet. Bake in a 350° oven for 12 to 14 minutes. Cool on a wire rack. Roll in powdered sugar. Makes about 60.

# Pecan Tassies

|     |                                         |
|-----|-----------------------------------------|
| ½   | cup butter *or* margarine               |
| 1   | 3-ounce package cream cheese            |
| 1   | cup all-purpose flour                   |
| 1   | egg                                     |
| ¾   | cup packed brown sugar                  |
| 1   | tablespoon butter *or* margarine, softened |
| 1   | teaspoon vanilla                        |
|     | Dash salt                               |
| ½   | cup coarsely chopped pecans    Oven 325° |

For pastry, in a mixer bowl beat the ½ cup butter or margarine and cream cheese. Add flour; beat well. Cover bowl; chill mixture about 1 hour.

In a small mixing bowl stir together egg, brown sugar, the 1 tablespoon butter, vanilla, and salt just till smooth; set aside.

Shape chilled pastry dough into 2 dozen 1-inch balls; place each ball in an *ungreased* 1¾-inch muffin cup. Press dough onto bottom and sides of cups. Spoon about 1 *teaspoon* of the pecans into *each* pastry-lined muffin cup; fill *each* with egg mixture. Bake in a 325° oven 25 minutes or till filling is set. Cool on wire racks; remove from pans. Makes 24.

## Spritz

| | |
|---|---|
| 3½ | **cups all-purpose flour** |
| 1 | **teaspoon baking powder** |
| 1½ | **cups butter *or* margarine** |
| 1 | **cup sugar** |
| 1 | **egg** |
| 1 | **teaspoon vanilla** |
| ½ | **teaspoon almond extract (optional)** |

Oven 400°

Stir together flour and baking powder. Beat butter or margarine for 30 seconds; add sugar and beat till fluffy. Add egg, vanilla, and almond extract, if desired; beat well. Gradually add dry ingredients to beaten mixture, beating till well combined. *Do not chill.* Force dough through a cookie press onto an ungreased cookie sheet. If desired, sprinkle with colored sugars or with ground almonds dyed red or green with food coloring. Bake in a 400° oven for 7 to 8 minutes. Cool on a wire rack. Makes about 60.

**Holiday Pineapple-Filled Spritz:** Prepare Spritz dough as above, *except* use ⅓ of dough and press dough onto the ungreased cookie sheet with a ribbon plate into eight 10-inch strips. Using a star plate and another ⅓ of the dough, press lengthwise rows of dough on top of each strip, making a rim along both edges. (Press remaining dough into any desired shapes and bake as above.)

For filling, in a saucepan stir together one 20-ounce can *crushed pineapple*, drained, and ⅔ cup *sugar*. Bring to boiling; reduce heat and simmer 30 to 35 minutes or till mixture is very thick, stirring often. Using a few drops of *food coloring*, tint half of the filling green and the other half red. Cool thoroughly. Spoon red or green pineapple filling between rims atop strips.

Bake in a 400° oven for 8 to 10 minutes. While hot, cut into 1¼-inch diagonals. Makes about 60.

---

## Berliner Kranser

     1  **cup butter *or* margarine**
     ½  **cup sifted powdered sugar**
     1  **hard-cooked egg yolk, sieved**
     1  **raw egg yolk**
     1  **teaspoon vanilla**
    2¼  **cups all-purpose flour**
     1  **slightly beaten egg white**
     ⅓  **cup sugar cubes, crushed
         (12 to 14)**                              Oven 325°

Beat butter for 30 seconds; add powdered sugar and beat till fluffy. Beat in egg yolks and vanilla. Stir in flour. Cover and chill 1 hour. Work with a small amount of dough at a time; keep the remainder chilled. Using about 1 tablespoon dough for each cookie, roll into 6-inch ropes. Shape each rope into a wreath, overlapping about 1 inch from ends. Brush with egg white; sprinkle with crushed sugar cubes. Place on an ungreased cookie sheet. Bake in a 325° oven for 15 to 17 minutes or till golden. Cool about 1 minute before removing to a wire rack. Makes about 36.

---

## Finnish Chestnut Fingers

     1  **cup all-purpose flour**
     ¼  **teaspoon ground cinnamon**
     6  **tablespoons butter *or* margarine**
     ¼  **cup sugar**
     1  **egg yolk**
     ½  **cup chestnut puree *or* canned chestnuts,
         drained and pureed**
     ½  **teaspoon vanilla**
     3  **squares (3 ounces) semisweet chocolate *or*
         ½ cup semisweet chocolate pieces,
         melted and cooled**                       Oven 350°

Lightly grease a cookie sheet. Combine flour, cinnamon, and ¼ teaspoon *salt*. Beat butter for 30 seconds; add the ¼ cup sugar and beat till fluffy. Add egg yolk; beat well. Beat in chestnut puree and vanilla. Add dry ingredients to beaten mixture, beating well. Using a scant tablespoon of dough for each cookie, roll into 2½-inch fingers. Place on a greased cookie sheet. Sprinkle with additional sugar. Bake in a 350° oven about 20 minutes or till slightly browned. When cool, dip one end of each cookie in melted chocolate; place on waxed paper. Chill 5 to 10 minutes. Makes 30.

# Rolled & Refrigerator Cookies

## Filled Sugar Cookies

|   |   |
|---|---|
| 1 | 8-ounce package (1⅓ cups) pitted dates, snipped |
| ⅓ | cup granulated sugar |
| 2 | tablespoons lemon juice |
| 1½ | teaspoons vanilla |
| 3 | cups all-purpose flour |
| ½ | teaspoon baking soda |
| ½ | cup butter or margarine |
| ½ | cup shortening |
| ½ | cup granulated sugar |
| ½ | cup packed brown sugar |
| 1 | egg |
| 3 | tablespoons milk |

Oven 375°

For filling, combine dates, ⅓ cup sugar, and ½ cup *water*; bring to boiling; reduce heat. Cook and stir till thickened. Add lemon juice and ½ *teaspoon* of the vanilla; cool.

Combine flour, soda, and ½ teaspoon *salt*. Beat butter and shortening for 30 seconds; add the ½ cup of granulated and brown sugar and beat till fluffy. Add egg, milk, and the remaining 1 teaspoon vanilla; beat well. Add dry ingredients to beaten mixture, beating well. Divide dough in half. Cover; chill 1 hour or till dough can be easily rolled. On a lightly floured surface, roll *each* portion to ⅛-inch thickness; cut with a 2½-inch round cutter. Place *1 teaspoon* of filling on each round; spread to within ½ inch of edge. Top with another round; seal edges with a fork. Repeat. Place on an ungreased cookie sheet. Bake in a 375° oven 10 to 12 minutes. Makes 36.

**Pinwheel Cookies:** Prepare Filled Sugar Cookies as above; chill dough. Working with ½ of the dough at a time, roll out on waxed paper into a 12x10-inch rectangle. Spread *each* rectangle with half of the date filling. Carefully roll up jelly roll style, beginning at long side; moisten and pinch edges to seal. Wrap each roll in waxed paper. Chill. Cut into ¼-inch slices. Place on a greased cookie sheet. Bake in a 375° oven about 12 minutes. Makes 72.

# Rolled Ginger Cookies

|   |   |
|---|---|
| 5 | **cups all-purpose flour** |
| 1½ | **teaspoons baking soda** |
| 2 | **teaspoons ground ginger** |
| 1 | **teaspoon ground cinnamon** |
| 1 | **teaspoon ground cloves** |
| 1 | **cup shortening** |
| 1 | **cup sugar** |
| 1 | **egg** |
| 1 | **cup molasses** |
| 2 | **tablespoons vinegar** |

Oven 375°

Grease a cookie sheet. Stir together flour, soda, spices, and ½ teaspoon *salt*. Beat shortening for 30 seconds. Add sugar; beat till fluffy. Add egg, molasses, and vinegar; beat well. Add dry ingredients to beaten mixture, beating well. Cover; chill 3 hours or overnight. Divide dough into thirds. On a lightly floured surface, roll *each* ⅓ of dough to ⅛-inch thickness. (Keep remainder chilled.) Cut into desired shapes. Place 1 inch apart on greased cookie sheet. Bake in a 375° oven for 5 to 6 minutes. Cool 1 minute; remove to a wire rack. Makes 60.

**Note:** Use the recipe above to make and cut out gingerbread men.

## Rolled Cream Cheese Cookies

|   |   |   |
|---|---|---|
| 2 | cups all-purpose flour | |
| ½ | teaspoon baking powder | |
| ½ | cup butter or margarine | |
| 1 | 3-ounce package cream cheese | |
| 1 | cup sugar | |
| 1 | egg | |
| 2 | squares (2 ounces) semisweet chocolate, melted and cooled | |
| ½ | teaspoon vanilla | Oven 375° |

Lightly grease a cookie sheet. Stir together flour and baking powder. Beat butter and cream cheese for 30 seconds; add sugar and beat till fluffy. Add egg, melted chocolate, and vanilla; beat well. Add dry ingredients to beaten mixture, beating till well combined. Cover and chill 2 hours or overnight. Working with ½ of the dough at a time, on a lightly floured surface roll to ⅛-inch thickness. (Keep remainder chilled.) Cut into desired shapes. Place on greased cookie sheet. Bake in a 375° oven for 8 to 10 minutes. Makes about 60.

**Note:** If desired, you can sandwich 2 cookies together with your favorite frosting.

# Lebkuchen

    **3** **cups all-purpose flour**
 **1¼** **teaspoons ground nutmeg**
 **1¼** **teaspoons ground cinnamon**
    **½** **teaspoon baking soda**
    **½** **teaspoon ground cloves**
    **½** **teaspoon ground allspice**
    **1** **egg**
    **¾** **cup packed brown sugar**
    **½** **cup honey**
    **½** **cup dark molasses**
    **½** **cup slivered almonds**
    **½** **cup diced mixed candied fruits and peels,**
        **finely chopped**
        **Lemon Glaze**                    Oven 375°

Grease a cookie sheet. Stir together flour, nutmeg, cinnamon, soda, cloves, and allspice. Beat egg; add brown sugar and beat till fluffy. Stir in honey and molasses. Add dry ingredients to molasses mixture, beating till well combined. Stir in nuts and fruits and peels. Chill several hours or overnight. On a floured surface roll into a 14-inch square. Cut into 3½x2-inch rectangles. Place 2 inches apart on greased cookie sheet. Bake in a 375° oven for 12 to 14 minutes. Cool about 1 minute before removing to a wire rack. While warm, brush with Lemon Glaze. Makes 28.

   ***Lemon Glaze:*** Combine 1 slightly beaten *egg white,* 1½ cups sifted *powdered sugar,* ½ teaspoon finely shredded *lemon peel,* 1 tablespoon *lemon juice,* and dash *salt;* mix well.

# Crisp Pecan Dainties

                                              Oven 375°

Stir together 2⅓ cups all-purpose *flour,* 1 teaspoon *baking powder,* and ½ teaspoon *salt.* Beat ¾ cup *butter* or *margarine* for 30 seconds; add 1 cup *sugar* and beat till fluffy. Add 1 *egg,* 1 teaspoon finely shredded *lemon peel,* and 1 tablespoon *lemon juice;* beat well. Add dry ingredients to beaten mixture, beating till well combined. Stir in 1 cup finely chopped *pecans.* Shape dough into two 7-inch rolls. Wrap in waxed paper or clear plastic wrap; chill thoroughly. If sides flatten, roll on a flat surface to make round. Cut into ⅛-inch slices. Place on an ungreased cookie sheet. Bake in a 375° oven for 6 to 8 minutes. Cool on a wire rack. Makes about 78.

## Refrigerator Cookies

| | |
|---|---|
| 2¼ | **cups all-purpose flour** |
| ½ | **teaspoon baking soda** |
| ½ | **teaspoon salt** |
| 1 | **teaspoon ground cinnamon** |
| ¼ | **teaspoon ground nutmeg** |
| ¼ | **teaspoon ground cloves** |
| ½ | **cup butter or margarine** |
| ½ | **cup shortening** |
| ½ | **cup granulated sugar** |
| ½ | **cup packed brown sugar** |
| 1 | **egg** |
| 2 | **tablespoons milk** |
| ½ | **teaspoon vanilla** |
| ½ | **cup finely chopped nuts** |

Oven 375°

Grease a cookie sheet. Stir together flour, baking soda, salt, cinnamon, nutmeg, and cloves. In a mixer bowl beat butter or margarine and shortening on medium speed of electric mixer for 30 seconds. Add sugars and beat till fluffy. Add egg, milk, and vanilla; beat well. Add dry ingredients to beaten mixture, beating till well combined. Stir in nuts.

Cover and chill 45 minutes for easier handling. Shape into two 7-inch rolls. Wrap in waxed paper or clear plastic wrap; chill at least 6 hours or overnight. Remove from refrigerator and reshape slightly to round out flattened side (chill longer if you have difficulty slicing). Remove wrap. Cut into ¼-inch slices. Place 1 inch apart on greased cookie sheet.

Bake in a 375° oven for 8 to 10 minutes or till lightly browned. Cool about 1 minute before removing from cookie sheet. Cool on a wire rack. Makes about 60.

**Peanut Butter Slices:** Prepare Refrigerator Cookies as above, *except* add ½ cup *peanut butter* with the shortening. Omit milk, spices, and nuts. Continue as directed.

**Whole Wheat Cookies:** Prepare Refrigerator Cookies as above, *except* use only 1½ cups all-purpose flour and add 1 cup *whole wheat flour*. Roll the shaped dough in ¼ cup *wheat germ* to coat surface before second chilling. Continue as directed.

---

# Orange-Chip Cookies

| | |
|---|---|
| 3 | cups all-purpose flour |
| ¼ | teaspoon baking soda |
| ½ | cup butter *or* margarine |
| ½ | cup shortening |
| ½ | cup granulated sugar |
| ½ | cup packed brown sugar |
| 1 | egg |
| 1 | tablespoon finely shredded orange peel |
| 2 | tablespoons orange juice |
| 1 | teaspoon vanilla |
| 1 | square (1 ounce) semisweet chocolate, coarsely shredded |

Oven 375°

Stir together flour, soda, and ¼ teaspoon *salt*. Beat butter and shortening for 30 seconds; add sugars and beat till fluffy. Add egg, orange peel, orange juice, and vanilla; beat well. Add dry ingredients to beaten mixture, beating till well combined. Stir in chocolate. Shape into two 8-inch rolls. Wrap in waxed paper or clear plastic wrap; chill thoroughly. Cut into ¼-inch slices. Place on an ungreased cookie sheet. Bake in 375° oven 10 to 12 minutes or till done. Makes about 60.

**Note:** For a cakelike cookie, drop *unchilled* dough by spoonfuls onto an ungreased cookie sheet. Bake in a 375° oven about 12 minutes.

## Santa's Whiskers

|       |                                              |            |
|-------|----------------------------------------------|------------|
| 1     | cup butter *or* margarine                    |            |
| 1     | cup sugar                                    |            |
| 2     | tablespoons milk                             |            |
| 1     | teaspoon vanilla                             |            |
| 2½    | cups all-purpose flour                       |            |
| 1     | cup finely chopped red *or* green candied cherries |      |
| ½     | cup finely chopped pecans                    |            |
| 1     | cup flaked coconut                           | Oven 375°  |

Beat butter for 30 seconds; add sugar and beat till fluffy. Add milk and vanilla; beat well. Stir in flour, then cherries and pecans. Shape into three 7-inch rolls. Roll dough in coconut to coat outside. Wrap in waxed paper or clear plastic wrap; chill thoroughly. Cut into ¼-inch slices. Place on an ungreased cookie sheet. Bake in a 375° oven 12 minutes or till edges are golden. Makes about 80.

## Rolled Sugar Cookies

|       |                                  |            |
|-------|----------------------------------|------------|
| 2     | cups all-purpose flour           |            |
| 1½    | teaspoons baking powder          |            |
| 6     | tablespoons butter *or* margarine |           |
| ⅓     | cup shortening                   |            |
| ¾     | cup sugar                        |            |
| 1     | egg                              |            |
| 1     | tablespoon milk                  |            |
| 1     | teaspoon vanilla                 | Oven 375°  |

Stir together flour, baking powder, and ¼ teaspoon *salt*. Beat butter and shortening for 30 seconds; add sugar and beat till fluffy. Add egg, milk, and vanilla; beat well. Add dry ingredients to beaten mixture, beating till well combined. Cover and chill at least 3 hours. Working with ½ of the dough at a time, on a lightly floured surface roll to ⅛-inch thickness. Cut into desired shapes. Place on an ungreased cookie sheet. Bake in a 375° oven for 8 minutes or till done. Makes 36 to 48.

## Oatmeal Refrigerator Cookies

1½   cups all-purpose flour
1   teaspoon salt
1   teaspoon baking soda
1   teaspoon ground cinnamon
⅛   teaspoon ground cloves (optional)
½   cup shortening
½   cup butter *or* margarine
1   cup packed brown sugar
2   eggs
1   teaspoon vanilla
1½   cups quick-cooking rolled oats
½   cup finely chopped walnuts          Oven 375°

Lightly grease a cookie sheet. Stir together flour; salt; baking soda; cinnamon; and cloves, if desired. Beat shortening and butter or margarine for 30 seconds; add brown sugar and beat till fluffy. Add eggs and vanilla; beat well. Add dry ingredients to beaten mixture, beating till well combined. Stir in oats and walnuts. Shape dough into two 8-inch rolls. Wrap in waxed paper or clear plastic wrap; chill thoroughly. Cut into ¼-inch slices. Place on greased cookie sheet. Bake in a 375° oven for 8 to 10 minutes. Makes about 60.

# Desserts

# Desserts

# Desserts

# Desserts

# Desserts

# Desserts

# Desserts

# Desserts

# Desserts

| Recipes | Servings (fraction of recipe) | Calories | Protein (grams) | Carbohydrate (grams) | Fat (grams) | Sodium (milligrams) | Potassium (milligrams) | Percent of U.S. RDA Per Serving | | | | | | | |
| --- | --- | --- | --- | --- | --- | --- | --- | --- | --- | --- | --- | --- | --- | --- | --- |
| | | | | | | | | Protein | Vitamin A | Vitamin C | Thiamine | Riboflavin | Niacin | Calcium | Iron |
| Apple Cobbler | 1/6 | 505 | 6 | 74 | 22 | 307 | 250 | 9 | 19 | 7 | 14 | 15 | 7 | 11 | 7 |
| Apple Dumplings | 1/6 | 755 | 6 | 112 | 33 | 416 | 189 | 9 | 9 | 4 | 22 | 14 | 13 | 6 | 10 |
| Applesauce | 1/10 | 144 | 0 | 36 | 1 | 2 | 200 | 1 | 3 | 12 | 4 | 2 | 1 | 1 | 3 |
| Apricot Angel Dessert | 1/12 | 248 | 4 | 42 | 7 | 80 | 225 | 6 | 31 | 6 | 3 | 5 | 2 | 3 | 2 |
| Baked Alaska | 1/8 | 557 | 10 | 85 | 21 | 364 | 226 | 15 | 9 | 1 | 3 | 17 | 1 | 2 | 3 |
| Baked Apples | 1/6 | 387 | 3 | 65 | 7 | 16 | 508 | 4 | 16 | 15 | 7 | 9 | 1 | 10 | 5 |
| Baked Coffee Custard | 1/6 | 173 | 7 | 21 | 7 | 171 | 179 | 11 | 10 | 1 | 4 | 14 | 2 | 12 | 5 |
| Baked Custard | 1/6 | 172 | 7 | 21 | 7 | 170 | 161 | 11 | 10 | 1 | 4 | 14 | 1 | 11 | 5 |
| Baked Rice Pudding | 1/6 | 496 | 12 | 49 | 29 | 413 | 449 | 19 | 27 | 4 | 12 | 27 | 4 | 28 | 8 |
| Basic Dessert Crepes | 1/16 | 67 | 2 | 9 | 2 | 37 | 49 | 4 | 2 | 0 | 4 | 5 | 2 | 2 | 2 |
| Basic Hard Sauce | 1/21 | 75 | 0 | 10 | 4 | 53 | 2 | 0 | 4 | 0 | 0 | 0 | 0 | 0 | 0 |
| Blueberry Melba Parfaits | 1/6 | 295 | 5 | 50 | 10 | 57 | 292 | 7 | 10 | 48 | 5 | 15 | 3 | 15 | 5 |
| Blueberry Shortcake | 1/8 | 460 | 6 | 50 | 27 | 479 | 163 | 10 | 24 | 18 | 16 | 15 | 10 | 10 | 10 |
| Brandy Hard Sauce | 1/11 | 112 | 0 | 9 | 8 | 102 | 3 | 0 | 7 | 0 | 0 | 0 | 0 | 0 | 0 |
| Bread Pudding | 1/6 | 207 | 8 | 28 | 7 | 236 | 235 | 13 | 10 | 1 | 8 | 16 | 3 | 13 | 8 |
| Brownie Pudding | 1/8 | 277 | 8 | 47 | 10 | 224 | 134 | 6 | 6 | 1 | 9 | 7 | 5 | 5 | 6 |
| Cheesecake Supreme w/Cherry Sauce | 1/12 | 482 | 8 | 49 | 29 | 272 | 173 | 12 | 37 | 9 | 8 | 15 | 4 | 6 | 5 |
| Cherries Jubilee | 1/6 | 248 | 4 | 39 | 7 | 43 | 208 | 6 | 7 | 5 | 3 | 9 | 2 | 11 | 2 |
| Cherry Cobbler | 1/6 | 485 | 7 | 64 | 24 | 332 | 321 | 10 | 41 | 18 | 14 | 16 | 8 | 12 | 7 |
| Cherry-Nut Ice Cream | 1/24 | 277 | 4 | 22 | 20 | 52 | 126 | 7 | 14 | 2 | 3 | 8 | 0 | 9 | 1 |

# Nutrition Analysis Chart

| Recipe | Serving | Calories | Protein (g) | Carbohydrate (g) | Fat (g) | Cholesterol (mg) | Sodium (mg) | Protein % | Vit. A % | Vit. C % | Thiamin % | Riboflavin % | Niacin % | Calcium % | Iron % |
|---|---|---|---|---|---|---|---|---|---|---|---|---|---|---|---|
| Cherry Torte | 1/8 | 290 | 3 | 50 | 10 | 103 | 103 | 5 | 9 | 6 | 2 | 6 | 1 | 4 | 2 |
| Choco-Coffee-Toffee Squares | 1/9 | 336 | 4 | 33 | 22 | 232 | 109 | 7 | 17 | 0 | 3 | 7 | 2 | 4 | 6 |
| Chocolate-Almond Ice Cream | 1/24 | 310 | 5 | 23 | 24 | 52 | 204 | 8 | 15 | 1 | 3 | 12 | 2 | 10 | 5 |
| Chocolate Chip Ice Cream | 1/24 | 261 | 4 | 20 | 19 | 52 | 127 | 6 | 14 | 1 | 2 | 8 | 0 | 9 | 5 |
| Chocolate Fondue w/angel cake | 1/8 | 527 | 11 | 89 | 16 | 250 | 369 | 17 | 5 | 1 | 4 | 22 | 2 | 20 | 4 |
| Chocolate Pots de Crème | 1/4 | 332 | 5 | 22 | 26 | 42 | 162 | 17 | 19 | 1 | 4 | 11 | 2 | 11 | 6 |
| Chocolate Pudding | 1/4 | 390 | 7 | 51 | 20 | 270 | 304 | 8 | 14 | 2 | 4 | 16 | 2 | 17 | 8 |
| Chocolate Soufflé | 1/6 | 342 | 8 | 26 | 25 | 224 | 202 | 11 | 21 | 1 | 5 | 14 | 2 | 9 | 8 |
| Choco-Mint Velvet | 1/8 | 403 | 6 | 52 | 22 | 110 | 213 | 12 | 17 | 1 | 3 | 11 | 1 | 12 | 8 |
| Choco-Velvet Ice Cream | 1/8 | 355 | 5 | 33 | 25 | 63 | 235 | 8 | 17 | 1 | 4 | 11 | 1 | 13 | 3 |
| Chunky Applesauce | 1/10 | 144 | 0 | 36 | 1 | 2 | 2 | 1 | 3 | 12 | 4 | 2 | 1 | 1 | 3 |
| Coffee Fondue w/angel cake | 1/8 | 528 | 11 | 89 | 16 | 251 | 390 | 17 | 5 | 1 | 4 | 22 | 3 | 20 | 5 |
| Coffee Ice Cream | 1/24 | 226 | 3 | 16 | 17 | 52 | 110 | 5 | 14 | 1 | 2 | 8 | 1 | 8 | 1 |
| Cream Puffs w/whipped cream | 1/10 | 279 | 5 | 11 | 24 | 204 | 81 | 8 | 22 | 2 | 7 | 9 | 3 | 5 | 5 |
| Crème Brûlée | 1/6 | 310 | 5 | 30 | 19 | 159 | 193 | 9 | 19 | 1 | 3 | 12 | 0 | 11 | 7 |
| Crêpes Suzette | 1/8 | 334 | 5 | 30 | 16 | 215 | 154 | 8 | 14 | 3 | 10 | 11 | 5 | 7 | 4 |
| Easy Vanilla Ice Cream | 1/12 | 268 | 2 | 20 | 21 | 55 | 90 | 3 | 17 | 1 | 1 | 6 | 0 | 7 | 0 |
| Eclairs w/pudding | 1/12 | 290 | 6 | 34 | 15 | 214 | 166 | 10 | 13 | 1 | 7 | 13 | 3 | 10 | 5 |
| Fluffy Hard Sauce | 1/21 | 79 | 0 | 10 | 5 | 56 | 5 | 1 | 4 | 0 | 0 | 0 | 0 | 0 | 0 |
| Fluffy Vanilla Sauce | 1/13 | 91 | 1 | 6 | 7 | 9 | 23 | 2 | 7 | 0 | 1 | 2 | 0 | 2 | 9 |
| Fresh Fruit Crisp | 1/6 | 348 | 3 | 59 | 13 | 122 | 320 | 5 | 12 | 11 | 9 | 8 | 3 | 8 | 2 |
| Fresh Strawberry Ice Cream | 1/12 | 207 | 3 | 20 | 13 | 69 | 92 | 4 | 12 | 25 | 1 | 5 | 1 | 4 | 5 |
| Frozen Yogurt Melba Bombe | 1/8 | 296 | 10 | 55 | 5 | 206 | 350 | 15 | 4 | 3 | 31 | 46 | 21 | 29 | 3 |
| Hot Fudge Sundaes | 1/8 | 251 | 4 | 28 | 15 | 95 | 181 | 6 | 9 | 1 | 13 | 9 | 1 | 10 | 7 |
| Individual Shortcakes | 1/8 | 221 | 4 | 25 | 12 | 367 | 58 | 6 | 10 | 0 | 12 | 5 | 7 | 5 | 4 |
| Lemon-Filled Crepes | 1/9 | 323 | 7 | 51 | 10 | 124 | 147 | 11 | 11 | 8 | 5 | 15 | 6 | 9 | 3 |
| Lemon Pudding Cake | 1/6 | 247 | 6 | 33 | 11 | 130 | 142 | 9 | 12 | 10 | 2 | 12 | 2 | 9 | 0 |
| Lemon Torte | 1/8 | 306 | 4 | 47 | 12 | 106 | 72 | 6 | 13 | 6 | 2 | 7 | 0 | 4 | 0 |
| Meringue Shells | 1/8 | 103 | 1 | 25 | 0 | 18 | 18 | 2 | 0 | 0 | 0 | 2 | 0 | 0 | 0 |

# Nutrition Analysis Chart

| Recipes | Servings (fraction of recipe) | Calories | Protein (grams) | Carbohydrate (grams) | Fat (grams) | Sodium (milligrams) | Potassium (milligrams) | Protein | Vitamin A | Vitamin C | Thiamine | Riboflavin | Niacin | Calcium | Iron |
|---|---|---|---|---|---|---|---|---|---|---|---|---|---|---|---|
| | | | | | | | | \<-- Percent of U.S. RDA Per Serving --\> | | | | | | | |
| Orange Hard Sauce | 1/8 | 100 | 0 | 13 | 6 | 70 | 6 | 0 | 5 | 2 | 0 | 0 | 0 | 0 | 0 |
| Orange Sauce | 1/9 | 79 | 0 | 17 | 1 | 16 | 83 | 0 | 3 | 34 | 2 | 2 | 1 | 1 | 1 |
| Orange Soufflé w/Orange Sauce | 1/8 | 222 | 5 | 31 | 9 | 110 | 181 | 7 | 13 | 48 | 7 | 9 | 9 | 2 | 4 |
| Peach-Cherry Ice Cream | 1/24 | 152 | 2 | 18 | 9 | 26 | 151 | 3 | 18 | 7 | 2 | 5 | 5 | 4 | 2 |
| Peach Cobbler | 1/6 | 443 | 6 | 54 | 24 | 336 | 418 | 10 | 50 | 16 | 13 | 13 | 16 | 12 | 11 |
| Peach Sauce | 1/16 | 64 | 0 | 15 | 1 | 10 | 64 | 0 | 5 | 7 | 1 | 1 | 5 | 2 | 0 |
| Peach Shortcake | 1/8 | 456 | 6 | 49 | 27 | 479 | 276 | 10 | 45 | 11 | 16 | 16 | 15 | 13 | 9 |
| Pineapple Sherbet | 1/12 | 82 | 2 | 19 | 0 | 58 | 82 | 4 | 0 | 3 | 2 | 2 | 5 | 5 | 0 |
| Praline Cheese Cups | 1/4 | 443 | 6 | 48 | 25 | 292 | 65 | 9 | 12 | 1 | 9 | 9 | 12 | 3 | 6 |
| Regal Plum Pudding w/Basic Hard Sauce | 1/8 | 553 | 6 | 94 | 19 | 334 | 652 | 10 | 8 | 27 | 18 | 18 | 14 | 9 | 18 |
| Rhubarb Sauce | 1/10 | 42 | 0 | 11 | 0 | 1 | 53 | 0 | 0 | 4 | 0 | 0 | 2 | 2 | 1 |
| Saucepan Rice Pudding | 1/6 | 208 | 6 | 33 | 6 | 176 | 252 | 8 | 5 | 2 | 8 | 8 | 13 | 15 | 4 |
| Sherried Fruit Compote | 1/6 | 320 | 2 | 73 | 2 | 404 | 553 | 4 | 48 | 14 | 6 | 6 | 6 | 6 | 17 |
| Sour Cream Cheesecake | 1/12 | 481 | 8 | 29 | 38 | 362 | 188 | 12 | 30 | 1 | 4 | 4 | 14 | 11 | 4 |
| Stirred Custard | 1/6 | 126 | 6 | 13 | 6 | 71 | 150 | 9 | 8 | 1 | 3 | 13 | 13 | 11 | 3 |
| Strawberry Shortcake | 1/8 | 457 | 6 | 48 | 27 | 480 | 288 | 10 | 24 | 111 | 17 | 17 | 17 | 12 | 12 |
| Summer Fruit Compote | 1/4 | 179 | 7 | 41 | 3 | 12 | 442 | 3 | 5 | 147 | 8 | 7 | 7 | 6 | 6 |
| Tapioca Fluff Pudding | 1/8 | 173 | 7 | 23 | 6 | 149 | 200 | 10 | 2 | 8 | 3 | 16 | 16 | 16 | 9 |
| Vanilla Ice Cream | 1/24 | 226 | 3 | 16 | 17 | 52 | 103 | 5 | 14 | 1 | 2 | 8 | 8 | 8 | 1 |
| Vanilla Pudding | 1/4 | 271 | 6 | 34 | 13 | 269 | 186 | 9 | 14 | 2 | 4 | 14 | 14 | 16 | 3 |

# Desserts

Whether quick and simple or elegant and impressive, a dessert should end the meal on a delicious note. While it shouldn't dominate the food that precedes it, it shouldn't be lost or ignored, either. Remember, if you've served a hearty meal, a light dessert is in order; likewise, a more filling dessert provides a nice contrast to a lighter entrée. A simple fruit cup or pudding can be as appropriate as crepes served in a chafing dish.

Some desserts are best served warm, while others should be eaten chilled. Don't make the mistake of serving your dessert too hot or too cold, however. In fact, frozen desserts are best if allowed to stand at room temperature for a few minutes before they are served.

## Saucepan Rice Pudding

|       |                                    |
| ----- | ---------------------------------- |
| 3     | **cups milk**                      |
| ½     | **cup long grain rice**            |
| ⅓     | **cup raisins**                    |
| 1     | **tablespoon butter** or **margarine** |
| ¼     | **cup sugar**                      |
| ¼     | **teaspoon ground cinnamon**       |

In a heavy medium saucepan bring milk to boiling; stir in *uncooked* rice, raisins, and ¼ teaspoon *salt*. Cover; cook over low heat, stirring occasionally, for 30 to 40 minutes or till most of the milk is absorbed. (Mixture may appear curdled.) Spoon into dessert dishes. Dot with butter and sprinkle with a mixture of the sugar and cinnamon. Serves 6.

## Tapioca Fluff Pudding

- ½ **cup sugar**
- ¼ **cup quick-cooking tapioca**
- ¼ **teaspoon salt**
- 4 **cups milk**
- 3 **slightly beaten egg yolks**
- 1½ **teaspoons vanilla**
- 3 **egg whites**

In a heavy large saucepan combine sugar, tapioca, and salt. Stir in milk; let stand 5 minutes. Stir in egg yolks. Bring mixture to a full boil, stirring constantly. Remove from heat (mixture will be thin). Stir in vanilla. Beat egg whites till stiff peaks form. Put ⅓ of the egg whites into a large bowl. Slowly stir in the tapioca mixture. Fold in remaining egg whites, leaving little fluffs of egg white. Cover and chill. Spoon tapioca mixture into individual sherbet or dessert dishes. If desired, serve with fresh or canned fruit. Makes 8 to 10 servings.

## Baked Rice Pudding

- 2 **cups milk**
- ½ **cup long grain rice**
- ½ **cup raisins**
- ¼ **cup butter or margarine**
- 3 **beaten eggs**
- 2 **cups milk**
- ½ **cup sugar**
- 1 **teaspoon vanilla**
- ½ **teaspoon salt**
  **Ground nutmeg or cinnamon**
  **Light cream or milk**                                    Oven 325°

In a heavy medium saucepan bring 2 cups milk, *uncooked* rice, and raisins to boiling; reduce heat. Cover and cook over very low heat about 15 minutes or till rice is tender. Remove from heat; stir in butter or margarine till melted. In a mixing bowl stir together the eggs, the 2 cups milk, sugar, vanilla, and salt.

Gradually stir rice mixture into egg mixture. Pour into a 10x6x2-inch baking dish. Bake in a 325° oven for 30 minutes. Stir well; sprinkle with nutmeg or cinnamon. Bake for 15 to 20 minutes more or till a knife inserted near center comes out clean. Serve warm or chilled with light cream or milk. Makes 6 servings.

## Vanilla Pudding

- ½ **cup sugar**
- 2 **tablespoons cornstarch**
- 2 **cups milk**
- 2 **beaten egg yolks or 1 beaten egg**
- 2 **tablespoons butter or margarine**
- 1½ **teaspoons vanilla**

In a heavy medium saucepan combine sugar, cornstarch, and ¼ teaspoon *salt*. Stir in milk. Cook and stir over medium heat till thickened and bubbly; cook and stir 2 minutes more. Remove from heat. Gradually stir about *1 cup* of the hot mixture into egg yolks or egg.

Return all to mixture in saucepan. Cook and stir 2 minutes more. Remove from heat. Stir in butter and vanilla till butter melts. Pour into a bowl. Cover surface with clear plastic wrap. Chill without stirring. To serve, spoon into individual sherbet dishes. Serves 4.

***Chocolate Pudding:*** Prepare Vanilla Pudding as above, *except* increase sugar to ¾ cup. Chop 2 squares (2 ounces) *unsweetened chocolate*. Add with milk. Continue as directed.

## Bread Pudding

Oven 325°

Beat together 4 *eggs*, 2 cups *milk*, ⅓ cup *sugar*, ½ teaspoon ground *cinnamon*, ½ teaspoon *vanilla*, and ¼ teaspoon *salt*. Place 2½ cups *dry bread cubes* (3½ slices) in an 8x1½-inch round baking dish. Sprinkle ⅓ cup *raisins* over bread. Pour egg mixture over all. Bake in a 325° oven for 40 to 45 minutes or till a knife inserted near center comes out clean. Cool slightly. Makes 6 servings.

---

### Pudding tip

To keep a "skin" from forming on the top of a pudding mixture while it cools, carefully place a piece of clear plastic wrap or waxed paper directly on the surface of the hot pudding. After the pudding has cooled, remove the wrap or paper and spoon the pudding into dessert dishes.

---

## Stirred Custard

**3 slightly beaten eggs**
**2 cups milk**
**¼ cup sugar**
**Dash salt**
**1 teaspoon vanilla**

In a heavy medium saucepan combine the eggs, milk, sugar, and salt. Cook and stir over medium heat. Continue cooking egg mixture till it coats a metal spoon. Remove from heat; cool at once by placing pan in a sink or bowl of ice water and stirring 1 to 2 minutes. Stir in vanilla. Pour custard mixture into a bowl. Cover surface with clear plastic wrap; chill till serving time. Makes 6 servings.

# Baked Custard

4 **eggs**
2 **cups milk**
½ **cup sugar**
1 **teaspoon vanilla**
¼ **teaspoon salt**
**Ground nutmeg (optional)** Oven 325°

In a medium bowl lightly beat eggs. Stir in milk, sugar, vanilla, and salt. Place one 1-quart casserole or six 6-ounce custard cups in a 13x9x2-inch baking pan on oven rack. Pour custard mixture into casserole or divide custard mixture among the custard cups. Sprinkle with nutmeg, if desired.

Pour boiling water into the pan around casserole or custard cups to a depth of 1 inch. Bake in a 325° oven for 50 to 60 minutes for the 1-quart casserole (30 to 40 minutes for individual cups) or till a knife inserted near center comes out clean. Serve warm or chilled. To unmold chilled individual custards, first loosen edges with a spatula or knife; slip point of knife down sides to let air in. Invert onto a serving plate. Makes 6 servings.

**Baked Coffee Custard:** Prepare Baked Custard as above, *except* add 4 teaspoons *instant coffee crystals* dissolved in 1 tablespoon *hot water* to eggs along with milk, sugar, vanilla, and salt. Continue as directed; omit sprinkling with nutmeg. If desired, serve topped with a dollop of whipped cream; sprinkle with toasted almonds.

# Chocolate Pots de Crème

1 **cup light cream**
1 **4-ounce package German sweet chocolate, coarsely chopped**
1 **tablespoon sugar**
**Dash salt**
3 **beaten egg yolks**
½ **teaspoon vanilla**
**Whipped cream (optional)**

In a heavy small saucepan combine light cream, chopped chocolate, sugar, and salt. Cook and stir over medium-low heat till smooth and *slightly thickened*. Gradually stir about *half* of the hot mixture into beaten egg yolks; return all to saucepan. Cook and stir over medium-low heat 2 to 3 minutes more. Remove from heat; stir in vanilla. Pour into 4 to 6 pots de crème cups or individual small sherbet dishes. Cover and chill several hours or overnight till firm. Garnish with whipped cream, if desired. Makes 4 to 6 servings.

## Crème Brûlée

   3  **slightly beaten eggs**
   2  **cups light cream**
   ¼  **cup granulated sugar**
   ¼  **teaspoon salt**
   ½  **teaspoon vanilla**
   ½  **cup packed brown sugar**

In a heavy 2-quart saucepan combine the beaten eggs, light cream, sugar, and salt; cook and stir over medium heat about 10 minutes or till custard coats a metal spoon. Remove from heat; cool at once by placing pan in a sink or bowl of ice water and stirring 1 to 2 minutes. Stir in vanilla. Pour into a 1-quart casserole; refrigerate at least 2 hours.

Press brown sugar through a sieve over custard. Set the casserole in a pan of ice cubes and cold water. Broil 4 to 5 inches from heat for 1 to 2 minutes or till sugar turns golden brown and a bubbly crust forms. Serve warm or chilled. Serves 6.

## Regal Plum Pudding

**3**   **slices bread, torn into pieces**
**1**   **5⅓-ounce can evaporated milk**
**2**   **ounces beef suet, ground**
**¾**   **cup packed brown sugar**
**1**   **beaten egg**
**¼**   **cup orange juice**
**½**   **teaspoon vanilla**
**1½**  **cups raisins**
**¾**   **cup snipped pitted dates**
**½**   **cup diced mixed candied fruits and peels**
**⅓**   **cup chopped walnuts**
**¾**   **cup all-purpose flour**
**1½**  **teaspoons ground cinnamon**
**¾**   **teaspoon baking soda**
**¾**   **teaspoon ground cloves**
**¾**   **teaspoon ground mace**
**¼**   **teaspoon salt**
    **Basic Hard Sauce (see recipe, page 363)**

In a large bowl soak torn bread in evaporated milk about 3 minutes or till softened; beat lightly to break up. Stir in ground suet, brown sugar, egg, orange juice, and vanilla. Add raisins, snipped dates, candied fruits and peels, and chopped nuts.

Stir together flour, cinnamon, baking soda, cloves, mace, and salt. Add to fruit mixture; stir till combined. Turn mixture into a well-greased 3-pound shortening can or 6½-cup tower mold. Cover with foil, pressing foil tightly against rim of the can or mold. Place on a rack in a deep kettle; add boiling water to a depth of 1 inch. Cover kettle; boil gently (bubbles break surface) and steam 4 hours or till done. Add more boiling water, if necessary. Cool 10 minutes before unmolding. Serve warm with Basic Hard Sauce. Makes 8 to 10 servings.

**Crockery cooker directions:** Prepare Regal Plum Pudding mixture as above. Turn mixture into a well-greased 3-pound shortening can. Place covered shortening can on a rack (use a metal jar lid or crumpled foil) in an electric slow crockery cooker. Cover and cook on high-heat setting for 4 hours or till done. Remove can from cooker; cool 10 minutes before unmolding. Serve as above.

## Brownie Pudding

|       |                                   |            |
|-------|-----------------------------------|------------|
| 1     | cup all-purpose flour             |            |
| ½     | cup sugar                         |            |
| 2     | tablespoons unsweetened cocoa powder |         |
| 2     | teaspoons baking powder           |            |
| ½     | teaspoon salt                     |            |
| ½     | cup milk                          |            |
| 2     | tablespoons cooking oil           |            |
| 1     | teaspoon vanilla                  |            |
| ½     | cup chopped walnuts               |            |
| ¾     | cup sugar                         |            |
| ¼     | cup unsweetened cocoa powder      | Oven 350°  |

In a large mixing bowl stir together flour, ½ cup sugar, the 2 tablespoons cocoa powder, baking powder, and salt. Add milk, oil, and vanilla; stir till smooth. Stir in nuts. Turn into an ungreased 8x8x2-inch baking pan. Combine ¾ cup sugar and ¼ cup cocoa powder; gradually stir in 1½ cups *boiling water*. Pour liquid mixture evenly over batter in pan. Bake in a 350° oven about 30 minutes or till cake tests done. Serve warm or chilled in individual dessert dishes. Makes 8 servings.

## Lemon Pudding Cake

|       |                                        |           |
|-------|----------------------------------------|-----------|
| ¾     | cup sugar                              |           |
| ¼     | cup all-purpose flour                  |           |
|       | Dash salt                              |           |
| 3     | tablespoons butter, melted             |           |
| 1½    | teaspoons finely shredded lemon peel   |           |
| ¼     | cup lemon juice                        |           |
| 3     | beaten egg yolks                       |           |
| 1½    | cups milk                              |           |
| 3     | egg whites                             | Oven 350° |

In a large mixing bowl combine sugar, flour, and salt. Stir in melted butter, lemon peel, and lemon juice. In a small bowl combine egg yolks and milk; add to flour mixture. In a mixer bowl beat egg whites to stiff peaks. Gently fold egg whites into lemon batter. Turn into an ungreased 8x8x2-inch baking pan. Place in a larger pan on oven rack. Pour hot water into larger pan to a depth of 1 inch. Bake in a 350° oven for 35 to 40 minutes or till top is golden and springs back when touched. Serve warm or chilled in individual dessert dishes. Makes 6 to 8 servings.

## Orange Soufflé

Oven 325°

Fit a 2-quart soufflé dish with a greased and sugared foil collar; set aside.

In a saucepan melt 3 tablespoons *butter or margarine*. Stir in ¼ cup all-purpose *flour* and dash *salt*. Add ⅔ cup *milk;* cook and stir till thick and bubbly. (Mixture will be very thick.) Remove from heat; stir in 1 teaspoon finely shredded *orange peel* and ⅓ cup *orange juice*. Mix well. Beat 4 *egg yolks* about 5 minutes or till thick and lemon colored. Gradually blend orange mixture into beaten egg yolks. Wash beaters thoroughly.

In a large mixer bowl beat 4 *egg whites* to soft peaks; gradually add ¼ cup *sugar,* beating to stiff peaks. Fold orange mixture into egg whites. Turn into ungreased soufflé dish. Bake in a 325° oven for 60 to 65 minutes or till a knife inserted near center comes out clean. Serve immediately with *Orange Sauce* (see recipe, page 364). Makes 8 servings.

## Chocolate Soufflé

Oven 325°

Fit a 1½-quart soufflé dish with a greased and sugared foil collar. (Or, use a 2-quart soufflé dish without collar.) In a small saucepan melt 3 tablespoons *butter or margarine*. Stir in ¼ cup all-purpose *flour* and ¼ teaspoon *salt*. Add ¾ cup *milk;*

cook and stir till thick and bubbly. Remove from heat. Beat 4 *egg yolks* about 5 minutes or till thick and lemon colored. Gradually stir saucepan mixture into yolks. Stir together 2 squares (2 ounces) *unsweetened chocolate*, melted and cooled; ¼ cup *sugar;* and 2 tablespoons *hot water.* Stir into egg yolk mixture. Wash beaters thoroughly.

In a large mixer bowl beat 4 *egg whites* and ½ teaspoon *vanilla* till soft peaks form; gradually add ¼ cup *sugar*, beating to stiff peaks. Fold chocolate mixture into egg whites. Turn into the ungreased soufflé dish. Bake in a 325° oven for 60 minutes (50 minutes for 2-quart dish) or till a knife inserted near center comes out clean. Quickly sprinkle top of soufflé with sifted *powdered sugar.* Serve immediately with *whipped cream.* Makes 6 servings.

## Meringue Shells

Oven 275°

Let 3 *egg whites* stand in a small mixer bowl about 1 hour or till they come to room temperature. Meanwhile, cover baking sheets with brown paper. Draw eight 3-inch circles or one 9-inch circle; set aside. Add 1 teaspoon *vanilla*, ¼ teaspoon *cream of tartar*, and dash *salt* to egg whites. Beat to soft peaks. Gradually add 1 cup *sugar*, beating till very stiff peaks form. Spread meringue over circles on paper to make 8 individual shells or one 9-inch meringue shell; use the back of a spoon to shape into shells. Bake either size in a 275° oven for 1 hour. Turn off oven and let dry in oven, with door closed, for at least 1 hour. Peel off paper. To serve, fill shells with ice cream or pudding and top with fruit or ice cream topping. If necessary to store shells before serving, place in a plastic bag or airtight container. Makes 8 servings.

## Sour Cream Cheesecake

| | |
|---|---|
| 1¾ | cups fine graham cracker crumbs |
| ¼ | cup finely chopped walnuts |
| ½ | teaspoon ground cinnamon |
| ½ | cup butter or margarine, melted |
| 2 | 8-ounce packages cream cheese, softened |
| 1 | cup sugar |
| 2 | teaspoons vanilla |
| ¼ | teaspoon almond extract |
| 3 | eggs |
| 3 | cups dairy sour cream |

Oven 375°

Combine crumbs, nuts, and cinnamon; add butter or margarine, stirring till well combined. Reserve ¼ cup for top; press remainder onto bottom and 2½ inches up sides of an 8-inch springform pan or 2 inches up sides of a 9-inch springform pan. In a large mixer bowl beat together cream cheese, sugar, vanilla, almond extract, and ¼ teaspoon *salt* just till smooth. *Do not overbeat.* Add eggs, beating at low speed of electric mixer just till combined. Stir in sour cream. Turn into prepared crust. Sprinkle reserved crumbs atop. Bake in a 375° oven for 50 to 55 minutes or till a knife inserted near center comes out almost clean. Cool on a wire rack; chill 4 to 5 hours. Makes 12 servings.

## Cheesecake Supreme

 ¾ **cup all-purpose flour**
 3 **tablespoons sugar**
 1 **teaspoon finely shredded lemon peel**
 6 **tablespoons butter or margarine**
 1 **slightly beaten egg yolk**
 ½ **teaspoon vanilla**
 3 **8-ounce packages cream cheese, softened**
 1 **cup sugar**
 2 **tablespoons all-purpose flour**
 ¼ **teaspoon salt**
 2 **eggs**
 1 **egg yolk**
 ¼ **cup milk**
   **Cherry Sauce**                                    Oven 400°

To prepare crust, combine the ¾ cup flour, the 3 tablespoons sugar, and ½ *teaspoon* of the lemon peel. Cut in butter or margarine till crumbly. Stir in 1 slightly beaten egg yolk and ¼ *teaspoon* of the vanilla. Pat ⅓ of the dough onto the bottom of an 8- or 9-inch springform pan (with sides removed). Bake in a 400° oven for 7 minutes or till golden; cool.

Butter the sides of pan; attach to bottom. Pat remaining dough onto sides of pan to a height of 1¾ inches; set aside.

For the filling, in a large mixer bowl beat together the softened cream cheese, remaining lemon peel, and remaining vanilla till fluffy. Stir together the 1 cup sugar, the 2 tablespoons flour, and the salt; gradually stir into cream cheese mixture. Add the 2 eggs and 1 *egg* yolk all at once, beating at low speed just till combined. Stir in milk. Turn into crust-lined pan. Bake in a 450° oven for 10 minutes. Reduce heat to 300°; bake 50 to 55 minutes more or till center appears set and a knife comes out clean. Cool 15 minutes. Loosen sides of cheesecake from pan with a spatula. Cool 30 minutes; remove sides of pan. Cool about 2 hours longer. Chill thoroughly. Top with Cherry Sauce. Serves 12.

***Cherry Sauce:*** In a saucepan combine ¾ cup *sugar*, 2 tablespoons *cornstarch*, and dash *salt*. Stir in ⅓ cup *water*. Stir in 4 cups fresh or frozen unsweetened pitted *tart red cherries*, thawed. Cook and stir till thickened and bubbly. Cook and stir 1 to 2 minutes more. Cover; chill without stirring. (*Or*, use one 21-ounce can *cherry pie filling* instead of sauce.)

---

## Lemon Torte

---

*A fancy dessert to climax that special dinner—*

>     4   **egg whites**
>     1   **teaspoon vanilla**
>    ¼   **teaspoon cream of tartar**
>    ¼   **teaspoon salt**
> 1⅓   **cups sugar**
>     4   **egg yolks**
>     2   **teaspoons finely shredded lemon peel**
>     3   **tablespoons lemon juice**
>    ½   **cup sugar**
>         **Dash salt**
>     1   **cup whipping cream**                    Oven 450°

Preheat oven to 450°. In a large mixer bowl beat egg whites, vanilla, cream of tartar, and the ¼ teaspoon salt at medium speed of electric mixer till soft peaks form. Gradually add the 1⅓ cups sugar, about a tablespoon at a time, beating at high speed about 12 minutes or till very stiff peaks form. Spread beaten egg whites in the bottom of a well-buttered 9-inch pie plate. Place in preheated oven; immediately turn heat off. Let stand in oven with *door closed* for 5 hours or overnight. *Do not open oven door.*

For lemon filling, in a small mixer bowl beat egg yolks about 5 minutes or till thick and lemon colored. Transfer to a small heavy saucepan. Stir in lemon peel, lemon juice, the ½ cup sugar, and dash salt. Cook and stir over low heat about 12 minutes or till thickened and bubbly. Remove from heat; cover. Cool without stirring.

To assemble torte, whip cream just to soft peaks. Spread a little less than half of the whipped cream in the bottom of baked torte shell. Top with cooled lemon filling, then with remaining whipped cream, spreading cream to cover entire shell. Chill 5 hours or overnight. Cut into wedges, using a wet knife. Makes 8 servings.

**Cherry Torte:** Prepare Lemon Torte as above, *except* omit lemon filling. For cherry filling, combine one 21-ounce can *cherry pie filling,* 1 tablespoon *lemon juice,* and several drops *almond extract.* Assemble torte as directed above.

## Cream Puffs

| | |
|---|---|
| ½ | **cup butter or margarine** |
| 1 | **cup water** |
| 1 | **cup all-purpose flour** |
| ¼ | **teaspoon salt** |
| 4 | **eggs** |

Oven 400°

In a medium saucepan melt butter. Add water; bring to boiling. Add flour and salt all at once; stir vigorously. Cook and stir till mixture forms a ball that doesn't separate. Remove from heat; cool slightly, about 5 minutes. Add eggs, one at a time, beating with a wooden spoon after each addition for 1 to 2 minutes or till smooth. Drop batter by heaping tablespoon 3 inches apart onto a greased baking sheet. Bake in a 400° oven about 30 minutes or till golden brown and puffy. Remove from oven; split, removing any soft dough inside. Cool on a wire rack. Fill with whipped cream, pudding, ice cream, or fruit mixture. Makes 10.

**Éclairs:** Prepare dough as for Cream Puffs. Spoon some of the dough into a pastry tube fitted with a number 10 or larger tip. Slowly pipe strips of dough through the tube onto a greased baking sheet, making each éclair about 4 inches long, ¾ inch wide, and ½ inch high. Bake in a 400° oven for 30 minutes. Split and cool as directed above. Fill with pudding or fruit filling; frost with a chocolate or vanilla icing. Makes 12 to 14 éclairs.

## Praline Cheese Cups

> 1 **4-ounce container whipped cream cheese**
> ¼ **cup dairy sour cream**
> 2 **tablespoons sugar**
> ½ **teaspoon vanilla**
> 4 **cake dessert cups**
> ¼ **cup pecan halves**
> ½ **cup caramel ice cream topping**
> 1 **tablespoon brandy**

Combine cream cheese, sour cream, sugar, and vanilla. With a fork remove a small amount of the center from each dessert cup. Fill centers of dessert cups with cream cheese mixture. Arrange pecans atop each. Chill till serving time. Just before serving, in a saucepan heat together ice cream topping and brandy till warm. Spoon atop filled dessert cups. Makes 4 servings.

## Apricot Angel Dessert

> 1 **17-ounce can unpeeled apricot halves,**
>    **drained**
> ¾ **cup sugar**
> 1 **envelope unflavored gelatin**
> 2½ **cups apricot nectar**
> 1 **teaspoon lemon juice**
> 2 **slightly beaten eggs**
> 1 **cup whipping cream**
> 9 **cups cubed angel cake**

Slice a few apricot halves; reserve for garnish. Chop remaining apricots; set aside. In a small saucepan combine sugar and gelatin; stir in nectar and lemon juice. Cook and stir till boiling. Stir about half of the hot mixture into beaten eggs; return all to remaining hot mixture. Cook and stir 1 to 2 minutes or till slightly thickened. Chill till partially set.

Whip cream to soft peaks. Fold whipped cream and chopped apricots into gelatin mixture. Fold into cake cubes. Turn mixture into a 13x9x2-inch baking dish. Cover; chill. Garnish with reserved apricot slices. Serves 12.

## Choco-Coffee-Toffee Squares

      1    **cup finely crushed chocolate wafers**
      3    **tablespoons butter, melted**
     ¾    **cup sugar**
     ½    **cup butter or margarine**
      4    **egg yolks**
      1    **square (1 ounce) unsweetened chocolate,**
             **melted and cooled**
      2    **teaspoons instant coffee crystals**
     ½    **teaspoon vanilla**
      4    **egg whites**
      2    **1¹⁄₁₆-ounce bars chocolate-coated English**
             **toffee, crushed (½ cup)**

Combine crushed wafers and melted butter; press onto bottom of an 8x8x2-inch baking dish. Cream together ½ *cup* of the sugar and ½ cup butter till fluffy. Add egg yolks, one at a time, beating well after each. Add chocolate, coffee crystals, and vanilla, beating till combined. Beat egg whites to soft peaks; gradually add remaining sugar, beating to stiff peaks. Fold egg whites into chocolate mixture; spread over crust. Sprinkle crushed toffee bars atop. Cover; freeze overnight or till firm. Let stand 5 minutes before serving. Serves 9.

# Strawberry Shortcake

|   |   |
|---|---|
| **6** | **cups fresh strawberries, sliced** |
| **¼** | **cup sugar** |
| **2** | **cups all-purpose flour** |
| **2** | **tablespoons sugar** |
| **1** | **tablespoon baking powder** |
| **½** | **teaspoon salt** |
| **½** | **cup butter *or* margarine** |
| **1** | **beaten egg** |
| **⅔** | **cup milk** |
| **3** | **tablespoons butter *or* margarine, softened (optional)** |
| **1** | **cup whipping cream** |
| **2** | **tablespoons sugar** |

Oven 450°

Stir together strawberries and ¼ cup sugar; set aside. For shortcake, thoroughly stir together flour, 2 tablespoons sugar, baking powder, and salt. Cut in the ½ cup butter or margarine till mixture resembles coarse crumbs. Combine beaten egg and milk; add all at once to dry ingredients and stir just to moisten. Spread dough in a greased 8x1½-inch round baking pan, building up edges slightly. Bake in a 450° oven for 15 to 18 minutes. Cool in pan 10 minutes. Remove from pan. Split into 2 layers; lift top off carefully. If desired, spread bottom layer with the softened butter or margarine. Whip cream with 2 tablespoons sugar just to soft peaks. Spoon berries and whipped cream between layers and over top. Serve warm. Makes 8 servings.

**Blueberry Shortcake:** Prepare Strawberry Shortcake as above, *except* omit the strawberries and ¼ cup sugar. Mash 2 cups whole *blueberries;* stir in ¼ cup *sugar.* Stir in 2 cups whole *blueberries;* set aside. Spoon berry mixture and whipped cream between layers and over top.

**Peach Shortcake:** Prepare Strawberry Shortcake as above, *except* omit the strawberries and ¼ cup sugar. Stir together 4 cups peeled sliced *peaches* and ⅓ cup *sugar;* set aside. Spoon peach mixture and whipped cream between layers and over top. (*Or,* substitute *Peach Sauce* (see recipe, page 364) for peach mixture.)

## Individual Shortcakes

> **2 cups all-purpose flour**
> **2 tablespoons sugar**
> **1 tablespoon baking powder**
> **½ teaspoon salt**
> **½ cup butter or margarine**
> **1 beaten egg**
> **½ cup milk** Oven 450°

In a large mixing bowl stir together flour, sugar, baking powder, and salt. Cut in butter or margarine till mixture resembles coarse crumbs. In a small bowl combine egg and milk; add all at once to dry ingredients and stir just to moisten. Knead gently on a lightly floured surface about 12 strokes. Pat or roll to ½-inch thickness. Cut into 9 biscuits with a floured 2½-inch biscuit cutter. Bake on an ungreased baking sheet in a 450° oven about 10 minutes or till golden. Split; butter bottom layers. Fill and top with fresh fruit and whipped cream. Serve warm. Makes 9 servings.

## Baked Apples

> **6 large baking apples**
> **¾ cup raisins or snipped pitted dates**
> **½ cup packed brown sugar**
> **½ cup water**
> **1 talespoon butter or margarine**
> **½ teaspoon ground cinnamon**
> **½ teaspoon ground nutmeg**
> **Light cream or vanilla ice cream** Oven 350°

Core apples; peel off a strip around top of each. Place apples in a 10x6x2-inch baking dish. Fill apples with raisins or dates. In a saucepan combine brown sugar, water, butter or margarine, cinnamon, and nutmeg; bring to boiling. Pour hot sugar mixture around apples. Bake, uncovered, in a 350° oven about 1 hour or till apples are tender, basting occasionally with the sugar mixture. Serve warm with light cream or ice cream. Makes 6 servings.

## Cherry Cobbler

| | |
|---|---|
| 4 | cups fresh or frozen unsweetened pitted tart red cherries |
| ¾ | cup granulated sugar |
| 1 | tablespoon quick-cooking tapioca |
| 1 | tablespoon butter or margarine |
| 1 | cup all-purpose flour |
| 2 | tablespoons granulated sugar |
| 1½ | teaspoons baking powder |
| ¼ | cup butter or margarine |
| 1 | slightly beaten egg |
| ¼ | cup milk |
| | Light cream or vanilla ice cream    Oven 400° |

For cherry filling, in a medium saucepan combine cherries, the ¾ cup granulated sugar, tapioca, and ⅓ cup *water*. Let stand 5 minutes, stirring occasionally. Cook and stir till slightly thickened and bubbly. Add the 1 tablespoon butter or margarine. Set aside; keep warm.

For biscuit topper, thoroughly stir together the 1 cup flour, 2 tablespoons granulated sugar, baking powder, and ¼ teaspoon *salt*. Cut in the ¼ cup butter or margarine till mixture resembles coarse crumbs. Combine beaten egg and milk; add all at once to dry ingredients, stirring just to moisten. Turn hot fruit filling into an 8x1½-inch round baking dish or 1½-quart casserole. Immediately spoon on biscuit topper in 8 mounds. Bake in a 400° oven about 20 minutes. Serve warm with light cream or ice cream. Makes 6 servings.

**Peach Cobbler:** Prepare Cherry Cobbler as above, *except* omit cherry filling. In a medium saucepan combine ½ cup packed *brown sugar*, 4 teaspoons *cornstarch*, and ¼ teaspoon ground *mace or nutmeg*. Add ½ cup *water*. Cook and stir till thickened and bubbly. Add 4 cups sliced fresh *peaches*, 1 tablespoon *lemon juice*, and 1 tablespoon *butter or margarine*. Heat through. Continue as directed.

**Apple Cobbler:** Prepare Cherry Cobbler as above, *except* omit cherry filling. In a large saucepan combine 1 cup granulated *sugar*, 2 tablespoons *all-purpose flour*, ½ teaspoon ground *cinnamon*, and ¼ teaspoon ground *nutmeg*. Gently stir in 6 cups sliced, peeled *apples*. Cook and stir over medium heat till boiling. Cover; cook about 5 minutes more or till apples are almost tender, stirring occasionally. Stir in 1 tablespoon *lemon juice*. Continue as directed.

## Fresh Fruit Crisp

|        |                                                         |
|--------|---------------------------------------------------------|
| ½      | **cup quick-cooking rolled oats**                       |
| ½      | **cup packed brown sugar**                              |
| ¼      | **cup all-purpose flour**                               |
| ½      | **teaspoon ground cinnamon**                            |
| ¼      | **cup butter or margarine**                             |
| 2      | **pounds apples (6 medium) or 2½ pounds peaches (10 medium)** |
| 2      | **tablespoons granulated sugar** |
|        | **Vanilla ice cream**         Oven 350° |

Combine oats, brown sugar, flour, cinnamon, and dash *salt*. Cut in butter till mixture resembles coarse crumbs; set aside. Peel, core, and slice fruit to make 5 to 6 cups. Place fruit in a 10x6x2-inch baking dish. Sprinkle with granulated sugar. Sprinkle crumb mixture over all. Bake in a 350° oven for 40 to 45 minutes. Serve with ice cream. Serves 6.

## Apple Dumplings

|        |                                    |
|--------|------------------------------------|
| 1½     | **cups sugar**                     |
| ½      | **teaspoon ground cinnamon**       |
| ½      | **teaspoon ground nutmeg**         |
| ¼      | **cup butter or margarine**        |
| 2¼     | **cups all-purpose flour**         |
| 2      | **teaspoons baking powder**        |
| ⅔      | **cup shortening**                 |
| ½      | **cup milk**                       |
| 6      | **small apples, peeled and cored** |
| ⅓      | **cup sugar**          Oven 375°   |

For syrup, in a saucepan combine 1½ cups sugar, ¼ *teaspoon* of the cinnamon, ¼ *teaspoon* of the nutmeg, and 2 cups *water*. Bring to boiling; reduce heat. Cook 5 minutes. Remove from heat; stir in butter. Set aside.

Combine flour, baking powder, and ½ teaspoon *salt*. Cut in shortening till mixture resembles coarse crumbs. Add milk all at once; stir just till all is moistened. Form into a ball. On a floured surface roll out into an 18x12-inch rectangle; cut into six 6-inch squares. Place an apple in center of each square. Sprinkle apple generously with a mixture of ⅓ cup sugar and remaining ¼ teaspoon *each* cinnamon and nutmeg; dot with additional butter. Moisten edges of dough; fold corners to center atop apple. Pinch the edges together. Place in a 13x9x2-inch baking dish. Pour syrup over dumplings. Bake in a 375° oven for 45 minutes or till apples are tender. Serves 6.

## Summer Fruit Compote

  ¼  **cup honey**
  1  **tablespoon lemon juice**
  ½  **teaspoon finely shredded orange peel**
  ¼  **teaspoon ground cinnamon**
  2  **oranges, peeled and sectioned**
1½  **cups cubed honeydew melon *or* cantaloupe**
  1  **cup fresh blueberries**
  1  **cup halved strawberries**
    **Toasted coconut**

Combine honey, lemon juice, orange peel, and cinnamon. Drizzle over orange sections in a bowl. Cover and chill several hours or overnight. Chill the remaining fruits.

To serve, drain orange sections, reserving the liquid. Arrange orange sections, melon, blueberries, and strawberries in 4 individual dessert dishes. Drizzle the reserved liquid over fruit mixture. Sprinkle with toasted coconut. Makes 4 servings.

## Sherried Fruit Compote

|       |                                            |
|-------|--------------------------------------------|
| 1     | 8¼-ounce can pineapple chunks             |
| 1     | cup dried apples                           |
| 1     | cup dried apricots                         |
| ¾     | cup packed brown sugar                     |
| ¾     | cup soft bread crumbs (1 slice)            |
| ½     | cup raisins                                |
| 2½    | cups water                                 |
| ½     | cup cream sherry *or* port                 |
| 1     | tablespoon lemon juice                     |
| 1½    | teaspoons ground cinnamon                  |
| 1     | teaspoon salt                              |
|       | Toasted coconut                            |

Oven 350°

In a 2-quart casserole combine *undrained* pineapple, apples, apricots, brown sugar, bread crumbs, and raisins. Stir together water, sherry, lemon juice, cinnamon, and salt. Pour over fruit mixture. Cover and bake in a 350° oven for 1½ hours, stirring several times. Serve warm in individual dessert dishes. Sprinkle toasted coconut atop. Makes 6 to 8 servings.

## Blueberry Melba Parfaits

|       |                                                                    |
|-------|--------------------------------------------------------------------|
| 1     | 10-ounce package frozen red raspberries, thawed                    |
| ¼     | cup sugar                                                          |
| 1     | tablespoon cornstarch                                             |
| 2     | cups fresh blueberries *or* one 16-ounce package frozen blueberries, thawed and drained |
| 2     | teaspoons lemon juice                                             |
| 1     | quart vanilla ice cream                                          |
| 2     | tablespoons frozen orange juice concentrate, thawed              |
| 1     | teaspoon ground cinnamon                                         |

Sieve raspberries with syrup; add enough water to make 1 cup. In a saucepan combine sugar and cornstarch; add raspberry puree. Cook and stir till thickened and bubbly. Remove from heat. Stir in blueberries and lemon juice; cover and chill. In a chilled bowl stir ice cream to soften. Combine ice cream, orange juice concentrate, and cinnamon; freeze 2 to 3 hours or till firm. To serve, alternately layer ice cream and fruit mixture in 6 parfait glasses, ending with ice cream mixture. Serve immediately. Makes 6 servings.

## Chocolate Fondue

> **8   squares (8 ounces) semisweet chocolate**
> **1   14-ounce can *sweetened condensed* milk**
> **⅓  cup milk**
> **Assorted fondue dippers (angel cake or pound cake squares, or banana or pineapple chunks, strawberries, or marshmallows)**

In a heavy saucepan melt chocolate over low heat. Stir in sweetened condensed milk and regular milk till well combined. Heat through. Transfer to a fondue pot; place over fondue burner. (If mixture becomes too thick, stir in a little more milk.) Spear desired fondue dipper with a fondue fork; dip into fondue. Makes 8 servings.

*Coffee Fondue:* Prepare Chocolate Fondue as above, *except* dissolve 2 tablespoons *instant coffee crystals* in the ⅓ cup milk; stir into chocolate mixture. Continue as directed.

## Crêpes Suzette

> **½  cup butter or margarine**
> **½  cup orange liqueur**
> **½  cup orange juice**
> **6  tablespoons sugar**
> **Basic Dessert Crêpes**
> **¼  cup brandy**

For sauce, in a skillet or chafing dish combine butter, liqueur, orange juice, and sugar; cook and stir till bubbly.

To assemble, fold a Basic Dessert Crêpe in half, browned side out; fold in half again, forming a triangle. Repeat with remaining crêpes. Arrange crêpes in sauce. Simmer till sauce thickens slightly, spooning sauce over crêpes as they heat. In a small saucepan heat the brandy over low heat till hot. Ignite and pour flaming brandy over crêpes. Serves 8.

**Basic Dessert Crêpes:** Combine 1½ cups *milk*, 1 cup *all-purpose flour*, *2 eggs*, 2 tablespoons *sugar*, 1 tablespoon *cooking oil*, and ⅛ teaspoon *salt*. Beat with a rotary beater till combined. Heat a lightly greased 6-inch skillet. Remove from heat. Spoon in 2 tablespoons batter; lift and tilt skillet to spread batter. Return to heat; brown on one side. (*Or*, cook on an inverted crêpe pan.) Invert pan over paper toweling; remove crêpe. Repeat to make 16 to 18 crêpes, greasing skillet occasionally.

# Lemon-Filled Crêpes

- **¾  cup sugar**
- **2  tablespoons cornstarch**
- **2  beaten egg yolks**
- **1  teaspoon grated lemon peel**
- **3  tablespoons lemon juice**
- **1  tablespoon butter *or* margarine**
- **9  Basic Dessert Crêpes (see recipe above)**

In a heavy saucepan combine sugar, cornstarch, and dash *salt;* stir in ¾ cup cold *water*. Stir in egg yolks, lemon peel, and juice. Cook and stir till thickened. Cook 1 minute more; remove from heat. Stir in butter. Cover; cool. To assemble, spread about *2 tablespoons* of the lemon filling over *unbrowned* side of a Basic Dessert Crêpe, leaving a ¼-inch rim around edge. Roll up jelly roll style. Repeat with remaining filling and crêpes. Cover and chill or serve immediately. Makes 9.

# Vanilla Ice Cream

1½ **cups sugar**
2 **envelopes unflavored gelatin**
8 **cups light cream**
2 **beaten eggs**
4 **teaspoons vanilla**

In a large saucepan combine sugar, gelatin, and ⅛ teaspoon *salt*. Stir in *half* of the light cream. Cook and stir over medium heat till mixture almost boils and sugar dissolves. Stir about *1 cup* of the hot mixture into beaten eggs; return all to saucepan. Cook and stir 2 minutes more. Cool. Add remaining cream and the vanilla. Freeze in a 4- or 5-quart ice cream freezer according to manufacturer's directions. Makes about 3 quarts ice cream (24 servings).

**Cherry-Nut Ice Cream:** Prepare Vanilla Ice Cream as above, *except* add 1 cup chopped *maraschino cherries*, 3 tablespoons *maraschino cherry juice*, and 1 cup chopped *walnuts* to cooled egg mixture. Continue as directed.

**Chocolate-Almond Ice Cream:** Prepare Vanilla Ice Cream as above, *except* increase sugar to *2 cups*. Add 6 squares (6 ounces) *unsweetened chocolate*, melted and cooled, to gelatin mixture after heating. Beat with rotary beater. Stir 1 cup chopped *toasted almonds* into cooled mixture. Continue as directed.

**Peach-Cherry Ice Cream:** Prepare a *half recipe* of Vanilla Ice Cream as above, *except* combine 2 pounds fully ripe peaches, peeled and mashed (3 cups), with ½ cup *sugar*. Add to cooled mixture along with 2 cups fresh *dark sweet cherries*, pitted and chopped, and ¼ teaspoon ground *mace* or ¼ teaspoon *almond extract*. Continue as directed.

**Coffee Ice Cream:** Prepare Vanilla Ice Cream as above, *except* stir 2 tablespoons *instant coffee crystals* into mixture just before cooling. Continue as directed.

**Chocolate Chip Ice Cream:** Prepare Vanilla Ice Cream as above, *except* stir one 6-ounce package *semisweet chocolate pieces*, chopped, into cooled mixture. Continue as directed.

# Fresh Strawberry Ice Cream

 2 cups fresh strawberries or 2 cups frozen
   unsweetened strawberries
 1 envelope unflavored gelatin
 ¼ cup cold water
 2 egg yolks
 2 cups whipping cream
 ¾ cup sugar
 1½ teaspoons vanilla
 ¼ teaspoon salt
 2 egg whites
 ¼ cup sugar

Thaw strawberries, if frozen. Crush strawberries; set aside. In a small bowl soften gelatin in cold water; place over hot water and stir to dissolve. In a small mixer bowl beat egg yolks till thick and lemon colored, about 4 minutes. In a large mixing bowl combine egg yolks, whipping cream, the ¾ cup sugar, the vanilla, salt, and crushed strawberries. Add gelatin; stir to mix well. Turn into a 13x9x2-inch pan. Cover and freeze till partially frozen. Beat egg whites to soft peaks; gradually add the ¼ cup sugar, beating to stiff peaks. Break frozen mixture into chunks. Turn into a chilled large mixer bowl. Beat with electric mixer till fluffy. Fold in beaten egg whites. Return to cold pan; cover and freeze till firm. Makes about 1½ quarts (12 servings).

# Choco-Velvet Ice Cream

 2 cups whipping cream
 ⅔ cup *sweetened condensed* milk (½ of a
   14-ounce can)
 ⅔ cup chocolate-flavored syrup
 ½ teaspoon vanilla
 ⅓ cup coarsely chopped walnuts

In a large mixer bowl combine whipping cream, sweetened condensed milk, chocolate syrup, and vanilla. Chill. Beat on high speed of electric mixer till soft peaks form. Fold in walnuts. Turn mixture into an 8x8x2-inch pan; freeze till firm. Makes 1 quart (8 servings).

**Choco-Mint Velvet:** Prepare Choco-Velvet Ice Cream as above, *except* substitute ⅓ cup crushed *buttermints* for the walnuts. Continue as directed.

---

## Easy Vanilla Ice Cream

- **2 cups light cream**
- **1 cup sugar**
- **4 teaspoons vanilla**
- **2 cups whipping cream**

In a large mixing bowl stir together light cream, sugar, vanilla, and ⅛ teaspoon *salt* till sugar dissolves. Stir in whipping cream. Turn into an 8x8x2-inch pan. Cover; freeze till partially frozen. Break mixture into chunks. Place in a chilled large mixer bowl. Beat with electric mixer 1 to 2 minutes or till smooth. Return the mixture to cold pan. Freeze till firm. Makes 1½ quarts (12 servings).

---

## Baked Alaska

*Use different flavors of ice cream and cake—*
- **2 pints *or* 1 quart brick-style ice cream***
- **1 1-inch-thick piece sponge cake *or* layer cake**
- **5 egg whites**
- **1 teaspoon vanilla**
- **½ teaspoon cream of tartar**
- **⅔ cup sugar**                    Oven 500°

Lay ice cream bricks side by side; measure length and width. Trim cake 1 inch larger on all sides than ice cream measurements. Place cake on a piece of foil. Center ice cream on cake. Cover; freeze till firm. At serving time, beat together egg whites, vanilla, and cream of tartar to soft peaks. Gradually add sugar, beating to stiff peaks. Transfer cake with ice cream to a baking sheet. Spread with egg white mixture, sealing to edges of cake and baking sheet all around. Swirl to make peaks. Place oven rack in lowest position. Bake in a 500° oven about 3 minutes or till golden. Slice; serve immediately. Serves 8.

**\*Note:** If you can't locate brick-style ice cream, reshape the ice cream you have to fit atop a round cake base. Select a mixing bowl with a diameter 2 inches smaller than the diameter of a 1-inch-thick round layer cake. Stir ice cream in mixing bowl just enough to soften. Cover; freeze till firm. Center ice cream on cake; continue as directed.

## Frozen Yogurt Melba Bombe

      **2    cups granola, crushed**
      **2    tablespoons butter, melted**
      **1    quart frozen lemon yogurt *or* lemon
             sherbet**
     **½    cup seedless red raspberry preserves**
      **1    pint frozen raspberry yogurt *or* raspberry
             sherbet**

Combine granola and melted butter. Pat about ¼ of the crumbs in bottom of a 6-cup bombe mold (or mixing bowl) lined with clear plastic wrap. Place in freezer for 10 minutes. Spoon *half* the frozen lemon yogurt evenly atop crumbs in mold. Spoon *half* the raspberry preserves atop, spreading to within ½ inch of edge. Sprinkle with another ¼ of crumb mixture. Return to freezer for 20 minutes or till firm. Spoon frozen raspberry yogurt evenly into mold. Spoon remaining preserves atop to within ½ inch of edge. Sprinkle with another ¼ of the crumbs. Return to freezer about 20 minutes. Top with remaining frozen lemon yogurt and crumbs. Freeze several hours or till firm. Remove from freezer 10 minutes before serving. To unmold, invert onto a serving plate; remove plastic wrap. Cut into wedges. Makes 8 servings.

## Pineapple Sherbet

1    **envelope unflavored gelatin**
2    **cups buttermilk**
¾   **cup sugar**
1    **8-ounce can crushed pineapple (juice pack)**
1    **teaspoon vanilla**
1    **egg white**
2    **tablespoons sugar**

Soften gelatin in ¼ cup *cold water;* dissolve over hot water. In a large mixing bowl combine buttermilk, the ¾ cup sugar, the *undrained* crushed pineapple, vanilla, and gelatin mixture. Turn into an 8x8x2-inch pan. Cover and freeze till firm. Beat egg white to soft peaks; gradually add 2 tablespoons sugar, beating to stiff peaks. Break frozen mixture into chunks with a wooden spoon; turn into a chilled mixer bowl. Beat with electric mixer till fluffy. Fold in egg white. Return mixture to cold pan. Cover; freeze till firm. Makes 1½ quarts (12 servings).

## Cherries Jubilee

1    **16-ounce can pitted dark sweet cherries**
¼   **cup sugar**
2    **tablespoons cornstarch**
¼   **cup brandy, cherry brandy,** *or* **Kirsch**
     **Vanilla ice cream**

Drain cherries, reserving syrup. Add cold water to syrup, if necessary, to make 1 cup. In a medium saucepan combine sugar and cornstarch; stir in syrup. Cook and stir till bubbly. Remove from heat; stir in cherries. Turn mixture into a heat-proof bowl or into the blazer pan of a chafing dish placed over hot water. Heat brandy in a small saucepan. (If desired, pour heated brandy into a large ladle.) Ignite and pour over cherry mixture. When flames die, stir to blend brandy into sauce. Serve at once over ice cream. Serves 6 to 8.

## Hot Fudge Sundaes

>     2    **squares (2 ounces) unsweetened chocolate**
>    ½    **cup sugar**
>     3    **tablespoons butter *or* margarine**
>    ¼    **teaspoon vanilla**
>         **Vanilla ice cream**

For sauce, in a heavy small saucepan combine chocolate and ⅓ cup *water*. Cook over low heat, stirring constantly, till chocolate is melted. Stir in sugar and dash *salt*. Cook over medium heat, stirring constantly, 8 minutes or till sugar is dissolved and mixture is slightly thickened. Remove from heat. Add butter or margarine and vanilla, stirring till smooth. Serve warm over ice cream. Makes about 1 cup sauce.

## Rhubarb Sauce

>    ½    **to ⅔ cup sugar**
>         **Orange peel strip (optional)**
>     3    **cups rhubarb cut into ½-inch pieces**

In a medium saucepan combine sugar, peel, and ¼ cup *water*. Bring to boiling; add rhubarb. Reduce heat. Cover; simmer 5 minutes or till tender. Remove peel. Makes 2 cups.

## Applesauce

>     4    **pounds cooking apples**
>     1    **to 1½ cups water**
>     6    **inches stick cinnamon (optional)**
>    ½    **to 1 cup sugar**

Cut apples into quarters. Core *each* of the quarters; peel. Place apples in a 4-quart Dutch oven; pour water over. Add stick cinnamon; bring to boiling. Reduce heat; cover and simmer 8 to 10 minutes or till tender. Uncover; remove cinnamon. Remove from heat; mash apples with a potato masher till smooth. Stir in sugar. Spoon applesauce into serving dishes, or cover and refrigerate. Makes about 5 cups (10 servings).

**Chunky Applesauce:** Prepare Applesauce as above, *except* add the sugar before cooking. Slightly mash cooked apple mixture. Continue as directed.

---

## Basic Hard Sauce

---

   ½  **cup butter or margarine, softened**
   2  **cups sifted powdered sugar**
   1  **teaspoon vanilla**

In a small mixer bowl cream together softened butter or margarine and powdered sugar with electric mixer. Beat in vanilla. Spread in a 7½x3½x2-inch loaf pan. Chill to harden. Cut into squares to serve. Serve with plum pudding or warm gingerbread. Makes 1⅓ cups (21 servings).

**Fluffy Hard Sauce:** Prepare Basic Hard Sauce as above, *except* beat 1 *egg yolk* into creamed mixture. Fold in 1 stiff-beaten *egg white* by hand. Turn into a serving bowl. Serve without chilling. Makes 1⅓ cups (21 servings).

**Brandy Hard Sauce:** Prepare Basic Hard Sauce as above, *except* decrease powdered sugar to 1 cup. Beat 1 to 2 tablespoons *brandy or rum* into creamed mixture with electric mixer. Spoon into a serving bowl; chill. To serve, sprinkle lightly with ground *nutmeg*. Makes ⅔ cup (11 servings).

**Orange Hard Sauce:** Prepare Basic Hard Sauce as above, *except* decrease butter to ¼ *cup* and decrease powdered sugar to *1 cup*. Beat ¼ teaspoon finely shredded *orange peel* and 1 tablespoon *orange juice* into creamed mixture. Spoon the mixture into a small serving bowl; chill. Makes ½ cup (8 servings).

## Orange Sauce

    ½   cup sugar
    2   tablespoons cornstarch
        Dash salt
  1½    cups orange juice
    1   tablespoon butter or margarine

In a medium saucepan combine sugar, cornstarch, and salt. Stir in orange juice. Cook and stir till thickened and bubbly. Cook 2 minutes more. Remove from heat; stir in butter or margarine. Serve warm. Makes 1¾ cups (9 servings).

## Peach Sauce

    1   29-ounce can peach slices
    ¼   cup sugar
    2   tablespoons cornstarch
    ½   teaspoon finely shredded orange peel
    ⅓   cup orange juice
    1   tablespoon butter or margarine

Drain peaches, reserving 1¼ cups syrup. Coarsely chop peaches. In a saucepan combine sugar and cornstarch; add reserved syrup. Cook and stir till thickened and bubbly; remove from heat. Stir in orange peel, orange juice, butter or margarine, and chopped peaches. Cover and chill without stirring. Serve over ice cream, pound cake, waffles, or filled crepes. Makes 3 cups sauce (16 servings).

## Fluffy Vanilla Sauce

    3   beaten egg yolks
    ¾   cup sifted powdered sugar
    ½   teaspoon vanilla
    ¼   teaspoon rum flavoring (optional)
        Dash salt
    1   cup whipping cream

In a mixing bowl combine egg yolks, powdered sugar, vanilla, rum flavoring, and salt. Whip cream to soft peaks; fold into egg yolk mixture. Cover; chill. Stir before serving. Serve over fresh fruit, chocolate cake, gingerbread, or plum pudding. Makes about 2½ cups (13 servings).

**Note:** Don't store this sauce for more than a few days because of the uncooked eggs.

# Eggs & Cheese

# Eggs & Cheese

# Eggs & Cheese

# Eggs & Cheese

# Eggs & Cheese

# Eggs & Cheese

# Eggs & Cheese

# Eggs & Cheese

# Eggs & Cheese

| Recipes | Servings (fraction of recipe) | Calories | Protein (grams) | Carbohydrate (grams) | Fat (grams) | Sodium (milligrams) | Potassium (milligrams) | Protein | Vitamin A | Vitamin C | Thiamine | Riboflavin | Niacin | Calcium | Iron |
|---|---|---|---|---|---|---|---|---|---|---|---|---|---|---|---|
| | | | | | | | | Percent of U.S. RDA Per Serving | | | | | | | |
| Bacon-Asparagus Omelet | 1/2 | 297 | 19 | 10 | 20 | 1191 | 482 | 30 | 47 | | 51 | 21 | 32 | 10 | 23 |
| Baked Eggs | 1/3 | 263 | 17 | 2 | 17 | 332 | 155 | 26 | 31 | 0 | 0 | 7 | 22 | 0 | 14 |
| Baked Omelet w/ Chicken Sauce | 1/6 | 307 | 24 | 9 | 18 | 659 | 393 | 37 | 19 | 4 | 7 | 7 | 25 | 25 | 9 |
| Beer Rabbit | 1/4 | 373 | 19 | 18 | 24 | 626 | 127 | 29 | 14 | 0 | 13 | 13 | 21 | 10 | 11 |
| Cheese and Herb Omelet | 1/2 | 474 | 22 | 8 | 37 | 709 | 269 | 34 | 44 | 2 | 2 | 8 | 33 | 1 | 12 |
| Cheese-Onion Scrambled Eggs | 1/3 | 320 | 18 | 3 | 23 | 621 | 190 | 28 | 37 | 2 | 2 | 8 | 25 | 22 | 14 |
| Cheese French Omelet | 1/1 | 379 | 20 | 2 | 20 | 737 | 156 | 31 | 40 | 0 | 0 | 8 | 25 | 0 | 15 |
| Cheese Soufflé | 1/6 | 468 | 23 | 10 | 23 | 801 | 207 | 36 | 38 | 1 | 1 | 8 | 33 | 3 | 9 |
| Classic Cheese Fondue | 1/10 | 449 | 23 | 31 | 23 | 749 | 172 | 36 | 16 | 0 | 3 | 14 | 24 | 9 | 11 |
| Classic Cheese Strata | 1/6 | 367 | 20 | 26 | 20 | 1252 | 271 | 31 | 20 | 3 | 3 | 15 | 31 | 7 | 12 |
| Classic Quiche Lorraine | 1/6 | 543 | 21 | 27 | 21 | 741 | 262 | 32 | 32 | 4 | 4 | 20 | 29 | 11 | 13 |
| Crab Mornay | 1/4 | 332 | 19 | 23 | 23 | 723 | 294 | 29 | 27 | 4 | 4 | 13 | 23 | 13 | 8 |
| Creamed Eggs | 1/4 | 367 | 17 | 25 | 17 | 527 | 268 | 26 | 28 | 2 | 2 | 17 | 29 | 7 | 15 |
| Creamy Cheese Fondue | 1/6 | 609 | 25 | 37 | 25 | 1255 | 174 | 38 | 29 | 7 | 7 | 4 | 24 | 3 | 8 |
| Creamy Cheese Scrambled Eggs | 1/3 | 355 | 16 | 3 | 16 | 478 | 191 | 25 | 39 | 0 | 0 | 8 | 24 | 1 | 14 |
| Creamy Poached Eggs | 1/4 | 413 | 18 | 26 | 18 | 929 | 256 | 28 | 27 | 2 | 2 | 18 | 28 | 7 | 14 |
| Curried Eggs | 1/4 | 534 | 22 | 22 | 39 | 1111 | 337 | 34 | 42 | 9 | 9 | 18 | 34 | 10 | 19 |
| Denver Scramble | 1/4 | 337 | 21 | 3 | 22 | 599 | 269 | 33 | 29 | 13 | 13 | 19 | 25 | 8 | 19 |
| Deviled Eggs | 1/12 | 74 | 3 | 0 | 3 | 86 | 35 | 5 | 6 | 0 | 0 | 2 | 4 | 0 | 4 |
| Easy Baked Cheese Omelet | 1/2 | 466 | 21 | 16 | 21 | 1203 | 231 | 32 | 48 | 1 | 1 | 7 | 32 | 1 | 10 |

# Nutrition Analysis Chart

| | Serving | Calories | Protein | Fat | Carbo | Sodium | | | | | | | | |
|---|---|---|---|---|---|---|---|---|---|---|---|---|---|---|
| Easy Cheese Eggs a la King | 1/4 | 397 | 18 | 24 | 25 | 308 | 28 | 31 | 36 | 14 | 26 | 7 | 32 | 15 |
| Egg and Whole Wheat Foldovers | 1/3 | 1020 | 23 | 42 | 86 | 2108 | 36 | 60 | 12 | 25 | 33 | 12 | 20 | 25 |
| Egg Foo Yong | 1/2 | 265 | 13 | 14 | 18 | 1536 | 20 | 20 | 68 | 12 | 20 | 4 | 8 | 18 |
| Egg-Rice Bake | 1/4 | 466 | 21 | 28 | 30 | 1364 | 32 | 32 | 22 | 13 | 29 | 7 | 31 | 17 |
| Eggs a la King | 1/4 | 396 | 19 | 29 | 29 | 353 | 29 | 34 | 18 | 22 | 35 | 11 | 22 | 18 |
| Egg-Sausage Casserole | 1/6 | 663 | 17 | 25 | 55 | 1135 | 27 | 32 | 6 | 31 | 26 | 15 | 13 | 14 |
| Eggs Benedict | 1/6 | 465 | 25 | 10 | 36 | 1770 | 38 | 32 | 4 | 51 | 24 | 20 | 6 | 24 |
| Eggs Florentine | 1/2 | 407 | 24 | 23 | 25 | 1308 | 37 | 213 | 37 | 15 | 36 | 4 | 36 | 28 |
| Eggs Goldenrod | 1/4 | 367 | 17 | 25 | 22 | 527 | 26 | 28 | 2 | 17 | 29 | 4 | 19 | 15 |
| Eggs in Spanish Sauce | 1/4 | 398 | 17 | 22 | 29 | 938 | 21 | 62 | 80 | 16 | 20 | 10 | 8 | 19 |
| Farmer's Breakfast | 1/4 | 387 | 19 | 14 | 28 | 767 | 29 | 27 | 24 | 21 | 19 | 12 | 7 | 18 |
| French Omelet | 1/1 | 266 | 13 | 1 | 23 | 540 | 20 | 33 | 0 | 7 | 18 | 0 | 6 | 13 |
| Fried Eggs | 1/2 | 215 | 13 | 1 | 17 | 192 | 20 | 28 | 0 | 7 | 18 | 0 | 6 | 13 |
| Fruited French Omelet | 1/1 | 395 | 14 | 21 | 28 | 556 | 22 | 38 | 74 | 9 | 23 | 3 | 11 | 20 |
| Gold Rush Brunch | 1/8 | 371 | 22 | 11 | 26 | 1367 | 33 | 23 | 7 | 39 | 26 | 15 | 15 | 18 |
| Ham and Cheese Omelet | 1/2 | 581 | 27 | 5 | 50 | 945 | 41 | 53 | 4 | 20 | 42 | 12 | 15 | 20 |
| Ham Egg Foo Yong | 1/7 | 105 | 6 | 4 | 7 | 514 | 9 | 9 | 19 | 7 | 7 | 3 | 5 | 7 |
| Hashed Brown Omelet | 1/4 | 385 | 19 | 21 | 25 | 752 | 29 | 20 | 56 | 14 | 22 | 10 | 32 | 14 |
| Herbed Scrambled Eggs | 1/3 | 250 | 14 | 2 | 20 | 407 | 22 | 33 | 4 | 8 | 20 | 1 | 9 | 14 |
| Huevos Rancheros | 1/3 | 466 | 26 | 35 | 25 | 892 | 40 | 63 | 71 | 23 | 35 | 14 | 33 | 27 |
| Individual Quiche Casseroles | 1/4 | 375 | 20 | 11 | 31 | 475 | 31 | 22 | 6 | 11 | 30 | 6 | 41 | 11 |
| Italian-Style Deviled Eggs | 1/12 | 62 | 3 | 1 | 5 | 109 | 5 | 5 | 0 | 2 | 4 | 0 | 1 | 3 |
| Macaroni and Cheese | 1/6 | 426 | 19 | 36 | 23 | 992 | 29 | 42 | 40 | 25 | 29 | 15 | 44 | 12 |
| Mushroom French Omelet | 1/1 | 375 | 14 | 2 | 35 | 683 | 21 | 42 | 1 | 9 | 24 | 5 | 6 | 14 |
| Mushroom-Sauced Eggs | 1/2 | 469 | 22 | 33 | 28 | 839 | 34 | 36 | 5 | 25 | 53 | 24 | 19 | 22 |
| Mushroom Scrambled Eggs | 1/3 | 257 | 14 | 4 | 20 | 413 | 22 | 33 | 4 | 4 | 25 | 4 | 9 | 15 |
| Old-Fashioned Cheese Bake | 1/4 | 313 | 17 | 22 | 17 | 714 | 27 | 19 | 2 | 13 | 28 | 6 | 36 | 10 |
| Omelet Sandwich Puff | 1/2 | 437 | 22 | 16 | 31 | 868 | 35 | 29 | 0 | 16 | 28 | 9 | 26 | 16 |
| Poached Eggs | 1/2 | 164 | 13 | 1 | 12 | 122 | 20 | 24 | 0 | 7 | 18 | 0 | 5 | 13 |

# Nutrition Analysis Chart

| Recipes | Servings (fraction of recipe) | Calories | Protein (grams) | Carbohydrate (grams) | Fat (grams) | Sodium (milligrams) | Potassium (milligrams) | Protein | Vitamin A | Vitamin C | Thiamine | Riboflavin | Niacin | Calcium | Iron |
|---|---|---|---|---|---|---|---|---|---|---|---|---|---|---|---|
| | | | | | | | | Percent of U.S. RDA Per Serving | | | | | | | |
| Puffy Omelet | 1/2 | 203 | 13 | 1 | 16 | 451 | 127 | 19 | 28 | 0 | 0 | 5 | 19 | 6 | 10 |
| Rosy Pickled Eggs | 1/12 | 98 | 7 | 5 | 5 | 151 | 6 | 11 | 10 | 0 | 2 | 4 | 9 | 3 | 8 |
| Scalloped Eggs and Bacon | 1/6 | 432 | 18 | 18 | 18 | 556 | 454 | 28 | 21 | 8 | 13 | 13 | 24 | 26 | 13 |
| Scrambled Eggs | 1/3 | 249 | 14 | 2 | 20 | 407 | 170 | 22 | 31 | 0 | 0 | 8 | 20 | 9 | 13 |
| Seafood Quiche | 1/6 | 496 | 22 | 27 | 33 | 965 | 258 | 34 | 26 | 11 | 3 | 17 | 27 | 38 | 12 |
| Shrimp-Egg Bake | 1/4 | 570 | 25 | 17 | 45 | 1233 | 295 | 39 | 32 | 8 | 1 | 11 | 29 | 28 | 20 |
| Shrimp Egg Foo Yong | 1/7 | 97 | 8 | 4 | 4 | 464 | 128 | 20 | 13 | 3 | 19 | 4 | 6 | 4 | 13 |
| Soft-Cooked or Hard-Cooked Eggs | 1/3 | 164 | 13 | 1 | 12 | 122 | 129 | 20 | 20 | 0 | 5 | 15 | 18 | 5 | 15 |
| Swiss Onion Bake | 1/6 | 389 | 20 | 28 | 22 | 1067 | 288 | 31 | 26 | 8 | 4 | 8 | 25 | 35 | 15 |
| Tuna Soufflé | 1/4 | 335 | 19 | 9 | 24 | 814 | 291 | 29 | 20 | 26 | 18 | 8 | 18 | 10 | 8 |
| Vegetable French Omelet | 1/1 | 332 | 15 | 4 | 28 | 624 | 217 | 24 | 50 | 18 | 1 | 8 | 21 | 13 | 15 |
| Welsh Rabbit | 1/4 | 295 | 16 | 18 | 18 | 493 | 146 | 25 | 15 | 5 | 1 | 9 | 22 | 40 | 8 |

# Eggs

Here's how to beat egg whites and identify the three phases. Place the egg whites in a deep, straight-sided bowl. Use a wire whisk, rotary beater, or electric mixer for beating air into the whites.

*Foamy-stage egg whites:* Slight whipping forms large air bubbles in the egg whites, making the mixture fluid and transparent.

*Soft-peak-stage egg whites:* With a bit more beating, the bubbles become smaller and the foam becomes less transparent. The foam turns white and becomes stiffer, so that soft peaks will form when the beaters are lifted out of the bowl. The tips of the peaks will bend over in soft curls.

*Stiff-peak-stage egg whites:* Use caution; this stage is reached quickly. With continued beating, the foam becomes whiter still and forms stiff peaks that stand straight when beaters are removed. The whites now contain all of the air they are capable of holding.

*Overbeaten egg whites:* More beating will give the egg whites a dull, dry look and cause small curd-like flakes to appear. That means the whites are too rigid for folding and you'll have to start over. Store the overbeaten whites in the refrigerator and add them to scrambled eggs.

# Cheese

Cheeses are available in natural and process forms. Here are the characteristics of the two types.

*Natural cheese:* Cheese made directly from the curd of milk and not reprocessed or blended is known as natural cheese. Although the storage quality of natural cheese varies greatly, in general, the lower the moisture content, the longer the cheese may be stored. As a result, firm or very hard ripened cheeses are less perishable than soft ripened varieties. Avoid too-high temperatures and prolonged cooking, which cause natural cheeses to become leathery and stringy.

*Pasteurized process cheese:* Made from natural cheeses, this type includes process cheese food, process cheese spread, cold-pack cheese, and cold-pack cheese food. Like natural cheese, process cheese should be stored in the refrigerator. It has a high moisture content and must be wrapped tightly in moisture-vaporproof wrap to prevent drying. Process cheese is very popular for use in cooking because it isn't likely to string, become rubbery, or to develop a grainy texture when heated.

## Fried Eggs

**Butter or margarine**
**4  eggs**

In a 10-inch skillet over medium heat melt a small amount of butter. (Or, use a 6- or 8-inch skillet for 1 or 2 eggs.) Add eggs; sprinkle with salt and pepper. When whites are set and edges cooked, add ½ *teaspoon water per egg.* Cover skillet; cook eggs to desired doneness (2 minutes for soft or 4 minutes for firm). For "over-easy" eggs, carefully lift eggs with a spatula and flip; cook briefly to set yolks. Serves 2.

## Soft-Cooked or Hard-Cooked Eggs

Place 6 *eggs* in shells in a large saucepan; add enough *water* to cover eggs. Bring to a rapid boil over high heat. Reduce heat so water is just below simmering; cover. For soft-cooked eggs, cook 4 to 6 minutes. For hard-cooked eggs, cook 15 to 20 minutes. Pour off water. Serves 3.

*For soft-cooked eggs,* add cold water just till eggs are cool enough to handle. Cut off tops and serve in egg cups. (*Or,* remove egg from shell by cutting egg in half and scooping out the egg into a dish.)

*For hard-cooked eggs,* fill a saucepan with cold water and let stand at least 2 minutes. To quickly cool, add a few *ice cubes.*

*To remove shells of hard-cooked eggs,* gently tap warm egg on a counter top; roll egg between palms. Peel off the eggshell, starting at large end.

## Egg-cooking tip

A greenish ring around the yolk of a hard-cooked egg is a common, harmless occurrence caused by the formation of iron sulfide. To lessen the possibility of such rings forming, carefully watch the cooking time and immediately cool eggs.

## Baked Eggs

*Baked eggs are also called shirred eggs. If desired, they may be baked in ramekins, which are individual baking dishes—*

**Butter or margarine**
6 **eggs**
2 **tablespoons light cream *or* milk**
6 **tablespoons shredded American cheese (optional)**

Oven 325°

Butter a custard cup for *each* egg. Carefully break eggs into the prepared custard cups; sprinkle with salt and pepper. Add *1 teaspoon* of the light cream or milk to *each* egg-filled cup. Set cups in a baking pan; place on oven rack. Pour hot water around cups in pan to a depth of 1 inch. Bake in a 325° oven about 20 minutes or till eggs are firm.

If desired, after 15 minutes of baking, top *each* egg with *1 tablespoon* of the shredded American cheese. Continue baking for 5 to 10 minutes more or till eggs are cooked and cheese is melted. Makes 3 servings.

## Poached Eggs

**Cooking oil or shortening**
**Eggs (2 eggs per serving)**

Lightly grease a 10-inch skillet to poach 2 to 4 eggs. (*Or*, use a small saucepan to poach 1 egg.) Add enough water to half-fill pan or skillet; bring to boiling. Reduce heat to simmer. Break 1 egg into a small dish. Carefully slide egg into water, holding lip of dish as close to water as possible. Repeat with remaining eggs so that each has an equal amount of space.

Simmer, uncovered, 3 to 5 minutes or to desired doneness. Remove with a slotted spoon. Season to taste with salt and pepper. Serve on buttered toast or English muffin, split and toasted, if desired.

*To cook eggs in poacher cups,* first grease each cup well. Place poacher in a pan of boiling water so that water is below bottom of poacher. Reduce heat to maintain water at a simmer. Break eggs into cups; insert cups into poacher. Cover and cook 3 to 5 minutes or to desired doneness (allow 4 minutes for soft eggs).

## Scrambled Eggs

        6   **eggs**
     1/3   **cup milk or light cream**
     1/4   **teaspoon salt**
             **Dash pepper**
        2   **tablespoons butter *or* margarine**

In a bowl beat together eggs, milk or light cream, salt, and pepper. Stir with a fork to mix. In a 10-inch skillet melt butter over medium heat; pour in egg mixture. Cook, without stirring, till mixture begins to set on the bottom and around edges. Using a large spoon or spatula, lift and fold partially cooked eggs so uncooked portion flows underneath. Continue cooking over medium heat about 4 minutes or till eggs are cooked throughout but are still glossy and moist. Remove from heat immediately. Season to taste. Makes 3 servings.

**Herbed Scrambled Eggs:** Prepare Scrambled Eggs as above, *except* add 1 tablespoon snipped *parsley* and 1/8 teaspoon dried *thyme,* crushed, to the uncooked egg mixture.

**Creamy Cheese Scrambled Eggs:** Prepare Scrambled Eggs as above, *except* cut up one 3-ounce package *cream cheese with chives;* add to the uncooked egg mixture.

**Cheese-Onion Scrambled Eggs:** Prepare Scrambled Eggs as above, *except* add 1/2 cup shredded *American or Swiss* *cheese* after the eggs begin to set. Continue cooking till eggs are firm and cheese melts. Sprinkle with 1 tablespoon sliced *green onion tops.*

**Mushroom Scrambled Eggs:** Prepare Scrambled Eggs as above, *except* in the skillet cook 1 tablespoon chopped *onion* in the 2 tablespoons butter or margarine. To the beaten egg mixture add one 2-ounce can chopped *mushrooms,* drained; 1 tablespoon snipped *parsley;* ½ teaspoon *dry mustard;* and ¼ teaspoon *Worcestershire sauce.* Pour into cooked onion in skillet. Continue as directed.

**Microwave directions:** In a nonmetal 1½-quart bowl melt the butter or margarine on high power in a counter-top microwave oven for 30 to 40 seconds. In another bowl beat the eggs, milk, salt, and pepper. Pour egg mixture into bowl with butter. Micro-cook, covered, on high power for 3 to 3½ minutes or till eggs are slightly softer than desired for scrambled eggs; stir through mixture two or three times during cooking. Let eggs stand for a few minutes, then stir before serving.

## Denver Scramble

> 1 **cup diced fully cooked ham**
> 1 **2-ounce can mushroom stems and pieces, drained**
> ¼ **cup chopped onion**
> 2 **tablespoons chopped green pepper**
> 2 **tablespoons butter or margarine**
> 8 **eggs**
> ⅓ **cup milk**

In a 10-inch skillet cook ham, mushrooms, onion, and green pepper in butter or margarine over medium heat about 5 minutes or till vegetables are tender but not brown. Beat together eggs, milk, ¼ teaspoon *salt,* and dash *pepper;* add to skillet. Cook, without stirring, till mixture begins to set on the bottom and around edges. Using a large spoon or spatula, lift and fold partially cooked egg mixture so uncooked portion flows underneath. Continue cooking over medium heat about

4 minutes or till eggs are cooked throughout but are still glossy and moist. Serve immediately. Serves 4.

## Farmer's Breakfast

  ¼  **cup chopped onion**
  ¼  **cup butter or margarine**
  2  **medium potatoes, peeled and finely
        chopped (2 cups)**
  1  **teaspoon water**
  6  **eggs**
  2  **tablespoons milk**
  1  **cup diced fully cooked ham**

In a 10-inch skillet cook onion in butter or margarine till tender. Add potatoes, water, and ¼ teaspoon *salt.* Cover and cook over medium heat about 10 minutes or till potatoes are tender, stirring occasionally. Beat together eggs, milk, ¼ teaspoon *salt,* and dash *pepper;* stir in ham. Pour over potato mixture. Cook, without stirring, till mixture begins to set on the bottom and around edges. Using a large spoon or spatula, lift and fold partially cooked egg mixture so uncooked portion flows underneath. Continue cooking over medium heat about 4 minutes or till eggs are cooked throughout but still glossy and moist. Serve immediately. Makes 4 servings.

## Egg Foo Yong

- ½ **cup finely chopped Chinese cabbage or cabbage**
- ¼ **cup chopped onion**
- ¼ **cup chopped green pepper**
- 1 **tablespoon cooking oil**
- 1 **tablespoon cornstarch**
- 1 **teaspoon instant beef bouillon granules**
- 1 **teaspoon sugar**
- 1 **cup cold water**
- 1 **tablespoon soy sauce**
- 3 **eggs**
- ½ **teaspoon salt**
- ⅛ **teaspoon pepper**
- 1 **cup fresh or canned bean sprouts, drained and rinsed**
- **Cooking oil for frying**

In a 10-inch skillet cook cabbage, onion, and green pepper in 1 tablespoon hot cooking oil for 2 minutes; remove from heat and cool.

Meanwhile, for sauce, in a small saucepan combine cornstarch, beef bouillon granules, and sugar. Stir in water and soy sauce. Cook and stir till thickened and bubbly. Cook and stir 1 to 2 minutes more. Keep sauce warm while frying egg foo yong mixture.

In a mixing bowl beat together eggs, salt, and pepper. Stir in the cooled cooked vegetables and the bean sprouts. In the same skillet heat about 2 tablespoons cooking oil. Using about ¼ cup of the mixture for each patty, fry patties in hot oil about 1 minute per side or till golden. (Spread the mixture to cover egg as egg spreads slightly while cooking.) Keep warm. Repeat till all the mixture is used, stirring mixture in bowl each time before frying. Add more oil as needed. Serve with warm sauce. Makes 2 servings.

**Ham Egg Foo Yong:** Prepare Egg Foo Yong as above, *except* add ½ cup diced *fully cooked ham* to beaten egg mixture. Continue as directed.

**Shrimp Egg Foo Yong:** Prepare Egg Foo Yong as above,

*except* add one 4½-ounce can *shrimp,* drained and chopped, to beaten egg mixture. Continue as directed.

## Eggs Benedict

> **6** slices Canadian-style bacon
> **6** eggs
> Classic Hollandaise Sauce (see recipe, page 712)
> **6** rusks *or* 3 English muffins, split, toasted, and buttered.

In a 12-inch skillet lightly brown bacon over medium heat for 3 minutes on each side. Cover; keep warm. Lightly grease a 10-inch skillet. Add water to half-fill the skillet; bring to boiling. Reduce heat to maintain a simmer. Break 1 egg into a small dish. Carefully slide egg into water, holding lip of dish as close to water as possible. Repeat with remaining eggs so that each has an equal amount of space. Simmer, uncovered, 3 to 5 minutes or till eggs are just soft-cooked. Remove with a slotted spoon; place eggs in a large pan of warm water to keep warm while preparing Classic Hollandaise Sauce. To serve, top each rusk or English muffin half with a bacon slice and an egg; spoon on sauce. Garnish with parsley or sprinkle lightly with paprika, if desired. Makes 6 servings.

## Creamy Poached Eggs

> **1** cup milk
> **¾** cup shredded American cheese (3 ounces)
> **1** tablespoon butter *or* margarine
> **1** tablespoon sliced green onion
> **1** tablespoon all-purpose flour
> **½** cup dairy sour cream
> **¼** cup sliced pimiento-stuffed olives
> **4** eggs
> **4** English muffins, split, toasted, and buttered

In an 8-inch skillet combine milk, cheese, butter, and green onion. Heat and stir till cheese is melted. Stir flour into sour cream; stir in about *half* of the hot cheese mixture. Return to skillet. Cook and stir till thickened and bubbly. Cook and stir 1 to 2 minutes more. Stir in olives. Break an egg into a small dish. Carefully slide egg into cheese mixture. Repeat with remaining eggs. Cover; cook over low heat 3 to 5 minutes or to desired doneness. Serve eggs in sauce on English muffins. Serves 4.

## Huevos Rancheros

| | |
|---|---|
| ¼ | **cup cooking oil** |
| 6 | **6-inch tortillas** |
| ½ | **cup chopped onion** |
| 1 | **16-ounce can tomatoes, cut up** |
| 2 | **canned green chili peppers, rinsed, seeded, and chopped** |
| ½ | **teaspoon chili powder** |
| ⅛ | **teaspoon garlic powder** |
| 6 | **eggs** |
| ¾ | **cup shredded Monterey Jack or American cheese** |

Oven 250°

In a 10-inch skillet heat oil. Fry tortillas, one at a time, in oil about 30 seconds per side or till crisp and golden; drain. Wrap in foil and keep warm in a 250° oven. In the same skillet cook onion in remaining oil till tender. Add *undrained* tomatoes, chili peppers, chili powder, garlic powder, and ¼ teaspoon *salt*. Simmer 5 to 10 minutes or till slightly thickened. Break 1 egg into a small dish. Carefully slide egg into hot tomato mixture. Repeat with remaining eggs. Season with salt and pepper. Cover; cook over low heat 3 to 5 minutes or to desired doneness. To serve, place eggs and some tomato mixture on warm tortillas. Sprinkle with cheese. Pass bottled hot pepper sauce, if desired. Makes 3 servings.

## Mushroom-Sauced Eggs

       2   **cups fresh mushrooms**
       4   **teaspoons all-purpose flour**
       2   **tablespoons butter *or* margarine**
     ¾   **cup milk**
    1½   **teaspoons Worcestershire sauce**
     ¾   **teaspoon dry mustard**
     ½   **teaspoon paprika**
       4   **Poached Eggs (see recipe, page 373)**
       2   **English muffins, split and toasted**

Chop mushrooms; sprinkle with flour. In a 1½-quart saucepan cook mushrooms in butter, covered, for 5 minutes, stirring occasionally. Stir in milk, Worcestershire sauce, mustard, paprika, ¼ teaspoon *salt*, and dash *pepper*. Cook and stir, uncovered, till thickened and bubbly. Cook and stir 1 minute more. Cover; keep warm. Prepare Poached Eggs. Place Poached Eggs on muffin halves. Spoon mushroom sauce over. Serves 2.

## Gold Rush Brunch

       1   **6-ounce package dry hashed brown
            potatoes with onion**
       3   **tablespoons butter *or* margarine**
       3   **tablespoons all-purpose flour**
       2   **cups milk**
       1   **cup dairy sour cream**
       2   **tablespoons snipped parsley**
       8   **slices Canadian-style bacon**
       8   **eggs**                                                    Oven 350°

Place dry potatoes in a bowl. Cover potatoes with very hot *water;* let stand 15 minutes. Drain potatoes; set aside. In a large saucepan melt butter; stir in flour, ½ teaspoon *salt*, and ⅛ teaspoon *pepper*. Add milk all at once. Cook and stir till thickened and bubbly. Cook and stir 1 to 2 minutes more. Remove from heat; stir in sour cream, parsley, and rehydrated potatoes. Spread in a 13x9x2-inch baking dish. Arrange bacon slices down center, overlapping as needed. Bake, uncovered, in a 350° oven for 20 minutes. Remove from oven. Make 4 depressions on each side of bacon. Break 1 egg into a small dish. Carefully slide each egg into one of the depressions.

Sprinkle with salt and pepper. Return to oven; bake 12 to 15 minutes more. Serves 8.

---

# Swiss Onion Bake

     2   **tablespoons butter or margarine**
   1½   **cups sliced onion**
     6   **hard-cooked eggs, sliced**
   1½   **cups shredded Swiss cheese (6 ounces)**
     1   **10¾-ounce can condensed cream of
           chicken soup**
    ¾   **cup milk**
    ½   **teaspoon prepared mustard**
          **French bread slices, toasted, or toast
           points**                                    Oven 350°

In a large skillet melt butter. Add onion; cover and cook 10 minutes or till tender. Spread onion in bottom of a 10x6x2-inch baking dish. Top with sliced eggs; sprinkle with shredded cheese. In a saucepan combine soup, milk, and mustard; heat and stir till smooth. Pour over casserole. Bake, covered, in a 350° oven for 30 minutes or till hot. Serve spooned over toasted bread. Sprinkle with paprika, if desired. Makes 6 servings.

---

# Eggs Florentine

     1   **10-ounce package frozen chopped spinach,
           cooked and drained**
     1   **11-ounce can condensed cheddar cheese
           soup**
     4   **eggs**
     2   **tablespoons milk**
     1   **teaspoon minced dried onion**
     1   **teaspoon prepared mustard**
    ½   **cup croutons**

Combine spinach and *half* of the cheese soup. Spoon into four 8-ounce individual casseroles; spread evenly on bottom and halfway up sides of casseroles. Break 1 egg into *each* dish. Bake in a 350° oven 20 to 25 minutes or till eggs are firm. In a saucepan heat together remaining soup, the milk, onion, and mustard. Spoon over eggs. Sprinkle *each* with some of the croutons. Makes 4 servings.

## Creamed Eggs

    3   **tablespoons butter or margarine**
    3   **tablespoons all-purpose flour**
  ½   **teaspoon dry mustard**
1¾   **cups milk**
    6   **hard-cooked eggs, coarsely chopped**
    4   **slices bread, toasted and buttered, or 2**
         **English muffins, split, toasted, and**
         **buttered**
      **Paprika or snipped parsley**

In a heavy saucepan melt butter or margarine. Stir in flour, dry mustard, ¼ teaspoon *salt,* and dash *pepper.* Add milk all at once. Cook and stir till mixture is thickened and bubbly. Cook and stir 1 to 2 minutes more. Carefully stir in eggs; heat through. Serve over toasted bread or English muffin halves. Sprinkle with paprika or parsley. Makes 4 servings.

    ***Eggs Goldenrod:*** Prepare Creamed Eggs as above, *except* reserve 3 of the egg yolks. Pour mixture over toast or English muffin halves. Press reserved yolks through a sieve atop each serving.

    ***Eggs a la King:*** Prepare Creamed Eggs as above, *except* increase milk to *2 cups;* decrease eggs to 4 and stir into the hot sauce along with one 3-ounce can chopped *mushrooms,* drained; ½ cup cooked *peas;* and 2 tablespoons chopped *pimiento.*

## Easy Cheese Eggs a la King

   ¼   **cup chopped celery**
   ¼   **cup chopped green pepper**
   ¼   **cup finely chopped onion**
   2   **tablespoons butter *or* margarine**
   1   **10¾-ounce can condensed cream of celery
       soup**
   1   **cup shredded American cheese (4 ounces)**
   ½   **cup milk**
   4   **hard-cooked eggs, sliced**
   2   **tablespoons chopped pimiento**
   4   **slices bread, toasted and buttered**

In a saucepan cover and cook celery, green pepper, and onion in butter or margarine till tender but not brown. Stir in celery soup, cheese, and milk; heat and stir till cheese melts. Gently stir in sliced eggs and pimiento. Serve spooned over buttered toast. Makes 4 servings.

## Curried Eggs

   ¼   **cup butter *or* margarine**
   2   **teaspoons curry powder**
   1   **medium apple, peeled and chopped**
   ½   **cup sliced green onion**
   2   **tablespoons all-purpose flour**
 1⅓   **cups milk**
   1   **cup shredded American cheese (4 ounces)**
   6   **hard-cooked eggs, quartered**
   1   **4-ounce can mushroom stems and pieces,
       drained**
       **Hot cooked rice**
       **Raisins (optional)**
       **Flaked *or* shredded coconut (optional)**
       **Chopped peanuts (optional)**

In a medium saucepan melt butter or margarine; stir in curry powder. Stir in chopped apple and green onion; cook about 4 minutes or till tender. Stir in flour. Add milk, ¼ teaspoon *salt*, and dash *pepper*. Cook and stir till thickened and bubbly. Cook and stir 1 to 2 minutes more.

Stir in cheese till melted. Gently stir in hard-cooked eggs and mushrooms; heat through. Serve over cooked rice. Pass raisins, coconut, and peanuts to sprinkle atop *each* serving, if desired. Makes 4 servings.

## Egg-Rice Bake

> ¼ **cup chopped onion**
> ¼ **cup chopped green pepper**
> 2 **tablespoons butter or margarine**
> 1 **10¾-ounce can condensed cream of**
>     **mushroom soup**
> ½ **cup milk**
> 2 **cups cooked rice**
> 6 **hard-cooked eggs, halved**
> 1 **cup shredded American cheese**
>     **(4 ounces)** Oven 350°

In a saucepan cook onion and green pepper in butter or margarine till tender but not brown. Add mushroom soup; stir in milk. Remove ½ *cup* of the soup mixture; set aside. Stir cooked rice into remaining mixture; spread in a 12x7x2-inch baking dish. Gently press hard-cooked egg halves, yolk side up, into the rice. Spoon reserved soup mixture over eggs. Cover and bake in a 350° oven for 25 minutes. Uncover; sprinkle shredded cheese over all. Return to oven and bake 5 minutes more or till cheese melts. Makes 4 servings.

## Egg-Sausage Casserole

       1  **pound bulk pork sausage**
      ¼  **cup butter** *or* **margarine**
      ¼  **cup all-purpose flour**
      ½  **teaspoon salt**
       2  **cups milk**
       4  **hard-cooked eggs, sliced**
       1  **17-ounce can whole kernel corn, drained**
      ¾  **cup soft bread crumbs (1 slice)**
       1  **tablespoon butter** *or* **margarine,
            melted**                         Oven 350°

In a skillet cook sausage till browned; drain off fat. In a saucepan melt the ¼ cup butter or margarine; stir in flour and salt. Add milk all at once. Cook and stir till mixture is thickened and bubbly. Cook and stir 1 to 2 minutes more. Stir in cooked sausage, sliced eggs, and drained corn. Pour mixture into a 1½-quart casserole. Toss bread crumbs with melted butter or margarine; sprinkle atop casserole. Bake, uncovered, in a 350° oven for 30 minutes or till heated through. Makes 6 servings.

## Scalloped Eggs and Bacon

      ¼  **cup chopped onion**
       2  **tablespoons butter** *or* **margarine**
       2  **tablespoons all-purpose flour**
     1½  **cups milk**
      ½  **cup shredded American cheese**
      ½  **cup shredded Swiss cheese**
       6  **hard-cooked eggs, sliced**
      10  **to 12 slices bacon, crisp-cooked and
            crumbled**
     1½  **cups crushed potato chips**           Oven 350°

Cook onion in butter till tender but not brown. Stir in flour. Add milk all at once. Cook and stir till thickened and bubbly. Cook and stir 1 to 2 minutes more. Add cheeses; stir till melted. Place *half* of the sliced eggs in the bottom of a

10x6x2-inch baking dish; pour *half* of the cheese sauce over. Sprinkle with *half* of the crumbled bacon and *half* of the crushed potato chips. Repeat layers. Bake in a 350° oven for 15 to 20 minutes. Makes 6 servings.

---

## Eggs in Spanish Sauce

  **6**   **hard-cooked eggs**
 **¼**   **cup mayonnaise or salad dressing**
  **1**   **teaspoon prepared mustard**
 **½**   **cup chopped onion**
 **¼**   **cup chopped green pepper**
  **2**   **tablespoons butter or margarine**
  **2**   **tablespoons all-purpose flour**
  **2**   **teaspoons sugar**
  **1**   **28-ounce can tomatoes, cut up**
  **1**   **bay leaf**
 **¼**   **cup fine dry bread crumbs**
  **1**   **tablespoon butter, melted**          Oven 350°

Halve eggs lengthwise. Remove yolks and mash; stir in mayonnaise, mustard, and ⅛ teaspoon *salt*. Stuff egg whites with yolk mixture. Arrange egg halves in a 10x6x2-inch baking dish. Cook onion and green pepper in 2 tablespoons butter till tender. Stir in flour, sugar, ½ teaspoon *salt,* and dash *pepper*. Add *undrained* tomatoes and bay leaf. Cook and stir till bubbly. Cook and stir 2 minutes more. Remove bay leaf; pour over eggs. Toss together crumbs and 1 tablespoon melted butter; sprinkle atop. Bake in a 350° oven about 25 minutes. Let stand 5 to 10 minutes. Serves 4.

## Shrimp-Egg Bake

      6 **hard-cooked eggs**
    ¼ **cup mayonnaise *or* salad dressing**
    ¼ **teaspoon paprika**
    ¼ **teaspoon curry powder**
    ¼ **teaspoon dry mustard**
      2 **tablespoons butter *or* margarine**
      2 **tablespoons all-purpose flour**
    ¼ **teaspoon curry powder**
      1 **10¾-ounce can condensed cream of shrimp
         soup**
    ¾ **cup milk**
      1 **cup fresh *or* frozen shelled shrimp, cooked
         and drained, *or* one 4½-ounce can
         shrimp, drained**
    ½ **cup shredded cheddar cheese**
      1 **tablespoon butter**
    ¾ **cup soft bread crumbs
         (1 slice)**                       Oven 350°

Cut hard-cooked eggs in half lengthwise; remove yolks and
mash. Combine mashed yolks with mayonnaise, paprika, the
¼ teaspoon curry powder, dry mustard, and ¼ teaspoon *salt.*
Stuff egg whites with yolk mixture. Arrange egg halves in a
10x6x2-inch baking dish. For shrimp sauce, in a saucepan
melt the 2 tablespoons butter; stir in flour and the ¼ teaspoon
curry powder. Stir in soup and milk. Cook and stir till thickened and bubbly. Cook and stir 1 to 2 minutes more. Add
shrimp and shredded cheese; stir till cheese melts. Pour sauce
over eggs. Melt the 1 tablespoon butter. Toss crumbs with
butter; sprinkle atop. Bake in a 350° oven 15 to 20 minutes.
Serves 4.

## Rosy Pickled Eggs

    1   cup juice from canned pickled beets
    1   cup vinegar
    1   clove garlic
    1   medium bay leaf
    2   teaspoons mixed pickling spices
   12   hard-cooked eggs
    1   small onion, sliced and separated into
          rings

In a large bowl combine beet juice, vinegar, garlic, bay leaf, pickling spices, 4 cups *water* and ½ teaspoon *salt;* mix well. Remove shells from the eggs. Add eggs and onion rings. Cover and refrigerate 3 to 4 days. Makes 12.

## Egg and Whole Wheat Foldovers

    6   hard-cooked eggs, finely chopped
    1   tablespoon finely chopped onion
    1   tablespoon snipped parsley
    1   tablespoon chopped pimiento
   ½   teaspoon celery salt
   ½   cup mayonnaise or salad dressing
    1   tablespoon horseradish mustard
    1   cup whole wheat flour
    6   tablespoons butter *or* margarine
   ⅓   cup dairy sour cream
    1   10¾-ounce can condensed cream of
          mushroom soup
   ½   cup dairy sour cream                    Oven 375°

In a mixing bowl combine chopped eggs, chopped onion, parsley, pimiento, celery salt, ½ teaspoon *salt,* and dash *pepper.* Add mayonnaise and horseradish mustard; mix well. For pastry, stir together whole wheat flour and ¼ teaspoon *salt.* Cut in butter till mixture resembles coarse crumbs. Add the ⅓ cup sour cream, mixing with hands, if necessary, till mixture forms a ball. Divide dough into 6 portions. On a lightly floured surface roll each portion into a 6-inch circle. Spoon about *3 tablespoons* of the egg filling just off-center on each pastry circle. Moisten edges of pastry. Fold in half, pressing with the tines of a fork to seal. Place foldovers on an ungreased baking sheet; prick tops. Bake in a 375° oven 30 to 35 minutes or till golden. Meanwhile, in a saucepan heat together the mushroom soup and ½ cup sour cream. Serve spooned over foldovers. Serves 3.

## Deviled Eggs

> **6** **hard-cooked eggs**
> **¼** **cup mayonnaise** *or* **salad dressing**
> **1** **teaspoon vinegar**
> **1** **teaspoon prepared mustard**

Halve hard-cooked eggs lengthwise; remove yolks and mash with a fork. Stir in mayonnaise, vinegar, mustard, and ⅛ teaspoon *salt*. Stuff egg whites with yolk mixture. Garnish with paprika or parsley, if desired. Makes 12 servings.

*Italian-Style Deviled Eggs:* Prepare Deviled Eggs as above, *except* omit mayonnaise, vinegar, and mustard. Add 3 tablespoons *creamy Italian salad dressing* to mashed yolks. Stuff egg whites with yolk mixture.

## Puffy Omelet

> **4** **egg whites**
> **2** **tablespoons water**
> **¼** **teaspoon salt**
> **4** **egg yolks**
> **1** **tablespoon butter** *or* **margarine**     Oven 325°

Beat egg whites till frothy. Add water and salt; continue beating about 1½ minutes or till stiff peaks form. Beat egg yolks at high speed of electric mixer about 5 minutes or till thick and lemon colored. Fold egg yolks into egg whites.

In a 10-inch skillet with an oven-proof handle, heat the butter or margarine till a drop of water sizzles. Pour in egg mixture, mounding it slightly higher at the sides. Cook over low heat for 8 to 10 minutes or till eggs are puffed and set, and the bottom is golden brown.

Place skillet in a 325° oven; bake for 10 minutes or till a knife inserted near center comes out clean. Loosen sides of omelet with a metal spatula. Make a shallow cut across the omelet, cutting slightly off-center. Fold the smaller (upper) portion of omelet over the larger portion. Slip omelet onto a warm platter. Makes 2 servings.

## Cheese and Herb Omelet

|       |                                        |
|-------|----------------------------------------|
| 1     | tablespoon butter *or* margarine       |
| 1     | tablespoon all-purpose flour           |
| ⅓     | cup milk                               |
| 1     | teaspoon snipped chives                |
| ¼     | teaspoon dried fines herbes            |
| ½     | cup shredded Gruyère cheese (2 ounces) |
| ¼     | cup dairy sour cream                   |
| 2     | tablespoons dry white wine             |
|       | Puffy Omelet                           |

In a small saucepan melt butter or margarine; stir in all-purpose flour. Stir in milk, snipped chives, and fines herbes. Cook and stir till mixture is thickened and bubbly. Cook and stir 1 to 2 minutes more. Stir in shredded cheese till melted. Stir in sour cream and wine; heat through but *do not boil*. To serve, pour over folded Puffy Omelet on a warm platter. Garnish with parsley, if desired. Makes 2 servings.

## Ham and Cheese Omelet

|       |                                            |
|-------|--------------------------------------------|
| ½     | cup diced fully cooked ham                 |
| 1     | 3-ounce can sliced mushrooms, drained      |
| 1     | tablespoon butter *or* margarine           |
| 1     | 3-ounce package cream cheese, softened     |
| ⅓     | cup milk                                   |
| 1     | beaten egg yolk                            |
| 1½    | teaspoons lemon juice                      |
| 1     | teaspoon prepared mustard                  |
|       | Dash salt                                  |
|       | Puffy Omelet                               |

In a small skillet heat ham and mushrooms in butter or margarine; keep warm. In a small saucepan stir together cream cheese and milk. Stir in egg yolk. Add lemon juice, mustard, and salt; beat well. Cook and stir over low heat till slightly thickened. Set aside; keep warm. To serve, fill Puffy Omelet with ham-mushroom mixture before folding. Slide onto a warm platter. Spoon cream cheese mixture over. Makes 2 servings.

## Bacon-Asparagus Omelet

  1    **8-ounce package frozen cut asparagus**
  2    **slices bacon**
  ¼    **cup chopped onion**
  ¼    **cup cold water**
  1    **tablespoon soy sauce**
  2    **teaspoons cornstarch**
       **Puffy Omelet**

Run hot water over frozen asparagus in a colander to break pieces apart; let excess water drain off. In a small skillet cook bacon till crisp; drain bacon, reserving drippings. Crumble bacon and set aside.

Cook onion in reserved drippings till tender but not brown. Add drained asparagus to skillet. Cook and stir 3 to 4 minutes. Combine cold water, soy sauce, and cornstarch; stir into asparagus mixture. Cook and stir till mixture is thickened and bubbly. Cook and stir 1 to 2 minutes more. Stir in bacon. To serve, fill Puffy Omelet before folding. Slide onto a warm platter. Makes 2 servings.

# Cheese Identification

**Soft**
White in color, these cheeses range from almost fluid in consistency to grainy and dry. Some are flaky, or have moist. delicate curds.

**Cottage**

**Farmer's**

**Feta**

**Limburger**

**Brie**

**Boursin**

**Ricotta**

**Camembert**

**Cream**

**Gourmandise**

**Very Hard**
These cheeses are usually grated for use in cooking. They have a dry, granular texture and a very pronounced flavor.

**Sapsago**

**Semi-Soft to Hard**
Curds are formed under a variety of conditions for specific types of cheeses. Salting improves the flavor of these compact, chewy curds. Edam is a mild, creamy yellow cheese with a red wax coating.

**Cheese Curds**

**Parmesan**

**Romano**

**Edam**

**Semi-Soft**
These smooth-textured cheeses are white or yellow in color, but Roquefort, blue/bleu, and Gorgonzola are marbled with blue-green mold.

**Havarti**

**Port du Salut**

**Muenster**

**Roquefort**

**Brick**

**Mozzarella**

**Gorgonzola**

**Monterey Jack**

**Blue/Bleu**

**Stilton**

**Asiago**

**Hard**
Smooth textured, these cheeses range in color from creamy white to golden. They're available in varied sizes and shapes.

**Fontina**

**Colby**

**Swiss**

**Gjetost**

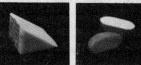

**Gruyère**

**Gouda**

**Cheddar**

**Provolone**

# French Omelet

**2   eggs**
**1   tablespoon water**
**⅛   teaspoon salt**
**Dash pepper**
**1   tablespoon butter *or* margarine**

Beat together the eggs, water, salt, and pepper with a fork till combined but not frothy. In a 6- or 8-inch skillet with flared sides, heat the butter till it sizzles and browns slightly. Lift and tilt the pan to coat the sides. Add egg mixture; cook over medium heat. As eggs set, run a spatula around edge of the skillet, lifting the eggs to allow the uncooked portion to flow underneath. When eggs are set but still shiny, remove from heat. Fold omelet in half. (If making a filled omelet, spoon the filling across center. Fold ⅓ of omelet over filling. Overlap remaining ⅓ atop filling.) Slide omelet to edge of pan. Tilt skillet, then invert to roll omelet out onto a warm serving plate. Makes 1 serving.

**Mushroom French Omelet:** Prepare French Omelet as above, *except* cook ⅓ cup sliced fresh *mushrooms* in 1 tablespoon *butter or margarine;* use to fill omelet. Continue as directed.

**Cheese French Omelet:** Prepare French Omelet as above, *except* sprinkle ¼ cup cheddar, Swiss, Monterey Jack, mozzarella, or American *cheese* in center of omelet. Continue as directed. If desired, top omelet with additional shredded cheese and snipped parsley.

**Fruited French Omelet:** Prepare French Omelet as above, *except* fill omelet with 2 tablespoons *dairy sour cream or yogurt*. Continue as directed. Top with ¼ cup halved *strawberries,* sliced *peaches,* or *blueberries;* sprinkle with 1 tablespoon *brown sugar.*

**Vegetable French Omelet:** Prepare French Omelet as above, *except* cook ⅓ cup sliced *green onion, asparagus, zucchini, celery, green pepper,* or *bean sprouts* in 1 tablespoon *butter or margarine.* Use to fill omelet. Continue as directed. Top with 1 tablespoon grated *Parmesan cheese.*

## Hashed Brown Omelet

>     3   **medium potatoes***
>     4   **slices bacon**
>    ¼   **cup chopped onion**
>    ¼   **cup chopped green pepper**
>    ¾   **teaspoon salt**
>     4   **beaten eggs**
>    ¼   **cup milk**
>    ¼   **teaspoon dried thyme, crushed**
>     1   **cup shredded Swiss cheese**

In a covered saucepan cook whole potatoes in enough boiling salted water to cover for 20 to 25 minutes or till almost tender. Drain and chill till cool enough to handle. Peel potatoes; shred to make 3 cups.

In a 10-inch skillet cook bacon till crisp; drain, reserving 2 tablespoons drippings in skillet. Crumble bacon; set aside. Combine potatoes, onion, green pepper, and ½ *teaspoon* of the salt; pat into skillet. Cook over low heat about 20 minutes or till underside is crisp and brown. Combine eggs, milk, thyme, the remaining ¼ teaspoon salt, and dash *pepper.* Stir in bacon and cheese; pour over potatoes. Cover; cook over low heat 8 to 10 minutes or till surface is set but still shiny. Loosen edges of omelet; cut into wedges. Serves 4.

*Note:** Or, substitute 3 cups cooked packaged hashed brown potatoes.

## Omelet Sandwich Puff

Oven 350°

Cook 4 slices *bacon* till crisp. Remove bacon; crumble and set aside. Beat together 2 *egg yolks,* 1 whole *egg,* 1 tablespoon *milk,* and ⅛ teaspoon *onion salt.* Add crumbled bacon. In a small skillet melt 2 teaspoons *butter.* Pour in egg mixture; cook over medium heat. As eggs set, run a spatula around edge of skillet, lifting the eggs to allow uncooked portion to flow underneath. When eggs are set but still shiny, fold in half; cut into 2 pieces crosswise.

On a baking sheet place *each* half of the egg mixture on 1 slice of toasted and buttered *bread*. Top *each* with 1 *cheese slice*. Beat 2 *egg whites* till stiff peaks form. Spread the beaten egg whites over both sandwiches. Sprinkle with salt and pepper. Bake in a 350° oven about 10 minutes or till golden. Serve immediately. Makes 2 sandwiches.

## Easy Baked Cheese Omelet

|   |   |   |
|---|---|---|
| **4** | **egg whites** | |
| **4** | **egg yolks** | |
| **1** | **11-ounce can condensed cheddar cheese soup** | |
| **½** | **cup dairy sour cream** | |
| **2** | **tablespoons milk** | Oven 400° |

Beat egg whites till stiff peaks form; set aside. Slightly beat egg yolks; add ½ *cup* of the cheddar cheese soup. Mix well. Fold yolk mixture into white mixture. Spread in an ungreased 8x1½-inch round baking dish. Bake in a 400° oven for 15 to 20 minutes or till puffy and golden brown. Meanwhile, in a small saucepan mix remaining cheddar cheese soup and sour cream. Stir in milk; heat through. Serve over omelet. Makes 2 servings.

# Baked Omelet with Chicken Sauce

|        |                                           |           |
| ------ | ----------------------------------------- | --------- |
| ½      | cup chopped onion                         |           |
| 3      | tablespoons butter *or* margarine         |           |
| 1      | cup sliced fresh mushrooms                |           |
| 3      | tablespoons all-purpose flour             |           |
| ⅛      | teaspoon dried rosemary, crushed          |           |
| 1¾     | cups milk                                 |           |
| 1½     | cups diced cooked chicken                 |           |
| 1      | cup shredded Swiss cheese                 |           |
| ¼      | cup dry sherry *or* milk                  |           |
| 4      | egg whites                                |           |
| ¼      | teaspoon cream of tartar                  |           |
| 4      | egg yolks                                 | Oven 375° |

For chicken sauce, in a medium saucepan cook onion in butter
or margarine till tender but not brown. Stir in mushrooms;
cook 2 minutes more. Stir in flour, rosemary, and ½ teaspoon
*salt*. Add milk all at once. Cook and stir till thickened and
bubbly. Cook and stir 1 to 2 minutes more. Stir in chicken, ¾
*cup* of the cheese, and the sherry or milk. Heat and stir till
cheese melts. Turn into an ungreased 10x6x2-inch baking
dish. Place in a 375° oven to keep hot.

Beat egg whites with cream of tartar till stiff peaks form. In a
small mixer bowl beat yolks till thick and lemon colored. Add
remaining ¼ cup cheese and ¼ teaspoon *salt;* fold into whites.
Spread over hot chicken sauce. Bake in a 375° oven 15 to 20
minutes or till golden brown. Makes 6 servings.

# Cheese Soufflé

|        |                                           |           |
| ------ | ----------------------------------------- | --------- |
| 6      | tablespoons butter *or* margarine         |           |
| ⅓      | cup all-purpose flour                     |           |
| ½      | teaspoon salt                             |           |
|        | Dash cayenne                              |           |
| 1½     | cups milk                                 |           |
| 3      | cups shredded cheddar cheese (12 ounces)  |           |
| 6      | egg yolks                                 |           |
| 6      | egg whites                                | Oven 300° |

Attach a foil collar to a 2-quart soufflé dish. For collar, measure enough foil to go around dish plus a 2- to 3-inch overlap. Fold foil into thirds lengthwise. Lightly butter one side. With buttered side in, position foil around dish, letting collar extend 2 inches above top of dish; fasten with tape. Set aside.

In a saucepan melt butter or margarine; stir in flour, salt, and cayenne. Add milk all at once. Cook and stir till thickened and bubbly. Cook and stir 1 to 2 minutes more. Remove from heat. Add shredded cheese, stirring till cheese is melted. Beat egg yolks till thick and lemon colored. *Slowly* add cheese mixture, stirring constantly. Cool slightly.

Using clean beaters, beat egg whites till stiff peaks form (tips stand straight). Gradually pour cheese-yolk mixture over beaten whites, folding to combine. Pour into the ungreased 2-quart soufflé dish. Bake in a 300° oven about 1½ hours or till a knife inserted near center comes out clean (see tip, page 398). Gently peel off collar; serve soufflé immediately. Serves 6.

---

### Serving a soufflé

Soufflés should be served *immediately* after they are removed from the oven, before they fall. It's true that it's better to have guests wait for the soufflé because the soufflé won't wait for the guests.

To serve, insert two forks, back to back, and gently pull the soufflé apart. Cut into servings in this manner. Use a large spoon to transfer soufflé to individual warm plates.

# Tuna Soufflé

- **3 tablespoons butter _or_ margarine**
- **¼ cup all-purpose flour**
- **¼ teaspoon paprika**
- **1 cup milk**
- **1 6½-ounce can tuna, drained and flaked, _or_ one 4½-ounce can shrimp, drained and chopped, _or_ one 7¾-ounce can salmon, drained and flaked, _or_ 1 cup finely chopped cooked chicken _or_ turkey**
- **1 tablespoon snipped parsley**
- **1 teaspoon grated onion**
- **3 egg yolks**
- **3 stiff-beaten egg whites**                    Oven 325°

In a saucepan melt the butter or margarine; stir in flour, paprika, ½ teaspoon _salt,_ and dash _pepper._ (_Or,_ if using the chopped cooked chicken or turkey, increase the salt to _1 teaspoon._) Add milk all at once. Cook and stir till thickened and bubbly. Cook and stir 1 to 2 minutes more. Remove from heat. Stir in tuna, shrimp, salmon, chicken, or turkey; parsley; and onion. Beat egg yolks till thick and lemon colored. Gradually add tuna mixture, stirring constantly. Cool slightly. Add gradually to egg whites, folding to combine. Turn into an ungreased 1½-quart soufflé dish. Bake in a 325° oven about

## Testing for doneness

Do not remove the soufflé from the oven to test for doneness. Insert a knife near the center and enlarge the hole slightly by moving knife from side to side. Otherwise the soufflé crust may "clean" the knife as it is pulled out. Test at the end of the suggested baking time; do not open oven door during baking.

40 minutes or till a knife inserted near center comes out clean. Serve immediately (see tip, page 398). Serves 4.

**Note:** If desired, serve soufflé with Dill, Lemon-Chive, or Curry Sauce (see recipes, pages 711 and 721).

## Old-Fashioned Cheese Bake

|   |   |
|---|---|
| 3 | beaten egg yolks |
| 1½ | cups milk |
| 1 | tablespoon snipped chives |
| ½ | teaspoon dry mustard |
| ¼ | teaspoon salt |
| ⅛ | teaspoon paprika |
|   | Dash pepper |
| 3 | cups soft bread crumbs (about 5 slices bread) |
| 1 | cup shredded American cheese (4 ounces) |
| 3 | egg whites          Oven 325° |

In a bowl thoroughly combine beaten egg yolks, milk, chives, dry mustard, salt, paprika, and pepper. Stir in bread crumbs and cheese.

In a small mixer bowl beat the egg whites at medium speed of electric mixer about 1½ minutes or till stiff peaks form. Gently fold egg whites into the egg yolk mixture.

Turn mixture into a 10x6x2-inch baking dish. Bake in a 325° oven for 30 to 35 minutes or till a knife inserted near center comes out clean. Serve immediately. Makes 4 servings.

# Crab Mornay

   ½ cup sliced fresh mushrooms
   2 tablespoons chopped onion
   2 tablespoons chopped celery
   2 tablespoons butter *or* margarine
   2 tablespoons all-purpose flour
     Dash cayenne
 1¼ cups milk
   1 cup shredded Swiss or Gruyère cheese (4 ounces)
   1 cup cooked crab meat *or* one 7-ounce can crab
     meat, drained, flaked, and cartilage removed
   2 tablespoons dry sherry *or* dry white wine
     Toast points

In a saucepan cook mushrooms, onions, and celery in butter till tender but not brown. Stir in flour, cayenne, and ⅛ teaspoon *salt*. Add milk all at once. Cook and stir till thickened and bubbly. Cook and stir 1 to 2 minutes more. Reduce heat. Add cheese and stir till melted. Stir in crab meat and sherry or white wine. Heat through; *do not boil*. Serve at once over toast points. Makes 4 servings.

# Classic Quiche Lorraine

Oven 450°

Cook 8 slices *bacon* till crisp; drain, reserving 2 tablespoons drippings. Crumble bacon; set aside. Cook 1 medium *onion*, thinly sliced, in reserved drippings till tender; drain. Stir together 4 beaten *eggs*, 1 cup *light cream*, 1 cup *milk*, 1 tablespoon *all-purpose flour*, ½ teaspoon *salt*, and dash ground *nutmeg*. Stir in the bacon, onion, and 1½ cups shredded *Swiss cheese*; mix well.

   Prepare *Pastry for Single-Crust Pie* (see recipe, page 569). To keep crust in shape, line the unpricked pastry shell with a double thickness of heavy-duty foil. Bake in a 450° oven for 5 minutes. Remove foil. Bake 5 to 7 minutes more or till pastry is nearly done. Remove from oven; reduce oven temperature to 325°. Pour cheese mixture into *hot* pastry shell. If necessary, cover edge of crust with foil to prevent overbrowning. Bake in a 325° oven for 45 to 50 minutes or till a knife inserted near center comes out clean. Let stand 10 minutes before serving. Makes 6 servings.

## Seafood Quiche

Oven 450°

Cook ½ cup chopped *onion* in 2 tablespoons *butter* till tender. Stir together 3 beaten *eggs*, ¾ cup *light cream*, ¾ cup *milk*, ½ teaspoon *salt*, ½ teaspoon finely shredded *lemon peel*, dash ground *nutmeg*, and the onion. Add one 7-ounce can *crab meat*, drained, flaked, and cartilage removed, *or* one 4½-ounce can *shrimp*, drained and chopped. Combine 1½ cups shredded *Swiss cheese* and 1 tablespoon *all-purpose flour*; add to egg mixture.

Prepare *Pastry for Single-Crust Pie* (see recipe, page 569). To keep crust in shape, line the unpricked pastry shell with a double thickness of heavy-duty foil. Bake in a 450° oven for 5 minutes. Remove foil. Bake 5 to 7 minutes more or till pastry is nearly done. Remove from oven; reduce oven temperature to 325°. Pour seafood mixture into *hot* pastry shell. Top with ¼ cup sliced *almonds*. If necessary, cover edge of crust to prevent overbrowning. Bake in a 325° oven 35 to 40 minutes or till a knife inserted near center comes out clean. Let stand 10 minutes before serving. Serves 6.

## Individual Quiche Casseroles

| | |
|---:|---|
| **4** | **slices bacon** |
| **½** | **cup chopped fresh mushrooms** |
| **½** | **cup finely chopped celery** |
| **¼** | **cup chopped onion** |
| **4** | **eggs** |
| **1½** | **cups milk** |
| **2** | **tablespoons all-purpose flour** |
| **1** | **cup shredded Swiss cheese** |
| | **Ground nutmeg** |

Oven 325°

Cook bacon till crisp; drain, reserving 2 tablespoons drippings. Crumble bacon; set aside. Cook mushrooms, celery, and onion in reserved drippings till tender; drain. Beat eggs, milk, flour, and ⅛ teaspoon *salt.* Stir in cooked vegetables, bacon, and cheese. Turn into four 8-ounce individual casseroles. Sprinkle lightly with nutmeg.

Place casseroles in a shallow baking pan on oven rack. Pour boiling water around casseroles in pan to a depth of 1 inch. Bake in a 325° oven 20 to 25 minutes or till a knife inserted near center comes out clean. Let stand 5 minutes. Makes 4 servings.

## Classic Cheese Strata

| | |
|---:|---|
| **8** | **slices day-old bread** |
| **8** | **ounces American *or* Swiss cheese, sliced** |
| **4** | **eggs** |
| **2½** | **cups milk** |
| **¼** | **cup finely chopped onion** |
| **½** | **teaspoon prepared mustard** |
| | **Paprika** |

Oven 325°

Trim crusts from 4 slices of the bread. Cut trimmed slices in half diagonally to make 8 triangles; set aside. Arrange trimmings and remaining 4 slices of untrimmed bread to cover bottom of a 9x9x2-inch baking pan. Place cheese slices over bread in pan. Arrange the reserved 8 bread triangles in 2 rows over cheese. (Points will slightly overlap bases of preceding triangles.) Beat eggs; stir in milk, chopped onion, mustard, 1½ teaspoons *salt,* and dash *pepper.* Pour over bread and cheese layers. Sprinkle with paprika. Cover; let chill in refrigerator several hours or overnight. Bake, uncovered, in a 325° oven 1¼ hours or till a knife inserted near center comes out clean. Let stand 5 minutes before serving. Serves 6.

# Classic Cheese Fondue

|       |                                                          |
|-------|----------------------------------------------------------|
| 6     | **cups coarsely shredded Gruyère or Swiss cheese (24 ounces)** |
| ¼     | **cup all-purpose flour**                                 |
| 1     | **clove garlic, halved**                                  |
| 2½    | **cups dry white wine**                                   |
| 2     | **tablespoons kirsch or dry sherry**                      |
|       | **Dash pepper**                                           |
|       | **Dash ground nutmeg**                                    |
|       | **French or Italian bread, cubed**                        |

Toss together cheese and flour; set aside. Rub bottom and sides of fondue pot with garlic cloves; discard garlic. Set fondue pot aside. In a large saucepan heat wine over low heat till small bubbles rise to surface. Just before wine boils, stir in cheese, little by little, making sure cheese has melted before adding more. (Stir *constantly* and continue to add cheese till all is mixed in.) Stir till fondue bubbles gently. Stir in kirsch or dry sherry, pepper, and nutmeg. Pour into a fondue pot; keep fondue bubbling gently over fondue burner. Serve with bread cubes (spear bread cubes with a fondue fork). Serves 10.

# Creamy Cheese Fondue

      4    cups shredded American cheese (16
           ounces)
      1    tablespoon all-purpose flour
      2    tablespoons finely chopped green pepper
      1    tablespoon butter *or* margarine
    1¼    cups dry white wine
      2    3-ounce packages cream cheese with
           chives, softened
      1    teaspoon prepared mustard
           Breadsticks *or* French bread, cubed

Toss together the shredded cheese and flour; set aside. In a
large saucepan cook green pepper in butter or margarine till
tender but not brown. Stir in wine; heat slowly just till bubbling.
Gradually add shredded cheese, stirring constantly, till smooth
and bubbly. Stir in cream cheese and mustard; cook and stir
over low heat till smooth. Transfer cheese mixture to fondue
pot; place over fondue burner. Serve with breadsticks or bread
cubes (dip breadsticks or spear bread cubes with a fondue
fork). Serves 6.

# Macaroni and Cheese

      6    ounces elbow macaroni (1½ cups)
      3    tablespoons butter *or* margarine
     ¼    cup finely chopped onion
      2    tablespoons all-purpose flour
     ½    teaspoon salt
           Dash pepper
      2    cups milk
      2    cups cubed American cheese
      1    medium tomato, sliced                 Oven 350°

Cook macaroni according to package directions; drain. For
cheese sauce, in a saucepan melt butter or margarine. Cook
onion in butter till tender but not brown. Stir in the flour, salt,
and pepper. Add milk all at once; cook and stir till thickened

and bubbly. Cook and stir 1 to 2 minutes more. Add cubed cheese; stir till melted.

Stir macaroni into cheese sauce. Turn into a 1½-quart casserole. Arrange tomato slices atop macaroni; sprinkle with a little salt. Bake in a 350° oven 30 to 35 minutes or till heated through. Makes 6 servings.

## Welsh Rabbit

1½  **cups shredded cheddar or American cheese (6 ounces)**
¾  **cup milk**
1  **teaspoon dry mustard**
1  **teaspoon Worcestershire sauce**
  **Dash cayenne**
1  **beaten egg**
4  **slices bread, toasted, *or poached* eggs**

For cheese sauce, in a heavy saucepan combine shredded cheese, milk, mustard, Worcestershire sauce, and cayenne. Cook over low heat, stirring constantly, till cheese melts. Slowly stir about *half* of the hot cheese mixture into 1 beaten egg; return all to remaining mixture in pan. Cook and stir over low heat till mixture thickens and just bubbles. Serve at once over toast or poached eggs. Makes 4 servings.

**Beer Rabbit:** Prepare Welsh Rabbit as above, *except* substitute *beer* for the milk. Top each serving with 2 slices of crisp-cooked *bacon,* halved crosswise.

**Fish & Seafood**

**Fish & Seafood**

**Fish & Seafood**

**Fish & Seafood**

**Fish & Seafood**

**Fish & Seafood**

**Fish & Seafood**

**Fish & Seafood**

# Fish & Seafood

Percent of U.S. RDA Per Serving

| Recipes | Servings (fraction of recipe) | Calories | Protein (grams) | Carbohydrate (grams) | Fat (grams) | Sodium (milligrams) | Potassium (milligrams) | Protein | Vitamin A | Vitamin C | Thiamine | Riboflavin | Niacin | Calcium | Iron |
|---|---|---|---|---|---|---|---|---|---|---|---|---|---|---|---|
| Baked Fillets and Steaks | 1/6 | 171 | 28 | 0 | 6 | 163 | 463 | 43 | 5 |  | 4 | 6 | 23 | 4 | 6 |
| Baked Fish a l'Orange | 1/6 | 294 | 32 | 4 | 17 | 440 | 762 | 50 | 16 | 25 | 9 | 7 | 64 | 3 | 7 |
| Baked Fish with Mushrooms | 1/4 | 240 | 20 | 2 | 17 | 316 | 423 | 31 | 12 | 8 | 7 | 10 | 20 | 3 | 6 |
| Baked Tuna Patties | 1/4 | 466 | 24 | 28 | 29 | 1099 | 332 | 36 | 22 | 3 | 16 | 18 | 42 | 14 | 14 |
| Boiled Crabs | 1/2 | 106 | 20 | 1 | 2 | 238 | 204 | 30 | 4 | 4 | 12 | 5 | 16 | 5 | 5 |
| Boiled Lobster | 1/2 | 138 | 27 | 0 | 2 | 305 | 261 | 42 | 0 | 0 | 10 | 2 | 11 | 9 | 7 |
| Boiled Lobster Tails | 1/4 | 104 | 21 | 2 | 1 | 160 | 251 | 33 | 2 | 0 | 2 | 2 | 18 | 7 | 10 |
| Boiled Scallops | 1/8 | 127 | 26 | 4 | 2 | 301 | 540 | 40 | 2 | 0 | 8 | 4 | 7 | 13 | 19 |
| Boiled Shrimp | 1/6 | 138 | 29 | 2 | 1 | 212 | 334 | 44 | 3 | 0 | 2 | 3 | 24 | 10 | 13 |
| Broiled Fish w/butter | 1/6 | 154 | 28 | 0 | 8 | 228 | 462 | 43 | 6 | 2 | 4 | 6 | 23 | 4 | 6 |
| Broiled Fish w/Dill Sauce | 1/6 | 188 | 28 | 0 | 8 | 364 | 467 | 43 | 6 | 4 | 4 | 6 | 23 | 4 | 4 |
| Broiled Shrimp | 1/6 | 162 | 19 | 2 | 8 | 325 | 233 | 30 | 4 | 6 | 1 | 2 | 16 | 7 | 9 |
| Bundled Fish | 1/4 | 434 | 30 | 41 | 17 | 929 | 701 | 46 | 76 | 18 | 23 | 24 | 32 | 13 | 15 |
| Company Creamed Tuna | 1/4 | 450 | 18 | 24 | 31 | 792 | 323 | 27 | 17 | 7 | 12 | 19 | 30 | 14 | 9 |
| Corn-Stuffed Fish | 1/6 | 289 | 24 | 17 | 14 | 613 | 441 | 37 | 60 | 24 | 14 | 12 | 22 | 4 | 6 |
| Crab Newburg | 1/4 | 534 | 23 | 22 | 38 | 1407 | 264 | 35 | 46 | 3 | 16 | 21 | 14 | 17 | 11 |
| Curried Fishwiches | 1/6 | 562 | 27 | 39 | 33 | 1009 | 503 | 42 | 35 | 4 | 20 | 16 | 28 | 31 | 12 |
| Easy Baked Fish Fillets | 1/8 | 322 | 27 | 19 | 15 | 511 | 482 | 41 | 9 | 6 | 12 | 14 | 23 | 9 | 10 |
| Fish and Chips | 1/4 | 492 | 29 | 43 | 22 | 370 | 851 | 45 | 4 | 35 | 25 | 20 | 33 | 8 | 14 |
| Fish Creole | 1/4 | 351 | 25 | 35 | 12 | 1107 | 725 | 39 | 36 | 83 | 16 | 9 | 27 | 6 | 15 |

# Nutrition Analysis Chart

| | | | | | | | | | | | | | | | |
|---|---|---|---|---|---|---|---|---|---|---|---|---|---|---|---|
| Fish Florentine | 1/6 | 240 | 19 | 14 | 12 | 583 | 459 | 29 | 63 | 14 | 4 | 9 | 8 | 11 | 7 |
| French-Fried Shrimp | 1/6 | 298 | 23 | 22 | 13 | 331 | 259 | 35 | 2 | 0 | 13 | 9 | 23 | 7 | 14 |
| Fried Clams | 1/4 | 284 | 21 | 19 | 13 | 482 | 324 | 33 | 8 | 19 | 18 | 21 | 13 | 10 | 30 |
| Fried Oysters | 1/4 | 309 | 21 | 24 | 14 | 573 | 276 | 32 | 17 | 90 | 27 | 29 | 28 | 19 | 64 |
| Fried Scallops | 1/4 | 318 | 32 | 21 | 12 | 742 | 598 | 49 | 8 | 0 | 18 | 13 | 13 | 15 | 27 |
| Individual Tuna Pies | 1/6 | 373 | 22 | 32 | 17 | 1091 | 399 | 34 | 42 | 13 | 16 | 20 | 40 | 13 | 14 |
| Lemon-Marinated Salmon Steaks | 1/6 | 331 | 29 | 4 | 22 | 436 | 516 | 44 | 74 | 34 | 15 | 11 | 23 | 5 | 5 |
| Lobster Newburg | 1/4 | 512 | 21 | 21 | 37 | 659 | 296 | 32 | 27 | 3 | 16 | 20 | 11 | 17 | 11 |
| Oven-Fried Fish | 1/3 | 351 | 32 | 13 | 18 | 516 | 525 | 50 | 16 | 4 | 9 | 14 | 27 | 7 | 12 |
| Pan-Fried Fish | 1/3 | 310 | 33 | 17 | 11 | 634 | 522 | 51 | 4 | 0 | 10 | 14 | 28 | 7 | 13 |
| Poached Fish w/Dill Sauce | 1/6 | 231 | 23 | 2 | 14 | 464 | 354 | 35 | 57 | 1 | 12 | 9 | 18 | 4 | 4 |
| Quick Fish-Potato Supper | 1/6 | 341 | 23 | 20 | 18 | 675 | 524 | 36 | 15 | 12 | 9 | 22 | 8 | 26 | 9 |
| Salmon-Broccoli Crepes | 1/6 | 517 | 27 | 31 | 32 | 927 | 514 | 42 | 48 | 43 | 19 | 41 | 21 | 55 | 13 |
| Salmon Loaf | 1/3 | 341 | 31 | 18 | 15 | 1063 | 559 | 48 | 12 | 3 | 8 | 24 | 54 | 32 | 12 |
| Sherry-Sauced Halibut | 1/6 | 321 | 33 | 3 | 21 | 553 | 714 | 50 | 20 | 1 | 10 | 10 | 65 | 4 | 7 |
| Shrimp Chow Mein | 1/4 | 455 | 31 | 48 | 17 | 2066 | 773 | 47 | 5 | 22 | 19 | 23 | 33 | 16 | 30 |
| Shrimp Newburg | 1/4 | 572 | 23 | 23 | 43 | 696 | 354 | 36 | 32 | 3 | 13 | 18 | 19 | 18 | 15 |
| Skillet Dilled Salmon Patties | 1/4 | 381 | 29 | 14 | 22 | 665 | 502 | 45 | 12 | 4 | 8 | 20 | 50 | 26 | 12 |
| Stacked Sole w/Shrimp Sauce | 1/6 | 225 | 32 | 3 | 9 | 324 | 732 | 49 | 10 | 10 | 8 | 13 | 21 | 14 | 17 |
| Steamed Clams | 1/2 | 523 | 20 | 2 | 49 | 611 | 349 | 31 | 40 | 24 | 15 | 15 | 9 | 11 | 27 |
| Stir-Fried Fish and Peppers | 1/4 | 477 | 25 | 69 | 11 | 1964 | 691 | 39 | 82 | 81 | 11 | 11 | 26 | 7 | 19 |
| Stuffed Flounder | 1/8 | 311 | 27 | 9 | 17 | 832 | 573 | 42 | 19 | 4 | 10 | 16 | 15 | 27 | 9 |
| Sweet-and-Sour Fish | 1/4 | 534 | 19 | 79 | 16 | 1080 | 533 | 30 | 33 | 62 | 12 | 7 | 14 | 3 | 11 |
| Trout Amandine | 1/4 | 528 | 27 | 15 | 40 | 427 | 458 | 41 | 71 | 6 | 20 | 19 | 23 | 8 | 8 |
| Tuna a la King | 1/6 | 524 | 23 | 21 | 38 | 1087 | 394 | 35 | 27 | 26 | 13 | 22 | 42 | 12 | 13 |
| Tuna-Noodle Casserole | 1/6 | 295 | 18 | 23 | 14 | 769 | 292 | 28 | 17 | 20 | 15 | 15 | 29 | 15 | 9 |
| Tuna-Vegetable Pie | 1/6 | 638 | 22 | 37 | 45 | 874 | 385 | 34 | 17 | 27 | 23 | 28 | 38 | 8 | 15 |
| Wild-Rice-Stuffed Fish | 1/6 | 355 | 26 | 18 | 20 | 722 | 495 | 40 | 65 | 21 | 22 | 20 | 28 | 5 | 11 |

# Fish

Add variety to your menus by including fish dishes often. Fish has a delicate flavor and tender texture. It's versatile and also cooks quickly. Use the following guidelines for buying, storing, and preparing fish.

## Buying

Before buying fish for any of the recipes in this chapter, become familiar with some of the more common forms. *Whole (or round) fish* are fish as they come from the water; they must be scaled and eviscerated (internal organs removed) before cooking. *Drawn fish* are eviscerated whole fish. *Dressed fish* have been eviscerated and scaled, with the head, tail, and fins usually removed; pan-dressed fish generally are smaller-size fish. *Fillets* are pieces of fish, usually boneless, cut lengthwise from the sides of the fish away from the backbone. *Steaks* are crosscut slices (⅝ to 1 inch thick) from a large, dressed fish with a cross-section of the backbone.

When buying fresh, whole fish, look for these characteristics: eyes should be clear, not cloudy; gills should be red; and flesh should be light pink to red and elastic, yet firm. Avoid fish with a strong odor and a dull, slimy skin. Ask to have the scales and fins removed if they're still present.

For fresh fillets and steaks, look for flesh with a firm, fresh appearance. Avoid pieces with a strong odor or dried edges.

When buying frozen fish, make sure the fish is solidly frozen and that the sides of a block of fish are straight, not curved in or out. The package should show no signs of frost and should be tightly sealed.

Canned fish is another market form, with tuna and salmon being most popular. Look on the can for the type of pack. Tuna is sold by size of pieces and may be labeled to indicate the packing medium, such as oil or water. Look on the salmon can for the variety. Check the tip on page 437 for suggested uses for the various packs of canned tuna and salmon.

To determine how much fish to buy, remember that an average serving consists of about 12 ounces whole fish, 8 ounces dressed or pan-dressed fish, 4 to 5 ounces fillets or steaks, or about 4 ounces fish sticks.

## Storing

Fresh fish is perishable and should be used as soon as possible after purchase. Tightly wrap in moisture-vaporproof material and refrigerate. Keep frozen fish at 0°F. or colder.

## Cooking

Baking, broiling, poaching, steaming, and frying are the popular ways of preparing fish. Almost any fish can be cooked by any of these methods if allowances are made for the fat content.

Fish are classified as lean (less than 5% fat) or fat fish. Lean fish include catfish, yellow perch, cod, haddock, flounder, sole, halibut, red snapper, sea and striped bass, and rockfish. To bake or broil these varieties, baste with melted butter or cook them in a sauce. Fat fish include lake and rainbow trout, whitefish, herring, mackerel, pompano, salmon, and tuna. These contain enough fat to make added moistening unnecessary.

### Test for doneness

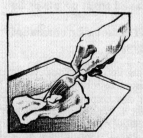

Insert fork tines into the fish at a 45-degree angle. Twist the fork gently (see illustration). If fish resists flaking and is still translucent, it's not done. If it flakes apart easily and is milky white, it's done. A dry and mealy texture indicates overcooked fish.

Cooking fish to the right doneness is important. Use the test in the tip below.

# Broiled Fish

*Broiled, 1-inch-thick salmon steaks, served with Dill Sauce.*
**2   pounds fresh or frozen fish fillets or steaks**
**2   tablespoons butter or margarine, melted,
       or Dill Sauce**

Thaw fish, if frozen. Preheat broiler. Cut fillets into 6 portions. Place fish in a single layer on a greased, unheated rack in a broiler pan or in a greased baking pan. Tuck under any thin edges. Brush *half* the melted butter or Dill Sauce over fish. Season buttered fish with salt and pepper. Broil fish 4 inches from heat until fish flakes easily when tested with a fork. Brush fish with remaining melted butter or Dill Sauce during cooking. Allow about 10 minutes for 1-inch-thick fillets or steaks. Makes 6 servings.
   ***Dill Sauce:*** In a small saucepan melt ¼ cup *butter;* stir in 1 tablespoon *lemon juice,* ½ teaspoon *salt,* ½ teaspoon dried *dillweed* or 1 teaspoon snipped *fresh dill,* and dash *pepper.*

# Pan-Fried Fish

**1   pound fresh or frozen fish fillets or steaks
       or three 10- to 12-ounce fresh or
       frozen pan-dressed trout or other fish**
**1   egg**
**⅔   cup fine dry bread crumbs or cornmeal
       Shortening for frying**

Thaw fish, if frozen. Cut fillets into 3 portions. Rinse pan-dressed fish; pat dry. In a shallow dish beat the egg; stir in 2 tablespoons *water.* In another dish combine bread crumbs or cornmeal, ½ teaspoon *salt,* and dash *pepper.* Dip fish into the egg mixture; coat both sides. Then roll fish in crumb mixture; coat evenly. In a large skillet heat ¼-inch-deep shortening.

Add the fish in a single layer. If fillets have skin on, fry skin side last. Fry fish on one side 6 to 7 minutes or till brown. Turn and fry 6 to 7 minutes longer. Fish is done when both sides are brown and crisp and when fish flakes easily when tested with a fork. (Thin fillets may require less total cooking time than pan-dressed fish.) Drain. Makes 3 servings.

## Oven-Fried Fish

    1   **pound fresh *or* frozen fish fillets *or* steaks**
            ***or* three 10- to 12-ounce fresh *or***
            **frozen pan-dressed trout *or* other fish**
    1   **beaten egg**
    ½   **cup fine dry bread crumbs**
    ¼   **cup butter *or* margarine, melted**
    1   **tablespoon lemon juice**                    Oven 500°

Thaw fish, if frozen. If using a fillet block, cut block into 3 portions. Dip fish into beaten egg, then into bread crumbs. Place coated fish in a well-greased, shallow baking pan. Sprinkle with salt and pepper. Drizzle a mixture of melted butter or margarine and lemon juice over fish. Bake in a 500° oven until golden and fish flakes easily when tested with a fork. Allow 5 to 6 minutes for each ½ inch of thickness. Makes 3 servings.

## Stir-Fried Fish and Peppers

    1   **pound fresh *or* frozen fish fillets**
    4   **tablespoons cornstarch**
    1   **medium sweet red *or* green pepper**
    1   **15¼-ounce can pineapple chunks (juice**
            **pack)**
    ¼   **cup soy sauce**
    ¼   **cup honey**
    ¼   **cup catsup**
    3   **tablespoons vinegar**
    3   **tablespoons dry sherry**
    3   **tablespoons cooking oil**
        **Hot cooked rice**

Thaw fish, if frozen. Cut into 1-inch pieces. Coat with *3 tablespoons* of the cornstarch; set aside. Cut pepper into ¾-inch squares; set aside. Drain pineapple, reserving juice. Combine pineapple juice, remaining 1 tablespoon cornstach, and dash *pepper.* Stir in soy, honey, catsup, vinegar, and sherry; set aside.

In a wok or electric skillet cook fish in hot oil about 1 minute on each side; remove from skillet. Add pepper squares; stir-fry 2 minutes. Remove peppers. Add pineapple juice mixture to pan; cook and stir till thickened and bubbly. Add pineapple to pan; stir in fish and pepper. Heat 1 minute. Serve over hot cooked rice. Makes 4 servings.

---

## Easy Baked Fish Fillets

**2  16-ounce packages frozen fish fillets**
**1  tablespoon cooking oil**
   **Bacon-Sour Cream Sauce**
   **Hot cooked noodles**
**¼  cup snipped parsley**                     Oven 450°

Let frozen blocks of fish stand at room temperature 20 minutes; cut each block into 4 portions. Place frozen fish in a greased shallow baking pan. Brush fish with the cooking oil. Sprinkle with salt. Bake, uncovered, in a 450° oven for 25 to 30 minutes or till fish flakes easily when tested with a fork. Meanwhile, prepare Bacon-Sour Cream Sauce. Serve fish and sauce over noodles. Sprinkle with parsley. Makes 8 servings.

**Microwave directions:** Cut fish into portions as above. Place frozen fish in a greased 12x7½x2-inch nonmetal baking dish. To thaw, cook, covered with waxed paper, in a counter-top microwave oven on high power for 2 minutes. Let stand 2 minutes. Micro-cook 1 minute; let stand 2 minutes. Again micro-cook 1 minute; let stand 2 minutes. Then, micro-cook about 30 seconds. (Turn fish over and give dish a half-turn halfway through defrosting.)

Brush thawed fish with cooking oil; sprinkle with salt. Micro-cook for 7 to 8 minutes or till fish flakes easily when tested with a fork, giving dish a half-turn after 4 minutes. Serve with sauce and noodles as above.

**Bacon-Sour Cream Sauce:** In a small saucepan heat one 10¾-ounce can condensed *cream of mushroom or celery soup* over low heat. Stir in 1 cup *dairy sour cream,* ¼ cup *milk,* and 6 slices *bacon,* crisp-cooked, drained, and crumbled. Heat sauce through.

---

## Baked Fillets and Steaks

Oven 450°

Use 2 pounds fresh *or* frozen *fish fillets or steaks.* Thaw fish, if frozen. Cut fillets into 6 portions. Place fish in a greased baking pan in a single layer with skin side down. Tuck under thin edges. Brush tops with 3 tablespoons melted *butter.* Season. Bake, uncovered, in a 450° oven until fish flakes easily when tested with a fork. Allow 5 to 6 minutes for each ½ inch of thickness. Makes 6 servings.

---

## Fish and Chips

- **1 pound fresh *or* frozen fish fillets**
- **1 pound potatoes, peeled (3)**
  **Shortening *or* cooking oil for deep-fat frying**
- **1 cup all-purpose flour**
- **½ cup milk**
- **1 egg**
- **2 tablespoons cooking oil**

Thaw fish, if frozen. Cut into 4 serving-size portions. Pat fish dry with paper toweling. Cut potatoes lengthwise into ⅜-inch-wide strips. Fry potatoes, about ¼ at a time, in deep hot fat (375°) for 7 to 8 minutes or till golden brown. Remove potatoes, drain, and keep warm while preparing fish.

Meanwhile, stir together ½ *cup* of the flour and ½ teaspoon *salt.* Add milk, egg, and the 2 tablespoons oil; beat till smooth. Dip fish into remaining ½ cup flour, then into batter.

Fry fish in deep hot fat (375°) about 2 minutes on each side or till golden brown. Drain. Sprinkle fish and chips with salt, if desired. To serve, sprinkle fish with malt vinegar, if desired. Makes 4 servings.

---

## Baked Fish with Mushrooms

---

**4**   **fresh or frozen fish fillets *or* steaks**
**2**   **slices bacon**
**1**   **cup sliced fresh mushrooms *or* one 6-ounce can sliced mushrooms, drained**
**½**   **cup green onion bias-sliced into 1-inch lengths**
**3**   **tablespoons butter *or* margarine**
**¼**   **teaspoon dried tarragon, crushed**
    **Paprika**            Oven 350°

Thaw fish, if frozen. In a skillet cook bacon; reserve drippings. Crumble bacon; set aside. Cook mushrooms and onion in drippings till tender. Place fish in a 12x7½x2-inch baking dish; sprinkle with salt. Combine mushrooms, onion, butter, and tarragon. Spread atop fish; sprinkle with paprika. Bake in a 350° oven 15 to 20 minutes or till fish flakes easily when tested with a fork. (Thin fillets will bake in less time.) Garnish with the crumbled bacon. Makes 4 servings.

---

## Stacked Sole

---

**2**   **pounds fresh or frozen sole fillets *or* other fish fillets**
**2**   **cups sliced fresh mushrooms**
**3**   **tablespoons sliced green onion**
**1**   **clove garlic, minced**
**2**   **tablespoons butter *or* margarine**
**1**   **6½-ounce can minced clams, drained**
**2**   **tablespoons snipped parsley**
**1**   **tablespoon lemon juice**
**¾**   **teaspoon dried oregano, crushed**
**¼**   **teaspoon salt**
    **Shrimp Sauce**           Oven 350°

Thaw fish, if frozen. In a skillet cook mushrooms, onion, and garlic in butter till tender but not brown. Remove from heat. Stir in drained clams, parsley, lemon juice, the oregano, salt, and ⅛ teaspoon *pepper*. In a 13x9x2-inch baking dish lay *half* of the fish fillets in a single layer. Spoon mushroom mixture over each fillet. Stack remaining fillets over top. Baked, covered, in a 350° oven for 25 minutes. Uncover; bake 10 to 15 minutes more or till fish flakes easily when tested with a fork. With a slotted spatula, transfer fish stacks to a serving platter. Spoon Shrimp Sauce over. Garnish with cherry tomatoes and endive or parsley, if desired. Serves 6 to 8.

**Shrimp Sauce:** In a saucepan melt 2 tablespoons *butter or margarine*. Stir in 1 tablespoon *lemon juice* and, if desired, 2 tablespoons snipped *parsley*. Drain one 4½-ounce can *tiny shrimp*; stir shrimp into butter mixture. Heat sauce through.

# Bundled Fish

|   |   |
|---|---|
| 1 | **16-ounce package frozen fish fillets** |
| 1 | **cup finely chopped onion** |
| 1 | **cup finely chopped carrot** |
| 1 | **cup thinly sliced fresh mushrooms** |
| 2 | **tablespoons butter or margarine** |
| ⅓ | **cup plain yogurt** |
| ½ | **teaspoon salt** |
| ½ | **teaspoon dried dillweed** |
| ¼ | **teaspoon pepper** |
| 1 | **package (8) refrigerated crescent rolls** |
| 1 | **beaten egg** |
| 1 | **tablespoon water** |

. . .

|   |   |   |
|---|---|---|
| ¼ | **cup chopped green onion** | |
| 2 | **tablespoons butter or margarine** | |
| 1 | **tablespoon cornstarch** | |
| 1 | **cup chicken broth** | |
| ¼ | **teaspoon finely shredded lemon peel** | |
| 2 | **teaspoons lemon juice** | Oven 350° |

Thaw fish fillets; drain well on paper toweling. In a shallow baking pan arrange fish pieces to make four portions, about 4x3 inches each.

In a saucepan cook onion, carrot, and mushrooms in 2 tablespoons butter or margarine, covered, about 5 minutes. Uncover; simmer 2 minutes or till liquid has evaporated. Stir in yogurt, salt, dillweed, and pepper.

Unroll crescent rolls. Press 2 triangles of dough together to form a 6x4-inch rectangle; repeat with remaining dough to make a total of 4 rectangles. Spoon ¼ of the vegetable mixture (about ⅓ cup) over each fish portion. Top each with a rectangle of dough. Brush dough with a mixture of egg and water. Cut slits in tops of dough for escape of steam. Bake in a 350° oven for 30 to 35 minutes or till browned.

Meanwhile, in a saucepan cook green onion in 2 tablespoons butter or margarine till tender but not brown. Stir in cornstarch. Add chicken broth all at once. Cook and stir till sauce is thickened and bubbly. Cook and stir 1 to 2 minutes more. Stir in the lemon peel and juice. Serve fish bundles with the lemon sauce. Makes 4 servings.

---

### Thawing fish

Place the frozen wrapped package in the refrigerator. A 16-ounce package takes about 24 hours to thaw. For faster thawing (1 to 2 hours per 1-pound package), set the wrapped package under cold running water. *Do not thaw the fish at room temperature or in warm water; do not refreeze fish. Also, do not thaw breaded fish portions.*

## Stuffed Flounder

*An elegant entrée for a special occasion—*

**2** **pounds fresh *or* frozen flounder fillets (8 fillets)***
**1** **3-ounce can chopped mushrooms**
**¼** **cup chopped onion**
**¼** **cup butter *or* margarine**
**1** **7-ounce can crab meat, drained, flaked, and cartilage removed**
**½** **cup coarsely crushed saltine crackers**
**2** **tablespoons snipped parsley**
**½** **teaspoon salt**
 **Dash pepper**

• • •

**3** **tablespoons butter *or* margarine**
**3** **tablespoons all-purpose flour**
**¼** **teaspoon salt**
 **Milk**
**⅓** **cup dry white wine**
**1** **cup shredded Swiss cheese (4 ounces)**
 **Paprika**                                   Oven 400°

Thaw fish, if frozen. Drain mushrooms, reserving liquid. In a skillet cook onion in ¼ cup butter or margarine about 3 minutes or till tender but not brown. Stir drained mushrooms into skillet with flaked crab, cracker crumbs, parsley, ½ teaspoon salt, and the pepper. Spread filling lengthwise over flounder fillets. Fold fillets over filling, tucking fish under. Place the filled fish fillets, seam side down, in a 12x7½x2-inch baking dish.

In a saucepan melt 3 tablespoons butter or margarine. Stir in flour and ¼ teaspoon salt. Add enough milk to mushroom liquid to make 1½ cups total liquid. Add liquid mixture with wine to saucepan. Cook and stir till sauce is thickened and bubbly. Pour sauce over fillets. Bake, uncovered, in a 400° oven about 30 minutes or till fish flakes easily when tested with a fork. Sprinkle with Swiss cheese and paprika. Return to oven. Bake 5 minutes longer or till cheese is melted. Makes 8 servings.

*If fish fillets are in pieces, press fish together to form 8 whole pieces.

## Fish Creole

1 **pound fresh or frozen fish fillets**
½ **cup chopped onion**
½ **cup chopped green pepper**
1 **clove garlic, minced**
¼ **cup butter or margarine**
1 **16-ounce can tomatoes, cut up**
1 **tablespoon dried parsley flakes**
1 **tablespoon instant chicken bouillon granules**
¼ **teaspoon bottled hot pepper sauce**
1 **tablespoon cornstarch**
1 **tablespoon cold water**
**Hot cooked rice**

Thaw fish, if frozen. In a 10-inch skillet cook onion, green pepper, and garlic in butter or margarine till tender but not brown. Add *undrained* tomatoes, parsley flakes, bouillon granules, and hot pepper sauce. Simmer, covered, for 10 minutes. Stir together cornstarch and cold water. Stir into tomato mixture. Cook and stir till thickened and bubbly. Cut fish into 1-inch pieces. Add fish to tomato mixture, stirring to coat. Return to boiling; reduce heat. Simmer, covered, for 5 to 7 minutes or till fish flakes easily when tested with a fork. Serve fish mixture over rice. Makes 4 servings.

**Microwave directions:** To thaw frozen fish, place unwrapped fish in a nonmetal dish or pie plate. Cook in a counter-top microwave oven on high power for 2 minutes or till nearly thawed, turning fish over once.

In a 2-quart nonmetal casserole combine onion, green pepper, garlic, and butter or margarine. Micro-cook, covered, for 2 minutes. Add *undrained* tomatoes, parsley flakes, bouillon granules, and hot pepper sauce. Micro-cook, covered, 5 minutes. Stir together cornstarch and cold water; stir into tomato mixture. Micro-cook, covered, 2 minutes more or till thick, stirring once. Cut fish into 1-inch pieces. Add fish to tomato mixture, stirring to coat. Micro-cook, covered, 3 to 4 minutes or till fish flakes easily when tested with a fork, stirring once. Serve fish mixture over rice.

## An alternate poaching pan

If a poaching pan and rack are not available, you can poach a whole fish in a large roasting pan. Just wrap the fish in the cheesecloth as direct-ed in the recipe. Then, lay the wrapped fish on two wide strips of dou-bled foil. Use the foil strips to transfer the fish to and from the roasting pan.

## Poached Fish with Dill Sauce

|   |   |
|---|---|
| 1 | **3-pound fresh *or* frozen dressed fish** |
| 2 | **cups water** |
| 3 | **lemon slices** |
| 1 | **bay leaf** |
| ¼ | **teaspoon dried tarragon, crushed** |
| 2 | **tablespoons butter *or* margarine** |
| 4 | **teaspoons all-purpose flour** |
| 2 | **teaspoons lemon juice** |
| ½ | **teaspoon sugar** |
| ½ | **teaspoon dried dillweed** |
| 1 | **beaten egg yolk** |

Thaw fish, if frozen. Place fish on a large piece of cheesecloth; overlap cheesecloth on top of fish. Place fish on rack of a poaching pan; place in pan. Add water, lemon slices, bay leaf, tarragon, and 1 teaspoon *salt*. Cover and simmer for 25 to 30 minutes. Fish is done when it flakes easily when tested with a fork (fold back cheesecloth to test). Remove fish from pan; wrap in foil to keep warm.

Reserve 1 cup cooking liquid for dill sauce; strain to remove herbs and lemon slices. In a saucepan melt butter. Stir in flour. Add reserved liquid, lemon juice, sugar, dillweed, and dash *salt*. Cook and stir till thickened and bubbly. Gradually stir about ½ *cup* of the mixture into beaten egg yolk; return all to hot mixture in saucepan. Cook and stir 1 to 2 minutes more. Set aside; keep warm.

Pull foil and cloth away from fish; carefully remove and discard skin. Transfer fish to a platter using 2 large spatulas. Top with some dill sauce; pass remaining. Serves 6.

## Corn-Stuffed Fish

    1   **3-pound fresh or frozen dressed whitefish**
        **or other fish, boned**
    1   **tablespoon butter or margarine**
    ¼   **cup chopped onion**
    3   **tablespoons chopped green pepper**
    1   **12-ounce can whole kernel corn, drained**
    1   **cup soft bread crumbs (1½ slices)**
    2   **tablespoons chopped pimiento**
    ½   **teaspoon salt**
    ¼   **teaspoon dried thyme, crushed**
                • • •
    1   **to 2 tablespoons cooking oil**       Oven 350°

Thaw fish, if frozen; pat dry with paper toweling. Place in a well-greased shallow baking pan; sprinkle cavity generously with salt.

For corn stuffing, in a medium saucepan melt the butter or margarine. Add onion and green pepper; cook about 5 minutes or till onion is tender. Stir in corn, bread crumbs, pimiento, salt, and thyme; mix well.

Stuff fish cavity loosely with corn mixture. Brush skin of fish with cooking oil. Cover loosely with foil. Bake in a 350° oven for 45 to 60 minutes or till fish flakes easily when tested with a fork. Use two large spatulas to transfer whole fish to a serving platter. Makes 6 servings.

*Wild-Rice-Stuffed Fish:* Prepare Corn-Stuffed Fish as above, *except* omit the corn stuffing ingredients. Instead, prepare wild rice stuffing. Cook one 4-ounce package (about ⅔ cup) *wild rice,* covered, according to package directions. Cook 1 cup sliced fresh *mushrooms* in ¼ cup *butter or margarine* till tender. Combine the cooked rice; cooked mushrooms; 1 cup frozen *peas,* thawed; ½ teaspoon finely shredded *lemon peel;* 2 tablespoons *lemon juice;* 2 tablespoons sliced *green onion;* 2 tablespoons chopped *pimiento;* 1 teaspoon *salt;* and ⅛ teaspoon *pepper*. Toss lightly. Fill fish cavity with *half* of the stuffing, patting stuffing to flatten evenly. (Place remaining stuffing in a 1-quart casserole and bake, covered, with the fish.) Brush skin of fish with cooking oil. Cover loosely with foil. Bake in a 350° oven and continue as directed.

# Trout Amandine

**4** **to 6 fresh *or* frozen pan-dressed trout (about 8 ounces each)**
**1** **beaten egg**
**¼** **cup light cream *or* milk**
**½** **cup all-purpose flour**
**2** **tablespoons cooking oil**
**6** **tablespoons butter *or* margarine**
**¼** **cup sliced almonds**
**2** **tablespoons lemon juice**

Thaw fish, if frozen. Bone trout, if desired. Season. Combine egg and cream or milk. Dip fish in flour, then in egg-cream mixture, and again in flour. In a large skillet heat together the oil and *2 tablespoons* of the butter. Fry trout in hot oil mixture for 5 to 6 minutes on each side or till golden and fish flakes easily with a fork. In a skillet cook almonds in remaining butter till nuts are golden brown. Remove from heat; stir in lemon juice. Place trout on a platter; pour almond mixture over. Serves 4 to 6.

## Sherry-Sauced Halibut

        2  **pounds fresh or frozen halibut steaks or**
           **other fish steaks**
        2  **tablespoons butter, melted**
      ¼  **cup finely chopped onion**
        1  **small clove garlic, minced**
        1  **tablespoon butter or margarine**
        1  **tablespoon all-purpose flour**
      ¼  **cup dairy sour cream**
      ½  **cup chicken broth**
        1  **2½-ounce jar sliced mushrooms**
        1  **tablespoon dry sherry**

Thaw fish, if frozen. Preheat broiler. Cut fish into 6 portions. Place in a single layer on a greased, unheated rack of broiler pan or in a greased baking pan. Brush with *half* of the melted butter; sprinkle with 1 teaspoon *salt* and dash *pepper*. Broil fish 4 inches from heat for 5 to 8 minutes; turn. Brush with remaining melted butter. Broil 5 to 8 minutes longer or till fish flakes easily with a fork.

In a saucepan cook onion and garlic in 1 tablespoon butter till tender. Stir flour into sour cream; stir in broth. Add to saucepan. Cook and stir till bubbly. Drain mushrooms. Stir mushrooms and sherry into sauce; heat through. Serve sauce over fish. Serves 6.

## Baked Fish a l'Orange

        2  **pounds fresh or frozen halibut steaks or**
           **other fish steaks**
      ½  **cup finely chopped onion**
        2  **cloves garlic, minced**
        2  **tablespoons cooking oil**
        2  **tablespoons snipped parsley**
      ½  **cup orange juice**
        1  **tablespoon lemon juice**                    Oven 400°

Thaw fish, if frozen. Arrange in a 12x7½x2-inch baking dish. Cook onion and garlic in oil till onion is tender but not brown. Stir in parsley, 1 teaspoon *salt,* and ⅛ teaspoon *pepper.* Spread mixture over fish. Combine orange and lemon juices; pour evenly over all. Bake, covered, in a 400° oven for 20 to 25 minutes or till fish flakes easily with a fork. If desired, arrange hard-cooked egg wedges atop fish, sprinkle with paprika, and garnish with orange slices. Makes 6 servings.

## Lemon-Marinated Salmon Steaks

**2 pounds fresh or frozen salmon steaks**
½ **cup lemon juice**
⅓ **cup sliced green onion**
¼ **cup cooking oil**
3 **tablespoons snipped parsley**
3 **tablespoons chopped green pepper**
1 **tablespoon sugar**
2 **teaspoons dry mustard**
⅛ **teaspoon cayenne**

Thaw fish, if frozen. Bring 1 cup *water* to boiling in a 10-inch skillet or fish poacher with tight-fitting cover. Sprinkle salmon with a little salt. Place *half* of the fish on a greased rack in a pan so fish does not touch water. Cover pan tightly and steam for 5 to 7 minutes or till fish flakes easily when tested with a fork. Carefully remove fish to a shallow dish. Repeat with remaining fish.

In a screw-top jar combine remaining ingredients and ¾ teaspoon *salt.* Shake vigorously to combine. Pour over fish. Cover; chill several hours or overnight, spooning mixture over fish several times. Drain before serving and spoon vegetables over fish. Serves 6.

## Quick Fish-Potato Supper

|       |                                                                        |           |
| ----- | ---------------------------------------------------------------------- | --------- |
| 1     | 12-ounce package frozen loose-pack hashed brown potatoes, thawed       |           |
| 4     | beaten eggs                                                            |           |
| 2     | cups milk                                                              |           |
| 1     | tablespoon minced dried onion                                         |           |
| 1¼    | teaspoons seasoned salt                                                |           |
| 1     | teaspoon dried dillweed                                                |           |
| ⅛     | teaspoon pepper                                                        |           |
| 1     | cup shredded American cheese                                          |           |
| 1     | 14-ounce package frozen fish sticks                                   | Oven 350° |

Break up potatoes; set aside. In a bowl combine eggs, milk, onion, seasoned salt, dillweed, and pepper. Stir in potatoes and cheese. Turn into a 12x7½x2-inch baking dish. Arrange fish sticks atop. Bake in a 350° oven for 55 to 60 minutes or till center is nearly set. Let stand 10 minutes before serving. Serves 6.

## Sweet-and-Sour Fish

|       |                                               |
| ----- | --------------------------------------------- |
| 1     | 14-ounce package frozen fish sticks          |
| ¾     | cup finely chopped green pepper               |
| ½     | cup finely chopped carrot                     |
| 1     | clove garlic, minced                          |
| 2     | tablespoons cooking oil                       |
| ¾     | cup sugar                                     |
| ½     | cup red wine vinegar                          |
| 1     | tablespoon soy sauce                          |
| 1½    | teaspoons instant chicken bouillon granules   |
| 3     | tablespoons cornstarch                        |
|       | Hot cooked rice                               |

Bake fish sticks following package directions; cut into 1-inch pieces. Meanwhile, in a 3-quart saucepan cook green pepper, carrot, and garlic in oil till tender. Add sugar, vinegar, soy, bouillon granules, and 1¾ cups *water*. Bring to boiling; boil rapidly 1 minute. Mix cornstarch and ¼ cup *cold water;* stir into hot mixture. Cook and stir till bubbly. Stir in fish. Serve over rice. Serves 4 to 6.

## Curried Fishwiches

>  2 **eggs**
>  6 **English muffins, split**
>    **Butter *or* margarine**
>  2 **8-ounce packages frozen fish sticks**
>  3 **tablespoons butter *or* margarine**
>  3 **tablespoons all-purpose flour**
>  ¾ **teaspoon curry powder**
>  ¾ **teaspoon dry mustard**
>  2¼ **cups milk**
>  1 **teaspoon minced dried onion**
>  1 **cup cubed *or* shredded American cheese (4 ounces)**
>  1 **tablespoon lemon juice**

Preheat broiler. In a saucepan cover eggs with cold water. Bring to boiling. Reduce heat to just below simmering. Cover; cook 15 minutes.

Meanwhile, toast muffins under broiler; remove and spread with butter. Broil fish sticks 4 inches from heat for 4 to 6 minutes.

Meanwhile, melt the 3 tablespoons butter. Stir in flour, curry, mustard, ½ teaspoon *salt,* and ⅛ teaspoon *pepper*. Add milk and onion. Cook and stir till mixture thickens. Stir in cheese; heat and stir till melted. Cool eggs under cold running water. Peel and chop eggs; stir into sauce. Drizzle fish with lemon juice. Place fish on muffin bottoms; spoon sauce over. Add muffin tops or serve open-faced. Makes 6 servings.

## Fish Florentine

|   |   |   |
|---|---|---|
| **6** | **frozen breaded fish portions** | |
| **1** | **10-ounce package frozen chopped spinach** | |
| **1** | **11-ounce can condensed cheddar cheese soup** | |
| **1** | **8-ounce can water chestnuts, drained and coarsely chopped** | |
| **3** | **tablespoons bacon bits** | Oven 350° |

Prepare fish following package directions. Cook spinach following package directions; drain well. In a saucepan stir soup, water chestnuts, and bacon bits into spinach; heat through. Turn into a 10x6x2-inch baking dish or 1½-quart casserole. Top with fish. Bake in a 350° oven for 10 minutes or till hot. Serve with halved lemon slices, if desired. Serves 6.

# Shellfish

Popular shellfish varieties include shrimp, lobster, crab, oysters, clams, scallops, and mussels. Below are some tips for buying, storing, and cooking the various types.

## Buying

Fresh shellfish may be sold live, partially prepared, or cooked and ready for eating. Shellfish also is available frozen and canned.

Fresh, live shellfish should show signs of life. Crabs and lobsters should actively move their legs, and live oysters and hard-shelled clams should close their shells when tapped lightly.

Partially prepared shellfish include shelled scallops, oysters, clams, and mussels packed in a clear liquid. Shrimp also are sold partially prepared (their heads have been removed).

Cooked shellfish are sold as whole cooked crab, lobster, and shrimp, as well as ready-to-eat meat in several forms.

Frozen shellfish is available cooked or uncooked, and in or out of the shell. Select tightly packaged shellfish without frost.

Canned shellfish is sold as whole shellfish, as pieces of meat, and as smoked meat. Shellfish may be vacuum-packed or packed in liquid.

An average shellfish portion consists of 15 to 20 clams in shells; ½ to 1 whole Dungeness crab; 1 whole lobster or an 8-ounce lobster tail; ½ to ¾ cup shucked clams or oysters; 4 to 5 ounces scallops; or 4 ounces shelled shrimp.

## Storing

Cook live shellfish at once and use the cooked meat as soon as possible. Keep shellfish refrigerated. See page 273 for freezing instructions.

## Cooking

Shellfish can be boiled, broiled, baked, steamed, or fried, following specific recipes. When done, shelled oysters, mussels, and clams will curl around the edges (or, if they're cooked in their shells, the shell will open). Lobster and shrimp will turn bright pink or red when properly cooked.

## Boiled Lobster

### 2  1- to 1½-pound live lobsters

In a large kettle combine 12 cups *water* and 1 tablespoon *salt*. Bring to boiling. Choose active live lobsters. Holding a lobster just behind the eyes, rinse in cold running water. Plunge it headfirst into boiling salted water. Repeat with other lobster. Return to boiling; reduce heat and simmer, uncovered, over low heat 20 minutes. Remove lobsters.

Place each cooked lobster on its back. With a sharp knife, cut lobsters in half lengthwise up to the tail section, leaving shell back intact, if desired. With kitchen shears or a knife, cut away membrane on tail. Remove back vein and body organs except the red coral roe and the liver. Crack open the large claws; break away from body. Serve lobster in shell with melted butter, if desired, or use meat for salads or other main dishes. Use a small fork or seafood fork to remove meat from claws, tail, and body. Pull smaller claws from body and gently suck out meat. Makes 2 servings or about 2 cups meat.

---

## Shellfish equivalents

You can substitute one kind of shellfish for another by using these equivalents:

**Clams:** 18 clams in shells = 1 pint shucked clams = two 7½-ounce cans minced clams

**Crab:** 1 pound crab legs in shell = one 6-ounce package frozen crab meat = one 7-ounce can crab meat = 1 cup cooked, flaked crab meat

**Lobster:** One 16-ounce whole lobster or 8-ounce tail = 4 to 5 ounces (1 cup) cooked lobster meat = one 5-ounce can lobster

**Oysters:** 24 oysters in shells = 1 pint shucked oysters

**Shrimp:** 12 ounces raw shrimp in shells = 8 ounces raw, shelled shrimp = one 4½-ounce can shrimp = 1 cup cooked, shelled shrimp

---

## Boiled Shellfish

*A basic way to prepare shellfish, especially when the meat will be used in other recipes—*

**Shrimp:** Heat 6 cups *water* and 2 tablespoons *salt* to boiling. Add 2 pounds fresh or frozen *shelled or unshelled shrimp;* simmer 1 to 3 minutes or till shrimp turn pink. Drain. Makes 6 to 8 servings.

**Scallops:** Heat 4 cups *water* and 2 teaspoons *salt* to

boiling. Add 2 pounds fresh or thawed frozen *scallops*. Simmer for 1 minute or till scallops are opaque. Drain. Serves 8.

**Lobster Tails:** Heat to boiling enough *salted water* to cover 2 pounds frozen *lobster tails*. Simmer the 3-ounce tails for 3 to 4 minutes; the 6-ounce tails for 8 minutes; or the 8-ounce tails for 11 minutes. Drain. Makes about 4 servings.

**Crabs:** Heat to boiling enough *salted water* to cover 2 pounds *crabs*. Plunge live, scrubbed Dungeness or hard-shell blue crabs into boiling water. Simmer Dungeness crabs 8 minutes per pound; simmer blue crabs for 15 minutes. Drain. Makes about 2 servings.

## Fried Clams, Oysters, or Scallops

> 2 **cups shucked clams *or* oysters, *or* fresh *or* frozen scallops, thawed**
> ⅓ **cup all-purpose flour**
> ½ **teaspoon salt**
> ⅛ **teaspoon pepper**
> 2 **beaten eggs**
> ¾ **cup finely crushed saltine crackers or fine dry bread crumbs**
> **Shortening *or* cooking oil for deep-fat frying**

Drain clams, oysters, or scallops. (If scallops are large, slice in half.) Gently pat dry with paper toweling. In a shallow bowl stir together flour, salt, and pepper. Roll seafood in seasoned flour. Dip coated seafood in a mixture of beaten eggs and 2 tablespoons *water,* then roll in cracker or bread crumbs. Fry in deep hot fat (375°) till golden. Allow about 1 minute for clams; about 1½ minutes for oysters; and about 2 minutes for scallops. Drain on paper toweling. Serve fried seafood with tartar sauce or cocktail sauce, if desired. Makes 4 servings.

# Broiled Shrimp

>   2   **pounds fresh *or* frozen large shrimp in
>        shells**
>  ¼   **cup butter *or* margarine, melted**
>   2   **tablespoons lemon juice**
>       **Dash bottled hot pepper sauce**

Thaw shrimp, if frozen. Remove shells and devein. Combine
butter, lemon juice, and hot pepper sauce. Brush some mixture over shrimp.

To broil in the oven, place shrimp on a well-greased broiler
rack and broil 4 to 5 inches from heat for 4 minutes. Turn and
brush with butter mixture. Broil 2 to 4 minutes more or till
shrimp are done. To cook on an outdoor grill, thread shrimp
on skewers and grill over *hot* coals for 4 minutes. Turn and
brush with butter mixture. Grill 4 to 5 minutes more or till
shrimp are done. Season shrimp lightly with salt. Makes 6
servings.

# French-Fried Shrimp

>   1   **cup all-purpose flour**
>  ½   **teaspoon sugar**
>   1   **beaten egg**
>   2   **tablespoons cooking oil**
>   2   **pounds fresh *or* frozen shrimp in shells**
>       **All-purpose flour**
>       **Shortening *or* cooking oil for deep-fat
>        frying**

For batter, stir together the 1 cup flour, the sugar, and ½
teaspoon *salt*. Make a well in the center. Combine egg, the 2
tablespoons oil, and 1 cup *cold water;* pour into dry ingredients. Beat with a rotary beater till smooth.

Peel shrimp, leaving last section and tail intact. With a sharp
knife, make a shallow slit along back of shrimp. If present,
remove sandy black vein. Make a deeper slit in the shrimp's
back, cutting almost all the way through the shrimp to butterfly

it. Pat dry with paper toweling. Dip shrimp in flour to coat. Dip flour-coated shrimp into batter.

In a saucepan or deep-fat fryer, heat shortening or oil to 375°. Fry a few shrimp at a time in the hot fat for 2 to 3 minutes or till golden. Remove from fat with a slotted spoon; drain on paper toweling. Keep hot in a warm oven while frying remaining shrimp. Serves 6 to 8.

## Shrimp Chow Mein

  1   **pound fresh or frozen shelled shrimp**
  ¼   **cup soy sauce**
  2   **tablespoons cornstarch**
  1½  **teaspoons instant chicken bouillon
        granules**
  1   **cup boiling water**
  2   **tablespoons cooking oil**
  1   **tablespoon cooking oil**
  1   **small onion, halved and sliced**
  1   **cup sliced fresh mushrooms**
  1   **clove garlic, minced**
  1   **16-ounce can bean sprouts, drained, or
        2 cups fresh bean sprouts**
  1   **8-ounce can water chestnuts, sliced**
  1   **6-ounce package frozen pea pods, thawed
        and halved crosswise**
  ⅓   **cup toasted slivered almonds
        Hot cooked rice or chow mein noodles**

Thaw shrimp, if frozen; halve large shrimp lengthwise. Stir soy sauce into cornstarch. Dissolve bouillon granules in the boiling water; stir into soy mixture. Set aside.

In a 10-inch skillet or wok heat the 2 tablespoons oil till hot. Stir-fry shrimp in hot oil 5 to 7 minutes or till almost done. Remove shrimp and set aside. Add remaining 1 tablespoon oil to pan. Add onion, mushrooms, and garlic. Stir-fry about 2 minutes or till crisp-tender. Remove vegetables. Add bean sprouts and water chestnuts; stir-fry about 1 minute. Return shrimp and the onion mixture to skillet. Stir soy sauce mixture and add to skillet or wok. Cook and stir till mixture is thickened and bubbly. Stir in pea pods and almonds; heat through. Serve over rice or chow mein noodles. Pass additional soy sauce, if desired. Makes 4 servings.

## Steamed Clams

- **24  soft-shelled clams in shells**
- **3  gallons cold water**
- **1  cup salt**
- **1  cup hot water**
   **Butter, melted**

Thoroughly wash clams. In a large kettle combine *1 gallon* of the cold water and ⅓ *cup* of the salt. Place clams in salt-water mixture and let stand 15 minutes. Rinse well. Repeat salt-water soaking and rinsing twice more. Place clams on a rack in a kettle with the hot water. Cover tightly and steam about 5 minutes or just till shells open. Discard any clams that do not open. Loosen clams from shells. Serve with melted butter. Serves 2 to 4.

## Lobster Newburg

- **¼  cup butter *or* margarine**
- **2  tablespoons all-purpose flour**
- **1½  cups light cream**
- **3  beaten egg yolks**
- **2  5-ounce cans lobster, drained, broken into large pieces, and cartilage removed, *or* 10 ounces cooked lobster**
- **3  tablespoons dry white wine**
- **2  teaspoons lemon juice**
- **¼  teaspoon salt**
   **Paprika**
- **4  baked patty shells**

Melt butter or margarine in a saucepan; stir in flour. Add cream all at once. Cook and stir till thickened and bubbly. Stir about *half* of the hot mixture into egg yolks; return to hot mixture. Cook and stir till thickened but *do not boil.* Add lobster; heat through. Stir in wine, lemon juice, and salt. Sprinkle with a little paprika. Spoon into patty shells. Garnish with fresh parsley sprigs, if desired. Serves 4.

**Crab Newburg:** Prepare Lobster Newburg as above, *except* substitute two 7-ounce cans *crab meat,* drained, flaked, and cartilage removed, *or* two 6-ounce packages frozen *crab meat,* thawed, for the lobster. Continue as directed.

**Shrimp Newburg:** Prepare Lobster Newburg as above, *except* substitute 1½ cups cooked shelled *shrimp or* two 4½-ounce cans *shrimp,* drained, for the lobster. Continue.

---

# Tuna-Noodle Casserole

---

*A home-style casserole—*

> **4** **ounces medium noodles (3 cups) *or* one**
>    **8-ounce package frozen noodles**
> **1** **cup chopped celery**
> **¼** **cup chopped onion**
> **2** **tablespoons butter *or* margarine**
> **2** **tablespoons all-purpose flour**
> **1** **11-ounce can condensed cheddar cheese**
>    **soup *or* one 10¾-ounce can condensed**
>    **cream of mushroom soup**
> **¾** **cup milk**
> **1** **9¼-ounce can tuna, drained and flaked**
> **¼** **cup chopped pimiento**
> **¼** **cup grated Parmesan cheese**          Oven 375°

Cook noodles according to package directions; drain and set aside.

Meanwhile, in a saucepan cook celery and onion in butter or margarine till tender but not brown. Stir in the flour; stir in condensed soup. Gradually stir in milk. Cook and stir till mixture is thickened and bubbly. Carefully stir in the tuna, pimiento, and the cooked and drained noodles.

Turn noodle mixture into a 1½-quart casserole. Sprinkle the Parmesan cheese over top of mixture. Bake, uncovered, in a 375° oven for 20 to 25 minutes. Garnish with sprigs of parsley, if desired. Makes 6 servings.

**Microwave directions:** On range top cook noodles according to package directions; drain and set aside. Meanwhile, in a 1½-quart nonmetal casserole cook celery and onion in butter, covered, in a counter-top microwave oven on high power for 4 to 5 minutes or till tender, stirring the mixture twice. Stir in flour; stir in condensed soup and the milk.

Micro-cook, uncovered, about 4 to 5 minutes or till mixture is thickened and bubbly, stirring after each minute. Carefully stir in tuna, pimiento, and cooked noodles. Micro-cook, uncovered, for 3 to 4 minutes or till mixture is heated through, stirring after 2 minutes. Stir. Sprinkle the Parmesan cheese over top.

---

## Individual Tuna Pies

|   |   |
|---|---|
| ½ | **cup chopped onion** |
| ¼ | **cup butter *or* margarine** |
| ½ | **cup all-purpose flour** |
| 2 | **teaspoons instant chicken bouillon granules** |
| ¼ | **teaspoon salt** |
| ¼ | **teaspoon dried thyme, crushed** |
| ⅛ | **teaspoon pepper** |
| 1¾ | **cups milk** |
| 1½ | **cups water** |
| 2 | **6½-ounce cans tuna, drained and flaked, or one 16-ounce can salmon, drained, bones and skin removed, and flaked** |
| 1 | **cup frozen mixed vegetables, cooked and drained** |
| 3 | **tablespoons snipped parsley** |
| 1 | **package (6) refrigerated biscuits** |

Oven 400°

Cook onion in butter till tender but not brown. Stir in flour, bouillon granules, salt, thyme, and pepper. Add milk and water. Cook and stir till thickened and bubbly. Stir in fish, cooked vegetables, and the parsley; heat till bubbly. Immediately pour mixture into 6 individual casseroles. Quarter biscuits; quickly place 4 pieces atop *hot* filling in each casserole.

(*Or,* pour mixture into a 1½-quart casserole. Halve biscuits; place pieces atop hot filling.) Bake in a 400° oven about 10 to 12 minutes or till biscuits are lightly browned. Makes 6 servings.

---

## Canned seafood

Canned tuna is packed in various-size pieces. Use fancy or solid pack when appearance is important. Chunk-style is good for casseroles, and grated or flaked tuna is appropriate for sandwich spreads.

Salmon is packed in cans according to species. The deeper red species, such as Chinook and sockeye, break into chunks and are good to use for salads. Chum and pink are best for loaves and patties because they break into smaller flakes.

---

## Baked Tuna Patties

¼ **cup finely chopped celery**
6 **tablespoons butter or margarine**
3 **tablespoons all-purpose flour**
¼ **teaspoon paprika**
¾ **cup milk**
1 **9¼-ounce can tuna, drained**
2 **cups soft bread crumbs**
2 **tablespoons chopped green onion**
1 **egg**
⅔ **cup finely crushed round cheese crackers (about 20)**                     Oven 350°

For sauce, in a saucepan cook celery in *3 tablespoons* of the butter till tender. Stir in flour, paprika, and ¼ teaspoon *salt.* Stir in milk. Cook and stir till thickened and bubbly. Cool slightly. Flake tuna. Mix into sauce with bread crumbs and onion. Form into eight 2½-inch patties. Beat together egg and 1 tablespoon *water.* Dip patties into egg mixture, then into crackers. Place in a lightly greased 11x7x1½-inch baking pan. Melt remaining butter. Drizzle over patties. Bake in a 350° oven for 20 to 25 minutes or till golden. Makes 4 servings.

## Tuna a la King

|   |   |
|---|---|
| 3 | beaten egg yolks |
| ¼ | cup butter or margarine, softened |
| ½ | teaspoon paprika |
| 1 | cup fresh mushrooms |
| ¼ | cup chopped green pepper |
| ¼ | cup chopped onion |
| 2 | tablespoons butter or margarine |
| 2 | tablespoons all-purpose flour |
| 2 | cups light cream |
| 2 | tablespoons chopped pimiento |
| 1 | tablespoon lemon juice |
| 2 | 7-ounce cans solid white pack tuna, drained and flaked |
| 2 | tablespoons dry sherry |
| 6 | to 8 baked patty shells |

Combine yolks, ¼ cup butter, and paprika; set aside. Thinly slice mushrooms. Cook mushrooms, green pepper, and onion in 2 tablespoons butter till tender. Stir in flour and ¾ teaspoon *salt*. Add cream; cook and stir till bubbly. Add pimiento and lemon juice; mix well. Add egg yolk mixture all at once; mix well. Stir in tuna and sherry; heat through. Spoon into patty shells. Makes 6 to 8 servings.

## Tuna-Vegetable Pie

      **Pastry for Double-Crust Pie (see recipe,
        page 569)**
 **1**  **tablespoon cooking oil**
 **2**  **cups chopped cabbage**
**1½**  **cups sliced fresh mushrooms**
 **½**  **cup chopped onion**
 **¼**  **teaspoon dried rosemary, crushed**
 **¼**  **teaspoon dried thyme, crushed**
 **⅓**  **cup milk**
 **1**  **8-ounce package cream cheese, softened**
 **2**  **hard-cooked eggs, sliced**
 **1**  **9¼-ounce can tuna, drained and
     flaked**                Oven 375°

Line a 9-inch pie plate with *half* of the pastry; set aside. In a 10-inch skillet heat oil. Add cabbage, mushrooms, onion, rosemary, thyme, ¼ teaspoon *salt*, and ⅛ teaspoon *pepper*. Cover; cook over low heat, stirring occasionally, for 10 minutes or till vegetables are tender. Remove from heat. Stir milk into cream cheese; stir into cabbage mixture. Set aside. Arrange egg slices in bottom of pie crust; top with tuna. Spoon in cabbage mixture. Adjust top crust; seal and flute edges. Cut slits in top crust for escape of steam. Bake in a 375° oven for 45 to 50 minutes. Serves 6.

## Company Creamed Tuna

 **2**  **tablespoons finely chopped onion**
 **3**  **tablespoons butter or margarine**
 **3**  **tablespoons all-purpose flour**
**1¼**  **cups milk**
 **½**  **cup dairy sour cream**
 **1**  **6½-ounce can tuna, drained**
 **3**  **tablespoons dry white wine**
 **2**  **tablespoons snipped parsley**
 **4**  **baked patty shells or buttered toast points**

In a saucepan cook onion in butter till tender. Stir in flour, ¼ teaspoon *salt*, and dash *pepper*. Add milk all at once; cook quickly, stirring constantly, until mixture thickens and bubbles. Stir about 1 *cup* of the hot milk mixture into sour cream; return all to saucepan. Add tuna, wine, and parsley. Heat through. Serve in patty shells or spoon over hot buttered toast points. Sprinkle with toasted almonds, if desired. Makes 4 servings.

## Salmon Loaf

    1   16-ounce can salmon, drained
    2   cups soft bread crumbs (about 2½ slices)
    2   tablespoons chopped green onion
    1   tablespoon butter or margarine, melted
   ½   teaspoon salt
   ⅛   teaspoon pepper
   ½   cup milk
    1   slightly beaten egg                    Oven 350°

Flake salmon, discarding skin and bones. In a bowl combine salmon, bread crumbs, chopped onion, butter or margarine, salt, and pepper. Mix well. Combine milk and egg; add to salmon mixture and mix thoroughly. Shape into a loaf in a greased shallow baking pan or in a greased 7½x3½x2-inch loaf pan. Bake in a 350° oven for 35 to 40 minutes. If desired, serve with Cheese Sauce (see recipe, page 711). Makes 3 or 4 servings.

## Skillet Dilled Salmon Patties

    1   16-ounce can salmon
   ½   cup chopped onion
    2   tablespoons butter or margarine
   ⅔   cup fine dry bread crumbs
    2   beaten eggs
    1   teaspoon dried dillweed
   ½   teaspoon dry mustard
    2   tablespoons shortening or cooking oil

Drain salmon, reserving ⅓ cup liquid. Discard bones and skin from salmon; flake meat. Cook onion in butter or margarine till tender but not brown. Remove from heat. Add reserved salmon liquid, ⅓ *cup* of the bread crumbs, beaten eggs, dillweed, mustard, and flaked salmon; mix well. Shape into 4 patties; coat with remaining crumbs.

In a skillet melt shortening or heat oil. Cook patties over medium heat about 3 minutes or till browned. Carefully turn; brown other side about 3 minutes more. If desired, spoon Lemon-Chive Sauce (see recipe, page 711) over patties or serve with lemon wedges or creamed peas. Makes 4 servings.

## Salmon-Broccoli Crepes

- ¼ **cup chopped onion**
- ¼ **cup butter *or* margarine**
- ¼ **cup all-purpose flour**
- ¼ **teaspoon salt**
- 2¼ **cups milk**
- 2 **cups shredded American cheese (8 ounces)**
- 1 **10-ounce package frozen chopped broccoli**
- 1 **7¾-ounce can salmon, drained, *or* one 6½-ounce can tuna, drained and flaked**
- 12 **Basic Crepes**
- 1 **hard-cooked egg, sliced**
  **Paprika**                    Oven 375°

For filling, in a saucepan cook onion in butter or margarine till tender but not brown. Stir in flour and salt. Add milk; cook and stir till sauce is thickened and bubbly. Add the shredded cheese; stir till melted. Remove saucepan from heat.

Cook broccoli according to package directions; drain. Cut up any large broccoli pieces. Flake salmon, discarding skin and bones. Fold salmon or tuna and ¾ *cup* of the sauce into broccoli. Spoon about *3 tablespoons* of the salmon-broccoli mixture onto the *unbrowned* side of *each* crepe; roll up. Place crepes, seam side down, in a 12x7½x2-inch baking dish; pour remaining sauce over crepes. Bake, covered, in a 375° oven for 20 to 25 minutes or till heated through. Arrange the hard-cooked egg slices over crepes lengthwise. Sprinkle with paprika. Makes 6 servings.

**Basic Crepes:** In a bowl combine 1 cup *all-purpose flour,* 1½ cups *milk,* 2 *eggs,* 1 tablespoon *cooking oil,* and ¼ teaspoon *salt.* Beat with a rotary beater till blended. Heat a lightly greased 6-inch skillet. Remove from heat. Spoon in about 2 tablespoons batter; lift and tilt skillet to spread batter. Return to heat; brown on one side only. (*Or,* cook on an inverted crepe pan.) Invert pan over paper toweling; remove crepe. Repeat to make 16 to 18 crepes, greasing skillet occasionally.

**Note:** Unfilled crepes freeze well, so if you have any remaining crepes, store them in your freezer. Just make a stack, alternating each crepe with 2 layers of waxed paper. Then overwrap the stack in a moisture-vaporproof bag. Freeze up to 4 months. Let crepes thaw at room temperature about 1 hour before using.

**Meat**

**Meat**

**Meat**

**Meat**

**Meat**

**Meat**

**Meat**

**Meat**

# Meat

Percent of U.S. RDA Per Serving

| Recipes | Servings (fraction of recipe) | Calories | Protein (grams) | Carbohydrate (grams) | Fat (grams) | Sodium (milligrams) | Potassium (milligrams) | Protein | Vitamin A | Vitamin C | Thiamine | Riboflavin | Niacin | Calcium | Iron |
|---|---|---|---|---|---|---|---|---|---|---|---|---|---|---|---|
| Apple-Stuffed Sausage Patties | 1/6 | 634 | 12 | 8 | 62 | 992 | 261 | 18 | 7 | 8 | 34 | 13 | 14 | 2 | 10 |
| Apricot-Ham Patties | 1/8 | 361 | 18 | 20 | 23 | 312 | 391 | 28 | 23 | 5 | 42 | 16 | 20 | 2 | 19 |
| Bacon | 1/1 | 151 | 2 | 0 | 16 | 154 | 29 | 3 | 0 | 0 | 5 | 1 | 2 | 0 | 2 |
| Barbecued Pork Sandwiches | 1/4 | 577 | 29 | 86 | 12 | 1263 | 374 | 44 | 17 | 29 | 61 | 31 | 41 | 6 | 31 |
| Basic Broiled Pork Chops | 1/1 | 406 | 23 | 0 | 34 | 81 | 373 | 36 | 0 | 0 | 75 | 16 | 30 | 1 | 20 |
| Basic Broiled Pork Steaks | 1/1 | 612 | 33 | 0 | 52 | 116 | 529 | 51 | 0 | 0 | 107 | 23 | 43 | 2 | 27 |
| Beef and Vegetable Stir-Fry | 1/4 | 513 | 32 | 48 | 21 | 1747 | 1175 | 49 | 167 | 187 | 32 | 31 | 43 | 5 | 40 |
| Beef au Jus (for juice only) | 1/6 | 22 | 0 | 0 | 2 | 45 | 22 | 0 | 0 | 0 | 0 | 0 | 0 | 0 | 0 |
| Beef Fondue w/Creamy Curry Sauce | 1/4 | 594 | 22 | 2 | 55 | 824 | 392 | 34 | 17 | 7 | 7 | 17 | 23 | 6 | 17 |
| Beef Fondue w/Wine Sauce | 1/4 | 532 | 20 | 10 | 43 | 1126 | 437 | 31 | 10 | 8 | 7 | 11 | 25 | 4 | 18 |
| Beef Pot Roast | 1/8 | 423 | 31 | 12 | 27 | 125 | 734 | 48 | 80 | 16 | 14 | 18 | 40 | 3 | 28 |
| Beef Stroganoff | 1/4 | 735 | 27 | 31 | 55 | 768 | 623 | 41 | 24 | 9 | 20 | 29 | 36 | 10 | 24 |
| Beef Wellington | 1/8 | 754 | 28 | 28 | 58 | 345 | 415 | 43 | 35 | 4 | 22 | 23 | 37 | 4 | 30 |
| Beer-Braised Rabbit | 1/4 | 502 | 33 | 45 | 20 | 569 | 1216 | 49 | 124 | 61 | 19 | 12 | 69 | 4 | 17 |
| Braised Pork Steaks | 1/4 | 621 | 33 | 2 | 52 | 306 | 529 | 51 | 5 | 3 | 108 | 23 | 44 | 3 | 28 |
| Breaded Pork Tenderloins | 1/6 | 423 | 18 | 17 | 31 | 464 | 280 | 27 | 5 | 0 | 49 | 17 | 24 | 7 | 16 |
| Brisket Carbonnade | 1/10 | 349 | 27 | 8 | 21 | 195 | 494 | 42 | 1 | 6 | 10 | 16 | 34 | 2 | 24 |
| Broiled Lamb Chops | 1/4 | 384 | 17 | 0 | 17 | 60 | 274 | 26 | 0 | 0 | 10 | 13 | 25 | 1 | 6 |
| Broiled Short Ribs | 1/6 | 517 | 21 | 18 | 40 | 394 | 581 | 33 | 12 | 15 | 9 | 13 | 27 | 3 | 22 |
| Broiling Beef Steaks | 1/2 | 802 | 30 | 0 | 75 | 104 | 475 | 46 | 3 | 0 | 8 | 16 | 36 | 2 | 25 |

| | | | | | | | | | | | | | | | |
|---|---|---|---|---|---|---|---|---|---|---|---|---|---|---|---|
| Canadian Bacon Pie | 1/6 | 733 | 30 | 43 | 49 | 2019 | 552 | 46 | 20 | 64 | 65 | 35 | 31 | 28 | 25 |
| Canadian-Style Bacon | 1/8 | 245 | 23 | 0 | 16 | 2144 | 445 | 35 | 0 | 0 | 63 | 15 | 27 | 1 | 19 |
| Chicken-Fried Round Steak | 1/6 | 363 | 24 | 9 | 25 | 395 | 384 | 38 | 3 | 0 | 11 | 16 | 29 | 2 | 23 |
| Chinese-Style Beef Ribs | 1/6 | 484 | 22 | 6 | 40 | 1843 | 446 | 34 | 2 | 3 | 7 | 15 | 25 | 3 | 23 |
| Choucroute Garni | 1/12 | 818 | 28 | 52 | 53 | 1779 | 1522 | 44 | 1 | 89 | 82 | 25 | 46 | 8 | 32 |
| Coney Islands | 1/6 | 373 | 17 | 20 | 25 | 1138 | 300 | 26 | 10 | 19 | 17 | 16 | 23 | 4 | 17 |
| Corn Dogs | 1/4 | 690 | 23 | 49 | 45 | 1943 | 420 | 35 | 6 | 1 | 32 | 29 | 26 | 10 | 21 |
| Creamed Bratwurst | 1/6 | 440 | 24 | 10 | 34 | 1796 | 402 | 37 | 2 | 32 | 12 | 23 | 27 | 6 | 21 |
| Creamed Dried Beef | 1/3 | 354 | 16 | 23 | 22 | 1601 | 249 | 25 | 16 | 2 | 11 | 21 | 12 | 16 | 12 |
| Creamed Sweetbreads | 1/6 | 503 | 28 | 31 | 29 | 782 | 557 | 44 | 15 | 16 | 26 | 24 | 23 | 14 | 17 |
| Curried Cranberry Glaze | 1/14 | 87 | 0 | 15 | 3 | 43 | 20 | 0 | 3 | 2 | 0 | 0 | 0 | 1 | 1 |
| Curried Lamb Madras | 1/6 | 618 | 26 | 34 | 41 | 805 | 472 | 41 | 0 | 5 | 25 | 20 | 40 | 4 | 15 |
| Curried Pork | 1/4 | 647 | 23 | 42 | 43 | 1104 | 488 | 35 | 20 | 13 | 35 | 25 | 24 | 17 | 19 |
| Deviled Beef Rolls | 1/4 | 299 | 24 | 3 | 21 | 477 | 398 | 37 | 5 | 1 | 7 | 15 | 30 | 3 | 21 |
| Double-Decker Burgers w/Tomato-Cucumber Relish | 1/8 | 523 | 24 | 29 | 34 | 903 | 472 | 37 | 11 | 12 | 18 | 18 | 32 | 6 | 24 |
| Easy Mustard Glaze | 1/6 | 71 | 0 | 18 | 0 | 6 | 73 | 0 | 4 | 0 | 0 | 0 | 2 | 2 | 4 |
| Fresh Pork Sausage | 1/4 | 565 | 11 | 0 | 58 | 839 | 159 | 16 | 0 | 0 | 33 | 11 | 13 | 1 | 9 |
| Hamburger-Corn Bake | 1/4 | 677 | 30 | 39 | 45 | 1164 | 606 | 46 | 25 | 18 | 25 | 27 | 37 | 14 | 26 |
| Hamburger Pie | 1/4 | 544 | 30 | 34 | 32 | 1520 | 1062 | 47 | 26 | 58 | 19 | 24 | 37 | 19 | 33 |
| Hamburgers | 1/4 | 304 | 20 | 0 | 24 | 71 | 325 | 31 | 1 | 0 | 6 | 11 | 24 | 1 | 17 |
| Ham Caribbean | 1/6 | 518 | 24 | 36 | 30 | 1173 | 655 | 37 | 3 | 53 | 70 | 17 | 29 | 6 | 25 |
| Ham Croquettes w/Cheese Sauce | 1/5 | 329 | 14 | 17 | 23 | 566 | 200 | 22 | 9 | 2 | 21 | 14 | 13 | 7 | 12 |
| Ham Loaf | 1/8 | 352 | 17 | 19 | 23 | 320 | 320 | 27 | 3 | 1 | 41 | 14 | 18 | 5 | 18 |
| Ham-Noodle Casserole | 1/4 | 513 | 21 | 35 | 32 | 1188 | 333 | 32 | 22 | 17 | 36 | 26 | 22 | 19 | 16 |
| Ham Slices | 1/6 | 425 | 28 | 0 | 34 | 998 | 312 | 43 | 0 | 0 | 42 | 14 | 24 | 1 | 19 |
| Harvest Pot Roast | 1/8 | 686 | 33 | 27 | 50 | 661 | 1137 | 51 | 92 | 45 | 106 | 28 | 48 | 6 | 32 |
| Hasenpfeffer | 1/4 | 371 | 28 | 29 | 16 | 1106 | 430 | 43 | 0 | 2 | 7 | 6 | 55 | 4 | 12 |
| Italian Lamb Chop Skillet | 1/4 | 416 | 17 | 17 | 31 | 367 | 620 | 27 | 7 | 53 | 15 | 15 | 28 | 4 | 11 |

# Nutrition Analysis Chart

| Recipes | Servings (fraction of recipe) | Calories | Protein (grams) | Carbohydrate (grams) | Fat (grams) | Sodium (milligrams) | Potassium (milligrams) | Protein | Vitamin A | Vitamin C | Thiamine | Riboflavin | Niacin | Calcium | Iron |
|---|---|---|---|---|---|---|---|---|---|---|---|---|---|---|---|
| | | | | | | | | Percent of U.S. RDA Per Serving | | | | | | | |
| Lamb Chops Supreme | 1/6 | 453 | 21 | 3 | 39 | 166 | 379 | 32 | 7 | 7 | 13 | 19 | 31 | 4 | 9 |
| Lamb Loin Chops w/Walnut Glaze | 1/4 | 401 | 17 | 19 | 29 | 58 | 317 | 26 | 3 | 9 | 11 | 13 | 24 | 2 | 9 |
| Lamb Patties w/Dill Sauce | 1/6 | 529 | 23 | 6 | 45 | 656 | 401 | 35 | 5 | 2 | 18 | 21 | 28 | 9 | 10 |
| Lasagna | 1/10 | 633 | 32 | 44 | 28 | 1339 | 505 | 49 | 39 | 31 | 33 | 33 | 18 | 57 | 16 |
| London Broil | 1/4 | 323 | 25 | 0 | 24 | 86 | 397 | 38 | 0 | 0 | 7 | 13 | 29 | 2 | 20 |
| Marinated Venison Chops | 1/4 | 287 | 24 | 6 | 18 | 596 | 443 | 37 | 5 | 4 | 19 | 33 | 37 | 2 | 11 |
| Meat Loaf | 1/6 | 417 | 25 | 16 | 25 | 644 | 480 | 38 | 11 | 8 | 10 | 19 | 28 | 8 | 23 |
| Mexicali Pork Chops | 1/4 | 622 | 31 | 48 | 31 | 767 | 896 | 47 | 30 | 110 | 90 | 23 | 44 | 5 | 35 |
| Moussaka | 1/4 | 597 | 27 | 14 | 32 | 965 | 559 | 41 | 20 | 12 | 12 | 29 | 30 | 19 | 14 |
| Mushroom Steak Sauce w/Steak | 1/4 | 901 | 32 | 4 | 83 | 335 | 673 | 49 | 10 | 6 | 12 | 26 | 44 | 3 | 28 |
| New England Boiled Dinner | 1/8 | 670 | 23 | 40 | 43 | 2258 | 1128 | 49 | 91 | 146 | 18 | 26 | 27 | 15 | 33 |
| Orange-Glazed Canadian Bacon | 1/4 | 349 | 23 | 20 | 20 | 2198 | 562 | 36 | 4 | 40 | 66 | 15 | 28 | 2 | 20 |
| Orange-Glazed Ribs | 1/6 | 756 | 27 | 27 | 60 | 757 | 473 | 42 | 7 | 60 | 86 | 20 | 35 | 5 | 26 |
| Oven-Baked Ribs and Kraut | 1/2 | 587 | 27 | 19 | 47 | 846 | 782 | 35 | 17 | 36 | 71 | 18 | 33 | 26 | 23 |
| Oven Hash | 1/4 | 478 | 28 | 28 | 29 | 917 | 699 | 42 | 184 | 66 | 13 | 30 | 23 | 9 | 19 |
| Oven Steak and Vegetables | 1/4 | 490 | 28 | 47 | 21 | 1178 | 1048 | 43 | 41 | 27 | 26 | 22 | 43 | 4 | 33 |
| Oven Swiss Steak | 1/6 | 409 | 26 | 34 | 18 | 936 | 645 | 40 | 3 | 0 | 19 | 15 | 36 | 2 | 27 |
| Panbroiling Beef Steaks | 1/2 | 802 | 30 | 0 | 75 | 104 | 475 | 46 | 0 | 0 | 8 | 16 | 36 | 0 | 25 |
| Pan Gravy | 1/6 | 82 | 1 | 4 | 4 | 176 | — | 1 | 0 | 0 | 0 | 1 | 1 | 1 | 1 |
| Pineapple-Glazed Canadian Bacon | 1/4 | 350 | 26 | 21 | 19 | 2198 | 532 | 35 | 3 | 12 | 65 | 16 | 27 | 2 | 21 |

# Nutrition Analysis Chart

| | | | | | | | | | | | | | | | |
|---|---|---|---|---|---|---|---|---|---|---|---|---|---|---|---|
| Pizza w/Tomato Sauce | 1/6 | 754 | 25 | 49 | 51 | 1714 | 352 | 38 | 20 | 31 | 50 | 34 | 29 | 30 | 19 |
| Porcupine Meatballs | 1/4 | 425 | 24 | 20 | 27 | 975 | 509 | 37 | 18 | 16 | 13 | 15 | 30 | 3 | 24 |
| Pork Burgers | 1/4 | 446 | 21 | 21 | 30 | 664 | 326 | 32 | 1 | 2 | 68 | 18 | 30 | 4 | 19 |
| Pork Chow Mein | 1/6 | 464 | 18 | 40 | 26 | 1576 | 594 | 28 | 8 | 19 | 51 | 20 | 31 | 6 | 22 |
| Pork Loaf | 1/6 | 411 | 21 | 13 | 30 | 563 | 401 | 33 | 8 | 8 | 61 | 17 | 26 | 4 | 21 |
| Pork w/Apple-Curry Sauce | 1/10 | 590 | 30 | 6 | 49 | 138 | 527 | 46 | 2 | 8 | 97 | 22 | 39 | 3 | 26 |
| Potato-Ham Scallop | 1/4 | 540 | 26 | 57 | 23 | 662 | 1310 | 39 | 9 | 84 | 45 | 29 | 34 | 18 | 21 |
| Pot Roast Gravy | 1/6 | 82 | 1 | 4 | 7 | 176 | 5 | 1 | 1 | 0 | 2 | 1 | 1 | 0 | 1 |
| Roast Pork w/Fennel | 1/8 | 412 | 23 | 3 | 33 | 347 | 371 | 35 | 1 | 1 | 74 | 16 | 30 | 2 | 20 |
| Roast w/Barbecue Gravy | 1/10 | 428 | 32 | 9 | 29 | 264 | 538 | 49 | 2 | 2 | 9 | 17 | 38 | 3 | 27 |
| Rump Roast w/Vegetables | 1/12 | 616 | 30 | 29 | 42 | 331 | 1098 | 46 | 81 | 51 | 19 | 19 | 44 | 4 | 28 |
| Salami-Bean Casserole | 1/4 | 372 | 15 | 47 | 14 | 1128 | 528 | 23 | 9 | 20 | 18 | 8 | 15 | 8 | 22 |
| Saucy Lamb Shanks | 1/4 | 517 | 25 | 34 | 27 | 1048 | 708 | 39 | 92 | 22 | 25 | 22 | 39 | 7 | 18 |
| Sauerbraten | 1/12 | 656 | 31 | 33 | 45 | 728 | 608 | 47 | 15 | 17 | 18 | 20 | 38 | 5 | 29 |
| Sauerbraten Burgers | 1/4 | 539 | 25 | 49 | 27 | 821 | 544 | 39 | 12 | 7 | 19 | 18 | 34 | 5 | 28 |
| Sausage and Corn Bread | 1/4 | 994 | 22 | 63 | 74 | 1748 | 647 | 34 | 34 | 51 | 56 | 30 | 29 | 13 | 25 |
| Sausage and Kraut | 1/4 | 465 | 11 | 36 | 36 | 2043 | 505 | 34 | 1 | 29 | 35 | 20 | 24 | 6 | 20 |
| Sausage-Apple Stuffed Squash | 1/4 | 700 | 19 | 32 | 57 | 930 | 1142 | 29 | 66 | 56 | 35 | 33 | 17 | 27 | 21 |
| Sausage-Macaroni Skillet | 1/5 | 637 | 19 | 26 | 50 | 1399 | 522 | 30 | 34 | 79 | 46 | 24 | 26 | 20 | 16 |
| Sautéed Liver and Onions | 1/4 | 318 | 30 | 8 | 18 | 297 | 459 | 47 | 1216 | 55 | 20 | 280 | 94 | 2 | 56 |
| Savory Lamburgers | 1/6 | 364 | 16 | 25 | 22 | 482 | 260 | 25 | 2 | 2 | 19 | 18 | 25 | 6 | 11 |
| Savory Stuffed Rib Roast | 1/8 | 967 | 35 | 1 | 90 | 304 | 564 | 54 | 4 | 4 | 12 | 19 | 42 | 3 | 30 |
| Sherried Veal Pot Roast | 1/6 | 243 | 19 | 10 | 13 | 566 | 500 | 30 | 83 | 11 | 13 | 18 | 33 | 4 | 18 |
| Skilletburgers | 1/7 | 456 | 19 | 52 | 18 | 1210 | 342 | 30 | 14 | 11 | 28 | 20 | 31 | 8 | 21 |
| Spaghetti and Meatballs | 1/6 | 586 | 30 | 47 | 31 | 1168 | 1276 | 46 | 65 | 151 | 31 | 27 | 44 | 8 | 38 |
| Spaghetti Sauce | 1/6 | 493 | 28 | 40 | 25 | 739 | 1228 | 42 | 63 | 150 | 27 | 22 | 42 | 5 | 35 |
| Spicy Apple-Pork Patties | 1/6 | 359 | 13 | 33 | 20 | 458 | 267 | 20 | 3 | 6 | 40 | 10 | 16 | 3 | 15 |
| Standing Rib Roast w/Yorkshire Pudding | 1/10 | 825 | 32 | 22 | 67 | 349 | 515 | 49 | 9 | 1 | 20 | 27 | 37 | 9 | 27 |

# Nutrition Analysis Chart

**Percent of U.S. RDA Per Serving**

| Recipes | Servings (fraction of recipe) | Calories | Protein (grams) | Carbohydrate (grams) | Fat (grams) | Sodium (milligrams) | Potassium (milligrams) | Protein | Vitamin A | Vitamin C | Thiamine | Riboflavin | Niacin | Calcium | Iron |
|---|---|---|---|---|---|---|---|---|---|---|---|---|---|---|---|
| Steak and Kidney Pie | 1/10 | 524 | 32 | 26 | 31 | 605 | 421 | 50 | 12 | 4 | 33 | 144 | 49 | 3 | 50 |
| Stuffed Cabbage Rolls | 1/6 | 314 | 16 | 17 | 20 | 821 | 453 | 25 | 12 | 42 | 26 | 13 | 20 | 7 | 16 |
| Stuffed Green Peppers | 1/6 | 386 | 22 | 25 | 22 | 749 | 781 | 34 | 33 | 374 | 20 | 21 | 26 | 17 | 23 |
| Sweet-Sour Pork | 1/4 | 670 | 23 | 47 | 44 | 874 | 475 | 35 | 37 | 90 | 64 | 19 | 19 | 3 | 21 |
| Swiss Steak | 1/6 | 409 | 26 | 34 | 18 | 936 | 645 | 40 | 41 | 27 | 19 | 15 | 36 | 4 | 27 |
| Swiss Veal Roast | 1/8 | 259 | 26 | 3 | 15 | 292 | 443 | 40 | 7 | 8 | 15 | 20 | 39 | 8 | 21 |
| Tacos con Carne | 1/6 | 462 | 24 | 32 | 26 | 887 | 512 | 37 | 23 | 25 | 18 | 22 | 27 | 21 | 22 |
| Teriyaki Roast Beef | 1/14 | 878 | 30 | 6 | 81 | 1619 | 594 | 46 | 25 | 0 | 9 | 18 | 35 | 4 | 31 |
| Texas Beef Skillet | 1/6 | 383 | 26 | 21 | 21 | 684 | 630 | 35 | 35 | 35 | 12 | 15 | 23 | 14 | 24 |
| Tongue and Lima Skillet | 1/4 | 354 | 24 | 25 | 17 | 563 | 541 | 37 | 12 | 29 | 9 | 18 | 21 | 4 | 23 |
| Veal Cordon Bleu | 1/4 | 458 | 29 | 19 | 29 | 638 | 381 | 45 | 18 | 3 | 21 | 26 | 37 | 21 | 24 |
| Veal Patties | 1/6 | 277 | 24 | 6 | 17 | 551 | 378 | 37 | 5 | 1 | 13 | 20 | 39 | 3 | 21 |
| Venison Pot Roast | 1/8 | 315 | 28 | 23 | 12 | 459 | 557 | 43 | 26 | 15 | 28 | 39 | 43 | 5 | 16 |

# Meat

When shopping for meat, there are several points to consider. First, think about how you plan to cook the meat. Then consider the amount of meat you'll need, and its price.

## Cooking Methods

There are two main methods of cooking meat—dry-heat cooking and moist-heat cooking. Dry heat cooking methods are used for the tender cuts, and include roasting (baking), broiling, frying, panfrying, and panbroiling. Moist-heat cooking methods are used for less-tender cuts and for some very lean, tender cuts. They include stewing, simmering in liquid, and braising. You will find these general cooking methods listed with the various cuts of meat on the meat identification pages that follow.

Generally, cuts of meat vary in tenderness depending on where they come from on the animal. Usually those cuts from the loin area (the part of the animal least exercised) are the most tender. Cuts of meat farther from this area are less tender.

While moist-heat cooking is one way to tenderize less-tender meat cuts, other ways include pounding, using meat tenderizers, and marinating. Pounding with a meat mallet breaks down some of the meat fibers. When using either seasoned or unseasoned powdered instant meat tenderizers, follow the package directions. Marinades add flavor to meats as well as tenderness. They consist of an acid (such as lemon juice, vinegar, or wine), cooking oil, and often other ingredients. The size and shape of the cut of meat determine the length of time it should be marinated. Marinating any meat too long may cause it to absorb too much marinade flavor.

Cooking meat in a microwave oven works well for many cuts. You may notice a difference in color and tenderness from meat prepared by conventional cooking methods. In addition to cooking meat, the microwave oven is handy for defrosting meat and speeding up barbecuing. Since microwave ovens vary with the manufacturer, consult your owner's manual for specific recommendations.

## Buying

Besides cooking methods, you'll want to consider the amount of meat to buy, as well as its cost. Price per pound is what you'll find on the label, but price per serving is what you need to consider. A boneless, well trimmed piece of meat may cost more per pound but may cost less per serving because there is more edible meat. Use the chart below as a guide to the number of servings per pound. When using this guide, also consider: What kinds and amounts of food are you serving with the meat? Do the people you plan to serve have light or hearty appetites? (Age as well as activity level make a difference.) Do you plan to have leftovers?

### *How much meat to buy*

| Type of Meat | Servings Per Pound |
|---|---|
| **Boneless meat—** ground, stew, or variety meat | 4 or 5 |
| **Cuts with little bone—** beef round or ham center cuts, lamb or veal cutlets | 3 or 4 |
| **Cuts with a medium amount of bone—** whole or end cuts of beef round, bone-in ham; loin, rump, rib, or chuck roasts; steaks and chops | 2 or 3 |
| **Cuts with much bone—** shank, spareribs, short ribs | 1 or 2 |

## Storing

Store meat properly to protect it against spoilage. Consult the storage times on page 840 or, for canned products, follow the label instructions if they are given. When there are no instructions on the can, cover the opened meat and refrigerate it. Fresh meat purchased precut and wrapped in clear flexible packaging may be refrigerated as purchased. If it's to be stored in the freezer, remove the clear-packaging material and tightly wrap the meat in moisture-vaporproof freezer paper.

---

### Using a meat thermometer

Because no two roasts are shaped exactly alike or have the same amount of bone or fat, a meat thermometer is your best guide to judging doneness. To use the thermometer correctly, insert it into a roast so that the bulb of the thermometer rests in the center of the thickest portion of meat. It should not rest in fat or on the bottom of the roasting pan, or touch bone.

Roast meat till the de-sired internal temperature is reached. To check the temperature, push the thermometer into the meat a little farther. If the temperature drops, continue cooking the meat to the desired temperature.

For easier carving, allow the meat to stand 15 minutes. During this time, the meat will continue cooking. Therefore, larger roasts should be removed from the oven when the meat thermometer registers about 5° below the specified internal temperature. However, the thermometer should register the correct temperature when you carve the meat.

# Beef

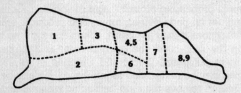

Locate the wholesale cuts on the drawing, identify the retail pieces in the same numbered pictures, and then note the cooking methods.

**1.** Boneless Chuck Eye Roast, upper left—*braise; roast high quality meat.* Chuck Arm Pot Roast, right—*braise.* Chuck Blade Roast, lower left—*braise; roast high quality meat.*

**2.** Boneless Beef Brisket, upper left—*cook in liquid.* Plate or Chuck Short Ribs, right. Shank Crosscuts, lower left—*braise, cook in liquid.*

**3.** Rib Roast, upper left. Boneless Rib Roast, right. Rib Eye Roast (Delmonico Roast), lower left—*roast.*

**4.** Boneless Top Loin Steak (New York Strip Steak, Kansas City Steak), upper left. Tenderloin Steak (Filet Mignon), right. Rib Eye Steak (from section 3 on drawing), lower left—*broil, panbroil.*

**5.** Porterhouse Steak, upper right. Top Loin Steak, lower right—*broil, panbroil.*

**6.** Scored Flank Steak, upper left—*braise; broil high quality meat.* Rolled Flank Steak, upper right—*braise.* Flank Steak Rolls, bottom—*broil, braise, panbroil.*

**7.** Sirloin Steak, upper right. Boneless Sirloin Steak, lower left—*broil, panbroil.*

**8.** Round Tip Roast, upper left—*braise; roast high quality meat.* Bottom Round Steak, center—*braise.* Top Round Steak, lower right—*braise, broil, panbroil.*

**9.** Boneless Round Rump Roast, upper right. Round Rump Roast, lower left—*braise; roast high quality meat.*

# Veal

Match the section number in
the photo caption to the number on the beef drawing on
page 452 to locate the origin
of a particular cut.

**1.** Boneless Shoulder Roast,
upper right. Shoulder Arm
Roast, left—*braise, roast*.
Shoulder Arm Steak, lower
right—*braise*. (Section 1 on
beef drawing.)

**2.** Loin Roast, upper right—
*roast*. Loin Kidney Chop, lower right. Loin Chop, left—
*braise*. (Section 4, 5 on beef
drawing).

**3.** Leg Round Roast, lower
left—*braise, roast*. Leg Round
Steak (cut thick), upper right—
*braise*. (Section 8, 9 on beef
drawing.)

## Pan Gravy

***Thickening combined with fat***—*for 2 cups gravy:* After
removing roasted meat to a platter, pour meat juices and fat
into a large glass measure. Skim off the fat, reserving 3 to 4
tablespoons. (If necessary, add cooking oil to equal the needed
amount of fat.) Return the reserved fat to the roasting pan.
Add enough *water, broth, or milk* to the reserved meat juices
to make 2 cups liquid; set aside.

Stir ¼ cup all-purpose *flour* into the reserved fat in the roasting pan, stirring in the crusty browned bits from the meat drippings. Cook and stir over low heat till bubbly. Remove pan from heat. Add liquid all at once to the fat-flour mixtures; stir to combine. Return pan to medium heat. Cook and stir till thickened and bubbly. Cook and stir 1 to 2 minutes more. If desired, add a few drops of Kitchen Bouquet. Season to taste with salt and pepper.

**Thickening combined with liquid**—*for 2 cups gravy:* After removing roasted meat to a platter, pour meat juices and fat into a large glass measure. Skim off excess fat. Add enough water to the meat juices to make 1½ cups liquid. Return juices to the roasting pan. Put ½ cup *cold water* in a screw-top jar. Add 2 tablespoons *cornstarch* or ¼ cup all-purpose *flour.* Shake well. Stir into juices. Cook and stir till thickened and bubbly. Cook and stir 1 to 2 minutes more. If desired, add a few drops of Kitchen Bouquet. Season to taste with salt and pepper.

# Roasting Beef & Veal

Season the roast by sprinkling with a little salt and pepper. Place meat, fat side up, on a rack in a shallow roasting pan. Insert a meat thermometer (see tip, page 451). Do not add water or other liquid, and do not cover the roasting pan. Except as noted below, roast meat in a 325° oven until meat thermometer registers the desired internal temperature.

For easier carving, let meat stand about 15 minutes. Allow for a rise of approximately 5°F. in internal temperature during standing time. Carve meat following the suggestions on pages 534–35. Remove string from rolled and tied roasts before carving.

Use the roasting times given in the chart on following page as a guide to the total cooking time for the cut of meat you're preparing, since individual cuts vary in size, shape, and tenderness.

| Beef or Veal Cut | Approximate Weight (pounds) | Internal Temperature on Removal from Oven | Approximate Cooking Time (total time) |
|---|---|---|---|
| **Roast meat at a constant 325° oven temperature unless otherwise indicated** | | | |
| **Beef** | | | |
| Rib Roast | 4 to 6 | 140° (rare) | 2 to 2½ hours |
| | | 160° (medium) | 2½ to 3¼ hours |
| | | 170° (well-done) | 2¾ to 4 hours |
| Rib Roast | 6 to 8 | 140° (rare) | 2½ to 3 hours |
| | | 160° (medium) | 3 to 3½ hours |
| | | 170° (well-done) | 3½ to 4¼ hours |
| Boneless Rib Roast | 5 to 7 | 140° (rare) | 2¾ to 3¾ hours |
| | | 160° (medium) | 3¼ to 4¼ hours |
| | | 170° (well-done) | 4 to 5½ hours |
| Boneless Round Rump Roast | 4 to 6 | 150° to 170° | 2 to 2½ hours |
| Round Tip Roast | 3½ to 4 | 140° to 170° | 2¼ to 2½ hours |
| Rib Eye Roast (Roast at 350°) | 4 to 6 | 140° (rare) | 1¼ to 1¾ hours |
| | | 160° (medium) | 1½ to 2 hours |
| | | 170° (well-done) | 1¾ to 2¼ hours |
| Tenderloin Roast (Roast at 425°) | 4 to 6 | 140° (rare) | ¾ to 1 hour |
| **Veal** | | | |
| Leg Round Roast | 5 to 8 | 170° (well-done) | 2¾ to 3¼ hours |
| Loin Roast | 4 to 6 | 170° (well-done) | 2¼ to 3 hours |
| Boneless Shoulder Roast | 4 to 6 | 170° (well-done) | 3 to 4 hours |

# Beef Wellington

| | |
|---|---|
| 1 | 2¼-pound beef tenderloin roast |
| 2 | cups all-purpose flour |
| ½ | teaspoon salt |
| ⅔ | cup shortening |
| ⅓ | to ½ cup cold water |
| 1 | 4¾-ounce can liver pâté |
| 1 | beaten egg |
| 1½ | cups water |
| 2 | teaspoons instant beef bouillon granules |
| ½ | cup cold water |
| ¼ | cup all-purpose flour |
| ⅓ | cup burgundy |
| ½ | teaspoon dried basil, crushed |
| | Parsley sprigs |

Oven 425°

Place meat on a rack in a shallow roasting pan. Insert a meat thermometer. Roast in a 425° oven about 45 minutes or till thermometer registers 130°. Remove from pan; cover and refrigerate while preparing pastry. Reserve drippings.

For pastry, combine 2 cups flour and salt. Cut in shortening till pieces are the size of small peas. Add ⅓ to ½ cup cold water, 1 tablespoon at a time, tossing with a fork till all is moistened. Form into a ball. On a floured surface roll into a 14x12-inch rectangle. Spread pastry with pâté to within ½ inch of edges.

Center meat atop pastry. Wrap pastry around meat, overlapping long sides. Brush with egg and seal. Trim excess pastry from ends; fold up. Brush with egg and seal. Place, seam down, on a greased baking sheet. Reroll trimmings; make cutouts. Place cutouts on pastry-covered meat; brush remaining egg over pastry. Bake in a 425° oven for 35 minutes.

To make gravy, in a saucepan heat and stir reserved drippings with 1½ cups water and bouillon granules till granules dissolve. Combine ½ cup cold water and ¼ cup flour; stir into hot bouillon mixture. Stir in burgundy and basil. Cook and stir till thickened and bubbly. Cook and stir 1 to 2 minutes more. Season to taste with salt and pepper. Garnish meat with parsley sprigs. Pass gravy. Serves 8.

## Standing Rib Roast with Yorkshire Pudding

|   |   |   |
|---|---|---|
| 1 | 4-pound beef rib roast | |
| 4 | eggs | |
| 2 | cups milk | |
| 2 | cups all-purpose flour | |
| 1 | teaspoon salt | Oven 325° |

Place meat, fat side up, in a 15½x10½x2-inch roasting pan. Sprinkle with a little salt and pepper. Insert a meat thermometer. Roast in a 325° oven 2¼ hours for rare or till thermometer registers 140°; 3 hours for medium (160°); or 3¼ hours for well-done (170°). Remove meat from pan. Cover with foil; keep warm.

Reserve ¼ cup drippings in roasting pan (Or, pour 2 tablespoons drippings into each of two 8x1½-inch round baking pans.) Set aside. Increase oven temperature to 400°. Beat eggs on low speed of electric mixer for ½ minute. Add milk; beat 15 seconds. Add flour and the 1 teaspoon salt; beat 2 minutes or till smooth. Pour batter over drippings in pan(s). Bake in a 400° oven about 35 to 40 minutes for roasting pan or about 30 to 35 minutes for round baking pans. Cut into squares or wedges to serve. Serve at once with roast. Makes 10 servings.

## Savory Stuffed Rib Roast

|   |   |
|---|---|
| **6** | **slices bacon** |
| **¼** | **cup chopped onion** |
| **1** | **clove garlic, minced** |
| **3** | **tablespoons chopped pimiento-stuffed olives** |
| **1** | **4- to 5-pound boneless beef rib roast** |

Oven 325°

Crisp-cook and crumble bacon; drain, reserving 1 tablespoon of the drippings. Set bacon aside. Cook onion and garlic in reserved drippings till tender. Remove from heat. Stir in olives and bacon. Unroll roast; spread bacon mixture over meat. Reroll roast; tie securely.

Place meat, fat side up, on a rack in a shallow roasting pan. Sprinkle with a little salt and pepper. Insert a meat thermometer. Roast in a 325° oven 2½ to 3 hours for rare or till thermometer registers 140°. Let roast stand covered with foil about 15 minutes. Remove strings and carve. Serves 8 to 10.

## Teriyaki Roast Beef

|   |   |
|---|---|
| **1** | **6- to 7-pound boneless beef rib roast** |
| **1** | **cup soy sauce** |
| **½** | **cup cooking oil** |
| **¼** | **cup light molasses** |
| **1** | **tablespoon ground ginger** |
| **1** | **tablespoon dry mustard** |
| **4** | **cloves garlic, minced** |

Oven 325°

Place meat in a plastic bag; set in a deep bowl. For marinade, combining remaining ingredients; pour over meat. Close bag. Chill overnight, turning occasionally.

Remove meat, reserving marinade. Place meat, fat side up, on a rack in a shallow roasting pan. Sprinkle with a little salt and pepper. Insert a meat thermometer. Roast in a 325° oven for 3 to 3¾ hours for rare or till thermometer registers 140°; 3½ to 4¼ hours for medium (160°); or 4 to 4¾ hours for well-done (170°). During roasting, baste several times with the reserved marinade.

Remove roast from oven; cover with foil. Let stand about 15 minutes. Remove strings and carve thinly across the grain. Serves 14.

---

## Marinating meat

Place roast, steaks, or meat cubes in a plastic bag and set in a deep bowl. Add marinade. Close the bag and turn to evenly distribute marinade.

---

## Rump Roast with Vegetables

|   |   |
|---|---|
| 1 | **4-pound boneless beef round rump roast** |
| ¼ | **teaspoon dried marjoram, crushed** |
| ¼ | **teaspoon dried thyme, crushed** |
| 12 | **medium potatoes, peeled and halved** |
| 6 | **medium carrots, cut up** |
| ¼ | **cup all-purpose flour** |
| 1 | **tablespoon snipped parsley** |
| 1 | **teaspoon instant beef bouillon granules** |

Oven 325°

Place meat, fat side up, on a rack in a shallow roasting pan. Combine marjoram, thyme, ¼ teaspoon *salt,* and dash *pepper;* rub onto meat. Insert a meat thermometer. Roast in a 325° oven about 2¼ hours or till the thermometer registers 150° to 170°. Meanwhile, in separates saucepans cook potatoes and carrots in boiling salted water for 15 minutes; drain. About 45 minutes before roast is done, place vegetables in drippings around roast, turning to coat. When done, transfer meat and vegetables to a serving platter; keep warm.

Pour meat juices and fat into a large glass measure. Skim off fat, reserving 3 tablespoons. (If necessary, add cooking oil to equal 3 tablespoons.) Return reserved fat to roasting pan. Add water to reserved meat juices to make 2 cups liquid; set aside. Stir flour into reserved fat in roasting pan. Cook and stir over low heat till bubbly. Remove from heat. Add meat juices all at once; stir to combine. Stir in parsley, bouillon, ¾ teaspoon *salt,* and dash *pepper.* Return pan to heat. Cook and stir till thickened and bubbly. Cook and stir 1 to 2 minutes more. Sprinkle vegetables with additional snipped parsley, if desired. Pass gravy with meat and vegetables. Serves 12.

## Beef au Jus

Cook *beef roast* according to chart on page 456. Remove to a platter; cover with foil. Leave crusty browned bits in the roasting pan; pour meat juices and fat into a glass measure. Skim off fat; reserve meat juices. Add 1 cup *boiling water* to roasting pan, stirring and scraping crusty bits off bottom of pan. Stir in meat juices. Cook and stir till bubbly. For a richer flavor, stir in instant beef bouillon granules (about ½ teaspoon per cup). Season. Pass with meat.

# Beef Pot Roast

| 1 | 3- to 4-pound beef chuck pot roast |
|---|---|
| | All-purpose flour |
| ¾ | cup water, beef broth, dry wine, beer, or tomato juice. |
| ½ | teaspoon dried basil *or* thyme, crushed |
| ½ | teaspoon Worcestershire sauce |
| 2 | medium potatoes *or* sweet potatoes, peeled and quartered |
| 4 | carrots, cut into 1½-inch pieces |
| | Pot Roast Gravy |

Oven 325°

Trim excess fat from meat; reserve trimmings. Coat all sides of meat with flour. In a Dutch oven heat trimmings till about 2 tablespoons hot fat accumulate. Discard trimmings. (If necessary, add cooking oil to equal the 2 tablespoons fat.) Brown meat slowly (about 10 minutes) on all sides in hot fat. Sprinkle with salt and pepper. Add water or desired liquid, basil or thyme, and Worcestershire. Cover; simmer for 1 to 1½ hours. Add vegetables. Sprinkle with salt and pepper. Cover; continue cooking about 45 minutes or till meat and vegetables are tender. Add additional water as needed to prevent sticking. (*Or,* after adding liquid and seasonings, cover and bake in a 325° oven for 1 to 1½ hours. Add vegetables; continue baking, covered, about 45 minutes or till tender.) Prepare Pot Roast Gravy. Makes 8 servings.

**Crockery cooker directions:** Prepare Beef Pot Roast as above, *except* cut meat, if necessary, to fit an electric slow crockery cooker. Brown meat as directed. If adding potatoes and carrots, thinly slice the vegetables and place in the *bottom* of the cooker; place meat atop. Generously salt and pepper meat and vegetables. Add liquid and seasonings (if desired, increase seasonings). Cover and cook on low-heat setting for 8 to 10 hours. Prepare Pot Roast Gravy in a saucepan.

# Pot Roast Gravy:

Remove meat and vegetables to a platter; keep warm. Pour meat juices and fat into a large glass measure. Skim off excess fat from pan juices. Measure 1½ cups juices (if necessary, and additional liquid to equal 1½ cups). Return juices to Dutch oven. Stir ½ cup *cold water* into ¼ cup all-purpose *flour;* stir into pan juices. Cook and stir until thickened and bubbly. Cook and stir 1 to 2 minutes more. If desired, add several drops Kitchen Bouquet. Season to taste.

## New England Boiled Dinner

|   |   |
|---|---|
| 1 | 3- to 4-pound corned beef brisket |
| 4 | medium potatoes, peeled |
| 4 | medium carrots |
| 8 | small onions |
| 3 | medium parsnips, peeled and cut into chunks |
| 2 | medium rutabagas, peeled and cut into chunks |
| 1 | small cabbage, cored |

Place meat in a Dutch oven; add juices and spices from package, if desired. Add water to cover meat. Bring to boiling; reduce heat and simmer, covered, about 2 hours or till meat is almost tender. Quarter potatoes and carrots; add to pan with onions, parsnips, and rutabagas. Cover; return to boiling. Reduce heat and simmer 15 minutes. Cut cabbage into wedges; add to pan. Cover; cook 15 to 20 minutes more or till meat and vegetables are tender. Transfer meat and vegetables to a platter. Season with salt and pepper. Serves 8.

## Brisket Carbonnade

|   |   |
|---|---|
| 1 | 3- to 4-pound fresh beef brisket |
| 3 | medium onions, sliced |
| 1 | 12-ounce can (1½ cups) beer |
| 1 | tablespoon brown sugar |
| 2 | teaspoons instant beef bouillon granules |
| 4 | whole black peppercorns *or* ⅛ teaspoon cracked pepper |
| 1 | clove garlic, minced |
| 1 | bay leaf |
| ¼ | teaspoon dried thyme, crushed |
| ¼ | cup all-purpose flour          Oven 350° |

Trim excess fat from brisket. Season meat with a little salt and pepper. Place in a 13x9x2-inch baking pan; cover with onion slices. Sprinkle lightly with salt. Reserve ⅓ cup beer. Combine remaining beer and next 6 ingredients; pour over meat. Cover with foil. Bake in a 350° oven for 3 to 3½ hours or till tender. Remove meat to a platter; keep warm. Skim off excess fat from pan juices; remove bay leaf.

In a saucepan cook juices down to 2 cups. Combine reserved beer and flour; stir into pan juices. Cook and stir until thickened and bubbly. Cook and stir 1 to 2 minutes more. Season. Slice meat across grain; pass gravy. Serves 10.

---

## Roast with Barbecue Gravy

   1   **4-pound beef chuck pot roast**
   2   **tablespoons cooking oil**
   ¾   **cup bottled barbecue sauce**
   ¼   **cup orange marmalade**
   1   **tablespoon vinegar**
   2   **tablespoons cornstarch**

Trim excess fat from meat. In a Dutch oven brown meat on all sides in hot oil. Sprinkle with salt and pepper. Combine barbecue sauce, marmalade, vinegar, and ½ cup *water*; pour over meat. Cover; simmer about 2¼ hours or till meat is tender. Remove meat to a platter; keep warm. Pour meat juices and fat into a large glass measure. Skim off excess fat. Measure 2 cups liquid (if necessary add water). Return to Dutch oven. Combine cornstarch and 2 tablespoons *cold water*; stir into pan juices. Cook and stir till bubbly. Cook and stir 1 to 2 minutes more. Spoon some gravy over meat; pass remaining gravy. Serves 10.

## Oven Steak and Vegetables

| | |
|---|---|
| 1 | to 1½ pounds beef round steak, cut ¾ inch thick |
| ¼ | cup all-purpose flour |
| 2 | tablespoons cooking oil |
| 1 | 16-ounce can tomatoes, cut up |
| ½ | cup chopped onion |
| ½ | teaspoon dried dillweed |
| 4 | medium carrots, cut into strips |
| 2 | medium zucchini, sliced (2 cups) |
| | Hot cooked rice                              Oven 350° |

Trim excess fat from meat. Cut meat into 6 serving-size pieces. In a plastic bag combine *half* of the flour, 1 teaspoon *salt,* and ⅛ teaspoon *pepper.* Shake meat in flour mixture to coat. In a skillet brown meat in hot oil. Transfer meat to a 12x7½x2-inch baking dish; reserve drippings in skillet. In the same skillet stir remaining flour into pan drippings. Stir in *undrained* tomatoes, onion, and dillweed. Cook and stir till thickened and bubbly. Pour mixture over meat. Add carrots. Cover; bake in a 350° oven for 1 hour. Add zucchini. Cover; continue baking 15 to 20 minutes more or till meat and vegetables are tender. Season with salt and pepper. Serve with hot cooked rice. Pass pan juices. Makes 4 to 6 servings.

## Sauerbraten

| | |
|---|---|
| | **Marinade** |
| 1 | 4-pound boneless beef round rump roast |
| 2 | tablespoons cooking oil |
| ½ | cup chopped onion |
| ½ | cup chopped carrot |
| ¼ | cup chopped celery |
| 1 | cup broken gingersnaps |
| | Hot buttered noodles *or* Spaetzle (see recipe, page 636) |

Prepare Marinade. Place meat in a plastic bag; set in a shallow pan. Pour Marinade over meat; close bag. Refrigerate 72 hours, turning meat occasionally. Remove meat; pat excess moisture from meat. Strain Marinade; set aside. In a Dutch oven brown meat on all sides in hot oil. Drain off fat. Add reserved Marinade, chopped onion, carrot, and celery. Cover; simmer about 2 hours or till meat is tender. Transfer meat to a platter; keep warm. Reserve 2 cups cooking liquid and vegetables in Dutch oven. Stir in gingersnaps and ⅔ cup *water*. Cook and stir till thickened and bubbly. Serve with meat and noodles or Spaetzle. Serves 12.

**Marinade:** Combine 1½ cups *water*; 1½ cups *red wine vinegar*; 2 medium *onions*, sliced; 1 *lemon*, sliced; 12 whole *cloves*; 6 whole *black peppercorns*, crushed; 4 *bay leaves*, crushed; 1 tablespoon *sugar*; 1 tablespoon *salt*; and ¼ teaspoon ground *ginger*.

---

## London Broil

---

   1   **1- to 1¼-pound beef flank steak**
  ⅓   **cup cooking oil**
   1   **teaspoon vinegar**
   1   **small clove garlic, minced**
       **Salt**
       **Freshly ground pepper**

Score steak on both sides. Place meat in a plastic bag; set in a deep bowl. Combine oil, vinegar, and garlic; pour over meat. Close bag. Let stand at room temperature 2 to 3 hours, turning several times. Remove meat from marinade; place on an unheated rack in a broiler pan. Broil 3 inches from heat 4 to 5 minutes. Sprinkle with salt and pepper. Turn; broil 4 to 5 minutes more for medium rare. Sprinkle with salt and pepper. Carve into very thin slices diagonally across grain. Serves 4 to 5.

## Swiss Steak

| | |
|---|---|
| 1½ | **pounds beef round steak, cut ¾ inch thick** |
| 3 | **tablespoons all-purpose flour** |
| 1 | **teaspoon salt** |
| 2 | **tablespoons shortening** |
| 1 | **16-ounce can tomatoes, cut up** |
| 1 | **small onion, sliced** |
| 1 | **stalk celery, sliced** |
| 1 | **medium carrot, thinly sliced** |
| ½ | **teaspoon Worcestershire sauce** |
| | **Hot cooked rice or noodles** |

Cut meat into 6 serving-size pieces. Combine flour and salt; pound 2 *tablespoons* of the flour mixture into meat. In a 10-inch skillet brown meat on both sides in hot shortening. Drain off excess fat. Add *undrained* tomatoes, onion, celery, carrot, and Worcestershire. Cover and cook over low heat about 1¼ hours or till meat is tender. Remove meat to a serving platter; keep warm. Skim off excess fat from tomato mixture. Combine ¼ cup *cold water* and the remaining flour mixture; stir into tomato mixture. Cook and stir till thickened and bubbly. Cook and stir 1 to 2 minutes more. Pass with meat. Serve meat and sauce with hot cooked rice or noodles. Makes 6 servings.

**Oven Swiss Steak:** Prepare Swiss Steak as above, *except* after browning meat in hot shortening, transfer meat to a 12x7½x2-inch baking dish. Stir remaining flour mixture into pan drippings in skillet. Stir in *undrained* tomatoes, onion, celery, carrot, and Worcestershire. Cook and stir till thickened and bubbly. Cook and stir 1 to 2 minutes more. Pour over meat in baking dish. Bake, uncovered, in a 350° oven for 1 hour 20 minutes or till meat is tender. Serve with hot cooked rice or noodles.

**Crockery cooker directions:** Prepare Swiss Steak as above, *except* cut meat to fit an electric slow crockery cooker. After browning meat in hot shortening, transfer meat to crockery cooker. Stir remaining flour mixture into pan drippings in skillet. Stir in *undrained* tomatoes, onion, celery, carrot, and Worcestershire. Cook and stir till thickened and bubbly; pour over meat in crockery cooker. Cover and cook on low-heat setting for 8 to 10 hours. Season with salt and pepper. Serve with hot cooked rice or noodles.

## Beef Stroganoff

    1   **pound beef tenderloin, sirloin, *or* round steak**
    1   **tablespoon all-purpose flour**
    2   **tablespoons butter *or* margarine**
 1½   **cups sliced fresh mushrooms**
  ½   **cup chopped onion**
    1   **clove garlic, minced**
    2   **tablespoons butter *or* margarine**
    3   **tablespoons all-purpose flour**
    1   **tablespoon tomato paste**
    1   **teaspoon instant beef bouillon granules**
    1   **cup dairy sour cream**
    2   **tablespoons dry white wine**
        **Hot cooked noodles**

Partially freeze meat; thinly slice across the grain into bite-size strips. Combine 1 tablespoon flour and ½ teaspoon *salt*; coat meat with flour mixture. In a skillet heat 2 tablespoons butter. Add meat; brown quickly on both sides. Add mushrooms, onion, and garlic; cook 3 to 4 minutes or till onion is crisp-tender. Remove meat and mushroom mixture from pan. Add 2 tablespoons butter to pan drippings; stir in 2 *tablespoons* of the flour. Add tomato paste, bouillon granules, and ¼ tea-spoon *salt*. Stir in 1¼ cups *water*. Cook and stir over medium-high heat till bubbly. Cook and stir 1 to 2 minutes longer. Combine sour cream and remaining 1 tablespoon flour. Return meat and mushrooms to skillet. Stir in sour cream mixture and wine. Heat through but *do not boil*. Serve over noodles. Serves 4.

# Chicken-Fried Round Steak

1½ **pounds beef round steak, cut ½ inch thick**
1 **beaten egg**
1 **tablespoon milk**
1 **cup finely crushed saltine crackers (28 crackers)**
¼ **cup cooking oil**

Pound steak to ¼-inch thickness; cut into 6 pieces. Stir together egg and milk; combine cracker crumbs, ½ teaspoon *salt,* and ¼ teaspoon *pepper.* Dip meat in egg mixture, then in crumbs. In a 12-inch skillet brown meat in hot oil, turning once. Cover; cook over low heat 45 to 60 minutes or till tender. Serves 6.

# Beef Fondue

1 **pound trimmed beef tenderloin *or* sirloin steak, cut into ¾-inch cubes**
**Cooking oil *or* peanut oil**
1 **teaspoon salt**
**Creamy Curry Sauce**
**Wine Sauce**

Bring meat to room temperature. Choose a deep, heavy metal fondue cooker that is smaller at the top than the bottom (this shape helps prevent spattering). Pour in oil to no more than half capacity or to a depth of 2 inches. Heat oil-filled cooker over range to 425°. Add salt to help reduce spattering. Transfer cooker to a fondue burner; keep hot.

Spear meat with a fondue fork or bamboo skewer, fry in hot oil to desired doneness (allow 15 seconds for rare; up to 1 minute for well-done). Transfer meat to a dinner fork and dip in either Creamy Curry Sauce or Wine Sauce. Makes 4 servings.

***Creamy Curry Sauce:*** In a mixing bowl combine one 3-ounce package *cream cheese,* softened; ½ cup *dairy sour cream;* 2 tablespoons *milk;* and 1 teaspoon *curry powder.* Stir in 2 tablespoons finely snipped *chives,* 2 tablespoons snipped parsley, 1 teaspoon *Worcestershire sauce,* and ¼ teaspoon *salt.* Makes about 1 cup.

**Wine Sauce:** In a small saucepan cook ¼ cup finely chopped *onion* and 1 clove minced *garlic* in 1 tablespoon *butter or margarine.* Stir in 1 tablespoon *cornstarch* and ¼ teaspoon *salt.* Stir in ½ cup *dry red wine,* ½ cup *water,* ⅓ cup *catsup,* and 1 teaspoon instant *beef bouillon granules.* Cook and stir till thickened and bubbly. Cook and stir 2 minutes more. Makes 1⅓ cups sauce.

## Mushroom Steak Sauce

*See Chapter 17 for other sauces to serve with steaks—*
In a medium saucepan cook 2 cups sliced fresh *mushrooms,* ½ cup chopped *onion,* and 1 clove *garlic,* minced, in 3 tablespoons *butter or margarine* about 5 minutes or till tender. Sprinkle with ⅛ teaspoon *salt,* ⅛ teaspoon *pepper,* and ⅛ teaspoon *celery salt.* Spoon over 4 broiled or panbroiled *beef steaks.* (See directions for cooking steaks at right.) Serves 4.

## Panbroiling Beef Steaks

Choose a beef T-bone, porterhouse, top loin, sirloin, or tenderloin steak cut 1 inch thick. Trim excess fat from steak. Continue using one of the following methods.

**Rub some of the trimmings** over the surface of a heavy skillet. Heat till skillet is *very hot.* Panbroil steak using the following timings to desired doneness, turning once. Season.

| Thickness | 1 inch |
| --- | --- |
| | (approx. total time) |
| Rare | 8–10 minutes |
| Medium | 13–14 minutes |
| Well-Done | about 20 minutes |

**Melt about 1 tablespoon butter** in a heavy skillet over *medium-high* heat. Add steak(s); panbroil using the timings below to desired doneness, turning once. Season. If necessary, keep 1 steak warm while cooking another in about 1 table-spoon butter.

| Thickness | 1 inch |
| --- | --- |
| | **(approx. total time)** |
| Rare | 10–12 minutes |
| Medium | 14–16 minutes |
| Well-Done | 20–22 minutes |

## Broiling Beef Steaks

Choose a beef T-bone, porterhouse, top loin, sirloin, or tenderloin steak cut 1 to 2 inches thick. Without cutting into meat, slash fat edge at 1-inch intervals. Place steak on an unheated rack in a broiler pan. Broil 1- to 1½-inch-thick steaks so surface of meat is 3 inches from heat. Broil 2-inch cuts 4 to 5 inches from heat. Broil on one side for about half of the time indicated for desired doneness. Season. Turn with tongs and broil to desired doneness. Season again.

| Thickness | 1 in. | 1½ in. | 2 in. |
| --- | --- | --- | --- |
| | **(approximate total time in minutes)** | | |
| Rare | 8–10 | 14–16 | 20–25 |
| Medium | 12–14 | 18–20 | 30–35 |
| Well-Done | 18–20 | 25–30 | 40–45 |

### Stir-frying

Use a wok or large skillet for stir-frying foods. Preheat the wok or skillet over high heat, then add the oil. Add the meat and/or vegetables to the hot oil. Using a long-handled spoon or spatula, frequently lift and turn the food with a folding motion as the food cooks. Maintain high heat so the food will cook quickly.

# Beef and Vegetable Stir-Fry

|       |                                                    |
|-------|----------------------------------------------------|
| 1     | pound beef top round steak                         |
| 1½    | cups broccoli cut into 1-inch pieces               |
| 3     | medium carrots, bias-sliced                        |
| 1     | teaspoon cornstarch                                |
| ½     | teaspoon sugar                                     |
| 2     | tablespoons soy sauce                              |
| 2     | tablespoons dry sherry                             |
| 2     | tablespoons cooking oil                            |
| 1     | medium onion, cut into thin wedges                 |
| ½     | of a 10-ounce package (1 cup) frozen peas, thawed  |
| ½     | cup water chestnuts, drained and thinly sliced     |
| ½     | cup bamboo shoots, halved lengthwise               |
|       | Hot cooked rice                                    |

Partially freeze beef; very thinly slice across the grain into bite-size strips. Cook broccoli and carrots, covered, in boiling salted water 2 minutes; drain. Mix cornstarch, sugar, and 1 teaspoon *salt*. Stir in soy and sherry. Set aside.

Preheat a wok or large skillet over high heat; add oil. Stir-fry broccoli, carrots, and onion in hot oil for 2 minutes or till crisp-tender. Remove from wok. (Add more oil, if necessary.) Add *half* the beef to *hot* wok; stir-fry 2 to 3 minutes or till browned. Remove beef. Stir-fry remaining beef 2 to 3 minutes. Return all meat to wok. Add peas, water chestnuts, and bamboo shoots. Stir soy mixture; stir into wok. Cook and stir till thickened and bubbly. Cook and stir 1 to 2 minutes more. Return broccoli, carrots, and onion to wok; cover and cook 1 minute more. Serve with rice. Serves 4 to 6.

## Broiled Short Ribs

  **4**   **pounds beef short ribs, cut into**
         **serving-size pieces**
 **⅔**   **cup catsup**
 **¼**   **cup light molasses**
 **¼**   **cup lemon juice**
  **1**   **tablespoon dry mustard**
 **½**   **teaspoon chili powder**
      **Dash garlic powder**

Trim excess fat from ribs. Sprinkle with some salt and pepper.
Place ribs in a Dutch oven; add water to cover. Simmer,
covered, about 2 hours or till meat is tender. Drain; place ribs
on an unheated rack in a broiler pan. Combine catsup, molasses, lemon juice, mustard, chili powder, and garlic powder;
brush some over ribs. Broil 4 to 5 inches from heat for 10 to
15 minutes, turning often and basting with catsup mixture.
Makes 6 servings.

## Chinese-Style Beef Ribs

  **4**   **pounds lean beef plate spareribs,**
         **cut into 2- to 3-rib portions**
 **½**   **cup soy sauce**
 **¼**   **cup dry white wine**
  **6**   **cloves garlic, minced**
  **2**   **tablespoons ground ginger**
  **1**   **tablespoon sugar**
  **1**   **tablespoon lemon juice**
 **½**   **teaspoon ground cloves**
 **½**   **teaspoon ground cinnamon**
 **¼**   **teaspoon aniseed, crushed**      Oven 350°

Place beef ribs in a plastic bag; set in a deep bowl. Combine
soy sauce, dry white wine, minced garlic, ground ginger, sugar,
lemon juice, ground cloves, ground cinnamon, and crushed
aniseed. Pour mixture over ribs in plastic bag. Close bag.

Marinate in refrigerator 4 hours or overnight, turning bag occasionally to distribute marinade evenly.

Remove ribs from bag and place ribs on a rack in a shallow roasting pan. Pour the marinade over the ribs. Cover and bake in a 350° oven for 1½ to 2 hours or till ribs are tender, basting with juices occasionally. Serves 6.

## Sherried Veal Pot Roast

    1   1½- to 2-pound veal shoulder blade roast
    2   tablespoons butter *or* margarine
    2   small onions, sliced
    1   bay leaf
    1   teaspoon instant beef bouillon granules
    ½   teaspoon dried thyme, crushed
    3   carrots, sliced
    3   tablespoons all-purpose flour
    ½   cup sliced fresh mushrooms
    3   tablespoons dry sherry

In a Dutch oven brown meat on all sides in butter. Add *half* of the onions. Add bay leaf, bouillon granules, thyme, 1 cup *water,* 1 teaspoon *salt,* and dash *pepper.* Cover and simmer for 45 minutes. Add remaining onions and the carrots. Simmer, covered, 25 to 30 minutes or till meat and vegetables are tender. Remove meat and vegetables to a platter; keep warm.

Pour meat juices and fat into a glass measure. Skim off excess fat. Measure 1 cup juices (if necessary, add water). Return juices to Dutch oven. Stir ⅓ cup *cold water* into flour; stir into pan juices. Add mushrooms. Cook and stir until thickened and bubbly. Cook and stir 1 to 2 minutes more. Stir in sherry. Season. Serve with veal. Makes 6 servings.

## Swiss Veal Roast

1   2½- to 3-pound veal leg sirloin roast
1   7½-ounce can tomatoes, cut up
¾   cup diced fully cooked ham
2   tablespoons dry white wine
2   tablespoons cornstarch
½   cup shredded process Swiss cheese (2
    ounces)                                    Oven 325°

Place meat, fat side up, on a rack in a shallow roasting pan.
Insert a meat thermometer. Roast in a 325° oven for 1¼ to 1¾
hours or till thermometer registers 170°. Remove meat to a
platter. Skim fat from pan juices, if necessary. Add *undrained*
tomatoes, ham, wine, and dash *pepper* to pan juices. Combine cornstarch and ½ cup *cold water*; stir into tomato mixture. Cook and stir till thickened and bubbly. Cook and stir 1
to 2 minutes more. Add cheese; stir till melted. Serve with
meat. Serves 8.

## Veal Cordon Bleu

2   slices boiled ham
2   slices Swiss cheese
1   pound veal leg round steak, cut ¼ inch
    thick
⅔   cup fine dry bread crumbs
1   teaspoon snipped parsley
⅛   teaspon pepper
¼   cup all-purpose flour
1   slightly beaten egg
¼   cup butter or margarine

Quarter ham and cheese slices. Cut veal into 4 pieces; pound
with a meat mallet to ⅛-inch thickness (each about 8x4 inches).
Cut each veal piece in half crosswise. On one half, place 2
quarters *each* of ham and cheese; trim or fold to fit. Cover
with second piece of veal; seal edges. Repeat with remaining
meats and cheese. Combine bread crumbs, parsley, and pep-

per. Dip meat in flour, then in beaten egg, then in crumb mixture.

In a skillet melt butter or margarine. Add meat; cook over medium-high heat about 4 minutes per side or till golden brown. Serve at once. Makes 4 servings.

## Veal Patties

- **1½ pounds ground veal**
- **1 teaspoon salt**
- **1 teaspoon lemon juice**
- **½ teaspoon paprika**
- **⅛ teaspoon ground nutmeg**
  **Dash pepper**
- **1 slightly beaten egg**
- **2 tablespoons water**
- **½ cup fine dry bread crumbs**
- **2 tablespoons butter or margarine**

Combine veal, salt, lemon juice, paprika, nutmeg, and pepper; mix well. Shape meat mixture into 6 patties. Combine the egg and water. Dip patties into egg mixture, then into bread crumbs. In a large skillet melt butter or margarine. Add patties; cook over medium-high heat to desired doneness, turning once (allow 12 to 15 minutes total time for medium). Makes 6 servings.

## Oven Hash

- **1 cup finely chopped cooked beef**
- **1 cup finely chopped cooked potato**
- **1 5⅓-ounce can evaporated milk**
- **¼ cup finely chopped onion**
- **2 tablespoons snipped parsley**
- **2 teaspoons Worcestershire sauce**
- **½ to 1 teaspoon salt**
  **Dash pepper**
- **¼ cup finely crushed rich round crackers**
- **1 tablespoon butter or margarine, melted**                    Oven 350°

Combine beef, potato, evaporated milk, onion, parsley, Worcestershire, salt, and pepper. Turn into a 1-quart casserole. Toss cracker crumbs with melted butter; sprinkle atop casserole. Bake in 350° oven about 30 minutes or till heated through. Makes 2 servings.

## Deviled Beef Rolls

- **2 tablespoons *regular* onion soup mix**
- **3 tablespoons horseradish mustard**
- **4 beef cubed steaks (1 pound total)**
- **1 4-ounce can sliced mushrooms, drained**
- **2 tablespoons butter, melted**

Mix dry soup mix and 4 teaspoons *water;* let stand 5 minutes. Stir in mustard. Sprinkle steaks with a little pepper. Spread one side of each steak with ¼ of the mustard mixture; top *each* with ¼ of the mushrooms. Roll up steaks and fasten with wooden picks. Brush with butter. Broil 4 to 5 inches from heat 6 minutes. Turn and brush with butter; broil 6 minutes more. Remove picks. Serves 4.

## Creamed Dried Beef

In a skillet cook one 3- or 4-ounce package *sliced dried or smoked beef,* snipped, in 2 tablespoons *butter* 3 minutes or till edges curl. Stir 2 tablespoons all-purpose *flour* into butter mixture; add 1⅓ cups *milk* all at once. Cook and stir till thickened and bubbly. Cook and stir 1 to 2 minutes more. Stir in ½ teaspoon *Worcestershire sauce* and dash *pepper.* Spoon over *buttered toast points.* Serves 3 or 4.

# Meat Loaf

      2   **eggs**
     ¾   **cup milk**
     ½   **cup fine dry bread crumbs**
     ¼   **cup finely chopped onion**
      2   **tablespoons snipped parsley**
      1   **teaspoon salt**
     ½   **teaspoon ground sage**
     1½  **pounds ground beef**
     ¼   **cup catsup**
      2   **tablespoons brown sugar**
      1   **teaspoon dry mustard**                  Oven 350°

Combine eggs and milk; stir in crumbs, onion, parsley, salt, sage, and ⅛ teaspoon *pepper*. Add beef; mix well. Pat into a 5½-cup ring mold; unmold in a shallow baking pan. Bake in a 350° oven for 50 minutes. (*Or*, pat mixture into an 8x4x2-inch loaf pan; bake for 1¼ hours.) Spoon off excess fat. Combine catsup, sugar, and mustard; spread over meat. Return to oven for 10 minutes. Makes 6 servings.

   **Microwave directions:** Prepare meat as above, *except* pat into a 5½-cup ring mold and invert into a 9- or 10-inch nonmetal pie plate; remove mold (Do not use a loaf pan.) Cover with waxed paper. Cook in a counter-top microwave oven on high power 12 to 13 minutes or till done; give dish a quarter-turn every 3 minutes. Spoon off excess fat. Combine catsup, sugar, and mustard; spread over meat. Let stand 5 minutes; transfer to a platter.

# Porcupine Meatballs

      1   **beaten egg**
      1   **10¾-ounce can condensed tomato soup**
     ¼   **cup long grain rice**
      2   **tablespoons finely chopped onion**
      1   **tablespoon snipped parsley**
      1   **pound ground beef**
      1   **teaspoon Worcestershire sauce**

In a bowl combine egg and ¼ cup of the soup. Stir in uncooked rice, onion, parsley, ½ teaspoon *salt*, and ⅛ teaspoon *pepper*. Add beef and mix well. Shape meat mixture into 20 small balls; place in a 10-inch skillet. Mix remaining soup with Worcestershire and ½ cup *water;* pour over meatballs. Bring to boiling; reduce heat. Cover and simmer 35 to 40 minutes; stir often. Makes 4 to 5 servings.

## Sauerbraten Burgers

| | |
|---|---|
| ½ | cup crushed gingersnaps (8 cookies) |
| 1 | 8-ounce can tomato sauce |
| ¼ | cup finely chopped onion |
| ¼ | cup raisins |
| ½ | teaspoon salt |
| 1 | pound ground beef |
| ⅓ | cup water |
| 2 | tablespoons brown sugar |
| 2 | tablespoons vinegar |
| 1 | teaspoon prepared mustard |
| | Dash pepper |
| | Hot cooked noodles or rice |

Reserve 2 *tablespoons* of the crushed gingersnaps. Mix remaining gingersnaps with 2 *tablespoons* of the tomato sauce, the onion, raisins, and salt. Add meat; mix well. Shape into four ¾-inch-thick patties; brown in a skillet. Drain off fat. Combine remaining tomato sauce, water, brown sugar, vinegar, mustard, and pepper. Pour over burgers. Cover; simmer 10 to 15 minutes, spooning sauce over meat. Remove burgers; keep warm.

Stir reserved crushed gingersnaps into sauce in skillet. Cook and stir till bubbly. Skim off excess fat. Pour some sauce over burgers; pass remaining sauce. Serve with noodles or rice. Makes 4 servings.

**Microwave directions:** Prepare meat patties as above, *except* place in an 8x8x2-inch nonmetal baking dish. Cook, covered with waxed paper, in a counter-top microwave oven on high power for 3 minutes. Give dish a half-turn; micro-cook 2 minutes more. Drain off excess fat and liquid. Combine remaining tomato sauce, reserved gingersnaps, water, brown sugar, vinegar, mustard, and pepper; pour over meat. Micro-cook, covered, 2 minutes. Stir the sauce and turn dish; micro-cook, covered, 3 minutes more.

## Hamburgers

Shape 1 pound *ground beef* into four ½-inch-thick patties. Panbroil, broil, or bake as directed below. Makes 4 servings.

**To panbroil:** Heat a heavy skillet till very hot. Sprinkle surface of skillet lightly with salt. Add patties. Cook over medium-high heat to desired doneness, turning once (allow about 6 minutes total time for rare; about 8 minutes for medium; about 10 minutes for well-done). Sprinkle both sides with salt and pepper. If necessary, partially cover the skillet to prevent spattering.

**To broil:** Place patties on an unheated rack in a broiler pan. Broil 3 inches from heat to desired doneness, turning once (allow about 8 minutes total time for rare; about 10 minutes for medium; about 12 mintues for well-done). Sprinkle both sides with salt and pepper.

**To bake:** Place patties in 8x8x2-inch baking pan. Cover and bake in a 350° oven to desired doneness (allow 20 to 25 minutes for rare; 25 to 30 minutes for medium; 30 to 35 minutes for well-done). Sprinkle with salt and pepper.

## Double-Decker Burgers

|   |   |
|---|---|
| 2 | **pounds ground beef** |
| 1½ | **teaspoons seasoned salt** |
| ⅛ | **teaspoon pepper** |
| 8 | **hamburger buns, split, toasted, and buttered** |
|   | **Tomato-Cucumber Relish** |

Combine meat, seasoned salt, and pepper; shape into sixteen 4-inch-diameter patties. Place 8 patties on an unheated rack in a broiler pan. Broil 3 inches from heat to desired doneness, turning once (allow 6 minutes total time for medium). Cover;

keep warm. Repeat with remaining patties. For each serving, stack 2 meat patties on bottom half of each bun, spooning Tomato-Cucumber Relish between and atop patties. Top with bun tops. Serves 8.

***Tomato-Cucumber Relish:*** Combine ¼ cup *vinegar*, ¼ cup *water*, 2 tablespoons *sugar*, 1 teaspoon *salt*, and ⅛ teaspoon *pepper*. Add 1 medium *tomato*, chopped (1 cup); ½ unpeeled *cucumber*, thinly sliced; and 1 medium *onion*, chopped (½ cup). Cover and refrigerate 1 to 2 hours. Before serving, drain well; stir in ¼ cup chopped *sweet pickle*.

## Skilletburgers

|   |   |
|---|---|
| 1 | **pound ground beef** |
| 1 | **cup chopped onion** |
| ½ | **cup chopped celery** |
| 1 | **15-ounce can tomato sauce** |
| 2 | **tablespoons quick-cooking rolled oats** |
| 1 | **tablespoon brown sugar** |
| 1 | **teaspoon Worcestershire sauce** |
| ½ | **teaspoon chili powder** |
|   | **Dash bottled hot pepper sauce** |
| 14 | **to 16 hamburger buns, split and toasted** |

In a skillet cook beef, onion, and celery till beef is browned and onion is tender; drain off excess fat. Stir in tomato sauce, oats, brown sugar, Worcestershire, chili powder, hot pepper sauce, ½ cup *water*, 1 teaspoon *salt*, and ⅛ teaspoon *pepper*. Simmer, uncovered, about 30 minutes or till mixture is of desired consistency. Spoon about ½ *cup* of the meat mixture into *each* bun. Makes 7 or 8 servings.

## Stuffed Green Peppers

    6   large green peppers
    1   pound ground beef
  ½   cup chopped onion
    1   16-ounce can tomatoes, cut up
  ½   cup long grain rice
  ½   cup water
    1   teaspoon salt
    1   teaspoon Worcestershire sauce
    1   cup shredded American cheese
        (4 ounces)                              Oven 350°

Cut tops from green peppers; discard seeds and membranes.
Chop enough of the tops to make ¼ cup; set aside. Cook the
whole green peppers, uncovered, in boiling water for 5 minutes; invert to drain well. Sprinkle insides of peppers lightly
with salt. In a skillet cook ground beef, onion, and the ¼ cup
chopped green pepper till meat is browned and vegetables are
tender. Drain off excess fat. Add *undrained* tomatoes, *uncooked*
rice, water, salt, Worcestershire, and dash *pepper*. Bring to
boiling; reduce heat. Cover and simmer 15 to 18 minutes or
till rice is tender. Stir in cheese. Stuff peppers with meat
mixture. Place in a 10x6x2-inch baking dish. Bake, covered, in
a 350° oven for 30 to 35 minutes. Serves 6.

# Spaghetti Sauce

1½   **pounds ground beef** *or* **bulk pork sausage**
1   **large onion, chopped (1 cup)**
1   **large green pepper, chopped (1 cup)**
2   **cloves garlic, minced**
3   **16-ounce can tomatoes, cut up**
1   **6-ounce can tomato paste**
2   **teaspoons brown sugar**
1½   **teaspoons dried oregano, crushed**
1   **teaspoon salt**
½   **teaspoon dried basil, crushed**
½   **teaspoon dried thyme, crushed**
1   **bay leaf**
2   **cups water**
    **Hot cooked spaghetti**

In a Dutch oven cook meat, onion, green pepper, and garlic till meat is browned and vegetables are tender. Drain off fat. Stir in *undrained* tomatoes, tomato paste, brown sugar, oregano, salt, basil, thyme, and bay leaf. Stir in the water. Bring to boiling; reduce heat. Simmer, uncovered, for 1½ to 2 hours or till sauce is of desired consistency, stirring occasionally. Remove bay leaf. Serve over hot cooked spaghetti. Pass grated Parmesan cheese, if desired. Makes 6 servings.

**Spaghetti and Meatballs:** Prepare Spaghetti Sauce as above, *except* omit the ground beef or pork sausage in the sauce. In a Dutch oven cook the onion, green pepper, and garlic in 1 tablespoon *cooking oil*. Continue cooking sauce as directed.

While the sauce is cooking, combine 1 beaten *egg* and ¼ cup *milk*; stir in 1½ cups soft *bread crumbs* (2 slices), ¼ cup finely chopped *onion*, and 1 teaspoon *salt*. Add 1½ pounds *ground beef*; mix well. With wet hands shape meat mixture into about 48 one-inch meatballs.

In a skillet slowly brown meatballs in 1 tablespoon hot *cooking oil*. Drain well. Add browned meatballs to the sauce the last 30 minutes of cooking. Serve meatballs and sauce over hot cooked spaghetti. Pass grated Parmesan cheese, if desired.

## Tacos con Carne

| | |
|---|---|
| **12** | **packaged taco shells** |
| **1** | **pound ground beef *or* bulk pork sausage** |
| **1** | **medium onion, chopped (½ cup)** |
| **1** | **clove garlic, minced** |
| **1** | **teaspoon chili powder** |
| **¾** | **teaspoon salt** |
| **2** | **tomatoes, chopped and drained** |
| | **Shredded lettuce** |
| **1** | **cup shredded sharp cheddar cheese (4 ounces)** |
| | **Bottled taco sauce** |

Oven 250°

Arrange taco shells on a baking sheet lined with paper toweling. Warm in a 250° oven while preparing meat mixture. In a skillet cook meat, onion, and garlic till meat is browned and onion is tender. Drain off fat. Season meat mixture with chili powder and the salt. Stuff *each* taco shell with some of the meat mixture, tomatoes, lettuce, and cheese; pass taco sauce. Makes 6 servings.

## Hamburger-Corn Bake

| | |
|---|---|
| **3** | **ounces medium noodles** |
| **1** | **pound ground beef** |
| **½** | **cup chopped onion** |
| **1** | **10¾-ounce can condensed cream of chicken soup or cream of mushroom soup** |
| **1** | **8¾-ounce can whole kernel corn, drained** |
| **1** | **cup dairy sour cream** |
| **¼** | **cup milk** |
| **2** | **tablespoons chopped pimiento** |
| **½** | **teaspoon salt** |
| | **Dash pepper** |
| **1** | **cup soft bread crumbs** |
| **1** | **tablespoon butter *or* margarine, melted** |

Oven 350°

Cook noodles according to package directions; drain. In a large skillet cook beef and onion till meat is browned and onion is tender. Drain off fat. Stir in soup, corn, sour cream, milk, pimiento, salt, and pepper; mix well. Stir in cooked noodles. Turn mixture into a 1½-quart casserole. Toss bread crumbs with melted butter; sprinkle atop casserole. Bake, uncovered, in a 350° oven about 50 minutes or till heated through. Makes 4 or 5 servings.

## Texas Beef Skillet

**1** **pound ground beef**
**¾** **cup chopped onion**
**1** **16-ounce can tomatoes, cut up**
**1** **15½-ounce can red kidney beans**
**½** **cup quick-cooking rice**
**3** **tablespoons chopped green pepper**
**1½** **teaspoons chili powder**
**½** **teaspoon garlic salt**
**¾** **cup shredded American cheese**
**Corn chips, crushed**

In a skillet cook ground beef and onion till meat is browned and onion is tender. Drain off fat. Stir in the *undrained* tomatoes, *undrained* beans, *uncooked* rice, green pepper, chili powder, garlic salt, ½ cup *water,* and ½ teaspoon *salt.* Bring to boiling; reduce heat. Simmer, covered, for 20 minutes, stirring occasionally. Top with cheese. Cover and heat about 3 minutes or till cheese melts. Sprinkle corn chips around the edge. Serves 6.

# Hamburger Pie

    1    **pound ground beef**
    ½    **cup chopped onion**
    1    **16-ounce can cut green beans, drained**
    1    **10¾-ounce can condensed tomato soup**
    3    **medium potatoes, peeled and quartered (1
          pound)**
    1    **beaten egg**
         **Milk**
    ½    **cup shredded American cheese
          (2 ounces)**                        Oven 350°

In a large skillet cook ground beef and onion till meat is
browned and onion is tender; drain off fat. Stir in beans, soup,
¼ cup *water,* ¾ teaspoon *salt,* and ⅛ teaspoon *pepper.* Turn
mixture into a 1½-quart casserole.

In a covered pan cook potatoes in boiling salted water about
20 minutes or just till tender; drain. Mash while hot; stir in egg.
Add enough milk to make potatoes fluffy, yet stiff enough to
hold their shape. Season with salt and pepper. Drop potatoes
in mounds atop meat mixture. Sprinkle with cheese. Bake,
uncovered, in a 350° oven for 25 to 30 minutes or till heated
through. Makes 4 to 6 servings.

# Pork and Ham

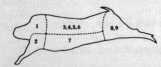

Locate the wholesale cuts on the drawing, identify the retail pieces in the same numbered picture, and then note the cooking methods.

**1.** Shoulder Blade Boston Roast, top—*roast*. Smoked Shoulder Roll, left—*roast, cook in liquid*. Shoulder Blade Steak, right—*braise, broil, panfry*.

**2.** Smoked Shoulder Picnic Whole, top—*roast, cook in liquid*. Canned Arm Picnic, left—*roast*. Smoked Pork Hocks (crosscut), right—*braise, cook in liquid*.

**3.** Rib Crown Roast, top—*roast*. Loin Center Loin Roast, right—*roast*. Loin Rib Chops for Stuffing, lower left—*roast, braise*.

**4.** Loin Sirloin Roast, upper right—*roast*. Tenderloin, left—*roast, braise, broil*. Loin Chop, lower right—*braise, broil*.

**5.** Pork Loin Rib Half, upper right—*roast*. Loin Back Ribs, left—*broil, roast, braise*. Loin Rib Chop, lower right—*braise, broil*.

**6.** Canadian-Style Bacon, upper left—*roast*. Sliced Canadian-Style Bacon, lower left—*broil, panbroil, panfry*. Boneless Loin Top Loin Roast, upper right—*roast*. Loin Butter-

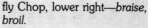

fly Chop, lower right—*braise, broil.*

**7.** Spareribs, left—*roast, braise, cook in liquid.* Salt Pork, upper right—*cook in liquid for seasoning, panfry.* Slab Bacon and Sliced Bacon, right—*broil, panbroil, panfry.*

**8.** Smoked Ham Shank Portion, left—*bake.* Smoked Ham Rump Portion, upper right—*bake.* Smoked Ham Center Slice, lower right—*broil, panfry, bake.*

**9.** Boneless Smoked Ham Roll, upper left—*bake.* Country-Style Ham, Shank Portion, right—*cook in liquid and bake.* Canned Ham, lower left—*bake.*

# Roasting Pork

Trim off excess fat from pork roast, leaving a thin layer of fat over the meat to protect the lean portion from drying out. Season fresh pork roasts by sprinkling with a little salt and pepper.

Place meat, fat side up, on a rack in a shallow roasting pan. The rack may be omitted when roasting meat with rib bones because the rib bones serve as a rack. Insert a meat thermometer, placing thermometer so its bulb rests in the center of the thickest portion of the meat and does not rest in fat or touch bone (see tip, page 451). Do not add water or other liquid, and do not cover the roasting pan. Roast the meat in a 325° oven until the meat thermometer registers the specified internal temperature.

For easier carving, let the meat stand about 15 minutes. Carve meat following the suggestions on pages 534–36. Remove string from rolled and tied roasts before carving.

Use the roasting times given in the chart below only as a guide to the total cooking time for the cut of meat you are preparing, since individual cuts of meat vary in size and shape.

## Roast Pork with Fennel

|   |   |
|---|---|
| 1 | 3- to 4-pound pork loin blade roast |
| ½ | teaspoon fennel seed |
| 2 | tablespoons sugar |
| 1 | teaspoon salt |
| 1 | teaspoon ground sage |
| 1 | teaspoon dried marjoram, crushed |
| ¼ | teaspoon celery seed |
| ¼ | teaspoon dry mustard |
| 1 | tablespoon snipped parsley |

Oven 325°

Stud roast with fennel seed by inserting the tip of a knife into the meat and pushing 4 or 5 seeds into a meat pocket as you remove the knife. Cut about 15 evenly spaced pockets on meat's surface. Combine sugar, salt, sage, marjoram, celery seed, dry mustard, and ⅛ teaspoon *pepper;* rub roast with mixture. Cover roast; let stand 4 hours in refrigerator.

Place meat on a rack in a shallow roasting pan. Insert a meat thermometer. Roast, uncovered, in a 325° oven for 2¼ to 2¾ hours or till meat thermometer registers 170°. Place on a platter; sprinkle with parsley. Serves 8 to 10.

| Pork Cut | Approximate Weight (pounds) | Internal Temperature on Removal from Oven | Approximate Cooking Time (total time) |
|---|---|---|---|
| | Roast meat at a constant 325° oven temperature | | |
| Shoulder Arm Picnic | 5 to 8 | 170° | 3 to 4 hours |
| Smoked Shoulder Picnic Whole | | | |
| cook-before eating | 5 to 8 | 170° | 3 to 4½ hours |
| fully cooked | 5 to 8 | 140° | 2½ to 3¼ hours |
| Shoulder Arm Roast | 3 to 5 | 170° | 2 to 3 hours |
| Shoulder Blade Boston Roast | 4 to 6 | 170° | 3 to 4 hours |
| Boneless Shoulder Blade | | | |
| Boston Roast | 3 to 5 | 170° | 2 to 3 hours |
| Smoked Shoulder Roll | 2 to 3 | 170° | 1¼ to 1¾ hours |
| Loin Blade Roast | 3 to 4 | 170° | 2¼ to 2¾ hours |
| Loin Center Loin Roast | 3 to 5 | 170° | 1¾ to 2½ hours |
| Loin Center Rib Roast | 3 to 5 | 170° | 1¾ to 2½ hours |
| Rib Crown Roast | 4 to 6 | 170° | 2¾ to 3½ hours |
| Boneless Loin Tip | | | |
| Loin Roast (double) | 3 to 5 | 170° | 2 to 3 hours |
| Boneless Loin Top Loin Roast | 2 to 4 | 170° | 1¼ to 2 hours |
| Loin Sirloin Roast | 3 to 5 | 170° | 2¼ to 3¼ hours |
| Tenderloin | 1 | 170° | ¾ to 1 hour |
| Leg (fresh ham) | 12 to 16 | 170° | 5 to 6 hours |
| Leg (fresh ham), half | 5 to 8 | 170° | 3¼ to 4¾ hours |

# Pork with Apple-Curry Sauce

**1** **5- to 8-pound fresh pork shoulder arm picnic *or* smoked pork shoulder picnic whole (cook-before-eating)**
**Milk *or* light cream**
**2** **teaspoons curry powder**
**2** **tablespoons butter *or* margarine**
**2** **medium apples, peeled, cored, and chopped (2 cups)**
**⅓** **cup finely chopped onion**
**2** **tablespoons all-purpose flour**          Oven 325°

Place meat on a rack in a shallow roasting pan. Insert a meat thermometer. Roast in a 325° oven for 3 to 4 hours or till thermometer registers 170°. Place meat on a serving platter; keep warm. Skim fat from pan juices; reserve 2 tablespoons juices. Add milk or cream to equal 1 cup liquid; set aside.

In a saucepan cook and stir curry powder in butter for 1 minute. Stir in apples and onions; cook, covered, till apples and onion are tender. Stir in flour. Add milk mixture all at once. Cook and stir over medium heat till thickened and bubbly. Cook and stir 1 to 2 minutes more. Season sauce for fresh roast with salt and pepper. If desired, spoon some sauce over roast. Pass remaining sauce. Serves 10 to 14.

## Orange-Glazed Ribs

      4  **pounds meaty pork spareribs, cut into**
         **serving-size pieces**
    2/3  **cup orange marmalade**
      3  **tablespoons soy sauce**
      2  **tablespoons lemon juice.**
    3/4  **teaspoon ground ginger**
         **Orange slices**                    Oven 450°

Place ribs, meaty side down, in a shallow roasting pan. Roast in a 450° oven for 30 minutes. Remove meat from oven; drain off excess fat. Turn ribs meaty side up. Reduce oven temperature to 350°; continue roasting 30 minutes longer. Meanwhile, prepare glaze. Combine marmalade, soy sauce, lemon juice, and ginger; mix well. Spoon *half* of the mixture over spareribs. Roast 30 minutes more or till tender, spooning remaining glaze over ribs occasionally. Garnish ribs on a serving platter with orange slices. Makes 6 servings.

# Harvest Pot Roast

|   |   |
|---|---|
| 1 | 4-pound pork shoulder arm roast |
| 2 | tablespoons cooking oil |
| 1 | medium onion, cut into thin wedges |
| 1 | teaspoon dried dillweed |
| 1 | medium acorn squash |
| 8 | small potatoes, peeled (1½ pounds) |
| 3 | large carrots, sliced |
| ¼ | cup all-purpose flour |
| ½ | teaspoon Kitchen Bouquet |

In a Dutch oven brown meat in hot oil. Spoon off fat. Add onion, dillweed, 2 cups *water*, 2 teaspoons *salt*, and ½ teaspoon *pepper*. Bring to boiling; reduce heat. Simmer, covered, 1 hour. Cut squash crosswise into 1-inch-thick slices; discard seeds. Halve slices. Add squash, potatoes, and carrots to meat. Simmer 30 minutes or till meat and vegetables are tender; remove to a platter. Skim fat from pan juices. Measure 1½ cups juices. Stir ½ cup *cold water* into the flour; stir into reserved juices. Cook and stir till bubbly. Stir in Kitchen Bouquet; cook and stir 1 to 2 minutes more. Pass with meat. Serves 8.

---

# Oven-Baked Ribs and Kraut

|   |   |   |
|---|---|---|
| 3 | pounds pork loin back ribs, cut into 2-rib portions | |
| 1 | 27-ounce can sauerkraut, drained | |
| 3 | medium potatoes, peeled and sliced | |
| ⅓ | cup chicken broth | |
| ¼ | cup chopped pimiento | |
| ½ | teaspoon celery seed | |
| 1 | medium onion, sliced | |
| ½ | cup bottled barbecue sauce | Oven 450° |

Place ribs, meaty side down, in a shallow roasting pan. Roast in a 450° oven for 20 minutes. Remove meat from oven; drain off excess fat. Reduce oven temperature to 350°. Combine sauerkraut, potatoes, broth, pimiento, and celery seed. Place in the bottom of a 13x9x2-inch baking dish. Separate onion into rings; place atop sauerkraut mixture. Place ribs, meaty side up, in center of dish; sprinkle with salt. Brush barbecue sauce over ribs. Cover; bake in a 350° oven for 1½ to 1¾ hours. Serves 6.

## Sweet-Sour Pork

In a bowl combine 1 beaten *egg,* ¼ cup *cornstarch,* ¼ cup all-purpose *flour,* ¼ cup *chicken broth,* and ½ teaspoon *salt.* Beat till smooth. Use 1 pound boneless pork, cut into 1-inch cubes; dip pork cubes into batter. Fry in deep hot *cooking oil* (365°) for 5 to 6 minutes or till golden. Drain; keep warm.

In a skillet cook 1 large *green pepper,* chopped; ½ cup chopped *carrot;* and 1 clove *garlic,* minced, in 2 tablespoons hot *cooking oil* till vegetables are tender but not brown. Stir in 1¼ cups *chicken broth,* ½ cup *sugar,* ⅓ cup *red wine vinegar,* and 2 teaspoons *soy sauce.* Bring to boiling; boil rapidly 1 minute. Stir ¼ cup *cold water* into 2 tablespoons *cornstarch.* Stir into vegetable mixture. Cook and stir till thickened and bubbly. Cook and stir 1 to 2 minutes more. Stir in pork cubes. Serve with hot cooked rice, if desired. Makes 4 to 6 servings.

## Pork Chow Mein

- **1 pound boneless pork**
- **3 tablespoons cooking oil**
- **1 cup sliced green onion**
- **1 cup sliced celery**
- **2 cups sliced fresh mushrooms**
- **1 8-ounce can water chestnuts, drained and sliced**
- **1 13¾-ounce can chicken broth**
- **¼ cup soy sauce**
- **1 16-ounce can chop suey vegetables, drained**
- **3 tablespoons cornstarch**
  **Hot cooked rice**

Partially freeze pork; slice thinly across the grain into bite-size strips. Preheat a large skillet or wok; add cooking oil. Add the pork; stir-fry 2 to 3 minutes (see tip, page 470). Remove meat. Add onion and celery to skillet or wok. Stir-fry 1 minute. Add mushrooms and water chestnuts; stir-fry 1 minute. Add 1¼ *cups* of the chicken broth, the soy sauce, and chop suey vegetables. Add meat to vegetable mixture. Stir remaining chicken broth into cornstarch. Stir into meat-vegetable mixture. Cook and stir till thickened and bubbly. Cook and stir 1 to 2 minutes more. Serve over hot cooked rice. Makes 6 servings.

---

## Curried Pork

- **1   large apple, cored and chopped**
- **¼   cup sliced green onion**
- **2   teaspoons curry powder**
- **1   tablespoon butter *or* margarine**
- **1   10¾-ounce can condensed cream of mushroom soup**
- **¾   cup milk**
- **2   tablespoons snipped parsley**
- **2   cups cubed cooked pork**
- **1   cup dairy sour cream**
  **Hot cooked rice**

In a saucepan cook chopped apple, green onion, and curry powder in butter or margarine till onion is tender. Stir in soup, milk, and parsley. Add pork; simmer, uncovered, 10 minutes. Stir in sour cream. Heat through but *do not boil*. Serve over hot cooked rice. Makes 4 servings.

## Barbecued Pork Sandwiches

|  |  |
|--|--|
| ½ | **pound cooked pork** |
| 1 | **8-ounce can tomato sauce** |
| ½ | **cup chopped onion** |
| ¼ | **cup finely chopped green pepper** |
| 1 | **clove garlic, minced** |
| 2 | **tablespoons vinegar** |
| 1 | **tablespoon brown sugar** |
| 1 | **tablespoon Worcestershire sauce** |
| 1½ | **teaspoons dry mustard** |
| 1 | **teaspoon chili powder** |
| 1 | **teaspoon dried basil, crushed** |
| ½ | **teaspoon paprika** |
| ¼ | **teaspoon celery seed** |
|  | **Dash bottled hot pepper sauce** |
| 4 | **individual French rolls, split** |
|  | **Coleslaw (optional)** |

Cut pork across the grain into very thin slices; set aside. In a large saucepan combine tomato sauce, onion, green pepper, garlic, vinegar, brown sugar, Worcestershire sauce, mustard, chili powder, basil, paprika, celery seed, and hot pepper sauce. Bring to boiling; reduce heat. Cover and simmer for 15 minutes. Add pork. Cover and simmer 15 minutes more. Toast rolls. Spoon meat mixture onto bottom half of each roll. Spoon some coleslaw atop meat filling, if desired. Top with other half of roll. Makes 4 sandwiches.

## Spicy Apple-Pork Patties

|   |   |
|---|---|
| 1 | beaten egg |
| ½ | cup cooked rice |
| ⅓ | cup finely chopped onion |
| 1½ | teaspoons salt |
| 1½ | teaspoons Worcestershire sauce |
| 1 | teaspoon ground sage |
| 1½ | pounds ground pork |
| 6 | spiced apple rings |
| ½ | cup syrup from spiced apple rings |
| 2 | teaspoons cornstarch |
| ¼ | cup light corn syrup |
| 1 | tablespoon lemon juice |

Oven 350°

Combine egg, rice, onion, salt, Worcestershire, and sage. Add ground pork; mix well. Shape into 6 patties. Place in a 13x9x2-inch baking pan. Press an apple ring into the top of each patty. Bake in a 350° oven for 35 minutes.

Meanwhile, in a saucepan stir the ½ cup spiced syrup into cornstarch. Stir in corn syrup and lemon juice. Cook and stir till thickened and bubbly. Cook and stir 1 to 2 minutes more. Spoon onto meat. Bake 5 minutes more. Serve patties atop hot corn bread squares, if desired. Spoon sauce over patties. Serves 6.

## Pork Loaf

|   |   |
|---|---|
| 2 | beaten eggs |
| 1 | 5½-ounce can tomato juice |
| ½ | cup fine dry bread crumbs |
| ¼ | cup chopped onion |
| 1 | teaspoon salt |
| 1 | teaspoon Worcestershire sauce |
| ½ | teaspoon dried oregano, crushed |
| ⅛ | teaspoon pepper |
| 1½ | pounds ground pork |
| 2 | tablespoons brown sugar |
| ½ | teaspoon dry mustard |

Oven 350°

In a bowl combine eggs and ½ cup of the tomato juice; stir in bread crumbs, onion, salt, Worcestershire sauce, oregano, and pepper. Add ground pork; mix thoroughly. Shape meat into an 8x4-inch loaf shape and place in an 11x7x1½-inch baking pan. Smooth the top. Bake in a 350° oven for 1¼ hours. Drain off fat. Combine brown sugar, dry mustard, and the remaining tomato juice (about 1½ tablespoons); spread over top of meat loaf. Bake 10 minutes more. Makes 6 servings.

## Pork Burgers

|   |   |
|---|---|
| **1** | **pound ground pork** |
| **2** | **tablespoons chopped green onion** |
| **¾** | **teaspoon salt** |
| **¼** | **teaspoon ground sage** |
| **⅛** | **teaspoon pepper** |
| **4** | **hamburger buns, split and toasted** |

Combine all ingredients except buns. Shape into four ½-inch-thick patties. Place patties on an unheated rack in a broiler pan. Broil patties 3 inches from heat for 8 minutes. Turn; broil 7 minutes more. (*Or*, panbroil patties. Preheat a heavy skillet. Cook patties over medium heat for 6 to 7 minutes per side, or till done. Partially cover skillet to prevent spattering.) Serve on toasted hamburger buns. Serves 4.

# Stuffed Cabbage Rolls

 1   beaten egg
 ½   cup milk
 ¼   cup finely chopped onion
 1   teaspoon Worcestershire sauce
 ¾   teaspoon salt
     Dash pepper
 ½   pound ground pork *and* ½ pound ground
       beef *or* 1 pound ground beef
 ¾   cup cooked rice
 6   large *or* 12 medium cabbage leaves
 1   10¾-ounce can condensed tomato soup
 1   tablespoon brown sugar
 1   tablespoon lemon juice                    Oven 350°

In a bowl combine egg, milk, onion, Worcestershire sauce, salt, and pepper; mix well. Add meat and cooked rice; mix well.

Remove center vein of cabbage leaves, keeping each leaf in 1 piece. Immerse leaves in boiling water about 3 minutes or till limp; drain. Place ½ cup meat mixture on each large leaf *or* ¼ cup mixture on each medium leaf; fold in sides. Starting at unfolded edge, roll up each leaf, making sure folded sides are included in roll. Arrange in a 12x7½x2-inch baking dish. Stir together condensed tomato soup, brown sugar, and lemon juice; pour sauce mixture over cabbage rolls. Bake, uncovered, in a 350° oven for 1¼ hours, basting once or twice with sauce. Makes 6 servings.

## Mexicali Pork Chops

| | |
|---|---|
| **4** | **pork loin chops, cut ¾ inch thick (1½ to 1¾ pounds)** |
| **½** | **cup chopped green pepper** |
| **¼** | **cup chopped onion** |
| **1** | **16-ounce can tomatoes, cut up** |
| **1** | **8-ounce can whole kernel corn, drained** |
| **1** | **8-ounce can red kidney beans, drained** |
| **½** | **cup long grain rice** |
| **½** | **cup water** |
| **1** | **4-ounce can mild green chili peppers, rinsed, seeded, and chopped** |
| | **Few dashes bottled hot pepper sauce** |

Oven 350°

Trim excess fat from chops; in a skillet cook fat trimmings till 2 tablespoons fat accumulate. Discard trimmings. Brown chops on both sides in hot fat. Season with salt and pepper. Set chops aside; reserve drippings in skillet. Cook green pepper and onion in reserved drippings till tender but not brown. Stir in *undrained* tomatoes, drained corn, drained kidney beans, *uncooked* rice, water, chili peppers, hot pepper sauce, and ¾ teaspoon *salt*. Bring to boiling. Turn mixture into a 12x7½x2-inch baking dish. Arrange pork chops atop. Cover and bake in a 350° oven for 35 minutes. Uncover and bake 10 to 15 minutes more or till meat is tender. Makes 4 servings.

## Braised Pork Steaks

| | |
|---|---|
| **4** | **pork shoulder blade steaks, cut ½ inch thick (2 to 2½ pounds)** |
| **½** | **cup tomato sauce** |
| **¼** | **teaspoon ground sage** |

Trim excess fat from steaks; in a large skillet cook fat trimmings till 2 tablespoons fat accumulate. Discard trimmings. Brown 2 steaks slowly on each side in hot fat; remove steaks. Repeat with remaining 2 steaks. Drain off excess fat. Return all steaks to skillet. Season with salt and pepper. Add tomato sauce and sage. Cover tightly; cook over low heat for 30 to 35 minutes or till meat is tender. Skim excess fat from juices. If necessary, cook down juices to thicken slightly; spoon over meat. Makes 4 servings.

## Basic Broiled Pork Chops and Steaks

Set the oven temperature to "broil" and preheat if desired (check instructions for your range). Place meat on a unheated rack in a broiler pan. Broil pork 3 to 4 inches from heat for half the suggested time. Season with salt and pepper. Turn meat using tongs; cook till done. Season again. Follow these times as guideline; pork rib or loin chops cut ¾ to 1 inch thick, 20 to 25 minutes total time; pork shoulder steaks cut ½ to ¾ inch thick, 20 to 22 minutes total time.

## Breaded Pork Tenderloins

| | |
|---|---|
| 1 | pound pork tenderloin, cut crosswise into 6 pieces |
| ⅓ | cup all-purpose flour |
| 1 | teaspoon seasoned salt |
| ¼ | teaspoon pepper |
| 1 | beaten egg |
| 2 | tablespoons milk |
| ¾ | cup fine dry bread crumbs |
| 1 | teaspoon paprika |
| 3 | tablepoons shortening |
| ¾ | cup chicken broth |
| 1 | tablespoon all-purpose flour |
| ¼ | teaspoon dried dillweed |
| ½ | cup dairy sour cream |

Pound pork to ¼- to ⅛-inch thickness. Cut small slits around edges to prevent curling. Coat meat with a mixture of the ⅓ cup flour, seasoned salt, and pepper. Combine egg and milk. Dip cutlets into egg mixture, then into a mixture of crumbs and paprika. In a large skillet cook 3 cutlets at a time in hot shortening for 2 to 3 minutes on each side. Remove from pan to a platter; keep warm.

For sauce, pour broth into skillet, scraping to loosen crusty drippings. Stir the 1 tablespoon flour and dillweed into sour cream. Stir sour cream mixture into broth. Cook and stir over low heat till mixture is thickened and bubbly. Cook and stir 1 to 2 minutes more. Pass sauce with pork. Serves 6.

# Baking Ham

Place meat, fat side up, on a rack in a shallow baking pan. If desired, score ham fat in a diamond pattern using a paper strip for a cutting guide. Make cuts only about ¼ inch deep. Insert a meat thermometer (see tip, page 451). Do not add water or other liquid and do not cover the baking pan. (Follow the label directions for heating canned hams.)

Bake the ham in a 325° oven until the meat thermometer registers the specified internal temperature. (Check the label to see whether the ham is a fully cooked or a cook-before-eating ham. If the ham is not marked, use the cook-before-eating temperatures and times.) Fully cooked and canned hams should be heated to 140° internal temperature. Cook-before-eating hams should be baked to an internal temperature of 160°.

If desired, prepare a glaze for the ham. To glaze the ham, spoon off fat from the baking pan 20 to 30 minutes before the end of the baking time. Brush the glaze over the meat. Continue baking and basting with the glaze till the thermometer registers the desired internal temperature.

Use the baking times given in the chart below as a guide to the total cooking time for a particular type and size of ham.

## Easy Mustard Glaze

    ½  cup packed brown sugar
    2  tablespoons orange or pineapple juice
    ½  teaspoon dry mustard

Combine sugar, fruit juice, and dry mustard. Spoon over ham 2 or 3 times during the last 30 minutes of baking time. Makes about ½ cup glaze.

## Curried Cranberry Glaze

- ½   **cup chopped onion**
- 4   **teaspoons curry powder**
- ¼   **cup butter or margarine**
- 1   **16-ounce can whole cranberry sauce**
- 2   **tablespoons light corn syrup**

Cook onion and curry powder in butter or margarine till onion is tender but not brown. Stir in cranberry sauce and corn syrup; heat through. Spoon some of the mixture over ham during the last 20 to 30 minutes of baking time. Reheat remaining mixture and pass with meat. Makes about 1¾ cups glaze.

| Ham Cut | Approximate Weight (pounds) | Internal Temperature on Removal from Oven | Approximate Cooking Time (total time) |
|---|---|---|---|
| | Bake meat at a constant 325° oven temperature | | |
| **Fully Cooked Ham** | | | |
| Whole, Bone In | 10 to 14 | 140° | 2½ to 3½ hours |
| Half, Bone In | 5 to 7 | 140° | 1¾ to 2¼ hours |
| Whole, Boneless | 10 to 12 | 140° | 3 to 3½ hours |
| Half, Boneless | 5 to 7 | 140° | 2 to 2¼ hours |
| Portion, Boneless | 3 to 4 | 140° | 1½ to 1¾ hours |
| Whole, Semi-Boneless | 10 to 12 | 140° | 3 to 3½ hours |
| Half, Semi-Boneless | 4 to 6 | 140° | 1¾ to 2½ hours |
| Canned Ham | 1½ to 3 | 140° | 1 to 1½ hours |
| | 3 to 7 | 140° | 1½ to 2 hours |
| | 7 to 10 | 140° | 2 to 2½ hours |
| **Cook-Before-Eating Ham** | | | |
| Whole | 10 to 14 | 160° | 3½ to 4 hours |
| Half | 5 to 7 | 160° | 3 to 3¼ hours |
| Shank Portion | 3 to 4 | 160° | 2 to 2½ hours |
| Rump Portion | 3 to 4 | 160° | 2 to 2½ hours |

## Cooking Ham Slices

Choose a fully cooked *ham center slice* cut 1 inch thick (about 2½ pounds). Broil or panfry as directed below. Makes 6 to 8 servings.

**To panfry:** In a large heavy skillet cook ham slice in about 2 tablespoons hot *cooking oil* over medium heat for 16 to 18 minutes total time, turning the meat occasionally.

**To broil:** Trim rind, if any; slash fat edge in several places. Place ham slice on an unheated rack in a broiler pan. Broil so surface of meat is 3 inches from heat. Broil ham for 16 to 18 minutes total time, turning once.

## Ham Croquettes with Cheese Sauce

    3    tablespoons butter *or* margarine
    ¼    to ½ teaspoon curry powder (optional)
    ¼    cup all-purpose flour
    ¾    cup milk
    2    cups coarsely ground fully cooked ham
    2    teaspoons prepared mustard
    1    teaspoon grated onion
    ⅔    cup fine dry bread crumbs
    1    beaten egg
    2    tablespoons water
         Cooking oil for deep-fat frying
         Cheese Sauce

In a saucepan melt butter with curry powder; stir in flour. Add milk all at once; cook and stir till thickened and bubbly. Cook and stir 1 to 2 minutes more. Remove from heat. Stir in ham, mustard, and onion. Chill thoroughly. Shape mixture into 8 cones. Roll in bread crumbs, handling lightly. Dip into mixture of egg and water; roll in crumbs again. Fry in deep hot fat (365°) about 2½ minutes or till golden. Drain. Serve with Cheese Sauce. Makes 4 servings.

**Cheese Sauce:** In a saucepan melt 2 tablespoons *butter or margarine*. Stir in 2 tablespoons all-purpose *flour*, ¼ teaspoon *salt*, and dash *pepper*. Add 1¼ cups *milk* all at once.

Cook and stir till thickened and bubbly. Cook and stir 1 to 2 minutes more. Stir in ½ cup shredded *American cheese* and ½ cup shredded *Swiss cheese*. Stir till smooth and cheese is melted.

---

## Cook-before-eating hams

Besides the more familiar whole, half, shank, and rump ham portions available (which are labeled "cook before eating" and must be baked to an internal temperature of 160°), there also are country or country-style hams that must be cooked before eating. These distinc- tively flavored, specially processed hams are dry-salt cured and are usually aged. Generally they are saltier than regular hams and often are named for the locality in which they are processed. Follow the label directions for preparing these specialty hams.

---

## Ham Caribbean

   1  **2-pound fully cooked ham center slice,
         cut 1 inch thick**
   2  **oranges**
      **Orange juice**
   1  **tablespoon whole cloves**
  ⅓  **cup packed brown sugar**
   4  **teaspoons cornstarch**
   2  **tablespoons rum**
   1  **tablespoon honey**
   1  **8¼-ounce can pineapple chunks, drained**
  ½  **cup light raisins**                    Oven 350°

Slash edge of ham slice; place on a rack in a shallow baking pan. Bake in a 350° oven for 30 minutes. Meanwhile, peel and section oranges over a bowl to catch juice. Set orange sections aside. Measure juice in bowl; add additional orange juice, if necessary, to make ⅓ cup liquid. In a saucepan combine orange juice and whole cloves; bring to boiling. Reduce heat; simmer gently, uncovered, for 5 minutes. Discard cloves. Combine brown sugar and cornstarch; stir in rum and honey. Stir mixture into orange juice. Cook and stir till thickened and bubbly. Cook and stir 1 to 2 minutes more. Stir in orange sections, pineapple chunks, and raisins. Heat through. Spoon over ham. Makes 6 servings.

## Apricot-Ham Patties

|        |                                          |           |
|--------|------------------------------------------|-----------|
| **2**  | **beaten eggs**                          |           |
| **¾**  | **cup milk**                             |           |
| **1½** | **cups soft bread crumbs (2 slices)**    |           |
| **½**  | **cup finely snipped dried apricots**    |           |
| **¼**  | **cup chopped onion**                    |           |
| **2**  | **tablespoons snipped parsley**          |           |
|        | **Dash pepper**                          |           |
| **1**  | **pound ground fully cooked ham**        |           |
| **1**  | **pound ground pork**                    |           |
| **⅓**  | **cup packed brown sugar**               |           |
| **1**  | **teaspoon all-purpose flour**           | Oven 350° |

Combine eggs, milk, bread crumbs, dried apricots, onion, parsley, and pepper. Add ground ham and pork; mix well. Shape meat mixture into eight ½-inch-thick patties. Combine brown sugar and flour; sprinkle in bottom of a 15x10x1-inch baking pan. Place patties in pan. Bake in a 350° oven for 40 to 45 minutes. Transfer patties to a serving platter. Stir together the pan juices and spoon over meat. Makes 8 servings.

# Ham Loaf

| | |
|---|---|
| 2 | beaten eggs |
| ½ | cup milk |
| ½ | cup finely crushed saltine crackers (4 crackers) |
| ½ | cup finely chopped onion |
| ½ | teaspoon dry mustard |
| ⅛ | teaspoon pepper |
| 1 | pound ground fully cooked ham |
| 1 | pound ground pork |
| ½ | cup packed brown sugar |
| 2 | tablespoons vinegar |
| ½ | teaspoon dry mustard |

Oven 350°

Combine eggs, milk, crushed crackers, onion, ½ teaspoon dry mustard, and pepper. Add ground ham and ground pork; mix well. Shape into a 8x4-inch loaf and place in a 13x9x2-inch baking pan. Bake in a 350° oven for 1 hour. For glaze, combine brown sugar, vinegar, and ½ teaspoon dry mustard. Spoon glaze over loaf. Bake 20 minutes more, basting with sauce occasionally. Makes 8 to 10 servings.

# Ham-Noodle Casserole

| | |
|---|---|
| 3 | ounces medium noodles |
| 1 | 11-ounce can condensed cheddar cheese soup |
| ½ | cup milk |
| ½ | cup dairy sour cream |
| ½ | cup thinly sliced celery |
| 1 | 2½-ounce can sliced mushrooms, drained |
| 2 | tablespoons chopped pimiento |
| 1 | tablespoon snipped parsley |
| 2 | cups ground fully cooked ham |
| ¾ | cup finely crushed rich round crackers |
| 1 | tablespoon butter or margarine, melted |

Oven 375°

Cook noodles in boiling, unsalted water till tender; drain. In a large bowl stir together soup, milk, and sour cream. Add celery, mushrooms, pimiento, and parsley. Stir in cooked noodles and ham. Turn mixture into a 2-quart casserole. Combine rich round cracker crumbs and melted butter; sprinkle over casserole. Bake, uncovered, in a 375° oven 30 to 35 minutes or till heated through. Serves 4 to 6.

## Potato-Ham Scallop

| | |
|---|---|
| 2 | **cups cubed fully cooked ham** |
| 6 | **medium potatoes, peeled and thinly sliced (2 pounds)** |
| ¼ | **cup finely chopped onion** |
| ⅓ | **cup all-purpose flour** |
| 2 | **cups milk** |
| 3 | **tablespoons fine dry bread crumbs** |
| 1 | **tablespoon butter or margarine, melted** |
| 2 | **tablespoons finely snipped parsley** |

Oven 350°

Place *half* of the ham in a 2-quart casserole. Cover with *half* of the potatoes and *half* of the onion. Stir *half* of the flour over; season with salt and pepper. Repeat layering ham, potatoes, and onion. Season with additional salt and pepper. Sift remaining flour atop. Pour milk over all. Bake, covered, in a 350° oven for 1 to 1¼ hours or till potatoes are nearly tender. Uncover. Combine bread crumbs and melted butter; sprinkle atop casserole. Top with parsley. Bake 15 minutes more. Serves 4 to 6.

## Cooking Bacon

**To bake:** Place bacon slices side by side on a rack in a shallow baking pan. Bake in a 400° oven 10 to 12 minutes or till done.

**To panfry:** Place bacon slices in an unheated skillet. Cook over medium-low heat for 6 to 8 minutes, turning often. Drain well on paper toweling to remove excess fat.

**To broil:** Place bacon slices side by side on an unheated rack in a broiler pan. Broil 5 inches from heat about 4 minutes or till done; turn once. Watch closely to prevent burning.

**To micro-cook:** Place bacon slices on paper toweling on a paper plate. Top with paper toweling. Cook in a counter-top microwave oven on high power to desired doneness (1 minute for 1 slice; 1¾ to 2 minutes for 2 slices; 3 to 3½ minutes for 4 slices; 4½ to 5 minutes for 6 slices; 5½ to 6 minutes for 8 slices.)

**Note:** For 8 slices, place 4 slices bacon on paper toweling. Cover with a single layer of paper toweling. Add 4 more bacon slices; cover with another single paper towel. To reserve drippings, omit paper toweling under bacon; cover with a single paper towel.

## Cooking Canadian-Style Bacon

**To bake:** Place on 2-pound piece *Canadian-style bacon* in a shallow baking pan. Spread some *Easy Mustard Glaze* (see recipe, page 500) atop. Bake, uncovered, in a 325° oven 1¼ to 1½ hours or till meat thermometer registers 160°. Baste often with remaining glaze. Slice to serve. Makes 8 servings.

**To panfry:** Slice Canadian-style bacon ¼ inch thick; slash edges. Preheat a skillet; brush lightly with cooking oil. Cook 2 to 3 minutes on the first side; turn. Cook 1 to 2 minutes on the second side or till browned.

**To broil:** Slice Canadian-style bacon ¼ inch thick; slash edges. Place on an unheated rack in a broiler pan. Broil 4 inches from heat 2 to 3 minutes on the first side; turn. Broil about 2 minutes on the second side.

**To micro-cook:** Slice Canadian-style bacon ¼ inch thick; slash edges. Arrange in a nonmetal baking dish and loosely cover with waxed paper. Cook in a counter-top microwave oven on high power for 1¼ minutes for 2 slices (cook 30 seconds longer for each additional slice). Turn dish once during cooking.

## Canadian Bacon Pie

> **Pastry for Double-Crust Pie (*see* recipe, page 569)**
> 1 **pound Canadian-style bacon**
> 1 **cup chopped green pepper**
> ½ **cup chopped onion**
> 1 **clove garlic, minced**
> 1 **tablespoon butter *or* margarine**
> 2 **tablespoons all-purpose flour**
> 1¼ **cups milk**
> 1 **3-ounce package cream cheese, softened**
> 1 **beaten egg**
> ¼ **cup snipped parsley**
> 1 **teaspoon dried marjoram, crushed**
> 1 **cup shredded Monterey Jack *or* Swiss cheese**                    Oven 350°

Prepare and roll out pastry. Line a 9-inch pie plate with *half* of the pastry; trim even with the pie plate rim. Chop bacon. Cook bacon, green pepper, onion, and garlic in butter till onion is tender. Stir in flour. Add milk and cream cheese. Cook, stirring constantly, till smooth and bubbly. Stir *1 cup* of the hot mixture into the beaten egg; return to remaining hot mixture. Stir in parsley, marjoram, and cheese.

Spoon mixture into pastry-lined pie plate. Cut slits in second pastry circle for escape of steam; place on filling. Seal; flute edge. Bake in a 350° oven for 40 to 45 minutes. Let stand 10 minutes before serving. Serves 6.

## Orange-Glazed Canadian Bacon

Lightly brown on both sides 8 slices *Canadian-style bacon,* cut ½ inch thick, half at a time, in 1 tablespoon *butter.* Return all to skillet. Combine ¼ cup *pineapple preserves;* 3 tablespoons frozen *orange juice concentrate,* thawed; 2 teaspoons *lemon juice;* 1 teaspoon *prepared mustard;* and ⅛ teaspoon ground *cloves;* pour over bacon. Bring to boiling; reduce heat slightly. Cook, uncovered, about 5 minutes. Transfer to a platter; spoon glaze over. Serves 4.

**Pineapple-Glazed Canadian Bacon:** Prepare Orange-Glazed Canadian Bacon as above, *except* substitute ¼ cup *orange marmalade* and 3 tablespoons frozen *pineapple juice concentrate,* thawed, for the pineapple preserves and orange juice concentrate. Continue as directed.

# Sausage

**1** Clockwise, starting at top: Cotto Salami with slices, Polish Sausage, Knackwurst, Beerwurst slice, Frankfurters.

**2** Hard Salami, Summer Sausage slices, Pepperoni with slices, Mortadella.

**3** Blood Sausage with slices, Salami, Bratwurst, Liver Cheese slices, Braunschweiger slices, Liver Sausage.

**4** Prosciutto, Head Cheese, Souse (folded slices), Dried Beef, Pastrami.

1.

2.

3.

4.

## Cooking Fresh Pork Sausage

***For Patties:*** Place sausage patties in an unheated skillet. Cook slowly, uncovered, 15 to 20 minutes or till thoroughly cooked, turning once. Drain well. (*Or*, arrange patties on an unheated rack in a shallow baking pan. Bake in a 400° oven for 20 to 25 minutes or till cooked.) One pound makes 4 or 5 servings.

***For Links:*** Do not prick sausages. Place uncooked pork sausage links in an unheated skillet. Add ¼ cup cold water per half pound sausage. Cover and cook slowly for 5 minutes; drain well. Cook slowly, uncovered, for 12 to 14 minutes more or till liquid from sausages has evaporated and sausages are thoroughly cooked; turn occasionally with tongs.

## Pizza

>     2½   **to 3 cups all-purpose flour**
>       1   **package active dry yeast**
>       1   **teaspoon salt**
>       1   **cup warm water (115° to 120°)**
>       2   **tablespoons cooking oil**
>           **Tomato Sauce**
>       1   **pound bulk Italian sausage *or* ground pork,**
>           **cooked and drained, *or* 6 ounces**
>           **sliced pepperoni**
>           **Sliced *or* chopped green onions, green**
>           **pepper, mushrooms, olives,**
>           ***and/or* canned green chili peppers**
>       2   **to 3 cups shredded mozzarella, Monterey**
>           **Jack, *or* Swiss cheese**              Oven 425°

For crust, in a large mixer bowl combine 1¼ *cups* of the flour, the yeast, and salt. Stir in warm water and oil. Beat at low speed of electric mixer for ½ minute, scraping bowl constantly. Beat 3 minutes at high speed. Stir in as much of the remaining flour as you can mix in with a spoon. Turn out onto a lightly floured surface. Knead in enough remaining flour to make a moderately stiff dough that is smooth and elastic (6 to 8 minutes total).

*For thin pizza crusts:* Cover dough and let rest 10 minutes. For 12-inch pizzas, divide dough in half. On a lightly floured surface roll each half into a 13-inch circle. (*Or,* for 10-inch pizzas, divide dough into thirds; roll each third into an 11-inch circle.) Transfer circles of dough to greased 12-inch pizza pans or baking sheets. Build up edges slightly. Bake in a 425° oven about 12 minutes or till lightly browned. Spread cooled Tomato Sauce over hot crust. Sprinkle meat, vegetables, and cheese atop. Return to the 425° oven; bake for 10 to 15 minutes longer or till bubbly. Makes two 12-inch or three 10-inch thin-crust pizzas.

*For pan pizza crusts:* Place dough in a greased bowl; turn once. Cover dough and let rise in a warm place till double (about 1 hour). Punch down. Divide dough in half. Cover; let rest 10 minutes. With greased fingers pat dough onto bottom and halfway up sides of two greased 11x7x1½-inch or 9x9x2-inch baking pans. Cover; let rise till nearly double (30 to 45 minutes). Bake in a 375° oven for 20 to 25 minutes or till lightly browned. Spread cooled Tomato Sauce over hot crust. Sprinkle meat, vegetables, and cheese atop. Return to the 375° oven; bake for 20 to 25 minutes longer or till bubbly. Let stand 5 minutes before serving. Makes two 11x7-inch or 9x9-inch pan pizzas.

*Tomato Sauce:* Combine one 8-ounce can *tomato sauce;* one 7½-ounce can *tomatoes,* cut up; 1 medium *onion,* chopped (½ cup); 2 cloves *garlic,* minced; 1 tablespoon dried *oregano,* crushed; 1 tablespoon dried *basil,* crushed; 1 teaspoon *sugar;* ½ teaspoon *salt;* and ⅛ teaspoon *pepper.* Bring to boiling. Reduce heat; cover and simmer 5 to 10 minutes or till onion is tender. Cool.

## Lasagna

|       |                                              |
|-------|----------------------------------------------|
| 1     | pound bulk pork sausage *or* ground beef     |
| ½     | cup chopped onion                            |
| 1     | clove garlic, minced                         |
| 1     | 16-ounce can tomatoes, cut up                |
| 1     | 8-ounce can tomato sauce                     |
| 1     | 6-ounce can tomato paste                     |
| 2     | teaspoons dried basil, crushed               |
| 1     | teaspoon salt                                |
| 8     | ounces lasagna noodles                       |
| 1     | tablespoon cooking oil                       |
| 2     | eggs                                         |
| 2½    | cups ricotta *or* cream-style cottage cheese |
| ¾     | cup grated Parmesan *or* Romano cheese       |
| 2     | tablespoons dried parsley flakes             |
| 1     | pound mozzarella cheese, thinly sliced       |

Oven 375°

Cook meat, onion, and garlic till meat is browned. Drain off fat. Stir in the *undrained* tomatoes and next 4 ingredients. Cover; simmer 15 minutes, stirring often. Meanwhile, cook noodles till tender in boiling salted water with cooking oil added to water. Drain; rinse noodles. Beat eggs; add ricotta, ½ *cup* of the Parmesan or Romano, the parsley, 1 teaspoon *salt*, and ½ teaspoon *pepper*. Layer *half* of the noodles in a 13x9x2-inch baking dish; spread with *half* of the ricotta filling. Add *half* of the mozzarella cheese and *half* of the meat sauce. Repeat layers. Sprinkle remaining Parmesan atop.

Bake in a 375° oven for 30 to 35 minutes or till heated through. (*Or,* assemble early and refrigerate; bake 45 minutes or till hot.) Let stand 10 minutes. Makes 10 servings.

# Apple-Stuffed Sausage Patties

    1½    pounds bulk pork sausage
    ½     cup finely chopped celery
    ¼     cup finely chopped onion
    2     tablespoons butter or margarine
    ¼     cup water
    1     cup packaged herb-seasoned stuffing mix
    1     medium cooking apple, peeled, cored, and
            finely chopped (1 cup)
    2     tablespoons snipped parsley
    2     tablespoons chili sauce
    ¼     teaspoon dry mustard
    ¼     teaspoon pepper                    Oven 375°

Shape sausage into eight ¼-inch-thick patties. In a saucepan cook celery and onion in butter or margarine till tender but not brown. Remove from heat. Add water. Add the stuffing mix, apple, parsley, chili sauce, dry mustard, and pepper; mix well. Place about ½ cup of the stuffing mixture atop each of four of the patties. Top with remaining patties; press around edges to seal. Place in a 13x9x2-inch baking pan. Bake in a 375° oven for 35 to 40 minutes or till done. Makes 4 servings.

# Sausage- and Apple-Stuffed Squash

    2     acorn squash, halved
    ¾     pound bulk pork sausage
    ¾     cup chopped celery
    3     tablespoons chopped onion
    1     medium cooking apple, peeled, cored, and
            chopped (1 cup)
    1     slightly beaten egg
    ½     cup dairy sour cream
    ¾     cup shredded American cheese
            (3 ounces)                       Oven 350°

Place squash halves, cut side down, in a baking pan. Bake in a 350° oven for about 45 minutes or till tender. Sprinkle cut side with salt. In a skillet cook sausage, celery, and onion till meat is browned. Stir in apple; cook 3 minutes more. Drain off fat. Combine egg and sour cream; stir into sausage mixture. Fill squash halves with sausage mixture. Bake 20 minutes. Sprinkle cheese atop. Bake 5 minutes more. Makes 4 servings.

## Sausage and Corn Bread

| | |
|---|---|
| 1 | 16-ounce can stewed tomatoes, cut up |
| 1 | 4-ounce can green chili peppers, rinsed, seeded, and chopped |
| 1 | teaspoon minced dried onion |
| ½ | teaspoon sugar |
| | Dash garlic powder |
| 3 | tablespoons cold water |
| 1 | tablespoon cornstarch |
| 1 | pound bulk pork sausage |
| ¾ | cup all-purpose flour |
| ¾ | cup yellow cornmeal |
| 2 | tablespoons sugar |
| 1 | tablespoon baking powder |
| ½ | teaspoon salt |
| 2 | beaten eggs |
| 1 | 8½-ounce can cream-style corn |
| ½ | cup milk |
| 3 | tablespoons cooking oil |

Oven 375°

In a saucepan combine the *undrained* tomatoes, chopped chili peppers, minced dried onion, the ½ teaspoon sugar, and the garlic powder; bring to boiling. Stir cold water into cornstarch; stir into tomato mixture. Cook and stir till mixture is thickened and bubbly. Cook and stir 1 to 2 minutes more. Remove from heat and set the mixture aside.

In a skillet cook sausage till browned, stirring occasionally to break meat into bits and to brown evenly; drain. Stir *half* of the tomato mixture into sausage; set sausage mixture and remaining tomato mixture aside.

In a mixing bowl stir together flour, cornmeal, the 2 tablespoons sugar, the baking powder, and salt. In another bowl combine eggs, cream-style corn, milk, and cooking oil; add to cornmeal mixture. Stir just till moistened. Spread *half* of the batter in a greased 9x9x2-inch baking pan. Spoon sausage mixture atop. Spread remaining batter over meat. Bake in a 375° oven about 30 minutes or till done. Let stand 5 minutes. Cut into squares. Heat remaining tomato mixture and spoon over corn bread squares. Makes 4 servings.

## Sausage-Macaroni Skillet

     1   **cup medium shell macaroni**
     1   **pound bulk Italian sausage**
    ½   **cup chopped green pepper**
     1   **16-ounce can tomatoes, cut up**
     1   **10-ounce can pizza sauce**
    ¼   **teaspoon salt**
     2   **cups thinly sliced zucchini**
     1   **cup shredded mozzarella cheese (4 ounces)**

Cook macaroni according to package directions; drain, rinse, and set aside. In a skillet cook sausage and green pepper till sausage is browned and pepper is tender; stir occasionally to break sausage into bits and to brown evenly. Drain off fat. Stir in *undrained* tomatoes, pizza sauce, and salt; bring to boiling. Stir in zucchini; cover and cook about 10 minutes or till zucchini is tender. Stir in cooked macaroni. Cook, uncovered, about 5 minutes more. Sprinkle with mozzarella cheese. Makes 5 or 6 servings.

## Salami-Bean Casserole

     1   **16-ounce can pork and beans in tomato**
          **sauce**
    ⅓   **cup catsup**
     2   **tablespoons brown sugar**
     2   **cups frozen hashed brown potatoes with**
          **onion and peppers**
     4   **ounces sliced salami**                    Oven 375°

Combine pork and beans, catsup, and brown sugar; stir in hashed brown potatoes. Turn into a 1-quart casserole. Bake, uncovered, in a 375° oven for 20 minutes; stir. Roll salami slices into logs; arrange atop casserole, pressing into bean mixture slightly. Bake, covered, 10 to 15 minutes more or till potatoes are done. Makes 4 servings.

**Microwave directions:** Prepare bean mixture as above, *except* turn into a 1-quart nonmetal casserole. Cover with waxed paper. Cook in a counter-top microwave oven on high power for 5 minutes; stir. Roll salami slices into logs; arrange atop casserole, pressing into bean mixture slightly. Micro-cook, covered, about 5 minutes more or till potatoes are done.

## Corn Dogs

 1 **cup all-purpose flour**
 ²/₃ **cup yellow cornmeal**
 2 **tablespoons sugar**
 1½ **teaspoons baking powder**
 1 **teaspoon salt**
 ½ **teaspoon dry mustard**
 2 **tablespoons shortening**
 1 **beaten egg**
 ¾ **cup milk**
 1 **pound frankfurters (8 to 10)**
   **Cooking oil**

In a bowl combine flour, cornmeal, sugar, baking powder, salt, and dry mustard. Cut in shortening till mixture resembles fine crumbs. Mix egg and milk. Add to dry ingredients; mix well. Insert wooden skewers in ends of frankfurters. Pour oil into skillet to a depth of 1 inch; heat to 375°. Coat franks with batter. (If batter is too thick, add 1 to 2 tablespoons *milk.*) Arrange coated franks 3 at a time in hot oil; turn franks with tongs after 10 seconds to prevent batter from sliding off. Cook 3 minutes, turning again halfway through cooking time. Serve hot with catsup and mustard, if desired. Makes 4 to 5 servings.

# Coney Islands

|       |                                         |
|-------|-----------------------------------------|
| ½     | pound ground beef                       |
| ½     | cup chopped onion                       |
| ¼     | cup chopped green pepper                 |
| 1     | 8-ounce can tomato sauce                |
| ½     | cup water                               |
| ½     | teaspoon chili powder                   |
| ½     | teaspoon paprika                        |
| ¼     | teaspoon salt                           |
| ⅛     | teaspoon ground red pepper (optional)   |
| 6     | frankfurters                            |
| 6     | warm frankfurter buns                   |

In a skillet cook ground beef, onion, and green pepper till meat is browned. Drain. Add tomato sauce, water, chili powder, paprika, salt, and ground red pepper. Simmer 15 minutes. In a saucepan cover frankfurters with cold water; bring to boiling. Simmer 5 minutes. To serve, place franks in buns and top each with meat mixture. Makes 6 servings.

---

# Creamed Bratwurst

In a 10-inch skillet brown 1½ pounds fully cooked *bratwurst* in 2 tablespoons hot *cooking oil* about 5 minutes; remove from skillet. Slice bratwurst into ½-inch-thick slices; set aside. Add 1 cup chopped *onion,* ½ cup chopped *green pepper,* and 1 teaspoon *dry mustard* to drippings in skillet. Cook and stir till onion is tender but not brown. Stir in 3 tablespoons *all-purpose flour* and ½ teaspoon *salt.* Add 1 cup *chicken broth* and ¾ cup *milk* all at once; cook and stir till thickened and bubbly. Cook and stir 1 to 2 minutes more. Add bratwurst slices. Reduce heat; cover and cook 5 minutes more. Serve with *hot cooked noodles,* if desired. Makes 6 servings.

## Sausage and Kraut

|        |                                                      |
|--------|------------------------------------------------------|
| **4**  | **slices bacon, cut into 1-inch pieces**             |
| **½**  | **pound boneless pork, cut into ½-inch cubes**       |
| **¼**  | **cup chopped onion**                                |
| **½**  | **pound Polish sausage, sliced**                     |
| **¼**  | **cup dry white wine**                               |
| **1**  | **4-ounce can sliced mushrooms**                     |
| **1½** | **teaspoons instant beef bouillon granules**         |
| **¾**  | **treaspoon paprika**                                |
| **1**  | **bay leaf**                                         |
| **1**  | **16-ounce can sauerkraut, drained and snipped**     |
| **2**  | **tablespoons cornstarch**                           |

In a 3-quart saucepan cook bacon till crisp. Drain, reserving
drippings; set aside. Brown pork cubes and onion in reserved
drippings. Stir in cooked bacon, sliced sausage, wine, *undrained*
mushrooms, beef bouillon granules, paprika, bay leaf, and 2½
cups *water*. Cover; simmer about 1 hour or till pork is tender.
Remove bay leaf; discard. Stir in sauerkraut. Stir ¼ cup *cold
water* into cornstarch. Add to sauerkraut mixture; cook and stir
till thickened and bubbly. Cook and stir 1 to 2 minutes more.
Makes 4 to 6 servings.

# Choucroute Garni

| | |
|---|---|
| 1 | medium onion, sliced |
| 1 | tablespoon bacon drippings |
| 3 | fresh pork hocks (1½ pounds) *or* 2 pounds pork spareribs, cut into 3-rib portions |
| 1 | 2-pound smoked pork shoulder roll *or* 3 or 4 smoked pork loin chops, cut ¾ inch thick (1½ pounds) |
| 3 | 16-ounce cans sauerkraut, rinsed and drained |
| 2 | cooking apples, peeled, cored, and cut into wedges |
| 2 | tablespoons brown sugar |
| 4 | whole cloves |
| 3 | juniper berries, crushed (optional) |
| 2 | small cloves garlic, minced |
| 1 | bay leaf |
| ⅛ | teaspoon pepper |
| 1½ | cups rhine wine |
| 1 | pound sausage links (use desired combination of fresh bratwurst, fresh bockwurst, fresh thuringer, precooked knackwurst, *and/or* precooked frankfurters) |
| | **Boiled potatoes**                                    Oven 375° |

In a 4½- or 5-quart Dutch oven cook onion in bacon drippings about 5 minutes or till tender; remove from heat. Add pork hocks or spareribs. Cut pork shoulder roll crosswise into ¾-inch-thick slices; add shoulder slices or loin chops to Dutch oven. In a large bowl stir together the sauerkraut and next 7 ingredients. Spoon over meats. Pour wine over all. Cover and bake in a 375° oven about 2½ hours or till meats are tender.

Meanwhile, prepare desired combination of sausages. For fresh bratwurst, bockwurst, and thuringer, place in an unheated skillet with 2 to 3 tablespoons *water;* cover and cook over low heat 5 to 8 minutes. Uncover; cook 5 to 8 minutes more or till water has evaporated and sausages are cooked through. For knackwurst and frankfurters, add to boiling water in a saucepan; cover and simmer 5 to 10 minutes or till heated through.

Mound sauerkraut mixture onto a deep, wide serving platter or in a large bowl. Arrange meats and sausages around and atop sauerkraut. Serve with boiled potatoes. Serves 12.

# Lamb

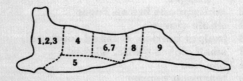

Locate wholesale cuts on the drawing, identify their retail pieces in the same numbered picture, and then note the cooking methods.

**1.** Whole Shoulder Square Cut, upper right—*roast*. Boneless Shoulder Roast (netted), lower left— *roast, braise.*

**2.** Boneless Shoulder Cushion Roast, top—*roast*. Boneless Shoulder Blade Chops, bottom—*broil, panbroil, braise.*

**3.** Shoulder Blade Chop, upper left—*broil, panbroil, braise.* Shoulder Arm Chop, lower left—*broil, panbroil, braise.* Lamb Shanks, right— *braise, cook in liquid.*

**4.** Frenched Rib Roast (contains up to 7 rib bones), upper

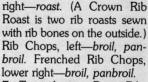

right—*roast*. (A Crown Rib Roast is two rib roasts sewn with rib bones on the outside.) Rib Chops, left—*broil, panbroil*. Frenched Rib Chops, lower right—*broil, panbroil*.

**5.** Top to bottom: Breast Riblets—*braise, cook in liquid, grill*. Breast Spareribs—*braise, roast*. Stuffed Chops—*roast, braise*.

**6.** Loin Roast, upper left—*roast*. Loin Chop, upper right—*broil, panbroil*. Loin Double (English) Chop, lower left—*broil, panbroil*.

**7.** Boneless Loin Double Roast, upper left—*roast*. Lamb Cubes for Kebabs, upper right—*broil*. Boneless Loin Double (English) Chop, lower left—*broil, panbroil, panfry*.

**8.** Leg Sirloin Half, upper left—*roast.* Leg Sirloin Chop, lower left—*broil, panbroil, roast.* Leg Center Slice, lower right (section 9 on the drawing) —*broil, panbroil, panfry.*

**9.** Leg American-Style Roast, upper left. Leg Frenched-Style Roast, right. Leg Roast Boneless (netted), lower left—*roast.*

# Roasting Lamb

**Roasting directions:** Season the lamb roast by sprinkling with a little salt and pepper. Place the meat, fat side up, on an unheated rack in a shallow roasting pan. Insert a meat thermometer (*see* tip box, page 451). *Do not add water or other liquid; do not cover the roasting pan.* Roast the meat in a 325° oven till the meat thermometer registers the desired internal temperature. For easier carving, let the meat stand about 15 minutes. Remove the string from rolled and tied roasts. Carve meat (see pages 534 and 535). Use the roasting times given in the chart on page 523 as a guide to the total cooking time for the cut of meat you are preparing.

## Broiled Lamb Chops

> 4   **lamb rib chops, loin chops, or leg sirloin chops, cut ¾ to 1 inch thick (1¼ pounds)**

Slash fat edge of lamb chops in several places to keep chops flat. Place chops on an unheated rack in a broiler pan.

For medium-done chops, broil 3 inches from heat for 5 to 6 minutes. Turn the chops; continue to broil 5 to 6 minutes more. For well-done chops, broil 3 inches from heat for 7 to 8 minutes. Turn the chops; continue to broil 7 to 8 minutes longer. Serves 4.

| Lamb Cut | Approximate Weight (pounds) | Internal Temperature on Removal from Oven | Approximate Cooking Time (total time) |
|---|---|---|---|
| **Roast meat at a constant 325° oven temperature** | | | |
| Leg, whole | 5 to 9 | 140° (rare)<br>160° (medium)<br>170° to 180° (well-done) | 2 to 3 hours<br>2½ to 3¾ hrs.<br>3 to 4½ hrs. |
| Leg, half | 3 to 4 | 160° (medium) | 1½ to 1¾ hrs. |
| Square Cut Shoulder | 4 to 6 | 160° (medium) | 2 to 2½ hrs. |
| Boneless Shoulder | 3 to 5 | 160° (medium) | 2 to 3 hrs. |
| Crown Roast | 3 to 4 | 140° (rare)<br>160° (medium)<br>170° to 180° (well-done) | 1¾ to 2 hrs.<br>2 to 2¼ hrs.<br>2¼ to 2¾ hrs. |

# Lamb Chops Supreme

In a large skillet brown 6 *lamb shoulder chops*, cut ½ inch thick, in 2 tablespoons hot *cooking oil*; sprinkle with salt and pepper. Drain off fat. Add ¾ cup *water*, ¼ cup finely chopped *celery*, ¼ cup sliced *green onion*, 1 teaspoon instant *beef bouillon granules*, and ½ teaspoon dried *thyme*, crushed. Cover; simmer 20 to 25 minutes or till tender. Remove chops to a platter; keep warm. Skim excess fat from drippings. Measure ½ cup drippings; set aside.

For sauce, combine ½ cup *dairy sour cream*, 1 tablespoon *all-purpose flour*, and dash *pepper*. Slowly stir in the reserved drippings. Return mixture to skillet. Add one 2½-ounce jar sliced *mushrooms*, drained, and 2 tablespoons snipped *parsley*. Cook and stir till thickened, just to boiling. Pass sauce with meat. Makes 6 servings.

## Italian Lamb Chop Skillet

|   |   |
|---|---|
| **4** | **lamb shoulder chops** |
| **¼** | **cup chopped onion** |
| **2** | **tablespoons cooking oil** |
| **¼** | **teaspoon dried basil, crushed** |
| **¼** | **teaspoon dried oregano, crushed** |
| **1** | **cup water** |
| **2** | **teaspoons instant chicken bouillon granules** |
| **2** | **medium potatoes, peeled and sliced (2 cups)** |
| **1** | **9-ounce package frozen Italian or cut green beans, partially thawed** |
| **¼** | **cup sliced pitted ripe olives** |
| **1** | **2-ounce jar sliced pimiento, drained and chopped** |
| **2** | **teaspoons cornstarch** |

In a large skillet brown lamb chops and chopped onion in hot oil. Drain off excess fat. Sprinkle meat with basil, oregano, and a little pepper. Stir in water and bouillon granules. Cover and simmer for 15 minutes. Arrange potatoes around chops; simmer, covered, about 15 minutes more or till potatoes are almost tender. Add beans, olives, and pimiento. Cover and simmer 5 to 10 minutes more or till beans are tender. Remove meat and vegetables to a platter; keep warm. Stir 1 tablespoon *cold water* into cornstarch; stir into cooking liquid. Cook and stir till thickened and bubbly. Cook and stir 1 to 2 minutes more. Serve with meat and vegetables. Serves 4.

## Saucy Lamb Shanks

Sprinkle 4 *lamb shanks* (3½ to 4 pounds total) with some salt and pepper. In a large skillet brown lamb in 2 tablespoons hot *cooking oil;* drain off excess fat. In a mixing bowl stir together 1 cup finely chopped *onion;* 1 cup finely chopped *carrot;* 1 cup chopped *celery;* one 8-ounce can *tomato sauce;* 1 cup *dry red wine;* ½ cup *water;* 1 clove *garlic,* minced; 1 *bay leaf;* 1

teaspoon *salt;* and ⅛ teaspoon *pepper.* Pour over lamb. Cover; simmer for 1½ hours or till meat is tender.

Place lamb shanks atop *hot cooked noodles* on a serving platter. Remove bay leaf from tomato sauce mixture; discard. Skim excess fat from sauce; spoon sauce over lamb shanks and noodles. Makes 4 servings.

---

## Curried Lamb Madras

     2   **pounds boneless lamb, cut into 1-inch**
         **cubes**
     2   **tablespoons cooking oil**
     1   **cup chopped peeled apple**
     1   **cup chopped onion**
     2   **to 3 tablespoons curry powder**
    2½   **cups water**
     2   **teaspoons instant chicken bouillon**
         **granules**
    ½   **teaspoon salt**
    ½   **teaspoon paprika**
    ½   **teaspoon dried oregano, crushed**
    ⅛   **teaspoon pepper**
    ½   **cup cold water**
    ¼   **cup all-purpose flour**
         **Hot cooked rice**
         **Condiments (optional)**

In a large saucepan or Dutch oven brown meat, half at a time, in hot oil. Remove meat and set aside. In the pan drippings cook chopped apple, onion, and curry powder till onion is tender but not brown. Add browned meat, 2½ cups water, chicken bouillon granules, salt, paprika, oregano, and pepper. Cover and simmer about 1 hour or till meat is tender. Stir ½ cup cold water into flour; stir into lamb mixture. Cook and stir till thickened and bubbly. Cook and stir 1 to 2 minutes more. Season to taste. Serve over hot cooked rice. If desired, pass condiments such as chutney, sliced green onion, raisins, shredded coconut, chopped peanuts, chopped cucumber, or crumbled crisp-cooked bacon. Makes 6 to 8 servings.

## Lamb Loin Chops with Walnut Glaze

  **4**   **lamb loin chops, cut ¾ inch thick**
  **¼**   **cup honey**
  **1**   **tablespoon lemon juice**
  **¼**   **cup finely chopped walnuts**
  **2**   **tablespoons snipped parsley**

Place lamb chops on an unheated rack in a broiler pan. Broil 3 inches from heat for 5 minutes. Season with salt and pepper. Turn; broil 5 to 6 minutes more. Combine honey and lemon juice; stir in walnuts and parsley. Spoon nut mixture over chops; broil 1 minute longer. Serves 4.

## Lamb Patties with Dill Sauce

  **6**   **slices bacon**
  **1**   **beaten egg**
  **¼**   **cup rolled oats**
  **¼**   **cup chopped onion**
  **1**   **teaspoon salt**
  **1½**   **pounds ground lamb**
  **1**   **tablespoon chopped onion**
  **1**   **tablespoon butter or margarine**
  **2**   **tablespoons grated Parmesan cheese**
  **1**   **tablespoon all-purpose flour**
  **½**   **teaspoon dried dillweed**
  **½**   **teaspoon paprika**
  **1**   **cup milk**

Partially cook the bacon; set aside. In a mixing bowl combine beaten egg, rolled oats, the ¼ cup chopped onion, salt, and dash *pepper*. Add ground lamb; mix well. Shape mixture into six ½-inch-thick patties. Wrap a partially cooked bacon slice around the side of each patty; fasten with a wooden pick. Place patties on an unheated rack in a broiler pan. Broil 4 to 5 inches from heat to desired doneness, turning once (allow 12 to 14 minutes total time for medium).

Meanwhile, in a saucepan cook 1 tablespoon chopped onion in the butter or margarine till tender but not brown. Stir in Parmesan cheese, flour, dillweed, paprika, and ⅛ teaspoon *salt*. Add milk all at once. Cook and stir till thickened and bubbly. Cook and stir 1 to 2 minutes more. Spoon over patties. Makes 6 servings.

## Savory Lamburgers

In a mixing bowl combine ¾ cup *soft bread crumbs* (1 slice); one 2-ounce can chopped *mushrooms,* drained; ⅓ cup *milk;* 2 tablespoons finely chopped *onion;* 2 tablespoons chopped *pimiento-stuffed olives;* 1 tablespoon snipped *parsley;* ¼ teaspoon *salt;* and dash *pepper.* Add 1 pound *ground lamb;* mix well. Shape into six ½-inch-thick patties. In a 10-inch skillet cook patties over medium heat for 5 to 7 minutes. Turn; cook 5 to 7 minutes more or till done. (*Or,* place lamb patties on an unheated rack in a broiler pan. Broil 4 to 5 inches from heat for 5 minutes; turn and broil 4 to 5 minutes longer.) Serve on 6 *hamburger buns,* split and toasted. Makes 6 servings.

## Moussaka

| | |
|---|---|
| 2 | large eggplants, peeled and cut into ½-inch slices |
| ¼ | cup cooking oil |
| 2 | pounds ground lamb *or* ground beef |
| 1 | cup chopped onion |
| 1 | clove garlic, minced |
| 1 | 8-ounce can tomato sauce |
| ¾ | cup dry red wine |
| 2 | tablespoons snipped parsley |
| 1 | teaspoon salt |
| ¼ | teaspoon dried oregano, crushed |
| ¼ | teaspoon ground cinnamon |
| 1 | beaten egg |
| ¼ | cup butter *or* margarine |
| ¼ | cup all-purpose flour |
| 1 | teaspoon salt |
| | Dash pepper |
| 2 | cups milk |
| 3 | beaten eggs |
| ½ | cup grated **Parmesan cheese** |
| | Ground cinnamon |

Oven 325°

Brush both sides of eggplant slices with the oil; sprinkle lightly with some salt. In a large skillet brown eggplant slices about 1½ minutes per side. Drain and set aside. In the same skillet cook ground lamb or beef, chopped onion, and garlic till meat is brown and onion is tender; drain off excess fat. Stir in tomato sauce, dry red wine, snipped parsley, the 1 teaspoon salt, oregano, and the ¼ teaspoon cinnamon. Simmer, uncovered, for 10 minutes. Gradually stir the tomato-meat mixture into the 1 beaten egg.

Meanwhile, in a medium saucepan melt butter or margarine; stir in flour, 1 teaspoon salt, and pepper. Add milk all at once; cook and stir till thickened and bubbly. Cook and stir 1 to 2 minutes more. Gradually stir the thickened milk mixture into the 3 beaten eggs. In a 13x9x2-inch baking dish arrange *half* of the browned eggplant slices. Pour all the tomato-meat mixture over; top with the remaining eggplant slices. Pour the hot milk-egg mixture over all. Top with Parmesan cheese and sprinkle with additional cinnamon. Bake in a 325° oven for 40 to 45 minutes. Top with additional parsley, if desired. Makes 8 to 10 servings.

# Variety Meats

## Tongue and Lima Skillet

| | |
|---|---|
| 2 | tablespoons chopped onion |
| 1 | tablespoon butter *or* margarine |
| 1⅓ | cups water |
| 1 | 10-ounce package frozen baby lima beans |
| 1 | teaspoon instant beef bouillon granules |
| 1 | teaspoon Worcestershire sauce |
| ¼ | teaspoon dried thyme, crushed |
| ⅓ | cup catsup |
| 1 | tablespoon cornstarch |
| 12 | ounces thinly sliced cooked tongue |

In a 10-inch skillet cook onion in butter till tender but not brown. Stir in water, lima beans, bouillon granules, Worcestershire, and thyme. Bring to boiling. Reduce heat; simmer, covered, for 10 minutes. Stir catsup into cornstarch. Stir into *undrained* lima mixture. Cook and stir till thickened and bubbly. Cook and stir 1 to 2 minutes more. Stir in sliced tongue; heat through. Makes 4 servings.

## Creamed Sweetbreads

> 1 **pound beef sweetbreads**
> 1 **tablespoon vinegar**
> ¼ **cup butter *or* margarine**
> 3 **tablespoons all-purpose flour**
> **Dash paprika**
> 2 **cups milk**
> 1 **10-ounce package frozen peas with sliced mushrooms, cooked and drained**
> **Patty shells *or* toast points**

In a 3-quart saucepan combine sweetbreads, vinegar, 4 cups *water*, and ½ teaspoon *salt*. Bring to boiling. Reduce heat; simmer, covered, for 20 minutes. Drain. Remove white membranes and cut sweetbreads into bite-size pieces; set aside. In a saucepan melt butter or margarine. Stir in flour, paprika, ½ teaspoon *salt*, and dash *pepper*. Add milk all at once. Cook and stir till bubbly; cook 1 minute more. Stir in sweetbreads and peas with mushrooms; heat through. Serve in patty shells or over toast points. Serves 6.

## Sautéed Liver and Onions

In a 10-inch skillet cook 1 medium *onion*, sliced, in 2 tablespoons *butter or margarine* till tender but not brown. Remove onion from skillet. Add 1 pound sliced *beef liver*, cut into 4 slices, to skillet; sprinkle with some salt and pepper. Cook over medium heat for 3 minutes; turn. Return onion to skillet; cook 2 to 3 minutes more. Remove liver and onions to a platter. Stir 2 teaspoons *water*, 2 teaspoons *lemon juice*, and 1 teaspoon *Worcestershire sauce* into pan drippings; pour over liver and onions. Makes 4 servings.

## Steak and Kidney Pie

| | |
|---|---|
| 1 | beef kidney (about 1 pound) |
| 1½ | pounds beef round steak, cut into 1-inch cubes |
| ⅓ | cup all-purpose flour |
| 3 | tablespoons shortening |
| 2 | cups water |
| 1 | large onion, sliced (1 cup) |
| 2 | teaspoons Worcestershire sauce |
| | Pastry for Single-Crust Pie (see recipe, page 569) |
| ¼ | cup all-purpose flour |
| 2 | tablespoons snipped parsley |

Oven 450°

Remove membrane and fat from kidney. In a 3-quart saucepan cover kidney with water. Bring to boiling. Simmer, covered, about 1½ hours or till kidney is tender. Drain; cut into ½-inch cubes. Set aside.

Toss beef steak cubes with ⅓ cup flour. In a large skillet brown beef in shortening. Add water, onion, and Worcestershire sauce. Cover and simmer about 30 minutes or till meat is tender. Meanwhile, prepare Pastry for Single-Crust Pie. Roll pastry into a circle 1-inch larger than a 2-quart casserole; set aside.

In a mixing bowl combine the ¼ cup flour, 1 teaspoon *salt,* and ⅛ teaspoon *pepper;* stir in ½ cup *cold water.* Stir into beef mixture in skillet. Stir in cubed kidney and parsley. Cook and stir till thickened and bubbly. Cook and stir 1 to 2 minutes more. Pour hot meat mixture into a 2-quart casserole. Place pastry atop meat mixture. Turn edges under and flute; cut slits for escape of steam. Bake in a 450° oven about 20 minutes or till crust is golden brown. Let stand 10 minutes before serving. Serves 10.

# Game

## Marinated Venison Chops

Place 4 *venison chops or steaks,* cut ¾ inch thick (about 1 pound), in a plastic bag; set in a shallow dish. For marinade, combine ¼ cup *wine vinegar;* ¼ cup *cooking oil;* ¼ cup *catsup;* 1 tablespoon *Worcestershire sauce;* 1 clove *garlic,* minced; ½ teaspoon *salt;* ½ teaspoon *dry mustard;* and dash *pepper.* Pour over meat in the plastic bag; close bag. Refrigerate 6 hours or overnight; turn occasionally.

Drain venison, reserving marinade; pat dry. Place marinated chops on an unheated rack in a broiler pan. Broil 4 inches from heat for 6 to 8 minutes; brush with some of the marinade. Turn and continue broiling to desired doneness. Brush with marinade again just before serving. (Allow about 12 minutes total time for medium-rare; 14 minutes for medium; and 16 minutes for well done.) Sprinkle with snipped *parsley.* If desired, heat remaining marinade and skim off fat; serve with chops. Makes 4 servings.

## Venison Pot Roast

Coat one 3- to 3½-pound *venison shoulder or rump roast* with about 2 tablespoons *all-purpose flour.* In a Dutch oven brown roast on all sides in 2 tablespoons hot *cooking oil.* Season with some salt and pepper. Add 1½ cups *tomato juice,* ½ cup finely chopped *onion,* ½ cup finely chopped *carrot,* and 2 teaspoons instant *beef bouillon granules.* Bring to boiling. Reduce heat; cover and simmer for 2 to 2½ hours or till meat is tender, adding water if necessary. Remove meat to a serving platter; keep warm.

For sour cream sauce, skim fat from pan juices. Measure juices; add enough water to measure 2 cups liquid. Return liquid to Dutch oven. Stir together ½ cup *dairy sour cream* and ¼ cup *cold water;* stir in ¼ cup *all-purpose flour.* Add to Dutch oven. Cook and stir till thickened and bubbly. Cook and stir 1 to 2 minutes more. Season to taste. Slice venison thinly; spoon sour cream sauce over. Serve with *hot cooked noodles*. Makes 8 servings.

## Beer-Braised Rabbit

Generously season one 1½- to 2-pound *rabbit,* cut up, with salt and pepper. In a 10-inch skillet brown rabbit in 3 table-spoons hot *cooking oil.* Add 3 medium *potatoes,* peeled and halved crosswise; 3 or 4 *carrots,* cut into 1-inch pieces (about 2 cups); and 1 medium *onion,* sliced (½ cup). Combine 1 cup *beer,* ¼ cup *chili sauce,* 1 tablespoon *brown sugar,* ½ tea-spoon *salt,* and 1 clove *garlic,* minced; pour over rabbit. Bring to boiling. Cover; reduce heat and simmer about 45 minutes or till rabbit is tender. Remove rabbit and vegetables to a serving platter; keep warm.

Measure pan juices, adding additional beer or water, if nec-essary, to make 1½ cups liquid. Return pan juices to skillet. Stir ⅓ cup *water* into 3 tablespoons *all-purpose flour;* stir into skillet. Cook and stir till thickened and bubbly. Cook and stir 1 to 2 minutes more. Serve with rabbit. Makes 4 servings.

## Hasenpfeffer

    3  cups water
    1  cup vinegar
    ⅓  cup sugar
    1  medium onion, sliced (½ cup)
    1  teaspoon mixed pickling spices
    1  1½-pound rabbit, cut up
    ¼  cup all-purpose flour
    2  tablespoons cooking oil
    2  tablespoons cold water
    1  tablespoon all-purpose flour

In a large bowl combine the 3 cups water, vinegar, sugar, onion, pickling spices, 2 teaspoons *salt,* and ¼ teaspoon *pep-per.* Add rabbit. Cover; refrigerate for 2 days. Remove rabbit from marinade; pat dry. Reserve the onion slices and *1 cup* of the marinade.

In a plastic bag shake rabbit pieces in the ¼ cup flour to coat. In a 10-inch skillet slowly brown rabbit in hot oil. Pour reserved marinade and onions over rabbit. Cover; simmer about 35 minutes or till meat is tender. Remove rabbit and onions to a serving platter; keep warm. Measure pan juices. Add water, if necessary, to make 1 cup liquid; return to skillet. Stir together the 2 tablespoons cold water and 1 tablespoon flour; stir into pan juices. Cook and stir till bubbly. Cook and stir 1 to 2 minutes more. Season to taste. Serves 4.

# Meat Carving

Carving meat can be baffling, especially when it comes to slicing a variety of meat cuts. To carve all meat successfully, keep the knife's cutting edge very sharp. For best results, sharpen knives with a hand-held sharpening steel or stone before each use. With the steel or stone in one hand, hold the knife in the other hand at a 20-degree angle to the sharpener. Draw the blade edge over the sharpener, using a motion that goes across and down at the same time. Turn the blade over, reverse directions, and sharpen the other side an equal number of times.

To keep knives clean, wipe them with a wet cloth after each use, then dry. And to keep knives in good condition, store them properly. Keep knives separated in a holder or rack to prevent blunting.

**Beef Rib Roast.** Carving the rib roast is easier if the chine bone (part of the back-

bone) is removed and the rib bones are cut short by the

butcher. Place the rib roast on a warm platter, largest end down, to form a solid base for carving. Insert a carving fork between the top two ribs. Starting on the fat side of the

meat, slice across the meat to the rib bone. Cut along the rib bone with the knife tip to loosen each slice, if the whole rib is not served. Keep knife as close to the rib bones as possible when cutting.

**Leg of Lamb.** With the shank on the carver's right, cut 2 or 3 slices from the thin side parallel to the leg bone;

turn leg to rest on this base. Steady with the carving fork. Beginning at the shank end, cut ¼-inch slices down to the leg bone. Cut until you reach the bone pointing upward.

Start at the shank end and cut along the leg bone to release slices.

**Shoulder Arm Picnic.** To carve a roasted shoulder arm picnic, remove a slice from the smaller side of the roast.

Place the roast on its side. Locate the elbow bone and cut down to the arm bone in front of the elbow bone. Cut along the arm bone.

Remove the boneless piece of meat and place it on a cutting board. Cut perpendicular slices.

With the boneless piece of meat placed cut side down on the cutting board, slice meat across the grain, as shown.

Remove the boneless pieces from both sides of the arm bone and cut into slices.

**Rump Half of Ham.** Place the cut side of the rump half of ham on a cutting board.

To carve the meat remaining on the bone, insert a fork into the meat next to the bone and make horizontal slices to the aitchbone, as shown. Cut away each slice from the bone using the tip of the knife and transfer each cut slice to a serving platter.

Notice that on one side of the ham there is a boneless piece that can be cut away from the bone. Cut along the bone from the top down to the cutting board. The piece can be on either side of the bone.

# Pies

# Pies

# Pies

# Pies

# Pies

# Pies

# Pies

# Pies

# Pies

Percent of U.S. RDA Per Serving

| Recipes | Servings (fraction of recipe) | Calories | Protein (grams) | Carbohydrate (grams) | Fat (grams) | Sodium (milligrams) | Potassium (milligrams) | Protein | Vitamin A | Vitamin C | Thiamine | Riboflavin | Niacin | Calcium | Iron |
|---|---|---|---|---|---|---|---|---|---|---|---|---|---|---|---|
| Apple Crumble Pie | 1/8 | 388 | 4 | 62 | 15 | 205 | 132 | 6 | 6 | 6 | 10 | 16 | 9 | 1 | 7 |
| Apple Pie | 1/8 | 424 | 4 | 62 | 19 | 286 | 124 | 6 | 3 | 6 | 6 | 16 | 9 | 1 | 7 |
| Apricot Pie | 1/8 | 438 | 5 | 65 | 19 | 286 | 337 | 7 | 59 | 19 | 19 | 17 | 11 | 3 | 9 |
| Baked Pastry Shell | 1/8 | 144 | 2 | 15 | 8 | 134 | 19 | 3 | 0 | 0 | 8 | 5 | 5 | 0 | 3 |
| Banana Cream Pie | 1/8 | 486 | 11 | 69 | 19 | 348 | 375 | 17 | 14 | 9 | 9 | 17 | 23 | 13 | 10 |
| Black Bottom Pie | 1/8 | 432 | 9 | 56 | 21 | 194 | 208 | 14 | 8 | 1 | 1 | 11 | 16 | 10 | 9 |
| Brandy Hard Sauce | 1/24 | 70 | 0 | 8 | 4 | 49 | 4 | 0 | 4 | 0 | 0 | 0 | 0 | 0 | 0 |
| Brown-Sugar-Rhubarb Pie | 1/8 | 343 | 7 | 56 | 11 | 251 | 314 | 10 | 6 | 6 | 11 | 13 | 14 | 10 | 14 |
| Cherry Pie | 1/8 | 485 | 4 | 78 | 18 | 287 | 179 | 4 | 17 | 6 | 9 | 16 | 9 | 2 | 7 |
| Chocolate Chiffon Pie | 1/8 | 276 | 5 | 38 | 13 | 221 | 98 | 8 | 2 | 0 | 9 | 16 | 8 | 1 | 7 |
| Chocolate Wafer Crust | 1/8 | 163 | 1 | 13 | 12 | 143 | 35 | 2 | 7 | 0 | 0 | 2 | 2 | 1 | 2 |
| Coconut Cream Pie | 1/8 | 523 | 11 | 62 | 27 | 353 | 265 | 18 | 12 | 12 | 3 | 16 | 22 | 13 | 10 |
| Coconut Crust | 1/8 | 108 | 1 | 2 | 11 | 57 | 52 | 1 | 4 | 0 | 1 | 1 | 0 | 0 | 2 |
| Coffee Angel Pie | 1/8 | 364 | 5 | 46 | 18 | 217 | 259 | 8 | 9 | 0 | 2 | 8 | 11 | 13 | 6 |
| Cornflake Piecrust | 1/8 | 142 | 1 | 15 | 9 | 212 | 15 | 1 | 17 | 17 | 6 | 9 | 6 | 0 | 1 |
| Custard Pie | 1/8 | 283 | 8 | 31 | 14 | 269 | 161 | 12 | 8 | 1 | 1 | 12 | 17 | 11 | 7 |
| Dark Chocolate Cream Pie | 1/8 | 526 | 12 | 69 | 25 | 348 | 298 | 18 | 12 | 2 | 2 | 16 | 23 | 14 | 12 |
| Deep-Dish Apple Pie | 1/10 | 317 | 2 | 55 | 11 | 205 | 168 | 4 | 5 | 9 | 9 | 11 | 6 | 2 | 5 |
| Deep-Dish Peach Pie | 1/8 | 310 | 3 | 49 | 12 | 170 | 290 | 5 | 36 | 18 | 18 | 11 | 9 | 2 | 7 |
| Electric Mixer Pastry | 1/8 | 265 | 3 | 21 | 19 | 200 | 26 | 4 | 0 | 0 | 6 | 7 | 6 | 1 | 4 |

# Nutrition Analysis Chart

| | | | | | | | | | | | | | | | |
|---|---|---|---|---|---|---|---|---|---|---|---|---|---|---|---|
| French Crunch Peach Pie | 1/8 | 469 | 6 | 65 | 22 | 248 | 319 | 10 | 22 | 9 | 13 | 15 | 13 | 4 | 11 |
| French Silk Pie | 1/10 | 382 | 5 | 34 | 27 | 294 | 109 | 7 | 15 | 0 | 8 | 7 | 5 | 2 | 8 |
| Fresh Blackberry Pie | 1/8 | 443 | 5 | 69 | 18 | 303 | 175 | 7 | 3 | 14 | 17 | 10 | 11 | 3 | 10 |
| Fresh Blueberry Pie | 1/8 | 439 | 4 | 66 | 19 | 285 | 110 | 7 | 3 | 22 | 17 | 11 | 12 | 2 | 11 |
| Fresh Cherry Pie | 1/8 | 425 | 4 | 63 | 19 | 287 | 180 | 7 | 17 | 13 | 16 | 10 | 10 | 2 | 7 |
| Fresh Pear Crumble Pie | 1/8 | 392 | 4 | 63 | 15 | 206 | 173 | 6 | 5 | 12 | 14 | 9 | 8 | 2 | 7 |
| Fresh Pineapple Pie | 1/8 | 397 | 4 | 56 | 18 | 286 | 147 | 6 | 2 | 23 | 18 | 9 | 9 | 2 | 7 |
| Fresh Raspberry Pie | 1/8 | 435 | 4 | 61 | 20 | 303 | 168 | 7 | 4 | 34 | 15 | 12 | 12 | 3 | 9 |
| Fudge Ribbon Pie | 1/8 | 524 | 9 | 73 | 29 | 256 | 281 | 13 | 10 | 1 | 11 | 20 | 6 | 16 | 7 |
| Gingersnap-Graham Crust | 1/8 | 132 | 1 | 16 | 7 | 174 | 75 | 2 | 5 | 0 | 2 | 2 | 2 | 1 | 2 |
| Gooseberry Pie | 1/8 | 380 | 4 | 50 | 18 | 286 | 151 | 7 | 6 | 41 | 20 | 10 | 20 | 2 | 8 |
| Graham Cracker Crust | 1/8 | 162 | 1 | 18 | 10 | 212 | 64 | 2 | 7 | 0 | 2 | 2 | 1 | 1 | 1 |
| Grasshopper Pie | 1/8 | 522 | 4 | 49 | 35 | 182 | 110 | 6 | 26 | 1 | 4 | 7 | 2 | 7 | 6 |
| Homemade Mincemeat Pie* | 1/8 | 565 | 8 | 83 | 24 | 379 | 471 | 12 | 1 | 20 | 20 | 12 | 14 | 4 | 16 |
| Lemon-Chess Pie | 1/8 | 439 | 7 | 56 | 21 | 256 | 110 | 11 | 15 | 4 | 11 | 13 | 6 | 4 | 8 |
| Lemon Meringue Pie | 1/8 | 410 | 6 | 67 | 14 | 210 | 80 | 10 | 7 | 8 | 11 | 11 | 6 | 2 | 6 |
| Lemon Pastry | 1/8 | 150 | 2 | 17 | 8 | 134 | 22 | 3 | 0 | 2 | 8 | 5 | 5 | 0 | 3 |
| Light Chocolate Cream Pie | 1/8 | 479 | 11 | 59 | 23 | 348 | 244 | 17 | 12 | 2 | 15 | 22 | 8 | 13 | 9 |
| Lime Parfait Pie | 1/8 | 354 | 5 | 33 | 23 | 198 | 136 | 8 | 12 | 6 | 10 | 11 | 5 | 8 | 3 |
| Meringue Crust | 1/8 | 103 | 2 | 14 | 5 | 79 | 56 | 2 | 0 | 0 | 4 | 2 | 0 | 0 | 1 |
| Meringue for Pie | 1/8 | 41 | 1 | 9 | 0 | 18 | 18 | 2 | 0 | 0 | 0 | 2 | 0 | 0 | 0 |
| Oil Pastry | 1/8 | 256 | 4 | 27 | 14 | 273 | 49 | 6 | 0 | 0 | 15 | 9 | 9 | 2 | 6 |
| Pastry for Double-Crust Pie | 1/8 | 260 | 3 | 24 | 17 | 267 | 30 | 5 | 0 | 0 | 13 | 7 | 8 | 1 | 5 |
| Pastry for Lattice-Top Pie | 1/8 | 260 | 3 | 24 | 17 | 267 | 30 | 5 | 0 | 0 | 13 | 7 | 8 | 1 | 5 |
| Pastry for Single-Crust Pie | 1/8 | 144 | 2 | 15 | 8 | 134 | 19 | 3 | 0 | 0 | 7 | 5 | 5 | 1 | 3 |
| Pecan Pastry | 1/8 | 162 | 2 | 15 | 10 | 134 | 35 | 4 | 0 | 0 | 8 | 5 | 5 | 1 | 3 |
| Pecan Pie | 1/10 | 420 | 5 | 52 | 23 | 222 | 109 | 7 | 9 | 0 | 14 | 7 | 5 | 4 | 14 |
| Pumpkin Pie | 1/8 | 304 | 7 | 41 | 13 | 323 | 264 | 11 | 79 | 5 | 12 | 15 | 5 | 10 | 7 |

**Note:** This recipe makes enough mincemeat for 3 pies, but analysis is based on ⅛ of 1 pie.

# Nutrition Analysis Chart

| Recipes | Servings (fraction of recipe) | Calories | Protein (grams) | Carbohydrate (grams) | Fat (grams) | Sodium (milligrams) | Potassium (milligrams) | Protein | Vitamin A | Vitamin C | Thiamine | Riboflavin | Niacin | Calcium | Iron |
|---|---|---|---|---|---|---|---|---|---|---|---|---|---|---|---|
| | | | | | | | | Percent of U.S. RDA Per Serving | | | | | | | |
| Raisin Crisscross Pie | 1/8 | 546 | 6 | 87 | 22 | 287 | 510 | 9 | 1 | 18 | 19 | 11 | 10 | 7 | 20 |
| Raspberry Chiffon Pie | 1/8 | 298 | 5 | 39 | 14 | 152 | 111 | 7 | 6 | 18 | 9 | 9 | 9 | 2 | 5 |
| Rhubarb Pie | 1/8 | 322 | 4 | 32 | 20 | 305 | 189 | 6 | 4 | 9 | 17 | 11 | 11 | 7 | 9 |
| Rum Cream Pie | 1/8 | 406 | 6 | 33 | 27 | 226 | 196 | 9 | 10 | 2 | 12 | 12 | 7 | 7 | 6 |
| Sour Cream-Raisin Pie | 1/10 | 410 | 7 | 59 | 18 | 259 | 262 | 10 | 11 | 1 | 12 | 15 | 6 | 10 | 9 |
| Strawberry Chiffon Pie | 1/8 | 271 | 4 | 32 | 14 | 152 | 123 | 7 | 5 | 47 | 10 | 9 | 9 | 3 | 6 |
| Strawberry Glacé Pie | 1/8 | 268 | 3 | 46 | 9 | 135 | 202 | 4 | 1 | 110 | 11 | 9 | 9 | 3 | 9 |
| Strawberry-Rhubarb Pie | 1/8 | 432 | 4 | 64 | 19 | 287 | 238 | 6 | 3 | 62 | 15 | 11 | 11 | 6 | 10 |
| Vanilla Cream Pie | 1/8 | 448 | 11 | 60 | 20 | 348 | 210 | 16 | 12 | 2 | 15 | 22 | 8 | 13 | 8 |
| Vanilla Wafer Crust | 1/8 | 146 | 1 | 11 | 11 | 143 | 13 | 1 | 7 | 0 | 2 | 2 | 2 | 1 | 1 |

# Pie-Making Basics

Simplify your pie making with the following equipment: a pastry blender to cut in shortening, a rolling pin with a stockinette cover, a pastry cloth (to prevent pastry from sticking), and a pastry wheel to cut pastry strips. For baking pies, use a glass pie plate or a dull metal pie plate. (Shiny metal pans keep the crust from browning properly). Cool baked pies on a wire rack. The rack allows air to circulate under the pie and helps prevent the crust from becoming soggy.

The "secret" of pastry making is measuring accurately. Before measuring flour, stir it in the canister to lighten it. Then gently spoon the flour into a dry measure and level off the top with a metal spatula. (Too much flour makes the pastry tough.) To measure solid shortening, pack it into a dry measure, running a spatula through it to make sure there are no air pockets. (Too much shortening makes pastry greasy and crumbly.) To measure water for pastry, fill a measuring tablespoon to the top. Sprinkle 1 tablespoon water at a time over the flour-shortening mixture. (Too much water makes pastry tough and soggy.)

When rolling out pastry, roll from center to edge with light, even strokes, forming a circle about 12 inches in diameter (about ⅛ inch thick). For easy transfer to the pie plate, wrap pastry around the rolling pin. (Lift the pastry cloth with pastry on it so that the pastry slides onto the rolling pin and rolls around it.) Loosely unroll the pastry onto a 9-inch pie plate. (Do not stretch the dough.) To repair tears, moisten edges and press together.

One method for fluting the edge of the pastry is to press the dough with a forefinger (from outside the pie plate) against the thumb and forefinger of the other hand (placed inside the pie plate). Continue around the dish till the entire edge is fluted. Hook the fluted edge over the side of the plate all the way around, or press it firmly against the rim of the pie plate.

If the pastry is to be baked without a filling, prick the bottom and sides all over with a fork. This helps prevent the crust from puffing up by allowing steam to escape. (Do not prick the pastry if filling is to be baked along with the crust.)

To prevent excessive browning on the edge of the pastry, cover it with foil. Fold a 12-inch square of foil into quarters; cut out a circle from the center. Unfold; mold over the edge of the pie. *Or*, mold long, narrow strips around the edge. (Pies that bake under 30 minutes do not need the foil shielding.)

# Fruit Pies

## Apple Pie

    6   cups thinly sliced, peeled cooking apples
            (2 pounds)
    1   cup sugar
    2   tablespoons all-purpose flour
    ½   to 1 teaspoon ground cinnamon
        Dash ground nutmeg
        Pastry for Double-Crust Pie*
    1   tablespoon butter                          Oven 375°

If apples lack tartness, sprinkle with 1 tablespoon lemon juice, if desired. Combine sugar, flour, cinnamon, and nutmeg. (For a very juicy pie, omit the flour.) Add sugar mixture to the sliced apples; toss to coat fruit. Fill a pastry-lined 9-inch pie plate with apple mixture; dot with butter. Adjust top crust. Seal and flute edge. Sprinkle some sugar atop, if desired. Cover edge of pie with foil. Bake in a 375° oven for 25 minutes. Remove foil; bake for 20 to 25 minutes more or till crust is golden. Cool. Serve with cheese, if desired. Serves 8.

**\*See recipe, page 569**

## Apple Crumble Pie

|      |                                                  |           |
| ---- | ------------------------------------------------ | --------- |
| 1    | cup sugar                                        |           |
| 2    | tablespoons all-purpose flour                    |           |
| 1    | teaspoon grated lemon peel                       |           |
| 6    | cups thinly sliced, peeled cooking apples        |           |
|      | (2 pounds)                                       |           |
| 3    | tablespoons lemon juice                          |           |
|      | Pastry for Single-Crust Pie*                     |           |
| ½    | cup all-purpose flour                            |           |
| ½    | teaspoon ground cinnamon                         |           |
| ¼    | teaspoon ground ginger                           |           |
| ⅛    | teaspoon ground mace                             |           |
| ¼    | cup butter                                       | Oven 375° |

Combine ½ *cup* of the sugar, the 2 tablespoons flour, and the lemon peel. Sprinkle apple slices with lemon juice; add sugar mixture and toss to coat. Fill a pastry-lined 9-inch pie plate with apple mixture. Combine remaining ½ cup of sugar, the ½ cup flour, and the spices. Cut in the butter till crumbly; sprinkle mixture atop apples. Cover edge of pie with foil. Bake in a 375° oven for 30 minutes. Remove foil; bake for 30 minutes more or till topping is golden. Serve warm. Makes 8 servings.

## Deep-Dish Apple Pie

|      |                                                  |           |
| ---- | ------------------------------------------------ | --------- |
|      | Pastry for Single-Crust Pie*                     |           |
| 1    | cup sugar                                        |           |
| ⅓    | cup all-purpose flour                            |           |
| 1    | teaspoon ground cinnamon                         |           |
| ½    | teaspoon ground allspice                         |           |
| ¼    | teaspoon salt                                    |           |
| 12   | cups thinly sliced, peeled cooking               |           |
|      | apples (4 pounds)                                |           |
| 3    | tablespoons butter or margarine                  |           |
|      | Milk *and* sugar                                 | Oven 375° |

*See recipe, page 569

Prepare Pastry for Single-Crust Pie, *except* roll out into a 13x8½-inch rectangle; cut slits in pastry. Combine sugar, flour, cinnamon, allspice, and salt. (For a very juicy pie, use ¼ cup all-purpose flour.) Add sugar mixture to apples; toss to coat fruit. Turn into a 12x7½x2-inch baking dish (apples will mound higher than sides). Dot with butter or margarine. Carefully place pastry atop apples; flute to the sides but not over the edge. Brush with milk and sprinkle with sugar. Cover edge of pie with foil. Bake in a 375° oven for 25 minutes. Remove foil; bake for 20 to 25 minutes more. Serve warm in dishes. Makes 10 servings.

---

### Tips for making fruit pies

Glaze the top of double-crust fruit pies to make them look and taste special. Brush the unbaked top crust with milk, water, or melted butter; then sprinkle lightly with sugar. Or, just brush the crust lightly with beaten egg or a light coating of milk before baking the pie.

To avoid messy spills in the oven, set the pie plate on a baking sheet on the oven rack. The pan will catch any juice if the pie bubbles over.

Fruit pies can be stored at room temperature for a short period of time. Cover and refrigerate any pies with fillings that contain eggs or dairy products.

# Fresh Cherry Pie

4 **cups fresh or frozen pitted tart red cherries (20 ounces)**
1 **cup sugar**
3 **tablespoons quick-cooking tapioca**
1 **tablespoon cherry brandy (optional)**
1 **teaspoon finely shredded lemon peel**
**Pastry for Double-Crust Pie***
1 **tablespoon butter or margarine**     Oven 375°

In a large bowl combine cherries; sugar; tapioca; brandy, if desired; lemon peel; and ⅛ teaspoon *salt*. Let stand 20 minutes, stirring occasionally. Fill a pastry-lined 9-inch pie plate with cherry mixture; dot with butter or margarine. Adjust top crust. Seal and flute edge high. Cover edge of pie with foil. Bake in a 375° oven for 30 minutes. Remove foil; bake for 25 to 30 minutes more or till golden. Cool pie on a wire rack before serving. Serves 8.

# Cherry Pie

2 **16-ounce cans pitted tart red cherries (water pack)**
1½ **cups sugar**
⅓ **cup cornstarch**
1 **tablespoon butter or margarine**
3 **or 4 drops almond extract**
10 **drops red food coloring (optional)**
**Pastry for Lattice-Top Pie***     Oven 375°

Drain cherries; reserve 1 cup liquid. In a saucepan combine ¾ *cup* of the sugar, the cornstarch, and dash *salt*. Stir in reserved cherry liqud. Cook and stir over medium heat till thickened and bubbly. Cook and stir 1 minute more. Remove from heat.

***See recipe, page 569**

Stir in remaining ¾ cup sugar, the cherries, butter or margarine, and almond extract. If desired, stir in red food coloring. Let stand while preparing pastry. Fill a pastry-lined 9-inch pie plate with cherry mixture. Adjust lattice crust; flute edge. Cover edge of pie with foil. Bake in a 375° oven for 25 minutes. Remove foil; bake for 25 to 30 minutes more or till crust is golden. Cool on a wire rack before serving. Makes 8 servings.

---

# Apricot Pie

 4 **cups sliced, pitted fresh or frozen apricots**
 1 **tablespoon lemon juice**
 1 **cup sugar**
 ¼ **cup all-purpose flour**
 ⅛ **teaspoon ground nutmeg**
   **Pastry for Double-Crust Pie***
 1 **tablespoon butter or margarine**       Oven 375°

In a large bowl sprinkle the apricots with lemon juice. Combine the sugar, flour, and nutmeg. Add sugar mixture to sliced apricots; toss to coat fruit. Fill a pastry-lined 9-inch pie plate with apricot mixture; dot with butter or margarine. Adjust top crust. Seal and flute edge. Cover edge of pie with foil. Bake in a 375° oven for 20 minutes. Remove foil; bake for 20 to 25 minutes more or till crust is golden. Cool on a wire rack before serving. Serves 8.

**\*See recipe, page 569**

## Raisin Crisscross Pie

1 cup packed brown sugar
2 tablespoons cornstarch
2 cups raisins
½ teaspoon finely shredded orange peel
½ cup orange juice
½ teaspoon finely shredded lemon peel
2 tablespoons lemon juice
½ cup chopped walnuts
Pastry for Lattice-Top Pie*          Oven 375°

In a saucepan combine brown sugar and cornstarch. Stir in raisins, orange peel and juice, lemon peel and juice, and 1⅓ cups cold *water*. Cook and stir over medium heat till thickened and bubbly; cook and stir 1 minute more. Remove from heat; stir in walnuts. Fill a pastry-lined 9-inch pie plate with raisin mixture. Adjust lattice crust; flute edge. Cover edge of pie with foil. Bake in a 375° oven for 20 minutes. Remove foil and bake about 20 minutes more or till crust is golden. Makes 8 servings.

## Deep-Dish Peach Pie

Pastry for Single-Crust Pie*
¾ cup sugar
3 tablespoons all-purpose flour
¼ teaspoon ground nutmeg
6 cups peeled, thickly sliced fresh peaches
    (3 pounds)
3 tablespoons grenadine syrup
2 tablespoons lemon juice
2 tablespoons butter *or* margarine    Oven 375°

Prepare Pastry for Single-Crust Pie, *except* roll out into an even 9-inch or 11-inch circle (depending on dish size). Cut slits

*See recipe, page 569

in pastry. Combine sugar, flour, and nutmeg. Add sugar mixture to peaches and toss to coat. Let stand 5 minutes. Stir in grenadine syrup and lemon juice. Turn mixture into a 1½-quart casserole or a deep 10-inch round baking dish, spreading peaches evenly; dot with butter. Place pastry over peach mixture in baking dish. Flute to side of dish but not over the edge. Cover edge with foil. Place dish on a baking sheet. Bake in a 375° oven for 25 minutes. Remove foil; bake for 30 to 35 minutes more or till crust is golden. Cool. Makes 8 servings.

---

# French Crunch Peach Pie

**Pastry for Single-Crust Pie***
2  **eggs**
1  **tablespoon lemon juice**
⅓  **cup sugar**
1  **29-ounce can *and* one 16-ounce can peach slices, drained**
1  **cup finely crushed vanilla wafers (22 wafers)**
½  **cup chopped toasted almonds**
¼  **cup butter, melted**                    Oven 450°

Bake pastry in a 450° oven for 5 minutes. Meanwhile, beat eggs and lemon juice till combined; stir in sugar. Fold in drained peaches. Turn peach mixture into the partially baked pastry shell. Stir together vanilla wafer crumbs, almonds, and butter; sprinkle over peach mixture. Cover edge of pie with foil. Reduce oven temperature to 375° and bake for 20 minutes. Remove foil; bake for 20 to 25 minutes more or till filling is set in center. Cool on a wire rack before serving. Cover; chill to store. Makes 8 servings.

**\*See recipe, page 569**

# Homemade Mincemeat Pie

>     1   pound beef stew meat
>     4   pounds cooking apples, peeled, cored, and
>           quartered (9 cups)
>     4   ounces suet
>   2½   cups sugar
>   2½   cups water
>     1   15-ounce package (about 2¾ cups) raisins
>     2   cups dried currants (9 ounces)
>     ½   cup diced mixed candied fruits and peels
>     1   teaspoon finely shredded orange peel
>     1   cup orange juice
>     1   teaspoon finely shredded lemon peel
>     ¼   cup lemon juice
>     1   teaspoon salt
>     ½   teaspoon ground nutmeg
>     ¼   teaspoon ground mace
>           Pastry for Double-Crust Pie*
>           Milk
>           Brandy Hard Sauce                    Oven 375°

In a large saucepan combine beef stew meat and enough water to cover. Cover and simmer for 2 hours or till tender. Drain; cool. Using the coarse blade of a food grinder, grind cooked beef, apples, and suet. In a large kettle combine sugar, the ½ cups water, raisins, currants, mixed candied fruits and peels, orange peel, orange juice, lemon peel, lemon juice, salt, nutmeg, and mace; stir in ground meat-apple mixture. Cover and simmer 45 minutes; stir mixture frequently.

Fill a pastry-lined 9-inch pie plate with 4 *cups* of the meat mixture. (Freeze remaining mincemeat in 4-cup portions.) Cut slits in top crust (or cut a design in pastry with a small cookie cutter). Adjust top crust. Seal and flute edge. Brush with a little milk. Cover edge of pie with foil. Bake in a 375° oven for 20 minutes. Remove foil; bake about 15 minutes more or till crust is golden. Cool on a wire rack before serving. Serve with Brandy Hard Sauce. Cover; chill to store. Makes 8 servings.

*See recipe, page 569

**Note:** This recipe makes enough mincemeat for three 9-inch pies.

**Brandy Hard Sauce:** Thoroughly stir together 2 cups sifted *powdered sugar*, ½ cup softened *butter or margarine*, and 1 teaspoon *brandy*. Stir in 1 beaten *egg yolk*; fold in 1 stiff-beaten *egg white*. Chill.

---

# Fresh Blueberry Pie

| | |
|---|---|
| 1 | **cup sugar** |
| ¼ | **cup all-purpose flour** |
| ½ | **teaspoon finely shredded lemon peel** |
| | **Dash salt** |
| 5 | **cups fresh blueberries or one 20-ounce package frozen unsweetened blueberries, thawed** |
| | **Pastry for Double-Crust Pie\*** |
| 2 | **teaspoons lemon juice** |
| 1 | **tablespoon butter or margarine**    Oven 375° |

In a mixing bowl combine sugar, flour, lemon peel, and salt. Add sugar mixture to blueberries; toss to coat fruit. Fill a pastry-lined 9-inch pie plate with blueberry mixture. Drizzle with lemon juice and dot with butter or margarine. Adjust top crust. Seal and flute edge. Cover edge of pie with foil. Bake in a 375° oven for 20 minutes. Remove foil and bake for 20 to 25 minutes more or till crust is golden. Cool on a wire rack. Makes 8 servings.

**Note:** If using frozen blueberries, increase the all-purpose flour to ⅓ cup.

**\*See recipe, page 569**

# Fresh Blackberry Pie

  1¼  **cups sugar**
  ¼  **cup all-purpose flour**
  ⅛  **teaspoon salt**
  4  **cups fresh blackberries**
     **Pastry for Double-Crust Pie\***     Oven 375°

Combine sugar, flour, and salt. Add sugar mixture to blackberries; toss to coat fruit. Fill a pastry-lined 9-inch pie plate
with berry mixture. Adjust top crust. Seal and flute edge.
Cover edge of pie with foil. Bake in a 375° oven for 20
minutes. Remove foil; bake for 25 to 30 minutes more or till
golden. Cool on a wire rack. Makes 8 servings.

# Gooseberry Pie

  4  **cups fresh gooseberries *or* two 16-ounce**
       **cans gooseberries**
  ⅔  **to 1 cup sugar**
  ¼  **cup all-purpose flour**
     **Dash salt**
     **Pastry for Double-Crust Pie\***
  1  **tablespoon butter *or* margarine**     Oven 375°

Stem and wash fresh gooseberries *or* drain canned berries.
Combine sugar, flour, and salt. Add sugar mixture to berries;
toss gently to coat fruit. Fill a pastry-lined 9-inch pie plate with
berry mixture; dot with butter or margarine. Adjust top crust.
Seal and flute edge. Cover edge of pie with foil. Bake in a
375° oven for 20 minutes. Remove foil; bake for 25 minutes
more or till golden. Cool on a wire rack. Makes 8 servings.

    **Note:** If using canned gooseberries, reduce the all-purpose
flour to 3 tablespoons.

**\*See recipe, page 569**

## Fresh Raspberry Pie

  1   **cup sugar**
  2   **tablespoons cornstarch**
      **Dash salt**
  2   **pints fresh or frozen red or black**
          **raspberries (1¼ pounds)**
      **Pastry for Double-Crust Pie***
  2   **tablespoons butter or margarine**    Oven 375°

In a mixing bowl combine sugar, cornstarch, and salt. Add sugar mixture to berries; toss gently to coat fruit. Fill a pastry-lined 9-inch pie plate with berry mixture; dot with butter or margarine. Adjust top crust. Seal and flute edge. Cover edge of pie with foil. Bake in a 375° oven for 20 minutes. Remove foil; bake for 20 to 30 minutes more. Cool on a wire rack. Makes 8 servings.

**Note:** If desired, serve blueberry, blackberry, gooseberry, or raspberry pie with vanilla ice cream.

## Strawberry Glacé Pie

  6   **cups fresh medium strawberries**
  ¾   **cup sugar**
  3   **tablespoons cornstarch**
  5   **drops red food coloring (optional)**
  1   **9-inch Baked Pastry Shell***

To prepare strawberry glaze, in a small saucepan crush *1 cup* of the smaller berries; add 1 cup *water*. Bring to boiling; simmer 2 minutes. Sieve berry mixture. In a saucepan combine sugar and cornstarch; stir in sieved berry mixture. Cook over medium heat, stirring constantly, till thickened and clear. Stir in red food coloring, if desired. Spread about ¼ *cup* of the strawberry glaze over bottom and sides of Baked Pastry Shell. Arrange *half* of the whole strawberries, stem end down, in pastry shell. Carefully spoon *half* of the remaining glaze over

*****See recipe, page 569**

berries, thoroughly covering each berry. Arrange remaining strawberries, stem end down, atop first layer; spoon on remaining glaze, covering each berry. Chill pie at least 3 to 4 hours. If desired, garnish with unsweetened whipped cream. Makes 8 servings.

## Rhubarb Pie

| | |
|---|---|
| 1¼ | **cups sugar** |
| ⅓ | **cup all-purpose flour** |
| 4 | **cups rhubarb cut into 1-inch pieces** |
| | **Pastry for Double-Crust Pie\*** |
| 2 | **tablespoons butter** |

Oven 375°

Stir together sugar, flour, and dash *salt*. Add sugar mixture to rhubarb pieces; toss to coat fruit. Let fruit mixture stand for 15 minutes. Fill a pastry-lined 9-inch pie plate with rhubarb mixture; dot with butter. Adjust top crust. Seal and flute edge. Cover edge of pie with foil. Bake in a 375° oven for 25 minutes. Remove foil and bake for 25 minutes more or till golden. Serve warm. Makes 8 servings.

**Strawberry-Rhubarb Pie:** Prepare Rhubarb Pie as above, *except* substitute 3 tablespoons quick-cooking *tapioca* for the flour and 3 cups *rhubarb* cut into ½-inch pieces plus 2 cups sliced fresh *strawberries* for the 4 cups rhubarb. Add ¼ teaspoon ground *nutmeg* to the tapioca mixture. Continue as directed.

## Fresh Pineapple Pie

| | |
|---|---|
| ¾ | **cup sugar** |
| 3 | **tablespoons quick-cooking tapioca** |
| 4 | **cups fresh pineapple cut into ¾-inch pieces** |
| 1 | **tablespoon lemon juice** |
| | **Pastry for Double-Crust Pie\*** |
| 1 | **tablespoon butter** |

Oven 375°

**\*See recipe, page 569**

Stir together sugar, tapioca, and dash *salt*. In a large bowl combine pineapple pieces and lemon juice. Add sugar mixture to pineapple; toss to coat fruit. Let stand 15 minutes. Fill a pastry-lined 9-inch pie plate with pineapple mixture; dot with butter. Adjust top crust. Seal and flute edge. Cover edge of pie with foil. Bake in a 375° oven for 20 minutes. Remove foil; bake for 25 to 30 minutes more or till crust is golden. Cool pie thoroughly on a wire rack before serving. Makes 8 servings.

---

## Fresh Pear Crumble Pie

    ½  cup sugar
    2  tablespoons all-purpose flour
    1  teaspoon finely shredded lemon peel
    5  cups sliced, peeled fresh pears (about
       2½ pounds)
    3  tablespoons lemon juice
       Pastry for Single-Crust Pie*
    ½  cup all-purpose flour
    ½  cup sugar
    ½  teaspoon ground ginger
    ½  teaspoon ground cinnamon
    ⅛  teaspoon ground mace
    ¼  cup butter                              Oven 375°

Combine ½ cup sugar, the 2 tablespoons flour, and the lemon peel. In a large bowl sprinkle pears with lemon juice. Add sugar mixture to pears; toss to coat fruit. Fill a pastry-lined 9-inch pie plate with pear mixture. In another bowl combine the ½ cup flour, ½ cup sugar, ginger, cinnamon, and mace. Cut in butter till mixture resembles coarse crumbs. Sprinkle crumb mixture over pear filling. Cover edge of pie with foil. Bake in a 375° oven for 25 minutes. Remove foil; bake for 25 to 30 minutes more or till pie is bubbly and crust is golden. Cool on a wire rack before serving. Serves 8.

**\*See recipe, page 569**

# Cream & Custard Pies

## Vanilla Cream Pie

    1    **cup sugar**
    ½    **cup all-purpose flour** *or* ¼ **cup cornstarch**
    ¼    **teaspoon salt**
    3    **cups milk**
    4    **eggs**
    3    **tablespoons butter** *or* **margarine**
    1½   **teaspoons vanilla**
    1    **9-inch Baked Pastry Shell***
         **Meringue for Pie****                    Oven 350°

For filling, in a medium saucepan combine sugar, flour or cornstarch, and salt; gradually stir in milk. Cook and stir over medium heat till thickened and bubbly. Reduce heat; cook and stir 2 minutes more. Remove from heat. Separate egg yolks from whites; set whites aside for meringue. Beat egg yolks slightly. Gradually stir *1 cup* of the hot mixture into yolks. Return egg mixture to saucepan; bring to a gentle boil. Cook and stir 2 minutes more. Remove from heat. Stir in butter or margarine and vanilla. Pour hot filling into Baked Pastry Shell. Spread meringue over hot filling; seal to edge. Bake in a 350° oven for 12 to 15 minutes or till golden. Cool. Cover; chill to store. Makes 8 servings.

   ***Coconut Cream Pie:*** Prepare Vanilla Cream Pie as above, *except* stir in 1 cup flaked *coconut* along with the vanilla. Sprinkle ⅓ cup flaked *coconut* over meringue and bake.

   ***Banana Cream Pie:*** Prepare Vanilla Cream Pie as above, *except* slice 3 *bananas* into bottom of Baked Pastry Shell. Pour hot filling over bananas. Continue as directed.

   ***Dark Chocolate Cream Pie:*** Prepare Vanilla Cream Pie as above, *except* increase sugar to 1¼ cups. Chop 3

**See recipe, page 569**
****See recipe, page 570**

squares (3 ounces) *unsweetened chocolate;* add to filling along with milk. Continue as directed.

**Light Chocolate Cream Pie:** Prepare Vanilla Cream Pie as above, *except* decrease sugar to ¾ cup. Chop 3 squares (3 ounces) *semisweet chocolate;* add to filling along with milk. Continue as directed.

---

## Tips for making cream pies

Cream pies must be thoroughly cool before serving, or the filling will be soft. After cooling to room temperature for 4 to 6 hours, cover and refrigerate.

To cover a meringue-topped cream pie, insert several toothpicks halfway into the surface of the meringue to hold wrap away from the pie. Loosely cover with clear plastic wrap and chill to store. (After the meringue is refrigerated, it will be somewhat rubbery.) Dip a knife in water before cutting the pie to prevent the meringue from sticking.

---

## Lemon Meringue Pie

| | |
|---|---|
| 1½ | **cups sugar** |
| 3 | **tablespoons cornstarch** |
| 3 | **tablespoons all-purpose flour** |
| 1½ | **cups water** |
| 3 | **eggs** |
| 2 | **tablespoons butter or margarine** |
| ½ | **teaspoon finely shredded lemon peel** |
| ⅓ | **cup lemon juice** |
| 1 | **9-inch Baked Pastry Shell\*** |
| | **Meringue for Pie\*\*** |

Oven 350°

**\*See recipe, page 569**
**\*\*See recipe, page 570**

In a medium saucepan combine sugar, cornstarch, flour, and dash *salt*. Gradually stir in water. Cook and stir over medium-high heat till thickened and bubbly. Reduce heat; cook and stir 2 minutes more. Remove from heat. Separate egg yolks from whites; set whites aside for meringue. Beat egg yolks slightly. Stir about *1 cup* of the hot mixture into the beaten yolks. Return mixture to saucepan; bring to a gentle boil. Cook and stir 2 minutes more. Remove from heat. Stir in butter or margarine and lemon peel. Gradually stir in lemon juice, mixing well. Pour hot filling into Baked Pastry Shell. Spread meringue over hot filling; seal to edge. Bake in a 350° oven for 12 to 15 minutes or till meringue is golden. Cool on a wire rack. Cover; chill to store. Makes 8 servings.

---

## Pumpkin Pie

        1    **16-ounce can pumpkin**
       ¾    **cup sugar**
        1    **teaspoon ground cinnamon**
       ½    **teaspoon ground ginger**
       ½    **teaspoon ground nutmeg**
        3    **eggs**
        1    **5⅓-ounce can (⅔ cup) evaporated milk**
       ½    **cup milk**
             **Pastry for Single-Crust Pie***          Oven 375°

In a large mixing bowl combine pumpkin, sugar, cinnamon, ginger, nutmeg, and ½ teaspoon *salt*. Add eggs; with a fork, lightly beat eggs into pumpkin mixture. Add the evaporated milk and milk; mix well. Place a pastry-lined 9-inch pie plate on oven rack; pour in pumpkin mixture. Cover edge of pie with foil. Bake in a 375° oven for 25 minutes. Remove foil; bake for 25 to 30 minutes more or till a knife inserted off-center comes out clean. Cool. Cover and chill to store. Serves 8.

***See recipe, page 569**

## Lemon-Chess Pie

|       | **Pastry for Single-Crust Pie\*** |           |
| ----- | ------------------------------------------ | --------- |
| 5     | **eggs**                                   |           |
| 1½    | **cups sugar**                             |           |
| 1     | **cup light cream or milk**                |           |
| ¼     | **cup butter or margarine, melted**        |           |
| 1     | **teaspoon finely shredded lemon peel**    |           |
| 2     | **tablespoons lemon juice**                |           |
| 1     | **tablespoon all-purpose flour**           |           |
| 1     | **tablespoon yellow cornmeal**             |           |
| 1½    | **teaspoons vanilla**                      | Oven 450° |

Bake pastry in a 450° oven for 5 minutes. Cool on a wire rack. For filling, in a mixing bowl beat eggs till well combined. Stir in sugar, light cream or milk, butter or margarine, lemon peel and juice, flour cornmeal, and vanilla. Mix well. Reduce oven temperature to 350°. Place pastry shell on oven rack. Pour filling into the partially baked pastry shell. Cover edge of pie with foil. Bake at 350° oven for 20 minutes. Remove foil from edge; bake for 20 to 25 minutes more or till a knife inserted off-center comes out clean. Cool pie on a wire rack. Cover and chill to store. Makes 8 servings.

## Pecan Pie

|       |                                       |           |
| ----- | ------------------------------------- | --------- |
| 3     | **eggs**                              |           |
| ⅔     | **cup sugar**                         |           |
|       | **Dash salt**                         |           |
| 1     | **cup dark corn syrup**               |           |
| ⅓     | **cup butter or margarine, melted**   |           |
| 1     | **cup pecan halves**                  |           |
|       | **Pastry for Single-Crust Pie\***     | Oven 350° |

In a mixing bowl beat eggs slightly with a rotary beater or fork. Add sugar and salt; stir till dissolved. Stir in dark corn syrup and melted butter or margarine; mix well. Stir in the pecan halves. Place a pastry-lined 9-inch pie plate on oven rack;

**\*See recipe, page 569**

pour in pecan mixture. Cover edge of pie with foil. Bake in a 350° oven for 25 minutes. Remove foil; bake about 25 minutes more or till a knife inserted off-center comes out clean. Cool on a wire rack. Cover; chill to store. Makes 10 servings.

## Sour Cream-Raisin Pie

| | |
|---|---|
| **1** | **cup raisins** |
| **3** | **eggs** |
| **1** | **cup sugar** |
| **6** | **tablespoons all-purpose flour** |
| **2¼** | **cups milk** |
| **½** | **cup dairy sour cream** |
| **¼** | **cup butter, cut into small pieces** |
| **1** | **9-inch Baked Pastry Shell\*** |
| | **Meringue for Pie\*\*** Oven 350° |

Cover raisins with 1 cup *boiling water;* let stand 5 minutes. Drain. Separate egg yolks from whites; set whites aside for meringue. For filling, in a saucepan combine sugar, flour, and ⅛ teaspoon *salt.* Gradually stir in milk. Cook and stir till thickened and bubbly. Reduce heat; cook and stir 2 minutes more. Remove from heat. Beat egg yolks slightly. Gradually stir about *1 cup* of the hot mixture into yolks. Return mixture to saucepan. Return to a gentle boil; cook and stir 2 minutes more. Remove from heat; add sour cream, butter, and drained raisins. Stir just till mixed; *do not over-mix.* Pour hot filling into Baked Pastry Shell. Make Meringue for Pie using the 3 reserved egg whites. Spread meringue over hot filling; seal to edge. Bake in a 350° oven for 12 to 15 minutes or till meringue is golden. Cool. Cover; chill to store. Makes 10 servings.

**\*See recipe, page 569**
**\*\*See recipe, page 570**

## Custard Pie

|       | **Pastry for Single-Crust Pie*** |           |
|-------|----------------------------------|-----------|
| 4     | eggs                             |           |
| ½     | cup sugar                        |           |
| ½     | teaspoon vanilla                 |           |
| ¼     | teaspoon salt                    |           |
| 2½    | cups milk                        |           |
|       | Ground nutmeg                    | Oven 450° |

Bake pastry in a 450° oven for 5 minutes. Cool on a wire rack. For filling, in a mixing bowl beat eggs slightly with a rotary beater or fork. Stir in the sugar, vanilla, and salt. Gradually stir in milk; mix well. Place pie shell on oven rack; pour filling into partially baked pastry shell. Sprinkle with a little nutmeg. Cover edge of pie with foil. Reduce oven temperature to 350° and bake for 30 minutes. Remove foil; bake for 30 to 35 minutes more or till a knife inserted off-center comes out clean. Cool pie on a wire rack before serving. Cover; chill to store. Makes 8 servings.

## Brown-Sugar-Rhubarb Pie

|   | **Pastry for Single-Crust Pie*** |           |
|---|----------------------------------|-----------|
| 1 | to 1¼ cups packed brown sugar    |           |
| ¼ | cup all-purpose flour            |           |
| ¼ | teaspoon salt                    |           |
| 4 | cups diced rhubarb (1 pound)     |           |
| 3 | eggs                             |           |
| 1 | tablespoon lemon juice           |           |
|   | **Meringue for Pie****           | Oven 450° |

Bake pastry in a 450° oven for 5 minutes. Cool. To prepare filling, combine brown sugar, flour, and salt. Add brown sugar mixture to rhubarb; toss to coat fruit. Let stand 15 minutes. Separate egg yolks from whites; set whites aside for meringue. Beat yolks slightly with a fork. Stir yolks and lemon juice into rhubarb mixture. Turn rhubarb filling into partially baked pastry

*See recipe, page 569
**See recipe, page 570

shell. Cover edge of pie with foil. Reduce oven temperature to 375° and bake for 25 minutes. Remove foil; bake for 20 to 25 minutes more or till nearly set. (*Pie appears soft in center but becomes firm after cooling.*) Spread meringue over hot filling; seal to edge. Reduce oven temperature to 350° and bake for 12 to 15 minutes. Cool. Cover; chill to store. Serves 8.

---

## Tips for making custard pies

Avoid messy spills by placing the pie shell on the oven rack before pouring in the pie filling.

To check for doneness after baking for the recommended time, insert a knife off-center; if it comes out clean with no custard filling clinging to it, the pie is done. Or, gently shake the pie. If the area that appears to be liquid is smaller than the size of a quarter, the pie is done. The filling will continue to set after it is removed from the oven.

After the pie cools, always cover and refrigerate it if it's to be held for any length of time before serving. Cover and chill to store after serving, as well.

---

## Rum Cream Pie

| 1   | 4-serving-size package *regular* vanilla pudding mix |
| 1¼ | cups milk |
| ¼  | cup light rum |
| 1   | teaspoon vanilla |
| ½  | cup finely chopped maraschino cherries |
| ½  | cup chopped Brazil nuts |
| 1   | cup whipping cream |
| 1   | 9-inch Baked Pastry Shell* |

*See recipe, page 569

In a saucepan cook pudding mix according to package directions, *except* use only the 1¼ cups milk. Remove from heat. Stir in rum and vanilla. Cover surface with clear plastic wrap; cool to room temperatrue without stirring. Drain chopped cherries thoroughly on paper toweling. Fold into pudding along with the nuts. Whip the cream till soft peaks form. Fold into pudding mixture. Turn into the Baked Pastry Shell. Cover and chill several hours. Garnish with additional unsweetened whipped cream, chocolate curls, and chopped nuts, if desired. Makes 8 servings.

# Refrigerated & Frozen Pies

## Strawberrry Chiffon Pie

| | |
|---|---|
| 2½ | cups fresh strawberries |
| ¼ | cup sugar |
| 1 | tablespoon lemon juice |
| ¼ | cup sugar |
| 1 | envelope unflavored gelatin |
| ¾ | cup water |
| 2 | egg whites |
| ¼ | cup sugar |
| ½ | cup whipping cream |
| 1 | 9-inch Baked Pastry Shell* |

Reserve a few strawberries for garnish; set aside. In a large mixing bowl crush enough of the remaining strawberries to measure 1¼ cups crushed berries. Stir in ¼ cup sugar and the lemon juice; let berry mixture stand 30 minutes.

Meanwhile, in a small saucepan stir together ¼ cup sugar and the gelatin. Stir in the water; heat and stir till sugar and gelatin dissolve. Cool. Stir the cooled gelatin mixture into the

*See recipe, page 569

strawberry mixture. Chill to the consistency of corn syrup, stirring occasionally. Remove from refrigerator (gelatin mixture will continue to set). Immediately begin beating the egg whites till soft peaks form. Gradually add ¼ cup sugar, beating till stiff peaks form. When gelatin is partially set (the consistency of unbeaten egg whites) fold in the stiff-beaten egg whites. Beat whipping cream till soft peaks form. Fold whipped cream into strawberry mixture. Chill till mixture mounds when spooned. Pile mixture into Baked Pastry Shell. Chill pie 8 hours or till firm. Garnish with reserved strawberries. Serve with additional whipped cream, if desired. Makes 8 servings.

**Raspberry Chiffon Pie:** Prepare Strawberry Chiffon Pie as above, *except* substitute 2½ cups fresh *raspberries* for the strawberries. Continue as directed.

---

## Chocolate Chiffon Pie

---

- **1 envelope unflavored gelatin**
- **3 egg yolks**
- **⅓ cup sugar**
- **1 teaspoon vanilla**
- **2 squares (2 ounces) unsweetened chocolate**
- **3 egg whites**
- **½ cup sugar**
- **1 9-inch Baked Pastry Shell***

Soften gelatin in ¼ cup cold *water*. Beat egg yolks on high speed of electric mixer about 5 minutes or till thick and lemon colored. Gradually beat in ⅓ cup sugar; stir in vanilla and ¼ teaspoon *salt*. In a saucepan combine chocolate and ½ cup *water*. Cook and stir over low heat till chocolate melts. Add to gelatin; stir to dissolve gelatin. Gradually beat gelatin mixture into egg yolk mixture. Chill to the consistency of corn syrup, stirring occasionally. Immediately beat egg whites till soft peaks form. Gradually add ½ cup sugar, beating till stiff peaks form. When gelatin is partially set (the consistency of unbeaten egg whites) fold in stiff-beaten egg whites. Chill till mixture mounds

*See recipe, page 569

when spooned. Turn into Baked Pastry Shell. Chill till set. Cover and chill. Serves 8.

## Tips for making chiffon pies

For a smooth pie, the gelatin must be of the proper consistency. Chill the gelatin mixture to the consistency of corn syrup, stirring occasionally. Remove from the refrigerator (the mixture will continue to set). Beat the egg whites to stiff peaks. When the gelatin mixture is the consistency of unbeaten egg whites (slightly thicker than corn syrup, but pourable), fold it into the stiff-beaten egg whites. Finally, fold whipped cream into the mixture. For a fluffy filling, chill the mixture till it mounds when spooned before turning it into the pastry shell.

## Lime Parfait Pie

    1   3-ounce package lime-flavored gelatin
    ½   cup boiling water
    ¾   teaspoon finely shredded lime peel
    ¼   cup lime juice
    1   pint vanilla ice cream
    1   cup whipping cream
    1   9-inch Baked Pastry Shell*

In a large bowl dissolve gelatin in boiling water. Stir in lime peel and lime juice. Add ice cream by spoonfuls, stirring till melted. Chill till partially set (the consistency of unbeaten egg whites). Whip the 1 cup whipping cream; fold into lime mixture. Chill till mixture mounds when spooned. Turn into Baked Pastry Shell. Chill several hours or overnight till set. To serve, top with unsweetened whipped cream and maraschino cherries, if desired. Cover and chill to store. Makes 8 servings.

**\*See recipe, page 569**

## French Silk Pie

    1    cup sugar
    ¾    cup butter (*not* margarine)
    3    squares (3 ounces) unsweetened
             chocolate, melted and cooled
    1½   teaspoons vanilla
    3    eggs
    1    9-inch Baked Pastry Shell*
         Unsweetened whipped cream (optional)
         Chocolate curls (optional)

In a small mixer bowl cream sugar and butter about 4 minutes or till fluffy. Stir in cooled chocolate and vanilla. Add eggs, one at a time, beating on medium speed of electric mixer after each addition and scraping sides of bowl constantly. Turn into Baked Pastry Shell. Chill several hours or overnight till set. Garnish with whipped cream and chocolate curls, if desired. Cover and chill. Makes 10 servings.

**Note:** Some brands of margarine produce a nonfluffy, sticky filling when used in this recipe. The results were so unsatisfactory that we recommend using only butter.

## Fudge Ribbon Pie

    1    5⅓-ounce can (⅔ cup) evaporated milk
    2    squares (2ounces) unsweetened chocolate
    1    cup sugar
    2    tablespoons butter *or* margarine
    1    teaspoon vanilla
    1    quart peppermint ice cream
    1    9-inch Baked Pastry Shell*
    3    egg whites
    ½    teaspoon vanilla
    ¼    teaspoon cream of tartar
    ⅓    cup sugar
    ¼    cup crushed peppermint candy      Oven 475°

*See recipe page, 569

For chocolate sauce, combine evaporated milk and chocolate. Cook and stir over low heat till chocolate is melted. Stir in the 1 cup sugar and the butter or margarine. Cook over medium heat for 5 to 8 minutes more or till thickened, stirring occasionally. Stir in the 1 teaspoon vanilla. Cool thoroughly.

In a mixing bowl soften ice cream using a wooden spoon to stir and press against sides of bowl. Soften till just pliable. Spoon *half* of the ice cream into the Baked Pastry Shell. Return remaining ice cream to freezer. Cover with *half* of the cooled chocolate sauce; freeze. Let remaining chocolate sauce stand at room temperature. Repeat layers with remaining ice cream and sauce, softening ice cream to spread, if necessary. Cover; freeze till firm.

Prepare meringue by beating egg whites, ½ teaspoon vanilla, and cream of tartar till soft peaks form. Gradually add ⅓ cup sugar, beating to stiff peaks. Fold *3 tablespoons* of the crushed candy into meringue.

Remove pie from freezer. Spread meringue over chocolate layer, carefully sealing to edge of pastry. Swirl the meringue in a circular motion to make decorative peaks. Place pie on a baking sheet. Bake in a 475° oven for 3 to 5 minutes or till meringue is golden. Sprinkle with remaining 1 tablespoon crushed candy. Serve immediately. Makes 8 servings.

## Black Bottom Pie

- 1 **cup sugar**
- 1 **tablespoon cornstarch**
- 2 **cups milk**
- 4 **slightly beaten egg yolks**
- 1 **teaspoon vanilla**
- 1 **6-ounce package (1 cup) semisweet chocolate pieces**
- 1 **9-inch Baked Pastry Shell (see recipe, page 569)**
- 1 **envelope unflavored gelatin**
- ½ **teaspoon rum extract**
- 4 **egg whites**

Combine ½ *cup* of the sugar and the cornstarch. Stir in milk and egg yolks. Cook and stir over medium heat till mixture thickens and coats a metal spoon. Remove from heat; stir in the vanilla. Stir chocolate into 1¼ *cups* of the thickened mixture till melted; pour into Baked Pastry Shell. Chill.

Soften gelatin in ¼ cup cold *water*. Stir into remaining *hot* thickened mixture till gelatin dissolves. Stir in rum extract. Chill to the consistency of corn syrup, stirring occasionally. Immediately beat egg whites till soft peaks form. Gradually add remaining ½ cup sugar, beating till stiff peaks form. When gelatin is partially set (the consistency of unbeaten egg whites) fold in stiff-beaten egg whites. Chill till mixture mounds when spooned; spread over chocolate layer. Cover and chill several hours or till set. Serves 8.

---

## Tips for making frozen pies

Remove ice cream pies from the freezer and allow to soften for 10 to 15 minutes before serving.

Baked-Alaska-type pies should be served immediately after baking.

---

## Coffee Angel Pie

| | |
|---|---|
| 1 | **pint coffee ice cream** |
| 1 | **pint vanilla ice cream** |
| | **Meringue Crust (see recipe, page 569)** |
| ½ | **cup packed brown sugar** |
| 1 | **tablespoon cornstarch** |
| ⅓ | **cup light cream** |
| 2 | **tablespoon light corn syrup** |
| ¼ | **cup coarsely chopped pecans** |
| 1 | **tablespoon butter *or* margarine** |
| 1 | **tablespoon rum *or* brandy** |

Arrange scoops of coffee and vanilla ice cream in baked and cooled Meringue Crust. Freeze several hours or overnight till firm.

About 1 hour before serving, prepare caramel sauce. In a heavy saucepan combine brown sugar, cornstarch, and ¼ teaspoon *salt*. Stir in ¼ cup *water*. Stir in light cream and corn syrup. Cook, stirring constantly, till thickened and bubbly (mixture may appear curdled during cooking). Stir in pecans, butter, and rum. Cover; cool to room temperature.

Let pie stand 10 minutes at room temperature before serving. Drizzle some of the caramel sauce over the ice cream. Slice pie and serve immediately with remaining sauce. Serves 8.

---

## Grasshopper Pie

    6½   cups tiny marshmallows
     ¼   cup milk
     ¼   cup crème de menthe liqueur
     2   tablespoons crème de cacao liqueur
     2   cups whipping cream
         Chocolate Wafer Crust (see recipe,
            page 574)

In a large saucepan combine marshmallows and milk. Cook over low heat, stirring constantly, till marshmallows are melted. Cool mixture, stirring every 5 minutes. Combine crème de menthe and crème de cacao; stir into marshmallow mixture. Whip 2 cups whipping cream till soft peaks form. Fold marshmallow mixture into whipped cream; turn into chilled Chocolate Wafer Crust. Freeze several hours or overnight till firm. If desired, garnish pie with additional unsweetened whipped cream and chocolate curls. Makes 8 servings.

# Piecrusts

## Pastry for Single-Crust Pie

  1¼   **cups all-purpose flour**
  ½   **teaspoon salt**
  ⅓   **cup shortening *or* lard**
  3   **to 4 tablespoons cold water**

In a mixing bowl stir together flour and salt. Cut in shortening or lard till pieces are the size of small peas. Sprinkle *1 table-spoon* of the water over part of the mixture; gently toss with a fork. Push to side of bowl. Repeat till all is moistened. Form dough into a ball. On a lightly floured surface flatten dough with hands. Roll dough from center to edge, forming a circle about 12 inches in diameter. Wrap pastry around rolling pin. Unroll onto a 9-inch pie plate. Ease pastry into pie plate, being careful not to stretch pastry. Trim to ½ inch beyond edge of pie plate; fold under extra pastry. Make a fluted, rope-shaped, or scalloped edge. Do not prick pastry. Bake as directed in individual recipe.

    ***Baked Pastry Shell:*** Prepare Pastry for Single-Crust Pie as above, *except* prick bottom and sides with the tines of a fork. Bake in a 450° oven for 10 to 12 minutes or till golden. Cool on a wire rack.

    ***Pastry for Double-Crust Pie:*** Prepare pastry for Single-Crust Pie as above, *except* use 2 cups *all-purpose flour,* 1 teaspoon *salt,* ⅔ cup *shortening or lard,* and 6 to 7 tablespoons *cold water.* Divide dough in half. Roll out half of dough as above. Fit into pie plate. Trim pastry even with rim. For top crust, roll out remaining dough. Cut slits for escape of steam. Place *desired pie filling* in pie shell. Top with pastry for top crust. Trim top crust ½ inch beyond edge of pie plate. Fold extra pastry under bottom crust; flute edge. Bake as directed in individual recipe.

    ***Pastry for Lattice-Top Pie:*** Prepare Pastry for Double-Crust Pie as above, *except* line a 9-inch pie plate with *half* of the pastry. Trim pastry to ½ inch beyond edge of pie plate. Turn filling into pastry-lined pie plate. Cut remaining pastry into ½-inch-wide strips. Weave strips atop filling to make a lattice crust. Press ends of strips into rim of crust. Fold bottom pastry over the lattice strips; seal and flute. Bake as directed in individual recipe.

## Meringue for Pie

**3** egg whites*
**½** teaspoon vanilla
**¼** teaspoon cream of tartar
**6** tablespoons sugar

In a small mixer bowl beat the egg whites, vanilla, and cream of tartar at medium speed of an electric mixer about 1 minute or till soft peaks form.

Gradually add the sugar, about 1 tablespoon at a time, beating at high speed of electric mixer about 4 minutes more or till mixture forms stiff, glossy peaks and sugar is dissolved. Immediately spread meringue over pie, carefully sealing to edge of pastry to prevent shrinkage. Bake as directed in individual pie recipe.

**\*Note:** While the 3-egg-white recipe makes an adequate amount of meringue, you can use the extra egg white from a 4-egg-yolk pie for a more generous meringue. Follow the directions above, *except* use 4 egg whites, *1 teaspoon* vanilla, *½ teaspoon* cream of tartar, and *½ cup* sugar. It may be necessary to beat the mixture slightly longer to achieve the proper consistency.

## Meringue Crust

**2** egg whites
**½** teaspoon vanilla
**¼** teaspoon salt
**¼** teaspoon cream of tartar
**½** cup sugar
**½** cup finely chopped pecans                    Oven 275°

In a mixer bowl beat together egg whites, vanilla, salt, and cream of tartar till soft peaks form. Gradually add sugar and beat to stiff peaks and till sugar is dissolved. Fold in chopped pecans. Spread mixture onto bottom and sides of a well-buttered 9-inch pie plate, building up the sides with a spoon to form a shell. Bake in a 275° oven for 1 hour. Turn off heat and let dry in oven with door closed for 1 hour more. Cool thoroughly on a wire rack.

## Oil Pastry

> 2¼ **cups all-purpose flour**
> 1 **teaspoon salt**
> ½ **cup cooking oil**
> 6 **tablespoons cold milk**

In a mixing bowl stir together flour and salt. Pour cooking oil and cold milk into a measuring cup (do not stir); add all at once to flour mixture. Stir lightly with a fork. Form into 2 balls; flatten slightly with hands.

Cut waxed paper into four 12-inch squares. Place each ball of dough between 2 squares of paper. Roll each ball of dough into a circle to edges of paper. (Dampen work surface with a little water to prevent paper from slipping.) Peel off top paper and fit dough, paper side up, into pie plate. Remove paper. Finish as for Pastry for Single- or Double-Crust Pie. Makes two 9-inch single-crust pastries or one 9-inch double-crust pastry.

## Electric Mixer Pastry

> 1¾ **cups all-purpose flour**
> ¾ **cup shortening**
> ⅓ **cup cold water**

Combine flour and ¾ teaspoon *salt;* add shortening. Beat at low speed of electric mixer till pieces are the size of small peas. Add water; beat at low speed just till a dough forms (15 to 20 seconds). Form dough into a ball with hands. Divide into 2 balls. Roll out and finish as for Pastry for Single- or Double-

Crust Pie. Makes two 9-inch single-crust pastries or one 9-inch double-crust pastry.

---

## Pecan Pastry

---

**Pastry for Single-Crust Pie**
**3** **tablespoons finely chopped pecans**

Prepare Pastry for Single-Crust Pie, *except* add the chopped pecans before adding the water. Bake as directed in individual recipe.

If individual recipe calls for a double-crust pecan pastry, prepare Pastry for Double-Crust Pie, *except* add ⅓ cup finely chopped pecans before adding water. Bake pastry as directed in individual recipe.

---

## Coconut Crust

---

**2** **cups flaked coconut**
**3** **tablespoons butter *or* margarine,**
**melted** Oven 325°

In a mixing bowl combine coconut and the melted butter or margarine. Turn the coconut mixture into a 9-inch pie plate. Spread the mixture evenly in the pie plate. Press onto bottom and sides to form a firm, even crust. Bake in a 325° oven about 20 minutes or till edge is golden. Cool piecrust thoroughly on a wire rack before filling.

---

## Lemon Pastry

---

**Pastry for Single-Crust Pie**
**1** **tablespoon sugar**
**½** **teaspoon finely shredded lemon peel**
**1** **tablespoon lemon juice**

Prepare Pastry for Single-Crust Pie, *except* add sugar and lemon peel to dry ingredients. Substitute lemon juice for *1 tablespoon* of the cold water. Bake as directed in individual recipe.

---

## Tips for making tart shells

Making tart shells is as easy as making piecrust. To make 10 baked tart shells, prepare Pastry for Double-Crust Pie. Roll *half* of the pastry at a time to ⅛-inch thickness. Cut each half into five 4½-inch circles. Fit over inverted muffin cups, pinching pleats at intervals to fit around the cups. Prick pastry with a fork. Bake in a 450° oven for 7 to 10 minutes or till golden. Cool.

Or, cut dough into 5-inch circles and fit into fluted tart pans. Prick pastry with a fork. Bake in a 450° oven for 10 to 12 minutes or till golden.

---

## Graham Cracker Crust

**18   graham cracker squares**
**¼   cup sugar**
**6   tablespoons butter *or* margarine, melted**

Place graham crackers in a plastic bag or between 2 sheets of plastic wrap or waxed paper. Crush into fine crumbs; measure 1¼ cups crumbs. (*Or*, crush crackers into fine crumbs in a blender.) In a mixing bowl combine crumbs and sugar. Stir in melted butter or margarine; toss to thoroughly combine. Turn the crumb mixture into a 9-inch pie plate. Spread the crumb mixture evenly into the pie plate. Press onto the bottom and sides to form a firm, even crust. Chill about 1 hour or till firm. (*Or*, bake in a 375° oven for 6 to 9 minutes or till edges are brown. Cool on a wire rack.)

## Vanilla Wafer Crust

  1½   **cups finely crushed vanilla wafers (36 wafers)**
   6   **tablespoons butter or margarine, melted**

In a mixing bowl combine crushed wafers and the melted butter or margarine; toss to thoroughly combine. Turn crumb mixture into a 9-inch pie plate. Spread the crumb mixture evenly in the pie plate. Press onto bottom and sides to form a firm, even crust. Chill about 1 hour or till firm.

## Chocolate Wafer Crust

  1½   **cups finely crushed chocolate wafers (25 wafers)**
   6   **tablespoons butter or margarine, melted**

In a mixing bowl combine crushed wafers and the melted butter or margarine; toss to thoroughly combine. Turn the chocolate crumb mixture into a 9-inch pie plate. Spread the crumb mixture evenly into the pie plate. Press onto bottom and sides to form a firm, even crust. Chill about 1 hour or till firm.

## Gingersnap-Graham Crust

  ¾   **cup finely crushed gingersnaps (12 cookies)**
  ½   **cup finely crushed graham crackers (7 crackers)**
  ¼   **cup butter or margarine, melted**
   2   **tablespoons sugar**          Oven 375°

In a mixing bowl combine crushed gingersnaps, crushed graham crackers, and sugar. Stir in melted butter; toss to thoroughly combine. Turn crumb mixture into a 9-inch pie plate. Spread the crumb mixture evenly in the pie plate. Press onto

bottom and sides to form a firm, even crust. Bake in a 375°
oven for 4 to 5 minutes. Cool on a wire rack before filling.

## Cornflake Piecrust

> **1** **cup crushed cornflakes *or* crisp rice cereal**
> ***or* cornflake crumbs**
> **¼ cup sugar**
> **6 tablespoons butter *or* margarine, melted**

Combine crushed cornflakes or crisp rice cereal or cornflake
crumbs with sugar and melted butter or margarine; toss to
thoroughly combine. Press mixture firmly into a 9-inch pie
plate. Chill 1 hour or till firm.

---

### Removing a piece of crumb-crust pie

Just before serving, rub
the outside of the filled
pie plate with a warm,
damp towel. This softens
the butter in the crust,
making it less likely to
stick to the pie plate.

To prepare the towel,
rinse it in very hot water,
then wring it well.

This procedure is not
necessary for crumb crusts
that have been baked,
since they slide out easily.

# Poultry

# Poultry

# Poultry

# Poultry

# Poultry

# Poultry

# Poultry

# Poultry

# Poultry

| Recipes | Servings (fraction of recipe) | Calories | Protein (grams) | Carbohydrate (grams) | Fat (grams) | Sodium (milligrams) | Potassium (milligrams) | Percent of U.S. RDA Per Serving — Protein | Vitamin A | Vitamin C | Thiamine | Riboflavin | Niacin | Calcium | Iron |
|---|---|---|---|---|---|---|---|---|---|---|---|---|---|---|---|
| Apricot Chicken | 1/6 | 403 | 31 | 47 | 10 | 562 | 309 | 48 | 35 | 9 | 19 | 15 | 61 | 4 | 17 |
| Arroz con Pollo | 1/6 | 408 | 29 | 45 | 11 | 683 | 233 | 45 | 34 | 38 | 26 | 33 | 48 | 4 | 27 |
| Barbecue-Style Broiled Chicken | 1/12 | 187 | 24 | 2 | 8 | 119 | 36 | 37 | 24 | 2 | 6 | 29 | 36 | 2 | 14 |
| Basic Broiled Chicken | 1/6 | 176 | 24 | 0 | 8 | 23 | 1 | 37 | 20 | 0 | 6 | 29 | 36 | 2 | 14 |
| Cassoulet | 1/8 | 424 | 31 | 31 | 20 | 750 | 770 | 47 | 64 | 23 | 26 | 31 | 37 | 9 | 34 |
| Cheesy Chicken a la King | 1/4 | 545 | 33 | 34 | 30 | 1149 | 525 | 51 | 29 | 25 | 18 | 34 | 42 | 29 | 15 |
| Chestnut Stuffing | 1/8 | 310 | 5 | 42 | 5 | 348 | 375 | 8 | 10 | 4 | 17 | 13 | 9 | 11 | 11 |
| Chicken a la King | 1/4 | 492 | 30 | 34 | 26 | 989 | 514 | 46 | 26 | 25 | 13 | 30 | 42 | 19 | 14 |
| Chicken and Dumplings | 1/12 | 255 | 27 | 14 | 9 | 439 | 110 | 41 | 35 | 6 | 13 | 18 | 40 | 5 | 18 |
| Chicken and Noodles | 1/12 | 283 | 28 | 23 | 8 | 363 | 228 | 44 | 88 | 9 | 18 | 38 | 43 | 5 | 20 |
| Chicken-Asparagus Stacks | 1/4 | 373 | 29 | 23 | 18 | 762 | 575 | 44 | 24 | 31 | 21 | 12 | 37 | 10 | 13 |
| Chicken Cacciatore | 1/6 | 327 | 27 | 27 | 11 | 1034 | 301 | 42 | 40 | 57 | 16 | 35 | 46 | 4 | 22 |
| Chicken-Cheese Crepes | 1/6 | 506 | 36 | 36 | 26 | 567 | 336 | 45 | 31 | 28 | 36 | 16 | 35 | 29 | 18 |
| Chicken Country Captain | 1/12 | 320 | 27 | 28 | 11 | 812 | 226 | 41 | 35 | 37 | 16 | 32 | 43 | 4 | 21 |
| Chicken Dijon | 1/4 | 415 | 33 | 13 | 33 | 674 | 82 | 50 | 12 | 1 | 1 | 17 | 62 | 6 | 16 |
| Chicken Divan | 1/6 | 337 | 24 | 13 | 21 | 537 | 506 | 37 | 52 | 124 | 10 | 19 | 35 | 20 | 9 |
| Chicken Enchilada Casserole | 1/6 | 535 | 29 | 35 | 31 | 1156 | 384 | 45 | 24 | 53 | 13 | 25 | 44 | 32 | 14 |
| Chicken Fricassee | 1/6 | 376 | 28 | 31 | 15 | 1021 | 140 | 43 | 22 | 13 | 13 | 16 | 44 | 5 | 21 |
| Chicken Italiano | 1/6 | 245 | 25 | 5 | 14 | 128 | 25 | 31 | 31 | 3 | 3 | 10 | 39 | 2 | 25 |
| Chicken Kiev | 1/8 | 334 | 30 | 9 | 25 | 194 | 14 | 46 | 15 | 3 | 3 | 9 | 56 | 3 | 12 |

# Nutrition Analysis Chart

| | | | | | | | | | | | | | | |
|---|---|---|---|---|---|---|---|---|---|---|---|---|---|---|
| Chicken Livers in Tomato Sauce | 1/5 | 351 | 30 | 30 | 12 | 999 | 623 | 46 | 261 | 57 | 43 | 153 | 83 | 8 | 51 |
| Chicken Livers Stroganoff | 1/5 | 457 | 30 | 24 | 24 | 228 | 386 | 47 | 231 | 29 | 23 | 158 | 63 | 8 | 49 |
| Chicken Paprikash | 1/6 | 329 | 28 | 16 | 16 | 81 | 104 | 42 | 23 | 5 | 12 | 34 | 40 | 5 | 17 |
| Chicken Pot Pies | 1/6 | 619 | 28 | 46 | 35 | 984 | 516 | 45 | 105 | 33 | 31 | 26 | 48 | 8 | 19 |
| Chicken Saltimbocca | 1/6 | 350 | 37 | 5 | 19 | 506 | 133 | 58 | 18 | 11 | 13 | 20 | 58 | 18 | 15 |
| Chicken Teriyaki Kebabs | 1/4 | 194 | 29 | 7 | 4 | 1329 | 136 | 45 | 4 | 19 | 6 | 16 | 54 | 4 | 15 |
| Chicken with Currant Glaze | 1/6 | 278 | 29 | 13 | 12 | 115 | 20 | 44 | 24 | 5 | 7 | 35 | 43 | 2 | 18 |
| Chicken with Walnuts | 1/4 | 502 | 32 | 35 | 26 | 1645 | 305 | 49 | 10 | 86 | 20 | 18 | 55 | 7 | 23 |
| Coq Au Vin | 3/12 | 271 | 9 | 9 | 11 | 204 | 180 | 40 | 36 | 10 | 10 | 35 | 40 | 4 | 17 |
| Corn Bread and Bacon Stuffing | 1/6 | 585 | 15 | 59 | 32 | 1078 | 359 | 24 | 14 | 12 | 30 | 23 | 17 | 16 | 17 |
| Cornmeal Batter Fried Chicken | 1/6 | 373 | 22 | 22 | 18 | 414 | 113 | 45 | 23 | 1 | 16 | 39 | 41 | 8 | 19 |
| Crab-Stuffed Chicken Breasts | 1/8 | 449 | 40 | 34 | 15 | 1046 | 136 | 62 | 17 | 4 | 17 | 24 | 85 | 20 | 19 |
| Cream Gravy for Fried Poultry | 1/6 | 114 | 3 | 6 | 9 | 386 | 92 | 4 | 2 | 1 | 7 | 7 | 1 | 8 | 1 |
| Crisp Fried Chicken | 1/6 | 218 | 4 | 4 | 11 | 533 | 5 | 38 | 19 | 0 | 8 | 30 | 37 | 8 | 14 |
| Crispy Baked Barbecued Chicken | 1/6 | 263 | 25 | 7 | 14 | 160 | 21 | 39 | 29 | 0 | 8 | 31 | 38 | 3 | 16 |
| Crowd-Size Chicken Bake | 7/24 | 298 | 21 | 25 | 12 | 479 | 118 | 32 | 10 | 5 | 18 | 19 | 31 | 10 | 9 |
| Cumberland-Style Broiled Chicken | 1/12 | 227 | 24 | 13 | 8 | 26 | 74 | 37 | 22 | 27 | 8 | 29 | 36 | 2 | 15 |
| Curried Chicken and Vegetables | 1/6 | 462 | 27 | 48 | 19 | 617 | 563 | 41 | 135 | 33 | 13 | 33 | 43 | 7 | 21 |
| Curry and Parsley Chicken | 1/6 | 263 | 25 | 6 | 15 | 450 | 30 | 38 | 29 | 7 | 13 | 31 | 37 | 2 | 17 |
| Dilled Chicken-Noodle Bake | 1/4 | 568 | 36 | 36 | 30 | 1228 | 70 | 48 | 30 | 36 | 24 | 32 | 41 | 25 | 13 |
| Fried Chicken with Crab Sauce | 1/6 | 222 | 25 | 7 | 10 | 877 | 72 | 39 | 15 | 9 | 5 | 13 | 42 | 4 | 9 |
| Giblet Gravy | 1/4 | 47 | 5 | 4 | 1 | 58 | 55 | 7 | 2 | 0 | 3 | 4 | 5 | 1 | 4 |
| Giblet Stuffing | 1/8 | 226 | 9 | 17 | 14 | 563 | 171 | 14 | 10 | 4 | 9 | 8 | 13 | 4 | 10 |
| Glazed Chicken and Rice | 1/6 | 340 | 27 | 22 | 15 | 934 | 120 | 41 | 24 | 8 | 14 | 32 | 41 | 4 | 22 |
| Golden Stuffed Cornish Hens | 1/8 | 385 | 24 | 14 | 24 | 374 | 133 | 37 | 53 | 12 | 13 | 29 | 36 | 4 | 17 |
| Harvest Stuffing | 1/10 | 260 | 18 | 22 | 18 | 430 | 244 | 8 | 33 | 7 | 7 | 4 | 6 | 5 | 9 |
| Hawaiian Broiled Chicken | 1/12 | 218 | 24 | 6 | 10 | 267 | 32 | 37 | 22 | 2 | 2 | 29 | 36 | 2 | 15 |
| Homemade Five-Spice Powder | 0 | 0 | 0 | 0 | 0 | 0 | 0 | 0 | 0 | 0 | 0 | 0 | 0 | 0 | 0 |
| Honey and Spice Duckling | 1/2 | 298 | 24 | 24 | 8 | 2302 | 38 | 48 | 24 | 0 | 7 | 39 | 46 | 4 | 22 |

# Nutrition Analysis Chart

The last eight columns show **Percent of U.S. RDA Per Serving**.

| Recipes | Servings (fraction of recipe) | Calories | Protein (grams) | Carbohydrate (grams) | Fat (grams) | Sodium (milligrams) | Potassium (milligrams) | Protein | Vitamin A | Vitamin C | Thiamine | Riboflavin | Niacin | Calcium | Iron |
|---|---|---|---|---|---|---|---|---|---|---|---|---|---|---|---|
| Mushroom Stuffing | 1/8 | 198 | 4 | 18 | 13 | 544 | 103 | 6 | 10 | 4 | 9 | 9 | 8 | 9 | 6 |
| Old-Fashioned Bread Stuffing | 1/8 | 194 | 4 | 17 | 13 | 544 | 103 | 6 | 10 | 4 | 8 | 8 | 5 | 7 | 5 |
| Oven Chicken Kiev | 1/8 | 354 | 30 | 9 | 22 | 264 | 35 | 47 | 19 | 3 | 3 | 9 | 16 | 56 | 12 |
| Oven-Crisped Orange Chicken | 1/6 | 291 | 27 | 14 | 13 | 670 | 172 | 41 | 28 | 50 | 12 | 12 | 33 | 39 | 19 |
| Oven-Fried Chicken | 1/6 | 275 | 25 | 11 | 14 | 219 | 17 | 38 | 37 | 7 | 15 | 15 | 39 | 43 | 15 |
| Oven-Fried Chicken Monterey | 1/8 | 343 | 24 | 19 | 24 | 694 | 330 | 30 | 38 | 4 | 8 | 14 | 11 | 13 | 10 |
| Oyster Stuffing | 1/8 | 232 | 6 | 19 | 19 | 661 | 222 | 10 | 14 | 32 | 14 | 8 | 12 | 5 | 23 |
| Pan- and Oven-Fried Chicken | 1/6 | 218 | 24 | 4 | 11 | 533 | 5 | 38 | 19 | 0 | 0 | 8 | 30 | 37 | 14 |
| Pan Gravy for Roast Poultry | 1/8 | 74 | 0 | 3 | 7 | 0 | 4 | 1 | 0 | 0 | 0 | 2 | 1 | 1 | 1 |
| Parmesan Chicken | 1/6 | 290 | 28 | 6 | 16 | 259 | 41 | 43 | 30 | 5 | 5 | 7 | 34 | 37 | 16 |
| Pheasant with Apples | 1/4 | 536 | 48 | 21 | 35 | 809 | 200 | 40 | 48 | 5 | 5 | 13 | 36 | 35 | 19 |
| Popover Chicken Tarragon | 1/6 | 414 | 33 | 27 | 18 | 328 | 150 | 50 | 27 | 27 | 22 | 22 | 46 | 44 | 11 |
| Potato-Chip Chicken | 1/6 | 341 | 25 | 10 | 22 | 161 | 228 | 39 | 25 | 25 | 5 | 8 | 30 | 40 | 16 |
| Raisin Stuffing | 1/8 | 233 | 4 | 27 | 13 | 548 | 206 | 6 | 10 | 4 | 4 | 7 | 6 | 7 | 8 |
| Roast Tarragon Chicken | 1/6 | 226 | 29 | 1 | 11 | 224 | 8 | 44 | 26 | 0 | 0 | 7 | 34 | 43 | 16 |
| Skillet-Fried Chicken | 1/6 | 218 | 24 | 2 | 4 | 533 | 5 | 38 | 38 | 0 | 0 | 8 | 30 | 37 | 14 |
| Stewed Chicken | 1/12 | 167 | 24 | 2 | 6 | 198 | 37 | 37 | 33 | 4 | 4 | 6 | 29 | 47 | 14 |
| Super Chicken Subs | 1/4 | 636 | 32 | 82 | 20 | 1503 | 601 | 49 | 25 | 68 | 68 | 42 | 33 | 47 | 28 |
| Turkey-Yam Kebabs | 1/4 | 682 | 26 | 82 | 29 | 95 | 824 | 40 | 294 | 25 | 68 | 19 | 18 | 28 | 18 |
| Wild-Rice-Chicken Casserole | 1/4 | 467 | 26 | 39 | 21 | 754 | 493 | 40 | 13 | 13 | 6 | 15 | 15 | 39 | 4 |

# Poultry

Include poultry in your meals often to help stretch your food budget. Poultry is high in protein and other nutrients, but low in calories and fat. Choose a large chicken or turkey for a greater proportion of meat to bone, and more value for the money. You can use the leftovers in soups, salads, sandwiches, and casseroles.

**Buying chicken for cooked meat in recipes:** Here are some handy rules of thumb to determine how much raw chicken to buy for a given amount of cooked chicken. Two whole chicken breasts (10 ounces each) yield about 2 cups of cubed or chopped cooked chicken. A 2½- to 3-pound broiler-fryer chicken yields about 2½ cups chopped cooked meat, and a 3½-pound roasting chicken provides about 3 cups cooked meat.

**Freezing chicken for longer storage:** For best results, rinse the chicken pieces and pat dry. Tightly wrap the pieces individually in plastic bags, then overwrap in moisture-vapor-proof material. Seal, label, and freeze the chicken for up to 6 months.

Save time and effort when cooking the frozen chicken—don't thaw it! When you're ready to cook, remove as many pieces from the freezer as you need. Place the packaged frozen chicken pieces under cold running water several minutes to loosen the plastic bag.

For skillet dishes, simply add 5 minutes to the browning time, then finish cooking. For oven dishes, bake the frozen chicken an extra 15 to 20 minutes.

## Cutting Up a Chicken

It may be more economical to buy a whole chicken and cut it up yourself. Here's how:

• Cut the skin between the body and thighs. Bend the legs until the bones break at the hip joints.

• Remove the leg and thigh pieces from the body by cutting

with a sharp knife between the hip joints as close to the backbone as possible.

• Separate the thighs and legs by first cutting through the skin at the knee joint. Break the joint, then cut the thigh and leg apart.

• To remove the wings from the body, cut through the skin on the inside of the wings at the joint. Break the joint, then cut the wings from the body.

• Divide the body. Cut along the breast end of the ribs to the neck to separate the breast and back sections. Bend the back piece in half to break it at the joint; cut through the broken joint. Cut off the tail, if desired.

• Divide the breast into 2 lengthwise pieces by cutting along the breastbone.

## Microwave-Thawed Poultry

Thaw poultry quickly using the *defrost setting* of your counter-top microwave oven. Leave the bird in the original plastic wrapping, but remove the metal clip. Place in a shallow non-metal baking dish.

**Chicken:** Broiler-fryer (2½- to 3-pound)—For *cut-up,* micro-thaw 18 to 20 minutes; separate after 12 minutes. For *whole,* micro-thaw, breast up, 10 minutes. Invert; micro-thaw 5 to 10 minutes. Let either stand 5 minutes.

Roasting chicken (4- to 5-pound)—Micro-thaw *whole* bird, breast up, 10 minutes; let stand 10 minutes. Micro-thaw, breast down, for 10 minutes; let stand 10 minutes. Micro-thaw, breast up, 5 to 10 minutes longer.

**Cornish Game Hens:** Micro-thaw one 1- to 1½-pound hen 12 to 15 minutes, 2 hens 16 to 20 minutes, or 4 hens 25 to 30 minutes. Micro-thaw, breast down, half the time. Invert; micro-thaw, breast up, remaining time. Let stand in cool water for 10 minutes.

**Turkey:** Micro-thaw one 7- to 8-pound *whole* turkey, breast up, 15 minutes; let stand 5 minutes. Give bird a quarter-turn. Repeat micro-thawing, standing, and turning for a total of 45 to 50 minutes. Let stand 30 minutes.

# Boning chicken breasts

Skin chicken breasts if directed in recipe. To skin, place chicken breast on a cutting board, skin side up. Pull the skin away from the meat; discard.

Using a large heavy knife or meat cleaver, split the chicken breast in half lengthwise. Hold a chicken breast half bone side down. Starting from the breastbone side of the breast, cut meat away from the bone using a thin sharp knife. Cut as close to the bone as possible.

Continue cutting, using a sawing motion. Press the flat side of the knife blade against the rib bones. As you cut, gently pull meat up and away from the bones, as shown above.

**Note:** To bone a whole chicken breast, skin if desired. Using a thin sharp knife, start cutting at the *outer* rib edge working toward the breastbone, back along the ribs. Proceed as above, gently pulling the meat away from the rib bones; discard the chicken bones.

# Range-Top & Oven

## Skillet-Fried Chicken

| | |
|---|---|
| 1 | 2½- to 3-pound broiler-fryer chicken, cut up |
| ¼ | cup all-purpose flour |
| 1½ | teaspoons salt |
| 1 | teaspoon paprika* |
| ¼ | teaspoon pepper |
| 2 | tablespoons cooking oil or shortening |

Rinse chicken pieces; pat dry with paper toweling. In a plastic or paper bag combine flour, salt, paprika, and pepper. Add a few chicken pieces at a time; shake to coat.

In a 12-inch skillet heat oil or shortening. Add chicken, with meaty pieces toward center of skillet. Cook, uncovered, over medium heat for 10 to 15 minutes, turning to brown evenly. Reduce heat; cover tightly. Cook 30 minutes. Uncover; cook 10 to 15 minutes more. Chicken is done when it is easily pierced with a fork. Drain chicken pieces on paper toweling. Makes 6 servings.

*Crisp Fried Chicken:* Prepare Skillet-Fried Chicken as above, *except* after the browning step, continue to cook chicken, uncovered, over medium-low heat for 45 minutes more or till chicken is tender. Turn occasionally. Drain on paper toweling before serving.

*Pan- and Oven-Fried Chicken:* Prepare Skillet-Fried Chicken as above, *except* brown chicken pieces in a 12-inch oven-going skillet. Transfer skillet to a 375° oven. (*Or,* remove chicken from skillet and place, skin side up, in an ungreased, large shallow baking pan.) Bake, uncovered, in a 375° oven for 35 to 45 minutes or till chicken is tender. Do not turn chicken pieces during baking time. Drain.

***Note:*** Add variety to the flavor of fried chicken by substituting other seasonings for the 1 teaspoon paprika in the seasoned flour mixture. Use either 1 teaspoon *curry powder;* 1 teaspoon *poultry seasoning;* 1 teaspoon *chili powder;* ½ teaspoon *garlic or onion powder;* 1 teaspoon dried *basil,* crushed; *or* 1 teaspoon dried *marjoram,* crushed.

# Cornmeal Batter Fried Chicken

|   |   |
|---|---|
| 1 | 2½- to 3-pound broiler-fryer chicken, cut up |
| ¾ | cup all-purpose flour |
| ½ | cup yellow cornmeal |
| 1 | teaspoon salt |
| ½ | teaspoon baking powder |
| ¼ | teaspoon poultry seasoning |
| ⅛ | teaspoon garlic powder |
|   | Dash cayenne |
| 1 | beaten egg |
| 1 | cup milk *or* 1¼ cups buttermilk |
| 2 | tablespoons cooking oil |
|   | Cooking oil for deep-fat frying |

In a large saucepan cover chicken with lightly salted water. Bring to boiling. Reduce heat. Cover and simmer for 20 minutes. Drain. Pat chicken dry with paper toweling.

In a mixing bowl combine flour, cornmeal, salt, baking powder, poultry seasoning, garlic powder, and cayenne. Stir together egg, milk, and 2 tablespoons oil. Combine with dry ingredients; beat till smooth. Dip chicken pieces, one at a time, into batter. Fry, a few at a time, in deep hot oil (365°) for 2 to 3 minutes or till golden. Drain well; keep warm while frying remaining chicken. Makes 6 servings.

# Chicken Paprikash

In a 12-inch skillet brown one 2½- to 3-pound *broiler-fryer chicken,* cut up, in 2 tablespoons hot *cooking oil* on all sides; season with salt and pepper. Remove browned chicken pieces from the skillet; set aside. Add 1 cup chopped *onion* to skillet; cook till tender but not brown. Stir in 1 tablespoon *paprika.* Return chicken to skillet, turning once to coat with paprika-onion mixture. Add ¼ cup *dry white wine* and ¼ cup *condensed chicken broth.* Bring to boiling. Reduce heat; cover and simmer 30 to 35 minutes or till chicken is tender. Remove chicken to a serving platter; keep warm. Boil skillet drippings about 2 minutes or till reduced to ½ cup liquid. Stir drippings into ½ cup *dairy sour cream;* return all to skillet. Heat through but *do not boil.* Pour sauce over chicken pieces. Serve over hot cooked *noodles.* Sprinkle with additional *paprika* and garnish with snipped *parsley,* if desired. Makes 6 servings.

## Chicken Dijon

> **2** **whole medium chicken breasts** **(1½ pounds)**
> **1** **teaspoon onion salt**
> **½** **teaspoon lemon pepper**
> **1** **6-ounce package regular long grain and** **wild rice mix** *or* **2 cups hot cooked rice**
> **3** **tablespoons butter** *or* **margarine** **Chicken broth**
> **½** **cup light cream**
> **2** **tablespoons all-purpose flour**
> **1** **tablespoon Dijon-style mustard** **Tomato wedges (optional)** **Parsley (optional)**

Skin, halve lengthwise, and bone chicken breasts (see tip, page 583). Sprinkle chicken with onion salt and lemon pepper. Prepare long grain and wild rice mix according to package directions.

Meanwhile, in a skillet over medium heat cook chicken in butter or margarine about 20 minutes or till tender. Remove to a platter; keep warm. Measure pan juices; add enough chicken broth to make 1 cup liquid. Return to skillet. Stir together light cream and flour; add to broth. Cook and stir till thickened and bubbly. Cook and stir 1 to 2 minutes more. Stir in Dijon-style mustard. Spoon some sauce over chicken; pass remainder. Garnish with tomato wedges and snipped parsley, if desired. Serve with hot cooked rice. Makes 4 servings.

**Microwave directions:** Skin, halve lengthwise, and bone chicken breasts (see tip, page 583). Prepare long grain and wild rice mix according to package directions. Meanwhile, in a 12x7½x2-inch baking dish, melt butter or margarine in a counter-top microwave oven on high power. Add chicken, turning to coat with the melted butter. Sprinkle with onion salt and lemon pepper. Micro-cook, covered, about 12 minutes or till tender, turning dish and rearranging chicken every 4 minutes. Remove chicken to a platter; keep warm. Measure pan juices; add enough chicken broth to make ¾ cup liquid. Return to dish. Stir together light cream and flour; add to broth. Micro-cook, uncovered, 1 minute; stir. Cook about 3 minutes more or till thickened and bubbly, stirring every 30 seconds. Stir in Dijon-style mustard. Serve as above.

---

## Chicken Kiev

*The classic version of Chicken Kiev is deep-fat fried, but you also can bake it in the oven—*

> **4  whole medium chicken breasts (3 pounds)**
> **2  tablespoons snipped parsley**
> **1  to 2 tablespoons chopped green onion**
> **1  ¼-pound stick of butter, chilled**
> **⅓  cup all-purpose flour**
> **1  beaten egg**
> **1  tablespoon water**
> **½  cup fine dry bread crumbs**
> **Cooking oil *or* shortening for deep-fat frying**

Skin, halve lengthwise, and bone chicken breasts (see tip, page 583). Place 1 piece of chicken between two pieces of clear plastic wrap. Working from center to edges, pound lightly with a meat mallet, forming a rectangle about ⅛ inch thick. Remove plastic wrap; sprinkle chicken with some parsley and onion. Season with salt and pepper. Repeat with remaining chicken.

Cut *chilled* butter into 8 sticks, each about 2 to 2½ inches long. Place 1 of the sticks on *each* chicken piece. Fold in sides; roll up jelly roll style, pressing all edges together gently with your fingers to seal.

Place flour in a shallow dish. In another shallow dish combine egg and water. Roll chicken in flour to coat, then dip in egg mixture. Coat with crumbs. Cover; chill at least 1 hour. Fry chicken rolls, a few at a time, in deep, hot oil (375°) for 5 minutes or till golden brown. Remove from hot oil with tongs or a slotted spoon; drain on paper toweling. Keep warm while frying remaining chicken rolls. Makes 8 servings.

**Oven Chicken Kiev:** Prepare Chicken Kiev as above, *except* omit deep-fat frying. Heat an additional ¼ cup *butter or margarine* in a large skillet. Fry chilled chicken rolls on all sides about 5 minutes or till brown. Transfer to a 12x7½x2-inch baking dish. Bake in a 400° oven for 15 to 18 minutes. Spoon pan drippings over individual servings.

## Fried Chicken with Crab Sauce

|  |  |
|--|--|
| 2 | **whole medium chicken breasts (1½ pounds)** |
| 1 | **tablespoon sugar** |
| 1 | **tablespoon cornstarch *or* all-purpose flour** |
| 1 | **teaspoon salt** |
| ¾ | **teaspoon Homemade Five-Spice Powder (see recipe, page 617)** |
| ⅛ | **teaspoon dry mustard** |
| 1 | **4-ounce can sliced mushrooms, drained** |
| 4 | **green onions, bias-sliced into 1½-inch lengths** |
| 1 | **teaspoon grated gingerroot** |
| 1 | **tablespoon cooking oil** |
| 1 | **cup chicken broth** |
| ¼ | **teaspoon salt** |
| ⅛ | **teaspoon pepper** |
| 1 | **7-ounce can crab meat, drained, flaked, and cartilage removed** |
| 1 | **tablespoon cold water** |
| 1 | **tablespoon cornstarch** |
|  | **Cooking oil for deep-fat frying** |
|  | **Green onion fans (optional)** |

Skin, halve lengthwise, and bone chicken breasts (see tip, page 583). Thoroughly rub the chicken breasts with a mixture of sugar, 1 tablespoon cornstarch or flour, the 1 teaspoon salt, Homemade Five-Spice Powder, and dry mustard. Cover chicken and let stand at room temperature for 30 to 40 minutes. Cut chicken into 1½-inch pieces.

Meanwhile, prepare the crab sauce. In a small saucepan cook mushrooms, sliced green onions, and gingerroot in the 1 tablespoon hot oil till onions are tender. Stir in chicken broth, the ¼ teaspoon salt, and pepper. Bring to boiling, stirring occasionally. Stir in crab meat. Slowly stir cold water into the 1 tablespoon cornstarch. Stir into crab mixture. Cook and stir till thickened and bubbly. Cook and stir 1 to 2 minutes more. Keep warm while frying chicken.

Fry chicken pieces, half at a time, in deep hot oil (365°) about 2 minutes or till golden brown. Using a slotted spoon or wire strainer, remove and drain on paper toweling.

To serve, arrange chicken pieces on a serving platter and pour the crab sauce over. Garnish with green onion fans, if desired. Serves 6.

## Oven-Fried Chicken Monterey

| | |
|---|---|
| ¼ | **cup all-purpose flour** |
| 1 | **1¼-ounce envelope taco seasoning mix** |
| 16 | **chicken thighs (4 pounds)** |
| ¼ | **cup butter *or* margarine** |
| 1 | **cup crushed tortilla chips** |
| 2 | **tablespoons finely chopped onion** |
| 1 | **tablespoon cooking oil** |
| 2 | **tablespoons all-purpose flour** |
| 1 | **13-ounce can evaporated milk** |
| ¼ | **teaspoon bottled hot pepper sauce** |
| 1 | **cup shredded Monterey Jack cheese (4 ounces)** |
| ¼ | **cup sliced pitted ripe olives** |
| 1 | **teaspoon lemon juice** |
| | **Lettuce** |

Oven 375°

Combine the ¼ cup flour and taco seasoning mix in a plastic bag. Add 2 or 3 chicken pieces at a time and shake to coat. Melt butter in a 15½x10½x2-inch baking pan. Place chicken in pan, turning once to butter surfaces. Roll *each* thigh in crushed chips and return to baking pan.

Bake in a 375° oven about 50 minutes or till tender. Meanwhile, for cheese sauce, cook onion in oil till tender but not brown. Stir in the 2 tablespoons flour and ¼ teaspoon *salt*. Add evaporated milk and pepper sauce all at once; cook and stir till thickened and bubbly. Cook and stir 1 to 2 minutes more. Add cheese, olives, and lemon juice, stirring just till cheese melts.

To serve, line a serving dish with leaf lettuce. Top with some shredded lettuce and chicken. Spoon some of the cheese sauce over chicken. Pass remaining sauce. Serves 8.

## Chicken with Walnuts

*Use a long-handled spoon or spatula to lift and turn the food with a folding motion. Be sure to maintain high heat so the food cooks quickly—*

| | |
|---|---|
| 1⅓ | **pounds whole chicken breasts** |
| 3 | **tablespoons soy sauce** |
| 2 | **teaspoons cornstarch** |
| 2 | **tablespoons dry sherry** |
| 1 | **teaspoon grated gingerroot** |
| 1 | **teaspoon sugar** |
| ½ | **teaspoon salt** |
| ½ | **teaspoon crushed red pepper** |
| 2 | **tablespoons cooking oil** |
| 2 | **medium green peppers, cut into ¾-inch pieces** |
| 4 | **green onions, bias-sliced into 1-inch lengths** |
| 1 | **cup walnut halves** |
| | **Fresh kumquats (optional)** |
| | **Hot cooked rice** |

Skin, halve lengthwise, and bone chicken breasts (see tip, page 583). Cut chicken into 1-inch pieces. Set aside.

In a small bowl stir soy sauce into cornstarch; stir in dry sherry, gingerroot, sugar, salt, and red pepper. Set aside. Preheat a wok or large skillet over high heat; add cooking oil. Stir-fry green peppers and green onions in hot oil for 2 minutes or till crisp-tender. Remove from wok or skillet. Add walnuts to wok or skillet; stir-fry 1 to 2 minutes or till just golden. Remove from wok or skillet. (Add more oil, if necessary.) Add *half* of the chicken to the hot wok or skillet; stir-fry 2 minutes. Remove from wok or skillet. Stir-fry remaining chicken 2 minutes. Return all chicken to wok or skillet. Stir soy mixture; stir into chicken. Cook and stir till thickened and bubbly. Stir in vegetables and walnuts; cover and cook 1 minute more. Serve chicken and vegetables at once. Garnish with fresh kumquats, if desired. Serve with hot cooked rice. Makes 4 to 6 servings.

---

## Using chicken broth

When a recipe calls for chicken broth, you can use the *homemade chicken broth* made from Stewed Chicken (see recipe, page 736), *canned chicken broth*, or *bouillon* (made from 1 teaspoon instant chicken bouillon granules for each 1 cup boiling water).

---

## Oven-Fried Chicken

   **3   cups corn flakes *or* ½ cup fine dry bread
          crumbs**
   **1   2½- to 3-pound broiler-fryer chicken, cut
          up**
   **¼   cup butter *or* margarine, melted**

Oven 375°

For the crumb mixture, crush corn flakes finely enough to make 1 cup crumbs or use the ½ cup bread crumbs; set aside.

Rinse chicken pieces; pat dry with paper toweling. Season chicken with salt and pepper. Brush *each* piece with melted butter. Place crushed corn flakes or bread crumbs on a sheet of waxed paper; roll chicken in crumbs to coat. Arrange chicken, skin side up and so pieces don't touch, in a shallow baking pan. Bake in a 375° oven about 50 minutes or till tender. *Do not turn.* (Chicken is done when it is easily pierced with a fork. Test the thigh or breast at a point near the bone, since these parts require the most cooking time.) Makes 6 servings.

**Potato-Chip Chicken:** Prepare Oven-Fried Chicken as above, *except* substitute 1½ cups crushed *potato chips or barbecue-flavored potato chips* for the crumb mixture. Do not season chicken with salt.

**Parmesan Chicken:** Prepare Oven-Fried Chicken as above, *except* substitute a mixture of ⅔ cup crushed *herb-seasoned stuffing mix,* ½ cup grated *Parmesan cheese,* and 3 tablespoons snipped *parsley* for the crumb mixture. Do not season chicken with salt.

**Curry and Parsley Chicken:** Prepare Oven-Fried Chicken as above, *except* substitute a mixture of ⅔ cup finely crushed *saltine crackers* (about 20 crackers), ¼ cup snipped *parsley,* 2 teaspoons *curry powder,* 1 teaspoon *onion salt,* and ⅛ teaspoon ground *ginger* for the crumb mixture. Do not season chicken with salt.

**Chicken Italiano:** Prepare Oven-Fried Chicken as above, *except* substitute a mixture of 1 cup coarsely crushed 40% *bran flakes,* 2 teaspoons *Italian or onion salad dressing mix,* and ½ teaspoon *paprika* for the crumb mixture.

---

## Crispy Baked Barbecued Chicken

   ½  **cup fine dry bread crumbs**
   1  **teaspoon brown sugar**
   1  **teaspoon chili powder**
   ½  **teaspoon garlic powder**
   ¼  **teaspoon dry mustard**
   ¼  **teaspoon celery seed**
   ⅛  **teaspoon cayenne**
   1  **2½- to 3-pound broiler-fryer chicken, cut up**
   ¼  **cup butter or margarine, melted**                    Oven 375°

Combine bread crumbs, brown sugar, chili powder, garlic powder, dry mustard, celery seed, and cayenne. Season chicken with salt and pepper. Brush *each* chicken piece with melted butter. Roll in crumb mixture to coat. Arrange chicken, skin side up and so pieces don't touch, in a shallow baking pan. Sprinkle with any remaining crumb mixture. Bake, uncovered, in a 375° oven about 50 minutes or till tender. *Do not turn.* Makes 6 servings.

## Oven-Crisped Orange Chicken

|     |                                                               |
| --- | ------------------------------------------------------------- |
| 1   | **beaten egg**                                                |
| ½   | **of a 6-ounce can (⅓ cup) frozen orange juice concentrate, thawed** |
| 2   | **tablespoons soy sauce**                                     |
| ½   | **cup fine dry bread crumbs**                                 |
| 1   | **teaspoon paprika**                                          |
| ¼   | **teaspoon salt**                                             |
| 3   | **tablespoons butter *or* margarine**                         |
| 1   | **2½- to 3-pound broiler-fryer chicken, cut up**   Oven 375°  |

Combine beaten egg, orange juice concentrate, and soy sauce; stir to mix well. In a small bowl thoroughly combine bread crumbs, paprika, and salt. Melt butter in a 13x9x2-inch baking pan. Dip chicken pieces in the orange-soy mixture, then coat with crumbs. Place chicken, skin side up and so pieces don't touch, in the baking pan. Sprinkle with any remaining crumb mixture. Bake, uncovered, in a 375° oven about 50 minutes or till tender. *Do not turn.* Makes 6 servings.

## Coq Au Vin

| | |
|---|---|
| 4 | slices bacon, cut up, *or* ¼ pound salt pork, finely chopped |
| 2 | 2½- to 3-pound broiler-fryer chickens, cut up |
| 2 | tablespoons all-purpose flour |
| ¾ | teaspoon salt |
| ¼ | teaspoon pepper |
| 2 | cups burgundy |
| 2 | tablespoons cognac *or* brandy |
| 2 | tablespoons snipped parsley |
| ½ | teaspoon dried marjoram, crushed |
| ½ | teaspoon dried thyme, crushed |
| 2 | bay leaves |
| 1 | pound shallots *or* small whole onions, peeled (16) |
| 2 | cups fresh whole mushrooms |
| ½ | cup thinly sliced carrot |
| 2 | cloves garlic, minced |
| 3 | tablespoons all-purpose flour |
| 3 | tablespoons butter *or* margarine, softened |
| | Snipped parsley (optional) |

In an 8-quart Dutch oven cook bacon or salt pork till crisp; remove from pan, reserving ¼ cup drippings. (If necessary, add cooking oil to drippings to measure ¼ cup.)

Brown the chicken, half at a time, over medium heat about 15 minutes, turning as necessary to brown evenly. Remove from Dutch oven. Repeat with remaining chicken. Remove; set aside.

Stir 2 tablespoons flour, salt, and pepper into remaining drippings in pan. Add burgundy and cognac or brandy all at once. Cook and stir till thickened and bubbly. Cook and stir 1 to 2 minutes more. Stir in 2 tablespoons parsley, marjoram, thyme, and bay leaves.

Return chicken to Dutch oven along with shallots or onions, mushrooms, carrot, garlic, and bacon or salt pork. Simmer, covered, for 40 minutes or till chicken is tender.

Remove chicken and vegetables from sauce mixture; arrange

on a serving plate and keep warm. Discard bay leaves. Stir the 3 tablespoons flour and butter or margarine to make a smooth paste. Using a wire whisk, stir into the hot sauce in pan. Cook and stir till thickened and bubbly. Cook and stir 1 to 2 minutes more. Season to taste with salt and pepper. To serve, top chicken with sauce mixture. Sprinkle with additional snipped parsley, if desired. Makes 12 servings.

## Chicken Saltimbocca

**3  whole medium chicken breasts
      (2¼ pounds)
6  thin slices boiled ham
6  thin slices Swiss cheese
1  medium tomato, peeled, seeded, and
      chopped
   Dried sage, crushed
⅓  cup fine dry bread crumbs
2  tablespoons grated Parmesan cheese
2  tablespoons snipped parsley
¼  cup butter or margarine,
      melted**                                Oven 350°

Skin, halve lengthwise, and bone chicken breasts (see tip, page 583). Place 1 piece of chicken, boned side up, between 2 pieces of clear plastic wrap. Working from the center to the edges, pound lightly with a meat mallet, forming a rectangle about ⅛ inch thick. Remove plastic wrap. Repeat with remaining chicken. Place a ham slice and a cheese slice on each cutlet, trimming to fit within ¼ inch of edges. Top with some chopped tomato; sprinkle lightly with sage. Fold in sides; roll up jelly roll style, pressing to seal. Combine bread crumbs, Parmesan cheese, and parsley. Dip chicken in butter, then roll in crumbs. Bake in a shallow baking pan in a 350° oven for 40 to 45 minutes. Remove to a serving platter. Stir mixture remaining in pan till smooth; spoon over chicken. Serves 6.

## Apricot Chicken

   **3    whole medium chicken breasts**
   **1    21-ounce can apricot pie filling**
   **1    tablespoon lemon juice**
   **½    teaspoon salt**
   **½    teaspoon ground nutmeg**
   **½    cup pecan halves**
        **Hot cooked rice**                    Oven 375°

Skin chicken breasts and halve lengthwise. Arrange in a
13x9x2-inch baking dish; sprinkle with a little salt and pepper.
In a mixing bowl combine apricot pie filling, lemon juice, ½
teaspoon salt, and nutmeg. Stir in pecans. Pour apricot mixture over chicken pieces. Cover and bake in a 375° oven for
55 to 60 minutes or till chicken is tender. Arrange chicken on
rice; spoon apricot mixture atop. Serves 6.

## Chicken Fricassee

In a plastic bag combine ½ cup *all-purpose flour*, 1 teaspoon
*salt*, 1 teaspoon *paprika*, and ¼ teaspoon *pepper*. Coat one
2½- to 3-pound *broiler-fryer chicken*, cut up, with flour mixture, 2 or 3 pieces at a time.

In a Dutch oven heat 2 tablespoons *cooking oil or shortening*. Brown chicken pieces over medium heat about 15 minutes, turning as necessary to brown evenly. Remove chicken.
In the same Dutch oven cook ½ cup chopped *celery* and ½
cup chopped *onion* till tender but not brown. Drain fat, if
necessary. Stir in one 10¾-ounce can of either condensed
*cream of mushroom soup, cream of celery soup, or cream of
chicken soup;* 1 cup *water;* 2 tablespoons chopped *pimiento;* 1
tablespoon *lemon juice;* and ½ teaspoon dried *rosemary or
thyme,* crushed.

Return chicken to Dutch oven. Cover; cook over medium
heat about 40 minutes or till chicken is tender; stirring occasionally. Serve with *hot cooked rice.* Makes 6 servings.

# Chicken Cacciatore

In a large skillet cook 2 medium *onions,* sliced, and 2 cloves *garlic,* minced, in 2 tablespoons hot *cooking oil* over medium heat till onions are tender. Remove onions; set aside. Add more cooking oil to skillet, if necessary. In the same skillet brown one 2½- to 3-pound *broiler-fryer chicken,* cut up, over medium heat about 15 minutes, turning to brown pieces evenly.

Return onions to skillet. Combine one 16-ounce can *tomatoes,* cut up; one 8-ounce can *tomato sauce;* 1 medium *green pepper,* cut into 1-inch pieces; one 2½-ounce jar sliced *mushrooms,* drained; 1 or 2 *bay leaves;* 2 teaspoons dried *oregano or basil,* crushed; 1 teaspoon *salt;* ½ teaspoon dried *rosemary,* crushed; and ¼ teaspoon *pepper.* Pour tomato mixture over chicken in skillet.

Cover and simmer for 30 minutes. Stir in ¼ cup *dry white wine.* Cook, uncovered, over low heat about 15 minutes more or till chicken is tender, turning occasionally. Skim off fat; discard bay leaves. Transfer chicken and sauce to a serving dish. Serve with *hot cooked rice or noodles.* Makes 6 servings.

---

# Stewed Chicken

In a large Dutch oven combine one 5- to 6-pound *stewing chicken,* cut up, *or* two 3-pound *broiler-fryer chickens,* cut up, and enough *water* to cover (about 6 cups). Add 4 stalks *celery with leaves,* cut up; 1 *carrot,* sliced; 1 small *onion,* cut up; 1 teaspoon *salt;* and ¼ teaspoon *pepper.* Cover; bring to boiling. Reduce heat; simmer 2 to 2½ hours for stewing chicken or about 1 hour for broiler-fryer chickens or till chicken is tender. Remove chicken; strain broth. Let chicken and broth cool.

When chicken is cool enough to handle, remove meat, discarding skin and bones. Store chicken and broth separately in tightly covered containers in the refrigerator. Lift fat from broth when chilled. (Broth and chicken may be frozen separately in 1-cup portions. Use the meat in recipes calling for cooked chicken; use the broth as directed in recipes.) Makes 6 cups broth and 6 cups cooked chicken. Serves 12.

## Chicken and Dumplings

      **Stewed Chicken (see recipe, page 597)**
1   **cup all-purpose flour**
2   **teaspoons baking powder**
2   **tablespoons snipped parsley**
1   **beaten egg**
¼   **cup milk**
2   **tablespoons cooking oil**
½   **cup all-purpose flour**

Prepare dumplings when Stewed Chicken is *almost tender*. For dumplings, combine 1 cup flour, baking powder, and ½ teaspoon *salt*; stir in parsley. Combine egg, milk, and oil. Add to flour mixture, stirring with a fork only till combined. Drop dough from a tablespoon directly onto chicken in bubbly broth. Return to boiling. Cover tightly Reduce heat; *do not lift cover*. Simmer 12 to 15 minutes. Remove dumplings and chicken to a warm serving platter; keep warm. Strain broth.

To thicken broth for gravy, in a saucepan bring 4 cups broth to boiling. Slowly stir 1 cup cold *water* into the ½ cup flour; gradually add to broth, mixing well. Cook and stir till bubbly. Cook and stir 2 minutes more. Season with ½ teaspoon *salt* and ⅛ teaspoon *pepper*. Pour some sauce over chicken and dumplings; pass remaining. Serves 12.

## Chicken and Noodles

Prepare *Stewed Chicken* (see recipe, page 597). When chicken is cool enough to handle, remove meat; discard skin and bones. Meanwhile, to make noodles, in a mixing bowl combine 2 beaten *eggs;* ¼ cup *milk;* ¾ teaspoon *salt;* and ¼ teaspoon dried *thyme or sage,* crushed. Stir in enough of 2 cups all-purpose *flour* to make a stiff dough. Cover; let rest 10 minutes. Divide dough in half. On a floured surface roll dough, half at a time, into a 16x12-inch rectangle. Let stand 20 minutes. Roll up loosely; cut into ¼-inch slices. Unroll; cut into desired lengths. Spread out and let dry on a rack 2 hours.

Bring chicken broth to boiling; add noodles, 2 cups thinly

sliced *carrots,* ½ cup chopped *celery,* and ½ cup chopped *onion.* Cover; simmer 10 minutes. Add chicken. Slowly stir ½ cup cold *water* into ¼ cup all-purpose *flour;* add to broth. Cook and stir till bubbly; continue cooking 1 to 2 minutes more. Serves 12.

## Pheasant with Apples

> ¼ **cup all-purpose flour**
> 2 **2- to 3-pound pheasants, halved *or*** **quartered**
> ¼ **cup butter *or* margarine**
> ¾ **cup dry white wine**
> ¾ **cup light cream**
> 3 **beaten egg yolks**
> 3 **tablespoons butter *or* margarine**
> 2 **medium apples, cored and cut into wedges**
> 1 **teaspoon sugar**

Combine flour, 1 teaspoon *salt,* and ¼ teaspoon *pepper* in a plastic bag. Add pheasant pieces one at a time; shake to coat. In a skillet brown birds in ¼ cup butter or margarine. Add wine; simmer, covered, 45 to 55 minutes or till tender. Remove to a platter; keep warm. For sauce, combine cream and egg yolks. Slowly stir into pan drippings; cook and stir over medium heat just till thickened; *do not boil.*

Meanwhile, for sautéed apples, in a skillet melt 3 tablespoons butter; add apple wedges. Sprinkle with sugar. Cook, turning often, about 5 minutes or till lightly browned. Pass sauce with pheasant; sprinkle with paprika, if desired. Serve with apples. Serves 4 to 6.

## Chicken Livers Stroganoff

In a 10-inch skillet cook 3 slices *bacon* till crisp. Drain, reserving drippings in skillet. Crumble bacon; set aside. Cook 1 pound *chicken livers,* cut up, in drippings over medium heat 5 minutes or till slightly pink in center. Remove from skillet; keep warm.

In the same skillet cook 1½ cups sliced fresh *mushrooms* and ½ cup chopped *onion* 2 to 3 minutes. Remove from skillet. Add ½ cup dry *sherry,* ½ cup *water,* and ½ teaspoon *instant chicken bouillon granules* to skillet; bring to boiling. Cook, uncovered, till liquid is reduced to ½ cup. Stir together 1 tablespoon all-purpose *flour* and 1 cup dairy *sour cream.* Gradually stir hot liquid into sour cream mixture; return all to saucepan. Stir in crumbled bacon, chicken livers, and mushrooms and onion. Cook slowly till heated through; *do not boil.* Serve over *hot cooked noodles.* Sprinkle with snipped *parsley,* if desired. Serves 5 or 6.

---

## Chicken Livers in Tomato Sauce

|   |   |
|---|---|
| 1 | **pound chicken livers, cut up** |
| 2 | **tablespoons cooking oil** |
| ⅓ | **cup chopped onion** |
| ⅓ | **cup chopped green pepper** |
| 1 | **clove garlic, minced** |
| 1 | **16-ounce can tomatoes, cut up** |
| 1 | **15-ounce can tomato sauce** |
| 1 | **tablespoon dried parsley flakes** |
| 1 | **teaspoon sugar** |
| 1 | **teaspoon dried oregano, crushed** |
| 1 | **teaspoon dried basil, crushed** |
| ½ | **teaspoon salt** |
|   | **Hot cooked spaghetti or noodles** |
|   | **Grated Parmesan cheese** |

In a 10-inch skillet cook chicken livers in hot cooking oil over medium heat for 5 minutes or till slightly pink in the center. Remove from skillet; keep warm.

In the same skillet combine chopped onion, green pepper, and garlic; cook till onions are tender but not brown. Stir in *undrained* tomatoes, tomato sauce, parsley, sugar, oregano, basil, salt, and ⅛ teaspoon *pepper.* Cover; simmer for 15 minutes. Stir in chicken livers; simmer, uncovered, for 5 minutes. Serve over hot cooked spaghetti or noodles. Pass Parmesan cheese. Makes 5 or 6 servings.

## Chicken Country Captain

| | |
|---|---|
| ½ | cup chopped onion |
| ½ | cup chopped green pepper |
| 1 | clove garlic, minced |
| 2 | tablespoons butter *or* margarine |
| 1 | 28-ounce can tomatoes, cut up |
| ¼ | cup dried currants *or* raisins |
| ¼ | cup snipped parsley |
| 2 | tablespoons curry powder |
| 1 | teaspoon salt |
| 1 | teaspoon ground mace |
| ½ | teaspoon sugar |
| ⅛ | teaspoon pepper |
| ½ | cup all-purpose flour |
| 1 | teaspoon salt |
| ¼ | teaspoon pepper |
| ¼ | teaspoon paprika |
| 2 | 2½- to 3-pound broiler-fryer chickens, cut up |
| 2 | tablespoons cooking oil |
| 2 | tablespoons cold water |
| 1 | tablespoon cornstarch |
| | Hot cooked rice |
| ¼ | cup sliced almonds (optional)       Oven 325° |

In a saucepan cook onion, green pepper, and garlic in butter or margarine till tender but not brown. Stir in *undrained* tomatoes, currants or raisins, parsley, curry powder, 1 teaspoon salt, mace, sugar, and ⅛ teaspoon pepper. Simmer, uncovered, for 15 minutes.

In a plastic bag combine flour, 1 teaspoon salt, ¼ teaspoon pepper, and paprika. Add 2 or 3 chicken pieces at a time; shake to coat. In a large skillet lightly brown chicken pieces on all sides in hot oil about 15 minutes. Arrange chicken in a 13x9x2-inch baking dish; top with tomato mixture. Cover and bake in a 325° oven about 1 hour or till chicken is tender.

Remove chicken from baking dish; keep warm. Skim excess fat from tomato mixture; transfer tomato mixture to a medium saucepan. Stir cold water into cornstarch; add to tomato mixture. Cook and stir till thickened and bubbly. Cook and stir 1 to 2 minutes more. Serve chicken and sauce with rice. Garnish with almonds, if desired. Makes 12 servings.

## Arroz con Pollo

| | |
|---|---|
| 1 | **2½- to 3-pound broiler-fryer chicken, cut up** |
| 2 | **tablespoons cooking oil** |
| 1½ | **cups long grain rice** |
| 1 | **cup chopped onion** |
| 2 | **cloves garlic, minced** |
| 3 | **cups water** |
| 1 | **7½-ounce can tomatoes, cut up** |
| 1 | **tablespoon instant chicken bouillon granules** |
| 1 | **teaspoon salt** |
| ¼ | **teaspoon thread saffron, crushed** |
| ¼ | **teaspoon pepper** |
| 1 | **cup frozen peas** |
| 1 | **2-ounce can sliced pimiento, drained and chopped** |

Sprinkle chicken lightly with salt. In a 12-inch skillet brown chicken in hot oil about 15 minutes. Remove chicken from skillet. In the remaining pan drippings cook and stir rice, onion, and garlic till rice is golden. Add water, *undrained* tomatoes, bouillon granules, salt, saffron, and pepper. Bring to boiling; stir well. Arrange chicken atop rice mixture. Cover and simmer 30 to 35 minutes or till chicken is tender. Stir in peas and pimiento; cover and cook 5 minutes more. Makes 6 servings.

## Chicken a la King

For sauce, in a saucepan melt 6 tablespoons *butter or margarine*. Stir in ½ cup all-purpose *flour*, ¾ teaspoon *salt,* and ⅛ teaspoon *pepper*. Add 2 cups *milk*, 1 cup *water*, and 1 teaspoon *instant chicken bouillon granules* all at once. Cook and stir over medium heat till thickened and bubbly. Cook and stir 1 to 2 minutes more. Stir in 2 cups cubed cooked *chicken or turkey;* one 4-ounce can *mushroom stems and pieces,* drained; and ¼ cup chopped *pimiento.* Heat through. Serve spooned over *toast points, toasted English muffins, or baked patty shells.* Makes 4 servings.

**Cheesy Chicken a la King:** Prepare Chicken a la King as above, *except* stir ½ cup shredded *American cheese* into the thickened sauce mixture. Cook and stir 2 minutes more. Continue as directed above.

---

## Chicken-Cheese Crêpes

---

  **6**   **tablespoons butter *or* margarine**
  **⅓**   **cup all-purpose flour**
          **Dash salt**
  **2**   **cups milk**
  **1**   **cup water**
  **1**   **tablespoon instant chicken bouillon granules**
  **½**   **cup shredded Swiss cheese *or* brick cheese (2 ounces)**
  **¼**   **cup dry white wine**
  **2**   **tablespoons snipped parsley**
          **Several dashes bottled hot pepper sauce**
  **1**   **2½-ounce jar sliced mushrooms, drained**
  **1**   **10-ounce package frozen peas**
  **2**   **cups chopped cooked chicken *or* turkey**
  **2**   **tablespoons chopped pimiento**
 **12**   **Basic Crêpes (see recipe, page 442)**
          **Paprika (optional)**                      Oven 375°

For cheese sauce, in a medium saucepan melt butter or margarine. Stir in flour and salt. Add milk, water, and chicken bouillon granules all at once. Cook and stir over medium heat till thickened and bubbly. Cook and stir 1 to 2 minutes more. Stir in cheese, wine, parsley, and hot pepper sauce. Remove *1 cup* of the cheese sauce; set aside. Stir drained mushrooms into remaining sauce.

For filling, cook peas according to package directions; drain.

Combine peas, chicken or turkey, pimiento, and the 1 cup reserved cheese sauce. Spread ¼ cup filling over the *unbrowned* side of *each* crêpe, leaving a ¼-inch rim around edge. Roll up crêpe. Place, seam side down, in a 12x7½x2-inch baking dish. Repeat with remaining crêpes. Pour the remaining cheese sauce over crêpes. Sprinkle with paprika, if desired. Cover; bake in a 375° oven for 18 to 20 minutes or till heated through. Let stand 10 minutes before serving. Makes 6 servings.

## Crab-Stuffed Chicken Breasts

| | |
|---|---|
| **4** | **whole medium chicken breasts (3 pounds)** |
| **3** | **tablespoons butter *or* margarine** |
| **¼** | **cup all-purpose flour** |
| **¾** | **cup milk** |
| **¾** | **cup chicken broth** |
| **⅓** | **cup dry white wine** |
| **¼** | **cup chopped onion** |
| **1** | **tablespoon butter *or* margarine** |
| **1** | **7-ounce can crab meat, drained, flaked, and cartilage removed** |
| **½** | **cup coarsely crumbled saltine crackers (10 crackers)** |
| **1** | **4-ounce can chopped mushrooms, drained** |
| **2** | **tablespoons snipped parsley** |
| **¼** | **teaspoon salt** |
| | **Dash pepper** |
| **1** | **cup shredded Swiss cheese (4 ounces)** |
| **½** | **teaspoon paprika** |
| | **Hot cooked rice** |

Oven 350°

Skin, halve lengthwise, and bone chicken breasts (see tip, page 583). Place 1 piece of chicken, boned side up, between 2 pieces of clear plastic wrap. Working from the center to the edges, pound lightly with a meat mallet, forming a rectangle about ⅛ inch thick. Remove plastic wrap; set aside. Repeat with remaining chicken.

For wine sauce, in a saucepan melt the 3 tablespoons butter or margarine; stir in flour. Add milk, chicken broth, and white wine all at once; cook and stir till mixture is thickened and bubbly. Cook and stir 1 to 2 minutes more. Set aside. In a skillet cook onion in the 1 tablespoon butter or margarine till tender but not brown. Stir in crab meat, cracker crumbs, mushrooms, snipped parsley, salt, and pepper. Stir in *2 table-spoons* of the wine sauce. Top *each* chicken piece with about ¼ *cup* of the crab mixture. Fold sides in; roll up. Place, seam side down, in a 12x7½x2-inch baking dish. Pour remaining wine sauce over all.

Bake, uncovered, in a 350° oven for 1 hour or till chicken is tender. Uncover; sprinkle with shredded Swiss cheese and paprika. Bake 2 minutes longer or till cheese melts. Transfer stuffed chicken breasts to a serving platter. Serve with sauce and rice. Makes 8 servings.

# Sandwiches

## Chicken-Asparagus Stacks

In a saucepan cook ⅓ cup finely chopped *green onion* in 1 tablespoon *butter or margarine* till tender but not brown. Stir on one 10¾-ounce can *condensed cream of chicken soup,* ½ cup dairy *sour cream,* and ⅓ cup *milk.* Add 2 cups chopped *cooked chicken or turkey.* Heat through; *do not boil.*

Cook one 8-ounce package frozen *asparagus spears* according to package directions; drain. To serve, top 4 *rusks* with *half* of the chicken mixture. Top with 4 *rusks,* asparagus, and remaining chicken mixture. Makes 4.

## Super Chicken Subs

½  **cup dairy sour cream**
2  **tablespoons thinly sliced green onion**
2  **teaspoons prepared mustard**
½  **teaspoon dried basil, crushed**
⅛  **teaspoon garlic salt**
4  **individual French rolls**
4  **lettuce leaves**
8  **slices cooked chicken *or* turkey**
4  **slices American, Swiss, cheddar, *or*
    Monterey Jack cheese**
2  **medium tomatoes, peeled and thinly sliced**
1  **small cucumber, sliced**
1  **small green pepper, sliced crosswise into
    rings**
¼  **cup sliced pimiento-stuffed olives or pitted
    ripe olives**
⅓  **cup alfalfa sprouts (optional)**

For sandwich spread, in a small mixing bowl combine sour cream, onion, mustard, basil, and garlic salt. Cover; chill thoroughly.

Split French rolls lengthwise, cutting to, but not through, the other side. Scoop out some of the center. Spread both halves of rolls generously with chilled spread mixture.

On the bottom half of *each* roll, arrange lettuce, chicken or turkey, cheese, and tomato. Top *each* with cucumber, green pepper, olives, and alfalfa sprouts, if desired. Place top halves of rolls atop. Anchor sandwiches with wooden picks, if desired. Makes 4 sandwiches.

# Broiling

## Basic Broiled Chicken

**1    2½- to 3-pound broiler-fryer chicken,
         halved lengthwise or quartered
         Melted butter or cooking oil**

Preheat broiler unit before cooking. (*Do not* preheat broiler pan or rack.) Break wing, hip, and drumstick joints of chicken so bird will remain flat during broiling. Twist wing tips under back. Brush chicken pieces with melted butter or oil and season with salt and pepper.

Place chicken, skin side down, on an unheated rack in a broiler pan; then place under unit with surface of chicken 5 to 6 inches from heat. (If your broiler compartment does not allow enough distance, remove rack and place chicken directly in broiler pan.) Broil about 20 minutes or till lightly browned. Brush occasionally with butter or cooking oil. Turn chicken, skin side up, and broil 15 to 20 minutes more or till tender, brushing occasionally. Serves 6.

**Cumberland-Style Broiled Chicken:** Prepare Basic Broiled Chicken as above, *except* use *two* 2½- to 3-pound broiler-fryer *chickens.* For sauce, in a small saucepan combine 1½ teaspoons *cornstarch,* ½ teaspoon ground *ginger,* and ¼ teaspoon ground *nutmeg.* Stir in ½ cup *currant jelly;* ½ of a 6-ounce can (⅓ cup) frozen *orange juice concentrate,* thawed; 3 tablespoons *water;* and 1 tablespoon *lemon juice.* Cook and stir till thickened and bubbly. Cook and stir 1 to 2 minutes more. Broil chicken 20 minutes. Turn chicken; broil 10 minutes more or till done, brushing occasionally with sauce. Makes 12 servings.

**Hawaiian Broiled Chicken:** Prepare Basic Broiled Chicken as above, *except* use *two* 2½- to 3-pound broiler-fryer *chickens.* For sauce, in a small saucepan combine 2 tablespoons *sugar* and 1 teaspoon *cornstarch.* Stir in one 8¼-ounce can crushed *pineapple,* 2 tablespoons *butter or margarine,* 2 tablespoons *soy sauce,* and 1 tablespoon finely chopped *onion*. Cook and stir till thickened and bubbly; continue 1 to 2 minutes more. Broil chicken for 20 minutes. Turn chicken; broil for 15 minutes. Brush with sauce. Broil 5 minutes more, brushing occasionally with sauce. Pass remaining sauce. Serves 12.

**Barbecue-Style Broiled Chicken:** Prepare Basic Broiled Chicken as above, *except* use *two* 2½- to 3-pound broiler-fryer *chickens*. For sauce, in a small saucepan combine ⅓ cup *catsup*, ¼ cup chopped *onion*, 1 tablespoon *water*, 1 tablespoon *prepared mustard*, ½ teaspoon *celery seed*, ½ teaspoon *chili powder*, and ¼ teaspoon *garlic powder*. Cook and stir till heated through. Broil chicken for 20 minutes. Brush with some of the sauce. Turn chicken; broil for 10 minutes. Brush again with some sauce. Broil 5 minutes more, brushing occasionally with sauce. Pass remaining sauce. Makes 12 servings.

## Turkey-Yam Kebabs

| | |
|---|---|
| 4 | medium yams *or* sweet potatoes |
| 1 | 8¼-ounce can pineapple slices |
| 2 | tablespoons brown sugar |
| 1 | teaspoon cornstarch |
| ½ | teaspoon ground cinnamon |
| ¼ | teaspoon dry mustard |
| ⅛ | teaspoon ground cloves |
| ½ | cup jellied cranberry sauce |
| ¼ | cup cooking oil |
| ¾ | pound frozen boneless turkey roast, thawed and cut into 12 pieces |
| 4 | spiced crab apples |

Cut off woody portion of yams or sweet potatoes. In a saucepan cook yams or sweet potatoes, covered, in enough boiling salted water to cover 25 to 30 minutes or till just tender. Drain; cool. Peel and cut into 1-inch chunks.

Drain pineapple slices, reserving ⅓ cup of the syrup. Quarter each pineapple slice. For sauce, in a small saucepan stir together brown sugar, cornstarch, cinnamon, dry mustard, and cloves. Stir in the reserved pineapple syrup, cranberry sauce, and cooking oil. Cook and stir till slightly thickened and bubbly. Cook and stir 1 to 2 minutes more.

On 4 skewers thread turkey pieces, yam pieces, pineapple pieces, and crab apples. Place the skewers on an unheated rack in a broiler pan; place under unit with surface of turkey 5 to 6 inches from heat. Broil 4 minutes. Brush occasionally with sauce. Turn skewers and broil about 4 minutes more, brushing with sauce; pass remaining sauce. Serves 4.

## Glazed Chicken and Rice

For basting sauce, in a small saucepan combine ¼ cup *soy sauce*, 2 tablespoons *water*, 2 tablespoons *dry sherry*, 1 teaspoon *sugar*, and ½ teaspoon grated *gingerroot or* ⅛ teaspoon ground *ginger*. Boil gently, uncovered, for 1 minute. Set aside.

Halve or quarter one 2½- to 3-pound *broiler-fryer chicken.* Break wing, hip, and drumstick joints so bird will remain flat. Twist wing tips under back. Brush poultry with *cooking oil.* Place chicken, skin side down, on an unheated rack in a broiler pan. Broil 5 to 6 inches from heat till poultry is tender, turning and brushing with cooking oil after half the cooking time. Brush poultry frequently with the basting sauce during the last 5 to 10 minutes, turning poultry as needed for even cooking.

Meanwhile, in a saucepan cook one 6-ounce package *long grain and wild rice mix* according to package directions. Stir in 1 cup fresh *or* canned *bean sprouts*, rinsed and drained; ¼ cup *green onion* bias-sliced into 1-inch lengths; and 2 tablespoons *butter or margarine*. Spoon rice mixture onto a warm serving platter; arrange poultry atop. Makes 6 servings.

## Chicken Teriyaki Kebabs

For marinade, in a bowl combine ½ teaspoon finely shredded *orange peel*, ⅓ cup *orange juice*, ¼ cup *soy sauce*, ¼ cup *dry sherry*, 2 tablespoons sliced *green onion*, 2 teaspoons grated *gingerroot or* ½ teaspoon *ground ginger*, 1 teaspoon toasted *sesame seed*, and 2 cloves *garlic*, minced.

Skin, halve lengthwise, and bone 2 whole medium *chicken breasts* (1½ pounds) (see tip, page 583). Pound chicken slightly to flatten; cut lengthwise into ½- to ¾-inch-wide strips. Add chicken pieces to marinade. Cover; let stand 30 minutes at room temperature. Drain chicken, reserving marinade. Thread chicken strips accordion style on wooden or metal skewers. Broil 4 to 5 inches from heat about 4 minutes per side, brushing occasionally with marinade. In a small saucepan combine ½ cup of the marinade, ¾ cup *water,* and 4 teaspoons *cornstarch.* Cook and stir till thickened and bubbly. Cook and stir 1 to 2 minutes more. Serve chicken and sauce over *hot cooked rice.* Makes 4 servings.

# Casseroles

## Chicken Pot Pies

| | |
|---|---|
| 1 | 10-ounce package frozen peas and carrots |
| ½ | cup chopped onion |
| ½ | cup chopped fresh mushrooms |
| ¼ | cup butter *or* margarine |
| ⅓ | cup all-purpose flour |
| ½ | teaspoon salt |
| ¼ | teaspoon ground sage |
| ⅛ | teaspoon pepper |
| 2 | cups water |
| ¾ | cup milk |
| 1 | tablespoon instant chicken bouillon granules |
| 3 | cups cubed cooked chicken *or* turkey |
| ¼ | cup chopped pimiento |
| ¼ | cup snipped parsley |
| | Pastry for Double-Crust Pie* (see recipe, page 569) Oven 450° |

Cook peas and carrots according to package directions; drain. In a saucepan cook onion and mushrooms in butter or margarine till tender but not brown. Stir in flour, salt, sage, and pepper. Add water, milk, and chicken bouillon granules all at once. Cook and stir till thickened and bubbly. Cook and stir 1 to 2 minutes more. Stir in drained cooked vegetables, chicken or turkey, pimiento, and parsley; heat till bubbly. Turn chicken mixture into 6 individual casseroles or a 12x7½x2-inch baking dish.

Roll pastry into a 15x10-inch rectangle. Cut into six 5-inch circles and place over individual casseroles; flute edges. (*Or,* roll pastry into a 13x9-inch rectangle. Place over the 12x7½x2-inch casserole; flute edges.) Cut slits in top for escape of steam. Bake in a 450° oven for 10 to 12 minutes or till crust is golden brown. Makes 6 servings.

**\*Note:** Instead of a pastry top, combine ½ cup *herb-seasoned stuffing croutons* and 1 tablespoon *butter or margarine,* melted. Sprinkle over casseroles; bake as directed above.

## Wild-Rice-Chicken Casserole

| | |
|---|---|
| 1 | **6-ounce package long grain and wild rice mix** |
| ½ | **cup chopped onion** |
| ½ | **cup chopped celery** |
| 2 | **tablespoons butter or margarine** |
| 1 | **10¾-ounce can condensed cream of mushroom soup** |
| ½ | **cup dairy sour cream** |
| ⅓ | **cup dry white wine** |
| ½ | **teaspoon curry powder** |
| 2 | **cups cubed cooked chicken or turkey** |

Oven 350°

Prepare rice mix according to package directions. Meanwhile, cook onion and celery in butter till tender. Stir in soup, sour cream, wine, and curry. Stir in chicken and cooked rice; turn into a 2-quart casserole or a 12x7½x2-inch baking dish. Bake, uncovered, in a 350° oven for 35 to 40 minutes. Stir before serving. Makes 4 to 6 servings.

## Chicken Divan

> **2**   **10-ounce packages frozen broccoli spears**
>     **or two 8-ounce packages frozen cut**
>     **asparagus**
> **¼**   **cup butter or margarine**
> **⅓**   **cup all-purpose flour**
> **⅛**   **teaspoon ground nutmeg**
> **1**   **cup light cream or milk**
> **1**   **cup chicken broth**
> **¼**   **cup dry white wine**
> **⅓**   **cup shredded Swiss cheese**
> **10**   **ounces sliced cooked chicken**
> **¼**   **cup grated Parmesan cheese**
>     **Paprika**                Oven 350°

Cook vegetable according to package directions; drain. Arrange crosswise in a 12x7½x2-inch baking dish. For sauce, in a saucepan melt butter; stir in flour, nutmeg, ½ teaspoon *salt,* and ⅛ teaspoon *pepper.* Add cream or milk and broth all at once. Cook and stir till bubbly; continue cooking 1 to 2 minutes more. Stir in wine. Add Swiss cheese; stir till melted.

Pour *half* of the sauce over broccoli or asparagus. Top with chicken. Pour remaining sauce over all. Sprinkle Parmesan and paprika atop. Bake in a 350° oven for 20 minutes or till heated through. Broil 3 or 4 inches from heat 1 to 2 minutes or till golden. Serves 6.

# Chicken Enchilada Casserole

|        |                                                           |
|--------|-----------------------------------------------------------|
| 1      | cup chopped onion                                         |
| ½      | cup chopped green pepper                                   |
| 2      | tablespoons butter or margarine                           |
| 2      | cups chopped cooked chicken or turkey                     |
| 1      | 4-ounce can green chili peppers, rinsed, seeded, and chopped |
| 3      | tablespoons butter or margarine                           |
| ¼      | cup all-purpose flour                                     |
| 1      | teaspoon ground coriander                                 |
| ¾      | teaspoon salt                                             |
| 2½     | cups chicken broth                                        |
| 1      | cup dairy sour cream                                      |
| 1½     | cups shredded Monterey Jack cheese (6 ounces)             |
| 12     | 6-inch tortillas                            Oven 350°     |

In a large saucepan cook onion and green pepper in the 2 tablespoons butter or margarine till tender. Combine onion mixture in a bowl with chopped chicken and green chili peppers; set aside.

For sauce, in the same saucepan melt 3 tablespoons butter or margarine. Stir in flour, coriander, and salt. Stir in chicken broth all at once; cook and stir till thickened and bubbly. Cook and stir 1 to 2 minutes more. Remove from heat; stir in sour cream and ½ *cup* of the cheese. Stir ½ *cup* of the sauce into the chicken mixture. Dip each tortilla into remaining sauce to soften; fill each with about ¼ cup of the chicken mixture. Roll up. Arrange rolls in a 13x9x2-inch baking dish; pour remaining sauce over. Sprinkle with remaining cheese. Bake, uncovered, in a 350° oven about 25 minutes or till bubbly. Serves 6.

## Popover Chicken Tarragon

Oven 350°

In a skillet brown one 2½- to 3-pound *broiler-fryer chicken*, cut up, in 2 tablespoons hot *cooking oil*; season with salt and pepper. Place in a well-greased 13x9x2-inch baking dish.

In a mixing bowl beat 3 *eggs*; add 1½ cups *milk* and 1 tablespoon *cooking oil*. Stir together 1½ cups all-purpose *flour*; ¾ to 1 teaspoon dried *tarragon*, crushed; and ¾ teaspoon *salt*. Add to egg mixture. Beat till smooth. Pour over chicken pieces in dish. Bake in a 350° oven for 55 to 60 minutes or till done. Serves 6.

## Crowd-Size Chicken Bake

Oven 350°

Cook 16 ounces *medium noodles* (12 cups) according to package directions; drain well. In a large kettle melt ½ cup *butter or margarine*. Stir in ½ cup all-purpose *flour*, 1½ teaspoons *salt*, and ¼ teaspoon *white pepper*. Add 7 cups *milk* all at once. Cook and stir till thickened and bubbly. Cook and stir 1 to 2 minutes more. Stir in four 10½-ounce cans *chicken gravy*. Stir in 8 cups chopped *cooked chicken or turkey*; one 2-ounce jar sliced *pimiento*, drained and chopped; and cooked noodles. Divide between two 13x9x2-inch baking dishes. Bake, covered, in a 350° oven about 35 minutes.

Toss together 1 cup fine dry *bread crumbs* and ¼ cup *butter or margarine*, melted. Sprinkle atop casseroles. Bake, uncovered, 10 minutes. Makes 2 casseroles, 12 servings each.

# Dilled Chicken-Noodle Bake

   **2**  **cups medium noodles**
   **1**  **cup chopped celery**
  **½**  **cup chopped onion**
  **¼**  **cup chopped green pepper**
   **3**  **tablespoons butter or margarine**
   **3**  **tablespoons all-purpose flour**
**1¾**  **cups milk**
   **2**  **tablespoons snipped parsley**
   **1**  **teaspoon dried dillweed**
   **1**  **cup dairy sour cream**
   **2**  **cups cubed cooked chicken or turkey**
  **½**  **cup coarsely crushed rich round crackers**
   **1**  **tablespoon butter or margarine,**
         **melted**                              Oven 350°

Cook noodles according to package directions; drain. In a large saucepan cook celery, onion, and green pepper, covered, in the 3 tablespoons butter till tender. Stir in flour, 1½ teaspoons *salt,* and ⅛ teaspoon *pepper.* Add milk all at once; cook and stir till thickened and bubbly. Cook and stir 1 to 2 minutes more. Stir in parsley and dillweed. Remove from heat; stir in sour cream. Stir in noodles and chicken. Turn into a 1½-quart casserole. Mix crumbs and 1 tablespoon melted butter; sprinkle around edge. Bake, uncovered, in a 350° oven for 35 to 40 minutes. Serves 4 to 6.

## Cassoulet

| | |
|---|---|
| 8 | cups water |
| 2 | cups dry navy beans (1 pound) |
| 1 | cup chopped celery |
| 1 | cup chopped carrot |
| 2 | teaspoons instant beef bouillon granules |
| 1 | teaspoon salt |
| 1 | 2½- to 3-pound broiler-fryer chicken with giblets, cut up |
| ½ | pound bulk pork sausage |
| 1 | cup chopped onion |
| 1 | clove garlic, minced |
| 1½ | cups tomato juice |
| 2 | tablespoons snipped parsley |
| 1 | tablespoon Worcestershire sauce |
| 2 | bay leaves |
| | Paprika (optional) |

Oven 325°

In an oven-going Dutch oven boil water and dry navy beans for 2 minutes. Remove from heat. *Do not drain.* Cover; let stand 1 hour. (*Or,* add water to beans. Cover and refrigerate overnight.)

Add chopped celery, carrot, beef bouillon granules, salt, and chicken neck and giblets to undrained beans. Simmer, covered, for 1 hour. Remove chicken neck and giblets. Discard neck; cut up giblets and add to beans, if desired. Drain beans, reserving liquid. Return beans to Dutch oven.

Shape pork sausage into small balls; brown in a large skillet. Remove browned sausage balls from skillet; set aside. Brown chicken pieces in the drippings over medium heat about 15 minutes, turning as necessary to brown evenly. Remove browned chicken pieces from skillet; set aside.

In the same skillet cook chopped onion and garlic till tender but not brown. Add to bean mixture along with sausage balls, tomato juice, parsley. Worcestershire sauce, and bay leaves. Arrange chicken pieces on top; add 1½ cups of the bean liquid. Sprinkle with a little paprika, if desired. Cover; bake in a 325° oven for 1 hour. (Add additional bean liquid, if necessary.) Remove and discard bay leaves; skim off *excess fat.* Makes 8 servings.

# Roasting

## Honey and Spice Duckling

| | |
|---|---|
| **2** | **teaspoons salt** |
| **2** | **teaspoons whole black pepper or Szechwan pepper, coarsely ground** |
| **1** | **teaspoon ground ginger** |
| **½** | **teaspoon Homemade Five-Spice Powder (see recipe below)** |
| **1** | **4- to 5-pound domestic duckling** |
| **¼** | **cup honey** |
| **2** | **tablespoons soy sauce** |

Oven 375°

In a bowl combine salt, pepper, ginger, and Homemade Five-Spice Powder. Sprinkle cavity of duck with some of the salt mixture; rub remaining on skin of duck. Skewer neck skin to back; tie legs to tail. Twist wing tips under back. Prick skin all over with a fork. Place duckling, breast-side up, on a rack in a shallow roasting pan. Roast in a 375° oven for 1¾ hours, spooning off fat occasionally. Mix honey and soy sauce; baste duckling with soy mixture. Roast 15 to 20 minutes more or till drumstick moves easily in socket, basting often with soy mixture. Makes 3 to 4 servings.

**Note:** To serve roast poultry with an Oriental flair, cut poultry in half lengthwise through the breast with a cleaver. Cut off the wings and legs close to the body; set aside.

Cut off the backbone on each half of the bird. Then cut each piece in half lengthwise. Cutting through meat and bone, cut the poultry into bite-size pieces and reassemble each half into its original shape on the serving platter. Cut each reserved wing and leg into two or three pieces and arrange on each side of the backbone.

## Homemade Five-Spice Powder

In a small bowl combine 1 teaspoon ground *cinnamon;* 1 teaspoon crushed *aniseed* or 1 star *anise,* ground; ¼ teaspoon crushed *fennel seed;* ¼ teaspoon freshly ground *pepper or* ¼ teaspoon crushed *Szechwan pepper;* and ¼ teaspoon ground *cloves.* Store in a covered container. (Or, purchase commercial five-spice powder at an Oriental foods store.)

## Curried Chicken and Vegetables

| | |
|---|---|
| ½ | cup honey |
| ¼ | cup prepared mustard |
| ¼ | cup butter or margarine |
| 2 | tablespoons finely chopped onion |
| 2 | tablespoons water |
| 1 | clove garlic, minced |
| 2 | teaspoons curry powder |
| 1 | teaspoon salt |
| ¼ | teaspoon crushed red pepper |
| ¼ | teaspoon ground ginger |
| 1 | 2½- to 3-pound broiler-fryer chicken or one 4- to 5-pound domestic duck or wild goose |
| | Cooking oil or melted butter |
| 2 | large potatoes, peeled and quartered, or 8 new potatoes |
| 6 | medium carrots, bias-sliced into ½-inch pieces |
| 2 | medium apples, cored and cut into wedges    Oven 375° |

In a small saucepan combine first 10 ingredients. Bring to boiling, stirring constantly. Remove from heat; set aside.

Rinse poultry and pat dry with paper toweling. Skewer neck skin to back. Tie legs to tail. Twist wing tips under back.

Place poultry, breast-side up, on a rack in a shallow roasting pan. Brush skin, except for duck, with cooking oil or melted butter. (Prick skin of domestic duck well all over to allow fat to escape. During roasting, remove excess fat.) Insert a meat thermometer. Roast chicken, uncovered, in a 375° oven for 1¼ to 1½ hours. (Roast domestic duck 1¾ to 2¼ hours; wild goose 2¼ to 2¾ hours.)

Meanwhile, in a covered saucepan cook potatoes and carrots in boiling salted water for 20 to 25 minutes or till nearly tender. Drain. The last 20 minutes of roasting time, discard any fat in roasting pan from poultry. Arrange vegetables and the uncooked apples around poultry in pan. Spoon honey mixture over poultry, vegetables, and apples. Roast about 20 minutes longer or till meat thermometer registers 185° and vegetables and apples are tender. Baste occasionally with honey mixture during roasting and again just before serving. Arrange poultry, vegetables, and apples on a serving platter. Makes 6 servings.

# Roasting Domestic Birds

| Poultry | Ready-to-Cook Weight | Oven Temp. | Guide Roasting Time | Special Instructions |
|---|---|---|---|---|
| **Chicken** | 1½-2 lbs. | 400° | 1-1¼ hrs. | Brush dry areas of skin occasionally with pan drippings. Cover chicken loosely with foil. |
| | 2½-3 lbs. | 375° | 1¼-1½ hrs. | |
| | 3½-4 lbs. | 375° | 1¾-2 hrs. | |
| | 4½-5 lbs. | 375° | 2¼-2½ hrs. | |
| **Capon** | 4-7 lbs. | 375° | 2-3 hrs. | Brush the dry areas with pan drippings. Roast as above. |
| **Cornish Game Hen** | 1-1½ lbs. | 375° | 1½ hrs. | Cover loosely with foil and roast for ½ hour. Uncover and roast about 1 hour or till done. If desired, baste occasionally the last hour. |
| **Turkey** | 6-8 lbs. | 325° | 3½-4 hrs. | Cover bird *loosely* with foil. Press lightly at the end of drumsticks and neck; leave an air space between bird and foil. Baste bird occasionally, if desired. Uncover the last 45 minutes of roasting. |
| | 8-12 lbs. | 325° | 4-4½ hrs. | |
| | 12-16 lbs. | 325° | 4½-5½ hrs. | |
| | 16-20 lbs. | 325° | 5½-6½ hrs. | |
| | 20-24 lbs. | 325° | 6½-7½ hrs. | |

| Poultry | Ready-to-Cook Weight | Oven Temp. | Guide Roasting Time | Special Instructions |
|---|---|---|---|---|
| **Foil-Wrapped Turkey** | 7-9 lbs. | 450° | 2¼-2½ hrs. | Place turkey, breast up, in the center of greased, wide, heavy foil. Bring ends of foil up over breast; overlap fold and press up against end of turkey. Place bird in a shallow roasting pan (no rack). Open foil for the last 20 minutes to brown the turkey. |
| | 10-13 lbs. | 450° | 2¾-3 hrs. | |
| | 14-17 lbs. | 450° | 3-3¼ hrs. | |
| | 18-21 lbs. | 450° | 3¼-3½ hrs. | |
| | 22-24 lbs. | 450° | 3¼-3¾ hrs. | |
| **Domestic Duckling** | 3-5 lbs. | 375° | 1½-2¼ hrs. | Prick skin well all over. During roasting, spoon off excess fat. Do not rub with oil. |
| **Domestic Goose** | 7-9 lbs. | 350° | 2½-3 hrs. | Prick skin well all over. During roasting, spoon off excess fat. Do not rub with oil. |
| | 9-11 lbs. | 350° | 3-3½ hrs. | |
| | 11-13 lbs. | 350° | 3½-4 hrs. | |
| **Guinea Hen** | 1½-2 lbs. | 375° | ¾-1 hr. | Lay bacon over breast. Roast, loosely covered with foil. Uncover guinea hen the last 20 minutes. |
| | 2-2½ lbs. | 375° | 1-1½ hrs. | |

**Preparation for roasting:** Rinse bird and pat dry with paper toweling. Rub inside of cavities with salt, if desired. Do not stuff the bird until just before cooking.

To stuff bird, spoon some of the stuffing loosely into the neck cavity; pull the neck skin to the back of the bird and fasten securely with a small skewer. Lightly spoon remaining stuffing into the body cavity. If the opening has a band of skin across the tail, tuck the drumsticks under the band; if the band of skin is not present, tie legs securely to the tail. Twist wing tips under back.

For an unstuffed bird, place quartered onions and celery in the body cavity, if desired. Prepare and roast. Discard vegetables after roasting bird, if desired.

**Roasting directions:** Place bird, breast-side up, on a rack in a shallow roasting pan. Brush skin of bird, *except* duckling and goose, with cooking oil. If a meat thermometer is used, insert it in the center of the inside thigh muscle, making sure the bulb does not touch bone.

Roast in an uncovered pan (unless specified) according to the chart at left. When bird is two-thirds done, cut the band of skin or string between the legs so thighs will cook evenly. Continue roasting until bird is done. Remove bird from oven; cover loosely with foil to keep warm. Let stand 15 minutes before carving.

**Test for doneness:** The meat thermometer inserted in the thigh should register 185°. Also, the thickest part of the drumstick should feel very soft when pressed between the fingers. The drumstick also should move up and down and twist easily in the socket. Remember, each bird differs in size, shape, or variety. Because of these differences, roasting times can be only approximate.

**To roast turkey in a covered roasting pan:** Rinse turkey and pat dry. Stuff, if desired; prepare for roasting as directed in the chart at left. Place turkey, breast side up, on a rack in a roasting pan. Brush bird with cooking oil or melted butter. Insert a meat thermometer in the center of the inside thigh muscle; make sure bulb does not touch bone. Do not add water. Cover pan with a lid or cover *tightly* with foil. Roast bird in a 350° oven till about three-quarters done (allow about 3 hours for an 11- to 12-pound turkey). Remove cover; cut the band of skin or string between the legs. Baste turkey with pan drippings. Continue roasting, uncovered, till done. When the bird is done, the meat thermometer should register 185° and drumstick should twist easily in socket. Turkey will not be as golden as when roasted loosely covered.

**To roast turkey in a commercial cooking bag:** Rinse turkey and pat dry. Stuff, if desired; prepare for roasting as directed at left. Place 1 tablespoon all-purpose *flour* in the commercial cooking bag; shake to coat interior. Place bag in a large roasting pan. Brush turkey with cooking oil or melted butter. Place turkey inside bag, breast side up. Close bag loosely with a twist tie. Make six ½-inch slits in the top of the bag to allow steam to escape. Roast according to manufacturer's directions. About 15 minutes before roasting time is up, cut the bag open. Insert a meat thermometer in the center of the inside thigh muscle of turkey, making sure bulb does not touch bone. When turkey is done, the meat thermometer should register 185° and drumstick should move up and down and twist easily in socket.

**Carving:** 1) Remove the bird from the oven and let stand 15 minutes before carving; cover to keep warm. Place bird on a carving board. Grasp the leg with your fingers; pull leg away from body. Cut through the meat between thigh and body. With the tip of the knife, disjoint the thigh bone from the backbone. 2) Holding the leg vertically, with large end down, slice meat parallel to the bone and under some tendons, turning the leg for even slices. *Or,* first separate the thigh and drumstick. Slice thigh meat by cutting slices parallel to the bone. 3) Before carving the white meat, make a deep horizontal cut into the breast close to the wing. Note that the wing tips have been twisted under the back before roasting so that carving can be done without removing wings. 4) Cut thin slices from the top of the breast down to the horizontal cut. Final smaller slices can follow the curve of the breastbone. Turn the bird and repeat each step to carve the other side of the bird.

---

# Chicken with Currant Glaze

|   |   |
|---|---|
| **1** | **3-pound whole roasting chicken** |
|   | **Cooking oil** |
| **⅓** | **cup red currant *or* raspberry jelly** |
| **2** | **tablespoons lemon juice** |
| **1** | **tablespoon butter *or* margarine** |
| **¼** | **teaspoon salt** |
|   | **Dash ground cinnamon** |
| **1** | **tablespoon cold water** |
| **2** | **teaspoons cornstarch** | Oven 375° |

Thoroughly rinse chicken; pat dry with paper toweling. Place chicken, breast side up, on a rack in a shallow roasting pan. Rub skin with oil. Insert a meat thermometer in the center of the inside thigh muscle but not touching bone. Roast, uncovered, in a 375° oven for 1¼ to 1½ hours or till thermometer registers 185°. In a small saucepan over low heat stir together jelly, lemon juice, butter or margarine, salt, and cinnamon till jelly melts. Combine water and cornstarch; stir into jelly mixture. Cook and stir over medium heat till thickened and bubbly. Cook and stir 1 to 2 minutes more. Brush on chicken several times during the last 15 minutes or roasting. Makes 6 servings.

## Roast Tarragon Chicken

| | |
|---|---|
| 1 | **3-pound broiler-fryer chicken** |
| 2 | **tablespoons lemon juice** |
| 2 | **tablespoons butter _or_ margarine** |
| 1½ | **teaspoons dried tarragon, crushed** |

Oven 375°

Brush chicken with lemon juice inside and out; rub with ½ teaspoon _salt_. Skewer neck skin to back; tie legs to tail. Twist wings under back. Place, breast side up, on a rack in a shallow roasting pan. Melt butter; stir in tarragon. Brush over chicken. Roast, uncovered, in a 375° oven for 1¼ to 1½ hours or till done. Baste occasionally with drippings. Serves 6.

## Golden Stuffed Cornish Hens

<pre>
  6  slices bacon
  1  cup finely chopped carrot
 ¼   cup snipped parsley
  1  teaspoon snipped fresh savory or ¼
       teaspoon dried savory, crushed
  3  cups dry bread cubes (4 slices)
 ½   teaspoon instant chicken bouillon granules
 ¼   cup hot water
  4  1- to 1½-pound Cornish game hens
     Cooking oil
 ½   cup dry red wine
  2  tablespoons butter or margarine, melted
  3  tablespoons orange juice
  2  tablespoons cornstarch
  2  tablespoons brown sugar
  1  teaspoon instant chicken bouillon granules
 ¼   teaspoon salt                          Oven 375°
</pre>

Cook bacon till crisp; drain, reserving 2 tablespoons drippings. Crumble bacon; set aside. Cook carrot in reserved drippings till tender; remove from heat. Stir in bacon, parsley, savory, and dash *pepper*. Stir in bread cubes. Dissolve ½ teaspoon bouillon granules in hot water; drizzle over bread mixture. Toss.

Season cavities of hens with salt. Lightly stuff hens with bread mixture. Pull neck skin, if present, to back of each hen. Twist wing tips under back, holding skin in place. Tie legs to tail. Place hens, breast side up, on a rack in a shallow roasting pan. Brush with cooking oil; cover loosely with foil. Roast in a 375° oven for 30 minutes.

Combine wine, melted butter, and orange juice. Uncover birds; brush with wine mixture. Roast, uncovered, about 1 hour longer or till drumstick can be twisted easily in socket, brushing with wine mixture once or twice. Remove to a warm serving platter; keep warm.

Pour drippings into a large measuring cup. Skim fat from pan drippings; stir in remaining wine mixture. Add water, if necessary, to make 1½ cups liquid. For sauce, in a small saucepan combine cornstarch, brown sugar, 1 teaspoon bouillon granules, and salt. Add cooking liquid all at once. Cook and stir till thickened and bubbly. Cook and stir 1 to 2 minutes more. Pass sauce with Cornish hens. Serves 8.

# Stuffings & Gravies

## Harvest Stuffing

- **1 cup shredded carrot**
- **1 cup chopped celery**
- **½ cup chopped onion**
- **½ cup butter or margarine**
- **1 teaspoon ground sage or poultry seasoning**
- **½ teaspoon salt**
- **¼ teaspoon ground cinnamon**
- **8 cups dry bread cubes**
- **2 cups finely chopped, peeled apple**
- **½ cup chopped walnuts**
- **¼ cup wheat germ**
- **½ to ¾ cup chicken broth**

In a skillet cook carrot, celery, and onion in butter or margarine till tender but not brown. Stir in sage or poultry seasoning, salt, cinnamon, and ⅛ teaspoon *pepper*. In a large mixing bowl combine bread cubes, chopped apple, walnuts, and wheat germ. Add cooked vegetable mixture. Drizzle with enough chicken broth to moisten, tossing lightly. Use to stuff one 10-pound turkey. Makes 10 servings.

## Old-Fashioned Bread Stuffing

> 1 **cup finely chopped celery**
> ½ **cup chopped onion**
> ½ **cup butter or margarine**
> 1 **teaspoon poultry seasoning or sage**
> ½ **teaspoon salt**
> ⅛ **teaspoon pepper**
> 8 **cups dry bread cubes**
> ¾ **to 1 cup chicken broth or water**

In a saucepan cook celery and onion in butter till tender but not brown; remove from heat and stir in poultry seasoning or sage, salt, and pepper. Place the dry bread cubes in a large mixing bowl. Add the onion mixture. Drizzle with enough broth or water to moisten, tossing lightly. Use to stuff one 10-pound turkey. Makes 8 to 10 servings.

*Mushroom Stuffing:* Prepare Old-Fashioned Bread Stuffing as above, *except* add two 4-ounce cans sliced *mushrooms,* drained, with the seasonings, *or* 1 cup sliced fresh *mushrooms* cooked with the celery-onion mixture.

*Raisin Stuffing:* Prepare Old-Fashioned Bread Stuffing as above, *except* add ¾ cup *raisins* with the seasonings.

*Giblet Stuffing:* Prepare Old-Fashioned Bread Stuffing as above, *except* use the *poultry giblets and neck.* Remove liver from giblets; set aside. In a small saucepan cover the giblets and neck with lightly salted water. Cover; simmer for 1 hour or till tender. Add the liver and simmer 5 to 10 minutes more. (Turkey livers may take 20 to 30 minutes to cook.) Cooking water may be reserved, if desired, and substituted for part of the broth or water. Chop the giblets and liver. Remove as much meat as possible from the neck bone; chop meat, discarding bones. Add chopped meats with the seasonings.

*Oyster Stuffing:* Prepare Old-Fashioned Bread Stuffing as above, *except* add 1 pint shucked *oysters,* drained and chopped, *or* two 8-ounce cans whole *oysters,* drained and chopped, with the seasonings. Reserve the drained oyster liquid, if desired, and substitute it for the chicken broth or water.

*Chestnut Stuffing:* Prepare Old-Fashioned Bread Stuffing as above, *except* slash shells of 1 pound fresh *chestnuts* (3 cups) with a sharp knife. Roast chestnuts on a baking sheet in a 400° oven for 15 minutes; cool. Peel and coarsely chop. Add with seasonings.

---

## Poultry choices for stuffings

Halve the recipe ingredients from Harvest Stuffing, Old-Fashioned Bread Stuffing, or Corn-Bread and Bacon Stuffing to use with one 5-pound whole roasting chicken or domestic duckling; *or* two 2- to 3-pound wild geese; *or* three 2-pound pheasants or wild ducks; *or* six 1- to 1½-pound Cornish game hens; *or* eight 4- to 6-ounce quail. Bake remaining stuffing, covered, in a 375° oven in a 2-quart casserole the last 20 to 30 minutes of roasting. (For turkey, bake in a 325° oven for 40 to 45 minutes.)

---

## Corn Bread and Bacon Stuffing

**Corn Bread (see recipe, page 155)**
**6  slices bread**
**6  bacon slices**
**1  cup chopped celery with leaves**
**1  cup chopped onion**
**2  beaten eggs**
**2  tablespoons snipped parsley**
**1  teaspoon poultry seasoning**
**¼  teaspoon salt**
**1  cup chicken broth**                    Oven 350°

Prepare Corn Bread; cool. Coarsely crumble enough corn bread to make 3 cups. Toast the bread slices; cut into cubes. Set aside.

In a skillet cook bacon till crisp; crumble and set aside. Cook celery and onion in the bacon drippings till tender but not brown.

In a mixing bowl combine eggs, crumbled bacon, cooked celery and onion, snipped parsley, poultry seasoning, and salt. Add crumbled corn bread and toasted bread cubes; toss lightly till well mixed. Add enough of the chicken broth to moisten; toss gently to mix. Bake, uncovered, in an ungreased 1½-quart casserole in a 350° oven for about 30 minutes. (*Or*, do not bake stuffing. Instead, use to stuff one 8-pound turkey or domestic goose.) Makes 6 to 8 servings.

## Cream Gravy for Fried Poultry

    **Fried poultry**
  **3**  **tablespoons fried poultry drippings**
 **¾**  **cup milk**
  **3**  **tablespoons all-purpose flour**
  **1**  **teaspoon salt**
    **Dash pepper**
 **¾**  **cup milk**

Remove fried poultry to a platter; keep warm. Reserve 3 tablespoons of the drippings in the skillet. In a screw-top jar combine the ¾ cup milk, flour, salt, and pepper; shake till well combined. Stir into drippings in the skillet. Stir in ¾ cup milk. Cook over medium heat, stirring constantly, till thickened and bubbly. Cook and stir 1 to 2 minutes more. If necessary, thin with a little additional milk. Makes 1½ cups.

## Pan Gravy for Roast Poultry

    **Roast poultry**
    **Hot drippings**
 **¼**  **cup all-purpose flour**
  **2**  **cups water or chicken broth**

Remove roast poultry to a serving platter; keep warm. Leaving crusty bits in the roasting pan, pour pan drippings into a large measuring cup. Skim off and reserve fat from the pan drippings. (To skim the fat from the drippings, tilt the measuring cup and spoon off the oily liquid that rises to the top.) Return ¼ *cup* of the fat to the roasting pan; discard any remaining. Stir in flour. Cook and stir over medium heat till bubbly. Remove pan from heat. Add enough water or chicken broth to the drippings in the liquid measuring cup to equal 2 cups total liquid. Add all at once to flour mixture in pan. Cook and stir till thickened and bubbly. Cook and stir 1 to 2 minutes more. Season to taste. Makes 2 cups.

## Giblet Gravy

|       |                                                |
| ----- | ---------------------------------------------- |
| ½     | **pound chicken *or* turkey giblets and neck** |
|       | **Celery leaves (optional)**                   |
|       | **Onion slices (optional)**                    |
| ½     | **cup all-purpose flour**                      |
|       | **Dash pepper**                                |
| 2     | **hard-cooked eggs, chopped (optional)**       |

Remove liver and set aside. In a saucepan place the giblets and neck in lightly salted water to cover; add a few celery leaves and onion slices, if desired. Cover; simmer for 1 hour or till tender. Add the liver, simmer 5 to 10 minutes or till tender (turkey livers will take 20 to 30 minutes). Remove and chop the cooked giblets. Discard neck.

For gravy, add enough water to reserved broth to measure 3 cups. (If making gravy with a roasting bird, add enough reserved broth to drippings from roast bird to measure 3 cups.) In a screw-top jar combine *1 cup* of the broth mixture, flour, and pepper; shake well. In a saucepan combine flour mixture and remaining broth. Cook and stir till thickened and bubbly. Cook and stir 1 to 2 minutes more. Stir in chopped giblets. If desired, stir in hard-cooked eggs. Heat through. Makes 3½ to 4 cups.

**Rice, Pasta,
& Cereal**

**Rice, Pasta,
& Cereal**

**Rice, Pasta,
& Cereal**

**Rice, Pasta,
& Cereal**

**Rice, Pasta,
& Cereal**

**Rice, Pasta,**

# Rice, Pasta, & Cereal

| Recipes | Servings (fraction of recipe) | Calories | Protein (grams) | Carbohydrate (grams) | Fat (grams) | Sodium (milligrams) | Potassium (milligrams) | Percent of U.S. RDA Per Serving | | | | | | | |
|---|---|---|---|---|---|---|---|---|---|---|---|---|---|---|---|
| | | | | | | | | Protein | Vitamin A | Vitamin C | Thiamine | Riboflavin | Niacin | Calcium | Iron |
| Baked Gnocchi | 1/6 | 359 | 14 | 23 | 23 | 754 | 240 | 21 | 21 | 2 | 10 | 24 | 5 | 42 | 55 |
| Brown Rice | 1/6 | 111 | 2 | 24 | 2 | 269 | 66 | 4 | 0 | 0 | 7 | 1 | 7 | 1 | 3 |
| Bulgur Sauté | 1/6 | 141 | 4 | 23 | 4 | 258 | 112 | 6 | 6 | 6 | 6 | 3 | 6 | 2 | 7 |
| Chinese Fried Rice | 1/4 | 340 | 12 | 37 | 12 | 1575 | 213 | 19 | 8 | 4 | 21 | 12 | 12 | 5 | 19 |
| Confetti Rice | 1/10 | 95 | 2 | 19 | 2 | 243 | 70 | 3 | 28 | 4 | 8 | 1 | 5 | 1 | 5 |
| Cornmeal Mush | 1/4 | 108 | 3 | 22 | 3 | 533 | 87 | 4 | 3 | 0 | 8 | 2 | 2 | 1 | 4 |
| Cottage Pasta Bake | 1/6 | 237 | 11 | 18 | 11 | 364 | 144 | 18 | 10 | 10 | 8 | 8 | 15 | 4 | 4 |
| Curried Bulgur Sauté | 1/6 | 141 | 4 | 23 | 4 | 258 | 112 | 6 | 6 | 6 | 6 | 3 | 6 | 2 | 7 |
| Curried Rice | 1/6 | 233 | 5 | 34 | 5 | 308 | 159 | 7 | 4 | 2 | 13 | 3 | 7 | 2 | 9 |
| Fried Mush | 1/6 | 106 | 2 | 15 | 2 | 402 | 59 | 3 | 5 | 0 | 5 | 1 | 1 | 2 | 3 |
| Fruit and Nut Brown Rice | 1/6 | 231 | 4 | 35 | 4 | 319 | 230 | 6 | 7 | 6 | 10 | 6 | 9 | 4 | 7 |
| Granola | 1/6 | 613 | 13 | 71 | 13 | 23 | 653 | 21 | 24 | 4 | 34 | 14 | 14 | 9 | 25 |
| Green Noodles | 1/7 | 95 | 4 | 17 | 4 | 168 | 77 | 6 | 18 | 8 | 11 | 8 | 6 | 2 | 6 |
| Grits | 1/4 | 145 | 3 | 31 | 3 | 533 | 32 | 5 | 4 | 0 | 12 | 6 | 6 | 1 | 6 |
| Herbed Rice | 1/6 | 130 | 3 | 25 | 2 | 363 | 30 | 3 | 2 | 0 | 9 | 1 | 5 | 5 | 5 |
| Homemade Noodles | 1/6 | 93 | 3 | 16 | 3 | 191 | 38 | 5 | 2 | 0 | 10 | 7 | 6 | 6 | 4 |
| Mushroom-Cereal Bake | 1/8 | 257 | 9 | 19 | 9 | 569 | 330 | 14 | 18 | 8 | 6 | 6 | 21 | 7 | 6 |
| Mushroom-Rice Bake | 1/8 | 289 | 9 | 26 | 9 | 723 | 307 | 14 | 18 | 8 | 10 | 10 | 21 | 8 | 8 |
| Oven Rice | 1/6 | 129 | 2 | 25 | 2 | 380 | 29 | 3 | 2 | 0 | 9 | 1 | 5 | 5 | 5 |
| Parsley Rice | 1/6 | 130 | 2 | 25 | 2 | 381 | 47 | 3 | 6 | 7 | 9 | 1 | 6 | 6 | 6 |

# Nutrition Analysis Chart

| | | | | | | | | | | | | | | | |
|---|---|---|---|---|---|---|---|---|---|---|---|---|---|---|---|
| Pasta, Cooking | 1/8 | 105 | 4 | 21 | 0 | 1 | 56 | 5 | 0 | 0 | 17 | 6 | 9 | 1 | 5 |
| Pasta with Carbonara Sauce | 1/12 | 293 | 12 | 30 | 14 | 201 | 140 | 19 | 13 | 4 | 15 | 14 | 8 | 14 | 10 |
| Pasta with Pesto | 1/8 | 286 | 8 | 34 | 13 | 43 | 193 | 13 | 20 | 32 | 15 | 10 | 8 | 10 | 11 |
| Polenta | 1/6 | 72 | 2 | 15 | 1 | 355 | 58 | 3 | 2 | 0 | 5 | 1 | 2 | 1 | 3 |
| Rice, Cooking | 1/6 | 129 | 2 | 25 | 2 | 380 | 29 | 3 | 2 | 0 | 9 | 1 | 5 | 1 | 5 |
| Skillet Barley | 1/6 | 125 | 2 | 20 | 4 | 306 | 61 | 4 | 5 | 5 | 2 | 1 | 4 | 1 | 3 |
| Southern Cheese Grits | 1/8 | 273 | 8 | 16 | 19 | 663 | 52 | 13 | 19 | 0 | 7 | 10 | 4 | 16 | 6 |
| Spaetzle | 1/8 | 224 | 7 | 30 | 9 | 410 | 90 | 10 | 8 | 0 | 16 | 13 | 10 | 5 | 8 |
| Spaghetti with Marinara Sauce | 1/8 | 195 | 6 | 34 | 4 | 536 | 582 | 9 | 76 | 62 | 16 | 9 | 13 | 3 | 11 |
| Spanish Rice | 1/6 | 217 | 5 | 29 | 9 | 648 | 393 | 8 | 29 | 67 | 15 | 6 | 11 | 3 | 11 |
| Spiced Porridge | 1/2 | 355 | 11 | 65 | 7 | 442 | 565 | 16 | 5 | 4 | 15 | 25 | 7 | 39 | 77 |
| Spicy Raisin Oatmeal | 1/4 | 222 | 5 | 49 | 2 | 543 | 382 | 8 | 0 | 1 | 15 | 4 | 2 | 4 | 15 |
| Toasted Barley Bake | 1/6 | 125 | 2 | 20 | 4 | 306 | 61 | 4 | 5 | 5 | 2 | 1 | 1 | 2 | 3 |
| Whole Wheat Noodles | 1/6 | 88 | 4 | 15 | 1 | 191 | 65 | 6 | 2 | 0 | 9 | 5 | 5 | 2 | 5 |
| Wild Rice | 1/6 | 108 | 5 | 21 | 1 | 355 | 59 | 8 | 0 | 0 | 8 | 10 | 12 | 2 | 6 |
| Wild Rice with Mushrooms | 1/6 | 163 | 6 | 22 | 6 | 408 | 126 | 10 | 2 | 3 | 11 | 14 | 15 | 1 | 7 |

# Pasta

Dozens of varieties of pasta are available both at the supermarket and at import shops. Some pieces are especially suited for stuffing, while other pastas carry sauces and blend well in casseroles. The tiniest ones make a pleasant addition to soups. Many of these varieties are shown on pages 639 and 640.

For best eating, pasta should be cooked to the point Italians call al dente (to the tooth), when the pasta is still a bit firm, but no longer starchy. The best way to test pasta for doneness is to taste it. When done, drain it immediately to prevent further cooking.

If you need to keep pasta hot for a short time, return drained pasta to the empty cooking pan, add a little butter, and cover with a lid. For longer periods, place the colander of pasta over a pan containing a small amount of boiling water. Coat pasta with a little butter to keep it from sticking, and cover the colander.

Reduce the cooking time by ⅓ for pasta that will be cooked again in a casserole. Plan to serve about 1 ounce of pasta per serving for a side dish and about 2 ounces for a main dish.

## Cooking Pasta

In a large kettle or Dutch oven bring 3 quarts water and 1 tablespoon salt to a rolling boil. If desired, add 1 tablespoon cooking oil to help keep the pasta separated. When the water boils, add 8 ounces pasta a little at a time so water does not stop boiling. (Hold long pasta, such as spaghetti, at one end and dip the other end into the water. As the pasta softens, gently curl it around in the pan till completely immersed.) Reduce heat slightly and continue boiling, uncovered, till pasta is tender but still slightly firm. Stir occasionally to prevent sticking. Taste often to test for doneness.

Cook very thin pasta (vermicelli and ancini de pepe) for 5 to 6 minutes. Cook medium-thin pasta (medium noodles, spaghetti, linguine, lasagne, and elbow macaroni) for 9 to 12 minutes. Medium-thick pasta (rigatoni, mostaccioli, and ziti) requires 14 to 15 minutes of cooking. Very thick pasta varieties (manicotti and jumbo shell macaroni) need 18 to 25 minutes of cooking time.

Immediately drain pasta in a colander; *do not rinse*. Transfer to a warm serving dish; serve at once. Makes about 4 cups cooked pasta.

---

# Homemade Noodles

- **1   beaten egg**
- **2   tablespoons milk**
- **½   teaspoon salt**
- **1   cup all-purpose flour**

In a mixing bowl combine egg, milk, and salt. Stir in enough of the flour to make a stiff dough. Cover and let rest for 10 minutes.

On a floured surface roll dough into a 16x12-inch rectangle. Let stand 20 minutes. Roll up loosely; cut into ¼-inch-thick slices. Unroll; cut into desired lengths. Spread out and let dry on a rack 2 hours. Store in an airtight container till ready to use.

Drop noodles into a large amount of boiling salted water or soup. Cook, uncovered, 10 to 12 minutes or till done. Makes about 3 cups.

**Whole Wheat Noodles:** Prepare Homemade Noodles as above, *except* substitute ½ cup *whole wheat flour* for ½ cup of the all-purpose flour. Continue as directed.

**Green Noodles:** In a saucepan combine 1¼ cups torn *spinach* leaves and 2 tablespoons *water*. Cover and cook till spinach is very tender. Cool slightly; place spinach and liquid in a blender container. Add 1 *egg* and ½ teaspoon *salt;* cover and blend till smooth. Transfer mixture to a bowl. Add about 1¼ cups all-purpose *flour* to make a stiff dough. Knead dough on a lightly floured surface for 1 minute. Roll out very thin; let stand, roll up, cut into slices, dry, and cook as directed above. Makes about 3½ cups.

## Spaetzle

    2   cups all-purpose flour
    1   teaspoon salt
    2   eggs
    ¾   cup milk
    ½   cup fine dry bread crumbs
    ¼   cup butter or margarine, melted

Stir together flour and salt. Combine eggs and milk; stir into the flour mixture. Pour batter into a colander with large holes (at least ³⁄₁₆-inch diameter) or spaetzle maker. Hold colander over a kettle of boiling salted water. Press batter through the colander to form the spaetzle. Cook and stir 5 minutes. Drain well. Combine the bread crumbs and melted butter or margarine; sprinkle over spaetzle. Makes 4 cups.

## Cottage Pasta Bake

    4   ounces fine noodles or medium noodles or
        elbow macaroni
    ¼   cup finely chopped onion
    1   clove garlic, minced
    1   tablespoon butter or margarine
 1½   cups cream-style cottage cheese
    1   cup dairy sour cream
    2   teaspoons poppy seed
    1   teaspoon Worcestershire sauce
    ½   teaspoon salt
        Dash pepper
        Dash bottled hot pepper sauce
        Paprika
        Grated Parmesan cheese
        (optional)                          Oven 350°

Cook noodles in a large amount of boiling salted water till tender; drain well. Cook onion and garlic in hot butter till tender. Combine noodles and onion mixture. Stir in cottage cheese, sour cream, poppy seed, Worcestershire sauce, salt, pepper, and hot pepper sauce. Turn into a 10x6x2-inch baking dish. Bake in a 350° oven 25 to 30 minutes or till hot. Sprinkle with paprika; pass Parmesan cheese, if desired. Makes 6 side-dish servings.

## Spaghetti with Marinara Sauce

> 1 **large onion, chopped**
> 2 **medium carrots, finely chopped**
> 2 **cloves garlic, minced**
> 2 **tablespoons cooking oil**
> 2 **28-ounce cans tomatoes, cut up**
> 1 **teaspoon sugar**
> 1 **teaspoon salt**
> 1 **teaspoon dried oregano, crushed**
> **Dash pepper**
> **Dash crushed red pepper**
> 8 **ounces spaghetti, linguine, *or* other pasta**

In a 3-quart saucepan cook onion, carrots, and garlic in hot oil till tender but not brown. Add *undrained* tomatoes, sugar, salt, oregano, pepper, and red pepper. Bring to boiling; reduce heat. Simmer, uncovered, for 45 to 60 minutes or to desired consistency.

Cook pasta in a large amount of boiling salted water till tender; drain well. Serve with tomato mixture. Makes 8 side-dish servings.

## Pasta with Pesto

*Try pesto on soups, vegetables, fish, or meats—*
> 1 **cup firmly packed snipped fresh basil**
> ½ **cup snipped parsley**
> ½ **cup grated Parmesan *or* Romano cheese (2 ounces)**
> ¼ **cup pine nuts, walnuts, *or* almonds**
> 1 **to 2 cloves garlic, quartered**
> ⅓ **cup olive oil *or* cooking oil**
> 12 **ounces spaghetti *or* other pasta**

Place basil, parsley, cheese, nuts, garlic, and ¼ teaspoon *salt* in a blender container or food processor bowl. Cover and blend or process with several on/off turns till a paste forms. With machine running slowly, gradually add oil and blend or process to the consistency of soft butter. Refrigerate or freeze till ready to use.

Thaw pesto, if frozen. Cook pasta in a large amount of boiling salted water; drain well. Toss pesto with hot, cooked pasta; serve immediately. Makes 8 to 12 side-dish servings.

---

## Pasta with Carbonara Sauce

- **4 eggs**
- **¼ cup butter *or* margarine**
- **¼ cup whipping cream**
- **½ pound bacon, cut up**
- **1 pound fettucine *or* spaghetti**
- **1 cup grated Parmesan *or* Romano cheese (4 ounces)**
- **¼ cup snipped parsley**
- **Pepper**                                   Oven 250°

Let eggs; butter or margarine, and cream stand at room temperature for 2 to 3 hours. In a skillet cook bacon till brown. Remove bacon and drain on paper toweling.

Heat an ovenproof serving dish in a 250° oven. Meanwhile, beat together eggs and cream just till combined. Add pasta to a large amount of boiling salted water. Cook 10 to 12 minutes or till tender but firm; drain well.

Turn hot pasta into the heated serving dish; toss pasta with butter. Pour egg mixture over and toss till pasta is well coated. Add bacon, cheese, and parsley; toss to mix. Season to taste with pepper. Serve immediately. Makes 12 side-dish servings.

# Pasta

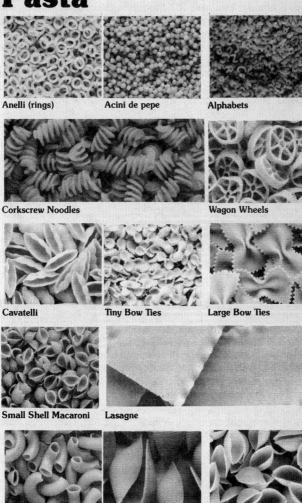

Anelli (rings)     Acini de pepe     Alphabets

Corkscrew Noodles                    Wagon Wheels

Cavatelli     Tiny Bow Ties     Large Bow Ties

Small Shell Macaroni     Lasagne

Elbow Macaroni     Jumbo Shell Macaroni     Large Shell Macaroni

Manicotti

Mostaccioli

Rigatoni

Ravioli

Spaghetti

Ziti

Nested Vermicelli

Fettucine

Linguine

Fusilli

Fine Noodles

Medium Noodles

Wide Noodles

# Rice

Of the many types of rice, regular milled rice is the most familiar. Its husk is removed, then the grain is cleaned and polished. Parboiled rice keeps more of its nutrients because it is steamed under pressure before milling. Quick-cooking rice is precooked then dehydrated, and requires less time to cook. Brown rice retains more fiber and nutrients than milled rice because less of the bran is removed. It must cook longer and remains chewy when done, although quick-cooking brown rice also is available. Slender, dark grains of wild rice have a nutty flavor and require longer cooking, too. Some rice varieties are shown on page 646.

To test rice for doneness, pinch a grain between your thumb and forefinger. If there's no hard core, the rice is done.

Cooked rice may be frozen or refrigerated. To reheat, add about 2 tablespoons water for each cup of cooked rice. Cover; simmer till hot.

## Oven Rice

    **1  tablespoon butter or margarine**
**2¼  cups boiling water**
    **1  cup long grain rice**
    **1  teaspoon salt**               Oven 350°

In a 1½-quart casserole stir butter into boiling water till melted. Add rice and salt. Cover; bake in a 350° oven 35 minutes or till done. Fluff with a fork after 15 minutes. Serves 6.

## Brown Rice

**2¼  cups water**
    **1  cup brown rice**
    **¾  teaspoon salt**

In a 2-quart saucepan mix water, rice, and salt. Bring to boiling. Reduce heat. Cover; simmer 40 to 50 minutes or till water is absorbed. (Rice will be chewy.) Serves 6.

***Fruit and Nut Brown Rice:*** Prepare Brown Rice as above. Meanwhile, in a skillet cook 1 large *apple,* peeled and chopped; ½ cup sliced *green onion;* and ½ cup sliced *almonds* in 2 tablespoons *butter or margarine* till onion is tender and almonds are toasted. Stir in ¼ cup *raisins* and ¼ teaspoon ground *cinnamon.* Toss with cooked rice. Serves 6.

## Cooking Rice

- **2 cups cold water**
- **1 cup long grain rice**
- **1 tablespoon butter or margarine**

In a saucepan mix water, rice, butter, and 1 teaspoon *salt.* Cover with a tight-fitting lid. Bring to boiling; reduce heat. Cook 15 minutes; do not lift cover. Remove from heat. Let stand, covered, for 10 minutes. Serves 6.

**Microwave directions:** In a 2-quart nonmetal casserole mix water, rice, and 1 teaspoon *salt.* Cook in a counter-top microwave oven on high power 6 minutes or till boiling. Stir; cover. Micro-cook 5 minutes. Stir; micro-cook, covered, 3 minutes longer. Stir; add butter. Cover and let stand several minutes.

***Parsley Rice:*** Prepare rice as above, *except* stir ¼ cup snipped *parsley* into cooked rice.

***Confetti Rice:*** Prepare rice as above, *except* cook one 10-ounce package frozen *mixed vegetables* according to package directions; drain well. Stir vegetables and ½ teaspoon dried *dillweed* into cooked rice. Serves 10.

***Herbed Rice:*** Prepare rice as above, *except* before cooking add 2 teaspoons instant *chicken bouillon granules* and 1 teaspoon dried *thyme,* crushed; decrease salt to ½ teaspoon.

**Note:** Prepare a rice ring with any above variation by pressing hot rice into a buttered 5½-cup ring mold. Unmold at once.

# Wild Rice

*Increase salt to ½ teaspoon when using water—*

> **1** **cup wild rice**
> **2** **cups chicken broth *or* water**
> **¼** **teaspoon salt**

Run cold water over rice in a strainer about 1 minute, lifting rice to rinse well. In a saucepan combine rice, chicken broth, and salt. Bring to boiling. Reduce heat. Cover; simmer 40 to 50 minutes or till done and most of the liquid is absorbed. Fluff with a fork. Serves 6.

**Wild Rice with Mushrooms:** Prepare Wild Rice as above. Meanwhile, cook 2 slices *bacon,* cut up; 1 cup sliced fresh *mushrooms;* ¼ cup sliced *green onion;* and ¼ teaspoon dried *thyme,* crushed, till bacon is done and mushrooms are tender. Stir into rice. Garnish with snipped parsley, if desired.

# Curried Rice

> **¼** **cup chopped onion**
> **¼** **cup thinly sliced celery**
> **2** **to 3 teaspoons curry powder**
> **2** **tablespoons butter or margarine**
> **1** **cup long grain rice**
> **2** **cups water**
> **¼** **cup raisins**
> **2** **teaspoons instant beef bouillon granules**
> **¼** **teaspoon salt**
> **½** **cup coarsely chopped cashews**

In a 2-quart saucepan cook onion, celery, and curry powder in butter or margarine till celery is tender but not brown. Add rice. Stir in water, raisins, bouillon granules, and salt. Cover pan and bring to boiling. Reduce heat; cover and simmer 15 minutes or till rice is done. Let stand, covered, for 10 minutes. Just before serving, stir in the chopped cashews and toss lightly to mix. Garnish with toasted coconut, if desired. Makes 6 servings.

# Spanish Rice

       6   **slices bacon**
       1   **medium onion, finely chopped**
       1   **small green pepper, finely chopped**
       1   **28-ounce can tomatoes, cut up**
       1   **cup water**
     ¾   **cup long grain rice**
       1   **tablespoon brown sugar**
       1   **tablespoon Worcestershire sauce**
       1   **teaspoon salt**
       1   **teaspoon chili powder**
     ⅛   **teaspoon pepper**
           **Dash bottled hot pepper sauce**

In a 10-inch skillet cook bacon till crisp. Drain on paper toweling; crumble and set aside. Drain fat from pan, reserving 2 tablespoons drippings in skillet. In the bacon drippings cook onion and green pepper till tender. Stir in *undrained* tomatoes, water, rice, brown sugar, Worcestershire sauce, salt, chili powder, pepper, and hot pepper sauce. Cover; simmer about 30 minutes or till rice is done and most of the liquid is absorbed. Top with the crumbled bacon. Sprinkle with shredded cheddar cheese, if desired. Makes 6 servings.

# Chinese Fried Rice

*Use long grain, quick-cooking, or brown rice—*
       3   **tablespoons cooking oil**
       2   **beaten eggs**
     ½   **cup diced fully cooked ham or raw pork**
     ¼   **cup finely chopped fresh mushrooms**
     ¼   **cup thinly sliced green onion**
       4   **cups cooked rice, chilled**
       3   **tablespoons soy sauce**

In a 10-inch skillet heat *1 tablespoon* of the oil. Add beaten eggs and cook without stirring till set. Invert skillet over a baking sheet to remove cooked eggs; cut them into short, narrow strips. In the same skillet heat the remaining oil. Cook ham or pork, mushrooms, and green onion in the hot oil for 4 minutes or till mushrooms and onion are tender. Stir in cooked rice and the egg strips; sprinkle with 3 tablespoons soy sauce. Heat through, tossing gently to coat with soy. Serve with additional soy sauce, if desired. Serves 4 to 6.

---

## Mushroom-Rice Bake

---

|   |   |
|---|---|
| 2 | cups sliced fresh mushrooms |
| ¼ | cup chopped onion |
| 2 | tablespoons butter or margarine |
| 2 | eggs |
| 2 | 3-ounce packages cream cheese, softened |
| 1 | 13-ounce can evaporated milk |
| 3 | cups cooked rice |
| ¼ | cup snipped parsley |
| 1 | teaspoon salt |

Oven 350°

In a skillet cook mushrooms and onion in butter or margarine till onion is tender but not brown. Beat together eggs and cream cheese till smooth. Stir in milk. Stir in cooked rice, parsley, salt, and cooked mushroom mixture. Turn mixture into a 10x6x2-inch baking dish. Bake, uncovered, in a 350° oven for 40 to 45 minutes or till a knife inserted off-center comes out clean. Let stand 10 minutes before serving. Makes 8 to 10 servings.

**Mushroom-Cereal Bake:** Prepare Mushroom-Rice Bake as above, *except* substitute 3 cups cooked *barley or bulgur* for the rice. Continue as directed.

# Rice

**Quick-Cooking Rice**

**Brown Rice**

**Long Grain White Rice**

**Wild Rice**

# Cereal

Cereals provide B vitamins and iron for good health, and whole-grain cereals add fiber to the diet. When combined with milk, cereal also is an excellent source of low-fat protein.

Whether ready-to-eat or uncooked, store cereal in a tightly covered container in a cool, dry place. In general, 1 ounce of ready-to-eat cereal makes 1 serving. For cooked cereal, plan on 1 cup uncooked cereal for about 4 servings.

For best results in cooking cereal, add the cereal to the boiling liquid in a slow stream. This allows each granule to be surrounded by liquid and prevents lumping. When cereal is done it will appear translucent and have no starchy taste. To keep cooked cereal warm, cover the pan and remove from heat. Reheat slowly, adding water if needed.

# Cornmeal Mush

2¾ **cups water**
1 **cup cornmeal**
1 **cup water**
1 **teaspoon salt**

In a medium saucepan bring the 2¾ cups water to boiling. In a bowl combine cornmeal, the 1 cup water, and salt; slowly add to the boiling water, stirring constantly. Cook and stir till boiling. Reduce heat; cover and cook over low heat 10 to 15 minutes, stirring occasionally. If desired, serve with milk, butter, sugar, or honey. Serves 4.

*Fried Mush:* Prepare Cornmeal Mush as above, *except* pour hot mush into an 8x4x2-inch loaf pan. Cool; chill several hours or overnight. Turn out of pan and cut into ½-inch-thick slices. Fry slowly in *butter or margarine* for 10 to 12 minutes on each side or till brown and crisp. If desired, serve with butter and syrup or honey. Serves 6.

*Polenta:* Prepare Cornmeal Mush as above, *except* pour hot mush into a 9-inch pie plate. Cover and chill 30 minutes or till firm. Bake in a 350° oven for 20 minutes or till hot. Cut into wedges. If desired, serve with tomato sauce or grated Parmesan cheese. Serves 6.

# Spicy Raisin Oatmeal

1½ **cups quick-cooking rolled oats**
1 **cup raisins**
1 **teaspoon salt**
1 **teaspoon ground cinnamon**
¼ **teaspoon ground nutmeg**

In a medium saucepan bring 3 cups *water* to boiling. Slowly add oats, raisins, salt, cinnamon, and nutmeg to boiling water, stirring constantly. Cook, stirring occasionally, for 1 minute. Cover. Remove from heat; let stand about 3 minutes. Pass sugar and cream or milk, if desired. Makes 4 servings.

## Spiced Porridge

  1½   **cups milk**
  ½   **cup raisins *or* currants**
  1   **tablespoon sugar**
  ¼   **teaspoon ground cinnamon**
  ⅓   **cup quick-cooking farina**

In a saucepan bring milk to boiling. Stir in raisins or currants, sugar, cinnamon, and ¼ teaspoon *salt*. Slowly add farina, stirring constantly. Cook and stir just to boiling. Reduce heat; cook and stir for 30 seconds. Cover and remove from heat; let stand 1 minute. Spoon into bowls. If desired, top each serving with butter and sugar; pass cream. Serves 2.

## Grits

  1   **cup quick-cooking hominy grits**
  1   **teaspoon salt**

In a saucepan bring 4 cups *water* to boiling. Slowly add grits and salt, stirring constantly. Cook and stir till boiling. Reduce heat; cook and stir 5 to 6 minutes or till all water is absorbed and mixture is thick. Serve with butter or milk, if desired. Serves 4.

***Southern Cheese Grits:*** Prepare Grits as above. Stir 1½ cups shredded *American cheese* and ½ cup *butter or margarine* into the hot grits till melted. Gradually stir about *1 cup* of the hot mixture into 2 beaten *eggs;* return all to saucepan. Turn into a greased 8x8x2-inch baking dish. Bake, uncovered, in a 325° oven for 35 minutes or till nearly set. Let stand 10 minutes. Makes 8 servings.

# Granola

2½　**cups regular rolled oats**
　1　**cup shredded coconut**
　½　**cup coarsely chopped almonds**
　½　**cup sesame seed *or* wheat germ**
　½　**cup shelled sunflower seed**
　½　**cup honey**
　¼　**cup cooking oil**
　½　**cup snipped dried apricots**
　½　**cup raisins**　　　　　　　　　　　Oven 300°

In a bowl stir together oats, coconut, almonds, sesame seed or wheat germ, and sunflower seed. Combine honey and oil; stir into oat mixture. Spread out evenly in a 13x9x2-inch baking pan. Bake in a 300° oven 45 to 50 minutes or till light brown; stir every 15 minutes.

Remove from oven; stir in apricots and raisins. Remove to another pan. Cool, stirring often to prevent lumping. Store in lightly covered jars or plastic bags. To keep more than 2 weeks, freeze in moisture-vaporproof bags. Makes 6½ cups.

---

# Baked Gnocchi

　2　**cups milk**
　¼　**cup butter *or* margarine**
　1　**cup milk**
　¾　**cup quick-cooking farina**
　2　**beaten eggs**
　½　**cup grated Parmesan cheese**
　3　**tablespoons butter *or* margarine, melted**
　½　**cup grated Parmesan cheese**　　　　Oven 425°

In a medium saucepan heat the 2 cups milk and ¼ cup butter to boiling. Meanwhile, mix 1 cup milk, the farina, and 1 teaspoon *salt* in a bowl. Slowly add farina mixture to boiling milk, stirring constantly. Cook and stir 5 minutes or till thick. Remove from heat; stir about *1 cup* hot mixture into eggs. Return all to pan; add ½ cup cheese. Pour into a buttered

8x8x2-inch baking pan. Chill 1 hour or till firm. Cut farina into 4x½-inch rectangles. Overlap pieces in a greased 13x9x2-inch baking pan. Brush with 3 tablespoons melted butter and sprinkle with ½ cup cheese. Bake in 425° oven for 25 to 30 minutes or till golden, Serves 6.

## Toasted Barley Bake

| | |
|---|---|
| **¾** | **cup quick-cooking barley** |
| **¼** | **cup finely chopped onion** |
| **2** | **tablespoons butter or margarine** |
| **2** | **cups water** |
| **1** | **teaspoon instant chicken bouillon granules** |
| **½** | **teaspoon salt** |
| **2** | **tablespoons snipped parsley**      Oven 325° |

In a large skillet cook barley and onion in butter or margarine over low heat about 15 minutes or till onion is tender and barley is golden ‧ brown, stirring frequently. Stir in water, bouillon granules, and salt. Bring to boiling. Pour into a 1-quart casserole. Bake, covered, in a 325° oven for 45 minutes, stirring once or twice. Uncover and bake 15 minutes more. Stir in snipped parsley. Serves 6.

***Skillet Barley:*** Prepare Toasted Barley Bake as above, *except* after adding water, bouillon granules, and salt, cover skillet and simmer for 25 minutes or till barley is done, stirring occasionally. Stir in parsley.

## Bulgur Sauté

| | |
|---|---|
| **1** | **cup bulgur wheat** |
| **⅓** | **cup chopped onion** |
| **⅓** | **cup thinly sliced celery** |
| **2** | **tablespoons butter or margarine** |
| **2** | **cups water** |
| **2½** | **teaspoons instant beef bouillon granules** |
| **2** | **tablespoons snipped parsley** |

In a medium skillet cook bulgur, onion, and celery in butter or margarine over low heat 10 to 15 minutes or till onion is tender, stirring frequently. Stir in water and beef bouillon granules. Bring to boiling. Reduce heat; cover and simmer for 15 minutes or till bulgur is done. Stir in snipped parsley. Makes 6 servings.

    ***Curried Bulgur Sauté:*** Prepare Bulgur Sauté as above, *except* stir 1 to 2 teaspoons *curry powder* into the bulgur-vegetable mixture before the first cooking step. Continue with recipe as directed.

# Salads & Dressings

# Salads & Dressings

# Salads & Dressings

# Salads & Dressings

# Salads &

# Salads & Dressings

| Recipes | Servings (fraction of recipe) | Calories | Protein (grams) | Carbohydrate (grams) | Fat (grams) | Sodium (milligrams) | Potassium (milligrams) | Protein | Vitamin A | Vitamin C | Thiamine | Riboflavin | Niacin | Calcium | Iron |
|---|---|---|---|---|---|---|---|---|---|---|---|---|---|---|---|
| | | | | | | | | Percent of U.S. RDA Per Serving | | | | | | | |
| Apricot Soufflé Salad | 1/4 | 261 | 3 | 32 | 15 | 182 | 233 | 4 | 21 | 16 | 2 | 2 | 2 | 1 | 2 |
| Asparagus Toss | 1/6 | 212 | 4 | 8 | 19 | 413 | 403 | 6 | 21 | 56 | 12 | 13 | 7 | 4 | 8 |
| Avocado Dressing | 1/12 | 67 | 1 | 2 | 6 | 2 | 146 | 2 | 4 | 6 | 2 | 2 | 4 | 3 | 1 |
| Blender Mayonnaise | 1/10 | 202 | 1 | 0 | 22 | 113 | 10 | 2 | 1 | 1 | 0 | 1 | 0 | 0 | 1 |
| Buttermilk Dressing | 1/14 | 81 | 1 | 1 | 8 | 96 | 38 | 1 | 3 | 1 | 1 | 1 | 1 | 0 | 0 |
| Caesar Croutons | 1/8 | 64 | 1 | 5 | 4 | 63 | 13 | 2 | 0 | 0 | 2 | 3 | 2 | 2 | 3 |
| Cheddar Macaroni Salad | 1/6 | 196 | 5 | 16 | 13 | 154 | 104 | 8 | 5 | 12 | 7 | 7 | 4 | 10 | 1 |
| Chef's Salad | 1/6 | 320 | 31 | 8 | 18 | 600 | 651 | 47 | 45 | 92 | 22 | 22 | 28 | 24 | 4 |
| Cherry-Cider Salad | 1/10 | 201 | 1 | 34 | 0 | 86 | 245 | 6 | 5 | 6 | 3 | 3 | 4 | 3 | 21 |
| Cherry-Lemon Ring | 1/8 | 154 | 4 | 36 | 0 | 85 | 171 | 6 | 1 | 3 | 1 | 1 | 1 | 5 | 5 |
| Chicken-Stuffed Tomatoes | 1/4 | 338 | 19 | 11 | 25 | 553 | 592 | 29 | 26 | 53 | 8 | 8 | 7 | 35 | 9 |
| Choose-a-Fruit Salad Platter w/Honey-Lime Dressing | 1/8 | 224 | 2 | 25 | 14 | 33 | 389 | 3 | 10 | 22 | 4 | 4 | 4 | 6 | 6 |
| Choose-a-Fruit Salad w/Spicy Nectar Dressing | 1/8 | 224 | 2 | 25 | 14 | 33 | 389 | 3 | 10 | 22 | 4 | 4 | 4 | 6 | 6 |
| Choose-a-Fruit Salad w/Strawberry-Cheese Dressing | 1/8 | 224 | 2 | 25 | 14 | 33 | 389 | 3 | 10 | 22 | 4 | 4 | 4 | 6 | 6 |
| Chunky Blue Cheese Dressing | 1/10 | 88 | 3 | 1 | 8 | 122 | 34 | 5 | 3 | 0 | 0 | 1 | 6 | 5 | 1 |
| Cider Waldorf Mold | 1/6 | 241 | 2 | 27 | 15 | 138 | 223 | 4 | 3 | 5 | 5 | 5 | 3 | 2 | 5 |
| Cinnamon Fruit Salad | 1/10 | 176 | 2 | 28 | 8 | 26 | 201 | 3 | 10 | 10 | 3 | 3 | 4 | 3 | 5 |

# Nutrition Analysis Chart

| Item | Serving | | | | | | | | | | | | | | | | |
|---|---|---|---|---|---|---|---|---|---|---|---|---|---|---|---|---|---|
| Citrus Vinaigrette | 1/12 | 165 | 0 | 1 | 18 | 267 | 19 | 0 | 0 | 10 | 0 | 0 | 0 | 0 | 0 | 6 | 0 |
| Coleslaw Vinaigrette | 1/4 | 139 | 4 | 10 | 10 | 573 | 172 | 6 | 17 | 43 | 3 | 6 | 5 | 3 | 5 | 1 | 6 |
| Cooked Dressing | 1/8 | 57 | 2 | 6 | 3 | 289 | 47 | 3 | 4 | 0 | 2 | 4 | 4 | 2 | 4 | 1 | 2 |
| Crab Louis | 1/4 | 642 | 23 | 17 | 55 | 509 | 734 | 35 | 67 | 84 | 18 | 19 | 19 | 16 | 12 | 16 | |
| Crab-Stuffed Tomatoes | 1/4 | 250 | 13 | 8 | 19 | 628 | 460 | 20 | 40 | 54 | 10 | 10 | 10 | 10 | 6 | 10 | |
| Cranberry Citrus Mold | 1/10 | 136 | 3 | 35 | 0 | 70 | 148 | 3 | 2 | 28 | 3 | 1 | 1 | 3 | 2 | 2 | |
| Cranberry Frost Salad | 1/8 | 304 | 4 | 25 | 22 | 83 | 237 | 6 | 21 | 28 | 4 | 8 | 8 | 4 | 6 | 4 | |
| Creamy Coleslaw | 1/8 | 119 | 1 | 5 | 11 | 162 | 149 | 1 | 17 | 47 | 2 | 2 | 2 | 2 | 3 | 2 | |
| Creamy French Dressing | 1/13 | 158 | 1 | 1 | 17 | 169 | 10 | 1 | 1 | 1 | 0 | 1 | 1 | 0 | 0 | 1 | |
| Creamy Fruit Dressing | 1/18 | 143 | 1 | 2 | 15 | 67 | 27 | 1 | 3 | 3 | 0 | 1 | 0 | 1 | 2 | 0 | |
| Creamy Fruit Salad | 1/8 | 227 | 6 | 20 | 15 | 94 | 262 | 9 | 15 | 31 | 6 | 8 | 2 | 6 | 7 | 5 | |
| Creamy Potato Salad | 1/8 | 367 | 5 | 24 | 29 | 706 | 532 | 7 | 6 | 32 | 8 | 6 | 8 | 8 | 3 | 7 | |
| Create a Tossed Salad | 1/6 | 90 | 4 | 6 | 6 | 85 | 312 | 6 | 20 | 24 | 5 | 8 | 4 | 4 | 10 | 5 | |
| Cucumber Ring Supreme | 1/10 | 300 | 4 | 14 | 26 | 382 | 187 | 6 | 14 | 22 | 3 | 6 | 1 | 3 | 4 | 4 | |
| Curried Chicken Salad | 1/6 | 582 | 28 | 50 | 32 | 301 | 911 | 43 | 13 | 54 | 15 | 19 | 45 | 15 | 13 | 16 | |
| Five-Cup Salad | 1/6 | 197 | 2 | 20 | 13 | 28 | 168 | 3 | 9 | 23 | 0 | 4 | 1 | 0 | 7 | 3 | |
| French Dressing | 1/6 | 165 | 0 | 1 | 18 | 178 | 12 | 0 | 0 | 4 | 0 | 0 | 0 | 0 | 0 | 0 | |
| Frosted Triple-Orange Squares | 1/12 | 246 | 4 | 42 | 8 | 106 | 277 | 5 | 11 | 65 | 8 | 5 | 2 | 8 | 8 | 3 | |
| Frozen Lemon Salad | 1/8 | 276 | 4 | 25 | 19 | 120 | 162 | 6 | 15 | 17 | 3 | 8 | 2 | 3 | 5 | 3 | |
| Fruit-and-Nut Tropical Slaw | 1/8 | 146 | 3 | 24 | 5 | 176 | 352 | 5 | 5 | 43 | 7 | 6 | 2 | 6 | 9 | 5 | |
| Fruit-Filled Melons | 1/6 | 299 | 18 | 58 | 28 | 288 | 1239 | 28 | 247 | 275 | 17 | 29 | 15 | 29 | 19 | 16 | |
| Fruit Medley Salad | 1/4 | 416 | 11 | 28 | 31 | 532 | 911 | 17 | 64 | 152 | 18 | 15 | 15 | 15 | 10 | 14 | |
| Fruit Strata Salad | 1/12 | 125 | 4 | 25 | 2 | 60 | 501 | 5 | 4 | 84 | 8 | 8 | 6 | 8 | 10 | 6 | |
| Fruity Ginger Ale Mold | 1/5 | 158 | 2 | 40 | 0 | 56 | 177 | 3 | 2 | 10 | 4 | 2 | 1 | 2 | 1 | 2 | |
| Garlic Olive Oil | 1/4 | 242 | 0 | 1 | 27 | 0 | 12 | 0 | 1 | 0 | 0 | 0 | 0 | 0 | 0 | 0 | |
| Gazpacho Salad | 1/4 | 182 | 3 | 14 | 14 | 283 | 510 | 5 | 27 | 111 | 8 | 7 | 5 | 7 | 6 | 10 | |
| German Potato Salad | 1/6 | 290 | 8 | 32 | 15 | 652 | 644 | 12 | 4 | 39 | 13 | 8 | 13 | 8 | 3 | 10 | |
| Greek Salad | 1/6 | 429 | 17 | 7 | 38 | 480 | 522 | 26 | 45 | 30 | 10 | 15 | 18 | 15 | 15 | 15 | |
| Green Goddess Dressing | 1/10 | 111 | 1 | 2 | 11 | 93 | 82 | 2 | 13 | 18 | 1 | 2 | 2 | 2 | 1 | 3 | |

# 656

# Nutrition Analysis Chart

| Recipes | Servings (fraction of recipe) | Calories | Protein (grams) | Carbohydrate (grams) | Fat (grams) | Sodium (milligrams) | Potassium (milligrams) | Percent of U.S. RDA Per Serving | | | | | | | |
|---|---|---|---|---|---|---|---|---|---|---|---|---|---|---|---|
| | | | | | | | | Protein | Vitamin A | Vitamin C | Thiamine | Riboflavin | Niacin | Calcium | Iron |
| Green Goddess Salad | 1/6 | 80 | 5 | 3 | 18 | 134 | 723 | 8 | 49 | 54 | 11 | 9 | 8 | 14 | 17 |
| Herb Dressing | 1/10 | 202 | 0 | 22 | 0 | 114 | 14 | 1 | 1 | 3 | 0 | 0 | 1 | 0 | 1 |
| Homemade Mayonnaise | 1/16 | 249 | 0 | 0 | 28 | 134 | 7 | 1 | 1 | 1 | 0 | 1 | 1 | 0 | 1 |
| Honey-Lime Dressing | 1/12 | 151 | 0 | 14 | 8 | 45 | 12 | 0 | 0 | 0 | 0 | 0 | 0 | 0 | 0 |
| Hot Five-Bean Salad | 1/10 | 293 | 10 | 43 | 10 | 594 | 418 | 16 | 4 | 7 | 10 | 7 | 7 | 6 | 22 |
| Italian Dressing | 1/14 | 188 | 0 | 1 | 21 | 407 | 10 | 0 | 0 | 0 | 0 | 0 | 0 | 0 | 0 |
| Jubilee Salad Mold | 1/8 | 185 | 3 | 41 | 0 | 71 | 209 | 5 | 3 | 23 | 2 | 2 | 3 | 2 | 3 |
| Lime Fruit Salad | 1/6 | 238 | 4 | 22 | 16 | 89 | 145 | 6 | 12 | 2 | 2 | 4 | 4 | 1 | 2 |
| Louis Dressing | 1/4 | 470 | 2 | 7 | 50 | 563 | 131 | 2 | 16 | 29 | 3 | 3 | 4 | 2 | 3 |
| Marinated Three-Bean Salad | 1/6 | 264 | 4 | 23 | 18 | 116 | 240 | 6 | 4 | 34 | 4 | 4 | 3 | 2 | 10 |
| Marinated Zucchini Salad | 1/4 | 213 | 3 | 13 | 13 | 274 | 495 | 4 | 20 | 59 | 8 | 8 | 12 | 11 | 6 |
| Meatless Meal-in-a-Bowl | 1/6 | 255 | 14 | 26 | 12 | 82 | 719 | 22 | 75 | 71 | 17 | 17 | 19 | 9 | 28 |
| Molded Shrimp Salad | 1/9 | 327 | 7 | 9 | 30 | 556 | 166 | 11 | 20 | 20 | 2 | 2 | 6 | 3 | 8 |
| Oriental Vegetable Toss | 1/8 | 123 | 2 | 10 | 9 | 181 | 322 | 4 | 14 | 39 | 5 | 5 | 8 | 3 | 8 |
| Original Caesar Salad | 1/8 | 217 | 6 | 11 | 17 | 123 | 380 | 10 | 51 | 42 | 8 | 8 | 12 | 4 | 13 |
| Potato Salad Nicoise | 1/8 | 149 | 8 | 27 | 4 | 139 | 816 | 14 | 17 | 67 | 13 | 13 | 10 | 12 | 15 |
| Quick Reuben Salad | 1/4 | 312 | 17 | 14 | 21 | 807 | 396 | 27 | 52 | 39 | 7 | 7 | 18 | 7 | 18 |
| Quick Three-Bean Salad | 1/6 | 283 | 4 | 16 | 24 | 935 | 219 | 6 | 6 | 34 | 4 | 4 | 4 | 3 | 10 |
| Raw Vegetable Antipasto | 1/4 | 355 | 4 | 15 | 33 | 488 | 607 | 7 | 73 | 136 | 10 | 10 | 12 | 12 | 15 |
| Red Wine Dressing | 1/13 | 156 | 0 | 1 | 17 | 14 | 41 | 0 | 0 | 0 | 0 | 0 | 0 | 0 | 0 |

# Nutrition Analysis Chart

| | | | | | | | | | | | | | | | |
|---|---|---|---|---|---|---|---|---|---|---|---|---|---|---|---|
| Russian Dressing | 1/14 | 118 | 0 | 7 | 10 | 207 | 44 | 0 | 3 | 5 | 1 | 0 | 1 | 0 | 1 |
| Rye Croutons | 1/8 | 76 | 1 | 8 | 5 | 140 | 24 | 2 | 4 | 0 | 3 | 2 | 2 | 1 | 2 |
| Salad Niçoise | 1/6 | 194 | 17 | 15 | 8 | 257 | 651 | 26 | 33 | 68 | 11 | 14 | 30 | 11 | 19 |
| Sausage Supper Salad | 1/5 | 403 | 16 | 14 | 32 | 639 | 418 | 24 | 10 | 10 | 16 | 13 | 13 | 7 | 18 |
| Scallop Toss | 1/6 | 238 | 22 | 10 | 13 | 275 | 354 | 34 | 50 | 25 | 6 | 18 | 4 | 30 | 20 |
| Shrimp-Avocado Salad | 1/6 | 295 | 24 | 12 | 18 | 492 | 818 | 37 | 32 | 54 | 12 | 19 | 20 | 29 | 14 |
| Sour Cream Cucumbers | 1/8 | 45 | 1 | 4 | 3 | 145 | 113 | 2 | 5 | 10 | 1 | 3 | 1 | 3 | 3 |
| South-of-the-Border Salad | 1/6 | 501 | 20 | 33 | 33 | 931 | 924 | 32 | 43 | 92 | 36 | 25 | 20 | 24 | 27 |
| Spicy Nectar Dressing | 1/16 | 101 | 0 | 3 | 10 | 8 | 33 | 1 | 1 | 1 | 0 | 3 | 6 | 2 | 0 |
| Spinach-Orange Toss | 1/6 | 175 | 4 | 9 | 15 | 119 | 382 | 7 | 64 | 51 | 7 | 16 | 6 | 8 | 12 |
| Strawberry-Banana Soufflé Salads | 1/6 | 241 | 3 | 36 | 11 | 191 | 297 | 5 | 4 | 54 | 4 | 4 | 3 | 2 | 5 |
| Strawberry-Cheese Dressing | 1/12 | 124 | 1 | 5 | 12 | 18 | 20 | 1 | 2 | 11 | 0 | 1 | 0 | 1 | 1 |
| Tangy Stuffed Pepper Salad | 1/4 | 137 | 13 | 13 | 4 | 589 | 519 | 19 | 39 | 210 | 21 | 16 | 11 | 11 | 12 |
| Taos Salad Toss | 1/8 | 177 | 8 | 17 | 9 | 194 | 403 | 13 | 14 | 19 | 8 | 9 | 5 | 15 | 11 |
| Thousand Island Dressing | 1/14 | 131 | 1 | 2 | 13 | 246 | 42 | 2 | 4 | 5 | 1 | 2 | 0 | 1 | 2 |
| Tomato Aspic | 1/8 | 52 | 3 | 11 | 0 | 536 | 365 | 5 | 21 | 51 | 5 | 3 | 5 | 2 | 8 |
| Tuna-Stuffed Tomatoes | 1/4 | 263 | 18 | 8 | 18 | 314 | 538 | 28 | 33 | 56 | 9 | 11 | 35 | 5 | 12 |
| 24-Hour Fruit Salad | 1/10 | 249 | 2 | 36 | 12 | 29 | 221 | 4 | 14 | 42 | 7 | 5 | 2 | 6 | 5 |
| 24-Hour Vegetable Salad | 1/10 | 288 | 11 | 6 | 25 | 356 | 167 | 17 | 17 | 14 | 12 | 13 | 5 | 16 | 10 |
| Vinaigrette Dressing | 1/12 | 164 | 0 | 1 | 18 | 267 | 13 | 0 | 0 | 0 | 0 | 0 | 0 | 0 | 0 |
| Waldorf Salad | 1/8 | 289 | 2 | 24 | 22 | 99 | 249 | 3 | 8 | 11 | 5 | 4 | 3 | 4 | 5 |
| Wilted Spinach Salad | 1/6 | 52 | 4 | 3 | 3 | 171 | 257 | 6 | 80 | 44 | 5 | 8 | 3 | 5 | 10 |
| Zucchini Salad Bowl | 1/6 | 21 | 1 | 4 | 0 | 13 | 265 | 2 | 41 | 25 | 4 | 6 | 4 | 4 | 5 |

# Salad Basics

On the next several pages you'll find a variety of delectable recipes for great tossed salads, molded vegetable and fruit salads, main-dish salads, and salad dressings. Whatever role the salad plays in your meal, combine these salad-making basics with a little ingenuity to create a tantalizing salad.

Probably the most familiar salad is the tossed green salad. But that doesn't mean it has to be commonplace. You can introduce interesting tastes and textures by combining a variety of salad greens. Besides the Basic Salad Greens (see the identification chart page 659), Swiss chard, mustard greens, beet tops, kale leaves, fennel, and dandelion greens make good additions to mixed green salads. Use full-flavored greens in small amounts.

A vegetable salad works as an appetizer or a side dish; a fruit salad functions as anything from a first course to a dessert. Either salad can be tossed, layered, or arranged however you please. For even more variety, combine fruits and vegetables.

### Salad Entrées

Turn a side-dish salad into an entrée by adding beans, soft or hard cheeses, and/or cooked seafood or poultry, hard-cooked eggs, or assorted cold cooked meats. But be sure there's adequate protein (at least 2 ounces per serving). And, when you're converting a side-dish salad to a main dish, double the amounts of the salad greens, vegetables, and/or fruits.

### Edible Salad "Bowls"

Pile your favorite tuna, chicken, or egg salad into a tomato cup, melon half, pineapple boat, or avocado half for a self-contained main dish. (See the tip on page 701. Making tomato cups.) Use the outer leaf from a large head of iceburg or Boston lettuce to hold a big salad, or Bibb lettuce for individual "cups."

### Cooked Vegetable Salads

You can turn almost any saucepan into a vegetable steamer with a self-adjusting stainless steel basket. A light steaming gives fresh vegetables a crisp-tender texture ideal for salads, and the vegetables retain their color.

## *Basic Salad Greens*

**Curly Endive**

**Romaine**

**Leaf Lettuce**

**Bibb Lettuce**

**Escarole**

**Iceberg Lettuce**

**Spinach**

**Boston Lettuce**

Bring a pan of water to boiling. Be sure the water doesn't touch the basket. Put vegetables in the steamer basket. Cover and reduce the heat. Steam till vegetables are just crisp-tender. Dress the cooked vegetables with Vinaigrette Dressing or other oil-based salad dressings (see recipes, page 703) while they're still hot so they'll absorb more flavor. Then chill till serving time to let them marinate.

Drain the excess dressing (you can reuse it) and arrange the vegetables on a platter or toss them with torn greens.

### Potato Salad Pointers

Boil potatoes in their jackets, then drain. Peel potatoes while still warm, using a fork to hold the warm potato; slice or cube the potatoes. To prevent sticking, toss lightly with a few tablespoons of oil, if desired. Cover and chill. Use in your favorite potato salad.

# Vegetable Salads

## Create a Tossed Salad

         6   **cups torn salad greens***
      1½   **cups desired salad ingredients****
             **Salad dressing (see recipes, pages
                701–5)**
             **Salad garnish*****

In a large salad bowl combine your choice of torn salad greens and a combination of 2 or more desired salad ingredients. Cover and chill till serving time. Toss salad lightly with desired salad dressing. Arrange a salad garnish on the top of the salad. Serve immediately. Makes 6 side-dish servings.

   ***Salad green suggestions:** Choose 2 or more of the following: iceberg lettuce, romaine, curly endive, leaf lettuce, spinach, Bibb lettuce, Boston lettuce, escarole, watercress, Chinese cabbage, Swiss chard, mustard greens, beet tops, kale leaves, dandelion greens, or fennel.

**\*\*Salad ingredient suggestions:** Choose 2 or more from the following categories:

*Fresh vegetables:* tomato wedges, sliced cucumber, sliced fresh mushrooms, chopped or sliced celery, sliced radishes, shredded carrot, sliced cauliflower flowerets, onion rings, green pepper strips or rings, sliced zucchini, halved cherry tomatoes, chopped red cabbage, bean sprouts, or sliced water chestnuts.

*Cooked vegetables:* chopped broccoli, brussels sprouts, peas, beans (garbanzo, cut green, lima, pinto, kidney), or artichoke hearts.

*Salad highlighters:* sliced avocado, sliced pitted ripe or pimiento-stuffed olives, anchovy fillets, coarsely chopped or sliced hard-cooked egg, snipped chives, sliced green onion, alfalfa sprouts, cubed tofu, or raisins.

*Cheeses:* cheddar, Monterey Jack, Swiss, Muenster, colby, American, brick, or Gruyère cheese cut into julienne strips or cubes, or crumbled feta or blue cheese.

**\*\*\*Salad garnishes:** Top the salad with 1 of the following: croutons, toasted pumpkin seeds, peanuts, broken pecans or walnuts, crumbled crisp-cooked bacon, parsley sprigs, sieved hard-cooked egg yolk, or carrot curls.

---

## Original Caesar Salad

> Garlic Olive Oil
> Ceasar Croutons
> 3 **medium heads romaine, torn into bite-size pieces (18 cups)**
> 2 **to 3 tablespoons wine vinegar**
> 1 **lemon, halved**
> 2 **eggs**
> Dash Worcestershire sauce
> Salt
> Whole black pepper
> ⅓ **cup grated Parmesan cheese**
> Rolled anchovy fillets (optional)

One or more days before serving the salad, prepare Garlic Olive Oil. Several hours before serving, prepare Ceasar Croutons. Chill a large salad bowl and dinner plates.

At serving time, place torn romaine in the chilled salad bowl. Drizzle romaine with about ⅓ *cup* of the Garlic Olive Oil and the vinegar; squeeze lemon over.

To coddle eggs, place eggs in shell in a saucepan of boiling water. Remove the saucepan from heat and let stand 1 minute. Remove eggs; let cool slightly.

Break coddled eggs over romaine. Add Worcestershire sauce; sprinkle with some salt. Grind a generous amount of pepper over all; sprinkle with grated Parmesan cheese. Toss salad lightly till dressing is combined and the romaine is well coated. Add Caesar Croutons; toss once or twice. Serve immediately on the chilled dinner plates. Garnish with anchovies, if desired. Makes 8 to 10 servings.

**Garlic Olive Oil:** Slice 6 cloves *garlic* lengthwise into quarters; combine with 1 cup *olive or salad oil*. Store in a covered jar in the refrigerator. Remove garlic before using oil.

**Ceasar Croutons:** Brush both sides of three ½-inch-thick slices of firm-textured *white bread or French bread* with some Garlic Olive Oil. Cut bread into ½-inch cubes. Spread out on a baking sheet. Bake in a 250° oven about 1 hour or till croutons are dry and crisp. Sprinkle with some grated *Parmesan cheese.* Cool. Store croutons in a covered jar in the refrigerator.

## Oriental Vegetable Toss

- ⅓ **cup salad oil**
- ¼ **cup vinegar**
- 1 **tablespoon sugar**
- 1 **tablespoon soy sauce**
- ¼ **teaspoon ground ginger**
- 1 **8-ounce can water chestnuts, drained and sliced**
- 6 **ounces fresh or frozen pea pods, thawed**
- 4 **cups sliced Chinese cabbage**
- 3 **cups torn leaf lettuce**
- 1 **cup fresh bean sprouts**
- 1 **cup sliced fresh mushrooms**
- 2 **tablespoons chopped pimiento**

For dressing, in a screw-top jar combine salad oil, vinegar, sugar, soy sauce, and ginger. Cover and shake well. In a large salad bowl combine water chestnuts, pea pods, Chinese cabbage, leaf lettuce, bean sprouts, mushrooms, and pimiento. Pour dressing over salad; toss lightly to coat vegetables. Serves 8.

## Asparagus Toss

| | |
|---|---|
| 1 | **pound fresh asparagus, cut into 2-inch pieces (2 cups)** |
| ½ | **cup salad oil** |
| ¼ | **cup finely chopped canned beets** |
| 2 | **tablespoons white wine vinegar** |
| 2 | **tablespoons lemon juice** |
| 1 | **teaspoon sugar** |
| 1 | **teaspoon salt** |
| 1 | **teaspoon paprika** |
| ½ | **teaspoon dry mustard** |
| 4 | **drops bottled hot pepper sauce** |
| 5 | **cups torn iceberg lettuce** |
| 1 | **cup sliced celery** |
| 1 | **hard-cooked egg, chopped** |
| ¼ | **cup sliced green onion** |

In a saucepan cook cut asparagus in boiling salted water 8 to 10 minutes or just till tender; drain well. Chill.

For dressing, in a screw-top jar combine salad oil, beets, vinegar, lemon juice, sugar, salt, paprika, dry mustard, and hot pepper sauce. Cover and shake well to mix. Chill.

In a large salad bowl combine chilled asparagus, lettuce, celery, egg, and green onion. Pour dressing over salad; toss lightly to coat vegetables. Makes 6 servings.

## 24-Hour Vegetable Salad

**6** cups iceberg lettuce, romaine, leaf lettuce,
   Bibb lettuce, *or* spinach
   Sugar
**1** 10-ounce package frozen peas, thawed, *or*
   2 cups sliced fresh cauliflower, broccoli,
   zucchini, carrots, mushrooms, *or*
   canned water chestnuts, drained and
   sliced
**4** hard-cooked eggs, sliced
**½** pound bacon, crisp-cooked, drained, and
   crumbled
**1½** cups shredded Swiss, American, cheddar,
   colby, Monterey Jack, *or* brick cheese
   (6 ounces)
**¾** cup mayonnaise *or* salad dressing
**1½** teaspoons lemon juice
**1** teaspoon paprika
**⅛** teaspoon ground red pepper
**2** tablespoons sliced green onion

Place lettuce or spinach in bottom of a large salad bowl;
sprinkle with a little salt, pepper, and sugar. Spoon desired
vegetable evenly atop. Arrange egg slices and bacon over
vegetable. Top with desired shredded cheese. Combine mayonnaise, lemon juice, paprika, and red pepper. Spread mayonnaise mixture over top of salad, sealing to edge of bowl.
Cover and chill salad in the refrigerator up to 24 hours. Garnish top of salad with sliced green onion. Before serving, toss
to coat the vegetables. Makes 10 to 12 servings.

## Zucchini Salad Bowl

    3   cups torn iceberg lettuce
    3   cups torn romaine
    1   cup thinly sliced zucchini
    ½   cup sliced radishes
    ½   cup sliced fresh mushrooms
    ½   cup thinly sliced carrots
    2   green onions, thinly sliced
        Italian Dressing (see recipe, page 702)

In a large salad bowl combine the first 7 ingredients. Sprinkle with a little salt and pepper. Toss; cover and chill. Pour Italian Dressing over salad; toss lightly to coat vegetables. Makes 6 servings.

## Green Goddess Salad

    1   medium head romaine, torn (6 cups)
    ½   medium head curly endive, torn (3 cups)
    1   9-ounce package frozen artichoke hearts,
          cooked, drained, and cooled, or one
          14-ounce can artichoke hearts, drained
    ½   cup sliced pitted ripe olives
    2   medium tomatoes, cut into wedges
        Green Goddess Dressing (see recipe, page
          704)

In a large salad bowl combine romaine, endive, artichoke hearts, ripe olives, and tomato wedges. Cover and chill. To serve, pour desired amount of Green Goddess Dressing over the salad. Toss lightly to coat vegetables. Makes 6 to 8 servings.

## Taos Salad Toss

  1   **medium head iceberg lettuce, chopped**
  1   **15-ounce can dark red kidney beans, chilled and drained**
  1   **cup shredded cheddar cheese (4 ounces)**
  ½   **cup sliced pitted ripe olives**
  1   **cup Avocado Dressing (see recipe, page 703)**
  1   **tablespoon chopped canned green chili peppers**
  2   **tablespoons finely chopped onion**
  ¾   **teaspoon chili powder**
  1   **medium tomato, cut into wedges**
1½   **cups tortilla chips**

In a large salad bowl combine lettuce, beans, ½ *cup* of the shredded cheese, and olives. Combine Avocado Dressing, green chili peppers, onion, and chili powder; mix well. Spoon dressing in center of salad. Arrange tomato wedges in a circle atop salad. Top with remaining shredded cheese. Trim edge of bowl with tortilla chips. Before serving, toss lightly to coat vegetables. Makes 8 servings.

## Wilted Spinach Salad

  8   **cups torn fresh spinach *or* leaf lettuce (about 10 ounces)**
  ¼   **cup sliced green onion**
      **Pepper**
  3   **slices bacon**
  1   **tablespoon white wine vinegar**
  2   **teaspoons lemon juice**
  ½   **teaspoon sugar**
  ¼   **teaspoon salt**
  1   **hard-cooked egg, chopped**

Place torn spinach or lettuce in a large bowl; add the sliced green onion. Sprinkle a generous amount of pepper over the torn greens.

Cut *uncooked* bacon into small pieces. In a 12-inch skillet cook bacon till crisp. *Do not drain off drippings.* Stir in wine vinegar, lemon juice, sugar, and salt. Remove skillet from heat; add torn spinach or lettuce and the green onion. Toss gently till well coated. Turn into a serving dish. Top with the chopped hard-cooked egg; serve immediately. Makes 6 servings.

## Spinach-Orange Toss

       6   cups torn fresh spinach (8 ounces)
       1   11-ounce can mandarin orange sections,
             drained
       1   cup sliced fresh mushrooms
       3   tablespoons salad oil
       1   tablespoons lemon juice
    ½   teaspoon poppy seed
    ¼   teaspoon salt
    ¾   cup toasted slivered almonds

Place torn spinach in a large salad bowl. Add mandarin orange sections and sliced fresh mushrooms. Toss lightly; cover and chill.

For dressing, in a screw-top jar combine salad oil, lemon juice, poppy seed, and salt. Cover and shake well. Chill. Shake again and pour the dressing over the spinach-orange mixture. Toss salad lightly to coat. Sprinkle toasted almonds over top. Serve immediately. Makes 6 servings.

## Cheddar Macaroni Salad

       1   cup elbow *or* shell macaroni
    ½   cup shredded cheddar cheese
    ⅓   cup chopped celery
       3   tablespoons chopped green pepper
       2   tablespoons chopped onion
    ¼   cup mayonnaise *or* salad dressing
    ¼   cup dairy sour cream
       2   tablespoons French Dressing (see recipe,
             page 704)
       1   tablespoon sweet pickle relish

Cook macaroni in a large amount of boiling salted water till tender; drain. Rinse with cold water; drain well. Toss with cheese, celery, green pepper, and onion. Combine mayonnaise, sour cream, French Dressing, and relish. Toss with macaroni mixture. Cover; chill several hours. Serve in a lettuce-lined bowl, if desired. Makes 6 servings.

## Potato Salad Niçoise

| | |
|---|---|
| 4 | **medium potatoes (1½ pounds)** |
| 1 | **7¾-ounce can artichoke hearts, drained and halved** |
| 1 | **small red onion, sliced and separated into rings** |
| 1 | **small green pepper, sliced into thin rings** |
| 1 | **cup cherry tomatoes** |
| ¼ | **cup pitted ripe olives** |
| | **Vinaigrette Dressing (see recipe, page 703)** |
| | **Leaf lettuce** |
| 3 | **hard-cooked eggs, chilled** |
| 1 | **2-ounce can anchovy fillets, drained** |
| ¼ | **cup snipped parsley** |

In a covered saucepan cook potatoes in boiling salted water for 25 to 30 minutes or till tender; drain well. Peel and cube potatoes. In a large bowl combine cubed potatoes and next 5 ingredients; toss with Vinaigrette Dressing. Cover; chill several hours or overnight, stirring gently once or twice. To serve, line a salad bowl with lettuce leaves. Using a slotted spoon, lift potato mixture to salad bowl, reserving dressing. Cut eggs into wedges. Arrange hard-cooked eggs and anchovies atop. Sprinkle with parsley. Pass reserved dressing. Serves 8 to 10.

# Creamy Potato Salad

|   |   |
|---|---|
| 6 | medium potatoes (2 pounds) |
| 1 | cup thinly sliced celery |
| ½ | cup finely chopped onion |
| ⅓ | cup chopped sweet pickle |
| 1¼ | cups mayonnaise *or* salad dressing |
| 2 | teaspoons sugar |
| 2 | teaspoons celery seed |
| 2 | teaspoons vinegar |
| 2 | teaspoons prepared mustard |
| 1½ | teaspoons salt |
| 2 | hard-cooked eggs, coarsely chopped |

In a covered saucepan cook potatoes in boiling salted water for 25 to 30 minutes or till tender; drain well. Peel and cube potatoes. Transfer to a large bowl. Add celery, onion, and sweet pickle. Combine mayonnaise or salad dressing, sugar, celery seed, vinegar, prepared mustard, and salt. Add mayonnaise mixture to potatoes. Toss lightly to coat potato mixture. Carefully fold in the chopped eggs. Cover and chill thoroughly. Makes 8 servings.

# German Potato Salad

|   |   |
|---|---|
| 6 | medium potatoes (2 pounds) |
| 6 | sliced bacon |
| ½ | cup chopped onion |
| 2 | tablespoons all-purpose flour |
| 2 | tablespoons sugar |
| 1½ | teaspoons salt |
| 1 | teaspoon celery seed |
|   | Dash pepper |
| 1 | cup water |
| ½ | cup vinegar |
| 2 | hard-coooked eggs, sliced |

In a covered saucepan cook potatoes in boiling salted water for 25 to 30 minutes or till tender; drain well. Peel and slice potatoes. In a large skillet cook bacon till crisp; drain and crumble, reserving ¼ cup drippings. Cook onion in the reserved drippings till tender but not brown. Stir in the flour, sugar, salt, celery seed, and pepper. Add water and vinegar. Cook and stir till thickened and bubbly. Cook and stir 1 to 2 minutes more. Stir in bacon and potatoes. Cook about 5 minutes or till heated through, tossing lightly. Add hard-cooked eggs; toss lightly just to mix. Makes 6 to 8 servings.

## Creamy Coleslaw

|       |                                    |
|-------|------------------------------------|
| 4     | cups shredded cabbage              |
| ½     | cup shredded carrot                |
| ¼     | cup finely chopped green pepper    |
| 2     | tablespoons finely chopped onion   |
| ½     | cup mayonnaise or salad dressing   |
| 1     | tablespoon vinegar                 |
| 2     | teaspoons sugar                    |
| 1     | teaspoon celery seed               |
| ¼     | teaspoon salt                      |

In a large bowl combine the cabbage, carrot, green pepper, and onion. To prepare dressing, stir together mayonnaise or salad dressing, vinegar, sugar, celery seed, and salt. Pour the dressing over the cabbage mixture; toss lightly to coat vegetables. Cover and chill. Makes 8 servings.

## Coleslaw Vinaigrette

|       |                              |
|-------|------------------------------|
| 2     | cups shredded cabbage        |
| ⅓     | cup sliced green pepper      |
| ¼     | cup snipped parsley          |
| 3     | tablespoons vinegar          |
| 2     | tablespoons sugar            |
| 2     | tablespoons salad oil        |
| 2     | hard-cooked eggs, chilled    |

In a bowl combine cabbage, green pepper, and parsley. Stir together vinegar, sugar, salad oil, and 1 teaspoon *salt* till sugar is dissolved. Pour vinegar mixture over vegetables; toss to coat. Cover and chill. Separate yolk from white of 1 of the hard-cooked eggs. Cut up white; toss with cabbage. Slice remaining egg; arrange atop salad. Sieve yolk over the egg slices. Serves 4.

## Sour Cream Cucumbers

> **2** **medium cucumbers, thinly sliced**
> **1** **small onion, thinly sliced**
> **½** **cup dairy sour cream**
> **1** **tablespoon vinegar**
> **1** **teaspoon sugar**
> **½** **teaspoon salt**

Combine the cucumbers and onion. Stir together sour cream, vinegar, sugar, and salt; toss with vegetables. Cover and chill, stirring occasionally. Makes 3 to 4 cups.

## Gazpacho Salad

In a bowl combine 3 medium *tomatoes,* cut into eighths; 1 medium *cucumber,* thinly sliced; 1 medium *green pepper,* coarsely chopped; 2 small *onions,* sliced and separated into rings; and 3 tablespoons snipped *parsley.*

For dressing, in a screw-top jar combine ¼ cup *salad oil;* 2 tablespoons *lemon juice;* 1 tablespoon *white wine vinegar;* 1 teaspoon dried *basil,* crushed; 1 clove *garlic,* minced; ½ teaspoon *salt;* and a few drops bottled *hot pepper sauce.* Cover and shake well. Pour the dressing over the tomato mixture. Toss lightly to coat vegetables. Cover and chill for 2 to 3 hours, stirring occasionally. Serve with *plain croutons,* if desired. Makes 4 to 6 servings.

## Marinated Zucchini Salad

|     |     |
| --- | --- |
| 3 | cups sliced zucchini |
| 2 | medium tomatoes, coarsely chopped |
| 1 | cup sliced fresh mushrooms |
| 2 | tablespoons thinly sliced green onion |
| ½ | cup white wine vinegar |
| ⅓ | cup olive oil or salad oil |
| 1 | tablespoon sugar |
| 1 | clove garlic, minced |
| ½ | teaspoon salt |
| ½ | teaspoon dried basil, crushed |
|   | Few dashes pepper |
|   | Lettuce leaves |
|   | Shredded mozzarella or Monterey Jack cheese (optional) |

Cook sliced zucchini in a small amount of boiling salted water about 3 minutes or till crisp-tender. Drain. In a shallow dish combine cooked zucchini, tomatoes, mushrooms, and onion. To make dressing, in a screw-top jar combine vinegar, oil, sugar, garlic, salt, basil, and pepper. Cover and shake well. Pour dressing over zucchini mixture; toss lightly. Cover and chill several hours or overnight, stirring occasionally. To serve, drain zucchini mixture, reserving dressing. Arrange zucchini mixture on lettuce-lined plates. Top with shredded cheese and pass additional dressing, if desired. Makes 4 to 6 servings.

# Raw Vegetable Antipasto

| | |
|---|---|
| 1 | tomato, peeled and thinly sliced |
| 1 | cup cauliflower flowerets |
| 1 | cup broccoli buds |
| 1 | cucumber, sliced |
| 1 | zucchini, cut into julienne strips |
| 1 | carrot, cut into julienne strips |
| 1 | small onion, sliced and separated into rings |
| ½ | cup olive oil or salad oil |
| ⅓ | cup wine vinegar |
| ½ | teaspoon dried oregano, crushed |
| ¼ | teaspoon salt |
| ¼ | teaspoon garlic salt |
| | Lettuce leaves |
| ½ | cup pitted ripe olives |

In a shallow dish combine tomato, cauliflower flowerets, broccoli, cucumber, zucchini, carrot, and onion rings. To make dressing, in a screw-top jar combine oil, wine vinegar, oregano, salt, garlic salt, and ¼ teaspoon *pepper*. Cover and shake to combine thoroughly. Pour dressing over the vegetables in dish. Cover and chill 2 to 3 hours, spooning dressing over vegetables occasionally. Drain. Serve vegetables on a lettuce-lined platter. Garnish the center of the salad with ripe olives. Makes 4 to 6 side-dish servings or 8 to 10 appetizer servings.

# Hot Five-Bean Salad

| | |
|---|---|
| 8 | slices bacon |
| ⅔ | cup sugar |
| 2 | tablespoons cornstarch |
| ¾ | cup vinegar |
| ½ | cup water |
| 1 | 16-ounce can cut green beans |
| 1 | 16-ounce can lima beans |
| 1 | 16-ounce can cut wax beans |
| 1 | 15½-ounce can red kidney beans |
| 1 | 15-ounce can garbanzo beans |

In a large skillet cook bacon till crisp; drain, reserving ¼ cup drippings in the skillet. Crumble bacon and set aside. Combine sugar, cornstarch, 1½ teaspoons *salt*, and dash *pepper;* stir into reserved drippings. Stir in vinegar and water; cook and stir till boiling. Drain all cans of beans; stir beans into the skillet. Cover and simmer for 15 to 20 minutes. Stir in crumbled bacon. Transfer to a serving dish. Makes 10 to 12 servings.

## Marinated Three-Bean Salad

> 1 **8½-ounce can lima beans**
> 1 **8-ounce can cut green beans**
> 1 **8-ounce can red kidney beans**
> 1 **medium onion, thinly sliced and separated**
> **into rings**
> ½ **cup chopped green pepper**
> ⅔ **cup vinegar**
> ½ **cup salad oil**
> ¼ **cup sugar**
> 1 **teaspoon celery seed**

Drain the canned beans. In a large bowl combine the lima beans, green beans, red kidney beans, onion rings, and green pepper. In a screw-top jar combine vinegar, salad oil, sugar, and celery seed; cover and shake well. Pour vinegar mixture over vegetables and stir lightly. Cover and chill at least 6 hours or overnight, stirring occasionally. Drain before serving. Makes 6 to 8 servings.

**Quick Three-Bean Salad:** Prepare Marinated Three-Bean Salad as above, *except* substitute one 8-ounce bottle *Italian salad dressing* for the vinegar, salad oil, sugar, and celery seed. Continue as directed; marinate in refrigerator for 1 to 1½ hours. Drain before serving.

# Tangy Stuffed Pepper Salad

     **2**  cups shredded cabbage
     **1**  cup diced fully cooked ham *or* cooked beef
    **½**  cup coarsely shredded carrot
    **¼**  cup sliced radish
    **¼**  cup chopped cucumber
     **1**  8-ounce carton plain yogurt
     **2**  teaspoons sugar
     **1**  teaspoon lemon juice
    **½**  teaspoon celery seed
    **¼**  teaspoon garlic salt
    **¼**  teaspoon onion salt
          **Dash pepper**
     **2**  large green peppers

In a bowl combine shredded cabbage, cooked meat, carrot, radish, and cucumber. Combine next 7 ingredients; mix well. Pour over vegetable mixture, tossing to coat. Cover and chill at least 1 hour. Remove tops from green peppers. Cut peppers in half lengthwise and remove seeds. Spoon vegetable mixture into pepper cups. Makes 4 servings.

# Tomato Aspic

     **2**  envelopes unflavored gelatin
     **1**  cup cold tomato juice *or* condensed beef
          broth
     **3**  cups tomato juice
    **⅓**  cup chopped onion
    **¼**  cup chopped celery
    **¼**  cup chopped green pepper
     **2**  tablespoons brown sugar
     **2**  teaspoons Worcestershire sauce
     **4**  whole cloves
     **2**  bay leaves
     **3**  tablespoons lemon juice
          **Lettuce**

To soften gelatin, add unflavored gelatin to the 1 cup tomato juice or beef broth; stir to combine. Let stand 5 minutes. Meanwhile, in a medium saucepan combine *2 cups* of the tomato juice, the onion, celery, green pepper, brown sugar, Worcestershire, cloves, bay leaves, and 1 teaspoon *salt*. (If using the beef broth, decrease salt to ½ teaspoon.) Simmer, uncovered, for 5 minutes. Strain into a bowl; discard vegetables and seasonings. Add softened gelatin to hot tomato juice mixture; stir to dissolve. Stir in remaining 1 cup tomato juice and the lemon juice. Pour into a 4½- or 5-cup ring or tower mold. Chill till firm. Unmold onto a lettuce-lined plate. Serves 8 to 10.

## Molded Shrimp Salad

In a mixing bowl soften 1 envelope *unflavored gelatin* in ½ cup *cold water*. Let stand 5 minutes. In a saucepan bring one 10¾-ounce can *condensed tomato soup* to a boil; add gelatin mixture and stir to dissolve. Remove from heat; turn into a large mixer bowl. Add one 8-ounce package *cream cheese*, cubed and softened, to soup mixture. Beat with a rotary beater or electric mixer till smooth. Stir in 1 cup *mayonnaise or salad dressing*. Chill till partially set (the consistency of unbeaten egg whites).

Fold in one 4½-ounce can small *shrimp*, drained; ½ cup chopped *celery;* ⅓ cup chopped *green pepper;* ⅓ cup chopped *onion;* and ¼ cup drained sweet *pickle relish.* Pour into an 8x8x2-inch dish or pan, or nine ½-cup molds. Cover and chill till firm. To serve, cut into squares or unmold onto lettuce-lined salad plates. Makes 9 servings.

# Cucumber Ring Supreme

|     |                                                    |
| --- | -------------------------------------------------- |
| 1   | 3-ounce package lemon-flavored gelatin             |
| 1   | cup boiling water                                  |
| ¾   | cup cold water                                     |
| 3   | tablespoons lemon juice                            |
| 1   | medium cucumber, thinly sliced                     |
| 2   | tablespoons sugar                                  |
| 1   | envelope unflavored gelatin                        |
| ¾   | teaspoon salt                                      |
| ¾   | cup water                                          |
| 2   | tablespoons lemon juice                            |
| 1   | 8-ounce package cream cheese, softened             |
| 3   | medium or 4 small cucumbers                        |
| 1   | cup mayonnaise or salad dressing                   |
| ¼   | cup snipped parsley                                |
| 3   | tablespoons finely chopped onion                   |
|     | Lettuce                                            |
|     | Cherry tomatoes (optional)                         |

In a mixing bowl dissolve the lemon-flavored gelatin in boiling water; add the ¾ cup cold water and 3 tablespoons lemon juice. Pour into a 6½-cup ring mold. Chill till partially set (the consistency of unbeaten egg whites). Overlap the thinly sliced cucumber atop gelatin mixture in mold; press into gelatin. Chill till almost firm.

Meanwhile, in a saucepan mix the sugar, unflavored gelatin, and salt. Add the ¾ cup water; stir over low heat till gelatin and sugar dissolve. Stir in the 2 tablespoons lemon juice. Gradually stir hot gelatin mixture into softened cream cheese till mixture is smooth.

Peel and halve the 3 or 4 cucumbers lengthwise; scrape out seeds and discard. Grind, using the fine blade of a food grinder, or finely shred cucumbers, Drain; measure about 1½ cups. Stir ground or shredded cucumber, mayonnaise or salad dressing, parsley, and onion into cream cheese mixture. Carefully spoon over the almost-firm gelatin in mold. Chill till firm. Unmold onto a lettuce-lined plate. Garnish with cherry tomatoes, if desired. Makes 10 to 12 servings.

# Fruit Salads

## Apricot Soufflé Salad

    **1**  **3-ounce package orange-flavored gelatin**
    **1**  **cup boiling water**
  **½**  **cup cold water**
    **2**  **tablespoons lemon juice**
  **⅓**  **cup mayonnaise *or* salad dressing**
    **2**  **tablespoons finely chopped celery**
    **4**  ***or* 5 apricots, peeled and sliced**
    **1**  **medium apple, thinly sliced**

In a mixing bowl dissolve gelatin in boiling water. Stir in cold water and lemon juice. Chill till partially set (the consistency of unbeaten egg whites); beat with a rotary beater till fluffy. Beat in mayonnaise or salad dressing. Fold in celery. Arrange apricot and apple slices in the bottom of a 5- to 5½-cup mold; carefully spoon in the whipped gelatin mixture. Chill till firm. Serves 4 to 6.

## Fruity Ginger Ale Mold

    **1**  **3-ounce package lemon-flavored gelatin**
    **1**  **cup ginger ale**
    **1**  **medium apple, cored and cut into wedges**
    **1**  **8¼-ounce can pineapple slices, drained and cut up**
    **1**  **small apple, cored, peeled, and chopped**
  **½**  **cup halved seedless green grapes**

Dissolve gelatin in 1 cup *boiling water*. Cool to room temperature. Slowly add ginger ale.

Arrange apple wedges and some pineapple in a 4½-cup mold. Pour in ¾ *cup* of the lemon gelatin mixture. Chill till almost firm. Meanwhile, chill remaining gelatin till partially set (the consistency of unbeaten egg whites). Fold in pineapple, chopped apple, and grapes. Pour over first layer. Chill till firm. Unmold onto a lettuce-lined platter, if desired. Serves 5 to 6.

## Frosted Triple-Orange Squares

> 1 **6-ounce package orange-flavored gelatin**
> 2 **cups boiling water**
> 1 **6-ounce can frozen orange juice concentrate**
> 1 **20-ounce can crushed pineapple**
> 1 **11-ounce can mandarin orange sections, drained**
> 1 **cup whipping cream**
> 1 **4-serving-size package *instant* lemon pudding mix**
> 1 **cup milk**
> **Lettuce (optional)**

Dissolve gelatin in boiling water; stir in orange juice concentrate till thawed. Stir in *undrained* pineapple. Chill till partially set (the consistency of unbeaten egg whites). Fold in oranges; pour into a 13x9x2-inch dish or pan. Chill till almost firm. Beat whipping cream to soft peaks; set aside. Beat pudding mix and milk with a rotary beater 1 to 2 minutes or just till smooth; fold in whipped cream. Spread over gelatin; chill 5 to 6 hours or overnight till firm. To serve, cut into squares. Serve on a lettuce-lined platter, if desired. Garnish each serving with additional orange sections, if desired. Makes 12 to 15 servings.

## Cherry-Lemon Ring

> 1 **3-ounce package lemon-flavored gelatin**
> 1 **3-ounce package cherry-flavored gelatin**
> 2 **cups boiling water**
> 1 **16-ounce can pitted dark sweet cherries**
> 1 **8-ounce carton lemon yogurt**

Dissolve lemon- and cherry-flavored gelatins in boiling water. Drain and halve cherries; reserve syrup. Add enough water to syrup to measure 1½ cups liquid; stir into gelatin mixture. Add lemon yogurt; beat with a rotary beater till smooth. Chill till partially set (the consistency of unbeaten egg whites). Fold in the halved cherries. Pour into a 5½-cup ring mold. Chill till firm. Makes 8 servings.

## Cherry-Cider Salad

**2**   **cups apple cider or apple juice**
**1**   **6-ounce package cherry-flavored gelatin**
**1**   **16-ounce can pitted dark sweet cherries**
**½**   **cup thinly sliced celery**
**½**   **cup chopped walnuts**
**1**   **3-ounce package cream cheese, softened**
**1**   **8½-ounce can (1 cup) applesauce**
    **Leaf lettuce**

Bring cider to boiling. Dissolve gelatin in boiling cider. Drain cherries, reserving syrup; halve cherries and set aside. Add enough water to reserved syrup to measure 1½ cups liquid; stir into gelatin. Set aside *2 cups* of the gelatin mixture; keep at room temperature. Chill remaining gelatin till partially set (the consistency of unbeaten egg whites).

Fold halved cherries, celery, and walnuts into the partially set gelatin. Pour into a 6½-cup ring mold. Chill till almost firm. Gradually add reserved gelatin to softened cream cheese, beating till smooth. Stir in applesauce. Spoon cream cheese mixture over cherry layer in mold. Chill till firm. Unmold onto a lettuce-lined platter. Serves 10 to 12.

# Cranberry Citrus Mold

  ½  **cup sugar**
  1  **3-ounce package cherry-flavored gelatin**
  1  **3-ounce package lemon-flavored gelatin**
2½  **cups boiling water**
  1  **8¼-ounce can crushed pineapple**
  1  **tablespoon lemon juice**
  1  **small whole orange, quartered and seeded**
  2  **cups fresh or frozen cranberries**
  1  **cup finely chopped celery**

Dissolve sugar and gelatins in boiling water. Add *undrained* pineapple and lemon juice; chill till partially set (the consistency of unbeaten egg whites). With a food grinder or the steel blade of a food processor coarsely grind orange and cranberries. Fold cranberry mixture and celery into gelatin. Pour into a 7-cup mold. Chill till firm. Serves 10 to 12.

# Strawberry-Banana Soufflé Salads

  1  **10-ounce package frozen sliced**
      **strawberries, thawed**
  1  **3-ounce package strawberrry-flavored**
      **gelatin**
  ¼  **teaspoon salt**
  1  **cup boiling water**
  2  **tablespoons lemon juice**
  ¼  **cup mayonnaise *or* salad dressing**
  ¼  **cup chopped walnuts**
  2  **ripe medium bananas, finely diced**
      **Lettuce**

Drain strawberries, reserving syrup; set strawberries aside. Add enough water to syrup to measure ¾ cup liquid. Dissolve gelatin and salt in boiling water. Stir in reserved strawberry syrup mixture and lemon juice. Add mayonnaise or salad dressing; beat with a rotary beater. Chill till partially set (the consistency of unbeaten egg whites). Whip gelatin mixture till fluffy. Fold in the reserved strawberries and the nuts. Divide banana slices among 6 individual molds. Divide gelatin mixture among molds. Chill till firm. Unmold onto a lettuce-lined platter. Serve with additional mayonnaise or salad dressing, if desired. Makes 6 servings.

## Jubilee Salad Mold

  1   **10-ounce package frozen red raspberries, thawed**
  1   **6-ounce package red raspberry-flavored gelatin**
1¾   **cups boiling water**
  ½   **cup cream sherry**
  ¼   **cup lemon juice**
  1   **16-ounce can pitted dark sweet cherries, drained and halved**
      **Lettuce**

Drain raspberries, reserving syrup; set raspberries aside. In a large mixing bowl dissolved gelatin in the boiling water. Stir in sherry, lemon juice, and reserved raspberry syrup. Chill till partially set (the consistency of unbeaten egg whites). Fold in raspberries and cherries. Pour into a 5½- or 6-cup ring mold. Chill till firm. Unmold onto a lettuce-lined platter. Makes 8 servings.

## Cider Waldorf Mold

  2   **cups apple cider or apple juice**
  1   **3-ounce package lemon-flavored gelatin**
  1   **cup finely chopped apple**
  ¼   **cup finely chopped celery**
  ¼   **cup finely chopped pecans**
      **Lettuce**
      **Mayonnaise or salad dressing**

In a saucepan bring *1 cup* of the apple cider to boiling. Dissolve gelatin in boiling cider, stirring constantly. Stir in the remaining apple cider. Chill till partially set (the consistency of unbeaten egg whites).

Fold in chopped apple, celery, and pecans. Pour into a 3-cup mold or spoon into 6 individual molds. Chill till firm. Unmold onto lettuce-lined plate(s). Serve with mayonnaise or salad dressing. Makes 6 servings.

---

## Unmolding a gelatin salad

Tower or ring gelatin salads aren't tricky to unmold if you follow these steps and helpful hints. To begin, with the tip of a small paring knife or spatula, loosen the edges of the gelatin from the mold (and around the center of the ring mold).

Then, dip the mold just to the rim in warm water for a *few seconds*. Tilt slightly to ease gelatin away from one side and let air in. Tilt and rotate mold so air can loosen gelatin all the way around.

Next, center an upside-down serving plate over the mold. Holding tightly, invert the plate and mold together. Shake mold gently. Lift off the mold, being careful not to tear the gelatin. If the salad doesn't slide out easily, repeat the process, beginning with the first step.

---

## Lime Fruit Salad

- 1   8¾-ounce can fruit cocktail
- ¾   cup water
- 1   3-ounce package lime-flavored gelatin
- 1   3-ounce package cream cheese, cubed and softened
- ½   cup whipping cream
- ¼   cup chopped walnuts

Drain fruit cocktail, reserving syrup. In a saucepan combine reserved fruit syrup, water, and the lime gelatin. Heat, stirring frequently, till gelatin is dissolved. Gradually add hot gelatin mixture to cream cheese; beat with a rotary beater till smooth. Chill till partially set (the consistency of unbeaten egg whites). Beat whipping cream till soft peaks form. Fold drained fruit cocktail, walnuts, and whipped cream into gelatin mixture. Pour into a 3½-cup mold. Chill till firm. Makes 6 servings.

## Creamy Fruit Salad

- **1   11-ounce can mandarin orange sections**
- **1   3-ounce package lemon-flavored gelatin**
- **½   cup orange juice**
- **2   beaten eggs**
- **1   cup dairy sour cream**
- **1   3-ounce package cream cheese, cubed and softened**
- **1   medium banana, sliced**
- **⅓   cup chopped walnuts**
      **Lettuce**

Drain orange sections, reserving syrup. Add enough water to syrup to measure 1 cup liquid. In a saucepan bring syrup-water mixture to boiling. Add gelatin, stirring to dissolve. Stir in orange juice. Gradually stir about *1 cup* of the hot mixture into eggs; return all to saucepan. Cook and stir 2 minutes more. Remove from heat. Add sour cream and cream cheese; beat with a rotary beater till smooth. Chill till partially set (the consistency of unbeaten egg whites).

Fold in orange sections, sliced banana, and nuts. Turn into a 10x6x2-inch dish. Chill till firm. Cut into squares. Serve on lettuce-lined salad plates. Makes 8 servings.

# Cranberry Frost Salad

> 1 **cup fresh *or* frozen cranberries, finely**
> **chopped**
> ⅓ **cup sugar**
> 2 **medium oranges**
> 1 **8-ounce package cream cheese, softened**
> 1 **teaspoon vanilla**
> 1 **medium apple, finely chopped**
> ½ **cup chopped dates**
> 1 **cup whipping cream**
> **Lettuce**

Combine cranberries and sugar; let stand 10 minutes. Meanwhile, peel and section 1 orange, reserving juice. Finely chop orange sections; set aside. Squeeze remaining orange to make a total of ⅓ cup juice. Combine the ⅓ cup orange juice, the cream cheese, and vanilla; beat with a rotary beater till fluffy. Stir in orange sections, cranberries, apple, and dates. Whip cream till soft peaks form. Fold whipped cream into cream cheese mixture.

Turn mixture into a 5-cup mold, 8x4x2-inch loaf pan, 8 or 9 individual molds, or into about 10 to 12 paper-bake-cup-lined muffin pans. Cover and freeze till firm. To serve, let stand at room temperature for 10 to 15 minutes to soften slightly. Unmold or peel off paper and serve on a lettuce-lined plate. Garnish with additional orange sections, if desired. Makes 8 or 9 servings.

# Five-Cup Salad

> 1 **11-ounce can mandarin orange sections,**
> **drained**
> 1 **8¼-ounce can pineapple chunks, drained**
> 1 **cup coconut**
> 1 **cup tiny marshmallows**
> 1 **cup dairy sour cream**

In a bowl combine mandarin orange sections, pineapple chunks, coconut, marshmallows, and sour cream. Cover and chill for several hours or overnight. Makes 6 to 8 servings.

## Frozen Lemon Salad

    1   8-ounce package cream cheese, softened
   ¼   cup mayonnaise or salad dressing
    1   pint lemon sherbet
    1   11-ounce can mandarin orange sections,
           drained and cut up
    1   8¾-ounce can peach slices, drained and
           chopped
   ¼   cup toasted slivered almonds
        Lettuce

In a large bowl stir together cream cheese and mayonnaise or salad dressing till smooth. Stir lemon sherbet to soften; quickly stir into cream cheese mixture. Stir in cut-up orange sections, chopped peaches, and almonds. Turn cream cheese-fruit mixture into an 8x8x2-inch dish. Cover and freeze till firm.

To serve, let stand at room temperature for 10 to 15 minutes. Cut into squares. Serve on lettuce-lined salad plates. Makes 8 to 9 servings.

## Waldorf Salad

    4   medium apples
    1   tablespoon lemon juice
   ½   cup chopped celery
   ½   cup halved seedless green grapes
   ½   cup chopped walnuts
   ¼   cup raisins
   ½   cup mayonnaise or salad dressing
    1   tablespoon sugar
   ½   teaspoon lemon juice
   ½   cup whipping cream
        Ground nutmeg

Core and dice apples (to make about 4 cups). In a large bowl sprinkle cut-up apples with 1 tablespoon lemon juice. Add celery, grapes, walnuts, and raisins.

For dressing, in a small bowl combine mayonnaise or salad

dressing, sugar, and ½ teaspoon lemon juice. Whip cream just till soft peaks form. Fold whipped cream into the mayonnaise mixture; spoon over the apple mixture. Sprinkle lightly with nutmeg. Cover and chill. To serve, fold dressing into fruit mixture. Makes 8 to 10 servings.

## Fruit-Filled Melons

- **1   16-ounce package frozen sliced strawberries**
- **1   8-ounce carton plain yogurt**
- **3   large cantaloupes**
  **Lettuce**
- **2   cups cream-style cottage cheese, drained**
- **1   cup fresh or frozen blueberries, thawed**

Partially thaw and drain frozen strawberries, reserving ¼ cup of the syrup. To prepare dressing, mix together yogurt and the reserved strawberry syrup. Cover and chill.

Meanwhile, cut each cantaloupe in half and remove the seeds. Use a melon baller to scoop out pulp. To make each melon half rest firmly on a salad plate, trim a thin slice from the bottom of each melon half. Line melon shells with lettuce. Allowing ⅓ cup of cottage cheese for *each* salad, begin layering with half of the cottage cheese in the bottom of each melon half. Continue layering with some of the strawberries, a few melon balls, remaining cottage cheese, remaining strawberries, the blueberries, and remaining melon balls. Top with chilled dressing. Serve immediately. Makes 6 servings.

## Fruit Strata Salad

> 3 cups shredded lettuce
> 1 honeydew melon, peeled, seeded, and cubed
> 1 20-ounce can pineapple chunks, drained
> 1 pint strawberries, halved
> 1 large banana, sliced
> 1 8-ounce carton pineapple, lemon, *or* vanilla yogurt
> ½ cup shredded Gruyère *or* Swiss cheese (2 ounces)

In a large salad bowl place *half* of the lettuce. Layer fruits atop lettuce. Top with remaining lettuce. Spread yogurt over top; sprinkle with shredded cheese. Cover and chill 2 to 3 hours. Toss gently to serve. Makes 12 servings.

## 24-Hour Fruit Salad

> 1 20-ounce can pineapple chunks
> 3 slightly beaten egg yolks
> 2 tablespoons sugar
> 2 tablespoons vinegar
> 1 tablespoon butter *or* margarine
> Dash salt
> 1 16-ounce can pitted light sweet cherries, drained
> 3 oranges, peeled, sectioned, and drained
> 2 cups tiny marshmallows
> 1 cup whipping cream

Drain pineapple; reserve 2 tablespoons syrup. To make custard, in a heavy small saucepan combine reserved pineapple syrup, egg yolks, sugar, vinegar, butter or margarine, and salt. Cook and stir over low heat about 6 minutes or till mixture thickens slightly and coats a metal spoon. Cool to room temperature. In a large bowl combine pineapple chunks, cherries, oranges, and marshmallows. Pour custard over; stir gently.

Beat the whipping cream till soft peaks form. Fold whipped cream into fruit mixture. Turn into a serving bowl. Cover and chill 24 hours or overnight. Makes 10 to 12 servings.

---

## Fruit-and-Nut Tropical Slaw

| | |
|---|---|
| 1 | **8¼-ounce can pineapple slices** |
| 1 | **tablespoon lemon juice** |
| 1 | **medium banana, sliced (1 cup)** |
| 3 | **cups finely shredded cabbage** |
| 1 | **cup thinly sliced celery** |
| 1 | **11-ounce can mandarin orange sections, drained** |
| ½ | **cup chopped walnuts** |
| ¼ | **cup raisins** |
| 1 | **8-ounce carton orange yogurt** |

Drain pineapple, reserving 2 tablespoons syrup. Cut up pineapple; set aside. Combine the reserved syrup and lemon juice. Toss banana slices with 1 tablespoon of the juice mixture; set aside remaining juice. In a large bowl combine pineapple, banana, cabbage, celery, oranges, nuts, and raisins. Combine the reserved juice mixture with the orange yogurt and ½ teaspoon *salt.* Add to pineapple-cabbage mixture; toss lightly to coat. Cover and chill. Makes 8 to 10 servings.

---

## Fruit Medley Salad

| | |
|---|---|
| ¼ | **cup dairy sour cream** |
| ¼ | **cup mayonnaise *or* salad dressing** |
| ¼ | **cup crumbled blue cheese** |
| 2 | **teaspoons milk** |
| 4 | **ounces prosciutto, thinly sliced and cut up** |
| ½ | **honeydew melon, cut into balls** |
| ½ | **cantaloupe, cut into balls** |
| 1 | **large peach, sliced** |
| 1 | **cup strawberries, halved** |
| | **Leaf lettuce** |

For dressing, in a small mixing bowl combine the sour cream, mayonnaise or salad dressing, blue cheese, and milk. Cover and chill.

Arrange prosciutto, honeydew and cantaloupe melon balls, peach slices, and halved strawberries on a lettuce-lined platter. Serve the chilled dressing with salad. Serves 4 to 6.

# Cinnamon Fruit Salad

        ¼   cup red cinnamon candies
        2   tablespoon vinegar
        2   tablespoons water
            Dash salt
        3   beaten egg yolks
        2   tablespoons honey
        1   tablespoon butter or margarine
        1   tablespoon lemon juice
        2   medium bananas, sliced (2 cups)
        3   medium apples, diced (3 cups)
        1   cup tiny marshmallows
        1   cup halved seedless green grapes
        ½   cup whipping cream

In a small saucepan combine cinnamon candies, vinegar, water, and salt. Cook and stir till candies are dissolved. In a small bowl combine egg yolks and honey. Gradually stir hot cinnamon mixture into egg yolk mixture; return all to saucepan. Add butter or margarine. Cook and stir 3 to 4 minutes or till thickened; cover and cool. In a large bowl sprinkle lemon juice over banana slices; let stand a few minutes. Add diced apples, marshmallows, and grapes. Fold in cinnamon mixture. Whip cream just to soft peaks; fold into fruit mixture. Cover and chill 4 to 6 hours. Makes 10 to 12 servings.

# Choose-a-Fruit Salad Platter

 8  **cups desired fresh fruits\***
    **Lemon juice**
    **Lettuce**
    **Honey-Lime Dressing, Strawberry-Cheese
    Dressing, or Spicy Nectar Dressing**

If necessary, brush fruits with some lemon juice to prevent
darkening. On a large lettuce-lined platter arrange the fresh
fruits. Serve with Honey-Lime Dressing, Strawberry-Cheese
Dressing, or Spicy Nectar Dressing. Makes 10 to 12 servings.

   *Honey-Lime Dressing:* In a small mixer bowl combine ⅓
cup *honey,* ½ teaspoon finely shredded *lime peel,* ⅓ cup *lime
juice,* ¼ teaspoon *salt,* and ¼ teaspoon ground *mace.* Gradually add ¾ cup *salad oil,* beating with an electric mixer or
rotary beater till mixture is smooth and thickened. Cover and
chill. Makes 1½ cups.

   *Strawberry-Cheese Dressing:* In a small mixer bowl
combine one 3-ounce package *cream cheese,* softened; ½ of
a 10-ounce package (½ cup) frozen *strawberries,* thawed; 1
tablespoon *sugar;* 1 tablespoon *lemon juice;* and dash *salt.*
Beat till smooth. Add ½ cup *salad oil* in a slow stream, beating
till thick. Cover and chill. Makes 1½ cups.

   *Spicy Nectar Dressing:* In a small mixer bowl combine
1 cup *dairy sour cream,* ½ cup *apricot nectar,* ½ cup *salad oil,*
2 tablespoons *sugar,* ½ teaspoon ground *cinnamon,* ½ teaspoon *paprika,* and dash *salt.* Beat till smooth. Cover and chill.
Makes 2 cups.

   **\*Fruit Options** (choose any combination): peeled and
sliced or cut-up avocados, bananas, kiwis, mangoes, melons,
papayas, peaches, or pineapples; sliced or cut-up apples, apricots, nectarines, pears, or plums; peeled and sectioned oranges,
tangerines, or grapefruits; berries (halve any large strawberries); halved and pitted dark sweet cherries; or halved seedless
green grapes.

# Main-Dish Salads

## Shrimp-Avocado Salad

- 1 small avocado, peeled, seeded, and cut up
- ½ cup buttermilk
- 1 3-ounce package cream cheese
- 1 tablespoon lemon juice
- 1 small clove garlic
- ¼ teaspoon bottled hot pepper sauce
- 6 cups torn lettuce
- 1 pound shelled shrimp, cooked and drained
- 18 cherry tomatoes, halved
- 4 ounces Swiss cheese, cut into julienne strips

In a blender container place the first 6 ingredients and ½ teaspoon *salt;* cover and blend till smooth. Arrange lettuce in a salad bowl. Arrange shrimp, tomatoes, and cheese atop. Sprinkle with a little pepper. Toss with avocado mixture to serve. Makes 6 servings.

## Chef's Salad

- 1 clove garlic, halved
- 6 cups torn iceberg lettuce
- 3 cups torn romaine
- 8 ounces Swiss or cheddar cheese
- 6 ounces fully cooked ham or cooked beef
- 6 ounces cooked chicken or turkey
- 4 hard-cooked eggs, sliced
- 3 medium tomatoes, cut into wedges
- 2 small green peppers, cut into rings and quartered
  Salad dressing (see recipes, pages 701–5)

Rub 6 large individual salad bowls with the cut surface of garlic clove. Place torn lettuce and romaine in salad bowls. Cut cheese, ham or beef, and chicken or turkey into julienne strips. Arrange cheese, meats, eggs, tomatoes, and green pepper over the greens. Serve with a salad dressing. Serves 6.

## Greek Salad

  **1**  **head curly endive, torn (6 cups)**
  **½**  **medium head iceberg lettuce, torn (3 cups)**
  **10**  **ounces cooked lamb *or* beef, cut into**
      **julienne strips (2 cups)**
  **2**  **tomatoes, peeled and chopped**
  **¾**  **cup cubed feta cheese**
  **¼**  **cup sliced pitted ripe olives**
  **¼**  **cup sliced green onion**
  **⅔**  **cup olive oil *or* salad oil**
  **⅓**  **cup white wine vinegar**
  **½**  **teaspoon salt**
  **¼**  **teaspoon dried oregano, crushed**
  **1**  **2-ounce can anchovy fillets, drained**

In a mixing bowl toss together endive and lettuce; mound onto 6 individual salad plates. Arrange lamb or beef, tomatoes, feta cheese, olives, and onion atop greens. To make dressing, in a screw-top jar combine oil, vinegar, salt, oregano, and ⅛ teaspoon *pepper*. Cover; shake well to mix. Pour dressing over salads. Top salads with the anchovy fillets. Serves 6.

# Curried Chicken Salad

    2  **large oranges**
    2  **medium bananas**
    7  **cups torn iceberg lettuce, romaine, leaf
         lettuce, Bibb lettuce, or spinach**
    3  **cups cubed cooked chicken or turkey**
    1  **8-ounce can jellied cranberry sauce, chilled
         and cut into ½-inch cubes**
    ½  **cup light raisins**
    ½  **cup salted peanuts**
    ¾  **cup mayonnaise or salad dressing**
    1  **8-ounce carton orange yogurt**
    2  **teaspoons curry powder**

Section oranges over a bowl to catch juice. Slice bananas diagonally and dip in the reserved orange juice. In a large salad bowl place lettuce. Arrange orange sections, banana slices, chicken, cranberry cubes, raisins, and peanuts atop lettuce. Cover; chill. To make dressing, combine mayonnaise or salad dressing, yogurt, and curry powder; cover and chill. Pass dressing with salad. Makes 6 servings.

# Scallop Toss

Cook one 12-ounce package frozen *scallops* according to package directions; drain. Halve any large scallops. In a bowl marinate scallops in ½ cup *Russian Dressing* (see recipe, page 704) in the refrigerator for 30 minutes or till thoroughly chilled.

Rub a large salad bowl with the cut side of 1 clove *garlic*, halved; discard. Add 2 cups torn *iceberg lettuce;* 2 cups torn *romaine;* 2 cups torn fresh *spinach;* 3 hard-cooked *eggs*, chilled and quartered; ½ cup chopped *celery;* and 6 ounces *mozzarella cheese,* cut into julienne strips. Toss lightly to mix. Add the chilled scallop mixture; toss to coat. Makes 6 servings.

## South-of-the-Border Salad

*If using hot sausage, decrease chili powder—*

- **1 pound bulk pork sausage, ground pork, or ground beef**
- **½ cup chopped onion**
- **1 clove garlic, minced**
- **1 tablespoon all-purpose flour**
- **1 8-ounce can tomato sauce**
- **1 7½-ounce can tomatoes, cut up**
- **1 4-ounce can green chili peppers, rinsed, seeded, and chopped**
- **2 teaspoons chili powder**
- **6 cups torn iceberg lettuce**
- **1 15-ounce can garbanzo beans, drained**
- **½ cup sliced pitted ripe olives**
- **1 cup shredded Monterey Jack or cheddar cheese (4 ounces)**
- **1 cup cherry tomatoes, halved**
- **1 medium green pepper, cut into julienne strips**
- **1 avocado, peeled, seeded, and sliced**

Cook meat, onion, and garlic till meat is browned and onion is tender; drain. Stir in flour, tomato sauce, *undrained* tomatoes, chili peppers, and chili powder. Cook and stir till thickened and bubbly. Meanwhile, in a salad bowl combine lettuce, beans, and olives; toss to mix. Place mixture on 6 individual salad plates. Top lettuce with meat mixture. Sprinkle cheese over. Top *each* salad with a few tomato halves and green pepper strips. Arrange avocado slices atop *each* salad. Serves 6.

## Salad Niçoise

½   medium head romaine, torn (3 cups)
1   head Bibb lettuce, torn (2 cups)
1   6½-ounce can water-pack tuna, drained
1   9-ounce package frozen cut green beans,
      cooked, drained, and chilled
1   cup cherry tomatoes, halved
1   small green pepper, cut into rings
1   small onion, sliced and separated into
      rings
3   hard-cooked eggs, chilled and cut into
      wedges
1   medium potato, cooked, chilled, and
      sliced
½   cup pitted ripe olives
1   2-ounce can anchovy fillets, drained
¾   cup Vinaigrette Dressing (see recipe, page
      703)

Line a large platter with torn romaine and Bibb lettuce. Break tuna into chunks; mound in center of torn lettuce. Arrange chilled green beans, tomatoes, green pepper, onion rings, egg wedges, potato, olives, and anchovy fillets atop the lettuce. Cover and chill. Just before serving, drizzle with Vinaigrette Dressing; toss. Makes 6 servings.

---

### How to julienne

Julienne meats and vegetables by cutting them into long thin strips. First cut a thin slice off one side of the meat or vegetable, if necessary, to make it lie flat on the cutting board. Placing the flat side down, cut off thin lengthwise slices.

Then cut each slice into narrow strips about ⅛ to ¼ inch thick.

# Quick Reuben Salad

8  cups torn leaf lettuce
1  cup chilled, cooked corned beef *or* two
       3-ounce packages sliced corned beef, cut
       into thin strips
1  8-ounce can sauerkraut, chilled, drained,
       and snipped
1  cup cubed Swiss cheese (4 ounces)
1  cup Rye Croutons
¾  cup Thousand Island Dressing (see recipe,
       page 704)
½  teaspoon caraway seed

In 4 individual salad bowls place torn lettuce. Arrange corned beef, sauerkarut, cheese, and Rye Croutons atop lettuce in each bowl. Combine Thousand Island Dressing and caraway seed; pour over salad. Makes 4 servings.

**Rye Croutons:** Brush both sides of 5 slices *rye bread* with 3 tablespoons *butter or margarine,* softened. Cut bread into ½-inch cubes. Spread out on a large shallow baking pan. Bake in a 300° oven for 20 to 25 minutes or till cubes are dry and crisp; stir at least once. Cool. Store in a covered container in the refrigerator. Makes 2 cups croutons.

# Meatless Meal-in-a-Bowl

4  hard-cooked eggs, chilled
4  cups torn fresh spinach
1  15-ounce can garbanzo beans, drained
1  cup cauliflower flowerets
1  cup sliced fresh mushrooms
1  cup cherry tomatoes, halved
1  small cucumber, thinly sliced
½  small red onion, thinly sliced and
       separated into rings
½  cup coarsely chopped walnuts
1  cup Avocado Dressing (see recipe, page
       703)

Slice 3 of the hard-cooked eggs. Cut the remaining egg into wedges; set aside.

In a salad bowl combine torn spinach, beans, cauliflower flowerets, mushrooms, tomatoes, cucumber, onion, walnuts, and the sliced hard-cooked eggs. Pour Avocado Dressing over salad; toss to coat. Garnish with the hard-cooked egg wedges. Makes 6 servings.

## Crab Louis

- 1 **medium head iceberg lettuce**
- 2 **7-ounce cans crab meat, chilled and drained**
- 2 **large tomatoes, cut into wedges**
- 2 **hard-cooked eggs, cut into wedges**
  **Louis Dressing**
  **Paprika**
- 1 **lemon, cut into wedges**

Line *each* of 4 individual salad plates with a large lettuce leaf. Tear remaining lettuce into bite-size pieces and pile atop lettuce-lined plates. Break crab meat into pieces, removing cartilage and reserving 4 large segments of crab meat. Place remaining crab meat on lettuce. Arrange tomato wedges and egg wedges around meat. Lightly salt tomatoes and eggs. Pour ¼ cup of the Louis Dressing over *each* salad. Sprinkle paprika atop. Top with reserved crab meat. To serve, pass the additional dressing and lemon wedges. Makes 4 servings.

***Louis Dressing:*** Combine 1 cup *mayonnaise or salad dressing,* ¼ cup *chili sauce,* ¼ cup finely chopped *green pepper,* ¼ cup finely chopped *green onion,* 1 teaspoon *lemon juice,* and dash *salt.* Beat ¼ cup *whipping cream* to soft peaks. Fold into mayonnaise mixture. Cover; chill. Makes 2 cups.

# Sausage Supper Salad

- **4** cups torn iceberg lettuce
- **8** ounces salami, pepperoni, summer sausage, *or* other dry sausage
- **1** cup cubed cheddar cheese
- **2** hard-cooked eggs, cut into wedges
- **½** of a 15-ounce can (1 cup) garbanzo beans, drained
- **1** cup sliced celery
- **½** cup chopped onion
- **½** cup mayonnaise *or* salad dressing
- **2** tablespoons milk
- **1½** teaspoons prepared horseradish
- **½** teaspoon dry mustard

Place lettuce in a large salad bowl. Cut sausage into thin slices, then into bite-size pieces. Arrange sausage, cheese, egg wedges, beans, celery, and onion atop lettuce. For dressing, combine remaining ingredients; pour over salad. Toss. Serves 6.

# Crab-Stuffed Tomatoes

- **2** hard-cooked eggs, coarsely chopped
- **½** cup chopped celery
- **¼** cup finely chopped cucumber
- **1** tablespoon lemon juice
- **1** 7-ounce can crab meat, drained and flaked
- **⅓** cup mayonnaise *or* salad dressing
- **1** teaspoon prepared mustard
- **4** tomato cups (see tip box)

Combine the first 4 ingredients and dash *pepper.* Stir in crab, mayonnaise, and mustard. Cover; chill. Fill *each* tomato cup with about ½ *cup* of the crab mixture. Makes 4 servings.

## Tuna-Stuffed Tomatoes

  ½   **cup chopped celery**
  ¼   **cup sliced green onion**
  1   **tablespoon lemon juice**
  ¼   **teaspoon salt**
  1   **6½-ounce can tuna, drained and flaked**
  ⅓   **cup mayonnaise *or* salad dressing**
  2   **hard-cooked eggs, chopped**
  4   **tomato cups (see tip box)**

Combine the first 4 ingredients and dash *pepper*. Stir in tuna, mayonnaise, and chopped eggs. (Add additional mayonnaise, if desired.) Cover; chill. Fill *each* tomato cup with about ½ *cup* of the tuna mixture. Makes 4 servings.

## Chicken-Stuffed Tomatoes

  ⅓    **cup finely chopped celery**
  ¼    **cup chopped sweet pickle**
  2    **teaspoons finely chopped onion**
  ½    **cup mayonnaise *or* salad dressing**
  1    **tablespoon lemon juice**
  ½    **teaspoon salt**
       **Dash pepper**
  1½   **cups chopped cooked chicken**
  4    **tomato cups (see tip box)**

Combine celery, pickle, and onion. Combine next 4 ingredients; fold into celery mixture along with chopped cooked chicken. Cover; chill. Fill *each* tomato cup with about ½ *cup* of the chicken mixture. Makes 4 servings.

## Making tomato cups

Fresh, red, ripe tomatoes make attractive containers for individual servings of main-dish salads.

To make decorative petal cups as shown above, place the tomatoes, stem end down, on a cutting surface. With a sharp knife, cut each tomato into 4 to 6 wedges, cutting to but not through the stem end of the tomato. Spread the wedges apart slightly; sprinkle in-side of tomato lightly with salt. Cover and chill.

When ready to serve, spread the wedges apart and spoon in the salad mixture. (*See* the recipes at left.)

To make plain cups, cut a small slice from the top of *each* tomato. Remove the core, if present. Use a spoon to scoop out the seeds, leaving a ½-inch-thick shell. Sprinkle the cups lightly with salt. Invert tomatoes; cover and chill. Fill tomato cups with salad mixture at serving time.

To dress up the plain tomato cups, carefully cut the edge into scallops or a sawtooth pattern.

# Salad Dressings

### Red Wine Dressing

In a screw-top jar combine 1 cup *salad oil*; ⅓ cup *vinegar*; ⅓ cup dry *red wine*; 1 teaspoon *sugar*; 1 teaspoon dried *thyme*, crushed; ½ teaspoon dried *oregano*, crushed; ¼ teaspoon *salt*;

and 1 clove *garlic*. Cover and shake well to mix. Chill. Remove garlic; shake again just before serving. Makes 1⅔ cups.

## Italian Dressing

In a screw-top jar combine 1⅓ cups *salad oil;* ½ cup *vinegar;* ¼ cup grated *Parmesan cheese,* if desired; 1 tablespoon *sugar;* 2 teaspoons *salt;* 1 teaspoon *celery salt;* ½ teaspoon *white pepper;* ½ teaspoon *dry mustard;* ¼ teaspoon *paprika;* and 1 clove *garlic,* minced. Cover; shake well to mix. Chill. Shake again just before serving. Makes 1¾ cups.

## Buttermilk Dressing

   ½   **cup mayonnaise *or* salad dressing**
   ½   **cup sour cream with chives**
   ½   **cup buttermilk**
   ¼   **cup tomato juice**
   2   **tablespoons grated Parmesan cheese**
   ½   **teaspoon dry mustard**
   ¼   **teaspoon paprika**
   ¼   **teaspoon celery seed**
   ⅛   **teaspoon garlic powder**

In a mixing bowl stir together mayonnaise, sour cream with chives, buttermilk, tomato juice, Parmesan cheese, dry mustard, paprika, celery seed, garlic powder, ⅛ teaspoon *salt,* and ⅛ teaspoon *pepper.* Store in a tightly covered jar in the refrigerator. Makes 1¾ cups.

## Creamy French Dressing

In a small mixer bowl combine 1 tablespoon *paprika,* 2 teaspoons *sugar,* 1 teaspoon *salt,* and dash ground *red pepper.* Add ¼ cup *vinegar* and 1 *egg;* beat well. Add 1 cup *salad oil* in a slow, steady stream, beating constantly with an electric mixer or a rotary beater till thick. Store in a tightly covered jar in the refrigerator. Makes about 1⅔ cups.

# Chunky Blue Cheese Dressing

In a blender container combine ½ cup *plain yogurt,* ¼ cup *cream-style cottage cheese,* ¼ cup *mayonnaise or salad dressing,* ¼ cup crumbled *blue cheese.* Cover and blend till nearly smooth. Transfer dressing to a storage container; stir in ½ cup crumbled *blue cheese.* Cover and chill. Makes 1⅓ cups.

# Avocado Dressing

Combine ¾ cup *dairy sour cream,* ⅓ cup *milk,* 1 tablespoon *lemon juice,* ½ teaspoon *celery salt,* and a few dashes bottled *hot pepper sauce.* Stir in 1 large *avocado,* seeded, peeled, and mashed. If necessary, stir in additional milk to achieve desired serving consistency. Cover and refrigerate and use within a few hours to prevent discoloration. Makes about 1⅔ cups dressing.

# Vinaigrette Dressing

> **1** **cup salad oil**
> **⅔** **cup vinegar**
> **2** **teaspoons snipped fresh herb or ½**
> **teaspoon dried herb, crushed***
> **1** **to 2 teaspoons sugar**
> **1½** **teaspoons salt**
> **1½** **teaspoons paprika (optional)**

In a screw-top jar combine all ingredients. Cover and shake well. Chill. Shake again just before serving. Makes about 1½ cups dressing.

**Citrus Vinaigrette:** Prepare Vinaigrette Dressing as above, *except* substitute *lemon juice or lime juice* for the vinegar.

***Note:** Vary the flavor by using different herbs. Choose from thyme, oregano, basil, tarragon, dillweed, and chives.

## French Dressing

In a screw-top jar combine ½ cup *salad oil*, 2 tablespoons *vinegar*, 2 tablespoons *lemon juice*, 1 teaspoon *sugar*, ¾ teaspoon *dry mustard*, ½ teaspoon *salt*, ⅛ teaspoon *paprika*, and dash ground *red pepper*. Cover; shake well. Chill. Shake before serving. Makes ¾ cup.

## Green Goddess Dressing

In a blender container combine 1 cup loosely packed *parsley leaves*; ½ cup *mayonnaise*; ½ cup *dairy sour cream*; 1 *green onion*, cut up; 2 tablespoons *tarragon vinegar*; 1 tablespoon *anchovy paste*; ½ teaspoon dried *basil*, crushed; and ¼ teaspoon *sugar*. Cover; blend till smooth. Store in a tightly covered jar in the refrigerator. Makes 1¼ cups.

## Thousand Island Dressing

Combine 1 cup *mayonnaise*, ¼ cup *chili sauce*, 2 finely chopped *hard-cooked eggs*, 2 tablespoons *each* finely chopped *green pepper*, *celery*, and *onion*, 1 teaspoon *paprika*, and ½ teaspoon *salt*; mix well. Store in a tightly covered jar in the refrigerator. Makes about 1¾ cups.

## Russian Dressing

In a screw-top jar combine ⅔ cup *salad oil*, ½ cup *catsup*, ¼ cup *sugar*, 3 tablespoons *lemon juice*, 2 tablespoons *Worcestershire sauce*, 2 tablespoons *vinegar*, 2 tablespoons *water*, 1 tablespoon grated *onion*, ½ teaspoon *salt*, and ½ teaspoon *paprika*. Cover; shake. Chill. Shake before serving. Makes 1¾ cups.

# Cooked Dressing

In a small saucepan combine 2 tablespoons *all-purpose flour,* 2 tablespoons *sugar,* 1 teaspoon *salt,* 1 teaspoon *dry mustard,* and dash ground *red pepper.* Stir in ¾ cup *milk.* Beat 2 *egg yolks* slightly; add to saucepan. Cook and stir over low heat till bubbly. Add ¼ cup *vinegar* and 1½ teaspoons *butter,* stirring till butter is melted. Cool. Store in a tightly covered jar in the refrigerator. Makes 1 cup.

# Homemade Mayonnaise

|   |   |
|---|---|
| ½ | **teaspoon dry mustard** |
| ¼ | **teaspoon paprika** |
|   | **Dash ground red pepper** |
| 2 | **egg yolks** |
| 2 | **tablespoons vinegar** |
| 2 | **cups salad oil** |
| 2 | **tablespoons lemon juice** |

In a small mixer bowl combine mustard, paprika, red pepper, and 1 teaspoon *salt.* Add egg yolks and vinegar; beat mixture at medium speed of electric mixer till combined. Add the oil, 1 teaspoon at a time, beating constantly. Continue adding oil 1 teaspoon at a time and beating mixture till ¼ *cup* oil has been added. While continuing to beat, add the remaining oil in a thin, steady stream, alternating the last ½ cup salad oil with the lemon juice. Store for up to 4 weeks in a tightly covered jar in the refrigerator. Makes about 2 cups.

***Creamy Fruit Dressing:*** In a mixing bowl combine 1 cup *mayonnaise or salad dressing,* 1 cup *dairy sour cream,* 1½ teaspoons shredded *orange peel,* 3 tablespoons *orange juice,* and 4 teaspoons *sugar.* Makes 2¼ cups dressing.

***Herb Dressing:*** In a mixing bowl combine 1 cup *mayonnaise or salad dressing;* 2 tablespoons finely chopped *onion;* 1 tablespoon *lemon juice;* 1 tablespoon *dry sherry;* 1 clove *garlic,* minced; 1 teaspoon *Worcestershire sauce;* and ½ teaspoon dried *mixed salad herbs,* crushed. Makes 1¼ cups dressing.

## Blender Mayonnaise

In a blender container combine 1 large *egg*, 1 tablespoon *vinegar*, ½ teaspoon *salt*, ¼ teaspoon *dry mustard*, ⅛ teaspoon *paprika*, and dash ground *red pepper*. Cover; blend about 5 seconds. With blender running slowly, gradually add ½ cup *salad oil*. (When necessary, stop blender and use a rubber spatula to scrape sides down.) Add 1 tablespoon *lemon juice*; pour ½ cup *salad oil* into the blender container with the blender running slowly. Store for up to 4 weeks in a tightly covered jar in the refrigerator. Makes about 1¼ cups.

# Sauces & Relishes

# Sauces & Relishes

# Sauces & Relishes

# Sauces & Relishes

# Sauces & Relishes

# Sauces &

# 708

# Sauces & Relishes

| Recipes | Servings (fraction of recipe) | Calories | Protein (grams) | Carbohydrate (grams) | Fat (grams) | Sodium (milligrams) | Potassium (milligrams) | Percent of U.S. RDA Per Serving — Protein | Vitamin A | Vitamin C | Thiamine | Riboflavin | Niacin | Calcium | Iron |
|---|---|---|---|---|---|---|---|---|---|---|---|---|---|---|---|
| Almond Sauce | 1/16 | 37 | 1 | 2 | 3 | 89 | 37 | 2 | 2 | 0 | 0 | 1 | 3 | 1 | 2 |
| Blender Hollandaise Sauce | 1/8 | 125 | 1 | 0 | 13 | 143 | 15 | 2 | 14 | 3 | 3 | 1 | 1 | 0 | 1 |
| Blue Cheese Sauce | 1/16 | 41 | 3 | 3 | 3 | 73 | 30 | 2 | 3 | 0 | 0 | 3 | 3 | 3 | 1 |
| Bordelaise Sauce | 1/8 | 34 | 0 | 3 | 1 | 138 | 20 | 2 | 1 | 1 | 2 | 0 | 0 | 0 | 0 |
| Brown Sauce | 1/4 | 67 | 1 | 6 | 3 | 250 | 6 | 1 | 5 | 0 | 2 | 2 | 4 | 1 | 1 |
| Cheese Sauce | 1/16 | 57 | 3 | 2 | 4 | 110 | 35 | 4 | 4 | 0 | 0 | 4 | 1 | 8 | 0 |
| Cinnamon Apple Rings | 1/12 | 61 | 0 | 15 | 0 | 2 | 51 | 0 | 0 | 3 | 1 | 1 | 1 | 0 | 1 |
| Classic Béarnaise Sauce | 1/4 | 264 | 3 | 1 | 28 | 289 | 37 | 4 | 30 | 0 | 3 | 3 | 4 | 0 | 5 |
| Classic Hollandaise Sauce | 1/8 | 132 | 1 | 1 | 14 | 144 | 17 | 2 | 15 | 3 | 1 | 1 | 2 | 0 | 3 |
| Cocktail Sauce | 1/8 | 29 | 0 | 7 | 0 | 361 | 106 | 1 | 7 | 10 | 0 | 1 | 1 | 2 | 1 |
| Confetti Sauce | 1/16 | 28 | 2 | 2 | 2 | 63 | 28 | 1 | 2 | 4 | 1 | 2 | 2 | 0 | 0 |
| Cranberry-Orange Relish | 1/14 | 149 | 0 | 35 | 0 | 1 | 77 | 1 | 1 | 25 | 2 | 1 | 2 | 1 | 2 |
| Cranberry Sauce | 1/10 | 155 | 0 | 40 | 0 | 1 | 37 | 0 | 0 | 8 | 1 | 1 | 1 | 0 | 1 |
| Creamy Mushroom Sauce | 1/6 | 103 | 2 | 4 | 9 | 249 | 80 | 3 | 7 | 2 | 2 | 2 | 7 | 2 | 1 |
| Cucumber or Zucchini Sauce | 1/16 | 27 | 1 | 2 | 2 | 59 | 29 | 1 | 1 | 2 | 0 | 1 | 2 | 2 | 0 |
| Curry Sauce | 1/16 | 26 | 1 | 2 | 2 | 58 | 23 | 1 | 2 | 2 | 0 | 0 | 2 | 2 | 0 |
| Dill Sauce | 1/4 | 18 | 0 | 1 | 1 | 48 | 2 | 2 | 0 | 0 | 0 | 0 | 0 | 0 | 0 |
| Easy Barbecue Sauce | 1/8 | 53 | 1 | 13 | 0 | 517 | 186 | 2 | 14 | 12 | 3 | 3 | 2 | 4 | 2 |
| Easy Dill Sauce | 1/10 | 41 | 1 | 3 | 3 | 243 | 43 | 2 | 2 | 1 | 1 | 0 | 3 | 1 | 1 |
| Easy Tomato-Pepper Relish | 1/16 | 26 | 0 | 2 | 0 | 79 | 58 | 2 | 4 | 26 | 1 | 1 | 0 | 0 | 1 |
| Flavored Butters | 1/12 | 68 | 0 | 0 | 8 | 93 | 2 | 0 | 6 | 0 | 0 | 0 | 0 | 0 | 0 |

# Nutrition Analysis Chart

| | | | | | | | | | | | | | | | | | | |
|---|---|---|---|---|---|---|---|---|---|---|---|---|---|---|---|---|---|---|
| Fluffy Horseradish Sauce | 1/16 | 11 | 1 | 1 | 6 | 70 | 42 | 1 | 0 | 8 | 0 | 1 | 0 | 1 | 0 | 2 | 0 | 0 |
| Fresh Cucumber Relish | 1/4 | 24 | 0 | 3 | 0 | 78 | 3 | 0 | 0 | 0 | 1 | 0 | 0 | 1 | 0 | 1 | 0 | 2 |
| Fresh Mint Sauce | 1/16 | 27 | 1 | 6 | 0 | 5 | 3 | 0 | 0 | 0 | 0 | 0 | 0 | 0 | 0 | 0 | 0 | 0 |
| Herb-Garlic Sauce | 1/16 | 27 | 2 | 2 | 2 | 59 | 24 | 1 | 2 | 0 | 1 | 2 | 2 | 2 | 2 | 0 | 2 | 2 |
| Herb Sauce | 1/16 | 26 | 1 | 2 | 2 | 58 | 23 | 1 | 2 | 0 | 1 | 2 | 2 | 2 | 2 | 0 | 2 | 0 |
| Herb-Seasoned Marinade | 1/8 | 68 | 0 | 2 | 7 | 159 | 38 | 0 | 0 | 1 | 0 | 0 | 0 | 0 | 2 | 0 | 2 | 1 |
| Honey Butter | 1/12 | 89 | 0 | 6 | 8 | 94 | 6 | 0 | 6 | 0 | 0 | 0 | 0 | 0 | 0 | 0 | 0 | 0 |
| Hot Chinese Mustard | 1/12 | 7 | 0 | 0 | 1 | 89 | 0 | 0 | 6 | 0 | 0 | 0 | 0 | 0 | 0 | 0 | 0 | 0 |
| Hot Curried Fruit | 1/14 | 64 | 0 | 15 | 1 | 11 | 130 | 1 | 13 | 5 | 2 | 1 | 1 | 1 | 1 | 1 | 1 | 0 |
| Lemon-Chive Sauce | 1/16 | 27 | 1 | 2 | 2 | 59 | 25 | 1 | 2 | 1 | 0 | 2 | 0 | 1 | 2 | 0 | 2 | 0 |
| Medium White Sauce | 1/16 | 26 | 1 | 2 | 2 | 58 | 23 | 1 | 2 | 0 | 0 | 2 | 0 | 1 | 2 | 0 | 2 | 0 |
| Mexicali Sauce | 1/16 | 27 | 1 | 2 | 2 | 60 | 35 | 1 | 3 | 3 | 1 | 2 | 0 | 1 | 2 | 0 | 2 | 0 |
| Mock Hollandaise Sauce | 1/4 | 131 | 3 | 2 | 14 | 98 | 28 | 1 | 1 | 1 | 0 | 2 | 0 | 2 | 2 | 1 | 2 | 1 |
| Orange-Grape Sauce | 1/10 | 63 | 0 | 7 | 5 | 129 | 51 | 1 | 5 | 19 | 1 | 2 | 1 | 2 | 1 | 1 | 1 | 1 |
| Parmesan or Romano Sauce | 1/16 | 31 | 1 | 2 | 2 | 68 | 25 | 2 | 2 | 0 | 0 | 1 | 0 | 2 | 3 | 0 | 3 | 0 |
| Pickled Beets | 1/8 | 39 | 0 | 10 | 0 | 85 | 98 | 1 | 0 | 4 | 1 | 1 | 1 | 1 | 1 | 1 | 1 | 2 |
| Quick Mushroom Sauce | 1/12 | 69 | 3 | 3 | 6 | 208 | 48 | 2 | 3 | 0 | 2 | 3 | 1 | 3 | 3 | 0 | 3 | 0 |
| Raisin Sauce | 1/12 | 58 | 0 | 15 | 0 | 5 | 113 | 1 | 0 | 2 | 1 | 1 | 0 | 1 | 2 | 1 | 2 | 3 |
| Sauce Diable | 1/4 | 45 | 3 | 3 | 3 | 134 | 30 | 1 | 5 | 4 | 1 | 1 | 1 | 1 | 1 | 1 | 1 | 1 |
| Sauce Provençale | 1/8 | 120 | 2 | 2 | 12 | 142 | 60 | 0 | 14 | 4 | 0 | 1 | 1 | 1 | 1 | 0 | 1 | 1 |
| Savory Wine Marinade | 1/12 | 92 | 0 | 1 | 9 | 90 | 26 | 0 | 1 | 5 | 0 | 0 | 0 | 0 | 0 | 1 | 0 | 0 |
| Sherry Sauce | 1/16 | 29 | 1 | 2 | 2 | 59 | 25 | 1 | 2 | 0 | 0 | 2 | 0 | 2 | 2 | 0 | 2 | 1 |
| Snappy Barbecue Sauce | 1/8 | 44 | 1 | 11 | 0 | 647 | 131 | 1 | 10 | 9 | 2 | 1 | 3 | 1 | 2 | 0 | 2 | 2 |
| Spicy Cherry Sauce | 1/16 | 54 | 0 | 14 | 0 | 1 | 49 | 0 | 4 | 7 | 1 | 0 | 0 | 0 | 1 | 0 | 1 | 0 |
| Sweet-Sour Sauce | 1/6 | 87 | 0 | 22 | 0 | 228 | 132 | 1 | 3 | 23 | 1 | 0 | 1 | 1 | 1 | 2 | 1 | 6 |
| Tangy Cranberry Sauce | 1/8 | 117 | 0 | 26 | 2 | 167 | 66 | 1 | 3 | 5 | 1 | 2 | 1 | 2 | 1 | 0 | 1 | 2 |
| Tartar Sauce | 1/16 | 100 | 0 | 1 | 11 | 117 | 15 | 0 | 2 | 3 | 0 | 0 | 0 | 0 | 0 | 1 | 0 | 1 |
| Teriyaki Marinade | 1/8 | 86 | 1 | 5 | 7 | 665 | 88 | 1 | 0 | 0 | 0 | 2 | 1 | 2 | 0 | 0 | 0 | 4 |
| Thin White Sauce | 1/16 | 18 | 1 | 1 | 1 | 50 | 23 | 1 | 0 | 1 | 0 | 2 | 1 | 2 | 2 | 1 | 2 | 0 |
| Wine-Mushroom Sauce | 1/6 | 61 | 1 | 3 | 4 | 219 | 86 | 1 | 7 | 6 | 1 | 4 | 3 | 4 | 3 | 2 | 3 | 2 |

# Sauces

Sauces are made by many methods, but egg yolk-, cornstarch-, or flour-thickened sauces are considered to be the most difficult. You can avoid the pitfalls of these thickened sauces by faithfully following the directions. Prevent lumps in cornstarch- or flour-thickened sauces by stirring constantly during cooking. If you must leave the sauce for a few seconds, remove it from the heat while you're gone. Any lumps that might form usually can be removed by beating the sauce with a wire whisk or a rotary beater.

Eggs will not tolerate high temperatures or long cooking times. So egg-yolk-thickened sauces are best cooked in the top of a double boiler over—but not touching—boiling water. Add egg yolks by first stirring some of the hot mixture into the beaten egg yolks and then returning it all to the hot mixture in the double boiler. Never let a sauce boil after egg yolks have been added.

---

## White Sauce

---

**Medium White Sauce:**
- 2 tablespoons butter or margarine
- 2 tablespoons all-purpose flour
- ¼ teaspoon salt
  Dash pepper
- 1 cup milk

**Thin White Sauce:**
- 1 tablespoon butter or margarine
- 1 tablespoon all-purpose flour
- ¼ teaspoon salt
  Dash pepper
- 1 cup milk

In a small saucepan melt butter or margarine. Stir in flour, salt, and pepper. Add milk all at once. Cook and stir over medium heat till thickened and bubbly. Cook and stir 1 to 2 minutes more. Makes about 1 cup.

***Almond Sauce:*** Prepare Medium White Sauce as above, *except* toast ¼ cup slivered *almonds* in the melted butter. Add 1 teaspoon instant *chicken bouillon granules.* Continue as directed. Serve with vegetables or fish.

***Blue Cheese Sauce:*** Prepare Medium White Sauce as above, *except* over low heat stir ¼ cup *dairy sour cream* and ¼ cup crumbled *blue cheese* into the cooked sauce. (*Do not boil.*) Serve with vegetables.

***Cheese Sauce*** Prepare Medium White Sauce as at left, *except* add ¼ cup additional *milk.* Continue as directed. Over low heat stir 1 cup shredded *cheddar, Swiss, American, or Gruyère cheese* into the cooked sauce, stirring to melt. Serve with vegetables.

***Confetti Sauce:*** Prepare Medium White Sauce as at left, *except* stir in 2 tablespoons finely chopped *green pepper or parsley,* 1 tablespoon finely chopped pitted black *or* green *olives,* and 1 tablespoon finely chopped *pimiento.* Serve with vegetables, beef, or fish.

***Cucumber or Zucchini Sauce:*** Prepare Medium White Sauce as at left, *except* stir in ½ cup shredded *or* finely chopped, unpeeled *cucumber or zucchini.* Serve with fish or seafood.

***Curry Sauce:*** Prepare Medium White Sauce as at left, *except* add 1 teaspoon *curry powder* to the melted butter; cook 1 minute. Continue as directed. If desired, stir 1 table-spoon chopped chutney into the cooked sauce. Serve with fish or poultry.

***Herb-Garlic Sauce:*** Prepare Medium White Sauce as at left, *except* cook 1 clove *garlic,* minced, in the butter or marga-rine for 1 minute. Continue as directed. Stir in ½ teaspoon dried *basil,* crushed, and ½ teaspoon dried *tarragon,* crushed, into the cooked sauce. Serve with vegetables.

***Herb Sauce:*** Prepare Medium White Sauce as at left, *except* stir in ½ *teaspoon* of one of the following herbs or spices: dried *basil,* crushed; *caraway seed; celery seed;* dried *marjoram,* crushed; dried *oregano,* crushed; dried *sage,* crushed; or dried *thyme,* crushed. Serve with vegetables or poultry.

***Lemon-Chive Sauce:*** Prepare Medium White Sauce as at left, except stir in 1 tablespoon snipped *chives* and 2 tea-spoons *lemon juice.* Serve with vegetables or fish.

***Mexicali Sauce:*** Prepare Medium White Sauce as at left, *except* stir in 2 tablespoons seeded, chopped *green chili peppers* and ½ teaspoon *chili powder.* Serve with beef or pork.

***Parmesan or Romano Sauce:*** Prepare Medium White Sauce as at left, *except* stir in ¼ cup grated *Parmesan cheese* or *Romano cheese.* Serve with vegetables, beef, sausage, poultry, pork, or burgers.

***Sherry Sauce:*** Prepare Medium White Sauce as at left, *except* stir in 2 tablespoons *dry sherry.* Cook 1 minute more. Serve with fish or veal.

## Classic Hollandaise Sauce

   **4    egg yolks**
   **½    cup butter *or* margarine, cut into thirds and
         at room temperature**
   **2    to 3 tablespoons lemon juice**
        **Dash salt**
        **Dash white pepper**

Place egg yolks and ⅓ of the butter in the top of a double boiler. Cook, stirring rapidly, over boiling water till butter melts. (Water in the bottom of the double boiler should not touch the top pan.) Add ⅓ more of the butter and continue stirring rapidly. As butter melts and mixture thickens, add the remaining butter, stirring constantly. When butter is melted, remove pan from water; stir rapidly for 2 more minutes. Stir in lemon juice, 1 teaspoon at a time; stir in salt and white pepper. Heat again over boiling water, stirring constantly, for 2 to 3 minutes or till thickened. Remove at once from heat. If sauce curdles, immediately beat in 1 to 2 tablespoons *boiling water.* Serve with vegetables, poultry, fish, or eggs. Makes about 1 cup.

## Blender Hollandaise Sauce

   **3    egg yolks**
   **½    cup butter *or* margarine**
   **2    tablespoons lemon juice**
        **Dash ground red pepper**

Place egg yolks in a blender container. Cover and blend about 5 seconds or till mixed. In a small saucepan heat butter or margarine, lemon juice, and red pepper till butter is melted and almost boiling. With lid ajar and blender running at high speed, slowly pour in butter mixture. Blend about 30 seconds or till thick and fluffy. Serve immediately with vegetables. Makes about 1 cup.

**Note:** To reheat, place Blender Hollandaise Sauce in a small saucepan over very low heat. Cook, stirring constantly, till warm. If mixture seems thick, stir in 1 tablespoon *water*. Serve immediately.

# Mock Hollandaise Sauce

- ¼   **cup dairy sour cream**
- ¼   **cup mayonnaise *or* salad dressing**
- 1   **teaspoon lemon juice**
- ½   **teaspoon prepared mustard**

In a small saucepan combine sour cream, mayonnaise or salad dressing, lemon juice, and mustard. Cook and stir over low heat till heated through. (*Do not boil.*) Serve with vegetables. Makes about ½ cup.

# Classic Béarnaise Sauce

- 3   **tablespoons white wine vinegar**
- 1   **teaspoon finely chopped shallot *or* green onion**
- 4   **whole black peppercorns, crushed**
      **Dash dried tarragon, crushed**
      **Dash dried chervil, crushed**
- 1   **tablespoon cold water**
- 4   **egg yolks**
- ½   **cup butter *or* margarine, softened**
- 1   **teaspoon snipped fresh tarragon *or* ¼ teaspoon dried tarragon, crushed**

In a saucepan combine vinegar, shallot or green onion, peppercorns, dash tarragon, and chervil. Bring to boiling; reduce heat and simmer about 30 seconds or till reduced to half volume (measure depth with a ruler at start and end of simmering time). Strain; discard solids. Add the cold water to herb liquid.

Beat egg yolks in the top of a double boiler (not over water). Slowly add herb liquid. Add *2 tablespoons* of the butter to the egg yolks; place over boiling water (upper pan should not touch water). Cook and stir till butter melts and sauce begins to thicken. Continue to add the remaining butter, 2 tablespoons at a time, while stirring constantly. Cook and stir till sauce is the consistency of thick cream. Remove from heat. Stir in the 1 teaspoon fresh tarragon or ¼ teaspoon dried tarragon. Season with salt to taste. Serve with beef, pork, poultry, or fish. Makes about ¾ cup.

## Sauce Provençale

    4  **small tomatoes, peeled, seeded, and cut up
       (1 pound)**
  ½  **teaspoon sugar**
  ¼  **cup sliced green onion**
    1  **clove garlic, minced**
    2  **tablespoons butter *or* margarine**
  ½  **cup dry white wine**
    6  **tablespoons butter *or* margarine**
    2  **tablespoons snipped parsley**

Sprinkle tomatoes with sugar; set aside. In a medium saucepan cook onion and garlic in the 2 tablespoons butter or margarine till tender but not brown. Add wine; cook over high heat, stirring occasionally, about 3 minutes or till liquid is slightly reduced. Stir in tomatoes, the 6 tablespoons butter or margarine, and parsley; heat through. Serve with beef or pork. Makes about 2 cups.

# Bordelaise Sauce

½   cup dry red wine
1   tablespoon chopped shallot *or* onion
½   teaspoon dried thyme *or* tarragon, crushed
1   small bay leaf
1   14½-ounce can beef broth
2   tablespoons cornstarch
1   tablespoon butter *or* margarine
1   tablespoon lemon juice
1   teaspoon snipped parsley
⅛   teaspoon pepper

In a small saucepan combine wine, shallot or onion, thyme or tarragon, and bay leaf; bring to boiling. Reduce heat and simmer briskly, uncovered, for 5 minutes or till mixture is reduced by half volume (measure depth with a ruler at start and end of simmering time). Remove bay leaf. Combine the beef broth and cornstarch; stir into wine mixture. Cook and stir till thickened and bubbly. Cook and stir 1 to 2 minutes more. Add butter or margarine, lemon juice, parsley, and pepper; reduce heat and simmer, covered, for 5 minutes. Serve with beef, veal, or poultry. Makes about 2 cups.

## Brown Sauce

> 2 **tablespoons butter or margarine**
> 2 **tablespoons all-purpose flour**
> 1½ **teaspoons instant beef bouillon granules***
> 1½ **cups hot water***

In a saucepan melt butter or margarine. Stir in flour. Cook and stir over medium-low heat for 15 to 20 minutes or till browned. Dissolve bouillon granules in hot water; add to flour mixture. Bring to boiling, stirring constantly. Boil for 3 to 5 minutes. Reduce heat and simmer about 30 minutes or till reduced to 1 cup liquid; stir frequently. Consistency of sauce should be slightly thinner than gravy. Serve with meat, or use instead of gravy, or use as a base for Sauce Diable. Makes about 1 cup.

**\*Note:** To substitute homemade Beef Stock for bouillon and hot water, see the recipe on page 737.

## Sauce Diable

> ¼ **cup sliced green onion**
> 3 **tablespoons dry white wine**
> 8 **to 10 whole black peppercorns, crushed**
> ½ **cup Brown Sauce (see recipe, above)**
> 1 **teaspoon snipped parsley**
> ½ **teaspoon Worcestershire sauce**

In a small saucepan combine green onion, wine, and crushed peppercorns. Boil about 2 minutes. Add Brown Sauce, parsley, and Worcestershire. Heat through. Serve with burgers or beef. Makes about ⅔ cup.

## Quick Mushroom Sauce

> 1 **10¾-ounce can condensed cream of**
>   **mushroom soup**
> 1 **cup dairy sour cream**

In a saucepan stir together soup and sour cream. Heat through over low heat but *do not boil.* Serve with vegetables, beef, or burgers. Makes about 2 cups.

**Note:** To reheat, cook and stir over low heat about 5 minutes. (*Do not boil.*)

## Wine-Mushroom Sauce

  **1  cup sliced fresh mushrooms**
  **¼  cup sliced green onion**
  **2  tablespoons butter *or* margarine**
  **1  tablespoon cornstarch**
  **½  cup dry red *or* dry white wine**
  **2  tablespoons snipped parsley**
  **1  teaspoon instant beef bouillon granules**
  **¼  teaspoon salt**

In a medium saucepan cook mushrooms and onion in butter or margarine 4 to 5 minutes or just till tender. Stir in cornstarch. Stir in wine, parsley, bouillon granules, salt, ½ cup *water,* and dash *pepper.* Cook and stir till thickened and bubbly. Cook and stir 1 to 2 minutes more. Serve with beef, lamb, veal, or pork. Makes about 1⅓ cups.

## Creamy Mushroom Sauce

  **¼  cup chopped onion**
  **2  tablespoons butter *or* margarine**
  **1  tablespoon all-purpose flour**
  **1  4-ounce can sliced mushrooms**
  **⅔  cup milk**
  **½  teaspoon salt**
  **⅛  teaspoon pepper**
  **½  cup dairy sour cream**

In a small saucepan cook onion in butter or margarine till tender but not brown. Stir in flour. Drain mushrooms. Stir in drained mushrooms, milk, salt, and pepper. Cook and stir till thickened and bubbly. Cook and stir 1 to 2 minutes more. Stir in sour cream; heat through. (*Do not boil.*) Serve with poultry, beef, pork, or burgers. Makes about 1½ cups.

## Hot Chinese Mustard

  ¼  **cup dry mustard**
  2  **teaspoons cooking oil**
  ½  **teaspoon salt**

In a small saucepan bring ¼ cup *water* to boiling. Combine dry mustard, cooking oil, and salt. Stir boiling water into dry mustard mixture. Serve with fried wontons, egg rolls, or burgers. Makes about ⅓ cup sauce.

## Fluffy Horseradish Sauce

  ½  **cup whipping cream**
  3  **tablespoons prepared horseradish**
  ⅛  **teaspoon salt**

Whip cream just to soft peaks; fold in horseradish and salt. Serve with beef, pork, burgers, ham, or vegetables. Makes about 1 cup.

## Snappy Barbecue Sauce

  1  **cup catsup**
  1  **cup water**
  ¼  **cup vinegar**
  1  **tablespoon sugar**
  1  **tablespoon Worcestershire sauce**
  1  **teaspoon salt**
  1  **teaspoon celery seed**
  2  *or* **3 dashes bottled hot pepper sauce**

In a saucepan combine catsup, water, vinegar, sugar, Worcestershire sauce, salt, celery seed, and bottled hot pepper sauce. Bring the catsup mixture to boiling; reduce heat and simmer, uncovered, for 30 minutes. Use to baste pork, beef, or poultry during the last 15 to 20 minutes of barbecuing. Pass any remaining sauce. Makes about 1½ cups.

## Easy Barbecue Sauce

| | |
|---|---|
| 1 | 14-ounce bottle hot-style catsup or one 12-ounce bottle chili sauce |
| 3 | tablespoons vinegar |
| 1 | teaspoon paprika |
| ¾ | teaspoon garlic powder |

In a bowl combine catsup or chili sauce, vinegar, paprika, and garlic powder. Cover; chill for several hours. Use to baste burgers or beef during the last 10 minutes of barbecuing. Makes about 1½ cups.

## Raisin Sauce

| | |
|---|---|
| ¼ | cup packed brown sugar |
| 2 | tablespoons cornstarch |
| 1½ | cups water |
| 1 | cup raisins |
| ½ | teaspoon finely shredded lemon peel |
| 2 | tablespoons lemon juice |
| 1 | tablespoon vinegar |

In a medium saucepan combine brown sugar and cornstarch. Gradually stir in water; add raisins, lemon peel, lemon juice, and vinegar. Cook and stir till thickened and bubbly. Cook and stir 1 to 2 minutes more. Serve with ham, pork, or poultry. Makes about 2 cups.

## Spicy Cherry Sauce

- ¾ **cup sugar**
- 2 **tablespoons cornstarch**
- ⅓ **cup orange juice**
- 1 **tablespoon lemon juice**
- 1 **16-ounce can pitted tart red cherries (water pack)**
- ¼ **teaspoon ground cinnamon**
  **Dash ground cloves**

In a medium saucepan combine about *half* of the sugar, the cornstarch, and dash *salt*; stir in orange juice and lemon juice. Stir in *undrained* cherries, cinnamon, and cloves. Cook and stir over medium heat till thickened and bubbly. Cook and stir 1 to 2 minutes more. Stir in the remaining sugar. Serve warm with ham or pork. Makes about 2⅔ cups.

## Tangy Cranberry Sauce

- 1 **16-ounce can jellied cranberry sauce**
- ⅓ **cup steak sauce**
- 1 **tablespoon brown sugar**
- 1 **tablespoon cooking oil**
- 2 **teaspoons prepared mustard**

In a mixer bowl combine cranberry sauce, steak sauce, brown sugar, oil, and mustard. Using an electric mixer or rotary beater, beat till smooth. Serve sauce warm or chilled with hamburgers, ham, pork, or poultry. Makes about 2 cups.

## Cranberry Sauce

- 2 **cups water**
- 1¾ **to 2 cups sugar**
- 4 **cups cranberries (16 ounces)**

In a large saucepan combine water and sugar. Bring to boiling, stirring to dissolve sugar. Boil rapidly for 5 minutes. Add cranberries; return to boiling. Cook, uncovered, over high heat 5 to 6 minutes or till skins pop. Remove from heat. Serve warm or chilled with poultry, pork, or beef. Makes about 5 cups.

**Note:** To mold Cranberry Sauce, cook 10 to 12 minutes more during the final cooking time or till a drop gels on a cold plate. Turn into a 4-cup mold; chill till firm. Unmold.

## Dill Sauce

|   |   |
|---|---|
| 2 | **tablespoons butter or margarine** |
| 2 | **tablespoons all-purpose flour** |
| 1 | **teaspoon instant chicken bouillon granules\*** |
| 1 | **cup hot water\*** |
| 1 | **teaspoon sugar** |
| 1 | **teaspoon dried dillweed** |
| 1 | **teaspoon lemon juice** |

In a saucepan melt butter. Stir in flour. Dissolve bouillon in hot water; add to flour mixture. Stir in sugar, dillweed, and lemon juice. Cook and stir till thickened and bubbly; continue cooking 1 to 2 minutes more. Serve warm with fish or lamb. Makes about 1 cup.

**\*Note:** To substitute homemade Chicken Stock for bouillon and hot water, see the recipe on page 736.

## Easy Dill Sauce

|   |   |
|---|---|
| 1 | **10¾-ounce can condensed cream of mushroom soup** |
| ½ | **cup milk** |
| 2 | **teaspoons dried dillweed** |
| 1½ | **teaspoons dry mustard** |
| 1 | **teaspoon lemon juice** |

In a saucepan combine all ingredients. Cook and stir till heated through. Serve with burgers, beef, or lamb. Makes about 1⅔ cups.

---

## Orange-Grape Sauce

---

> **1**    **medium orange**
> **½**    **cup water**
> **¼**    **cup butter or margarine**
> **2**    **tablespoons vinegar**
> **1**    **tablespoon honey**
> **1½**   **teaspoons instant chicken bouillon granules**
>       **Dash ground ginger**
> **1**    **tablespoon cornstarch**
> **½**    **cup red grapes, halved and seeded**
> **2**    **teaspoons orange liqueur**

Using a vegetable peeler, remove the orange portion of the peel. Slice enough peel into julienne strips to measure 1 tablespoon. Section the orange over a bowl to catch juice; add orange sections to juice and set aside. In a saucepan simmer the orange peel strips, covered, in a small amount of water for 15 minutes; drain well. Set aside.

In a saucepan combine the ½ cup water, butter or margarine, vinegar, honey, bouillon granules, and ginger. Bring to boiling, stirring constantly. Combine cornstarch and 1 tablespoon cold *water;* stir into vinegar mixture. Cook and stir till thickened and bubbly. Cook and stir 1 to 2 minutes more. Stir in orange sections and juice, orange peel, red grapes, and orange liqueur. Heat to boiling. Serve with poultry or pork. Makes about 1⅔ cups.

## Sweet-Sour Sauce

- ½   **cup packed brown sugar**
- 1   **tablespoon cornstarch**
- ⅓   **cup red wine vinegar**
- ⅓   **cup unsweetened pineapple juice**
- ¼   **cup finely chopped green pepper**
- 2   **tablespoons chopped pimiento**
- 1   **tablespoon soy sauce**
- ¼   **teaspoon garlic powder**
- ¼   **teaspoon ground ginger**

In a small saucepan combine brown sugar and cornstarch. Stir in vinegar, pineapple juice, green pepper, pimiento, soy sauce, garlic powder, and ginger. Cook, stirring constantly, till thickened and bubbly. Cook and stir 1 to 2 minutes more. Serve warm with spareribs, egg rolls, or fried wontons. Makes about 1¼ cups.

## Fresh Mint Sauce

- 1½   **teaspoons cornstarch**
- ¼   **cup cold water**
- ¼   **cup snipped fresh mint leaves**
- 3   **tablespoons light corn syrup**
- 1   **tablespoon lemon juice**
- 1   **drop green food coloring (optional)**

In a small saucepan combine cornstarch and cold water; stir in mint leaves, corn syrup, and lemon juice. Cook and stir till thickened and bubbly. Cook and stir 1 to 2 minutes more. Strain. If desired, stir in green food coloring. Serve with lamb or pork. Makes about ½ cup.

## Tartar Sauce

 1 **cup mayonnaise *or* salad dressing**
 ¼ **cup finely chopped dill pickle, finely
     chopped sweet pickle, *or* sweet pickle
     relish, drained**
 1 **tablespoon finely chopped onion**
 1 **tablespoon snipped parsley**
 1 **tablespoon chopped pimiento**
 1 **teaspoon lemon juice**

In a bowl combine mayonnaise, pickle or pickle relish, onion,
parsley, pimiento, and lemon juice. Cover and chill for several
hours. Serve with fish or seafood. Makes about 1 cup.

## Cocktail Sauce

 ¾ **cup chili sauce**
 2 **tablespoons lemon juice**
 1 **tablespoon prepared horseradish**
 2 **teaspoons Worcestershire sauce**
 ½ **teaspoon finely chopped onion**
    **Few dashes bottled hot pepper sauce**

In a small bowl combine chili sauce, lemon juice, horseradish,
Worcestershire sauce, onion, and hot pepper sauce. Mix well;
cover and chill for several hours. Serve with fish or seafood.
Makes about 1 cup.

## Teriyaki Marinade

 ¼ **cup cooking oil**
 ¼ **cup soy sauce**
 ¼ **cup dry sherry**
 1 **teaspoon ground ginger**
 1 **clove garlic, minced**
 2 **tablespoons molasses**

To make marinade, combine oil, soy sauce, dry sherry, ginger, and garlic. Place chicken, beef, or pork in a baking dish or in a plastic bag set in a deep bowl. Pour marinade over meat. Cover dish or close bag; chill for 4 to 6 hours or overnight. Turn bag or spoon marinade over meat occasionally to coat evenly. Drain, reserving marinade. Stir molasses into reserved marinade. Use to baste meat during the last 10 minutes of barbecuing. Makes about 1 cup marinade (enough for 2 pounds meat).

## Herb-Seasoned Marinade

Combine ¼ cup finely chopped *onion;* ¼ cup cooking *oil;* ¼ cup *wine vinegar;* 1 tablespoon *Worcestershire sauce;* ½ teaspoon *salt;* ½ teaspoon dried *basil,* crushed; ½ teaspoon dried *rosemary,* crushed; ¼ teaspoon *pepper;* and ⅛ teaspoon *bottled hot pepper sauce.* Place beef, pork, or chicken in a baking dish or in a plastic bag set in a deep bowl. Pour marinade over meat. Cover dish or close bag; chill for 4 to 6 hours or overnight. Turn bag or spoon marinade over meat occasionally to coat evenly. Makes about ¾ cup marinade (enough for 2 pounds meat).

## Savory Wine Marinade

Combine ½ cup cooking *oil,* ½ cup dry white *wine,* ¼ cup *lime juice or lemon juice,* 2 tablespoons snipped *parsley,* ½ teaspoon *salt,* and ¼ teaspoon *bottled hot pepper sauce.* Thinly slice 1 small *onion;* separate into rings. Add onion to oil mixture. Place fish or chicken in a baking dish or in a plastic bag set in a deep bowl. Pour onion mixture over meat. Cover dish or close bag; chill for 4 to 6 hours or overnight. Occasionally turn bag or spoon marinade over meat to coat evenly. Makes about 1½ cups marinade (enough for 3 pounds meat).

# Flavored butters

Flavored butters are an easy way to dress up ordinary vegetables, meats, or breads. To flavor ½ cup *butter or margarine*, soften butter by cutting it into pieces and placing it in a heat-proof bowl in a cool oven. Turn the oven to 350°; heat for 3 minutes. Transfer butter to a cool bowl so it won't melt. Then stir in any of the seasonings listed below to obtain the desired flavor.

***Orange Butter:*** Stir in 1 tablespoon *powdered sugar* and ½ teaspoon grated *orange peel*. Serve with bread.

***Garlic Butter:*** Stir in 2 cloves *garlic*, minced, or ½ teaspoon *garlic powder*. Serve with bread or beef.

***Parsley Butter:*** Stir in 1 tablespoon snipped *parsley;* 1 teaspoon *lemon juice;* ¼ teaspoon dried *savory,* crushed; ⅛ teaspoon *salt;* and dash *pepper*. Serve with potatoes or bread.

***Onion Butter:*** Stir in ¼ cup finely chopped *onion,* 2 teaspoons *Worcestershire sauce,* ½ teaspoon *dry mustard,* and ¼ teaspoon *pepper*. Serve with beef or burgers.

***Herb Butter:*** Stir in ½ teaspoon dried *thyme,* crushed, and ½ teaspoon ground *sage*. Serve with vegetables.

***Tarragon Butter:*** Stir in 2 teaspoons *lemon juice* and 1 teaspoon dried *tarragon,* crushed. Serve with fish, beef, chicken, or vegetables.

## Honey Butter

- **½ cup butter or margarine, cut up**
- **¼ cup honey**
- **½ teaspoon finely shredded lemon peel**

Place butter in a heat-proof bowl in a cool oven. Turn oven to 350°; heat 3 minutes. Transfer butter to a cool bowl. Stir in honey and peel. Serve with bread. Makes ½ cup.

# Relishes

## Cinnamon Apple Rings

- ½ cup red cinnamon candies
- ¼ cup sugar
- 2 cups water
- 4 small cooking apples, peeled (if desired), cored, and cut crosswise into ½-inch rings

In a 10-inch skillet combine candies and sugar; add water. Cook and stir over medium heat till liquid boils. Add apple rings to candy mixture. Simmer gently, uncovered, for 15 to 20 minutes or till tender. Stir occasionally and spoon candy mixture over apples. Cool apple rings in candy mixture. Drain. Makes about 3 cups.

## Cranberry-Orange Relish

- 2 medium oranges
- 4 cups fresh cranberries (1 pound)
- 2 cups sugar
- ¼ cup finely chopped walnuts

With a vegetable peeler, remove the orange portion of the peel of one orange; set aside. Completely peel and section both oranges. Using a food grinder with a coarse blade or a food processor, grind reserved orange peel, orange sections, and cranberries. Stir in sugar and nuts. Chill for several hours. Serve with poultry or ham. Makes about 3½ cups.

# Hot Curried Fruit

  1  **17-ounce can unpeeled apricot halves**
  1  **16-ounce can pear slices**
  1  **8¼-ounce can pineapple chunks**
  2  **tablespoons brown sugar**
  1  **tablespoon butter, melted**
  1  **teaspoon curry powder**          Oven 350°

Drain all fruits. In a 1½-quart casserole combine fruits. Stir together brown sugar, melted butter, and curry powder; dot over fruits. Cover and bake in a 350° oven about 25 minutes or till heated through, stirring gently once. Serve warm as an accompaniment to poultry, pork, or ham. Makes 3½ cups.

# Pickled Beets

  ⅓  **cup vinegar**
  ¼  **cup sugar**
  ¼  **cup water**
  ½  **teaspoon ground cinnamon**
  ¼  **teaspoon salt**
  ¼  **teaspoon ground cloves**
  2  **cups sliced, cooked beets *or* one 16-ounce
       can sliced beets, drained**

In a medium saucepan combine vinegar, sugar, water, cinnamon, salt, and cloves. Bring to boiling, stirring occasionally; add sliced beets. Return to boiling; reduce heat. Cover and simmer 5 minutes. Cool, then chill in liquid 8 hours or overnight. Drain before serving. Makes about 2 cups.

# Fresh Cucumber Relish

**3**   **medium cucumbers (1½ pounds)**
**½**   **medium onion**
**¼**   **cup vinegar**
**1**   **tablespoon sugar**
**½**   **teaspoon salt**
**¼**   **teaspoon dried dillweed**

Slice cucumbers in half lengthwise; scoop out seeds and discard. Grind cucumbers and onion using a food grinder with a
coarse blade *or* finely chop by hand; drain. Stir in vinegar,
sugar, salt, and dried dillweed. Chill for 8 hours or overnight.
Serve on frankfurters or hamburgers. Makes about 4 cups.

# Easy Tomato-Pepper Relish

**2**   **medium tomatoes, finely chopped (1⅓ cups)**
**1**   **large green pepper, seeded and chopped**
     **(1 cup)**
**¼**   **cup Italian salad dressing**

Place chopped tomatoes in a colander for 30 minutes to drain
off the juices. In a bowl combine tomatoes and green pepper;
add salad dressing. Cover; chill several hours, stirring occasionally. Makes 2½ cups.

# Soups & Stews

# Soups & Stews

| Recipes | Servings (fraction of recipe) | Calories | Protein (grams) | Carbohydrate (grams) | Fat (grams) | Sodium (milligrams) | Potassium (milligrams) | Percent of U.S. RDA Per Serving | | | | | | | |
|---|---|---|---|---|---|---|---|---|---|---|---|---|---|---|---|
| | | | | | | | | Protein | Vitamin A | Vitamin C | Thiamine | Riboflavin | Niacin | Calcium | Iron |
| Beef-Barley Soup | 1/8 | 343 | 19 | 21 | 21 | 929 | 631 | 30 | 76 | 50 | 11 | 11 | 12 | 26 | 20 |
| Beef Bourguignonne | 1/10 | 572 | 33 | 32 | 31 | 622 | 846 | 50 | 98 | 16 | 22 | 8 | 31 | 47 | 32 |
| Beef Stew | 1/6 | 385 | 25 | 20 | 22 | 808 | 1028 | 39 | 80 | 44 | 17 | 4 | 17 | 37 | 26 |
| Beef Stock | 1/8 | 2 | 0 | 0 | 0 | 480 | 2 | 1 | 0 | 0 | 0 | 0 | 0 | 0 | 0 |
| Bouillabaisse | 1/6 | 184 | 32 | 6 | 7 | 943 | 518 | 32 | 48 | 25 | 11 | 11 | 9 | 18 | 15 |
| Cheese Soup | 1/4 | 234 | 12 | 17 | 13 | 620 | 372 | 19 | 90 | 10 | 8 | 8 | 22 | 4 | 4 |
| Cheesy Chicken-Corn Chowder | 1/4 | 228 | 17 | 18 | 10 | 937 | 223 | 26 | 17 | 20 | 4 | 4 | 15 | 23 | 8 |
| Chicken Stock | 1/4 | 2 | 0 | 0 | 0 | 540 | 2 | 1 | 0 | 0 | 0 | 0 | 0 | 0 | 0 |
| Chicken Vegetable-Noodle Soup | 1/10 | 295 | 34 | 17 | 10 | 658 | 498 | 52 | 19 | 27 | 7 | 7 | 13 | 56 | 13 |
| Chili con Carne | 1/4 | 481 | 30 | 35 | 25 | 892 | 1026 | 47 | 47 | 105 | 21 | 21 | 20 | 36 | 37 |
| Cider Stew | 1/6 | 538 | 32 | 33 | 30 | 851 | 1080 | 50 | 107 | 38 | 18 | 18 | 21 | 44 | 33 |
| Cioppino | 1/6 | 255 | 29 | 9 | 9 | 841 | 558 | 44 | 60 | 57 | 12 | 12 | 12 | 22 | 22 |
| Cream of Asparagus Soup | 1/3 | 176 | 6 | 15 | 11 | 557 | 423 | 10 | 25 | 57 | 15 | 15 | 21 | 9 | 7 |
| Cream of Broccoli Soup | 1/3 | 169 | 14 | 14 | 11 | 562 | 361 | 9 | 34 | 100 | 8 | 8 | 17 | 16 | 5 |
| Cream of Carrot Soup | 1/3 | 163 | 4 | 13 | 11 | 567 | 260 | 7 | 64 | 13 | 6 | 6 | 11 | 4 | 5 |
| Cream of Cauliflower Soup | 1/3 | 168 | 6 | 14 | 11 | 562 | 337 | 9 | 10 | 80 | 9 | 9 | 13 | 4 | 5 |
| Cream of Celery Soup | 1/3 | 164 | 5 | 13 | 11 | 631 | 392 | 7 | 16 | 22 | 6 | 6 | 11 | 3 | 4 |
| Cream of Chicken Soup | 1/4 | 282 | 20 | 10 | 18 | 563 | 312 | 31 | 14 | 1 | 7 | 7 | 11 | 33 | 5 |
| Cream of Green Bean Soup | 1/3 | 170 | 5 | 15 | 11 | 559 | 304 | 8 | 15 | 23 | 6 | 6 | 14 | 3 | 4 |
| Cream of Mushroom Soup | 1/3 | 159 | 5 | 12 | 11 | 558 | 267 | 7 | 9 | | 6 | 6 | 16 | 7 | 3 |

# Nutrition Analysis Chart

| | | | | | | | | | | | | | | | | |
|---|---|---|---|---|---|---|---|---|---|---|---|---|---|---|---|---|
| Cream of Onion Soup | 1/4 | 150 | 3 | 18 | 6 | 433 | 270 | | | | | | | | | |
| Cream of Pea Soup | 1/3 | 235 | 10 | 21 | 13 | 624 | 428 | 18 | 15 | 39 | 25 | 8 | 17 | 14 | 13 | 11 |
| Cream of Potato Soup | 1/3 | 191 | 5 | 19 | 11 | 556 | 373 | 9 | 8 | 23 | 8 | 7 | 6 | 6 | 3 |
| Cream of Spinach Soup | 1/3 | 162 | 5 | 12 | 11 | 581 | 342 | 68 | 8 | 37 | 7 | 14 | 14 | 3 | 14 | 8 |
| Cream of Tomato Soup | 1/3 | 189 | 6 | 18 | 11 | 560 | 570 | 38 | 9 | 69 | 11 | 14 | 8 | 13 | 6 |
| Cream of Zucchini Soup | 1/3 | 164 | 5 | 13 | 11 | 555 | 301 | 13 | 8 | 27 | 7 | 14 | 5 | 13 | 3 |
| Creamy Borscht | 1/6 | 134 | 5 | 17 | 6 | 847 | 613 | 75 | 7 | 66 | 8 | 9 | 5 | 8 | 9 |
| Creole Gumbo | 1/6 | 293 | 20 | 36 | 7 | 1093 | 418 | 30 | 31 | 68 | 8 | 10 | 18 | 12 | 19 |
| Dilled Lamb Ragout | 1/6 | 667 | 28 | 15 | 53 | 722 | 589 | 14 | 43 | 19 | 28 | 25 | 41 | 16 | 16 |
| Easy Chicken-Curry Soup | 1/3 | 327 | 18 | 14 | 22 | 1315 | 374 | 19 | 28 | 9 | 5 | 21 | 18 | 16 | 8 |
| Easy Pork Cassoulet | 1/6 | 482 | 20 | 35 | 29 | 1101 | 588 | 4 | 30 | 11 | 36 | 12 | 17 | 11 | 25 |
| Fish Chowder | 1/6 | 301 | 20 | 18 | 16 | 849 | 616 | 57 | 31 | 22 | 16 | 17 | 18 | 13 | 6 |
| French Onion Soup | 1/6 | 283 | 12 | 33 | 12 | 1514 | 222 | 9 | 18 | 19 | 12 | 10 | 7 | 14 | 8 |
| Fresh Corn Chowder | 1/6 | 250 | 10 | 30 | 11 | 672 | 494 | 17 | 16 | 21 | 14 | 25 | 9 | 21 | 5 |
| Gazpacho | 1/10 | 93 | 2 | 10 | 6 | 328 | 419 | 26 | 3 | 72 | 7 | 5 | 6 | 3 | 7 |
| German Sausage Chowder | 1/6 | 428 | 22 | 23 | 27 | 1571 | 704 | 10 | 34 | 59 | 18 | 30 | 16 | 36 | 14 |
| Ham and Bean Vegetable Soup | 1/10 | 252 | 15 | 36 | 6 | 342 | 832 | 32 | 23 | 15 | 34 | 10 | 13 | 8 | 25 |
| Ham Hodgepodge | 1/6 | 329 | 16 | 43 | 11 | 984 | 1106 | 25 | 25 | 100 | 36 | 14 | 21 | 13 | 22 |
| Herbed Lamb Stew | 1/6 | 459 | 20 | 14 | 36 | 469 | 628 | 188 | 31 | 17 | 16 | 18 | 29 | 10 | 10 |
| Herbed Tomato Soup | 1/8 | 98 | 2 | 10 | 6 | 589 | 450 | 111 | 4 | 56 | 7 | 4 | 7 | 3 | 7 |
| Lentil Soup | 1/8 | 247 | 15 | 38 | 5 | 801 | 630 | 33 | 23 | 23 | 18 | 9 | 8 | 6 | 24 |
| Manhattan Clam Chowder | 1/4 | 276 | 21 | 25 | 10 | 849 | 1049 | 55 | 32 | 89 | 21 | 18 | 19 | 12 | 30 |
| Meatball Stew w/Spinach Dumplings | 1/4 | 725 | 36 | 51 | 43 | 1827 | 988 | 82 | 55 | 120 | 27 | 41 | 36 | 30 | 37 |
| Minestrone | 1/8 | 256 | 12 | 39 | 6 | 693 | 800 | 55 | 19 | 56 | 23 | 11 | 12 | 9 | 23 |
| Mulligatawny | 1/6 | 116 | 16 | 9 | 2 | 725 | 444 | 26 | 25 | 41 | 5 | 5 | 30 | 2 | 7 |
| New England Clam Chowder | 1/6 | 327 | 17 | 33 | 14 | 552 | 876 | 8 | 26 | 51 | 18 | 24 | 15 | 23 | 36 |
| Old-Fashioned Vegetable-Beef Soup | 1/10 | 498 | 22 | 17 | 38 | 940 | 727 | 44 | 33 | 39 | 14 | 15 | 30 | 4 | 21 |

# Nutrition Analysis Chart

Percent of U.S. RDA Per Serving

| Recipes | Servings (fraction of recipe) | Calories | Protein (grams) | Carbohydrate (grams) | Fat (grams) | Sodium (milligrams) | Potassium (milligrams) | Protein | Vitamin A | Vitamin C | Thiamine | Riboflavin | Niacin | Calcium | Iron |
|---|---|---|---|---|---|---|---|---|---|---|---|---|---|---|---|
| Oven-Baked Pork Stew | 1/6 | 578 | 24 | 46 | 33 | 495 | 369 | 37 | 221 | 107 | 81 | 23 | 36 | 7 | 29 |
| Oyster Stew | 1/4 | 276 | 16 | 13 | 18 | 625 | 400 | 25 | 200 | 63 | 15 | 31 | 16 | 33 | 37 |
| Quick Beans-and-Franks Soup | 1/6 | 424 | 19 | 37 | 22 | 1672 | 666 | 30 | 10 | 15 | 17 | 19 | 14 | 19 | 22 |
| Quick Beef Goulash Stew | 1/4 | 438 | 26 | 26 | 25 | 604 | 628 | 40 | 144 | 31 | 28 | 19 | 37 | 4 | 27 |
| Quick Cabbage-Cheese Soup | 1/4 | 341 | 17 | 21 | 21 | 1047 | 563 | 26 | 54 | 41 | 7 | 34 | 5 | 56 | 4 |
| Quick Cheesy Tuna Soup | 1/4 | 320 | 16 | 13 | 22 | 1127 | 444 | 25 | 36 | 36 | 6 | 11 | 27 | 7 | 7 |
| Quick Tomato-Rice Soup | 1/4 | 126 | 3 | 25 | 2 | 983 | 195 | 5 | 13 | 15 | 8 | 2 | 7 | 2 | 6 |
| Scotch Broth | 1/6 | 383 | 19 | 15 | 27 | 616 | 531 | 30 | 53 | 15 | 15 | 7 | 29 | 3 | 10 |
| Sherry-Pea Soup Elegante | 1/8 | 230 | 5 | 13 | 18 | 773 | 169 | 7 | 17 | 5 | 3 | 3 | 3 | 8 | 3 |
| Shrimp-Rice Soup | 1/6 | 189 | 13 | 19 | 5 | 455 | 389 | 20 | 7 | 7 | 7 | 8 | 17 | 5 | 10 |
| South American Pork Soup | 1/8 | 357 | 16 | 18 | 25 | 588 | 681 | 25 | 73 | 43 | 50 | 16 | 24 | 3 | 18 |
| Split Pea Soup | 1/10 | 233 | 15 | 31 | 6 | 292 | 573 | 24 | 34 | 5 | 34 | 11 | 12 | 3 | 17 |
| Swedish Fruit Soup | 1/8 | 206 | 1 | 53 | 0 | 75 | 359 | 2 | 8 | 26 | 5 | 5 | 4 | 4 | 9 |
| Turkey Frame Soup | 1/10 | 149 | 18 | 12 | 3 | 717 | 443 | 27 | 37 | 31 | 7 | 7 | 23 | 4 | 9 |
| Vegetable-Oyster Stew | 1/4 | 336 | 17 | 15 | 23 | 737 | 500 | 26 | 56 | 67 | 16 | 31 | 16 | 34 | 38 |
| Vichyssoise | 1/4 | 416 | 8 | 28 | 32 | 915 | 693 | 12 | 27 | 45 | 11 | 17 | 9 | 18 | 5 |

# Soup-Making Basics

**Stock making:** A good stock is the basic ingredient in a great soup. In this chapter, you'll find recipes for making beef and chicken stocks from scratch, as well as a few shortcuts for giving them home-style flavor. When you're making stock, remember that it's not necessary to peel or trim vegetables, since they'll be strained out. Just wash and cut them up. Always start your stocks with cold water to extract the most flavor from the meat and vegetables. Simmer stocks slowly for best flavor—bubbles should form slowly and burst before reaching the surface. Use a sieve lined with one or two layers of cheesecloth to remove small particles when straining stocks. (To avoid spills, ladle the stock into the strainer; don't pour it.)

**Storing stock:** To store a stock for future use, ladle the finished stock into pint or quart jars or other nonplastic containers while it's still hot. Cover and refrigerate to chill quickly. Stock may be stored in the refrigerator for a few days or in the freezer for up to six months. Be sure to label each container with the contents, quantity, and date. If you frequently use stock in small quantities, freeze it in ice cube trays. Then place the frozen stock cubes in a plastic bag and return them to the freezer. Measure the volume of a melted cube to determine the exact amount in each cube (approximately 2 tablespoons).

**Appliance shortcuts:** Use your small kitchen appliances to simplify making soups and stews. For instance, use your blender or food processor to puree, chop, or blend foods; a food processor can slice and shred, as well. A counter-top microwave oven speeds single preparation steps—such as melting butter, cooking onion in butter, or cooking bacon—as well as entire recipes. An electric slow crockery cooker is another natural, since it lets you start soups and stews early in the day to be ready to serve for the evening meal. Once the food goes in the cooker, it usually cooks for several hours, depending on the recipe, and often needs no attention. You can even leave the crockery cooker operating while you're away from home.

## Chicken Stock

|      | **Bony chicken pieces (backs, necks, and wings) from 2 chickens** |
|------|------|
| 3    | **stalks celery with leaves, cut up** |
| 1    | **carrot, cut up** |
| 1    | **large onion, quartered** |
| 1½   | **teaspoons salt** |
| ¼    | **teaspoon pepper** |
| 3    | **whole cloves** |
| 6    | **cups cold water** |

In a large stockpot or Dutch oven place chicken pieces, celery, carrot, onion, salt, pepper, and cloves. Add the water. Bring to boiling. Reduce heat; cover and simmer for 1 hour. Remove chicken. Strain stock. Discard vegetables. Clarify stock; if desired (see tip box). If using the stock while hot, skim fat. (*Or*, chill stock and lift off fat.) Makes about 4½ cups stock.

**Crockery cooker directions:** Use ingredients as above, *except* use only 4 cups water. Combine all ingredients in an electric slow crockery cooker. Cover; cook on low-heat setting for 8 to 10 hours. Strain stock. Discard vegetables. Continue as directed. Makes about 4½ cups stock.

### Stock substitutions

When a recipe calls for beef or chicken broth, use one of the stock recipes on this page. Or, if you're in a hurry, use one of the commercial substitutes that are available. Instant bouillon granules and cubes can be purchased in beef, chicken, vegetable, and onion flavors. These should be mixed with water according to package directions before being used as a broth substitute.

Canned beef and chicken broths are ready to use straight from the can. Canned condensed beef and chicken broths also are available, but must be diluted according to can directions.

# Beef Stock

6   **pounds meaty beef soup bones (neck bones, arm bones, shank bones, or marrow bones)**
3   **carrots, cut up**
1   **large onion, sliced**
2   **stalks celery with leaves, cut up**
1   **large tomato, cut up (optional)**
1   **small head cabbage, cut up**
8   **whole black peppercorns**
4   **sprigs parsley**
1   **bay leaf**
1   **tablespoon salt**
2   **teaspoons dried thyme, crushed**
1   **clove garlic, halved**
12  **cups cold water**                          Oven 450°

In a large shallow roasting pan place soup bones, carrots, and onion. Bake, uncovered, in a 450° oven about 30 minutes or till the bones are well browned, turning occasionally. Drain off fat. In a large stockpot or Dutch oven place the browned bones, carrots, and onion. Pour ½ cup *water* into the roasting pan and rinse. Pour this liquid into the stockpot. Add the celery; tomato, if desired; cabbage; peppercorns; parsley; bay leaf; salt; thyme; and garlic. Add the 12 cups cold water. Bring

## Clarifying stock

Clarify beef or chicken stock for a clear soup. Clarifying removes solid flecks that are too small to be strained out with cheesecloth, but that will muddy a soup's appearance. To clarify, combine ¼ cup cold water, 1 egg white, and 1 eggshell, crushed. Add to strained stock; bring to boiling. Remove from heat; let stand 5 minutes. Strain again through a sieve lined with cheesecloth.

mixture to boiling; reduce heat. Cover and simmer for 5 hours. Strain stock. Discard meat, vegetables, and seasonings. Clarify stock, if desired (see tip box). If using the stock while hot, skim fat. (*Or,* chill stock and lift off fat.) Makes about 8 cups stock.

# Main-Dish Soups & Stews

## Beef Bourguignonne

Cut 3 slices *bacon* into small pieces. In a Dutch oven cook bacon till crisp; remove bacon and set aside. Add ¼ cup *cooking oil* to bacon drippings. Cut 3 pounds boneless *beef chuck* into 1-inch cubes. Combine ⅓ cup all-purpose *flour*, 2 teaspoons *salt*, and ¼ teaspoon *pepper*. Toss beef cubes with flour mixture to coat.

Cook *half* of the beef; 2 medium *onions*, chopped; and 1 clove *garlic*, minced, in the hot oil mixture till beef is brown. Remove; set aside. Cook remaining beef in hot oil mixture till brown. Drain off fat; return beef-onion mixture to Dutch oven. In a small saucepan heat ¼ cup *cognac or brandy*; set aflame and pour over beef. Stir in 1 cup *burgundy*, 1 cup *beef broth*, and 2 *bay leaves*. Bring to boiling; reduce heat. Cover; simmer 1 hour or till meat is nearly tender.

Add 8 small *carrots*, cut up, and ½ pound tiny *onions*. Cover; cook 20 minutes more. Add 16 whole fresh *mushrooms*; cook 10 minutes more. Remove bay leaves. Stir in bacon. Garnish with snipped *parsley*. Serve with hot, cooked *noodles*. Serves 10.

## Cider Stew

Cut 2 pounds *beef stew meat* into 1-inch cubes. Combine 3 tablespoons all-purpose *flour*, 2 teaspoons *salt*, ¼ teaspoon *pepper*, and ¼ teaspoon dried *thyme*, crushed. Coat meat with flour mixture. In a Dutch oven brown meat, half at a time, in 3 tablespoons hot *cooking oil*. Drain off fat. Return all meat to Dutch oven. Stir in 2 cups *apple cider or apple juice*, ½ cup *water*, and 1 to 2 tablespoons *vinegar*. Bring to boiling; reduce heat. Cover and simmer about 1¼ hours or till meat is nearly tender. Stir in 3 medium *potatoes*, peeled and quartered; 4 medium *carrots*, quartered; 2 medium *onions*, sliced; and 1 stalk *celery*, sliced. Cover; simmer 30 minutes more or till meat and vegetables are done. Serves 6 to 8.

## Beef Stew

|   |   |
|---|---|
| **3** | **tablespoons all-purpose flour** |
| **1½** | **pounds beef stew meat or boneless pork, cut into 1-inch cubes** |
| **2** | **tablespoons cooking oil** |
| **½** | **cup chopped onion** |
| **1** | **clove garlic, minced** |
| **½** | **teaspoon dried thyme, crushed** |
| **3** | **cups vegetable juice cocktail** |
| **1** | **teaspoon instant beef bouillon granules** |
|   | **Few dashes bottled hot pepper sauce** |
| **2** | **medium potatoes, peeled and cubed** |
| **1½** | **cups sliced celery** |
| **1½** | **cups sliced carrot** |

In a plastic bag combine flour and 1 teaspoon *salt*. Add meat cubes, a few at a time, shaking to coat. In a large saucepan brown meat, half at a time, in hot oil. Return all meat to saucepan; add onion, garlic, and thyme. Stir in vegetable juice, bouillon, hot pepper sauce, and 1 cup *water*. Bring to boiling; reduce heat. Cover; simmer 1¼ hours for beef (30 minutes for pork) or till meat is nearly tender. Stir in potatoes, celery, and carrot. Cover; simmer 30 minutes more. Skim off fat. Serves 6.

## Old-Fashioned Vegetable-Beef Soup

In a large kettle or Dutch oven combine 3 pounds *beef shank crosscuts;* 8 cups *water;* 4 teaspoons *salt;* ½ teaspoon dried *oregano,* crushed; ¼ teaspoon dried *marjoram,* crushed; 5 whole black *peppercorns;* and 2 *bay leaves.* Bring mixture to boiling; reduce heat. Cover; simmer for 2 hours. Remove beef; when cool enough to handle, cut off meat and coarsely chop. Discard bones. Strain broth; skim excess fat. Return broth to kettle. Cut corn from 4 fresh ears of *corn.* (Or, use one 10-ounce package frozen whole kernel corn.) Stir the chopped meat; corn; 3 *tomatoes,* peeled and cut up; 2 medium *potatoes,* peeled and cubed; 1 cup fresh or frozen cut *green beans;* 2 medium *carrots,* sliced; 2 stalks *celery,* sliced; and 1 medium *onion,* chopped, into broth. Cover; simmer for 1 hour. Season to taste with salt and pepper. Serves 10 to 12.

## Beef-Barley Soup

|   | |
|---|---|
| 2½ | **pounds beef short ribs** |
| 2 | **tablespoons cooking oil** |
| 7 | **cups water** |
| 1 | **16-ounce can tomatoes, cut up** |
| 1 | **large onion, sliced** |
| 2 | **tablespoons instant beef bouillon granules** |
| 1½ | **teaspoons salt** |
| 1 | **teaspoon dried basil, crushed** |
| ½ | **teaspoon Worcestershire sauce** |
| 2 | **cups sliced carrot** |
| 1 | **cup sliced celery** |
| ⅔ | **cup quick-cooking barley** |
| ½ | **cup chopped green pepper** |
| ¼ | **cup snipped parsley** |

In a large kettle or Dutch oven brown short ribs in hot oil over low heat; drain well. Stir in water, *undrained* tomatoes, onion, bouillon granules, salt, basil, and Worcestershire sauce. Cover; simmer for 1½ hours. Stir in carrot, celery, barley, green pepper, and parsley. Cover, simmer for 45 minutes. Remove ribs; when cool enough to handle, cut off any meat and coarsely chop. Discard bones. Skim fat from soup. Return meat to soup; heat through. Season to taste with salt and pepper. Makes 8 servings.

## Meatball Stew with Spinach Dumplings

In a mixing bowl combine 1 beaten *egg*, ¾ cup *soft bread crumbs* (1 slice), and 1 teaspoon *garlic salt*. Add 1 pound *ground beef*; mix well. Shape mixture into 1-inch meatballs. In a 12-inch skillet heat 1 tablespoon *cooking oil*; brown meatballs in hot oil. Stir in ½ cup chopped *onion;* cook 5 minutes. Drain off fat. Combine one 11-ounce can condensed *cheddar cheese soup* and 1 soup can (1¼ cups) *milk;* stir into skillet mixture. Cover; simmer 10 minutes. Stir in one 16-ounce can diced *beets,* drained, and one 10-ounce package frozen *brussels sprouts.* Cover; simmer 5 minutes more.

Meanwhile, in a bowl combine one 8-ounce can *spinach,* well drained and chopped; 1 cup packaged *biscuit mix;* and ¼ cup *milk.* Drop spinach mixture atop bubbling-hot soup mixture to make eight dumplings. Cover; simmer 10 minutes (do not lift lid). Makes 4 servings.

## Chili con Carne

    1   **pound ground beef**
    1   **cup chopped onion**
    ¾   **cup chopped green pepper**
    1   **clove garlic, minced**
    1   **16-ounce can tomatoes, cut up**
    1   **16-ounce can dark red kidney beans,**
        **drained**
    1   **8-ounce can tomato sauce**
    2   **teaspoons chili powder**
    ½   **teaspoon dried basil, crushed**

In a large kettle cook ground beef, onion, green pepper, and garlic till meat is browned. Drain off fat. Stir in *undrained* tomatoes, kidney beans, tomato sauce, chili powder, basil, ½ teaspoon *salt,* and ¼ teaspoon *pepper.* Bring to boiling; reduce heat. Cover and simmer about 20 minutes. Makes 4 to 6 servings.

**Microwave directions:** In a 2-quart nonmetal casserole combine onion, green pepper, garlic, and 1 tablespoon *cooking oil.* Cook, covered with waxed paper, in a counter-top microwave oven on high power 4 minutes or till tender. Add crumbled ground beef. Cook, covered, 5 minutes more or till meat is browned. Stir several times to break up meat. Drain. Stir in *undrained* tomatoes, kidney beans, tomato sauce, chili powder, basil, ½ teaspoon *salt,* and ¼ teaspoon *pepper.* Cook, covered, 8 minutes or till heated through, stirring twice.

**Crockery cooker directions:** In a skillet cook ground beef, onion, and garlic till meat is browned; drain off fat. Transfer mixture to an electric slow crockery cooker. Stir in green pepper, *undrained* tomatoes, kidney beans, tomato sauce, chili powder, basil, ½ teaspoon *salt,* and ¼ teaspoon *pepper.* Cover; cook on low-heat setting for 8 to 10 hours.

---

## Quick Beef Goulash Stew

In a large saucepan cook 1 pound *ground beef* and ½ cup chopped *onion* till meat is browned and onion is tender. Drain off fat. Stir in one 10¼-ounce can *beef gravy;* one 7½-ounce can *tomatoes,* cut up; ½ cup *water;* and 1 teaspoon *Worcestershire sauce.* Bring to boiling. Add one 10-ounce package frozen *peas and carrots* and 1 cup uncooked fine *noodles.* Return to boiling. Cover; simmer for 10 minutes or till vegetables and noodles are tender. Serves 4.

# German Sausage Chowder

 1 **pound fully cooked bratwurst *or* knackwurst, cut into ½-inch pieces (8 links)**
 2 **medium potatoes, peeled and chopped (2 cups)**
 1 **medium onion, chopped (½ cup)**
 1 **small head cabbage, shredded (4 cups)**
 3 **cups milk**
 3 **tablespoons all-purpose flour**
 1 **cup shredded Swiss cheese (4 ounces)**
   **Snipped parsley**

In a large saucepan or Dutch oven combine sausage, potatoes, onion, 1½ teaspoons *salt*, and dash *pepper*. Add 2 cups *water*. Bring to boiling; reduce heat. Cover; simmer for 20 minutes or till potatoes are nearly tender. Stir in cabbage; cook 10 minutes more or till vegetables are tender. Stir in 2½ *cups* of the milk. Stir remaining ½ cup milk into flour; stir into soup. Cook and stir till thickened and bubbly. Stir in cheese till melted. Garnish with parsley. Makes 6 servings.

# Scotch Broth

 1½ **pounds boneless lamb, cut into 1-inch cubes**
  4 **cups water**
  1 **medium onion, chopped (½ cup)**
  3 **sprigs parsley**
  2 **whole cloves**
  1 **bay leaf**
  ¼ **cup pearl barley**
  2 **medium carrots, chopped (1 cup)**
  1 **medium potato, peeled and chopped (1 cup)**
  1 **stalk celery, chopped (½ cup)**
  ¼ **teaspoon dried thyme, crushed**
  ¼ **teaspoon dried rosemary, crushed**

In a large saucepan combine lamb, water, onion, parsley, cloves, bay leaf, 1½ teaspoons *salt,* ¼ teaspoon *pepper.* Bring to boiling; reduce heat. Cover; simmer for 30 minutes. Remove parsley, cloves, and bay leaf. Stir in pearl barley; cover and cook 30 minutes more. Stir in carrots, potato, celery, thyme, and rosemary. Cover and cook about 30 minutes more or till barley and vegetables are tender. Serves 6.

## Dilled Lamb Ragout

Oven 375°

Cut 2 pounds boneless *lamb* into ¾-inch cubes. Combine ⅓ cup all-purpose *flour,* 1½ teaspoons *salt,* ½ teaspoon *dried dillweed,* and dash *pepper.* Coat lamb with flour mixture. In an oven-proof Dutch oven heat ¼ cup *cooking oil;* brown lamb, half at a time, in hot oil. Return all meat to pan. Stir in any remaining flour mixture. Stir in 2 cups *water.* Bake, covered, in a 375° oven for 45 minutes. Stir in one 10-ounce package frozen *peas,* 1 cup sliced *celery,* and ½ cup *rosé wine.* Cover and bake 45 minutes more. Skim off fat. Stir about *1 cup* of the hot mixture into 1 cup dairy *sour cream;* return to remaining hot mixture. Cook and stir on top of range till heated through (*do not boil*). Makes 6 servings.

# Herbed Lamb Stew

  1½  **pounds boneless lamb *or* beef stew meat,**
       **cut into ¾-inch cubes**
  2  **tablespoons cooking oil**
  1  **clove garlic, minced**
  1  **bay leaf**
  2  **teaspoons instant beef bouillon granules**
  ½  **teaspoon dried thyme, crushed**
  ½  **teaspoon dried oregano, crushed**
  ½  **teaspoon dried marjoram, crushed**
  4  **medium carrots, sliced ½ inch thick**
  4  **stalks celery, sliced 1 inch thick**
  2  **medium onions, cut into wedges**
  ½  **cup dairy sour cream**
  ¼  **cup all-purpose flour**

In a Dutch oven brown meat, half at a time, in hot oil; remove from heat. Return all meat to pan. Add next 6 ingredients, 2 cups *water*, ½ teaspoon *salt*, and ¼ teaspoon *pepper*. Bring mixture to boiling; reduce heat. Cover; simmer for 30 minutes. Stir in carrots, celery, and onions. Cover; simmer about 25 minutes more or till meat and vegetables are tender. Remove bay leaf. Combine sour cream, flour, and 2 tablespoons *water*. Stir about ½ *cup* of the hot mixture into sour cream mixture; return to remaining hot mixture. Cook and stir till thickened and bubbly. Serves 6.

# South American Pork Soup

Cut 1½ pounds boneless *pork or beef stew meat* into ½-inch cubes. In a Dutch oven heat 2 tablespoons *cooking oil*. Cook half of the meat in hot oil till browned; remove meat and set aside. Cook remaining meat with ½ cup finely chopped *onion;* 2 cloves *garlic,* minced; and 1 teaspoon *paprika* till meat is brown. Return meat to pan. Stir in 4 cups *water* and 1 table-spoon instant *beef bouillon granules.* Bring to boiling; reduce heat. Cover; simmer for 1 hour. Add 2 medium *potatoes,* peeled and cut into ½-inch cubes; 2 medium *carrots,* chopped;

½ pound *winter squash or sweet potatoes,* peeled and cut into ½-inch cubes; one 8-ounce can whole kernel *corn, undrained;* 1 medium *tomato,* peeled and chopped; 1 teaspoon *salt;* and ¼ teaspoon ground *red pepper.* Cover; simmer 15 to 20 minutes more or till meat and vegetables are tender. Stir in 2 cups torn fresh *spinach;* simmer 3 to 5 minutes more. Skim off fat, if necessary. Season. Serves 8.

## Ham Hodgepodge

In a Dutch oven combine 5 cups chopped *cabbage;* 6 large *carrots,* cut into 1-inch pieces (1 pound); 2 large *potatoes,* peeled and chopped (3 cups); 3 cups *water;* 2 cups diced *ham* (10 ounces); ½ cup chopped *onion;* ½ teaspoon *salt;* ½ teaspoon *seasoned salt;* and ⅛ teaspoon *pepper.* Bring to boiling; reduce heat. Cover; simmer 1 hour. Stir in one 15-ounce can *garbanzo beans, undrained;* cover and cook 10 to 15 minutes more. (Add more water, if needed.) Makes 6 to 8 servings.

## Easy Pork Cassoulet

Oven 350°

In a skillet cook ½ pound bulk *pork sausage;* 1 medium *onion,* sliced; and 1 clove *garlic,* minced, till meat is browned and onion is tender. Drain off fat. Add 1½ cups cubed fully cooked *ham,* 2 tablespoons snipped *parsley,* and 1 *bay leaf;* mix well. Stir in two 15-ounce cans *navy beans, undrained;* ¼ cup dry white *wine;* and dash ground *cloves.* Turn into a 1½-quart casserole. Bake, covered, in a 350° oven for 45 minutes. Remove bay leaf. Serves 6.

# Oven-Baked Pork Stew

| | |
|---|---|
| 1½ | **pounds boneless pork, cut into 1-inch cubes** |
| 2 | **tablespoons cooking oil** |
| 3 | **tablespoons all-purpose flour** |
| 1 | **16-ounce can tomatoes, cut up** |
| 1 | **clove garlic, minced** |
| 1 | **bay leaf** |
| 1 | **teaspoon sugar** |
| 1 | **teaspoon instant beef bouillon granules** |
| ½ | **teaspoon dried thyme, crushed** |
| ½ | **teaspoon dried oregano, crushed** |
| ¼ | **teaspoon bottled hot pepper sauce** |
| 4 | **medium sweet potatoes, peeled and sliced ¾ inch thick (4 cups)** |
| 1 | **large onion, cut into wedges** |
| 1 | **medium green pepper, cut into thin strips** |
| 1 | **10-ounce package frozen peas, thawed** |

Oven 350°

In a large skillet brown meat, half at a time, in hot oil. Remove meat from skillet, reserving drippings. Stir flour into drippings. Stir in *undrained* tomatoes, garlic, bay leaf, sugar, bouillon granules, thyme, oregano, pepper sauce, ¼ cup *water,* and ½ teaspoon *salt.* Cook and stir till thickened and bubbly. In a 3-quart casserole combine meat, sweet potatoes, onion, and green pepper. Stir in tomato mixture. Bake, covered, in a 350° oven about 1½ hours or till meat and vegetables are tender, stirring occasionally. Remove bay leaf. Stir in peas. Bake 5 to 10 minutes more. Serves 6.

---

# Quick Beans-and-Franks Soup

In a saucepan combine ¾ cup chopped *celery,* ¾ cup chopped *onion,* ½ cup *water,* ½ teaspoon *salt,* and dash *pepper.* Cook 10 minutes or till vegetables are tender. Stir in two 16-ounce cans *pork and beans in tomato sauce;* mash slightly. Stir in 2 cups *milk* and ¼ cup *chili sauce.* Stir in 12 ounces *frankfurters,* sliced; heat through. Makes 6 servings.

## New England Clam Chowder

      1   **pint shucked clams, chopped, *or* two**
          **6½-ounce cans minced clams**
      4   **ounces salt pork, diced, *or* 2 slices bacon,**
          **cut up**
      4   **medium potatoes, peeled and diced**
     ½   **cup chopped onion**
     2½  **cups milk**
      1   **cup light cream**
      3   **tablespoons all-purpose flour**
     ½   **teaspoon Worcestershire sauce**

Drain clams, reserving liquid. Add enough water to reserved liquid to measure 2 cups liquid; set aside. In a large saucepan fry salt pork or bacon till crisp; remove bits of pork or bacon and set aside. Add reserved liquid, potatoes, and onion to fat in saucepan. Cook, covered, about 15 minutes or till potatoes are tender. Stir in clams, *2 cups* of the milk, and the light cream. Stir remaining ½ cup milk into flour; stir into chowder. Cook and stir till bubbly. Cook 1 minute more. Add Worcestershire, ¾ teaspoon *salt,* and dash *pepper.* Sprinkle pork or bacon atop. Serves 6.

## Creole Gumbo

In a large saucepan cook ½ cup chopped *onion* and 1 clove *garlic,* minced, in 3 tablespoons *butter or margarine* till onion is tender. Blend in 3 tablespoons all-purpose *flour.* Cook, stirring constantly, till flour is golden brown. Stir in one 16-ounce can *tomatoes,* cut up; 1½ cups *water;* ½ cup chopped *green pepper;* 2 *bay leaves;* 1 teaspoon dried *oregano,* crushed; 1 teaspoon dried *thyme,* crushed; ½ teaspoon *salt;* and ¼ to ½ teaspoon bottled *hot pepper sauce.* Bring to boiling; reduce heat. Cover; simmer for 20 minutes.

Remove bay leaves. Stir in 10 ounces fresh *or* frozen *okra,* cut up (2 cups). Bring mixture to boiling; reduce heat. Simmer for 5 minutes. Drain two 4½-ounce cans *shrimp.* Stir shrimp and one 7-ounce can *crab meat,* drained, flaked, and cartilage removed, into okra mixture; cook about 5 minutes or till heated through. Serve the gumbo mixture over *hot cooked rice* in soup plates. (Traditionally, rice is mounded in a heated soup plate and the gumbo is spooned around it.) Serves 6.

## Bouillabaisse

| | |
|---|---|
| 1 | **or 2 8-ounce fresh *or* frozen lobster tails** |
| 1 | **pound fresh *or* frozen fish fillets** |
| 8 | **clams in shell** |
| 2½ | **cups chicken broth *or* water** |
| 1 | **16-ounce can tomatoes, cut up** |
| ½ | **cup dry white wine** |
| 1 | **large onion, cut up** |
| 2 | **sprigs parsley** |
| 1 | **clove garlic, halved** |
| 1 | **bay leaf** |
| 1 | **teaspoon dried thyme, crushed** |
| ¼ | **teaspoon thread saffron, crushed** |

Partially thaw lobster and fish, if frozen. Split lobster tails in half lengthwise, then in half crosswise. Cut fish into 1-inch pieces. Thoroughly wash clams. Cover clams with salted water (3 tablespoons *salt* to 8 cups cold *water*); let stand 15 minutes. Rinse. Repeat twice. Combine remaining ingredients. Stir in 1½ teaspoons *salt* and ⅛ teaspoon *pepper*. Bring to boiling; reduce heat. Simmer, covered, for 30 minutes. Strain; reserve broth. Discard vegetables and herbs. Bring to boiling. Stir in lobster, fish, and clams. Cook 5 minutes or till fish flakes and clams open. Serves 6.

## Manhattan Clam Chowder

  **1**   **pint shucked clams, chopped, or two**
             **6½-ounce cans minced clams**
  **2**   *or* **3 slices bacon, cut up**
  **1**   **cup finely chopped celery**
  **1**   **cup chopped onion**
  **1**   **16-ounce can tomatoes, cut up**
  **2**   **medium potatoes, peeled and diced**
  **½**   **cup finely chopped carrots**
  **½**   **teaspoon dried thyme, crushed**

Drain clams, reserving liquid. Add enough water to liquid to measure 3 cups. In a large saucepan partially cook bacon; stir in celery and onion. Cook till celery and onion are tender. Stir in liquid mixture, *undrained* tomatoes, potatoes, carrots, thyme, 1 teaspoon *salt,* and ⅛ teaspoon *pepper.* Bring to boiling; reduce heat. Cover; simmer 30 to 35 minutes or till vegetables are tender. Mash slightly to thicken. Stir in clams; heat through. Serves 4.

## Shrimp-Rice Soup

  **2**   **cups sliced fresh mushrooms**
  **¼**   **cup sliced green onion**
  **1**   **clove garlic, minced**
  **2**   **tablespoons butter or margarine**
  **4**   **cups chicken broth**
  **¾**   **cup dry white wine**
  **½**   **teaspoon dried thyme, crushed**
  **½**   **cup long grain rice**
  **2**   **tablespoons cornstarch**
**12**   **ounces fresh or frozen shelled shrimp**
  **2**   **tablespoons snipped parsley**

In a saucepan cook mushrooms, onion, and garlic in butter till onion is tender but not brown. Stir in broth, wine, and thyme. Bring to boiling; stir in rice. Reduce heat; cover and simmer for 15 minutes. Blend 2 tablespoons *cold water* into cornstarch;

stir into hot broth mixture. Cook and stir till bubbly. Stir in shrimp. Bring to boiling; reduce heat. Cover; simmer 1 to 2 minutes more or till shrimp are done. Stir in parsley. Serves 6.

## Cioppino

1 **pound fresh** *or* **frozen fish fillets**
1 **small green pepper, cut into ½-inch squares**
2 **tablespoons finely chopped onion**
1 **clove garlic, minced**
1 **tablespoon cooking oil**
1 **16-ounce can tomatoes, cut up**
1 **8-ounce can tomato sauce**
½ **cup dry white** *or* **red wine**
3 **tablespoons snipped parsley**
¼ **teaspoon dried oregano, crushed**
¼ **teaspoon dried basil, crushed**
2 **4½-ounce cans shrimp, drained,** *or* **one 12-ounce package frozen shelled shrimp**
1 **6½-ounce can minced clams**

Thaw fish, if frozen. Cut fish into 1-inch pieces. In a large saucepan cook green pepper, onion, and garlic in hot oil till onion is tender. Add next 6 ingredients, ½ teaspoon *salt,* and dash *pepper.* Bring to boiling; reduce heat. Cover; simmer 20 minutes. Add fish, shrimp, and *undrained* clams. Bring just to boiling; reduce heat. Cover; simmer 5 to 7 minutes or till fish is done. Serves 6.

## Oyster Stew

1 **pint shucked oysters**
2 **cups milk**
1 **cup light cream**
    **Dash bottled hot pepper sauce (optional)**
    **Paprika**
    **Butter** *or* **margarine**

In a medium saucepan combine the *undrained* oysters and ¾ teaspoon *salt*. Cook over medium heat about 5 minutes or till edges of oysters curl. Stir in milk, cream, and hot pepper sauce. Heat through. Season to taste with additional salt and pepper. Sprinkle *each* serving with paprika and top with a pat of butter or margarine. Makes 4 servings.

**Vegetable-Oyster Stew:** Prepare Oyster Stew as above, *except* in a small saucepan cook ½ cup finely chopped *carrots* and ½ cup finely chopped *celery* in 2 tablespoons *butter*, covered, 10 to 15 minutes or until vegetables are tender but not brown. Stir vegetable mixture and 1 teaspoon *Worcestershire sauce* into oyster-milk mixture. Heat through.

## Fish Chowder

- **1 pound fresh or frozen fish fillets**
- **2 medium potatoes, peeled and cubed (2 cups)**
- **1 medium carrot, diced (½ cup)**
- **2 teaspoons salt**
- **⅛ teaspoon pepper**
- **4 slices bacon**
- **½ cup chopped onion**
- **2 cups milk**
- **3 tablespoons all-purpose flour**
- **¼ teaspoon dried thyme, crushed**

Thaw fish, if frozen. Cut fish into 2-inch squares. In a large saucepan bring 2 cups *water* to boiling; add potatoes and carrots. Reduce heat. Cover; simmer for 5 minutes. Stir in fish, salt, and pepper. Simmer, covered, 10 minutes. Meanwhile, in a skillet cook bacon till crisp. Drain bacon, reserving 2 tablespoons of the drippings in skillet; crumble bacon. Cook onion in drippings till tender. Blend ½ cup of the milk into the flour; stir into fish mixture along with crumbled bacon, onion mixture, thyme, and remaining 1½ cups milk. Cook and stir till bubbly; cook 1 minute more. Serves 6.

# Mulligatawny

>        4    **cups chicken broth (see tip, page 736)**
>        2    **cups chopped cooked chicken**
>        1    **16-ounce can tomatoes, cut up**
>        1    **medium cooking apple, peeled and**
>             **chopped (1 cup)**
>       ¼    **cup finely chopped onion**
>       ¼    **cup chopped carrot**
>       ¼    **cup chopped celery**
>       ¼    **cup green pepper**
>        1    **tablespoon snipped parsley**
>        2    **teaspoons lemon juice**
>        1    **teaspoon sugar**
>        1    **teaspoon curry powder**
>       ⅛    **teaspoon ground cloves**

In a large saucepan combine broth, chicken, *undrained* tomatoes, apple, onion, carrot, celery, green pepper, parsley, lemon juice, sugar, curry, ground cloves, ¾ teaspoon *salt,* and dash *pepper.* Bring to boiling; reduce heat. Cover; simmer for 20 minutes, stirring occasionally. Makes 6 to 8 servings.

---

# Chicken Vegetable-Noodle Soup

>        6    **cups water**
>        1    **5- to 6-pound stewing chicken, cut up**
>       ⅓    **cup chopped onion**
>        1    **bay leaf**
>        1    **16-ounce can tomatoes, cut up**
>        1    **16-ounce can cream-style corn**
>        2    **small zucchini, thinly sliced**
>     1½    **cups uncooked medium noodles**

In a large kettle combine water, chicken pieces, onion, bay leaf, 2 teaspoons *salt,* and ¼ teaspoon *pepper.* Bring to boiling; reduce heat. Cover; simmer about 2 hours or till chicken is tender. Remove chicken. When chicken is cool enough to handle, cut off meat and cube chicken. Discard bones and skin. Skim fat from broth; remove bay leaf and discard.

Add *undrained* tomatoes, corn, and zucchini to broth. Bring to boiling. Stir in noodles. Reduce heat. Cover; simmer about 8 minutes or till noodles are almost tender. Stir in the cubed chicken. Cover; simmer till noodles are tender and mixture is heated through. Season with salt and pepper. Serves 10.

## Turkey Frame Soup

| | |
|---|---|
| 1 | meaty turkey frame |
| 3 | quarts water (12 cups) |
| 1 | onion, quartered |
| 2 | teaspoons salt |
| 1 | 16-ounce can tomatoes, cut up |
| 1 | tablespoon instant chicken bouillon granules |
| 1½ | teaspoons dried oregano, crushed |
| 1 | teaspoon dried thyme, crushed |
| ⅛ | teaspoon pepper |
| 4 | cups fresh vegetables (any combination of uncooked sliced celery, sliced carrot, chopped onion, chopped rutabaga, sliced mushrooms, chopped broccoli, and cauliflower flowerets) |
| 1½ | cups uncooked medium noodles |

Break turkey frame or cut in half with kitchen shears; place in a large Dutch oven with water, onion, and salt. Bring to boiling; reduce heat. Cover; simmer for 1½ hours. Remove turkey frame; when cool enough to handle, cut off meat and coarsely chop. Discard bones. Strain broth; discard solids. Return broth to Dutch oven. Stir in cup-up turkey meat, *undrained* tomatoes, bouillon granules, oregano, thyme, and pepper. Stir in fresh vegetables. Bring to boiling; reduce heat. Cover; simmer for 45 minutes. Stir in uncooked noodles; simmer, uncovered, 8 to 10 minutes or till noodles are done. Season to taste with salt and pepper. Makes 10 servings.

## Cream of Chicken Soup

- ¼ cup butter or margarine
- ¼ cup all-purpose flour
- ½ cup milk
- ½ cup light cream
- 3 cups chicken broth (see tip, page 736)
- 1½ cups finely chopped cooked chicken
  Dash pepper

In a large saucepan melt butter or margarine; stir in flour. Stir in milk, cream, and broth. Cook and stir till mixture is slightly thickened and bubbly; reduce heat. Stir in chicken and pepper; heat through. Garnish with snipped chives and parsley, if desired. Makes 4 servings.

# Meal-Mate Soups

## Minestrone

- 1½ cups dry navy beans
- 2 medium carrots, chopped (1 cup)
- 6 slices bacon
- 1 large onion, chopped (1 cup)
- 2 stalks celery, chopped (1 cup)
- 1 clove garlic, minced
- 2 16-ounce cans tomatoes, cut up
- 2 cups finely shredded cabbage
- 1 medium zucchini, sliced
- 1 17-ounce can peas, drained
- 1 teaspoon dried basil, crushed
- ½ teaspoon ground sage
- 1½ cups uncooked fine noodles

Rinse beans. Combine beans and 9 cups *water*. Bring to boiling; reduce heat. Simmer 2 minutes. Remove from heat.

Cover; let stand 1 hour. (*Or*, soak beans in the water overnight.) *Do not drain.* Add carrots. Cover; simmer 2½ to 3 hours. Cook bacon till crisp. Drain, reserving 2 tablespoons drippings. Crumble bacon; set aside. Cook onion, celery, and garlic in reserved drippings till almost tender; drain. Stir into beans along with *undrained* tomatoes, cabbage, zucchini, peas, basil, sage, 2 teaspoons *salt*, and ¼ teaspoon *pepper*. Bring to boiling; stir in noodles. Reduce heat; simmer 25 minutes more. Stir in bacon. Serves 8.

---

### Soaking dry beans

Dry beans and dry whole peas need soaking before cooking, but split peas and lentils do not. Rinse and drain all of these dried products before cooking. To soak, combine dry beans with the specified amount of water in a Dutch oven. Bring to boiling; reduce heat and simmer 2 minutes. Remove from heat. Cover; let stand 1 hour. *Or*, instead of heating, soak beans in water overnight.

---

## Split Pea Soup

Rinse 2¼ cups dry *green split peas* (1 pound). In a Dutch oven combine peas; 8 cups cold *water;* 1 teaspoon *instant chicken bouillon granules;* 1 meaty *ham bone* (1½ pounds); 1 medium *onion*, chopped; ¼ teaspoon *pepper;* and ¼ teaspoon dried *marjoram*, crushed. Bring to boiling; reduce heat. Cover; simmer for 1 hour. Stir occasionally. Remove ham bone; when cool enough to handle, cut off meat and coarsely chop. Discard bone. Return meat to soup; stir in 2 medium *carrots*, chopped, and 2 stalks *celery*, chopped. Cover; simmer 30 minutes more. Season. Serves 10.

# Ham and Bean Vegetable Soup

Rinse 1 pound dry *navy beans* (2½ cups). In a Dutch oven combine beans and 8 cups *water*. Bring to boiling; reduce heat and simmer 2 minutes. Remove from heat. Cover; let stand 1 hour. (*Or*, soak beans in the water overnight in a covered pan.) *Do not drain.*

Bring beans and liquid to boiling. Add 1½ pounds meaty *smoked pork hocks* (ham hocks); reduce heat. Cover; simmer for 1 hour or till beans are nearly tender. Remove pork hocks; when cool enough to handle, cut off meat and coarsely chop. Discard bones. Return meat to pan. Add 2 medium *potatoes*, peeled and cubed; 2 medium *carrots*, chopped; 2 stalks *celery*, sliced; 1 medium *onion*, chopped; ¾ teaspoon dried *thyme*, crushed; ½ teaspoon *salt*; ¼ teaspoon *pepper*; and several dashes bottled *hot pepper sauce*. Cover; simmer 30 minutes or till vegetables are tender. Season. Serves 10.

# Lentil Soup

Rinse 1 pound dry *lentils* (2⅓ cups). In a Dutch oven combine lentils; 8 cups *cold water*; one 16-ounce can *tomatoes*, cut up; 2 slices *bacon*, cut up; 1 medium *onion*, chopped (½ cup); 1 medium *carrot*, chopped (½ cup); 3 tablespoons snipped *parsley*; 2 tablespoons *wine vinegar*; 1 clove *garlic*, minced; 2½ teaspoons *salt*; ½ teaspoon dried *oregano*, crushed; and ¼ teaspoon *pepper*. Bring to boiling; reduce heat. Cover; simmer 45 minutes. Serves 8 to 10.

# Fresh Corn Chowder

|   |   |
|---|---|
| 6 | **fresh medium ears of corn** |
| ¼ | **cup chopped onion** |
| 4 | **cups milk** |
| 2 | **tablespoons butter *or* margarine** |
| 3 | **tablespoons all-purpose flour** |
| 1 | **slightly beaten egg** |

Using a sharp knife, cut tips of corn kernels off cobs. Scrape cobs. In a saucepan combine the corn, onion, ½ cup *water*, and ½ teaspoon *salt*. Bring to boiling; reduce heat. Cover; simmer about 15 minutes or till corn is barely done, stirring occasionally. Stir in 3½ cups of the milk, the butter or margarine, 1 teaspoon *salt*, and ¼ teaspoon *pepper*.

Combine the remaining ½ cup milk and the flour. Add milk-flour mixture to corn mixture. Cook and stir till thickened and bubbly. Gradually stir about *1 cup* of the hot mixture into beaten egg. Return to hot mixture in saucepan. Cook over low heat for 2 minutes more, stirring constantly (*do not boil*). If desired, garnish soup with snipped chives and paprika or crumbled bacon. Serves 6.

## Herbed Tomato Soup

In a large saucepan heat ¼ cup *butter* till melted. Add 2 medium *onions*, sliced (1 cup); cook till tender but not brown. Peel, core, and coarsely chop 6 medium *tomatoes* (about 4 cups); add to saucepan. (*Or*, use one 28-ounce can *undrained* whole peeled *tomatoes*, cut up.) Stir in one 6-ounce can *tomato paste;* 1 tablespoon snipped *fresh basil* or 1 teaspoon *dried basil*, crushed; 2 teaspoons snipped *fresh thyme* or ½ teaspoon *dried thyme*, crushed; 1 teaspoon *salt;* and ⅛ teaspoon *pepper*. Stir in 4 cups *chicken broth* (see tip, page 736). Bring to boiling; reduce heat. Cover; simmer for 30 to 40 minutes. Press through a food mill. (*Or*, place about *half* at a time in a blender container; cover and blend till pureed. Blending leaves more seeds in the tomato mixture than sieving.) Return to saucepan. Heat through. Makes 8 servings.

# Creamy Borscht

    **4**   **cups beef broth (see tip, page 737)**
    **4**   **medium beets, peeled and cubed (3 cups)**
    **2**   **medium carrots, chopped (1 cup)**
    **1**   **medium onion, chopped (½ cup)**
    **1**   **bay leaf**
    **1**   **tablespoon vinegar**
    **1**   **teaspoon sugar**
    **1**   **teaspoon salt**
   **¼**   **teaspoon pepper**
   **½**   **small head cabbage, shredded (3 cups)**
    **1**   **16-ounce can tomatoes, cut up**
    **2**   **slightly beaten egg yolks**
   **½**   **cup dairy sour cream**

In a Dutch oven combine beef broth, beets, carrots, onion, bay leaf, vinegar, sugar, salt, and pepper. Bring to boiling; reduce heat. Cover; simmer for 40 minutes. Stir in cabbage and *undrained* tomatoes. Cover and cook 30 to 35 minutes more or till vegetables are tender. Remove bay leaf.

Stir together egg yolks and sour cream; gradually stir in about *1 cup* of the hot mixture. Return to Dutch oven; heat through, stirring constantly over low heat. *Do not boil.* Serve immediately. Makes 6 to 8 servings.

# French Onion Soup

 **1½**   **pounds onions, thinly sliced (6 cups)**
   **¼**   **cup butter *or* margarine**
    **3**   **10½-ounce cans *condensed* beef broth**
    **1**   **teaspoon Worcestershire sauce**
    **6**   **to 8 slices French bread, toasted**
        **Shredded Swiss cheese**

In a large saucepan cook onions, covered, in butter about 20 minutes or till tender. Add condensed beef broth, Worcestershire sauce, ¼ teaspoon *salt,* and dash *pepper;* bring to boiling. Sprinkle toasted bread with cheese; place under broiler till cheese is lightly browned. Ladle soup into bowls and float bread atop. (*Or*, place a bread slice on soup in each broiler-proof soup bowl; sprinkle with cheese. Broil till cheese is lightly browned.) Makes 6 to 8 servings.

## Cream of Fresh Vegetable Soup

  1½  **cups chicken broth (see tip, page 736)**
  ½  **cup chopped onion**
    **Desired vegetable and seasonings (see chart below)**
  2  **tablespoons butter or margarine**
  2  **tablespoons all-purpose flour**
  ¼  **teaspoon salt**
    **Few dashes white pepper**
  1  **cup milk**

In a saucepan combine chicken broth, chopped onion, and one of the vegetable-seasoning combinations from the chart. (*Or*, substitute an equal amount of frozen vegetable, if desired.) Bring mixture to boiling. Reduce heat; cover and simmer for the time indicated in the chart or till vegetable is tender. (Remove bay leaf if using broccoli.)

  Place *half* of the vegetable mixture in a blender container or food processor. Cover and blend 30 to 60 seconds or till smooth. Pour into a bowl. Repeat with remaining vegetable mixture; set all aside.

  In the same saucepan melt the butter. Stir in flour, salt, and pepper. Add the milk all at once. Cook and stir till mixture is thickened and bubbly. Stir in the blended vegetable mixture. Cook and stir till soup is heated through. Season to taste with additional salt and pepper. Makes 3 or 4 servings.

| Vegetable | Seasonings | Cooking Time | Yield |
|---|---|---|---|
| 2 cups cut asparagus | 1 teaspoon lemon juice<br>⅛ teaspoon ground mace | 8 minutes | 3½ cups |
| 1½ cups cut green beans | ½ teaspoon dried savory, crushed | 20 to 30 minutes | 3 cups |
| 2 cups cut broccoli | ½ teaspoon dried thyme, crushed<br>1 small bay leaf<br>Dash garlic powder | 10 minutes | 3½ cups |

| Vegetable | Seasonings | Cooking Time | Yield |
|---|---|---|---|
| 1 cup sliced carrots | 1 tablespoon snipped parsley<br>½ teaspoon dried basil, crushed | 12 minutes | 3½ cups |
| 2 cups sliced cauliflower | ½ to ¾ teaspoon curry powder | 10 minutes | 3½ cups |
| 1½ cups chopped celery | 2 tablespoons snipped parsley<br>½ teaspoon dried basil, crushed | 15 minutes | 3 cups |
| 1 cup sliced fresh mushrooms | ⅛ teaspoon ground nutmeg | 5 minutes | 2⅔ cups |
| 2½ cups chopped onions | ½ teaspoon Worcestershire sauce<br>1 small clove garlic, minced | 5 minutes | 4 cups |
| 1½ cups shelled peas | ¼ cup shredded lettuce<br>2 tablespoons diced fully cooked ham<br>¼ teaspoon dried sage, crushed | 8 minutes | 3½ cups |
| 1 cup sliced potatoes | ½ teaspoon dried dillweed | 10 minutes | 3 cups |
| 2 cups chopped spinach | ⅛ teaspoon dried thyme, crushed<br>Dash ground nutmeg | 3 minutes | 2½ cups |
| 4 medium tomatoes, peeled, quartered, and seeded | ¼ teaspoon dried basil, crushed | 15 minutes | 3⅓ cups |
| 1½ cups cut unpeeled zucchini | Several dashes ground nutmeg | 5 minutes | 3⅓ cups |

# Gazpacho

> **6  large tomatoes (2½ pounds)**
> **2  cups tomato juice**
> **1  medium cucumber, seeded and chopped (1¼ cups)**
> **1  medium onion, finely chopped (½ cup)**
> **1  small green pepper, finely chopped (½ cup)**
> **1  small clove garlic, minced**
> **¼  cup olive oil or cooking oil**
> **2  tablespoons vinegar**
> **Few drops bottled hot pepper sauce**
> **Croutons or toasted bread cubes**

Plunge tomatoes in boiling water for 30 seconds to loosen skins, then immerse in cold water. Slip skins off; core and coarsely chop tomatoes (measure about 6 cups).

In a large mixing bowl combine tomatoes, tomato juice, cucumber, onion, green pepper, garlic, oil, vinegar, hot pepper sauce, 1 teaspoon *salt,* and ⅛ teaspoon *pepper.* Cover and chill. If desired, add an ice cube to each serving. Top with croutons or toasted bread cubes. Makes 10 to 12 appetizer servings.

## Swedish Fruit Soup

|   |   |
|---|---|
| 1 | 8-ounce package mixed dried fruits |
| ½ | cup raisins |
| 3 | to 4 inches stick cinnamon |
| 2 | cups unsweetened pineapple juice |
| 2 | tablespoons quick-cooking tapioca |
| 1 | medium orange, thinly sliced and halved and quartered |
| ½ | cup currant jelly |
| ¼ | cup sugar |

Halve large pieces of fruit. In a large saucepan combine mixed fruits, raisins, cinnamon, and 4 cups *water.* Bring to boiling; reduce heat. Simmer, covered, for 10 minutes. Meanwhile, combine pineapple juice and tapioca; let stand 5 minutes. Add to cooked fruit mixture along with orange, jelly, sugar, and ¼ teaspoon *salt.* Bring to boiling; reduce heat. Cover; simmer for 5 minutes, stirring occasionally. Remove stick cinnamon. Serve warm or chilled. Makes 8 to 10 dessert servings.

## Cheese Soup

|   |   |
|---|---|
| 1 | cup finely chopped carrot |
| ¼ | cup finely chopped celery |
| ¼ | cup finely chopped onion |
| 1¾ | cups chicken broth (see tip, page 736) |
| 2 | cups milk |
| ¼ | cup all-purpose flour |
|  | Dash paprika |
| 1 | cup shredded American cheese (4 ounces) |

In a medium saucepan combine carrot, celery, and onion; add chicken broth. Heat to boiling; reduce heat. Cover; simmer for 15 minutes or till vegetables are done. Combine milk, flour, paprika, and dash *salt;* stir into chicken broth mixture. Cook and stir till thickened and bubbly. Add cheese, stirring till melted. Makes 4 to 6 servings.

## Vichyssoise

> **2  leeks**
> **1  small onion, sliced**
> **2  tablespoons butter *or* margarine**
> **3  small potatoes, peeled and sliced (2½**
>    **cups)**
> **2  cups chicken broth (see tip, page 736)**
> **1½  cups milk**
> **1  cup whipping cream**
>    **Snipped chives**

Trim green tops from leeks; thinly slice the white portion of the leeks (measure about ⅔ cup). In a medium saucepan cook leeks and onion in butter till vegetables are tender but not brown. Stir in sliced potatoes, chicken broth, and 1 teaspoon *salt.* Bring to boiling; reduce heat. Cover; simmer for 35 to 40 minutes or till potatoes are very tender.

Place *half* of the mixture in a blender container or food processor; cover and blend till mixture is smooth. Pour into a bowl. Repeat with remaining mixture. Return all mixture to saucepan; stir in milk. Season to taste with additional salt and white pepper. Bring to boiling, stirring frequently. Cool. Stir in whipping cream. Cover and chill thoroughly before serving. Garnish with snipped chives. Makes 4 to 6 servings.

# Quick Soups

### Easy Chicken-Curry Soup

In a saucepan cook ¼ cup chopped *onion* and ½ teaspoon *curry powder* in 2 tablespoons *butter* till onion is tender. Stir in one 10¾-ounce can condensed *cream of chicken soup;* gradually blend in 1¼ cups *milk*. Stir in one 4-ounce can *mushroom stems and pieces, undrained*. Bring to boiling; reduce heat. Cover; simmer for 5 to 10 minutes. Stir in one 5-ounce can boned *chicken*, drained and cut up; heat through. Makes 3 or 4 main-dish servings.

## Cheesy Chicken-Corn Chowder

| | |
|---|---|
| 1 | **whole small chicken breast** |
| ¼ | **cup chopped onion** |
| ¼ | **cup chopped celery** |
| 1 | **10¾-ounce can condensed cream of chicken soup** |
| 1 | **8¾-ounce can whole kernel corn** |
| ½ | **cup milk** |
| ½ | **cup shredded American cheese** |
| 2 | **tablespoons chopped pimiento** |

In a saucepan combine chicken, onion, celery, and ½ cup *water*. Bring to boiling; reduce heat. Cover; simmer 15 to 20 minutes. Remove chicken; when cool enough to handle, cut off meat and chop. Discard skins and bones. Return meat to broth; stir in remaining ingredients. Cook, uncovered, for 10 minutes. Makes 4 main-dish servings.

## Quick Tomato-Rice Soup

| | |
|---|---|
| 1 | **10¾-ounce can condensed tomato soup** |
| 3 | **cups chicken broth (see tip, page 736)** |
| ¾ | **cup quick-cooking rice** |
| ½ | **cup finely chopped celery** |
| | **Few drops bottled hot pepper sauce** |

Combine soup, broth, rice, celery, and pepper sauce. Bring to boiling; reduce heat. Cover; simmer for 8 to 10 minutes or till rice is tender. Makes 4 to 6 side-dish servings.

# Quick Cheesy Tuna Soup

In a saucepan cook 2 tablespoons chopped *onion* in 2 table-spoons *butter or margarine* till tender but not brown. Stir in one 11-ounce can condensed *cheddar cheese soup;* gradually stir in ½ cup *milk.* Stir in one 16-ounce can *tomatoes,* cut up; one 6¾-ounce can *tuna,* drained and broken into chunks; 1 tablespoon snipped *parsley;* and dash *pepper.* Bring to boiling; reduce heat. Cover; simmer for 10 minutes. Makes 4 side-dish servings.

# Sherry-Pea Soup Elegante

|       |                                              |
|-------|----------------------------------------------|
| 1     | 11¼-ounce can condensed green pea soup        |
| 1     | 10¾-ounce can condensed cream of chicken soup |
| 1     | 14½-ounce can beef broth (about 2 cups)       |
| 2     | cups light cream or milk                      |
| ¼     | cup dry sherry                                |
| 2     | tablespoons butter or margarine              |

In a saucepan combine green pea and cream of chicken soups; stir in beef broth and light cream or milk. Cook and stir till heated through. Stir in sherry and butter or margarine; heat through. Makes 8 to 10 appetizer servings.

# Quick Cabbage-Cheese Soup

|       |                                                  |
|-------|--------------------------------------------------|
| 3½    | cups milk                                        |
| 1     | 10¾-ounce can condensed cream of potato soup     |
| 2     | cups coarsely chopped cabbage                    |
| 1     | medium carrot, coarsely shredded (½ cup)         |
| 1     | cup shredded process Swiss cheese (4 ounces)     |
| ¼     | teaspoon caraway seed                            |
| ¼     | teaspoon pepper                                  |

In a saucepan stir milk into soup. Cook and stir till bubbly; stir in cabbage and carrot. Cover and simmer 5 minutes or till cabbage is done. Stir in Swiss cheese, caraway seed, and pepper. Heat and stir till cheese melts. Makes 4 main-dish servings.

# Vegetables

# Vegetables

# Vegetables

# Vegetables

# Vegetables

# Vegetables

# Vegetables

# Vegetables

# Vegetables

## Percent of U.S. RDA Per Serving

| Recipes | Servings (fraction of recipe) | Calories | Protein (grams) | Carbohydrate (grams) | Fat (grams) | Sodium (milligrams) | Potassium (milligrams) | Protein | Vitamin A | Vitamin C | Thiamine | Riboflavin | Niacin | Calcium | Iron |
|---|---|---|---|---|---|---|---|---|---|---|---|---|---|---|---|
| American-Fried Potatoes | 1/4 | 166 | 3 | 23 | 7 | 271 | 349 | 4 | 0 | 45 | 9 | 3 | 10 | 1 | 4 |
| Artichokes Velvet | 1/6 | 143 | 7 | 9 | 11 | 377 | 273 | 11 | 9 | 8 | 5 | 12 | 7 | 20 | 6 |
| Artichokes with Butter Sauce | 1/2 | 232 | 3 | 11 | 23 | 311 | 331 | 5 | 25 | 24 | 5 | 3 | 4 | 6 | 7 |
| Asparagus-Tomato Stir-Fry | 1/6 | 55 | 3 | 7 | 2 | 239 | 373 | 4 | 21 | 56 | 12 | 15 | 11 | 3 | 7 |
| Au Gratin Vegetables (green beans) | 1/4 | 300 | 12 | 19 | 20 | 686 | 275 | 18 | 26 | 20 | 15 | 21 | 6 | 33 | 8 |
| Baked Acorn Squash Halves | 1/2 | 97 | 3 | 25 | 0 | 2 | 843 | 5 | 53 | 51 | 7 | 14 | 7 | 7 | 11 |
| Baked Bean Quintet | 1/12 | 363 | 17 | 65 | 5 | 635 | 868 | 25 | 8 | 17 | 16 | 9 | 11 | 14 | 37 |
| Baked Potatoes | 1/1 | 145 | 4 | 33 | 0 | 6 | 782 | 6 | 0 | 51 | 10 | 4 | 14 | 1 | 6 |
| Baked Tomatoes | 1/6 | 90 | 2 | 11 | 5 | 123 | 309 | 3 | 25 | 47 | 7 | 4 | 6 | 2 | 5 |
| Beets with Pineapple | 1/4 | 125 | 1 | 25 | 1 | 304 | 263 | 3 | 3 | 15 | 4 | 2 | 3 | 3 | 5 |
| Broccoli-Onion Casserole | 1/8 | 201 | 7 | 15 | 13 | 305 | 327 | 11 | 48 | 93 | 8 | 14 | 4 | 16 | 6 |
| Broccoli Oriental | 1/6 | 59 | 3 | 7 | 3 | 260 | 246 | 5 | 51 | 110 | 5 | 8 | 3 | 6 | 5 |
| Broccoli Soufflé | 1/6 | 263 | 14 | 11 | 19 | 473 | 412 | 21 | 58 | 143 | 10 | 27 | 5 | 29 | 10 |
| Broiled Tomatoes | 1/6 | 61 | 1 | 6 | 4 | 50 | 301 | 2 | 25 | 47 | 5 | 3 | 4 | 2 | 3 |
| Brussels Sprouts Soufflé | 1/6 | 256 | 13 | 10 | 19 | 467 | 270 | 20 | 24 | 65 | 8 | 20 | 7 | 22 | 8 |
| Candied Squash | 1/2 | 164 | 3 | 33 | 4 | 52 | 875 | 5 | 56 | 51 | 5 | 14 | 7 | 8 | 13 |
| Candied Squash Rings | 1/4 | 301 | 3 | 51 | 12 | 150 | 941 | 5 | 62 | 51 | 8 | 15 | 7 | 9 | 16 |
| Carrot-Rice Bake | 1/6 | 301 | 15 | 27 | 15 | 676 | 361 | 23 | 136 | 13 | 11 | 19 | 7 | 35 | 10 |
| Cauliflower Soufflé | 1/6 | 247 | 12 | 8 | 19 | 465 | 206 | 18 | 20 | 38 | 7 | 18 | 6 | 22 | 7 |
| Cheddar-Squash Puff | 1/8 | 239 | 11 | 10 | 18 | 258 | 319 | 17 | 21 | 36 | 8 | 19 | 8 | 24 | 7 |

# Nutrition Analysis Chart

| | | | | | | | | | | | | | | | |
|---|---|---|---|---|---|---|---|---|---|---|---|---|---|---|---|
| Cheese-Frosted Cauliflower | 1/5 | 252 | 7 | 7 | 23 | 357 | 358 | 11 | 7 | 147 | 9 | 11 | 4 | 15 | 9 |
| Cheesy Scalloped Potatoes | 1/4 | 362 | 10 | 43 | 17 | 756 | 934 | 15 | 14 | 61 | 18 | 21 | 16 | 20 | 7 |
| Chinese Spinach | 1/4 | 109 | 4 | 9 | 7 | 743 | 604 | 7 | 184 | 99 | 8 | 15 | 4 | 12 | 23 |
| Company Cabbage with Pecans | 1/6 | 104 | 2 | 7 | 9 | 336 | 259 | 3 | 48 | 53 | 7 | 3 | 2 | 5 | 4 |
| Corn Custard Pudding | 1/6 | 159 | 7 | 18 | 7 | 642 | 215 | 11 | 9 | 9 | 5 | 13 | 4 | 9 | 5 |
| Corn on the Cob w/butter | 1/1 | 172 | 3 | 16 | 12 | 140 | 154 | 4 | 16 | 12 | 6 | 5 | 4 | 1 | 3 |
| Creamed Peas and New Potatoes | 1/4 | 277 | 10 | 42 | 8 | 240 | 958 | 16 | 18 | 88 | 29 | 16 | 23 | 11 | 13 |
| Creamed Spinach with Nutmeg | 1/4 | 66 | 3 | 5 | 4 | 91 | 296 | 5 | 115 | 35 | 5 | 10 | 2 | 12 | 8 |
| Creamed Vegetables (peas) | 1/4 | 158 | 9 | 19 | 5 | 200 | 326 | 14 | 17 | 41 | 24 | 14 | 15 | 10 | 12 |
| Creamy Curried Corn | 1/4 | 241 | 5 | 21 | 18 | 303 | 202 | 8 | 21 | 21 | 7 | 6 | 6 | 4 | 4 |
| Creamy Succotash | 1/4 | 123 | 5 | 21 | 3 | 273 | 359 | 8 | 8 | 24 | 8 | 6 | 7 | 4 | 4 |
| Deluxe Peas and Mushrooms | 1/4 | 126 | 5 | 13 | 6 | 343 | 328 | 8 | 16 | 41 | 18 | 11 | 14 | 3 | 9 |
| Dilly Panned Summer Squash | 1/3 | 94 | 2 | 6 | 8 | 273 | 316 | 3 | 18 | 51 | 5 | 8 | 8 | 5 | 4 |
| Duchess Potatoes | 1/6 | 175 | 4 | 24 | 7 | 178 | 581 | 7 | 7 | 46 | 10 | 6 | 10 | 3 | 6 |
| Easy Baked Beans | 1/6 | 326 | 12 | 39 | 14 | 943 | 423 | 18 | 6 | 8 | 11 | 5 | 7 | 10 | 19 |
| Eggplant Parmigiana w/Homemade Tomato Sauce | 1/6 | 306 | 14 | 17 | 21 | 671 | 555 | 21 | 35 | 45 | 12 | 16 | 10 | 30 | 12 |
| French-Fried Onion Rings | 1/6 | 352 | 7 | 30 | 23 | 398 | 270 | 10 | 4 | 20 | 14 | 14 | 8 | 9 | 8 |
| French Fries | 1/1 | 250 | 5 | 39 | 9 | 135 | 916 | 7 | 0 | 75 | 15 | 5 | 17 | 2 | 7 |
| Fried Eggplant | 1/6 | 205 | 6 | 20 | 11 | 296 | 150 | 9 | 4 | 3 | 11 | 10 | 7 | 5 | 8 |
| Fried Green Tomatoes | 1/6 | 207 | 6 | 20 | 11 | 297 | 191 | 9 | 9 | 17 | 11 | 10 | 7 | 5 | 8 |
| Fried Ripe Tomatoes | 1/6 | 208 | 6 | 21 | 11 | 297 | 215 | 9 | 15 | 24 | 11 | 10 | 8 | 5 | 8 |
| Fried Zucchini | 1/6 | 214 | 7 | 22 | 11 | 296 | 294 | 10 | 12 | 36 | 13 | 15 | 12 | 7 | 9 |
| Garden Vegetable Stir-Fry | 1/6 | 94 | 3 | 11 | 5 | 459 | 352 | 4 | 59 | 62 | 6 | 7 | 4 | 5 | 7 |
| Glazed Carrots | 1/6 | 111 | 1 | 19 | 4 | 86 | 305 | 1 | 170 | 12 | 3 | 3 | 2 | 4 | 5 |
| Glazed Onions | 1/4 | 106 | 2 | 13 | 6 | 81 | 180 | 3 | 3 | 19 | 2 | 3 | 1 | 3 | 3 |
| Golden Crumb Broccoli | 1/6 | 198 | 7 | 14 | 14 | 569 | 493 | 10 | 60 | 218 | 9 | 21 | 8 | 18 | 9 |
| Gourmet Onions | 1/4 | 134 | 2 | 9 | 9 | 399 | 155 | 3 | 8 | 14 | 2 | 3 | 1 | 6 | 3 |
| Green Bean Bake with Onion | 1/6 | 124 | 3 | 12 | 8 | 432 | 202 | 5 | 12 | 22 | 4 | 8 | 3 | 5 | 6 |

# Nutrition Analysis Chart

| Recipes | Servings (fraction of recipe) | Calories | Protein (grams) | Carbohydrate (grams) | Fat (grams) | Sodium (milligrams) | Potassium (milligrams) | Protein | Vitamin A | Vitamin C | Thiamine | Riboflavin | Niacin | Calcium | Iron |
|---|---|---|---|---|---|---|---|---|---|---|---|---|---|---|---|
| Green Beans Amandine | 1/6 | 73 | 2 | 6 | 5 | 52 | 205 | 3 | 12 | 25 | 4 | 6 | 2 | 5 | 4 |
| Green Beans Especial | 1/4 | 83 | 3 | 5 | 6 | 42 | 184 | 5 | 13 | 20 | 7 | 5 | 4 | 3 | 6 |
| Harvard Beets | 1/4 | 104 | 2 | 19 | 3 | 173 | 392 | 3 | 3 | 19 | 2 | 3 | 2 | 2 | 5 |
| Hashed Brown Potatoes | 1/4 | 158 | 2 | 18 | 9 | 376 | 431 | 4 | 7 | 36 | 7 | 3 | 8 | 1 | 4 |
| Hawaiian-Style Parsnips | 1/6 | 193 | 2 | 38 | 5 | 331 | 792 | 4 | 5 | 56 | 10 | 5 | 2 | 8 | 7 |
| Herbed Green Beans | 1/6 | 65 | 2 | 7 | 4 | 60 | 227 | 3 | 13 | 27 | 5 | 5 | 2 | 5 | 4 |
| Herbed Lima Bean Bake | 1/6 | 373 | 12 | 32 | 23 | 543 | 600 | 18 | 21 | 37 | 10 | 14 | 8 | 18 | 13 |
| Italian Bean Bake | 1/6 | 78 | 4 | 10 | 3 | 730 | 170 | 7 | 17 | 15 | 5 | 6 | 4 | 12 | 11 |
| Lemon-Parsleyed Potatoes | 1/4 | 220 | 3 | 27 | 12 | 146 | 659 | 5 | 16 | 65 | 11 | 4 | 12 | 2 | 6 |
| Lemon-Parsleyed Turnips | 1/4 | 56 | 1 | 7 | 3 | 83 | 273 | 2 | 3 | 63 | 3 | 3 | 4 | 3 | 3 |
| Mashed Potatoes | 1/8 | 108 | 2 | 18 | 3 | 109 | 427 | 4 | 3 | 34 | 7 | 3 | 3 | 3 | 3 |
| Mashed Sweet Potato Bake | 1/6 | 266 | 5 | 49 | 6 | 262 | 462 | 7 | 291 | 62 | 12 | 9 | 5 | 8 | 8 |
| Minted New Peas | 1/4 | 146 | 5 | 13 | 9 | 240 | 262 | 7 | 21 | 40 | 17 | 6 | 11 | 3 | 8 |
| Mushrooms Elegante | 1/4 | 267 | 6 | 7 | 24 | 231 | 320 | 9 | 24 | 7 | 7 | 23 | 12 | 11 | 6 |
| New England Baked Beans | 1/6 | 508 | 20 | 80 | 14 | 508 | 1352 | 30 | 0 | 5 | 41 | 14 | 13 | 22 | 48 |
| Orange-Glazed Beets | 1/4 | 131 | 2 | 21 | 6 | 113 | 234 | 2 | 5 | 13 | 2 | 4 | 1 | 2 | 3 |
| Orange-Glazed Carrots | 1/4 | 94 | 1 | 16 | 1 | 222 | 419 | 2 | 252 | 28 | 5 | 4 | 5 | 5 | 3 |
| Oven-Browned Potatoes | 1/4 | 211 | 5 | 39 | 5 | 7 | 916 | 7 | 0 | 75 | 15 | 5 | 17 | 2 | 7 |
| Oven Candied Sweet Potatoes | 1/6 | 378 | 4 | 73 | 4 | 298 | 569 | 6 | 386 | 76 | 14 | 8 | 7 | 8 | 11 |
| Pea Pods with Almonds | 1/3 | 128 | 3 | 7 | 11 | 827 | 223 | 5 | 13 | 10 | 4 | 12 | 5 | 4 | 6 |

# Nutrition Analysis Chart

| | Serving | Calories | Protein (g) | Carbohydrate (g) | Fat (g) | Sodium (mg) | Potassium (mg) | Protein | Vitamin A | Vitamin C | Thiamine | Riboflavin | Niacin | Calcium | Iron |
|---|---|---|---|---|---|---|---|---|---|---|---|---|---|---|---|
| Potato Patties | 1/6 | 187 | 4 | 24 | 9 | 108 | 488 | 6 | 25 | 55 | 5 | 12 | 7 | 21 | 6 |
| Potluck Vegetable Casserole | 1/12 | 195 | 9 | 23 | 6 | 574 | 236 | 14 | 25 | 56 | 5 | 12 | 7 | 21 | 7 |
| Rutabaga and Apple | 1/4 | 176 | 9 | 31 | 6 | 80 | 289 | 2 | 17 | 50 | 5 | 5 | 5 | 9 | 6 |
| Saucy Brussels Sprouts | 1/6 | 182 | 6 | 13 | 13 | 445 | 411 | 9 | 18 | 132 | 7 | 13 | 4 | 11 | 7 |
| Saucy Celery Casserole | 1/6 | 192 | 7 | 8 | 15 | 586 | 402 | 11 | 19 | 28 | 4 | 13 | 4 | 22 | 4 |
| Scalloped Corn | 1/6 | 173 | 5 | 27 | 6 | 449 | 187 | 8 | 13 | 20 | 6 | 10 | 7 | 6 | 7 |
| Scalloped Potatoes | 1/4 | 362 | 10 | 43 | 17 | 1022 | 934 | 15 | 14 | 61 | 18 | 21 | 16 | 20 | 7 |
| Scalloped Tomatoes | 1/6 | 146 | 4 | 22 | 5 | 362 | 441 | 7 | 29 | 56 | 11 | 8 | 9 | 7 | 7 |
| Scalloped Vegetables (spinach) | 1/4 | 177 | 7 | 14 | 11 | 379 | 538 | 11 | 228 | 64 | 11 | 19 | 6 | 21 | 18 |
| Sesame Asparagus | 1/6 | 57 | 3 | 3 | 4 | 49 | 186 | 4 | 16 | 32 | 8 | 8 | 6 | 2 | 6 |
| Skillet Candied Sweet Potatoes | 1/6 | 360 | 4 | 69 | 8 | 296 | 569 | 6 | 386 | 76 | 14 | 8 | 7 | 8 | 10 |
| Spicy Stuffed Eggplant | 1/4 | 299 | 8 | 13 | 25 | 488 | 341 | 12 | 24 | 45 | 8 | 9 | 6 | 19 | 8 |
| Squash and Applesauce | 1/2 | 155 | 3 | 40 | 0 | 6 | 921 | 5 | 53 | 52 | 8 | 15 | 7 | 8 | 14 |
| Squash and Sausage | 1/2 | 302 | 6 | 42 | 15 | 213 | 894 | 9 | 52 | 52 | 16 | 18 | 10 | 7 | 14 |
| Squash with Onions | 1/6 | 309 | 5 | 51 | 12 | 117 | 992 | 8 | 59 | 72 | 10 | 16 | 8 | 11 | 20 |
| Sweet-Potato-Cashew Bake | 1/6 | 360 | 4 | 66 | 10 | 271 | 550 | 7 | 294 | 59 | 13 | 8 | 7 | 7 | 12 |
| Tomatoes and Okra | 1/6 | 74 | 2 | 9 | 4 | 230 | 263 | 3 | 18 | 66 | 6 | 6 | 4 | 4 | 3 |
| Twice-Baked Potatoes | 1/4 | 256 | 8 | 34 | 11 | 243 | 812 | 12 | 8 | 52 | 11 | 9 | 14 | 13 | 7 |
| Vegetable Tempura w/Tempura Sauce | 1/4 | 297 | 9 | 37 | 12 | 2920 | 393 | 13 | 10 | 33 | 18 | 19 | 12 | 8 | 21 |
| Volcano Potatoes | 1/6 | 214 | 6 | 24 | 11 | 255 | 585 | 9 | 46 | 46 | 10 | 7 | 7 | 10 | 5 |
| Whipped Parsnip Puff | 1/4 | 204 | 6 | 25 | 9 | 423 | 581 | 9 | 27 | 27 | 9 | 11 | 7 | 8 | 9 |
| Whipped Rutabaga Puff | 1/4 | 170 | 5 | 18 | 9 | 416 | 249 | 8 | 23 | 51 | 9 | 10 | 10 | 9 | 7 |
| Whipped Turnip Puff | 1/4 | 160 | 5 | 15 | 9 | 459 | 321 | 8 | 11 | 60 | 7 | 10 | 5 | 7 | 8 |

# Vegetables

From artichokes to zucchini, choose fresh, frozen, canned, or dried vegetables as versatile meal accompaniments. Cook them in several different ways following these suggestions.

**Cooking fresh and dried vegetables in water:** Prepare and cook the vegetables according to the charts on the following pages. Begin timing when the water returns to boiling, and cook at a gentle boil till done.

**Heating canned vegetables:** Heat the vegetables in their own liquid in a saucepan till heated through. Drain off liquid, season, and add butter. Or, follow label directions.

**Cooking frozen vegetables:** Follow label.

**Steaming fresh vegetables:** Prepare fresh vegetables as for cooking in water. Place vegetables in a steamer basket; place over, but not touching, boiling water. Cover; reduce heat. Steam 3 to 5 minutes longer than for cooking in water (see chart), or till tender. Drain; season to taste. For a vegetable combination, start with the longest-cooking vegetable and add others at the appropriate time.

**Microwave cooking vegetables:** Micro-cook fresh or frozen vegetables, and micro-heat canned vegetables. Follow timings given in your microwave oven owner's manual. Remember to cook vegetables only till they are almost done since their stored heat completes the cooking.

**Stir-frying vegetables:** Use a wok or large heavy skillet to stir-fry fresh vegetables in hot oil. (Certain vegetables need some precooking; follow recipe recommendations.) Quickly cook over high heat and use a long-handled spoon or spatula to lift and turn the food with a folding motion. Generally, stir-fried vegetables are cooked just till crisp-tender.

**Butter-baking frozen vegetables:** Place one 8- to 10-ounce package (about 2 cups) frozen unseasoned vegetables—asparagus, broccoli, brussels sprouts, sliced carrots, cauliflower, whole kernel corn, green beans, green peas, lima beans*, small onions, mixed vegetables, or spinach—in a 2½- to 4-cup casserole. Season. Dot with butter.

Cover tightly. Bake in a 350° oven for 40 to 50 minutes or till done. (*Or*, bake, covered, in a 325° oven for 50 to 60 minutes or till done.) Stir vegetables once or twice during cooking to break up large pieces. Stir again before serving. Makes 4 to 6 servings.

**\*Note:** Add 2 tablespoons water with butter.

## Creamed Vegetables

For sauce, in a saucepan melt 1 tablespoon *butter or margarine;* stir in 1 tablespoon all-purpose *flour,* ¼ teaspoon *salt,* and dash *pepper.* Add 1 cup *milk* all at once. Cook and stir over medium heat till thickened and bubbly. Cook and stir 1 to 2 minutes more. Add 3 cups *cooked or canned vegetables,* drained. Heat through. Makes 4 to 6 servings.

*Scalloped Vegetables:* Prepare Creamed Vegetables as above, *except* pour into a 1-quart casserole. Combine ¾ cup *soft bread crumbs* and 2 tablespoons melted *butter;* sprinkle atop. Bake, uncovered, in a 350° oven for 20 to 25 minutes. Makes 4 to 6 servings.

*Au Gratin Vegetables:* Prepare sauce for Creamed Vegetables as above, *except* stir in 1 cup shredded *American cheese* (4 ounces) till melted. Stir in vegetables. Pour into a 1-quart casserole. Combine ½ cup *fine dry bread crumbs* and 2 tablespoons melted *butter;* sprinkle atop. Bake, uncovered, in a 350° oven for 20 to 25 minutes. Makes 4 to 6 servings.

## Pan-Fried Vegetable Slices

*Fried Ripe Tomatoes:* Cut 3 medium unpeeled firm *ripe tomatoes* into about ½-inch-thick slices. Dip slices in ¼ to ⅓ cup *milk,* then in a mixture of ½ cup all-purpose *flour,* ½ teaspoon *salt,* and ¼ teaspoon *pepper.* Then dip in 2 beaten *eggs,* and finally in ¾ cup *fine dry bread crumbs.* In a 10-inch skillet fry *half* of the slices at a time in ¼ cup hot *shortening or cooking oil* over medium heat 3 or 4 minutes on each side or till brown. Add more shortening if needed to fry remaining slices. Season. Makes 6 servings.

*Fried Green Tomatoes:* Prepare Fried Ripe Tomatoes as above, *except* slice *green tomatoes,* coat, and fry over medium-low heat 8 to 10 minutes on each side or till brown.

**Fried Eggplant:** Prepare Fried Ripe Tomatoes as above, *except* use 1 small *eggplant* instead of tomatoes. Halve the eggplant lengthwise, then cut crosswise into ½-inch-thick slices. Continue as directed above.

**Fried Zucchini:** Prepare Fried Ripe Tomatoes as above, *except* use 3 medium unpeeled *zucchini* instead of tomatoes. Slice zucchini crosswise into ½-inch-thick slices. Continue as directed above.

# Cooking Vegetables

| Vegetable | Preparation | Cooking Directions | Cooking Time |
|---|---|---|---|
| **Artichokes** | Wash; trim stems; cut off 1 inch of top. Remove loose outer leaves; snip off sharp leaf tips. Brush cut edges of leaves with lemon juice. | In a large covered kettle simmer in a large amount of boiling salted water till a leaf pulls out easily. Drain upside down. | 20-30 minutes |
| **Asparagus** | Wash and scrape off scales. Break off woody bases where spears snap easily. Leave spears whole. | Cook whole spears, covered, in a small amount of boiling salted water. Prop tips up out of water with crumpled foil. (Or, fasten spears in a bundle; stand upright in a deep kettle so tips extend 2 to 3 inches above boiling salted water.) | 10-15 minutes (whole) |
| | Or, cut up asparagus spears. | Cook, covered, in a small amount of boiling salted water. | 8-10 minutes (cut-up) |
| **Beans, Green and Wax, fresh** | Wash; remove ends and strings. Leave whole or cut into 1-inch pieces. (Or, slice end-to-end for French-style beans.) | Cook, covered, in a small amount of boiling salted water till crisp-tender. | 20-30 minutes (whole or cut-up- 10-12 minutes (French-style) |
| **Lima, fresh** | Shell and wash. | Cook, covered, in a small amount of boiling salted water till tender. | 25-30 minutes |

| Vegetable | Preparation | Cooking Directions | Cooking Time |
|---|---|---|---|
| **Lima, Navy Northern, dried** | Rinse; add 3 times as much water as beans. Cover; soak overnight. (Or, bring to boiling; simmer 2 minutes. Remove from heat. Cover; soak 1 hour.) Do not drain. | Add salt. Bring to boiling. Cover; reduce heat and simmer in water used for soaking till beans are tender. | ¾-1 hour (lima) 1¼-1½ hours (navy and northern) |
| **Beets** | Cut off all but 1 inch of stems and roots. Wash. Do not peel whole beets. | Cook, covered, in boiling salted water till tender. Cool slightly; slip off skins. | 35-50 minutes (whole) |
| | Or, peel beets; slice or cube. | Cook, covered, in a small amount of boiling salted water till tender. | 20 minutes (sliced or cubed) |
| **Broccoli** | Wash; remove outer leaves and tough parts of stalks. Cut lengthwise into uniform spears, following the branching lines. | Cook, covered, in 1 inch of boiling salted water till crisp-tender. | 10-15 minutes (spears) |
| | Or, cut off buds; set aside. Cut remaining stalk into 1-inch pieces. | Cook, covered, in boiling salted water for 5 to 8 minutes. Add reserved buds; cook 5 minutes. | 10-13 minutes total (cut-up) |
| **Brussels Sprouts** | Trim stems. Remove wilted leaves, wash. Cut large sprouts in half lengthwise. | Cook, covered, in a small amount of boiling salted water till crisp-tender. | 10-15 minutes |
| **Cabbage** | Remove wilted outer leaves; wash. Cut into wedges; remove center core. (Or, shred.) | Cook, uncovered, in a small amount of boiling salted water for the first few minutes. Cover; cook till crisp-tender. | 10-12 minutes (wedges) 5-7 minutes (shredded) |
| **Carrots** | Wash, trim, and peel or scrub. Leave tiny carrots whole; for larger carrots, slice, dice, shred, or cut into strips. | Cook, covered, in 1 inch of boiling salted water just till carrots are tender. | 10-20 minutes (whole or cut-up) 5 minutes (shredded) |
| **Cauliflower** | Wash. Remove leaves and woody stem. Leave whole or break into flowerets. | Cook, covered, in a small amount of boiling salted water just till tender. | 15-20 minutes (whole) 10-15 minutes (flowerets) |
| **Celery** | Cut off leaves. Separate stalks. Slice. | Cook, covered, in a small amount of boiling salted water just till tender. | 10-15 minutes |
| **Corn** | For cut corn, cut off the tips of kernels. Scrape cobs with the dull edge of a knife. Or, cook on the cob. | Cook, covered, in a small amount of boiling salted water till done. See directions, page 796. | 12-15 minutes |

| Vegetable | Preparation | Cooking Directions | Cooking Time |
|---|---|---|---|
| **Eggplant** | Wash; cut off cap. Peel, if desired. Cut crosswise into ½-inch-thick slices. | Sauté on both sides in hot cooking oil. | About 2 minutes per side |
| **Greens** | Thoroughly wash in cool water. Cut off any roots; remove damaged portions and large veins. Tear or cut up large leaves. | Cook, covered, in boiling salted water just till tender. | 10-75 minutes, depending on type and maturity |
| **Kohlrabi** | Cut off leaves; wash, peel, and chop or slice. | Cook, covered, in a small amount of boiling salted water till tender. | About 25 minutes |
| **Lentils, dried** | Rinse; add 2½ times as much water as lentils. Don't soak. | Bring to boiling. Simmer, covered, till tender. | 35-45 minutes |
| **Mushrooms** | Rinse gently in cold water; pat dry. Leave whole, chop, or slice through cap and stem. | Cook in butter, uncovered, over medium-high heat till tender; stir often. Season. | 4 to 5 minutes (sliced) |
| **Okra** | Wash pods. Cut off stems. | Cook, covered, in a small amount of boiling salted water. | 8-15 minutes |
| **Onions** | Peel; cut into quarters. (*Or,* leave small boiling onions whole; cut off ends.) | Cook, covered, in boiling salted water till tender. | 25-30 minutes |
| **Parsnips** | Wash; peel or scrape. Leave whole, cut in half, slice, or cut into strips. | Cook, covered, in a small amount of boiling salted water till tender. | 25-40 minutes (whole) 15-20 minutes (cut-up) |
| **Peas, Green, fresh** | Shell and wash. | Cook, covered, in a small amount of boiling salted water just till tender. | 10-12 minutes |
| **Black-Eyed, fresh** | Shell and wash. | Cook, covered, in a small amount of boiling salted water till tender. | 15-18 minutes |
| **Black-Eyed, dried** | Rinse; add 4 times as much water as peas. Cover; soak overnight. (*Or,* bring to boiling; simmer 2 minutes. Remove from heat. Cover; soak 1 hour.) Do not drain. | Add salt. Bring to boiling. Cover; reduce heat and simmer in water used for soaking till peas are done. | 1¼-1½ hours |
| **Potatoes** | Scrub thoroughly; remove any sprouts or green areas. Cook with skins on. (*Or,* wash and peel. Cook whole, quartered, or cubed.) Or, bake potatoes. | Cook, covered, in boiling salted water till tender.<br><br>See directions, page 802. | 25-40 minutes (whole) 20-25 minutes (quartered) 10-15 minutes (tiny new) |

| Vegetable | Preparation | Cooking Directions | Cooking Time |
|---|---|---|---|
| **Sweet Potatoes** | Scrub; cut off woody portions and ends. Peel or cook in jackets, depending on use. | Cook, covered, in enough boiling salted water to cover till tender. (*Or*, bake whole in jackets in a 375° oven.) | 25-35 minutes (boiled)<br>40-45 minutes (baked) |
| **Rutabagas** | Wash; peel. Slice or cube. | Cook in small amount of boiling salted water till tender. | 25-35 minutes. |
| **Spinach** | Wash several times in a pan of lukewarm water, lifting out of the water each time and discarding the water. | Cook, covered, in a very small amount of water. Reduce heat when steam forms. Turn frequently with a fork. | 3-5 minutes after steam forms |
| **Squash, Winter**<br><br><br><br><br>**Summer (cook as Zucchini)** | Wash; cut in half; remove seeds and strings. Cut each half into serving-size pieces. | Place, cut side down, in a baking pan. Cover; bake in a 350° oven 30 minutes. Turn cut side up; bake, covered, 20 to 30 minutes more for acorn, buttercup, or butternut squash; 45 to 50 minutes more for hubbard, banana, or spaghetti squash. | 50-80 minutes (total) |
| **Tomatoes** | Wash; remove stems. Core. Peel. Cut up or cook whole. | In a tightly covered pan cook slowly without added water. | 10-15 minutes |
| **Turnips** | Wash; peel. Slice or cube. | Cook in small amount boiling salted water till tender. | 10-20 minutes |
| **Zucchini** | Wash; do not peel. Cut off ends. Slice. | Cook in small amount boiling salted water till crisp-tender. | 5-10 minutes |

## Vegetable Tempura

Cut assorted *fresh vegetables* (such as asparagus, green beans, green onions, cauliflower, peeled eggplant, mushrooms, parsley, and zucchini) into 2-inch lengths, ½-inch-thick slices, or 1-inch cubes. Stir together 1 cup all-purpose *flour*, 2 tablespoons *cornstarch,* and ½ teaspoon *salt*. Combine 1 *egg yolk* and 1 cup *cold water;* add to dry ingredients. Stir slowly just till moistened; do not overbeat but leave a few lumps. Fold in 1 stiff-beaten *egg white*. Do not allow batter to stand more than a few minutes before starting to use.

Dip vegetables into batter. Fry a few pieces at a time in deep hot *cooking oil* (400°) for 2 to 3 minutes or till light brown. Drain. Serve with Tempura Sauce and condiments, such as grated *gingerroot*, grated *radish or daikon*, and a mixture of ¼ cup *prepared mustard* and 3 tablespoons *soy sauce*. Makes 2 cups tempura batter.

**Tempura Sauce:** Mix 1 cup *water*, ¼ cup *dry sherry*, ¼ cup *soy sauce*, 1 teaspoon *sugar*, and 1 teaspoon instant *chicken bouillon granules*. Heat and stir till boiling.

---

### Vegetable toppers

**Quick Sauce:** Stir ¼ cup *milk* into 1 can of condensed *cream of mushroom soup, cheddar cheese soup, or cream of celery soup*. Heat. Serve over plain, cooked vegetables.

**Polonaise Topping:** Stir together 2 tablespoons *butter*, browned; ¼ cup *fine dry bread crumbs*; 1 *hard-cooked egg*, finely chopped; and 2 tablespoons snipped *parsley*. Sprinkle atop buttered or sauced cauliflower, broccoli, or asparagus.

**Butter-Crumb Topping:** Combine ¼ cup *fine dry seasoned bread crumbs* with 1 tablespoon melted *butter*. Sprinkle atop vegetables.

**For Buttered and/ or Sauced Vegetables:** Sprinkle with toasted *sesame seed, walnuts*, or other toasted nuts; crumbled crisp-cooked *bacon*; canned *french-fried onions*; or slightly crushed *seasoned croutons*.

## Artichokes with Butter Sauce

   2   artichokes (about 10 ounces each)
   ¼   cup butter *or* margarine
   1   tablespoon snipped parsley
   1   tablespoon lemon juice

Prepare, cook, and drain artichokes as directed on page 774.
Melt butter; stir in parsley and lemon juice. After draining
artichokes upside down, turn right side up and serve with the
butter sauce. Makes 2 servings.

**Microwave directions:** Prepare artichokes for cooking
as directed on page 774. Place artichokes in a covered 2-quart
nonmetal casserole or wrap in waxed paper. Cook in a counter-
top microwave oven on high power for 6 to 7 minutes or till
done. In a nonmetal bowl melt butter or margarine on high
power about 1 minute. Stir in parsley and lemon juice. Drain
artichokes and serve as above.

**Note:** To eat, pull off one leaf at a time and dip the base of
the leaf in butter sauce. Turn the leaf upside down and draw
through the teeth, eating only the tender flesh. Discard remainder of leaf. Continue removing leaves until the fuzzy "choke"
appears. Scoop out and discard the "choke." Eat the remaining heart with a fork, dipping each piece in sauce.

## Artichokes Velvet

   2   cups sliced fresh mushrooms
   2   tablespoons butter *or* margarine
   2   9-ounce packages frozen artichoke hearts,
         cooked and drained
   1   1-ounce envelope chicken gravy mix
   ⅛   teaspoon dried thyme, crushed
   ⅛   teaspoon dried marjoram, crushed
   1   cup shredded Swiss cheese
   1   tablespoon dry white wine          Oven 350°

Cook mushrooms in butter about 5 minutes or till tender.
Combine mushrooms and artichokes in a 1½-quart casserole.

Prepare gravy mix according to package directions. Remove from heat. Add herbs and ¾ cup of the cheese; stir till melted. Stir in wine. Pour over vegetables. Cover; bake in a 350° oven for 25 to 30 minutes. Sprinkle with remaining cheese; bake 2 to 3 minutes more or till melted. Serves 6 to 8.

## Asparagus-Tomato Stir-Fry

       1   **tablespoon water**
       1   **teaspoon cornstarch**
       2   **teaspoons soy sauce**
      ¼   **teaspoon salt**
       1   **pound asparagus**
       1   **tablespoon cooking oil**
       4   **green onions, bias-sliced into 1-inch
              lengths**
     1½   **cups sliced fresh mushrooms**
       2   **small tomatoes, cut into thin wedges**

Stir water into cornstarch; stir in soy sauce and salt. Set aside. Snap off and discard the woody bases from asparagus. Bias-slice asparagus crosswise into 1½-inch lengths. (If asparagus is not slender young stalks, precook for 4 to 5 minutes.)

Preheat a wok or large skillet over high heat; add cooking oil. Stir-fry asparagus and green onions in hot oil for 4 minutes. Add mushrooms; stir-fry 1 minute more. Stir soy mixture; stir into vegetables. Cook and stir till thickened and bubbly. Add tomatoes and heat through. Serve at once. Makes 6 servings.

## Sesame Asparagus

       2   **8-ounce packages frozen cut asparagus**
       1   **2½-ounce jar sliced mushrooms, drained**
       2   **tablespoons butter *or* margarine**
       1   **teaspoon lemon juice**
       1   **teaspoon sesame seed, toasted**

Cook frozen asparagus according to package directions. Drain well. Season to taste with salt and pepper. Gently stir in mushrooms, butter, and lemon juice. Cook until heated through. Turn mixture into a serving bowl; sprinkle with sesame seed. Makes 6 servings.

**Microwave directions:** Place frozen asparagus in a 1½-quart nonmetal casserole. Cook, covered, in a counter-top microwave oven on high power about 10 minutes or till tender, stirring twice. Drain well. Season. Gently stir in mushrooms, butter, and lemon juice. Micro-cook, covered, about 2 minutes or till heated through, stirring once. Turn into a serving bowl; sprinkle with sesame seed.

---

# Green Beans Amandine

-   1 **pound green beans or two 9-ounce**
         **packages frozen French-style green**
         **beans**
-   2 **tablespoons slivered almonds**
-   2 **tablespoons butter or margarine**
-   1 **teaspoon lemon juice**

Cut fresh beans French-style and cook as directed on page 774. (*Or*, cook frozen beans according to package directions.) Drain. Cook almonds in butter over low heat, stirring occasionally, till golden. Remove from heat; add lemon juice. Pour over beans. Serves 6.

---

# Herbed Green Beans

-    1 **pound green beans or two 9-ounce**
          **packages frozen cut green beans**
-   ½ **cup chopped onion**
-   ¼ **cup chopped celery**
-    1 **clove garlic, minced**
-    2 **tablespoons butter or margarine**
-   ¼ **teaspoon dried rosemary, crushed**
-   ¼ **teaspoon dried basil, crushed**

Cut fresh green beans into 1-inch pieces and cook as directed on page 774. (Or, cook frozen beans according to package directions.) Drain. Cook onion, celery, and garlic in butter till vegetables are tender. Stir in herbs. Add beans; toss lightly. Cover; heat through. Season with salt. Makes 6 to 8 servings.

## Green Beans Especial

    1   **9-ounce package frozen French-style green
            beans** *or* **one 16-ounce can
            French-style green beans**
    ¼   **cup diced fully cooked ham**
    2   **tablespoons finely chopped onion**
    1   **tablespoon butter** *or* **margarine**
    1   **small tomato, peeled, cored, and coarsely
            chopped**

Cook frozen beans according to package directions; drain. (Or, drain canned beans.) In a saucepan cook ham and onion in butter, stirring occasionally, till onion is tender. Stir in drained cooked or canned beans, tomato, and dash *pepper*. Cover; heat through. Serves 4.

## Italian Bean Bake

    2   **16-ounce cans cut Italian green beans,
            drained**
    1   **8-ounce can tomato sauce**
    1   **tablespoon prepared mustard**
    2   **teaspoons minced dried onion**
    ⅛   **teaspoon garlic salt**
    ⅛   **teaspoon pepper**
    ½   **cup shredded provolone cheese**   Oven 350°

Combine drained beans, tomato sauce, mustard, dried onion, garlic salt, and pepper. Turn mixture into a 1-quart casserole. Cover and bake in a 350° oven 30 minutes. Sprinkle cheese atop. Bake, uncovered, 1 to 2 minutes more or till cheese is melted. Makes 6 servings.

**Microwave directions:** In a 1-quart nonmetal casserole combine beans, tomato sauce, mustard, dried onion, garlic salt, and pepper. Cook, covered, in a counter-top microwave oven on high power for 6 minutes or till hot, turning and stirring once. Sprinkle cheese atop. Micro-cook, uncovered, 1 minute longer.

## Green Bean Bake with Onion

    2  **9-ounce packages frozen French-style green
       beans** or **two 16-ounce cans French-style
       green beans**
    1  **10¾-ounce can condensed cream of
       mushroom soup**
    2  **tablespoons chopped pimiento**
    1  **teaspoon lemon juice**
    ½  **of a 3-ounce can french-fried
       onions**                              Oven 350°

Cook frozen beans according to package directions; drain. (Or, drain canned beans.) Combine the cooked frozen or the canned beans, mushroom soup, pimiento, and lemon juice. Turn mixture into a 1-quart casserole. Bake, uncovered, in a 350° oven for 35 minutes. Sprinkle with french-fried onions. Continue baking, uncovered, about 5 minutes more or till onions are heated through. Serves 6.

## Herbed Lima Bean Bake

    2  **10-ounce packages frozen lima beans**
    ¼  **cup chopped onion**
    3  **tablespoons butter or margarine**
    1  **cup herb-seasoned stuffing mix**
    ⅓  **cup water**
    1  **cup dairy sour cream**
    1  **tablespoon all-purpose flour**
    ⅔  **cup milk**
    ½  **cup shredded American cheese
       (2 ounces)**                          Oven 350°

Cook lima beans according to package directions. Meanwhile, in a small saucepan cook onion in butter or margarine till tender. Add stuffing mix and water; toss to mix. Set aside. Drain lima beans. Combine sour cream and flour; stir in milk. Stir into beans along with cheese. Add about ⅔ of the stuffing mix mixture; mix well. Turn into a 1½-quart casserole; sprinkle with remaining stuffing mixture. Bake, uncovered, in a 350° oven for 18 to 20 minutes or till heated through. Makes 6 to 8 servings.

## Creamy Succotash

  **1**   **10-ounce package frozen lima beans**
 **½**   **cup water**
 **½**   **teaspoon salt**
 **⅛**   **teaspoon pepper**
  **1**   **10-ounce package frozen whole kernel corn**
 **½**   **cup milk**
  **4**   **teaspoons all-purpose flour**
  **1**   **tablespoon butter *or* margarine**

Cook lima beans, covered, in the water seasoned with the salt and pepper for 10 minutes. Add frozen corn. Return to boiling. Reduce heat; cover and cook 5 minutes more or till tender. *Do not drain.* Gradually stir milk into flour; stir into vegetable mixture in saucepan. Add butter or margarine. Cook and stir till thickened and bubbly. Cook and stir 1 to 2 minutes more. Makes 6 servings.

## New England Baked Beans

    **1   pound dry navy beans *or* dry great northern beans (2⅓ cups)**
    **¼   pound salt pork, cut up**
    **1   large onion, chopped (1 cup)**
    **½   cup molasses**
    **⅓   cup packed brown sugar**
    **1   teaspoon dry mustard**
    **½   teaspoon salt**
    **⅛   teaspoon pepper**                 Oven 300°

Rinse beans. In a heavy 3-quart saucepan combine beans and 8 cups *cold water*. Soak as directed on page 775. Add ½ teaspoon *salt* to beans and soaking water. Cook as directed on page 775 till beans are tender.

    Drain beans, reserving liquid. In a 2½-quart bean pot or casserole combine the beans, salt pork, and onion. Stir in *1 cup* of the reserved bean liquid, molasses, brown sugar, dry mustard, ½ teaspoon salt, and pepper. Cover and bake in a 300° oven for 2½ hours or to desired consistency, stirring occasionally. Add additional reserved bean liquid, if necessary. Makes 6 to 8 servings.

    **Crockery cooker directions:** Rinse beans. In a saucepan bring beans, 8 cups *water,* and ½ teaspoon *salt* to boiling; reduce heat. Simmer, covered, 1½ hours. Pour beans and liquid into a bowl; cover. Chill overnight. Drain beans, reserving 1 cup liquid; place in an electric slow crockery cooker. Add 1 cup reserved cooking liquid. Stir in salt pork, onion, molasses, sugar, dry mustard, ½ teaspoon salt, and pepper. Cover; cook on low-heat setting for 12 to 14 hours. Stir before serving.

## Easy Baked Beans

                                                      Oven 350°

Cook 4 slices *bacon* till crisp. Remove bacon, reserving about 3 tablespoons drippings in skillet. Drain and crumble bacon; set aside. Cook ½ cup chopped *onion* in reserved drippings till tender. Stir in two 16-ounce cans *pork and beans in tomato sauce,* 2 tablespoons *brown sugar,* 2 tablespoons *catsup,* 1 tablespoon *Worcestershire sauce,* and 1 tablespoon *prepared mustard.* Turn into a 1½-quart casserole. Bake, uncovered, in a 350° oven for 1½ to 1¾ hours. Stir; top with bacon. Let stand a few minutes before serving. Makes 6 servings.

---

## Baked Bean Quintet

---

 - **6 slices bacon**
 - **1 cup chopped onion**
 - **1 clove garlic, minced**
 - **1 16-ounce can butter beans, drained**
 - **1 16-ounce can lima beans, drained**
 - **1 16-ounce can pork and beans in tomato sauce**
 - **1 15½-ounce can red kidney beans, drained**
 - **1 15-ounce can garbanzo beans, drained**
 - **¾ cup catsup**
 - **½ cup light molasses**
 - **¼ cup packed brown sugar**
 - **1 tablespoon Worcestershire sauce**
 - **1 tablespoon prepared mustard**
 - **¼ teaspoon pepper**
   **Onion, sliced and separated into rings (optional)**                         Oven 375°

In a skillet cook bacon till crisp. Remove bacon, reserving 2 tablespoons drippings in skillet. Drain and crumble bacon; set aside. Cook onion and garlic in reserved bacon drippings till onion is tender but not brown; drain. In a large bowl combine crumbled bacon, onion, garlic, butter beans, lima beans, pork and beans in tomato sauce, kidney beans, and garbanzo beans. Stir in catsup, molasses, brown sugar, Worcestershire sauce, prepared mustard, and pepper. Turn into a 2½-quart bean pot or casserole.

Cover and bake in a 375° oven for 1 hour or till heated through. Garnish with onion rings, if desired. Makes 12 to 14 servings.

## Orange-Glazed Beets

>   **2** **cups sliced beets** *or* **one 16-ounce can
>      sliced beets**
>   **2** **tablespoons butter** *or* **margarine**
>   **¼** **cup orange marmalade**

Prepare and cook fresh beets as directed on page 775; drain.
(*Or*, drain canned beets.) In a small skillet melt butter or
margarine over medium-low heat; stir in orange marmalade till
combined. Add drained cooked or canned beets; cook and stir
till beets are glazed and heated through. Makes 4 servings.

## Harvard Beets

>   **4** **medium beets** *or* **one 16-ounce can sliced
>      *or* diced beets**
>   **2** **tablespoons sugar**
>   **2** **teaspoons cornstarch**
>   **3** **tablespoons vinegar**
>   **1** **tablespoon butter** *or* **margarine**

Prepare, peel, slice or cut into ½-inch cubes, and cook fresh
beets as directed on page 775. Drain, reserving ⅓ cup liquid.
(*Or*, drain canned beets, reserving ⅓ cup liquid.) Combine sugar,
cornstarch, and ⅛ teaspoon *salt*. Stir in reserved beet liquid,
vinegar, and butter. Cook and stir till thickened and bubbly.
Cook and stir 1 to 2 minutes more. Stir in cooked or canned
beets. Cook and stir about 5 minutes or till beets are heated
through. Serves 4.

## Beets with Pineapple

    2   cups sliced beets *or* one 16-ounce can
          sliced beets
    1   tablespoon brown sugar
    2   teaspoons cornstarch
    1   8¼-ounce can crushed pineapple
    1   tablespoon butter *or* margarine
    1   tablespoon lemon juice

Prepare and cook fresh beets as directed on page 775; drain.
(*Or,* drain canned beets.) In a saucepan combine brown sugar,
cornstarch, and dash *salt.* Stir in *undrained* pineapple. Cook
and stir until mixture is thickened and bubbly. Cook and stir 1
to 2 minutes more. Add butter, lemon juice, and cooked or
canned beets. Cook and stir over medium heat about 5 minutes or till heated through. Serves 4.

## Broccoli Oriental

    2   10-ounce packages frozen broccoli spears
    1   tablespoon butter *or* margarine
    1   tablespoon sugar
    1   tablespoon soy sauce
    2   teaspoons sesame seed, toasted

Cook broccoli according to package directions. Drain; keep
warm. Combine butter, sugar, soy, and 1 tablespoon *water;*
heat till butter melts. Pour over broccoli; top with seeds. Serves 6.

## Golden Crumb Broccoli

| | |
|---|---|
| 1½ | **pounds broccoli** *or* **three 10-ounce packages frozen cut broccoli** |
| 1 | **10¾-ounce can condensed cream of mushroom soup** |
| ¼ | **cup mayonnaise** *or* **salad dressing** |
| ¼ | **cup shredded American cheese** |
| 1 | **tablespoon chopped pimiento** |
| 1½ | **teaspoons lemon juice** |
| ⅓ | **cup crushed round cheese crackers** |

Oven 350°

Cut up fresh broccoli to make about 6 cups and cook as directed on page 775. (*Or*, cook frozen broccoli according to package directions.) Drain well. Turn into a 1½-quart casserole. Mix soup, mayonnaise, cheese, pimiento, and lemon juice. Pour over broccoli. Top with crushed crackers. Bake, uncovered, in a 350° oven for 35 minutes. Serves 6 to 8.

## Broccoli-Onion Casserole

| | |
|---|---|
| 2 | **10-ounce packages frozen cut broccoli** |
| 2 | **cups frozen small whole onions** *or* **3 medium fresh onions, cut into wedges** |
| 2 | **tablespoons butter** *or* **margarine** |
| 2 | **tablespoons all-purpose flour** |
| ¼ | **teaspoon salt** |
| 1 | **cup milk** |
| 1 | **3-ounce package cream cheese, cut up** |
| ½ | **cup shredded American cheese** |
| 2 | **tablespoons butter** *or* **margarine** |
| 1 | **cup soft bread crumbs** |

Oven 350°

Cook broccoli according to package directions. Drain well; set aside. Cook frozen or fresh onions in boiling salted water about 10 minutes or till tender. Drain; set aside.

In the same saucepan melt the 2 tablespoons butter. Stir in flour, salt, and dash *pepper*. Add milk. Cook and stir till thickened and bubbly. Cook and stir 1 to 2 minutes more. Add cream cheese; stir till melted. Stir in broccoli and onions. Turn into a 1½-quart casserole. Top with American cheese. Melt the remaining 2 tablespoons butter; toss with crumbs. Sprinkle over casserole. Bake in a 350° oven for 35 to 40 minutes. Makes 8 servings.

## Saucy Brussels Sprouts

Prepare and cook 2 pints *brussels sprouts* as directed on page 775. (*Or*, cook two 10-ounce packages frozen *brussels sprouts* according to package directions.) Drain.

In a saucepan cook ½ cup chopped *onion* in 2 tablespoons *butter or margarine* till tender but not brown. Stir in 1 tablespoon all-purpose *flour*, 1 tablespoon *brown sugar*, 1 teaspoon *salt*, and ½ teaspoon *dry mustard*. Stir in ½ cup *milk*. Cook and stir till thickened and bubbly. Cook and stir 1 to 2 minutes more. Stir in 1 cup dairy *sour cream*. Add the cooked brussels sprouts. Stir gently to combine. Cook till heated through, but *do not boil*. Serves 6 to 8.

## Brussels Sprouts Soufflé

|   |   |   |
|---|---|---|
| **1** | **pint brussels sprouts *or* one 10-ounce package frozen brussels sprouts** | |
| **¼** | **cup butter *or* margarine** | |
| **¼** | **cup all-purpose flour** | |
| **1** | **cup milk** | |
| **1** | **cup shredded cheddar cheese** | |
| **4** | **eggs** | Oven 350° |

Prepare and cook fresh brussels sprouts till tender as directed on page 775. (*Or*, cook frozen brussels sprouts according to package directions.) Drain well. Chop finely. In a saucepan melt butter; stir in flour and ½ teaspoon *salt*. Add milk. Cook and stir till thickened and bubbly. Cook and stir 1 to 2 minutes more. Stir in cheese till melted. Remove from heat. Stir in finely chopped brussels sprouts.

Separate eggs. Beat yolks till thick and lemon colored; slowly stir in hot mixture. Wash beaters. Beat egg whites till stiff peaks form; fold into vegetable mixture. Turn into an *ungreased* 2-quart soufflé dish. Bake in a 350° oven 35 to 40 minutes or till a knife inserted near center comes out clean. Serve at once. Serves 6.

**Broccoli Soufflé:** Prepare Brussels Sprouts Soufflé as above, *except* omit brussels sprouts. Cook 2 cups *broccoli* in a small amount of boiling salted water, covered, 8 to 10 minutes. Drain; chop finely. Continue as above.

**Cauliflower Soufflé:** Prepare Brussels Sprouts Soufflé as above, *except* omit sprouts. Cook 2 cups *cauliflower flowerets* in a small amount of boiling salted water for 10 minutes. Drain; chop finely. Continue as above.

---

## Company Cabbage with Pecans

- **1 teaspoon instant beef bouillon granules**
- **5 cups coarsely shredded cabbage**
- **1 cup coarsely shredded carrots**
- **½ cup sliced green onion**
- **2 tablespoons butter *or* margarine, melted**
- **⅓ cup chopped pecans**
- **1 teaspoon prepared mustard**
  **Paprika**

In a large saucepan heat bouillon granules in ¼ cup *water* till dissolved. Add cabbage, carrots, onion, ½ teaspoon *salt*, and ¼ teaspoon *pepper*. Toss to mix. Cook, covered, over medium heat 5 to 10 minutes or till tender, stirring once during cooking. Drain, if necessary. Combine butter, pecans, and mustard. Pour over vegetables; toss to mix. Spoon into a dish. Sprinkle with paprika. Serves 6 to 8.

---

## Pennsylvania Red Cabbage

Heat 2 tablespoons *bacon drippings or cooking oil* in a skillet. Stir in ¼ cup packed *brown sugar*, ¼ cup *vinegar*, ¼ cup *water*, 1¼ teaspoons *salt*, ½ to 1 teaspoon *caraway seed*, and dash *pepper*. Add 4 cups shredded *red cabbage* and 2 cups cubed unpeeled *apple,* stirring to coat. Cover and cook over medium-low heat, stirring occasionally. For crisp cabbage, cook 15 minutes; for tender cabbage, cook about 30 minutes. Makes 5 or 6 servings.

## Glazed Carrots

> **6** **medium carrots (1 pound)**
> **2** **tablespoons butter *or* margarine**
> **⅓** **cup packed brown sugar**
> **1** **tablespoon snipped parsley**

Cut carrots in half crosswise then lengthwise into 2 or 3 sticks. Simmer, covered, in a small amount of boiling salted water about 10 minutes or till crisp-tender. Drain.

Melt the butter; stir in brown sugar till dissolved. Add carrots. Cook over medium-low heat about 10 minutes, turning often. Sprinkle with snipped parsley. Makes 6 servings.

## Orange-Glazed Carrots

> **3** **cups carrots sliced into 1-inch pieces (about 1 pound)**
> **1** **tablespoon sugar**
> **1** **teaspoon cornstarch**
> **¼** **teaspoon salt**
> **¼** **teaspoon ground ginger**
> **¼** **cup orange juice**
> **1** **tablespoon butter *or* margarine**

Cook carrots as directed on page 775. Drain. In a small saucepan combine sugar, cornstarch, salt, and ginger. Add orange juice. Cook and stir till thickened and bubbly. Cook and stir 1 to 2 minutes more. Stir in butter or margarine. Pour over hot carrots, stirring lightly to coat. Makes 4 to 6 servings.

**Microwave directions:** In a 1½-quart nonmetal bowl combine carrots with 2 tablespoons *water.* Cook, covered, in a counter-top microwave oven on high heat for 8 to 9 minutes or till tender, stirring once. Drain. In a 1-cup glass measure combine sugar, cornstarch, salt, and ginger. Stir in orange juice. Cook, uncovered, on high power for 1 minute, stirring once. Stir in butter till melted. Pour sauce over carrots, stirring lightly to coat.

## Carrot-Rice Bake

3 cups shredded carrots (1 pound)
1½ cups water
⅔ cup long grain rice
½ teaspoon salt
2 cups shredded American cheese (8 ounces)
1 cup milk
2 beaten eggs
2 tablespoons minced dried onion
¼ teaspoon pepper                    Oven 350°

In a saucepan combine carrots, water, rice, and salt. Bring to boiling. Reduce heat and simmer, covered, about 15 minutes or till rice is done. Do not drain. Stir in 1½ *cups* of the shredded cheese, milk, eggs, onion, and pepper. Turn into a 10x6x2-inch baking dish. Bake, uncovered, in a 350° oven for 20 to 25 minutes. Top with remaining ½ cup shredded cheese. Return to oven about 2 minutes longer to melt cheese. Cut into squares. Serves 6.

## Cheese-Frosted Cauliflower

1 medium head cauliflower (about 1¼ pounds)
½ cup mayonnaise *or* salad dressing
1½ teaspoons prepared mustard
¾ cup shredded American cheese (3 ounces)                    Oven 375°

Prepare and cook whole cauliflower as directed on page 775. Drain well. Place cooked head of cauliflower in an 8x8x2-inch baking pan. Stir together mayonnaise or salad dressing and mustard; spread over cauliflower. Top with the shredded cheese.

Bake in a 375° oven about 5 minutes or till cheese melts. Makes 5 or 6 servings.

## Saucy Celery Casserole

  **4**  **cups thinly sliced celery**
  **¼**  **cup butter or margarine**
  **2**  **tablespoons all-purpose flour**
  **¼**  **teaspoon salt**
  **1**  **cup milk**
  **1**  **cup shredded American cheese (4 ounces)**
  **1**  **4-ounce can chopped mushrooms, drained**
  **2**  **tablespoons chopped green pepper**
  **2**  **tablespoons chopped pimiento**      Oven 350°

In a saucepan cook celery in butter or margarine, covered, about 15 minutes or till crisp-tender; stir in flour and salt. Add milk; cook and stir till thickened and bubbly. Cook and stir 1 to 2 minutes more. Add ¾ *cup* of the cheese; stir till melted. Stir in mushrooms, green pepper, and pimiento. Turn into a 1-quart casserole. Bake, uncovered, in a 350° oven for 20 minutes. Sprinkle with remaining ¼ cup shredded cheese. Makes 6 servings.

**Microwave directions:** In a 1-quart nonmetal casserole cook celery in butter, covered, in a counter-top microwave oven on high power for 6 to 7 minutes or till crisp-tender; stir after 3 minutes. Stir in flour and salt. Add milk, ¾ *cup* of the cheese, mushrooms, green pepper, and pimiento; mix well. Micro-cook, uncovered, 4 to 5 minutes or till thickened and bubbly, stirring after every minute. Sprinkle with remaining ¼ cup cheese.

## Scalloped Corn

1    beaten egg
1    cup milk
1    cup coarsely crushed saltine crackers (22 crackers)
1    17-ounce can cream-style corn
¼    cup finely chopped onion
3    tablespoons chopped pimiento
1    tablespoon butter or margarine, melted                Oven 350°

Combine egg, milk, ⅔ cup cracker crumbs, ¼ teaspoon *salt,* and dash *pepper.* Stir in corn, onion, and pimiento; mix well. Turn into a 1-quart casserole. Toss butter with remaining crumbs; sprinkle atop corn mixture. Bake, uncovered, in a 350° oven 1 hour or till a knife inserted near center comes out clean. Serves 6.

## Corn Custard Pudding

⅓    cup finely chopped onion
1    tablespoon butter or margarine
1    17-ounce can whole kernel corn
3    slightly beaten eggs
1½   cups milk
1    teaspoon sugar                          Oven 350°

In a small saucepan cook onion in butter till tender but not brown. Drain corn. In a bowl combine eggs, corn, milk, sugar, and 1 teaspoon *salt.* Add the onion mixture. Turn into an 8x1½-inch round baking dish. Place in a larger baking pan. Place on oven rack. Pour boiling water into larger baking pan to a depth of 1 inch. Bake, uncovered, in a 350° oven for 25 to 30 minutes or till a knife inserted near center comes out clean. Makes 6 servings.

## Creamy Curried Corn

In a saucepan melt 3 tablespoons *butter*. Add 2 cups cut *fresh corn* or one 10-ounce package frozen *whole kernel corn*, 2 tablespoons chopped *green pepper*, 2 tablespoons chopped *onion*, ¼ to ½ teaspoon *curry powder*, ¼ teaspoon *salt*, and dash *pepper*. Cover; cook over medium heat 8 to 10 minutes or till corn is just tender. Add one 3-ounce package *cream cheese*, cut into cubes, and ⅓ cup *milk*; stir over low heat till combined. Makes 4 servings.

## Corn on the Cob

Remove husks from fresh *ears of corn;* scrub with a brush. Rinse. Cook according to one of the following methods. Serve with *plain or a flavored butter* (see recipe, page 726).
   ***Kettle-Cooked Corn:*** Cook, covered, in a small amount of boiling salted water (*or,* cook, uncovered, in enough boiling water to cover) for 6 to 8 minutes.
   ***Foil-Baked Corn:*** Spread ears of corn with *butter* and sprinkle with *salt* and *pepper*. Wrap *each* ear in foil. Bake in a 450° oven about 30 minutes; turn several times during baking.
   ***Micro-Cooked Corn:*** Wrap each ear in waxed paper; place on paper toweling. (*Or,* place corn in a nonmetal baking dish; cover.) Cook in a counter-top microwave oven on high power. Micro-cook 1 ear 2 minutes; 2 ears 3 to 4 minutes; 3 ears 5 to 7 minutes; 4 ears 8 to 10 minutes; 5 ears 10 to 12 minutes; 6 ears 12 to 14 minutes. Halfway through cooking time, rearrange the ears of corn.

# Spicy Stuffed Eggplant

|   |   |
|---|---|
| 1 | medium eggplant (about 1 pound) |
| 1/3 | cup chopped onion |
| 1 | clove garlic, minced |
| 1 | tablespoon snipped parsley |
| 3 | tablespoons butter *or* margarine |
| 3/4 | cup soft bread crumbs |
| 1/4 | cup chopped pitted ripe olives |
| 2 | tablespoons chopped canned green chili peppers |
| 2 | tablespoons cooking oil |
| 2 | tablespoons lemon juice |
| 1/4 | teaspoon dried basil, crushed |
| 3/4 | cup shredded provolone cheese |
| 4 | to 6 tomato slices     Oven 350° |

Halve eggplant lengthwise; scoop out and reserve pulp, leaving a 1/4-inch shell. Cook shells, covered, in enough boiling water to cover for 2 minutes or till tender; drain. Chop uncooked pulp finely. Cook pulp with onion, garlic, and parsley in butter till tender. Stir in bread crumbs, olives, chili peppers, oil, lemon juice, basil, and 1/4 teaspoon *salt*. Stir in 1/2 *cup* of the cheese. Pile into shells. Bake, covered, in a 350° oven 20 minutes. Top with tomato slices; brush with *cooking oil*. Top with remaining cheese. Bake, uncovered, 5 to 10 minutes. Serves 4.

## Eggplant Parmigiana

¼   **cup all-purpose flour**
1   **medium eggplant, peeled and cut crosswise into ½-inch slices**
1   **beaten egg**
¼   **cup cooking oil**
⅓   **cup grated Parmesan cheese**
    **Homemade Tomato Sauce or one 16-ounce jar Italian cooking sauce**
6   **ounces sliced mozzarella cheese**                    Oven 400°

Combine flour and ½ teaspoon *salt*. Dip eggplant into egg, then into flour mixture. Brown eggplant, half at a time, in hot oil about 3 minutes per side, adding additional oil as needed. Drain well on paper toweling. Using *half* of the eggplant, place in a single layer in a 10x6x2-inch baking dish, cutting slices to fit. Sprinkle with *half* of the Parmesan. Top with *half* of the sauce and *half* of the mozzarella. Cut remaining mozzarella into triangles. Repeat layers. Bake, uncovered, in a 400° oven for 15 to 20 minutes or till hot. Serves 6.

   ***Homemade Tomato Sauce:*** Cook ⅓ cup chopped *onion;* ¼ cup chopped *celery;* and 1 small clove *garlic,* minced, in 2 tablespoons *cooking oil* till tender. Stir in one 16-ounce can *tomatoes,* cut up; ⅓ cup *tomato paste;* 1 teaspoon dried *parsley flakes;* ½ teaspoon *salt;* ½ teaspoon dried *oregano,* crushed; ¼ teaspoon *pepper;* and 1 *bay leaf.* Boil gently, uncovered, about 15 minutes or to desired consistency; stir occasionally. Remove bay leaf.

## Mushrooms Elegante

Toss 3 cups sliced fresh *mushrooms* (8 ounces) and 2 tablespoons chopped *onion* with 1 tablespoon all-purpose *flour.* Cook mushrooms and onion in 3 tablespoons *butter or margarine,* covered, over low heat 8 to 10 minutes or till tender, stirring occasionally. Add 1 cup *light cream or milk,* 2 tablespoons grated *Parmesan cheese,* ⅛ teaspoon *salt,* and ⅛ teaspoon *pepper*. Cook and stir till slightly thickened and bubbly; cook 2 minutes more.

Stir about 1 cup of the hot mixture into 2 beaten *egg yolks;* return to saucepan. Cook and stir 2 minutes more or just till bubbly. Remove from heat; stir in 1 tablespoon *lemon juice.* Serve in sauce dishes. Makes 4 servings.

---

## French-Fried Onion Rings

- **6 medium Bermuda *or* mild white onions, sliced ¼ inch thick**
- **1 slightly beaten egg**
- **1 cup milk**
- **3 tablespoons cooking oil**
- **1 cup plus 2 tablespoons all-purpose flour**
  **Cooking oil for deep-fat frying**

Separate onions into rings; set aside. In a bowl combine egg, milk, the 3 tablespoons oil, flour, and ½ teaspoon *salt*. Beat just till well moistened. Using a fork, dip onion rings into batter; drain off excess batter. Add to deep hot fat (375°). Fry onion rings in a single layer, stirring once with a fork to separate rings. When onions are golden brown, about 2 to 3 minutes, remove from fat and drain on paper toweling. Sprinkle with salt and serve. Makes 6 to 8 servings.

---

## Gourmet Onions

- **3 cups sliced onions (6 medium)**
- **3 tablespoons butter *or* margarine**
- **¼ cup dry sherry**
- **½ teaspoon sugar**
- **2 tablespoons grated Parmesan cheese**

In a 10-inch covered skillet cook onions in butter about 10 minutes or until tender but not brown, stirring occasionally. Add sherry, sugar, ½ teaspoon *salt,* and dash *pepper*. Cook, uncovered, 2 to 3 minutes. Turn into a serving dish. Sprinkle with Parmesan. Serves 4.

## Glazed Onions

> 1 **pound boiling onions**
> 2 **tablespoons butter** *or* **margarine**
> 1 **tablespoon sugar**

Prepare and cook onions as directed on page 776 about 15 minutes or till nearly tender. Drain well, reserving ¼ cup liquid. In a medium skillet combine butter, sugar, and reserved liquid. Cook and stir till combined; add onions. Cook, uncovered, over medium-low heat about 15 minutes or until onions are nicely glazed; stir often. Makes 4 servings.

## Hawaiian-Style Parsnips

> 2 **pounds parsnips (10 medium)**
> 2 **tablespoons brown sugar**
> 1 **tablespoon cornstarch**
> 1 **8¼-ounce can crushed pineapple**
> ½ **teaspoon finely shredded orange peel**
> ½ **cup orange juice**
> 2 **tablespoons butter** *or* **margarine**

Peel and slice parsnips. Cook as directed on page 776; drain well. In a large saucepan combine sugar, cornstarch, and ¾ teaspoon *salt;* stir in *undrained* pineapple, orange peel, and juice. Cook and stir till thickened and bubbly. Cook and stir 1 to 2 minutes more. Add butter; stir till melted. Add parsnips. Cover; heat through, about 5 minutes. Serves 6 to 8.

## Pea Pods with Almonds

Combine ½ cup *water,* 1 tablespoon *soy sauce,* 1½ teaspoons *cornstarch,* and 1 teaspoon instant *chicken bouillon granules;* set aside.

Melt 2 tablespoons *butter* in a 10-inch skillet. Add 2 tablespoons slivered *almonds;* stir-fry 2 minutes or till lightly browned.

Add one 6-ounce package frozen *pea pods;* stir-fry 2 minutes more. Stir in one 4-ounce can sliced *mushrooms,* drained. Stir cornstarch mixture; add to pea pods in skillet. Cook and stir till thickened and bubbly. Cook and stir 1 to 2 minutes more. Serves 3 or 4.

## Deluxe Peas and Mushrooms

- **2   cups shelled peas *or* one 10-ounce package frozen peas**
- **1   cup sliced fresh mushrooms**
- **¼   cup chopped onion**
- **2   tablespoons butter *or* margarine**
- **1   teaspoon sugar**
- **1   tablespoon chopped pimiento**

Cook fresh peas as directed on page 776. (*Or,* cook frozen peas according to package directions.) Drain well. Cook mushrooms and onion in butter till tender. Stir in sugar, ½ teaspoon *salt,* and dash *pepper.* Add cooked peas and pimiento. Cover; heat through. Serves 4.

## Minted New Peas

- **½   cup chopped green onion**
- **3   tablespoons butter *or* margarine**
- **2   cups shelled peas *or* one 10-ounce package frozen peas**
- **2   tablespoons water**
- **1   tablespoon finely chopped fresh mint leaves *or* 1 teaspoon dried mint**
- **1   teaspoon sugar**
- **1   teaspoon lemon juice**
- **¼   teaspoon salt**
- **¼   teaspoon dried rosemary, crushed**

Cook green onion in butter till tender. Add fresh or frozen peas, water, mint, sugar, lemon juice, salt, and rosemary. Cover and cook 10 to 12 minutes or till peas are just tender;

add more water as necessary. Garnish with a lemon twist and fresh mint leaves, if desired. Serves 4.

## Creamed Peas and New Potatoes

| | |
|---|---|
| 1½ | **pounds tiny new potatoes (about 15)** |
| 2 | **cups shelled peas or one 10-ounce package frozen peas** |
| ¼ | **cup sliced green onion** |
| 2 | **tablespoons butter or margarine** |
| 1 | **tablespoon all-purpose flour** |
| ¼ | **teaspoon salt** |
| | **Dash white pepper** |
| 1 | **cup milk** |

Scrub potatoes; remove a narrow strip of peel around center of each. Cook potatoes as directed on page 776 till tender; drain. Meanwhile, cook fresh peas till tender as directed on page 776. (Or, cook frozen peas according to package directions.) Drain peas. Cook onion in butter or margarine till tender. Stir in flour, salt, and pepper. Add milk. Cook and stir till thickened and bubbly. Cook and stir 1 to 2 minutes more. Combine vegetables and onion mixture. Makes 4 to 6 servings.

## Baked Potatoes

Oven 425°

Scrub *baking potatoes* with a brush. For soft skins, rub with shortening. Prick potatoes with a fork. Bake in a 425° oven for 40 to 60 minutes or in a 350° oven for 70 to 80 minutes. When done, roll gently under your hand. Cut a crisscross in the top with a knife. Press ends; push up.

**Foil-Baked Potatoes:** Scrub potatoes; prick with a fork. Wrap each in foil. Bake in a 350° oven for 1½ hours or till done.

**Micro-Baked Potatoes:** Scrub potatoes; prick with a fork. In a counter-top microwave oven arrange potatoes on paper toweling, leaving at least 1 inch between potatoes. Micro-cook, uncovered, on high power till potatoes are done. Allow

6 to 8 minutes for 2 potatoes, 13 to 15 minutes for 4 potatoes, and 17 to 19 minutes for 6 potatoes. Halfway through cooking time, rearrange potatoes and turn over.

## French Fries

Peel *baking potatoes*. To prevent darkening, immerse the peeled potatoes in a bowl of cold water till ready to cut. Cut potatoes lengthwise into ⅜-inch-wide strips using a knife or french-fry cutter. Return potato strips to bowl of cold water till ready to fry. Heat *shortening or cooking oil* in a deep sauce-pan or deep-fat fryer to 375°. Dry potatoes *thoroughly* with paper toweling. Fry potatoes, a few at a time, in deep hot fat (375°) for 6 to 7 minutes or till crisp and golden brown. Remove with a slotted spoon and drain on paper toweling. Sprinkle with salt; serve at once.

## American-Fried Potatoes

**2   cups thinly sliced peeled potatoes**
**2   tablespoons bacon drippings *or* cooking oil**

In a large skillet add potatoes to hot bacon drippings or oil. Season with salt and pepper. Cover and cook over medium heat for 10 minutes. Turn potatoes and cook, *uncovered,* over medium-high heat about 5 minutes, loosening once or twice. Makes 4 servings.

## Twice-Baked Potatoes

**4   medium baking potatoes**
**2   tablespoons butter or margarine**
    **Milk**
**2   slices American cheese, halved diagonally**
    **Paprika**                                      Oven 425°

Prepare and bake potatoes as directed at left. Cut a lengthwise slice from the top of each baked potato; discard skin from slice. Reserving potato shells, scoop out the insides and add to potato portions from top slices; mash. Add butter. Beat in enough milk to make of stiff consistency. Season to taste with salt and pepper. Pile mashed potato mixture into potato shells. Place in a 10x6x2-inch baking dish. Bake in a 425° oven for 20 to 25 minutes or till lightly browned. Place cheese atop potatoes; sprinkle with paprika. Bake 2 to 3 minutes longer or till cheese melts. Makes 4 servings.

**Microwave directions:** Prepare and bake potatoes as directed at left in a microwave oven. Prepare potato shells and mashed potato mixture as above. Pile mashed potato mixture into potato shells. Place in a 10x6x2-inch nonmetal baking dish. Micro-cook, uncovered, on high power about 5 minutes or till potatoes are heated through, rearranging potatoes twice. Place cheese atop potatoes. Sprinkle with paprika. Micro-cook 30 seconds longer.

## Hashed Brown Potatoes

    3   medium potatoes
    3   tablespoons butter or margarine
    ¼   cup finely chopped onion or green onion
    ½   teaspoon salt
        Dash pepper

Prepare and cook whole potatoes as directed on page 776 for 20 to 25 minutes or till potatoes are *almost* tender. Drain and chill. Peel potatoes; shred to make 3 cups. In a medium skillet melt butter. Combine potatoes, onion, salt, and pepper; pat into skillet. Cook over low heat about 15 to 20 minutes or till underside is crisp. Cut with a spatula to make 4 wedges; turn. Cook about 5 minutes more or till other side is golden. Makes 4 servings.

**Note:** If desired, the onion may be omitted.

## Mashed Potatoes

> 6    **medium potatoes (2 pounds)**
> 2    **tablespoons butter or margarine**
> ¼    **teaspoon salt**
>      **Dash pepper**
>      **Milk, heated (about ¼ cup)**

Prepare, peel, and cook potatoes as directed on page 776. Drain. Mash with a potato masher or on low speed of electric mixer. Add butter or margarine, salt, and pepper. Gradually beat in enough of the hot milk to make light and fluffy. Makes 8 servings.

**Volcano Potatoes:** Prepare Mashed Potatoes as above, *except* mound potatoes into a greased 8x1½-inch round baking dish. Make a shallow crater in the center. Whip ¼ cup *whipping cream*. Fold ½ cup shredded *American cheese* into the whipped cream. Spoon into crater. Bake in a 350° oven about 20 minutes or till lightly browned. Makes 6 to 8 servings.

**Duchess Potatoes:** Prepare Mashed Potatoes as above, *except* let potatoes cool slightly. Beat in 1 *egg*. Using a pastry bag with a large star tip, pipe potatoes around a hot broiled beef steak or ham steak on a wooden plank. Brush with 1 tablespoon melted *butter or margarine*. Broil till potatoes are lightly browned. (*Or*, spoon into 6 or 8 mounds on a greased baking sheet and shape with the back of a spoon into nests. Brush with melted butter and bake in a 500° oven for 10 to 12 minutes.) Makes 6 to 8 servings.

## Lemon-Parsleyed Potatoes

> 1½   **pounds tiny new potatoes, scrubbed, or**
>      **medium potatoes, peeled and quartered**
> ¼    **cup butter or margarine**
> ¼    **cup snipped parsley**
> 1    **tablespoon lemon juice**

Scrub potatoes; if desired, remove a narrow strip of peel around the center of each new potato. Cook potatoes till tender as directed on page 776; drain. Place in a serving bowl; keep warm. Meanwhile, melt butter; stir in parsley and lemon juice. Pour over potatoes; stir lightly to coat. Makes 4 to 6 servings.

## Potato Patties

> **2** tablespoons finely chopped onion
> **¼** cup butter or margarine
> **3** medium potatoes, cooked, mashed, and chilled (2 cups mashed)
> **1** slightly beaten egg
> **¼** cup all-purpose flour

In a 10-inch skillet cook onion in *1 tablespoon* of the butter. Drain onion, reserving drippings in skillet. Combine onion, mashed potatoes, and egg. Shape into six 3-inch patties. Dip in flour. Add the remaining *3 tablespoons* butter or shortening to skillet. Heat over medium heat. Add potato patties and cook about 5 minutes on each side or till browned. Serves 6.

## Oven-Browned Potatoes

Peel 4 or 5 medium *potatoes*. Quarter and cook in boiling salted water about 10 minutes; drain. About 40 minutes before roast is done, place potatoes in drippings around roast, turning to coat. If necessary, add ½ cup *water* to pan to make enough drippings.

## Scalloped Potatoes

*Try the Potato-Ham Scallop recipe on page 506—*
> **¼** cup chopped onion
> **¼** cup butter or margarine
> **¼** cup all-purpose flour
> **2½** cups milk
> **5** large potatoes, peeled and thinly sliced (5 cups)                Oven 350°

To make sauce, cook onion in butter or margarine till tender but not brown. Stir in flour, 1½ teaspoons *salt,* and ⅛ teaspoon *pepper.* Add milk. Cook and stir till thickened and bubbly. Cook and stir 1 to 2 minutes more. Remove from heat. Place *half* of the sliced potatoes in a greased 2-quart casserole. Cover with *half* of the sauce. Repeat layers. Bake, covered, in a 350° oven 45 minutes, stirring once. Uncover, bake about 30 minutes more or till potatoes are done. Makes 4 to 6 servings.

    ***Cheesy Scalloped Potatoes:*** Prepare Scalloped Potatoes as above, *except* reduce salt to 1 teaspoon; stir ¾ cup shredded *American cheese* into sauce till melted.

## Sweet-Potato-Cashew Bake

    **6  medium sweet potatoes (2 pounds)**
    **½  cup packed brown sugar**
    **⅓  cup broken cashews**
    **¼  teaspoon ground ginger**
    **1  8¾-ounce can peach slices**
    **3  tablespoons butter**              Oven 350°

Prepare and cook whole sweet potatoes in water as directed on page 777. Drain, peel, and cut crosswise into thick pieces. Combine brown sugar, cashews, ginger, and ½ teaspoon *salt.* Drain peaches well. In a 10x6x2-inch baking dish layer *half each* of the sweet potatoes, peach slices, and brown sugar mixture. Repeat layers. Dot with butter. Bake, covered, in a 350° oven for 30 minutes. Uncover; bake about 10 minutes longer. Spoon brown sugar syrup over before serving. Serves 6 to 8.

## Oven Candied Sweet Potatoes

    **8  medium sweet potatoes**
    **⅓  cup packed brown sugar**
    **¼  cup butter *or* margarine**
    **½  teaspoon salt**
    **¾  cup tiny marshmallows**          Oven 375°

Prepare and cook whole sweet potatoes in water *just* till tender as directed on page 777. Drain, peel, and cut into ½-inch-thick slices. In a 1½-quart casserole layer *half each* of the potatoes, brown sugar, butter, and salt. Repeat layers. Bake, uncovered, in a 375° oven for 30 to 40 minutes or till glazed. Sprinkle marshmallows over top. Bake about 5 minutes longer or till lightly browned. Serves 6.

**Skillet Candied Sweet Potatoes:** Use ingredients for Oven Candied Sweet Potatoes as above. Cook the potatoes. Melt butter in a 12-inch skillet. Stir in brown sugar, ¼ cup *water,* and salt. Add cooked, sliced potatoes. Cook, uncovered, over medium heat 10 to 15 minutes or till glazed, basting and turning gently 2 or 3 times. Omit the marshmallows.

---

## Mashed Sweet Potato Bake

|   |   |   |
|---|---|---|
| 6 | medium sweet potatoes | |
| ½ | teaspoon grated orange peel | |
| 2 | tablespoons orange juice | |
| 2 | tablespoons brown sugar | |
| 2 | tablespoons butter or margarine | |
| ½ | teaspoon salt | |
| ¼ | teaspoon ground cinnamon | |
| 1 | egg | |
| ½ | cup milk | Oven 350° |

Prepare and cook whole sweet potatoes in water as directed on page 777. Drain, peel, and cut up. Mash with a potato masher or on low speed of electric mixer. Add orange peel, orange juice, brown sugar, butter, salt, and cinnamon. Add egg and milk; beat till fluffy. Add additional milk, if necessary. Turn into a greased 1-quart casserole. Cover; bake in a 350° oven for 45 to 50 minutes. Serves 6 to 8.

---

## Rutabaga and Apple

|   |   |   |
|---|---|---|
| 1 | medium rutabaga, peeled and cubed | |
| 1 | medium apple, peeled, cored, and sliced | |
| ⅓ | cup packed brown sugar | |
| 2 | tablespoons butter | Oven 350° |

Cook rutabaga as directed on page 777; drain well. Place *half* of the rutabaga and *half* of the apple in a 1-quart casserole. Sprinkle with *half* of the sugar; dot with *half* of the butter. Season with salt. Repeat layers. Bake, covered, in a 350° oven about 30 minutes. Serves 4 to 6.

## Mashed vegetables

For sweet potatoes, prepare and cook potatoes as directed on page 777. Drain. Peel and mash hot potatoes. Beat till fluffy, gradually adding hot milk as needed. Add butter, salt, and pepper to taste.

For mashed rutabagas or turnips, prepare and cook vegetable as directed on page 777. Drain. Mash. Add butter, salt, and pepper to taste.

## Creamed Spinach with Nutmeg

    1   **10-ounce package frozen chopped spinach**
    1   **tablespoon butter *or* margarine**
   ½    **cup milk**
  1½    **teaspoons cornstarch**
        **Dash ground nutmeg**

Cook frozen spinach according to package directions using ½ cup *water*. Remove from heat. *Do not drain*. Add butter. Stir milk into cornstarch and nutmeg; add to spinach. Cook and stir till thickened and bubbly. Cook and stir 1 to 2 minutes more. Serve in sauce dishes. Makes 4 servings.

## Chinese Spinach

        1    **pound spinach (12 cups)**
        2    **tablespoons cooking oil**
        ½    **teaspoon sugar**
        2    **tablespoons soy sauce**
        ½    **cup sliced water chestnuts**
        2    **tablespoons chopped onion**

Cut fresh spinach stems into 1-inch pieces; tear leaves into bite-size pieces. Cook spinach as directed on page 777 for 3 minutes; drain well. Heat oil, sugar, and soy sauce in a skillet; add spinach, water chestnuts, and onion. Cook, tossing lightly, 2 to 3 minutes or till spinach is coated and heated. Serves 4.

## Dilly Panned Summer Squash

        1    **pound zucchini _or_ yellow crookneck squash**
        2    **tablespoons butter _or_ margarine**
        1    **tablespoon snipped parsley**
        ¼    **teaspoon salt**
        ¼    **teaspoon dried dillweed**
             **Dash pepper**

Slice unpeeled squash to make 3 cups. In a medium skillet melt butter or margarine. Add squash; sprinkle squash with parsley, salt, dillweed, and pepper. Cover and cook over medium-low heat 8 to 10 minutes or till tender, stirring frequently. Makes 3 or 4 servings.

## Cheddar-Squash Puff

    2  **pounds zucchini or yellow crookneck**
         **squash**
    1  **cup dairy sour cream**
    2  **beaten egg yolks**
    2  **tablespoons all-purpose flour**
    2  **stiff-beaten egg whites**
 1½  **cups shredded cheddar cheese**
    4  **slices bacon, crisp-cooked, drained, and**
         **crumbled**
   ¼  **cup fine dry bread crumbs**
    1  **tablespoon butter or margarine,**
         **melted**                                   Oven 350°

Thinly slice unpeeled squash to make 6 cups. Cook as directed
on page 777; drain well. Thoroughly combine sour cream, egg
yolks, and flour; fold in the beaten egg whites.

In a 12x7½x2-inch baking dish layer *half each* of the squash,
egg mixture, and cheese; sprinkle with all of the bacon. Repeat
layers of remaining squash, egg mixture, and cheese. Combine
bread crumbs and butter; sprinkle over all. Bake, uncovered,
in a 350° oven for 20 to 25 minutes. Makes 8 to 10 servings.

## Candied Squash Rings

    2  **acorn squash**
   ½  **cup packed brown sugar**
   ¼  **cup butter or margarine**
    2  **tablespoons water**                           Oven 350°

Cut squash crosswise into 1-inch-thick slices; discard seeds.
Arrange in a single layer in a shallow baking pan. Season with
salt and pepper. Cover; bake in a 350° oven about 40 minutes. In a saucepan combine brown sugar, butter, and water;
cook and stir till bubbly. Spoon over squash. Continue baking,
uncovered, about 15 minutes more or till squash is tender;
baste often. Serves 4 to 6.

**Microwave directions:** Pierce squash with a metal skewer

or long-tined fork in several places. Cook in a counter-top microwave oven on high power 8 to 10 minutes or till soft. Let stand 5 minutes. Cut crosswise into 1-inch-thick slices; discard seeds. Place squash in a 12x7½x2-inch nonmetal baking dish. Season. In a glass measuring cup combine remaining ingredients. Micro-cook 15 seconds. Spoon over squash. Cover with waxed paper. Micro-cook 3 to 5 minutes or till hot. Baste once.

## Baked Acorn Squash Halves

Oven 350°

Halve and seed *acorn squash.* Place cut side down in a shallow baking pan. Bake in a 350° oven for 30 minutes. Turn cut side up; sprinkle with *salt.* Fill, if desired, with following suggestions below. Bake 20 to 30 minutes longer. One whole squash makes 2 servings.

**Squash and Sausage:** Prepare Baked Acorn Squash Halves as above. After turning, drizzle *each half* with about 1 tablespoon *honey* and fill with 1 *pork sausage link,* sliced and browned. Continue baking as directed.

**Squash and Applesauce:** Prepare Baked Acorn Squash Halves as above. After turning cut side up, in *each half* spoon ¼ to ⅓ cup *applesauce* combined with 2 teaspoons *brown sugar.* Continue baking as directed.

**Candied Squash:** Prepare Baked Acorn Squash Halves as above. After turning, in *each half* put 1 teaspoon *butter* and 2 teaspoons *brown sugar.* Continue baking as directed.

**Squash with Onions:** Prepare 6 Baked Acorn Squash Halves (3 whole) as above. After turning and sprinkling with salt, fill with 2 cups cooked fresh *or* frozen *pearl onions* and ⅓ cup chopped *walnuts.* Mix ½ cup *dark corn syrup,* ¼ cup melted *butter,* and ¼ teaspoon ground *cinnamon;* spoon over onions. Continue as directed. Serves 6.

## Fresh Tomato Fix-Ups

*Broiled Tomatoes:* Halve 3 large unpeeled ripe *tomatoes* or cut a slice from the tops of 6 medium unpeeled ripe *tomatoes.* Place, cut side up, in a shallow baking pan. Season with salt and pepper. If desired, sprinkle each with ⅛ to ¼ teaspoon dried *basil or thyme,* crushed, *or* 1 teaspoon snipped *fresh parsley or chives.* Dot each with about 1 teaspoon *butter or margarine.* Broil 3 inches from heat about 5 minutes or till heated through. Makes 6 servings.

*Baked Tomatoes:* Halve 3 large unpeeled ripe *tomatoes* or cut a slice from tops of 6 medium unpeeled ripe *tomatoes.* Place, cut side up, in a shallow baking pan. Season with salt and pepper. Combine ½ cup crushed *saltine crackers,* 2 tablespoons melted *butter,* and 1 teaspoon dried *basil,* crushed; sprinkle atop tomatoes. Bake, uncovered, in a 375° oven about 20 minutes. Serves 6.

## Scalloped Tomatoes

| | |
|---|---|
| 6 | medium tomatoes, peeled and cut up (2 pounds) *or* one 28-ounce can tomatoes, cut up |
| 1 | cup sliced celery |
| ½ | cup chopped onion |
| 2 | tablespoons all-purpose flour |
| 1 | tablespoon sugar |
| ½ | teaspoon dried marjoram, crushed |
| 2 | tablespoons butter *or* margarine |
| 4 | slices bread, toasted |
| 2 | tablespoons grated Parmesan cheese |

Oven 350°

In a saucepan combine tomatoes, celery, and onion. Simmer, covered, about 10 minutes or till celery is tender. Combine flour, sugar, marjoram, ½ teaspoon *salt,* and dash *pepper.* Stir in ¼ cup *water;* add to tomatoes. Cook and stir till thickened and bubbly. Cook and stir 1 to 2 minutes more. Stir in butter till melted.

Cut *3 slices* toast into cubes; stir into tomato mixture. Pour into a 1½-quart casserole or a 10x6x2-inch baking dish. Bake in a 350° oven for 30 minutes. Cut the remaining slice of toast into 4 triangles. Arrange triangles down center of tomato mixture, overlapping slightly. Sprinkle with Parmesan cheese. Bake 20 minutes longer. Serve scalloped tomatoes in sauce dishes. Makes 6 servings.

## Tomatoes and Okra

| | |
|---|---|
| 1½ | cups okra cut into ½-inch-thick slices *or* one-half of a 20-ounce package frozen cut okra |
| ½ | cup chopped onion |
| ½ | cup chopped green pepper |
| 2 | tablespoons butter *or* margarine |
| 1 | tablespoon sugar |
| 1 | teaspoon all-purpose flour |
| 3 | medium tomatoes, peeled and coarsely chopped (1 pound) |

Cook okra as directed on page 776 about 10 minutes or till *almost* tender; drain. (*Or*, cook frozen okra according to package directions; drain.) Cook onion and green pepper in butter till tender but not brown; stir in sugar, flour, ½ teaspoon *salt*, and dash *pepper*. Add tomatoes. Cook and stir till slightly thickened and bubbly. Add cooked okra; heat through. Makes 6 servings.

## Whipped Turnip Puff

| | |
|---|---|
| 1 | pound turnips, peeled and cut up (3 cups) |
| ¼ | cup chopped onions |
| 2 | tablespoons butter *or* margarine |
| 1 | tablespoon sugar |
| ½ | teaspoon salt |
| | Dash pepper |
| ¾ | cup soft bread crumbs (1 slice) |
| 2 | eggs |

Oven 375°

Cook turnips and onion as directed on page 777 for turnips till tender. Drain. Add butter or margarine, sugar, salt, and pepper; beat well with electric mixer or mash with a potato masher. Add bread crumbs and eggs; beat well. Turn into a lightly greased 1-quart casserole. Bake, uncovered, in a 375° oven for 35 to 40 minutes. Makes 4 to 6 servings.

**Whipped Rutabaga Puff:** Prepare Whipped Turnip Puff as above, *except* substitute 1 medium *rutabaga* (1 pound), peeled and cut up, for turnips. Cook rutabaga and onion as directed on page 777 for rutabaga. Continue as directed.

**Whipped Parsnip Puff:** Prepare Whipped Turnip Puff as above, *except* substitute 1 pound parsnips (4 medium), cut up, for the turnips. Remove any woody portions from the parsnips. Cook parsnips and onion as directed on page 776 for parsnips. Continue as directed.

## Lemon-Parsleyed Turnips

- 1 **pound turnips (3 medium), peeled and cut into strips, cubes, or slices**
- 1 **tablespoon butter or margarine**
- 1 **tablespoon snipped parsley**
- 2 **teaspoons lemon juice**
- 1 **teaspoon finely chopped onion**

Cook turnips as directed on page 777 just till tender. Drain well. Add butter or margarine, parsley, lemon juice, and onion. Season with salt and pepper. Stir gently to coat. Makes 4 servings.

## Potluck Vegetable Casserole

>   1   **17-ounce can whole kernel corn**
>   1   **10-ounce package frozen cauliflower,**
>        **cooked**
>   1   **10-ounce package frozen cut broccoli,**
>        **cooked**
>   1   **4-ounce can sliced mushrooms**
>   1   **17-ounce can cream-style corn**
>   2   **cups shredded Swiss cheese**
>   1   **10¾-ounce can condensed cream of celery**
>        **soup**
>   2   **tablespoons butter**
>  1½   **cups soft rye or white bread**
>        **crumbs**                          Oven 375°

Drain whole kernel corn, cooked cauliflower, cooked broccoli,
and mushrooms. Cut up large pieces of cauliflower. Combine
cream-style corn, cheese, and soup. Fold in drained vegetables. Turn into a 12x7½x2-inch baking dish. Melt butter; toss
with crumbs. Sprinkle atop mixture. Bake, uncovered, in a
375° oven 30 to 35 minutes or till hot. Serves 12 to 15.

## Garden Vegetable Stir-Fry

>   2   **medium carrots, cut into thirds**
>   2   **cups green beans bias-sliced into 1-inch**
>        **lengths**
>   2   **cups sliced cauliflower**
>  1½   **teaspoons cornstarch**
>   2   **tablespoons soy sauce**
>   1   **tablespoon dry sherry**
>   2   **teaspoons sugar**
>   2   **tablespoons cooking oil**
>   1   **medium onion, cut into thin wedges**
>   1   **cup sliced zucchini**

Cut carrots into thin sticks. In a covered saucepan cook carrots and green beans in boiling salted water for 3 minutes. Add cauliflower; cover and cook 2 minutes more. Drain well. Stir 2 tablespoons cold *water* into cornstarch; stir in soy, sherry, sugar, and dash *pepper*. Set aside. Preheat a wok or large skillet over high heat; add cooking oil. Stir-fry onion in hot oil for 1 minute. Add carrots, beans, cauliflower, and zucchini; stir-fry 2 minutes more or till vegetables are crisp-tender. Push vegetables from center of wok. Stir soy mixture; stir into vegetables. Cook and stir 3 to 4 minutes or till thickened and bubbly. Serve at once. Serves 6.

# Special Helps

Special Helps

Special Helps

Special Helps

Special Helps

Special Helps

Special Helps

Special Helps

# Meal Planning

To make your meal planning easier, read over the nutrition-wise planning and shopping tips on the next several pages. Besides good nutrition, you'll need to consider your family food preferences and budget, the family's mealtime schedule, and the meal preparation time. Also, consider what food storage space you have available.

If you're watching your food budget, keep in mind current good food buys, taking advantage of seasonal foods and specials whenever you can. (Check the chart on page 845 to learn when fresh fruits and vegetables are plentiful.) Another way to save is by cutting your meat expenditures. Occasionally, substitute less expensive protein foods for meat, such as cooked legumes or eggs. Also, serve no more than the suggested 2- to 3-ounce portions of cooked meat if economizing is important.

Mealtime schedules are another important consideration. With busy workdays and even busier evening schedules for some family members, you might consider planning menus around make-ahead foods (both the refrigerated and frozen types), and jiffy, quick-to-cook dishes. Or, consider enlisting family members to pitch in at mealtime. And don't forget to use work- and timesaving appliances for food preparation.

One efficient way to plan menus is to plan for several days or a week at a time. Equipped with recipes, newspaper food ads, and a knowledge of good nutrition (a review of the basic food groups follows on the next few pages), write out your menus, thinking about the entire day's variety of foods. At the same time, write out a detailed shopping list—it saves looking up all the recipes again. One well-planned trip to the grocery store with shopping list in hand should save you both time and money.

## Planning Nutritious Meals

To help you plan nutritious meals incorporating foods from the basic food groups, follow this seven-step guideline, keeping in mind all the day's menus:

1. Plan the protein main dish from the meat group.

2. Add a bread or cereal product to complement the main dish.

3. Choose a hot or cold vegetable.

4. Select a fruit or vegetable salad to complement the main dish.

5. Add a dessert that's appropriate to the rest of the meal. Fruits make a good dessert, as do milk-based desserts, such as pudding. Remember that a light dessert is best after a heavy meal and vice versa.

6. Choose a beverage. This is an excellent place for a serving from the milk group.

7. After the first four food group requirements are met, you can add extras from the fifth "fats-sweets" group to complement the meal and suit your family's tastes. Remember to include these foods in moderation.

Perhaps not every meal will include all seven steps. Just make sure that all the days's menus include the proper amounts from the basic food groups, and that they include a wide variety of foods.

To get you started with your own menu plans, use the generic three-meal plan or five-meal plan listed at right. The three-meal plan includes some snacks that help round out the food selections.

Simply plug in a specific food for each food group serving listed. If five meals a day fit into your schedule, follow that plan. (Allowances for pregnant women or nursing mothers have not been included in the menu planner.) Combination foods—those that include foods from more than one food group—short-cut meal preparation. For example, a casserole may include a serving from the meat group, a serving from the vegetable group, and a bread/cereal serving, such as pasta or rice. Determine the foods in the dish, then determine what groups they come from to calculate the servings from the Basic Five Food Groups.

# Other Considerations

Although nutrition is a top consideration when planning meals, it's not everything. If you want to be sure that well-planned nutrients are eaten and are enjoyed, you must consider the aesthetic appeal of the food as well. Foods must have eye and taste appeal and should look and taste good together. Likewise, the table setting should provide a pleasing background for the food. Not only should you plan a variety of foods in the day's menus, you also should plan for a variety of color, form, flavor, texture, and temperature. Proper seasoning also is important.

• Variety in color—Add a colorful yet simple garnish to a food that lacks color. A sprig of parsley, bright red radishes, cherry tomatoes, or a spiced crab apple can do wonders for plain meat and potatoes. But avoid color clashes.

• Variety in the form of food—Don't serve too many small pieces, too many similar shapes, or too many mixtures. Plan a contrast in sizes and shapes. Leave some foods whole and serve others sliced, cubed, mashed, or cut into matchstick-size strips.

• Variety in flavor— Complement a bland food with a tart or zippy food. Usually plan only one highly seasoned food per menu.

• Variety in texture—Serve some soft foods with some crisp ones. Breadsticks, croutons, and lettuce are some of the common foods that add "crunch."

• Variety in temperatures— Plan a balance of hot and cold foods. Be sure to serve hot foods piping hot and cold foods well chilled.

• Season foods carefully so that their flavor isn't hidden by the seasoning.

• Try new foods and new seasonings, but don't serve more than one new food at the same meal, especially when young children are being served.

• To shortcut meal preparations, make at least one of the courses a simple food rather than a recipe. Lettuce with a bottled dressing and ice cream or sherbet with a prepared topping are examples of timesavers.

• Serve only one starchy food at a meal. The exception to this rule is bread or rolls, which can be served with almost any meal.

# Menu Planner

**3-Meal Plan**

**Meal #1** 1 milk serving
1 citrus fruit serving
1 bread/cereal
serving

**Meal #2** 1 meat serving
1 vegetable serving
1 bread/cereal
serving

**Snack** 1 milk serving
*(children and
teens)*
1 bread/cereal
serving

**Meal #3** 1 meat serving
1 vegetable serving
*(deep green or
yellow every
other day)*
1 bread/cereal
serving
1 fruit serving
1 milk serving

**Snack** 1 milk serving *(for
teens)*

**5-Meal Plan**

**Meal #1** 1 milk serving
1 bread/cereal
serving

**Meal #2** ½ meat serving
1 citrus fruit serving
1 bread/cereal
serving

**Meal #3** ½ meat serving
1 milk serving
1 vegetable serving
*(deep green or
yellow every
other day)*

**Meal #4** 1 milk serving
*(for children
and teens)*
1 vegetable serving
1 bread/cereal
serving

**Meal #5** 1 meat serving
1 milk serving
*(for teens)*
1 bread/cereal
serving
1 fruit serving

# Use the Basic Five Food Groups

As you plan menus using these nutrition basics, the five food groups listed on page 827, and the generic menu planner, be sure to consider any medical problems in your family that require special menus. Your doctor is the best source of information for a special diet.

The serving sizes recommended in the first four food groups should provide adequate protein and most of the vitamins and minerals needed daily by the body. If you need to consume fewer calories, cut down on foods in the fifth "fats-sweets" group, then choose items in the other four groups that have fewer calories. To gain weight, increase the number of servings or portion sizes from the first four groups

and add some foods from the "fats-sweets" group.

# Nutrition Basics

When we eat food, we obtain nutrients essential for maintaining the body. Food is made up of protein, carbohydrates, fats, vitamins, minerals, and water. Most foods contain several nutrients, but no single food contains them all. Therefore, to get all the needed nutrients, eat a variety of foods daily for a balanced diet.

To help you plan nutritious, well-balanced meals, use the Basic Five Food Group system in menu preparation. The food choices within the groups let you plan a variety of food combinations. The five groups are listed on page 827.

## Nutrient Descriptions

**Protein** (amino acids) is needed for building,

maintaining, and repairing the body. It is necessary for the production of antibodies that ward off disease and of enzymes and hormones that regulate many of the body processes. If there is not enough carbohydrate or fat in the diet, protein will be used for energy instead of its other more important jobs.

Proteins may come from animal and from plant sources. Animal protein provides complete protein, whereas most plant protein is incomplete. You can make the plant protein nutritionally equivalent to animal protein by combining it with other protein sources, such as small amounts of high-quality animal protein or by adding another plant protein that provides the missing essentials. Plant protein combinations must be eaten at the same meal to perform effectively.

**Carbohydrates** (sugars and starches) provide energy. If too little carbohydrate is consumed, the body will use protein for energy, possibly causing a protein shortage.

**Fats** provide a highly concentrated form of energy and are essential to the diet. Fats carry the fat-soluble vitamins A, D, E, and K throughout the body. They also help insulate the body and provide a cushion around vital organs.

Fats also give "staying power" to the meal, so you won't get hungry too soon after eating. Some fats also supply essential fatty acids.

**Vitamins** are very important to the body. We obtain them only from foods that we eat, since they are not manufactured by the body.

An important vitamin is *Vitamin A*, which promotes growth and the development of normal skin, and aids night vision and the prevention of eye disease. *Vitamin C* (ascorbic acid) is needed for the framework of bones and teeth. It plays a part in the formation of collagen, which binds the body's cells together. *Vitamin D* aids in the proper utilization of calcium. *Vitamin K* is important for the normal clotting of blood.

The *B-complex vitamins* include thiamine, riboflavin, niacin, and others, including vitamin $B_6$, vitamin $B_{12}$, and folacin. *Thiamine* (vitamin $B_1$) helps regulate the appetite and digestion, maintains a healthy nervous system, and helps release energy from carbohydrates. *Riboflavin* (vitamin $B_2$) aids in food metabolism, promotes healthy skin, helps cells use oxygen, and aids vision in bright light. *Niacin* is involved in the conversion of sugars to energy, tissue respiration, and fat synthesis. *Vitamins $B_6$, $B_{12}$, and folacin* are important in maintaining hemoglobin.

**Minerals** are also important in the daily diet. *Calcium* gives strength to bones and rigidity and permanence to teeth. Calcium also aids in blood clotting and muscle contraction. *Iron* is an important part of every red blood cell and is found in the hemoglobin. It carries oxygen throughout the body and also helps the body resist infections.

# Nutrition Analysis

All of these nutrients, plus others, are important to the body and must be consumed in the foods we eat. Throughout this book, you will find a nutrition analysis included with each recipe chapter, giving the values of certain nutrients for an individual serving as well as the percentages of the United States Recommended Daily Allowances (U.S. RDAs) for certain nutrients. Read the introduction on page 825 for more information on the nutrition analysis of recipes. Use this information, as well as the guidelines for the Basic Five Food Groups on the next page, to ensure that your nutritional needs are met.

# The Basic Five Food Groups

| Vegetables and Fruits | Breads and Cereals | Milk and Cheeses | Meats, Fish, Poultry, and Beans | Fats, Sweets, and Alcohol |
|---|---|---|---|---|
| **Foods in this group include:** | | | | |
| All vegetables and fruits (fresh, canned, frozen, or dried) and their juices. | All foods based on whole grains or enriched flour or meal. Includes breads, biscuits, muffins, waffles, pancakes, pasta, rice, barley, bulgur, and cereals. | All types of milk, yogurt, cheese, ice milk, ice cream, and foods prepared with milk (milk shakes, puddings, and creamed soups). | Beef, veal, lamb, pork, poultry, fish, shellfish, variety meats, dry beans or peas, soybeans, lentils, eggs, peanuts and other nuts, peanut butter, and seeds. | All fats and oils; mayonnaise and salad dressings; all concentrated sweets; highly sugared beverages; alcoholic beverages; unenriched, refined flour products. |
| **Number of servings suggested daily** | | | | |
| Everyone—4 servings. (For vitamin C, use citrus fruits, melons, berries, tomatoes, or dark green vegetables daily. For vitamin A, use dark green or deep-yellow vegetables.) | Everyone—4 servings. (For fiber, include some whole grain bread or cereal every day.) | Children, under 9—2 to 3 servings. Children, 9 to 12—3 servings. Teens—4 servings. Adults—2 servings. Pregnant women—3 servings. Nursing mothers—4 servings. | Everyone—2 servings. | No serving number is recommended. In moderation, these foods can be used to round out meals, as long as requirements from the other categories are satisfied. |

| Vegetables and Fruits | Breads and Cereals | Milk and Cheeses | Meats, Fish, Poultry, and Beans | Fats, Sweets, and Alcohol |
|---|---|---|---|---|
| **A serving consists of:** | | | | |
| ½ cup or a typical portion such as 1 medium orange, ½ medium grapefruit, 1 medium potato, or 1 wedge of lettuce. | 1 slice bread; 1 biscuit or muffin; 1 pancake or waffle; ½ to ¾ cup cooked pasta, rice, bulgur, or cereal; or 1 ounce ready-to-eat cereal. | 1 cup milk or yogurt, 2 cups cottage cheese, 1⅓ ounces cheese, 2 ounces process cheese food or spread, ¼ cup Parmesan cheese, or 1½ cups ice cream. | 2 to 3 ounces lean cooked meat, poultry, or fish; 1 to 1½ cups cooked dry beans, peas, or lentils; 2 eggs; ½ to 1 cup nuts or seeds; or ¼ cup peanut butter. | No specific serving size is recommended. |
| **Major nutrients supplied:** | | | | |
| Carbohydrates, fiber, and vitamins A and C. Dark green vegetables are good sources of riboflavin, folacin, iron, and magnesium. Certain greens are valued for calcium. | Carbohydrates, protein, B vitamins, and iron. Whole grain products provide magnesium, folacin, and fiber. | Protein, calcium, riboflavin, and vitamins A, $B_6$, and $B_{12}$. When fortified, these products also provide vitamin D. | Protein, phosphorus, and vitamin $B_6$. Foods of animal origin provide vitamin $B_{12}$. Meats, dry beans, and dry peas provide iron. Liver and egg yolks provide vitamin A. Dry beans, peas, and nuts provide magnesium. | These foods provide very few nutrients in proportion to the number of calories they contain. Vegetable oils provide vitamin E and essential fatty acids. |

# Calorie Tally

The foods we eat furnish energy, which is measured in heat units called calories. A certain number of calories is necessary for basic body functions and activity. However, if more calories are consumed than the body needs, the excess is stored away as body fat. Each pound of excess body fat is produced by 3,500 extra calories.

To figure your daily caloric needs, follow these steps:

1. Estimate your desirable weight by consulting a height-weight chart.

2. Multiply your desirable or ideal weight by 18 for

women or 21 for men to calculate the number of calories you need to maintain that weight. (This is for moderately active people. Multiply by 14 for women or 16 for men if you lead a sedentary life.) Use this amount as a *guide* to your desirable caloric intake.

**Remember that these are maintenance calories. To lose weight, you'll need to consume fewer calories than this amount. Make sure that any diet you follow is nutritionally sound. Use these caloric counts to make wise food choices.**

## A-B

**Anchovies,** canned; 5
  fillets . . . . . . . . . . . . . . . . . 35
**Apple**
  fresh; 1 medium . . . . . . . . 80
  juice, canned; 1 cup . . . . .117
**Applesauce,** canned
  sweetened; ½ cup . . . . . . .116
  unsweetened; ½ cup . . . . . 50
**Apricots**
  canned, in syrup, ½ cup .111
  dried, cooked, unsweetened,
    in juice; ½ cup . . . . . . . .106
  fresh; 3 medium . . . . . . . . 55
  nectar; 1 cup . . . . . . . . . . .143
**Asparagus**
  cooked, drained; 4 spears. . 12
  fresh spears; 1 cup . . . . . . 35
**Avocado,** peeled;
  ½ avocado . . . . . . . . . . .188
**Bacon**
  2 crisp strips, medium
    thickness . . . . . . . . . . . . 86
  Canadian-style; cooked;
    1 slice . . . . . . . . . . . . . . 58
**Banana;** 1 medium . . . . . . .101
**Barbecue Sauce\*,** bottled;
  ½ cup . . . . . . . . . . . . . . . . .114

**Beans**
  baked, with tomato sauce and
    pork, canned; ½ cup . .155
  green snap, canned;
    ½ cup . . . . . . . . . . . . . . 21
  green snap, frozen;
    ½ cup . . . . . . . . . . . . . . 17
  lima, cooked; ½ cup . . . . . 95
  red kidney, canned;
    ½ cup . . . . . . . . . . . . . . .115
  yellow or wax, cooked;
    ½ cup . . . . . . . . . . . . . . 14
**Bean Sprouts,** fresh,
  ½ cup . . . . . . . . . . . . . . . . . 18
**Beef Cuts**
  corned, canned; 3
    ounces . . . . . . . . . . . . . .184
  ground beef, cooked,
    21% fat; 3 ounces . . . . .233
  pot roast, cooked lean and
    fat; 3 ounces . . . . . . . . . .246
    lean only; 3 ounces . . . .164
  rib roast, cooked
    lean and fat; 3 ounces .375
    lean only; 3 ounces . . . .205
  round steak, cooked; 3
    ounces . . . . . . . . . . . . . .161
  sirloin steak, broiled;
    3 ounces . . . . . . . . . . . . .329

**\*Recipe appears in this book.**

**Beef,** dried, chipped;
2 ounces . . . . . . . . . . . . . . 116
**Beef liver,** fried; 2 ounces . 130
**Beets,** cooked, diced;
½ cup . . . . . . . . . . . . . . . . 13
**Beverages,** alcoholic
beer; 1 cup . . . . . . . . . . . . . 101
dessert wine; 1 ounce . . . . 41
gin, rum, vodka—80-proof
1 jigger . . . . . . . . . . . . . . . 97
table wine; 1 ounce . . . . . . 25
**Biscuit\*,** enriched baking
powder, 1 . . . . . . . . . . . . . . 195
**Blackberries,** fresh;
½ cup . . . . . . . . . . . . . . . . 42
**Blueberries,** fresh;
½ cup . . . . . . . . . . . . . . . . 45
**Bouillon,**
instant granules;
1 teaspoon . . . . . . . . . . . 2
**Boysenberries,** frozen,
unsweetened; ½ cup . . . . . 30
**Bread**
Boston brown\*; 1 slice . . . 53
breadstick, plain; 1
(7¾ inches long) . . . . . . 19
bun, frankfurter or hamburger,
1 . . . . . . . . . . . . . . . . . . . . 119
corn bread\*; 1 piece . . . . . 238
crumbs, dry; ¼ cup . . . . . . 98
crumbs, soft; ¼ cup . . . . . 30
cubes; 1 cup . . . . . . . . . . . 81
French; 1 slice (½ inch
thick) . . . . . . . . . . . . . . . . 44
Italian; 1 slice (½ inch
thick) . . . . . . . . . . . . . . . . 28
pumpernickel; 1 slice . . . . . 79
raisin; 1 slice . . . . . . . . . . . 66
rye; 1 slice . . . . . . . . . . . . . 61
white; 1 slice . . . . . . . . . . . 68
whole wheat; 1 slice . . . . . 56
**Broccoli**
cooked; 1 medium stalk . . 47
frozen chopped, cooked;
½ cup . . . . . . . . . . . . . . . . 24

**Brussels Sprouts,** cooked;
½ cup . . . . . . . . . . . . . . . . 28
**Butter;** 1 tablespoon . . . . . . 102

# C

**Cabbage**
Chinese, raw, ½ cup . . . . . 6
common varieties, raw,
shredded; 1 cup . . . . . . . 17
red, raw, shredded;
1 cup . . . . . . . . . . . . . . . . 22
**Cake**
angel\*, no icing; 1/12 cake . 157
dark fruitcake\*; 1 slice . . . 266
devil's food\*, seven-minute
frosting\*; 1/12 cake . . . . . . . 415
pound\*, no icing; 1/12 cake 303
sponge\*, no icing; 1/12 cake 186
white\*; butter frosting\*;
1/12 cake . . . . . . . . . . . . . . . 503
yellow\*, chocolate icing\*;
1/12 cake . . . . . . . . . . . . . . 439
**Candy**
caramel; 1 ounce
(3 medium) . . . . . . . . . . . 113
chocolate bar, milk;
1 ounce . . . . . . . . . . . . . . 147
fudge\*; ½-ounce piece . . . 64
gumdrops; 1 ounce (2½ large
or 20 small) . . . . . . . . . . 98
hard; 1 ounce . . . . . . . . . . 109
jelly beans; 1 ounce (10) . 104
peanut brittle\*; ½ ounce . 64
**Cantaloupe;** ¼ (5-inch
diameter) . . . . . . . . . . . . . . 41
**Carrots**
cooked, diced; ½ cup . . . . 22
raw; 1 large or 2 small . . . 30
**Catsup;** 1 tablespoon . . . . . 16
**Cauliflower**
cooked; ½ cup . . . . . . . . . . 14
raw; whole flowerets;
1 cup . . . . . . . . . . . . . . . . 27

**\*Recipe appears in this book.**

**Celery,** raw, chopped;
½ cup . . . . . . . . . . . . . . . . 10
**Cereal,** cooked
oatmeal; ½ cup . . . . . . . . 66
wheat, rolled; ½ cup . . . . . 90
**Cereal,** ready-to-eat
bran flakes; ½ cup . . . . . . 53
cornflakes; ½ cup . . . . . . . 47
oats, puffed; ½ cup . . . . . 50
rice, crisp cereal with sugar,
½ cup . . . . . . . . . . . . . . 70
rice, puffed; ½ cup . . . . . . 30
wheat flakes; ½ cup . . . . . 53
wheat, puffed; ½ cup . . . . 27
**Cheese**
American, process;
1 ounce . . . . . . . . . . . . . . 105
blue; 1 ounce . . . . . . . . . . 104
brick; 1 ounce . . . . . . . . . . 105
Camembert; 1 ounce . . 85
cheddar; 1 ounce . . . . . . . 113
cottage, dry; 1 cup . . . . . 125
cottage, from skim milk,
cream-style; 1 cup . . . . . 223
cream cheese; 1 ounce . . 106
Edam; 1 ounce . . . . . . . . . 105
Neufchâtel; 1 ounce . . . . . 70
Parmesan, grated; 1
tablespoon . . . . . . . . . . . 23
spread, American;
1 ounce . . . . . . . . . . . . . . 82
Swiss (natural); 1 ounce . . 105
**Cherries**
canned (heavy syrup), tart
or sweet, pitted; ½ cup . 104
canned (water pack), tart or
sweet, pitted; ½ cup . . . 52
fresh, sweet, whole;
½ cup . . . . . . . . . . . . . . . 41
**Chewing Gum,** candy-coated;
1 piece . . . . . . . . . . . . . . . . 5
**Chicken**
dark meat, skinned, roasted;
4 ounces . . . . . . . . . . . . 209

dark meat, with skin, fried;
4 ounces . . . . . . . . . . . . 263
light meat, skinned, roasted;
4 ounces . . . . . . . . . . . . 206
light meat, with skin, fried;
4 ounces . . . . . . . . . . . . 234
**Chili Sauce;** 1
tablespoon . . . . . . . . . . . . . 16
**Chives,** chopped; 1
tablespoon . . . . . . . . . . . . . 1
**Chocolate**
bitter; 1 ounce . . . . . . . . . 143
semisweet; 1 ounce . . . . . 144
sweet plain; 1 ounce . . . . . 150
syrup, fudge-type; 1
tablespoon . . . . . . . . . . . 62
syrup, thin-type; 1
tablespoon . . . . . . . . . . . 46
**Clams,** canned in liquor;
½ cup . . . . . . . . . . . . . . . . 57
**Cocoa Powder,** unsweetened;
1 tablespoon . . . . . . . . . . . 14
**Cocoa*;** 6 ounces . . . . . . . . 177
**Coconut,** shredded;
½ cup . . . . . . . . . . . . . . . . 138
**Coffee** . . . . . . . . . . . . . . . . . 2
**Cola,** carbonated beverage;
1 cup . . . . . . . . . . . . . . . . 96
**Cookies**
chocolate chip*; 1 . . . . . . . 93
cream sandwich, chocolate;
1 . . . . . . . . . . . . . . . . . . 49
fig bars; 1 . . . . . . . . . . . . . 50
gingersnap; 1 . . . . . . . . . . 29
sugar*; 1 . . . . . . . . . . . . . 77
vanilla wafer; 3 . . . . . . . . . 42
**Corn**
cream style; ½ cup . . . . . . 105
sweet, cooked; 1 ear
(5x1¾ inches) . . . . . . . . 80
whole kernel; ½ cup . . . . . 137
**Cornstarch;** 1
tablespoon . . . . . . . . . . . . 29
**Corn Syrup;** 1
tablespoon . . . . . . . . . . . . 59

**\*Recipe appears in this book.**

**Crab Meat,** canned;
½ cup .................. 68

**Crackers**
butter, rectangular; 1 ..... 17
cheese, round; 1 ........ 15
graham; 4 small squares .. 58
oyster; 10 ............. 33
rye wafer, crisp; 2
(1⅞x3½ inches) ...... 45
saltine; 2 (2-inch
square) ............. 24

**Cranberry Juice Cocktail;**
1 cup ................. 164

**Cranberry-Orange Relish;**
1 cup ................. 490

**Cranberry Sauce,** sweetened,
canned; 1 cup ......... 404

**Cream**
half-and-half; 1
tablespoon ........... 20
heavy or whipping;
1 tablespoon ......... 53
light; 1 tablespoon ...... 32

**Cucumber;** 6 large slices,
(1 ounce)............. 4

---

# D-G

**Dates,** fresh or dried, pitted;
10 ................... 219

**Doughnut**
cake, with chocolate glaze*;
1..................... 240
yeast*; 1 ............. 167

**Egg**
fried; 1 large .......... 99
scrambled, plain; made with
1 large egg .......... 111
poached, hard- or soft-
cooked; 1 medium .... 72
whole; 1 large ......... 82
whole; 1 medium....... 72

**Eggplant,** cooked, diced;
½ cup ................ 19

**Endive,** raw; 1 cup ...... 10

**Figs**
canned, in syrup; ½ cup .109
dried; 1 large .......... 52
raw; 3 small .......... 96

**Fish**
bass, baked; 3 ounces....219
flounder, baked; 3
ounces...............171
haddock, fried; 3 ounces .141
halibut, broiled; 3 ounces .144
herring, pickled; 3
ounces...............189
ocean perch, fried;
3 ounces.............192
salmon, broiled or baked;
3 ounces ............156
salmon, canned, pink;
½ cup ...............155
sardines, canned, in oil,
drained; 3 ounces .....174
swordfish, broiled; 3
ounces...............138
tuna, canned, in oil,
drained; ½ cup .......158
tuna, canned, in water,
drained; ½ cup .......126

**Fish Stick,** breaded; 1 .... 50

**Frankfurter,** cooked; 1 ...139

**Fruit Cocktail**
canned, in syrup;
½ cup ............... 97
canned, water-pack;
½ cup ...............45

**Garbanzo Beans,** cooked;
½ cup ...............129

**Garlic,** peeled; 1 clove .... 4

**Gelatin Dessert,** plain, ready-
to-serve; ½ cup ......... 71

**Gelatin,** dry, unflavored;
1 envelope ............ 23

**Ginger Ale;** 1 cup ....... 72

**Gooseberries,** raw;
2 cups ................ 59

**Goose,** cooked; 3 ounces .198

**\*Recipe appears in this book.**

## Grapefruit
canned sections, in syrup;
½ cup .............. 89
fresh; ½ medium ........ 45
juice, canned, sweetened;
1 cup ................133
juice, canned, unsweetened;
1 cup ................101
juice, fresh; 1 cup ....... 96
juice, frozen, sweetened,
reconstituted; 1 cup ....117
juice, frozen, unsweetened,
reconstituted; 1 cup ....101

## Grapes
concord, fresh; ½ cup.... 35
green, fresh; ½ cup...... 52
juice, canned; 1 cup ..... 167

---

# H-O

**Ham,** fully cooked, lean;
3 ounces ...............159
**Honey;** 1 tablespoon...... 64
**Honeydew Melon;**
¼ medium (6½-inch
diameter) .............124
**Horseradish,** prepared;
1 tablespoon ........... 6
**Ice Cream,** vanilla
10% fat; 1 cup .........257
ice milk; 1 cup ..........199
soft-serve; 1 cup .......266
**Jam;** 1 tablespoon ........ 54
**Jelly;** 1 tablespoon ....... 49
**Kale,** cooked; ½ cup ...... 22
**Kohlrabi,** cooked; ½ cup . 20
**Lamb,** cooked
loin chop, lean; 3 ounces .159
rib chop, lean; 3 ounces ..180
roast leg, lean; 3 ounces ..158
**Lard;** 1 tablespoon .......117
**Lemon;** 1 medium ....... 20
**Lemonade,** frozen, sweetened,
reconstituted; 1 cup ......107

**Lemon Juice,** 1
tablespoon ........... 4
**Lentils,** cooked; ½ cup ...106
**Lettuce**
Boston; ¼ medium head . 4
iceberg, ¼ medium
compact head ........ 18
leaves; 2 large or 4 small . 10
**Lime;** 1 medium ......... 19
**Lime Juice;** 1 tablespoon . 4
**Liverwurst;** 2 ounces (3¼-
inch diameter, ¼ inch
thick) ................175
**Lobster,** canned; ½ cup ... 69
**Luncheon Meat**
bologna; 1 ounce........ 79
ham, boiled; 1 ounce .... 66
salami, cooked; 1 ounce.. 88
**Macaroni,** cooked; ½ cup. 78
**Malted Milk;** 1 cup .....244
**Maple Syrup;**
1 tablespoon .............50
**Margarine;** 1 tablespoon ..102
**Marshmallows;** 1
ounce ................. 90
**Melba Toast;** 1 slice ..... 15
**Milk**
buttermilk; 1 cup ........ 88
chocolate drink; 1 cup ...190
condensed, sweetened,
undiluted; 1 cup.......982
dried nonfat, instant,
reconstituted; 1 cup.... 81
evaporated, undiluted;
1 cup ................345
skim; 1 cup ............. 88
skim, 2% fat; 1 cup ......145
whole; 1 cup ...........159
**Molasses,** light; 1
tablespoon ............. 50
**Muffin**
bran; 1 ................104
blueberry*; 1 ...........200
plain*; 1 ..............184
**Mushrooms,** raw; 1 cup .. 20

**\*Recipe appears in this book.**

**Mustard Greens,** cooked;
½ cup . . . . . . . . . . . . . . . . 16
**Mustard,** prepared; 1
tablespoon . . . . . . . . . . . . 12
**Nectarine,** fresh; 1
(2½-inch diameter) . . . . . . 88
**Noodles,** chow mein, canned;
1 cup . . . . . . . . . . . . . . . . . 220
**Noodles,** cooked; ½ cup . . 100
**Nuts**
　almonds, shelled, chopped;
　　1 tablespoon . . . . . . . . . . 48
　Brazil nuts; 3 . . . . . . . . . . . 89
　cashews, roasted; 4 or 5 . . 75
　peanuts, roasted, shelled,
　　chopped; 1 tablespoon . 52
　pecans, chopped; 1
　　tablespoon . . . . . . . . . . . 52
　pistachio; 1 ounce . . . . . . . 168
　walnuts, chopped;
　　1 tablespoon . . . . . . . . . . 52
**Oil,** corn; 1 tablespoon . . . . 120
**Okra**
　fresh, cooked; 10 pods
　　(3x⅝ inch) . . . . . . . . . . . 31
　frozen, cooked; ¼ cup . . . 35
**Olives,** green; 4 medium . . 15
**Olives,** ripe; 3 small . . . . . . 15
**Onion**
　cooked; ½ cup . . . . . . . . . 30
　green, without tops;
　　6 small . . . . . . . . . . . . . . 14
　mature, raw, chopped;
　　1 tablespoon . . . . . . . . . . 4
**Orange**
　fresh; 1 medium . . . . . . . . 64
　juice, canned, unsweetened;
　　1 cup . . . . . . . . . . . . . . . 120
　juice, fresh; 1 cup . . . . . . . 112
　juice, frozen concentrate,
　　reconstituted; 1 cup . . . . 122
**Oysters**
　fried; 1 ounce . . . . . . . . . . 68
　raw; ½ cup (6 to 10
　　medium) . . . . . . . . . . . . . 79

***Recipe appears in this book.**

# P-S

**Pancakes**
　buckwheat*; 1 . . . . . . . . . . 127
　plain*; 1 . . . . . . . . . . . . . . 129
**Parsley,** raw; 1
tablespoon . . . . . . . . . . . . . 2
**Parsnips,** cooked; ½ cup . 51
**Peaches**
　canned, in syrup; 1 half and
　　2 tablespoons syrup . . . 96
　canned, water-pack;
　　½ cup . . . . . . . . . . . . . . 35
　fresh; 1 medium . . . . . . . . 38
　frozen, sweetened;
　　½ cup . . . . . . . . . . . . . . 110
**Peanut Butter;** 1
tablespoon . . . . . . . . . . . . . 94
**Pears**
　canned, in syrup; 2 halves
　　and 2 tablespoons
　　syrup . . . . . . . . . . . . . . 91
　fresh; 1 medium . . . . . . . . 100
**Peas,** green, cooked;
½ cup . . . . . . . . . . . . . . . . 57
**Pepper,** green, sweet,
chopped; ½ cup . . . . . . . . 16
**Pickle Relish,** sweet;
1 tablespoon . . . . . . . . . . . 21
**Pickles**
　dill; 1 large (4x1¾
　　inches) . . . . . . . . . . . . . . 15
　sweet; 1 medium
　　(2¾x¾ inch) . . . . . . . . . 30
**Pie** (⅛ of a 9-inch pie)
　apple* . . . . . . . . . . . . . . . 424
　blueberry* . . . . . . . . . . . . 439
　cherry* . . . . . . . . . . . . . . 485
　custard* . . . . . . . . . . . . . . 283
　lemon meringue* . . . . . . . 410
　mincemeat* . . . . . . . . . . . 565
　pumpkin* . . . . . . . . . . . . 304
**Pimiento;** 2 tablespoons . . 7
**Pineapple**
　canned, in syrup; ½ cup . 86

**Pineapple cont'd.**
 canned, water-pack;
  ½ cup . . . . . . . . . . . . . . 48
 fresh, diced; ½ cup . . . . . . 40
 juice, canned, unsweetened;
  1 cup . . . . . . . . . . . . . . . 138
**Plums**
 canned, syrup-pack;
  ½ cup . . . . . . . . . . . . . . . 107
 fresh; 1 (2-inch diameter) . 6
**Pomegranate,** fresh;
 1 medium . . . . . . . . . . . . . 97
**Popcorn,** plain; 1 cup . . . . 23
**Pork,** cooked
 chop, loin center cut, lean
  only; 3 ounces . . . . . . . . 198
 picnic shoulder, fresh, lean;
  3 ounces . . . . . . . . . . . . . 180
 sausage, links or patty;
  3 ounces . . . . . . . . . . . . . 291
**Potato Chips;** 10
 medium . . . . . . . . . . . . . . . 114
**Potatoes**
 baked; 1 medium . . . . . . . 145
 boiled; 1 medium . . . . . . . 173
 French fries*;
  1 medium potato . . . . . . 250
 French fries, frozen, oven
  heated; 10 medium . . . 172
 hashed brown*; ¾ cup . . . 158
 mashed with milk; ½ cup . 108
 sweet, baked; 1 medium . 148
 sweet, canned, vacuum-pack;
  ½ cup . . . . . . . . . . . . . . 108
**Pretzels;** 10 small sticks . . . 23
**Prune Juice,** canned;
 1 cup . . . . . . . . . . . . . . . . . 197
**Prunes,** dried
 cooked, unsweetened;
  ½ cup . . . . . . . . . . . . . . 127
 uncooked, pitted; 1 cup . . 459
**Pudding,** cornstarch
 chocolate*; ½ cup . . . . . . 390
 vanilla*; ½ cup . . . . . . . . 271
**Pumpkin,** canned; 1 cup . . 81
*Recipe appears in this book.*

**Rabbit,** domestic, cooked;
 3 ounces . . . . . . . . . . . . . . 185
**Radishes,** raw; 5 medium . 5
**Raisins;** 1 cup . . . . . . . . . . 419
**Raspberries**
 black, fresh; ½ cup . . . . . . 49
 red, fresh; ½ cup . . . . . . . . 35
 red, frozen, sweetened;
  ½ cup . . . . . . . . . . . . . . . 122
**Rice**
 brown, cooked; ½ cup . . . 116
 quick-cooking, cooked;
  ½ cup . . . . . . . . . . . . . . . 90
 white, cooked; ½ cup . . . . 112
**Roll**
 hard; 1 medium . . . . . . . . 156
 plain; 1 medium . . . . . . . . 119
 sweet; 1 medium . . . . . . . 179
**Rusk;** 1 (3¾-inch diameter,
 ½ inch thick) . . . . . . . . . . 38
**Rutabagas,** cooked;
 ½ cup . . . . . . . . . . . . . . . . . 30
**Salad Dressing**
 blue cheese; 1 tablespoon 76
 French; 1 tablespoon . . . . 66
 Italian; 1 tablespoon . . . . . 83
 mayonnaise; 1
  tablespoon . . . . . . . . . . . 101
 mayonnaise-type; 1
  tablespoon . . . . . . . . . . . 65
 Russian; 1 tablespoon . . . . 74
 Thousand Island; 1
  tablespoon . . . . . . . . . . . 80
**Sauerkraut,** canned;
 ½ cup . . . . . . . . . . . . . . . . . 21
**Scallops,** cooked; 3
 ounces . . . . . . . . . . . . . . . . 99
**Sherbet,** orange; ½ cup . . 130
**Shortening;** 1 tablespoon . 111
**Shrimp**
 canned; 3 ounces . . . . . . . 100
 French-fried; 3 ounces . . . 192
 boiled; 3 ounces . . . . . . . . 98
**Soup,** condensed, canned,
 diluted with water unless

## Soup cont'd.

specified otherwise

beef bouillon broth,
consommé; 1 cup ... 31
beef noodle; 1 cup .... 67
chicken noodle; 1 cup.. 62
clam chowder, Manhattan-
style; 1 cup ........ 81
cream of celery, diluted
with milk; 1 cup .....169
cream of mushroom, diluted
with milk; 1 cup .....216
split pea; 1 cup .......145
tomato; 1 cup........ 88
tomato, diluted with milk;
1 cup .............173
vegetable with beef broth;
1 cup ............. 78

**Soy Sauce;** 1 tablespoon . 12

**Spinach**

frozen, chopped, cooked;
½ cup ............... 23
raw, torn; 1 cup ........ 14

**Squash**

summer, cooked, diced;
½ cup ............. 15
winter, baked, mashed;
½ cup ............. 65

**Strawberries**

fresh, whole; ½ cup ..... 28
frozen, sweetened, whole;
½ cup ...............117

**Sugar**

brown, packed; 1
tablespoon .......... 34
granulated; 1 tablespoon . 46
powdered; 1 tablespoon .. 31

# T-Z

**Tangerine;** 1 medium .... 39

**Tartar Sauce;** 1
tablespoon ............ 74

**Tea** ...................... 0

**Tomatoes**

canned; ½ cup ......... 25
fresh; 1 medium ......... 27
juice, canned; 1 cup ..... 46
sauce; 1 cup ........... 70

**Turkey,** roasted; 3 slices
(4x2x¼ inch) ...........162

**Turnip Greens,** cooked;
½ cup ................ 15

**Turnips,** cooked, diced;
½ cup ................ 18

**Veal,** cooked
cutlet; 3 ounces .........184
loin chop; 3 ounces ......198

**Vegetable Juice Cocktail;**
1 cup ................ 41

**Vinegar;** 1 tablespoon .... 2

**Waffle*;** 1 (9x9-inch) .....734

**Water Chestnuts;** 4 ..... 55

**Watermelon;** 1 wedge
(8x4 inches) ............111

**Yogurt**

low-fat fruit-flavored;
½ cup ...............115
plain, made from skim milk;
½ cup ............... 61

**Zwieback;** 1 piece ....... 30

**\*Recipe appears in this book.**

# Food Shopping Tips

## Shopping List

One of the best times to make out your shopping list is when you plan menus. By doing so, you will have the ingredients you need to prepare recipes, and you also can check your cupboards for ingredients that you already have. Use your newspaper's food ads to help you make out your shopping list. Not only can the ads spark ideas for menus, but you may be able to plan several meals around the weekly "good buys."

Divide your shopping list so that you group like items, perhaps even listing them in the order in which they appear in your favorite grocery store. Besides the food items and the specified amounts needed, list any special advertised prices and the brands of these specials. Also, if you have coupons for any of the foods on your list, be sure to note this information, too. However, when you get to the store, compare prices to see if the "special" or the coupon brand is really the best buy.

Perhaps you're the type of grocery shopper who lists only food items that you know you need and then buys a variety of foods around which you plan the daily meals. This method has its advantages and disadvantages. One advantage is that you can compare food costs at the store and plan meals around the best buys that you see. Also, you might see something that may create a menu idea. A disadvantage is that you may find an essential recipe ingredient missing as you start to prepare the dish, necessitating another trip to the store.

## Budget Thoughts

If you're watching your food budget, you can cut down on the cost of groceries without cutting out good nutrition. Become a comparison shopper. For example, compare canned fruits and vegetables with fresh and frozen items to see which is the most economical in terms of cost per serving. You may find that canned items cost less.

And when considering cost per serving or per unit, compare foods in various-size packages. If buying in quantity, consider storage space—shelf, freezer, and refrigerator. It's not a bargain if part of the item is discarded. So, make sure that leftovers are planned into other meals.

Cost per serving is especially important with a high-ticket item such as meat. The cheapest price per pound is not always the best meat buy, because you may get fewer servings due to more fat and bone, depending on the cut. Besides figuring cost per serving to cut down on your meat costs, you might plan smaller portions. Remember, two to three ounces of cooked meat is a nutritionally adequate serving. To make a serving of meat seem like more, prepare it in casseroles and stews. Also, vary the diet by including meatless main dishes in your menus.

Stick to a shopping list and avoid impulse purchases. However, keep your eyes open for *useful* unadvertised specials. Plan to buy fruits and vegetables in season and items sold at lower prices during peak periods of the normal production cycle.

## Shopping Trips

Choose a time of the week when the store isn't crowded, yet the shelves are fully stocked. It's best not to shop when you're hungry or you may come home with some unnecessary food that you just couldn't pass up.

Take your time at the store and be a label reader. Besides the nutrition information, you should consider the grade and quality of the canned goods you buy, keeping in mind their intended use. Compare the store and generic (no-name) brands of canned or packaged food with national brands; if they meet your quality needs, you can save money by using them.

## Nutrition Labeling

Read the labels on packaged foods. The Food and Drug Administration requires that some labels include nutrition information and percentages of U.S. Recommended Daily Allowances (U.S. RDAs) for certain nutrients. This is required on foods to which a nutrient has been added and that are advertised as having special nutritional qualities. The U.S. RDAs are based on the levels of protein, vitamins, and minerals needed by most people to maintain good health.

# Storage

Use the freezer for long-term storage and keep it set at 0°F. or lower for maximum food preservation. The best place to thaw frozen foods is in the refrigerator or in a microwave oven. Or, thaw food in a sealed bag under cold running water.

For perishable foods that are to be used within a few days, use the refrigerator for storage. Set the refrigerator temperature between 36°F. and 40°F.

Store staples such as flour and sugar and sturdy foods such as canned goods in a cool, dry, well ventilated place away from sunlight. The best storage temperature is between 50°F. and 70°F.

## Preparing Food for Storage

Keep all utensils and counters clean. And make sure that cooked meat or poultry doesn't touch equipment used for raw meat.

**Cooked foods:** Cover and chill or freeze cooked foods and leftovers promptly. For freezing, use moisture-vaporproof materials such as freezer paper or heavy foil, or use freezer containers.

**Fresh fruits and vegetables:** Store these

in the refrigerator crisper. Keep items such as potatoes and dry onions in a cool, well ventilated place.

**Meat, poultry, and fish:** Chill meat and poultry as purchased in clear packaging. To freeze, remove the clear packaging; wrap tightly in moisture-vaporproof material. (Prepackaged meat and poultry can be frozen for one to two weeks without rewrapping.) Tightly wrap fresh fish in moisture-vaporproof material before freezing or refrigerating.

**Eggs:** Keep eggs in the covered egg carton in the refrigerator. You can chill leftover separated eggs in tightly covered containers (cover yolks with cold water). To freeze eggs, break into a bowl, stir to combine, and add 1½ teaspoons sugar *or* corn syrup *or* ⅛ teaspoon salt per ¼ cup whole eggs (two whole) or ¼ cup yolks (four yolks). Egg whites require no additions. Use freezer containers. Thaw in the refrigerator; use within 24 hours. Allow for any added sugar, corn syrup, or salt when using in recipes.

**Dairy products:** Store cheese, milk, and butter, tightly covered in the refrigerator. Chill strong-flavored cheese in a tightly covered glass container.

| Food | Maximum Storage Times | |
|---|---|---|
| | **Refrigerator** (36°F. to 40°F.) | **Freezer** (0°F. or lower) |
| **Meat** | | |
| Beef | 2 to 4 days | 6 to 12 months |
| Pork | 2 to 4 days | 3 to 6 months |
| Ground Meats | 1 to 2 days | 3 months |
| Ham | 7 days | 2 months |
| Bacon | 5 to 7 days | 1 month |
| Frankfurters | 4 to 5 days | 1 month |
| Fresh Pork Sausage | 7 days | 2 months |
| Luncheon Meats | 7 days | Do not freeze |
| Lamb | 2 to 4 days | 6 to 9 months |
| Veal | 2 to 4 days | 6 to 9 months |
| Variety Meats | 1 to 2 days | 3 to 4 months |
| Cooked Meats | 4 to 5 days | 2 to 3 months |

| Food | Maximum Storage Times | |
|------|-----------------------|---|
| | Refrigerator (36°F. to 40°F.) | Freezer (0°F. or lower) |
| **Poultry** | | |
| Chicken, whole | 1 to 2 days | 12 months |
| Chicken, pieces | 1 to 2 days | 9 months |
| Turkey, whole | 1 to 2 days (thawed) | 12 months |
| Poultry, cooked (without liquid) | 1 to 2 days | 1 month |
| **Fish** | | |
| Fat fish | 1 to 2 days | 4 months |
| Lean fish | 1 to 2 days | 8 months |
| **Eggs (see above)** | | |
| Whole eggs | 4 weeks | 9 to 12 months |
| Whites | 7 days | 9 to 12 months |
| Yolks | 2 to 3 days | 9 to 12 months |
| **Cheese** | | |
| Hard cheese | Several months | 6 months |
| Soft cheese | 2 weeks | 4 months |
| Cottage cheese | 5 days | Do not freeze |
| **Ice Cream** | | 1 to 3 months |
| **Butter** | 7 days | 3 to 6 months |

# Freezing Cooked Food

Use your freezer to store all types of prepared foods. Keep an inventory of items in the freezer and use foods within their recommended storage times.

Here are a few tips to guide you with recipe selection and preparation:

• For "wet" vegetables such as spinach, drain well, pressing out excess moisture.

• **Use fat sparingly in sauces—it doesn't combine well when reheated. Stirring may help during reheating.**

• **Freeze most casseroles before baking, especially when ingredients are cooked. Exceptions include dishes that contain uncooked rice, raw vegetables, or uncooked meat that has been frozen and thawed.**

• **Add crumb toppers at reheating time.**

• **Cool foods quickly before wrapping for the freezer. Place the pan of cooked food in ice water to cool to room temperature.**

• **Package foods properly. Use freezer containers or moisture-vaporproof material such as freezer paper, heavy foil, or plastic freezer bags. Or, cover other containers with a lid; fix tape around edges to make a leakproof seal. Allow headspace (room for food to expand) when packing liquid or semiliquid foods.**

• **Be sure to label packages with their contents and the date. Freeze at 0°F.**

• **Prepare foods for serving following the directions below, or check your microwave oven cook book for directions.**

| Food | Preparation for Freezing | How to Serve | Storage Time |
|---|---|---|---|
| **Breads** | | | |
| Biscuits and Muffins | Bake as usual; cool. Seal in a freezer container or wrap with moisture-vaporproof material; seal and label. | Thaw in a package at room temperature 1 hour or reheat in foil in a 300° oven 20 minutes. | 2 months |
| Yeast breads and rolls | Bake as usual; cool. Wrap with moisture-vaporproof material; seal and label. (Frost sweet rolls after thawing and heating, if desired.) For Brown-and-Serve Rolls, see page 125. | Thaw in package at room temperature or reheat yeast rolls in foil in a 300° oven about 15 minutes and the bread about 40 minutes. | 4 to 8 months |

| Food | Preparation for Freesing | How to Serve | Storage Time |
|------|--------------------------|--------------|--------------|
| **Cakes** | | | |
| General | Bake cake or cupcakes as usual. Remove from pan; cool. (If cake is frosted, freeze it before wrapping.) Wrap in a moisture-vaporproof material; seal and label. (Unfrosted cakes and cupcakes freeze better frosted and filled cakes may become soggy.) | Thaw at room temperature (allow 3 hours for a large cake, 1 hour for layers, and 40 minutes for cupcakes). Thaw frosted or filled cakes in the refrigerator. | 6 months |
| Cake frostings and fillings | *Recommended for freezing:* Cream cheese and butter cream frostings and fillings. Seal in freezer containers; label. *Not recommended for freezing:* Soft frostings, frostings made with egg whites, and cream fillings. | Thaw, covered, in the refrigerator. | 6 months |
| **Cookies** | | | |
| Unbaked, general | Pack unbaked dough in freezer containers; seal and label. *Not recommended for freezing:* Meringue-type cookies. | Thaw in container at room temperature till dough is soft. Bake as usual. | 6 months |
| Refrigerator cookies | Shape unbaked dough into a roll. Wrap in moisture-vaporproof material. | Thaw slightly. Slice roll; bake. | 6 months |
| Baked, general | Bake as usual; cool. Pack in containers with waxed paper between layers. | Thaw in package at room temperature. | 6 to 12 months |
| **Pastry** | Pastry and graham cracker piecrusts freeze satisfactorily. Prepare pastry; fit into pie plate. Bake, if desired. Wrap with moisture-vaporproof material. Seal; label. | Thaw baked pastry in a 325° oven 8 to 10 minutes. For unbaked frozen pastry shells, bake as for fresh shells. | 2 months |
| **Pies** | | | |
| Fruit, general two-crust | *Unbaked:* Treat light-colored fruits with ascorbic acid color keeper to prevent the fruit from darkening. Prepare pie as usual but do not slit top crust. Use a freezer-to-oven or metal pie plate. Cover top with an inverted paper plate to protect crust. Wrap with moisture-vaporproof material; seal and label. If desired, place in a sturdy container. | Unwrap; cut vent holes in top crust. Cover edge of crust with foil. Without thawing, bake in a 450° oven for 15 minutes, then in a 375° oven for 15 minutes. Uncover edge and bake about 30 to 35 minutes longer or till done. | 3 months |
| | *Baked:* Bake as usual in a glass or metal pie plate. Cool and package as above for unbaked pies. | Thaw in package at room temperature or covered with foil in a 300° oven. | 2 to 3 months |

| Food | Preparation for Freezing | How to Serve | Storage Time |
|------|--------------------------|--------------|--------------|
| **Main Dishes** | | | |
| Casseroles: Poultry, fish, or meat with vegetables or pasta | Cool mixture quickly. Turn into a freezer-to-oven casserole dish. Cover tightly. Seal and label. | Bake, covered, in a 400° oven for half of baking time; uncover for second half of baking time. Allow 1¾ hours for one quart. | 3 to 6 months |
| Meatballs with tomato sauce | Cook till done; cool quickly. Ladle into freezer jars or containers, allowing headspace (don't use metal or foil for acidic foods). Seal and label. | Heat in a heavy saucepan, over low heat, stirring frequently. Or, defrost overnight in the refrigerator. Heat. | 3 months |
| Stews and soups | Select vegetables that freeze well. Omit potatoes. Green pepper and garlic become more intense in flavor. Omit salt and thickening if stew is to be kept longer than 2 months. Do not completely cook vegetables. Cool quickly; turn into a freezer container. Cover tightly. Seal and label. | Heat from the frozen state in a heavy saucepan over low heat. Separate with a fork during thawing. Do not overcook. Season and thicken heated stew before serving. | 6 months |
| Sandwiches | These freeze well: Cream cheese, egg, meat and poultry, tuna or salmon, and peanut butter. Spread bread with softened butter; fill. Wrap tightly. Not recommended: Lettuce, celery, tomatoes, cucumber, watercress, jelly, and mayonnaise. | Thaw sandwiches in wrapping at room temperature about 3 hours. | 1 month |

# Fruits & Vegetables

**Use this guide when planning fresh fruits and vegetables for your daily meals. Take advantage of best buys during peak seasons to stretch your food budget. Buy extras when they're most plentiful, and can or freeze them for off-season enjoyment.**

| Fruits | Plentiful or Near Peak | Vegetables | Plentiful or Near Peak |
|---|---|---|---|
| Apples | October through December | Beets | June through September |
| Apricots | June and July | Broccoli | November through March |
| Cantaloupe | June through September | Cauliflower | October and November |
| Cherries | June and July | Celery | October through June |
| Cranberries | October through December | Corn | June through September |
| Grapefruit | January through April | Cucumbers | May through August |
| Grapes | August through November | Green beans | May through August |
| Lemons | June and July | Mushrooms | November through January |
| Oranges | December through May | Peppers, green | June through August |
| Peaches | June through September | Potatoes, sweet | October through December |
| Pears | August through November | Radishes | March through May |
| Rhubarb | February through June | Rutabagas, Turnips | November through January |
| Strawberries | April through June | Spinach | March and April |
| Tangerines | November through January | Squash, summer | June through August |
| Watermelons | May through August | Squash, winter | September through November |
| Bananas, cabbage, carrots, onions, lettuce, and potatoes usually are in good supply year-round. | | Tomatoes | May through August |

Sources: U.S. Department of Agriculture;
United Fresh Fruit and Vegetable Association.

# Ingredient Equivalents

**Many foods change measure when you crumble, cook, shred, or chop them. Use this guide to determine ingredient equivalents and to convert a weight or item into a measured product. Listed below are some common before and after measurements.**

| Food | Amount Before Preparation | Approximate Measure After Preparation |
|---|---|---|
| **Cereals** | | |
| Macaroni | 1 cup (3½ ounces) | 2½ cups cooked |
| Noodles, medium | 3 cups (4 ounces) | 3 cups cooked |
| Spaghetti | 8 ounces | 4 cups cooked |
| Long grain rice | 1 cup (7 ounces) | 3 cups cooked |
| Quick-cooking rice | 1 cup (3 ounces) | 2 cups cooked |
| Popcorn | ¼ cup | 5 cups cooked |

| Food | Amount Before Preparation | Approximate Measure After Preparation |
|---|---|---|
| **Crumbs** | | |
| Bread | 1 slice | ¾ cup soft or ¼ cup fine dry crumbs |
| Saltine crackers | 28 squares | 1 cup finely crushed |
| Rich round crackers | 24 crackers | 1 cup finely crushed |
| Graham crackers | 14 squares | 1 cup finely crushed |
| Gingersnaps | 15 cookies | 1 cup finely crushed |
| Vanilla wafers | 22 cookies | 1 cup finely crushed |
| **Fruits** | | |
| Apples | 1 medium | 1 cup sliced |
| Apricots | 1 medium | ¼ cup sliced |
| Avocados | 1 medium | 1¼ cups sliced |
| Bananas | 1 medium | ⅓ cup mashed |
| Cherries, red | 1 pound | 2 cups pitted |
| Lemons | 1 medium | 3 tablespoons juice; 2 teaspoons shredded peel |
| Limes | 1 medium | 2 tablespoons juice; 1 teaspoon shredded peel |
| Oranges | 1 medium | ¼ to ⅓ cup juice; 4 teaspoons shredded peel |
| Peaches, Pears | 1 medium | ½ cup sliced |
| Strawberries | 4 cups whole | 4 cups sliced |
| **Vegetables** | | |
| Beans and peas, dried | 1 pound (about 2½ cups) | 6 cups cooked |
| Cabbage | 1 pound (1 small) | 5 cups shredded |
| Carrots, without tops | 1 pound (6 to 8 medium) | 3 cups shredded or 2½ cups diced |
| Celery | 1 medium bunch | 4½ cups chopped |
| Corn | 1 medium ear | ½ cup cut from cob |
| Green beans | 1 pound (3 cups) | 2½ cups cooked, cut up |
| Green onions | 1 bunch (7) | ½ cup sliced |
| Green peppers | 1 large | 1 cup diced |
| Mushrooms | 1 pound (6 cups) | 6 cups sliced or 2 cups cooked |
| Onions | 1 medium | ½ cup chopped |
| Potatoes | 1 medium | ⅔ cup cubed or ½ cup mashed |
| Spinach | 1 pound (12 cups) | 1½ cups cooked |
| Tomatoes | 1 medium | ½ cup cooked |
| **Nuts** | | |
| Almonds | 1 pound in shell | 1¼ cups shelled |
| Pecans | 1 pound in shell | 2 cups shelled |
| Walnuts | 1 pound in shell | 1½ cups shelled |
| **Miscellaneous** | | |
| Cheese, Swiss or American | 4 ounces | 1 cup shredded or cubed |
| Eggs | 1 large | 3 tablespoons egg |
| Egg whites | 1 large | 2 tablespoons white |
| Egg yolks | 1 large | 1 tablespoon yolk |
| Whipping cream | 1 cup | 2 cups whipped |
| Ground beef | 1 pound raw | 2¾ cups cooked |
| Boneless meat | 1 pound raw | 2 cups cooked, cubed |
| Cooked meat | 1 pound | 3 cups diced |

# Preparation Helps

Before you begin your recipe preparation, read through the recipe to make sure you understand it. If any cooking terms are unfamiliar, look them up on pages 864–68 before you start. Next, gather all the ingredients you'll need for the recipe, making sure that you have enough of each ingredient. Do any necessary preparations— chopping, draining, toasting, etc.—and assemble the cooking equipment you'll need.

Here are some preparation tips that will make your cooking easier and more fun.

## Tips for Baked Products

Proper preparation techniques, accurately measured ingredients, a carefully followed recipe, and correct pan sizes all contribute to perfect baked products.

**Cakes:** When a recipe calls for shortening, don't use butter, margarine, lard, or oils. If a recipe calls for butter, margarine may be used.

• Place cake pans as near to the center of the oven as possible. Don't let pans touch each other or the oven sides.

**Cookies:** Cool cookies on racks to prevent sogginess.

• Use a cool cookie sheet to bake each batch. This helps prevent spreading.

**Breads:** To test a yeast loaf for doneness, tap the crust with your finger. If you hear a hollow sound, this is an indication that the bread is done.

• After baking, immediately remove a yeast bread loaf from the pan; place it on a wire rack to cool. This keeps the loaf from steaming.

Many quick bread loaves should cool in the pan about 10 minutes before removing to a wire rack.

• For evenly shaped, straight-sided baking powder biscuits, press the biscuit cutter straight down through the dough. Do not twist the cutter or flatten

the edges of cut biscuits.
• To keep baked muffins
from steaming and becoming
soggy, tip them to one
side in the muffin pan after
baking.

**Pies:** For two-crust pies,
cut slits in the top crust in
a decorative design, or, for a
fancier design, cut out
small pieces of pastry with
hors d'oeuvre cutters or
small cookie cutters. The cuts
allow steam to escape,
keep the underside of the
crust from becoming
soggy, and prevent steam
pressure from tearing the
crust.

# Crumbs and Croutons

**Soft bread crumbs:** Tear
slices of fresh bread into
crumbs. Or, tear bread into
quarters. Place a few at a
time in a blender container,
cover and blend till
coarsely chopped.

**Fine dry bread
crumbs:** Toast bread slices
in a 300° oven till crisp and
dry. Crush with a rolling pin.
Or, place in a blender
container; cover and blend
till finely crushed.

**Buttered crumbs:** Add
1 tablespoon melted butter
or margarine to each ¼ cup
dry crumbs or ¾ cup soft

bread crumbs. Toss to coat
the crumbs with butter.

**Croutons:** Brush bread
slices lightly with cooking
oil or melted butter, if
desired. Cut into ½-inch
cubes. For seasoned
croutons, sprinkle with
garlic powder or crushed
dried herbs. Spread bread
cubes in a shallow baking
pan. Bake in a 300° oven
for 20 to 25 minutes or till
cubes are dry; stir at least
once.

# Using a Pastry Cloth

Use a pastry cloth for rolling
out cookies and kneading
bread dough, as well as for
rolling out pastry. To
prepare the cloth, sprinkle it
with flour, then rub the
flour in. As you work, you
can add more flour, but
only if the dough is sticking.
After using, wash the
pastry cloth. Or, if it doesn't
appear fat soaked, store it
in a tightly closed plastic bag
in a cool place or in the
refrigerator.

# Preheating the Oven

At one time, all recipes
recommended preheating the

oven. But with rising energy costs, avoiding this step is often a good idea. Cakes, breads, cookies, and piecrusts generally are best when baked in a preheated oven. However, for casseroles and roasts, preheating is not necessary. *(The recipe timings in this cook book are based on a preheated oven, so you may need to add several extra minutes to the baking time if you do not preheat your oven.)*

# Basic Techniques

**Understanding some basic cooking techniques is essential for preparing successful recipes. On this and the next few pages are illustrated directions for some basic cooking tasks. By mastering these techniques, you'll make your cooking easier and more enjoyable.**

**Clarifying butter:** Melt the butter over low heat in a heavy saucepan without stirring. When the butter is completely melted, you will see a clear oily layer atop a milky layer. Slowly pour the clear liquid into a dish, as shown, leaving the milky layer in the saucepan. Discard the milky pan liquid. The clear liquid is the clarified butter.

**Separating eggs:** Gently crack the egg in the center with a knife. Over a bowl, slip yolk back and

forth from one shell half to the other, as shown, allowing the white to fall into the bowl. If the yolk breaks into the whites, remove all yolk traces, since they can prevent the whites from whipping.

Cold eggs are easier to separate; bring to room temperature before beating.

onion slices together with one hand, as shown, carefully slice in the other direction. Use a very sharp chef's knife to make the job easier. This technique also works well for chopping other vegetables, such as potatoes and carrots.

**Melting chocolate** (unsweetened, semisweet, or sweet): Melt chocolate over low heat in a small heavy saucepan, as shown. Stir the chocolate often to avoid scorching it. If the recipe calls for cooled chocolate, simply remove pan from heat and let it stand till lukewarm. Scrape the chocolate from the saucepan with a rubber spatula.

**Chopping onions:** Cut onions in half, then use the cut side as a stable base. Slice the onion in one direction. Then, holding

**Peeling tomatoes:** Spear a tomato with a fork and plunge it into boiling water for 30 seconds. The skin will split. Immediately dip the tomato into cold water. Using a sharp paring knife, pull off the tomato skin, as shown. Use this method of peeling tomatoes only when you are going to cook the

tomatoes, since it softens the flesh.

Peel peaches and apricots in a similar manner.

**Caramelizing sugar:**
Sugar will melt into a golden liquid as it is heated. Place the sugar in a heavy skillet or saucepan. Heat and stir over low heat till the sugar melts and turns a golden brown.

To make a syrup from this melted sugar (it will harden when cooled), add hot water *very slowly,* stirring constantly and using the specified proportions.

**Sectioning grapefruit or oranges:** Begin by cutting off the peel and the

white membrane, using a very sharp utility knife, or a serrated knife for peeling citrus fruits. Remove the sections by cutting into the center of the fruit between one section and the membrane. Then turn the knife and slide the knife down the other side of the section next to the membrane, as shown.

Remove any seeds. Allow the grapefruit or orange sections to fall into a bowl along with any juice.

**Steaming vegetables:**
Place desired vegetables in a steamer basket. The steamer basket will prevent the vegetables from coming in contact with the water.

Then, place the basket of vegetables over (but not touching) boiling water in a saucepan, as shown. Cover the saucepan and steam vegetables for the time specified in the recipe or till tender.

**Cutting up a fresh pineapple:** First, remove the crown by holding the pineapple in one hand and the crown in the other; twist in opposite directions.

Next, trim the top and the base. Cut off wide strips of peel with a knife, starting at the top of the fruit and working down.

Remove the eyes by making narrow wedge-shaped grooves in the pineapple, as shown. Cut diagonally around the fruit, following the pattern of the eyes. Cut into spears or chunks.

**Using fresh garlic:** Mince or crush a garlic clove so that its strong flavor and aroma are evenly distributed throughout a food. The finer the pieces, the stronger the flavor. To crush garlic, place a peeled garlic clove in a garlic press, as shown, then clamp the handles together. Be sure to clean the press thoroughly after each use. To mince garlic, use a sharp utility knife to cut it into very tiny, irregularly shaped pieces.

**Cutting up apples:** Wash apples. Halve, and then cut into quarters. Remove the section of core from each quarter; slice fruit.

To keep apple slices (or any fruit) from turning brown after being cut, dip the fruit into a bowl of lemon juice, as shown. Or, use orange juice, grapefruit juice, or an ascorbic acid color keeper. Then drain the fruit on paper toweling.

**Stir-frying:** To use a traditional Oriental cooking wok, place the wok ring stand over the largest

burner on your range. *For gas ranges,* place the ring with the wide end down. *For electric ranges,* place the ring with the wide end up. Set the wok securely on the ring stand; warm over high heat.

Stir-fry the food over high heat using a long-handled spoon or spatula to frequently lift and turn the food with a folding motion, as shown. Maintain high heat so the food cooks quickly.

**Using a whisk:** Foods become frothy and smooth when beaten with a whisk. Most whisks are made of wire loops fastened to a handle, but some are

made of wood. Whisks range in size from tiny ones, suitable for beating one egg, to large balloon-shaped whisks for beating doughs. A whisk is especially useful in preparing smooth egg-thickened sauces, as shown. This utensil also is used to beat egg whites in a copper bowl.

**Using whole spices:** Allspice, cinnamon, cloves, black pepper, and nutmeg are available in whole form. Whole spices are ideal for foods that cook slowly. To use whole spices, place them in a cheesecloth bag for easy removal. Grate whole nutmeg before using. A special nutmeg grater is available for this job, as shown. Use freshly grated nutmeg just as you would ground nutmeg.

**Using a chef's knife:** Any chopping job becomes easier with proper use of a chef's knife. The knife is

designed with enough room to grasp the handle so that the fingers don't touch the chopping board while you chop. Grasp the handle firmly; lightly place the fingers of the other hand on the tip of the blade. To efficiently chop, rock the knife handle up and down, keeping the tip of the knife on the cutting board.

**Using a mortar and pestle:** Dried herbs, aromatic seeds, garlic cloves, and nuts will release more of their flavor when crushed with a mortar and pestle. The mortar is a deep bowl in which the ingredients are placed. The tool used for

crushing is the pestle. For a uniform grind, crush a small amount at a time. These tools also are useful for blending together several different seasonings.

**Snipping fresh herbs:** Put the fresh herb in a container, such as a 1-cup glass measure, and snip it with kitchen shears. To substitute fresh herbs for dried, use three times more of the fresh herb. To freeze fresh herbs, wash young tender leaves thoroughly in several changes of cool water. Pat the leaves dry with paper toweling. Seal small amounts of the leaves in freezer bags, foil, or clear plastic wrap. Staple all packages of the same herb to cardboard; label and freeze.

**Using a pastry bag:** This flexible cone-shaped bag, often fitted with a

fancy tip, can be filled with frosting or whipped cream for decorating foods. The

bag also can be filled with a soft dough to form various shapes for baking.

Neatly fill the pastry bag by folding back the top of the bag about 1½ inches. Spoon the desired mixture into the bag, filling it only about two-thirds full. Unfold the top, twist closed, and squeeze to release the contents.

# Ingredients & How to Use Them

Here's a glossary of some basic ingredients and the role they play in the foods you prepare.

## Flour

**All-purpose flour** is a blend of hard- and soft-wheat flours. The combination allows it to be used in all types of baked goods, as well as for thickening.

**Self-rising flour** is an all-purpose flour that contains added leavening and salt. It may be substituted for all-purpose flour in quick bread recipes, but the salt, baking powder, and baking soda must be omitted.

**Cake flour** is a flour made from a softer wheat. It is used for making tender, delicate cakes.

Other types of flour include whole wheat, rye, and buckwheat flours.

## Thickeners

**Flour** (all-purpose) may be used to thicken gravies, sauces, and puddings. It gives sauces an opaque appearance.

**Cornstarch** is used to

thicken sauces and puddings when a translucent product is desired. Its thickening power is about twice that of flour.

**Tapioca** may be used to thicken pie fillings and puddings.

**Eggs** may be used to thicken mixtures and to add richness.

## Fats and Oils

Fats and oils differ in consistency and function. Fats are solid at room temperature, while oils are liquid. Both make baked products tender, add flavor, and can be used for frying.

**Hydrogenated shortenings** (referred to in recipes as shortening) are composed of vegetable or animal fat or a combination of the two. They are processed to give the desired flavor, consistency, storage quality, and functional characteristics. This makes them solid at room temperature and ideal for baking, but less suitable for frying.

**Lard** is a rendered pork fat. It is good for pastry and biscuits.

**Butter** is made from milk fat. Since it is 80% fat and 20% moisture and solids, it has different characteristics from other fats. Butter lends flavor to baked goods as well as some shallow-fried foods. However, butter is not suitable for deep-fat frying.

**Margarine,** like butter, is only 80% fat. It is made from vegetable oil to simulate the characteristics of butter.

**Oils** are fats that are liquid at room temperature. They are a good choice for frying, but should not be interchanged with solid fats for baking purposes, since they cannot be creamed to hold air. However, certain recipes for baked goods are designed specifically for oil.

## Sweeteners

Besides adding flavor, sweeteners affect the tenderness of baked goods and the consistency of puddings and sauces.

**Granulated sugar** is a basic sweetener made from sugar cane or sugar beets.

**Powdered sugar or confectioners' sugar** is granulated sugar crushed and screened till grains are tiny. Starch is then added to keep lumping to a minimum. It's designed for use in uncooked frostings and to dust over baked products.

**Brown sugar** is a less-refined form of granulated sugar. It derives a special flavor and moistness from the molasses that clings to the granules. Dark brown sugar has a stronger flavor than light brown sugar. A granulated form is available, but it can't be substituted for regular brown sugar because its moisture content is lower.

**Honey** is made by bees from the nectar of flowers. It is sweeter than sugar, and adds a characteristic flavor.

**Syrups** include corn, cane, sorghum, maple, and maple-flavored syrups, and molasses. They are used as toppings as well as recipe ingredients.

**Artificial sweeteners** sweeten foods without the use of natural sugars. They cannot be substituted for sugar in baked foods because they do not have the other properties of sugar. However, they are widely used to sweeten beverages and breakfast cereals.

# Leavenings

Leavenings are ingredients that cause a food to rise in the oven or on the griddle.

**Baking soda** reacts with the acid in food to form carbon dioxide gas. The soda and acid begin to react as soon as liquid is added, so a product containing soda should be baked immediately.

**Baking powder** is a combination of baking soda and an acidic ingredient. It does not produce its full degree of leavening until heated, so the unbaked product is more stable than one with soda.

**Yeast** is a microscopic plant that produces carbon dioxide from starch or sugar when placed in suitable conditions for growth. It can be purchased in the active dry or compressed form.

# Dairy Products

**Homogenized whole milk** has been processed. Its fat content is at least 3.25%. **Skim milk** has less than 0.5% fat. **Low-fat milk** has 0.5% to 2% fat.

**Nonfat dry milk** is milk with both fat and water removed. It's processed to mix easily with water.
**Evaporated milk** has 60% of the water removed, and is processed in cans.
**Sweetened condensed milk** has about half the water removed and a large amount of sugar added.

**Buttermilk** is the liquid left after butter-making. More common is cultured buttermilk, a product made by adding a bacteria to skim milk.

**Yogurt** is a creamy product made by fermenting milk.

**Whipping cream** contains 30% to 40% fat.
**Light cream** (half-and-half) contains 10% to 30% fat. **Dairy sour cream** is a commercially cultured light cream.

form streaks of white and yellow.

**Beaten eggs** are whole eggs beaten with a fork till the whites and yolks are blended and no streaks of white and yellow remain.

**Well-beaten eggs** are whole eggs beaten with an electric mixer or rotary beater till they are very light in color and texture.

## Eggs

Eggs have many functions in cooking. They can thicken mixtures, bind ingredients, or form a structure in baked goods.

**Slightly beaten eggs** are whole eggs beaten with a fork just long enough to break up the yolks and

**Egg whites beaten to soft peaks** are whites beaten with an electric mixer or rotary beater till they form peaks with tips that curl over when the beaters are lifted.

**Thick and lemon-colored yolks** are yolks beaten with an electric mixer till very thick and lemon colored. They flow in a thick stream when the beaters are lifted.

**Egg whites beaten to stiff peaks** are whites beaten with an electric mixer or rotary beater till they form peaks that stand straight when the beaters are lifted.

# How to Measure

**Measurements are important for consistent results, but all ingredients are not measured in the same way. Learn to measure properly and accurately to guarantee a successful product every time.**

**To measure liquids,**
use a standard glass or clear
plastic measuring cup.
Place it on a level surface
and bend down so your
eye is level with the marking
you wish to read, as
shown. Fill the cup to the
marking.

Don't lift the cup off the
counter to your eye, since
your hand is not as steady or
as level as a counter top.

measure butter or margarine
is to use a quarter-pound
stick for ½ cup, half of a
stick for ¼ cup, or an
eighth of a stick for 1
tablespoon.

**To measure dry
ingredients,** use a dry
measure with exactly the
capacity you wish to
measure. Pile the ingredient
lightly into the cup with a
spoon, then level off with a
metal spatula, as shown.

Never pack dry ingredients
except brown sugar, which
must be packed into the cup
so that it holds the shape
of the measure when turned
out. See at right for tips on
measuring flour.

**To measure solid
shortening,** pack it into
a dry measure using a
spatula, as shown. Run the
spatula through the
shortening in the cup to
make sure there are no air
pockets remaining.

The easiest way to

**To measure dried
herbs,** lightly fill a
measuring spoon to the
top—it's not necessary to
level with a spatula—
keeping the level as close to
the top as possible. Then
empty the spoon into your
hand and crush the herb

with your other hand. (*Or*, to use a mortar and pestle, see page 854.) This breaks the leaves to better release their flavor.

### Is sifting necessary?
In years past, it was essential to sift all-purpose flour to lighten it for accurate measurement and to remove any lumps. But today's flour is no longer lumpy and compact. Stirring it before measuring is sufficient.

To measure flour, stir it in the canister to lighten it. Then gently spoon it into a dry measure, as shown, and level off the top with a metal spatula. Two products that should be sifted are *cake flour*, which is very soft and tends to pack down, and *powdered sugar*.

### What's a dash?
Recipes often call for a dash of an ingredient. It's a measure of less than ⅛ teaspoon (the smallest amount you can accurately measure using standard measuring spoons). When a dash is used, it is for seasoning, and the actual amount is up to you. However, as a guide, consider a dash to be about ¹⁄₁₆ teaspoon.

# What's the Difference?

**Understanding the differences between similar cooking terms can be essential to a** **recipe's success. Here's an explanation of some often-confused terms.**

**Cube:** To cut a food into pieces ½ inch or larger on each side. Use a chef's knife to make lengthwise cuts of the desired width, then cut crosswise to make cubes.

**Mince:** To cut a food into very tiny, irregularly shaped pieces. A utility knife is the right utensil to use for mincing. Mincing is primarily used for garlic.

**Grate:** To rub a food across a rough grating surface to make very fine particles. Grate potent seasonings such as gingerroot, and hard cheeses such as Parmesan.

**Dice:** To cut a food into pieces ⅛ to ¼ inch on each side. Use a chef's knife to cut into strips of the desired width. Pile strips together and cut crosswise into cubes.

**Finely shred:** To rub a food across a fine shredding surface to form very narrow strips. This is used when tiny pieces of potent seasonings are needed.

**Simmer:** To cook just below boiling. A few bubbles form slowly and burst before they surface. Simmering usually takes place between 185°F. (85°C) and 210°F. (99°C).

**Chop:** To cut a food into irregularly shaped pieces about the size of a pea. Use a chopper, blender, food processor, or a chef's knife.

**Shred:** To cut a food into long, narrow strips, usually by rubbing it across a shredding surface. Use a shredder for most vegetables and for cheeses.

**Boil:** To cook in liquid kept at the temperature at which bubbles rise to the surface of the liquid and break. At sea level, water boils at 212°F. (100°C).

# Cooking Terms

Here's a collection of commonly used cooking terms you'll find referred to throughout this cook book. Whether you're an experienced cook or a novice, knowing and understanding basic cooking terminology will make more efficient use of your kitchen time.

**Baste**—To moisten foods during cooking with pan

drippings or a special sauce to add flavor and to prevent drying.

**Beat**—To make a mixture smooth by adding air with a brisk whipping or stirring motion, using a spoon or an electric mixer.

**Blanch**—To precook in boiling water or steam to prepare foods for canning or freezing, or to loosen their skins.

**Blend**—To process food

in an electric blender. Or, to thoroughly combine two or more ingredients by hand with a stirring motion to make a smooth and uniform mixture.

**Boil**—To cook in liquid at boiling temperature (212°F. or 100°C. at sea level) where bubbles rise to the surface and break. For a full rolling boil, bubbles form rapidly throughout the mixture.

**Bouillon**—A clear soup made by cooking meat, usually beef, together with vegetables and seasonings, and then straining the resulting stock. It can also be prepared from bouillon granules or bouillon cubes.

**Bouquet garni**—A combination of several herbs, such as parsley, thyme, and bay leaf, either tied in a bunch or put in a small cheesecloth bag and added to stews, soups, and sauces. It can easily be removed at any stage in the cooking.

**Braise**—To cook slowly with a small amount of liquid in a tightly covered pan on top of the range or in the oven.

**Bread**—To coat with bread crumbs before cooking.

**Broil**—To cook by direct heat under a broiler in an electric or gas range.

**Broth**—Any clear soup, usually made with meat or fish stock.

**Butterfly**—To split foods such as shrimp and steak through the middle without completely separating sections and then spreading the sections to resemble a butterfly.

**Can**—To preserve food by sealing it in airtight containers. The food is processed either in a water bath or pressure canner.

**Candy**—To cook in sugar or syrup, when applied to sweet potatoes and carrots. For fruit or fruit peel, to cook in heavy syrup till translucent and well coated.

**Caramelize**—To melt sugar slowly over low heat until it becomes brown in color.

**Chop**—To cut into pieces about the size of peas with a knife, chopper, blender, or food processor.

**Clarify**—To make liquids clear by filtering, such as stock or broth, or butter.

**Coat**—To evenly cover food with crumbs, flour, or a batter.

**Coddle**—To cook food in water just below the boiling point, as in coddled eggs.

**Cool**—To remove from heat and let stand at room temperature. When a recipe says, "cool quickly," the food should be chilled or set in a bowl of ice water to quickly reduce its temperature.

**Cream**—To beat a mixture with a spoon or electric mixer till it becomes soft and smooth. When applied to combining shortening and sugar, the mixture is beaten till light and fluffy, depending on the proportion of sugar to shortening.

**Crisp-tender**—To cook food to the stage where it is tender but still crisp.

**Cube**—To cut into pieces that are the same size on each side—at least ½ inch.

**Cut in**—To mix shortening with dry ingredients using a pastry blender or two knives.

**Dice**—To cut food into small cubes of uniform size and shape—between ⅛ and ¼ inch.

**Dollop**—To add a small amount, such as a scoop or spoonful, of a semiliquid food to garnish another food.

**Dot**—To distribute small bits of food over another food, such as dotting an apple pie with butter before baking.

**Dust**—To sprinkle foods lightly with sugar, flour, etc.

**Fillet**—To cut lean meat or fish into pieces without bones.

**Finely shred**—To rub food across a fine shredding surface to form very narrow strips.

**Flake**—To break food lightly into small pieces.

**Flute**—To make small decorative impressions in food. Piecrusts are fluted by pressing the pastry edge into various shapes.

**Fold**—To add ingredients gently to a mixture. Using a spatula, cut down through the mixture; cut across the bottom of the bowl, and then up and over, close to the surface. Turn the bowl frequently for even distribution.

**Freeze**—To reduce the temperature of foods so that the liquid content becomes solidified.

**Fry**—To cook in hot fat. To panfry, cook food in a small amount of fat. To deep-fat fry, cook the food immersed in a large amount of fat.

**Garnish**—To decorate the served dish with small pieces of food that have distinctive texture or color, such as parsley.

**Glaze**—To brush a mixture on a food to give it a glossy appearance or a hard finish.

**Grate**—To rub food across a grating surface that separates the food into very fine particles.

**Grill**—To cook food over hot coals.

**Grind**—To use a food grinder to cut a food into very fine pieces.

**Julienne**—To cut vegetables, fruits, or meats into matchlike strips.

**Knead**—To work dough with the heel of your hand in a pressing and folding motion.

**Marinate**—To allow a food to stand in a liquid to add flavor.

**Mince**—To chop food into very small, irregularly shaped pieces.

**Mull**—To heat beverages such as red wine and cider with spices and sugar.

**Panbroil**—To cook uncovered, removing fat as it accumulates.

**Panfry**—To cook food in a small amount of hot fat.

**Partially set**—To chill gelatin mixtures to the point in setting when the consistency resembles raw egg whites.

**Peel**—To remove the outer layer or skin from a fruit or vegetable.

**Pickle**—To preserve or flavor meat, fish, vegetables, etc. in a brine, or a solution made of vinegar, spices, and other seasonings.

**Pit**—To remove the seed from a piece of fruit.

**Poach**—To cook food in hot liquid, being careful that the food holds its shape while cooking.

**Precook**—To cook food partially or completely before the final cooking or reheating.

**Preserve**—To prepare meat, fruit, vegetables, etc. for future use by salting, boiling in syrup, soaking in a brine, dehydrating, curing, smoking, canning, or freezing.

**Puree**—To use a blender, food processor, or food mill to convert a food into a liquid or heavy paste.

**Reduce**—To rapidly boil a mixture to evaporate liquid so that the mixture becomes thicker.

**Render**—To separate solid fat such as suet or lard from meat tissue by melting.

**Roast**—To cook a meat, uncovered, in the oven. Pot-roasting refers to braising a meat roast.

**Sauté**—To brown or cook food in a small amount of hot fat.

**Scald**—To bring food to a temperature just below boiling so that tiny bubbles form at the edges of the pan.

**Scallop**—To bake food, usually in a casserole, with a sauce or other liquid.

**Score**—To cut narrow grooves or slits partway through the outer surface of a food.

**Shred**—To rub food on a shredder to form long, narrow pieces.

**Sift**—To put one or more dry ingredients through a sieve or sifter to incorporate air and break up lumps.

**Simmer**—To cook food in liquid over low heat at a temperature of 185°F. (85°C.) to 210°F. (99°C.) where bubbles form at a slow rate and burst before reaching the surface.

**Steam**—To cook food in steam. A small amount of boiling water is used, and more water is added during steaming if necessary.

**Steep**—To extract color, flavor, or other qualities from a substance by leaving it in liquid just below the boiling point.

**Sterilize**—To destroy microorganisms by boiling, dry heating, or steaming.

**Stew**—To simmer food slowly in small amount of liquid.

**Stiff peaks**—To beat egg whites till peaks stand up straight when the beaters are lifted from the mixer bowl, but are still moist and glossy.

**Stir**—To mix ingredients with a spoon in a circular or figure-eight motion till well blended.

**Stir-fry**—To cook food quickly in a small amount of hot fat, stirring constantly.

**Toss**—To mix ingredients lightly by lifting and dropping them with a spoon or a spoon and fork.

**Whip**—To beat food lightly and rapidly, incorporating air into the mixture to make it light and to increase its volume.

# Seasoning Guide

Use the following suggestions as a guide when experimenting with seasonings. Start with ¼ teaspoon for each 4 servings; then taste before adding more. Crush dried herbs (see page 854) or snip fresh herbs before using. To substitute fresh for dried, use three times more fresh herbs than dried.

**Allspice**—fruits, desserts, soups, meat dishes, egg dishes, vegetables.

**Anise**—beef and pork dishes, carrots, beets, mixed vegetable salads, cakes, cookies, pastries.

**Basil**—broiled and roasted meat and poultry, stews, stuffing, fish, vegetables, pasta, salads, salad dressings, stewed fruit, breads, egg dishes, dips, sauces.

**Bay leaf**—corned beef, stews, fish, dried bean dishes, potatoes, rice, salads, egg dishes, gravies, marinades.

**Caraway**—meat loaves, pot roasts, stews, poultry stuffing, fish stews, vegetables, salads, breads, egg dishes, dips, sauces, spreads.

**Cardamom**—fruit salads and dressings, pastries, breads, meats, poultry, fish.

**Cayenne** (red pepper) —egg dishes, Mexican dishes, dips and spreads, cream soups, French dressing.

**Celery** (salt, flakes, seed)—salads, roasts, sauces, stews, stuffings, relishes, spreads, egg dishes, breads.

**Chervil**—roasted meats and poultry, fish, vegetables, salads, dressings, egg dishes.

**Chili powder**—spreads, dips, stews, French dressing, vegetables, egg dishes, meats, poultry, fish, croutons.

**Cinnamon**—fruit, salad dressings, vegetables, French toast, barbecue sauce, pork chops, boiled beef, stewed chicken, pastries, breads, desserts, beverages, puddings.

**Cloves**—cookies, pastries, pork and lamb dishes, marinades, fruit salads, dressings, vegetables.

**Coriander**—curries, roast poultry and stuffing, pork stews, artichokes, bean dishes, fruit salads, cookies, pastries, gingerbread.

**Curry powder**—dips, cheese spreads, seafood salads, dressings, creamed vegetables, rice, egg dishes, lamb, pork, beef, sauces, poultry, fish, fruit compotes.

**Dill** (weed, seed)—beef, lamb, veal, stews, poultry, fish, seafood, vegetables, salads, dressings, breads, egg dishes, sauces.

**Fennel**—meat roasts, stews, poultry, fish, seafood, vegetables, salads, dressings, cakes, pastries, breads, sauces, egg dishes.

**Ginger**—Oriental dishes, meats, poultry, fruit, desserts, cookies, breads, pastries, marinades, salad dressings, vegetables.

**Lemon or orange peel**—spreads, relishes, fruit soup, fruit salads, dressings, vegetables, meats, stuffings, marinades, fish, seafood, poultry, breads, pastries, desserts, sauces.

**Marjoram**—roasted meats and poultry, meat and poultry pies, stews, casseroles, fish, seafood, vegetables, salads, breads, egg dishes, gravies, sauces.

**Mace**—veal and fish dishes, cakes, cookies, chowders, fondues.

**Mint**—roast beef, lamb, poultry, fish, vegetables, salads, stewed fruits, marinades, sauces.

**Mustard**—pickles, corned beef, sauerkraut, marinades, sauces, dips, macaroni salads, dressings, egg dishes, sauces, biscuits.

**Nutmeg**—sauces, egg dishes, desserts, cookies, pastries, breads, fruits.

**Oregano**—broiled and roasted meat, meat and poultry pies, stews, casseroles, fish, seafood, vegetables, salads, egg dishes.

**Rosemary**—roasted meat and poultry, meat pies, stews, casseroles, fish, vegetables, salads, breads, egg dishes.

**Saffron**—cakes, breads, poultry, fish stews and casseroles, rice, seafood salads.

**Sage**—roasted meat and poultry, meat loaves, stews, stuffing, fish, vegetables, egg dishes, breads, fondues, gravies, sauces.

**Savory**—meat and poultry

pies, stews, casseroles, stuffing, hamburgers, chops, fish, vegetables, salads, egg dishes, gravies, sauces.
**Tarragon**—steaks, roasted meats and poultry, casseroles, stews, fish, seafood, vegetables, salads, dressings, cheese spreads, sauces.

**Thyme**—roasted meat and poultry, meat loaves, meat and poultry pies, stews, casseroles, fish, seafood, vegetables, salads, breads, egg dishes, sauces, spreads.
**Turmeric**—curries, pickles, relishes, dips.

# Emergency Substitutions

**For best results, use the ingredients specified in the recipe. But when** **you're in a bind, this chart can help you find an acceptable substitute.**

| If you don't have: | Substitute: |
|---|---|
| 1 cup cake flour | 1 cup minus 2 tablespoons all-purpose flour |
| 1 tablespoon cornstarch (for thickening) | 2 tablespoons all-purpose flour |
| 1 teaspoon baking powder | ¼ teaspoon baking soda plus ½ cup buttermilk or sour milk (to replace ½ cup of the liquid called for) |
| 1 package active dry yeast | 1 cake compressed yeast |
| 1 cup granulated sugar | 1 cup packed brown sugar or 2 cups sifted powdered sugar |
| 1 cup honey | 1¼ cups granulated sugar plus ¼ cup liquid |
| 1 cup corn syrup | 1 cup granulated sugar plus ¼ cup liquid |

| If you don't have: | Substitute: |
| --- | --- |
| 1 square (1 ounce) unsweetened chocolate | 3 tablespoons unsweetened cocoa powder plus 1 tablespoon butter or margarine |
| 1 cup whipping cream, whipped | 2 cups whipped dessert topping |
| 1 cup buttermilk | 1 tablespoon lemon juice or vinegar plus enough whole milk to make 1 cup (let stand 5 minutes before using) *or* 1 cup whole milk plus 1¾ teaspoons cream of tartar *or* 1 cup plain yogurt |
| 1 cup whole milk | ½ cup evaporated milk plus ½ cup water *or* 1 cup reconstituted nonfat dry milk (plus 2 teaspoons butter or margarine, if desired) |
| 1 cup light cream | 2 tablespoons butter plus 1 cup minus 2 tablespoons milk |
| 1 whole egg | 2 egg yolks (for most uses) |
| 2 cups tomato sauce | ¾ cup tomato paste plus 1 cup water |
| 1 cup tomato juice | ½ cup tomato sauce plus ½ cup water |
| 1 clove garlic | ⅛ teaspoon garlic powder or minced dried garlic |
| 1 small onion | 1 teaspoon onion powder *or* 1 tablespoon minced dried onion, rehydrated |
| 1 teaspoon dry mustard | 1 tablespoon prepared mustard |
| 1 teaspoon finely shredded lemon peel | ½ teaspoon lemon extract |

# Stocking Your Kitchen

An organized and well-supplied kitchen can reduce the time and effort you spend preparing your meals, no matter how simple or elaborate they may be. Follow these hints for organizing your kitchen, stocking basic groceries, using canned foods, selecting kitchen tools, and choosing basic kitchen equipment.

## Organizing your kitchen

Place utensils and staples near the areas where they're used most often. Store seldom-used utensils and appliances in an out-of-the-way place and move frequently used items to handy locations. Organize canned goods and packaged mixes on shelves by types so you can find them easily and quickly.

## Basic groceries

Most foods you buy are matters of preference, but there are some food staples you can't cook without. Buy these things in quantities you can use up within a reasonable period of time.

When buying perishable foods, choose the form—fresh, canned, dried, or frozen—that best fits your needs and storage facilities. When you start to run low on an item, note it for your next shopping trip.

*Keep these foods on hand:* Sugar, all-purpose flour, salt, pepper, baking powder, baking soda, coffee and/or tea, shortening, cooking oil, butter and/or margarine, herbs and spices, vanilla, unsweetened cocoa powder, mayonnaise and/or salad dressing, prepared mustard, Worcestershire sauce, catsup, bread, cereals, pasta, eggs, meat, salad greens, vegetables, fruits, cheese, juices, and milk.

## Using canned foods

*Health life versus shelf life:* The *health life* of canned foods (the length of time they're safe to eat) is extensive. That's because the food has been sterilized. As long as the seal stays airtight, the food won't spoil.

Processors usually say the *shelf life* of canned foods (when the food tastes its best) is about one year. You don't need to toss the can after a year, but canned food loses some flavor and nutrients in prolonged storage.

*Selecting canned foods:* Avoid buying badly dented cans. Small dents on the can body generally are harmless, but reject a can with dented side seams or end seams, visible leaks, or swollen ends.

*Storing canned foods:* Keep canned foods in a cool (below 70°F.), dry, dark place. Discard any can that's very rusty.

Once a can is opened, store it, covered, in the refrigerator. You can keep food in its original can for up to two days. For longer storage, transfer food to a covered container.

## Selecting kitchen tools

Any cook who has never stocked a kitchen or who is trimming down on kitchen

equipment faces the "how many pots and pans do I need?" dilemma. The following guidelines will help you stock your kitchen with the essentials:

• Choose pieces you can use for more than one job, such as freezer-to-oven-to-table baking dishes and casseroles, and oven-going skillets.

• Every saucepan and skillet should have a secure cover. Make sure that the cover knobs and handles don't conduct heat.

• If buying new equipment, purchase the best quality that you can afford. However, remember that high price doesn't always mean good quality. Make sure that each item you buy is durable and easy to clean.

## Basic equipment

The equipment needed to prepare food can be broken down into four groups— preparation and cooking utensils, bakeware, top-of-the-range cookware, and equipment for food storage. Concentrate first on the basic utensils listed. Purchase other less-essential equipment as the need arises.

*Preparation and cooking utensils:* Set of mixing bowls; nested set of dry measuring cups; clear glass liquid measuring cup; set of standard measuring spoons; wooden spoons; rubber spatulas; flexible metal spatula; serrated knife for bread, tomatoes, and citrus fruits; paring knife with 3-inch blade; utility knife with 6-inch blade; French cook's or chef's knife; vegetable peeler; meat mallet; long-handled fork; long-handled spoon; ladle; slotted spoon; pancake turner; tongs; kitchen scissors; bottle opener; can opener; rotary beater and/or electric mixer; grater or shredder; small and large strainers; colander; kitchen timer; cutting board; rolling pin with cover; and pastry cloth.

*Bakeware:* Baking sheet or jelly roll pan; wire cooling racks; 6-ounce custard cups; muffin pan; pie plate; loaf baking pan; various sizes of oblong, round, and square baking dishes (non-metal) and pans (metal); various sizes of casserole dishes; roasting pan with rack; and meat thermometer.

*Top-of-the-range cookware:* Select 1-, 2-, and 3-quart covered saucepans and a 4- to 6-quart covered kettle or Dutch oven. (For more even cooking, it's best to use about ⅔ of the pan's capacity.) A 6- to 8-inch and a 10-inch covered skillet will fill most any need.

*Food storage:* For storing food, stock up on assorted refrigerator-freezer dishes, foil, clear plastic wrap, waxed paper, and assorted canisters.

# Tips about Equipment

Certain pieces of kitchen equipment can be real assets when preparing recipes. In the following hints you'll find out how to use appliances for shortcutting recipe preparations. You'll also read about the various types of kitchen thermometers and how they can aid in successful cooking results. And finally, you'll discover some make-do cooking equipment that you can substitute if you are missing a specific item.

## Appliance shortcuts

While many of the time-saving appliances available are not essential to preparing good meals in a hurry, they can be handy tools.

*Blender:* Put your blender to work for you. Use it to blend bread into bread crumbs. When you're making a vanilla wafer or graham cracker crust, let the blender crush the cookies or crackers. Prepare fruit juice concentrates or dissolve gelatin by whirling them in the blender. Make quick and easy milk shakes and other beverages. The blender also is great for combining salad dressings, pureeing vegetables and fruits, and grating hard cheeses.

*Food processor:* This appliance does many of the same chores as the blender in addition to

shredding cheese, slicing vegetables, and making peanut butter or almond paste. Use your food processor to chop large quantities of nuts to store in the freezer, or to blend meat loaf mixtures.

*Counter-top oven appliances:* These handy portable ovens save time by heating up faster than your large regular oven, without heating up the kitchen. Use your counter-top oven along with your range oven to prepare recipes with different baking temperatures at the same time.

*Microwave oven:* While you can prepare entire dishes in a microwave oven, you can also use this appliance to quicken certain recipe steps of conventionally cooked food. Use it to melt butter or margarine, toast nuts, melt chocolate, dry fresh herbs, toast coconut, make croutons, cook bacon, or cook onions in butter.

*Pressure saucepan:* These pans help you cook foods in about ⅓ the normal time. Because of the short cooking time and the small amount of water used, cooking vegetables in a pressure cooker helps retain nutrients as well as color. And it saves time with normally slow-cooking foods such as stews, pot roasts, or ribs.

# Kitchen thermometer tips

Thermometers can help you cook a roast to just the right doneness. They can tell you when a candy recipe is at the correct stage, and they can tell you when the cooking oil is at the proper temperature for frying. There are also thermometers to check oven and freezer temperatures.

*Meat thermometers:* This type is usually a needle-shaped instrument with a tube of mercury in the center. To get an accurate temperature reading, make sure the tip of the thermometer isn't resting on a meat bone, fat, gristle, or the pan bottom.

*Candy/deep-fat frying thermometers:* These have different temperature ranges than meat thermometers and the gauges are sometimes marked for special foods. Test the thermometer occasionally for accuracy in boiling water (see page 207). To get an accurate temperature read-ing, be sure to look at the thermometer at eye level.

*Appliance thermometers:* Use an oven thermometer to check the temperature of the oven and a freezer thermometer to make sure that your freezer is holding food at the proper temperature.

# Make-do cookware

The time may come when you start to prepare a recipe and discover that you don't have the recommended cooking equipment on hand. Here are some ideas for spur-of-the-moment substitutions.

• Create a covered casserole by covering a baking pan with foil.
• Cook a pizza on a baking sheet instead of a pizza pan. Build up crust edges so the filling will stay corralled.
• Substitute any straight-sided casserole for a soufflé dish as long as volumes are the same.
• When a recipe calls for putting food through a food mill, you can generally achieve the same results by sieving the food through a strainer.

# Tips for Saving Time

Cooking nutritious appetizing meals quickly and without fuss is easy if you plan ahead. And when you're short on time, you can speed up your food preparation even more by using the following hints.

## General tips

• For a quick garnish or for use in recipes, toast chopped nuts or coconut in a shallow baking pan in a 350° oven for 5 to 10 minutes or till browned, stirring once or twice. Cool the nuts or coconut; seal in plastic bags or freezer containers; label and freeze.

• Shred American, cheddar, Swiss, or mozzarella cheese in batches to save time and effort. Plan your menus ahead and shred the amount of cheese you'll need all at once. Seal it in plastic bags, then label and chill.

• Chill foods quickly by placing them in your freezer for 20 to 30 minutes.

• Keep a supply of hard-cooked eggs in your refrigerator to use in recipes. Hard-cooked eggs will remain fresh for up to 1 week in your refrigerator.

• When you need a sauce on the spur of the moment, heat a can of undiluted condensed cream of mushroom, cream of celery, cream of chicken, cream of shrimp, cream of onion, cheddar cheese, or tomato soup.

## Main-dish tips

• Cut the cooking time of meat loaves by shaping them into small round loaves in a baking pan, or by baking the meat in muffin cups.

• Shape ground meat into patties. Place two pieces of waxed paper between each patty; wrap, label, and freeze. The next time you need burgers in a hurry, you can remove just the number you need from the freezer. Individual patties thaw faster than 1-pound packages of ground meat, too.

• If making meatballs is a

bother, here are two ways to make shaping them fast and simple. Shape the meat mixture into a log and cut off slices. These slices will roll easily into balls. Or, pat the meat into a square and cut it into cubes. The cubes also roll easily into evenly sized meatballs.

• Skip last-minute food preparation by making casseroles ahead. Most casseroles can be made and chilled up to 24 hours before cooking. Just add 15 to 20 minutes to the normal cooking time.

• Serve one-dish meals such as meat and vegetable combinations frequently. They save cooking, serving, and cleanup time.

• Before freezing meat and poultry leftovers, cut up the meat as specified in the recipe you intend to use; measure out the correct amount. Wrap, seal, and label with recipe use.

## Salad tips

• Shortcut salad making by serving lettuce wedges rather than torn salad greens.

• Make gelatin salads in a hurry by spooning your favorite gelatin salad mixture into individual molds, custard cups, or plastic cups and chilling them in the freezer for 20 to 25 minutes.

• Wash lettuce and remove the core before refrigerating in a plastic container.

## Vegetable tips

• Avoid the time-consuming chore of chopping onion and green pepper or mincing garlic by using commercially frozen chopped onion or green pepper, minced dried onion or garlic, onion powder, or garlic powder.

• If frozen chopped onion or green pepper costs too much for your budget, chop and freeze your own.

• To separate frozen vegetables quickly, place them in a colander and pour boiling water over them. You can add the vegetables to casseroles or top-of-the-range dishes to finish cooking.

## Bread tips

• For biscuits on the double, use a drop biscuit recipe rather than kneading, rolling, and cutting regular biscuits.

• Slice a loaf of French bread to, but not through, the bottom crust. Spread the cut edges with softened butter or garlic butter. Wrap the loaf in foil, label, and freeze. Simply heat the loaf in the oven in its foil wrapping.

# Cooking at High Altitudes

If you are having difficulties with certain types of recipes and live 1,000 feet or more above sea level, your altitude may be responsible for your problems. Unfortunately, there is no one formula that will adjust recipes for high altitude cooking. Your best bet is to become familiar with how altitude affects food, then experiment with recipes to find a balance suitable to your location.

## Baking

Almost every ingredient in baked goods is affected by lower air pressure at high altitudes, especially leavenings, liquids, and sugar.

Leavenings: With less air pressure to control expansion, baked products rise too quickly and textures are coarse and crumbly.

Liquids: Evaporation is accelerated at high elevations, causing foods to dry.

Sugar: As liquid evaporates, sugar becomes more concentrated. This weakens the cell structure of cakes and breads, causing them to fall.

**Cakes** leavened by air, such as angel cake, expand too much if egg whites are beaten according to sea-level directions. Beat whites only to *soft* peaks. Cakes leavened with baking powder or soda need more adjustment. Use the chart below to compensate for altitude.

**Cookies, biscuits, and muffins** are more stable than cakes and need little

## High Altitude Adjustments for Cakes

When making cakes, use this chart as a guide. Adjust all ingredients listed. You may need to experiment with each recipe to discover the best formula; where two amounts appear, try the smaller first, and adjust ingredients next time, if necessary.

| Ingredients | 3,000 feet | 5,000 feet | 7,000 feet |
| --- | --- | --- | --- |
| Liquid: Add for each cup | 1 to 2 tablespoons | 2 to 4 tablespoons | 3 to 4 tablespoons |
| Baking powder: Decrease for each teaspoon | ⅛ teaspoon | ⅛ to ¼ teaspoon | ¼ teaspoon |
| Sugar: Decrease for each cup | 0 to 1 tablespoon | 0 to 2 tablespoons | 1 to 3 tablespoons |

adjustment. Experiment by reducing sugar and baking powder and increasing liquid.

**For cakes and cookies,** increase oven temperature about 20°F. and decrease time. This allows cakes to set before leavening expands them too much, and keeps cookies from drying out.

**Yeast doughs** rise quickly at high altitudes, resulting in a weaker structure. To compensate, shorten rising time and add extra liquid.

## Range-Top Cooking

Liquids boil at lower temperatures at high altitudes, which means foods take longer to cook. Increase cooking time rather than heat, since doing the latter can scorch food. Also increase the liquid, as it will evaporate more quickly.

**Deep-fat fry** foods at a lower temperature for a longer time. Since moisture in the food has a lower boiling point, food fried at recommended sea-level temperature will be crusty but underdone. Lower the temperature of the fat 3°F. for each 1,000 feet above sea level.

**Candies, syrups, and jellies** become more concentrated at high altitudes. The cold water test and sheet test are reliable to determine doneness, but if you use a candy thermometer, decrease temperature about 2°F. for each 1,000 feet above sea level.

**Processing time for canning** must be adjusted at high altitudes for safe processing. When water-bath processing, increase processing time 1 minute for each 1,000 feet above sea level when processing 20 minutes or less. Increase the time 2 minutes per 1,000 feet when processing more than 20 minutes. In pressure canners, the steam pressure must be increased 1 pound for every 2,000 feet above sea level when using a canner with a spring-dial gauge.

For more information on cooking at high altitudes write to: Colorado State University Experiment Station Bulletin Room, Fort Collins, Colorado 80523.

# The Metric System

The metric system or System Internationale (SI) is far from new. It was conceived in 1790 as a standard to simplify measurement throughout the world. As of now, the United States is the only major country that has not converted to SI.

But the change is coming, however slowly. Because SI is easier to learn and use and will simplify world trade, the United States is moving toward adopting the metric system. Presently, however, the changeover is voluntary and many questions are yet to be decided.

Based on the experience of Canada and other countries already using SI, here is some information to acquaint you with metrics.

Because it is based on multiples of 10, the metric system is easy to learn. Once you know the basic units (meter for length, liter for volume, etc.), you can convert to convenient units

| Putting Metric Units into Perspective | | |
|---|---|---|
| **Measurement** | **Unit** | **Example** |
| **Volume** | milliliter (ml) | A dash of salt is about 1 ml |
| | | 1 teaspoon equals 5 ml |
| | | 1 quart equals 946.4 ml |
| | liter (1) | 1.06 quarts equal 1 l |
| **Weight (mass)** | gram (g) | A paper clip weighs 1 g |
| | | A saltine cracker weighs 3 g |
| | | 1 g equals 0.035 ounces |
| | | 1 ounce equals 28.35 g |
| | kilogram (kg) | 1 kg equals 2.2 lbs. |
| **Length** | millimeter (mm) | The thickness of a dime is 1 mm |
| | centimeter (cm) | 1 cm equals 0.4 inch |
| | | 30 cm equals 1 foot |
| | meter (m) | 1 m is about 1.1 yards |
| | kilometer (km) | 1 km is about 0.6 mile |
| | | National speed limit is 90 km/hour. |
| **Temperature** | degrees Celsius (°C) | Water freezes at 0°C |
| | | Water boils at 100°C |
| | | Room temperature is 20° to 25°C |

simply by moving the decimal point.

The smaller and larger units are named by adding a prefix to the basic unit. Thus, a meter becomes a kilometer (1,000 meters), a centimeter (0.01 meter), or a millimeter (0.001 meter).

**Volume:** The metric system is quite simple since there are fewer units of measure to remember. You'll be trading teaspoons, fluid ounces, pints, and gallons for milliliters and liters.

Measuring cups will change slightly, but measuring techniques should remain the same. Liquid measures will probably be sized 250 ml, 500 ml, and 1,000 ml (1 liter)—only slightly larger than the present 1-cup, 2-cup, and 4-cup measures.

Dry measures will

probably be sized 50 ml (just under ¼ cup), 125 ml (just over ½ cup), and 250 ml (just over 1 cup).

Measuring spoons will include spoons with 1 ml, 2 ml, 5 ml, 15 ml, and 25 ml capacities, a range from just under ¼ teaspoon to the size of a coffee measure.

**Weight:** Rather than pounds and ounces, you'll be seeing grams and kilograms on products.

**Length:** Pan sizes also will change to correspond with the new system, with most measured in centimeters.

**Temperature:** You're probably already familiar with the SI method of measuring heat. Measured in degrees Celsius, water freezes at 0°C and boils at 100°C (at sea level). Although the conversion from degrees Fahrenheit is oversimplified here, for the range of cooking temperatures, the reading in degrees Fahrenheit is nearly double that in degrees Celsius. Recipes in this book are stated in degrees Fahrenheit.

# Garnishes

**Garnishes "frame" the food, providing a contrast of color and texture. Learn how to prepare simple garnishes that will add flair and appeal to your favorite foods.**

**Frosted grapes:** Cut grapes into small clusters of about 3 to 5 grapes each. Combine 1 slightly beaten egg white with a little water; brush over grape clusters. Sprinkle with sugar; place on a rack to dry.

**Citrus cartwheels and twists:** Thinly slice lemons, limes, and oranges. For cartwheels, cut V-shaped notches on rind. For twists, cut into center of slice; twist ends in opposite directions.

**Onion brushes:** Slice off roots from ends of green onions; remove most of the top portion. Make slashes at both ends to make a fringe. Place in ice water to curl back ends.

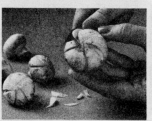

**Radish accordions:** Trim ends of long narrow radishes. In each radish make 8 to 10 narrow crosswise cuts ⅛ inch wide, cutting partially through the radish. Place in ice water so slices fan out.

**Fluted mushrooms:** Begin at the tip of the mushroom cap and carve an inverted "V" strip out of the cap. Turn the mushroom and in spiral fashion, cut out 5 to 6 inverted "V" strips.

**Carrot curls/zigzags:**
Make thin lengthwise strips
of carrot, using a vegetable
peeler. For curls, roll up;
secure with a wooden
pick. For zigzags, thread on a
wooden pick accordion
style.

**Pepper flower:** Make
several lengthwise slashes
through a 2- to
3-inch-long Serrano chili
pepper to make a fringe.
Do not cut through stem.
Place in ice water to curl
ends.

**Tomato roses:** Cut a
"base" from the stem end of
tomato (do not sever). Cut
a continuous narrow strip in
spiral fashion, tapering the
end to remove. Curl the strip
onto its base in a rose
shape.

**Chocolate curls/grated
chocolate:** Use a bar of
sweet chocolate at room
temperature. Shave into curls
with a vegetable peeler.
To grate, rub chocolate
across the rough surface of
a grater.

# Index

# Index

# Index

# Index

# Index

# Index

# Index

# Index

# INDEX

## A

Almond Cookies, **8**. 316

Almond Opera Fudge, **6**. 206

Almond Sauce, **17**. 711

American-Fried Potatoes, **19**. 803

Anadama Bread, **4**. 110

Angel Cake, **5**. 185

Antipasto, Raw Vegetable, **16**. 673

Any-Fruit Coffee Cake, **4**. 143

Appetizers

  Appetizer Clam Shells, **1**. 5

  Appetizer Fruit Combo, **1**. 7

  Baked Ham-Stuffed Mushrooms, **1**. 10

  Beer-Cheese Fondue, **1**. 19

  Blue Cheese Onion Dip, **1**. 21

  Broiled Grapefruit Halves, **1**. 18

  Cheese Ball, **1**. 8

  Cheese-Ham Ball, **1**. 12

  Cheese-Wine Log, **1**. 9

  Chicken and Crab Wontons, **1**. 16

  Chicken Liver Pâté, **1**. 14

  Chili con Queso, **1**. 22

  Cocktail Meatballs, **1**. 7

  Crab-Bacon Bites, **2**. 70

  Crab Cocktail, **1**. 13

  Creamy Dill Dip, **1**. 20

  Creamy Onion Dip, **1**. 21

  Crunch Party Mix, **1**. 18

  Dilled Salmon Dip, **1**. 8

  Egg Rolls, **1**. 16–17

  Egg Salad Triangles, **1**. 14

  Fluffy Fruit Dip, **1**. 21

  Fruit-Crab Cocktail, **1**. 10

  Guacamole, **1**. 22

  Hot Broccoli Dip, **1**. 19

  Italian Appetizer Artichokes, **1**. 17

  Marinated Shrimp Appetizers, **2**. 69

  Oyster Cocktail, **1**. 13

  Oysters Rockefeller, **1**. 4

  Party Ham Sandwiches, **1**. 15

  Pineapple-Orange Ice, **1**. 8

  Salmon Mousse, **1**. 11

  Saucy Lamb Riblets, **2**. 62–63

  Shrimp Cocktail, **1**. 13

  Shrimp-Cucumber Appetizer Spread, **1**. 13

  Smoky Cheese Ball, **1**. 12

  Swedish Meatballs, **1**. 6

  Swiss Cheese-Ham Spread, **1**. 9

  Teriyaki Appetizer Ribs, **2**. 69

  Tomato-Chili Guacamole, **1**. 22

Apples

  Apple Butter, canning and freezing, **7**. 243

  Apple Cobbler, **9**. 351–52

  Apple Crumble Pie, **13**. 543

  Apple Dumplings, **9**. 352–53

  Apple-Filled Oatmeal Cookies, **8**. 309

  Apple Fritter Rings, **4**. 150–51

  Apple Jelly, **7**. 284

  Apple Juice, canning and freezing, **7**. 244

  Apple-Peanut-Buttered Pork Steaks, **2**. 52–53

  Apple Pie, **13**. 542

  Apple-Raisin Muffins, **4**. 157

  Apples, canning and freezing, **7**. 242

  Apple-Stuffed Sausage Patties, **12**. 513

  Baked Apples, **9**. 350

  Caramel Apples, **6**. 213

  Cinnamon Apple Rings, **4**. 150

  Date-Apple Coffee Bread, **4**. 137–38

  Deep-Dish Apple Pie, **13**. 543–44

  Fresh-Fruit Crisp, **9**. 352

  Peanut Caramel Apples, **6**. 213

  Pheasant with Apples, **14**. 599

  Pork with Apple-Curry Sauce, **12**. 489

  Rutabaga and Apple, **19**. 808–9

  Sausage- and Apple-Stuffed Squash, **12**. 513–14

**Boldface numbers
indicate chapters.**

Apples (continued)
  Sherried Fruit Compote, **9.** 354
  Waldorf Salad, **16.** 686
Applesauce
  Applesauce, **9.** 362
  Applesauce, canning and freezing, **7.** 243–44
  Applesauce Coffee Cake, **4.** 147
  Applesauce Spice Cake, **5.** 176–77
  Chunky Applesauce, **9.** 963
  Squash and Applesauce, **19.** 812
Apricots
  Apricot Angel Dessert, **9.** 347
  Apricot Chicken, **14.** 596
  Apricot-Filled Oatmeal Bars, **8.** 297
  Apricot Glaze, **2.** 53
  Apricot-Ham Patties, **12.** 504
  Apricot Nectar, canning and freezing, **7.** 246
  Apricot-Orange Bread, **4.** 139
  Apricot Pie, **13.** 546
  Apricots, canning and freezing, **7.** 244–45
  Apricot Soufflé Salad, **16.** 678
  Apricot Swizzle, **3.** 82
  Sherried Fruit Compote, **9.** 354
Arroz con Pollo, **14.** 602
Artichokes
  Artichokes Velvet, **19.** 779–80
  Artichokes with Butter Sauce, **19.** 779
  Italian Appetizer Artichokes, **1.** 17
Asparagus
  Asparagus, canning and freezing, **7.** 255
  Asparagus-Tomato Stir-Fry, **19.** 780
  Asparagus Toss, **16.** 663
  Bacon-Asparagus Omelet, **10.** 391
  Chicken-Asparagus Stacks, **14.** 605
  Chicken Divan, **14.** 612
  Sesame Asparagus, **19.** 780–81
Au Gratin Vegetables, **19.** 773

Avocados
  Avocado Dressing, **16.** 703
  Guacamole, **1.** 22
  Fruit-Crab Cocktail, **1.** 10
  Tomato-Chili Guacamole, **1.** 22

**B**

Bacon
  Bacon-Asparagus Omelet, **10.** 391
  Bacon-Sour Cream Sauce, **11.** 415
  Bacon-Wrapped Franks, **2.** 46
  Canadian Bacon Pie, **12.** 508
  Cooking Bacon, **12.** 506
  Cooking Canadian-Style Bacon, **12.** 507
  Orange-Glazed Canadian Bacon, **12.** 508
  Pineapple-Glazed Canadian Bacon, **12.** 509
Bagels
  Bagels, **4.** 127
  Herb Bagels, **4.** 128
  Light Rye Bagels, **4.** 128
  Onion Bagels, **4.** 128
  Poppy Seed or Sesame Seed Bagels, **4.** 128
Baked Acorn Squash Halves, **19.** 812
Baked Alaska, **9.** 359
Baked Apples, **9.** 350
Baked Bean Quintet, **19.** 786
Baked Beans, Easy, **19.** 785
Baked Beans, New England, **19.** 785
Baked Coffee Custard, **9.** 337
Baked Custard, **9.** 337
Baked Eggs, **10.** 373
Baked Fillets and Steaks, **11.** 415
Baked Fish a l'Orange, **11.** 424
Baked Fish with Mushrooms, **11.** 416
Baked Gnocchi, **15.** 649
Baking Ham-Stuffed Mushrooms, **1.** 10
Baked Omelet with Chicken Sauce, **10.** 397
Baked Pastry Shell, **13.** 569
Baked Potatoes, **19.** 802
Baked Rice Pudding, **9.** 334

**Boldface numbers
indicate chapters.**

Baked Tomatoes, **19.** 813
Baked Tuna Patties, **11.** 437
Baking Ham, **12.** 500
Bananas
  Banana Butter Frosting, **8.** 308
  Banana Cake, **5.** 171
  Banana Cream Pie, **13.** 555
  Banana Drop Cookies, **8.** 308
  Banana Nut Bread, **4.** 140
  Banana-Nut Muffins, **4.** 157
  Slushy Punch, **3.** 78
  Strawberry-Banana Soufflé Salads, **16.** 681
Barbecue Breadsticks, **4.** 129
Barbecued Pork Sandwiches, **12.** 494
Barbecue Recipes
  Apple-Peanut-Buttered Pork Steaks, **2.** 52
  Bacon-Wrapped Franks, **2.** 46
  Barbecued Bacon Burgers, **2.** 40
  Basic Grilled Burgers, **2.** 38
  Basted Poultry-on-a-Spit, **2.** 43
  Beef Teriyaki, **2.** 34
  Blue Cheese Burgers, **2.** 40
  Calico Rice Bake, **2.** 68
  Cheesy Potato-Carrot Foil Bake, **2.** 65
  Company Pork Loin Roast, **2.** 52
  Corn-Stuffed Pork Chops, **2.** 50
  Country-Style Barbecued Ribs, **2.** 54
  Crab-Bacon Bites, **2.** 70
  Fiesta Beef Kebabs, **2.** 37
  Fish in a Basket, **2.** 57
  Foil-Barbecued Shrimp, **2.** 58
  Foil-Wrapped Clambake, **2.** 65
  Frank-Vegetable Kebabs, **2.** 47
  Glazed Ham Slice, **2.** 49
  Grilled Acorn Squash, **2.** 66
  Grilled Bread Fix-Ups, **2.** 63
  Grilled Rock Lobster Tails, **2.** 59
  Grilled Salmon Steaks, **2.** 57
  Grilled Turkey Pieces, **2.** 42
  Grilled Whole Potatoes, **2.** 65
  Herb-Butter Basting Sauce, **2.** 45
  Herb-Seasoned Vegetables, **2.** 67
  Italian-Seasoned Vegetable Kebabs, **2.** 66
  Lamb Shish Kebabs, **2.** 62
  Lemon-Marinated Chuck Roast, **2.** 37
  Marinated Fish Kebabs, **2.** 58
  Marinated Leg of Lamb, **2.** 60
  Marinated Shrimp Appetizers, **2.** 69
  Meat and Potato Bake, **2.** 50
  Onion-Stuffed Steak, **2.** 36
  Pineapple-Glazed Chicken, **2.** 42
  Pizza Burgers, **2.** 39
  Pizza-Frank Sandwiches, **2.** 47
  Polish Sausage-Krauters, **2.** 45
  Quick Garlic Cubed Steaks, **2.** 38
  Roasted Corn on the Cob, **2.** 64
  Roasted Pork Chops, **2.** 51
  Saucy Lamb Riblets, **2.** 62
  Skillet-Fried Fish, **2.** 56
  Smoked Mustard-Glazed Ribs, **2.** 54
  Smoked Short Ribs, **2.** 34
  Spiced Orange-Apricot Ribs, **2.** 53
  Spicy Barbecued Chicken, **2.** 41
  Steak and Shrimp Kebabs, **2.** 35
  Sweet-Sour Basting Sauce, **2.** 44
  Sweet-Sour Ham, **2.** 48
  Teriyaki Appetizer Ribs, **2.** 69
  Wine Basting Sauce, **2.** 44
  Wine-Sauced Shoulder Chops, **2.** 61
Barbecue Sauce, Easy, **17.** 719
Barbecue Sauce, Snappy, **17.** 718
Barbecue-Style Broiled Chicken, **14.** 608
Bar Cookies, **8.** 294
Barley Bake, Toasted, **15.** 650
Barley, Skillet, **15.** 650
Barley Soup, Beef-, **18.** 740
Basic Broiled Chicken, **14.** 607
Basic Broiled Pork Chops, **12.** 499
Basic Broiled Pork Steaks, **12.** 499
Basic Crêpes, **11.** 442
Basic Dessert Crêpes, **9.** 356
Basic Drop Cookies, **8.** 305
Basic Grilled Burgers, **2.** 38
Basic Hard Sauce, **9.** 363

**Boldface numbers
indicate chapters.**

Basic Muffins, **4.** 157
Basted Poultry-on-a-Spit, **2.** 43
Batter Rolls, **4.** 133
Beans
 Baked Bean Quintet, **19.** 786
 Easy Baked Beans, **19.** 785
 Ham and Bean Vegetable Soup, **18.** 757
 Hot Five-Bean Salad, **16.** 673
 Marinated Three-Bean Salad, **16.** 674
 New England Baked Beans, **19.** 785
 Quick Beans-and-Franks Soup, **18.** 747
 Quick Three-Bean Salad, **16.** 674
 Salami-Bean Casserole, **12.** 515
 Tongue and Lima Skillet, **12.** 529
Beans, Green
 Beans—Green or Wax, canning and freezing, **7.** 256
 Green Bean Bake with Onion, **19.** 783
 Green Beans Amandine, **19.** 781
 Green Beans Especial, **19.** 782
 Herbed Green Beans, **19.** 781
 Italian Bean Bake, **19.** 782
Beans, Lima
 Beans—Lima or Butter, canning and freezing, **7.** 257
 Creamy Succotash, **19.** 784
 Herbed Lima Bean Bake, **19.** 783
Béarnaise Sauce, Classic, **17.** 713
Beef
 Beef Bourguignonne, **18.** 738
 Beef Stew, **18.** 739
 Beef Stock, **18.** 737
 Brisket Carbonnade, **12.** 462
 Cheese-Wine Log, **1.** 9
 Cider Stew, **18.** 739
 Creamed Dried Beef, **12.** 476
 Herbed Lamb Stew, **18.** 745
 Meat identification, **12.** 452
 New England Boiled Dinner, **12.** 462
 Old-Fashioned Vegetable-Beef Soup, **18.** 740

**Boldface numbers indicate chapters.**

South American Pork Soup, **18.** 745
Beef, Cooked
 Chef's Salad, **16.** 692
 Greek Salad, **16.** 693
 Oven Hash, **12.** 475
Beef, Ground
 Barbecued Bacon Burgers, **2.** 40
 Basic Grilled Burgers, **2.** 38
 Blue Cheese Burgers, **2.** 40
 Chili con Carne, **18.** 741
 Cocktail Meatballs, **1.** 7
 Coney Islands, **12.** 517
 Double-Decker Burgers, **12.** 479
 Hamburger-Corn Bake, **12.** 483
 Hamburger Pie, **12.** 485
 Hamburgers, **12.** 479
 Lasagna, **12.** 512
 Meatball Stew with Spinach Dumplings, **18.** 741
 Meat Loaf, **12.** 477
 Moussaka, **12.** 528
 Pizza Burgers, **2.** 39
 Pizza-Frank Sandwiches, **2.** 47
 Porcupine Meatballs, **12.** 477
 Quick Beef Goulash Stew, **18.** 742
 Sauerbraten Burgers, **12.** 478
 Skilletburgers, **12.** 480
 South-of-the-Border Salad, **16.** 695
 Spaghetti and Meatballs, **12.** 482
 Spaghetti Sauce, **12.** 482
 Stuffed Cabbage Rolls, **12.** 497
 Stuffed Green Peppers, **12.** 481
 Swedish Meatballs, **1.** 6
 Tacos con Carne, **12.** 483
 Texas Beef Skillet, **12.** 484
Beef, Ribs
 Beef-Barley Soup, **18.** 740
 Broiled Short Ribs, **12.** 472
 Chinese-Style Beef Ribs, **12.** 472
 Smoked Short Ribs, **2.** 34
Beef, Roasts
 Beef au Jus, **12.** 460
 Beef Pot Roast, **12.** 461
 Beef Wellington, **12.** 456
 Lemon-Marinated Chuck Roast, **2.** 37

Roasting Beef, **12.** 455
Roast with Barbecue Gravy, **12.** 463
Rump Roast with Vegetables, **12.** 459
Sauerbraten, **12.** 464
Savory Stuffed Rib Roast, **12.** 458
Standing Rib Roast with Yorkshire Pudding, **12.** 457
Teriyaki Roast Beef, **12.** 458
Beef, Steak
Beef and Vegetable Stir-Fry, **12.** 471
Beef Fondue, **12.** 468
Beef Stroganoff, **12.** 467
Beef Teriyaki, **2.** 34
Broiling Beef Steaks, **12.** 470
Chicken-Fried Round Steak, **12.** 468
Deviled Beef Rolls, **12.** 476
Fiesta Beef Kebabs, **2.** 37
London Broil, **12.** 465
Onion-Stuffed Steak, **2.** 36
Oven Steak and Vegetables, **12.** 466
Oven Swiss Steak, **12.** 466
Panbroiling Beef Steaks, **12.** 469
Quick Garlic Cubed Steaks, **2.** 38
Steak and Kidney Pie, **12.** 531
Steak and Shrimp Kebabs, **2.** 35
Swiss Steak, **12.** 466
Beer-Braised Rabbit, **12.** 533
Beer-Cheese Fondue, **1.** 19
Beer-Cheese Triangles, **4.** 152
Beer Rabbit, **10.** 406
Beets
Beets, canning and freezing, **7.** 258
Beets with Pineapple, **19.** 788
Harvard Beets, **19.** 787
Orange-Glazed Beets, **19.** 787
Pickled-Beets, **17.** 728
Berliner Kranser, **8.** 319
Berries
Berries, canning and freezing, **7.** 246
Blueberry Melba Parfaits, **9.** 354
Summer Fruit Compote, **9.** 353
Beverages

Apricot Swizzle, **3.** 82
Bloody Marys, **3.** 80
Café Almond, **3.** 90
Café Benedictine, **3.** 90
Café Columbian, **3.** 90
Café Israel, **3.** 90
Champagne Fruit Punch, **3.** 77
Chocolate Milk Shake, **3.** 85
Chocolate Soda, **3.** 87
Choco-Nutty Milk Shake, **3.** 86
Citrus Rum Punch, **3.** 77
Cocoa, **3.** 83
Coffee, **3.** 90
Coffee-and-Cream Milk Shake, **3.** 86
Coffee Chocolate, **3.** 85
Creamy Reception Punch, **3.** 80
Dessert Coffee, **3.** 90
Double Chocolate Soda, **3.** 87
Drip Coffee, **3.** 90
Easy Sherbet Punch, **3.** 80
Eggnog, **3.** 83
Frisky Sours, **3.** 88
Frosty Cranberry Cocktail, **3.** 88
Fruit Cooler, **3.** 81
Fruit-Flavored Float, **3.** 82
Grenadine Punch, **3.** 81
Hot Buttered Rum Mix, **3.** 86
Hot Chocolate, **3.** 84
Hot Mulled Cider, **3.** 87
Iced Tea, **3.** 91
Individual Cocktails, **3.** 79
Irish Coffee, **3.** 90
Lemonade or Limeade, **3.** 87
Nonalcoholic Punch, **3.** 79
Orange-Grape Cooler, **3.** 85
Orange Spiced Tea, **3.** 91
Party Punch Base, **3.** 79
Pastel Punch, **3.** 80
Percolator Coffee, **3.** 89
Quantity Fruit Punch, **3.** 77
Sangria, **3.** 84
Slushy Punch, **3.** 78
Spicy Chocolate, **3.** 85
Spiked Party Punch, **3.** 79
Spiked Slushy Punch, **3.** 79

**Boldface numbers
indicate chapters.**

Beverages (continued)
Strawberry Milk Shake, **3.** 86
Strawberry Spritzer, **3.** 89
Sun Tea, **3.** 91
Tea, **3.** 90
Vanilla Milk Shake, **3.** 85
Vanilla Soda, **3.** 86
White Wine Punch, **3.** 79
Yogurt Sip, **3.** 89
Biscuits
Beer-Cheese Triangles, **4.** 152
Biscuits Supreme, **4.** 153
Buttermilk Biscuits, **4.** 153
Cornmeal Biscuits, **4.** 153
Garden Biscuits, **4.** 154
Homemade Biscuit Mix Biscuits,
**4.** 151
Pecan Biscuit Spirals, **4.** 152
Sesame Swirls, **4.** 154
Sour Cream Biscuits, **4.** 154
Bismarcks, **4.** 124
Blackberry Pie, Fresh, **13.** 551
Black Bottom Pie, **13.** 566
Black Forest Cake, **5.** 180
Blender Hollandaise Sauce, **17.** 712
Blender Mayonnaise, **16.** 706
Blonde Brownies, **8.** 296
Bloody Marys, **3.** 80
Blueberries
Blueberry Buckle, **4.** 145
Blueberry Melba Parfaits, **9.** 354
Blueberry Muffins, **4.** 157
Blueberry Shortcake, **9.** 349
Fresh Blueberry Pie, **13.** 550
Blue Cheese Burgers, **2.** 40
Blue Cheese-Onion Dip, **1.** 21
Blue Cheese Sauce, **17.** 711
Boiled Crabs **11.** 431
Boiled Lobster, **11.** 429
Boiled Lobster Tails, **11.** 431
Boiled Scallops, **11.** 430
Boiled Shellfish, **11.** 430
Boiled Shrimp, **11.** 430
Bordelaise Sauce, **17.** 715
Boston Brown Bread, **4.** 136
Bouillabaisse, **18.** 749

**Boldface numbers
indicate chapters.**

Braised Pork Steaks, **12.** 498
Brandy Hard Sauce, **9.** 363
**13.** 550
Bread and Butter Pickles, canning,
**7.** 279
Breaded Pork Tenderloins, **12.** 499
Bread Pudding, **9.** 335
Breads, Quick,
Any-Fruit Coffee Cake, **4.** 143
Apple Fritter Rings, **4.** 150
Apple-Raisin Muffins, **4.** 157
Applesauce Coffee Cake, **4.** 147
Apricot-Orange Bread, **4.** 139
Banana Nut Bread, **4.** 140
Banana-Nut Muffins, **4.** 157
Basic Muffins, **4.** 157
Beer-Cheese Triangles, **4.** 152
Biscuits, **4.** 151
Biscuits Supreme, **4.** 153
Blueberry Buckle, **4.** 145
Blueberry Muffins, **4.** 157
Boston Brown Bread, **4.** 136
Buckwheat Pancakes, **4.** 159
Buttermilk Biscuits, **4.** 153
Buttermilk Doughnuts, **4.** 150
Buttermilk Pancakes, **4.** 159
Cake Doughnuts, **4.** 149
Cheese Muffins, **4.** 157
Cheese-Nut Bread, **4.** 142
Cheese Spoon Bread, **4.** 156
Cherry-Pecan Bread, **4.** 140
Chocolate Cake Doughnuts, **4.**
149
Cocoa Ripple Ring, **4.** 146
Corn Bread, **4.** 155
Cornmeal Biscuits, **4.** 153
Corn Sticks, **4.** 156
Cranberry Muffins, **4.** 157
Cranberry-Orange Bread, **4.** 138
Date-Apple Coffee Bread, **4.** 137
Date-Nut Muffins, **4.** 157
French Toast, **4.** 160
Garden Biscuits, **4.** 154
Homemade Biscuit Mix, **4.** 151
Homemade Biscuit Mix Pancakes,
**4.** 151
Honey-Wheat Muffins, **4.** 158
Hush Puppies, **4.** 155
Jelly Muffins, **4.** 157

Muffins, **4.** 151
Nut Bread, **4.** 142
Orange-Date Coffee Cake, **4.** 144
Orange Sticky Rolls, **4.** 148
Pancakes, **4.** 159
Pecan Biscuit Spirals, **4.** 152
Popovers, **4.** 161
Pumpkin Muffins, **4.** 157
Pumpkin Nut Bread, **4.** 141
Sesame Swirls, **4.** 154
Sour Cream Biscuits, **4.** 154
Spicy Buttermilk Coffee Cake, **4.** 144
Spoon Bread, **4.** 156
Sticky Nut Rolls, **4.** 148
Streusel Coffee Cake, **4.** 146
Sunflower Seed Muffins, **4.** 158
Sunshine Muffins, **4.** 158
Three-C Bread, **4.** 141
Waffles, **4.** 160
Zucchini Nut Loaf, **4.** 139
Breadsticks, **4.** 128
Breads, Yeast
Anadama Bread, **4.** 110
Bagels, **4.** 127
Barbecue Breadsticks, **4.** 129
Batter Rolls, **4.** 133
Bismarcks, **4.** 124
Breadsticks, **4.** 128
Brioche, **4.** 130
Brown-and-Serve Rolls, **4.** 125
Caramel-Pecan Rolls, **4.** 120
Cardamom Braid, **4.** 115
Cheese Bread, **4.** 108
Chocolate Swirl Coffee Cake, **4.** 118
Chocolate Yeast Doughnuts, **4.** 122
Cinnamon Crisps, **4.** 119
Cinnamon Rolls, **4.** 121
Cinnamon Swirl Bread, **4.** 113
Croissants, **4.** 129
Dinner Rolls, **4.** 125
Easy-Mix White Bread, **4.** 102
Egg Bread, **4.** 113
French Bread, **4.** 104
German Stollen, **4.** 107
Hamburger and Frankfurter Buns, **4.** 125

Herb Bagels, **4.** 128
Hot Cross Buns, **4.** 123
Individual French Loaves, **4.** 104
Julekage, **4.** 114
Kuchen, **4.** 116
Light Rye Bagels, **4.** 128
Molasses-Oatmeal Bread, **4.** 105
Onion Bagels, **4.** 128
Orange-Cinnamon Sourdough Rolls, **4.** 135
Parmesan Breadsticks, **4.** 129
Party Pita Bread, **4.** 133
Peasant Bread, **4.** 115
Pita Bread, **4.** 132
Poppy Seed or Sesame Seed Bagels, **4.** 128
Potato Bread, **4.** 112
Prune Kuchen, **4.** 118
Pumpernickel, **4.** 109
Raisin Bread, **4.** 114
Russian Black Bread, **4.** 111
Rye Bread, **4.** 106
Soft Pretzels, **4.** 131
Sourdough Bread, **4.** 134
Sourdough Starter, **4.** 134
Swedish Limpa, **4.** 109
Sweet Rolls, **4.** 120
White Bread, Conventional Method, **4.** 103
Whole Wheat Bread, **4.** 106
Whole Wheat Pita Bread, **4.** 133
Yeast Doughnuts, **4.** 121
Brioche, **4.** 130
Brisket Carbonnade, **12.** 462
Broccoli
Broccoli, freezing, **7.** 259
Broccoli-Onion Casserole, **19.** 789
Broccoli Oriental, **19.** 788
Broccoli Soufflé, **19.** 791
Chicken Divan, **14.** 612
Golden Crumb Broccoli, **19.** 789
Hot Broccoli Dip, **1.** 19
Broiled Coconut Topping, **5.** 197
Broiled Fish, **11.** 412
Broiled Grapefruit Halves, **1.** 18
Broiled Lamb Chops, **12.** 522

**Boldface numbers
indicate chapters.**

Broiled Short Ribs, **12.** 472
Broiled Shrimp, **11.** 432
Broiled Tomatoes, **19.** 813
Broiling Beef Steaks, **12.** 470
Brown-and-Serve Rolls, **4.** 125
Browned Butter Frosting, **8.** 311
Brownie Pudding, **9.** 340
Brownies
   Blonde Brownies, **8.** 296
   Chocolate Cake Brownies, **8.** 296
   Chocolate-Cream Cheese
     Brownies, **8.** 294
   Chocolate Syrup Brownies, **8.** 295
   Fudge Brownies, **8.** 294
Brown Rice, **15.** 641
Brown Sauce, **17.** 716
Brown Sugar Nut Brittle, **6.** 215
Brown-Sugar-Rhubarb Pie, **13.** 560
Brussels Sprouts
   Brussels Sprouts Soufflé, **19.** 790
   Frank-Vegetable Kebabs, **2.** 47
   Saucy Brussels Sprouts, **19.** 790
Buckwheat Pancakes, **4.** 159
Bulgur Sauté, **15.** 650
Busy-Day Cake, **5.** 170
Butter Frosting, **5.** 195
Buttermilk Biscuits, **4.** 153
Buttermilk Doughnuts, **4.** 150
Buttermilk Dressing, **16.** 702
Buttermilk Pancakes, **4.** 159
Butters
   Herbed Butter, **2.** 64
   Honey Butter, **17.** 726
   Flavored Butters, **17.** 726
Butterscotch Filling, **4.** 124
Butterscotch Marble Cake, **5.** 190

---

# C

Cabbage
   Company Cabbage with Pecans,
     **19.** 791
   Pennsylvania Red Cabbage, **19.**
     791

**Boldface numbers
indicate chapters.**

   Quick Cabbage-Cheese Soup, **18.**
     765
   Stuffed Cabbage Rolls, **12.** 497
Caesar Croutons, **16.** 662
Caesar Salad, Original, **16.** 661
Café Almond, **3.** 90
Café Benedictine, **3.** 90
Café Columbian, **3.** 90
Café Israel, **3.** 90
Cake Doughnuts, **4.** 149
Cakes
   Applesauce Spice Cake, **5.** 176
   Banana Cake, **5.** 171
   Black Forest Cake, **5.** 180
   Busy-Day Cake, **5.** 170
   Butterscotch Marble Cake, **5.** 190
   Carrot Cake, **5.** 173
   Chocolate Chip Cake, **5.** 168
   Chocolate Marble Cake, **5.** 189
   Dark Fruitcake, **5.** 184
   Date Cake, **5.** 177
   Devil's Food Cake, **5.** 179
   Feathery Fudge Cake, **5.** 181
   German Chocolate Cake, **5.** 178
   Gingerbread, **5.** 175
   Italian Cream Cake, **5.** 191
   Lady Baltimore Cake, **5.** 168
   Lemon Pudding Cake, **9.** 340
   Light Fruitcake, **5.** 183
   Nutmeg Cake with Toasted
     Meringue Topping, **5.** 174
   Pineapple Upside-Down Cake, **5.** 171
   Poppy Seed Cake, **5.** 189
   Pound Cake, **5.** 172
   Pumpkin Molasses Cake, **5.** 173
   Sour Cream Chocolate Cake, **5.**
     182
   Spice Nut Cake, **5.** 176
   White Cake Supreme, **5.** 168
   White Cake Supreme Petits Fours,
     **5.** 168
   Yellow Cake, **5.** 170
   Yellow Citrus Cake, **5.** 169
Cakes, Angel
   Angel Cake, **5.** 185
   Apricot Angel Dessert, **9.** 347
Cakes, Chiffon
   Golden Chiffon Cake, **5.** 185
Cakes, Sponge

Chocolate Cake Roll, **5.** 188
Hot Milk Sponge Cake, **5.** 187
Jelly Roll, **5.** 187
Orange Sponge Cake, **5.** 186
Calico Rice Bake, **2.** 68
Canadian Bacon Pie, **12.** 508
Candied Squash, **18.** 812
Candied Squash Rings, **18.** 811
Candies
Caramel Apples, **6.** 213
Carob Candy Squares, **6.** 220
Cherry Divinity, **6.** 209
Cream Cheese Mints, **6.** 221
Divinity, **6.** 209
Easy Walnut Penuche, **6.** 219
Fondant, **6.** 208
Fondant Mint Patties, **6.** 209
Old-Fashioned Molasses Taffy, **6.** 216
Peanut Caramel Apples, **6.** 213
Penuche, **6.** 206
Peppermint Bonbons, **6.** 218
Saltwater Taffy, **6.** 213
Seafoam Candy, **6.** 210
Southern Pralines, **6.** 208
Toffee Butter Crunch, **6.** 215
Walnut Divinity, **6.** 210
Candies, Caramels
Caramels, **6.** 212
Chocolate Caramels, **6.** 212
Candies, Chocolate
Chocolate-Covered Cherries, **6.** 210
Chocolate Nut Balls, **6.** 217
Choco-Scotch Crunchies, **6.** 220
Easy Fudge, **6.** 217
Old-Time Fudge, **6.** 204
Remarkable Fudge, **6.** 205
Rocky Road, **6.** 221
Candies, Fudge
Almond Opera Fudge, **6.** 206
Cherry Opera Fudge, **6.** 206
Easy Fudge, **6.** 217
Old-Time Fudge, **6.** 204
Opera Fudge, **6.** 205
Remarkable Fudge, **6.** 205
Candies, Nut
Brown Sugar Nut Brittle, **6.** 215
Chocolate Nut Balls, **6.** 217

Glazed Nuts, **6.** 214
Nut Brittle, **6.** 214
Candies, Popcorn
Caramel Corn, **6.** 218
Old-Time Popcorn Balls, **6.** 216
Sugared Popcorn, **6.** 219
Canning
Bread and Butter Pickles, **7.** 279
Canning basics, **7.** 229–38
Corn Relish, **7.** 277
Dill Pickles. **7.** 279
Fish, **7.** 272
Grape Jam, **7.** 287
Kosher Dill Pickles, **7.** 280
Meat, **7.** 271
Mixed Pickles, **7.** 280
Orange Marmalade, **7.** 288
Peach-Banana Jam, **7.** 286
Peach Jam, **7.** 286
Peach-Plum Jam, **7.** 286
Pickles and Relishes, **7.** 275
Plum Jam, **7.** 287
Poultry, **7.** 273
Quick Mustard Pickles, **7.** 281
Strawberry Jam, **7.** 286
Sweet Pickle Slices, **7.** 278
Vegetable Relish, **7.** 276
Canning, Fruit
Apple Butter, **7.** 243
Apple Juice, **7.** 244
Apples, **7.** 242
Applesauce, **7.** 243
Apricot Nectar, **7.** 246
Apricots, **7.** 244–45
Berries, **7.** 246
Canning basics, **7.** 229–38
Cherries, **7.** 247
Grape Juice Concentrate, **7.** 249
Peaches, **7.** 250
Pears, **7.** 252
Plums, **7.** 253
Rhubarb, **7.** 254
Spiced Peaches, **7.** 251
Whole Cranberry Sauce, **7.** 249
Canning Vegetables
Asparagus, **7.** 255

**Boldface numbers
indicate chapters.**

Canning (continued)
Beans—Green or Wax, **7.** 256
Beans—Lima or Butter, **7.** 257
Beets, **7.** 258
Carrots, **7.** 259
Corn—Cream-Style, **7.** 261
Corn—Whole Kernel, **7.** 263
Peas (Green), **7.** 264
Peppers (Sweet), **7.** 265
Sweet Potatoes, **7.** 265
Tomato Catsup, **7.** 269
Tomatoes, **7.** 266
Tomato Juice, **7.** 268
Tomato Juice Cocktail, **7.** 268
Winter Squash or Pumpkin, **7.** 270
Capon, Roasting, **14.** 619
Caramel Apples, **6.** 213
Caramel Corn, **6.** 218
Caramel-Pecan Rolls, **4.** 120
Caramels, **6.** 212
Caraway-Cheese Spread, **2.** 64
Cardamom Braid, **4.** 115
Carob Candy Squares, **6.** 220
Carrots
Carrot Cake, **5.** 173
Carrot-Rice Bake, **19.** 793
Carrots, canning and freezing, **7.** 259
Cheesy Potato-Carrot Foil Bake, **2.** 65
Glazed Carrots, **19.** 792
Orange-Glazed Carrots, **19.** 792
Casseroles
Classic Cheese Strata, **10.** 403
Cottage Pasta Bake, **15.** 636
Egg-Rice Bake, **10.** 384
Egg-Sausage Casserole, **10.** 385
Eggs Florentine, **10.** 381
Gold Rush Brunch, **10.** 380
Individual Quiche Casseroles, **10.** 403
Macaroni and Cheese, **10.** 405
Mushroom-Cereal Bake, **15.** 645
Mushroom-Rice Bake, **15.** 645
Old-Fashioned Cheese Bake, **10.** 400

Salami-Bean Casserole, **12.** 515
Scalloped Eggs and Bacon, **10.** 385
Swiss Onion Bake, **10.** 381
Toasted Barley Bake, **15.** 650
Casseroles, Beef
Hamburger-Corn Bake, **12.** 483
Hamburger Pie, **12.** 485
Casseroles, Fish and Seafood
Baked Fish with Mushrooms, **11.** 416
Bundled Fish, **11.** 417
Fish Florentine, **11.** 428
Individual Tuna Pies, **11.** 436
Quick Fish-Potato Supper, **11.** 426
Seafood Quiche, **10.** 402
Shrimp-Egg Bake, **10.** 387
Tuna Noodle Casserole, **11.** 435
Casseroles, Ham
Ham-Noodle Casserole, **12.** 505
Potato-Ham Scallop, **12.** 506
Casseroles, Pork
Egg-Sausage Casserole, **10.** 385
Sausage and Corn Bread, **12.** 514
Scalloped Eggs and Bacon, **10.** 385
Casseroles, Poultry
Arroz con Pollo, **14.** 602
Cassoulet, **14.** 616
Chicken-Cheese Crêpes, **14.** 603
Chicken Country Captain, **14.** 601
Chicken Divan, **14.** 612
Chicken Enchilada Casserole, **14.** 613
Chicken Pot Pies, **14.** 610
Crowd-Size Chicken Bake, **14.** 614
Dilled Chicken-Noodle Bake, **14.** 615
Popover Chicken Tarragon, **14.** 614
Wild-Rice-Chicken Casserole, **14.** 611
Casseroles, Vegetable
Artichokes Velvet, **19.** 779
Baked Bean Quintet, **19.** 786
Broccoli-Onion Casserole, **19.** 789

Carrot-Rice Bake, **19.** 793
Cheddar-Squash Puff, **19.** 811
Cheesy Scalloped Potatoes, **19.** 807
Corn Custard Pudding, **19.** 795
Easy Baked Beans, **19.** 785
Eggplant Parmigiana, **19.** 798
Golden Crumb Broccoli, **19.** 789
Green Bean Bake with Onion, **19.** 783
Herbed Lima Bean Bake, **19.** 783
Italian Bean Bake, **19.** 782
Mashed Sweet Potato Bake, **19.** 808
New England Baked Beans, **19.** 785
Oven Candied Sweet Potatoes, **19.** 807
Potluck Vegetable Casserole, **19.** 817
Rutabaga and Apple, **19.** 808
Saucy Celery Casserole, **19.** 794
Scalloped Corn, **19.** 795
Scalloped Potatoes, **19.** 806
Scalloped Tomatoes, **19.** 813
Spicy Stuffed Eggplant, **19.** 797
Sweet-Potato-Cashew Bake, **19.** 807
Whipped Parsnip Puff, **19.** 815
Whipped Rutabaga Puff, **19.** 815
Whipped Turnip Puff, **19.** 814
Cassoulet, **14.** 616
Cauliflower
Cauliflower, freezing, **7.** 260
Cauliflower Soufflé, **19.** 791
Cheese-Frosted Cauliflower, **19.** 793
Celery Casserole,
Saucy, **19.** 794
Cereal
Baked Gnocchi, **15.** 649
Bulgur Sauté, **15.** 650
Cornmeal Mush, **15.** 647
Curried Bulgur Sauté **15.** 651
Fried Mush, **15.** 647
Granola, **15.** 649
Grits, **15.** 648
Mushroom-Cereal Bake, **15.** 645
Polenta, **15.** 647

Skillet Barley, **15.** 650
Southern Cheese Grits, **15.** 648
Spiced Porridge, **15.** 648
Spicy Raisin Oatmeal, **15.** 647
Toasted Barley Bake, **15.** 650
Champagne Fruit Punch, **3.** 77
Cheddar Macaroni Salad, **16.** 667
Cheddar-Squash Puff, **19.** 811
Cheese
Beer-Cheese Fondue, **1.** 19
Beer-Cheese Triangles, **4.** 152
Cheese and Herb Omelet, **10.** 390
Cheese Ball, **1.** 8
Cheese Bread, **4.** 108
Cheese French Omelet, **10.** 394
Cheese-Frosted Cauliflower, **19.** 793
Cheese-Ham Ball, **1.** 12
Cheese identification, **10.** 392–93
Cheese Muffins, **4.** 157
Cheese-Nut Bread, **4.** 142
Cheese-Onion Scrambled Eggs, **10.** 374
Cheese Sauce, **12.** 502, **17.** 711
Cheese Soufflé, **10.** 397
Cheese Soup, **18.** 762
Cheese Spoon Bread, **4.** 156
Cheese-Wine Log, **1.** 9
Cheesy Potato-Carrot Foil Bake, **2.** 65
Chicken-Cheese Crêpes, **14.** 603
Chocolate-Cream Cheese Brownies, **8.** 294
Classic Cheese Fondue, **10.** 404
Classic Cheese Strata, **10.** 403
Cottage Pasta Bake, **15.** 636
Creamy Cheese Fondue, **10.** 405
Easy Baked Cheese Omelet, **10.** 396
Easy Cheese Eggs a la King, **10.** 383
Ham and Cheese Omelet, **10.** 390
Macaroni and Cheese, **10.** 405
Old-Fashioned Cheese Bake, **10.** 400

**Boldface numbers
indicate chapters.**

Cheese (continued)

    Quick Cabbage-Cheese Soup, **18.** 765

    Quick Cheesy Tuna Soup, **18.** 765

    Rolled Cream Cheese Cookies, **8.** 322

    Smoky Cheese Ball, **1.** 12

    Southern Cheese Grits, **15.** 648

    Welsh Rabbit, **10.** 406

Cheesecake

    Cheesecake Supreme, **9.** 344

    Sour Cream Cheesecake, **9.** 343

Cheesy Butter Spread, **2.** 64

Cheesy Chicken a la King, **14.** 603

Cheesy Chicken Corn Chowder, **18.** 764

Cheesy Potato-Carrot Foil Bake, **2.** 65

Cheesy Scalloped Potatoes, **19.** 807

Chef's Salad, **16.** 692

Cherries

    Cherries, canning and freezing, **7.** 247

    Cherries Jubilee, **9.** 361

    Cherry-Cider Salad, **16.** 680

    Cherry Cobbler, **9.** 351

    Cherry Divinity, **6.** 209

    Cherry Filling, **5.** 181

    Cherry-Lemon Ring, **16.** 679

    Cherry-Nut Ice Cream, **9.** 357

    Cherry Opera Fudge, **6.** 206

    Cherry-Pecan Bread, **4.** 140

    Cherry Pie, **13.** 545

    Cherry Sauce, **9.** 344

    Cherry Torte, **9.** 346

    Fresh Cherry Pie, **13.** 545

    Peach-Cherry Ice Cream, **9.** 357

    Spicy Cherry Sauce, **17.** 720

Chestnut Stuffing, **14.** 626

Chicken

    Apricot Chicken, **14.** 596

    Arroz con Pollo, **14.** 602

    Barbecue-Style Broiled Chicken, **14.** 608

**Boldface numbers indicate chapters.**

Basic Broiled Chicken, **14.** 607

Basted Poultry-on-a-Spit, **2.** 43

Cassoulet, **14.** 616

Cheesy Chicken Corn Chowder, **18.** 764

Chicken and Crab Wontons, **1.** 16

Chicken and Dumplings, **14.** 598

Chicken and Noodles, **14.** 598

Chicken Cacciatore, **14.** 597

Chicken Country Captain, **14.** 601

Chicken Dijon, **14.** 586

Chicken Fricassee, **14.** 596

Chicken Italiano, **14.** 592

Chicken Kiev, **14.** 587

Chicken Liver Pâté, **1.** 14

Chicken Livers in Tomato Sauce, **14.** 600

Chicken Livers Stroganoff, **14.** 599

Chicken Paprikash, **14.** 585

Chicken Saltimbocca, **14.** 595

Chicken Stock, **18.** 736

Chicken Teriyaki Kebabs, **14.** 609

Chicken Vegetable-Noodle Soup, **18.** 753

Chicken with Currant Glaze, **14.** 622

Chicken with Walnuts, **14.** 590

Coq Au Vin, **14.** 594

Cornmeal Batter Fried Chicken, **14.** 585

Crab-Stuffed Chicken Breasts, **14.** 604

Crisp-Fried Chicken, **14.** 584

Crispy Baked Barbecue Chicken, **14.** 592

Cumberland-Style Broiled Chicken, **14.** 607

Curried Chicken and Vegetables, **14.** 618

Curry and Parsley Chicken, **14.** 592

Foil-Wrapped Clambake, **2.** 55

Fried Chicken with Crab Sauce, **14.** 588

Giblet Gravy, **14.** 629

Glazed Chicken and Rice, **14.** 609

Hawaiian Broiled Chicken, **14.** 607

Oven Chicken Kiev, **14.** 588
Oven-Crisped Orange Chicken, **14.** 593
Oven-Fried Chicken, **14.** 591
Oven-Fried Chicken Monterey, **14.** 589
Pan- and Oven-Fried Chicken, **14.** 584
Parmesan Chicken, **14.** 592
Pineapple-Glazed Chicken, **2.** 42
Popover Chicken Tarragon, **14.** 614
Potato-Chip Chicken, **14.** 592
Roasting Chicken, **14.** 617
Roast Tarragon Chicken, **14.** 623
Skillet-Fried Chicken, **14.** 584
Spicy Barbecued Chicken, **2.** 41
Stewed Chicken, **14.** 597
Chicken, Cooked
Baked Omelet with Chicken Sauce, **10.** 397
Cheesy Chicken a la King, **14.** 603
Chef's Salad, **16.** 692
Chicken a la King, **14.** 602
Chicken and Dumplings, **14.** 598
Chicken and Noodles, **14.** 598
Chicken-Asparagus Stacks, **14.** 605
Chicken-Cheese Crêpes, **14.** 603
Chicken Divan, **14.** 612
Chicken Enchilada Casserole, **14.** 613
Chicken Pot Pies, **14.** 610
Chicken-Stuffed Tomatoes, **16.** 700
Cream of Chicken Soup, **18.** 755
Crowd-Size Chicken Bake, **14.** 614
Curried Chicken Salad, **16.** 694
Dilled Chicken-Noodle Bake, **14.** 615
Easy Chicken-Curry Soup, **18.** 763
Mulligatawny, **18.** 753
Super Chicken Subs, **14.** 606
Tuna Soufflé, **10.** 399
Wild-Rice-Chicken Casserole, **14.** 611
Chicken-Fried Round Steak, **12.** 468

Chili con Carne, **18.** 741
Chili con Queso, **1.** 22
Chinese Fried Rice, **15.** 644
Chinese Mustard, Hot, **17.** 718
Chinese Spinach,**19.** 810
Chinese-Style Beef Ribs, **12.** 472
Choco-Coffee-Toffee Squares, **9.** 348
Chocolate
Black Bottom Pie, **13.** 566
Black Forest Cake, **5.** 180
Brownie Pudding, **9.** 340
Café Columbian, **3.** 90
Café Israel, **3.** 90
Choco-Coffee-Toffee Squares, **9.** 348
Chocolate-Almond Ice Cream, **9.** 357
Chocolate Butter Frosting, **5.** 195
Chocolate Cake Brownies, **8.** 296
Chocolate Cake Doughnuts, **4.** 149
Chocolate Cake Roll, **5.** 188
Chocolate Caramels, **6.** 212
Chocolate Chiffon Pie, **13.** 563
Chocolate Chip Cake, **5.** 168
Chocolate Chip Cookies, **8.** 306
Chocolate Chip Ice Cream, **9.** 357
Chocolate-Covered Cherries, **6.** 210
Chocolate-Cream Cheese Brownies, **8.** 294
Chocolate Filling, **4.** 124
Chocolate Fondue, **9.** 355
Chocolate Frosting, **8.** 296
Chocolate Glaze, **4.** 149
Chocolate Icing, **5.** 199
Chocolate Marble Cake, **5.** 189
Chocolate Milk Shake, **3.** 85
Chocolate Nut Balls, **6.** 217
Chocolate-Peanut Cookies, **8.** 305
Chocolate Pots de Crème, **9.** 337
Chocolate Pudding, **9.** 335
Chocolate Revel Bars, **8.** 299
Chocolate Soda, **3.** 87

**Boldface numbers
indicate chapters.**

Chocolate (continued)
Chocolate Soufflé, **9.** 341
Chocolate Sour Cream Frosting, **5.** 182
Chocolate Swirl Coffee Cake, **4.** 118
Chocolate Syrup Brownies, **8.** 295
Chocolate Wafer Crust, **13.** 574
Chocolate Yeast Doughnuts, **4.** 122
Choco-Mint Velvet, **9.** 359
Choco-Nutty Milk Shake, **3.** 86
Choco-Scotch Crunchies, **6.** 220
Choco-Velvet Ice Cream, **9.** 358
Cocoa, **3.** 83
Cocoa Ripple Ring, **4.** 146
Coffee Chocolate, **3.** 85
Coffee Fondue, **9.** 355
Crispy Chocolate-Peanut Butter Bars, **8.** 303
Dark Chocolate Cream Pie, **13.** 555
Devil's Food Cake, **5.** 179
Double Chocolate Drops, **8.** 310
Double Chocolate Soda, **3.** 87
Feathery Fudge Cake, **5.** 181
French Silk Pie, **13.** 565
Fudge Brownies, **8.** 294
Fudge Ribbon Pie, **13.** 565
German Chocolate Cake, **5.** 178
Hot Chocolate, **3.** 84
Italian Cream Cake, **5.** 191
Light Chocolate Cream Pie, **13.** 554
Mocha Butter Frosting, **5.** 195
Quick Chocolate Glaze, **8.** 295
Sour Cream Chocolate Cake, **5.** 182
Spicy Chocolate, **3.** 85
Choco-Mint Velvet, **9.** 359
Choco-Nutty Milk Shake, **3.** 86
Choco-Scotch Crunchies, **6.** 220
Choco-Velvet Ice Cream, **9.** 358
Choose-a-Fruit Salad Platter, **16.** 691
Choucroute Garni, **12.** 519
Chowders

Cheesy Chicken-Corn Chowder, **18.** 764
Fish Chowder, **18.** 753
Fresh Corn Chowder, **18.** 757
German Sausage Chowder, **18.** 743
Manhattan Clam Chowder, **18.** 750
New England Clam Chowder, **18.** 748
Chow Mein, Shrimp, **11.** 433
Chunky Applesauce, **9.** 363
Chunky Blue Cheese Dressing, **16.** 703
Cider Stew, **18.** 739
Cider Waldorf Mold, **16.** 682
Cinnamon
Cinnamon-Apple Jelly, **7.** 284
Cinnamon Apple Rings, **17.** 727
Cinnamon Crisps, **4.** 119
Cinnamon Fruit Salad, **16.** 690
Cinnamon Rolls, **4.** 121
Cinnamon Swirl Bread, **4.** 113
Orange-Cinnamon Sourdough Rolls, **4.** 135
Cioppino, **18.** 751
Citrus Rum Punch, **3.** 77
Citrus Vinaigrette, **16.** 703
Clams
Appetizer Clam Shells, **1.** 5
Bouillabaisse, **18.** 749
Cioppino, **18.** 751
Foil-Wrapped Clambake, **2.** 55
Fried Clams, Oysters, or Scallops, **11.** 431
Manhattan Clam Chowder, **18.** 750
New England Clam Chowder, **18.** 748
Steamed Clams, **11.** 434
Classic Béarnaise Sauce, **17.** 713
Classic Cheese Fondue, **10.** 404
Classic Cheese Strata, **10.** 403
Classic Hollandaise Sauce, **17.** 712
Classic Quiche Lorraine, **10.** 401
Cobblers
Apple Cobbler, **9.** 351
Cherry Cobbler, **9.** 351
Peach Cobbler, **9.** 351

**Boldface numbers
indicate chapters.**

Cocktail Meatballs, **1.** 7
Cocktails
  Bloody Marys, **3.** 80
  Citrus Rum Punch, **3.** 77
  Eggnog, **3.** 83
  Frisky Sours, **3.** 88
  Frosty Cranberry Cocktail, **3.** 88
  Hot Buttered Rum Mix, **3.** 86
  Individual Cocktails, **3.** 79
  Spiked Party Punch, **3.** 79
  Spiked Slushy Punch, **3.** 79
  Yogurt Sip, **3.** 89
Cocktail Sauce, **17.** 724
Cocoa, **3.** 83
Cocoa Ripple Ring, **4.** 146
Coconut
  Coconut Cream Pie, **13.** 555
  Coconut Crust, **13.** 572
  Coconut Macaroons, **8.** 311
  Coconut-Pecan Frosting, **5.** 197
  Pineapple-Coconut Drops, **8.** 305
Coffee
  Baked Coffee Custard, **9.** 337
  Café Almond, **3.** 90
  Café Benedictine, **3.** 90
  Café Columbian, **3.** 90
  Café Israel, **3.** 90
  Choco-Coffee-Toffee Squares, **9.** 348
  Coffee, **3.** 89
  Coffee-and-Cream Milk Shake, **3.** 86
  Coffee Angel Pie, **13.** 567
  Coffee Chocolate, **3.** 85
  Coffee Fondue, **9.** 355
  Coffee Ice Cream, **9.** 357
  Dessert Coffee, **3.** 90
  Drip Coffee, **3.** 90
  Irish Coffee, **3.** 90
  Percolator Coffee, **3.** 89
Coffee Cakes
  Any-Fruit Coffee Cake, **4.** 143
  Applesauce Coffee Cake, **4.** 147
  Blueberry Buckle, **4.** 145
  Chocolate Swirl Coffee Cake, **4.** 118
  Cocoa Ripple Ring, **4.** 146
  Date-Apple Coffee Bread, **4.** 137
  Kuchen, **4.** 116

Orange-Date Coffee Cake, **4.** 144
  Spicy Buttermilk Coffee Cake, **4.** 144
  Streusel Coffee Cake, **4.** 146
Coleslaw, Creamy, **16.** 670
Coleslaw, Vinaigrette, **16.** 670
Company Cabbage with Pecans, **19.** 791
Company Creamed Tuna, **11.** 439
Company Pork Loin Roast, **2.** 52
Coney Islands, **12.** 517
Confetti Rice, **15.** 642
Confetti Sauce, **17.** 711
Cooked Dressing, **16.** 705
Cookies, Bar
  Apricot-Filled Oatmeal Bars, **8.** 297
  Blonde Brownies, **8.** 296
  Chocolate Cake Brownies, **8.** 296
  Chocolate-Cream Cheese Brownies, **8.** 294
  Chocolate Revel Bars, **8.** 299
  Chocolate Syrup Brownies, **8.** 295
  Crispy Chocolate-Peanut Butter Bars, **8.** 303
  Date-Orange Bars, **8.** 298
  English Toffee Bars, **8.** 298
  Fudge Brownies, **8.** 294
  Lemon Squares, **8.** 301
  Meringue-Topped Bars, **8.** 304
  Old-Fashioned Raisin Bars, **8.** 300
  Peanut Butter-Oatmeal Bars, **8.** 302
  Prune-Filled Oatmeal Bars, **8.** 297
  Pumpkin Bars, **8.** 303
  Raisin-Filled Oatmeal Bars, **8.** 297
  Seven-Layer Bars, **8.** 300
  Toffee Bars, **8.** 298
Cookies, Drop
  Apple-Filled Oatmeal Cookies, **8.** 309
  Banana Drop Cookies, **8.** 308
  Basic Drop Cookies, **8.** 305
  Chocolate Chip Cookies, **8.** 306
  Chocolate-Peanut Cookies, **8.** 305
  Coconut Macaroons, **8.** 311

**Boldface numbers indicate chapters.**

Cookies, Drop (continued)
Double Chocolate Drops, **8.** 310
Hermits, **8.** 309
Lemon Tea Cookies, **8.** 312
Lemon-Yogurt Cookies, **8.** 305
Orange-Chip Cookies, **8.** 306
Pineapple-Coconut Drops, **8.** 305
Pumpkin Drop Cookies, **8.** 307
Ranger Cookies, **8.** 307
Sour Cream Nut Drops, **8.** 311
Spicy Oatmeal-Raisin Cookies, **8.** 305
Cookies, Refrigerated
Crisp Pecan Dainties, **8.** 323
Crispy Chocolate-Peanut Butter Bars, **8.** 303
Oatmeal Refrigerator Cookies, **8.** 327
Orange-Chip Cookies, **8.** 325
Peanut Butter Slices, **8.** 325
Pinwheel Cookies, **8.** 321
Refrigerator Cookies, **8.** 324
Santa's Whiskers, **8.** 326
Whole Wheat Cookies, **8.** 325
Cookies, Rolled
Filled Sugar Cookies, **8.** 320
Lebkuchen, **8.** 323
Pinwheel Cookies, **8.** 321
Rolled Cream Cheese Cookies, **8.** 322
Rolled Ginger Cookies, **8.** 321
Rolled Sugar Cookies, **8.** 326
Cookies, Shaped
Almond Cookies, **8.** 316
Berliner Kranser, **8.** 319
Finnish Chestnut Fingers, **8.** 319
Ginger Crinkles, **8.** 316
Holiday Pineapple-Filled Spritz, **8.** 318
Jam Thumbprints, **8.** 313
Oatmeal Cookies, **8.** 314
Peanut Butter Cookies, **8.** 313
Pecan Tassies, **8.** 317
Pfeffernuesse, **8.** 317
Sandies, **8.** 315
Snickerdoodles, **8.** 315

**Boldface numbers
indicate chapters.**

Spritz, **8.** 318
Cooking Bacon, **12.** 506
Cooking Canadian-Style Bacon, **12.** 507
Cooking Fresh Pork Sausage, **12.** 510
Cooking Ham Slices, **12.** 502
Cooking Pasta, **15.** 634
Cooking Pork Sausage Links, **12.** 510
Cooking Pork Sausage Patties, **12.** 510
Cooking Rice, **15.** 642
Coq Au Vin, **14.** 594
Corn
Cheesy Chicken-Corn Chowder, **18.** 764
Corn—Cream-Style, canning and freezing, **7.** 261
Corn Custard Pudding, **19.** 795
Corn on the Cob, **19.** 796
Corn—On the Cob, freezing, **7.** 262
Corn Relish, canning, **7.** 277
Corn-Stuffed Fish, **11.** 422
Corn-Stuffed Pork Chops, **2.** 50
Corn—Whole Kernel, canning and freezing, **7.** 263
Creamy Curried Corn, **19.** 796
Creamy Succotash, **19.** 784
Foil-Baked Corn, **19.** 796
Foil-Wrapped Clambake, **2.** 55
Fresh Corn Chowder, **18.** 757
Hamburger-Corn Bake, **12.** 483
Kettle-Cooked Corn, **19.** 796
Roasted Corn on the Cob, **2.** 64
Scalloped Corn, **19.** 795
Steak and Shrimp Kebabs, **2.** 35
Corn Bread, **4.** 155
Corn Bread and Bacon Stuffing, **14.** 627
Corn Bread, Sausage and, **12.** 514
Corn Dogs, **12.** 516
Cornflake Piecrust, **13.** 575
Cornish Game Hens
Basted Poultry-on-a-Spit, **2.** 43
Golden Stuffed Cornish Hens, **14.** 624
Roasting Cornish game hen, **14.** 619

Cornmeal
  Cheese Spoon Bread, **4.** 156
  Corn Bread, **4.** 155
  Cornmeal Batter-Fried Chicken,
    **14.** 585
  Cornmeal Biscuits, **4.** 153
  Cornmeal Mush, **15.** 647
  Corn Sticks, **4.** 156
  Fried Mush, **15.** 647
  Polenta, **15.** 647
  Spoon Bread, **4.** 156
Corn Sticks, **4.** 156
Cottage Pasta Bake, **15.** 636
Country-Style Barbecued Ribs, **2.** 54
Crab
  Boiled Crabs, **11.** 431
  Chicken and Crab Wontons, **1.** 16
  Crab-Bacon Bites, **2.** 70
  Crab Cocktail, **1.** 13
  Crab Louis, **16.** 698
  Crab Mornay, **10.** 401
  Crab Newburg, **11.** 435
  Crab-Stuffed Chicken Breasts, **14.**
    604
  Crab-Stuffed Tomatoes, **16.** 699
  Creole Gumbo, **18.** 748
  Fried Chicken with Crab Sauce,
    **14.** 588
  Fruit-Crab Cocktail, **1.** 10
  Seafood Quiche, **10.** 402
  Stuffed Flounder, **11.** 419
Cranberries
  Cranberry Citrus Mold, **16.** 681
  Cranberry Frost Salad, **16.** 685
  Cranberry Muffins, **4.** 157
  Cranberry-Orange Bread, **4.** 138
  Cranberry-Orange Relish, **17.** 727
  Cranberry Sauce, **17.** 720
  Curried Cranberry Glaze, **12.** 501
  Frosty Cranberry Cocktail, **3.** 88
  Tangy Cranberry Sauce, **1.** 7, **17.**
    720
  Whole Cranberry Sauce, canning
    and freezing, **7.** 249
Cream Cheese Frosting, **5.** 197
Cream Cheese Mints, **6.** 221
Creamed Bratwurst, **12.** 517
Creamed Dried Beef, **12.** 476
Creamed Eggs, **10.** 382

Creamed Peas and New Potatoes,
  **19.** 802
Creamed Spinach with Nutmeg, **19.**
  809
Creamed Sweetbreads, **12.** 530
Creamed Vegetables, **19.** 773
Cream Gravy for Fried Poultry, **14.**
  628
Cream of Asparagus Soup, **18.** 760
Cream of Broccoli Soup, **18.** 760
Cream of Carrot Soup, **18.** 761
Cream of Cauliflower Soup, **18.** 761
Cream of Celery Soup, **18.** 761
Cream of Chicken Soup, **18.** 755
Cream of Fresh Vegetable Soup,
  **18.** 760
Cream of Green Bean Soup, **18.**
  760
Cream of Mushroom Soup, **18.** 761
Cream of Onion Soup, **18.** 761
Cream of Pea Soup, **18.** 761
Cream of Potato Soup, **18.** 761
Cream of Spinach Soup, **18.** 761
Cream of Tomato Soup, **18.** 761
Cream of Zucchini Soup, **18.** 761
Cream Puffs, **9.** 346
Creamy Borscht, **18.** 759
Creamy Butter Frosting, **5.** 195
Creamy Cheese Fondue, **10.** 405
Creamy Cheese Scrambled Eggs,
  **10.** 374
Creamy Coleslaw, **16.** 670
Creamy Curried Corn, **19.** 796
Creamy Curry Sauce, **12.** 468
Creamy Dill Dip, **1.** 20
Creamy French Dressing, **16.** 702
Creamy Fruit Dressing, **16.** 705
Creamy Fruit Salad, **16.** 684
Creamy Mushroom Sauce, **17.** 717
Creamy Onion Dip, **1.** 21
Creamy Poached Eggs, **10.** 378
Creamy Potato Salad, **16.** 669
Creamy Reception Punch, **3.** 80
Creamy Succotash, **19.** 784
Creamy White Frosting, **5.** 193
Create a Tossed Salad, **16.** 660

**Boldface numbers
indicate chapters.**

Crème Brûlée, **9.** 338
Creole Gumbo, **18.** 748
Crêpes
    Basic Crêpes, **11.** 442
    Basic Dessert Crêpes, **9.** 356
    Chicken-Cheese Crêpes, **14.** 603
    Crêpes Suzette, **9.** 355
    Lemon-Filled Crêpes, **9.** 356
    Salmon-Broccoli Crêpes, **11.** 441
Crisp Fried Chicken, **14.** 584
Crisp Pecan Dainties, **8.** 323
Crispy Baked Barbecued Chicken,
    **14.** 592
Crispy Chocolate-Peanut Butter
    Bars, **8.** 303
Crockery cooking
    Beef Pot Roast, **12.** 461
    Chicken Stock, **18.** 736
    Chili con Carne, **18.** 741
    New England Baked Beans, **19.** 785
    Regal Plum Pudding, **9.** 339
    Swiss Steak, **12.** 466
Croissants, **4.** 129
Croquettes with Cheese Sauce,
    Ham, **12.** 502
Croutons, Caesar, **16.** 662
Croutons, Rye, **16.** 697
Crowd-Size Chicken Bake, **14.** 614
Crunch Party Mix, **1.** 18
Cucumbers
    Cucumber Ring Supreme, **16.** 677
    Cucumber or Zucchini Sauce, **17.**
        711
    Fresh Cucumber Relish, **17.** 729
    Shrimp-Cucumber Appetizer
        Spread, **1.** 13
    Sour Cream Cucumbers, **16.** 671
Cumberland-Style Broiled Chicken,
    **14.** 607
Cupcakes
    White Cake Supreme Cupcakes,
        **5.** 168
    Yellow Cake Cupcakes, **5.** 170
Curried Bulgur Sauté, **15.** 651
Curried Chicken and Vegetables, **14.**
    618

Curried Chicken Salad, **16.** 691
Curried Cranberry Glaze, **12.**
    501
Curried Eggs, **10.** 383
Curried Fishwiches, **11.** 417
Curried Fruit, Hot, **17.** 728
Curried Lamb Madras, **12.** 525
Curried Pork, **12.** 493
Curried Rice, **15.** 643
Curry and Parsley Chicken, **14.**
    592
Curry Sauce, **17.** 711
Custards
    Baked Coffee Custard, **9.** 337
    Baked Custard, **9.** 337
    Chocolate Pots de Crème, **9.** 337
    Corn Custard Pudding, **19.** 795
    Crème Brûlée, **9.** 338
    Custard Pie, **13.** 560
    Stirred Custard, **9.** 336

# D

Dark Chocolate Cream Pie, **13.** 555
Dark Fruitcake, **5.** 184
Dates
    Date-Apple Coffee Bread, **4.** 137
    Date Cake, **5.** 177
    Date-Nut Muffins, **4.** 157
    Date-Orange Bars, **8.** 298
    Filled Sugar Cookies, **8.** 320
    Orange-Date Coffee Cake, **4.** 144
    Pinwheel Cookies, **8.** 321
Deep-Dish Apple Pie, **13.** 543
Deep-Dish Peach Pie, **13.** 547
Deluxe Peas and Mushrooms, **19.**
    801
Denver Scramble, **10.** 375
Desserts (see also Cakes, Cookies,
    Pies)
    Apple Cobbler, **9.** 351
    Apple Dumplings, **9.** 352
    Applesauce, **9.** 362
    Apricot Angel Dessert, **9.** 347
    Baked Alaska, **9.** 359
    Baked Apples, **9.** 350
    Baked Coffee Custard, **9.** 337

Baked Custard, **9.** 337
Baked Rice Pudding, **9.** 334
Basic Dessert Crêpes, **9.** 356
Basic Hard Sauce, **9.** 363
Blueberry Melba Parfaits, **9.** 354
Blueberry Shortcakes, **9.** 349
Brandy Hard Sauce, **9.** 363
Bread Pudding, **9.** 335
Brownie Pudding, **9.** 340
Cheesecake Supreme, **9.** 344
Cherries Jubilee, **9.** 361
Cherry Cobbler, **9.** 351
Cherry-Nut Ice Cream, **9.** 357
Cherry Torte, **9.** 346
Choco-Coffee-Toffee Squares, **9.** 348
Chocolate-Almond Ice Cream, **9.** 357
Chocolate Chip Ice Cream, **9.** 357
Chocolate Fondue, **9.** 355
Chocolate Pots de Crème, **9.** 337
Chocolate Pudding, **9.** 335
Chocolate Soufflé, **9.** 341
Choco-Mint Velvet, **9.** 359
Choco-Velvet Ice Cream, **9.** 358
Chunky Applesauce, **9.** 363
Coffee Fondue, **9.** 355
Coffee Ice Cream, **9.** 357
Cream Puffs, **9.** 346
Crème Brûlée, **9.** 338
Crêpes Suzette, **9.** 355
Dessert Coffee, **3.** 90
Easy Vanilla Ice Cream, **9.** 359
Éclairs, **9.** 346
Fluffy Hard Sauce, **9.** 363
Fluffy Vanilla Sauce, **9.** 364
Fresh Fruit Crisp, **9.** 352
Fresh Strawberry Ice Cream, **9.** 358
Frozen Yogurt Melba Bombe, **9.** 360
Hot Fudge Sundaes, **9.** 362
Individual Shortcakes, **9.** 350
Lemon-Filled Crêpes, **9.** 356
Lemon Pudding Cake, **9.** 340
Lemon Torte, **9.** 345
Meringue Shells, **9.** 342
Orange Hard Sauce, **9.** 363
Orange Sauce, **9.** 364

Orange Soufflé, **9.** 341
Peach-Cherry Ice Cream, **9.** 357
Peach Cobbler, **9.** 351
Peach Sauce, **9.** 364
Peach Shortcake, **9.** 349
Pineapple Sherbet, **9.** 361
Praline Cheese Cups, **9.** 347
Regal Plum Pudding, **9.** 339
Rhubarb Sauce, **9.** 362
Saucepan Rice Pudding, **9.** 333
Sherried Fruit Compote, **9.** 354
Sour Cream Cheesecake, **9.** 343
Stirred Custard, **9.** 336
Strawberry Shortcake, **9.** 349
Summer Fruit Compote, **9.** 353
Tapioca Fluff Pudding, **9.** 334
Vanilla Ice Cream, **9.** 357
Vanilla Pudding, **9.** 335
Deviled Beef Rolls, **12.** 476
Deviled Eggs, **10.** 389
Devil's Food Cake, **5.** 179
Dill
    Creamy Dill Dip, **1.** 20
    Dilled Chicken-Noodle Bake, **14.** 615
    Dilled Lamb Ragout, **18.** 744
    Dilled Salmon Dip, **1.** 8
    Dill Pickles, **7.** 279
    Dill Sauce, **11.** 412, **17.** 721
    Dilly Panned Summer Squash, **19.** 810
    Easy Dill Sauce, **17.** 721
Dinner Rolls, **4.** 125
Dips
    Blue Cheese-Onion Dip, **1.** 21
    Chili con Queso, **1.** 22
    Creamy Dill Dip, **1.** 20
    Creamy Onion Dip, **1.** 20
    Dilled Salmon Dip, **1.** 8
    Fluffy Fruit Dip, **1.** 21
    Guacamole, **1.** 22
    Hot Broccoli Dip, **1.** 19
    Tomato-Chili Guacamole, **1.** 22
Divinity, **6.** 209
Double Chocolate Drops, **8.** 310
Double Chocolate Soda, **3.** 87

**Boldface numbers
indicate chapters.**

Double-Decker Burgers, **12.** 479
Doughnuts
  Apple Fritter Rings, **4.** 150
  Bismarcks, **4.** 124
  Buttermilk Doughnuts, **4.** 150
  Cake Doughnuts, **4.** 149
  Chocolate Cake Doughnuts, **4.**
    149
  Chocolate Yeast Doughnuts, **4.**
    122
  Yeast Doughnuts, **4.** 121
Duchess Potatoes, **19.** 805
Duck
  Curried Chicken and Vegetables,
    **14.** 618
  Honey and Spice Duckling, **14.**
    617
  Roasting Domestic Duckling, **14.**
    620
Dumplings
  Apple Dumplings, **9.** 352
  Chicken and Dumplings, **14.** 598
  Meatball Stew with Spinach
    Dumplings, **18.** 741

E

Easy Baked Beans, **19.** 785
Easy Baked Cheese Omelet, **10.** 396
Easy Baked Fish Fillets, **11.** 414
Easy Barbecue Sauce, **17.** 719
Easy Cheese Eggs a la King, **10.** 383
Easy Chicken-Curry Soup, **18.** 763
Easy Dill Sauce, **17.** 721
Easy Fudge, **6.** 217
Easy-Mix White Bread, **4.** 102
Easy Mustard Glaze, **12.** 500
Easy Pork Cassoulet, **18.** 746
Easy Sherbet Punch, **3.** 80
Easy Tomato-Pepper Relish, **17.** 729
Easy Vanilla Ice Cream, **9.** 359
Easy Walnut Penuche, **6.** 219
Éclairs, **9.** 346
Egg Bread, **4.** 113

**Boldface numbers
indicate chapters.**

Eggplant
  Eggplant Parmigiana, **19.** 798
  Fried Eggplant, **19.** 774
  Spicy Stuffed Eggplant, **19.** 797
Egg Rolls, **1.** 16
Eggs
  Bacon-Asparagus Omelet, **10.** 391
  Baked Eggs, **10.** 373
  Baked Omelet with Chicken
    Sauce, **10.** 397
  Cheese and Herb Omelet, **10.**
    390
  Cheese French Omelet, **10.** 394
  Cheese-Onion Scrambled Eggs,
    **10.** 374
  Cheese Soufflé, **10.** 397
  Classic Quiche Lorraine, **10.** 401
  Creamed Eggs, **10.** 382
  Creamy Cheese Scrambled Eggs,
    **10.** 374
  Creamy Poached Eggs, **10.** 378
  Curried Eggs, **10.** 383
  Denver Scramble, **10.** 375
  Deviled Eggs, **10.** 389
  Easy Baked Cheese Omelet, **10.**
    396
  Easy Cheese Eggs a la King, **10.** 383
  Egg and Whole Wheat Foldovers,
    **10.** 388
  Egg Bread, **4.** 113
  Egg Foo Yong, **10.** 377
  Eggnog, **3.** 83
  Egg-Rice Bake, **10.** 384
  Egg Salad Triangles, **1.** 14
  Eggs a la King, **10.** 382
  Egg-Sausage Casserole, **10.** 385
  Eggs Benedict, **10.** 378
  Eggs Florentine, **10.** 381
  Eggs Goldenrod, **10.** 382
  Eggs in Spanish Sauce, **10.** 386
  Farmer's Breakfast, **10.** 376
  French Omelet, **10.** 394
  Fried Eggs, **10.** 372
  Fruited French Omelet, **10.** 394
  Gold Rush Brunch, **10.** 380
  Ham and Cheese Omelet, **10.** 390
  Ham Egg Foo Yong, **10.** 377
  Hashed Brown Omelet, **10.** 395
  Herbed Scrambled Eggs, **10.** 374

Huevos Rancheros, **10.** 379
Individual Quiche Casseroles, **10.** 403
Italian-Style Deviled Eggs, **10.** 389
Mushroom French Omelet, **10.** 394
Mushroom-Sauced Eggs, **10.** 380
Mushroom Scrambled Eggs, **10.** 375
Old-Fashioned Cheese Bake, **10.** 400
Omelet Sandwich Puff, **10.** 395
Poached Eggs, **10.** 373
Puffy Omelet, **10.** 389
Rosy Pickled Eggs, **10.** 388
Scalloped Eggs and Bacon, **10.** 385
Scrambled Eggs, **10.** 374
Seafood Quiche, **10.** 402
Shrimp-Egg Bake, **10.** 387
Shrimp Egg Foo Yong, **10.** 377
Soft-Cooked or Hard-Cooked Eggs, **10.** 372
Swiss Onion Bake, **10.** 381
Tuna Soufflé, **10.** 399
Vegetable French Omelet, **10.** 394
Electric Mixer Pastry, **13.** 571
English Toffee Bars, **8.** 299

**F**

Farmer's Breakfast, **10.** 376
Feathery Fudge Cake, **5.** 181
Fiesta Beef Kebabs, **2.** 37
Filled Sugar Cookies, **8.** 320
Finnish Chestnut Fingers, **8.** 319
Fish
Baked Tuna Patties, **11.** 437
Company Creamed Tuna, **11.** 439
Fish, canning and freezing, **7.** 272
Individual Tuna Pies, **11.** 436
Salmon-Broccoli Crêpes, **11.** 441
Salmon Loaf, **11.** 440
Skillet Dilled Salmon Patties, **11.** 440
Tuna a la King, **11.** 438

Tuna-Noodle Casserole, **11.** 435
Tuna-Vegetable Pie, **11.** 439
Fish, Dressed
Corn-Stuffed Fish, **11.** 422
Fish in a Basket, **2.** 57
Oven-Fried Fish, **11.** 413
Pan-Fried Fish, **11.** 412
Poached Fish with Dill Sauce, **11.** 421
Skillet-Fried Fish, **2.** 56
Trout Amandine, **11.** 423
Wild-Rice-Stuffed Fish, **11.** 422
Fish Fillets
Baked Fillets and Steaks, **11.** 415
Baked Fish with Mushrooms, **11.** 416
Bouillabaisse, **18.** 749
Broiled Fish, **11.** 412
Bundled Fish, **11.** 417
Cioppino, **18.** 751
Easy Baked Fish Fillets, **11.** 414
Fish and Chips, **11.** 415
Fish Chowder, **18.** 752
Fish Creole, **11.** 420
Marinated Fish Kebabs, **2.** 58
Oven-Fried Fish, **11.** 413
Pan-Fried Fish, **11.** 412
Stacked Sole, **11.** 416
Stir-Fried Fish and Peppers, **11.** 413
Stuffed Flounder, **11.** 419
Fish Portions or Sticks
Curried Fishwiches, **11.** 427
Fish Florentine, **11.** 428
Quick Fish-Potato Supper, **11.** 426
Sweet-and-Sour Fish, **11.** 426
Fish Steaks
Baked Fillets and Steaks, **11.** 415
Baked Fish a l'Orange, **11.** 424
Baked Fish with Mushrooms, **11.** 416
Broiled Fish, **11.** 412
Grilled Salmon Steaks, **2.** 57
Lemon-Marinated Salmon Steaks, **11.** 425

**Boldface numbers
indicate chapters.**

Fish Steaks (continued)
  Oven-Fried Fish, **11**. 413
  Pan-Fried Fish, **11**. 412
  Sherry-Sauced Halibut, **11**. 425
Five-Bean Salad Hot, **16**. 673
Five-Cup Salad, **16**. 685
Five-Spice Powder, Homemade, **14**. 617
Fluffy Fruit Dip, **1**. 21
Fluffy Hard Sauce, **9**. 363
Fluffy Horseradish Sauce, **17**. 718
Fluffy Vanilla Sauce, **9**. 364
Fluffy White Frosting, **5**. 196
Foil-Baked Corn, **19**. 796
Foil-Baked Potatoes, **19**. 802
Foil-Barbecued Shrimp, **2**. 58
Foil-Wrapped Clambake, **2**. 55
Fondant, **6**. 208
Fondant Mint Patties, **6**. 209
Fondues
  Beef Fondue, **12**. 468
  Beer-Cheese Fondue, **1**. 19
  Chocolate Fondue, **9**. 355
  Classic Cheese Fondue, **10**. 404
  Coffee Fondue, **9**. 355
  Creamy Cheese Fondue, **10**. 405
Frankfurters
  Bacon-Wrapped Franks, **2**. 46
  Coney Islands, **12**. 517
  Corn Dogs, **12**. 516
  Frank-Vegetable Kebabs, **2**. 47
  Pizza-Frank Sandwiches, **2**. 47
  Polish Sausage-Krauters, **2**. 45
  Quick Beans-and-Franks Soup, **18**. 747
Freezer Jam, **7**. 285
Freezing
  Fish, **7**. 272
  Freezer Jam, **7**. 285
  Freezing basics, **7**. 238
  Meat, **7**. 271
  Poultry, **7**. 273
  Shellfish, **7**. 273
  Vegetable Relish, **7**. 276
Freezing, Fruit
  Apple Butter, **7**. 243

Apple Juice, **7**. 244
Apples, **7**. 242
Applesauce, **7**. 243
Apricot Nectar, **7**. 246
Apricots, **7**. 244
Berries, **7**. 246
Cherries, **7**. 247
Grape Juice Concentrate, **7**. 249
Melons, **7**. 250
Peaches, **7**. 250
Plums, **7**. 253
Rhubarb, **7**. 254
Whole Cranberry Sauce, **7**. 249
Freezing, Vegetables
Asparagus, **7**. 255
Beans—Green or Wax, **7**. 256
Beans—Lima or Butter, **7**. 257
Beets, **7**. 258
Broccoli, **7**. 259
Carrots, **7**. 259
Cauliflower, **7**. 260
Corn—Cream-Style, **7**. 261
Corn—On-the-Cob, **7**. 262
Corn—Whole Kernel, **7**. 263
Peas (Green), **7**. 264
Peppers (Sweet), **7**. 265
Sweet Potatoes, **7**. 265
Tomato Catsup, **7**. 269
Tomatoes, **7**. 266
Tomato Juice, **7**. 268
Tomato Juice Cocktail, **7**. 268
Turnips and Rutabagas, **7**. 270
Winter Squash or Pumpkin, **7**. 270
French Bread, **4**. 104
French Crunch Peach Pie, **13**. 548
French Dressing, **16**. 704
French Dressing, Creamy, **16**. 702
French-Fried Onion Rings, **19**. 799
French-Fried Shrimp, **11**. 432
French Fries, **19**. 803
French Omelet, **10**. 394
French Onion Soup, **18**. 759
French Silk Pie, **13**. 565
French Toast, **4**. 160
Fresh Blackberry Pie, **13**. 551
Fresh Blueberry Pie, **13**. 550
Fresh Cherry Pie, **13**. 545
Fresh Corn Chowder, **18**. 757

**Boldface numbers
indicate chapters.**

Fresh Cucumber Relish, **17.** 729
Fresh Fruit Crisp, **9.** 352
Fresh Mint Sauce, **17.** 723
Fresh Pear Crumble Pie, **13.** 554
Fresh Pineapple Pie, **13.** 553
Fresh Raspberry Pie, **13.** 552
Fresh Strawberry Ice Cream, **9.** 358
Fresh Tomato Fix-Ups, **19.** 813
Fried Chicken with Crab Sauce, **14.** 588
Fried Clams, Oysters or Scallops, **11.** 431
Fried Eggplant, **19.** 774
Fried Eggs, **10.** 372
Fried Green Tomatoes, **19.** 773
Fried Mush, **15.** 647
Fried Ripe Tomatoes, **19.** 773
Fried Zucchini, **19.** 774
Frisky Sours, **3.** 88
Frosted Triple-Orange Squares, **16.** 679
Frostings
   Banana Butter Frosting, **8.** 308
   Broiled Coconut Topping, **5.** 197
   Browned Butter Frosting, **8.** 311
   Butter Frosting, **5.** 195
   Chocolate Butter Frosting, **5.** 195
   Chocolate Frosting, **8.** 296
   Chocolate Icing, **5.** 199
   Chocolate Sour Cream Frosting, **5.** 199
   Coconut-Pecan Frosting, **5.** 197
   Cream Cheese Frosting, **5.** 197
   Creamy Butter Frosting, **5.** 195
   Creamy White Frosting, **5.** 193
   Fluffy White Frosting, **5.** 196
   Fudge Frosting, **5.** 199
   Golden Butter Frosting, **5.** 181
   Mocha Butter Frosting, **5.** 195
   Mocha Frosting, **8.** 310
   Orange or Lemon Butter Frosting, **5.** 195
   Peanut Butter Frosting, **5.** 195
   Penuche Frosting, **5.** 198
   Peppermint Frosting, **5.** 194
   Peppermint-Stick Frosting, **5.** 194
   Petits Fours Icing, **5.** 196
   Powdered Sugar Icing, **5.** 195
   Rocky Road Frosting, **5.** 198

   Seafoam Frosting, **5.** 194
   Seven-Minute Frosting, **5.** 194
Frosty Cranberry Cocktail, **3.** 88
Frozen Lemon Salad, **16.** 686
Frozen Yogurt Melba Bombe, **9.** 360
Fruitcake, Dark, **5.** 184
Fruitcake, Light, **5.** 183
Fruits (see also individual fruits)
   Appetizer Fruit Combo, **1.** 7
   Fluffy Fruit Dip, **1.** 21
   Fresh Fruit Crisp, **9.** 352
   Fruit and Nut Brown Rice, **15.** 642
   Fruit-and-Nut Tropical Slaw, **16.** 689
   Fruit Cooler, **3.** 81
   Fruit-Crab Cocktail, **1.** 10
   Fruited French Omelet, **10.** 394
   Fruit-Filled Melons, **16.** 687
   Fruit-Flavored Float, **3.** 82
   Fruit Juice Jelly, **7.** 285
   Fruit Medley Salad, **16.** 689
   Fruit Strata Salad, **16.** 688
   Fruity Ginger Ale Mold, **16.** 678
   Sherried Fruit Compote, **9.** 354
   Summer Fruit Compote, **9.** 353
   Swedish Fruit Soup, **18.** 762
Fudge Brownies, **8.** 294
Fudge Cake, Feathery, **5.** 181
Fudge Frosting, **5.** 199
Fudge Ribbon Pie, **13.** 565

## G

Game
   Beer-Braised Rabbit, **12.** 533
   Hasenpfeffer, **12.** 533
   Marinated Venison Chops, **12.** 532
   Pheasant with Apples, **14.** 599
   Venison Pot Roast, **12.** 532
Garden Biscuits, **4.** 154
Garden Vegetable Stir-Fry, **19.** 816
Garlic Cubed Steaks, Quick, **2.** 38
Garlic Olive Oil, **16.** 662

**Boldface numbers
indicate chapters.**

Garlic Spread, **2.** 63
Gazpacho, **18.** 761
Gazpacho Salad, **16.** 671
German Chocolate Cake, **5.** 178
German Potato Salad, **16.** 669
German Sausage Chowder, **18.** 743
German Stollen, **4.** 107
Giblet Gravy, **14.** 629
Giblet Stuffing, **14.** 626
Gingerbread, **5.** 175
Ginger Cookies, Rolled, **8.** 321
Ginger Crinkles, **8.** 316
Gingersnap-Graham Crust, **13.** 574
Glazed Carrots, **19.** 792
Glazed Chicken and Rice, **14.** 609
Glazed Ham Slice, **2.** 49
Glazed Nuts, **6.** 214
Glazed Onions, **19.** 800
Golden Butter Frosting, **5.** 181
Golden Chiffon Cake, **5.** 185
Golden Crumb Broccoli, **19.** 789
Golden Stuffed Cornish Hens, **14.** 624
Gold Rush Brunch, **10.** 380
Gooseberry Pie, **13.** 551
Goose, roasting domestic, **14.** 620
Gourmet Onions, **19.** 799
Graham Cracker Crust, **13.** 573
Granola, **15.** 649
Grapefruit
  Broiled Grapefruit Halves, **1.** 18
  Fruit-Crab Cocktail, **1.** 10
Grapes
  Grape Jam, **7.** 287
  Grape Juice, Concentrate, canning and freezing, **7.** 249
  Orange-Grape Cooler, **3.** 85
  Orange-Grape Sauce, **17.** 722
Grasshopper Pie, **13.** 568
Gravies
  Cream Gravy for Fried Poultry, **14.** 628
  Giblet Gravy, **14.** 629
  Pan Gravy for Roast Poultry, **14.** 628
  Pot Roast Gravy, **12.** 461

Greek Salad, **16.** 693
Green Bean Bake with Onion, **19.** 783
Green Beans Amandine, **19.** 781
Green Beans Especial, **19.** 782
Green Goddess Dressing, **16.** 704
Green Goddess Salad, **16.** 665
Green Noodles, **15.** 635
Grenadine Punch, **3.** 81
Grilled Acorn Squash, **2.** 66
Grilled Bread Fix-Ups, **2.** 63
Grilled Rock Lobster Tails, **2.** 59
Grilled Salmon Steaks, **2.** 57
Grilled Turkey Pieces, **2.** 42
Grilled Whole Potatoes, **2.** 65
Grilling chart, barbecue, **2.** 30–31
Grits, **15.** 648
Grits, Southern Cheese, **15.** 648
Guacamole, **1.** 22
Guinea Hen, Roasting, **14.** 620

# H

Ham
  Apricot-Ham Patties, **12.** 504
  Baked Ham-Stuffed Mushrooms, **1.** 10
  Baking Ham, **12.** 500
  Cheese-Ham Ball, **1.** 12
  Chef's Salad, **16.** 692
  Cooking Ham Slices, **12.** 502
  Glazed Ham Slice, **2.** 49
  Ham and Bean Vegetable Soup, **18.** 757
  Ham and Cheese Omelet, **10.** 390
  Ham Caribbean, **12.** 503
  Ham Croquettes with Cheese Sauce, **12.** 502
  Ham Egg Foo Yong, **10.** 377
  Ham Hodgepodge, **18.** 746
  Ham Loaf, **12.** 505
  Ham-Noodle Casserole, **12.** 505
  Party Ham Sandwiches, **1.** 15
  Potato-Ham Scallop, **12.** 506
  Sweet-Sour Ham, **2.** 48
  Swiss Cheese-Ham Spread, **1.** 9
  Swiss Veal Roast, **12.** 474

**Boldface numbers
indicate chapters.**

Hamburger and Frankfurter Buns, **4.** 125

Hamburger-Corn Bake, **12.** 483

Hamburger Pie, **12.** 485

Hamburgers, **12.** 479

Harvard Beets, **19.** 787

Harvest Pot Roast, **12.** 491

Harvest Stuffing, **14.** 625

Hasenpfeffer, **12.** 533

Hashed Brown Omelet, **10.** 395

Hashed Brown Potatoes, **19.** 804

Hawaiian Broiled Chicken, **14.** 607

Hawaiian-Style Parsnips, **19.** 800

Herb Bagels, **4.** 128

Herb-Butter Basting Sauce, **2.** 45

Herb Dressing, **16.** 705

Herbed Butter, **2.** 64

Herbed Green Beans, **19.** 781

Herbed Lamb Stew, **18.** 745

Herbed Lima Bean Bake, **19.** 783

Herbed Rice, **15.** 642

Herbed Scrambled Eggs, **10.** 374

Herbed Spread, **2.** 64

Herbed Tomato Soup, **18.** 758

Herb-Garlic Sauce, **17.** 711

Herb Sauce, **17.** 711

Herb-Seasoned Marinade, **17.** 725

Herb-Seasoned Vegetables, **2.** 67

Hermits, **8.** 309

Holiday Pineapple-Filled Spritz, **8.** 18

Hollandaise Sauce, Blender, **17.** 712

Hollandaise Sauce, Classic, **17.** 712

Hollandaise Sauce, Mock, **17.** 713

Homemade Biscuit Mix, **4.** 151

Homemade Biscuit Mix Biscuits, **4.** 151

Homemade Biscuit Mix Muffins, **4.** 151

Homemade Biscuit Mix Pancakes, **4.** 151

Homemade Five-Spice Powder, **14.** 617

Homemade Mayonnaise, **16.** 705

Homemade Mincemeat Pie, **13.** 549

Homemade Noodles, **15.** 635

Homemade Tomato Sauce, **19.** 798

Honey and Spice Duckling, **14.** 617

Honey Butter, **17.** 726

Honey-Lime Dressing, **16.** 691

Honey-Wheat Muffins, **4.** 158

Horseradish Sauce, Fluffy, **17.** 718

Hot Broccoli Dip, **1.** 19

Hot Buttered Rum Mix, **3.** 86

Hot Chinese Mustard, **17.** 718

Hot Chocolate, **3.** 84

Hot Cross Buns, **4.** 123

Hot Curried Fruit, **17.** 728

Hot Five-Bean Salad, **16.** 673

Hot Fudge Sundaes, **9.** 362

Hot Milk Sponge Cake, **5.** 187

Hot Mulled Cider, **3.** 87

Huevos Rancheros, **10.** 379

Hush Puppies, **4.** 155

# I

Ice Cream

  Cherry-Nut Ice Cream, **9.** 357

  Chocolate-Almond Ice Cream, **9.** 357

  Chocolate Chip Ice Cream, **9.** 357

  Choco-Mint Velvet, **9.** 359

  Choco-Velvet Ice Cream, **9.** 358

  Coffee Ice Cream, **9.** 357

  Easy Vanilla Ice Cream, **9.** 359

  Fresh Strawberry Ice Cream, **9.** 358

  Peach-Cherry Ice Cream, **9.** 357

  Vanilla Ice Cream, **9.** 357

Individual Cocktails, **3.** 79

Individual French Loaves, **4.** 104

Individual Quiche Casseroles, **10.** 403

Individual Shortcakes, **9.** 350

Individual Tuna Pies, **11.** 436

Irish Coffee, **3.** 90

Italian Appetizer Artichokes, **1.** 17

Italian Bean Bake, **19.** 782

Italian Cream Cake, **5.** 191

Italian Dressing, **16.** 702

Italian Lamb Chop Skillet, **12.** 524

Italian-Seasoned Vegetable Kebabs, **2.** 66

Italian-Style Deviled Eggs, **10.** 389

**Boldface numbers indicate chapters.**

## J

Jams
  Freezer Jam, **7.** 285
  Grape Jam, **7.** 287
  Jellies and Jams, **7.** 282
  Peach-Banana Jam, **7.** 286
  Peach Jam, **7.** 286
  Peach-Plum Jam, **7.** 286
  Plum Jam, **7.** 287
  Strawberry Jam, **7.** 286
Jam Thumbprints, **8.** 313
Jellies
  Apple Jelly, **7.** 284
  Cinnamon-Apple Jelly, **7.** 284
  Fruit Juice Jelly, **7.** 285
  Jellies and Jams, **7.** 282
  Mint-Apple Jelly, **7.** 284
Jelly Muffins, **4.** 157
Jelly Roll, **5.** 187
Jubilee Salad Mold, **16.** 682
Julekage, **4.** 114

## K

Kebabs
  Chicken Teriyaki Kebabs, **14.** 609
  Fiesta Beef Kebabs, **2.** 37
  Frank-Vegetable Kebabs, **2.** 47
  Lamb Shish Kebabs, **2.** 62
  Steak and Shrimp Kebabs, **2.** 35
  Turkey-Yam Kebabs, **14.** 608
Kettle-Cooked Corn, **19.** 796
Kosher Dill Pickles, canning, **7.** 280
Kuchen, **4.** 116

## L

Lady Baltimore Cake, **5.** 168
Lamb
  Blue Cheese Burgers, **2.** 40
  Broiled Lamb Chops, **12.** 522

**Boldface numbers
indicate chapters.**

Curried Lamb Madras, **12.** 525
Dilled Lamb Ragout, **18.** 744
Herbed Lamb Stew, **18.** 745
Italian Lamb Chop Skillet, **12.** 524
Lamb Chops Supreme, **12.** 523
Lamb Loin Chops with Walnut
  Glaze, **12.** 526
Lamb Patties with Dill Sauce, **12.**
  526
Lamb Shish Kebabs, **2.** 62
Marinated Leg of Lamb, **2.** 60
Meat identification, **12.** 520–22
Moussaka, **12.** 528
Roasting Lamb, **12.** 522
Saucy Lamb Riblets, **2.** 62
Saucy Lamb Shanks, **12.** 524
Savory Lamburgers, **12.** 527
Scotch Broth, **18.** 743
Wine-Sauced Shoulder Chops, **2.**
  61
Lamb, Cooked
  Greek Salad, **16.** 693
Lasagna, **12.** 512
Lebkuchen, **8.** 323
Leg of Lamb, Marinated, **2.** 60
Lemons
  Cherry-Lemon Ring, **16.** 679
  Frozen Lemon Salad, **16.** 686
  Lemonade or Limeade, **3.** 87
  Lemon-Chess Pie, **13.** 558
  Lemon-Filled Crêpes, **9.** 356
  Lemon Filling, **5.** 169
  Lemon Glaze, **8.** 312, 323
  Lemon-Marinated Chuck Roast, **2.**
    37
  Lemon-Marinated Salmon Steaks,
    **11.** 425
  Lemon Meringue Pie, **13.** 556
  Lemon-Parsleyed Potatoes, **19.**
    805
  Lemon-Parsleyed Turnips, **19.**
    815
  Lemon Pastry, **13.** 572
  Lemon Pudding Cake, **9.** 340
  Lemon Sauce, **17.** 711
  Lemon Squares, **8.** 301
  Lemon Tea Cookies, **8.** 312
  Lemon Torte, **9.** 345
  Lemon-Yogurt Cookies, **8.** 305

Orange or Lemon Butter Frosting, **5.** 195
Sangria, **3.** 84
Lentil Soup, **18.** 757
Light Chocolate Cream Pie, **13.** 556
Light Fruitcake, **5.** 183
Light Rye Bagels, **4.** 128
Lima Bean Bake, Herbed, **19.** 783
Lima Skillet, Tongue and, **12.** 529
Limes
  Lemonade or Limeade, **3.** 87
  Lime Fruit Salad, **16.** 683
  Lime Parfait Pie, **13.** 564
Liver, Beef
  Sautéed Liver and Onions, **12.** 530
Liver, Chicken
  Chicken Liver Pâté, **1.** 14
  Chicken Livers in Tomato Sauce, **14.** 600
  Chicken Livers Stroganoff, **14.** 599
Lobster
  Boiled Lobster, **11.** 429
  Boiled Lobster Tails, **11.** 431
  Bouillabaisse, **18.** 749
  Grilled Rock Lobster Tails, **2.** 59
  Lobster Newburg, **11.** 434
London Broil, **12.** 465
Louis Dressing, **16.** 698

### M

Macaroni and Cheese, **10.** 405
Macaroons, Coconut, **8.** 311
Manhattan Clam Chowder, **18.** 750
Marinated Fish Kebabs, **2.** 58
Marinated Leg of Lamb, **2.** 60
Marinated Shrimp Appetizers, **2.** 69
Marinated Three-Bean Salad, **16.** 674
Marinated Venison Chops, **12.** 532
Marinated Zucchini Salad, **16.** 672
Marmalade, Orange, **7.** 288
Mashed Potatoes, **19.** 805
Mashed Sweet Potato Bake, **19.** 808
Mayonnaise, Blender, **16.** 706

Mayonnaise, Homemade, **16.** 705
Meat (see also Beef, Ham, Lamb, Pork, Veal)
  Buying, **12.** 450
  Cooking Methods, **12.** 449
  Meat and Potato Bake, **2.** 50
  Meat, canning and freezing, **7.** 271
  Meat, carving, **12.** 534–36
  Storing, **12.** 451
Meatballs
  Cocktail Meatballs, **1.** 7
  Meatball Stew with Spinach Dumplings, **18.** 741
  Porcupine Meatballs, **12.** 477
  Spaghetti and Meatballs, **12.** 482
  Swedish Meatballs, **1.** 6
Meatless Meal-in-a-Bowl, **16.** 697
Meat Loaves
  Ham Loaf, **12.** 505
  Meat Loaf, **12.** 477
  Pork Loaf, **12.** 495
Melon
  Appetizer Fruit Combo, **1.** 7
  Fruit-Filled Melons, **16.** 687
  Melons, freezing, **7.** 250
  Summer Fruit Compote, **9.** 353
Meringue Crust, **13.** 570
Meringue for Pie, **13.** 570
Meringue Shells, **9.** 342
Meringue-Topped Bars, **8.** 304
Mexicali Pork Chops, **12.** 498
Mexicali Sauce, **17.** 712
Microwave cooking
  Artichokes with Butter Sauce, **19.** 779
  Candied Squash Rings, **19.** 811
  Chicken Dijon, **14.** 586
  Chili con Carne, **18.** 741
  Choco-Scotch Crunchies, **6.** 220
  Cooking Bacon, **12.** 506
  Cooking Canadian-Style Bacon, **12.** 507
  Cooking Rice, **15.** 642
  Easy Baked Fish Fillets, **11.** 414
  Fish Creole, **11.** 420
  Italian Bean Bake, **19.** 783
  Micro-Baked Potatoes, **19.** 802

**Boldface numbers indicate chapters.**

Microwave cooking (continued)
Micro-Cooked Corn, **19.** 796
Orange-Glazed Carrots, **19.** 792
Rocky Road, **6.** 221
Salami-Bean Casserole, **12.** 515
Saucy Celery Casserole, **19.** 794
Sauerbraten Burgers, **12.** 478
Scrambled Eggs, **10.** 375
Sesame Asparagus, **19.** 781
Tuna-Noodle Casserole, **11.** 435
Twice-Baked Potatoes, **19.** 804
Milk
Chocolate Milk Shake, **3.** 85
Choco-Nutty Milk Shake, **3.** 86
Coffee-and-Cream Milk Shake, **3.** 86
Hot Milk Sponge Cake, **5.** 187
Strawberry Milk Shake, **3.** 86
Vanilla Milk Shake, **3.** 85
Mincemeat Pie, Homemade, **13.** 549
Minestrone, **18.** 755
Mint
Choco-Mint Velvet, **9.** 359
Cream Cheese Mints, **6.** 221
Fresh Mint Sauce, **17.** 723
Mint-Apple Jelly, **7.** 284
Minted New Peas, **19.** 801
Mixed Pickles, canning, **7.** 281
Mocha Butter Frosting, **5.** 195
Mocha Frosting, **8.** 310
Mock Hollandaise, **17.** 713
Molasses-Oatmeal Bread, **4.** 105
Molded Shrimp Salad, **16.** 676
Moussaka, **12.** 528
Mousse, Salmon, **1.** 11
Muffins
Apple-Raisin Muffins, **4.** 157
Banana-Nut Muffins, **4.** 157
Basic Muffins, **4.** 157
Blueberry Muffins, **4.** 157
Cheese Muffins, **4.** 157
Cranberry Muffins, **4.** 157
Date-Nut Muffins, **4.** 157
Homemade Biscuit Mix Muffins, **4.** 151
Honey-Wheat Muffins, **4.** 158

Jelly Muffins, **4.** 157
Pumpkin Muffins, **4.** 157
Sunflower Seed Muffins, **4.** 158
Sunshine Muffins, **4.** 158
Mulligatawny, **18.** 753
Mushrooms
Baked Ham-Stuffed Mushrooms, **1.** 10
Creamy Mushroom Sauce, **17.** 717
Deluxe Peas and Mushrooms, **19.** 801
Mushroom-Cereal Bake, **15.** 645
Mushroom Omelet, **10.** 394
Mushroom-Rice Bake, **15.** 645
Mushroom-Sauced Eggs, **10.** 380
Mushrooms Elegante, **19.** 798
Mushroom Scrambled Eggs, **10.** 375
Mushroom Steak Sauce, **12.** 469
Mushroom Stuffing, **14.** 626
Quick Mushroom Sauce, **17.** 716
Wine-Mushroom Sauce, **17.** 717
Mustard Glaze, Easy, **12.** 500
Mustard, Hot Chinese, **17.** 718
Mustard-Parsley Spread, **2.** 63

## N

New England Baked Beans, **19.** 785
New England Boiled Dinner, **12.** 462
New England Clam Chowder, **18.** 748
Nonalcoholic Punch, **3.** 79
Noodles
Chicken and Noodles, **14.** 598
Chicken Vegetable-Noodle Soup, **18.** 753
Dilled Chicken-Noodle Bake, **14.** 615
Green Noodles, **15.** 635
Ham-Noodle Casserole, **12.** 505
Homemade Noodles, **15.** 635
Whole Wheat Noodles, **15.** 635
Nut Bread, **4.** 142
Nut Brittle, **6.** 214
Nutmeg Cake with Toasted Meringue

**Boldface numbers
indicate chapters.**

Topping, **5.** 174
Nutrition Analysis
    Appetizers and Snacks, **1.** 32
    Barbecue, **2.** 26
    Beverages, **3.** 74
    Breads, **4.** 96
    Cakes, **5.** 164
    Candy, **6.** 202
    Canning and Freezing, **7.** 224
    Cookies, **8.** 290
    Desserts, **9.** 330
    Eggs and Cheese, **10.** 368
    Fish and Seafood, **11.** 408
    Meat, **12.** 444
    Pies, **13.** 538
    Poultry, **14.** 578
    Rice, Pasta, and Cereal, **15.** 632
    Salads and Dressings, **16.** 654
    Sauces and Relishes, **17.** 708
    Soups and Stews, **18.** 732
    Vegetables, **19.** 768

## O

Oatmeal
    Apple-Filled Oatmeal Cookies, **8.**
        309
    Apricot-Filled Oatmeal Bars, **8.**
        297
    Granola, **15.** 649
    Molasses-Oatmeal Bread, **4.** 105
    Oatmeal Cookies, **8.** 314
    Oatmeal Refrigerator Cookies, **8.**
        327
    Peanut Butter-Oatmeal Bars, **8.**
        302
    Prune-Filled Oatmeal Bars, **8.** 297
    Raisin-Filled Oatmeal Bars, **8.** 297
    Spicy Oatmeal-Raisin Cookies, **8.**
        305
    Spicy Raisin Oatmeal, **15.** 647
Oil Pastry, **13.** 571
Okra, Tomatoes and, **19.** 814
Old-Fashioned Bread Stuffing, **14.**
    626
Old-Fashioned Cheese Bake, **10.**
    400

Old-Fashioned Molasses Taffy, **6.**
    216
Old-Fashioned Raisin Bars, **8.** 300
Old-Fashioned Vegetable-Beef Soup,
    **18.** 740
Old-Time Fudge, **6.** 204
Old-Time Popcorn Balls, **6.** 216
Omelets
    Bacon-Asparagus Omelet, **10.** 391
    Baked Omelet with Chicken Sauce,
        **10.** 397
    Cheese and Herb Omelet, **10.** 390
    Cheese French Omelet, **10.** 394
    Easy Baked Cheese Omelet, **10.**
        396
    French Omelet, **10.** 394
    Fruited French Omelet, **10.** 394
    Ham and Cheese Omelet, **10.** 390
    Hashed Brown Omelet, **10.** 395
    Mushroom French Omelet, **10.**
        394
    Omelet Sandwich Puff, **10.** 395
    Puffy Omelet, **10.** 389
    Vegetable French Omelet, **10.** 394
Onions
    Broccoli-Onion Casserole, **19.** 789
    Creamy Onion Dip, **1.** 21
    French-Fried Onion Rings, **19.** 799
    French Onion Soup, **18.** 759
    Glazed Onions, **19.** 800
    Gourmet Onions, **19.** 799
    Green Bean Bake with Onions,
        **19.** 783
    Onion Bagels, **4.** 128
    Onion-Stuffed Steak, **2.** 36
    Sautéed Liver and Onions, **12.**
        530
    Squash with Onions, **19.** 812
Opera Fudge, **6.** 205
Oranges
    Apricot-Orange Bread, **4.** 139
    Cranberry-Orange Bread, **4.** 138
    Date-Orange Bars, **8.** 298
    Frosted Triple-Orange Squares,
        **16.** 679
    Orange-Chip Cookies, **8.** 325

**Boldface numbers
indicate chapters.**

Oranges (continued)
Orange-Cinnamon Sourdough
Rolls, **4.** 135
Orange-Date Coffee Cake, **4.** 144
Orange Glaze, **4.** 149
Orange-Glazed Beets, **19.** 787
Orange-Glazed Canadian Bacon,
**12.** 508
Orange-Glazed Carrots, **19.** 792
Orange-Glazed Ribs, **12.** 490
Orange-Grape Cooler, **3.** 85
Orange-Grape Sauce, **17.** 722
Orange Hard Sauce, **9.** 363
Orange Marmalade, **7.** 288
Orange or Lemon Butter Frosting,
**5.** 195
Orange Sauce, **9.** 364
Orange Soufflé, **9.** 341
Orange Spiced Tea, **3.** 91
Orange Sponge Cake, **5.** 186
Orange Sticky Rolls, **4.** 148
Spinach-Orange Toss, **16.** 667
Oriental Vegetable Toss, **16.** 662
Original Caesar Salad, **16.** 661
Oven-Baked Pork Stew, **18.** 747
Oven-Baked Ribs and Kraut, **12.** 491
Oven-Browned Potatoes, **19.** 806
Oven Candied Sweet Potatoes, **19.**
807
Oven Chicken Kiev, **14.** 588
Oven-Crisped Orange Chicken, **14.**
593
Oven-Fried Chicken, **14.** 591
Oven-Fried Chicken Monterey, **14.**
589
Oven-Fried Fish, **11.** 413
Oven Hash, **12.** 475
Oven Rice, **15.** 641
Oven Steak and Vegetables, **12.** 464
Oven Swiss Steak, **12.** 466
Oysters
Fried Clams, Oysters, or Scallops,
**11.** 431
Oyster Cocktail, **1.** 13
Oysters Rockefeller, **1.** 4
Oyster Stew, **18.** 751

Oyster Stuffing, **14.** 626
Vegetable-Oyster Stew, **18.** 752

---

# P-Q

Pan- and Oven-Fried Chicken, **14.**
584
Panbroiling Beef Steaks, **12.** 469
Pancakes
Buckwheat Pancakes, **4.** 159
Buttermilk Pancakes, **4.** 159
Homemade Biscuit Mix Pancakes,
**4.** 151
Pancakes, **4.** 159
Pan-Fried Fish, **11.** 412
Pan-Fried Vegetable Slices, **19.** 773
Pan Gravy, **12.** 454
Pan Gravy for Roast Poultry, **14.** 628
Parmesan Breadsticks, **4.** 129
Parmesan Chicken, **14.** 592
Parmesan or Romano Sauce, **17.**
712
Parmesan Spread, **2.** 63
Parsleyed Potatoes, Lemon-, **19.** 805
Parsley Rice, **15.** 642
Parsnips
Hawaiian-Style Parsnips, **19.** 800
Whipped Parsnip Puff, **19.** 815
Party Ham Sandwiches, **1.** 15
Party Pita Bread, **4.** 133
Party Punch Base, **3.** 79
Pasta
Cooking Pasta, **15.** 634
Cottage Pasta Bake, **15.** 636
Green Noodles, **15.** 635
Homemade Noodles, **15.** 635
Pasta with Carbonara Sauce, **15.**
638
Pasta with Pesto, **15.** 637
Spaetzle, **15.** 636
Spaghetti with Marinara Sauce, **15.**
637
Whole Wheat Noodles, **15.** 635
Pastel Punch, **3.** 80
Pastries
Baked Pastry Shell, **13.** 569
Electric Mixer Pastry, **13.** 571

**Boldface numbers
indicate chapters.**

Lemon Pastry, **13.** 572
Oil Pastry, **13.** 571
Pastry for Double-Crust Pie, **13.** 569
Pastry for Lattice-Top Pie, **13.** 569
Pastry for Single-Crust Pie, **13.** 569
Pecan Pastry, **13.** 572
Peaches
    Deep-Dish Peach Pie, **13.** 547
    French Crunch Peach Pie, **13.** 548
    Fresh Fruit Crisp, **9.** 352
    Peach-Banana Jam, **7.** 286
    Peach-Cherry Ice Cream, **9.** 357
    Peach Cobbler, **9.** 351
    Peaches, canning and freezing, **7.** 250
    Peach Jam, **7.** 286
    Peach-Plum Jam, **7.** 286
    Peach Sauce, **9.** 364
    Peach Shortcake, **9.** 349
    Spiced Peaches, **7.** 251
Peanut Butter
    Peanut Butter Cookies, **8.** 313
    Peanut Butter Frosting, **5.** 195
    Peanut Butter-Oatmeal Bars, **8.** 302
    Peanut Butter Slices, **8.** 325
Peanut Caramel Apples, **6.** 213
Pea Pods with Almonds, **19.** 800
Pears
    Fresh Pear Crumble Pie, **13.** 554
    Pears, canning, **7.** 252
Peas
    Creamed Peas and New Potatoes, **19.** 802
    Deluxe Peas and Mushrooms, **19.** 801
    Minted New Peas, **19.** 801
    Peas (Green), canning and freezing, **7.** 264
    Sherry-Pea Soup Elegante, **18.** 765
    Split Pea Soup, **18.** 756
Peasant Bread, **4.** 115
Pecan Biscuit Spirals, **4.** 152
Pecan Pastry, **13.** 572
Pecan Pie, **13.** 558
Pecan Tassies, **8.** 317

Pennsylvania Red Cabbage, **19.** 791
Penuche, **6.** 206
Penuche Frosting, **5.** 198
Peppermint Bonbons, **6.** 218
Peppermint Frosting, **5.** 194
Peppermint-Stick Frosting, **5.** 194
Peppers
    Easy Tomato-Pepper Relish, **17.** 729
    Peppers (Sweet), canning and freezing, **7.** 265
    Stuffed Green Peppers, **12.** 481
    Tangy Stuffed Pepper Salad, **16.** 675
Pesto, Pasta with, **15.** 637
Petits Fours, **5.** 168
Petits Fours Icing, **5.** 196
Pfeffernuesse, **8.** 317
Pheasant with Apples, **14.** 599
Pickled Beets, **17.** 728
Pickled Eggs, Rosy, **10.** 388
Pickles
    Bread and Butter Pickles, **7.** 279
    Dill Pickles, **7.** 279
    Kosher Dill Pickles, **7.** 280
    Mixed Pickles, **7.** 281
    Quick Mustard Pickles, **7.** 281
    Sweet Pickle Slices, **7.** 278
Piecrusts
    Baked Pastry Shell, **13.** 569
    Chocolate Wafer Crust, **13.** 574
    Coconut Crust, **13.** 572
    Cornflake Piecrust, **13.** 575
    Electric Mixer Pastry, **13.** 571
    Gingersnap-Graham Crust, **13.** 574
    Graham Cracker Crust, **13.** 573
    Lemon Pastry, **13.** 572
    Meringue Crust, **13.** 570
    Oil Pastry, **13.** 571
    Pastry for Double-Crust Pie, **13.** 569
    Pastry for Lattice-Top Pie, **13.** 569
    Pastry for Single-Crust Pie, **13.** 569
    Pecan Pastry, **13.** 572

**Boldface numbers
indicate chapters.**

Piecrusts (continued)
  Vanilla Wafer Crust, **13.** 574
Pies, Cream and Custard
  Banana Cream Pie, **13.** 555
  Brown-Sugar-Rhubarb Pie, **13.**
    560
  Coconut Cream Pie, **13.** 555
  Custard Pie, **13.** 560
  Dark Chocolate Cream Pie, **13.**
    555
  Lemon-Chess Pie, **13.** 558
  Lemon Meringue Pie, **13.** 556
  Light Chocolate Cream Pie, **13.**
    556
  Pecan Pie, **13.** 558
  Pumpkin Pie, **13.** 557
  Rum Cream Pie, **13.** 561
  Sour Cream-Raisin Pie, **13.** 559
  Vanilla Cream Pie, **13.** 555
Pies, Fruit
  Apple Crumble Pie, **13.** 543
  Apple Pie, **13.** 542
  Apricot Pie, **13.** 546
  Brown-Sugar-Rhubarb Pie, **13.**
    560
  Cherry Pie, **13.** 545
  Deep-Dish Apple Pie, **13.** 543
  Deep-Dish Peach Pie, **13.** 547
  French Crunch Peach Pie, **13.** 548
  Fresh Blackberry Pie, **13.** 551
  Fresh Blueberry Pie, **13.** 550
  Fresh Cherry Pie, **13.** 545
  Fresh Pear Crumble Pie, **13.** 554
  Fresh Pineapple Pie, **13.** 553
  Fresh Raspberry Pie, **13.** 552
  Gooseberry Pie, **13.** 551
  Homemade Mincemeat Pie, **13.**
    549
  Raisin Crisscross Pie, **13.** 547
  Rhubarb Pie, **13.** 553
  Sour Cream-Raisin Pie, **13.** 559
  Strawberry Glacé Pie, **13.** 552
  Strawberry-Rhubarb Pie, **13.** 553
Pies, Main-Dish
  Canadian Bacon Pie, **12.** 508
  Chicken Pot Pies, **14.** 610

**Boldface numbers
indicate chapters.**

  Hamburger Pie, **12.** 485
  Individual Tuna Pies, **11.** 436
  Steak and Kidney Pie, **12.** 531
  Tuna-Vegetable Pie, **11.** 439
Pies, Refrigerated and Frozen
  Black Bottom Pie, **13.** 566
  Chocolate Chiffon Pie, **13.** 563
  Coffee Angel Pie, **13.** 567
  French Silk Pie, **13.** 565
  Fudge Ribbon Pie, **13.** 565
  Grasshopper Pie, **13.** 568
  Lime Parfait Pie, **13.** 564
  Raspberry Chiffon Pie, **13.** 563
  Strawberry Chiffon Pie, **13.** 562
Pineapple
  Appetizer Fruit Combo, **1.** 7
  Beets with Pineapple, **19.** 788
  Fresh Pineapple Pie, **13.** 553
  Holiday Pineapple-Filled Spritz, **8.**
    318
  Pineapple-Coconut Drops, **8.** 305
  Pineapple-Glazed Canadian Bacon,
    **12.** 509
  Pineapple-Glazed Chicken, **2.** 42
  Pineapple-Orange Ice, **1.** 8
  Pineapple Sherbet, **9.** 361
  Pineapple Upside-Down Cake, **5.**
    171
  Sherried Fruit Compote, **9.** 354
Pinwheel Cookies, **8.** 321
Pita Bread, **4.** 132
Pizza, **12.** 510
Pizza Burgers, **2.** 39
Pizza-Frank Sandwiches, **2.** 47
Plum Pudding, Regal, **9.** 339
Plums
  Plum Jam, **7.** 287
  Plums, canning and freezing, **7.**
    253
Poached Eggs, **10.** 373
Poached Fish with Dill Sauce, **11.**
    421
Polenta, **15.** 647
Polish Sausage-Krauters, **2.** 45
Popcorn
  Caramel Corn, **6.** 218
  Old-Time Popcorn Balls, **6.** 216
  Sugared Popcorn, **6.** 219
Popover Chicken Tarragon, **14.** 614

Popovers, **4.** 161
Poppy Seed Bagels, **4.** 128
Poppy Seed Cake, **5.** 189
Porcupine Meatballs, **12.** 477
Pork
  Apple-Peanut-Buttered Pork
    Steaks, **2.** 52
  Basic Broiled Pork Chops and
    Steaks, **12.** 499
  Braised Pork Steaks, **12.** 498
  Breaded Pork Tenderloins, **12.**
    499
  Choucroute Garni, **12.** 519
  Meat identification, **12.** 486–87
  Oven-Baked Pork Stew, **18.** 747
  Pork Chow Mein, **2.** 492
  Pork with Apple-Curry Sauce, **12.**
    489
  Sausage and Kraut, **12.** 518
  South American Pork Soup, **18.**
    745
  Sweet-Sour Pork, **12.** 492
Pork Chops
  Basic Broiled Pork Chops and
    Steaks, **12.** 499
  Choucroute Garni, **12.** 519
  Corn-Stuffed Pork Chops, **2.** 50
  Mexicali Pork Chops, **12.** 498
  Roasted Pork Chops, **2.** 51
Pork, Cooked
  Barbecued Pork Sandwiches, **12.**
    494
  Curried Pork, **12.** 493
Pork, Ground
  Apricot-Ham Patties, **12.** 504
  Pizza, **12.** 510
  Pork Burgers, **12.** 496
  Pork Loaf, **12.** 495
  Ham Loaf, **12.** 505
  South-of-the-Border Salad, **16.** 695
  Spicy Apple-Pork Patties, **12.** 495
  Stuffed Cabbage Rolls, **12.** 497
  Swedish Meatballs, **1.** 6
Pork Ribs
  Country-Style Barbecued Ribs, **2.**
    54
  Orange-Glazed Ribs, **12.** 490
  Oven-Baked Ribs and Kraut, **12.**
    491

  Smoked Mustard-Glazed Ribs, **2.**
    54
  Spiced Orange-Apricot Ribs, **2.** 53
  Teriyaki Appetizer Ribs, **2.** 69
Pork Roast
  Company Pork Loin Roast, **2.** 52
  Harvest Pot Roast, **12.** 491
  Pork with Apple-Curry Sauce, **12.**
    489
  Roasting Pork, **12.** 488
  Roast Pork with Fennel, **12.** 488
Pork Sausage, Cooking Fresh, **12.**
  510
Porridge, Spiced, **15.** 648
Potatoes
  American-Fried Potatoes, **19.** 803
  Baked Potatoes, **19.** 802
  Cheesy Potato-Carrot Foil Bake,
    **2.** 65
  Cheesy Scalloped Potatoes, **19.**
    807
  Creamed Peas and New Potatoes,
    **19.** 802
  Creamy Potato Salad, **16.** 669
  Duchess Potatoes, **19.** 805
  Fish and Chips, **11.** 415
  Foil-Baked Potatoes, **19.** 802
  French Fries, **19.** 803
  German Potato Salad, **16.** 669
  Grilled Whole Potatoes, **2.** 65
  Hashed Brown Omelet, **10.** 395
  Hashed Brown Potatoes, **19.** 804
  Lemon-Parsleyed Potatoes, **19.**
    805
  Mashed Potatoes, **19.** 805
  Meat and Potato Bake, **2.** 50
  Oven-Browned Potatoes, **19.** 806
  Potato Bread, **4.** 112
  Potato-Chip Chicken, **14.** 592
  Potato-Ham Scallop, **12.** 506
  Potato Patties, **19.** 806
  Potato Salad Niçoise, **16.** 668
  Quick Fish-Potato Supper, **11.**
    426
  Scalloped Potatoes, **19.** 806
  Twice-Baked Potatoes, **19.** 803

**Boldface numbers
indicate chapters.**

Potatoes (continued)
Volcano Potatoes, **19.** 805
Potluck Vegetable Casserole, **19.** 816
Pot Roast, Beef, **12.** 461
Pot Roast Gravy, **12.** 461
Pot Roast, Harvest, **12.** 491
Pot Roast, Sherried Veal, **12.** 473
Pot Roast, Venison, **12.** 532
Poultry, canning and freezing, **7.** 273
Pound Cake, **5.** 172
Powdered Sugar Icing, **4.** 121, **5.** 195
Praline Cheese Cups, **9.** 347
Prune-Filled Oatmeal Bars, **8.** 297
Prune Kuchen, **4.** 118
Puddings
Baked Rice Pudding, **9.** 334
Bread Pudding, **9.** 335
Brownie Pudding, **9.** 340
Chocolate Pudding, **9.** 335
Corn Custard Pudding, **19.** 795
Lemon Pudding Cake, **9.** 340
Regal Plum Pudding, **9.** 339
Saucepan Rice Pudding, **9.** 333
Tapioca Fluff Pudding, **9.** 334
Vanilla Pudding, **9.** 335
Puffy Omelet, **10.** 389
Pumpernickel, **4.** 109
Pumpkin Bars, **8.** 303
Pumpkin, canning and freezing, **7.** 270
Pumpkin Drop Cookies, **8.** 307
Pumpkin Molasses Cake, **5.** 173
Pumpkin Muffins, **4.** 157
Pumpkin Nut Bread, **4.** 141
Pumpkin Pie, **13.** 557
Punches
Citrus Rum Punch, **3.** 77
Creamy Reception Punch, **3.** 80
Easy Sherbet Punch, **3.** 80
Grenadine Punch, **3.** 81
Nonalcoholic Punch, **3.** 78
Party Punch Base, **3.** 78
Pastel Punch, **3.** 80
Quantity Fruit Punch, **3.** 77
Slushy Punch, **3.** 78

**Boldface numbers
indicate chapters.**

Spiked Party Punch, **3.** 78
Spiked Slushy Punch, **3.** 78
White Wine Punch, **3.** 78
Quantity Fruit Punch, **3.** 77
Quiches
Classic Quiche Lorraine, **10.** 401
Individual Quiche Casseroles, **10.** 403
Seafood Quiche, **10.** 402
Quick Beans-and-Franks Soup, **18.** 747
Quick Beef Goulash Stew, **18.** 742
Quick Breads, **4.** 136
Quick Cabbage-Cheese Soup, **18.** 765
Quick Cheesy Tuna Soup, **18.** 765
Quick Chocolate Glaze, **8.** 295
Quick Fish-Potato Supper, **11.** 426
Quick Garlic Cubed Steaks, **2.** 38
Quick Mushroom Sauce, **17.** 716
Quick Mustard Pickles, **7.** 281
Quick Reuben Salad, **16.** 697
Quick Three-Bean Salad, **16.** 674
Quick Tomato-Rice Soup, **18.** 764

# R

Rabbit
Beer-Braised Rabbit, **12.** 533
Hasenpfeffer, **12.** 533
Raisins
Apple-Raisin Muffins, **4.** 157
Old-Fashioned Raisin Bars, **8.** 300
Raisin Bread, **4.** 114
Raisin Crisscross Pie, **13.** 547
Raisin-Filled Oatmeal Bars, **8.** 297
Raisin Sauce, **17.** 719
Raisin Stuffing, **14.** 626
Sour Cream-Raisin Pie, **13.** 559
Spicy Oatmeal-Raisin Cookies, **8.** 305
Spicy Raisin Oatmeal, **15.** 647
Ranger Cookies, **8.** 307
Raspberries
Blueberry Melba Parfaits, **9.** 354
Fresh Raspberry Pie, **13.** 552
Raspberry Chiffon Pie, **13.** 563

Raw Vegetable Antipasto, **16.** 673
Red Wine Dressing, **16.** 701
Refrigerator Cookies, **8.** 324
Regal Plum Pudding, **9.** 339
Relishes
   Cinnamon Apple Rings, **17.** 727
   Corn Relish, **7.** 277
   Cranberry-Orange Relish, **17.** 727
   Easy Tomato-Pepper Relish, **17.** 729
   Fresh Cucumber Relish, **17.** 729
   Hot Curried Fruit, **17.** 728
   Pickled Beets, **17.** 728
   Tomato-Cucumber Relish, **12.** 480
   Vegetable Relish, **7.** 276
Remarkable Fudge, **6.** 205
Reuben Salad, Quick, **16.** 697
Rhubarb
   Brown-Sugar-Rhubarb Pie, **13.** 560
   Rhubarb, canning and freezing, **7.** 254
   Rhubarb Pie, **13.** 553
   Rhubarb Sauce, **9.** 362
   Strawberry-Rhubarb Pie, **13.** 553
Rice
   Baked Rice Pudding, **9.** 334
   Brown Rice, **15.** 641
   Calico Rice Bake, **2.** 68
   Chinese Fried Rice, **15.** 644
   Confetti Rice, **15.** 642
   Cooking Rice, **15.** 642
   Curried Rice, **15.** 643
   Egg-Rice Bake, **10.** 384
   Fruit and Nut Brown Rice, **15.** 642
   Herbed Rice, **15.** 642
   Mushroom-Rice Bake, **15.** 645
   Oven Rice, **15.** 641
   Parsley Rice, **15.** 642
   Rice Rings, **15.** 642
   Saucepan Rice Pudding, **9.** 333
   Spanish Rice, **15.** 644
   Wild Rice, **15.** 643
   Wild Rice with Mushrooms, **15.** 643
Roasted Corn on the Cob, **2.** 64
Roasted Pork Chops, **2.** 51
Roasting Beef, **12.** 455

Roasting Lamb, **12.** 522
Roasting Pork, **12.** 488
Roasting Veal, **12.** 455
Roast Pork with Fennel, **12.** 488
Roast Tarragon Chicken, **14.** 623
Roast with Barbecue Gravy, **12.** 463
Rocky Road, **6.** 221
Rocky Road Frosting, **5.** 198
Rolled Cream Cheese Cookies, **8.** 322
Rolled Ginger Cookies, **8.** 321
Rolled Sugar Cookies, **8.** 326
Rosy Pickled Eggs, **10.** 388
Rum Cream Pie, **13.** 561
Rump Roast with Vegetables, **12.** 459
Russian Black Bread, **4.** 111
Russian Dressing, **16.** 704
Rutabagas
   Rutabaga and Apple, **19.** 808
   Turnips and Rutabagas, freezing, **7.** 270
   Whipped Rutabaga Puff, **19.** 815
Rye Bread, **4.** 106
Rye Croutons, **16.** 697

---

## S

Salad Dressings
   Avocado Dressing, **16.** 703
   Blender Mayonnaise, **16.** 706
   Buttermilk Dressing, **16.** 702
   Chunky Blue Cheese Dressing, **16.** 703
   Citrus Vinaigrette, **16.** 703
   Cooked Dressing, **16.** 705
   Creamy French Dressing, **16.** 702
   Creamy Fruit Dressing, **16.** 705
   French Dressing, **16.** 704
   Garlic Olive Oil, **16.** 662
   Green Goddess Dressing, **16.** 704
   Herb Dressing, **16.** 705
   Homemade Mayonnaise, **16.** 705
   Honey-Lime Dressing, **16.** 691

**Boldface numbers
indicate chapters.**

Salad Dressings (continued)
Italian Dressing, **16.** 702
Louis Dressing, **16.** 698
Red Wine Dressing, **16.** 701
Russian Dressing, **16.** 704
Spicy Nectar Dressing, **16.** 691
Strawberry-Cheese Dressing, **16.** 691
Thousand Island Dressing, **16.** 704
Vinaigrette Dressing, **16.** 703
Salad greens identification, basic, **16.** 659
Salad Niçoise, **16.** 696
Salads, Fruit
Apricot Soufflé Salad, **16.** 678
Cherry-Cider Salad, **16.** 680
Cherry-Lemon Ring, **16.** 679
Choose-a-Fruit Salad Platter, **16.** 691
Cider Waldorf Mold, **16.** 682
Cinnamon Fruit Salad, **16.** 690
Cranberry Citrus Mold, **16.** 681
Cranberry Frost Salad, **16.** 685
Creamy Fruit Salad, **16.** 684
Five-Cup Salad, **16.** 685
Frosted Triple-Orange Squares, **16.** 679
Frozen Lemon Salad, **16.** 686
Fruit-and-Nut Tropical Slaw, **16.** 689
Fruit-Filled Melons, **16.** 687
Fruit Medley Salad, **16.** 689
Fruit Strata Salad, **16.** 688
Fruity Ginger Ale Mold, **16.** 678
Jubilee Salad Mold, **16.** 682
Lime Fruit Salad, **16.** 683
Strawberry-Banana Soufflé Salads, **16.** 681
24-Hour Fruit Salad, **16.** 688
Waldorf Salad, **16.** 686
Salads, Main-Dish
Chef's Salad, **16.** 692
Chicken-Stuffed Tomatoes, **16.** 700
Crab Louis, **16.** 698

Crab-Stuffed Tomatoes, **16.** 699
Curried Chicken Salad, **16.** 694
Greek Salad, **16.** 693
Meatless Meal-in-a-Bowl, **16.** 697
Quick Reuben Salad, **16.** 697
Salad Niçoise, **16.** 696
Sausage Supper Salad, **16.** 699
Scallop Toss, **16.** 694
Shrimp-Avocado Salad, **16.** 692
South-of-the-Border Salad, **16.** 695
Tuna-Stuffed Tomatoes, **16.** 700
Salads, Vegetable
Asparagus Toss, **16.** 663
Cheddar Macaroni Salad, **16.** 667
Coleslaw Vinaigrette, **16.** 670
Creamy Coleslaw, **16.** 670
Creamy Potato Salad, **16.** 669
Create a Tossed Salad, **16.** 660
Cucumber Ring Supreme, **16.** 677
Gazpacho Salad, **16.** 671
German Potato Salad, **16.** 669
Green Goddess Salad, **16.** 665
Hot Five-Bean Salad, **16.** 673
Marinated Three-Bean Salad, **16.** 674
Marinated Zucchini Salad, **16.** 672
Molded Shrimp Salad, **16.** 676
Oriental Vegetable Toss, **16.** 662
Original Caesar Salad, **16.** 661
Potato Salad Niçoise, **16.** 668
Quick Three-Bean Salad, **16.** 674
Raw Vegetable Antipasto, **16.** 673
Sour Cream Cucumbers, **16.** 671
Spinach-Orange Toss, **16.** 667
Tangy Stuffed Pepper Salad, **16.** 675
Taos Salad Toss, **16.** 666
Tomato Aspic, **16.** 675
24-Hour Vegetable Salad, **16.** 664
Wilted Spinach Salad, **16.** 666
Zucchini Salad Bowl, **16.** 665
Salami-Bean Casserole, **12.** 515
Salmon
Dilled Salmon Dip, **1.** 8
Grilled Salmon Steaks, **2.** 57
Lemon-Marinated Salmon Steaks, **11.** 425
Salmon-Broccoli Crêpes, **11.** 441

Salmon Loaf, **11.** 440
Salmon Mousse, **1.** 11
Skillet Dilled Salmon Patties, **11.** 440
Tuna Soufflé, **10.** 399
Saltwater Taffy, **6.** 213
Sandies, **8.** 315
Sandwiches
  Bacon-Wrapped Franks, **2.** 46
  Barbecued Bacon Burgers, **2.** 40
  Barbecued Pork Sandwiches, **12.** 494
  Basic Grilled Burgers, **2.** 38
  Blue Cheese Burgers, **2.** 40
  Corn Dogs, **12.** 516
  Curried Fishwiches, **11.** 427
  Double-Decker Burgers, **12.** 479
  Omelet Sandwich Puff, **10.** 395
  Party Ham Sandwiches, **1.** 15
  Pizza Burgers, **2.** 39
  Pizza-Frank Sandwiches, **2.** 47
  Polish Sausage-Krauters, **2.** 45
  Pork Burgers, **12.** 496
  Savory Lamburgers, **12.** 527
  Skilletburgers, **12.** 480
  Super Chicken Subs, **14.** 606
  Tacos con Carne, **12.** 483
Sangria, **3.** 84
Santa's Whiskers, **8.** 326
Saucepan Rice Pudding, **9.** 333
Sauces
  Almond Sauce, **17.** 711
  Bacon-Sour Cream Sauce, **11.** 415
  Basic Hard Sauce, **9.** 363
  Blender Hollandaise Sauce, **17.** 712
  Blue Cheese Sauce, **17.** 711
  Bordelaise Sauce, **17.** 715
  Brandy Hard Sauce, **9.** 363, **13.** 550
  Brown Sauce, **17.** 716
  Cheese Sauce, **12.** 502, **17.** 711
  Cherry Sauce, **9.** 344
  Classic Béarnaise Sauce, **17.** 713
  Classic Hollandaise Sauce, **17.** 712
  Cocktail Sauce, **17.** 724
  Confetti Sauce, **17.** 711
  Cranberry Sauce, **17.** 720
  Creamy Curry Sauce, **12.** 468
  Creamy Mushroom Sauce, **17.** 717
  Cucumber or Zucchini Sauce, **17.** 711
  Curry Sauce, **17.** 711
  Dill Sauce, **11.** 412, **17.** 721
  Easy Barbecue Sauce, **17.** 719
  Easy Dill Sauce, **17.** 721
  Fluffy Hard Sauce, **9.** 363
  Fluffy Horseradish Sauce, **17.** 718
  Fluffy Vanilla Sauce, **9.** 364
  Fresh Mint Sauce, **17.** 723
  Herb-Butter Basting Sauce, **2.** 45
  Herb-Garlic Sauce, **17.** 711
  Herb Sauce, **17.** 711
  Homemade Tomato Sauce, **19.** 798
  Hot Chinese Mustard, **17.** 718
  Lemon-Chive Sauce, **17.** 711
  Medium White Sauce, **17.** 710
  Mexicali Sauce, **17.** 712
  Mock Hollandaise Sauce, **17.** 713
  Mushroom Steak Sauce, **12.** 469
  Orange-Grape Sauce, **17.** 722
  Orange Hard Sauce, **9.** 363
  Orange Sauce, **9.** 363
  Parmesan or Romano Sauce, **17.** 711
  Peach Sauce, **9.** 364
  Quick Mushroom Sauce, **17.** 716
  Raisin Sauce, **17.** 719
  Rhubarb Sauce, **9.** 362
  Sauce Diable, **17.** 716
  Sauce Provençale, **17.** 714
  Sherry Sauce, **17.** 711
  Shrimp Sauce, **11.** 417
  Snappy Barbecue Sauce, **17.** 718
  Spicy Cherry Sauce, **17.** 720
  Sweet-Sour Basting Sauce, **2.** 44
  Sweet-Sour Sauce, **17.** 723
  Tangy Cranberry Sauce, **1.** 7, **17.** 720
  Tartar Sauce, **17.** 724

**Boldface numbers
indicate chapters.**

Sauces (continued)
Tempura Sauce, **19.** 778
Thin White Sauce, **17.** 710
Tomato Sauce, **12.** 511
White Sauce, **17.** 710
Wine Basting Sauce, **2.** 44
Wine-Mushroom Sauce, **17.** 717
Wine Sauce, **12.** 469
Saucy Brussels Sprouts, **19.** 790
Saucy Celery Casserole, **19.** 794
Saucy Lamb Riblets, **2.** 62
Saucy Lamb Shanks, **12.** 524
Sauerbraten, **12.** 464
Sauerbraten Burgers, **12.** 478
Sausage
Apple-Stuffed Sausage Patties, **12.** 513
Bacon-Wrapped Franks, **2.** 46
Choucroute Garni, **12.** 519
Coney Islands, **12.** 517
Cooking Fresh Pork Sausage, **12.** 510
Corn Dogs, **12.** 516
Creamed Bratwurst, **12.** 517
Easy Pork Cassoulet, **18.** 746
Egg-Sausage Casserole, **10.** 385
Frank-Vegetable Kebabs, **2.** 47
German Sausage Chowder, **18.** 743
Lasagna, **12.** 512
Meat identification, **12.** 509
Pizza, **12.** 510
Pizza-Frank Sandwiches, **2.** 47
Polish Sausage-Krauters, **2.** 45
Salami-Bean Casserole, **12.** 515
Sausage- and Apple-Stuffed Squash, **12.** 513
Sausage and Corn Bread, **12.** 514
Sausage and Kraut, **12.** 518
Sausage-Macaroni Skillet, **12.** 515
Sausage Supper Salad, **16.** 699
South-of-the-Border Salad, **16.** 695
Spaghetti and Meatballs, **12.** 482
Spaghetti Sauce, **12.** 482
Squash and Sausage, **19.** 812

Tacos con Carne, **12.** 483
Sautéed Liver and Onions, **12.** 530
Savory Lamburgers, **12.** 527
Savory Stuffed Rib Roast, **12.** 458
Savory Wine Marinade, **17.** 725
Scalloped Corn, **19.** 795
Scalloped Eggs and Bacon, **10.** 385
Scalloped Potatoes, **19.** 806
Scalloped Tomatoes, **19.** 813
Scalloped Vegetables, **19.** 773
Scallops
Boiled Scallops, **11.** 430
Fried Clams, Oysters, or Scallops, **11.** 431
Scallop Toss, **16.** 691
Scotch Broth, **18.** 743
Scrambled Eggs, **10.** 374
Sea Foam Candy, **6.** 210
Seafoam Frosting, **5.** 194
Seafood Quiche, **10.** 402
Sesame Asparagus, **19.** 780
Sesame Seed Bagels, **4.** 128
Sesame Swirls, **4.** 154
Seven-Layer Bars, **8.** 300
Seven Minute Frosting, **5.** 194
Shellfish (see also Clams, Crab, Lobster, Oysters, Scallops, Shrimp)
Boiled Shellfish, **11.** 430
Shellfish, freezing, **7.** 273
Sherried Fruit Compote, **9.** 354
Sherried Veal, **12.** 473
Sherry-Pea Soup Elegante, **18.** 765
Sherry Sauce, **17.** 712
Sherry-Sauced Halibut, **11.** 424
Shortcake, Blueberry, **9.** 349
Shortcake, Peach, **9.** 349
Shortcakes, Individual, **9.** 350
Shortcake, Strawberry, **9.** 349
Shrimp
Boiled Shrimp, **11.** 430
Broiled Shrimp, **11.** 432
Cioppino, **18.** 751
Creole Gumbo, **18.** 748
Foil-Barbecued Shrimp, **2.** 58
French-Fried Shrimp, **11.** 432
Marinated Shrimp Appetizers, **2.** 69
Molded Shrimp Salad, **16.** 676
Seafood Quiche, **10.** 402
Shrimp-Avocado Salad, **16.** 692

Shrimp Chow Mein, **11.** 433
Shrimp Cocktail, **1.** 13
Shrimp-Cucumber Appetizer
   Spread, **1.** 13
Shrimp-Egg Bake, **10.** 387
Shrimp Egg Foo Yong, **10.** 377
Shrimp Newburg, **11.** 435
Shrimp-Rice Soup, **18.** 750
Shrimp Sauce, **11.** 417
Steak and Shrimp Kebabs, **2.** 35
Tuna Soufflé, **10.** 399
Skillet Barley, **15.** 650
Skilletburgers, **12.** 480
Skillet Candied Sweet Potatoes, **19.**
   808
Skillet Dilled Salmon Patties, **11.**
   440
Skillet-Fried Chicken, **14.** 584
Skillet-Fried Fish, **2.** 56
Slushy Punch, **3.** 78
Smoked Mustard-Glazed Ribs, **2.** 54
Smoked Short Ribs, **2.** 34
Smoky Cheese Ball, **1.** 12
Snappy Barbecue Sauce, **17.** 718
Snickerdoodles, **8.** 315
Soft-Cooked or Hard-Cooked Eggs,
   **10.** 372
Soft Pretzels, **4.** 131
Soufflés
   Apricot Soufflé Salad, **16.** 678
   Broccoli Soufflé, **19.** 791
   Brussels Sprouts Soufflé, **19.** 790
   Cauliflower Soufflé, **19.** 791
   Cheese Soufflé, **10.** 397
   Chocolate Soufflé, **9.** 341
   Orange Soufflé, **9.** 341
   Strawberry-Banana Soufflé Salads,
   **16.** 681
   Tuna Soufflé, **10.** 399
Soups
   Beef Stock, **18.** 737
   Chicken Stock, **18.** 736
Soups, Main-Dish
   Beef-Barley Soup, **18.** 740
   Cheesy Chicken-Corn Chowder,
   **18.** 764
   Chicken Vegetable-Noodle Soup,
   **18.** 753
   Chili con Carne, **18.** 741

Cream of Chicken Soup, **18.** 755
Creole Gumbo, **18.** 748
Easy Chicken-Curry Soup, **18.**
   763
Fish Chowder, **18.** 752
German Sausage Chowder, **18.**
   743
Ham Hodgepodge, **18.** 746
Manhattan Clam Chowder, **18.**
   750
Mulligatawny, **18.** 753
New England Clam Chowder, **18.**
   748
Old-Fashioned Vegetable-Beef
   Soup, **18.** 740
Oyster Stew, **18.** 751
Quick Beans-and-Franks Soup,
   **18.** 747
Quick Cabbage-Cheese Soup, **18.**
   765
Scotch Broth, **18.** 743
Shrimp-Rice Soup, **18.** 750
South American Pork Soup, **18.**
   745
Turkey Frame Soup, **18.** 754
Vegetable-Oyster Stew, **18.** 752
Soups, Meal-Mate
   Cheese Soup, **18.** 762
   Cream of Fresh Vegetable Soup,
   **18.** 760
   Creamy Borscht, **18.** 759
   French Onion Soup, **18.** 759
   Fresh Corn Chowder, **18.** 757
   Gazpacho, **18.** 761
   Ham and Bean Vegetable Soup,
   **18.** 757
   Herbed Tomato Soup, **18.** 758
   Lentil Soup, **18.** 757
   Minestrone, **18.** 755
   Quick Cheesy Tuna Soup, **18.**
   765
   Quick Tomato-Rice Soup, **18.** 764
   Sherry-Pea Soup Elegante, **18.** 765
   Split Pea Soup, **18.** 756
   Swedish Fruit Soup, **18.** 762
   Vichyssoise, **18.** 763

**Boldface numbers
indicate chapters.**

Sour Cream
  Sour Cream Biscuits, **4.** 154
  Sour Cream Cheesecake, **9.** 343
  Sour Cream Chocolate Cake, **5.** 182
  Sour Cream Cucumbers, **16.** 671
  Sour Cream Nut Drops, **8.** 311
  Sour Cream-Raisin Pie, **13.** 559
Sourdough Bread, **4.** 134
Sourdough Starter, **4.** 134
South American Pork Soup, **18.** 745
Southern Cheese Grits, **15.** 648
Southern Pralines, **6.** 208
South-of-the-Border Salad, **16.** 695
Spaetzle, **15.** 636
Spaghetti and Meatballs, **12.** 482
Spaghetti Sauce, **12.** 482
Spaghetti with Marinara Sauce, **15.** 637
Spanish Rice, **15.** 644
Special helps
  Appliance shortcuts, **20.** 876
  Basic equipment, **20.** 874
  Basic five food groups, **20.** 827
  Basic groceries, **20.** 873
  Basic techniques, **20.** 849
  Budget thoughts, **20.** 837
  Calorie tally, **20.** 828
  Caramelizing sugar, **20.** 851
  Chopping onions, **20.** 850
  Clarifying butter, **20.** 849
  Cooking at high altitudes, **20.** 880
  Cooking terms, **20.** 864
  Crumbs and croutons, **20.** 848
  Cutting up a fresh pineapple, **20.** 852
  Cutting up apples, **20.** 852
  Dairy products, **20.** 857
  Eggs, **20.** 858
  Emergency substitutions, **20.** 871
  Fats and oils, **20.** 856
  Flour, **20.** 855
  Food shopping tips, **20.** 837
  Freezing cooked food, **20.** 841
  Fruits and vegetables chart, **20.** 845

Garnishes, **20.** 884
High altitude adjustments for cakes, **20.** 881
How to measure, **20.** 859
Ingredient equivalents, **20.** 845
Ingredients and how to use them, **20.** 855
Is sifting necessary?, **20.** 861
Kitchen thermometer tips, **20.** 877
Leavenings, **20.** 857
Make-do cookware, **20.** 877
Meal planning, **20.** 821
Measurements, 924
Melting chocolate, **20.** 850
Metric system, the, **20.** 882
Nutrient descriptions, **20.** 825
Nutrition analysis, **20.** 827
Nutrition basics, **20.** 825
Nutrition labeling, **20.** 839
Organizing your kitchen, **20.** 873
Peeling tomatoes, **20.** 850
Planning nutritious meals, **20.** 822
Preheating the oven, **20.** 848
Preparation helps, **20.** 847
Preparing food for storage, **20.** 839
Putting metric units into perspective, **20.** 883
Seasoning guide, **20.** 869
Sectioning grapefruit or oranges, **20.** 851
Selecting kitchen tools, **20.** 874
Separating eggs, **20.** 849
Snipping fresh herbs, **20.** 854
Steaming vegetables, **20.** 851
Stir-frying, **20.** 852
Stocking your kitchen, **20.** 873
Storage, **20.** 839
Sweeteners, **20.** 856
Thickeners, **20.** 855
Tips about equipment, **20.** 875
Tips for baked products, **20.** 847
Tips for saving time, **20.** 878
Use the basic five food groups, **20.** 824
Using a chef's knife, **20.** 853
Using a mortar and pestle, **20.** 854
Using a pastry bag, **20.** 854
Using a pastry cloth, **20.** 848

**Boldface numbers
indicate chapters.**

Using a whisk, **20.** 853
Using canned foods, **20.** 873
Using fresh garlic, **20.** 852
Using whole spices, **20.** 853
What's a dash?, **20.** 861
What's the difference?, **20.** 862
Spiced Orange-Apricot Ribs, **2.** 53
Spiced Peaches, **7.** 251
Spiced Porridge, **15.** 648
Spice Nut Cake, **5.** 176
Spicy Apple-Pork Patties, **12.** 495
Spicy Barbecued Chicken, **2.** 41
Spicy Buttermilk Coffee Cake, **4.** 144
Spicy Cherry Sauce, **17.** 720
Spicy Chocolate, **3.** 85
Spicy Nectar Dressing, **16.** 691
Spicy Oatmeal-Raisin Cookies, **8.** 305
Spicy Raisin Oatmeal, **15.** 647
Spicy Stuffed Eggplant, **19.** 797
Spiked Party Punch, **3.** 79
Spiked Slushy Punch, **3.** 79
Spinach
  Chinese Spinach, **19.** 810
  Creamed Spinach with Nutmeg, **19.** 809
  Meatball Stew with Spinach Dumplings, **18.** 741
  Spinach-Orange Toss, **16.** 667
  Wilted Spinach Salad, **16.** 666
Spit-Roasting Chart, **2.** 32–33
Split Pea Soup, **18.** 756
Spoon Bread, **4.** 156
Spritz, **8.** 318
Squash
  Baked Acorn Squash Halves, **19.** 812
  Candied Squash, **19.** 812
  Candied Squash Rings, **19.** 811
  Cheddar-Squash Puff, **19.** 811
  Dilly Panned Summer Squash, **19.** 810
  Grilled Acorn Squash, **2.** 66
  Sausage- and Apple-Stuffed Squash, **12.** 513
  Squash and Applesauce, **19.** 812
  Squash and Sausage, **19.** 812
  Squash with Onions, **19.** 812

Stacked Sole, **11.** 416
Standing Rib Roast with Yorkshire Pudding, **12.** 457
Steak and Kidney Pie, **12.** 531
Steak and Shrimp Kebabs, **2.** 35
Steamed Clams, **11.** 434
Stewed Chicken, **14.** 597
Stews, Beef
  Beef Bourguignonne, **18.** 738
  Beef Stew, **18.** 739
  Cider Stew, **18.** 739
  Meatball Stew with Spinach Dumplings, **18.** 741
  Quick Beef Goulash Stew, **18.** 742
Stews, Fish and Seafood
  Bouillabaisse, **18.** 749
  Cioppino, **18.** 751
  Oyster Stew, **18.** 751
  Vegetable-Oyster Stew, **18.** 752
Stews, Lamb
  Dilled Lamb Ragout, **18.** 744
  Herbed Lamb Stew, **18.** 745
Stews, Pork
  Easy Pork Cassoulet, **18.** 746
  Oven-Baked Pork Stew, **18.** 747
Sticky Nut Rolls, **4.** 148
Stir-Fried Fish and Peppers, **11.** 413
Stirred Custard, **9.** 336
Stock
  Beef Stock, **18.** 737
  Chicken Stock, **18.** 736
Strata, Classic Cheese, **10.** 403
Strawberries
  Appetizer Fruit Combo, **1.** 7
  Fresh Strawberry Ice Cream, **9.** 358
  Strawberry-Banana Soufflé Salads, **16.** 681
  Strawberry-Cheese Dressing, **16.** 691
  Strawberry Chiffon Pie, **13.** 562
  Strawberry Glacé Pie, **13.** 552
  Strawberry Jam, **7.** 286
  Strawberry Milk Shake, **3.** 86
  Strawberry-Rhubarb Pie, **13.** 553

**Boldface numbers indicate chapters.**

Strawberries (continued)
   Strawberry Shortcake, **9.** 349
   Strawberry Spritzer, **3.** 89
Streusel Coffee Cake, **4.** 146
Stuffed Cabbage Rolls, **12.** 497
Stuffed Flounder, **11.** 419
Stuffed Green Peppers, **12.** 481
Stuffings
   Chestnut Stuffing, **14.** 626
   Corn Bread and Bacon Stuffing,
     **14.** 627
   Giblet Stuffing, **14.** 626
   Harvest Stuffing, **14.** 625
   Mushroom Stuffing, **14.** 626
   Old-Fashioned Bread Stuffing,
     **14.** 626
   Oyster Stuffing, **14.** 626
   Raisin Stuffing, **14.** 626
Succotash, Creamy, **19.** 784
Sugar Cookies, Filled, **8.** 320
Sugar Cookies, Rolled, **8.** 326
Sugared Popcorn, **6.** 219
Summer Fruit Compote, **9.** 353
Sunflower Seed Muffins, **4.** 158
Sunshine Muffins, **4.** 158
Sun Tea, **3.** 91
Super Chicken Subs, **14.** 606
Swedish Fruit Soup, **18.** 762
Swedish Limpa, **4.** 109
Swedish Meatballs, **1.** 6
Sweet-and-Sour Fish, **11.** 426
Sweetbreads, Creamed, **12.** 530
Sweet Pickle Slices, **7.** 278
Sweet Potatoes
   Mashed Sweet Potato Bake, **19.**
     808
   Oven Candied Sweet Potatoes,
     **19.** 807
   Skillet Candied Sweet Potatoes, **19.**
     808
   Sweet-Potato-Cashew Bake, **19.**
     807
   Sweet Potatoes, canning and
     freezing, **7.** 265
   Turkey-Yam Kebabs, **14.** 608
Sweet Rolls, **4.** 120

**Boldface numbers
indicate chapters.**

Sweet-Sour Basting Sauce, **2.** 44
Sweet-Sour Ham, **2.** 48
Sweet-Sour Pork, **12.** 492
Sweet-Sour Sauce, **17.** 723
Swiss Cheese-Ham Spread, **1.** 9
Swiss Onion Bake, **10.** 381
Swiss Steak, **12.** 466
Swiss Veal Roast, **12.** 474

---

# T

---

Tacos con Carne, **12.** 483
Tangy Cranberry Sauce, **1.** 7, **17.**
   720
Tangy Stuffed Pepper Salad, **16.**
   675
Taos Salad Toss, **16.** 666
Tapioca Fluff Pudding, **9.** 334
Tartar Sauce, **17.** 724
Tea
   Iced Tea, **3.** 91
   Orange Spiced Tea, **3.** 91
   Sun Tea, **3.** 91
   Tea, **3.** 90
Tempura Sauce, **19.** 778
Teriyaki Appetizer Ribs, **2.** 69
Teriyaki Marinade, **17.** 724
Teriyaki Roast Beef, **12.** 458
Texas Beef Skillet, **12.** 484
Thousand Island Dressing, **16.** 704
Three-Bean Salad, Marinated, **16.**
   674
Three-C Bread, **4.** 141
Tips
   An alternate poaching pan, **11.**
     421
   Appetizer juices, **1.** 5
   Arranging coals for barbecuing, **2.**
     71
   Basic guide for cooking foods on
     the grill, **2.** 30–31
   Basic salad greens, **16.** 659
   Beef identification, **12.** 452–53
   Beverage dress-ups, **3.** 76
   Boning chicken breasts, **14.** 583
   Candy testing, **6.** 207
   Canned seafood, **11.** 437

Cheese identification, **10.** 392–93

Clarifying stock, **18.** 737

Cook-before-eating hams, **12.** 503

Cooking vegetables, **19.** 774

Cutting up a chicken, **14.** 581

Dipping chocolates, **6.** 211

Easy-mix method, **4.** 102

Egg-cooking tip, **10.** 373

Flavored butters, **17.** 726

Fondue dippers, **1.** 20

Grilling chart, **2.** 30–31

Grilling frozen vegetables, **2.** 67

Headspace in canning, **7.** 235

High altitude chart, **5.** 178

How much meat to buy, **12.** 450

How to braid breads, **4.** 117

How to frost and cut cakes the professional way, **5.** 192

How to julienne, **16.** 696

Jelly roll pointers, **5.** 188

Jelly test, **7.** 283

Lamb identification, **12.** 520–22

Making sour milk, **4.** 137

Making tomato cups, **16.** 701

Marinating meat, **12.** 459

Mashed vegetables, **19.** 809

Meat carving, **12.** 534–35

Microwave-thawed poultry, **14.** 582

Mounting birds on a spit, **2.** 44

Pasta identification, **15.** 639–40

Pork identification, **12.** 486–87

Poultry choices for stuffings, **14.** 627

Pressure canning altitude adjustment, **7.** 237

Processing pickles and relishes, **7.** 278

Pudding tip, **9.** 336

Removing a piece of crumb-crust pie, **13.** 575

Rice identification, **15.** 646

Roasting domestic birds, **14.** 619

Roast on a spit, **2.** 61

Safety reminder, **7.** 231

Sausage identification, **12.** 509

Serving a soufflé, **10.** 398

Shaping dinner rolls, **4.** 126

Shellfish equivalents, **11.** 430

Soaking dry beans, **18.** 756

Spit-roasting chart, **2.** 32–33

Stir-frying, **12.** 470

Stock substitutions, **18.** 736

Syrups for canning and freezing fruit, **7.** 234

Test fish for doneness, **11.** 411

Testing soufflés for doneness, **10.** 399

Thawing fish, **11.** 418

Tips for making chiffon pies, **13.** 564

Tips for making cream pies, **13.** 556

Tips for making custard pies, **13.** 561

Tips for making frozen pies, **13.** 567

Tips for making fruit pies, **13.** 544

Tips for making tart shells, **13.** 573

Tips for using the nutrition analysis chart, **5.** 167

Unmolding a gelatin salad, **16.** 683

Using a meat thermometer, **12.** 451

Using chicken broth, **14.** 591

Veal identification, **12.** 452–54

Vegetable toppers, **19.** 778

Water-bath canning altitude adjustment, **7.** 232

Wine guide, **3.** 92

Wrap for freezing, **7.** 274

Toasted Barley Bake, **15.** 650

Toasted Meringue Topping, **5.** 175

Toffee Bars, **8.** 298

Toffee Butter Crunch, **6.** 215

Tomatoes

    Asparagus-Tomato Stir-Fry, **19.** 780

    Baked Tomatoes, **19.** 813

    Broiled Tomatoes, **19.** 813

    Chicken-Stuffed Tomatoes, **16.** 700

**Boldface numbers indicate chapters.**

Tomatoes (continued)
  Chili con Queso, **1.** 22
  Crab-Stuffed Tomatoes, **16.** 699
  Easy Tomato-Pepper Relish, **17.** 729
  Fresh Tomato Fix-Ups, **19.** 813
  Fried Green Tomatoes, **19.** 773
  Fried Ripe Tomatoes, **19.** 773
  Herbed Tomato Soup, **18.** 758
  Homemade Tomato Sauce, **19.** 798
  Quick Tomato-Rice Soup, **18.** 764
  Scalloped Tomatoes, **19.** 813
  Tomato Aspic, **16.** 675
  Tomato Catsup, **7.** 269
  Tomato-Chili Guacamole, **1.** 22
  Tomato-Cucumber Relish, **12.** 480
  Tomatoes and Okra, **19.** 814
  Tomatoes, canning and freezing, **7.** 266
  Tomato Juice, **7.** 268
  Tomato Juice Cocktail, **7.** 268
  Tomato Sauce, **12.** 511
  Tuna-Stuffed Tomatoes, **16.** 700
Tongue and Lima Skillet, **12.** 529
Tortes
  Cherry Torte, **9.** 346
  Lemon Torte, **9.** 345
Trout Amandine, **11.** 423
Tuna
  Baked Tuna Patties, **11.** 437
  Company Creamed Tuna, **11.** 439
  Individual Tuna Pies, **11.** 436
  Quick Cheesy Tuna Soup, **18.** 765
  Salmon-Broccoli Crêpes, **11.** 441
  Salmon Mousse, **1.** 11
  Salad Niçoise, **16.** 696
  Tuna a la king, **11.** 438
  Tuna-Noodle Casserole, **11.** 435
  Tuna Soufflé, **10.** 399
  Tuna-Stuffed Tomatoes, **16.** 700
  Tuna-Vegetable Pie, **11.** 439
Turkey

Giblet Gravy, **14.** 629
Roasting Turkey, **14.** 619
Turkey Frame Soup, **18.** 754
Turkey-Yam Kebabs, **14.** 608
Turkey, Cooked
  Chef's Salad, **16.** 692
  Chicken-Asparagus Stacks, **14.** 605
  Chicken Enchilada Casserole, **14.** 613
  Crowd-Size Chicken Bake, **14.** 614
  Curried Chicken Salad, **16.** 694
  Super Chicken Subs, **16.** 606
  Tuna Soufflé, **10.** 399
Turnips
  Lemon-Parsleyed Turnips, **19.** 815
  Turnips and Rutabagas, freezing, **7.** 270
  Whipped Turnip Puff, **19.** 814
24-Hour Fruit Salad, **16.** 688
24-Hour Vegetable Salad, **16.** 664
Twice-Baked Potatoes, **19.** 803

# V

Vanilla Cream Pie, **13.** 555
Vanilla Ice Cream, **9.** 357
Vanilla Ice Cream, Easy, **9.** 359
Vanilla Milk Shake, **3.** 85
Vanilla Pudding, **9.** 335
Vanilla Sauce, Fluffy, **9.** 364
Vanilla Soda, **3.** 86
Vanilla Wafer Crust, **13.** 574
Variety Meats
  Creamed Sweetbreads, **12.** 530
  Sautéed Liver and Onions, **12.** 530
  Steak and Kidney Pie, **12.** 531
  Tongue and Lima Skillet, **12.** 529
Veal
  Meat identification, **12.** 454
  Roasting Veal, **12.** 455
  Sherried Veal Pot Roast, **12.** 473
  Swedish Meatballs, **1.** 6
  Swiss Veal Roast, **12.** 474

**Boldface numbers
indicate chapters.**

Veal Cordon Bleu, **12.** 474
Veal Patties, **12.** 475
Vegetables (see also individual vegetables)
  Au Gratin Vegetables, **19.** 773
  Beef and Vegetable Stir-Fry, **12.** 471
  Chicken Vegetable-Noodle Soup, **18.** 753
  Cooking Vegetables, **19.** 774
  Creamed Vegetables, **19.** 773
  Cream of Fresh Vegetable Soup, **18.** 760
  Curried Chicken and Vegetables, **14.** 618
  Frank-Vegetable Kebabs, **2.** 47
  Garden Vegetable Stir-Fry, **19.** 816
  Ham and Bean Vegetable Soup, **18.** 757
  Herb-Seasoned Vegetables, **2.** 67
  Italian-Seasoned Vegetable Kebabs, **2.** 66
  Old-Fashioned Vegetable-Beef Soup, **18.** 740
  Oriental Vegetable Toss, **16.** 622
  Oven Steak and Vegetables, **12.** 464
  Potluck Vegetable Casserole, **19.** 816
  Raw Vegetable Antipasto, **16.** 673
  Scalloped Vegetables, **19.** 773
  Tuna-Vegetable Pie, **11.** 439
  24-Hour Vegetable Salad, **15.** 664
  Vegetable Omelet, **10.** 394
  Vegetable-Oyster Stew, **18.** 752
  Vegetable Relish, **7.** 276
  Vegetable Tempura, **19.** 777
Venison
  Marinated Venison Chops, **12.** 532
  Venison Pot Roast, **12.** 532
Vichyssoise, **18.** 763
Vinaigrette Dressing, **16.** 703
Volcano Potatoes, **19.** 805

Waldorf Salad, **16.** 686
Walnut Divinity, **6.** 210
Welsh Rabbit, **10.** 406
Whipped Parsnip Puff, **19.** 815
Whipped Rutabaga Puff, **19.** 815
Whipped Turnip Puff, **19.** 814
White Bread, **4.** 103
White Cake Supreme, **5.** 168
White Cake Supreme Cupcakes, **5.** 168
White Sauce, **17.** 710
White Wine Punch, **3.** 79
Whole Cranberry Sauce, **7.** 249
Whole Wheat Bread, **4.** 106
Whole Wheat Cookies, **8.** 325
Whole Wheat Noodles, **15.** 635
Whole Wheat Pita Bread, **4.** 133
Wild Rice, **15.** 643
Wild-Rice-Chicken Casserole, **14.** 611
Wild-Rice-Stuffed Fish, **11.** 422
Wild Rice with Mushrooms, **15.** 643
Wilted Spinach Salad, **16.** 666
Wine
  Cheese-Wine Log, **1.** 9
  Red Wine Dressing, **16.** 701
  Sangria, **3.** 84
  Savory Wine Marinade, **17.** 725
  White Wine Punch, **3.** 79
  Wine Basting Sauce, **2.** 44
  Wine Guide, **3.** 92
  Wine-Mushroom Sauce, **17.** 717
  Wine Sauce, **12.** 469
  Wine-Sauced Shoulder Chops, **2.** 61
Winter Squash or Pumpkin, canning and freezing, **7.** 270

**Y-Z**

Yeast Doughnuts, **4.** 121
Yellow Cake, **5.** 170
Yellow Cake Cupcakes, **5.** 170
Yellow Citrus Cake, **5.** 169

**W**

Waffles, **4.** 160

**Boldface numbers
indicate chapters.**

Yogurt
  Frozen Yogurt Melba Bombe,
    **9.** 360
  Lemon-Yogurt Cookies, **5.** 305
  Yogurt Sip, **3.** 89
Zucchini
  Cucumber or Zucchini Sauce,
    **17.** 711

Fried Zucchini, **19.** 774
Italian-Seasoned Vegetable
  Kebabs, **2.** 66
Marinated Zucchini Salad, **16.**
  672
Steak and Shrimp Kebabs, **2.** 35
Zucchini Nut Loaf, **4.** 139
Zucchini Salad Bowl, **16.** 665

# Measurements

## Broiling

| | Total Time in Minutes |
|---|---|
| **Beef steaks** | |
| 1-inch | |
| Rare | 8–10 |
| Medium | 12–14 |
| Well-done | 18–20 |
| 1½-inch | |
| Rare | 14–16 |
| Medium | 18–20 |
| Well-done | 25–30 |
| 2-inch | |
| Rare | 20–25 |
| Medium | 30–35 |
| Well-done | 40–45 |

### Hamburgers
| | |
|---|---|
| ½-inch | |
| Rare | 8 |
| Medium | 10 |
| Well-done | 12 |
| 1-inch | |
| Rare | 15 |
| Medium | 20 |
| Well-done | 25 |

### Pork chops
¾- to 1-inch ..... 20–25

### Pork steaks
½- to ¾-inch ..... 20–22

### Ham center slice
Fully cooked, bone-in
| | |
|---|---|
| ½-inch | 10–12 |
| 1-inch | 16–18 |

### Lamb Chops
| | |
|---|---|
| ¾-inch | |
| Medium | 10–12 |
| Well-done | 13–15 |
| 1-inch | |
| Medium | 11–13 |
| Well-done | 16–18 |
| 1½-inch | |
| Medium | 15–18 |
| Well-done | 20–22 |

### Chicken
Halved lengthwise or quartered ...... 35–40

### Fish fillets, steaks
| | |
|---|---|
| ½-inch | 5–6 |
| 1-inch | 10–12 |

*Broil ¾- to 1½-inch-thick steaks and chops so surface of meat is 3 inches from heat. Broil thicker cuts 4 to 5 inches from heat. (Check your range instruction booklet.) Broil on one side for about *half* of the time indicated in the chart for desired doneness. Turn with tongs; broil for remaining time.

## Weights and Measures

3 teaspoons = 1 tablespoon
4 tablespoons = ¼ cup
5⅓ tablespoons = ⅓ cup
8 tablespoons = ½ cup
10⅔ tablespoons = ⅔ cup

12 tablespoons = ¾ cup
16 tablespoons = 1 cup
1 ounce = 28.35 grams
1 pound = 453.59 grams
1 gram = 0.035 ounces
1 kilogram = 2.2 pounds
1 tablespoon = ½ fluid ounce
1 cup = 8 fluid ounces
1 cup = ½ pint
2 cups = 1 pint
4 cups = 1 quart
2 pints = 1 quart
4 quarts = 1 gallon
8 quarts = 1 peck
2 gallons = 1 peck
4 pecks = 1 bushel
1 tablespoon = 14.79 milliliters
1 cup = 236.6 milliliters
1 quart = 946.4 milliliters
1 liter = 1.06 quarts

## Internal Temperature of Meat on Removal from Oven*

| | Temp. of Meat |
|---|---|
| **Beef** | |
| Rare | 140° |
| Medium | 160° |
| Well-done | 170° |
| **Veal** | 170° |
| **Pork** | 170° |
| **Ham** | |
| Fully cooked | 140° |
| Cook-before-eating | 160° |
| **Lamb** | |
| Rare | 140° |
| Medium | 160° |
| Well-done | 170°–180° |
| **Poultry** | 185° |

*For meat, insert a meat thermometer into the center of the roast so that the bulb reaches the thickest part of the lean meat. Make sure that the bulb does not rest in fat or touch bone. For poultry, insert a meat thermometer in the center of the inside thigh muscle, making sure that the bulb does not touch bone.

## White Sauce

**Thin (1 cup)**
  1 tablespoon butter
  1 tablespoon all-purpose flour
  ¼ teaspoon salt
  1 cup milk
**Medium (1 cup)**
  2 tablespoons butter
  2 tablespoons all-purpose flour
  ¼ teaspoon salt
  1 cup milk

In a saucepan melt butter. Stir in flour, salt, and dash *pepper*. Add milk all at once. Cook and stir over medium heat till thickened and bubbly. Cook and stir 2 minutes more.

## Pastry for Pie

**Single-crust**
  **1¼ cups all-purpose flour**
  **½ teaspoon salt**
  **⅓ cup shortening or lard**
  **3 to 4 tablespoons cold water**
**Double-crust or lattice-top**
  **2 cups all-purpose flour**
  **1 teaspoon salt**
  **⅔ cup shortening or lard**
  **6 to 7 tablespoons cold water**

Stir together flour and salt. Cut in shortening or lard till pieces are the size of small peas. Sprinkle *1 tablespoon* of the water over part of the mixture; gently toss with a fork. Push to side of bowl. Repeat till all is moistened. Form dough into a ball. On a lightly floured surface, flatten dough with hands. Roll dough from center to edge, forming a circle about 12 inches in diameter. Ease pastry into a 9-inch pie plate, being careful not to stretch pastry. Trim pastry.

## Emergency Substitutions

For best results, use the ingredients specified in the recipe. But when you're in a bind, this chart can help you find a substitute.

| If you don't have: | Substitute: |
| --- | --- |
| 1 cup cake flour | 1 cup minus 2 tablespoons all-purpose flour |
| 1 tablespoon cornstarch (for thickening) | 2 tablespoons all-purpose flour |
| 1 teaspoon baking powder | ¼ teaspoon baking soda plus ½ cup buttermilk or sour milk (to replace ½ cup of the liquid called for) |
| 1 package active dry yeast | 1 cake compressed yeast |
| 1 cup granulated sugar | 1 cup packed brown sugar or 2 cups sifted powdered sugar |
| 1 cup honey | 1¼ cups granulated sugar plus ¼ cup liquid |
| 1 cup corn syrup | 1 cup granulated sugar plus ¼ cup liquid |
| 1 square (1 ounce) unsweetened chocolate | 3 tablespoons unsweetened cocoa powder plus 1 tablespoon butter or margarine |
| 1 cup whipping cream, whipped | 2 cups whipped dessert topping |
| 1 cup buttermilk | 1 tablespoon lemon juice or vinegar plus enough whole milk to make 1 cup (let stand 5 minutes before using) or 1 cup whole milk plus 1¾ teaspoons cream of tartar or 1 cup plain yogurt |
| 1 cup whole milk | ½ cup evaporated milk plus ½ cup water or 1 cup reconstituted nonfat dry milk (plus 2 teaspoons butter or margarine, if desired) |
| 1 cup light cream | 2 tablespoons butter plus 1 cup minus 2 tablespoons milk |

| If you don't have: | Substitute: |
|---|---|
| 2 cups tomato sauce | ¾ cup tomato paste plus 1 cup water |
| 1 cup tomato juice | ½ cup tomato sauce plus ½ cup water |
| 1 clove garlic | ⅛ teaspoon garlic powder or minced dried garlic |
| 1 small onion | 1 teaspoon onion powder or 1 tablespoon minced dried onion, rehydrated |
| 1 teaspoon dry mustard | 1 tablespoon prepared mustard |
| 1 teaspoon finely shredded lemon peel | ½ teaspoon lemon extract |

## Ingredient Equivalents

| Food | Amount Before Preparation | Approximate Measure After Preparation |
|---|---|---|
| **Cereals** | | |
| Macaroni | 1 cup (3½ oz.) | 2½ cups cooked |
| Noodles, medium | 3 cups (4 oz.) | 3 cups cooked |
| Spaghetti | 8 oz. | 4 cups cooked |
| Long grain rice | 1 cup (7 oz.) | 3 cups cooked |
| Quick-cooking rice | 1 cup (3 oz.) | 2 cups cooked |
| Popcorn | ¼ cup | 5 cups popped |
| **Crumbs** | | |
| Bread | 1 slice | ¾ cup soft or ¼ cup fine dry crumbs |
| Saltine crackers | 28 crackers | 1 cup finely crushed |
| Rich round crackers | 24 crackers | 1 cup finely crushed |
| Graham crackers | 14 squares | 1 cup finely crushed |
| Gingersnaps | 15 cookies | 1 cup finely crushed |
| Vanilla wafers | 22 cookies | 1 cup finely crushed |
| **Fruits** | | |
| Apples | 1 medium | 1 cup sliced |
| Bananas | 1 medium | ⅓ cup mashed |
| Lemons | 1 medium | 3 tbsp. juice; 2 tsp. shredded peel |
| Limes | 1 medium | 2 tbsp. juice; 1½ tsp. shredded peel |
| Oranges | 1 medium | ¼ to ⅓ cup juice; 4 tsp. shredded peel |

| Food | Amount Before Preparation | Approximate Measure After Preparation |
|------|---------------------------|----------------------------------------|
| Peaches, Pears | 1 medium | ½ cup sliced |
| Strawberries | 4 cups whole | 4 cups sliced |
| **Vegetables** | | |
| Beans, dried | 1 pound (2½ cups) | 6 cups cooked |
| Cabbage | 1 pound (1 small) | 5 cups shredded |
| Carrots, without tops | 1 pound (6 to 8 medium) | 3 cups shredded or 2½ cups chopped |
| Celery | 1 medium bunch | 4½ cups chopped |
| Green beans | 1 pound (3 cups) | 2½ cups cooked |
| Green peppers | 1 large | 1 cup chopped |
| Mushrooms | 1 pound (6 cups) | 2 cups cooked |
| Onions | 1 medium | ½ cup chopped |
| Potatoes | 1 medium | ⅔ cup cubed or ½ cup mashed |
| Spinach | 1 pound (12 cups) | 1½ cups cooked |
| Tomatoes | 1 medium | ½ cup cooked |
| **Nuts** | | |
| Almonds | 1 pound in shell | 1¼ cups shelled |
| Pecans | 1 pound in shell | 2 cups shelled |
| Walnuts | 1 pound in shell | 1½ cups shelled |
| **Miscellaneous** | | |
| Cheese | 4 ounces | 1 cup shredded |
| Whipping cream | 1 cup | 2 cups whipped |
| Boneless meat | 1 pound raw | 2 cups cooked |
| Cooked meat | 1 pound | 3 cups chopped |